An Introduction to Counselling

Fifth Edition

Fifth Edition

An Introduction to Counselling

John McLeod

Open University Press

Open University Press
McGraw-Hill Education
McGraw-Hill House
Shoppenhangers Road
Maidenhead
Berkshire
SL6 2QL

email: enquiries@openup.co.uk
world wide web: www.openup.co.uk

and Two Penn Plaza, New York, NY 10121–2289, USA

First Published 1993
Reprinted 1994 (twice), 1996 (twice), 1997
Second Edition published 1998
Reprinted 1999, 2000 and 2001
Third Edition published 2003
Reprinted 2003, 2004
Fourth Edition published 2009
Reprinted 2009, 2010, 2011 and 2012
First published in this Fifth Edition 2013

A catalogue record of this book is available from the British Library

ISBN-13: 978-0-335-24722-6
ISBN-10: 0-335-24722-9
eISBN: 978-0-335-24723-3

Library of Congress Cataloging-in-Publication Data
CIP data has been applied for

Typeset by RefineCatch Limited, Bungay, Suffolk

Praise for this book

"John McLeod's An Introduction to Counselling not only provides a definitive review of the field, but is also at the cutting edge of new developments. It offers a radical, progressive vision of what counselling can be – an invaluable resource, not only for new students coming into the field, but for any counsellor wishing to understand where we are at and where we are going."

Mick Cooper, Professor of Counselling, University of Strathclyde, UK

"It is my pleasure to endorse a textbook that has been so widely used within the field of counselling. John McLeod's Introduction to Counselling has influenced so many budding counsellors in the past (myself included) and I have no doubt that this updated edition will continue adding to this legacy. It has been updated to account for new developments in the field and remains an informed and accessible point of reference."

Terry Hanley, Editor of Counselling Psychology Review and Programme Director of the Doctorate in Counselling Psychology, University of Manchester, UK

"This wonderfully comprehensive introduction to counselling tells you all you need to know about counselling, whether you are thinking of training in counselling, are a newcomer or an established counsellor. Beautifully written and richly illustrated with clinical vignettes, the book amounts to a concise encyclopaedia of counselling. I know of no other book that successfully covers the history of counselling, different theoretical perspectives and approaches as well as research in a single volume. It contains scholarly insights and useful resources whilst tackling fundamental and interesting questions. It is an indispensable survival guide for would-be counsellors, trainees and experienced therapists. A gem of a book carried through with rigour and love."

Maria Luca, Reader in Psychotherapy and Counselling Psychology and Head of Reflections Research Centre, Regent's University, London, UK

"This latest edition of John McLeod's Introduction to Counselling is a masterpiece, weaving theory and practice in a readable and comprehensive manner. Practical examples and case studies, along with the latest research, address the many contemporary issues facing students and professionals in the field. The additional chapters including 'Art-making as a therapeutic practice', 'Therapy in nature', 'Integrating approaches' and 'Pluralism: an organizing framework for counselling practice', are essential reading not only for counsellors in training, but also for practitioners who wish to deepen their understanding and enhance their on-going professional development. John McLeod's vast experience and wisdom, which he brings to his writing, makes this work one of the best textbooks available, and I highly recommend it and will certainly use it in our training programmes."

Dr Ann Moir-Bussy, Program Leader and Senior Lecturer in Counselling, University of Sunshine Coast, Queensland, Australia

"This robust new edition gives a thorough overview of contemporary approaches to counselling and psychotherapy. As a practitioner, lecturer or student this book offers a wide application of theory to practice presented in a very clear and easily readable format. The use of text boxes highlighting topics for reflection and discussion, implications for practice and examples from case studies together with the in-depth suggestions for further reading provide an excellent book for counselling training and continuous professional development."

Sharon Vesty, Psychotherapist (UKCP Reg) and Senior Lecturer at
Nottingham Trent University, UK

"This is an excellent text which goes beyond being a technical handbook for trainee counsellors and gives a comprehensive overview of the profession offering 'food for thought' to both new and the experienced counsellors. I welcome the new four-part format which is clear, accessible and offers ample examples of counselling practice alongside indications for further reading. Part 4 in particular explores and asks critical questions about fundamental issues within the profession – the politics of counselling, values and ethics, the role of research in counselling and psychotherapy: For me a key text for those entering the profession."

Clare Walker, Psychotherapist and Senior Lecturer, Anglia Ruskin University, UK

"The first edition of this book was superb, an easily accessible, well-crafted presentation of counselling theory and practice. Each edition has been updated with new developments in the field. This fourth edition brings even more to our attention. With new sections and chapters on such topics as the political context of counselling, evidence-based practice, pluralism and the future of counselling, students and experienced practitioners will find all they need to bring them up to date with therapy as understood and practiced not only in the UK but worldwide. John McLeod writes beautifully and does the research for his books impeccably. He does the hard work that enables the rest of us to keep up to date effortlessly by reading this book."

Sue Wheeler, Institute of Lifelong Learning, University of Leicester, UK

Dedication

For Julia

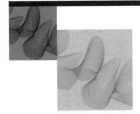

Contents

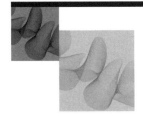

How to use this book

Counselling is an activity that is at the same time simple yet also vastly complicated. What can be simpler than talking to a concerned and interested listener about your problems? But it is what is involved in the telling and listening, knowing and being known, reflecting and acting, that can be so complex. In counselling, people talk about anything and everything. The relationship between the counsellor and the person seeking counsel is simultaneously taking place at a physical, bodily level, and through language, and in the thoughts, feelings and memories of each participant. This is what makes it so complicated, and this is what makes counselling a big topic. Counselling is an interdisciplinary activity, which contains different traditions and schools of thought, and spreads itself across the multiple discourses of theory, research and practice. Counselling has generated a rich and fascinating literature, and a range of powerful theories and research studies. I believe that it is vital for counsellors to be able to find their way around this literature, to tap into all these different knowledges.

Reading a book like this is somewhat similar to looking through a window into a room. In the room there are people doing something, but their world is always on the other side of the glass. Counselling is a practical activity, and can only be grasped through the experience of doing it, as client and counsellor. Real knowledge about counselling can never be gained through reading a book. It requires immersion in an oral tradition, physically being there and doing it and – crucially – *feeling* what is happening, rather than merely looking at words on a page. Given these inevitable limitations, in attempting to provide an introduction that does justice to its topic matter, this book has been organized around a set of guiding principles. What the book tries to do is:

- provide a comprehensive overview of as many aspects as possible of the rich array of ideas and practices that constitutes contemporary counselling;
- within each specific topic that is covered, to offer enough information to give the reader an initial understanding, and 'feel' for the issue, and then to provide clear suggestions for further reading through which readers can explore topics in greater depth;
- invite readers to adopt a critical, questioning stance in relation to the field of counselling, by placing theory and practice within a historical, social and political context;
- exemplify and reinforce the role of research and inquiry, by adopting a research-informed approach throughout;
- provide sufficient case vignettes and examples to enable readers to develop a sense of the 'lived experience' of counselling.

This is a book that is intended to be used by students who are engaging in degree-level (advanced undergraduate or Masters) study of counselling, and by experienced practitioners who are interested in updating their knowledge around recent developments in the field. It may be useful to think about the book as comprising four distinct parts:

- Part 1 (Chapters 1–3) defines and introduces counselling, and locates counselling in the context of social, historical and intellectual factors that have shaped its nature and development;

- Part 2 (Chapters 4–16) discusses the main theoretical perspectives and traditions that currently inform counselling training and practice. This part of the book begins with a chapter that considers the role of theory in counselling, and provides a framework for 'reading' theory that can be applied to the chapters that follow. The sequence of substantive chapters within this part of the book starts off by examining the 'big three' therapy approaches that dominate the contemporary scene: psychodynamic, person-centred/experiential and cognitive–behavioural therapy (CBT). The sequence ends by considering other therapy traditions that are less widely used at present but have nevertheless had a significant impact on theory and practice, and some emergent approaches that are likely to become more important in the future;

- Part 3 considers the issue of how best the different approaches can be combined or integrated. Chapter 17 introduces and discusses strategies for integration, and Chapter 18 provides an outline of a pluralistic perspective. Chapters 19 and 20 explore the ways that different perspectives can be brought together to create an integrated understanding of the therapeutic relationship and the process of therapy.

- Part 4 focuses on a broad range of professional issues in counselling, encompassing such topics as: ethical decision-making; organizational factors; different delivery systems; meeting the needs of specific groups of clients; counsellor training; supervision and professional development; and making use of research findings.

Throughout the book, there are cross-references to sections in different chapters that consider related aspects of the topic that is being discussed on that specific page. The book closes with a brief chapter that looks at counselling from a global perspective, and identifies some of the main challenges facing counselling in future decades.

There is a lot of signposting throughout the book, to indicate subtopics within chapters, to encourage topic-hopping and selective sampling of material that seems most relevant. Each chapter, and the book as whole, has been constructed to be a 'good read', in the sense of telling a coherent story. However, it is clear that we are in the era of the download, the hyper-link and the drop-down menu. It is certainly possible to access the book in a non-linear fashion: *An Introduction to Counselling* is intended to be a resource for students and practitioners of counselling and allied fields.

It is important to emphasize that this book is an introduction, or an invitation, to key aspects of counselling. It makes no claim to be exhaustive or comprehensive. Hopefully, it includes sufficient suggestions for further reading to enable users of the book to find comprehensive and authoritative sources if that is what they need.

As well as containing many suggestions for further and broader reading, *An Introduction to Counselling* is supported by two companion texts. *The Counsellor's Workbook: Developing a Personal Approach* (McLeod 2010a) includes a wide range of self-exploration learning tasks and group exercises that are linked to particular topics covered in *An Introduction*. A further text, *Counselling Skills* (McLeod and McLeod 2011) is a book that focuses primarily on 'how to do' counselling, and is intended not only to be read by counsellors, but also by practitioners whose counselling function is embedded in another professional role (teacher, nurse, social worker, doctor).

It may be relevant to some readers to know about my own background, in order to become more aware of the biases that have shaped my treatment of certain topics. My initial educational experience was in psychology, followed by a primary training in person-centred counselling/psychotherapy and additional training experiences in psychodynamic, cognitive–behavioural therapy (CBT), narrative therapy and other approaches. A significant part of my career has involved doing research, and encouraging others to do research (McLeod 2010a, 2011, 2013a). My practice has involved work with a range of different client groups. I believe that, in as far as I can be aware of such things, there are five positions with which I strongly identify, in respect of counselling theory and practice, and which I feel sure have influenced the writing of this book.

First, I believe that good counselling is based, in a fundamental way, on the personal integrity of the therapist, and his or her willingness to 'go the extra mile' in terms of responding to each client as a unique person and creating a relationship of value to that person. Although specific therapy techniques and interventions can be useful, a technique will not be effective if the recipient does not trust the provider. Conversely, if a client and counsellor have a good enough relationship (and if the latter is not shackled by adherence to a therapeutic ideology), most of the time they will be able to improvise the procedures that are necessary in order to tackle any problem.

Second, I feel frustrated and annoyed by the territorial wars that exist within the counselling and psychotherapy professions, regarding the relative merits of different approaches (CBT versus psychodynamic versus person-centred, and so on). I believe that these inter-school arguments are inward looking, distract attention from the needs of clients, and are a waste of time. I take a historical perspective on the question of 'pure schools' as against integrated approaches: the profession began its existence organized around discrete schools of therapy, but now it is time to move on. I am personally interested in all approaches to counselling/psychotherapy, and believe that each one of them has something valuable to offer. The frequent references to the concept of 'pluralism', through this book and in my other writing, are a reflection of this attitude.

My third source of personal bias concerns the relationship between counselling and psychotherapy. In my initial training, I was taught that counselling and psychotherapy are basically the same thing. I later encountered the widespread (but typically unvoiced) attitude that counselling is a 'little sister' profession – it is what you do while you are waiting to be accepted on to a psychotherapy training programme. I no longer believe either of these positions (although acknowledging that each of them is 'true' in the sense that many people would endorse them). Increasingly, I see counselling as an activity and occupation that has strong links with psychotherapy, but is nevertheless different from it in significant ways. The distinctive features of counselling are that it views the person with his or her social context, and that it does not seek to impose any one theoretical model on to the experience of the person seeking help.

My fourth source of bias is that I think that research is interesting and important. I have spent my career in a UK counselling environment in which the majority of colleagues are indifferent, sceptical or even hostile about the value of research. There is a great deal of research evidence woven into *An Introduction to Counselling,* because I believe that it is a central source of knowledge and understanding, alongside personal knowledge (such as life experience and personal therapy), theoretical knowledge and clinical knowledge. As counsellors, we work alongside colleagues from other professions, such as nursing and education, that have embraced evidence-based practice.

My final source of personal bias is that I believe that it is essential to acknowledge that we are cultural beings, and that what we do as counsellors needs to be understood as a form of 'cultural work'. Certainly the hard-wired, biological aspects of our beings are important too, but relationships, language and shared history have allowed human beings to control and channel these biological 'givens' in many different ways. A worry that I have about counselling is that sometimes it can support the movement toward self-contained individualism, and undermines the forces that bind us together and allow us to be strong.

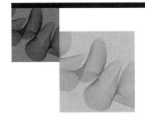

Acknowledgements

Any author knows that what he or she writes does not come freshly minted from their own personal and private thoughts about things, but is in fact an assemblage of words and ideas borrowed from other people. I have been fortunate to be in a position to learn from many people. Among those I would particularly like to thank are a number of generous friends and colleagues who have helped me in many ways: Lynne Angus, Joe Armstrong, Lucia Berdondini, Sophia Balamoutsou, Kirsten Bennun, Ronen Berger, Tim Bond, Julia Buckroyd, Anne Chien, Mick Cooper, Edith Cormack, Angela Couchman, Windy Dryden, Robert Elliott, Kim Etherington, Marcella Finnerty, Soti Grafanaki, Hanne Haavind, Margrethe Halvorsen, Robin Ion, Colin Kirkwood, Noreen Lillie, Thomas Mackrill, Dave Mearns, John Mellor-Clark, Judith Moore, Denis O'Hara, Vanja Orlans, Campbell Purton, Marit Rabu, Andrew Reeves, David Rennie, Helge Ronnestad, Brian Rogers, Nancy Rowland, Alison Rouse, Margot Schofield, John Sherry, Alison Shoemark, Hanne Stromme, Rolf Sundet, Laco Timulak, Mhairi Thurston, Biljana van Rijn, Dot Weaks, William West, Sue Wheeler, and Mark Widdowson.

I also thank, in a different way, my wife Julia, who has provided unfailing support and encouragement, and my daughters Kate, Emma and Hannah, who have constantly reminded me of how much else there is to life. I owe them more than I can say.

Part 1
Introduction to counselling

What is counselling?

Introduction

Counselling is an activity that emerged during the twentieth century, and reflects the pressures and values of modern life. We live in a complex, busy, changing world. In this world, there are many different types of experience that are difficult for people to cope with. Most of the time, we get on with life, but sometimes we are stopped in our tracks by an event or situation that we do not, at that moment, have the resources to sort out. Most of the time, we find ways of dealing with such problems in living by talking to family, friends, neighbours, priests or our family doctor. But occasionally their advice is not sufficient, or we are too embarrassed or ashamed to tell them what is bothering us, or we just do not have an appropriate person to turn to. Counselling is a really useful option at these moments. In most places, counselling is available fairly quickly, and costs little or nothing. A counsellor is someone who does his or her best to listen to you and work with you to find the best ways to understand and resolve your problem. Counsellors do not diagnose or label people, but instead do their best to work within whatever framework of understanding makes most sense for each client. For some people, one conversation with a counsellor is sufficient to make a real difference to them. Other people need to see their counsellor on a regular basis for months or years. These can be precious hours. Where else in our society is there the opportunity to be heard, taken seriously, understood, to have the focused attention of a caring other for hours at a time without being asked to give anything in return?

Being a counsellor is also a satisfying and rewarding work role. There are times when, as a counsellor, you *know* that you have made a profound difference to the life of another human being. It is always a great privilege to be allowed to be a witness and companion to someone who is facing their own worst fears and dilemmas. Being a counsellor is endlessly challenging. There is always more to learn. The role of counsellor lends itself to flexible work arrangements. There are excellent counsellors who are full-time paid staff; others who work for free in the evenings for voluntary agencies; and some who are able sensitively to offer a counselling relationship within other work roles, such as nurse, doctor, clergy, social worker or teacher.

This book is about counselling. It is a book that celebrates the creative simplicity of counselling as a cultural invention which has made a huge contribution to the quality of life of millions of people. The aim of this book is to provide a framework for making sense of all of the different aspects of counselling that exist in contemporary society, while not losing sight of its ordinary simplicity and direct human value.

The focus of this introductory chapter is on asking some basic questions about counselling: Who needs it? What is it? Who does it? Where is it available?

Counselling in action

The following paragraphs reflect some typical examples of counselling, in terms both of different problems in living that can be tackled through counselling, and the different counselling processes that can occur.

Donald's story: coming to terms with the pressures of work

As a manager in a local government department, Donald continually felt himself to be under pressure, but able to cope. Following a series of absences for minor illnesses, the occupational health nurse within the authority suggested to Donald that it might be helpful for him to see one of the counsellors contracted to the occupational health service. Initially, Donald thought that it would be a sign of weakness to see a counsellor. He was also worried that other people in the organization might view him as having mental health problems, and begin to see him as unreliable. Following further discussion with the occupational health nurse, Donald accepted that counselling was completely confidential and might have something to offer. In the eight counselling sessions that he attended, Donald made two important discoveries about himself. First, he realized the extent to which he was driven by his father's ambition for him, to the extent of never being satisfied with his own achievements, and as a result being very reluctant to take holidays from work. He also reflected, with the help of his counsellor, on his unwillingness to accept support from other people, not only at work but also in the context of his family life. With the encouragement of his counsellor, Donald began to make some shifts in his behaviour, in relation to arranging time off, and making opportunities to speak about his concerns to his wife, and to another close colleague. At the end of the counselling, he described it as having given him an opportunity to 'sort himself out'.

Maria's story: moving on from abuse

At the age of 25, Maria's emotional life, and relationships, were still dominated by her memories of having been subjected to physical and sexual abuse in her childhood. She found it very hard to trust other people, or to speak up in social situations. For the most part, Maria had decided that the best course of action for survival was to be as invisible as possible. Although at various stages in her life she had tried to talk about her experiences to various doctors, psychiatrists and nurses, she had always felt that they did not really want to know what had happened to her, and were more interested in prescribing various forms of drug treatment to control her anxiety and self-harming behaviour. However, she had made enough progress in her recovery to decide to go to university to train as a nurse. Once started on her course, she found herself confronted by a variety of frightening situations – talking in seminar groups, making new friends, being on placement in busy hospital wards. Maria decided to visit the university student counselling service. This was the first time in her life that she had ready access to any form of psychological therapy. Maria formed a strong relationship with her counsellor, who she occasionally described as 'the mother I never had', and attended counselling weekly throughout the entire three years of her training. Together, Maria and her counsellor developed strategies that allowed her to deal with the many demands of nurse training. As Maria gradually built up a sense of herself as competent, likeable and strong, she became more able to leave behind much of her fearfulness and tendency to engage in binge eating.

Arva's story: whether to leave a marriage

Having been married for five years to a man whose family were prominent members of a leading family within the Asian community in her city, the idea of marital separation and divorce was terrifying for Arva. Although she was no longer willing to accept the physical violence of her husband, she was at the same time unable to envisage that any other life might be open to her if, as she put it, she 'walked away' from her community. Eventually, Arva made an appointment to speak to a counsellor at a domestic violence helpline. Reassured by the acceptance she felt from the counsellor, she agreed to come in for a face-to-face appointment. Initially, Arva was very unsure about whether her counsellor could help her, because it did not seem that the counsellor understood the meaning and implications, within Arva's cultural group, of leaving a marriage or publicly accusing a husband of mistreating his wife. Over time, the counsellor developed a sufficient understanding of Arva's experience, to allow the counselling to proceed. The counsellor also helped Arva to make contact with an Asian women's support group and a legal advice centre, both of which were helpful to her in providing a broader perspective on her position. Eventually, Arva courageously confronted her husband about his behaviour. To her surprise, he agreed to join her in joint counselling in which they agreed on some better ways to resolve the conflicts that sometimes arose between them.

Anita's story: dealing with loss

Married to Bill for 40 years, Anita was devastated by his sudden death, within 6 months of his retirement. Although Anita felt herself to be fortunate, in enjoying regular contact with her son and daughter and several grandchildren, she increasingly felt that her life was meaningless, and that she would never get over the loss of her beloved Bill. Nine months after his death, she visited her general practitioner (GP), who suggested a course of antidepressants. Unhappy about the idea of possibly becoming dependent on drugs, Anita asked if there were any other alternatives. The GP then referred her to a bereavement counselling service. Anita only attended the counselling on two occasions, and did not find it helpful. When asked, afterwards, about why she thought that the counselling had not been useful for her, she said: 'he was a nice man, but he just sat and listened, and I felt worse and worse. I couldn't see any point in it'.

Simon's story: creating a new self-image

By the age of 13, Simon had acquired a reputation as a 'difficult' student. Often required to attend detention because of aggressive and uncooperative behaviour, Simon was on the edge of being suspended from school. His form teacher persuaded him that it would do no harm to see the school counsellor. In his first counselling session, Simon sat with his arms crossed, reluctant to talk. However, on the basis that speaking to someone who genuinely seemed interested in his side of things was better than attending maths class, he gradually allowed himself to open up. From Simon's perspective, he felt trapped in an image that other people had of him. Physically strong and mature for his age, and from a family that believed in the value of standing up for yourself, Simon felt that he had made the mistake, early in his career at the school, of challenging one teacher who had (in Simon's eyes) unfairly accused him of a misdemeanour. Ever since that day, it seemed, not only other teachers, but also his classmates, seemed to expect him to 'rise to the bait' whenever a teacher reprimanded him. He admitted that he felt 'fed up and stuck' with this pattern, but could not find any way to change it. With the counsellor's help, Simon identified some key trigger situations, and ways of responding differently when they occurred. He also began to cultivate a subtly different image within the school, and within his own imagination – the 'joker' rather than the 'troublemaker'.

Defining counselling

The case vignettes presented above give some brief examples of what can happen when someone goes to see a counsellor. But what is counselling? What are the ideas and principles that link together the very different experiences of these counselling clients? How can we understand and define counselling? There are many definitions of 'counselling' formulated by professional bodies and leading figures in the field:

> . . . a professional relationship between a trained counsellor and a client . . . designed to help clients to understand and clarify their views of their lifespace, and to learn to reach their self-determined goals through meaningful, well-informed choices and through resolution of problems of an emotional or interpersonal nature.
>
> (Burks and Stefflre 1979: 14)

> . . . a principled relationship characterised by the application of one or more psychological theories and a recognised set of communication skills, modified by experience, intuition and other interpersonal factors, to clients' intimate concerns, problems or aspirations.
>
> (Feltham and Dryden 1993: 6)

> Counselling and psychotherapy are umbrella terms that cover a range of talking therapies. They are delivered by trained practitioners who work with people over a short or long term to help them bring about effective change or enhance their wellbeing.
>
> (British Association for Counselling and Psychotherapy website 2013)

> Counseling is a professional relationship that empowers diverse individuals, families, and groups to accomplish mental health, wellness, education, and career goals.
>
> (American Counseling Association website 2013)

These definitions share one important feature in common: they are primarily framed from the point of view of the *counsellor*. They are definitions that primarily seek to define counselling as 'something done by a counsellor'. In taking this perspective, these definitions reflect the aim of professional bodies to establish counselling as a professional specialism within contemporary society. However, a profession-centred definition of counselling runs the risk of ignoring the basic fact that counselling is always a two-person (or multiperson) activity, which arises when one person seeks the help of another. In order to reflect a more inclusive meaning of the term 'counselling', this book espouses a *user-centred* definition:

> Counselling is a purposeful, private conversation arising from the intention of one person (couple or family) to reflect on and resolve a problem in living, and the willingness of another person to assist in that endeavour.

The key assumptions that underpin, and are implied by, this definition include:

1 Counselling is an activity that can only happen if the person seeking help, the client, wants it to happen. Counselling takes place when someone who is troubled invites and allows another person to enter into a particular kind of relationship with them. If a person is not ready to extend this invitation, they may be exposed to the best efforts of expert counsellors for long periods of time, but what will happen will not be counselling. The person seeking counselling is regarded as actively engaged in finding ways of overcoming his or her problems, and as a co-participant in the counselling process, rather than as a passive recipient of interventions.

2 A person seeks a counselling relationship when they encounter a 'problem in living' that they have not been able to resolve through their everyday resources, and that has resulted in their exclusion from some aspect of full participation in social life. The concept of 'problem in living' can be understood to refer to any situation or perceived difficulty or impediment that prevents a person from getting on with his or her life. Counselling is not focused on symptom reduction, but on enabling the person to live their life in a way that is most meaningful and satisfying to him or her.

3 Counselling is fundamentally based on conversation, on the capacity of people to 'talk things through' and to generate new possibilities for action through dialogue.

4 Counselling depends on the creation of a relationship between two people, which is sufficiently secure to allow the person seeking help to explore issues that are painful and troubling.

5 The person seeking counselling possesses strengths and resources that can be channelled in the service of resolving a problem in living. The act of seeking counselling is not viewed as an indicator of personal deficiency or pathology.

6 The person in the role of counsellor does not necessarily possess special training or knowledge of psychological theories – counselling is grounded in ordinary human qualities such as a capacity to listen, sensitivity to the experience of others, personal integrity and resourcefulness in solving the difficulties that arise in everyday life.

7 The person seeking counselling invites another person to provide him or her with time and space characterized by the presence of a number of features that are not readily available in everyday life: permission to speak, respect for difference, confidentiality and affirmation.

   a *Encouragement and permission to speak.* Counselling is a place where the person can tell their story, where they are given every encouragement to give voice to aspects of their experience that have previously been silenced, in their own time and their own way, including the expression of feeling and emotion.

   b *Respect for difference.* The counsellor sets aside, as far as they are able, their own position on the issues brought by the client, and his or her needs in the moment, in order to focus as completely as possible on helping the client to articulate and act on his or her personal values and desires.

   c *Confidentiality.* Whatever is discussed is confidential: the counsellor undertakes to refrain from passing on what they have learned from the person to any others in the person's life world.

   d *Affirmation.* The counsellor enacts a relationship that is an expression of a set of core values: honesty, integrity, care, belief in the worth and value of individual persons, commitment to dialogue and collaboration, reflexivity, the interdependence of persons, a sense of the common good.

Counselling practice is therefore grounded in a distinctive set of values, and moral position, based on respect and affirmation of the worth of the individual person.

8 Counselling represents an arena for support, reflection and renewal that is unique within modern societies. Within this arena, the client and counsellor make use of whatever cultural resources come to hand (conversation, ideas, theories, rituals, altered states of consciousness, problem-solving algorithms, discourses, technologies) to achieve a satisfactory resolution of the initial problem in living that initiated the decision to engage in counselling.

9 The potential outcomes of counselling can be understood as falling into three broad categories:

   a *Resolution* of the original problem in living. Resolution can include: achieving an understanding or perspective on the problem, arriving at a personal acceptance of the problem or dilemma and taking action to change the situation in which the problem arose.

   b *Learning.* Engagement with counselling may enable the person to acquire new understandings, skills and strategies that make them better able to handle similar problems in future.

   c *Social inclusion.* Counselling stimulates the energy and capacity of the person as someone who can contribute to the well-being of others and the social good.

10 Counselling always exists within a social and cultural context: 'counsellor' and 'client' are social roles, and the ways in which participants make sense of the aims and work of counselling are shaped by the broad cultural and specific community and organizational contexts within which they live. The practice of counselling is informed by awareness and appreciation of social, cultural, historical and economic factors. The meaning of 'counselling', and the forms of practice associated with this term, continually evolve in response to social and cultural change.

11 Counselling is readily accessible. It is a 'frontline' service, this is located within the community or organization where the person lives, works or studies. There is minimal 'gatekeeping' that needs to be negotiated in order to see a counsellor.

It can be seen that a user-centred description of counselling highlights a range of factors that are partially hidden in profession-centred definitions. User-centred language characterizes the person seeking counselling as active and resourceful, and purposefully seeking to resolve problems in living, rather than merely a recipient of 'treatment'. It also emphasizes the connection between counselling and the social world of which the person is a member. It characterizes counselling as a relationship, a space, or an opportunity that is sought by a troubled person, rather than as any particular form of practice (e.g., two people sitting talking to each other face to face) – thereby inviting creativity and exploration in relation to how this space and opportunity might be constructed. It makes no claim that a professional qualification, or formal knowledge of psychology, is necessary in order to practice counselling – effective counselling can take place both within and outside professionalized networks.

How does counselling help?

The concept of *diversity* is central to an understanding of what counselling is about. Counselling is a form of helping that does its best to respect and work with the diverse needs and learning styles of different clients. Because counselling is a frontline service, counsellors are not specialists in one single approach to therapy. Instead, counsellors need to be able to work with whatever and whoever walks through the door, or make contact by phone or other means. Effective counsellors are responsive and creative in their capacity to find out what will be most helpful for each individual client. There are many ways in which counselling can help people to move on in their lives:

- *Insight.* The acquisition of an understanding of the origins and development of emotional difficulties, leading to an increased capacity to take rational control over feelings and actions.
- *Relating with others.* Becoming better able to form and maintain meaningful and satisfying relationships with other people: for example, within the family or workplace.
- *Self-awareness.* Becoming more aware of thoughts and feelings that had been blocked off or denied, or developing a more accurate sense of how self is perceived by others.
- *Self-acceptance.* The development of a positive attitude towards self, marked by an ability to acknowledge areas of experience that had been the subject of self-criticism and rejection.
- *Self-actualization or individuation.* Moving in the direction of fulfilling potential or achieving an integration of previously conflicting parts of self.
- *Enlightenment.* Assisting the client to arrive at a higher state of spiritual awakening.
- *Problem-solving.* Finding a solution to a specific problem that the client had not been able to resolve alone. Acquiring a general competence in problem-solving.
- *Psychological education.* Enabling the client to acquire ideas and techniques with which to understand and control behaviour.
- *Acquisition of social skills.* Learning and mastering social and interpersonal skills such as maintenance of eye contact, turn-taking in conversations, assertiveness or anger control.
- *Cognitive change.* The modification or replacement of irrational beliefs or maladaptive thought patterns associated with self-destructive behaviour.
- *Behaviour change.* The modification or replacement of maladaptive or self-destructive patterns of behaviour.
- *Systemic change.* Introducing change into the way in that social systems (e.g., families) operate.
- *Empowerment.* Working on skills, awareness and knowledge that will enable the client to take control of his or her own life.
- *Restitution.* Helping the client to make amends for previous destructive behaviour.

- *Generativity and social action.* Inspiring in the person a desire and capacity to care for others and pass on knowledge (generativity) and to contribute to the collective good through political engagement and community work.

Counselling should be flexible enough to make it possible for the client to use the therapeutic relationship as an arena for exploring whatever dimension of life is most relevant to their well-being at that point in time.

What is the difference between counselling and psychotherapy?

The degree of similarity and difference between counselling and psychotherapy has been the focus of considerable debate. This issue is made more complex by the fact that, although all English-language societies employ both terms, there are many countries in which only the term 'psychotherapy' is used (e.g., Sweden) and other countries in which 'psychotherapy' is mainly used but where there are ongoing attempts to create a distinction between counselling and psychotherapy (e.g., Germany, where there is a movement to use 'Beratung' as the equivalent to 'counselling'). Within the English language community, two contrasting positions have dominated this debate:

- *A clear distinction can be made between counselling and psychotherapy.* The argument here is that, although there is a certain amount of overlap between the theories and methods of counsellors and psychotherapists, and the type of clients that they see, there is nevertheless a fundamental difference between the two, with psychotherapy representing a deeper, more fundamental level of work, over a longer period, usually with more disturbed clients.
- *Counsellors and psychotherapists are basically doing the same kind of work*, using identical approaches and techniques, but are required to use different titles in response to the demands of the agencies that employ them. For example, traditionally psychotherapy has been the term used in medical settings such as psychiatric units, and counselling the designation for people working in educational settings such as student counselling services.

One of the difficulties with both of these positions is that each of them portrays counselling in a 'little sister' role in relation to psychotherapy. In the 'clear distinction' position, counselling is explicitly described as less effective. In the 'no difference' position, counselling is still placed in a lesser position, by dint of the fact that psychotherapy jobs are higher status and better paid than counselling posts, even when they involve doing equivalent work.

Many people who work as counsellors are dissatisfied with the 'little sister' image of their professional role, because they know that they work with some of the most damaged people in society, and believe that what they do is as effective as any form of psychotherapy. In recent years there has emerged a view that counselling and psychotherapy comprise alternative approaches to responding to the needs of people who experience problems in living. Some key points of contrast between counselling and psychotherapy are summarized in Table 1.1.

TABLE 1.1 Similarities and differences between counselling and psychotherapy

Psychotherapy	Counselling
Similarities	
Provides the person with a confidential space in which to explore personal difficulties	Provides the person with a confidential space in which to explore personal difficulties
Effective practice depends to a great extent on the quality of the client–psychotherapist relationship	Effective practice depends to a great extent on the quality of the client–counsellor relationship
Self-awareness and personal psychotherapy are valued elements of training and ongoing development	Self-awareness and personal therapy are valued elements of training and ongoing development
Differences	
A wholly professionalized occupation	An activity that includes specialist professional workers, but also encompasses paraprofessionals, volunteers and those whose practice is embedded within other occupational roles
Public perception: inaccessible, expensive, middle class	Public perception: accessible, free, working class
Perception by government/state: given prominent role in mental health services; strongly supported by evidence-based practice policies	Perception by government/sate: largely invisible
Conceptualizes the client as an individual with problems in psychological functioning	Conceptualizes the client as a person in a social context
Training and practice focuses on delivering interventions	Training and practice involves not only delivering interventions, but also working with embedded colleagues, and promoting self-help
Psychotherapy agencies are separate from the communities within which they are located	Counselling agencies are part of their communities – e.g., a student counselling service in a university
Treatment may involve the application of interventions defined by a protocol, manual or specific therapy model	The helping process typically involves counsellor and client working collaboratively, using methods that may stretch beyond any single protocol or manual
Treatment has a theory-derived brand name (e.g., interpersonal therapy, CBT, solution-focused therapy)	Often has a context-derived title (e.g., workplace counselling, bereavement counselling, student counselling)
Many psychotherapists have a psychology degree, which functions as a key entrance qualification	Counsellors are likely to be drawn from a wide variety of backgrounds; entrance qualification is life experience and maturity rather than any particular academic specialism
Predominant focus on the pathology of the person	Predominant focus on personal strengths and resources

It is essential to acknowledge that none of the statements of difference in Table 1.1 represent an *absolute* difference between counselling and psychotherapy. In reality, the domains of counselling and psychotherapy are fragmented and complex, and embrace a multiplicity of forms of practice. It would not be hard to find examples of psychotherapy practice that correspond to characteristics attributed in Table 1.1 to counselling (and vice versa); there is a huge degree of overlap between counselling and psychotherapy. It is best to regard these differences between counselling and psychotherapy as indicative of a direction of travel that is occurring within the therapy professions, rather than as constituting any kind of fixed map of what is happening now. Nevertheless, a conception of counselling as distinctively contextually oriented, strengths based and as a pragmatic form of frontline, community-based practice reflects a trajectory that is clearly visible within the international counselling community. The present book seeks to acknowledge the substantial similarities and overlap between counselling and psychotherapy, while at the same time reinforcing the distinctive nature of counselling.

Where can I find a counsellor?

There are several occupational titles that refer to people who are practising counselling. A term that is sometimes used is *counselling psychologist*. This refers to a counsellor who has initial training in psychology, and whose work is specifically informed by psychological methods and models. There are also several labels that refer to counsellors who work with particular client groups: for example, *mental health counsellor, marriage/couple counsellor, bereavement counsellor* or *student counsellor*. These practitioners possess specialist training and expertise in their particular field in addition to general counselling training. There are also many instances where counselling is offered in the context of a relationship that is primarily focused on other, non-counselling concerns. For example, a student may use a teacher as a person with whom it is safe to share worries and anxieties. A community nurse may visit a home to give medical care to a patient who is terminally ill, but finds herself also providing emotional support. In these situations it seems appropriate to describe what is happening as *embedded counselling* (McLeod and McLeod 2011). Embedded counselling is, or can be, an aspect of a wide range of professional roles: clergy, teaching, health, social work and community work, legal and justice work, personnel, human resources and management, and much else. Embedded counselling also takes place in a variety of peer self-help networks, such as Alcoholics Anonymous and Weightwatchers. In recent years, some counsellors have started to describe their work as *life coaching* or *executive coaching*. Coaching is an activity that draws on much of the skill and knowledge of counselling, but is focused on the promotion of positive effectiveness and achievement, rather than on the amelioration of problems. Finally, there is a large degree of overlap between the use of the terms 'counselling' and 'psychotherapy', as discussed in the preceding section of this chapter.

There also exists a wide diversity in counselling practice, with counselling being delivered through one-to-one contact, in groups, with couples and families, over the telephone and internet, and through written materials such as books and self-help manuals. Counselling is practiced in a range of different settings, and offered to a wide array of client groups.

This diversity of theory and practice can be attributed to the fact that counselling emerged and grew during the twentieth century in response to a mix of cultural, economic and social forces. In essence, because it is targeted at individuals and small groups, and focuses on the personal needs of each client, counselling represents a highly flexible means of responding to societal problems. For example, many counselling agencies are funded by, or attached to, organizations that have a primary task of providing medical and health care. These range from mental health/psychiatric settings, which typically deal with highly disturbed or damaged clients, through to counselling available in primary care settings, such as GP surgeries, and from community nurses. There has also been a growth in specialist counselling directed towards people with particular medical conditions such as AIDS, cancer and various genetic disorders. Counselling has also played an important role in many centres and clinics offering alternative or complementary health approaches. One of the primary cultural locations for counselling and psychotherapy can therefore be seen to be alongside medicine. Even when counsellors and counselling agencies work independently of medical organizations they will frequently establish some form of liaison with medical and psychiatric services, to enable referral of clients who may require medical or nursing care. These areas of counselling practice reflect the increasing medicalization of social life (Turner 1995), and the pressure to create a space for personal contact and relationship within technologically driven health care.

Counselling also has a place in the world of work. A variety of counselling agencies exist for the purpose of helping people through difficulties, dilemmas or anxieties concerning their work role. These agencies include vocational guidance, student counselling services and employee-assistance programmes or workplace counselling provided by large organizations in industry and the public sector. Whether the work role is that of executive, postal worker or college student, counsellors are able to offer help with stress and anxiety arising from the work, coping with change and making career decisions.

A number of counselling agencies have evolved to meet the needs of people who experience traumatic or sudden interruptions to their life development and social roles. Prominent among these are agencies and organizations offering counselling in such areas as marital breakdown, rape and bereavement. The work of the counsellor in these agencies can very clearly be seen as arising from social problems. For example, changing social perceptions of marriage, redefinitions of male and female roles, new patterns of marriage and family life, and legislation making divorce more available represent major social and cultural changes of the past century. Counselling provides a way of helping individuals to negotiate this changing social landscape.

A further field of counselling activity lies in the area of addictions. There exists a range of counselling approaches developed to help people with problems related to drug and alcohol abuse, food addiction and smoking cessation. The social role of the counsellor can be seen particularly clearly in this type of work. In some areas of addiction counselling, such as with hard drug users, counsellors operate alongside a set of powerful legal constraints and moral judgements. The possession and use of heroin, for example, is seen by most people as morally wrong, and has been made a criminal offence. The counsellor working with a heroin addict, therefore, is not merely exploring ways of living more satisfyingly and resourcefully, but is mediating between competing social definitions of what an acceptable 'way of living' entails. In other fields of addiction counselling, such as food, alcohol and cigarette abuse, the behaviour in question is heavily reinforced by advertising paid for by the slimming, drink and tobacco industries. The incidence of alcohol- and smoking-related diseases would be more effectively reduced by tax increases than by increases in the number of counsellors, an insight that raises questions about the role of counselling in relation to other means of control of behaviour.

The significance of paying attention to the context within which counselling takes place arises from an appreciation that counselling is not merely a process of individual learning. It is also a social activity that has a social meaning. Often, people turn to counselling at a point of transition, such as the transition from child to adult, married to divorced, addict to straight, or when they are struggling to adapt to social institutions. Within these contexts, counsellors are rarely managers or executives who hold power in colleges, businesses or communities. Counsellors, instead, have a more 'liminal' role, being employed at the edge of these institutions to deal with those in danger of falling off or falling out.

Conclusions

The aim of this chapter has been to provide an image of the complex mosaic of contemporary counselling practice. From the point of view of the user or client, counselling can be understood as a relationship and a conversational space that enables problems in living to be explored and resolved. Counselling is a flexible form of helping, that respects diversity and strives to understand problems from the point of view of the client, rather than trying to fit the client to a pre-existing diagnostic system. At its best, counselling is a frontline, community-based service that is readily accessible to people who need it. As a result, counselling is available in a wide range of community settings. The implications of this image of counselling, and the ways in which it has been interpreted and articulated by practitioners and organizations, are explored in the following chapters.

Topics for reflection and discussion

1   Read through the definition of counselling presented in this chapter. Does it capture the meaning of counselling, as you understand it? What might you wish to add to this definition, or delete? How might this definition come across to you if you were someone in extreme need of emotional help and support? How might it come across if you were a member of an ethnic minority group, were gay or lesbian, or disabled (in other words, not part of the dominant cultural way of looking at things)?

2   Make a list of all the different counselling and psychotherapy services that are available in the city or community where you live. Identify the groups of people who are most likely to use each service. What does this tell you about the links between counselling and social class, age, gender and ethnicity? What does your analysis indicate about the different functions that are fulfilled by counselling, and by psychotherapy, in your community?

Suggested further reading

This chapter is intended to introduce the general issues and topics that weave through subsequent chapters, so in a sense the further reading is the remainder of the book. However, many of the specific issues raised in this chapter are discussed with great insight in *What Is Counselling?* by Colin Feltham (1995). Some of the flavour of the (sometimes almost overwhelming) diversity of contemporary theory and practice in counselling is captured in journals such as *Therapy Today* and the *Journal of Counseling and Development*. The former is a British publication, while the latter is American.

CHAPTER 2

The social and historical origins of counselling

Introduction

To understand the nature and diversity of contemporary counselling it is necessary to look at the ways in which counselling has developed and evolved over the past 200 years. The differences and contradictions that exist within present-day counselling have their origins in the social and historical forces that have shaped modern culture as a whole.

People in all societies, at all times, have experienced emotional or psychological distress and behavioural problems. Each culture has its own, well-established indigenous ways of helping people to deal with these difficulties. The Iroquois Indians, for example, believed that one of the causes of ill-health was the existence of unfulfilled wishes, some of which were only revealed in dreams (Wallace 1958). When someone became ill and no other cause could be determined, diviners would discover what his or her unconscious wishes were, and arrange a 'festival of dreams' at which other members of the community would give these objects to the sick person. There seems little reason to suppose that modern-day counselling is any more valid, or effective, than the Iroquois festival of dreams.

The most that can be said is that it is seen as valid, relevant or effective by people in this culture at this time.

This chapter begins with a discussion of some of the fundamental changes in Western society, in the eighteenth century, that laid the groundwork for the emergence of counselling and psychotherapy. We then look, in turn, at how counselling and psychotherapy developed within the twentieth century. From a historical perspective, counselling and psychotherapy can be viewed as separate, yet closely interlinked, traditions of theory and practice. The chapter closes by considering the contemporary implications of these historical factors.

The social and historical origins of counselling and psychotherapy

Counselling is a form of emotional support and personal learning that has developed within Western industrial societies, and can be considered as a healing practice that is indigenous to Western culture. Although counselling and psychotherapy only become widely available to people, within that cultural context, during the second half of the twentieth century, their origins can be traced back to the beginning of the eighteenth century, which in many respects can be regarded as a major turning point in the way that people thought about things, and lived their lives. Prior to the eighteenth century, society was primarily based on small rural communities, who lived according to religious principles. In Europe, the Industrial Revolution brought about a fundamental shift, from traditional to modern ways of living and thinking. Increasingly, people moved to cities, worked in factories, and were influenced by scientific rather than religious belief systems. This shift was accompanied by major changes in the way that society responded to the needs of people who had problems in their lives. Before this, the problems in living that people encountered were primarily dealt with from a religious perspective, implemented at the level of the local community (McNeill 1951; Neugebauer 1978, 1979). Anyone who was seriously disturbed or insane was essentially tolerated as part of the community. Less extreme forms of emotional or interpersonal problems were dealt with by the local priest: for example, through the Catholic confessional. McNeill (1951) refers to this ancient tradition of religious healing as 'the cure of souls'. An important element in the cure of souls was confession of sins followed by repentance. McNeill (1951) points out that in earlier times, confession of sins took place in public, and was often accompanied by communal admonishment, prayer and even excommunication. The earlier Christian rituals for helping troubled souls were, like the Iroquois festival of dreams, communal affairs. Only later did individual private confession become established. McNeill (1951) gives many examples of clergy in the sixteenth and seventeenth centuries acting in a counselling role to their parishioners.

As writers such as Foucault (1967), Rothman (1971), Scull (1979, 1981a, 1989) and Porter (1985) have pointed out, all this began to change as the Industrial Revolution took effect, as capitalism began to dominate economic and political life, and as the values of science began to replace those of religion. The fundamental changes in social structure and in social and economic life that took place at this point in history were accompanied by basic changes in relationships and in the ways people defined and dealt with emotional and psychological needs. Albee (1977: 154) has written that:

> Capitalism required the development of a high level of rationality accompa-
> nied by repression and control of pleasure seeking. This meant the strict
> control of impulses and the development of a work ethic in which a majority
> of persons derived a high degree of satisfaction from hard work. Capitalism
> also demanded personal efforts to achieve long-range goals, an increase in
> personal autonomy and independence . . . The system depended on a heavy
> emphasis on thrift and ingenuity and, above all else, on the strong control
> and repression of sexuality.

The key psychological shift that occurred, according to Albee (1977), was from a 'tradition-
centred' (Riesman *et al.* 1950) society to one in which 'inner direction' was emphasized.
In traditional cultures, people live in relatively small communities in which everyone
knows everyone else, and behaviour is monitored and controlled by others. There is direct
observation of what people do, and direct action taken to deal with social deviance
through scorn or exclusion. The basis for social control is the induction of feelings of
shame. In urban, industrial societies, on the other hand, life is much more anonymous,
and social control must be implemented through internalized norms and regulations,
which result in guilt if defied. In an important sense, the psychology of being a person,
and the sense that people had of who they were and how they related to others, were
gradually transformed as a result of the Industrial Revolution and its impact on all aspects
of social life.

At the same time, there was a fundamental transformation of the structure of workplace, the kinds of jobs that were available to people, and the type of education that was
required in order to undertake these roles. Before the eighteenth century, there were a
limited range of occupations that were available to individuals, and access to these occupations was largely determined by social class, religion and geographical location. As
industrialization and urbanization rolled out across Europe and North America, a vast
range of new work roles were created. In the new industrial and commercial enterprises
that took shape, it was no longer possible to select job candidates on the basis of personal
acquaintance. In addition, more and more jobs required specialist training. In the earlier
era, there were few universities, dedicated in the main to producing physicians, clergy and
lawyers. People stayed at school longer (leading to a new perception of the meaning of
'childhood'; Aries 1962) and more people attended college and universities. The sociologist Anthony Giddens (1991) has argued that the emergence of the new 'modern' world
created massive dilemmas for people in terms of planning the course of their lives. No
longer was a personal future mapped out for a person by their family and community.
Within a period of one or two generations, a vast array of personal choices came into
being, in respect of the capacity, and pressure, to construct a personal identity and career
trajectory. Inevitably, the existence of these choices were associated with a growth in
anxiety ('am I making the right decision?' 'can I cope with this role?') and depression ('I
have failed', 'I am not achieving as much as other people').

From this analysis, it is possible to see how the central elements of urban, industrial,
capitalist culture created a need for new sources of help, guidance and support that
addressed the confusions and dilemmas experienced by individuals. What then happened
was the parallel development, in separate arenas of social life, of something that came to

be described as 'counselling' or 'psychotherapy'. How all this happened is a complex story, which for reasons of space can only be sketched out here. Basically, one form of personal support, that became 'psychotherapy', emerged within and out of the world of medicine. A similar form of helping practice, that became known as 'counselling' emerged from non-medical spheres such as education and social work.

The emergence of psychotherapy

The historical account pieced together by Scull (1979, 1993) indicates that during the years 1800–90 the proportion of the population of England and Wales living in towns larger than 20,000 inhabitants increased from 17 to 54 per cent. People were leaving the land to come to the city to work in the new factories. Even on the land, the work became more mechanized and profit-oriented. These large-scale economic and social changes had profound implications for all disadvantaged or handicapped members of society. Previously there had been the slow pace of rural life, the availability of family members working at home and the existence of tasks that could be performed by even the least able. Now there was the discipline of the machine, long hours in the factory and the fragmentation of the communities and family networks that had taken care of the old, sick, poor and insane. There very quickly grew up, from necessity, a system of state provision for these non-productive members of the population, known as the work-house system. Inmates of workhouses were made to work under conditions of strict discipline.

Gradually these 'separate apartments', the asylums, began to be built, beginning slowly in the middle of the eighteenth century and given further encouragement in Britain by the 1845 Asylums Act, which compelled local justices to set up publicly run asylums. A similar pattern can be traced in other European countries.

The development of 'asylums' marked the first systematic involvement of the state in the care and control of the insane in European society. At first, the asylums were seen as places where lunatics could be contained, and attempts at therapeutic intervention were rare. In a few asylums run by Quakers – for example, Tuke at the York Asylums – there evolved what was known as 'moral treatment' (Scull 1981b). In most institutions, however, lunatics were treated like animals and kept in appalling conditions. The Bethlem Hospital in London, for instance, was open to the public, who could enter to watch the lunatics for a penny a time. During this early period of the growth of the asylums movement, at the beginning of the nineteenth century, the medical profession had relatively little interest in the insane. From the historical investigations carried out by Scull (1975), it can be seen that the medical profession gradually came to recognize that there were profits to be made from the 'trade in lunacy', not only from having control of the state asylums, which were publicly funded, but also from running asylums for the insane members of the upper classes. The political power of the medical profession allowed them, in Britain, to influence the contents of Acts of Parliament that gave the medical profession control over asylums. The defeat of moral treatment can be seen as a key moment in the history of psychotherapy: science replaced religion as the dominant ideology underlying the treatment of the insane.

During the remainder of the nineteenth century the medical profession consolidated its control over the 'trade in lunacy'. Part of the process of consolidation involved rewriting the history of madness. Religious forms of care of the insane were characterized as 'demonology', and the persecution of witches was portrayed, erroneously, as a major strand in the pre-scientific or pre-medical approach to madness (Szasz 1971; Kirsch 1978; Spanos 1978). Medical and biological explanations for insanity were formulated, such as phrenology (Cooter 1981) and sexual indulgence or masturbation (Hare 1962). Different types of physical treatment were experimented with, such as hypodermic injections of morphine, the administration of bromides, amyl nitrate, the application of electricity, and the use of Turkish baths (Scull 1979). An important theme throughout this era was the use of the asylum to oppress women, who constituted the majority of inmates (Appignanesi 2008; Showalter 1985). Towards the end of the century, the medical specialism of psychiatry had taken its place alongside other areas of medicine, backed by the system of classification of psychiatric disorders devised by Kraepelin, Bleuler and others. Many of these developments were controversial at the time. For example, there was considerable debate over the wisdom of locking up lunatics in institutions, since contact with other disturbed people was unlikely to aid their rehabilitation. Several critics of psychiatry during the nineteenth century argued that care in the community was much better than institutionalization. There was also a certain amount of public outcry over the cruelty with which inmates were treated, and scepticism over the efficacy of medical approaches.

The issues and debates over the care of the insane in the nineteenth century may seem very familiar to us from our vantage point over a century later. We are still arguing about the same things. But an appreciation of how these issues originally came into being can help us by bringing into focus a number of very clear conclusions about the nature of care offered to emotionally troubled people in modern industrial society. When we look at the birth of the psychiatric profession, and compare it with what was happening before the beginning of the nineteenth century, we can see that:

1 Emotional and behavioural 'problems in living' became medicalized.
2 There emerged a 'trade in lunacy', an involvement of market forces in the development of services.
3 There was an increased amount of rejection and cruelty in the way the insane were treated, and much greater social control.
4 The services that were available were controlled by men and used to oppress women.
5 Science replaced religion as the main framework for understanding madness.

None of these factors was evident to any extent before the Industrial Revolution and all are still with us today. They can be seen as fundamental to the way that any industrialized, urbanized, secularized society responds to the question of madness. The French social philosopher Foucault (1967) has pointed out that one of the central values of the new social order that emerged in the nineteenth century was reason or rationality. For a society in which a rational, scientific perspective on life was all-important, the irrational lunatic, who had lost his reason, would readily become a scapegoat, a source of threat to be banished to an asylum somewhere outside the city. Foucault (1967) describes this era as an age of 'confinement', in which society developed means of repressing or imprisoning representatives of unreason or sexuality.

The earliest forms of psychotherapy: hypnosis and psychoanalysis

By the end of the nineteenth century psychiatry had achieved a dominant position in the care of the insane, now recategorized as 'mentally ill'. From within medicine and psychiatry, there now evolved a new specialism of psychotherapy. The earliest physicians to call themselves psychotherapists had been Van Renterghem and Van Eeden, who opened a Clinic of Suggestive Psychotherapy in Amsterdam in 1887 (Ellenberger 1970). Van Eeden defined psychotherapy as: '. . . all curative methods which use psychic agents to combat illness through the intervention of psychic functions' (Shamdasani 2005: 6). This definition is still relevant today, as a description of the fundamental aim and purpose of psychotherapy.

Hypnosis was a phenomenon of great interest to the European medical profession in the nineteenth century. Originally discovered by the pioneers of 'animal magnetism', Johann Joseph Gassner (1727–79) and Franz Anton Mesmer (1734–1815), hypnotism came to be widely used as an anaesthetic in surgical operations before the invention of chemical anaesthetics. During the 1880s, the influential French psychiatrists Charcot and Janet began to experiment with hypnosis as a means of treating 'hysterical' patients. There were two aspects of their hypnotic technique that have persisted to this day as key concepts in contemporary counselling and psychotherapy. First, they emphasized the importance of the relationship between doctor and patient. They knew that hypnosis would not be effective in the absence of what they called 'rapport'. Second, they argued that the reason why hypnosis was helpful to patients was that it gave access to an area of the mind that was not accessible during normal waking consciousness. In other words, the notion of the 'unconscious' mind was part of the apparatus of nineteenth-century hypnotism just as much as it is part of twentieth- and twenty-first-century psychotherapy.

The part played by hypnosis in the emergence of psychotherapy is of great significance. Bourguignon (1979), Prince (1980) and many others have observed that primitive cultures employ healing rituals that rely on trance states or altered states of consciousness. The appearance of Mesmerism and hypnosis through the eighteenth and nineteenth centuries in Europe, and their transformation into psychotherapy, can be viewed as representing the assimilation of a traditional cultural form into modern scientific medicine. Cushman (1995: 119) has written about the huge popularity of mesmerism in the USA in the mid-nineteenth century: 'in certain ways, mesmerism was the first secular psychotherapy in America, a way of ministering psychologically to the great American unchurched'.

The key figure in the process of transition from hypnosis to psychotherapy was, of course, Sigmund Freud. Having spent four months with Charcot in Paris during 1886–87, Freud went back to Vienna to set up in private practice as a psychiatrist. He soon turned his back on the specific techniques of hypnosis, choosing instead to develop his own technique of psychoanalysis based on free association and the interpretation of dreams. Freud became, eventually, an enormously powerful figure not only in medicine and psychotherapy, but in European cultural history as a whole. Without denying the genius and creativity of Freud, it is valuable to reflect on some of the ways in which his approach reflected the intellectual fashions and social practices of his time. For example:

1 Individual sessions with an analyst were an extension of the normal practice of one-to-one doctor–patient consultations prevalent at that time.

2 Freud's idea of a unitary life–force (libido) was derived from nineteenth-century biological theories.

3 The idea that emotional problems had a sexual cause was widely accepted in the nineteenth century.

4 The idea of the unconscious had been employed not only by the hypnotists, but also by other nineteenth-century writers and philosophers.

The distinctive contribution of Freud can probably be regarded as his capacity to assimilate all of these ideas into a coherent theoretical model that has proved of great value in many fields of work.

The cultural significance of Freudian ideas can be seen to lie in the implicit assumption that we are all neurotic, that behind the facade of even the most apparently rational and successful person there lie inner conflicts and instinctual drives. The message of Freud was that psychiatry is relevant not just for the mad man or woman in the asylum, but for everyone. The set of ideas contained in psychoanalysis also reflected the challenges faced by members of the European middle classes making the transition from traditional to modern forms of relationship. Sollod (1982: 51–2) writes that in Victorian society:

> it was quite appropriate to view elders as father figures and experience oneself as a respectful child in relationship to them. In the [modern] secular world, impersonal economic and employment arrangements rather than traditional ties bind one to authority, so such transferential relationships to authority figures could be inappropriate and maladaptive rather than functional.

Freudian ideas had a somewhat limited impact in Britain and Europe during his lifetime, where up until quite recently psychoanalysis was acceptable and accessible only to middle-class intellectuals and artists. In Britain, for example, the early development of psychoanalysis was associated with the literary elite of the 'Bloomsbury group' (Kohon 1986). It was not until psychoanalysis emigrated to the USA that psychotherapy, and then counselling, became more widely available.

Box 2.1: *Critical perspectives on the role of counselling and psychotherapy in contemporary society*

A central theme in this chapter is the idea that counselling and psychotherapy can be viewed as necessary and valuable strategies for coping with the impact of personal and family life of modern industrialized, bureaucratized and capitalist forms of social organization. However, there are also several writers who have argued that therapy represents a false and destructive response to these pressures. Furedi (2004), Morrall (2008), Smail

(1991, 2001, 2005) and others have drawn attention to the overblown personal transformation and cure claims made by some therapists, and the proliferation of psychiatric jargon and diagnostic categories in everyday conversation. These critics argue that the spread of 'therapy culture' has led to an individualization of problems that has made it harder for people to identify, and tackle, the social factors that lie behind these issues. Other critics, such as Masson (1992) and the contributors to Bates (2006) argue that the apparently benign image of therapy conceals a significant amount of exploitative and damaging practice, arising from the power imbalance between therapists and their clients.

Psychotherapy comes of age in the USA

One of the most influential writers on the history of psychotherapy has been Philip Cushman (1990, 1992, 1995), who has argued that underlying cultural factors in American culture and society in the nineteenth and twentieth centuries represented ideal conditions for the expansion of psychotherapy. America was a new nation in which in the nineteenth century people were subjected to massive social change and transformation. The early precursors of psychotherapy in the USA, such as mesmerism or the revivalist movement, were attempts to find meaning and stability at a time of enormous social uncertainty. At the same time, the capitalist system, much more dominant in America than in European countries, demanded that individuals mould themselves to the requirements of particular niches in the economic system. People had to learn how to sell not only goods and services, but them*selves*. Self-improvement books and pamphlets were very popular, but psychotherapy offered a more effective way of achieving the right kind of personality.

The extent of social mobility in America meant that traditional social structures, such as family and community, became eroded and the sense of purpose and belonging associated with these structures was lost. A core experience of many Americans, Cushman (1990) has argued, has been that of the 'empty self':

> . . . our terrain has shaped a self that experiences a significant absence of community, tradition and shared meaning. It experiences these social absences . . . as a lack of personal conviction and worth, and it embodies the absences as a chronic, undifferentiated emotional hunger. The post-World War II self thus yearns to acquire and consume as an unconscious way of compensating for what has been lost. It is empty.
>
> (Cushman 1990: 600)

The two major cultural responses to the empty self, according to Cushman, were psychotherapy and consumerism/advertising. In order to assuage 'undifferentiated emotional hunger', the citizen of an advanced capitalist economy has the choice of making an appointment with a therapist, or, perhaps, buying a new car. The link between the emergence of psychotherapy in twentieth-century America, and the development of a consumer society, has been discussed by other historical writers, such as Caplan (1998) and Pfister (1997). A key theme in these historical accounts has been the extent to which psychotherapy approaches have consistently diverted attention from the social conditions that trigger personal problems in living, by promising solutions to these problems that are based on the identification of dysfunctional aspects of the individual psyche (Cushman 1995). The result of this movement in the direction of self-contained individualism is argued, by these authors, to erode the basis of social solidarity and cultural capital that might in fact make it possible for people to mount a collective response to the demands of capitalist economic forces. These writers invite us to consider psychotherapy not simply as forms of applied psychological or medical science, but as manifestations of broader social and cultural forces that influence all aspects of social life. For example, Pfister (1997) makes the point that certain strands of popular music in the 1970s and 1980s (a time of massive expansion and popularity of psychotherapy) reinforced the self-focused individualized ethos of psychotherapy.

An essential catalyst, that captured the imagination of Americans, and paved the way for the growth of psychotherapy in the USA, was the visit of Sigmund Freud in 1909. Freud had a great loathing of American society. He did not enjoy his one and only trip to the USA, with Carl Jung and Sandor Ferenczi, to give some lectures and receive an honorary degree at Clark University (Gay 1988). But American culture resonated to the ideas of psychoanalysis, and when the rise of fascism in Europe led to prominent analysts like Otto Rank and Erik Erikson moving to New York and Boston, they found a willing clientele. Psychoanalytic ideas also had a significant impact on popular debates around the nature of family life, parenting and child-rearing (Demos 1997).

The idea of psychoanalysis held a great attraction for Americans, but for it to become assimilated into the culture required an Americanization of Freud's thinking. Freud had lived in a hierarchically organized, class-dominated society, and had written from a world-view immersed in classical scholarship and biological science, informed by a pessimism arising from being a Jew at a time of violent anti-Semitism. There were, therefore, themes in his writing that did not sit well with the experience of people in the USA. As a result there emerged in the 1950s a whole series of writers who reinterpreted Freud in terms of their own cultural values. Foremost among these were Carl Rogers, Eric Berne, Albert Ellis, Aaron Beck and Abraham Maslow. Many of the European analysts who went to the USA, such as Erikson and Erich Fromm, were also prominent in reframing psychoanalysis from a wider social and cultural perspective, thus making it more acceptable to an American clientele.

One of the strongest sources of resistance to psychoanalysis in American culture lay in academic psychology. Although William James (1890), who had been one of the first scholars to make psychology academically respectable in American universities, had given close attention to Freudian ideas, in the first half of the twentieth century American academic psychologists had become deeply committed to a behaviourist approach. Behaviourism emphasized the use of scientific methods such as measurement and laboratory experiments, and was primarily oriented to the study of observable behaviour rather than obscure internal processes, such as dreams, fantasies and impulses. The behaviourist academic establishment was consequently fiercely opposed to psychoanalysis, and refused to acknowledge it as worthy of serious study. Although some academic departments of psychiatry did show some limited interest in psychoanalysis, most practitioners and writers were forced to work in private practice or within the hospital system, rather than having an academic base.

When Rogers, Berne and Ellis developed distinctive American brands of therapy in the 1950s and 1960s there was initially only very limited academic discussion of their work and ideas. One of the distinctive contributions of Rogers was to invent systematic methods of carrying out research into the processes and outcomes of therapy. The effect of this innovation was to reinforce the legitimacy of therapy as a socially acceptable enterprise by giving it the respectability and status of an applied science. In 1947 Rogers became the first therapist to be made President of the American Psychological Association (Whiteley 1984). The confirmation of therapy as an applied science was given further impetus by the entry into the therapy arena of cognitive–behavioural approaches in the 1960s, bringing with them the language and assumptions of behavioural psychology, and the image of the 'scientist-practitioner' (see Chapter 6).

The impact of World War II on the USA resulted in a substantial number of soldiers returning home with psychological injuries, particularly from the Pacific theatre. In turn, this led to pressure from the Veterans' Administration, the government organization responsible for the health and social welfare of former service personnel, and from society more widely, for some kind of psychotherapy to be made available. The client-centred therapy of Carl Rogers represented the most credible contender for a form of psychotherapy that was relatively brief and affordable, and for which new therapists could be trained fairly rapidly. The consequence was that there was major investment in client-centred therapy in the late 1940s, which meant that, for a time in the 1950s it became the dominant therapeutic approach in the USA and then worldwide (Barrett-Lennard 1998; Kirschenbaum 2007). Client-centred therapy was similar to psychoanalysis in that it was built around an exploration of self, or a search for a 'real' self, but was less time-consuming, more egalitarian in its philosophy, and more optimistic – whereas psychoanalysis was well suited to the emotional needs of the European middle classes, client-centred therapy was better attuned to the lives and aspirations of those in the USA.

It is possible to see, therefore, that there were many factors that contributed to the rapid growth of psychotherapy in American society in the middle of the twentieth century. Because of the global influence of the USA in the post-war years, this had the effect of triggering an expansion of psychotherapy in other countries too. The particular cultural circumstances that prevailed in mid-twentieth-century USA had a big impact on the shape of psychotherapy practice, which has persisted to the present day. The relative weakness of state-funded health care in the USA meant that psychotherapy largely took the form of a private practice model, rather than a more community-based approach. The competitive capitalist ethos of the USA meant that innovative therapists were rewarded for producing new 'brand name' therapies, rather than for contributing to a more collective pooling of wisdom – thus contributing to a proliferation in therapy approaches and theories. And the growth of psychology, as an emergent academic discipline, meant that the legitimacy of psychotherapy became increasingly dependent on its capacity to undergo the trial of rigorous objective research.

The secularization of society

There are many links between organized religion and the historical development of psychotherapy. Halmos (1965) has documented the correspondence in the twentieth century in Britain between the decline in numbers of clerical personnel and the rise in numbers of therapists. He argues that religious faith was gradually replaced by a set of beliefs and values that he calls the 'faith of the counsellors'. Nelson and Torrey (1973) have described some of the ways in which therapy has taken over from religion in such areas of life as offering explanations for events that are difficult to understand, offering answers to the existential question 'what am I here for?', defining social values and supplying ritual ways of meeting other people. Holifield (1983) has documented the process through which some of the first 'psychotherapists' were in fact part of the Church in the USA, but gradually became transformed into a separate profession. Myers-Shirk (2000) has discussed the role of the Protestant churches in the USA in disseminating counselling approaches in the 1920s and 1930s, in the form of pastoral care.

The origins of counselling and psychotherapy in the religious 'cure of souls' were discussed at the beginning of this chapter. The parallels between therapy and, for example, the use of the confessional in the Catholic Church are striking. It is also clear that in traditional, non-industrialized societies, emotional and psychological healing is largely carried out within a religious framework. However, until recently, few therapists would acknowledge that religion and spirituality had any relevance for counselling and psychotherapy. It was as if the pressure to establish therapy as a separate, independent profession meant that therapists had to make a clear-cut boundary between what they were doing and what a priest or minister might do. Of course, there are important differences. Yet there are also significant areas of convergence. In order to locate itself as a product in the twentieth-century marketplace, in order to build up a mental health 'industry' (Kovel 1981), therapy differentiated itself from religion. In general, mainstream theories of counselling and psychotherapy have had little to say about religious or spiritual dimensions of life. Therapy is embedded in a scientific world-view, even if, as Halmos (1965) has argued, theories of therapy can be seen as a form of 'faith'. It is only in recent years that a rapprochement between psychotherapy and religion has begun to be forged (Richards and Bergin 2000, 2004, 2005; West 2000, 2004).

The role of Carl Rogers

In many ways, Carl Rogers was a pivotal figure in the development of counselling and psychotherapy. The story of the early life of Carl Rogers (1902–87), founder of the client-centred or person-centred approach to therapy (see Chapter 7), contains many of the themes already explored in this chapter. The early background of Rogers (Rogers 1961; Kirschenbaum 1979, 2007) was that he was brought up in a rural community in the American Midwest, a member of a strictly religious Protestant family in which there was active disapproval of leisure activities such as gambling or theatre-going. As a substitute for forbidden leisure pursuits, Rogers displayed a strong interest in scientific agriculture, by the age of 14 conducting his own experiments on crops and plants. He decided to become a minister, and at the age of 20 in preparation for this vocation was a delegate to the World Student Christian Federation Conference in China. This exposure to other cultures and beliefs influenced him to break away from the rigid religious orientation of his parents, and when he entered theological college he chose one of the most liberal seminaries, the Union Theological Seminary. However, following exploration of his faith in the equivalent of a student-led 'encounter group', Rogers decided to change career and began training as a psychologist at Columbia University, where he was exposed to the ideas of the progressive education movement, which emphasized a trust in the freedom to learn and grow inherent in each child or student.

This account of Rogers' early life shows how the dual influences of religion and science came together in a career as a therapist. The respect for scientific rigour was expressed in his involvement in research, where he was one of the first to make recordings of therapy sessions, and developed a wide range of methods to investigate aspects of the therapy process. The influence of Protestant thought on client-centred theory is apparent in the emphasis on the capacity of each individual to arrive at a personal understanding of his or her destiny, using feelings and intuition rather than being guided by doctrine or reason. The client-centred approach is also focused on behaviour in the present, rather than on what has happened in the past. Sollod (1978: 96) argues that the Protestantism of client-centred therapy can be compared with psychoanalysis, where 'the trust is in the trained reason of the therapist (rabbi) and in his Talmudic interpretations of complex phenomena'.

Following his qualification as a clinical psychologist, Rogers worked mainly with disturbed children and adolescents, and their families, in the child study department of the Society for the Prevention of Cruelty to Children, in Rochester, New York. Although he received further training in psychodynamically oriented therapy from Jessie Taft, a follower of Otto Rank (Sollod 1978), and was also influenced by the ideas of Alfred Adler (Watts 1998), he did not identify himself as a student of any particular approach. During his time at Rochester (1928–40) he largely evolved his own distinctive approach, guided by his sense of what seemed to help his clients. Rogers was, in his clinical work, and earlier in his experience at Columbia, immersed in the values of American culture, and his theory contains many elements of that cultural context. Meadow (1964), for example, has suggested that client-centred therapy has adopted 'basic American cultural norms', such as distrust of experts and authority figures, emphasis on method rather than theory, emphasis on individuals' needs rather than shared social goals, lack of interest in the past and a valuing of independence and autonomy. Barrett-Lennard (1998) has drawn attention to the similarities between Rogers' approach and the philosophy of the 'New Deal' political movement in the USA in the 1930s.

Psychotherapy in its cultural context

The emergence of psychotherapy has been driven by powerful cultural forces and historical events within European and North American societies, and has then followed the pathway of globalization and established itself within other cultural settings. The key cultural themes that have stimulated the historical development of psychotherapy in Western societies are:

- the increase in individualism within modern societies, accompanied by an erosion of collective/communal ways of life;
- for individuals, a sense of fragmentation in their sense of self;
- pressure on individuals to act rationally and control their emotions;
- in a postmodern world, individuals are reflexively aware of choices open to them around identity – psychotherapy is one way of constructing an identity;
- the replacement of spiritual/religious systems of making sense of life, by scientific models;
- an increasing emphasis on medical solutions to social and personal problems;
- the growth of consumerism as a source of meaning and identity, in response to capitalist economic pressures for expanding markets.

For further exploration of these sociological themes, readers are invited to consult the work of Bauman (2004), Gergen (1991) and Giddens (1991). Psychotherapy can be regarded as a mirror of society, in that the work of psychotherapists has highlighted aspects of social life that have been particularly problematic at various times. For example, Freud brought into the open the sexual oppression of the Victorian era, Rogers and many other therapists in the 1950s wrote about the confusion around self and identity that was triggered by post-World War II economic expansion, and currently many therapists are drawing attention to the depression and hopelessness that seems endemic in contemporary society. These are just some of the many ways in which psychotherapy has functioned as a kind of existential barometer for society. However, psychotherapy has also had an active role within society, in shaping people to become the type of citizens, workers or consumers that are required at any specific time and place. For example, psychoanalysis, with its emphasis on the potentially destructive impact of parents on their children, was just what was needed around the beginning of the twentieth century, when economic and scientific progress required people to take on quite different work roles from those held by their parents. In the 1960s, the new consumerism required people who could reflect and choose – qualities that were promoted by both client-centred and cognitive therapies. The threat of global warming and economic domination by China, in the first decade of the twenty-first century, have stimulated calls for a return to spiritual values and practices, and to more collective ways of life – trends that are exhibited in the popularity of mindfulness therapies and narrative therapy. The mode of delivery of psychotherapy has also been determined by social factors. In Freud's time, when users of therapy were upper–middle-class individuals with plenty of leisure time and money, it made perfect sense to provide interminable therapy on a daily basis. In modern times, when psychotherapy is provided by health organizations seeking to assist people back to work, brief time-limited therapy has become dominant.

Behind the social and cultural construction of psychotherapy there are two basic assumptions. The first assumption is that unhappiness is bad, and that we all deserve to be happy. This assumption is reflected within psychotherapy research, in the universal use of symptom change (i.e., unhappiness indicators) to assess the effectiveness of therapy. The second assumption is that unhappiness can be fixed and sorted by changing the individual. In the main, psychotherapy has emerged from a long historical journey, on the part of Western societies, in the direction of self-contained *individualism* (Baumeister 1987; Logan 1987; Cushman 1990, 1995). This assumption is reflected in the ideas and practices of the majority of schools of psychotherapy, and in the proliferation of what Gergen (1990) has characterized as the 'language of deficit' – the capacity of psychologists, psychiatrists and psychotherapists to describe a myriad of patterns of psychological dysfunction within individual persons.

Psychotherapy has become institutionally powerful and influential within Western societies. Partly this is because it has allied itself, from the start, with the status and prestige of medicine. But it is also partly because the leaders, the dominant elite, of Western societies, recognize themselves in at least some of the psychotherapy ideas that circulate within their awareness. Currently, politicians and health managers like the look of CBT because it promotes the idea that, to get ahead, it is necessary to be rational and to be able to control one's emotions. This makes perfect sense to them, because it perfectly describes the basis on which their individual success in life has been built. As we shall see, later in this chapter, although, historically, counselling and counsellors have been strongly influenced by psychotherapy, counselling reflects a rather different cultural tradition, based on somewhat different assumptions.

Box 2.2: *The concept of postmodernity: a perspective on the nature of contemporary social life*

Among sociologists and philosophers, there is a broad agreement that the past 30 years have marked a significant shift in culture and society, and the ways in which people relate to each other and view the world. It is possible to characterize European culture as having passed through two broad phases in its development. Initially, society was largely governed by religious and traditional ways of life, in which there was relatively little social change or movement. Around the seventeenth and eighteenth centuries, the writings of Enlightenment philosophers, the advances of science and technology, and the movement of populations into cities, contributed to the erosion of traditional hierarchical and religious beliefs, and their replacement by a system of thought that emphasized rationality, scientific evidence and social progress. It was within this *modern* era (the nineteenth and twentieth centuries) that counselling and psychotherapy developed. Toward the end of the twentieth century, however, it began to be apparent to many people that there was an emptiness to modern ideas about progress, and that perhaps the sweeping away of traditional truths had resulted in a world in which everything could be questioned and nothing could be believed. The French philosopher Jean Francois Lyotard (1984) was the first to use the term *postmodern* to capture this new cultural movement, and observed that a central characteristic of postmodern attitudes is a sceptical stance towards what he called 'grand narratives', or totalizing truth claims, such as Marxism, psychoanalysis, Christianity and so on, and their replacement by more relativistic, nuanced, local knowledges. Although there are lively debates within sociology around the meaning of 'postmodernity', there is agreement that, in a world in which ideas and information circulate at a global level, 'grand theories' such as communism and psychoanalysis, which offer a single, monolithic, author-itative version of reality, have become less convincing for many people. In place of these grand theories, there appears to be a movement towards a pragmatic knitting together of ideas that work, within groups and communities. The implications for counselling and psychotherapy of this cultural shift have been explored by Kvale (1992), Downing (2000), Loewenthal and Snell (2003) and others, and are explored at various points throughout this book. The transition from modernity to postmodernity has had a major impact on counsel-ling and psychotherapy. The monolithic 'brand name' therapies that have dominated the field, such as psychoanalysis and CBT, are very much part of the modernist project. By contrast, more recent initiative such as narrative and constructivist therapy, feminist therapy, multicultural counselling and therapeutic pluralism, represent the first stirrings of a turn in the direction of a postmodern perspective.

Box 2.3: *From psychotherapy to psychotechnology: the bureaucratization of therapy*

Counselling and psychotherapy can be viewed as having undergone a continuous process of reconstruction in response to social, political and technological change. One of the most important dimensions of social change in the past 30 years has been the demand on health budgets resulting from an ageing population, increasingly expensive medical treatments associated with advances in technology and the general public expectation for improve-ment in health care standards and quality. These factors have led to pressure to control or 'ration' the amount of health care that is provided in a number of areas. In the USA, this policy is known as 'managed care'. For example, in relation to the provision of psycho-therapy, health insurance companies rigidly control the number of sessions of therapy that are available, closely monitor the performance of therapists and only reimburse therapists where clients have specific diagnosed disorders that have been shown in research studies to be effectively treatable by the approach to therapy adopted by the practitioner. Many writers within the American psychotherapy profession have been highly critical of what they regard as a significant shift away from professional autonomy, and an ethical 'client-centred' approach, towards a style of therapy that could be described as the application of *psycho-technology* (techniques and measures) rather than the development of a healing relationship (Cushman and Gilford 1999). In Britain, a similar process has taken place under the auspices of the Improving Access to Psychological Therapies (IAPT) programme (Clark 2011).

The emergence of counselling

The history of psychotherapy has been much more fully documented than has the history of counselling. Counselling, as a distinct profession, came of age only in the 1940s. One of the public markers of the emergence of counselling at that time was that Carl Rogers, in the face of opposition from the medical profession to the idea that anyone without medical training could call himself a 'psychotherapist', began to use the term 'counselling and psychotherapy' to describe his approach (Rogers 1942). Although in many respects counselling, both then and now, can be seen as an extension of psychotherapy, a parallel activity or even a means of 'marketing' psychotherapy to new groups of consumers, there are also at least two important historical strands that differentiate counselling from psychotherapy: involvement in the educational system and the role of the voluntary sector. The American Personnel and Guidance Association, which was later to become the American Counselling Association was formed in 1952, through the merger of a number of vocational guidance professional groupings that were already well established by that time. The membership of American Personnel and Guidance Association consisted of counsellors who worked in schools, colleges, and career advisory services. In Britain, the Standing Council for the Advancement of Counselling, which was later to become the British Association for Counselling was inaugurated in 1971, by a network of people who were primarily based in social services, social work and the voluntary sector.

The precursors to the formation of these organizations can be understood in terms of a sense of crisis within society, or 'moral panic', around various areas of social life. In effect, what happened was that there was a sense of unease around some aspect of the breakdown of social order, or the identification of groups of individuals who were being unfairly treated in some way. These crises were characterized by widespread publicity about the problem, debate in newspapers and magazines, and efforts to bring about political or legislative change. At some point in this process, someone would have the idea that the best means of helping was to treat each person needing assistance as an individual, and that the most effective way to proceed was to sit down with that individual, discuss the matter, and find the best way forward for that person in terms of his or her unique needs and circumstances. The idea of 'counselling' appears to have emerged more or less simultaneously, in many different fields of social action, in this manner.

Probably the first recorded example of this kind of 'invention of counselling' was in the work of the American social reformer Frank Parsons (1854–1908). In his earlier years, Parsons had been employed as an engineer, lawyer and writer, before turning to lecturing, at Boston University. He was well known, internationally, for his writing and lecturing that argued against the uncontrolled capitalism of the time, and proposed that it should be replaced by a philosophy of *mutualism* – 'the replacement of competition by cooperation, and lust for money by concern for humanity' (Gummere 1988: 403). He campaigned for votes for women, and public ownership of key industries. In the final years of his life, Parsons came to be particularly interested in the issue of helping young people to be matched with jobs that were right for them. He established a 'Vocation Bureau' in an immigrant district of Boston, where young people were interviewed and assessed, provided with information about possible career choices, and provided with opportunities to explore their feelings around the work they would like to do. The philosophy of the Bureau was clearly grounded in what we now consider to be a counselling approach: 'no person shall decide for another what occupation he should choose, but it is possible to help him so to approach the problem that he shall come to a wise conclusion for himself' (Parsons 1909: 4). The Vocation Bureau operated as an example and catalyst for the expansion of counselling provision in schools, and vocational guidance services, throughout the USA (O'Brien 2001). Counselling of various kinds came to be offered within the school and college systems in the 1920s and 1930s, as careers guidance and also as a service for young people who were having difficulties adjusting to the demands of school or college life. Psychological testing and assessment was bound up with these activities, but there was always an element of discussion or interpretation of the student's problems or test results (Whiteley 1984).

In Britain, counselling had strong roots in the voluntary sector. For example, the largest single counselling agency in Britain, the National Marriage Guidance Council (now RELATE), dates back to 1938, when a clergyman, Dr Herbert Gray, mobilized the efforts of people who were concerned about the threat to marriage caused by modern life (Tyndall 1985). The additional threat to married life introduced by World War II led to the formal establishment of the Marriage Guidance Council in 1942. A comprehensive historical analysis of the growth of the National Marriage Guidance Council, in response to societal and governmental alarm about divorce rates and marital breakdown, has been published by Lewis *et al.* (1992). Since that time, many other groups of volunteers have set up counselling services as a response to perceived social breakdown and crisis in areas such as rape, bereavement, gay and lesbian issues and child abuse. As with the National Marriage Guidance Council, many of these initiatives were led by Church groups. For example, in Scotland, many counselling agencies owe their existence to the pioneering work of the Board of Social Responsibility of the Church of Scotland.

A further early example of the use of a counselling approach in response to a social problem can be found in the employee counselling scheme introduced in 1936 in the Hawthorne plant of the Western Electric manufacturing company (Dickson 1945; Dickson and Roethlisberger 1966; Levinson 1956; Wilensky and Wilensky 1951). In this project, counsellors were available to employees on the shop floor, to talk about any issues (both work based and personal) that might be affecting their capacity to do their job. The rationale for the provision of counselling was that the management of the company acknowledge the pressures of working on a production line, and sought to maintain workforce well-being both as a welfare response, and also as a means of maximizing productivity and reducing staff turnover. The acceptability and popularity of this service, on the part of workers, was documented in an evaluation of the scheme by Dickson and Roethlisberger (1966), which found that over a three-month period, 37 per cent of the workforce made use of counselling, with 10 per cent of those who used it reporting that it had been very helpful.

These examples of critical moments in the emergence of counselling illustrate the existence of a distinct historical tradition, which has primarily arisen from a social action perspective rather than an individual pathology orientation. Although there has been much mutual interaction and influence across counselling–psychotherapy professional communities, from a historical vantage point it is possible to see that they are each culturally positioned in somewhat different territories.

From these beginnings, counselling expanded rapidly in the latter half of the twentieth century, in terms of the membership of counselling professional bodies, the range, scope and number of counselling agencies and the ease of public access to counselling. There would appear to be a number of factors responsible for this growth:

- The success of the earliest counselling services, in the areas of education, marital and bereavement work, inspired groups of people to develop counselling services for a wide array of other social issues, such as suicide prevention, domestic abuse, sexual violence, drug and alcohol abuse, disability and affirmation of sexual orientation.

- We live in a fragmented society, in which there are many people who lack emotional and social support systems that might assist them in coping with stressful problems in living – counselling fulfils a vital role in society, as a means of assisting individuals effectively to negotiate transition points in their lives.

- Counselling agencies are generally located within the communities of those whom they serve, and are networked with other caring organizations – members of the public usually know about the counselling that is available in their community, and do not feel stigmatized in making use of it.

- Counselling regularly receives publicity in the media, most of which is positive. The media image of counselling is low-key and reassuring, in contrast to, for example, the cartoon representation of the psychoanalyst.

- The legitimacy of counselling has never relied on research evidence or government policy initiatives, but instead is based on word-of-mouth recommendation from users.

- Caring and 'people' professions, such as nursing, medicine, teaching and social work, which had previously performed a quasi-counselling role, were financially and managerially squeezed during the 1970s and 1980s. Members of these professions no longer have time to listen to their clients. Many of them have sought training as counsellors, and have created specialist counselling roles within their organizations, as a way of preserving the quality of contact with clients.

- Many thousands of people who work in caring professions have received training in counselling skills, as part of their basic professional education, and use these skills within an 'embedded counselling' role. There are also a large number of part-time volunteer counsellors, who combine some counselling work alongside other occupational and family responsibilities. All this creates an enormous reservoir of awareness within society of counselling methods (such as empathic listening) and values (such as non-judgemental acceptance);

- There is an entrepreneurial spirit in many counsellors, who will actively sell their services to new groups of consumers. For example, any human resource or occupational health director of a large company will have a filing cabinet full of brochures from counsellors and counselling agencies eager to provide employee counselling services.

- Counselling is a highly diverse activity, which is delivered in a broad range of contexts (voluntary/not-for-profit, statutory, private practice, social care, health, education); this diversity has allowed counselling to continue to expand at times when funding pressures might have resulted in cuts in provision in any one sector.

The emergence of counselling needs to be understood in relation to the parallel growth of psychotherapy. There have been many practitioners, from Carl Rogers onwards, who have spanned the counselling–psychotherapy divide. The majority of counselling agencies draw heavily on ideas from psychotherapy, to shape their training, supervision and practice policies. In the UK, and other countries, there are organizations, such as the British Association for Counselling and Psychotherapy, that seek to emphasize the convergence of the two professional traditions and communities. Nevertheless, counselling has retained its own identity as a distinctive practice with its own history.

Box 2.4: *Moral treatment – an early example of a form of practice that embodied the spirit of counselling*

In the eighteenth and nineteenth centuries, the development of treatment for people who had severe and enduring problems in living, largely comprised a punitive, institutionalized and medicalized form of practice that had the effect of restraining troubled individuals, and keeping them out of sight. An exception to this was the York Retreat, which along with some other centres such as the Crichton Royal Hospital in Dumfries, Scotland, evolved a more holistic, collaborative and socially oriented form of care. The Retreat was founded in 1796 by a Quaker family, the Tukes. At the Retreat, residents were introduced to an environment characterized by 'mutual solidarity' and a 'tradition of empathy with marginalized members of society', where they might 'begin to take responsibility for their own emotions and conduct, in order that they might come into clearer focus with their own personal truth and their responsibility towards others' (Borthwick *et al.* 2001: 428). In practice, daily life at the Retreat was structured around a set of key principles: the value of good diet, exercise and contact with the external community; a physical setting that was tranquil, light and welcoming; active involvement in domestic and other roles, so that socially acceptable behaviour could be encouraged; exploration and resolution of problems by talking them through. Underlying these practices was a philosophy that highlighted the healing power of everyday relationships, and a spiritual perspective that espoused the belief that there is an inner light in every individual (Borthwick *et al.* 2001). The approach developed by the Tukes became known as *moral treatment* (in the sense of seeking to promote *morale*). Scull (1993: 98) has commented that moral treatment was 'emphatically not a specific technique' – over the space of 20 years the Tukes experimented with several medical and physical interventions that were then fashionable and found them to be 'very inadequate' in the cure of insanity (Tuke 1813/1964: 111). Rather, moral treatment was a common-sense approach, focused on pragmatic problem-solving and caring rather than reliance on ideology or technology. Over time, the Retreat and other similar establishments were marginalized by domination of medically based treatments. However, for many practitioners in the field of mental health and social care, they remain a symbol of the possibilities of a collaborative, strengths-based, socially-oriented approach to healing.

The professionalization of counselling

Counselling is not just something that happens between two people. It is also a social institution that is embedded in the culture of modern industrialized societies. As an autonomous profession, counselling has relatively recent origins. In Britain, the Standing Council for the Advancement of Counselling was formed in 1971, and became the British Association for Counselling in 1976. The membership of the British Association for Counselling grew from 1,000 in 1977 to 8,556 in 1992 (British Association for Counselling

1977, 1992). Renamed the British Association for Counselling and Psychotherapy in 2001, at the time of publication this organization reported over 30,000 members. The American Counselling Association was formed in 1962, and now has around 50,000 members. Division 17 (Counselling Psychology) of the American Psychological Association was founded in 1945, and now has in the region of 2,600 members (Munley *et al.* 2004). These figures indicate only the extent of the growth in numbers of more highly trained or professionalized counsellors in each country. There are, in addition, many people active in voluntary organizations who provide non-professional counselling and who are not represented in these statistics. And the majority of people now working in the 'human service' professions, including nursing, teaching, the clergy, the police and many others, would consider counselling skills to be part of their work role.

It has proved difficult in many countries, including the UK, for counselling to attain full professional status in the form of state regulation and control of title. Partly this is because it has been hard to define counselling, as a separate activity from psychotherapy or psychology, and also because members of other established professions, such as nursing or social work, can claim that they fulfil a counselling role. A study of the history of the professionalization of counselling in Britain concluded that the counselling profession can be viewed as a 'self-effacing' occupational group (Aldridge 2011). Other professions, such as law, medicine and the clergy, are highly assertive in claiming their possession of specialist knowledge, and their right to be sole providers of specific services. Counselling, on the other hand, consists of a set of skills and ideas that are shared by all 'people-facing' occupations.

Implications for counselling theory and practice

The historical account given here is inevitably incomplete and partial. However, from even this limited discussion of historical factors it can be seen that the form and shape of contemporary theory and practice has been strongly influenced by cultural forces. However, what are the contemporary implications of these historical factors? What do they mean for us *now*, in terms of theory and practice?

One important area of learning concerns an appreciation of counselling as a continuing tradition, that reflects a distinctive set of values and practices. Although counselling and psychotherapy are closely aligned practices, that share a great deal of common ground in terms of ways of working and ways of thinking, an historical account highlights the visibility of a distinctive tradition of practice, associated with counselling, which is largely non-medical, focused on the social world, pragmatically oriented rather than theory-driven, and which has its own 'moral vision' (Christopher 1996). The hegemony of psychotherapy, in terms of official recognition, has served to obscure the contribution of counselling and counsellors; further attention to the history of counselling is necessary if the values of counselling are to be effectively maintained.

A further area of learning lies in the acceptance that contemporary knowledge is incomplete in the absence of a historical perspective. We live in a world that is in thrall to the ideal of progress, and it is all too easy to assume that new knowledge, for example the most recent research findings, and new techniques, are necessarily more valid than what has gone before. In the field of counselling, the assumption of the inevitable validity of the new is undermined by an awareness of historical developments. For example, close study of each of the key moments in the emergence of counselling described earlier in this chapter – the vocational counselling of Frank Parsons, the Western Electric experiment, the work of Marriage Guidance, and the flowering of moral treatment in the nineteenth century – has a lot to offer any contemporary practitioner working in these areas. In similar fashion, the real meaning and significance of the writings of seminal figures such as Freud and Rogers cannot be gleaned from textbooks (such as this one) but require close reading of their early cases, which illustrate the radical nature of what it was they actually did (rather than the tidied-up version that has become part of accepted wisdom).

A final lesson that can be drawn from analysis of the history of counselling and psychotherapy is a reminder that therapy always treads a fine line between control and liberation. It is very easy for therapists to believe that their approach (whatever it may be) is fully committed to the empowerment of the client, rather than operating as a means of social control. However, therapists have always believed this, and it is only with the benefit of historical hindsight that it becomes apparent that there are pressures in the direction of social conformity and control that exist in all counselling situations. The counsellor–client relationship has modelled itself on the doctor–patient and priest–parishioner relationships. Traditionally, doctors and priests have been seen as experts and authority figures, and the people who consulted them expected to be told what to do. Theories of therapy reflect cultural norms and values, and the application of these theories in counselling or psychotherapy can be seen as a way of shaping individual lives and behaviour in the direction of socially acceptable outcomes.

Box 2.5: *Where have we got to now? How much counselling is there?*

It is hard to measure the amount of counselling that is available within society, and it is probably even harder to estimate the potential demand for counselling. There have been attempts to estimate the proportion of the population using therapy (for example, Kirkwood 2000; Olfson and Pincus 1999; McLeod 2008). Although the proportion of the population who use therapy varies across gender, social class and ethnicity, it would appear that around 4 per cent of people make use of counselling in any one year. How large is the potential demand for counselling? Research carried out by Goldberg and Huxley (1992), Wittchen and Jacobi (2005) and others suggest that at any one time, around 25 per cent of the population describe themselves as suffering from psychological problems. A national survey carried out by Anderson and Brownlie (2011) in the UK reported that around one in three of the population regarded counselling or psychotherapy as something that they might use if they had a problem. Around one in three reported that they would be very unlikely to use a counsellor under any circumstances, and the remainder held mixed views (see also Anderson, S. *et al.* 2009).

Another means of estimating the demand for counselling and other psychological therapies is to monitor waiting times. In the UK, it is not uncommon for National Health Service (NHS) specialist psychotherapy services to have waiting times of over 12 months, or for voluntary sector counselling agencies to decide to close their waiting lists as a means of controlling demand. Putting all these figures together, it seems likely that in modern Western industrialized societies, there is about one full-time counsellor or psychotherapist for every 2,000 of the population, and that there is an unmet demand for counselling services because of cost, waiting times and other obstacles.

Conclusions

In this chapter, it has been suggested that an understanding of the ways in which counselling is defined and practiced requires an appreciation of the history of counselling and its role in contemporary society. Members of the public, or clients arriving for their first appointment, generally have very little idea of what to expect. Few people can tell the difference between a psychiatrist, psychologist, counsellor and psychotherapist, never mind differentiate between alternative approaches to counselling that might be on offer. But behind that lack of specific information, there resonates a set of cultural images, which may include a fear of insanity, shame at asking for help, the ritual of the confessional and the image of doctor as healer. In a multicultural society the range of images may be very wide indeed. The counsellor is also immersed in these cultural images, as well as being socialized into the language and ideology of a particular counselling approach or into the implicit norms and values of a counselling agency. To understand counselling requires moving the horizon beyond the walls of the interview room, to take in the wider social environment within which the interview room has its own special place.

Topics for reflection and discussion

1   Select a counselling agency with which you are familiar. What do you know about the historical development of that agency? To what extent can its creation be understood in terms of the themes discussed in this chapter? What is the social role of the agency within its community?

2   Ask people you know to give you their definition of terms such as 'counsellor', 'psychotherapist', 'hypnotherapist' and 'psychiatrist'. Invite them to tell you what they believe happens when someone consults one of these professionals. What are the origins of the images and ideas you elicit?

3   What is the relationship between religious beliefs and counselling in your own life, and in the lives of other counsellors you know or have read about?

4   The historical studies reviewed in this chapter have largely focused on factors that shaped the development of counselling and psychotherapy in the USA. What are the different historical factors and events that have shaped the development of therapy in other societies with which you are familiar, and what are the implications of these historical perspectives for current policy and practice in these countries?

Suggested further reading

The book that brings together many of the themes of this chapter in a compelling and authoritative manner is Phillip Cushman's (1995) *Constructing the Self, Constructing America: A Cultural History of Psychotherapy*. This is possibly the only book currently available that offers an overview of the historical development of therapy. It is largely American oriented, and has little to say about Europe, or indeed about counselling. But it is a rattling good read – thought-provoking and horizon-widening. There are a number of useful collections of historical and autobiographical chapters written by therapists (see, for example, Dryden and Spurling 1989; Dryden 1996; Goldfried 2001) which are worth reading. The biography of Carl Rogers by Howard Kirschenbaum (2007) gives a very full account of a key period in the emergence of the counselling profession. A well-informed and stimulating critical perspective on the role of therapy in society is provided in *Therapy Culture: Cultivating Vulnerability in an Uncertain Age*, by Frank Furedi (2004).

The interdisciplinary knowledge base for counselling theory and practice

Introduction

A new client, Alec, arrives for his first meeting. One of my main objectives in this situation is to begin to develop an understanding of who a client is – where and how they have developed a niche within society, and the kinds of experiences that have shaped their approach to life. It is important for me to get a sense of Alec as a person, before he begins to tell me about the problem that brings him to counselling. What I learn is that Alec is 60 years old. He is married and has two grown-up children and four grandchildren. His mother came from Ireland to work in a factory in Glasgow, and his father was a policemen who had 'traditional attitudes'. His mother was often ill, and his recollection of family life was that he was left to his own devices a lot of the time. Alec left home to join the army at the earliest opportunity. He saw active service in Northern Ireland during the troubles. On leaving the army he trained as a plumber and had his own business. Five years ago he began to developed more and more physical symptoms – back pain, headaches, fatigue – for which his doctor was not able to find a satisfactory diagnosis. He believes that there is something organically wrong with him. He is angry that his doctor has advised him to come to counselling, because he interprets his doctor's advice as implying that 'its all in my head'. He acknowledges that he feels depressed, and increasingly obsessed with monitoring his symptoms and searching for medical information on the internet.

What does this information mean to me? When I listen to Alec talking about his life, I find myself making connections between his story, and various domains of knowledge that are available to me. I am curious about the cultural influences that have contributed to Alec's way of being in the world such as his exposure to rural Irish traditions, and the relevance of hierarchical, uniformed organizations. I begin to get an inkling of a philosophical worldview built around facts, truths and physical causes. I experience Alec as a man who has lived in a man's world. I wonder about the bodily nature of his problems – could it be that his body 'remembers' things (Beatings from his Dad? Atrocities in Northern Ireland?) that his mind has buried? I am mindful of the economic realities of his situation – he is unemployed, and this is a hard place to be for someone who has always been the breadwinner. At the same time, I am aware of my own position in relation to these domains. I do not really understand what traditional life in Ireland is like, or what it means to serve in the army and aim a gun at another human being. My worldview is a bit different, and my experience of being a man is a bit different to that of Alec. My work role, as a counsellor, is probably something he has never come across before. My task, in relation to Alec, is to use my counselling skills and knowledge to help him to understand what is happening in his life, and make any adjustments that he decides are necessary. But I cannot connect with him effectively unless I am able to engage to a sufficient extent with the various layers of meaning that make up his experience of life.

The aim of the present chapter is to offer an overview of the various domains of knowledge that are relevant to counselling theory and practice. The chapter reflects the view that counselling is an interdisciplinary activity. Although psychological theories and research represent highly important sources of knowledge for counsellors, there are also several additional domains of knowledge that need to be taken into account if a counsellor is to be able to respond to the client as a whole person. One of the strengths of counselling as a profession is that the majority of counsellors enter training after they have gained knowledge and experience in other areas of life. The life stories of members of any counselling training course reveal a group of people who are usually at least 30 years of age (sometimes much older), who have prior learning and experience in all walks of life. Almost all counsellors are able to critically evaluate the counselling theories and skills they are taught against other sources of knowledge.

It is unrealistic and unnecessary to expect a counsellor to possess a comprehensive knowledge of all of the knowledge domains that might be relevant to their work with a client. What is important is to be aware that these domains are significant, to have given them some thought, and to have an active curiosity in terms of ongoing learning.

The following sections of this chapter offer an introduction to five key areas of knowledge that need to be considered in counsellor training and continuing professional development: philosophy, psychology, biological sciences, social science and the humanities. It is not possible, in the available space, to provide a comprehensive overview of all of the ideas and topics within these discipline areas that might be relevant to counsellors. Instead, the intention is to highlight some of the more immediately relevant topics, and explore their implications for counselling theory and practice.

> ## Box 3.1: *Support for the idea that therapy is an interdisciplinary activity*
>
> In recent years, counselling and psychotherapy have increasingly been defined as branches of psychology. The use of the term 'psychological therapies', and the expansion of counselling psychology have reinforced this trend. Textbooks on the psychology of personality mainly consist of chapters on different theories of therapy. However, there does exist a longstanding tradition that acknowledges the multi- or interdisciplinary nature of counselling and psychotherapy. In the late 1940s, the American Psychological Association set up a number of committees and conferences to discuss the training syllabus for the newly-emerging profession of clinical psychology. A major report (American Psychological Association 1947) recommended that the undergraduate psychology curriculum should include coverage of sociology, anthropology, economics, political science, history of civilization, comparative literature, comparative religion, philosophy and 'psychology as revealed in literature'. In respect of postgraduate training, the committee observed that '(the clinical psychologist) works in a setting with medical specialists of many kinds: psychiatrists, physiologists, neurologists, to mention the most prominent, and with representatives of other disciplines such as social workers and educators' and that training needs to provide an ability to 'meet colleagues on common ground' (American Psychological Association 1947: 550). The appreciation of the value of this kind of breadth of knowledge has been gradually squeezed out of training syllabuses that have become more and more narrowly focused.

The relevance for counselling of the study of philosophy

Philosophy is the original academic discipline. Philosophers examine the underlying assumptions that inform any and all aspects of human life. There is a sense, therefore, that implicit philosophical ideas underpin everything that we think and do. However, the immense scope and range of philosophical writing can make it hard for counsellors to make meaningful use of philosophy as a resource. Professional philosophers undergo many years of scholarly training in order to achieve a mastery of their discipline, and even then will tend to specialize in a particular area. In terms of understanding what philosophy has to offer, it is important to appreciate that philosophy does not aim to generate a set of 'findings' or fixed 'truths', but instead operates as a kind of open-ended conversation about the ultimate questions of human existence. It is useful to think about the role of philosophy in terms of an active process (philosophiz*ing*) of questioning existing ideas and arriving at a more nuanced or differentiated ways of understanding.

It is possible to identify several areas of philosophy that are relevant to counsellors:

- *Classical Greek philosophy*. The thought of Greek philosophers such as Aristotle, Socrates and Plato can be considered as the intellectual bedrock of Western civilization. Philosophy was used and respected in Greek civic life, and the issues and debates that concerned classical philosophers, and the methods they used to examine these issues, remain relevant today.

- *Enlightenment philosophy*. Around the seventeenth and eighteenth centuries, Europe was in the process of moving from a traditional social system based on religion, feudalism and an agricultural economy, to an era of modernity characterized by cities, literacy, democracy and scientific values. The key figures here are Descartes, Locke, Hume and Kant. The central concern of these philosophers was exploring how it is possible to achieve knowledge, and behave morally, in a world that is no longer dominated by religious certainties and traditional prejudices.

- *Phenomenology*. The German nineteenth-century philosopher, Edmund Husserl, developed a method of inquiry, which he called 'phenomenology', which was designed to allow exploration of the underlying meaning or 'essence' of aspects of human experience. The techniques of phenomenological reduction and bracketing-off of assumptions have proved to be hugely valuable for counsellors and psychotherapists and influences a wide range of therapy traditions in providing a means of getting beyond the client's immediate description of his or her problem and inviting exploration of underlying layers of meaning.

- *Critics of modernity*. In the twentieth century, the place of scientific rationality became so firmly established that some philosophers were drawn in the direction of analysing the limitations and contradictions of modern ways of life and thought. Wittgenstein, who argued that human realities are constructed through our 'form of life', and Heidegger, who sought to uncover the meaning of the dimensions of being and existence that lay behind everyday activities, have probably been the main influences on this branch of contemporary philosophy. Among the many other important writers who have questioned the assumptions of modernity are Taylor, MacIntyre, Macmurray and Rorty. A very significant subgroup within this movement has been the existentialists – such as Sartre and Merleau-Ponty – who were influenced by the nineteenth-century pioneer of existentialism, Kierkegaard. Another important subgroup has been made up of postmodern thinkers such as Derrida, Foucault and Lyotard.

- *Ethics and moral philosophy*. Counselling inevitably engages with a variety of moral issues. These range from professional ethics, in terms of understanding the meaning and implications of concepts of confidentiality and informed consent, through to the capacity to be accepting and responsive to the moral choices made by clients in their lives.

- *Philosophy of science*. It has become increasingly important for counselling, alongside other professions in contemporary society, to be publically accountable and able to demonstrate that there is a scientific evidence base to support its activities. At the same time, there are fierce debates around the question of the type of knowledge and evidence that is most relevant to counselling. The field of philosophy of science provides a means of making sense of these issues.

- *Non-Western philosophical traditions*. The main non-Western philosophical tradition that has been influential within the development of Western counselling and psychotherapy is Buddhism. There have also been attempts to apply, within therapy, ideas from Vedantic, Sufi and other philosophical systems.

There have always been multiple points of contact between philosophy and therapy. Some of the most important ideas in counselling and psychotherapy have originated in philosophy. The concept of the 'unconscious' had been used in nineteenth-century philosophy (Ellenberger 1970) some time before Freud began to use it in his theory. The concepts of phenomenology and authenticity had been developed by existential philosophers such as Heidegger and Husserl long before they were picked up by Rogers, Perls and other humanistic therapists. The field of moral philosophy also makes an input into counselling, by offering a framework for making sense of ethical issues (see Chapter 22). Many counsellors have sought to develop an understanding of the implications of postmodern concepts for their practice (Chapter 11). There are some therapists who base their entire approach on philosophical principles (see Box 3.2)

The concept of 'worldview' represents a particularly valuable point of context between philosophy and counselling. It seems clear that different people, and groups of people at different points in history, possess quite different ideas about how to make sense of the complex flow of human experience and social interaction. For example, probably the majority of people in contemporary Western society believe that everyday experience is underpinned by an objective physical reality that can be uncovered through the methods of modern science. A smaller set of people within the same society espouse a quite different position, which can be described as constructivist, social constructionist or postmodern in orientation. From this alternative perspective, there is no objective reality and no single truth that can be known. Instead, groups of people live their lives in accordance with co-constructed myths and beliefs, expressed in a language system and built on a kind of 'archaeology of knowledge' that can be understood as comprising layers of meaning deposited during earlier periods of history. Yet another large group of people, mainly (but not only) in traditional societies believe that everyday experience is underpinned and determined by some form of spiritual or transcendent dimension.

Describing and analysing worldviews and epistemologies (beliefs about what counts as true knowledge) constitutes a core task of philosophy. For example, philosophical debates around the existence of God can be seen as an effort to determine whether it is possible to reconcile an objectivist–realist worldview (there is no God, only a physical reality can exist) and a spiritual one.

The relevance of worldviews for counselling and psychotherapy theory and practice has been explored in several research studies. There is evidence that counsellors are drawn to espouse theoretical orientations that reflect their preferred worldview. For example, a student with a realist worldview is more likely to choose to be trained in CBT, and a student with a romantic worldview is more likely to be drawn to a training programme in a humanistic therapy such as person-centred counselling. In addition, there is also evidence that clients are more satisfied with therapies that match their worldview. Further information about research in this area can be found in the work of Lyddon (1989a,1989b, 1991; Lyddon and Adamson 1992; Lyddon and Bradford 1995). One of the implications of taking worldviews seriously, is the realization that an effective counsellor needs to be able to understand and engage with the entire range of worldviews that might be espoused by his or her clients. The challenge for counsellors is therefore to be able to step outside their own preferred worldview or core beliefs. Hansen (2004, 2006) has suggested that it is easier for counsellors to do this if they are able to adopt a postmodern position in which multiple realities and 'truths' coexist.

Box 3.2: *Philosophical counselling as a form of therapeutic practice*

The origins of the philosophical counselling movement are generally attributed to the German philosopher Gerd Achenbach (see Jongsma 1995; Lahav 1995a), who opened the first philosophical counselling practice in Bergisch Gladbach, near Cologne, in 1981. The German Association for Philosophical Practice was formed in 1982. In 1984, a group of students at the University of Amsterdam became interested in the application of philosophy in counselling; their efforts led to the opening of the Hotel de Filosoof (The Philosopher Hotel) in Amsterdam in 1988, and the establishment of the Dutch Association for Philosophical Practice in 1989. There are now philosophical counsellors practising in most European countries, North America and Australia. The development of philosophical counselling has been supported by the publication of key texts such as Lahav and da Venza Tillmanns (1995), Schuster (1999) and Raabe (2001, 2006), as well as a number of training programmes, websites and conferences. One of the main strategies used by philosophical counsellors is to encourage clients to explore their underlying assumptions about the world:

> It is possible to interpret everyday problems and predicaments – such as meaning crises, feelings of boredom and emptiness, difficulties in interpersonal relationships, anxiety, etc. – as expressing problematic aspects of one's worldview: contradictions or tensions between two conceptions about how life should be lived, hidden presuppositions that have not been examined, views that fail to take into account various considerations, over-generalizations, expectations that cannot realistically be satisfied, fallacious interpretations, and so on.
>
> (Lahav 1995b: 9)

An additional strategy can be described as a process of *entering into dialogue*. The use of dialogue as a way of exploring assumptions and opening up alternative ways of viewing the world is associated with the work of Socrates and many other philosophers down the centuries. One of the goals of dialogue is to demonstrate that there are always different ways of looking at an issue or problem (Achenbach 1995).

Suggested further reading

Accessible introductory texts for those who are new to philosophy include Blackburn (1999), Howard (2000) and Magee (2010). An introductory overview of philosophy of science can be found in McLeod (2013a, Chapter 3). The collections of essays edited by Mace (1999) and King-Spooner (1999) and Kirkwood (2012) also include stimulating and thoughtful contributions on a range of philosophical topics. Sass (1988) provides an excellent philosophical critique of humanistic psychology and therapy. *Sources of the Self: The Making of Modern Identity*, by Charles Taylor (1989), is an important book that should be read by all therapists at some point in their careers. However, it is a complex and demanding piece of writing.

Psychology as a foundational discipline for counselling theory and practice

It may seem strange to highlight the relevance of psychology for the practice of counselling. After all, the ideas of leading figures in the history of psychotherapy, such as Freud and Rogers, are heavily featured in most psychology textbooks. In some contexts, counselling and psychotherapy are described as 'psychological therapies', and regarded as fields of applied psychology. Many counselling training programmes are based in university psychology departments, and are taught by psychologists. An important group of practitioners describe themselves as 'counselling psychologists'. In some European countries, there is no distinction between counselling, psychotherapy and psychology – all these activities are simply considered as 'psychology'. Nevertheless, despite the strong links between counselling and psychology, there are important areas of psychological research and practice that are rarely referred to within the counselling literature or on counsellor training programmes. These include the following.

- *Contemporary developmental psychology*. Most counsellors possess, and make practical use of, some level of knowledge of lifespan development, often influenced by the ideas of Freud and Erikson. However, more recent advances in research in developmental psychology have opened up new understandings that have been integrated into counselling theory and practice to only a very limited extent. One example from this body of work, is the research carried out by Colwyn Trevarthen into early mother–infant interaction (Malloch and Trevarthen 2010). Moment-by-moment analysis of video recordings of mother–infant interaction in the weeks following birth, reveals two phenomena that are potentially significant for counsellors. First, in these interactions the baby leads and the adult follows. Second, the adult draws the baby into a rhythmic interaction that resembles a piece of music. These observations have important implications for our understanding of how learning occurs.

- *The psychology of personality*. The ideas of Freud, Jung, Rogers and others represent theories of personality. However, they are theories that have arisen from clinical practice, rather than being informed by research on the behaviour of people in real-life contexts. The findings of such research suggest that therapy theories tend to focus on only one 'slice' of personality. The work of McAdams (2009) offers an understanding of personality that reflects the totality of current research evidence. This literature suggests that making sense of the uniqueness or individual identity of a person requires taking account of three broad levels of functioning (McAdams and Pals 2006). There is a bedrock of biologically hard-wired traits, such as the extent to which the person is introverted or sociable, impulsive or controlled, and so on. It is then also possible to identify a set of adaptations that have occurred, as these underlying dispositions bump against the person's social environment over the course of their life. This is the level of analysis that is reflected in most therapy theories. Finally, there is a personal narrative, that is shaped by the cultural narratives that are available in the society within which the person lives. For example, many people currently living in the USA are likely to frame their lives along the lines of what McAdams (2006) has described as a 'redemption' narrative (making a mistake and then doing good). The lives of recent Presidents such as Bill Clinton and George W. Bush represent well-known stories of redemption. McAdams and Pals (2006) suggest that therapists need to learn to accept that the fundamental traits exhibited by their clients are largely impervious to change, whereas their personal narratives are much more open to change.

- *Occupational psychology*. Despite Freud's famous statement that the aim of psycho-analysis was to enable the patient 'to love and to work', theories of therapy have paid little attention to the personal significance of work in relation to the problems reported by their clients. The subdiscipline of occupational psychology addresses all aspects of the psychology of work. One topic that is clearly relevant for counselling, is the psychology of stress. In reviews of theory and research on work stress, Dewe and Cooper (2004) and Dewe *et al.* (2010) identify many dimensions of stress that are potentially relevant for counselling, such as the meaning and impact of different work environments, and the effect of different coping mechanisms that people use to survive within these environments.

These examples, from developmental, personality and occupational psychology, are not intended to be comprehensive. Instead, the aim has been to highlight some of the many areas of current psychological knowledge that could be useful for counsellors.

Neuroscience and interpersonal neurobiology

Recent decades have seen a massive expansion in research into the way that the brain functions. New methods of brain scanning and imaging, and tracking of biochemical processes, have allowed researchers to move to a stage at which biological knowledge can be used to inform the practice of counselling and psychotherapy. Acquiring an understanding of brain function is becoming increasingly important for therapists, both as a means of possessing a richer and more holistic perspective on the person, and as a source of ideas around specific therapeutic strategies for clients with particular kinds of problems. Being able to develop a critical appreciation of neurobiology and its implications for therapy is a massive task, because of the substantial technical complexity of this field. The coverage of this topic within the present section makes no claim to be comprehensive. Instead, the intention is to provide an introduction to some of the key themes and issues within this domain.

The application of neuroscience in therapy needs to begin with an understanding of some basic aspects of brain functioning. Diagrams of brain structure tend to emphasize two key features. Vertically, the brain can be broadly divided into the limbic system, situated at the base of the brain and top of the spinal cord, which is covered by the cortex – a large area that fills most of the skull. Horizontally, it can be seen that the cortex is divided into two hemispheres. The role and functioning of these parts of the brain, and the way they interact with each other, is highly complex. Nevertheless, it is possible to identify certain functions that are primarily located in certain areas. The limbic system is the 'old' (in evolutionary terms) part of the brain. It deals with rapid emotional reactions to events, for example the activation of the 'fight–flight' response. The cortex, by contrast is a more recent evolutionary development, and deals with thinking, language use, and conscious control and planning. Within the cortex, each hemisphere broadly specializes in a different function. The left hemisphere controls the right hand and the right side of the body, and the use of language. The right hemisphere controls the left hand and left side of the body, and specializes in processing information in terms of images. Another important aspect of brain functioning, from a psychotherapeutic perspective, is the existence within the cortex of 'mirror neurons'. Neurons are the basic cell-level 'building blocks' of the brain. Mirror neurons seem to have a specific function of replicating, in one individual, a pattern of action being observed in another individual. For example, very young babies will smile in response to a smile directed at them, from someone in their field of view. It is clear that a baby is not capable of consciously interpreting the meaning of a smile. What seems to be happening is that an automatic neural response is being triggered. The significance of mirror neurons is that they demonstrate that sensitivity to relationships with others is an integral part of the way that the brain works.

Further information on these topics can be found in introductory neuroscience texts, written for therapists, such as Montgomery (2013) and Siegel (2012). Shorter, article-length accounts are available in Siegel (2006, 2009) and Oliver and Ostrofsky (2007).

Counselling does not directly intervene to change the way that a client's brain is functioning. Counselling involves talking, reflection and trying out new behaviours. Why, then, is neuroscience important? The significance of neuroscience lies in the fact that certain possibilities and tendencies are 'hard-wired' into the physical fabric of human beings. These biological structures shape how human beings respond to different types of situations. They do not *determine* how a person will respond, because there is a certain amount of plasticity in the brain and nervous system, resulting in a capacity to 'work around' these structures and establish alternative pathways (Doidge 2007). Human beings also have capacity to be selective in what they attend to and what they do, which results in a multiplicity of strategies for modifying or regulating basic neural processes. However, in the end, plasticity and choice operate in relation to fixed parameters. It is possible to move the furniture around in many different configurations. But it is still the same furniture in the same room.

There are many ways in which knowledge of neurobiology can be useful in counselling. Basically, neurobiology acts as a reminder that clients (and counsellors) are embodied entities as well as being cognitive and linguistic entities. One of the simple ways in which a biological perspective can be helpful is to pay attention to the breathing patterns of a client. Shallow breathing exacerbates anxiety and panic, while breath-holding is often a sign of an attempt to control painful or terrifying emotions. On the other hand, deep breathing into the abdomen can produce energy and a sense of positivity. The relevance of 'breath work' in counselling is discussed by Young *et al.* (2010). Other physical signs, such as a flushed face or agitated movement may indicate that the client is close to being aware of emotional states that have been long suppressed (Minton *et al.* 2006; Ogden and Fisher 2012; Ogden and Minton 2000). The technique of eye movement desensitization (Shapiro 2001) has been devised to activate both hemispheres of the brain at the same time, as a means of facilitating the cognitive assimilation of traumatic memories that have been 'trapped' or stored as terrifying visual and sensory images. At a general level, these approaches reflect a position that 'the body remembers' (Rothschild 2000) – the effort to maintain self-control in the face of emotionally threatening experiences leads to a variety of types of stress in the body. When a person arrives at a point in their life when he or she wishes to confront these memories, and come to terms with them, the concomitant body 'armouring' begins to fragment, which is manifested in many different types of bodily symptom. There are many therapy approaches that specifically focus on somatic or bodily intervention (Heller and Duclos 2012). Similar interventions are found in yoga and other traditional healing systems. However, many counsellors who work with clients primarily through conversational methods, have also found it meaningful to be aware of the physical or embodied dimension of their work with clients.

Another facet of neurobiology that counsellors need to understand is psychopharmacology. Many clients who make use of counselling are also taking prescribed medication to control anxiety, depression or mood swings. Further information about this topic can be found in Daines *et al.* (2007), Gitlin (2007), King and Anderson (2004), Patterson *et al.* (2009) and Sinacola and Peters-Strickland (2011). Issues and possibilities arising from the combined use of counselling and antidepressants are also discussed by Feldman and Feldman (1997), Peterson (2006) and Sparks *et al.* (2006). Finally, there are specific conditions from which clients may suffer, that have a major neurological component, such as brain injury, Asperger's syndrome and Alzheimer's disease. Counsellors who work with such clients may find it valuable to develop an understanding of how neurological factors may have an impact on their client's behaviour and emotions.

Box 3.3: *The experience of taking antidepressants*

Research into client experiences of using antidepressants acts as a reminder that the impact of biological processes (such as changing brain chemistry through medication) on human behaviour is usually shaped by the meaning that the person attributes to the biological event. Garfield *et al.* (2003) interviewed people who had taken antidepressant medication to treat their depression. Almost all of them talked about ways in which the meaning of taking the drug influenced their recovery. For example, deciding to take medication helped some individuals to feel that they were taking control of their problems:

> I would know that I was taking steps to do something about it, not to just keep going and it would go on affecting me. I wanted to actually change the situation and it was one way I felt I was able to do it.
>
> I was clinging onto that one hope and I wanted, I wanted it to work.
>
> (Garfield *et al.* 2003: 524)

For other participants in this study, taking an antidepressant was associated with a sense of shame and stigma that impeded their recovery. The strength of these types of reaction to antidepressant use is so significant that Ankarberg and Falkenstrom (2008) have suggested that prescribing an antidepressant should be regarded as a psychological intervention rather than a pharmacological one.

Religion

The importance of the connection between counselling and religion was mapped out in Chapter 2. Historically, counselling and psychotherapy can be regarded as secularized adaptations of various practices that had been in existence for many hundreds of years within faith communities. In recent years, there has been a resurgence of interest in the relevance for counselling of concepts and techniques from different spiritual traditions, expressed through an expanding literature on the psychotherapeutic implications of forgiveness, compassion, mindfulness, yoga and prayer. These developments are discussed further in Chapter 17 and at various points throughout this book.

The social sciences and humanities

There are many ways in which humanities disciplines, such as literary criticism, history, art and media studies, can inform the theory and practice of counselling. Some examples of ways in which this can be accomplished are explored in Chapter 15, in the context of the use of art-making and writing as therapeutic methods. Hansen (2012) offers a strong argument in favour of a greater use of humanities and arts-based perspectives in counselling training and practice. For example, it is possible to learn a great deal about human motivation and experience, family dynamics, relationship patterns and cultural differences, through the study of fiction, drama and cinema.

Social science disciplines such as sociology, economics, political science and social anthropology also have a lot to offer. Narrative therapy (Chapter 11) grew out of the ideas of the French social theorist Michel Foucault. The work of leading contemporary sociologists such as Anthony Giddens (1991) and Zygmunt Bauman (2004) provide a basis for understanding how the struggles presented by individual counselling clients reflect broader social themes and movements. Madeline Bunting (2004) and Richard Sennett (1998, 2003) write about the changing meaning of work in a globalized world economy, in a way that will immediately make sense to any therapy client suffering from work stress or unable to see a positive future. The discipline of social anthropology, which studies the way people live within different cultures, has had a major influence on the field of multicultural counselling (Chapter 13). The investigations of indigenous shamanic healing by Victor Turner (1964, 1982), one of the leading figures in twentieth-century social anthropology, did a great deal to promote awareness of the degree to which psychotherapeutic practices reflect their cultural context.

Social science disciplines have been at the forefront of developing methods of qualitative research. One of the areas of qualitative research that is highly relevant for counselling has been the literature around the experiences of people who are suffering from particular disorders or conditions. The pioneer of much of this work was Arthur Kleinman (1988). Examples of recent qualitative social research into health experience include studies by Rice *et al.* (2011) and Ridge and Ziebland (2006, 2011) of what it is like to be depressed and recover from depression. These investigations are not 'therapy-focused', but instead try to capture the everyday lived experience of people who are trying to cope with depression. As such, they offer invaluable insights for counsellors, in providing an appreciation of the multiple ways in which depressed people draw on their own resources to enable them to move on in their lives.

The functioning of the economic system may seem far removed from the world of counselling. However, there is considerable evidence that the level of mental health problems in society is exacerbated by the degree of social and economic inequality in that society (Marmot 2004; Wilkinson and Pickett 2010) and by the position of the economy on an expansion–contraction cycle (Warner 2003). Some of the implication of these factors are explored further in Chapter 21.

Conclusions: the importance of an interdisciplinary perspective

Counselling needs to have an interdisciplinary base because as a profession it is committed to respecting diversity of experience, and because counsellors are committed to working with whatever issues their clients want to talk about. Attempts to fuse counselling and psychotherapy into a single *psychological* therapy will never be successful because they have the effect of cutting off the powerful mix of ideas and practices that have enabled counselling to provide a flexible response to many different types of human dilemma. At the same time, it needs to be acknowledged that maintaining an interdisciplinary orientation represents a major challenge to the counselling profession. Contemporary academic life is largely organized in terms of single disciplines. Psychology is a particularly powerful, internationally recognized discipline, and it has been all too easy for counselling to try to establish an academic niche within it. Not enough attention has been given, in the form of books and articles, research studies, and practice development, to the contribution that can be made to counselling by disciplines other than psychology.

The interdisciplinary nature of counselling also represents a challenge for counsellor training. The ideas outlined in this chapter provide no more than a preliminary indication of the range and scope of potentially useful sources of knowledge for counselling theory and practice. There is a lot more out there. It would be impossible to include all of this in a counselling training course, and it would be completely unrealistic to expect a counsellor to possess an in-depth knowledge of philosophy, neuroscience, literary criticism, sociology and so on. What would be helpful, in my view, would be two things. People who become counsellors already have at least some of this knowledge, through life experience or previous occupational roles. It would be helpful, therefore, in training and throughout later careers, to offer encouragement and permission for counsellors to express their pre-existing knowledge in their counselling work, in whatever way is appropriate to them. It would also be helpful to adopt a collectivist approach to interdisciplinarity, by the profession as a whole inviting representatives of various disciplines to share their knowledge, and making it possible for counsellors to learn from each other.

Topics for reflection and discussion

1 What are the knowledge disciplines that are of particular interest to you, or that you have studied? In what ways has the knowledge that you possess as a result of that interest or studying been useful to you in your role as a counsellor (or might potentially be useful in the future)?

2 Having read this chapter, what are the areas of knowledge that you would like to know more about? What can you do to pursue that goal over the next six months?

3 Mainstream counselling theory and practice is based on psychological theory and research. However, there are some counsellors and psychotherapists, notably art therapists, narrative therapists and philosophical counsellors, who mainly base their practice on non-psychological theories. What might be the advantages and disadvantages of adopting of non-psychological stance toward clients?

4 Identify a counselling agency or service with which you are familiar. In what ways is the work of that service informed by an interdisciplinary approach? In what ways might the quality of the service that is offered to clients be improved by further consideration of what can be learned from specific disciplines that are currently not given much attention?

5 A major focus for counselling research, over several decades, has been the question of effectiveness. Does it work? To what extent, and in what ways, do clients benefit from the counselling they receive? At the present time, counselling is dominated by ideas and methods from psychology and psychiatry. What would a counselling outcome/effectiveness study look like if it was conducted by a philosopher or a social anthropologist or an artist?

Suggested further reading

Indications for further reading are provided within each section of this chapter. In addition, *Counselling: Interdisciplinary Perspectives*, edited by Brian Thorne and Windy Dryden (1993), includes chapters written by counsellors whose initial training and career was in a different discipline (e.g., English literature, ecology), describing about how they have used their discipline-based knowledge and learning to inform their psychotherapeutic work.

Part 2
Counselling approaches

Theory in counselling: using conceptual tools to facilitate understanding and guide action

Introduction

During the twentieth century, psychotherapy came to be organized around a number of distinct theoretical models or 'approaches'. Historically, the most important of these approaches or 'schools' of therapy have been psychodynamic, cognitive–behavioural and humanistic. However, these are merely the most popular of a wide range of theoretical orientations presently in use. The current situation in both counselling and psychotherapy is one of great theoretical diversity and creativity. Just as quickly as new theories are spawned, new attempts are enjoined to unify, combine or integrate them. The proliferation of theories and approaches is often confusing for people learning about counselling, whether clients or students. The aim of this chapter is to make sense of the diversity of approaches that exist. The topic is tackled by first establishing just what is meant by a counselling 'approach', then looking more closely at the concept of 'theory', and the *uses* of theorizing in counselling (Why do we need theory? How is theory used in practice?).

It is important to understand theories within their social and historical context. Chapters 5 to 16, which follow, review the most widely used theories that are used by contemporary counsellors, ranging from the beginnings of psychotherapy in the work of Sigmund Freud, to the most recent developments in narrative therapy, philosophical counselling, nature therapy and feminist approaches. The ideas introduced in the present chapter are intended to make it possible to look at these established approaches with a spirit of open inquiry and questioning. Theories of therapy do not represent immutable truths, but are perhaps better regarded as providing tools for practice and understanding. In the end, it is not enough merely to accept the ideas and methods associated with any particular approach to therapy: instead, it is essential for each counsellor to develop his or her own *personal* approach, consistent with his or her own life experience, cultural values and work setting.

This chapter, and this book as a whole, is written from the standpoint that *psychotherapy* is a practice that is (mainly) based on the application of a single approach. Thus, for instance, psychotherapy practitioners tend to describe themselves in terms of their core orientation, such as 'psychodynamic', 'cognitive–behavioural' or 'transactional analysis'. By contrast, *counselling* is a practice that draws on a range of theoretical approaches, which are selected on the basis of their relevance to a particular client or group. So, for instance, a counsellor would describe himself or herself as a 'bereavement counsellor' or a 'primary care counsellor', rather than use a label derived from a theoretical orientation. This distinction is not, of course, set in stone with clearly defined boundaries – there is a great deal of overlap between what psychotherapists do, and the work roles of counsellors. Nevertheless, it is a distinction that has important implications for counsellors, both those in training and those in practice. Whereas a psychotherapist only needs to learn the theory that he or she has chosen, a counsellor needs to learn not only about (some) theories, but also to develop a framework for choosing between theories, and to select the best ideas for accomplishing whatever the therapeutic task in hand might be at any particular moment. A central aim of this chapter, therefore, is to provide readers with a perspective from which they can critically evaluate the relevance, for them and their clients, of the theories that are introduced in the following chapters.

The concept of an 'approach'

The field of counselling and psychotherapy can be characterized as comprising a complex set of interlocking *traditions* (MacIntyre 2007). These traditions can be viewed as consisting of accumulated knowledge and wisdom, assembled over a long period of time, concerning how best to assist people who are experiencing problems in living. During training, each counsellor needs to learn how to position himself or herself somewhere within this spectrum of traditions. Because the concept of 'tradition' has on old-fashioned sound to it, and therapists usually wish to regard themselves as engaged in cutting-edge practices, the term 'approach' tends to be used in place of the word 'tradition'. Like any cultural tradition, a counselling/psychotherapy approach can be regarded as a complex system of ideas and behaviours. Some of the elements that make up a counselling approach are:

- *An organized and coherent set of concepts, or theory.* The distinguishing feature of competing approaches to counselling is that each of them is built around a small set of key ideas, that mark them out as different and unique. On closer examination, it is always possible to see that the concepts that comprise a theory are structured in terms of three levels of abstraction. At the most abstract level are underlying philosophical or 'metapsychological' assumptions (for example, in psychoanalysis, the idea of 'the unconscious'). At an intermediate level of abstraction are specific theoretical propositions, that predict connections between observable events (i.e., in psychoanalysis, the posited causal association between certain childhood events and adult psychopathology). Finally, at the most concrete level are concepts that function as 'labels' for discrete observable events (e.g., in psychoanalysis, concepts such as 'transference' or 'denial'). Each of these levels of conceptual abstraction serves a different function in relation to the approach as a whole. Concrete label-type concepts represent the routine language or terminology used by adherents of an approach in communication with each other. The philosophical level of conceptualization embodies the core values of an approach. Finally, specific theoretical propositions correspond to the ground for debate and dialogue – the intellectual cutting edge of the approach.

- *A language or way of talking.* Each approach provides a language for talking about clients, and the work of therapy, and is characterized by its own particular style of talking. For example, one of the distinctive features of the way that practitioners of an approach to counselling talk relates to their use of evidence to support what they say. Different approaches have very different ideas about what counts as evidence. Within the person-centred approach, a counsellor is likely to make frequent reference to feelings and personal experience. By contrast, a CBT therapist is more likely to back up his or her arguments by reference to research evidence or behavioural observation.

- *A distinctive set of therapeutic procedures or interventions.* Linked to the theory that is used within an approach are a range of practical procedures, techniques or methods. For example, systematic desensitization is a distinctive CBT procedure, and interpretation of transference is a distinctive psychoanalytic procedure. In addition to the existence of these procedures or methods, a practitioner within an approach will possess a framework for deciding which procedures are most appropriate for specific counselling situations, presenting problems and client groups.

- *A knowledge community.* It is a mistake to think of a counselling approach as being merely a set of ideas that can be described in a book. An approach is a dynamic network of people and institutions that sustain it as a form of practice – journals, training courses, conference, meetings, websites, etc. This knowledge community is itself structured and organized in terms of subgroups of people who represent contrasting standpoints or subtraditions within the approach. It is important to acknowledge, here, the essential role of conflict and debate in sustaining a tradition over time. A tradition that does not change in response to the creativity of its members, and the shifting demands of the external environment, will eventually die: tensions within its knowledge community are to be expected in any intellectually healthy and vibrant approach to counselling.

- *Set of values*. Behind each approach to counselling lies a constellation of guiding assumptions about what constitutes the 'good life'. Although all approaches to counselling and psychotherapy can be understood as sharing a broad set of 'humanistic' values (i.e., based on humanism), each of them places special emphasis on certain values or virtues above others. For example, the person-centred approach highlights the virtue of self-fulfilment, whereas CBT place special emphasis on the virtue of rational action.

- *Mythology*. The ideas, values and practices that make up an approach are encapsulated within its mythology – the account that is shared among adherents of the personal, social, cultural and historical context within which the approach has been developed. Specifically, contemporary approaches to counselling and psychotherapy tend to be strongly associated with 'hero' figures (people such as Sigmund Freud and Carl Rogers), whose personal qualities symbolize the core characteristics of the approaches they founded.

This way of understanding counselling and psychotherapy as cultural entities, reflects the social analysis of scientific knowledge carried out by the philosopher Thomas Kuhn (1962). It is a perspective that has a number of important implications in terms of the way that the therapy professions have developed, and how they currently function. One of the crucial implications, for anyone learning to become a counsellor, is that it is easy to see that counselling training is about much more than intellectual or academic 'book' learning, but involves socialization into a mythology, language, value system and knowledge community. A further implication is that the core beliefs and practices of an approach are not easily changed through rational argument or research evidence, because the approach is built around a thick web of relationships, history and personal commitment, rather than just being a set of ideas. A third implication is that a counselling approach is more than just theory – it consists of a network of institutions and relationships, a language and a set of values. A final implication is that an approach or tradition is a dynamic system, that involves debate and disagreement – an approach needs constantly to adapt and change in order to stay alive and relevant in the face on new challenges. When studying theory, therefore, it is always necessary to take account of the fact that a theory is only one part of a broader network of belief and behaviour.

What is a theory?

The following chapters introduce and explain a number of counselling theories. To be able to arrive at an informed critical evaluation of these theories, to be able to use them creatively in the service of clients, it is important to understand what a theory is. The word 'theory' is itself a multifaceted concept. This is not the place to attempt to develop a comprehensive account of debates around the role of theory in psychology and social science. Nevertheless, for the purposes of understanding theories of therapy it is helpful to look briefly at three aspects of the concept of a theory. These are: a theory as a structured set of ideas; theory as a set of social practices; and the practical function or purpose of theory.

Theory as a structured set of ideas

The obvious way of looking at a 'theory' is to think about it as a set of ideas or concepts that are used to make sense of some dimension of reality: for example, Einstein's 'theory of relativity' is a set of ideas that explain the relationship between time and space. A theory is different from everyday, common-sense ideas in that it is stated formally, with clearly defined terms, has been tested or critically evaluated in some way, and is consistent with other scientific ideas.

In relation to theories of counselling, it is essential to acknowledge that the set of ideas that makes up a theory is not only all of these things (useful, clearly defined, critically tested etc.), but is also *structured*. In other words, a counselling theory operates at different levels of abstraction, and the implications for a counsellor of using any particular theory depend a great deal on which level of abstraction he or she is employing.

A useful analysis of the structure of counselling theories has been carried out by the psychoanalytic writers Rapaport and Gill (1959), who argued that there are three levels to any theoretical model used in counselling and therapy. First, there are statements about *observational* data. Second, there are theoretical *propositions*, which make connections between different observations. Third, there are statements of *philosophical assumptions*, or 'metapsychology'. Rapaport and Gill (1959) looked at the theoretical structure of psychoanalysis, and came to the conclusion that statements about, for example, defence mechanisms such as projection or denial were fundamentally simple observations of behavioural events. Psychoanalytic concepts such as 'anal personality', on the other hand, went beyond mere observation, and made inferences about the connectedness of events separated by time and space. For example, the idea of anal personality implies a link between childhood events (potty training) and adult behaviour (obsessionality), and this association is inferred rather than directly observed. However, in principle, given good enough research, the truth of the inference could be tested through research. Finally, concepts such as the 'unconscious' and 'libido' referred to philosophical abstractions that could not be directly observed but were used as general explanatory ideas. In psychoanalysis, the reason why potty training can result in obsessional adult patterns of behaviour is because potty training operates to shape or fixate certain libidinal impulses, which then unconsciously determine the way that the person behaves in adult life. However, 'libido' and 'the unconscious' are not factors that can be measured or researched, but represent a level of highly abstract, philosophical theorizing about the meaning of being a person.

Rapaport and Gill's (1959) discussion of these issues has a number of implications for the application of theory in practice. The use of lower-level, observational constructs can be seen to carry relatively little in the way of theoretical 'baggage'. For example, describing a client as 'using the defence mechanism of projection' might be an effective shorthand means of giving information to a supervisor or colleagues in a case conference. However, it would be a straightforward matter to use everyday ordinary language to communicate the same information. Different counselling theories tend to include their own uniquely phrased observational labels, and counsellors often find it helpful to use these labels. In doing so, they are not necessarily using the theoretical model from which the label is taken, but may be merely borrowing a useful turn of phrase. At the same time, it is important to recognize that there may be times when using observational constructs may result in making assumptions about the client, and missing useful information. Categorizing a client's behaviour as 'resistance', for example, may prevent a counsellor from reflecting in a more open-ended way about different possible meanings of what the client might be doing, and why. The danger of using 'observational' concepts, therefore, can be that they can result in jumping to conclusions (by just 'labelling' a phenomenon) rather than thinking more deeply, or with more curiosity, about what might be happening.

Higher-level constructs and concepts, by contrast, cannot be as easily taken out of the context of the theoretical model within which they fit. A term such as 'libido' (Freudian theory) or 'self-actualization' (Rogerian/person-centred theory) cannot be used without making a substantial number of philosophical assumptions about what it means to be a person. As a result, any attempt to combine 'libido' and 'self-actualization' in the same conversation, case study or research project is likely to lead to confusion. Thinking about people as basically driven by libidinous desires (Freud) or as basically driven by a drive to wholeness and fulfilment (Rogers) are very different philosophical positions.

The 'middle' level of theory, which involves theoretical propositions such as Freud's explanation of the 'anal personality', or Rogers' model of the 'core conditions' for therapeutic change, is potentially the most useful level of theory for practitioners, because it deals in supposedly tangible cause-and-effect sequences that give the counsellor a 'handle' on how to facilitate change. The difficulty here is whether the particular explanation offered by a theoretical model can be believed to be true, or be viewed as just one among many competing interpretations. For example, psychoanalysts claim that rigid patterns of potty training produce obsessional people (this is an oversimplification of the theory). However, if a link can be demonstrated between potty training and adult behaviour, this connection could be explained in many ways, such as being a result of obsessional attitudes being reinforced by obsessional parents (behavioural explanation), or by the acquisition of 'conditions of worth' around tidiness (Rogerian explanation).

It can be seen, therefore, that learning and using a theory of counselling involves different kinds of tasks and challenges. On the one hand, to become familiar with a theory it is necessary to learn how to detect or label observational phenomena such as 'defences', 'transference', 'empathy', 'irrational beliefs' and so on. On the other hand, it is also necessary to become immersed enough in the underlying 'image of the person' or philosophy of a theory to appreciate what is meant by 'the unconscious', 'self-actualization' or 'reinforcement'. Finally, there is the task of understanding how observational and philosophical concepts are brought together in the form of specific theoretical propositions. All this is made even more difficult because few theories of counselling and psychotherapy are ever formulated in a manner that allows their structure to be clearly identified. For example, writers such as Rogers or Freud conveyed their ideas through case studies, through essays on specific topics and (in Rogers' case) in research papers. The structures of therapy theories are often more clearly explained not in therapy and counselling books, but in personality textbooks such as those by Monte (1998) and Pervin and Johns (2000).

Theory as a set of social practices

There is no doubt that a theory of counselling can be written out in the form of a scientific formula, with all constructs being operationally defined, and cause-and-effect sequences clearly specified. In the 1950s, Carl Rogers, the founder of client-centred and person-centred counselling, and one of the leading figures in humanistic psychology, was invited to do just this by the American psychologist Sigmund Koch. The resulting scientific statement was published (Rogers 1957), and comprises a set of fundamental theoretical propositions. If this can be done for a humanistic theory that emphasizes the freedom of the person to make choices, it can certainly be done for other therapy theories. It is interesting, however, that few other leading counselling and psychotherapy theorists have opted to follow the example of Rogers and write up their theories in the form of testable hypotheses and propositions.

Despite the undeniable fact that theories exist as sets of ideas, there is an increasing appreciation that there is a human, or social, side to any theory, not only in psychology and social sciences, but also in the physical sciences such as physics, chemistry and biology. The social dimension of science has been highlighted in the writings of the philosopher Thomas Kuhn (1962). At the heart of his argument is the idea that theories are created and sustained by *scientific communities*, and that it is impossible fully to understand a theory without participating in the activities of that community. Kuhn noticed that, when scientists are trained, they do not just learn about ideas, but are socialized into a way of seeing the world, and a way of doing things. Learning about theory in chemistry, for example, involves doing experiments, learning how to interpret the results produced by particular equipment, knowing when results 'feel wrong' and learning about which problems or issues are understandable and solvable by the theory, and which are anomalous or viewed as irrelevant. A scientific community is organized around textbooks, journals and conferences. In other words, there is a whole *community of practice* that physically embodies and perpetuates the theory. The philosopher Polanyi (1958) introduced the term 'implicit knowledge' to refer to the kind of knowing used by people who belong in a community of scientists. Implicit or 'tacit' knowledge is picked up informally and unconsciously rather than being explicitly written down.

The social dimension is extremely important for an understanding of theories of counselling. Learning about counselling involves seeing, hearing and doing. Participating in a training course, or receiving supervision, represents the transmission of an *oral tradition* that is passed on from one practitioner to another. There are many concepts that, it can be argued, can only be understood by being experienced. For example, many psychoanalysts would say that a real understanding of the idea of 'transference' could only be obtained by undergoing personal psychoanalysis (a 'training analysis'). Many person-centred counsellors would assert that a full appreciation of the meaning of 'congruence' within person-centred theory requires participating in person-centred 'encounter' groups. There are aspects of personal presence, ways of talking and ways of being that can only be conveyed through actually meeting experienced practitioners or trainers. Certainly, these implicit or tacit dimensions of theory cannot be adequately communicated in a textbook (such as this one) or research report.

There are several implications of a social perspective that are significant for understanding how theory is created and used in counselling. First, the oral tradition is always broader than what is written about it. Writers such as Freud and Rogers were influential because they were able to put into words, better than anyone else at the time, the ways of understanding and working with clients that were being generated in their oral communities. But, even in their cases, there was always more that could be said. Both Freud and Rogers struggled, throughout their careers, to find the best ways to articulate in words what they *knew* at an implicit level. Some of the apparent theoretical debates and differences in counselling and psychotherapy can therefore be viewed not so much as arguments over the substance of what is happening in therapy, but as disputes around the best language to use in talking about these happenings.

Another key implication is that, much of the time, it is more accurate to talk about counselling *approaches* rather than theories. The idea of an 'approach' is a reminder that there is more to a way of doing counselling than merely applying a set of ideas: an approach embraces philosophical assumptions, style, tradition and tacit knowing.

The third, and in some ways most important, implication of a social perspective is to suggest that in many ways a theory is like a *language*: psychodynamic theory is the language used by one group of practitioners, cognitive–behavioural theory is a language used by another group and so on. The idea of theory as language is a fertile metaphor. It does not imply that one theory is right and another one is wrong. However, it does admit the possibility that it is easier to talk about some things in certain languages rather than others. Learning a language involves knowing about formal rules, acquiring everyday idioms and practising with other speakers. And it also introduces the issue of *translating* between different languages, in order to communicate with colleagues in other communities: to be able to translate practitioners need to know about different theories, rather than remaining monolingual. There is also the question as to whether it might ever be possible, or desirable, to develop a common language for all therapies (a kind of counsellors' Esperanto?), as suggested by Ryle (1978, 1987).

Finally, by regarding a theory as a language-system, it becomes easier to appreciate how processes of power and oppression can occur in counselling. If, for example, a theory does not contain language for talking about homosexuality in positive terms, then gay and lesbian counsellors and clients are silenced and excluded. If a theory does not include words to describe spiritual experience, then it becomes much harder to talk about that dimension of life in counselling or supervision. In fact, both homosexuality and religion/spirituality were largely suppressed in the language of mid-twentieth-century therapy, and it has been a long and hard struggle to allow these voices to be heard.

The purpose of theory: explanation or understanding?

There are differences in the way that the *purpose* or function of theory can be understood. From a traditional, scientific–technological standpoint, a good theory represents as close as we can get to nature, to objective external reality. A theory allows us to *explain* events, by specifying a single set of causal factors responsible for the event, and to *predict* (and therefore control) future events by applying this causal framework to the design of machines and technology. For instance, the design of a car engine is based on very precise predictions about what will happen when petrol is sparked in a cylinder etc. There is, however, another way of looking at theory. From this alternative perspective, a theory provides a way of interpreting events, with the aim of *understanding* them. A theoretical understanding involves a kind of sensitive appreciation of the multiple factors that could plausibly have contributed to an event. The possession of such an understanding can never give certain prediction, but can provide a capacity to anticipate what will happen in the future, at least in terms of considering possibilities. Theory-as-understanding opens out the possible *reasons* why something might have happened. Note here that the idea of a 'reason' allows for the possibility of human intentionality and purpose, whereas the idea of 'cause' refers to a mechanical or automatic process, with no space for human willingness or choice.

Does counselling theory provide an explanation or understanding? In many cases, it would appear that counselling and psychotherapy theories would appear to claim the status of scientific explanations. Many people who support particular theories often behave as if they believe that their ideas reflect objective truths, and singular, true explanations for the problems that people have in their lives. Some theorists have sought confirmation in 'hard' scientific research in biology, genetics and neurology to back up their claims of objective, explanatory truth. One of the approaches that has been active in trying to secure objective scientific confirmation, since the days of Freud, has been psychoanalysis. Within the psychoanalytic and psychodynamic approach, an important and influential essay was published by Rycroft (1966). In this paper, Rycroft suggested that there are profound differences between theories of therapy and scientific theories in fields such as physics and chemistry. The latter can yield cause-and-effect statements that can be used to predict future events. The former are used by people largely to attribute meaning to events that have already taken place. Rycroft argued that, despite his genius, Freud was caught between two incompatible goals: that of establishing an objective psychology, and that of creating a rich and powerful interpretive framework. Rycroft concluded that, when looked at closely, none of Freud's ideas stood scrutiny in terms of scientific criteria for causal explanations, but that his ideas did provide a solid framework for understanding. Rycroft suggested that psychoanalytic theory is all about the *reasons* why people behave in the ways that they do, not about the *causes* of their behaviour. For example, Freud's classic work is called *The Interpretation of Dreams* (1900/1997) not the '*causes* of dreams'.

Another psychoanalyst who arrived at a similar conclusion was Donald Spence (1982), who introduced the distinction between *narrative truth* and *historical truth*. Historical truth results from inquiry into past events that uncovers objective evidence of earlier events that preceded later events. Spence argued that, although they might believe that their methods revealed evidence of what had taken place in a client's childhood, psychodynamic thera- pists were very rarely (if ever) able to collect objective evidence. The best that could be hoped for, according to Spence, was a believable story, a 'narrative truth' that enabled the client to understand their life better by providing a plausible account of some of the possible reasons for their current difficulties.

The philosopher Richard Rorty (1979) offers another way of looking at the explanation versus understanding debate. He suggests that scientific theorists have been too much caught up in thinking about their work in terms of trying to create theories that function as 'mirrors of nature'. Rorty proposes that a more fruitful metaphor is that of the *conversation*: a theory is better viewed as an ongoing conversation, in which those involved in constructing, testing and using a theory continually discuss, debate and refine their ideas. The idea of a theory as an agreement between interested stakeholders around what 'works', in a pragmatic sense, rather than as an 'objective truth', also lies behind the writings of Fishman (1999).

The trend in recent years within the field of counselling and psychotherapy has been in the direction of regarding theories as interpretive frameworks, or 'lens' through which people and therapy might be viewed and understood more clearly, rather than as consti- tuting explanatory models in a traditional scientific sense. For some people, however, the drift towards an interpretive or 'constructivist' stance in relation to theory is worrying, because it raises the spectre of relativism: is everything true? Is there no objective reality at all? Some of the most important current debates within the field have focused on this dilemma (Fishman 1999; Downing 2000; Rennie 2000a). However, it would be reason- able to conclude that, even if some therapists and psychologists believe that it *should* be possible to construct a scientific–explanatory theory of therapy, there seems little doubt that none of the theories presently available are able, at this point in time, to provide such a level of theoretical certainty. The theories we have, for now, are ones that generate *understanding* rather than explanation.

Box 4.1: *The cultural specificity of theories of therapy*

Theories of therapy have evolved within a Western/European tradition of thought and practice. It is essential to acknowledge that other cultures have generated quite different theoretical systems for understanding human distress and healing. The validity or applicability of Western theories of therapy cannot be assumed in relation to work with clients from Western cultural backgrounds. Even in Western societies it could be argued that theories of therapies reflect the assumptions of dominant social class groups. The question of the cultural specificity of theory is discussed in more detail in Chapter 13.

Why do we need theory? The uses of conceptualization in counselling practice

What do counsellors do when they make use of theory? Do we need theory? What is theory *for*? These are fundamental questions, which open up an appreciation of the relationship between theory and practice.

Something to hang on to: structure in the face of chaos

The experience of being a counsellor is, typically, one of attempting to respond adequately and helpfully to complex and confusing sources of information. A client makes an appointment for a counselling session, apparently a wish to engage in a therapeutic process, and then sits slumped in his chair and says nothing. A highly successful professional woman enters counselling to deal with issues around work stress but soon talks about, and exhibits, the fear she feels about anything that reminds her of powerful memories of being a victim of violence. These are two examples of the sometimes dramatic contradictions that can be encountered in the counselling room. On some occasions, too, clients move beyond contradictions and beyond any attempt to maintain a coherent and consistent social self. In exploring painful experiences, control can be lost. Often, a client will report being stuck and hopeless, unable to see any way forward or to imagine any viable future. It is at these moments that a counsellor needs to draw deeply on a belief in his or her capacity to be helpful, and in the general capacity of human beings to learn and develop. But it can also be vital to be able to use a theoretical framework so as to begin to place what is happening into some kind of context. At difficult moments, theory gives a counsellor a basis for reflecting on experience, and a language for sharing that experience with others (for example, colleagues, a supervisor) and thus enlisting support and guidance.

Offering the client a way of making sense

One of the striking themes within the development of counselling in recent years has been the increasing emphasis given to didactic learning. Traditionally, counselling approaches such as psychodynamic and person-centred have largely relied on experiential learning and on insights or new understandings that are framed in the client's own language and the dialogue between counsellor and client. Recently, more and more counsellors and therapists have found that it is valuable for clients to acquire a theoretical framework within which they can make sense of their difficulties. Transactional analysis (TA) is one example of a therapy approach that has generated a wide range of client-oriented books and pamphlets, and that encourages therapists to explain TA concepts to clients. Many cognitive–behavioural therapists operate in a similar manner, and claim that the best evidence of whether a client has gained from therapy is when they can quote the theory back to the therapist and explain how they apply it in their everyday life. Even in therapies that do not overtly encourage clients to learn the theory there is no doubt that many clients do, on their own initiative, carry out a certain amount of background reading and study.

Constructing a case formulation

One of the early tasks for a counsellor, when beginning to work with a client, is to arrive at an overall 'formulation' of the case. A formulation usually comprises a set of hypotheses that make potential connections between the immediate problems being presented by a client, the underlying factors and processes that are responsible for these problems, and through which they are maintained, the factors in the client's life that might facilitate or impede therapy, and the therapeutic interventions or strategies that might be used in working to resolve the client's problems. Some counsellors and psychotherapists construct written formulations, which may be shared with their client. Other practitioners engage in formulation in a more implicit way, for example by talking through the elements of a formulation with their supervisor. In either scenario, a useful formulation is one in which theoretical ideas are used to make links between observations – a case formulation that does not incorporate a theoretical understanding ends up being no more than a list of presenting problems.

Establishing professional status

One of the characteristics of professions (such as law, medicine, the Church), as opposed to less formally established occupational groups, is that they can claim privileged access to a specialist body of theory and knowledge. Counsellors and psychotherapists who operate within professional networks would almost certainly be regarded as lacking in status and credibility if they lacked the 'special' knowledge and insight provided by a good theory.

Providing a framework for research

Research can be regarded as a pooling of insight and understanding, by bringing together the observations and conclusions of a wide network or community of investigators. Research can also be seen as a way of building knowledge, by testing the validity of ideas and methods. It is very difficult to carry out productive research in the absence of theoretical frameworks. Although there may be some areas of knowledge building in which it is sufficient merely to identify instances of phenomena, and itemize or classify them, the majority of scientific studies involve testing hypotheses derived from theory, or developing ways of theoretically conceptualizing patterns of events. The points in the history of counselling and psychotherapy at which the most significant advances in understanding and practice were achieved, for example in the group of client-centred therapists led by Carl Rogers at the University of Chicago in the early 1950s, occurred when communities of inquirers managed to operate simultaneously across the domains of theory, research, practice and training (McLeod 2002). At these times, it was the possession of fertile theoretical ideas that made progress possible.

Box 4.2: *Metaphors for theory*

The many different ways in which 'theory' is understood in our culture can be explored by reflecting on the multiplicity of metaphors that can be applied to the process of using a theory. These include:

- *building* an understanding or explanation; an explanatory *structure* or *framework*;
- *illuminating/shining* a light on something that is unclear;
- a *lens* that focuses on certain pieces of information;
- a *mirror* of nature;
- a *tool* for action; getting a *handle* on a confusing issue;
- a *map* of knowledge;
- a *net*work of ideas;
- a *conversation* or *dialogue* between different perspectives.

These metaphors begin to capture the different ways in which theory-making and theory-using is an essential part of everyday life.

Why are there so many theories? The diversity of theorizing about therapy

A major challenge for everyone who enters training as a counsellor or psychotherapist is the number of different therapy theories that are in circulation. One widely publicized survey, by Karasu (1986), found more than 400 different named approaches to therapy. It is clear that, in reality, there are not 400 unique ways to practice therapy. But then, why are there are so many theories? How can we understand the existence of such a degree of theoretical diversity? The proliferation of therapy theories arises from a number of factors, which are discussed in the following sections.

The historical unfolding of theories of psychotherapy

One of the reasons for the ever-expanding number of therapy theories is that different therapy theories emerged at different times in response to different social and cultural conditions. An overview of the historical unfolding of competing approaches to psycho-therapy is provided in Table 4.1. In the interest of simplicity and intelligibility, the list of theories included in this table is not complete – the aim is merely to indicate the broad historical pattern. Further discussion of the conditions under which each of these approaches came to prominence is given in later chapters. One of the striking aspects of this list is that none of the main models of psychotherapy that have been developed has ever disappeared – even forms of therapy that were created in the very different social

TABLE 4.1 Key landmarks in the development of theories of psychotherapy

Decade of first emergence	Psychotherapy approach
1890	Psychoanalysis
1910	Post-Freudian
1940	Client-centred
	Behavioural
	Psychodynamic/object relations
	Existential
1950	Psychodynamic/self theory
1960	Cognitive, rational emotive
	Family/systemic
	Gestalt, transactional analysis
1970	Cognitive–behavioural therapy (CBT)
	Feminist
	Multicultural
1980	Psychodynamic integrative: cognitive analytic, psychodynamic–interpersonal
	Philosophical counselling
1990	Narrative
	Third-wave CBT
	Emotion focused
2000	Postmodern

conditions associated with pre-World War I upper-class culture (psychoanalysis and the Jungian, Adlerian and Reichian post-Freudian therapies) are still widely practiced today, because they retain meaning and relevance for at least some practitioners and clients, and because they have adapted in response to contemporary life issues. The adaptation of theory can be seen most vividly in the case of psychoanalytic theory, which has evolved in the direction of a more socially oriented approach (object relations theory) and then assimilated ideas from cognitive therapy (cognitive analytic therapy) and humanistic therapies (psychodynamic–interpersonal therapy) that made it possible to forge a time-limited, brief therapy variant of psychoanalysis.

It can be helpful to think of psychotherapy as a form of helping that is continually 'reconstructed' in response to changing social and cultural forces. In Chapter 2, some of the important social factors responsible for the invention of psychotherapy in the nineteenth century were mentioned: the secularization of society, the movement away from authority-base relationships, the moves in the direction of greater individuality. All of these factors helped to determine the shape of psychoanalytic therapy. In more recent times, the increasing economic pressures facing health care systems have stimulated the development of brief therapies, such as CBT, and the political momentum of equal opportunities advocacy has lead to the emergence of feminist and multicultural approaches. Most recently, the popularity of narrative therapy can be viewed as a reflection of a broad cultural shift away from competitive individualism and in the direction of a more collectivist, community-based set of values for living.

Finally, some approaches to therapy can be understood in terms of the influence on the therapy world of ideas and practices from other fields. The best example of such an influence is family therapy, which originated in social work and gradually became a psychotherapeutic specialism. Other examples are arts-based therapies, nature therapy, and 'third-wave' CBT (the importation of spiritual practices such as mindfulness meditation).

A basic reason for the multiplicity of theories of therapy, therefore, is that counselling and psychotherapy does not exist in an intellectual, social or professional vacuum, but instead is constantly being reconstructed in response to external influences.

The mental health industry: brand names and special ingredients

Theoretical diversity in therapy can be understood in commercial terms. It can be argued that all therapists are essentially offering clients the same basic product (i.e., someone to talk to). The exigencies of the marketplace, however, mean that there are many pressures leading in the direction of product diversification. It is obvious to anyone socialized into the ways of the market economy that in most circumstances it is not a good idea merely to make and sell 'cars' or 'washing powder'. Who would buy an unbranded car or box of detergent? Products that are on sale usually have 'brand names', which are meant to inform the customer about the quality and reliability of the commodity being sold. To stimulate customer enthusiasm and thereby encourage sales, many products also boast 'special ingredients' or 'unique selling features', which are claimed to make the product superior to its rivals.

This analogy is applicable to counselling and therapy. The evidence from research implies that there exists a set of 'common therapeutic factors' that operate in all forms of therapy; counsellors and therapists are, like car manufacturers, all engaged in selling broadly similar products. But for reasons of professional identity, intellectual coherence and external legitimacy there have emerged a number of 'brand name' therapies. The best known of these brand name therapies have been reviewed in earlier chapters. Psychodynamic, person-centred and cognitive–behavioural approaches are widely used, generally accepted and universally recognized. They are equivalent to the Mercedes, Ford and Toyota of the therapy world. Other, smaller, 'firms' have sought to establish their own brand names. Some of these brands have established themselves in a niche in the marketplace.

The main point of this metaphor is to suggest the influence of the marketplace, the 'trade in lunacy', on the evolution of counselling theory. The huge expansion in therapies was associated with the post-war expansion of modern capitalist economies. This economic growth has slowed and stopped, as the costs of health and welfare systems, struggling to meet the needs of an ageing population and an increasing demand for more costly and sophisticated treatments, have had to be kept within limits. At this time, when counselling and therapy services are under pressure to prove their cost-effectiveness, there are strong pressures in the direction of consolidating around the powerful brand names, and finding ways to combine resources through merger or integration.

Box 4.3: *Client perspectives on counselling theory*

It is a mistake to assume that an interest in therapy theory is solely a matter for practitioners. There are many situations in which counselling clients actively engage with theoretical ideas and concepts. For example, there is a huge commercial market in therapeutic self-help books, the majority of them providing readers with a CBT-based set of explanations for the problems. Even before the recent growth in sales of self-help books, the distribution of 'academic' books written by therapy writers such as Carl Rogers, Erik Erikson and Erik Fromm, stretched far beyond the professional community. The theoretical assumptions held by clients, or the ideas that they find most credible, may also have an impact on their commitment to therapy. Bragesjo *et al.* (2004) carried out a survey of the general public in Sweden, in which participants were asked to read and comment on brief, one-page descriptions of the key ideas of psychodynamic, cognitive, and cognitive–behavioural theories of therapy. Although these approaches were rated as broadly equivalent by members of the public, in terms of their credibility and potential usefulness, there were wide variations regarding their evaluations of the theories, with some individuals strongly agreeing with certain ideas and strongly disagreeing with other therapeutic concepts. It seems likely that clients may be disappointed or confused when their therapist operates on the basis of a set of assumptions about life that are different from those that they hold themselves. Van Deurzen-Smith (1988: 1) has suggested that: 'Every approach to counselling is founded on a set of ideas and beliefs about life, about the world, and about people . . . Clients can only benefit from an approach in so far as they feel able to go along with its basic assumptions'.

   In recognition of the significance of the client's ideas and beliefs, Duncan *et al.* (2010) suggest that one of the first tasks of a counsellor or psychotherapist, on starting work with a client, is to learn about the client's theory of change, and to build their therapeutic strategy around the client's own ideas as far as possible. Similarly Stiles *et al.* (1998) argue that effective therapists do not rigidly apply theory to individual cases, but are flexible in everything they do, in a manner that is *responsive* to the preferences of their client.

The movement toward theoretical integration

The fact that so many competing theoretical models of psychotherapy have been developed can be regarded as both a strength and a weakness. It is a strength in that the field of psychotherapy encompasses a wealth of good ideas about how to understand problems, and how to help people with problems. However, it is also a weakness in that the profession as a whole is highly fragmented. On the whole, practitioners trained in one theoretical approach are unlikely to understand or appreciate the hard-won theoretical insights generated by those who espouse other approaches. Most psychotherapy approaches operate within their own professional space, and pay little attention to research or theoretical advances in other approaches. Many students or trainees of therapy, who are asked by their tutors to compare different therapy models, are surprised to find that there is very little to read on this topic. There is a huge amount of theoretical repetition across the field, because each approach develops its own theoretical language to explain the therapy relationship, the process of change, the role of emotion, and so on. Concerns around the proliferation and fragmentation of theories within psychotherapy has meant that, even in the 1930s, the issue of *theoretical integration* was being discussed (Duncan 2010). Even though the main therapy approaches that were most widely used in the 1930s and 1940s – psychoanalytic and behavioural – were so different from each other, several efforts were made to find ways to bring them together. As time went on, the search for a satisfactory means of reconciling theoretical differences, and integrating ideas and methods, remained an important intellectual pursuit within the counselling and psycho-therapy professional community (see Chapter 17). Nevertheless, at the present time the field is still largely organized around 'brand name' approaches.

The personal dimension of theory

In other disciplines, theories and ideas tend to be identified in terms of conceptual labels, rather than being known through the name of their founder. Even in mainstream psychology, theoretical terms such as behaviourism or cognitive dissonance are employed, rather than the names of their founders (J. B. Watson, Leon Festinger). In counselling and psychotherapy, by contrast, there is a tradition of identifying theories very much with their founders. Terms such as Freudian, Jungian, Adlerian, Rogerian or Lacanian are commonplace. There are probably many reasons for this. However, one factor is certainly the recognition that theories of therapy typically reflect, to a greater or lesser extent, the personality and individual worldview of the founder. Huge amounts have been written, for instance, about the links between Freud's own life and circumstances, and the ideas that came together in his psychoanalytic theory. It may be that theories of therapy are neces-sarily so personal, that it is impossible to write and formulate them without importing one's own personal experience and biases. The connections between theorizing in therapy and the personality of the theorist is explored in a classic book by Atwood and Stolorow (1993).

The biographical research carried out by Magai and Haviland-Jones (2002) has added further depth to the analysis of therapy theories as expressions of the subjectivity of their authors. Magai and Haviland-Jones (2002) carefully analysed biographical and autobio-graphical material, and video recordings of practice, relating to three key figures in the history of psychotherapy – Carl Rogers (client-centred/person-centred therapy), Albert Ellis (rational emotive therapy) and Friz Perls (gestalt therapy). Specifically, they sought to develop an understanding between the lives of these therapists, their theoretical writings and a micro-analysis of their moment-by-moment emotional states when interacting with a client.

Carl Rogers grew up in a privileged, Christian-religious family in a suburb of Chicago. Magai and Haviland-Jones (2002) concluded that Carl Rogers had experienced what they describe as an 'imperfectly secure' attachment, arising from a close early relationship with his mother, followed later by the experience of not being fully accepted by his family, which left him with a sense of vulnerability in his later relationships with others. His adult life and work was characterized by themes of commitment to healing, through interpersonal closeness and communication, and commitment to achievement. His emotional profile was organized around avoiding anger and excitement, accompanied by consistent expression of both shame and interest.

By contrast, Magai and Haviland-Jones (2002) described Albert Ellis as a person who received little attention or affirmation from either his mother or father, and experienced and extended period of hospital care between the ages of five and seven, with only infrequent visits from his parents. Magai and Haviland-Jones summarized the childhood pattern of Ellis in the following terms:

> . . . a child who is a de facto orphan and whose worries are unarticulated or fall on deaf ears . . . a four-year-old child dropped off at school with little psychological preparation and thrown in with older children, a child left to cross dangerous intersections on his own, a child who must face the uncertainties of surgery with little preparation or support, a child who is left to deal with virtual abandonment in the anonymous corridors of a big city hospital for a prolonged period of time . . .
>
> (Magai and Haviland-Jones 2002: 113).

It is little surprise that Ellis, even as early as the age of four, began to develop the cognitive strategies (e.g., 'what does happen could always be worse', 'hassles are never terrible unless you make them so') that were the precursors of his later theory of therapy. Magai and Haviland-Jones sum up his therapeutic philosophy as 'how to finesse negative emotion'.

Magai and Haviland-Jones (2002) report that Fritz Perls was born into a lower middle-class Jewish family in Berlin in 1893. With two older sisters, he was indulged by his mother, and was described as spoiled and unruly. His father, whom he hated, was frequently away on business, and had many affairs. Throughout his upbringing, he was also subjected to anti-Semitism. He found solace from family and external tensions in visiting the theatre and circus:

> . . . .what impressed him most about the actors was that they could be something other than what they were . . . In later years . . . his work in group therapy involved stripping away masks, props and roles with the goal of returning the individual to his or her real self. Concerns with masks, real and false selves, phoniness and authenticity turned out to be preoccupations that he carried throughout his life.
>
> (Magai and Haviland-Jones 2002: 156)

Later in life, Perls served in the German Army in the trenches, and was traumatized. After the war, he trained as a doctor and then as a psychoanalyst. His Jewishness and socialist political activities meant that ne was forced to flee Germany in 1933, moving first to South Africa and then to the USA. Magai and Haviland-Jones (2002) argue that these life experiences meant that Perls developed a stance of emotional self-sufficiency, and:

> could not afford to connect with the plight of helpless others . . . (he) did not, and likely could not, nurture his patients or cultivate a warm therapeutic alliance; he could not sustain long treatments with patients . . . He badgered his patients in a way that left them with no recourse but to capitulate or leave treatment
>
> (Magai and Haviland-Jones 2002: 173).

The biographical accounts constructed by Magai and Haviland-Jones (2002) concentrate mainly on psychological and interpersonal dimensions of the development of these three major theorists. However, the historical material that they present can also be viewed from a social class perspective. It is very evident that Rogers grew up in a privileged and stable upper middle-class world that was largely protected from encounter with poverty, racism and injustice. By contrast, both Ellis and Perls, in different ways, were directly exposed, from an early age, to a world in which cruelty and despair were unavoidable. These dimensions of social experience, it could be argued, have contributed to the marked contrast that exists between the moral universe portrayed in Rogers' writings – a world of basic goodness, sense of entitlement and possibility of fulfilment – and the moral universes depicted by both Ellis and Perls, which convey a sense that the best that can be achieved is individual survival, or at best temporary contact with another, in the face of unremitting threat.

This brief account of the work of Magai and Haviland-Jones (2002) does not do justice to the closely argued, uniquely detailed analysis of the links between personality formation and theoretical formulation that they have constructed. What their writing (along with that of Atwood and Stolorow 1993) does, is to demonstrate the extent to which theories of therapy are intimately grounded in the lives of the theorists, and represent the attempts of these theorists to make sense and resolve key issues in their lives. Of course, the theories that they generate will inevitably possess some degree of universal validity, because they are grappling with life issues that are common to everyone. Yet, at the same time, their theories, particularly in respect of the emotional focus that they adopt, are also inevitably slanted in the direction of one particular perspective on these core life issues.

The 'subjectivity' of therapy theories provides a partial explanation for the multiplicity of therapy theories that have been published. It seems likely that many individual therapists and counsellors find that the personal tenor of established theories does not quite chime with their own experience, with the result that they are driven to write down, and articulate through practice, training and research, their own, personal 'version' of the theory. In time, some of the next generation of therapists to be trained in this new theory will in turn be drawn towards making their own personal statement of theory, in reaction to what they have been taught. And so the theory production line continues.

Box 4.4: *Choosing a theory: a key theme in counsellor development*

A recurring task within the working lives of counsellors, is that of finding a blend of theory that is both personally meaningful and professionally effective (Fitzpatrick *et al.* 2010). A collection of biographical accounts of the change and transformation in therapists, over the course of their careers, has been produced by Goldfried (2001). It is possible to see, in this group of experienced therapists, that the majority of them engaged in a 'theory search' during at least the first 20 years of their professional lives, only arriving at a settled theoretical framework for practice after much experimentation and exploration. Skovholt and Jennings (2004) carried out intensive interviews with a set of 'master therapists' – practitioners who were considered by their colleagues to be the 'best of the best'. A central theme within the descriptions generated by these informants, of the beliefs and attitudes that shaped their approach, was an insatiable curiosity about new ideas. A pattern that is often seen in the therapists studied by Goldfried (2001) and Skovholt and Jennings (2004), but also in the lives of counsellors whose accomplishments have not been celebrated in print, is the experience of finding a theoretical 'home' fairly early in a career. Typically, a practitioner's intellectual home is provided by the initial training programme they have completed, or by a mentor with whom they have worked closely. However, the 'home theory' is rarely felt to be sufficient in itself, and the majority of practitioners will eventually embark on a quest to expand their theoretical understanding into new areas, by learning about new theories and models, before finally arriving at a theoretical synthesis or integration with which they are satisfied.

A postmodern perspective: theory as narrative

Underlying the ideas that have been introduced in this chapter, there lies a fundamental tension regarding the attitudes practitioners have in relation to theory. Essentially, there exists a split between those who regard theories as reflecting an ultimate *truth* about the way that the world operates, and those who view theory as a practical *tool* for understanding. Because psychotherapy has largely developed in a professional and academic context, within psychology and medicine, that emphasizes the value of rigorous scientific method (which involves creating and testing theories), there has been a tendency for the leading figures in the therapy world to explain their work in scientific terms, and construct formal theories that took the form of 'truths'. The Western societies in which psychotherapy evolved during the twentieth century placed great emphasis on progress and the achievement of objective truth. As a result, all of the mainstream therapy approaches that emerged in the early- and mid-twentieth century were built around core ideas that their founders believed to be objectively and universally true.

For Freud, the unconscious mind and the relationship between childhood events and adult neuroses were objective truths, which in the fullness of time would be shown to have biological and neurological correlates. For behaviourists such as Skinner, learning through stimulus–response reinforcement was an objective truth. For Rogers, the self-concept and the actualizing tendency were objective realities that could in principle be observed and measured. One consequence of believing in the ultimate validity of such 'truths' was the conclusion that people who did not share the chosen belief were wrong and mistaken. These others then needed to be converted to the one truth, or their heresies needed to be defended against, or, as a last resort, they could be ignored. The legacy of these attitudes has been that, to this day, the world of psychotherapy (and to some extent also, the world of counselling) remains divided – between major schools or approaches that dispute the validity of each other's work, and then into many smaller sects.

The alternative to the 'objectivist' approach to theory is to adopt a postmodern perspective, informed by philosophical ideas from constructivism and social constructionism (Lock and Strong 2010; Mahoney 2003). From this perspective, a theory is viewed as a set of conceptual tools, that allow the theory-user to make connections between different observations, gain understanding and insight, communicate with others and plan actions. The touchstone of good theory, from a postmodern point of view, is not the metaphysical question 'is it true', but instead is the pragmatic question 'does it work?' Adopting a postmodern perspective allows therapy theories to be understood as comprising plausible stories that circulate within a culture, regarding what it means to be a person, how problems arise in people's lives, and how these problems can be healed. The aim of counsellor training, according to Hansen (2006: 295), is therefore:

> . . . not . . . for the student to absorb transcendental truths from the enlightened university intelligentsia; rather, counselor education provides prospective counselors with a repertoire of narrative possibilities for reframing the lives of their future clients. That is, clients typically enter counseling with meaning systems that have failed to support adaptive functioning. In order to reconstruct these systems so optimal living is enhanced, counselors must be prepared with a variety of reconstructive, narrative possibilities. If counselors did not enter the counseling situation with narrative tool kits, or theories, to counter and enrich the maladaptive narratives of their clients, counselors would have little to contribute to a coconstruction of new meanings within the counseling process. Education, therefore, under the postmodern vision of counselling can be reconceptualized as narrative preparation.

A narrative, postmodern approach invites counsellors to celebrate the powerful transformational possibilities of a wide range of theories of therapy. It places theory, understood as a 'narrative toolkit', right at the heart of the therapy process, functioning as a resource that clients can use to change their lives.

Conclusions: the role of theory in counselling

In the past, most psychotherapy training and practice has been based on immersion in and socialization into one theoretical approach. Although the field of psychotherapy has become more open to theoretical integration in recent years, it is still the case that psychotherapy research is overwhelmingly based on the evaluation of the effectiveness of single-theory interventions for particular clinical conditions (e.g., CBT for social anxiety, interpersonal therapy for depression), and in some clinical psychology settings the practice of psychotherapy is organized around the delivery of manualized, protocol-drive single-therapy interventions. Within the domain of psychotherapy, therefore, it makes sense for training and practice to engage with theory at the level of discrete 'pure' models.

The situation in counselling is quite different. The areas in which counselling differs from psychotherapy, from a theory-using point of view are:

1 A substantial amount of counselling is provided my minimally trained volunteers or paraprofessionals, or practitioners of other professions (e.g., teaching, social work), whose theoretical knowledge is not sufficient for anyone to believe that what they are doing is informed to any significant degree by formal theories of therapy.

2 Counselling services tend to be built around particular social problems and issues, for example bereavement, domestic violence and marital problems, rather than (as in psychotherapy) psychological problems such as depression, anxiety or personality disorder. This means that counsellors (unlike psychotherapists) need to acquire theoretical frameworks for understanding and explaining the 'social problem' aspect of their work, as well as frameworks for understanding the psychological processes that happen with clients. In other words, a marriage/couple counsellor needs to have a theoretical grasp of the nature of marriage in contemporary society, a bereavement counsellor needs to have a grasp of how society copes with death, and a work stress counsellor needs to know about employment law and organizational structures. The implication here is that a counsellor needs to acquire and use: (a) a wide repertoire of theory, encompassing sociological perspectives; and (b) some kind of 'meta-theory' through which sociological ideas can be used alongside psychological concepts from therapy theories.

3 On the whole, the history, tradition and ethos of counselling is antithetical to any kind of obedience to fixed ideologies. What is important in counselling is to work with the person or group in ways that make sense to them – to start from wherever the client is. Often, people (mostly women) enter counselling training as a second career, following plentiful life experience, and are sceptical about the meaningfulness or practical value of purist theories.

As a consequence of these factors, the tendency in the counselling world is for trainees and practitioners to read widely, in terms of theory, and assemble a theoretical framework that makes sense to them personally, and which has practical utility in terms of the client group with which they work. Similarly, counselling agencies and services tend to evolve their own idiosyncratic set of theoretical 'readings', and conceptual language that is used in communicating between colleagues – often it can take new recruits some time before they learn how to decipher the theoretical code being used in a new place of work. A postmodern perspective, which takes the view that therapy theories are best understood as well-loved stories and conversation resources, fits well with the nature of everyday counselling practice.

Finally, it may be helpful to look at how the concept of 'theory' is used in the context of music. If someone is learning to play a musical instrument, and goes to classes on 'music theory', then what they acquire is a capacity to understand and follow a set of instructions for performing a musical score in the correct manner. But it is possible to be a creative and entertaining musician without knowing any music 'theory'. And being expert in music theory does not guarantee a satisfying performance – a good player needs to be able to interpret the score, appreciate the composer's intentions and the tradition he or she was composing within, make human contact with the audience and fellow players, and so on.

The following chapters present a series of alternative theoretical perspectives from which counselling and psychotherapy can be practised. In reading this theory, it is necessary, as with music, to interpret the text in the light of the composer, his or her intentions and the tradition that he or she worked within, and to remember that the theory is merely a vehicle for making contact with the audience (client) and fellow players (colleagues).

Topics for reflection and discussion

1 Make a list of the theoretical terms and concepts you routinely use in talking about counselling. Identify which you employ as 'observational' labels and which refer to more abstract theoretical assumptions. What does this tell you about the theoretical model(s) you use in practice?

2 What is the theoretical 'language' used in the agency in which you do your work as a counsellor (or attend as a client)? Alternatively, what is the theoretical 'language' of the training course you are, or have been, participating in? To what extent is this language coherent (i.e., are apparently contradictory ideas used alongside each other)? How are new people socialized into the language? What happens if, or when, someone uses a different language?

3 Focus on the theory that was constructed by a major therapy writer who has influenced you. Find out about the early life of this person, and the social world in which his or her attitudes to life were formed. In what ways has the theory of therapy associated with this person been shaped by these personal and subjective factors? What are the implications of this aspect of the theory, in terms of its general applicability and validity?

4 Take any two theories of therapy that interest you, and that you know about. Reflect on: (a) what topics and experiences are easy to talk about using each 'theoretical language', and (b) which topics and experiences are difficult or impossible to talk about? What are the implications of each 'theoretical vocabulary' for the practice of counselling/psychotherapy carried out from the basis of each approach?

5 The social psychologist Kurt Lewin believed that 'there is nothing as practical as a good theory' (Lewin 1952: 169; Marrow 1969). How valid is this statement, in the context of counselling?

Suggested further reading

A series of fascinating biographical accounts of the role of theory in the lives of well-known therapy writers, can be found in *The Hidden Genius of Emotion* (Magai and Haviland-Jones 2002) and *How Therapists Change* (Goldfried 2001). The complex and sometimes contradictory philosophical assumptions that inform theories of therapy are discussed in an accessible manner in the writings of Brent Slife (Slife 2004; Slife and Williams 1995) and James Hansen (2004, 2006, 2007). Philosophical issues associated with the use of theory in therapy are discussed in depth by Downing (2000).

CHAPTER

5

Themes and issues in the psychodynamic approach to counselling

Introduction

The psychodynamic approach represents one of the major traditions within contemporary counselling and psychotherapy. Psychodynamic counselling places great emphasis on the counsellor's ability to use what happens in the immediate, unfolding relationship between client and counsellor to explore the types of feelings and relationship dilemmas that have caused difficulties for the client in his or her everyday life. The aim of psychodynamic counselling is to help clients to achieve insight and understanding around the reasons for their problems, and translate this insight into a mature capacity to cope with current and future difficulties. To enable this process to take place, the counsellor needs to be able to offer the client an environment that is sufficiently secure and consistent to permit safe expression of painful or shameful phantasies, impulses and memories.

Although psychodynamic counselling has its origins in the ideas of Sigmund Freud, current theory and practice have gone far beyond Freud's initial formulation. Whereas Freud was convinced that repressed sexual wishes and memories lay at the root of the patient's problems, later generations of practitioners and theorists have developed a more social, relationship-oriented approach. Psychodynamic methods have been applied to understanding and treating a wide range of problems, and have been adapted to a variety of ways of working, including brief therapy, group therapy and marital/couples counselling.

The aim of this chapter is to introduce some of the main ideas and methods involved in the theory and practice of psychodynamic counselling. The chapter begins with an account of Freud's ideas. Freud remains a key point of reference for the majority of psychodynamic counsellors and psychotherapists, and later developments in psychodynamic counselling can all be viewed as an ongoing debate with Freud – sometimes disagreeing markedly with his positions, but always returning to his core ideas. Subsequent sections in the chapter review the significance of object relations and attachment theory, and other important themes in psychodynamic thinking.

The origins of psychodynamic counselling: the work of Sigmund Freud

Sigmund Freud (1856–1939) is widely regarded as being not only one of the founders of modern psychology, but also a key influence on Western society in the twentieth century. As a boy Freud had ambitions to be a famous scientist, and he originally trained in medicine, becoming in the 1880s one of the first medical researchers to investigate the properties of the newly discovered coca leaf (cocaine). However, anti-Semitism in Austrian middle-class society at that time meant that he was unable to continue his career at the University of Vienna, and he was forced to enter private practice in the field that would now be known as psychiatry. Freud spent a year in Paris studying with the most eminent psychiatrist of the time, Charcot, who taught him the technique of hypnosis. Returning to Vienna, Freud began seeing patients who were emotionally disturbed, many of them suffering from what was known as 'hysteria'. He found that hypnosis was not particularly effective for him as a treatment technique, and gradually evolved his own method, called 'free association', which consisted of getting the patient to lie in a relaxed position (usually on a couch) and to 'say whatever comes to mind'. The stream-of-consciousness material that emerged from this procedure often included strong emotions, deeply buried memories and childhood sexual experiences, and the opportunity to share these feelings and memories appeared to be helpful for patients. One of them, Anna O., labelled this method 'the talking cure'. Further information about the development of Freud's ideas, and the influence on his thought of his own early family life, his Jewishness, his medical training and the general cultural setting of late nineteenth-century Vienna, can be found in a number of books and articles (e.g., Wollheim 1971; Gay 1988; Jacobs 1992; Langman 1997).

Freud's method of treatment is called psychoanalysis. From the time his theory and method became known and used by others (starting from about 1900) his ideas have been continually modified and developed by other writers on and practitioners of psychoanalysis. As a result, there are now many counsellors and psychotherapists who would see themselves as working within the broad tradition initiated by Freud, but who would call themselves *psychodynamic* in orientation rather than psychoanalytic. Counsellors working in a psychodynamic way with clients all tend to make similar kinds of assumptions about the nature of the client's problems, and the manner in which these problems can best be worked on. The main distinctive features of the psychodynamic approach are:

1 An assumption that the client's difficulties have their ultimate origins in childhood experiences.

2 An assumption that the client may not be consciously aware of the true motives or impulses behind his or her actions.

3 The use in counselling and therapy of interpretation of the transference relationship.

These features will now be examined in more detail.

The childhood origins of emotional problems

Freud noted that, in the 'free association' situation, many of his patients reported remembering unpleasant or fearful sexual experiences in childhood, and, moreover, that the act of telling someone else about these experiences was therapeutic. Freud could not believe that these childhood sexual traumas had actually happened in reality (although today we might disagree), and made sense of this phenomenon by suggesting that what had really happened had its roots in the child's own sexual needs.

It is important to be clear here about what Freud meant by 'sexual'. In his own writing, which was of course in German, he used a concept that might more accurately be translated as 'life force' or, more generally, 'emotional energy' (Bettelheim 1983). Although this concept has a sexual aspect to it, it is unfortunate that its English translation focuses only on this aspect.

Freud surmised, from listening to his patients talk about their lives, that the sexual energy, or libido, of the child develops or matures through a number of distinct phases. In the first year of life, the child experiences an almost erotic pleasure from its mouth, its oral region. Babies get satisfaction from sucking, biting and swallowing. Then, between about two and four years of age, children get pleasure from defecating, from feelings in their anal region. Then, at around five to eight years of age, the child begins to have a kind of immature genital longing, which is directed at members of the opposite sex. Freud called this the phallic stage. (Freud thought that the child's sexuality became less important in older childhood, and he called this the latency stage.)

The phases of psycho-sexual development set the stage for a series of conflicts between the child and its environment, its family and, most important of all, its parents. Freud saw the parents or family as having to respond to the child's needs and impulses, and he argued that the way in which the parents responded had a powerful influence on the later personality of the child. Mainly, the parents or family could respond in a way that was too controlling or one that was not controlling enough. For example, little babies cry when they are hungry. If the mother feeds the baby immediately every time, or even feeds before the demand has been made, the baby may learn, at a deep emotional level, that it does not need to do anything to be taken care of. It may grow up believing, deep down, that there exists a perfect world and it may become a person who finds it hard to accept the inevitable frustrations of the actual world. On the other hand, if the baby has to wait too long to be fed, it may learn that the world only meets its needs if it gets angry or verbally aggressive. Somewhere in between these two extremes is what the British psychoanalyst D. W. Winnicott (1964) has called the 'good enough' mother, the mother or caretaker who responds quickly enough without being over-protective or smothering.

Freud suggests a similar type of pattern for the anal stage. If the child's potty training is too rigid and harsh, it will learn that it must never allow itself to make a mess, and may grow up finding it difficult to express emotions and with an obsessive need to keep everything in its proper place. If the potty training is too permissive, on the other hand, the child may grow up without the capacity to keep things in order.

The third developmental stage, the phallic stage, is possibly the most significant in terms of its effects on later life. Freud argues that the child at this stage begins to feel primitive genital impulses, which are directed at the most obvious target: its opposite-sex parent. Thus at this stage little girls are 'in love' with their fathers and little boys with their mothers. But, Freud goes on, the child then fears the punishment or anger of the same-sex parent if this sexual longing is expressed in behaviour. The child is then forced to repress its sexual feelings, and also to defuse its rivalry with the same-sex parent by identifying more strongly with that parent. Usually, this 'family drama' would be acted out at a largely unconscious level. The effect later on, in adulthood, might be that people continue to repress or distort their sexuality, and that in their sexual relationships (e.g., marriage) they might be unconsciously seeking the opposite-sex parents they never had. The basic psychological problem here, as with the other stages, lies in the fact that the person's impulses or drives are 'driven underground', and influence the person unconsciously. Thus, someone might not be consciously aware of having 'chosen' a marriage partner who symbolically represents his or her mother or father, but his or her behaviour towards the partner may follow the same pattern as the earlier parent–child relationship. An example of this might be the husband who as a child was always criticized by his mother, and who later on seems always to expect his wife to behave in the same way.

It may be apparent from the previous discussion that, although Freud in his original theory emphasized the psycho-sexual nature of childhood development, what really influences the child emotionally and psychologically as he or she grows up is the quality of the relationships he or she has with his or her parents and family. This realization has led more recent writers in the psychodynamic tradition to emphasize the psycho-social development of the child rather than the sexual and biological aspects.

One of the most important of these writers is the psychoanalyst Erik Erikson, whose book *Childhood and Society* (1950) includes a description of eight stages of psycho-social development, covering the whole lifespan. His first stage, during the first year or so of life, is equivalent to Freud's 'oral' stage. Erikson, however, suggests that the early relationship between mother and child is psychologically significant because it is in this relationship that the child either learns to trust the world (if his or her basic needs are met) or acquires a basic sense of mistrust. This sense of trust or mistrust may then form the foundation for the type of relationships the child has in later adult life.

Another writer who stresses the psycho-social events of childhood is the British psychoanalyst John Bowlby (1969, 1973, 1980, 1988). In his work, he examines the way that the experience of attachment (the existence of a close, safe, continuing relationship) and loss in childhood can shape the person's capacity for forming attachments in adult life.

Although subsequent theorists in the psychodynamic tradition have moved the emphasis away from Freud's focus on sexuality in childhood, they would still agree that the emotions and feelings that are triggered by childhood sexual experiences can have powerful effects on the child's development. However, the basic viewpoint that is shared by all psychoanalytic and psychodynamic counsellors and therapists is that to understand the personality of an adult client or patient it is necessary to understand the development of that personality through childhood, particularly with respect to how it has been shaped by its family environment.

The importance of the 'unconscious'

Freud did not merely suggest that childhood experiences influence adult personality; he suggested that the influence occurred in a particular way – through the operation of the unconscious mind. The 'unconscious', for Freud, was the part of the mental life of a person that was outside direct awareness. Freud saw the human mind as divided into three regions:

- The id ('it'), a reservoir of primitive instincts and impulses that are the ultimate motives for our behaviour. Freud assumed that there were two core drives: life/love/sex/Eros and death/hate/aggression/Thanatos. The id has no time dimension, so that memories trapped there through repression can be as powerful as when the repressed event first happened. The id is governed by the 'pleasure principle', and is irrational.

- The ego ('I'), the conscious, rational part of the mind, which makes decisions and deals with external reality.

- The superego ('above I'), the 'conscience', the store-house of rules and taboos about what you should and should not do. The attitudes a person has in the superego are mainly an internalization of his or her parents' attitudes.

There are two very important implications of this theory of how the mind works. First, the id and most of the superego were seen by Freud as being largely unconscious, so that much of an individual's behaviour could be understood as being under the control of forces (e.g., repressed memories, childhood fantasies) that the person cannot consciously acknowledge. The psychodynamic counsellor or therapist, therefore, is always looking for ways of getting 'beneath the surface' of what the client or patient is saying – the assumption is that what the person initially says about himself or herself is only part of the story, and probably not the most interesting part.

Second, the ego and the other regions (the id and superego) are, potentially at any rate, almost constantly in conflict with each other. For example, the id presses for its primitive impulses to be acted upon ('I hate him so I want to hit him') but the ego will know that such behaviour would be punished by the external world, and the superego tries to make the person feel guilty because what he or she wants to do is wrong or immoral. It is, however, highly uncomfortable to live with such a degree of inner turmoil, and so Freud argued that the mind develops defence mechanisms – for example, repression, denial, reaction formation, sublimation, intellectualization and projection – to protect the ego from such pressure. So, not only is what the person consciously believes only part of the story, it is also likely to be a part that is distorted by the operation of defence mechanisms.

Box 5.1: *The concept of transference*

The concept of transference represents one of the fundamental cornerstones of psychodynamic theory and practice. Freud discovered that as soon as he began to encourage his patients to express whatever it was that they were thinking and feeling (free association) that their view of him was not based on an objective or rational response to his actual behaviour and demeanour. Instead, they developed strong positive or negative feelings about him that had no apparent basis in reality. What he soon realized was that it was as if his patients were perceiving him through a lens or filter constructed from previous relationships in their lives. They were experiencing him as if he was a harsh father, or loving mother, or seductive governess, or whatever mix of significant early attachments had shaped their way of being with other people. He also began to appreciate that this process occurs in everyday life (someone immediately falls in love with a person they know nothing about, or feels like a little child when their boss speaks to them), but is less readily detected because so much else is happening within a relationship. By contrast, the unique environment of the therapy relationship, in which the therapist maintains rigorously neutral, allows these underlying ways of being with others gradually to come into focus.

Within psychodynamic theory, the general everyday manifestations of distortions in the ways in which people relate to each other are discussed under the heading of *defence mechanisms*. Within the setting of the therapy room, the same phenomena are described as *transference*. The concept of transference has been defined by two leading figures in contemporary psychodynamic practice in the following terms:

> the conscious and unconscious responses – both affective and cognitive – of the patient to the therapist.
>
> (Maroda 2004: 66)

> 'transference': the unconscious transferring of past relationship into the present, especially as it appears in the psychoanalytic or psychotherapeutic setting. Transference is both positive, with the patient feeling love and

dependency on the analyst as the giving, nurturing, perhaps sexually exciting parent; and also negative, with the analyst being experienced as the with-holding, forbidding and cruel parent.

(Gomez 1997: 26)

Over the years, psychodynamic therapy has consistently moved in the direction of regarding the exploration of transference reactions (and the *counter-transference* response of the therapist) as a central component of the therapeutic endeavour. If the client can arrive at a point of displaying what he or she really feels for the therapist (whether love, hate or anything else), then the stage is set for a re-enactment of the original scenarios that laid down their basic emotional attitudes towards other people. The task of the therapist, when these critical moments arise, is to 'behave differently from the original characters in the patient's life drama' (Maroda 2004: 4). If this happens, the client begins to become aware of new and different possibilities around relationships with others.

The therapeutic techniques used in psychoanalysis

The Freudian or psychodynamic theory described in the previous sections originally emerged out of the work of Freud and others on helping people with emotional problems. Many aspects of the theory have, therefore, been applied to the question of how to facilitate therapeutic change in clients or patients. Before we move on to look at the specific techniques used in psychoanalytic or psychodynamic therapy and counselling, however, it is essential to be clear about just what the aims of such treatment are. Freud used the phrase 'where id was, let ego be' to summarize his aims. In other words, rather than being driven by unconscious forces and impulses, people after therapy will be more rational, more aware of their inner emotional life and more able to control these feelings in an appropriate manner. A key aim of psychoanalysis is, then, the achievement of insight into the true nature of one's problems (i.e., their childhood origins). But genuine insight is not merely an intellectual exercise – when the person truly understands, he or she will experience a release of the emotional tension associated with the repressed or buried memories. Freud used the term 'catharsis' to describe this emotional release.

Box 5.2: *The mechanisms of defence*

Anne Freud, the youngest child of Sigmund Freud, trained as a psychoanalyst and went on to be one of the pioneers of child analysis. Anna Freud also made a major theoretical contribution to psychoanalysis by elaborating and refining her father's ideas about the role of *defence mechanisms*. This increasing attention to the ways in which the ego defends itself against emotionally threatening unconscious impulses and wishes represents an important step away from the original biologically oriented psychoanalystic 'drive' theory, in the direction of an 'ego' psychology that gave more emphasis to cognitive processes. The key defence mechanisms described by Anna Freud (1936/1966) in her book *The Ego and the Mechanisms of Defence* included:

- *Repression* (motivated forgetting): the instant removal from awareness of any threatening impulse, idea or memory.

- *Denial* (motivated negation): blocking of external events and information from awareness.

- *Projection* (displacement outwards): attributing to another person one's own unacceptable desires or thoughts.

- *Displacement* (redirection of impulses): channelling impulses (typically aggressive ones) on to a different target.

- *Reaction formation* (asserting the opposite): defending against unacceptable impulses by turning them into the opposite.

- *Sublimation* (finding an acceptable substitute): transforming an impulse into a more socially acceptable form of behaviour.

- *Regression* (developmental retreat): responding to internal feelings triggered by an external threat by reverting to 'child-like' behaviour from an earlier stage of development.

Although it may often be straightforward to identify these kinds of patterns of behaviour in people who seek counselling (and in everyday life), it is less clear just how best a counsellor might respond to such defences. Is it best to draw the client's attention to the fact that they are using a defence mechanism? Is it more effective to attempt gently to help the person to put into words the difficult feelings that are being defended against? Is it useful to offer an interpretation of how the defensive pattern arose in the person's life, and the role it plays? Or is it better to respond in the 'here-and-now', perhaps by reflecting on how the counsellor feels when, for example, certain assumptions are projected on to him or her? From a psychodynamic perspective, there are many issues and choices involved in knowing how to use an awareness of the mechanisms of defence in the interests of the client. The writings of the British analyst David Malan (1979) provide an invaluable guide to ways of using the interpretation of defences to help clients to develop insight and, eventually, more satisfying relationships.

There are a number of therapeutic techniques or strategies used in psychoanalytic or psychodynamic therapy.

1 *Systematic use of the relationship between the counsellor and client.* Psychoanalytic counsellors and therapists tend to behave towards their clients in a neutral manner. It is unusual for psychoanalytically trained counsellors to share much of their own feelings or own lives with their clients. The reason for this is that the counsellor is attempting to present himself or herself as a 'blank screen' on to which the client may project his or her fantasies or deeply held assumptions about close relationships. The

therapist expects that as therapy continues over weeks or months, the feelings clients hold towards him or her will be similar to the feelings they had towards significant, authority figures in their own past. In other words, if the client behaved in a passive, dependent way with her own mother as a child, then she could reproduce this behaviour with her therapist. By being neutral and detached, the therapist ensures that the feelings the client has towards him or her are not caused by anything the therapist has done, but are a result of the client projecting an image of his or her mother, father etc. on to the therapist. This process is called transference and is a powerful tool in psychoanalytic therapy, since it allows the therapist to observe the early childhood relationships of the client as these relationships are re-enacted in the consulting room. The aim would be to help the client to become aware of these projections, first in the relationship with the therapist but then in relationships with other people, such as his or her spouse, boss, friends and so on.

2 *Identifying and analysing resistances and defences.* As the client talks about his or her problem, the therapist may notice that he or she is avoiding, distorting or defending against certain feelings or insights. Freud saw it as important to understand the source of such resistance, and would draw the patient's attention to it if it happened persistently. For example, a student seeing a counsellor for help with study problems, who then persistently blames tutors for his difficulties, is probably avoiding his own feelings of inadequacy, or dependency, by employing the defence mechanism of projection (i.e., attributing to others characteristics you cannot accept in yourself).

3 *Free association or 'saying whatever comes to mind'.* The intention is to help the person to talk about himself or herself in a fashion that is less likely to be influenced by defence mechanisms. It is as though in free association the person's 'truth' can slip out.

4 *Working on dreams and fantasies.* Freud saw the dream as 'the royal road to the unconscious', and encouraged his patients to tell him about their dreams. Again the purpose is to examine material that comes from a deeper, less defended, level of the individual's personality. It is assumed that events in dreams symbolically represent people, impulses or situations in the dreamer's waking life. Other products of the imagination – for example, waking dreams, fantasies and images – can be used in the same way as night dreams in analysis.

5 *Interpretation.* A psychoanalytic counsellor or therapist will use the processes described above – transference, dreams, free association etc. – to generate material for interpretation. Through interpreting the meaning of dreams, memories and transference, the therapist is attempting to help clients to understand the origins of their problems, and thereby gain more control over them and more freedom to behave differently. However, effective interpretation is a difficult skill. Some of the issues that the therapist or counsellor must bear in mind when making an interpretation are:

● Is the timing right? Is the client ready to take this idea on board?

● Is the interpretation correct? Has enough evidence been gathered?

● Can the interpretation be phrased in such a way that the client will understand it?

6 *Other miscellaneous techniques.* When working with children as clients it is unrealistic to expect them to be able to put their inner conflicts into words. As a result, most

child analysts use toys and play to allow the child to externalize his or her fears and worries. Some therapists working with adults also find it helpful to use expressive techniques, such as art, sculpture and poetry. The use of projective techniques, such as the Rorschach Inkblot Test or the Thematic Apperception Test (TAT), can also serve a similar function. Finally, some psychodynamic therapists may encourage their clients to write diaries or autobiographies as a means of exploring their past or present circumstances.

Although the number of actual psychoanalysts in Britain is small, the influence on counselling in general of psychoanalysis and the psychodynamic tradition has been immense. It is probably true to say that virtually all counsellors have been influenced at some level by psychoanalytic ideas. It should be acknowledged that the understanding of Freud in Britain and the USA is a version filtered through his translators. Bettelheim (1983) has suggested that the ideas and concepts introduced by Freud in his original writings (in German) have been made more 'clinical' and more mechanical through translation into English.

The account of Freudian theory and practice given here can provide no more than a brief introduction to this area of literature. The interested reader who would wish to explore psychoanalytic thinking in more depth is recommended to consult Freud's own work. *The Introductory Lectures* (Freud 1917/1973), *New Introductory Lectures* (Freud 1933/1973) and the case studies of the *Rat Man* (Freud 1909/1979), *Schreber* (Freud 1910/1979) and *Dora* (Freud 1901/1979) represent particularly accessible and illuminating examples of the power of Freudian analysis in action.

The post-Freudian evolution of the psychodynamic approach

It is well documented that Freud demanded a high level of agreement with his ideas from those around him. During his lifetime, several important figures in psychoanalysis who had been his students or close colleagues were involved in disputes with Freud and subsequently left the International Association for Psycho-Analysis. The best known of these figures is Carl Jung, who was regarded as Freud's 'favourite son' within the psychoanalytic circle, and was expected in time to take over the leadership of the psychoanalytic movement. The correspondence between Freud and Jung has been collected and published, and illustrates a growing split between the two men which became irrevocable in 1912. The principal area of disagreement between Freud and Jung centred on the nature of motivation. Jung argued that human beings have a drive towards 'individuation', or the integration and fulfilment of self, as well as more biologically based drives associated with sexuality. Jung also viewed the unconscious as encompassing spiritual and transcendental areas of meaning.

Other prominent analysts who broke off from Freud included Ferenczi, Rank, Reich and Adler. Ferenczi and Rank were frustrated with the lack of interest Freud showed in the question of technique, of how to make the therapy a more effective means of helping patients. Reich left to pursue the bodily, organismic roots of defences, the ways in which the sexual and aggressive energy that is held back by repression, denial and other defences is expressed through bodily processes such as muscle tension, posture and illness. The theme that Adler developed was the significance of social factors in emotional life: for example, the drive for power and control, which is first experienced in situations of sibling rivalry.

The disagreements between Freud and his followers are misunderstood if they are regarded as mere personality clashes, examples of Freud's irrationality or attributable to cultural factors such as the Austrian Jewishness of Freud as against the Swiss Protestantism of Jung. These disagreements and splits represent fundamental theoretical issues within the psychodynamic approach, and although the personalization of the debate during the early years can obscure the differences over ideas and technique, it also helps by making the lines of the debate clear. The underlying questions being debated by Freud and his colleagues were:

- What happens in the early years of life to produce later problems?
- How do unconscious processes and mechanisms operate?
- What should the therapist do to make psychoanalytic therapy most effective for patients or clients (the question of technique)?

While Freud was alive he dominated psychoanalysis, and those who disagreed with him were forced to set up separate and independent institutes and training centres. The results of these schisms in psychoanalysis persist to this day, in the continued existence of separate Jungian, Adlerian and Reichian approaches. After the death of Freud in 1939, it became possible to re-open the debate in a more open fashion, and to reintegrate some of the ideas of the 'heretics' into a broader-based psychodynamic approach. It would be impossible to review here all the interesting and useful elements of contemporary psychodynamic thinking about counselling and psychotherapy. However, three of the most important directions in which the approach has evolved since Freud's death have been through the development of a theoretical perspective known as the 'object relations' approach, the work of the British 'Independents' and the refinements to technique necessary to offer psychodynamic counselling and therapy on a time-limited basis.

Box 5.3: *The Jungian tradition in psychodynamic counselling and psychotherapy*

The Jungian approach, also known as *analytic psychology*, was created by C. G. Jung (1875–1961). Jung was a Swiss psychiatrist who was one of the earliest members of the circle around Freud, the 'favourite son' who was predicted to take over from Freud as leader of the psychoanalytic movement. Jung split with Freud in 1912 through disagreement over theoretical differences. In particular, Jung diverged from the Freudian position on the predominance of sexual motives in the unconscious. Jung developed a concept of the 'collective unconscious', which he saw as structured through 'archetypes', symbolic representations of universal facets of human experience, such as the mother, the trickster, the hero. Perhaps the best known of the Jungian archetypes is the 'shadow', or animus (in women) or anima (in men), which represents those aspects of the self that are denied to conscious awareness. Another difference between Freud and Jung was highlighted in their views on development. Freudian thinking on development is restricted largely to events in childhood, particularly the oral, anal and Oedipal stages. Jung, on the other hand, saw human development as a lifelong quest for fulfilment, which he called 'individuation'. Jung also evolved a system for understanding personality differences, in which people can be categorized as 'types' made up of sensation/intuition, extraversion/introversion and thinking/feeling.

There is substantial common ground between psychodynamic approaches to counselling and the 'analytic' approach of Jung, in the shared assumptions regarding the importance of unconscious processes and the value of working with dreams and fantasy. There are, however, also significant areas of contrast, centred on the understanding of the unconscious and ideas of development and personality. Jung was also highly influenced by religious and spiritual teachings, whereas Freud was committed to a more secular, scientific approach. In recent years there has been a strong interest in Jungian approaches within the counselling and psychotherapy community. There has been a proliferation of new texts elaborating Jungian concepts and methods. The application of a Jungian perspective to gender issues has been a particularly successful area of inquiry. Although the process of Jungian analysis is lengthy, and more appropriate for the practice of psychotherapy than for counselling (at least as counselling is defined in most agencies), many counsellors have read Jung or interpreters of his work (such as Kopp 1972, 1974) and have integrated ideas such as the 'shadow' into their own way of making sense of therapy. The Jungian model of personality type has also influenced many counsellors through the use in personal development work of the Myers–Biggs Type Indicator (MBTI), a questionnaire devised to assess personality type in individuals.

The most accessible of Jung's writings are his autobiography, *Memories, Dreams, Reflections* (Jung 1963), and *Man and His Symbols* (Jung 1964). Other valuable introductory texts are Fordham (1986), Kaufmann (1989) and Carvalho (1990).

The object relations school

The 'object relations' approach to psychoanalysis and psychodynamic counselling and psychotherapy has been highly influential. It is based on direct observation of the behaviour of babies and infants, and its application involves a relationship-oriented approach to therapy (Gomez 1997).

The origins of object relations theory in child observation. The originator of the object relations movement within the psychodynamic approach is usually accepted to be Melanie Klein. Born in Austria, Klein trained with a student of Freud, Sandor Ferenczi, in Hungary, and eventually moved to Britain in 1926, becoming an influential member of the British Psycho-Analytical Society. The work of Klein was distinctive in that she carried out psychoanalysis with children, and placed emphasis on the relationship between mother and child in the very first months of life, whereas Freud was mainly concerned with the dynamics of Oedipal conflicts, which occurred much later in childhood. For Klein, the quality of the relationship that the child experienced with human 'objects' (such as the mother) in the first year set a pattern of relating that persisted through adult life. The original writings of Klein are difficult, but H. Segal (1964), J. Segal (1985, 1992) and Sayers (1991) present accessible accounts of her life and work.

Before Klein, very few psychoanalysts had worked directly with children. Using drawings, toys, dolls and other play materials, Klein found that she was able to explore the inner world of the child, and discovered that the conflicts and anxieties felt by children largely arose not from their sexual impulses, as Freud had assumed, but from their relationships with adults. The relationship with the mother, in particular, was a centrally important factor. A young child, in fact, cannot survive without a caretaker, usually a mother. Another child psychoanalyst working within this tradition, D. W. Winnicott (1964), wrote that 'there is no such thing as a baby', pointing out that 'a baby cannot exist alone, but is essentially part of a relationship'.

From the point of view of the baby, according to Klein, the mother in the first months is represented by the 'part-object' of the breast, and is experienced as either a 'good object' or a 'bad object'. She is 'good' when the needs of the baby are being met through feeding. She is 'bad' when these needs are not being met. The baby responds to the bad object with feelings of destructive rage. The first few months are described by Klein as a 'paranoid–schizoid' period, when the baby feels very little security in the world and is recovering from the trauma of birth. Over time, however, the baby begins to be able to perceive the mother as a more realistic whole object rather than as the part-object of the breast, and to understand that good and bad can coexist in the same person. The early phase of splitting of experience into 'good' and 'bad' begins to be resolved.

The next phase of development, according to Klein, is characterized by a 'depressive' reaction, a deep sense of disappointment and anger that a loved person can be bad as well as good. In the earlier phase, the baby was able to maintain the fantasy of the 'good mother' as existing separate from the 'bad'. Now he or she must accept that the bad and the good go together. There is a primitive sense of loss and separation now that the possibility of complete fusion with the 'good' mother has been left behind. There may be a sense of guilt that it was the child himself or herself who was actually responsible for the end of the earlier, simpler, phase of the relationship with the mother.

It is essential to recognize that the infant is not consciously aware of these processes as they happen. The awareness of the child is seen as dream-like and fragmented rather than logical and connected. Indeed, it is hard for adults to imagine what the inner life of a child might be like. In her effort to reconstruct this inner life, Klein portrays a world dominated by strong impulses and emotions in response to the actions of external 'objects'. The assumption is that the emotional inner world of the adult is built upon the foundations of experience of these earliest months and years.

One of the key characteristics of this inner world, according to the object relations perspective (and other theories of child development, such as that of Piaget), is the inability of the child to differentiate between what is self and what is the rest of the world. In the beginning, the child is egocentric in the sense that it believes it has power over everything that happens in its world; for example, that food arrives because I cry, it is morning because I wake up, or Granddad died because I did not take care of him. It is this 'self-centredness', which may become expressed in grandiose or narcissistic patterns of relating to others, that forms the underlying cause of many of the problems that the person may encounter in adult life.

The application of an object relations perspective in therapy. It should be apparent, from the discussion of Klein's ideas presented here, that her work represents a subtle but highly significant shift in psychoanalytic thinking. Rather than focusing their attention primarily on the operation of biological/libidinal impulses, Klein and her colleagues were beginning to take seriously the quality of the *relationships* between the client/patient and others:

> within object relations theory, the mind and the psychic structures that comprise it are thought to evolve out of human interactions rather than out of biologically derived tensions. Instead of being motivated by tension reduction, human beings are motivated by the need to establish and maintain relationships. It is the need for human contact, in other words, that constitutes the primary motive within an object relations perspective.
>
> (Cashdan 1988: 18)

Object relations theorists adopted the term 'object' in acknowledgement of the fact that the person's emotionally significant relationships could be with an actual person, with an internalized image or memory of a person with *parts* of a person or with a physical object:

> an approximate synonym for 'Object Relations' is 'Personal Relationships'. The reason why the latter, more readily understandable phrase is not used is because psychodynamic theory also attaches significance to the *object* of a person's feelings or desires, which may be non-human (as Winnicott used the term 'transitional object') or part of a person (the breast, for example, in the earliest mother–baby relationship). Apart from relationships to whole persons, the psychodynamic therapist and counsellor is therefore concerned to understand the relationships the client has to her or his internal objects (. . . internalised aspects of the personality . . .); to what are known as 'part-objects' (parts of the body, as well as persons who are perceived only partially, and not as a whole); and to non-human objects (such as a child's security blanket as in some sense 're-presenting' the nurturing, but temporarily absent, parent).
>
> (Jacobs 1999: 9)

The use of the term 'object' also implies that the client may be relating to another person not in a 'real' or 'authentic' way, but in a way that is selective or objectifying.

One of the most fundamental of the dysfunctional patterns by which people relate to 'objects' is *splitting*. The idea of splitting refers to a way of defending against difficult feelings and impulses that can be traced back to the very first months of life. Klein, it will be recalled, understood that babies could only differentiate between the wholly 'good' and wholly 'bad' part-object of the breast. This object was experienced by the baby as one associated with pleasurable and blissful feelings while feeding, or with feelings of rage when it was absent or taken away. Correspondingly, the psychological and emotional world of the baby at this very early stage consisted only of things that were good or bad;

there were no shades of feelings in between. The fundamental insecurity and terror evoked by the feelings of 'bad' led Klein to characterize this as a 'paranoid–schizoid' position.

As the child grows and develops, it becomes able to perceive that good and bad can go together, and therefore it can begin to distinguish different degrees of goodness and badness. When this development does not proceed in a satisfactory manner, or when some external threat re-evokes the insecurity of these early months, the person may either grow up with a tendency to experience the world as 'split' between objects which are all good or all bad, or use this defence in particular situations.

It is not difficult to think of examples of splitting in everyday life, as well as in the counselling room. Within the social and political arena, many people see only good in one political party, soccer team, religion or nationality, and attribute everything bad to the other. Within relationships and family life, people have friends and enemies, parents have favourite and disowned children, and the children may have perfect mothers and wicked fathers. Within an individual personality, sexuality may be bad and intellect good, or drinking reprehensible and abstinence wonderful.

For the psychodynamic counsellor, the client who exhibits splitting is defending against feelings of love and hate for the same object. For example, a woman who idealizes her counsellor and complains repeatedly in counselling of the misdeeds and insensitivity of her husband may have underlying strong feelings of longing for closeness in the marriage and rage at the way he abuses her, or an underlying need to be taken care of by him coupled with anger at his absences at work. As with the other defences described earlier in the chapter, the task of the counsellor is first of all to help the client to be aware of the way she is avoiding her true feelings through this manoeuvre, then gently to encourage exploration and understanding of the emotions and impulses that are so hard to accept. From a psychodynamic perspective, the reason why the person needs to use the defence is that some aspects of the current situation are similar to painful childhood situations, and are bringing to the surface long buried memories of early events. Although the client may be a socially and professionally successful and responsible adult, the inner emotional turmoil she brings to counselling is the part of her that is still a child, and only has available to it infantile ways of coping, such as splitting. So, in the case of the woman who idealizes her counsellor and scorns her husband, it may eventually emerge that, perhaps, the grandfather who was supposed to look after her when mum was out actually abused her sexually, and she could only deal with this by constructing a 'good' granddad object and a 'bad' one.

The defence mechanism of splitting is similar to the classic Freudian ideas of defence, such as repression, denial and reaction formation, in that these are all processes that occur within the individual psyche or personality. The Kleinian notion of projective identification, however, represents an important departure, in that it describes a process of emotional defence that is interpersonal rather than purely intrapersonal. Being able to apply the idea of projective identification is therefore a uniquely valuable strategy for psychodynamic counsellors who view client problems as rooted in relationships.

The concept of 'projection' has already been introduced as a process whereby the person defends against threatening and unacceptable feelings and impulses by acting as though these feelings and impulses only existed in other people, not in the person himself or herself. For example, a man who accuses his work colleagues of always disagreeing with his very reasonable proposals may be projecting on to them his own buried hostility and competitiveness. The counsellor who persists in assuming that a depressed client really needs to make more friends and join some clubs may be projecting her own fear of her personal inner emptiness.

Projective identification occurs when the person to whom the feelings and impulses are being projected is manipulated into believing that he or she actually has these feelings and impulses. For instance, the man who accuses his colleagues may unconsciously set up circumstances where they have little choice but to argue with him: for example, by not explaining his ideas with enough clarity. And the counsellor may easily persuade the depressed client that she herself does want to make friends.

From an object relations perspective, the dynamics of projective identification have their origins in very early experience, in the time when the child was unable to tell the difference between self and external objects. In projective identification, this blurring of the self–other boundary is accompanied by a need to control the other, which comes from the early state of childhood grandiose omnipotence.

Cashdan (1988) has identified four major patterns of projective identification, arising from underlying issues of dependency, power, sexuality and ingratiation. He describes projective identification as a process that occurs in the context of a relationship. In the case of dependency, the person will actively seek assistance from other people who are around by using phrases such as 'What do you think?' or 'I can't seem to manage this on my own'. The person is presenting a relationship stance of helplessness. Usually, however, these requests for help are not based on a real inability to solve problems or cope, but are moti-vated by what Cashdan (1988) calls a 'projective fantasy', a sense of self-in-relationship origi-nating in disturbed object relations in early childhood. The dependent person might have a projective fantasy that could be summarized as a fundamental belief that 'I can't survive'. The great reservoir of unresolved childhood need or anger contained within this fantasy is what gives urgency and force to what may otherwise appear to be reasonable requests for assistance. The recipient of the request is therefore under pressure, and may be induced into taking care of the person. Similar processes take place with other unconscious needs. In any patterns of projective identification, the outcome is to re-create in an adult relationship the type of object relations that prevailed in childhood. The dependent person, for instance, may possibly have had a mother who needed to look after him or her all the time.

The idea of projective identification provides psychodynamic counsellors with a useful conceptual tool for disentangling the complex web of feelings and fantasies that exist in troubled relationships. The unconscious intention behind projective identification is to induce or entice the other to behave towards the self as if the self was in reality a dependent, powerful, sexual or helpful person. This interpersonal strategy enables the person to deny that the dependency, for example, is a fantasy which conceals behind it a multiplicity of feelings, such as resentment, longing or despair. There may be times when the projection is acceptable to the person on the receiving end, perhaps because it feeds his or her fantasy of being powerful or caring. But there will be times when the recipient becomes aware that there is something not quite right, and resists the projection. Or there may be times when the projector himself or herself becomes painfully aware of what is happening. Finally, there will be occasions in counselling when projective identification is applied to the counsellor, who will be pressured to treat the client in line with fantasy expectations. These times provide rich material for the counsellor to work with.

Box 5.4: *The goal of therapy, from an object relations perspective*

The Scottish psychoanalyst Ronald Fairbairn (1889–1964) was one of the leading figures in the development of an object relations approach within psychoanalysis. Fairbairn was particularly interested in the difficulties that many of his patients had in making 'real' contact either with him or with anyone else in their lives. He came to describe the inner worlds of such patients as 'closed systems'. Towards the end of his career, he characterized the aim of psychoanalysis in the following terms: 'the aim of psychoanalytic treatment is to effect breaches of the closed system which constitutes the patient's inner world, and thus to make this world accessible to the influence of outer reality' (Fairbairn 1958: 380).

Fairbairn pointed out that the idea of 'transference' implied a process taking place within a closed system. If a person was able to make genuine contact with another, then he or she would treat that other person as a unique individual, and no transference would occur. However, for a person trapped inside a 'closed' psychological world, contact with another person can only be made by acting as though that person was treated as an 'internal object' (i.e., an internalized representation of a pattern of childhood experience). Fairbairn believed that his view held important implications for the practice of therapy:

> The implication of these considerations is that the interpretation of transference phenomena in the setting of the analytic situation is not in itself enough to promote a satisfactory change in the patient. For such a change to accrue, it is necessary for the patient's relationship with the analyst to undergo a process of development in which a relationship based on transference becomes replaced by a realistic relationship between two persons in the outer world. Such a process of development represents the disruption of the closed system within which the patient's symptoms have developed and are maintained, and which compromises his relationships with external objects. It also represents the establishment of an open system in which the distortions of inner reality can be corrected by outer reality and true relationships with external objects can occur.
>
> (Fairbairn 1958: 381)

> . . . psycho-analytical treatment resolves itself into a struggle on the part of the patient to press-gang his relationship with the analyst into the closed system of the inner world through the agency of transference, and a determination on the part of the analyst to effect a breach in this closed system.
>
> (Fairbairn 1958: 385)

These passages from Fairbairn capture the enormity of the shift in psychoanalytic practice represented by the object relations approach. The significance of this shift can too easily be lost in the abstract language used by the majority of psychodynamic/psychoanalytic theorists. It is clear that what Fairbairn is referring to is an *active* therapist, who is seeking to move beyond transference and use a 'realistic relationship' to 'breach' the closed system of the client's inner world.

The British Independents: the importance of counter-transference

The psychodynamic approach to counselling in the post-Freudian era has been marked by the emergence of a range of different writers who have developed the theory in different directions. One of the significant groupings of psychodynamic therapists has been the British 'Independent' group. The origins of the Independents can be traced back to the beginnings of psychoanalysis in Britain. The British Psycho-Analytical Society was formed in 1919, under the leadership of Ernest Jones. In 1926, Melanie Klein, who had been trained in Berlin, moved to London and became a member of the British Society. From the beginning Klein was critical of conventional psychoanalysis. She pioneered child analysis, insisted on the primary importance of destructive urges and the death instinct, and paid more attention to early development than to Oedipal issues. The contrast between the views of Klein and her followers, and those of more orthodox Freudians, came to a climax with the emigration of Freud and his daughter Anna Freud, along with several other analysts from Vienna, to London in 1938. Anna Freud represented the mainstream of Freudian theory, and in the years immediately following the death of Freud in 1939, the relationship between her group and the Kleinians became tense. In the 1940s there were a series of what came to be known as 'controversial discussions' in the Society. The drama of this period in psychoanalysis is well captured by Rayner:

> by 1941 the atmosphere in scientific meetings was becoming electric . . . It is puzzling that there should be such passion on matters of theory in the midst of a world war. The situation was that London was being bombed nearly every night, and many did not know whether they would survive, let alone what would happen to analysis – to which they had given their lives. They felt they were the protectors of precious ideas which were threatened not only by bombs but from within their colleagues and themselves. Also, it was hardly possible to go on practising analysis, which is vital to keep coherent analytic ideas alive. Ideological venom and character assassination were released under these circumstances. Where many people found a new communality under the threats of war, the opposite happened to psychoanalysts in London.
>
> (Rayner 1990: 18–19)

In what can be seen as a reflection of the British capacity for compromise, the Society decided by 1946 to divide, for purposes of training, into three loose groups: the Kleinians, the Anna Freud group and the 'middle' group, who later became known as the Independents. The rule was introduced that analysts in training must be exposed to the ideas and methods of more than one group. This principle has resulted in a tradition of openness to new ideas within the British psychodynamic community. The influence of the 'independent mind' in psychoanalysis has been documented by Kohon (1986) and Rayner (1990).

Although the Independents have inevitably generated new ideas across the whole span of psychodynamic theory (Rayner 1990), the group is particularly known for its reappraisal of the concept of counter-transference. It is not without significance that a group of therapists who had gone through the kind of personal and professional trauma described by Rayner (1990) should become particularly sensitive to the role of the personality and self of the therapist in the therapeutic relationship. The contribution of the Independents has been to draw attention to the value of the feelings of the counsellor in the relationship with the client.

Previously, counter-transference had been regarded with some suspicion by analysts, as evidence of neurotic conflicts in the analyst. Heimann (1950) argued, by contrast, that counter-transference was 'one of the most important tools' in analysis. Her position was that 'the analyst's unconscious understands that of the patient. This rapport on a deep level comes to the surface in the form of feelings which the analyst notes in response to [the] patient' (p. 82). Another member of the Independent group, Symington (1983: 286), suggested that 'at one level the analyst and patient together make a single system'. Both analyst and patient can become locked into shared illusions or fantasies, which Symington (1983) argues can only be dissolved through an 'act of freedom' by the analyst. In other words, the analyst needs to achieve insight into the part he or she is playing in maintaining the system. The approach to counter-transference initiated by the Independents involved a warmer, more personal contact between client and therapist (Casement 1985, 1990), and anticipated many of the developments associated with time-limited psychodynamic counselling. However, there still exist many debates over the nature of counter-transference and how it can be used in counselling and psychotherapy (see Box 5.5).

Box 5.5: *What are the sources of therapists' counter-transference feelings?*

In the early years of psychoanalysis, the analyst or therapist was generally regarded as a neutral, *blank screen* upon which the patient projected his or her fantasies based on unresolved emotional conflicts from the past (the 'transference neurosis'). In the recent writings on psychoanalytic and psychodynamic counselling and psychotherapy, however, it has become widely accepted that the emotional response of the therapist to the client, the 'counter-transference', is an essential source of data about what is happening in the therapy. But where does counter-transference come from? Holmqvist and Armelius (1996) suggest that within the psychoanalytic literature there are three competing perspectives on counter-transference.

First, there is the classical Freudian view of counter-transference, which is that it derives from the personality of the therapist, in particular from unresolved conflicts that the therapist has not analysed and understood, which therefore interfere with the therapeutic process. This is the view that counter-transference is a distortion in the blank screen.

The second perspective is to explain counter-transference as the response of the therapist to the patient's characteristic ways of relating to other people. The feelings that the therapist experiences in relation to the client or patient are, from this perspective, invaluable clues to the client's relationship style or inner life.

Third, some contemporary psychodynamic writers have argued that counter-transference is a *shared* interpersonal reality that client and therapist create between them.

Some research by Holmqvist and Armelius (1996) and Holmqvist (2001) throws new light on this debate. They used a checklist of feeling words to assess the emotional reactions of therapists to their patients. The therapists were employed in treatment units for severely disturbed people, and each patient in the unit was seen by several therapists in the team. The checklist asked therapists to think about a specific client and then to choose from a list of adjectives to indicate their response to the trigger question 'when I talk with (this client), I feel . . .' Data were gathered on several occasions for each group of therapists and patients. The hypothesis was that if these therapist emotional reactions were dominated by patient transference projections (Perspective 2), then different therapists would rate each individual patient in the same way (i.e., the ratings would be dominated by a fixed way in which the patient reacted with everyone). If, on the other hand, the emotional response of a therapist to a patient was dominated by therapist personal style or unresolved conflicts (Perspective 1), then individual therapists would rate each of their patients in the same way. Finally, if counter-transference was indeed a uniquely new emotional reality with each patient (Perspective 3), then there would be what are known as statistical 'interaction effects' in the pattern of ratings.

Analysis of the data showed some support for all three perspectives. In other words, there was evidence that the way that a therapist felt about a specific patient would be influenced by the patient, by the therapist and by a combination of the two. However, the single most important factor determining the therapist's emotional response was the personal style of the therapist (Perspective 1). Holmqvist (2001: 115) has concluded from his research that 'the therapist's reactions [belong] primarily to his or her own emotional universe'. This research suggests that it is a mistake to oversimplify the notion of counter-transference (evidence for all three sources of counter-transference was found) but that the therapist's 'habitual feeling style' lies at the heart of the way he or she responds emotionally to clients.

The American post-Freudian tradition: ego psychology and self-theory

The development in Britain, by Klein, Fairbairn and others, of an object relations approach that emphasized the importance of the client's relationships, rather than his or her libido-based drives, was matched in the USA by the writings of Margaret Mahler, Heinz Kohut and their colleagues, who were beginning to take a similar line.

The model of child development provided by Klein can usefully be supplemented by that offered by Margaret Mahler (1968; Mahler *et al.* 1975), whose approach is generally described as 'ego psychology'. Mahler views the child in the first year of life as being autistic, without any sense of the existence of other people. Between two and four months is the 'symbiotic' stage, in which there is the beginning of recognition of the mother as an object. Then, from about four months through to three years of age, the infant undergoes a gradual process of separation from the mother, slowly building up a sense of self independent from the self of the mother. At the beginning of this process the infant will experiment with crawling away from the mother then returning to her. Towards the end of the period, particularly with the development of language, the child will have a name and a set of things that are 'mine'.

By observing both 'normal' and disturbed children, Klein, Mahler and other post-Freudian practitioners have been able to piece together an understanding of the emotional life of the child that is, they would assert, more accurate than that reconstructed by Freud through interpretation of the free associations of adult patients in therapy. However, like Freud they regard the troubles of adult life as being derived ultimately from disturbances in the developmental process in childhood. Winnicott (1964) used the phrase 'good enough' to describe the type of parenting that would enable children to develop effectively. Unfortunately, many people are subjected to childhood experiences that are far from 'good enough', and result in a variety of different patterns of pathology.

It can be seen here that the theoretical framework being developed by Mahler and her colleagues includes a strong emphasis on the idea of 'self', a concept which was not extensively used by Freud. Where Freud, influenced by his medical and scientific training, saw personality as ultimately determined by the biologically driven stages of psycho-sexual development and biologically based motives, theorists such as Klein and Mahler came to view people as fundamentally social beings.

Another important strand of recent psychoanalytic thinking is represented by the work of Kohut (1971, 1977) and Kernberg (1976, 1984), whose ideas are referred to as 'self' theory. Kohut (1971) and Kernberg (1975) initiated a re-evaluation of the problem of narcissism within psychoanalysis. The concept of narcissism was originally introduced by Freud, who drew upon the Greek legend of Narcissus, a youth who fell in love with his own reflection. Freud viewed over-absorption in self as a difficult condition to treat through psychoanalysis, since it was almost impossible for the analyst to break through the narcissism to reach the underlying conflicts. Kohut (1971) argued that the narcissistic person is fundamentally unable to differentiate between self and other. Rather than being able to act towards others as separate entities, in narcissism other people are experienced as 'self-objects', as little more than extensions of the self. Other people only exist to aggrandize and glorify the self. For Kohut, the solution to this lay in the transference relationship between client and therapist. If the therapist refrained from directly confronting the falseness and grandiosity of the client, but instead empathized with and accepted the client's experience of things, a situation would be created that paralleled the conditions of early childhood.

Kohut (1971) argued that, just as the real mother is never perfect, and can only hope to be 'good enough', the therapist can never achieve complete empathy and acceptance. The client therefore experiences, at moments of failure of empathy, a sense of 'optimal frustration'. It is this combination of frustration in a context of high acceptance and warmth that gradually enables the client to appreciate the separation of self and other. Although the model proposed by Kohut (1971, 1977) has much more to say on the matter than is possible here, it should be apparent that his approach has made a significant contribution to psychodynamic theory and practice around this issue.

Another important area of advance has been in work with 'borderline' clients. This label is used to refer to people who exhibit extreme difficulties in forming relationships, have been profoundly emotionally damaged by childhood experiences and express high levels of both dependency and rage in the relationship with the therapist. One of the meanings of 'borderline' in this context refers to the idea of 'borderline schizophrenic'. Traditionally, people with this kind of depth and array of problems have not been considered as viable candidates for psychodynamic therapy, and have generally been offered long-term 'supportive' therapy rather than anything more ambitious. The work of Kernberg

(1975, 1984) and others from an object relations/self perspective has attributed the problems of borderline clients to arrested development in early childhood. These people are understood to be emotionally very young, dealing with the world as if they were in the paranoid–schizoid stage described by Klein, where experience is savagely split between 'good' and 'bad'. The task of the therapist is to enable the client to regress back to the episodes in childhood that presented blocks to progress and maturity, and to discover new ways of overcoming them. This type of therapy can be seen almost as providing a second chance for development with a special kind of parenting, with the therapeutic relationship acting as a substitute for the nuclear family.

Therapy with borderline clients is often conducted over several years, with the client receiving multiple sessions each week. The intensity and challenge of this kind of therapeutic work, and the generally moderate success rates associated with it, mean that practitioners are often cautious about taking on borderline clients, or limit the number of such clients in their case load at any one time (Aronson 1989).

Box 5.6: *The influence of D.W. Winnicott*

One of the key figures in the development of the object relations approach to psychodynamic therapy was D.W.Winnicott (1896–1971). Born into an upper-class family in Plymouth, Donald Winnicott trained in medicine and specialized in paediatrics, and used his early professional experience in working with children as the basis of many of his most influential contributions to psychoanalysis. Winnicott described the therapy relationship as providing a 'holding environment' within which the client could feel safe to examine painful experiences. He observed that it was necessary for any child to have a 'good enough' mother in order to thrive emotionally, and was the first to describe the existence of 'transitional objects' – blankets, toys and other articles that unconsciously functioned to remind the child, when away from the mother, of the security of the parental relationship. Winnicott also introduce the distinction between the 'true self' (the core of the personality) and 'false self' (the mask that adapts to the demands of others). Winnicott's concept of the true/false self had an impact on the thinking of many other important therapy theorists, such as Eric Berne and R. D. Laing. For Winnicott, the ideal form of therapy was one in which he could help the client to enter a state of playfulness, as a means of re-evoking positive childhood experience: the work of the therapist is directed towards bringing the client from a state of not being able to play into a state of being able to play. He believed that '. . . it is in the space between inner and outer world, which is also the space between people – the transitional space – that intimate relationships and creativity occur' (Winnicott 1958: 233).

Winnicott remains essential reading for any counsellor who is interested in developing an in-depth understanding of the use of psychodynamic concepts in practice. Key books by Winnicott include: *The Child, the Family and the Outside World* (1964), *Maturational Processes and the Facilitating Environment* (1965) and *The Piggle. An Account of the Psychoanalytic Treatment of a Little Girl* (1977). Excellent biographical accounts of his life and work have been published by Jacobs (1995), Phillips (2007) and Rodman (2003).

The European tradition

It is important to recognize that there exists an important European tradition in psycho-analytic psychotherapy. For example, psychodynamic and psychoanalytic approaches to therapy dominate therapy provision in Germany, Sweden and France, and are represented in all other European countries. The tradition of psychodynamic therapy that has developed in Germany and Sweden has reflected the influence of British and American writers discussed earlier in this chapter. However, Germany is unusual in the respect to which its psychological therapy service has developed psychodynamic therapy for patients with psychosomatic disorders. The majority of these patients are treated on an inpatient basis – Germany is unique in having more than 8,000 short-term inpatient psychotherapy beds (Kachele *et al.* 1999). The generosity of the German health care system is also reflected in the number of sessions of publicly funded psychodynamic therapy that are available to patients: 'analytic psychotherapy should as a rule achieve a satisfactory result in 160 sessions, and special cases, up to 240 sessions. Further extension to 300 sessions is possible under exceptional circumstances, but must be supported by detailed arguments' (Kachele *et al.* 1999: 336). German and Swedish researchers have been responsible for a substantial number of studies of psychoanalytic therapy. One of the most important recent research studies into the effectiveness of psychoanalysis and psychoanalytic psychotherapy has been carried out in Stockholm (see Box 5.7).

The development of psychoanalysis in France has, however, followed a different pathway. The French analyst Jacques Lacan (1901–81) drew heavily on concepts from philosophy and linguistics, as well as advocating a return to what he perceived to be some of the basic ideas of Freud. Lacan (1977, 1979) placed a great deal of emphasis on the concept of *desire*, and the categorization of consciousness into three modes of apprehending the world: the *imaginary*, the *symbolic* and the *real*. For Lacan the task of therapy was to use language (the symbolic) to bridge the gap between two fundamentally non-linguistic realms: the imaginary and the real. Lacan also advocated innovations in technique, such as the use of short sessions. A key theme in Lacanian theory is the limits of an understanding that is based solely on language, and much of his work explores the limitations of language. An accessible example of the application of a Lacanian framework can be found in Shipton (1999).

Box 5.7: *Are psychoanalysis and psychodynamic therapy effective? The Stockholm study*

There have been many research studies into the effectiveness of various types of psycho-dynamic counselling and psychotherapy. A comprehensive review of this research can be found in Shedler (2010). However, the majority of these studies reflect situations where the therapy that is provided has been set up by a research team in a clinic, and delivered and monitored under tightly defined conditions. It can be argued that such 'controlled' studies may not fully represent what happens in everyday practice. The *Stockholm Outcome of Psychoanalysis and Psychotherapy Project* (STOPPP) is a research study that was set up to evaluate the effectiveness of psychoanalysis and psychodynamic psychotherapy as it is delivered in ordinary conditions (Sandell *et al.* 2000). There is a strong tradition of psychodynamic therapy in Sweden, and the health authorities subsidize long-term therapy delivered by private-practice therapists. The STOPPP study was designed to track the progress of *all* clients receiving either classical psychoanalysis or psychodynamically oriented psychotherapy within Stockholm County over a period of several years.

Information on clients, at the waiting list stage and then during and after treatment, was collected through questionnaires that measured psychiatric symptoms, quality of social relationships/adjustment, optimism/morale and various demographic factors. Some clients participated in in-depth open-ended interviews following completion of therapy. Data on absence from work and health care utilization were collected from health service records. All therapists completed questionnaires on their training, attitude and approach to therapy, and use of personal therapy and supervision.

The report by Sandell *et al.* (2000) draws on information collected over an eight-year period from 554 clients at the waiting list stage, 408 people who had completed therapy (331 in psychodynamic psychotherapy, 74 in psychoanalysis) and 209 therapists. All the clients in the study received long-term therapy. The psychoanalysis clients received, on average, 3.5 sessions each week over 54 months, whereas the psychodynamic therapy clients received an average of 1.5 sessions per week over 46 months. In general, clients were people with fairly severe problems, with many having made previous use of inpatient, drug treatment and other types of psychological therapy. The clients in analysis and those in therapy reported equal levels of symptoms at the waiting list stage, but those who had chosen to enter analysis were slightly older and better educated, and more likely to be male, than those who had opted for psychotherapy.

How effective was the therapy received by these clients? The STOPPP project team collected a great deal of data, which can be analysed in many different ways. However, the main findings reported by Sandell *et al.* (2000) were that major positive gains were found in levels of symptoms, and morale, for both groups of clients. The extent of benefit was equivalent to that found in other studies of the effectiveness of therapy: at the beginning of therapy all clients showed high levels of symptoms, whereas at the final follow-up period the majority were within the range of symptoms/problems exhibited by the 'normal', non-clinical population. Improvement in social functioning was less dramatic, with only moderate benefits found in quality of social relationship/adjustment and general health. The clients who had received psychoanalysis did better than those who had been in psychodynamic therapy, particularly at follow-up. Both groups had improved significantly by the end of treatment, but the clients who had received psychoanalysis continued to improve several months after treatment had concluded. At follow-up interviews, psychoanalysis clients were much less likely than psychotherapy clients to be interested in seeking further therapy.

The research team also looked at the factors associated with good outcomes, in terms of the characteristics of therapists who had worked with high-gain clients, and those who had moderate or low-gain cases. Better results were associated with analysts and therapists who were older and more experienced, and were female. Poorer results were associated with analysts and therapists who had undergone *more* personal therapy and supervision – the researchers speculated that some of these practitioners were people who understood that they were not operating effectively, and were seeking ways of compensating for their limitations. For psychoanalysts, the personal style and attitudes of the analysts did not appear to make a difference to outcome – it appeared as though the 'discipline' and structure of the analytic session were more important than the personal qualities of the analyst. However, for psychotherapists, style and attitude had a major influence on outcome. Psychodynamic therapists who were more kindly, supportive, involved and self-disclosing, and who emphasized coping strategies (i.e., were more like humanistic and cognitive–behavioural therapists in style and attitude), were more effective than those who displayed the more classically psychoanalytic value of neutrality. In other words, the more *eclectic* the psychotherapists (but not the analysts) were, the better they did. Sandell *et al.* (2000: 940) suggested that: 'We are led to the conclusion that there is a negative transfer of the psychoanalytic stance into psychotherapeutic practice, and that this negative transfer *may be* especially pronounced when the psychoanalytic stance is not backed up by psychoanalytic training'.

The Stockholm study therefore raises important questions about the relationship between psychoanalysis and psychodynamic therapy, and points towards significant differences in the processes involved in each of these approaches. The implication from this study is that a 'pure' psychoanalytic approach can be very effective with clients who have chosen to engage in it on a four-sessions-per-week basis, but that the majority of clients, who opt for once-per-week therapy, appear to need a more 'sociable' and supportive stance on the part of their therapists. It would also seem that therapists who behave in an 'over-analytic' manner in once-per-week therapy are significantly less effective than those who deliver a form of psychodynamic therapy that combines psychoanalytic ideas with a relationship style and practice that is also informed by other therapeutic approaches.

Attachment theory

The ideas of the British psychoanalyst John Bowlby (1969, 1973, 1980, 1988) have become increasingly influential within psychodynamic counselling and psychotherapy in recent years. Although trained as an analyst, Bowlby was also an active researcher. The main focus of his work was around the process of *attachment* in human relations. In his research and writing, Bowlby argued that human beings, like other animals, have a basic need to form attachments with others throughout life, and will not function well unless such attachments are available. The capacity for attachment is, according to Bowlby, innate, but is shaped by early experience with significant others. For example, if the child's mother is absent, or does not form a secure and reliable bond, then the child will grow up with a lack of trust and a general inability to form stable, close relationships. If, on the other hand, the mother or other family members have provided the child with what Bowlby calls a 'secure base' in childhood, then later close relationships will be possible.

Similarly, according to Bowlby, early experiences of loss can set an emotional pattern that persists into adulthood. Bowlby and colleagues (1952) observed that children separated from their parents – for example, through hospitalization – initially respond through protest and anger, then with depression and sadness, and finally by behaving apparently normally. This normality, however, masks a reserve and unwillingness to share affection with new people. If the parents return, there will be reactions of rejection and avoidance before they are accepted again. For the young child, who is unable to understand at a cognitive level what is happening, this kind of experience of loss may instil a fear of abandonment that makes him or her either cling on to relationships in later life or even avoid any relationship that might end in loss or abandonment. For the older child, the way he or she is helped (or not) to deal with feelings of grief and loss will likewise set up patterns that will persist. For example, when parents divorce it is quite common for a child to end up believing that he or she caused the split and subsequent loss, and that consequently he or she is a 'bad' person who would have a destructive impact on any relationship. Such a person might then find it hard to commit to relationships later in their life.

Bowlby (1973) suggested that the person develops an 'internal working model' to describe his or her internal representation of the social world, his or her main attachment figures within that world, himself or herself and the links between these elements. It can be seen that the idea of the 'internal working model' is similar to the notion of internalized 'object relations' used by Klein and Fairbairn and other 'object relations' theorists. There were, however, three important differences in emphasis between Bowlby and the object relations theorists. First, he argued that a biologically based mechanism of attachment had a central part to play in the inner life of the person. Second, he always maintained that attachments were the result of actual behaviour by another person (i.e., not solely internal). Third, Bowlby strongly believed that evidence from scientific research was just as important as insight derived from clinical practice.

Inspired by Bowlby, researchers in different parts of the world have sought to develop deeper understandings of the way that attachment operates, and how this idea can be applied in therapy. The most important lines of research are associated with the work of Mary Ainsworth, Mary Main and Peter Fonagy.

With the aim of looking more closely at attachment behaviour in young children, Mary Ainsworth carried out a series of studies using the 'strange situation' procedure (Ainsworth *et al.* 1978; Bretherton and Waters 1985). The 'strange situation' is a laboratory laid out like a playroom, where infants can be systematically observed from behind a mirror while the mother twice leaves, and then returns. The behaviour of infants in this situation has been shown to be similar to their behaviour in real-life (home) situations when they are left alone. Infant responses can be categorized into four types.

- *Secure.* The child shows signs of missing the parent, then seeks contact when she returns and settles back into playing normally.
- *Insecure–avoidant.* The infant shows few signs of missing the parent, and avoids her upon reunion.
- *Insecure–ambivalent.* The child is highly distressed and angry when the parent leaves, and cannot be settled when she returns.
- *Insecure–disoriented.* The child shows a range of stereotyped and frozen patterns of behaviour.

Ainsworth found that the behaviour of infants in the strange situation experiment could be explained by the behaviour of their mothers. For example, 'secure' children had mothers who were sensitive to their emotional signals, whereas 'insecure' children had mothers who could be observed to be insensitive, rejecting or unpredictable.

Although Ainsworth's research provided a convincing picture of the powerful nature of attachment patterns in early childhood, it is not possible to observe adult patterns in such a clear-cut manner in a laboratory experiment. Mary Main therefore developed the *Adult Attachment Interview (AAI)* as a means of assessing patterns of attachment later in life (Main 1991; Hesse 1999). The AAI consists of a 15-item clinical interview, which will normally take around two hours to complete. The questions asked in the interview (Table 5.1) are intended to surprise the unconscious. In other words, the person will find himself or herself saying things, or contradicting themselves, in ways that are beyond their conscious control. For participants, the interview is similar to a therapy session, in they are invited to talk openly, and at length, about childhood experiences and memories that may be quite painful. Analysis of the interview depends less on the content of what the person says, but is largely derived from the style or manner in which the person tells the story of their early life.

Coding of the AAI yields four types of attachment pattern that are broadly similar to the categories used in the 'strange situation' test:

- *Secure/autonomous*. The person's story is coherent, consistent and objective. He or she is able to collaborate with the interviewer.

- *Dismissing*. The story is not coherent. The person tends to be dismissive of attachment-related experiences and relationships. Tendency to describe parents as 'normal' or ideal.

TABLE 5.1 Questions asked in the Adult Attachment Interview

---

1   Who was in your immediate family? Where did you live?
2   Describe your relationship with your parents, starting as far back as you can remember.
3   Can you give me five adjectives or phrases to describe your relationship with your mother and father during childhood?
4   What memories and experiences led you to choose these adjectives?
5   To which parent did you feel closer, and why?
6   When you were upset as a child, what did you do, and what would happen?
7   Could you describe your first separation from your parents?
8   Did you ever feel rejected as a child? What did you do?
9   Were your parents ever threatening toward you?
10   How do you think your early experiences may have affected your adult personality?
11   Why do you think your parents behaved as they did in your childhood?
12   Who were the other adults who were close to you in your childhood?
13   Did you experience the loss of a parent, or other close loved one as a parent, or in adulthood?
14   Were there many changes in your relationships with your parents between childhood and adulthood?
15   What is your relationship with your parents like for you currently?

Note: This is an abbreviated list of questions. The actual AAI is based on an extensive protocol, with follow-up questions.
Source: Hesse 1999.

- *Preoccupied*. The story is incoherent, and the speaker may appear angry, passive or fearful, and preoccupied with past relationships. Sentences often long, vague and confusing.
- *Unresolved disorganized*. Similar to dismissive or preoccupied, but may include long silences or overtly erroneous statements (for example, talking as though someone who died is still alive).

A large amount of research has been carried out using the AAI, and has found strong correlations between the attachment styles of parents and their children, and differences in the process of counselling with people exhibiting different attachment styles (Hesse 1999).

From the point of view of counselling and psychotherapy, one of the most significant aspects of research using the AAI was the discovery by Mary Main that people who had experienced secure attachments, and who functioned well in their lives, were able to talk about their past in a coherent and collaborative way. Main suggested that 'securely attached' people are able to do this because they are able to engage in 'metacognitive monitoring': they are able to 'step back' from the situation and reflect on what they are saying. It is as though the person is able to look objectively at their own thought processes. This is only possible, according to Main and other AAI researchers, because the person has been able to develop a single, coherent 'internal working model', rather than multiple models:

> Multiple models of attachment are formed when the acknowledgement of disturbing feelings or memories threatens the self or current relationships; distortion and incoherence are the cognitive and linguistic manifestations of multiple contradictory models . . . coherence is also a critical element in the intergenerational transmission of attachment: the mother who is able to openly acknowledge, access and evaluate her own attachment experiences will be able to respond to her child's attachment needs in a sensitive and nurturing way.
>
> (Slade 1999: 580)

The contribution of Peter Fonagy and his colleagues has been to elaborate on the implications of Main's notion of metacognitive monitoring for the practice of counselling and psychotherapy. Fonagy (1999) argues that it is the capacity to learn how to *reflect* on experience that lies at the heart of effective therapy. The development within therapy of what Fonagy calls the 'reflexive function', the ability to think about and talk about painful past events, helps the person to protect himself or herself against the raw emotional impact of these events, without having to use defences such as denial or repression.

Bowlby's ideas on attachment have not resulted in the creation of a specific 'attachment therapy'. The impact of attachment theory on psychodynamic counselling and psychotherapy has taken a number of forms. A knowledge of attachment theory helps practitioners to become more aware of the possible origins of patterns of relationships described by their clients, and assists them to their way of being with clients (i.e., their own characteristic attachment styles, which may be differentially triggered by different clients). A series of research studies (Kivlighan *et al.* 1998; Tyrrell *et al.* 1999; Eames and Roth

2000; Kilmann *et al.* 1999; Rubino *et al.* 2000) have provided convincing evidence for the role of both client and therapist attachment style in shaping the process of therapy. Research has also established the biological mechanisms responsible for patterns of attachment behaviour (Cassidy and Shaver 1999), which has enhanced the scientific plausibility of psychoanalytically oriented theories of therapy. Most important of all, perhaps, attachment theory and AAI research enable counsellors to become more sensitive to the ways in which their clients tell their story – it opens up links between the style of telling the story and broader patterns of relating with others. Particularly useful accounts of how attachment theory can be applied in therapy practice can be found in the writings of the British psychodynamic therapist Jeremy Holmes (2000, 2001).

Box 5.8: *The concept of mentalization*

There has been a great deal of interest in recent years within psychoanalytic and psychodynamic circles in the idea of *mentalization* (Fonagy *et al.* 2002; Allen and Fonagy 2006). The concept of mentalization refers to a process of implicitly or explicitly interpreting the actions of others as meaningful in terms of the operation of intentional mental states (states of mind, desires, needs, feelings, reasons). It can be regarded as a form of imaginative activity, because it involves imagining what another person might be thinking or feeling. A reduced capacity to engage in mentalization has been found to be characteristic of individuals suffering from severe forms of psychological difficulties, such as borderline personality disorder (Fonagy and Target 2006; Fonagy and Bateman 2006). In the absence of mentalization, it is very hard for a person to develop satisfactory relationships with other people – he or she never really understands why these people behave in the way they do (and may not even understand his or her own personal responses to others). It is difficult for such a person to reflect on action, and it is therefore almost impossible for them to benefit from any form of psychotherapeutic process that relies on reflection. An example of a therapeutic interaction with a client who had difficulties around mentalization is provided by Holmes:

> Peter was an in-patient on an acute psychiatric admission ward . . . he had been detained in hospital for several months because of his tendency to cut himself repeatedly, especially when drunk . . . He described a typical episode. He was on the ward wanting some medication . . . his request was refused. He felt an upsurge of rage . . . and stormed off the ward and out of the hospital. As he walked down the road he found himself crying and feeling utterly miserable and desolate. Then an idea formed in his mind. He went to the nearest shop, bought some razor blades, made for the public toilets where he locked himself in and cut his wrists. Eventually the police, who had been alerted to his disappearance, found him and he was returned to hospital. [His psychotherapist] reflected his story back to him as follows: 'You want something badly, relief from tension; you can't get it; you fly into a rage with your depriver; beneath the rage you feel utterly alone and abandoned; then your

anger focuses in on yourself and your body, the only thing that seems to be within your control; you go somewhere where you are alone, a place of primitive bodily needs; finally your plight is recognized, at least partially, and you are rescued' . . .

'Yep, that just about sums it up,' he replies . . .

[The psychotherapist] asked him if he felt anyone on the ward understood him. No one, he insisted. What about his 'key worker'?

'Oh, she just thinks I'm a waste of space just like everyone else' he replies.

'Do you really mean that?'

'Well, I don't suppose she *really* does, its just the way I feel about it most of the time.'

Here, at last, is Peter mentalizing.

(Holmes 2005: 189–90)

This brief case example illustrates the essence of therapy, from a mentalization perspective. First, the client is deeply troubled, and enacts a sequence of self-destructive behaviour, but without being able to reflect on any of it. His therapist – Jeremy Holmes – summarizes the client's experience in a manner that demonstrates mentalization. In a moment of intimacy, the client himself takes a small step in the direction of mentalizing; he needed to feel secure enough, with a sense of being accepted and understood, before he was able to be capable of reflecting on his emotional experience. This brief case example illustrates the potential contribution that the concept of mentalization can make to therapeutic practice, by sensitizing counsellors and psychotherapists to the absence of mentalization in some clients, and the conditions that need to be in place in order to allow mentalization to take place.

In elaborating the concept of mentalization, Peter Fonagy and his colleagues have brought together strands of research and clinical experience from psychoanalysis, attachment theory, developmental psychology, and neuropsychology. A poor capacity for mentalization appears to be associated with negative attachment experiences in early childhood. Although mentalization is a concept whose implications are only just beginning to be realized, it seems that it has particular relevance in work with clients experiencing borderline personality disorder or psychosomatic disorders. In some respects mentalization is similar to the cognitive–behavioural concept of metacognition, and the humanistic and constructivist idea of 'meaning-making'. It remains to be seen whether the convergence between these ideas will prove to be a fertile ground for theoretical integration.

Psychodynamic counselling within a time-limited framework

In the early years of psychoanalysis, it was not assumed by Freud or his colleagues that patients need necessarily be in treatment for long periods of time. For example, Freud is reported to have carried out, in 1908, successful therapy of a sexual problem in the composer Gustav Mahler in the course of four sessions (Jones 1955). However, as psychoanalysts became more aware of the problem of resistance in patients, and more convinced of the intractable nature of the emotional problems they brought to therapy, they began to take for granted the idea that psychoanalysis in most cases would be a lengthy business, with patients attending therapy several times a week, perhaps for years.

Among the first psychoanalysts, however, there were some critics of this trend, who argued for a more active role for the therapist, and definite time limits for the length of therapy. The two most prominent advocates of this view were Sandor Ferenczi and Otto Rank. There was strong opposition to their ideas from Freud and the inner circle of analysts, and eventually both men were forced to leave. Within psychoanalytic circles, the ideas of Ferenczi appear to have been neglected for many years, but have recently received an increasing amount of attention from counsellors and psychotherapists interested in developing a more collaborative, active approach to working with clients.

A further important event in the progress of the debate about psychoanalytic technique came with the publication in 1946 of a book by Alexander and French, which advocated that psychoanalysts take a flexible approach to treatment. Over a period of seven years at the Chicago Institute for Psychoanalysis, they had experimented with a range of variations of standard psychoanalytic technique: for example, trying out different numbers of sessions each week, the use of the couch or chair and the degree of attention paid to the transference relationship. The Alexander and French book was highly influential and, in the spirit of openness to new ideas that followed the death of Freud in 1939, it stimulated many other analysts to tackle the issues of the technique involved in offering psychodynamic therapy or counselling on a time-limited basis. The main figures in the subsequent development of what is often known as 'brief therapy' are Mann (1973), Malan (1976, 1979), Sifneos (1979) and Davanloo (1980).

It is essential to recognize that the emergence of brief psychodynamic therapy and counselling arose as much from the pressures of social need and client demand as from the deliberations of therapists themselves. In the 1940s in the USA, for example, counsellors and psychotherapists were being expected to help large numbers of members of the armed forces returning from war with emotional problems. In the 1960s there was substantial political pressure in the USA to move mental health facilities into the community, and to make them more readily available for large numbers of clients. Even clients seeing therapists in private practice did not want 'interminable' therapy. For example, Garfield (1986), in a review of studies of the length of treatment in a variety of therapy settings, found that the largest group of clients were those who came for five or six sessions, with the majority seeing their counsellor or therapist on fewer than 20 occasions. These factors led counsellors and therapists from all orientations to examine closely the problem of time-limited interventions, and the literature on brief psychodynamic work is paralleled by writings on brief cognitive, client-centred and other modes of work.

Writers on brief psychodynamic therapy have different ideas about what they mean by 'brief', which can refer to anything between 3 and 40 sessions. Most are agreed that brief treatment is that involving fewer than 25 sessions. More fundamental, however, is the idea that the number of sessions is rationed, and that a contract is made at the start of counselling that there will only be a certain number of sessions. Although there are many styles of brief psychodynamic work that have been evolved by teams of therapists in different clinics (see Gustafson (1986) for a review of some of the main currents of thought within this movement), there is general agreement that brief work is focused on three discrete stages: beginning, the active phase and termination (Rosen 1987). If the time to be spent with a client is limited, then the maximum use must be made of each and every client–counsellor interaction. The beginning phase is therefore a site for a variety of different kinds of counsellor activity, encompassing assessment, preparing the client, establishing a therapeutic alliance, starting therapeutic work and finding out about the life history and background of the client. The first meeting with the client, and indeed the first words uttered by the client, can be of great significance. This point is well made by Alexander and French:

> The analyst during this period may be compared to a traveller standing on top of a hill overlooking the country through which he is about to journey. At this time it may be possible for him to see his whole anticipated journey in perspective. When once he has descended into the valley, this perspective must be retained in the memory or it is gone. From this time on, he will be able to examine small parts of this landscape in much greater detail than was possible when he was viewing them from a distance, but the broad relations will no longer be so clear.
>
> (Alexander and French 1946: 109)

It is generally assumed that time-limited counselling is appropriate only for particular kinds of clients. For example, clients who are psychotic or 'borderline' are usually seen as unlikely to benefit from time-limited work (although some practitioners, such as Budman and Gurman (1988), would dispute this, and would view all clients as potentially appropriate for time-limited interventions). In brief counselling or therapy it is therefore necessary to carry out an assessment interview. The objectives of the assessment session might cover exploration of such issues as:

- the attitude of the client towards a time-limited treatment contract;
- motivation for change and 'psychological-mindedness';
- the existence of a previous capacity to sustain close relationships;
- the ability to relate with the therapist during the assessment interview;
- the existence of a clearly identifiable, discrete problem to work on in therapy.

Positive indications in all, or most, of these areas are taken to suggest a good prognosis for brief work. Techniques for increasing the effectiveness of the assessment interview include asking the client to complete a life-history questionnaire before the interview, recording the interview on video and discussing the assessment with colleagues, and engaging in 'trial therapy' during the interview. The last refers to the practice of the interviewer offering some limited interpretation of the material offered by the client during the interview (Malan 1976), or devoting a segment of the assessment time to a very short therapy session (Gustafson 1986).

It is, of course, important that care is taken with clients who are assessed as unsuitable for brief work, and that alternative referrals and forms of treatment are available. Special training is usually considered necessary for those carrying out assessment interviews. The beginning stage of brief work also encompasses negotiation with the client over the aims and duration of the counselling or therapy contract, and preparation of the client for what is to follow by explaining to the client the nature of his or her therapeutic responsibilities and tasks.

One of the principal tasks of the brief therapist is to find a focus for the overall therapy, and for each particular session. The therapist is active in seeking out a focus for the work, and in this respect differs from the traditional psychoanalyst, who would wait for themes to emerge through free association. In finding a focus, the counsellor brings to the session some assumptions about the type of material with which he or she is seeking to work. These assumptions are derived from psychoanalytic and object relations theory, and guide the counsellor in the choice of which threads of the client's story to follow up.

For example, Budman and Gurman (1988) describe an 'IDE' formula that they use in deciding on a focus for a session. They view people as inevitably grappling with developmental (D) issues arising from their stage of psycho-social development, involved in interpersonal (I) issues arising from relationships and faced with existential (E) issues such as aloneness, choice and awareness of death. Gustafson (1986: 26) emphasizes the central importance of finding a focus when he writes that 'I will not go a step until I have the "loose end" of the patient's preoccupation for today's meeting'.

It is often valuable, in finding the focus for client work, to consider the question 'Why now?' In brief psychodynamic work it is assumed that the problem the client brings to therapy is triggered off by something currently happening in his or her life. The client is seen as a person who is having difficulties coping with a specific situation, rather than as a fundamentally 'sick' individual. The question 'Why now?' helps to begin the process of exploring the roots of the troublesome feelings that are evoked by current life events. Sometimes the precipitating event can be something that happened many years ago, which is being remembered and relived because of an anniversary of some kind. For example, a woman who requested counselling because of a general lack of satisfaction with her relationship with her husband reported that what seemed to be happening now somehow seemed to be associated with her daughter, who was 16 and starting to go out to parties and have boyfriends. The client found herself remembering that, when she had been 16, she had become pregnant and quickly found herself with all the responsibilities of a wife and mother. Her daughter was now at that same stage in life, and bringing home to the client her buried feelings about the stage of development in her life she had missed out on. This case illustrates how the question 'Why now?' can open up developmental issues.

Another set of central issues that are often the focus for brief work arise from experiences of loss. The case just mentioned in fact included a component of grieving for the loss of youth and adolescence. The events that stimulate people to seek counselling help encompass many different types of loss. The death of someone in the family, being made redundant, leaving home or the surgical removal of a body part are all powerful loss experiences. Usually, loss themes in counselling encompass both interpersonal and existential dimensions. Most experiences of loss involve some kind of change in relationships as well as change in the way the person experiences self. The experience of loss particularly challenges the illusion of self as invulnerable and immortal (Yalom 1980). The other existential facet of loss is that it can throw the person into a state of questioning the meaningfulness of what has happened: 'nothing makes sense any more'. Finally, current experiences of loss will reawaken dormant feelings about earlier losses, and may thereby trigger off strong feelings related to early childhood events.

The aims of the counsellor or therapist working with loss from within a brief psychodynamic approach will include uncovering and working through. The uncovering part of the counselling will involve the client exploring and expressing feelings, and generally opening up this whole area of inner experience for exploration. Techniques for assisting uncovering may include retelling the story of the loss, perhaps using photographs or visits to evoke memories and feelings. The working through phase involves becoming aware of the implications of what the loss event has meant, and how the person has coped with it personally and interpersonally. In the latter phase, the counsellor may give the client information about the 'normal' course of reactions to loss.

It can be seen that, although the active phase of brief psychodynamic therapy involves the use of interpretation of current feelings in terms of past events, it also includes encouragement from the therapist or counsellor to express feelings in the here-and-now setting of the counselling room. The aim is to allow the client to undergo what Alexander and French (1946) called a 'corrective emotional experience'. They saw one of the principal aims of therapy as being 'to reexpose the patient, under more favorable circumstances, to emotional situations which he/she could not handle in the past' (Alexander and French 1946: 66). So, for example, a client who had always been afraid to express his anger at the loss of his job, in case his wife could not handle it, can allow this feeling to be shown in the presence of the counsellor, and then, it is hoped, become more able to have this type of emotional experience with his wife or other people outside the counselling room. Part of the active stance of the brief therapist is therefore to assist the communication of feelings that are 'under the surface' by using questions such as 'What do you feel right now?' and 'How do you feel inside?' (Davanloo 1980).

In any kind of time-limited counselling, the existence of a definite date after which therapy will no longer be available raises a whole range of potential issues for clients. The ending of counselling may awaken feelings associated with other kinds of endings, and lead the client to act out in the relationship with the counsellor the ways he or she has defended against previous feelings of loss. The end of counselling may similarly have a resonance for the client of the separation/individuation stage of development (Mahler 1968), the stage of leaving the protective shell of the parental relationship and becoming a more autonomous individual. There may also be a sense of ambivalence about the end of a counselling relationship, with feelings of satisfaction at what has been achieved and frustration at what there still is to learn. The fact of a time limit may bring into focus the client's habitual ways of living in time: for example, by existing only in a future-orientation (in this case, being obsessed with how much time there is left) and being unwilling to be in the present or with the past. The intention of the brief therapist is to exploit the time-limited format by predicting that some of these issues will emerge for the client, and actively challenging the client to confront and learn from them when they do.

The ending of a counselling relationship can also raise issues for the counsellor, such as feelings of loss, grandiosity at how important the therapy has been for the client or self-doubt over how little use the therapy has been. Dealing with termination is therefore a topic that receives much attention in the counsellor's work with his or her supervisor.

It should already be clear that the role of the counsellor in brief psychodynamic work is subtly different from that in traditional psychoanalysis. In the latter, the therapist takes a passive role, acting as a 'blank screen' on to which may be projected the transference reactions of the client. In brief work, by contrast, the therapist is active and purposeful, engaging the client in a therapeutic alliance in which they can work together. The use that is made of the transference relationship is therefore of necessity quite different.

In long-term analysis, the therapist encourages the development of a strong transference reaction, sometimes called a 'transference neurosis', in order to allow evidence of childhood relationship patterns to emerge. In brief work, strategies are used to avoid such deep levels of transference: for example, by identifying and interpreting transferences as soon as they arise, even in the very first session, and by reducing client dependency by explaining what is happening and maintaining a clear focus for the work. In brief therapy, the here-and-now feeling response of the client towards the therapist or counsellor, the transference, is used instead as the basis for making links between present behaviour with the therapist and past behaviour with parents (Malan 1976).

Some useful principles for the interpretation of transference behaviour have been established by Malan (1979) and Davanloo (1980). The triangle of insight (Davanloo 1980) refers to the links between the behaviour of the client with the therapist (T), with other current relationship figures (C) and with past figures such as parents (P). Clients can be helped to achieve insight by becoming aware of important T–C–P links in their lives. For example, a woman who treats her counsellor with great deference, depending on him to solve her problems, may make the connection that her mother was someone who had a strong need to take care of her. The next step might be to unravel the ways in which she is deferential and dependent with her husband and work colleagues. The triangle of insight would allow this client to understand where her behaviour pattern came from, how it operates (through careful, detailed exploration of how she is in relationship to her counsellor) and what effects the pattern has in her current life.

It can be seen here that the basic techniques of psychoanalysis – transference, resistance and interpretation – are used in brief psychodynamic work, but with important modifications. Just as in any kind of psychoanalytic work, the effectiveness of these techniques will depend on the skill of the therapist.

Box 5.9: *The concept of 'thirdness'*

Thinking in terms of 'threes' represents an important principle of psychodynamic practice. In his earliest writings, Freud suggested that many of the emotional problems that people experience in adult life can be traced back to the interplay between the Oedipal threesome of child, mother and father. More recently, Malan (1979) and other therapists used the idea of 'triangular' relationships to inform their use of transference interpretation. For example, the relationship between the client and therapist could be influenced by the client's relationship with authority figures from earlier periods in their life, or could replicate the dynamics of their relationship with their current husband, wife or partner. Pointing out these links to the client, in the form of interpretation, can lead to insight and change. Jessica Benjamin (2004: 7) has taken this approach further, in arguing that awareness that there can be a 'third' point of view is an essential element of the process of learning about relationships:

. . . to the degree that we ever manage to grasp two-way directionality, we do so only from the place of the *third,* a vantage point outside the two. . . . The concept of the third means a variety of things to different thinkers, and has been used to refer to the profession, the community, the theory one works with – anything one holds in mind that creates another point of reference outside the dyad.

The way this can operate is explained by Britton (1989: 86–7) in the following passage:

The acknowledgement by the child of the parents' relationship with each other unites his psychic world, limiting it to one world shared with his two parents in which different object relationships can exist. The closure of the oedipal triangle by the recognition of the link joining the parents provides a limiting boundary for the internal world. It creates what I call a 'triangular space', i.e., a world bounded by the three persons of the oedipal situation and all their potential relationships. It includes, therefore, the possibility of being a partici-pant in a relationship and observed by a third person as well as being an observer of a relationship between two people . . . if the link between the parents perceived in love and hate can be tolerated in the child's mind, it provides him for a prototype for an object relationship of a third kind in which he is a witness and not a participant. A third position then comes into existence from which object relationships can be observed. Given this, we can also envisage being observed. This provides us with a capacity for seeing ourselves in interaction with others and for entertaining another point of view while retaining our own, for reflecting on ourselves while being ourselves, this is a capacity we hope to find in ourselves and in our patients in analysis.

The concept of 'thirdness' represents a valuable means of making sense of the nature of human consciousness. When a person is in contact with someone else, their awareness of that other person rarely consists of only the information that they directly perceive. Instead, it is as though there is always someone else present.

Narrative psychodynamic approaches: working with stories

Psychoanalytic and psychodynamic therapists and counsellors have always shown a great deal of interest in narrative, and have looked at this phenomenon in two main ways. First, the stories told by clients or patients have been seen as conveying information about the person's habitual ways of relating to others. Second, the role of the therapist has been viewed as that of helping the client to arrive at an alternative, and more satisfactory, way of telling their life story.

The first of these topics, the value of the client's story as a source of information about recurring patterns of conflict within their relationships, has been explored by Strupp and Binder (1984) and by Luborsky and Crits-Christoph (1990). Although Strupp and Luborsky have taken broadly similar approaches to this issue, the work of Luborsky's research group, based at the University of Pennsylvania, is better known and more extensive. The key source for these studies is Luborsky and Crits-Christoph (1990), although Luborsky *et al.* (1992, 1994) have compiled excellent short reviews of their research programme and its clinical implications.

The Luborsky group has observed that although clients in therapy tell stories about their relationships with many different people (for instance, their spouse/partner, family members, friends, the therapist), it is nevertheless possible to detect consistent themes and conflicts running through all, or most, of the stories produced by an individual. Luborsky labels this the core conflictual relationship theme (CCRT). Moreover, Luborsky suggests that these stories are structured in a particular way, around three structural elements. The story expresses the wish of the person in relation to others, the response of the other and finally the response of self. This model allows the meaning of what might be a convoluted and complex story told by a client to be summarized in a relatively simple form. An example of a CCRT analysis of a client's story is given in Box 5.10. In general, the most frequently reported client wishes are 'to be close and accepted', 'to be loved and understood' and 'to assert self and be independent'. The most common responses from others are 'rejecting and opposing' and 'controlling', and the most frequent responses of self are 'disappointed and depressed', 'unreceptive' and 'helpless' (Luborsky *et al.* 1994). In their research studies, Luborsky and his colleagues have found that clients tell an average of four stories in each session, usually about events that have taken place in the past two weeks, and that around 80 per cent of the responses from others and of self are clearly negative, but become more positive as therapy progresses.

Box 5.10: *Analysing a core conflictual relationship theme: the case of Miss Smithfield*

To illustrate the application of the CCRT method, Luborsky *et al.* (1994) have published their analysis of the relationship themes expressed in a pre-therapy interview by a young woman, Miss Smithfield. Some examples of the stories told by this client are given below.

Story 1

I met him at the end of my [university] programme, and I was staying, I stayed longer than the programme, but I met him at the end of my programme in Jakarta, and everything just clicked, perfectly. Both of us politically had the same mind set, emotionally had very similar mind sets, and culturally we just fascinated each other because of the differences . . . so we spent the rest of our time together . . . we married, and I returned to this country [the USA] not too long afterwards. The plan was that he was going to finish writing his thesis . . . come to this country till I graduated, and then we would both have gone back over . . . but he disappeared six months after I came back . . . actually I don't know exactly what has happened to him . . . Nobody knows what has happened . . . I don't know . . . I think its better for my own sanity that I don't. I decided from after about a year from the time he disappeared that it was, I needed to get on with my own life and live it as best I could.

Story 2

I've been raped a total of five times. Four times in the past few years though. They're all knowledge rapes. People that I thought I knew, in one sense or another, and that's really put a damper on my trust . . . one of the rapes . . . happened in Indonesia. It was with a man that I had once been seeing before I met my husband, and I'd broken up with him . . . but he was still willing to help me out when I got sick, so I went down to Bandung to heal myself, and I was very weak at the time, and he expected because he was caring for me he would have sexual rights as well, and I could not fight him physically because I was very weak . . . he forced me into this position . . . he had been with another woman who had VD . . . and he knowably gave it to me because he was mad at me for breaking off with him . . .

Story 3

I was the 'school scapegoat' and was avoided and picked on . . . my parents are both highly intelligent individuals . . . they're good people, and now I'm beginning to have a better relationship with them . . . there's less pressure, there's less pressure now . . . they never really had any specific goals, but they wanted me to make it . . . I mean they did push me in my music because I was a talented oboe player for quite a while . . . they helped and supported me . . . but at times they forced me to practise an hour and a half per day or whatever to keep me going . . . I wanted to go out and play and run around in the woods with my friends and what friends I did have at that point.

On the basis of these stories, and several other stories told by this client in a lengthy and detailed interview, Luborsky *et al.* (1994: 178) arrived at a CCRT formulation: 'I wish to resist domination and not to be forced to submit or to be overpowered. But the other person dominates, takes control and overpowers me. Then I feel dominated, submissive, helpless and victimized'.

They suggest that underlying this relationship pattern there may have been a less conscious desire to submit to another, to be controlled. Such a wish can be seen to have its origins in early childhood experience: for example, in issues around separation from the mother. The analysis of Miss Smithfield's narrative shows how the CCRT approach strips the narrative from its context, and rigorously focuses in on core themes associated with emotionally very basic early object relationships. It is also worth noting that the CCRT method tends to highlight conflictual aspects of the person's story, in contrast to the approach taken by White and Epston (1990) of focusing on what the story conveys about the positive, life-enhancing capabilities of the person.

The research carried out by Luborsky and his collaborators has established the importance of the CCRT as a unit for analysing therapy process. However, their model also has many implications for practice. Luborsky's main aim has been to provide therapists with a straightforward and easy-to-use method of both making interpretations and analysing transference. It has been shown (Luborsky and Crits-Christoph 1990) that interpretations accurately based on CCRT elements are highly effective in promoting insight, although overall the accuracy of therapist interpretations assessed by this technique tend to be low, and the relationship with the therapist (the transference) tends to correspond to the CCRT pattern found in stories about other people. The CCRT model therefore serves as a highly practical method for improving the effectiveness of psychodynamic counselling, by acting as a conceptual tool that counsellors and psychotherapists can use to enhance the accuracy of their interpretations.

Several other psychoanalytic theorists have made important contributions to an understanding of the role of narrative in therapy. Spence (1982) has argued for a distinction between narrative truth and historical truth. Whereas Freud and other early psychoanalytic therapists believed that free association and dream analysis were unearthing evidence about early childhood conflicts that actually occurred, Spence points out that it is seldom possible to verify in an objective sense whether or not these childhood events took place. He suggests that what therapists do is to help the client to arrive at a narrative truth, a story that makes sense and has sufficient correspondence with the historical data that are available. Another significant psychoanalytic writer on narrative has been Schafer (1992), who regards the interpretations made by the therapist over a period of time as comprising a 're-telling' of the client's story in the form of a psychoanalytic narrative. Eventually, the client comes to see his or her life in psychoanalytic terms. In similar fashion, Schafer would argue, a client of person-centred counselling would develop a Rogerian narrative account of their life, and a cognitive–behavioural client would acquire a cognitive–behavioural story. Finally, McAdams (1985, 1993) has explored the underlying or unconscious narrative structures, such as myths, that people use to give shape to their life as a whole.

The psychoanalytic or psychodynamic tradition has generated a wealth of powerful and applicable ideas about the role of narrative in therapy. However, for psychodynamic writers and practitioners an interest in narrative is only an adjunct to the real business of identifying unconscious material, interpreting the transference and so on. Luborsky, Schafer and others have aimed not to create a narrative therapy, but to practise psychodynamic therapy in a narrative-informed fashion.

The psychodynamic–interpersonal model

Another significant development within psychodynamic counselling in recent years has been the evolution of what was originally described as the *conversational* model, but more recently has been termed a *psychodynamic–interpersonal* approach. This version of psychodynamic counselling was initially developed in Britain by Bob Hobson and Russell Meares (Hobson 1985), and has become increasingly influential. There are three key features of the conversational model, which, taken together, distinguish it from other psychodynamic approaches. First, it is based on contemporary ideas about the meaning and role of language that are quite different from the assumptions and concepts of mainstream psychodynamic theory. Second, it is intended to be applied within a limited number of sessions. Third, the effectiveness of the model is supported by the results of research. Whereas other psychodynamic models can claim achievements in one or perhaps two of these domains, the psychodynamic–interpersonal model is the only current psychodynamic approach to have been simultaneously innovative in the areas of theory, service delivery and research. In addition, there has been research into how best to train people in this approach (Goldberg *et al.* 1984; Maguire *et al.* 1984).

The main text for the conversational/psychodynamic–interpersonal model is *Forms of Feeling: The Heart of Psychotherapy* by Hobson (1985). This is an unusual and creative book, in which Hobson draws on lengthy case descriptions and makes frequent use of literary sources. It is clear from the way the book is written that Hobson is presenting the approach not as an abstract theoretical or intellectual system, but as a set of principles that can help to focus the task of constructing what he terms the 'special friendship' that is therapy. It also appears as though Hobson is unwilling to present the theory as a fixed and definitive set of ideas. Tentativeness and uncertainty are highly valued. Knowledge and understanding are to be achieved through dialogue rather than by authoritative assertion.

At the core of the approach is the idea that people need to be able to talk about their feelings. The troubles that people bring to therapy stem from an inability to engage in dialogue with others around their feelings. The dialogue or conversation is crucial to well-being because it is through conversation that a person can act on feelings (language is a form of action; words 'do things'), and because the dialogue with another person dissolves the loneliness that is associated with holding feelings to oneself: for example, grieving in isolation. A primary task of the counsellor or psychotherapist is to develop a mutual 'feeling language' through which client and therapist can conduct a conversation about how the client feels. The counsellor does this by paying attention to the actual or implicit feeling words and metaphors employed by the client.

The counsellor also uses 'I' statements as a way of communicating the presence of another person, and therefore extending an invitation to dialogue. Here, the counsellor eschews neutrality and 'owns' what he or she says to the client, and through this way of talking hopes to act as a model for the client, thereby encouraging the client to 'own' their feelings too. The counsellor suggests tentative hypotheses that suggest possible links between the feelings of the client and the events or relationships in his or her life. All of this is built around the idea of the mutual conversation. The client has a 'problem' because in that area of their life they are unable to engage in a mutual conversation with anyone. Therapy offers the chance to open up such a mutual conversation, with the possibility that it might extend after therapy into other relationships.

Hobson, Meares and many of their colleagues involved in the development of the psychodynamic–interpersonal model had a background in psychoanalytic and Jungian psychotherapy, and versions of many key psychodynamic and psychoanalytic concepts can be found in the model. However, these concepts are restated and reworked to fit with the more interpersonally and linguistically oriented assumptions underlying the psychodynamic–interpersonal approach. For example, the Freudian notion of defence appears as 'avoidance'; transference becomes 'direct enactment'; insight becomes 'personal problem-solving'; an interpretation is a 'hypothesis'. Although the concept of counter-transference does not appear in the index of the Hobson (1985) book, the whole of the conversational approach relies on the counsellor's awareness of his or her input to the relationship. Meares and Hobson (1977) have also discussed negative aspects of counter-transference in terms of their concept of the 'persecutory therapist'. The goals of therapy in the psychodynamic–interpersonal approach are defined as:

to facilitate growth by removing obstructions . . . the reduction of fear associated with separation, loss and abandonment . . . an aspiration toward an ideal state of aloneness–togetherness . . . an increase of individual awareness with 'inner' conversations between 'I' and many 'selves' in a society of 'myself' . . . the discovery of a 'true voice of feeling'.

(Hobson 1985: 196)

Quite apart from the established psychodynamic concepts of separation and loss, also apparent here are traces of the influence of humanistic theory ('growth', 'awareness'), existentialism ('aloneness–togetherness') and personal construct theory: for example, Mair's (1989) notion of a 'community of selves'. A discussion of the distinctive integration of therapeutic ideas and methods that is found in psychodynamic–interpersonal therapy, is available in Blagys and Hilsenroth (2000).

An example of how the psychodynamic–interpersonal approach works in practice is given in Box 5.11. This case vignette is taken from a study of the effectiveness of the psychodynamic–interpersonal model with hospital patients suffering from chronic irritable bowel syndrome (IBS). Chronic IBS is a debilitating condition that is believed to have a strong psychosomatic component, but that has proved in previous studies to have been fairly intractable to counselling or psychotherapy. Guthrie, however, found that a limited number of sessions of psychodynamic–interpersonal therapy could significantly help these patients.

Box 5.11: *'I can't keep it in . . . my guts are churning': psychodynamic conversations about bowel problems*

Irritable bowel syndrome (IBS) is a condition that consists of abdominal pain and distension, and altered bowel habits, in the absence of any identifiable underlying organic cause. Many of those suffering from IBS respond well to medical treatment, but about 15 per cent are not helped by drugs or dietary regimes. It seems likely that the problems of many of these 'refractory' IBS patients are psychosomatic in nature, and that counselling may be of value to them. Guthrie (1991) carried out a study of the effectiveness of psychodynamic–interpersonal therapy with 102 hospital outpatients diagnosed as having refractory IBS. Half of the patients received therapy, which comprised one long (3–4 hour) initial session, followed by six sessions of 45 minutes spread over the following 12 weeks. The other half were allocated to a control group, and met with the therapist on five occasions over the same period of time to discuss their symptoms, but without receiving actual therapy. The results of the study demonstrated the effectiveness of psychodynamic–interpersonal counselling with this group of people. The account of one case described by Guthrie (1991) offers a good illustration of the way that the conversational model operates in practice.

Bob was 49, and had suffered from abdominal pain and loose motions for several years. He had been unable to work for the previous three years. Bob was an only child, brought up by a 'strict and unaffectionate' mother; his father had left home when he was six. He saw himself as a 'loner', and he was far from convinced that counselling could help him. He spoke for a long time in the first session about his symptoms:

'My guts are always churning.'
'I can't work, I always have to keep rushing to the loo.'
'It's awful, everything just explodes away from me.'
'I just have to go, it's awful, I'm frightened to go out.'
The counsellor did little more than feed back his words:
'Can't keep things in.'
'When things come out . . . no control.'
'Frightened . . . no control . . . awful . . . just have to go.'
Guthrie (1991: 178) comments that:

> gradually Bob came to realise that, although I was using virtually the same words that he was using to describe bowel symptoms, I was actually talking about feelings. After he had made this connection, he began to talk more freely about himself. He described in some depth how humiliated he felt by his first wife, who had particularly belittled his sexual performance, and how dominated he had felt by his mother. After a long pause I tentatively enquired whether he was worried that I would humiliate him in some way. At this point he suddenly got up and rushed out of the room saying he had to go to the toilet.

When he returned to the counselling room, Bob acknowledged that he had been feeling frightened of the counsellor, and then 'smiled with relief'. Over the following sessions, he became more able to see his bowel symptoms as a metaphor for how he felt inside. As a result of making this connection, he began to talk to his wife about his fear, and his symptoms improved. Soon, he was able to return to work, even though his symptoms had not completely disappeared.

The case of Bob captures the way that the psychodynamic–interpersonal approach works. The counsellor engages in a conversation around whatever is most meaningful for the client, in this instance bowel symptoms. The counsellor and client develop a mutual feeling language, and through being able to use this language the client is enabled to stop avoiding what is difficult or painful in his or her life. The counsellor is tentative, yet direct and personal.

The other main studies of the conversational model have been carried out in the context of the Sheffield Psychotherapy Project, a large-scale comparison of the efficacy of time-limited psychodynamic–interpersonal (i.e., conversational) and cognitive–behavioural therapies for people who were depressed. Because of factors associated with the politics of psychotherapy research in these studies the conversational model was given the more generic title of 'psychodynamic–interpersonal'. The results of this research programme strongly confirmed the effectiveness of conversational therapy for this group of clients (Shapiro et al. 1994).

The psychodynamic–interpersonal model is an approach to counselling and psychotherapy that is likely to grow in importance over the next few years. Its use of philosophical, literary and constructivist concepts has revitalized psychodynamic theory and practice, and it is attractive to many counsellors eager to espouse a broadly integrative approach that draws on the humanistic/existential as well as psychodynamic traditions (Mackay *et al.* 2001). Recent developments in theory, research, practice and training in relation to the conversational model are reviewed in Barkham *et al.* (1998), and include the application of this approach in work in cases of deliberate self-harm (Guthrie *et al.* 2001) and with people with longstanding mental health difficulties (Guthrie *et al.* 1998, 1999; Davenport *et al.* 2000).

Research into psychodynamic therapy

Despite Freud's somewhat negative attitude to research – he believed that the only way to understand psychoanalysis was to participate in it – there exists an extensive research literature on all aspects of psychoanalytic and psychodynamic counselling and psychotherapy. A straightforward summary of research into the effectiveness of psychodynamic therapy can be found in Shedler (2010). Further discussion of specific themes and topics within this research literature is available within the present chapter, as well as in Chapter 25.

Conclusion: an appraisal of the psychodynamic approach to counselling

Psychoanalysis has provided a set of concepts and methods that have found application in a wide variety of contexts. Psychodynamic ideas have proved invaluable not only in individual therapy and counselling, but also in groupwork, couples counselling and the analysis of organizations. The ideas of Freud have been robust and resilient enough to withstand critique and reformulation from a number of sources. Psychodynamic perspectives have made a significant contribution to research into the process of counselling and therapy. Throughout this book there are many examples of the ways psychodynamic ideas have been used in different contexts and settings. All counsellors and therapists, even those who espouse different theoretical models, have been influenced by psychodynamic thinking and have had to make up their minds whether to accept or reject the Freudian image of the person.

There are clearly innumerable similarities and differences between psychodynamic and other approaches. The most essential difference, however, lies in the density of psychodynamic theory, particularly in the area of the understanding of development in childhood. Cognitive–behavioural theory is largely silent on child development, and the person-centred approach, in its use of the concept of 'conditions of worth', is little more than silent. Psychodynamic counsellors, by contrast, have at their disposal a highly sophisticated set of concepts with which to make sense of developmental issues.

In practice, psychodynamic counselling involves a form of therapeutic helping that draws on the theories of psychoanalysis, as a means of deepening and enriching the relationship between counsellor and client, rather than being dominated by these theories. The use of these ideas in counselling can be summarized in terms of a set of key principles:

1 People have troubled relationships because they are repeating a destructive relationship pattern from the past. When a person meets someone new, there is a tendency to treat that person not as an individual, but as if they represented someone from the person's past (transference). People in authority (counsellors, nurses, teachers) often find that their clients project or transfer on to them their images of their father, mother, uncle etc.

2 The person may seek to control or hide difficult or unacceptable internal desires, memories and feelings by defending against them. 'Defence mechanisms', such as transference, projection, denial, repression, sublimation, splitting and projective identification, are used to divert attention from threatening 'internal' material.

3 It is important for helpers to be aware of their feelings, fantasies and impulses in relation to the person they are helping. This inner response (counter-transference) is evidence of (a) the kind of feelings that the person typically evokes in others, and/or (b) the kind of emotional world in which the person lives their life. In either case, 'counter-transference' feelings are valuable sources of evidence concerning the inner life, and relationship patterns, of a person seeking help.

4 The person's problems can often be understood as representing unresolved developmental tasks (for example, separating from the mother/parents). Freud proposed a

series of biologically focused stages of development: oral, anal, Oedipal. Erikson suggested more socially oriented stages: trust, autonomy, initiative, industry, identity, intimacy, generativity, integrity. However, the underlying theory is the same: if a person has an unsatisfactory experience at one stage, they will continue to try to deal with this developmental issue for the rest of their lives (or until they gain some insight into it).

5 People have a need for secure, consistent emotional attachments. If a person's attachments are disrupted in early life (parental absence, illness etc.) they may grow up being insecure about forming attachments, and exhibit a pattern of difficulty in committing to relationships, ambivalence within a relationship, difficulty in parenting consistently etc.

These principles provide a powerful set of strategies for helping people first to understand and then to change conflictual and self-defeating ways of relating to others. For counsellors who find these ideas meaningful, the psychodynamic literature, and associated training opportunities, represent hugely valuable resources.

Topics for reflection and discussion

1 Coltart (1986: 187) has written of 'the need to develop the ability to tolerate not knowing, the capacity to sit it out with a patient, often for long periods, without any real precision as to where we are, relying on our regular tools and our faith in the process, to carry us through the obfuscating darkness of resistance, complex defences, and the sheer unconsciousness of the unconscious'. What might be the advantages and disadvantages of adopting a 'not knowing' stance in relation to a client's problems?

2 To what extent does time-limited counselling dilute or undermine the distinctive aims and meaning of psychodynamic work?

3 What are the main similarities and differences between psychodynamic counselling and the other approaches introduced in the following chapters?

4 Strupp (1972: 276) has suggested that the psychodynamic counsellor or psychotherapist 'uses the vantage point of the parental position as a power base from which to effect changes in the patient's interpersonal strategies in accordance with the principle that *in the final analysis the patient changes out of love for the therapist*'. Do you agree?

5 Think about your relationship with someone you have found difficult to deal with at an interpersonal level. Make some brief notes about what happened, and what was difficult about your contact with this person. Analyse what you have written about this relationship in psychodynamic terms, using concepts such as transference, countertransference and mechanisms of defence. What were the psychodynamic processes occurring in the patient, and in you, that made this relationship problematic? In what ways might the psychodynamic perspective on what happened help you in dealing with a similar situation in the future?

Suggested further reading

Anyone who is seriously interested in making sense of what psychodynamic counselling is really about needs to read some of Freud's original writings, rather than rely on second-hand textbook accounts. Freud was a wonderfully vivid and persuasive writer, who inexorably draws the reader into his search for psychoanalytic truth. A good place to start might be the *Five Lectures on Psycho-analysis* (Freud 1910/1963), first delivered at Clark University in Massachusetts in 1909. Here, Freud was trying to explain his ideas to an enthusiastic, but also sceptical, audience of American psychologists and psychiatrists. Beyond the *Five Lectures*, it is worth looking at one of the classic case studies – Dora, the Rat Man, the Wolf Man, Schreber – all of which are included in the widely available *Standard Edition of Freud's Works* (1976).

The literature on psychodynamic counselling is so wide and varied that it is not easy to recommend specific books without generating an endless list. An accessible, jargon-free introduction to contemporary psychodynamic thought can be found in *That Was Then, This Is Now: Psychoanalytic Psychotherapy for the Rest of Us* by Jonathan Shedler (2006; available at http:// psychsystems.net/shedler.html). Gomez (1997), Jacobs (2010) and Spurling (2009) provide easy-to-read introductions to this approach. The movement in psychoanalysis and psychodynamic therapy in the direction of a more 'relational' approach is discussed well by Kahn (1997) and Mitchell (1986). The journals *Psychodynamic Practice* and *British Journal of Psychotherapy* contain stimulating combinations of clinical material, theoretical papers and research articles that reflect the broad scope of psychodynamic work. Books that perhaps communicate the spirit of contemporary psychodynamic thought are *On Learning from the Patient* by Patrick Casement (1985), *Mothering Psychoanalysis* by Janet Sayers (1991), *Cultivating Intuition* by Peter Lomas (1994) and *Psychodynamic Techniques: Working with Emotion in the Therapeutic Relationship* by Karen Maroda (2010).

CHAPTER

6

The cognitive–behavioural approach to counselling

Introduction

The *cognitive–behavioural* tradition represents an important approach to counselling, with its own distinctive methods and concepts. This approach has evolved out of behavioural psychology and has three key features: a problem-solving, change-focused approach to working with clients; a respect for scientific values; and close attention to the cognitive processes through which people monitor and control their behaviour. In recent years cognitive–behavioural therapy (CBT) has been widely adopted as the intervention model most likely to be offered to clients within health care systems in North America and Europe. This chapter begins by reviewing the roots of CBT in academic behavioural and cognitive psychology, and offers on overview of the further development of this approach. The chapter then examines in more detail the specific concepts and methods associated with cognitive–behavioural counselling.

The origins and development of the cognitive–behavioural approach

To understand the nature of cognitive–behavioural counselling, it is necessary to examine its historical emergence from within the discipline of academic psychology. It is widely accepted that the development of CBT has passed through three main phases. The earliest stage in the emergence of CBT was represented by the application of principles of behavioural psychology into *behaviour therapy*. The second stage was characterized by the addition of cognitive perspectives and techniques, and the use of the term *cognitive–behavioural* therapy. The third, current phase in the development of CBT has seen the assimilation of a broader range of ideas, such as acceptance, mindfulness and compassion, into basic CBT procedures.

The roots of CBT in behaviour therapy

Ultimately, the cognitive–behavioural approach to therapy has its origins in behavioural psychology, which is widely seen as having been created by J. B. Watson, particularly through the publication in 1919 of *Psychology from the Standpoint of a Behaviorist*. Watson was a psychology professor at the University of Chicago at a time when psychology as an academic discipline was in its infancy. It had only been in 1879 that Wilhelm Wundt, at the University of Leipzig, had first established psychology as a field of study separate from philosophy and physiology. The method of research into psychological topics, such as memory, learning, problem-solving and perception, that Wundt and others such as Titchener had used was the technique known as 'introspection', which involved research subjects reporting on their own internal thought processes as they engaged in remembering, learning or any other psychological activity. This technique tended to yield contradictory data, since different subjects in different laboratories reported quite dissimilar internal events when carrying out the same mental tasks. The weakness of introspection as a scientific method, argued Watson, was that it was not open to objective scrutiny. Only the actual subject could 'see' what was happening, and this would inevitably result in bias and subjective distortion. Watson made the case that, if psychology was to become a truly scientific discipline, it would need to concern itself only with observable events and phenomena. He suggested that psychology should define itself as the scientific study of actual, overt behaviour rather than invisible thoughts and images, because these behaviours could be controlled and measured in laboratory settings.

Watson's 'behavioural' manifesto convinced many of his colleagues, particularly in the USA, and for the next 30 years mainstream academic psychology was dominated by the ideas of the behavioural school. The main task that behaviourists like Guthrie, Spence and

Skinner set themselves was to discover the 'laws of learning'. They took the position that all the habits and beliefs that people exhibit must be learned, and so the most important task for psychology is to find out how people learn. Moreover, they suggested that the basic principles of learning, or acquisition of new behaviour, would be the same in any organism. Since there were clearly many ethical and practical advantages in carrying out laboratory research on animals rather than human beings, the behaviourists set about an ambitious programme of research into learning in animal subjects, mainly rats and pigeons.

Behavioural psychologists were eager to identify ways to apply their ideas to the explanation of psychological and emotional problems. Probably the first theorist to look at emotional problems from a behavioural perspective was Pavlov, a Russian physiologist and psychologist working at the end of the nineteenth century, who noted that when he set his experimental dogs a perceptual discrimination task that was too difficult (for example, they would be rewarded with food for responding to a circle, but not when the stimulus was an ellipse) the animals would become distressed, squeal and 'break down'. Later, Liddell, carrying out conditioning experiments at Cornell University, coined the phrase 'experimental neurosis' – a pattern of behaviour characterized by swings from somnolence and passivity to hyperactivity – to describe the behaviour of his experimental animals exposed to monotonous environments. Watson himself carried out the well known 'Little Albert' experiment, where a conditioned fear of animals was induced in a young boy by frightening him with a loud noise at the moment he had been given a furry animal to hold. Masserman, in a series of studies with cats, found that 'neurotic' behaviour could be brought about by creating an approach–avoidance conflict in the animal: for example, by setting up a situation where the animal had been rewarded (given food) and punished (given an electric shock) in the same area in the laboratory.

Skinner (1953) found that when animals were rewarded or reinforced at random, with there being no link between their actual behaviour and its outcome in terms of food, they began to acquire 'ritualistic' or obsessional behaviour. Seligman (1975) conducted studies of the phenomenon of 'learned helplessness'. In Seligman's studies, animals restrained in cages and unable to escape or in any other way control the situation are given electric shocks. After a time, even when they are shocked in a situation where they are able to escape, they sit there and accept it. They have learned to behave in a helpless or depressed manner. Seligman views this work as giving some clues to the origins of depression. Further documentation of the origins of behaviour therapy in experimental studies can be found in Kazdin (1978).

To behaviourists, these studies provided convincing evidence that psychological and psychiatric problems could be explained, and ultimately treated, using behavioural principles. However, the strong identification of the behavioural school with the values of 'pure' science meant that they restricted themselves largely to laboratory studies. It was not until the years immediately after World War II, when there was a general expansion of psychiatric services in the USA, that the first attempts were made to turn behaviourism into a form of therapy. The earliest applications of behavioural ideas in therapy drew explicitly upon Skinner's operant conditioning model of learning, which found practical expression in the behaviour modification programmes of Ayllon and Azrin (1968), and on Pavlov's classical conditioning model, which provided the rationale for the systematic desensitization technique devised by Wolpe (1958).

Box 6.1: *The cultural origins of CBT*

When leading figures in the world of CBT write about how this approach was initially developed, they tend to place a strong emphasis on its origins in scientific research in behavioural psychology. However, it is also important to acknowledge that many of the techniques that are used in CBT can be traced back to methods of emotional self-control of 'mind training' that were in existence in Victorian nineteenth century society, and even in earlier times (Ablow 2008; Stearns and Stearns 1986; Thomson 2007), long before the advent of scientific psychology. The current high levels of public acceptance of CBT as a method of therapy can be understood, in part, as a consequence of the degree to which CBT taps in to longstanding and deep-rooted ideas about conduct and relationships.

Behavioural methods in counselling

Behaviour modification is an approach that takes as its starting point the Skinnerian notion that in any situation, or in response to any stimulus, the person has available a repertoire of possible responses, and emits the behaviour that is reinforced or rewarded. This principle is known as *operant conditioning*. For example, on being asked a question by someone, there are many possible ways of responding. The person can answer the question, he or she can ignore the question, he or she can run away. Skinner (1953) argued that the response that is emitted is the one that has been most frequently reinforced in the past. So, in this case, most people will answer a question, because in the past this behaviour has resulted in reinforcements such as attention or praise from the questioner, or material rewards. If, on the other hand, the person has been brought up in a family in which answering questions leads to physical abuse and running away leads to safety, his or her behaviour will reflect this previous reinforcement history. He or she will run off. Applied to individuals with behavioural problems, these ideas suggest that it is helpful to reward or reinforce desired or appropriate behaviour, and ignore inappropriate behaviour. If a behaviour or response is not rewarded it will, according to Skinner, undergo a process of extinction, and fade out of the behavioural repertoire of the person.

Ayllon and Azrin (1965, 1968) applied these principles in psychiatric hospital wards, with severely disturbed patients, using a technique known as 'token economy'. With these patients specific target behaviours, such as using cutlery to eat a meal or talking to another person, were systematically rewarded by the ward staff, usually by giving them tokens that could be exchanged for rewards such as cigarettes or visits, or sometimes by directly rewarding them at the time with chocolate, cigarettes or praise. At the beginning of the programme, in line with Skinner's research on reinforcement schedules, the patient would be rewarded for very simple behaviour, and the reward would be available for every performance of the target behaviour. As the programme progressed, the patient would only be rewarded for longer, more complex sequences of behaviour, and would be rewarded on a more intermittent basis. Eventually, the aim would be to maintain the desired behaviour through normal social reinforcement.

The effectiveness of behaviour modification and token economy programmes is highly dependent on the existence of a controlled social environment, in which the behaviour of the learner can be consistently reinforced in the intended direction. As a result, most behaviour modification has been carried out within 'total institutions', such as psychiatric and mental handicap hospitals, prisons and secure units. The technique can also be applied, however, in more ordinary situations, like schools and families, if key participants such as teachers and parents are taught how to apply the technique. It is essential, however, that whoever is supplying the behaviour modification is skilled and motivated so that the client is not exposed to contradictory reinforcement schedules. Furthermore, because behaviour modification relies on the fact that the person supplying the reinforcement has real power to give or withhold commodities that are highly valued by the client, there is the possibility of corruption and abuse. It is not unusual for people with only limited training in behavioural principles to assume that punishment is a necessary component of a behaviour modification regime. Skinner, by contrast, was explicit in stating that punishment would only temporarily suppress undesirable behaviour, and that in the long term behaviour change relies on the acquisition of new behaviour, which goes hand-in-hand with the extinction of the old, inappropriate behaviour.

Behaviour modification does not sit easily within a counselling relationship, which is normally a collaborative, one-to-one relationship in which the client can talk about his or her problems. Nevertheless, the principles of behaviour modification can be adapted for use in counselling settings, by explaining behavioural ideas to the client and working with him to apply these ideas to bring about change in his own life. This approach is often described as 'behavioural self-control', and involves functional analysis of patterns of behaviour, with the aim not so much of 'knowing thyself' as of 'knowing thy controlling variables' (Thoresen and Mahoney 1974). The assumption behind this way of working is that, following Skinner, any behaviour exhibited by a person has been elicited by a stimulus, and is reinforced by its consequences. The client can then be encouraged to implement suitable change at any, or all, of the steps in a sequence of behaviour.

Box 6.2: *Behaviour modification in a case of bulimia*

Binge eating followed by self-induced vomiting is characteristic of the condition labelled as *bulimia nervosa*. This pattern of behaviour lends itself to behavioural intervention, since the behaviours in question are overt and take place over a relatively extended period of time on a regular, predictable basis. There are thus multiple opportunities to disrupt the sequence of behaviour and introduce new responses and reinforcers. In addition, clients suffering from this condition are often desperate to change, and are therefore highly motivated to comply with a behavioural regime. In a case study reported by Viens and Hranchuk (1992), a 35-year-old woman with longstanding difficulties in eating was offered behavioural treatment. She had previously undergone surgery for weight reduction, and now was compulsively bingeing and vomiting her food. She had lost any capacity to control her eating behaviour, which was negatively reinforced by the effect that it kept her overall body weight at a personally acceptable level. However, disapproval of her eating by significant others in her life had resulted in an increasing problem of social isolation.

The initial phase of the treatment involved rigorous self-monitoring of her eating behaviour for a period of three weeks. She wrote down what she ate, how many mouthfuls she took each meal and how many times she vomited her food during and after each meal. On the basis of this information, a behavioural regime was set up, which included:

- at mealtimes, eating two spoonfuls, then resting for 30 seconds while practising a relaxation exercise, then another two spoonfuls;
- weighing herself daily in the morning, entering the weight data on a graph and reporting the results to her therapist once each week;
- continued self-monitoring of what was eaten, mouthfuls and vomiting episodes;
- engaging in some kind of physical activity every day, and reporting her progress to the therapist at their weekly meeting;
- her boyfriend was briefed on the rationale for the therapy.

This client's vomiting reduced markedly within six weeks, and remained low over the six-month period of treatment. These gains had been maintained at a one-year follow-up interview. Viens and Hranchuk (1992) suggest that this case demonstrates that behavioural change in an eating disorder can be achieved in the absence of any cognitive intervention. Moreover, there was only minimal therapist involvement, mainly comprising being available on a weekly schedule to reinforce the client's gains and progress. They ascribe the effectiveness of the behavioural intervention not only to the fact that the client's actual eating behaviour was modified, but to the fact that this set of changes led to secondary reinforcement of the new eating pattern as she became more willing to socialize, and as people she met commented favourably on her weight loss.

A simple example of what is known as *functional analysis* (Cullen 1988) of problem behaviour might involve a client who wishes to stop smoking. A behaviourally oriented counsellor would begin by carrying out a detailed assessment of where and when the person smokes (the stimulus), what he does when he smokes (the behaviour) and the rewards or pleasures he experiences from smoking (the consequences). This assessment will typically identify much detailed information about the complex pattern of behaviours that constitutes 'smoking' for the client, including, for example, the fact that he always has lunch with a group of heavy smokers, that he offers round his cigarettes and that smoking helps him to feel relaxed. This client might work with the counsellor to intervene in this pattern of smoking behaviour by choosing to sit with other, non-smoking colleagues after lunch, never carrying more than two cigarettes so he cannot offer them to others and carrying out an 'experiment' where he smokes one cigarette after the other in a small room with other members of a smoking cessation clinic, until he reaches a point of being physically sick, thus learning to associate smoking with a new consequence: sickness rather than relaxation. Further information on recent developments in functional analysis can be found in Sturmey (2007).

The other technique that represented the beginning of a behavioural approach to counselling and therapy was the *systematic desensitization* method pioneered by Wolpe (1958). This approach relies on Pavlov's classical conditioning model of learning. Pavlov had demonstrated, in a series of experiments with dogs, that the behaviour of an animal or organism includes many reflex responses. These are unlearned, automatic reactions to particular situations or stimuli (which he called 'unconditioned stimuli'). In his own research he looked at the salivation response. Dogs will automatically salivate when presented with food. Pavlov discovered, however, that if some other stimulus is also presented at the same time as the 'unconditioned' stimulus, the new stimulus comes to act as a 'signal' for the original stimulus, and may eventually evoke the same reflex response even when the original, unconditioned stimulus is not present. So Pavlov rang a bell just as food was brought in to his dogs, and after a time they would salivate to the sound of the bell even when there was no food around. Furthermore, they would begin to salivate to the sound of other bells (generalization) and would gradually lessen their salivation if they heard the bell on a number of occasions in the absence of any association with food.

Wolpe saw a parallel between classical conditioning and the acquisition of anxiety or fear responses in human beings. For a vivid example, imagine a person who has been in a car crash. Like one of Pavlov's dogs, the crash victim can only passively respond to a situation. Similarly, he experiences an automatic reflex response to the stimulus or situation, in this case a reflex response of fear. Finally, the fear response may generalize to other stimuli associated with the crash: for instance, travelling in a car or even going out of doors. The crash victim who has become anxious or phobic about travelling, therefore, can be understood as suffering from a conditioned emotional response. The solution is, again following Pavlov, to re-expose the person to the 'conditioned' stimuli in the absence of the original fear-inducing elements. This is achieved through a process of systematic desensitization. First of all, the client learns how to relax. The counsellor either carries out relaxation exercises during counselling sessions, or gives the client relaxation instructions and tapes to practise at home. Once the client has mastered relaxation, the client and counsellor work together to identify a hierarchy of fear-eliciting stimuli or situations, ranging from highly fearful (for example, going for a trip in a car past the accident spot) to minimally fearful (for example, looking at pictures of a car in a magazine). Beginning with the least fear-inducing, the client is exposed to each stimulus in turn, all the while practising his relaxation skills. This procedure may take some time, and in many cases the counsellor will accompany the client into and through fear-inducing situations, such as taking a car journey together. By the end of the procedure, the relaxation response rather than the fear response should be elicited by all the stimuli included in the hierarchy.

Although systematic desensitization takes its rationale from classical conditioning, most behavioural theorists would argue that a full account of the development of maladaptive fears and phobias requires the use of ideas from operant, or Skinnerian, as well as classical conditioning. They would point out that although the initial conditioned fear response may have been originally acquired through classical conditioning, in many cases it would have been extinguished in the natural course of events as the client allowed himself to re-experience cars, travel and the outside world. What may happen is that the person actively avoids these situations, because they bring about feelings of anxiety. As a result, the person is being reinforced for avoidance behaviour – he is rewarded or reinforced by feeling more relaxed in the home rather than outside, or walking rather than going in a car. This 'two-factor' model of neurosis views the anxiety of the client as a conditioned emotional response that acts as an avoidance drive. Through systematic desensitization, the counsellor can help the client to overcome his avoidance.

The limitations of a purely behavioural perspective

It was argued by behaviour therapists that the techniques of behavioural self-control and systematic desensitization are explicitly derived from behavioural 'laws of learning' (i.e., operant and classical conditioning). However, in a process that reflected the general movement within psychology during the 1960s in the direction of a more cognitivist approach, critics such as Breger and McGaugh (1965) and Locke (1971) began to question whether the therapeutic processes involved in these techniques could actually be fully understood using behaviourist ideas. In the words of Locke (1971), the issue was: 'Is behaviour therapy "behaviouristic"?' Locke (1971) pointed out that behavioural therapists and counsellors typically asked their clients to report on and monitor their inner emotional experiences, encouraged self-assertion and self-understanding, and aimed to help them to develop new plans or strategies for dealing with life. These activities encompass a wide variety of cognitive processes, including imagery, decision-making, remembering and problem-solving.

In summary, it can be seen that the 'behavioural' stage in the development of CBT demonstrated that principles of behaviour change, derived from conditioning theories of learning, could be used to generate useful therapeutic techniques, and that methods of scientific research were of value in monitoring change in therapy clients. However, it became apparent that, in practice, behavioural techniques draw heavily upon the capacity of clients to make sense of things, to process information cognitively, and that a more cognitive theory was needed in order to understand what was going on. There arose an increasing acceptance among behaviourally oriented counsellors and therapists of the need for an explicit cognitive dimension to their work. Initially, the social learning theory approach of Bandura (1971, 1977), which demonstrated that learning could occur through observation and imitation, as well as through processes of operant and classical conditioning, made an important contribution to the developments of a more cognitively oriented form of therapy. This interest in cognitive aspects of therapy coincided with the emergence of the cognitive therapies, such as rational emotive therapy (RET; Ellis 1962) and Beck's (1976) cognitive therapy. These influences came together, during the 1970s and 1980s, to form what became know as cognitive behaviour therapy or cognitive–behavioural therapy.

Box 6.3: *Combining behavioural and cognitive techniques in a case of competitive sport performance anxiety*

Houghton (1991) published a case report on his work with an elite athlete suffering from performance-related anxiety. The athlete was a male archer who had represented his country at Olympic and World Championship competitions. On several occasions, when left needing a high scoring final arrow to complete a competition successfully, he 'froze' on the signal to shoot, waited too long, went through his routine up to five times without shooting and then hurriedly released three arrows in quick succession. He reported feeling 'anxious and negative' when needing a 'gold' (ten points) on his final arrow, and always said to himself 'Why couldn't it be a nine instead of ten?' This athlete received 12 sessions of counselling from a sport psychologist, using a combination of behavioural and cognitive techniques.

First, his behaviour during competitions was carefully observed. Following an analysis of this baseline information, he was introduced to the method of progressive relaxation, and was taught a technique of visualization that involved cognitive rehearsal of a successful performance. Finally, he was encouraged to make positive self-statements. These techniques were practised during training and at competition. Finally, he made an audiotape recording of his elation following a successful shot, and played it back daily. Following this cognitive–behavioural intervention, his scores during competition increased significantly, even in important events being covered on national television. As well as demonstrating the way in which behavioural (relaxation) and cognitive (visualization) techniques can be used together, this case also illustrates the preference of therapists using this approach for trying to find objective measures of change in key target behaviours. This archer was not asked whether he felt better about himself as a result of the treatment: the proof of effectiveness lay in his actual performance.

The emergence of cognitive approaches to therapy

The development of the 'cognitive' strand of cognitive–behavioural counselling is well described in Ellis (1989). The earliest attempts to work in a cognitive mode with clients took place, Ellis (1989) points out, within the field of sex therapy. The pioneers of sex therapy found that, of necessity, they needed to give their clients information about sexuality and the varieties of sexual behaviour. In other words, they needed to challenge the inappropriate fantasies and beliefs that their clients held about sex. The aim of helping clients to change the way they think about things remained the central focus of all cognitive approaches.

Both Albert Ellis, the founder of rational emotive behaviour therapy, and Aaron Beck, the founder of cognitive therapy, began their therapeutic careers as psychoanalysts. Both became dissatisfied with psychoanalytic methods, and found themselves becoming more aware of the importance of the ways in which their clients thought about themselves.

The story of his conversion to a cognitive therapeutic perspective is recounted by Beck (1976) in his book *Cognitive Therapy and the Emotional Disorders*. He notes that he had 'been practising psychoanalysis and psychoanalytic psychotherapy for many years before I was struck by the fact that a patient's cognitions had an enormous impact on his feelings and behavior' (Beck 1976: 29). He reports on a patient who had been engaging in free association, and had become angry, openly criticizing Beck. When asked what he was feeling, the patient replied that he felt very guilty. Beck accepted this statement, on the grounds that, within psychoanalytic theory, anger causes guilt. But then the patient went on to explain that while he had been expressing his criticism of Beck, he had 'also had continual thoughts of a self-critical nature', which included statements such as 'I'm wrong to criticize him . . . I'm bad . . . He won't like me . . . I have no excuse for being so mean' (Beck 1976: 30–1). Beck concluded that 'the patient felt guilty because he had been criticizing himself for his expressions of anger to me' (Beck 1976: 31), and realized that it was not the guilt that was the problem, so much as the way the client *thought* about being guilty ('I'm bad and mean for feeling like this').

Beck (1976) described these self-critical cognitions as 'automatic thoughts', and began to see them as one of the keys to successful therapy. The emotional and behavioural difficulties that people experience in their lives are not caused directly by events but by the way they interpret and make sense of these events. When clients can be helped to pay attention to the 'internal dialogue', the stream of automatic thoughts that accompany and guide their actions, they can make choices about the appropriateness of these self-statements, and if necessary introduce new thoughts and ideas, which lead to a happier or more satisfied life. From the beginning, Beck highlighted commonalities between cognitive and behavioural approaches to therapy: both employ a structured, problem-solving or symptom-reduction approach, with a highly active therapist style, and both stress the 'here-and-now' rather than making 'speculative reconstructions of the patient's childhood relationships and early family relationships' (Beck 1976: 321).

A further element in the Beck (1976) model is the idea of *cognitive distortion*. Beck argued that the experience of threat resulted in a loss of ability to process information effectively:

> Individuals experience psychological distress when they perceive a situation as threatening to their vital interests. At such times, there is a functional impairment in normal cognitive processing. Perceptions and interpretations of events become highly selective, egocentric and rigid. The person has a decreased ability to 'turn off' distorted thinking, to concentrate, recall or reason. Corrective functions, which allow reality testing and refinements of global conceptualisations, are weakened.
>
> (Beck and Weishaar 1989: 23)

Beck (1976) has identified a number of different kinds of cognitive distortion that can be addressed in the counselling situation. These include *overgeneralization*, which involves drawing general or all-encompassing conclusions from very limited evidence. For example, if a person fails her driving test at the first attempt she may overgeneralize by concluding that it is not worth bothering to take it again because it is obvious that she will never pass. Another example of cognitive distortion is *dichotomous thinking*, which refers to the tendency to see situations in terms of polar opposites. A common example of dichotomous thinking is to see oneself as 'the best' at some activity, and then to feel a complete failure if presented with any evidence of less than total competence. Another example is to see other people as either completely good or completely bad. A third type of cognitive distortion is *personalization*, which occurs when a person has a tendency to imagine that events are always attributable to his actions (usually to his shortcomings), even when no logical connection need be made. For example, in couple relationships it is not unusual to find that one of the partners believes that the mood of the other partner is always caused by his or her conduct, despite ample proof that, for instance, the irritation of the partner is caused by work pressures or other such external sources.

Box 6.4: *The roots of rational emotive behaviour therapy in the early life experience of Albert Ellis*

Albert Ellis is the founder of rational emotive behaviour therapy, one of the cornerstones of contemporary CBT practice. Ellis was born in Pittsburgh 1913, the eldest of three children in a Jewish family, and grew up in New York. His father was frequently absent, and his mother was neglectful, and physically and emotionally unavailable to her children. His parents divorced during his childhood. Ellis was sent to school at the age of four, and was expected to cross busy roads without adult assistance in order to get there. He was seriously ill for much of his childhood, and was hospitalized for long periods with infrequent parental visits (Magai and Haviland-Jones 2002; Weiner 1988). Ellis has described how he responded to this neglect by reframing it as an opportunity to develop autonomy and independence, and claims that at the age of four he began to formulate a number of rules that were to guide him for the remainder of his life, such as 'hassles are never terrible unless you make them so', 'making a fuss about problems makes them worse', and 'use your head in reactions as well as your heart'. When he left school, he worked in business for ten years before paying himself through graduate school in clinical psychology. Initially trained in psychoanalysis, he quickly found himself reverting in his work with patients to his own rules for rational living, and by the early 1950s had developed his own approach. The story of the life of Albert Ellis encapsulates many of the factors that make CBT attractive to so many people. Fundamentally, Ellis evolved a set of procedures for overcoming fear, in situations where it was not possible to rely on the support of other people. He devised a set of simple rules for effective living, designed to meet the needs of people who wanted to get ahead in their lives, to be prosperous, successful and effective rather than to explore an 'inner self'.

Albert Ellis had, a decade earlier, followed much the same path as Beck. Also trained in psychoanalysis, he evolved a much more active therapeutic style characterized by high levels of challenge and confrontation designed to enable the client to examine his or her 'irrational beliefs'. Ellis (1962) argued that emotional problems are caused by 'crooked thinking' arising from viewing life in terms of 'shoulds' and 'musts'. When a person experiences a relationship, for example, in an absolutistic, exaggerated manner, he or she may be acting upon an internalized, irrational belief, such as 'I *must* have love or approval from all the significant people in my life'. For Ellis, this is an irrational belief because it is exaggerated and overstated. A rational belief system might include statements such as 'I enjoy being loved by others' or 'I feel most secure when the majority of the people in my life care about me'. The irrational belief leads to 'catastrophizing', and feelings of anxiety or depression, if anything goes even slightly wrong in a relationship. The more rational belief statements allow the person to cope with relationship difficulties in a more constructive and balanced fashion.

The set of 'irrational beliefs', as identified by Ellis, provide the counsellor with a starting point for exploring the cognitive content of the client.

I *must* do well at all times.

I am a bad or worthless person when I act in a weak or stupid manner. I *must* be approved or accepted by people I find important.

I am a *bad, unlovable* person if I get rejected.

People *must* treat me fairly and give me what I need.

People who act immorally are undeserving, rotten people. People *must* live up to my expectations or it is terrible.

My life *must* have few major hassles or troubles. I *can't stand* really bad things or difficult people. It is awful or horrible when important things don't turn out the way I want them to.

I *can't* stand it when life is really unfair.

I *need* to be loved by someone who matters to me a lot.

I *need* immediate gratification and always feel awful when I don't get it.

The belief statements used in RET reflect the operation of a number of distorted cognitive processes. For example, overgeneralization is present if the client believes he or she *needs* to be loved *at all times*. Cognitive therapists would dispute the rationality of this statement, inviting the client perhaps to reframe it as 'I enjoy the feeling of being loved and accepted by another person, and if this is not available to me I can sometimes feel unhappy'. Other cognitive distortions, such as dichotomous thinking ('if people don't love me they must hate me'), arbitrary inference ('I failed that exam today so I must be totally stupid'), personalization ('the gas man was late because they all hate me at that office') are also evident in irrational beliefs.

The ideas that underpin the cognitive therapies of Beck and Ellis are familiar ones within the broader field of cognitive psychology. For example, it has been demonstrated in many studies of problem-solving that people frequently make a 'rush to judgement', or overgeneralize on the basis of too little evidence, or stick rigidly to one interpretation of the facts to the point of avoiding or denying contradictory evidence. The concept of 'personalization' is similar to the Piagetian notion of egocentricity, which refers to the tendency of children younger than about four years old to see everything that happens only from their own perspective – they are unable to 'decentre' or see things from the point of view of another person. It is to some degree reassuring that the phenomena observed by cognitive therapists in clinical settings should also have been observed by psychological researchers in other settings.

The cognitive distortion model of cognitive processing is similar in many respects to the Freudian idea of 'primary process' thinking. Freud regarded human beings as capable of engaging in rational, logical thought ('secondary process' thinking), but also as highly prone to reverting to the developmentally less mature 'primary process' thinking, in which thought is dominated by emotional needs. The crucial difference between the primary process and cognitive distortion models is that in the former emotion controls thought, whereas in the latter thought controls emotion.

Another important dimension of cognitive distortion lies in the area of *memory*. Williams (1996) has carried out research that shows that people who are anxious, or who have undergone difficult life experiences, often find it difficult to remember painful events in detail. Their memories are overgeneralized, so they recall that 'something happened', but they are unable to fill in the detail. Williams (1996) argues that this kind of memory distortion is due to the linkage between recalled events and negative emotions. Since it may often be necessary in cognitive–behavioural counselling to construct detailed micro-analyses of specific events, counsellors need to be aware of the difficulties that clients can have with this type of recall task.

A further approach to understanding cognitive process within cognitive counselling and therapy is concerned with the operation of *metacognition* (Meichenbaum 1977, 1985, 1986) This refers to the ability of people to reflect on their own cognitive processes, to be aware of how they are going about thinking about something, or trying to solve a problem. A simple example to illustrate metacognition is to reflect on your experience of completing a jigsaw puzzle. You will find that you do not just 'do' a jigsaw in an automatic fashion (unless it is a very simple one) but that you will be aware of a set of strategies from which you can choose as needed, such as 'finding the corners', 'finding the edges' or 'collecting the sky'. An awareness of, and ability to communicate, metacognitive strategies is very important in teaching children how to do a jigsaw, rather than just doing it for them. Metacognition is a topic widely researched within developmental psychology in recent years. The principle of metacognitive processing is in fact central to the work of Ellis, Beck and other cognitive–behavioural practitioners.

For example, Ellis (1962) has devised an A–B–C theory of personality functioning. In this case, A refers to the activating event, which may be some action or attitude of an individual, or an actual physical event. C is the emotional or behavioural consequence of the event, the feelings or conduct of the person experiencing the event. However, for Ellis A does not cause C. Between A and C comes B, the person's beliefs about the event. Ellis contends that events are always mediated by beliefs, and that the emotional consequences of events are determined by the belief about the event rather than the event itself. For example, one person may lose her job and, believing that this event is 'an opportunity to do something else', feel happy. Another person may lose her job and, believing that 'this is the end of my usefulness as a person', feel deeply depressed. The significance of the A–B–C formula in relation to metacognition is that the RET counsellor will teach the client how to use it as a way of monitoring cognitive reactions to events. The client is then able to engage in metacognitive processing of his or her thoughts in reaction to any event, and is, ideally, more able to make choices about how he or she intends to think about that event.

Cognitive therapists have been active in cataloguing a wide variety of problematic cognitive contents, referred to by different writers as irrational beliefs (Ellis 1962), dysfunctional or automatic thoughts (Beck 1976), self-talk or internal dialogue (Meichenbaum 1986) or 'hot cognitions' (Zajonc 1980), that punctuate everyday activities, and introduce disruptive emotional responses that undermine effective behaviour. A central aim of much cognitive work is to replace beliefs that contribute to self-defeating behaviour with beliefs that are associated with self-acceptance and constructive problem-solving. However, many cognitive therapists also believe that there exists a deeper layer of cognition that underpins and maintains irrational beliefs and automatic thoughts. Beck *et al.* (1979) characterized the underlying structures as *cognitive schema* – deeply held general statements that sum up the assumptions the client holds about the world. For lasting change to occur, or in more serious cases, it seems to be necessary to move beyond the stage of identifying and challenging irrational beliefs and automatic thoughts, and deal with the schema within which they are embedded. More recently, the concept of schema has been elaborated more fully in the *schema therapy* developed by Jeffery Young (Young *et al.* 2003). Young defines schema as broad patterns or themes of cognition, memory, behaviour and emotion, that arise when basic childhood needs are not met. An example of a maladaptive schema is *abandonment*: a fundamental assumption that others people will not provide ongoing support or protection because they are emotionally unstable, unpredictable, unreliable, will die imminently, or abandon the person as soon as they meet someone 'better'. For Young, the concept of schema provides a means of linking current dysfunctional thoughts to childhood experiences of dysfunctional relationships.

Over the past 20 or 30 years, cognitive therapy has remained a distinctive approach that has built on the early work of Beck and Ellis in devising cognitive strategies for working with an increasing range of client groups (see Leahy 2003; Neenan and Dryden 2004; Wills and Sanders 1997). However, probably the most significant contribution of the cognitive therapy tradition has been in the combination of cognitive and behavioural ideas and methods, within what became known as cognitive behaviour therapy or cognitive–behavioural therapy (CBT). There are many examples of the fusion of cognitive therapy and CBT. For instance, the authors of a leading CBT textbook by Westbrook *et al.* (2011: 1) acknowledge that their work is based in a 'Beckian' model. Further, the rational emotive therapy (RET) developed by Ellis is now known as rational emotive *behaviour* therapy (REBT; Dryden 2004a, 2004b).

The development of CBT

Following the emergence of cognitive approaches to therapy, pioneered by Beck, Ellis and others, it quickly became apparent to practitioners, theorists and researchers within both the behavioural and cognitive traditions that their existed a natural affinity between the two perspectives. Significant turning points were the publication of *Cognition and Behavior Modification* by Michael Mahoney in 1974, and *Cognitive-Behavior Modification: An Integrative Approach*, by Donald Meichenbaum in 1977. The combination of a structured approach to behaviour change, alongside attention to irrational or dysfunctional thoughts as a critical focus for change, led to a hugely productive stage within the history of counselling and psychotherapy, which saw a wide range of new techniques being developed for an increasing array of client populations (for further information of these achievements, see: Dobson and Craig 1996; Dobson 2001; Scott *et al.* 1995). The key therapeutic principles that underpin CBT have been defined by Westbrook *et al.* (2011) as:

- therapy is regarded as a *collaborative* project between client and counsellor;
- the work is problem-focused and structured;
- therapy is time-limited and brief;
- practice is informed by research.

Dobson and Dozois (2001) identified three theoretical principles that inform all CBT:

- cognitive activity affects behaviour;
- cognitive activity may be monitored and altered;
- desired behaviour change may be affected through cognitive change.

Behind these core ideas lies a philosophical commitment to the application of scientific methods. There is a strong emphasis in CBT on measurement, assessment and experimentation. Training and practice are grounded in what has been called the 'scientist–practitioner' model (Barlow *et al.* 1984), also known as the 'Boulder model', since it emerged from a conference held at Boulder, Colorado, in 1949 to decide the future shape of training in clinical psychology in the USA. The basic assumption of the scientist–practitioner model is that therapists should be trained in methods of systematic research, and routinely collect quantitative data on the outcomes of their work with clients. This has resulted in high levels of research productivity from adherents of CBT, with the consequence that there is much more evidence in respect of the efficacy of CBT than there is in relation to other models of counselling and psychotherapy. Some of this research has employed '$N=1$' single case studies, which have made it possible to rapidly evaluate innovative interventions, whereas other CBT research has involved large-scale controlled trials. At a time when health care systems around the world are increasingly seeking to implement evidence-based practice policies (i.e., only funding the delivery of interventions that are backed by valid research evidence), this has given CBT therapists a major competitive advantage in the therapy marketplace.

Over the past 30 years, CBT has made a massive contribution to mental health care. It is important to recognize that CBT represents a broad tradition, with some practitioners operating more at the 'cognitive' end of the CBT spectrum, and others at the 'behavioural' end. Further discussion of discrete 'schools' of CBT can be found in Dobson (2001) and Dobson and Katri (2000).

Using CBT treatment protocols for specific disorders

The establishment and consolidation of CBT as a leading therapeutic modality was facilitated by the development and use of treatment manuals that provided detailed guidelines around how to apply CBT principles and techniques to address specific client problems. Among the dozens of CBT protocols that are available are widely used manuals for the treatment of panic (Barlow and Cerny 1988), anxiety disorders (Beck and Emery 1985), personality disorders (Beck and Freeman 1990), depression (Beck et al. 1979), substance abuse (Beck et al. 1993) and obesity (Cooper et al. (2004a). These manuals have contributed to the success of CBT in a number of different ways. They provide therapists with ideas about how to structure therapy for particular clients, in a step-by-step manner. They include examples of change techniques, and assessment scales that can be used to gauge progress in therapy. The existence of clinical manuals gives a clear focus to training and supervision, and helps therapists to feel confident that they know what they are doing. Manuals can be used to carry out rigorous outcome research, because it is possible to specify and evaluate whether competent therapy is being delivered. The development of specific interventions for specific disorders makes sense to colleagues in the medical profession, who operate on a 'diagnose then treat' model, and has enabled CBT to be widely adopted within health care systems around the world. Finally, client versions of many treatment manuals have been produced, in the form of self-help books. These publications have served to reinforce public understanding and acceptance of CBT, as well as functioning as adjuncts to face-to-face therapy.

Expanding the cognitive–behavioural tradition: the third wave

From the 1990s, the success and confidence of the CBT community created the conditions for the emergence of what Hayes has termed a 'third wave' of CBT innovation in theory and practice:

> the third wave of behavioral and cognitive therapy . . . tends to emphasize contextual and experiential change strategies in addition to more direct and didactic ones . . . These treatments tend to seek the construction of broad, flexible and effective repertoires over an eliminative approach to narrowly defined problems, and to emphasize the relevance of the issues they examine for clinicians as well as clients.
>
> (Hayes 2004: 658)

Within this body of work, four new approaches of particular import can be identified, each of which reflects the holistic, reflexive and experiential themes identified by Hayes (2004):

- dialectical behaviour therapy (DBT);
- acceptance and commitment therapy (ACT);
- mindfulness-based cognitive therapy (MBCT); and
- constructivist therapy.

One of the most important accomplishments within the psychotherapy field as a whole, within the past 20 years, has been the development by Marsha Linehan and her colleagues of *dialectical behaviour therapy* (DBT). A key reason for the impact of this form of CBT is that it has been devised as a means of helping people diagnosed with borderline personality disorder, a condition that has proved extremely hard to treat (by any method). Individuals with 'borderline' characteristics tend to have difficulty in forming lasting relationships (including with therapists), are troubled by strong, fluctuating emotional states, exhibit many forms of self-harm, and are prone to suicide. The approach taken by Linehan (1993a, 1993b, 1994) has been to address the needs of these individuals by assembling a comprehensive treatment package, incorporating intensive individual therapy, skills training in groups, regular supportive telephone contact, an explicit treatment contract, and structured support for the therapists involved in delivering the programme. Borderline personality disorder is conceptualized by Linehan (1993a) as ultimately grounded in a biological sensitivity to strong emotional responses to threat, exacerbated by childhood experiences (such as emotional abuse) in which the emotional reality of the person has been systematically invalidated by others.

The key therapeutic principles of DBT encompass validation/acceptance of the person's emotional distress and troubled life, coupled with resolute and consistent emphasis on learning new life skills in such areas as self-regulation and self-control of emotion, and coping with relationships. In the expectation that the client will not find it easy to participate in therapy, a variety of methods are utilized to provide a secure environment: contracting, long-term treatment, multiple helpers and telephone support. For Linehan (1993a, 1994) the concept of the *dialectic* lies at the heart of the approach; the aim is to maintain a dialectical tension between acceptance of the client's suffering versus demanding that the client change his or her behaviour in the present moment.

Acceptance and Commitment Therapy (ACT – said as a single word, not as initials) is a CBT that has been applied to many different problem areas (Batten 2011; Hayes *et al.* 1999, 2006). A distinctive aspect of this approach is the extent to which it is grounded in a specific philosophical position, known as functional contextualism. The underlying assumption in ACT is that a person's problems arise from use of language that fails to acknowledge the contextual basis of meaning (i.e., the person behaves as though his or her statements are objectively true for all time, rather than merely being true in specific contexts), which results in cognitive inflexibility. Hayes *et al.* (2006) have developed a range of strategies for enabling clients to develop enhanced cognitive flexibility. These include: *acceptance* of thoughts and feelings, rather than trying to void them or defend against them; *cognitive defusion*, or altering the undesirable functions of thoughts – for example a person might learn calmly to reflect that 'I am having the thought that I am no good', rather than getting locked into a struggle to eradicate the 'I am no good' cognition; *being present* – learning to experience the world more directly; an appreciation of the person's sense of self or identity as a flow, rather than as a 'thing' (*self as context*); action based on consciously chosen *values; committed action* – the development of effective patterns of behaviour, which reflect personal values. These strategies can be summarized in terms of a simple formula: 'Accept, Choose, and Take Action'. Implicit in the model is the idea that it is helpful for clients to extend their awareness and repertoire of possible actions; concentrating solely on a single problem, or dysfunctional cognition merely increases the importance of that 'node' within the overall consciousness of the person, and as a result reduces cognitive flexibility. Hayes *et al.* (1999) openly acknowledge the extent to which their approach has been influenced by a range of perspectives – experiential, humanistic and gestalt therapies, feminist psychology, social constructionism, narrative psychology. Nevertheless, they are clear that they have integrated these ideas into a therapeutic framework that is firmly located within the cognitive–behavioural tradition.

Mindfulness-based cognitive therapy (MBCT) is a form of CBT that integrates mindfulness meditation with Beck's cognitive therapy (Segal *et al.* 2001). Mindfulness is a meditation technique, taken from Buddhist practices (described in more detail in a later section of this chapter). Some writers have recently used the term mindfulness-*informed* cognitive therapy to describe this approach. The founders of MBCT, Zindel Segal, Mark Williams and John Teasdale, have been leading figures in the development of cognitive/CBT approaches to depression and suicidal behaviour, argue that although CBT techniques are effective in helping people to recover from an episode of depression, there remains a high chance of recurrence of depression at a future time. This seems to be because once someone has suffered depression a further episode of depression can be triggered by a relatively minor degree of negative mood. The person then finds that they are 'back to square one', and starts to question their own well-being, which in turn exacerbates the depressive state they are in. A capacity to engage in mindfulness meditation, by contrast, has the effect of protecting the person against a susceptibility to depression, by enabling them to become more aware of what is happening, stay in the present moment rather than ruminating on negative past events, and accepting feelings and emotions rather than trying to suppress them. Research evidence has shown that MBCT is effective in reducing the risk of relapse in depression (Teasdale *et al.* 2000). The MBCT group has produced a self-help book and compacted disc (CD), to disseminate wider use of their methods (Williams *et al.* 2007).

Constructivist therapy probably represents the most radical strand of the 'third wave' in CBT. Constructivism is a philosophical movement that is influential in many areas of the arts, social sciences and education, which is based on the position that there is no fixed 'objective' reality, but that individual human beings actively construct the realities within which they live their lives. Applied to counselling and psychotherapy, constructivism draws attention to the ways in which people construct personal worlds through their use of language, metaphor and narrative. Some constructivist therapists adopt the view that people (and clients) can be thought of as behaving as 'personal scientists', with theories about self and relationships that are constantly being tested out in their behaviour.

In many respects, constructivist therapy is a much broader approach than CBT. Indeed, it is possible to conceive all counselling and psychotherapy theories in constructivist terms. Nevertheless, in practice there exists a strong link between CBT and contemporary constructivist approaches to therapy. This is because two of the seminal figures in the early emergence of CBT – Michael Mahoney and Donald Meichenbaum – actively espoused constructivism in the later stages of their careers: *Treating Post-traumatic Stress Disorder* (Meichenbaum 1994) and *Constructive Psychotherapy* (Mahoney 2003) represent probably the most convincing examples of how constructivist philosophy can be translated into clinical practice. The complex links between constructivist therapies and CBT are explored in Mahoney (1995) and Neimeyer and Raskin (2001).

The third wave in the development of CBT has reflected a willingness to expand the boundaries of CBT theory and practice. Each of the third-wave approaches described here have looked beyond psychology, into the realm of philosophy, to find a deeper rationale for practical interventions that offer clients opportunities for life-changing experiences. Each of the approaches has shifted the emphasis of cognitive–behavioural work somewhat away from a sole focus on patterns of behaviour and cognition in problem situations and towards an appreciation and acceptance of here-and-now experiencing. At the same time, these approaches have retained the core CBT values of brief therapy, providing clients with structure and clear guidelines around what is expected of them, and a commitment to evaluate outcome and process using rigorous methods of research. The extent to which third-wave approaches actually represent new techniques, or just adaptations of established CBT techniques, has been the focus of debate (Hofmann *et al.* 2010).

The practice of cognitive–behavioural counselling

Unlike the psychodynamic and person-centred approaches to counselling, which place a great deal of emphasis on exploration and understanding, the cognitive–behavioural approach is less concerned with insight and more oriented towards client action to produce change. Although different practitioners may have different styles, the tendency in cognitive–behavioural work is to operate within a structured stage-by-stage programme, in which the problem behaviour that has been troubling the client is identified and then modified in a systematic, step-by-step manner. The attraction of CBT, for many clients, is that it is experienced as purposeful and that it makes sense – it is made clear to the client what is expected from him or her, and how his or her efforts will lead to desired outcomes. The main areas of focus within cognitive–behavioural work are:

1 The therapeutic relationship: establishing rapport and creating a working alliance between counsellor and client; explaining the rationale for treatment.

2 Assessment: identifying and quantifying the frequency, intensity and appropriateness of problem behaviours and cognitions.

3 Case formulation: arriving at an agreed conceptualization of the origins and maintenance of current problems, and setting goals or targets for change that are specific and attainable.

4 Intervention: application of cognitive and behavioural techniques.

5 Monitoring: using ongoing assessment of target behaviours to evaluate the effectiveness of interventions.

6 Relapse prevention: attention to termination and planned follow-up to reinforce generalization of gains.

The following sections examine each of these areas of therapeutic activity in more detail.

The therapeutic relationship: establishing rapport and creating a working alliance

The creation of a relationship of safety and trust is an essential first step in CBT, as in any form of therapy. A central theme in the cognitive–behavioural literature and training is the notion of client–counsellor *collaboration:* the aim is for the client and CBT counsellor to be able to work together on identifying problems and implementing interventions. In contrast to forms of therapy, such as psychodynamic or person-centred therapy, that regard the therapeutic relationship as itself a vehicle for change, CBT practitioners tend to view the relationship as necessary for the delivery of CBT interventions, but not necessarily as a focus of therapeutic work. For example, a CBT counsellor would be unlikely to want to analyse or interpret a transference reaction on the part of the client, or to seek to create relational depth as a means of facilitating authentic engagement. The early behavioural, cognitive therapy and CBT literature tended to devote relatively little attention to the issue of the therapeutic relationship within this form of therapy. This lack of emphasis may have been influenced, in part, by a wish to distance CBT from other types of therapy. However, the absence of a published literature on the therapeutic relationship in CBT should not be taken to mean that, in practice, CBT counsellors and psychotherapists do not value the establishment of a relational bond with clients. There is high levels of acceptance and empathy toward their clients. In recent years there has been a growing interest within the CBT community into the characteristics of the therapeutic relationship in CBT (Gilbert and Leahy 2007). A widely used checklist that has been designed to evaluate the capacity of cognitive therapists (Barber *et al.* 2003) includes items that reflect core CBT relational competencies:

- socialization of the client to a cognitive model;
- warmth, genuineness and congruence;
- being accepting, respectful and non-judgemental;
- attentiveness to the client;
- accurate empathy;
- collaboration – sharing responsibility for defining problems and solutions.

The idea that effective practice of CBT necessarily incorporates a capacity to form a supportive and collaborative relationship with the client is also reflected in the CBT competency framework developed by Roth and Pilling (2007). A research study carried out by Borrill and Foreman (1996; Box 6.5) illustrates the way in which the quality of the relationship between a CBT therapist and her clients can underpin the effective use of CBT interventions.

Box 6.5: *Overcoming fear of flying: what helps?*

Cognitive–behavioural methods are well suited to helping people who are experiencing overwhelming fears in specific areas of their life. Fear of flying is a good example of the type of problem that can often be addressed effectively from a cognitive–behavioural approach. But when a client receives a cognitive–behavioural intervention to combat fear of flying, what is it that helps? Does change occur because irrational beliefs about air travel have been altered? How important is the fact that the client has acquired a new repertoire of behaviours: for example, relaxation skills? And how significant is the relationship with the cognitive–behavioural counsellor? Do people get better because they trust the counsellor, or want to please him or her? Borrill and Foreman (1996) explored these issues in a series of interviews with clients who had successfully completed a cognitive–behavioural fear of flying programme.

The programme comprised an initial session where the origins of the fear for the individual client were explored, and they were taught about the nature of anxiety. The second session was an accompanied return flight on a normal scheduled service. When asked about their experience of therapy, these clients had a lot to say about the process of mastering their fear and panic. They reported that therapy had helped them to be able to understand their emotional arousal, and to apply a cognitive–behavioural model of anxiety in a way that made a real difference to how they felt. They became able cognitively to re-label difficult emotions. Fear and anxiety now became discomfort or excitement, or both. They became able to think rationally about their experience of flying. Actually facing up to fear, by undertaking a flight, was also a valuable source of confidence. For example, one client recalled that:

> then she [the psychologist] said 'I want you to walk the length of the plane'. Normally I've got superglue on the bottom of my shoes. I went up there and I was so proud that I had done it.
>
> (Borrill and Foreman 1996: 69)

These experiences are consistent with cognitive–behavioural theory. Coping skills, cognitive reframing and self-efficacy are central features of the cognitive–behavioural model. However, these clients also reported that their *relationship* with the therapist had been crucial to the success of their therapy. The therapist was perceived as trustworthy, open and warm, and also *informal*. One client stated that:

> she comes over as being very casual and relaxed and enjoying it all immensely . . . it was all terribly laid back. It's just that she doesn't give the impression that there is anything to worry about.
>
> (Borrill and Foreman 1996: 65)

The therapist legitimized their fear, she accepted that they were terrified, in contrast to friends or family members who had dismissed their feelings. However, what seemed crucial was the sense that clients had of the therapist as being in control. This enabled them to feel confidence in her, and thus to feel confidence in themselves. As one client put it:

> what got me through it is this thing of someone having trust in you – her saying 'of course you can do it'. It's like *borrowing someone's belief in you to actually believe in yourself.*
>
> (Borrill and Foreman 1996: 66)

The authors of this study conclude that a strong therapeutic relationship was a necessary component of this treatment, but that this relationship operated in a somewhat paradoxical way: 'empowerment comes from being prepared to relinquish power and control, to trust the psychologist and follow her instructions' (Borrill and Foreman 1996: 66).

Assessment: identifying and quantifying problem behaviours and cognitions

An early task for any cognitive–behavioural counsellor is to assess the problem that the client is seeking to change. This process will usually elicit information in four key domains:

- *cognitions:* the words, phrases or images that are in the mind of the client when he or she is experiencing a problematic situation;
- *emotions*: the different feeling states that occur around the manifestation of the problem;
- *behaviour*: what the person actually does;
- *physical*: physiological or bodily symptoms associated with the problem.

Cognitive–behavioural assessment is grounded in client descriptions, or narratives, of specific events that have been experienced – generalized accounts of 'what usually happens' do not yield information that is sufficiently precise for cognitive–behavioural work. During the assessment phase, the counsellor invites the client to talk about problematic events, and aims to use these descriptions to find out as much as possible about the *content* that is present within each of the four domains (i.e., precisely *what* is being thought and felt), the *intensity* of the client's experience (e.g., how strong is an emotion, how much is a disturbing belief considered to be true), and the *sequencing* of elements, or their re-occurrence in repeating cycles of dysfunctional activity. Informed by the stimulus–response basis of early behavioural psychology, much of the power of CBT assessment lies in the capacity of the counsellor and client, working together, to identify sequences of cognition, emotion, behaviour/action and bodily states.

For example, a woman who came to counselling for help with controlling her anger was asked to describe a recent situation in which anger was a problem for her. She talked about an episode in which she lost her temper with her husband. Over a period of about 20 minutes, the counsellor encouraged the client to describe what had happened during that incident, in as much detail as possible. During this activity, the counsellor was primarily using empathic listening and reflecting to draw out the story, but was also occasionally asking questions to clarify what had been taking place within each of the four assessment domains. At the end of this interview, the counsellor was able, with the assistance of the client, to map out on a flipchart the sequence of actions that constituted an 'anger episode'. In brief, the episode began with a state of physical exhaustion and fatigue, where the client had been engaged in child care. Her response to that physical state was to 'carry on making the evening meal' while feeling resentment. When her husband came home from work, she did not look at him, did not report her tiredness to him, and interpreted his actions as undermining. When he made a negative comment about the meal, she had an 'automatic' cognitive response ('nothing I do is good enough') and initiated an argument, during which she felt overwhelming rage. By being able to construct an understanding of how cognitions, emotions, actions and physical states are linked together, it becomes possible for the therapist and client to begin to consider the points in the chain at which the sequence can be broken, and the different cognitions or behaviour that might be introduced at each point.

It is not always easy for a client to report on problem sequences in the kind of detail that is required by a cognitive–behavioural therapist. In some cases, a sensitive interview, of the type outlined in the previous paragraph, may be sufficient for assessment purposes. In other cases, the counsellor may need to use additional assessment techniques to augment the basic interview material that has been collected. There exists a large number of questionnaires and rating scales that are used by CBT practitioners, to assess not only global levels of distress (e.g., intensity of depression or anxiety) but also specific areas of problem functioning (e.g., intensity of panic, obsessive–compulsive thinking, dysfunctional eating patterns, etc). Clients may also be invited to engage in self-observation or *self-monitoring* during the assessment phase, for instance through being provided with charts or worksheets to fill in at home that require them to describe their thoughts, emotions, actions and symptoms during specific problem incidents. Further information about these assessment tools can be found in CBT texts such as Westbrook *et al.* (2011) and Ledley *et al.* (2005).

The assessment phase of CBT counselling not only sets the scene for treatment planning and the implementation of interventions, but can be therapeutic in itself. During assessment, the client is given an opportunity to tell his or her story to a listener who validates his or her experience. In reflecting in detail on specific events, the client learns to differentiate between different thoughts and emotions that occur, and begins to develop a closer understanding of how he or she is actively engaged in constructing sequences of problem behaviour. Finally, assessment represents a task around which the client and counsellor can work collaboratively, and begin to develop a relationship of understanding and trust.

Case formulation: arriving at an agreed conceptualization of the origins and maintenance of current problems

One of the critical steps in CBT practice involves creating a case formulation, and sharing this framework with the client. The case formulation comprises a kind of mini-theory of the individual client and his or her problems. Within the formulation, the particular circumstances of the client's life and problems are explained in terms of CBT theory and concepts – the formulation statement can therefore be viewed as an application of CBT theory. The collaborative stance of CBT is reinforced through a process in which the formulation is explained to the client, the response of the client is used to sharpen the formulation, and the client is provided with a written copy of the formulation that will serve as a guide for subsequent work. Within the CBT professional community, there exist a number of different ideas about what makes an effective formulation. One of the leading figures in contemporary CBT, Jacqueline Persons, advocates that a good formulation might include the following elements (Persons 1993; Persons *et al.* 1991; Persons and Davidson 2001; Persons and Tompkins 2007):

- problem list – itemizing the client's difficulties in terms of cognitive, behavioural and emotional components;
- hypothesized mechanisms – one or two psychological mechanisms underlying the client's difficulties;
- account/narrative of how the hypothesized mechanisms lead to the overt difficulties;
- current precipitants – events or situations that are activating the client's vulnerability at this time;
- origins of the underlying vulnerability;
- treatment plan;
- obstacles to treatment.

By contrast, Dudley and Kuyken (2006) suggest that a cognitive–behavioural case formulation should be constructed around 'five Ps':

- presenting issues;
- precipitating factors;
- perpetuating factors;
- predisposing factors;
- protecting factors (person's resilience, strengths and safety activities).

Whatever format is used to structure the case formulation, it is clear that it needs to incorporate explanatory accounts of both the current problem (what it is and how it is maintained) and the underlying personality predispositions or vulnerability that has created the conditions for the problem to emerge. It is also valuable to use the formulation to highlight the factors that might impede therapeutic progress (obstacles), or will be likely to facilitate it (sources of support, personal strengths).

In so far as the construction of a formulation, and its discussion with the client, represents the application of CBT thinking to the specific conditions of the client's own life, the formulation also opens up a space within therapy where the client can begin to learn about CBT concepts. This is a significant aspect of cognitive–behavioural work – ultimately, the aim is for the client to become his or her own therapist, and to become able to deal with future occurrences of problems areas by initiating CBT strategies on their own.

Being able to put together a convincing case formulation and communicate it to a client is a key competence within CBT work. This is a somewhat controversial aspect of CBT, because it is clear that this aspect of cognitive–behavioural practice can never be fully based in scientific method; a good formulation requires imagination, literary skill and clinical wisdom.

Bieling and Kuyken (2003) have raised the question of the extent to which case formulation is 'science or science fiction'. They point out that little research has been carried out into the reliability and validity of case formulations, or the links between formulation templates and outcome, and call for further research to be carried on these questions. Another area around which there has been some debate in the CBT literature concerns the relationship between case formulation and diagnosis (see, for example, Persons and Tomkins 2007). Traditionally, CBT therapists have eschewed the use of diagnostic categories, arguing that individualized accounts of problem behaviour have more practical utility, in terms of treatment planning. On the other hand, there now exist many CBT treatment planning 'packages' or manuals that are based on diagnostic groupings, and some CBT therapists see advantages in devising formulations that allow them to access these materials in the interest of selecting interventions for their clients that are maximally supported by research evidence.

Intervention strategies: the application of cognitive and behavioural techniques

A cognitive–behavioural counsellor has access to a range of intervention techniques to achieve the behavioural objectives agreed with the client, and specified in the case formulation. Techniques that are frequently used include the following.

Socratic dialogue. During the assessment phase of CBT, and then throughout the course of therapy, the counsellor is on the lookout for irrational beliefs, automatic thoughts, negative self-statements, dichotomous (all or nothing) thinking, and other forms of cognitive processing associated with the emotional and relational difficulties being experienced by the client. The client is recruited to this endeavour, and may be provided with worksheets and exercises designed to enable him or her to develop skill and awareness in monitoring his or her own cognitive activity in problem situations. Once key cognitive processes have been identified, a CBT therapist engages in the activity of Socratic questioning (or Socratic dialogue) in order to facilitate further exploration of this material. This method is ultimately derived from descriptions of the approach taken by the Greek philosopher, Socrates, who was highly effective in asking questions that enabled his students to explore the underlying assumptions, and logical contradictions, that were inherent in their way of making sense of the world (Overholser 2010). Socratic questioning has two aims: (a) to lead the client in the direction of making connections between their thoughts and the behavioural consequences of these thoughts; (b) opening a creative, reflective space within which new possibilities (i.e., different ways of thinking about things) might be realized. Examples of Socratic questions are:

- How much do you believe what you say about yourself?
- What evidence is there to support this belief?
- What evidence is there that contradicts your conclusions?
- What is the worst thing that could happen?
- What would happen if you were to . . .?
- What would you advise someone else to do in this situation?

Effective facilitation of Socratic dialogue requires genuine curiosity, allied to empathy and sensitivity: the questions that are asked need to reflect the 'track' of the client's own exploration of the issue, and must avoid any sense that the therapist is patronizing the client. Carey and Mullan (2004) in a valuable review of the literature on Socratic questioning/dialogue in therapy, conclude that there exist many contrasting ideas about this procedure, reflecting the different aims and therapeutic styles of leading CBT writers. This suggests that Socratic questioning is more of a clinical skill (or art), rather than necessarily being grounded in scientific research. In terms of the process of cognitive–behavioural therapy, the fruits of Socratic dialogue lead to therapeutic activities that seek to reinforce cognitive shifts that may have occurred. For instance, within a session in which Socratic technique has been employed, the therapist may work with the client to practice new ways of thinking, such as reframing (e.g., perceiving internal emotional states as excitement rather than fear) or actively rehearsing the use of different self-statements in role-play scenarios with the counsellor. Beyond this, new cognitive shifts may be tested out in homework assignments. Westbrook *et al.* (2011) provide a useful discussion of problems that can arise when using Socratic questions.

Mindfulness. A method that is increasingly used within CBT is *mindfulness meditation*. Originally derived from Buddhist teaching, mindfulness is viewed within CBT as a cognitive skill, or mode of attention, in which the person learns to accept and be aware of his or her experiencing. Mindfulness has been defined as 'bringing one's attention to the present experience on a moment-by-moment basis' (Marlatt and Kristeller 1999: 68) or as 'paying attention in a particular way; on purpose, in the present moment, and nonjudgementally' (Kabat-Zinn 1994: 4). Mindfulness was first adapted for use in Western therapy by Kabat-Zinn (1990). Typically, counselling or psychotherapy clients attend a structured mindfulness class over a number of weeks, often augmented by CDs for home study. For clients, the development of competence in mindfulness facilitates curiosity about inner states, makes it possible to avoid being locked into 'automatic thoughts' and emotions, and increases the appreciation of positive experiences.

Mindfulness has been integrated into formal CBT protocols, such as MBCT (Williams *et al.* 2006, 2007), DBT (Linehan 1993a, 1993b) and ACT (Hayes *et al.* 1999), as well as being used as an adjunct to other forms of therapy (e.g., Weiss *et al.* 2005). Theoretically, mindfulness represents a significant shift in relation to the therapeutic goals of CBT. The founders of CBT, such as Beck, Ellis, Mahoney and Meichenbaum, developed a range of techniques that aimed to help a client to *change* the content of their thoughts. By contrast, the emphasis in mindfulness is not on forcing change to take place, but on promoting awareness and acceptance.

Behaviour experiments. An important aspect of CBT practice is that, unlike most other therapies, it does not merely involve talking about difficulties – CBT can also encompass enacting sequences of behaviour. Bennett-Levy *et al.* (2004) describe this practice as 'behavioural experiments', and their book contains many examples of different types of experiments used with clients with different problems and at different stages in treatment. Some of these experiments are carried out in the counselling room. For example, a client who has issues around personal boundaries in relationships may be invited to sit closer to the therapist, or further away. A client who experiences agoraphobic panic attacks may be encouraged to be in the therapy room with the door locked. Other experiments can take place in the wider world. For instance, a client who is afraid to travel on his own might experiment with different lengths of bus journey. In some circumstances, clients may engage in experiments on their own; in other cases, the therapist may accompany them.

Behaviour experiments give clients opportunities to practice new skills and ways of coping, or can involve confronting (rather than avoiding) feared situations or stimuli. As with all aspects of CBT, the effective design, planning and implementation of behaviour experiments requires the establishment of a strong collaborative relationship between client and therapist. In practice, behaviour experiments are similar to, and overlap with, other categories of CBT intervention that are described below: social skills training, exposure techniques, and homework assignments.

Assertiveness or social skills training. In the 1960s and 1970s, a group of social psychologists in the UK, led by Michael Argyle, began to develop some practical clinical applications of research into social interaction. Their approach became known as *social skills training* (Argyle and Kendon 1967; Trower *et al.* 1978). Similar developments in the USA are usually described as *assertiveness training*. The central idea in social skills training is that people can develop psychological problems because they are not very good at engaging in micro-level social interaction sequences, that require appropriate and well-timed use of eye contact, conversational turn-taking, self-disclosure, voice quality and volume, touch, gesture and proxemics.

For example, a person may have grown up in a family in which no-one engaged in eye contact or personal disclosure. On leaving home to go to college, the person then has great trouble in making friends, which in turn may result in social anxiety and depression. For such an individual, a therapeutic focus solely on cognitive processes is unlikely to be helpful – what he or she needs is to learn the 'rules' of everyday social interaction. Social skills training protocols provide useful guidelines on how to structure this kind of learning. For instance, it is essential that the person learns how to collect accurate feedback on his or her social performance. In recent years, social skills and assertiveness training has largely disappeared as a distinct form of therapy. However, the ideas and methods of these approaches have been incorporated into the intervention repertoires of many CBT practitioners.

Exposure techniques. From a CBT perspective, many of the problems that people develop are a result of a tendency to *avoid* threatening situations. Where many other therapies encourage clients to try to understand the nature of their fear and avoidance, CBT encourages clients to face the fear directly. This general technique is known as *exposure*. The assumption is that when a person purposefully engages with fearful situations, in a context in which they feel supported by a therapist, he or she will either realize that their fears are illusory (nothing bad happens to me when I hold a spider in my hand) or that they possess coping skills that are adequate to allow them to tolerate the situation (I feel terrified being on an aircraft, but I know that if I practice my breathing and relaxation techniques and positive self-talk then I will survive it). Conditioning theory predicts that, if a person continues to be exposed to a situation or stimuli in the absence of frightening consequences the fear that has become a conditioned response to that stimulus will gradually fade or extinguish. (By contrast, continued avoidance only serves to maintain the fear.) The aim is the eventual replacement of anxiety or fear responses by a learned relaxation response. (The technique of *systematic desensitization*, in which clients learn relaxation skills that are then applied in fearful situations, is an example of this principle.) In most cases, it is not sensible to begin by exposing the client to whatever is the most terrifying situation they can imagine – usually, the counsellor takes the client through a graded hierarchy of fear-eliciting situations, that have been discussed and planned in advance.

Imagery rescripting. The technique of *imagery rescripting* can be used if a client is bothered by intrusive memories of traumatic past events. The client is invited to keep the distressing image in mind and tell the story of what happened. Following a phase of reflection on the event, the client is asked to 'rescript' the event by imagining what would need to have happened to have made the original event less distressing. Alternatively, the client may be invited to observe the event from the point of view of their 'adult self'. Examples of how this process operates can be found in Wheatley and Hackman (2011) and Wild and Clark (2011).

Homework. Homework assignments in CBT involve the practice of new behaviours and cognitive strategies, engagement in behavioural experiments and collection of self-monitoring data between therapy sessions. A typical homework assignment might invite a client suffering from social anxiety to initiate a conversation with at least one new person every day, and write in a worksheet about the type and intensity of feelings that were elicited by these actions. Homework activity in CBT is firmly based in basic principles of behavioural psychology: a new behaviour may be acquired in one situation (i.e., elicited by a specific set of stimuli), but will rapidly be extinguished if it does not generalize to (i.e., be reinforced in) a range of other situations. For example, a client with social anxiety may fairly quickly develop confidence and fluency in speaking to their therapist – but the big test is to be able to reproduce that capability in everyday life settings. The potential advantages of homework are that it expands the impact of counselling beyond the therapy hour, creates a structure for the active participation of the client, and provides the possibility of success experiences for the client. The disadvantages of homework are that the client may become confused about what he or she has agreed to do, may not be able to fulfil the task and as a result may become disillusioned with therapy. In a review of research into the use of homework in CBT, Kazantzis *et al.* (2005) specified the following principles for successful use of homework assignments in therapy:

- a rationale for homework assignments should be provided in the first session of therapy;
- homework should be relevant to the client's goals and aligned with their existing coping strategies;
- the homework task should be specific rather than vague;
- the therapist should check out that the client understands what is expected;
- written instructions should be provided;
- the assignment should not be discussed if the client is highly distressed;
- the outcome of a homework task should be discussed at the following session.

In addition, Kazantzis *et al.* (2005) suggest that counsellors should accept that homework non-completion is a common occurrence, and refrain from becoming irritated or demotivated if the client does not appear to engage effectively with homework tasks. A comprehensive model of homework implementation has been devised by Scheel *et al.* (2004). Kazantzis *et al.* (2005) provide a useful brief checklist that clients and counsellors can use to evaluate the effectiveness of homework in therapy.

Self-help learning materials. CBT therapists often supply clients with information sheets and worksheets that enable them to learn how to apply CBT ideas and use CBT methods to make changes in their lives. There are also a wide range of CBT-oriented self-help books that can be 'prescribed' to clients, on such topics as social anxiety (Butler 1999), panic (Silove and Manicavasagar 1997), obsessive–compulsive disorder (Veale and Wilson 2005), low self-esteem (Fennell 1999), depression (Gilbert 2000; Greenberger and Padesky 1995), chronic fatigue (Burgess 2005) and general anxiety (Kennerley 1997). There are also some CBT-based online packages that can be used in a similar fashion (for example, Grime 2004). A key objective in using self-help materials is to enable the client to 'become their own therapist' and to become actively involved in treatment. The wide availability of CBT self-help books in bookshops and public libraries also has the effect of creating public awareness of CBT, so that at least some clients are informed about what to expect before they even meet their therapist, and have positive expectations for benefit.

Further information on cognitive–behavioural methods can be found in a wide range of texts, including Fennell (1999), Freeman *et al.* (1989), Granvold (2004), Greenberger and Padesky (1995), Kanfer and Goldstein (1986), Kuehnel and Liberman (1986) Lam and Gale (2004), Leahy (2003), Salkovskis (1996) and Seiser and Wastell (2002).

Monitoring: ongoing assessment of target behaviours

Influenced by its origins in behavioural psychology, CBT makes considerable use of measurement techniques to assess the severity of problems, and to monitor change. A technique that is often used within sessions is the Subjective Units of Distress Scale (SUDS), where clients are asked to rate their level of anxiety or panic on a scale of 0–100. The SUDS technology provides a convenient shorthand means for clients and counsellors to communicate around severity of emotional distress, and the magnitude of change that may have resulted from therapy interventions or life events.

There are also a large number of standardized measurement instruments and scaling strategies that have been developed for therapy in relation to specific disorders. For example, there is good evidence that CBT is a particularly effective way of working with obsessive–compulsive disorder (OCD) (Salkovskis 1985; Whittal and O'Neill 2003). Typically, somewhere within the ritualized sequence of actions that are characteristic of OCD there are some automatic thoughts, and beliefs about the validity of these thoughts, that serve to maintain an obsessional way of living. However, these cognitions may be ephemeral and hard to keep in focus – the use of scaling helps both client and therapist to keep a handle on what is happening. A case study published by Guay *et al.* (2005, Box 6.6) illustrates the variety of scaling and monitoring techniques that can be drawn upon by CBT practitioners working with this type of problem. A key aspect of the development of competence as a CBT therapist involves building up a resource bank of measures that are revenant to the client group with whom one is working.

Box 6.6: *Quantification as a means of maintaining therapeutic focus in a case of a person experiencing obsessional rituals*

A case report by Guay *et al.* (2005) demonstrates some of the ways that monitoring is integrated into CBT treatment. The client was a married man of 38 years who had been diagnosed with severe OCD, high levels of anxiety, suicidal thoughts, and sleep disturbance. He had suffered from obsessive–compulsive symptoms for 30 years. The story behind these problems indicated the severity of his difficulties:

> As a child, his father who was an alcoholic . . . abused him psychologically, physically and sexually. At age 7, during an episode of physical abuse against his mother, he hid in a wardrobe and started counting and singing aloud so he would not hear his mother's screams . . . At the beginning of his adolescence, he acquired the belief that he was at-risk of becoming like his father, and this thought produced very high levels of anxiety. He recalled from that day onward how he decided to do everything to protect himself from becoming a violent and abusive person. Consequently, he started to perform rituals that were contrary to his father's personality. For example, he became perfectionist and extremely organized which he perceived as contrary to his father's disorganized personality. This perfectionist behaviour was reinforced by his teachers at school and maintained up to university level. He also developed superstitious rituals such as stepping over sidewalk lines and always passing around posts to his right. These formed a counterpart to his obsessively organized self-control . . . these superstitions were intended to prevent a misfortune. Over time, his compulsions permeated all aspects of his life including work, family and leisure.
>
> (Guay *et al.* 2005: 370)

In order to track the overall effectiveness of therapy, a set of questionnaires measures of anxiety, depression and obsessional beliefs, were administered on a regular basis. To track micro-changes in specific areas of obsessional behaviour, the client was asked to generate a list of rituals (for instance: read aloud road signs when driving, check that the front door is locked, check if the oven rings are off), and rate each one of them on a series of scales to assess his strength of conviction in respect of (a) how likely it was that the thought would arise, (b) the likelihood of feared consequences if the ritual was not performed, and (c) the usefulness of the ritual. He also made ratings of his capacity to resist each ritual, and kept a diary of the amount of time each day engaged in OCD rituals. Therapy (seven sessions) was very effective with this client. It emerged that all of his obsessive thoughts and rituals stemmed from a core schema that 'I must keep things under control . . . to avoid becoming like my father'. The careful measurement of key dimensions of his obsessional cycles enabled the client and therapist to tackle different aspects of belief and behaviour one at a time, and monitor the extent of change. For example, one homework assignment concentrated on finding examples of the inutility of his behaviour, and how it prevented him from living as he wished. Monitoring was also reassuring for the client, in reminding him of the progress he had made at times in therapy when he felt insecurity due to the loss of his obsessional coping mechanisms at a point where new, more adaptive coping mechanisms had still to be developed. Finally, the existence of a set of measures that depicted his level of dysfunction at the start of therapy, made it possible to be confident, at three-year follow-up, that real changes had been achieved and maintained.

Relapse prevention: termination and planned follow-up

A set of ideas and techniques that have come to be widely used by cognitive–behavioural counsellors is associated with the concept of *relapse prevention*. Marlatt and Gordon (1985) observed that although many clients who are helped, through therapy, to change their behaviour may initially make good progress, they may at some point encounter some kind of crisis, which triggers a resumption of the original problem behaviour. This pattern is particularly common in clients with addictions to food, alcohol, drugs or smoking, but can be found in any behaviour-change scenario. Marlatt and Gordon (1985) concluded that it is necessary in cognitive–behavioural work to prepare for this eventuality, and to provide the client with skills and strategies for dealing with relapse events. The standard approaches to relapse prevention involve the application of cognitive–behavioural techniques. For example, the 'awful catastrophe' of 'relapse' can be redefined as a 'lapse'. The client can learn to identify the situations that are likely to evoke a lapse, and acquire social skills in order to deal with them. Marlatt and Gordon (1985) characterize three types of experience as being associated with high rates of relapse: 'downers' (feeling depressed), 'rows' (interpersonal conflict) and 'joining the club' (pressure from others to resume drinking, smoking etc.). Clients may be given written instructions on what action to take if there is a threat of a lapse, or a phone number to call. Wanigaratne *et al.* (1990) and Antony *et al.* (2005) describe many other ways in which the relapse prevention concept can be applied in counselling.

Box 6.7: *How 'cognitive' is CBT?*

Cognitive–behavioural therapy consists of a combination of cognitive and behavioural interventions, in the context of a secure therapeutic relationship. But how important are the respective cognitive and behavioural elements? One of the advantages of the research-oriented nature of CBT is that there exist researchers with the skills and resources to address this kind of issue. There have been two studies that have looked at the specific role of cognitive interventions in CBT. Jacobson *et al.* (1996) argued that there were three main components in Beck's cognitive therapy for depression (Beck *et al.* 1979). Following assessment, clients initially engage in a phase of *behavioural activation*, which involves self-monitoring of behaviour and the prescription of behavioural techniques. There then follows a phase of *modification of dysfunctional thoughts*, in which automatic thoughts are identified and monitored, and interventions are introduced to change them. Finally, there is a phase of working with underling *schemas*, which represent core beliefs and assumptions that are regarded as the ultimate cause of depressed behaviour.

Jacobson *et al.* (1996) recruited 150 people diagnosed with severe depression, who were randomly allocated to three intervention conditions. The first group only received behavioural activation therapy. The second group received behavioural activation and modification of dysfunctional thoughts. The final group received the whole Beck cognitive therapy package. Therapists were carefully trained and supervised, to ensure that they delivered only the interventions specified by the research design. Standardized measures were used to assess change in client outcomes, and a two-year follow-up was conducted (Gortner *et al.* 1998). Analysis of outcome showed quite clearly that all three groups benefited to an equal extent from the therapy they had received. In other words, there did not appear to be any additional gain from including cognitive techniques on top of the initial behavioural interventions.

These findings support the results of a literature review carried out by Ilardi and Craighead 1994, 1999). Their review looked at studies in which session-by-session symptom change was assessed in clients receiving CBT. What they found was that the majority of symptomatic improvement occurred within the first few weeks of treatment. Given that the opening sessions of CBT are devoted to assessment and case formulation, the results of Ilardi and Craighead's (1994) review implied that CBT clients tended to improve *before* they received any cognitive interventions.

How can these results be understood, in the light of the emphasis that CBT practitioners place on the necessity for using cognitive techniques? Snyder *et al.* (2000) have suggested that these findings can be interpreted as evidence for the potency of non-specific factors (i.e., processes that occur in all therapies). They particularly highlight the role of the non-specific factor of *hope*, and argue that CBT approaches provide a structure that promotes hopefulness in clients, by offering a clearly understandable pathway to desired personal goals and a sense of active agency in the form of guidance on what they can do to achieve these goals. From this perspective, working therapeutically with dysfunctional thoughts and schema are helpful not so much because they address the cognitive roots of depression, but because they continue, over a number of sessions, to give opportunities for hope-engendering structured activity.

An appraisal of the cognitive–behavioural approach to counselling

Cognitive–behavioural concepts and methods have made an enormous contribution to the field of counselling. Evidence of the energy and creativity of researchers and practitioners in this area can be gained by inspection of the ever-increasing literature on the topic. Cognitive–behavioural approaches appeal to many counsellors and clients because they are straightforward and practical, and emphasize action. The wide array of techniques provide counsellors with a sense of competence and potency. The effectiveness of CBT for a wide range of conditions is amply confirmed in the research literature.

Box 6.8: *Is CBT more effective than other approaches to therapy?*

The widespread adoption of CBT as the therapy most likely to be offered within health care systems, such as the NHS in the UK, is largely due to the substantial research evidence that has accumulated concerning the effectiveness of CBT for a variety of disorders. The volume and quality of this research evidence has led some adherents of CBT to claim that their approach is the single most effective therapy model currently available. For example, the introductory CBT textbook by Westbrook *et al.* (2011) reviews the evidence for the efficacy of different approaches to therapy for a list of problem categories, such as depression, panic, anxiety, etc. and concludes that, CBT is the treatment of choice for all of these conditions.

But how valid is this kind of analysis? When interpreting conclusions from accumulated outcome studies, it needs to be kept in mind that the historical roots of CBT in academic psychology mean that there are many more CBT researchers than there are researchers into other therapies. There is therefore *more* evidence regarding the effectiveness of CBT than there is for other approaches, which means that reviewers such as Roth and Fonagy (2005) or the National Institute for Health and Clinical Excellence (NICE; the UK government body that evaluates evidence around health interventions) can have a high degree of confidence in recommending CBT as a 'proven' treatment. However, there remains substantial evidence for the effectiveness of other types of therapy. For example, the review of person-centred and experiential therapies carried out by Elliott (2002; Elliott *et al.* 2004) has demonstrated levels of effectiveness that are equivalent to, and some cases greater than, those achieved by CBT. A review by Cuijpers *et al.* (2011) found that there is little difference in effectiveness for depression across any of the established therapy approaches. Lynch *et al.* (2010) came to similar conclusions in a review of the efficacy of CBT for major psychiatric problems such as schizophrenia. In a study of several thousand clients receiving counselling in the NHS, Stiles *et al.* (2006) found no differences in outcome between clients who had received CBT, person-centred counselling or psychodynamic counselling.

The evidence base for CBT also needs to be interpreted in the light of the fact that many CBT studies have focused on the effectiveness of specific CBT protocols designed to treat highly specific disorders, such as panic or obsessive–compulsive rituals. By contrast, the majority of clients or patients seen in routine practice settings have multiple problems, in which panic attacks may be mixed in with relationship difficulties, low self-esteem, and other issues. On balance, it seems reasonable to conclude that CBT is an affective form of therapy, which is well-received by clients. But is it more effective than other forms of therapy? For very specific behaviour problems such as panic and OCD – possibly yes. For more generalized depression, relationship difficulties and anxiety – probably not.

It is possible to identify some areas of tension within the current overall structure of CBT theory and practice. One of these areas of tension arises from a disparity between a reliance by some practitioners (and trainers) on treatment manuals or protocols that outline highly specified treatment programmes for specific disorders, and the complex lives and realities represented by individual clients. This tension is reflected in the difference between the number of therapy sessions offered in research studies (where clients are carefully selected in terms of strict inclusion and exclusion criteria) and the number of sessions offered by therapists in private practice settings, working with complex cases. Westen *et al.* (2004) analysed these data, and found that the average number of sessions in research studies that looked at CBT for depression was significantly higher than the average number of sessions conducted in private practice by CBT therapists working with depressed clients. A contributory factor in relation to what might be termed the simplicity–complexity issue has been the enthusiasm among the majority of CBT theorists, researchers and practitioners for operating within the framework provided by psychiatric categories. There are, of course, major debates within the counselling/psychotherapy field regarding the value of psychiatric diagnosis as a guide to treatment choice and delivery in psychotherapy. The big advantage of operating within a psychiatric nosology is that it strengthens the link between counselling and mainstream health care. But it can be argued that CBT is, in a fundamental sense, an approach that is not conceptually consistent with the use of psychiatric categories. This is because CBT interventions are ultimately always individualized, and based on a detailed analysis of patterns of cognition, behaviour and emotion that are linked to specific situations in the context of individual lives – it is not clear what is added to CBT case formulation by including a psychiatric diagnosis (see, for example, the discussion of this issue in Persons and Tomkins 2007).

Another critical issue in relation to CBT theory practice concerns the question of just *how* CBT works: what are the active therapeutic ingredients? There is a lot happening in CBT. There are a whole host of non-specific or common factors in operation, such as the induction of hope and positive expectations, the development of a relationship with a socially sanctioned healer, a set of healing rituals, acquiring an explanatory framework within which to make sense of one's difficulties, and so on. Beyond these common factors, shared by all approaches to therapy, CBT also includes an impressive list of specific techniques. But how important are these techniques? For example, there is some research that seems to suggest that the specific cognitive change interventions used by CBT therapists may not in fact be having much effect on clients, compared with the impact of somewhat simpler behavioural change strategies that are offered (see Box 6.2).

Another intriguing dimension of CBT practice concerns the role of emotional expression in CBT. Traditionally, CBT has always been regarded as a form of therapy that operates through rational, cognitive analysis, reflection, and planning (as opposed to humanistic and experiential therapies, that are often characterized as strongly 'emotion-focused'). The sense that, in CBT, the aim is to control emotion, rather than to allow it to be felt, is captured in the statement by Ellis (1973: 56) that 'there are virtually no legitimate reasons for people to make themselves terribly upset, hysterical or emotionally disturbed, no matter what kind of psychological or verbal stimuli are impinging on them'. But, from a different perspective, what could be more emotional than the behaviour experiments described by Bennett-Levy *et al.* (2004). What could be more terrifying, for someone with a fear of flying, than mounting the stairs to enter a Boeing 737 (even if accompanied by their therapist)? There is a paradoxical sense that, of all the therapies, CBT is the one that is most willing to plunge clients right into directly experienced strong emotion (not thinking about it or talking about it – actually feeling it in the moment). The issue that is at stake here is whether CBT is effective in terms of its own rationale (the skilled delivery of cognitive and behavioural change techniques) or whether it is, in the end, more like other therapies, and effective because it offers people a trusting relationship and other non-specific factors.

It may be that in the end the single most distinctive aspect of CBT is its commitment to the canons of scientific method – formulating hypotheses about how to initiate change in individual behaviour, running behaviour 'experiments', viewing the client as a fellow scientist, using measures to monitor change, using numbers to give precision to statements about emotional states. The historical account of the evolution of CBT, and its origins in behaviourism, provided in the early sections of this chapter, demonstrates a deeply scientistic basis for CBT practice. However, it seems clear that the scientific foundation of CBT is softening. Ultimately, mindfulness is not a scientific construct. Socratic questioning is an unexamined practice, lacking adequate definition or a research base (Carey and Mullan 2004). It can be argued that the basis for CBT casework, the construction of a case formulation, is an activity that relies as much on artistry and clinical experience as it does on scientific principles. And, of course, an increasing appreciation of the importance of the therapeutic relationship brings with it a haunting realization of the significance of the domain of the personal, and the subjective. Another way of making sense of this tension is to celebrate the unique capacity of CBT (in practice if not in theory) to continue to be willing and able to bring together personal and creative facets of human experience, and objective/rational ones, in the service of effective therapy.

Box 6.9: *Drop-out from CBT*

Clients who drop out of therapy without any negotiation with their therapist can be found in all therapy approaches (Barkham *et al.* 2006; Defife *et al.* 2010). Controlled research studies invest a lot of effort in recruiting and taking care of clients, to ensure that attrition is as low as possible. By contrast, in routine practice, on average around one in three clients quits therapy by the fifth session. There appears to be some evidence for particularly high drop-out rates in the routine practice of CBT. Studies have reported rates ranging from 22 per cent (Westbrook and Kirk 2005) to 44 per cent (Bados *et al.* 2007). Although there are many reasons why clients quit therapy, it seems reasonable to interpret high 'no-show' rates as an indicator of lack of client satisfaction. Given the relatively high success rates reported in CBT, with clients who stay the course, these drop-out figures suggest that there may be some clients who are looking for a different type of therapeutic experience, and who realize early on that CBT may not represent the best path for them to follow.

Box 6.10: *The emergence of a transdiagnostic perspective in CBT*

Over the past 40 years, influenced by the success of Beck's treatment protocols outlining cognitive interventions targeted at specific disorders such as anxiety and depression, the bulk of research and practice development within the CBT community has focused on disorder-oriented interventions (e.g., distinct CBT packages for clients with eating disorders, marital problems, post-traumatic stress disorder (PTSD)). This approach has been highly successful in terms of generating a strong research base demonstrating the efficacy of CBT for these disorders. However, it has led to problems in the field of routine practice. Typically, clients seen by frontline therapists report multiple problems. Treatment protocols that have been developed in the context of carefully selected 'single disorder' clients are hard to apply with clients who have comorbid conditions, because it is difficult to know where to start, and which condition should take priority. More recently, some CBT researchers and practitioners have evolved an alternative, *transdiagnostic* approach (Barlow *et al.* 2004; Egan *et al.* 2011; Mansell *et al.* 2009; McManus *et al.* 2011).

A transdiagnostic perspective seeks to identify maladaptive cognitive and behavioural processes that are found in all, or most disorders. The transdiagnostic processes that have been studied so far include self-focused attention, perfectionism, avoidance behaviour, thought suppression, rumination and safety-seeking behaviours. In practice, adopting a transdiagnostic approach allows the therapist to build a case formulation and treatment plan around the particular 'CBT common factors' that are most significant for each individual client, and then make use of evidence-based interventions that have been developed and validated for each transdiagnostic theme.

Conclusions

The cognitive–behavioural tradition represents an enormous resource for counsellors and clients. The practical and pragmatic nature of this approach means that there exists a wealth of therapeutic techniques and strategies that can be applied to different clients and their problems. The creativity of the cognitive–behavioural tradition can be seen in its recent embrace of constructivist thinking and spiritual practices, and in the willingness on the part of many writers and therapists from this perspective to dialogue with others in a search for integration. An important theme in all the CBT models discussed in this chapter, from behaviour modification to mindfulness training, is a consistent focus on the strengths of the client, and his or her capacity to change, rather than on lengthy exploration of 'problems'. These therapies are in the vanguard of a newly emerging emphasis on *positive psychology* (Seligman and Csikszentmihalyi 2000).

In addition, the cognitive–behavioural approach has always had a healthy respect for the value of research as a means of improving practice, and this has enabled practitioners to be critical and questioning in a constructive way, and to learn quickly from the discoveries of their colleagues. Finally, of all of the therapies currently available, CBT is possibly the approach that is best suited to the social and political environment of our time. It does not promise to reveal much in the way of personal meaning or cultural transformation. It does not seek to challenge the disconnectedness and alienation of contemporary life. What it does do, is to help people to get back on track, to make the best of the life that is available to them.

Topics for reflection and discussion

1 What are the strengths and weaknesses of CBT, in comparison with other counselling approaches you have studied? Are there specific strengths/weaknesses of CBT in relation to working with certain types of client problem, or certain categories of client?

2 What are the advantages and disadvantages of the strongly scientific emphasis of the cognitive–behavioural approach?

3 What are the advantages and disadvantages of using treatment manuals or protocols designed for specific client groups or disorders?

4 To what extent do 'third wave' concepts such as mindfulness and constructivism represent a radically new departure from the basic concepts of behavioural and cognitive–behavioural therapies?

5 Select one of the CBT-informed self-help books listed in this chapter, or available in your local library. How effective do you think it would be to rely on this book as a source of therapeutic assistance? What might be the advantages (and disadvantages) of using the book in conjunction with regular meetings with a therapist?

6 How culture-bound is CBT? Is it an approach to counselling that would work best (or at all) with people who hold a Western set of values and worldview? Or is it universally applicable? Based on your knowledge of different cultures, reflect on some of the ways in which CBT might either be consistent with the norms, beliefs and values of that culture, or might be culturally alien?

Suggested further reading

One of the most consistently interesting and thought-provoking writers in the cognitive–behavioural tradition is Donald Meichenbaum. His book on PTSD (Meichenbaum 1994) is an excellent illustration of the application of cognitive–behavioural and constructivist ideas and methods to a difficult clinical problem. Westbrook *et al.* (2011) and Ledley *et al.* (2005) have written highly readable introductory textbooks on CBT, which examine in more detail many of the issues discussed in the present chapter. An excellent brief introduction to CBT is Salkovskis (2010). Scott *et al.* (1995) and Dobson (2001) are valuable in exploring more advanced issues in CBT theory and practice. The discussion of case formulation in Kuyken *et al.* (2009) represents valuable insight into how to 'think CBT' and how to communicate these ideas to clients. A good way to learn about how CBT works in practice is to read through a CBT-informed self-help book, such as Butler (1999), Silove and Manicavasagar (1997), Veale and Wilson (2005), Greenberger and Padesky (1995) or Williams *et al.* (2007). There are many excellent CBT journals. Counsellors might find it particularly useful to browse *Cognitive and Behavioral Practice,* a stimulating source of new ideas in CBT, and to learn about how CBT is applied in action through reading some of the well-documented case examples in the journal *Clinical Case Studies.*

Theory and practice of the person-centred approach

Introduction

The brief account in Chapter 2 of the social and cultural background that shaped the work of Carl Rogers gives some indication of the extent to which his approach to counselling was rooted in the values of American society. The approach associated with Rogers, called at various times 'non-directive', 'client-centred', 'person-centred' or 'Rogerian', has not only been one of the most widely used orientations to counselling and therapy over the past 50 years, but has also supplied ideas and methods that have been integrated into other approaches (Thorne and Sanders 2012). As with other mainstream approaches to counselling, such as psychodynamic and cognitive–behavioural, it encompasses a number of distinct yet overlapping groupings (Bohart 1995). Warner (2000a) and Sanders (2004) have described the person-centred approach as being similar to a therapeutic 'nation', comprising a number of 'tribes'. These 'tribes' include classical client-centred/person-centred therapy, focusing approaches, experiential therapy such as emotion focused therapy (EFT), and some versions of existential therapy. There are probably two basic therapeutic principles that define membership of the person-centred nation. The first principle is that person-centred practitioners seek to create a *relationship* with clients that is characterized by a high degree of respect, equality and authenticity. The client is regarded as the expert on his or her own life and problems, and it is within the context of a facilitative relationship that the person can come to identify and accept his or her own personal solutions to the challenges of life. The second key therapeutic principle is an assumption that it is particularly helpful to work with clients in ways that enable them to become more aware of their moment-by-moment or 'here-and-now' experiencing. The idea is that patterns of thought and feeling that are associated with difficulties in everyday life situations are being continually re-created, wherever the client might be, and that a willingness to enter the *now* provides the client and therapist with opportunities to learn about these patterns, and change them. Another way of looking at this form of therapeutic activity is to view it as *process*-oriented work – the concept of process is a central construct in all forms of person-centred practice.

The aim of this chapter is to provide an overview of the person-centred approach to counselling. Primarily, this is achieved by examining the theory and practice of 'classical' person-centred counselling (Mearns and Thorne 2013). The contribution to this tradition of the focusing approach (Gendlin 1981), EFT (Greenberg *et al.* 1993) and 'pre-therapy' (Prouty *et al.* 2002) are also examined. The chapter closes with an appraisal of the person-centred approach to counselling.

Box 7.1: *The humanistic tradition in counselling*

The emergence of client-centred therapy in the 1950s was part of a broader movement in American psychology to create a 'humanistic' alternative to the two theories that at that time dominated the field: psychoanalysis and behaviourism. This movement became known as the 'third force' (in contrast to the other main forces represented by the ideas of Freud and Skinner). Apart from Rogers, the central figures in early humanistic psychology included Abraham Maslow, Charlotte Buhler and Sydney Jourard. These writers shared a vision of a psychology that would have a place for the human capacity for creativity, growth and choice, and were influenced by the European tradition of existential and phenomenological philosophy, as well as by Eastern religions such as Buddhism. The image of the person in humanistic psychology is of a self striving to find meaning and fulfilment in the world. Bugental (1964) formulated five 'basic postulates' for humanistic psychology:

1 Human beings, as human, supersede the sum of their parts. They cannot be reduced to components.

2 Human beings have their existence in a uniquely human context, as well as in a cosmic ecology.

3 Human beings are aware and aware of being aware – i.e., they are conscious. Human consciousness always includes an awareness of oneself in the context of other people.

4 Human beings have some choice and, with that, responsibility.

5   Human beings are intentional, aim at goals, are aware that they cause future events, and seek meaning, value and creativity.

Humanistic psychology has always consisted of a broad set of theories and models connected by shared values and philosophical assumptions, rather than constituting a single, coherent, theoretical formulation (Rice and Greenberg 1992; Cain 2002; McLeod 2002). Within counselling and psychotherapy, the most widely used humanistic approaches are person-centred and gestalt, although psychosynthesis, transactional analysis and other models also contain strong humanistic elements. Following a period in which the humanistic tradition appeared to be waning as a source of influence and inspiration in counselling and psychotherapy, there are signs of a revival in this approach. The edited collections by Greenberg *et al.* (1998) and Cain and Seeman (2002) bring together an impressive body of research into person-centred, experiential and humanistic therapies. The *Handbook of Humanistic Psychology*, edited by Schneider *et al.* (2001), provides a valuable overview of the many different strands of contemporary humanistic theory and practice. The recent decision by the editors of *Psychotherapy,* a mainstream journal, to publish a special issue on 'the renewal of humanism in psychotherapy' (Schneider and Längle 2012) is indicative of a resurgence of interest in this approach. The continuing vitality of journals such as the *Journal of Humanistic Psychology*, and *The Humanistic Psychologist,* attest to the ongoing relevance of the humanistic tradition not only within psychotherapy and counselling but also in relation to other fields such as education, peace studies and human ecology. Mearns (2004) characterizes humanistic psychology as comprising a 'potentiality paradigm' that has a major contribution to make in the resolution of contemporary social problems.

The evolution of the person-centred approach

The birth of the person-centred approach is usually attributed to a talk given by Rogers in 1940 on 'new concepts in psychotherapy' to an audience at the University of Minnesota (Barrett-Lennard 1979). In this talk, which was subsequently published as a chapter in *Counseling and Psychotherapy* (Rogers 1942), it was suggested that the therapist could be of most help to clients by allowing them to find their own solutions to their problems. The emphasis on the client as expert and the counsellor as source of reflection and encouragement was captured in the designation of the approach as 'non-directive' counselling. In the research carried out at that time by Rogers and his students at the University of Ohio, the aim was to study the effect on the client of 'directive' and 'non-directive' behaviour on the part of the counsellor. These studies were the first pieces of psychotherapy research to involve the use of direct recording and transcription of actual therapy sessions.

In 1945 Rogers was invited to join the University of Chicago, as Professor of Psychology and Head of the Counseling Center. At this time, the ending of the war and the return from the front line of large numbers of armed services personnel, many of them traumatized by their experiences, meant that there was a demand for an accessible, practical means of helping these people to cope with the transition back to civilian life. At that time, the dominant form of psychotherapy in the USA was psychoanalysis, which would have been too expensive to provide for large numbers of soldiers, even if there had been enough trained analysts to make it possible. Behavioural approaches had not yet emerged. The 'non-directive' approach of Rogers represented an ideal solution, and a whole new generation of American counsellors was trained at Chicago, or by colleagues of Rogers at other colleges. It was in this way that the Rogerian approach became quickly established as the main non-medical form of counselling in the USA. Rogers was also successful in attracting substantial funding to enable a continuing programme of research. It is important to note, however, that the new approach to therapy being advocated by Rogers in the 1940s was widely criticized by many within the profession, on a variety of grounds. A special issue of the *Journal of Clinical Psychology,* published in 1948, brought together a collection of critiques of non-directive therapy, from leading figures within the profession. A summary of the key objections to Rogers' approach, highlighted in this special issue, can be found in Hill and Nakayama (2000).

These developments in the 1940s were associated with a significant evolution in the nature of the approach itself. The notion of 'non-directiveness' had from the beginning implied a contradiction. How could any person in a close relationship fail to influence the other, at least slightly, in one direction or another? Studies by Truax (1966) and others suggested that supposedly non-directive counsellors in fact subtly reinforced certain statements made by clients, and did not offer their interest, encouragement or approval when other types of statement were made. There were, therefore, substantial problems inherent in the concept of non-directiveness.

At the same time, the focus of research in this approach was moving away from a concern with the behaviour of the counsellor, to a deeper consideration of the process that occurred in the client, particularly in relation to changes in the self-concept of the client. This change of emphasis was marked by a renaming of the approach as 'client-centred'. The key publications from this period are *Client-centered Therapy* by Rogers (1951) and the Rogers and Dymond (1954) collection of research papers.

The third phase in the development of client-centred counselling came during the latter years at Chicago (1954–7), and can be seen as representing an attempt to consolidate the theory by integrating the earlier ideas about the contribution of the counsellor with the later thinking about the process in the client, to arrive at a model of the therapeutic relationship. Rogers' 1957 paper on the 'necessary and sufficient' conditions of empathy, congruence and acceptance, later to become known as the 'core conditions' model, was an important landmark in this phase, as was his formulation of a 'process conception' of therapy. The book that remains the single most widely read of all of Rogers' writings, *On Becoming a Person* (Rogers 1961), is a compilation of talks and papers produced during this phase.

In 1957 Rogers and several colleagues from Chicago were given an opportunity to conduct a major research study based at the University of Wisconsin, investigating the process and outcome of client-centred therapy with hospitalized schizophrenic patients. One of the primary aims of the study was to test the validity of the 'core conditions' and 'process' models. This project triggered a crisis in the formerly close-knit team around Rogers (see Kirschenbaum (1979) for a lively account of this episode). Barrett-Lennard

(1979: 187), in his review of the historical development of the person-centred approach, notes that 'the research team suffered internal vicissitudes'. The results of the study showed that the client-centred approach was not particularly effective with this type of client. There were also tensions between some of the principal members of the research group, and, although the project itself came to an end in 1963, the final report on the research was not published until 1967 (Rogers *et al.* 1967).

Several significant contributions emerged from the schizophrenia study. New instruments for assessing concepts such as empathy, congruence, acceptance (Barrett-Lennard 1962; Truax and Carkhuff 1967) and depth of experiencing (Klein *et al.* 1986) were developed. Gendlin began to construct a model of the process of experiencing that was to have a lasting impact. The opportunity to work with highly disturbed clients, and the difficulties in forming therapeutic relationships with these clients, led many of the team to re-examine their own practice, and in particular to arrive at an enhanced appreciation of the role of congruence in the therapy process. Client-centred therapists such as Shlien discovered that the largely empathic, reflective mode of operating, which had been effective with anxious college students and other clients at Chicago, was not effective with clients locked into their own private worlds. To make contact with these clients, the counsellor had to be willing to take risks in being open, honest and self-disclosing. The increase in emphasis given to congruence was also stimulated by the phase of the project where the eight therapists involved made transcripts of sessions available to other leading practitioners, and engaged in a dialogue. In the section of the Rogers *et al.* (1967) report that gives an account of this dialogue, it can be seen that these outside commentators were often highly critical of the passive, 'wooden' style of some of the client-centred team. The fruits of these more experiential sources of learning from the schizophrenia study are included in Rogers and Stevens (1968).

The Wisconsin project has more recently been criticized by Masson (1988), who argues that the acceptance and genuineness of the client-centred therapists could never hope to overcome the appalling institutionalization and oppression suffered by these patients:

> [The] patients lived in a state of oppression. In spite of his reputation for empathy and kindness, Carl Rogers could not perceive this. How could he have come to terms so easily with the coercion and violence that dominated their everyday existence? Nothing [written by Rogers] indicates any genuinely human response to the suffering he encountered in this large state hospital.
>
> (Masson 1988: 245)

In defence, it can be pointed out that Rogers *et al.* (1967) discuss in great detail the issues arising from working in a 'total institution', and were clearly attempting to deal with the problem that Masson (1988) describes. Rogers *et al.* (1967: 93) commented that:

> one of the unspoken themes of the research, largely evident through omission, is that it was quite unnecessary to develop different research procedures or different theories because of the fact that our clients were schizophrenic. We found them far more similar to, than different from, other clients with whom we have worked.

This passage would indicate that at least one of the elements in the power imbalance, the existence of labelling and rejection, was not an important factor. The end of the Wisconsin experiment also marked the end of what Barrett-Lennard (1979) has called the 'school' era in client-centred therapy. Up to this point, there had always been a definable nucleus of people around Rogers, and an institutional base, which could be identified as a discrete, coherent school of thought. After the Wisconsin years, the client-centred approach fragmented, as the people who had been involved with Rogers moved to different locations, and pursued their own ideas largely in isolation from each other.

Rogers himself went to California, initially to the Western Behavioral Sciences Institute, and then, in 1968, to the Center for Studies of the Person at LaJolla. He became active in encounter groups, organizational change and community-building and, towards the end of his life, in working for political change in East–West relations and in South Africa (Rogers 1978, 1980). He did not engage in any further developments of any significance regarding his approach to one-to-one therapy. The extension of client-centred ideas to encompass groups, organizations and society in general meant that it was no longer appropriate to view the approach as being about clients as such, and the term 'person-centred' came increasingly into currency as a way of describing an approach to working with larger groups as well as with individual clients (Mearns and Thorne 2007).

Of the other central figures at that time, Gendlin and Shlien went back to Chicago, the former to continue exploring the implications of his experiential approach, the latter to carry out research in the effectiveness of time-limited client-centred therapy. Barrett-Lennard eventually returned to Australia, and remained active in theory and research. Truax and Carkhuff (1967) were key figures in creating new approaches for training people in the use of counselling skills. In Toronto, Rice was the leader of a group that explored the relationship between client-centred ideas and the information-processing model of cognitive psychology. Various individuals, such as Gendlin, Gordon, Goodman and Carkhuff, were instrumental in setting up programmes with the aim of enabling ordinary, non-professional people to use counselling skills to help others (see Larson 1984).

The post-Wisconsin developments in client-centred theory and practice are summarized by Lietaer (1990), who notes that while there have been many useful new directions, the approach as a whole has lacked coherence and direction in the absence of the powerful, authoritative voice provided by Rogers. So, although the periodic reviews of client-centred and person-centred theory, research and practice compiled by Hart and Tomlinson (1970), Wexler and Rice (1974), Levant and Shlien (1984) and Lietaer *et al.* (1990) contain much useful material, there is also a sense of a gradual drifting apart and splitting, and consequent reduction in impact. The client-centred or person-centred approach has been becoming less influential in the USA, partly because its central ideas have been assimilated into other approaches, although it remains a major independent force in Britain, Belgium, Germany and Holland (Lietaer 1990).

The evolution of the person-centred approach over a 50-year period illustrates many important social and cultural factors. Client-centred therapy was created from a synthesis of European 'insight' therapy and American values (Sollod 1978). The emphasis in the model on self-acceptance and its theoretical simplicity made it wholly appropriate as a therapy for soldiers returning from war, and allowed it to gain a peak of influence at that time. In the post-war years in the USA, the increasing competitiveness of the 'mental health industry' resulted in the gradual erosion of this influence, as other therapies that could claim specific techniques, special ingredients and rapid cures became available. Moreover, the insistence of insurance companies in the USA that clients receive a diagnosis before payments for therapy could be authorized went against the grain of the client-centred approach. Finally, the failure to maintain a solid institutional base, either in the academic world or in an independent professional association, contributed further to its decline. In other countries, and, for example, in Europe, counsellors and therapists working in state-funded educational establishments and in voluntary agencies were largely protected from these pressures, enabling the person-centred approach to thrive. In these other countries there have also been Rogerian institutes and training courses.

The basic theoretical framework of the person-centred approach

The summary of person-centred theory that is offered here is primarily informed by the writings of Carl Rogers, who was unusual, in comparison with other significant counselling/psychotherapy theorists, in that he sought to produce a formal statement of this theoretical position (see, for example, Rogers 1957, 1959) in terms of a set of propositions. Further propositions, that reflect subsequent theorizing within the person-centred approach have been added by Mearns and Thorne (2013).

The person-centred approach begins and ends with experiencing. Because of this, the set of ideas and practices that comprise the person-centred approach build on a *phenomenological* approach to knowledge. Phenomenology is a method of philosophical inquiry evolved by Husserl and other thinkers (see Moran 2000; Moran and Mooney 2002), which is widely employed in existential philosophy, and which takes the view that valid knowledge and understanding can be gained by exploring and describing the way things are experienced by people (rather than trying to construct knowledge through abstract theorizing). The aim of phenomenology is to depict the nature and quality of personal experience. Phenomenology has been applied to many areas of study other than therapy: for example, the experience of the social world. The technique of phenomenology involves 'bracketing off' the assumptions one holds about the phenomenon being investigated, and striving to describe it in as comprehensive and sensitive a manner as possible. The act of 'bracketing off' or 'suspending' assumptions is carried out to ensure that, as far as possible, the phenomenological researcher (or therapist) does not impose his or her theoretical assumptions on experience on to the phenomena (events, process, experiences) that are the object of inquiry.

The adoption of a phenomenological stance has a number of implications. It yields concepts that are 'experience-near', that serve to capture the directly lived feel of what happens, rather than being abstract and distanced from experience. It places emphasis on rich, detailed descriptions, that capture all facets of a phenomenon (including how it changes), rather than seeking to use broad 'labels'. Finally, a phenomenological stance regards meaning as being actively constructed through the intentionality of the knower – there is no assumption that there can be one fixed, 'objective' reality that is the same for everyone. Although Rogers, and other researchers within the person-centred tradition, carried out research studies that aimed to define and measure key concepts within person-centred theory, such as empathy, congruence, self-concept and experiential processing, the instruments (e.g., questionnaires) used in these studies were always based on descriptions of how people actually experienced these constructs.

The phenomenological stance is important because the concept of *experiencing* is absolutely central to the person-centred approach – the person is viewed as responding to the world on the basis of his or her flow of moment-by-moment experiencing. The concept of experience can be defined as an amalgam of bodily sensed thoughts, feelings and action tendencies, which is continually changing. The person-centred approach therefore positions itself differently from cognitive–behavioural therapy, which makes a firm distinction between cognition and emotion, and psychodynamic theory, which makes a firm distinction between conscious and unconscious. Within the person-centred approach, cognition and emotion, and conscious/unconscious material, are always interwoven within the 'phenomenal field' (i.e., the flow of experiencing) of the person.

The person, in the person-centred approach, is viewed as acting to fulfil two primary needs. The first is the need for self-actualization. The second is the need to be loved and valued by others. Both these needs are, following Maslow (1943), seen as being independent of biological survival needs. However, the person is very much seen as an embodied being, through the concept of 'organismic valuing' (i.e., the person has an inner 'gut' sense of what is right or wrong for them).

The idea of the 'self-concept' has a central place in person-centred theory. The self-concept of the person is understood as those attributes or areas of experiencing about which the person can say 'I am . . .' For example, a client in counselling may define himself or herself in terms such as 'I am strong, I can be angry, I sometimes feel vulnerable'. For this person, strength, anger and vulnerability are parts of a self-concept, and when he or she feels vulnerable, or angry, there will usually be a *congruence* between feelings and resulting words and actions. But if this person does not define himself or herself as 'nurturing', and is in a situation where a feeling of care or nurturance is evoked, he or she will not be able to put that inner sense or feeling accurately into words, and will express the feeling or impulse in a distorted or inappropriate way. Someone who is not supposed to be nurturing may, for instance, become very busy 'doing things' for someone who needs no more than companionship, comforting or a human touch. Where there is a disjunction between feelings and the capacity for accurate awareness and symbolization of these feelings, a state of *incongruence* is said to exist. Incongruence is the very broad term used to describe the whole range of problems that clients bring to counselling.

Why does incongruence happen? Rogers argued that, in childhood, there is a strong need to be loved or valued, particularly by parents and significant others. However, the love or approval that parents offer can be conditional or unconditional. In areas of unconditional approval, the child is free to express his or her potential and accept inner feelings. Where the love or acceptance is conditional on behaving only in a certain way, and is withdrawn when other behaviour or tendencies are exhibited, the child learns to define himself or herself in accordance with parental values. Rogers used the phrase *conditions of worth* to describe the way in which the self-concept of the child is shaped by parental influence. In the example above, the person would have been praised or accepted for being 'useful', but rejected or scorned for being 'affectionate' or 'soft'. Incongruence, therefore, results from gaps and distortions in the self-concept caused by exposure to conditions of worth.

Another idea that is linked to the understanding of how the self-concept operates is the notion of *locus of evaluation.*. Rogers observed that, in the process of making judgements or evaluations about issues, people could be guided by externally defined sets of beliefs and attitudes, or could make use of their own internal feelings on the matter, their *organismic valuing process*. An over-reliance on external evaluations is equivalent to continued exposure to conditions of worth, and person-centred counselling encourages people to accept and act on their own personal, internal evaluations. Rogers had a positive and optimistic view of humanity, and believed that an authentic, self-aware person would make decisions based on an internal locus of evaluation that would be valid not only for himself or herself, but for others too. Although it is perhaps not explicitly articulated in his writings, his underlying assumption was that each person carried a universal morality, and would have a bodily sense of what was right or wrong in any situation.

It is perhaps worth noting that the simple phrase 'conditions of worth' encompasses the entirety of the person-centred model of child development. The person-centred counsellor does not possess a model of developmental stages into which to fit the experience of the client. The simple idea of conditions of worth merely points the counsellor in the direction of anticipating that some unresolved childhood process may be around for the client. The task is not to go looking for these childhood episodes, but to allow the client to pursue an understanding of them if he or she chooses to do so. Also of interest is the fact that childhood experiences are seen as leaving an enduring influence in the form of internalized values and self-concepts. This is clearly different from the psychodynamic idea that people grow up with internalized images of the actual people who were formative in childhood, usually the mother and father (see Chapter 4).

The person-centred theory of the self-concept suggests that the person possesses not only a concept or definition of self 'as I am now', but also a sense of self 'as I would ideally like to be'. The 'ideal self' represents another aspect of the consistent theme in Rogers' work concerning the human capacity to strive for fulfilment and greater integration. One of the aims of person-centred therapy is to enable the person to move in the direction of his or her self-defined ideals.

One of the distinctive features of the person-centred image of the person is its attempt to describe the *fully functioning* person. The idea of the 'actualized' or fully functioning individual represents an important strand in the attempt by humanistic psychologists to construct an alternative to psychoanalysis. Freud, reflecting his background in medicine and psychiatry, created a theory that was oriented towards understanding and explaining pathology or 'illness'. Rogers, Maslow and the 'third force' regarded creativity, joyfulness and spirituality as intrinsic human qualities, and sought to include these characteristics within the ambit of their theorizing. The main features of the fully functioning person were described by Rogers (1963: 22) in the following terms:

> he is able to experience all of his feelings, and is afraid of none of his feelings. He is his own sifter of evidence, but is open to evidence from all sources; he is completely engaged in the process of being and becoming himself, and thus discovers that he is soundly and realistically social; he lives completely in this moment, but learns that this is the soundest living for all time. He is a fully functioning organism, and because of the awareness of himself which flows freely in and through his experiences, he is a fully functioning person.

The person envisioned here is someone who is congruent, and is able to accept and use feelings to guide action. The person is also autonomous rather than dependent on others: 'the values of being and becoming himself'.

One of the difficulties involved in grasping the person-centred image of the person is that textbook versions of what is meant are inevitably incomplete. This is an area of counselling theory where the gap between the lived, oral tradition and the written account is particularly apparent. For Rogers, the actualizing tendency or formative tendency is central, the person is always in process, always becoming, ever-changing. The task for psychological theory was not to explain change, but to understand what was happening to arrest change and development. The idea of 'becoming a person' captures this notion. From a person-centred perspective, any conceptualization of the person that portrays a static, fixed entity is inadequate. The aim is always to construct a process conceptualization. In this respect, it could well be argued that some of the earlier elements in the theory, such as the idea of the self-concept, place too much emphasis on static structures. It would be more consistent to talk about a 'self-process'. The image of the fully functioning person can similarly give an impression that this is an enduring structure that can be permanently attained, rather than part of a process that can include phases of incongruence and despair. The process orientation of the model is also expressed through the absence of any ideas about personality traits or types, and the strong opposition in person-centred practitioners to any attempts to label or diagnose clients.

The significance of the image of the person employed by this approach is underlined by the fact that this orientation attaches relatively little importance to the technical expertise of the counsellor, and concentrates primarily on the attitude or philosophy of the counsellor and the quality of the therapeutic relationship (Combs 1989). For example, the key introductory textbook of person-centred theory and practice, written by Mearns and Thorne (2013) places great emphasis on the personal challenge for the counsellor of offering the core conditions, and the 'work on self' that is necessary in order to be able to achieve a person-centred relationship on a consistent basis.

Key aspects of the person-centred theory of therapy are discussed in more detail in the following sections.

The therapeutic relationship

Person-centred counselling is a relationship therapy. People with emotional 'problems in living' have been involved in relationships in which their experiencing was denied, defined or discounted by others. What is healing is to be in a relationship in which the self is fully accepted and valued. The characteristics of a relationship that would have this effect were summarized by Rogers (1957: 95) in his formulation of the 'necessary and sufficient conditions of therapeutic personality change', which postulates that:

> For constructive personality change to occur, it is necessary that these conditions exist and continue over a period of time:
>
> 1 Two persons are in psychological contact.
>
> 2 The first, whom we shall term the client, is in a state of incongruence, being vulnerable and anxious.
>
> 3 The second person, whom we shall term the therapist, is congruent or integrated in the relationship.
>
> 4 The therapist experiences unconditional positive regard for the client.
>
> 5 The therapist experiences an empathic understanding of the client's internal frame of reference, and endeavours to communicate this to the client.
>
> 6 The communication to the client of the therapist's empathic understanding and unconditional positive regard is to a minimal extent achieved.
>
> No other conditions are necessary. If these six conditions exist, and continue over a period of time, this is sufficient. The process of constructive personality change will follow.

This formulation of the therapeutic relationship has subsequently become known as the 'core conditions' model. It specifies the characteristics of an interpersonal environment that will facilitate actualization and growth.

The three ingredients of the therapeutic relationship that have tended to receive most attention in person-centred training and research are the counsellor qualities of acceptance, empathy and genuineness. In the statement above, the term 'unconditional positive regard' is used, rather than the everyday idea of 'acceptance'.

The core conditions model represented an attempt by Rogers to capture the essence of his approach to clients. It also represented a bold challenge to other therapists and schools of thought, in claiming that these conditions were not just important or useful, but sufficient in themselves. The view that no other therapeutic ingredients were necessary invited a head-on confrontation with psychoanalysts, for example, who would regard interpretation as necessary, or behaviourists, who would see techniques for inducing behaviour change as central. The model stimulated a substantial amount of research, which has broadly supported the position taken by Rogers (Patterson 1984). However, many contemporary counsellors and therapists would regard the 'core conditions' as components of what has become known as the 'therapeutic alliance' (Bordin 1979) between counsellor and client.

Box 7.2: *Pre-therapy: a method of making contact with individuals who find relationships difficult*

The theory of 'necessary and sufficient conditions' proposed by Rogers (1957) has generally been interpreted as highlighting the importance of empathy, congruence and unconditional positive regard as basic ingredients of a productive therapeutic relationship. Less attention has been given to the opening statement in Rogers' model: 'two persons are in psychological contact'. In a great many counselling situations, it may be reasonable to take for granted the existence of a sufficient degree of basic psychological connectedness. No matter how anxious or depressed a person is, usually he or she will retain some capacity to take account of the psychological reality represented by whoever else is in their immediate proximity, whether this be a counsellor or someone else. However, there are some people for whom basic contact with another human being is hugely problematic. These may be people who have been damaged by life experiences, who are profoundly anxious, institutionalized or sedated, or who suffer from cognitive impairment. Persons regarded as schizophrenic or learning disabled may fall into this category. Few attempts have been made to provide counselling to clients from these groups. Within the person-centred approach, the pioneering work carried out at the University of Wisconsin by Rogers and his colleagues into the process of counselling with hospitalized schizophrenic patients (Rogers *et al.* 1967) has been continued in the form of the approach to pre-therapy developed by Garry Prouty (1976, 1990; Prouty and Kubiak 1988; Prouty *et al.* 2002). Rogers (1968: 188) wrote that the Wisconsin project taught him that 'schizophrenic individuals tend to fend off relationships either by an almost complete silence . . . or by a flood of overtalk which is equally effective in preventing a real encounter'. Prouty has designed ways of counteracting that degree of 'fending-off' by reflecting back to the client, in very simple ways, the counsellor's awareness of the client's external world, self and feelings, and communication with others. The aim is to restore the client's capacity to be in psychological contact, and as a result to enable them to enter conventional therapy. Two examples from van Werde (1994: 123–4) illustrate how this technique functions in practice:

> Christiane walks into the nurses' office, stands still, and stares straight ahead. She is obviously in a kind of closed, locked-up position, but nevertheless she has come to the office or to the nurses. Instead of immediately telling her to go back to her room or pedagogically instructing her first to knock at the door and then come in, one of the nurses empathically reflects what is happening: 'You are standing in the office. You look in the direction of the window. You are staring'. These reflections seem to enable Christiane to contact her feelings and free herself from whatever had been on her mind in a way that she could not master. She now says: 'I am afraid that my mother is going to die!' Then she turns herself around and walks toward the living room. The semi-psychotic mood is processed and she is once again in control of herself.
>
> [At] the twice-weekly patient-staff meeting . . . approximately twenty people are sitting in a large circle. Suddenly a patient, Thierry, comes in with

a Bible in his hand, walks straight up to me, shows me a page and says 'I can make the words change'. I make eye contact, also point at the Bible and reflect 'I can make the words change. Thierry, we are sitting in a circle. You're standing up next to me and are showing me the Bible'. Reflecting all this enables Thierry to realise that he is doing something odd, given the context of the situation, and he is able to anchor himself back into the shared reality by taking a chair and sitting quietly at the edge of the circle.

Although pre-therapy has been used mainly in work with severely damaged individuals, it is equally applicable during moments when more fully functioning individuals withdraw from the relationship. Pre-therapy draws on core person-centred principles of respect, acceptance, willingness to enter the frame of reference of the other and belief in a process of actualization. Further sources of information on pre-therapy include Peters (1999, 2005) and Sanders (2006).

In the person-centred approach there is considerable debate over the accuracy and comprehensiveness of the necessary and sufficient conditions model. For example, Rogers (1961: Chapter 3) himself described a much longer list of characteristics of a helping relationship:

- Can I be in some way which will be perceived by the other person as trustworthy, as dependable or consistent in some deep sense?
- Can I be expressive enough as a person that what I am will be communicated unambiguously?
- Can I let myself experience positive attitudes towards this other person – attitudes of warmth, caring, liking, interest, respect?
- Can I be strong enough as a person to be separate from the other?
- Am I secure enough within myself to permit his or her separateness?
- Can I let myself enter fully into the world of his or her feelings and personal meanings and see these as he or she does?
- Can I accept each facet of this other person when he or she presents it to me?
- Can I act with sufficient sensitivity in the relationship that my behaviour will not be perceived as a threat?
- Can I free the other from the threat of external evaluation?
- Can I meet this other individual as a person who is in the process of becoming, or will I be bound by his past and by my past?

This list includes the qualities of empathy, congruence and acceptance, but also mentions other important helper characteristics, such as consistency, boundary awareness, interpersonal sensitivity and present-centredness. Later, Rogers was also to suggest that therapist 'presence' was an essential factor (Rogers 1980), and Thorne (1991) has argued that 'tenderness' should be considered a core condition. These modifications of the model may be seen as attempts to articulate more clearly what is meant, or to find fresh ways of articulating the notion of a uniquely 'personal' relationship (van Balen 1990), but do not change the basic relational framework outlined by the 'core conditions' model, which has remained the cornerstone of person-centred practice (Mearns and Thorne 2013).

Box 7.3: *The enduring influence of Carl Rogers*

In recent years, the fifth anniversaries of various key publications of Carl Rogers has stimulated the counselling and psychotherapy profession to engage in a reappraisal of the continued influence and relevance of his ideas, with major review articles on the general legacy of Rogers, by Hill and Nakayama (2000) and Orlinsky and Ronnestad (2000), and a cluster of papers revisiting the significance of the Rogers (1957) 'necessary and sufficient conditions' paper (Brown 2007; Elliott and Freire 2007; Farber 2007; Goldfried 2007; Hill 2007; Lazarus 2007; Mahrer 2007; Samstag 2007; Silberschatz 2007, Wachtel 2007; Watson 2007). On the whole, these commentaries confirm the continuing relevance of client-centred ideas and methods. The only contemporary theorist who argues that Rogers got it *wrong* is Mahrer (2007). The feminist psychotherapist, Laura Brown (2007: 258) reflects a general theme in contemporary perspectives on client-centred theory in observing that 'much of what Rogers proposed 50 years ago remains true today'. Orlinsky and Ronnestad (2000) document the extent to which the currently highly influential concept of the 'working alliance' owes to the original formulation by Rogers of the characteristics of the facilitative relationship. On the other hand, the majority of these commentators also argue that there are significant factors that are missing in Rogers' writings, for instance an appreciation of the different requirements of clients with different preferred modes of feeling and problem-solving (Lazarus 2007; Silberschatz 2007), and an appreciation of the realities of social power and control (Brown 2007). It is striking that the critiques of Rogers' ideas that are put forward in the early years of the twenty-first century are broadly similar to the critiques that were published in the 1940s (see Hill and Nakayama 2000).

Empathy

The importance attributed to empathic responding has been one of the distinguishing features of the person-centred approach to counselling. It is considered that, for the client, the experience of being 'heard' or understood leads to a greater capacity to explore and accept previously denied aspects of self. However, there were a number of difficulties apparent in the conception of empathy contained within the 'core conditions' model. When researchers attempted to measure the levels of empathic responding exhibited by counsellors, they found that ratings carried out from different points of view produced different patterns of results. A specific counsellor statement to a client would be rated differently by the client, the counsellor and an external observer (Kurtz and Grummon 1972). It was difficult to get raters to differentiate accurately between empathy, congruence and acceptance: these three qualities all appeared to be of a piece in the eyes of research assistants rating therapy tapes. Finally, there were philosophical difficulties arising from alternative interpretations of the concept. Rogers characterized empathy as a 'state of being'. Truax and Carkhuff defined empathy as a communication skill, which could be modelled and learned in a structured training programme.

Box 7.4: *How did Carl Rogers do therapy?*

One of the significant contributions made by Carl Rogers and his colleagues was to initiate the practice of taping counselling sessions, so that they could later be used for purposes of research and teaching. An important by-product of this policy is that there exist several tapes of Carl Rogers doing therapy. These tapes are an invaluable archive, which has been widely used by scholars and researchers interested in the nature of person-centred counselling and psychotherapy. Farber *et al.* (1996) have compiled a book in which ten of Rogers' cases are presented, alongside commentary from both person-centred practitioners and representatives of other schools of therapy. Brink and Farber (1996), offer an analysis of the different kinds of responses that Rogers made to the clients in these cases.

These are as follows.

Providing orientation. Rogers tended to start sessions by giving himself and the client an opportunity to orient themselves to the task. For example, Rogers started one counselling session by saying, 'Now, if you can get your chair settled . . . I need to take a minute or two to kind of get with myself somehow, okay? . . . Then let's just be quiet for a minute or two. [Pause] Do you feel ready?'

Affirming attention. Rogers frequently let his client know that he was present and listening, by leaning towards the client, saying 'm-hm, m-hm' or nodding affirmatively.

Checking understanding. Often Rogers would check whether he had correctly understood the meaning of what the client was saying.

Restating. Sometimes Rogers' words seemed directly to mirror what the client had said. On other occasions, a restatement would take the form of a short statement that clarified the core of what the client was expressing, as in the example below.

Client:	And I allow myself to, and I don't regret caring, and I don't regret loving or whatever, but you know, like, I'm like a kid, you know, I'm a kid in a way, I like to be loved too, some reciprocity. And I'm going to start, I think, expecting that, you know, without being cold or anything like that. But I have to, you know, start getting something back in return.
Carl Rogers:	You want love to be mutual.
Client:	For sure, for sure.

There would be times when Rogers would phrase a restatement in the first person, as if speaking as the client.

Acknowledging clients' unstated feelings. This response involved making reference to feelings that were expressed in either non-verbal behaviour or voice quality, but were not explicitly verbalized by the client.

Providing reassurance. In the widely known Gloria case, there are several moments of reassurance. For example:

Gloria: I don't get that as often as I like . . . I like that whole feeling, that's real precious to me.

Carl Rogers: I suspect none of us get it as often as we'd like.

There were times, too, when Rogers would convey reassurance by touching a client, or responding to a request to hold the client's hand.

Interpreting. On rare occasions Rogers made interpretations, defined as venturing beyond the information being immediately offered by the client.

Confronting. Sometimes Rogers would confront clients who appeared to be avoiding a difficult or painful issue.

Direct questioning. An example of this response was made to a client who had mentioned feeling different. Rogers invited further exploration of the topic by asking her: 'and what are some of those differences?'

Turning pleas for help back to the client. When a client asked for guidance or answers, Rogers would often turn the request back to the person. For example:

Gloria: I really know you can't answer for me – but I want you to guide me or show me where to start or so it won't look so hopeless . . .

Carl Rogers: I might ask, what is it you wish I could say to you?

Maintaining and breaking silences. In some sessions Rogers could be seen to allow silences to continue (in one instance for as long as 17 minutes!). On other occasions he appeared to be willing to interrupt a silence.

Self-disclosing. For example, with one client Rogers stated: 'I don't know whether this will help or not, but I would just like to say that – I think I can understand pretty well – what it's like to feel that you're just no damned good to anyone, because there was a time when – I felt that way about myself. And I know it can be really tough'.

Accepting correction. When a client indicated that one of Rogers' responses was not accurate, he would accept the correction, try again to get it right and then move on.

Brink and Farber (1996) do not claim that this list of responses represents an exhaustive or comprehensive analysis of all of the therapeutic strategies or techniques used by Rogers. They do suggest, however, that the list illustrates some of the different forms through which the facilitative conditions of empathy, congruence and acceptance can be expressed within a relationship. They also observe that Rogers behaved differently with different clients. He was able to adapt his style to the needs and communication styles of specific clients. Finally, it is clear that the Brink and Farber taxonomy includes responses that are not strictly consistent with person-centred therapy, notably reassurance and interpretation. The lesson here is that perhaps it is more important to be human than it is to adhere rigorously to the dictates of a theoretical model.

Many of these issues associated with the concept of empathy are addressed in the 'empathy cycle' model proposed by Barrett-Lennard (1981):

Step 1: *Empathic set by counsellor*. Client is actively expressing some aspect of his or her experiencing. Counsellor is actively attending and receptive.

Step 2: *Empathic resonation*. The counsellor resonates to the directly or indirectly expressed aspects of the client's experiencing.

Step 3: *Expressed empathy*. The counsellor expresses or communicates his or her felt awareness of the client's experiencing.

Step 4: *Received empathy*. The client is attending to the counsellor sufficiently to form a sense or perception of the counsellor's immediate personal understanding.

Step 5: *The empathy cycle continues*. The client then continues or resumes self-expression in a way that provides feedback to the counsellor concerning the accuracy of the empathic response and the quality of the therapeutic relationship.

In this model, empathy is viewed as a process that involves intentional, purposeful activity on the part of the counsellor. It can be seen that the perceptions of different observers reflect their tendency to be aware of what is happening at particular steps in the process rather than others. The counsellor will consider himself or herself to be in good empathic contact with the client if he or she is 'set' and 'resonating' in response to what the client has expressed (Steps 1 and 2). An external observer will be most aware of the actual behaviour of the counsellor (expressed empathy – Step 3). The client, on the other hand, will be most influenced by the experience of 'received' empathy (Step 4). The Barrett-Lennard (1981) model also makes sense of the definition of empathy as communication skill or way of being. In so far as the counsellor needs to be able to receive and resonate to the expressed feelings of the client, empathy is like a state of being. But in so far as this understanding must be offered back to the client, it is also a communication skill.

The empathy cycle raises the question of the interconnectedness of the core conditions. The Barrett-Lennard model describes a process that includes non-judgemental openness to and acceptance of whatever the client has to offer. It also describes a process in the counsellor of being congruently aware of his or her inner feelings, and using these in the counselling relationship. In the flow of the work with the client the effective person-centred counsellor is not making use of separate skills, but is instead offering the client a wholly personal involvement in the relationship between them. There is a sense of mutuality, or an 'I–thou' relationship described by Buber (van Balen 1990). Bozarth (1984) has written that, at these points in counselling, an empathic response to a client may bear little resemblance to the wooden 'reflection of meaning' statements much favoured in the early years of client-centred therapy. For Bozarth (1984), the ideal is to respond empathically in a manner that is 'idiosyncratic' and spontaneous.

Another important development in relation to empathy has been to examine the impact of an accurate, well timed and sensitive empathic response. Barrett-Lennard (1993: 6) observes that:

> the experience of being literally heard and understood deeply, in some personally vital sphere, has its own kind of impact – whether of relief, of

> something at last making sense, a feeling or inner connection or somehow
> being less alone, or of some other easing or enhancing quality.

Vanaerschot (1990, 1993) has examined the therapeutic 'micro-processes' released by effective empathic responses. These include: feeling valued and accepted; feeling confirmed in one's own identity as an autonomous, valuable person; learning to accept feelings; reduction in alienation ('I am not abnormal, different and strange'); learning to trust and get in touch with one's own experiencing; cognitive restructuring of chaotic experiencing; and facilitating recall and organization of information.

Finally, there has been some intriguing research into the way that the counsellor or psychotherapist formulates an empathic communication. Bohart *et al.* (1993) carried out a study that suggests that it can be helpful to employ empathic reflections that are future-oriented in meaning, that link current concerns with future directions and intentions.

These recent contributions to the person-centred theory of empathy have moved the emphasis away from a definition of empathy as a trainable skill, and back towards a wider meaning of empathy, understood as a component of an authentic commitment to be engaged in the world of the other. This notion implies more of a unity of the 'core condi-tions', and is to some extent a return to the very earliest formulation of the principles of client-centred therapy. Before Rogers and his colleagues began to use terms like empathy, congruence and unconditional regard, they described the approach as an attitude or philos-ophy of 'deep respect for the significance and worth of each person' (Rogers 1951: 21).

Congruence and presence

In practice, possibly the single most distinctive aspect of the person-centred approach to counselling lies in the emphasis that is placed on congruence. The influence of Rogers' ideas has meant that versions of such classic person-centred notions of empathy, self, therapeutic relationship and experiencing have entered the vocabularies of other approaches. However, no other approach gives as much importance to the realness, authenticity and willingness to be known of the counsellor as do person-centred therapy and other contemporary humanistic therapies. In the early years of client-centred therapy, Rogers and his colleagues based their way of doing counselling on principles of non-directiveness, respect for the internal frame of reference and locus of evaluation of the client, and acceptance of self. It was largely as a result of the Wisconsin project, during which Rogers, Shlien, Gendlin and their colleagues struggled to find ways of communi-cating with deeply withdrawn schizophrenic inpatients, that it became apparent that the therapist's contribution to the process, his or her ability to use self in the service of the relationship, was crucial to the success of therapy (see Gendlin 1967). Perhaps because of his own training and professional socialization, the concept of congruence only really entered Rogers' language in the late 1950s, and tended, at least initially, to be explained in a somewhat technical manner (Rogers 1961). Lietaer (1993, 2001) gives an excellent account of the evolution of the concept of congruence in Rogers' writings. Congruence was believed by Rogers (1961: 61) to occur when:

> the feelings the therapist is experiencing are available to him, to his aware-
> ness, and he is able to live these feelings, be them, and to communicate them

if appropriate. No one fully achieves this condition, yet the more the therapist is able to listen acceptantly to what is going on within himself, and the more he is able to be the complexity of his feelings, without fear, the higher the degree of his congruence.

Mearns and Thorne (2007: 75) defined congruence as 'the state of being of the counsellor when her outward responses to the client consistently match the inner feelings and sensations which she has in relation to the client'. Gendlin (1967: 120–1) describes congruence as a process that requires a deliberate act of attention on the part of the counsellor:

> At every moment there occur a great many feelings and events in the therapist. Most of these concern the client and the present moment. The therapist need not wait passively till the client expresses something intimate or therapeutically relevant. Instead, he can draw upon his own momentary experiencing and find there an ever present reservoir from which he can draw, and with which he can initiate, deepen and carry on therapeutic interaction even with an unmotivated, silent or externalised person . . . to respond truly from within me I must, of course, pay some attention to what is going on within me . . . require a few steps of self-attention, a few moments in which I attend to what I feel.

The research carried out by Barrett-Lennard (1986) led to an appreciation of the counsellor's *willingness to be known* as an important element of congruence. All of these writers emphasize, in their different ways, the idea that congruence is not a skill to be deployed ('I used a lot of congruence in that session . . .') but is something that is much more central to the therapeutic endeavour – a basic value or attitude, or a 'way of being'. The various strands of thinking around the concept of congruence, within the person-centred approach, are represented in Wyatt (2001).

Why is congruence therapeutic? In what ways is it helpful for clients to work with a counsellor who is congruent, genuine and willing to be known? Counsellor congruence can have a number of valuable effects on therapy:

- it helps to develop trust in the relationship;
- if the counsellor expresses and accepts his or her own feelings of vulnerability and uncertainty, then it becomes easier for the client to accept their own;
- it models one of the intended outcomes of therapy (straightforward, honest relating to others);
- if cues from speech, tone and gesture are unified or consistent, then communication is clearer and more understandable;
- the counsellor is able to draw upon unsaid or 'subvocal' (Gendlin 1967) elements in the relationship;
- it can facilitate the positive flow of energy in the relationship;
- it helps to develop trust in the relationship;
- if the counsellor expresses and accepts his or her own feelings of vulnerability and uncertainty, then it becomes easier for the client to accept their own;

- it models one of the intended outcomes of therapy (straightforward, honest relating to others);
- if cues from speech, tone and gesture are unified or consistent, then communication is clearer and more understandable;
- the counsellor is able to draw upon unsaid or 'subvocal' (Gendlin 1967) elements in the relationship;
- it can facilitate the positive flow of energy in the relationship.

By contrast, if a counsellor is consistently incongruent, the client is likely to become confused, and lack confidence in the counselling relationship as a safe place within which he or she might explore painful or shameful experiences. On the whole, clients seek counselling because the other people in their life have responded to their 'problems in living' in a silencing, judgemental manner. An important factor in the possibility of counselling making a difference is the client's belief that their counsellor is really listening, and really accepts them as a person, and that there is no hidden condemnation waiting to be unleashed. If a counsellor appears to be open and genuine, but then tenses up or seems preoccupied whenever the counsellor touches on a sensitive subject, without offering any explanation, then the chances are that the client will learn that this subject is 'out of bounds' for the counsellor, and not to be broached.

In recent years, there has been an increasing recognition within the person-centred approach that the concept of congruence offers an over-individualized means of understanding what is a key dimension of their practice. Essentially, Rogers' idea of congruence was grounded in the extent to which inner experiences (feelings, emotions, impulses and images) were either available to the person's awareness (i.e., not suppressed or repressed) or could be expressed verbally. Useful though this formulation has been, many therapists believe that it does not take sufficient account of the interpersonal, relational quality of what can take place during significant moments in therapy. Towards the end of his career, Rogers himself opened up the possibility of a more holistic understanding of congruence when he wrote that:

> when I am at my best, as a group facilitator or as a therapist, I discover another characteristic. I find that when I am closest to my inner, intuitive self, when I am somehow in touch with the unknown in me, when perhaps I am in a slightly altered state of consciousness, then whatever I do seems to be full of healing. Then, simply my *presence* is releasing and helpful to the other.
>
> Rogers (1980: 129, emphasis added)

Mearns (1994, 1996) has elaborated this sense of being 'at my best' in terms of the presence of the counsellor. Mearns (1996: 307) quotes from reports written by clients:

> it felt as though she was right inside me – feeling me in the same moment that I was feeling myself.

> the space she created for me was huge. It made me realise how little space I usually felt in other relationships.

Mearns (1996: 309) observes that this degree of presence is risky for counsellors: 'it is one thing to have my surface relational competencies judged, but can I risk my congruent self being judged?' He compares the congruent person-centred counsellor to a 'method' actor who projects or immerses himself or herself fully in their role. In research into client and counsellor experiences during moments of congruence and incongruence, Grafanaki and McLeod (1999, 2002) were able to identify times when both participants were engaged in a process of mutual flow, and fully present to each other. Greenberg and Geller (2001) interviewed therapists (from a range of theoretical orientations) about their experience of presence, and found that presence was typically described as comprising a series of stages.

First, these therapists were consciously committed to the practice of presence in their everyday lives and relationships. Second, within a counselling session the therapist allows herself to 'respond to whatever presents itself in the moment' (Greenberg and Geller 2001: 144). Third, the therapist then allows herself to meet, and remain engaged with, the client. Schneider (1998: 111), an existential psychotherapist, has argued that 'presence is the *sina qua non* of experiential liberation. It is the beginning and the end of the approach, and it is implicated in every one of its aspects . . . presence is palpable . . . it is a potent sign that one is "here" for the other'.

The central emphasis placed on congruence and presence by person-centred practitioners is reflected in the types of training and supervision that have evolved within this approach. For example, person-centred training typically involves substantial periods working within large groups. The large experiential group offers an environment in which most people find it difficult to be congruent, present and empathic, and in which there are plentiful opportunities for other group members to identify and feed back their perceptions of incongruent and avoidance patterns of behaviour that they witness in each other. The emphasis on congruence and presence also underscores the basic assumption of person-centred counselling, that it is within moments of authentic encounter between client and therapist that the most meaningful and significant learning takes place.

Box 7.5: *The debate over non-directiveness*

In his early writings, Carl Rogers used the term 'non-directive' to describe his new approach to therapy. However, this idea was soon regarded by Rogers and his colleagues as contributing to potential misunderstanding of their practice, in so far as it defined their method as an 'absence' (rather than emphasizing what it was striving to achieve), and because the concept of non-directiveness tended to trigger unhelpful debates around the impossibility of being with another person without influencing them. For many years, therefore, the concept of non-directiveness was employed only by those who wished to discount the client-centred/person-centred approach as a potent form of therapy (the concept is hardly mentioned in the core person-centred text of Mearns and Thorne 2007). In 1999, Edwin Kahn published a paper in the *Journal of Humanistic Psychology,* titled 'A critique of nondirectivity'. In this article he agreed that the principle of non-directivity was central to good practice, but argued that it was impossible for any practitioner to be consistently nondirective, because of 'unavoidable subjective biases in the therapist' (Kahn 1999: 95), and suggested that the spirit of the person-centred tradition called for a willingness to be flexible and to work in whatever way was most helpful for any specific client. Kahn offered examples of his own use of *empathic interpretation* to illustrate one of the forms that person-centred directivity might take, and concluded that it might be more appropriate to think in terms of a non-directive *attitude* as opposed to non-directiveness as a pattern of behaviour.

Kahn's (1999) paper triggered some strong responses from the person-centred community (Bozarth 2002; Merry and Brodely 2002; Sommerbeck 2002), vigorously re-asserting the primacy of non-directivity in person-centred theory and practice, and claiming that Kahn misunderstood what the person-centred approach was all about. This debate has continued, in the form of an edited collection of further papers (Levitt 2005). What is this debate about? And why has it taken place some 50 years after Rogers stopped using the concept? It may be relevant to consider the cultural context of counselling and psychotherapy at the turn of the century, as a contributory factor to the debate. This is a time when there is a global emphasis on brief therapy, the use of evidence-based interventions, and an explosion in the use of didactic methods such as self-help manuals and online packages. The common themes across all of these trends is that each of them represents a direct threat to the kind of rigorously *person*-centred work that Rogers had devised. Perhaps the debate around Kahn's (1999) article is less to do with practice (he is probably describing the kinds of things that most person-centred counsellors do, at least some of the time) than to do with the core values that underpin the sense of identity of the person-centred network.

The therapeutic process

From a person-centred perspective, the process of therapeutic change in the client is described in terms of a process of greater openness to experience. Rogers (1951) characterized the direction of therapeutic growth as including increasing awareness of denied experience, movement from perceiving the world in generalizations to being able to see things in a more differentiated manner and greater reliance on personal experience as a source of values and standards. Eventually, these developments lead to changes in behaviour, but the 'reorganization of the self' (Rogers 1951) is seen as a necessary precursor to any new behaviour.

Rogers (1961) conceptualized the process of counselling as a series of stages, and his model formed the basis for subsequent work by Gendlin (1974) and Klein *et al.* (1986) and the concept of 'depth of experiencing'. In successful counselling the client will become able to process information about self and experiencing at greater levels of depth and intensity. The seven stages of increasing client involvement in his or her inner world (Rogers 1961; Klein *et al.* 1986) are summarized as follows:

1 Communication is about external events. Feelings and personal meanings are not 'owned'. Close relationships are construed as dangerous. Rigidity in thinking. Impersonal, detached. Does not use first-person pronouns.

2 Expression begins to flow more freely in respect of non-self topics. Feelings may be described but not owned. Intellectualization. Describes behaviour rather than inner feelings. May show more interest and participation in therapy.

3 Describes personal reactions to external events. Limited amount of self-description. Communication about past feelings. Beginning to recognize contradictions in experience.

4 Descriptions of feelings and personal experiences. Beginning to experience current feelings, but fear and distrust of this when it happens. The 'inner life' is presented and listed or described, but not purposefully explored.

5 Present feelings are expressed. Increasing ownership of feelings. More exactness in the differentiation of feelings and meanings. Intentional exploration of problems in a personal way, based in processing of feelings rather than reasoning.

6 Sense of an 'inner referent', or flow of feeling that has a life of its own. 'Physiological loosening', such as moistness in the eyes, tears, sighs or muscular relaxation, accompanies the open expression of feelings. Speaks in present tense or offers vivid representation of past.

7 A series of felt senses connecting the different aspects of an issue. Basic trust in own inner processes. Feelings experienced with immediacy and richness of detail. Speaks fluently in present tense.

Research using this seven-stage model has shown that clients who begin therapy at Stage 1 are less likely to be able to benefit from the process. Mearns and Thorne (1988) have commented on the importance of the 'readiness' of the client to embark on this type of self-exploration. Rogers (1961) also comments that the changes associated with Stage 6 appear to be irreversible, so the client may be able to move into Stage 7 without the help of the counsellor.

The process in the client is facilitated by the empathy, congruence and acceptance of the counsellor. For example, sensitive empathic listening on the part of the counsellor enables him or her to reflect back to the client personal feelings and meanings implicit in Stage 1 statements. The acceptance and genuineness of the counsellor encourages the growth of trust in the client, and increased risk-taking regarding the expression of thoughts and feelings that would previously have been censored or suppressed. Then, as this more frightening material is exposed, the fact that the counsellor is able to accept emotions that had been long buried and denied helps the client to accept them in turn. The willingness of the counsellor to accept the existence of contradictions in the way the client experiences the world gives the client permission to accept himself or herself as both hostile and warm, or needy and powerful, and thus to move towards a more differentiated, more complex sense of self.

This process is also influenced by the growing capacity of the client to operate from a sense of their own value as a person, to employ an internal locus of evaluation. Mearns (1994) has argued that at the beginning of therapy it is likely that a client will interact with others from a perspective of an external locus of evaluation. He or she will be looking for guidance and advice from others: they know best. At this stage, the counsellor needs to be rigorous in following the client, maintaining a disciplined empathic and accepting focus on the client's frame of reference. Later, however, when the client becomes stronger in his or her locus of evaluation, becomes more internal and integrated with self, it is possible for the counsellor to be more congruent, to take risks in using his or her own experience in the counselling room. Thus it can be seen that the 'core conditions' are not static, but are expressed in response to who the client is, and their stage of the process of change.

Experiential focusing

An important framework that is widely employed in the person-centred approach as a means of understanding process is Gendlin's model of experiential focusing, which represents perhaps the single most influential development in person-centred theory and practice in the post-Wisconsin era (Lietaer 1990). The technique of focusing and the underlying theory of experiencing are supported by thorough philosophical analysis (Gendlin 1962, 1984a) and considerable psychological research (Gendlin 1969, 1984b).

The focusing process is built on an assumption that the fundamental meanings that events and relationships have for people are contained in the 'felt sense' experienced by the person. The felt sense is an internal, physical sense of the situation. In this inner sense the person knows there is more to the situation than he or she is currently able to say. According to Gendlin (1962), this 'inner referent' or felt sense holds a highly differentiated set of implicit meanings. For these meanings to be made explicit, the person must express the felt sense in a symbol, such as a word, phrase, statement, image or even bodily movement. The act of symbolizing an area of meaning in the felt sense allows other areas to come to attention. Accurate symbolization therefore brings about a 'shift' in the inner felt sense of a situation or problem.

Gendlin takes the view that the experiential process described here is at the heart of not only person-centred counselling but all other therapies too. He regards the therapeutic movement or shifts brought about by interpretation, behavioural methods, gestalt interventions and so on to be reducible to episodes of effective experiential focusing. This experiential process is also a common feature of everyday life. The problems that bring people to counselling are caused by an interruption of the process, an unwillingness or inability of the person to achieve a complete and accurate picture of the felt sense of the problem. The basic tasks of the counsellor are therefore to help the client to stay with the inner referent rather than avoiding it, and to facilitate the generation of accurate symbols to allow expression of implicit meanings.

The process of 'focusing on a problem' can be broken into a number of stages or steps:

1 Clearing a space. Taking an inventory of what is going on inside the body.
2 Locating the inner felt sense of the problem. Letting the felt sense come. Allowing the body to 'talk back'.
3 Finding a 'handle' (word or image) that matches the felt sense.
4 Resonating handle and felt sense. Checking symbol against feeling. Asking 'does this really fit?'
5 A felt shift in the problem, experiencing either a subtle movement or 'flood of physical relief'.
6 Receiving or accepting what has emerged.
7 Stop, or go through process again.

These steps can occur, or be helped to occur, in the dialogue or interaction between counsellor or client, or the counsellor can intentionally instruct and guide the client through the process. Leijssen (1993, 1998) has provided some very clear accounts of how she integrates the use of experiential focusing into a conventional person-centred counselling session with a client (see Box 7.6). The technique has been taught to clients and used in peer self-help groups. Cornell (1993) reviews the issues involved in teaching focusing. Guidelines on how to learn practical skills in experiential focusing can be found in Gendlin (1981, 1996) and Cornell (1996). A comprehensive exploration of all aspects of the use of focusing in counselling can be found in Purton (2004).

Box 7.6: *Using experiential focusing in a counselling session: two examples*

Sonia, in her twenty-fourth session of therapy, felt tense, even though it was the first day of her holidays. At the start of the session, she described herself as 'having an awful lot of things to do'. The therapist understood this statement as indicating, in terms of focusing theory, that Sonia was 'too close' to her problems to be able usefully to explore her 'felt sense' of any one of them. The therapist then initiated a simple strategy for 'clearing a space' within which Sonia could gain a clearer sense of what were the main issues for her. The therapist suggested:

> You have a notepad . . . each problem that makes you tense will receive a name, which you will write down on a sheet of notepaper, and next, you will assign the sheet – and thus the problem – a place in this room here, at a comfortable distance from yourself.

Sonia wrote and placed notes referring to each of her concerns – the carpenter coming to do some work, the heating system needing fixing, washing curtains, making an appointment with her dentist, talking to her cleaning lady . . . her loneliness, facing up to her father. In this way, the client was enabled to step back from what had seemed an overwhelming inner pressure, and to clear an emotional space in which she could discover that the underlying issue that was making her tense at the beginning of her holiday was that she no longer had an excuse to avoid visiting her father. She was then ready to look more closely at this specific issue.

Oskar was a client who tended to talk about past events in a highly rational way. He was consistently 'too far' from his feelings to be able to focus effectively on any specific issue in his life. In one session, he told a long story about how he 'thinks' he 'should' feel angry with someone he knows. The next few minutes in the session proceeded in the following manner.

Therapist: You think you should feel furious, but you don't feel any contact with it . . . Now, could you set aside for a moment everything you thought and we will start with your body and see what comes from there . . . Take your time to close your eyes and take a few deep breaths . . . [*The therapist invites the client to fully feel his body, from the feet up, asking 'what are you aware of in that part of the body?'*] . . . Just . . . What strikes you when you have covered the whole body?

Client: That feeling in the pit of my stomach . . . that tension there . . . that is the most powerful.

Therapist: There you experience something powerful . . . Why don't you remain there and look what else will come out of it . . .

Client: It wants to jump out of it, as a devil out of a box . . .

Therapist: Something wants to jump out . . . [*silence*].

Client: Hate . . . but that would be very unusual for me.

Therapist: You hesitate to use the word 'hate', but that is what jumps out at you?

Client: It gives me power!

Therapist: You notice that your hate is accompanied by a feeling of power.

Client: I always withdraw from my friend because he has hurt me so often [*tells therapist about an incident in which he felt deeply humiliated*].

Therapist: You don't want this to happen again . . . Something in you wants to keep facing him with power?

Client: Yes. That feels good . . . that is it . . . [*sighs, sits more relaxed; silence*]. This was the last time that I'll give him so much power over me . . . I see him tomorrow, and will make it very clear that I won't let myself be pushed aside any more . . . [*client sits up straight and considers further what he wants to tell his friend*].

These examples are taken from Leijssen (1998: p. 145 and p. 148, respectively), who provides a detailed discussion of the experiential processes that are involved in each case. It is worth noting that, although the therapist in these cases is clearly following a focusing approach, she is also drawing upon a wide range of skills and competencies that can be found in other therapeutic approaches: for example, the use of empathic reflection, metaphor and symbol, ritual and externalization. The difference lies in the fact that, here, the therapist is employing all of these skills with reference to the bodily felt sense of the client (and presumably her own felt sense in relationship with the client). The aim of experiential focusing can be seen to be that of exploring and unfolding the implicit meanings that are held in bodily feeling.

Emotion focused therapy

Another important development within the broad person-centred or humanistic tradition has been the approach to counselling and psychotherapy created by Les Greenberg, Laura Rice, Robert Elliott and others, in the 1990s. This approach was originally described as *process-experiential* therapy (Greenberg *et al.* 1993) but has subsequently been 're-badged' as *emotion focused therapy* (EFT) (Greenberg 2002; Elliott *et al.* 2003). The emotion focused approach is an integration of ideas and techniques from person-centred and gestalt therapies, and contemporary cognitive psychology. One of the distinctive features of the approach is its emphasis on significant events within counselling sessions. Whereas Rogers' conditions of empathy, congruence and acceptance refer to interpersonal processes, or a relationship environment, that exists throughout the therapy, Greenberg and his colleagues have suggested that it can be useful to give particular attention to creating highly meaningful moments of change. A central assumption in emotion focused counselling is that the problems people have are based on an inability to engage in effective emotional processing. Emotions provide vital information about relationships, and are guides to action. When a person fails to express or communicate emotion, his or her capacity to interact with others is impaired. The goal of therapy is therefore to facilitate emotional processing, to enable the person to integrate how they feel into how they experience things. Greenberg *et al.* (1993) suggest that, as a client talks about his or her problems, he or she will communicate clues or *markers* to the therapist concerning blocked or distorted emotions. The task of the therapist is to listen out for these markers and initiate an appropriate sequence of emotional processing.

An example of this kind of approach can be found in Rice's (1974, 1984) model of stages in the resolution of 'problematic incidents'. These are incidents in the client's life when he or she felt as though his or her reaction to what happened was puzzling or inappropriate. Rice (1984) has found that effective counselling in these situations tends to follow four discrete stages. First, the client sets the scene for exploration, by labelling an incident as problematic, confirming what it was that made the reaction to the incident unacceptable and then reconstructing the scene in general terms. The second stage involves the client and counsellor working on two parallel tasks. One task is to tease out different facets of the feelings experienced during the incident; the other is to search for the aspects of the event that held the most intense meaning or significance. This second stage is centred on the task of discovering the meanings of the event for the client. In the third phase, the client begins to attempt to understand the implications for his or her 'self-schema' or self-concept of what has merged earlier. The final phase involves the exploration of possible new options. Rice (1984: 201) describes this whole process as being one of 'evocative unfolding', in which 'the cognitive-affective reprocessing of a single troubling episode can lead into a widening series of self-discoveries'.

Greenberg *et al.* (1993) have conducted a substantial amount of research into emotional processing tasks in counselling and psychotherapy and have, to date, compiled protocols to guide therapists in working effectively with six types of emotional processing event:

1 Systematic evocative unfolding at a marker of a problematic reaction point.

2 Experiential focusing for an unclear felt sense.

3 Two-chair dialogue at a self-evaluative split.

4 Two-chair enactment for self-interruptive split.

5 Empty-chair work to resolve emotional 'unfinished business'.

6 Empathic affirmation at a marker of intense vulnerability.

There is evidence of the effectiveness of process-experiential therapy in marital therapy (Greenberg and Johnson 1988), with people who are depressed (Elliott *et al.* 1990; Greenberg *et al.* 1990; Greenberg and Watson 2005), and with PTSD (Elliott *et al.* 1996, 1998); research is currently being conducted into the impact of this approach in people suffering from social anxiety.

The emotion focused approach is a variant of person-centred counselling that builds on the principles described by Rogers (1961) and by Mearns and Thorne (2007) but that also makes use of the practice, employed in gestalt therapy and psychodrama, of creating highly emotionally charged moments of change. There is no doubt that EFT is in tune with the spirit of the times. It is highly specified and trainable. It is research based. It can be readily adapted for use with clients selected according to diagnostic categories such as depression or PTSD. It is applicable within a limited number of sessions. It extends the repertoire of the counsellor, adds to the number of different ways the counsellor has of being emotionally responsive to the client by using markers to indicate the introduction of different interventions (see Watson 2006). Yet, at the same time, at the heart of the Rogerian approach there has always been a profound respect for the capacity of the person to change at their own pace. There is a basic assumption about how vital it is to support the agency of the client (Rennie 1998), rather than the counsellor becoming the agent who does things to the client. Some person-centred traditionalists worry that the methods of process-experiential therapy may turn out to threaten this key feature of the person-centred approach.

Box 7.7: *Is person-centred counselling culturally specific?*

Carl Rogers was fascinated by cultural difference, and at different points in his life visited all areas of the world and worked with people from many different cultural backgrounds. Despite this, person-centred theory does not make any specific reference to the significance of cultural factors, and person-centred practice does not usually include any kind of accommodation to different cultural values and behaviours. Further, many commentators have observed that the optimism, egalitarianism and focus on the individual self that are central aspects of person-centred philosophy, are highly characteristic of mid-twentieth century American culture, and as a result the approach inevitably lacks relevance and resonance for people from other cultural groups (see, for example, MacDougall 2002).

The case of the adoption of the person-centred approach in Japan provides an alternative perspective on the way that a therapy approach can be applied in a cultural setting that is radically different from the one in which it was originally developed. Hayashi *et al.* (1998) explain that the Japanese psychologist Fujio Tomoda discovered the writings of Carl Rogers in 1948, and was immediately convinced that they had a great deal to offer in his home country. He later studied with Rogers in Chicago, and translated many of Rogers' books and articles into Japanese. However, in the process of using person-centred ideas with a range of client groups in Japan, and running training courses, Tomoda and his colleagues began to evolve a version of person-centred counselling that was essentially Japanese in orientation. For example, Tomoda argued that envisaging self in terms of the idea of a *self-concept* ran the risk of overdefining an entity that, in Japanese culture, would be understood in a more ambiguous way, as something that can ultimately never be put into words. Tomoda also argued that moments of change occurred when the person is able to be 'utterly alone', and that it is the task of the counsellor to be an empathic partner who can handle the 'inner strangers' who are 'restraining the person's mind' and allow the person to arrive at a state of alone-ness where self-realization was possible. These ideas were further articulated in a distinctive approach to training that incorporated the use of Japanese traditional renku poetry. The adoption of person-centred ideas in Japan, and their development over a 60-year period, show that the use of a therapy approach by practitioners in diverse cultural settings is more than just a matter of imposing ideas and methods from one culture into another. Ideally, the use of therapy ideas across culture should involve a fusion of cultural horizons, where each set of participants learns from, and is changed by, the other.

Motivational interviewing

Motivational interviewing is an approach to counselling that was developed by Stephen Rollnick and William R. Miller in the 1980s (Miller 1983; Miller and Rollnick 1991, 2002). The main area of application for motivational interviewing has been in the area of addictions, in working with people with drug and alcohol problems around making a decision or commitment to change their behaviour, and in the field of lifestyle change for people with life-threatening health conditions. William R. Miller was originally trained in client-centred therapy, and the theoretical basis of motivational interviewing draws heavily on Carl Rogers' ideas about the qualities of a facilitative relationship. However, while a person-centred counsellor adopts a rigorously non-directive stance, in the sense of following the client's 'track' in respect of whatever topic the client wishes to explore, motivational interviewing takes a more directive approach. In counselling that is informed by a motivational interviewing approach, the counsellor already has an idea of a desirable change that they would like the client to make (e.g., giving up illegal drug-taking). The focus of motivational work is to help the client to overcome his or her ambivalence and resistance about making necessary changes in their life.

Motivational interviewing relies on four basic principles:

1 *Empathy*: the counsellor seeks to view the issue from the frame of reference of the client;

2 *Developing discrepancy*: the counsellor explores with the client tensions between how the client wants his or her life to be (the ideal) and their current behaviour (the actual);

3 *Acceptance* or 'rolling with resistance': the counsellor does not try to pressure the client to make a decision, but instead accept that a reluctance to change is natural, and invites exploration of this resistance;

4 *Client autonomy*: the counsellor respects the client as someone who has the capacity to arrive at the right decision for himself/herself in the present circumstances.

When these principles are implemented, a counselling space is constructed in which the client feels that he or she is in a relationship in which it is possible to talk honestly about all aspects of a decision, and as a result to be able eventually to make a genuine commitment to a new course of action that is grounded in a comprehensive exploration of all possible aspects of the issue. Rollnick and Allison (2004: 104) characterize the essence of motivational interviewing as 'an atmosphere of constructive conversation about behaviour change, in which the counsellor uses empathic listening . . . to understand the client's perspective and minimize resistance'.

There has been a substantial amount of research into the effectiveness of motivational interviewing, both as an intervention in itself and as an adjunct to other approaches (Westra and Arkowitz 2011). There have also been studies of the use of motivational techniques by doctors, nurses and other health professionals. These studies have generated strong evidence that motivational interviewing is well-received by clients, and as effective as any other method in facilitating change in hard-to-treat client groups (Burke *et al.* 2003; Lundahl *et al.* 2010; Miller and Rose 2009).

Research seems to show that there are two main active therapeutic elements in motivational interviewing. The first of these elements comprises the 'core conditions' of empathy and acceptance. The second element is that the directive focus of the counsellor means that the client engages in more 'change talk', which eventually translates into 'change behaviour'. Miller and Rose (2009) suggest that whereas core conditions on their own are useful for the client, there is a tendency for people struggling with addictions to avoid talking about difficult choices. They also argue that merely requiring the client to talk about such issues in the absence of an empathic relationship is unlikely to be effective because the client will feel unsafe and unsupported.

Motivational interviewing is controversial among person-centred counsellors who believe that non-directiveness represents a central value and therapeutic principle that underpins their work. Motivational interviewing is explicitly directive:

> . . . counsellors need to provide clear structure to the session. They frequently also have a clear view about what direction they would like the client to take. Typically this involves gently coaching the client to explore the conflicts and contradictions so prevalent in addiction problems. By summarizing these for the client, and giving the person room to reflect, it is assumed that motivation to change is more likely to be enhanced.
>
> (Rollnick and Allison 2004: 105)

At the same time, Miller and Rollnick (2009) are clear that motivational interviewing does not involve trying to pressurize or persuade the client – the idea is to create a space for reflection. They are also clear that what they are doing is not the same as person-centred or client-centred therapy, even if it draws heavily on that tradition. The existence, and success, of motivational interviewing represents a dilemma for adherents of the person-centred approach. On the one hand, the effectiveness of motivational interviewing is testimony to the validity of Rogers' ideas and methods. On the other hand, the harnessing of these ideas and methods in the service of a pre-determined, socially acceptable outcome is hard to reconcile with a belief in authenticity and actualization. There is then, maybe, also a further worrying possibility: to what extent do person-centred practitioners already work in a 'motivational' way, steering their clients toward particular answers? It is hard to answer this question, because there is little or no research into the non-directiveness of typical person-centred practice. Person-centred counsellors may declare an allegiance to the principle of non-directiveness, but to what extent is this ethos demonstrated in practice – particularly in tough situations where the client is behaving in a highly self-destructive manner?

Further developments in person-centred theory

The bedrock of person-centred theory is based on the set of ideas that were generated by Rogers and his colleagues in a highly productive period up to the end of the 1950s (Rogers 1961). The classic 'manual' of person-centred practice written by Mearns and Thorne (2013) is largely based on this early body of knowledge. These foundational ideas have been debated and elaborated by many writers and researchers. However, as the level of interest in the person-centred approach grew in the 1990s, a number of influential new ideas also began to emerge, which have now achieved widespread acceptance across most of the person-centred community. The key concepts that have been brought forward during this time are: the pluralistic self; the nature of relational depth; and the concept of difficult process. These ideas are discussed below.

The pluralistic self. The idea that there exist different 'parts' of the self, representing separate aspects of the experience or identity of a person, has been central to the practice of a number of different approaches to therapy, ranging from object relations theory to transactional analysis and gestalt therapy. However, Carl Rogers tended to describe the self as, essentially, a unitary structure that may shift in the direction of growth, fulfilment and self-actualization, but is not characterized by internal conflict. Mearns and Thorne (2000) have revisited this aspect of person-centred theory, and have argued that there has always been an implicit 'self-split' in the way that person-centred practitioners and theorists view the self. The split is between the 'growthful' part of the self and the 'not-for-growth' part. Mearns and Thorne (2000) use the term 'configurations' to describe these parts, to emphasize the individual, active and changing nature of the person's process in relation to these elements of the self. They draw out some of the implications of this new perspective for the practice of person-centred counselling, particularly in relation to the necessity for the counsellor to accept and empathize with each 'configuration', rather than favouring the vulnerable 'growing' parts of the self. From this standpoint, it is the living *dialogue* between parts of the self that constitutes growth. Their use of the term 'configuration' is intended to imply a sense of how self-plurality is experienced within therapy, as a separation of contrasting clusters of thought, feeling and action *in the moment*; there is no assumption that configurations arise from permanent structures or 'parts' of the self.

A further example of how the concept of self-plurality has been articulated within the person-centred approach has been the work on the *inner critic* by a number of person-centred theorists (see, for example, Stinckens *et al.* 2002a, 2002b). One of the themes in counselling with people who might describe themselves as 'depressed' is that they frequently criticize their own thoughts, actions and feelings, sometimes in a very harsh manner. With some clients, it can be helpful to understand these actions as comprising an 'inner critic', to enable the client to become more aware of this pattern as a specific 'part' of the self.

Finally, the work of Bill Stiles and his research group has established a valuable resource of research and practice around the idea that the self can be envisaged as a community of *voices*. Although the voice concept is intended as an integrative concept, applicable in all therapy approaches (Stiles 2002), it has been found to have particular relevance within the person-centred tradition (Stiles and Glick 2002). Other examples of self-pluralism within person-centred and experiential therapy practice can be found in Cooper *et al.* (2004b) and Elliott and Greenberg (1997).

The nature of relational depth. The 'core conditions' model proposed by Rogers (1957) has acted as a cornerstone for person-centred theory and practice for 50 years. Despite the undoubted value of this set of ideas, it can be argued that the 'necessary and sufficient' conditions described by Rogers (1957) represent a fairly limited description of the nature of the therapeutic relationship – even if the core conditions are valid, do they represent the final word in thinking about relationships in therapy? The counselling/psychotherapy field as a whole has largely incorporated Rogers' ideas into the somewhat broader conceptualization of the therapeutic relationship provided by Bordin's (1979) *therapeutic alliance* model, which identifies three dimensions of relationship: bond, goals and tasks. However, neither the core conditions nor working alliance models of the therapeutic relationship attempt to come to terms with a key question: what does a *really good* therapy relationship look like? They offer useful models of adequate, or good-enough, client–counsellor relating. But, given that much research suggests that the quality of the therapeutic relationship is central to the effectiveness of counselling (Cooper 2004), it is worthwhile to seek to go further, and attempt to develop a more comprehensive understanding of what constitutes a highly productive therapy relationship.

From within the person-centred approach, this issue has been tackled from two angles. First, Mearns and Cooper (2005) reviewed both the research and clinical literature, to arrive at an analysis of *relational depth* – a state of profound engagement and contact in which each person is fully real with the other, and in which there is an enduring sense of contact and connectedness between client and therapist. Mearns and Cooper (2005) identify a number of strategies that therapists can adopt to facilitate the emergence of relational depth: letting go of expectations and agendas; 'knocking on the door' of deeper experiences; being open to being affected by the client; transparency; working in the here-and-now. Research by McMillan and McLeod (2006), in which clients were interviewed about their experiences of relational depth, found that although the qualities described by Mearns and Cooper (2005) were reported as being quite rare within therapy, they were nevertheless experienced as highly meaningful. From the client perspective, relational depth is definitely a mutual activity; they described themselves as needing to be 'willing to let go' in order to enter such an intense and impactful relationship.

The idea that strong therapeutic relationships are grounded in a sense of mutuality is reinforced by the work of the Austrian person-centred therapist Peter Schmid. In a series of papers, Schmid (Schmid 2001, 2007a, 2007b) has carried out a careful philosophical analysis of the meaning of relationships in therapy (similar, in some respects, to the influential philosophical analysis of the concept of experiencing conducted by Gendlin 1962). The central theme within this analysis is that it limits the potential of a relationship to consider it as taking place between two separate, individual persons. Schmid (2001) argues that an essential aspect of being human involves understanding and accepting a sense of the 'we' – there is a collective or shared reality that transcends the individual perceptions or lives of any one of us. To acknowledge the 'we' involves the therapist being open to the 'otherness' of the client, and seeking to establish a 'Thou–I' relationship (I realize myself through my effort and struggle to understand and be with you). For Schmid (Schmid 2001, 2007a, 2007b) the aim of therapy is to engage in dialogue in which each participant can be fully present to the other. This kind of agenda is intellectually, morally and personally challenging, but for Schmid (Schmid 2007a, 2007b) it underpins any possibility of relational depth. An overview of recent developments in theory, research and practice around the topic of relational depth can be found in Knox *et al.* (2012) and and Knox and Cooper (2011).

The concept of difficult process. Running through this chapter is the idea that, from a person-centred perspective, it is useful to think about therapy in terms of the way that the person experiences the world, and the way that he or she processes different elements of experience (thoughts, feelings, bodily phenomena, action tendencies). The idea of 'process', in this context, can be defined as an activity, involving paying attention to, and regulating the intensity of, different facets of experiencing. Person-centred counsellors, of whatever 'tribe' they belong to, have always been trained to work with process. However, the models of process that have been used within the person-centred approach – for example the Rogers (1961), Klein *et al.* (1986) model of depth of experiencing, or the stages of experiential focusing model, both described earlier in this chapter – have always described a generalized process, that would in principle be the same for any person in any situation.

   In an important body of work, Margaret Warner has begun to develop a framework for understanding different *types* of experiential processing that are characteristic of people with different types of problem. She uses the term *difficult process* to encompass this set of ideas. Warner (2000b; 2002a) has described two main types of difficult process. *Fragile process* occurs when the person has difficulty in maintaining the flow of processing of experiential material. In fragile processing, the person may be unable to 'stay with' a thought or feeling that is problematic for them, with the result that the 'track' of their conversation is punctuated by silences or gaps – they get lost, or the feeling that they were exploring seems to dissolve. *Dissociated process* occurs when the person abruptly shifts from one area of experiencing to another. For example, a person may be talking about a troubling episode in his relationship with his partner, and abruptly moves away from this topic, and starts to talk instead about how he feels about a painting on the wall of the counselling room. What has happened with this client could be interpreted as an example of a dissociative process in which he protected himself against potentially painful emotions and memories by refocusing his attention on something soothing and trivial – a safety procedure learned early in life.

Mearns and Thorne (2007: 30) have described Warner's work as 'the most significant contribution in recent years'. Mearns and Thorne (2007) themselves have identified a further example of difficult process. *Ego-syntonic process* happens when a person is so afraid of social relationships that he or she consistently perceives all issues in terms of their pay off for self (this is like being 'self-centred'). A further example of a different type of difficult process (as yet uncategorized) has been described by Warner (2002b) in her work with a man diagnosed as schizophrenic. The capacity to identify distinct patterns of difficult process in clients is only part of the problem: what does a counsellor do in response to such processes? Vanaerschot (2004) makes a powerful case for the view that difficult processes arises because of a failure of empathy in the early social world of the person, and that careful attention to empathic engagement, and the use of pre-therapy strategies (Prouty *et al.* 2002) can make it possible for a person to begin to emerge from difficult process, and gradually to be able to engage more fully with the totality of his or her experiencing.

The three topics outlined above – self-pluralism, relational depth, and difficult process – represent areas of major advance in person-centred theory and practice. It is worth noting that, in each of these areas, person-centred theorists have made considerable use of ideas from other approaches to counselling and psychotherapy, primarily from psychodynamic theory, and also from theory and research in social and developmental psychology. It is probably fair to say that these innovative perspectives have yet to be fully integrated into mainstream person-centred theory and practice. Just as, in the 1950s, new concepts such as empathy and experiencing underwent thorough examination in the form of research and practice, these contemporary new concepts need to undergo a similar process.

Can the person-centred approach be combined with other approaches?

The person-centred approach to counselling represents a philosophically coherent and practically robust approach to therapy, which has remained largely unchanged since the 1960s. At least two generations of counsellors have found meaning and satisfaction in working solely within the approach, and have been able to offer effective help to a wide range of clients. On the other hand, many counsellors are drawn in the direction of integrationism, and in acquiring new ideas and models that can extend their therapeutic repertoire. Where does the person-centred approach stand in relation to therapy integration? Over the years, a spectrum of views articulated around the issue of combining person-centred and other methods. At one end of the continuum, Mearns and Thorne (2013: 202) argue that the distinctive characteristics of the person-centred tradition 'rule out for us the possibility of combining the approach with other orientations that are based on quite different or even contrary assumptions'. The key point here is that anyone who seeks to work in a person-centred manner is committed to some basic philosophical assumptions about the nature of the person, which are not shared by other approaches, and that the adoption of an alternative position would inevitably dilute the quality of that commitment. Bozarth (1998) takes a similar stance, but concedes that he would be willing to use specific techniques if the impetus to try them had emerged from the client's own frame of reference.

Analysis of therapy sessions conducted by Carl Rogers has been carried out by Hayes and Goldfried (1996) and Tursi and Cochran (2006). They found that his interventions with clients could be described as forms of cognitive restructuring techniques, similar to those used by practitioners of cognitive therapy and CBT. Tursi and Cochran (2006) argued, on the basis of this, that a greater knowledge of CBT methods might allow person-centred counsellors to be more effective in respect of this kind of cognitive intervention. In similar fashion, several types of 'fusion' between person-centred therapy and other therapy methods have been described, for instance in relation to play therapy (Axline 1971), body therapy (Leijssen 2006), solution-focused therapy (Jaison 2002), feminist approaches (Lovering 2002), psychodrama (Wilkins 1994) and art therapy (Rogers 1993; Silverstone 1997).

A more radical strategy for combining person-centred and other approaches has been advocated by Boy and Pine (1982), who suggested that although a person-centred way of working with a client is required in the early stage of therapy, in order to develop a strong client–counsellor relationship, it is helpful to adopt active change techniques in the latter stages of treatment. An example of this two-stage strategy can be found in a case study by Cepeda and Davenport (2006), which describes the combination of person-centred and solution-focused methods with a client. The approach advocated by Boy and Pine (1982) is characteristic of that of many counsellors who use the person-centred perspective as a basis for integration. The end product is a way of working that is perhaps better understood as *a* person-centred approach rather than *the* person-centred approach. There is support for this kind of endeavour in Rogers' writings. He suggested in relation to the core conditions that empathy, congruence and unconditional positive regard could be communicated to the client in many different ways, for example through psychoanalytic interpretation (Rogers 1957).

Yet another integrative strategy can be seen in EFT (Greenberg *et al.* 1993; Watson 2006), which specifies that a person-centred relationship provides a context for the implementation of more 'active' techniques (such as two-chair work) that are initiated in response to client 'markers' of different forms of underlying emotional difficulty. Beyond these specific examples of combining person-centred and other approaches, there sits a much wider literature reflecting the extent to which Rogers' ideas about the therapeutic relationship, and the importance of empathy, have been assimilated into the work of many writers and practitioners within the psychodynamic and CBT traditions.

In summary, it can be seen that there are many ways in which a person-centred approach can be combined with other approaches to therapy. On the other hand, there is the danger that counsellors seeking to integrate person-centred and other models may end up merely using person-centred ideas as a gloss beneath which they are operating in a quite different fashion. For example, a rigorous interpretation of person-centred principles involves a reliance on the actualizing tendency of the client, and continual use of self in the relationship. These are characteristics that can easily become lost when ideas from other approaches are introduced.

Conclusions: an appraisal of the person-centred approach

The early phase of the development of the person-centred approach, particularly the 'Chicago' years (Barrett-Lennard 1979), represents a unique achievement in the history of counselling and psychotherapy (McLeod 2002). Between 1940 and 1963, Rogers and others evolved a consistent, coherent body of theory and practice that was informed and shaped by ongoing research, and which remains a powerful strand of thought in the contemporary counselling world. Further developments within the person-centred approach have resulted in both a deeper understanding of some of Rogers' key concepts, and an extension of the approach to embrace new concepts. The person-centred approach has been applied in work with a wide range of client groups, and is supported by a substantial body of research that indicates levels of therapeutic effectiveness equivalent to that achieved by any other form of therapy, including CBT (Elliott *et al.* 2013; Mearns and Thorne 2013).

The ideas that have been introduced in this chapter give some indication of the continuing intellectual health of the person-centred tradition, which has been able to accommodate constructive debate, for example around the concept of non-directivity, the cultural biases within the approach, the active role of the therapist, and the issue of integrationism. The person-centred approach has also provided a platform for a continuing programme of research. A further debate, not dealt with in this chapter, has emerged in person-centred counselling over the role of spiritual or transcendent dimensions of experience. Although Rogers himself had originally intended to join the ministry, for most of his career his psychological theorizing was conducted within a strictly secular humanistic framework. It was only towards the end of his life that Rogers (1980) wrote of his experience of 'transcendent unity' and 'inner spirit'. These ideas have been both welcomed (Thorne 2012) and criticized (van Belle 1990; Mearns 1996) within the person-centred movement.

There are many counsellors who have made successful and satisfying careers supported by the ideas, methods and institutions of the person-centred approach. There are many other counsellors who do not define themselves as 'person-centred', but whose practice is informed at a deep level by person-centred values and the person-centred way of relating to others.

Topics for reflection and discussion

1   How valid do you find the 'necessary and sufficient conditions' model? Are there other 'conditions' you would want to add to Rogers' list?

2   What are the strengths and weaknesses of the person-centred approach, in comparison with the psychodynamic and cognitive–behavioural approaches described in previous chapters?

3   Kahn (1997: 38) has written that: 'Rogers spent forty years developing his view of therapy. And perhaps it would not be far off the mark to view his whole forty years' work as an attempt to shape an answer to a single question: What should a therapist do

to convey to a client that at last he or she is *loved*?' In your view, how valid is Kahn's assertion?

4 To what extent can EFT and/or motivational interviewing be seen as merely an extension of Rogers' ideas? Are there ways in which EFT and motivational interviewing models are in conflict with basic, non-negotiable person-centred ideas and assumptions? If they are, why does it matter?

Suggested further reading

There is no substitute for reading the work of important original thinkers in the field of counselling. In this field, Carl Rogers has been a dominant figure, and his key books, *Client-centered Therapy* (Rogers 1951) and *On Becoming a Person* (Rogers 1961) remain as fresh and relevant as ever. Kirschenbaum and Henderson (1990) have brought together a collection of Rogers' work from all phases of his career.

The contemporary texts that best represent current person-centred theory and practice are Mearns and Thorne (2013) and Merry (1999). The Thorne and Sanders (2012) book on Rogers supplies a useful overview of the approach, as well as discussing the various criticisms of person-centred counselling that have been made. Rennie (1998) offers a distinctive perspective on person-centred theory and practice. The range and scope of contemporary thinking around person-centred and experiential theory, research and practice is comprehensively represented in Cooper *et al.* (2013) and in the journal *Person-Centred and Experiential Psychotherapies*.

A book that is a pleasure to read and conveys the spirit of the person-centred approach is *Dibs*, by Virginia Axline (1971). This is an account of a version of client-centred play therapy carried out by Axline with a young boy, Dibs. More than any other piece of writing, *Dibs* communicates the deep respect for the person, and the capacity of the person to grow, that is so central to effective person-centred work.

The collections edited by Cain and Seeman (2002) and Schneider *et al.* (2001) venture beyond the person-centred approach, to encompass the many strands of contemporary humanistic therapy. Each provides a rich resource, and evidence that the 'third force' remains a potent presence. There are three journals that consistently publish interesting and stimulating articles on humanistic themes: *The Humanistic Psychologist*, the *Journal of Humanistic Psychology*, and the *Journal of Humanistic Counseling*.

CHAPTER 8

Transactional analysis: a comprehensive theoretical system

Introduction

Transactional analysis (TA) is a social psychological theory, developed by the psychiatrist and psychoanalyst Eric Berne in the 1960s (1961/2001). Transactional analysis has been applied in a number of areas of social life: counselling and psychotherapy, education, organization and management studies. It is of particular interest to counsellors because it represents a theoretical framework that is both comprehensive and integrative – TA is an invaluable source of concepts and ideas, even for those therapists who do not use the approach directly in their practice. This chapter is organized in two main sections. First, an overview is provided of the main elements of TA theory. Second, the application of these ideas in counselling is explored, in relation to four main traditions of TA practice. The chapter closes with some reflections on the strengths and weaknesses of the TA approach, and the contribution that it has made to the field of counselling as a whole.

The theoretical foundations of TA

Eric Berne (1910–70) was born and brought up in Montreal, Canada, as Eric Lennard Bernstein. His father was a doctor and his mother a writer, both from Polish/Russian immigrant backgrounds. His father, with whom he had a close relationship, died in 1921. Berne qualified as a doctor and psychiatrist, and shortened his name when he moved to the USA and took up American citizenship in 1939. He worked in private practice and in the US army, before entering psychoanalytic training with Paul Federn and Erik Erikson, and made contributions to the psychoanalytic literature with his writing on intuition. He eventually settled in Carmel, California. He hosted a weekly seminar from 1951, in which the key ideas of what was to become his new approach, were formulated. A key life event for Berne was the rejection of his application in 1956 for full membership of the San Francisco Psychiatric Institute, which stimulated him to develop his own model of therapy. The biographical sketch provided by Stewart (1992) portrays Berne as a man who was perhaps difficult to know, and who found it hard to sustain intimate relationships.

Virtually all of the key ideas and principles of TA were generated by Berne and a group of close colleagues in the period 1958–70. This was a time of great innovation more generally within the field of counselling and psychotherapy within the USA, particularly in relation to humanistic alternatives to psychoanalysis (e.g., the client-centred therapy of Carl Rogers). The theory and practice of TA that evolved during these years can be seen as representing a creative fusion of psychoanalytic and humanistic concepts and values, alongside some ideas from social psychology. It is important to note that most of Berne's clinical practice consisted of group psychotherapy, rather than individual therapy. Transactional analysis is probably the only mainstream therapy approach that has its origins in groupwork, and this explains the high level of emphasis within the theory on understanding patterns of interaction between people, and on being able to observe the behavioural and non-verbal manifestations of underlying psychological states.

Box 8.1: *The radical tradition in TA*

The period during which TA theory and practice was beginning to become established, in the 1960s, was also a time of political upheaval, with protests against the Vietnam war, racism and capitalist systems. This radical agenda had an impact on the development of TA through the influence of Claude Steiner, a close colleague of Eric Berne. From 1968, Steiner was a leading figure in the *Radical Psychiatry* group in the USA, a regular contributor to the journals *Radical Therapist* and *Issues in Radical Therapy*, and co-author of *Readings in Radical Psychiatry* (Steiner and Wyckoff 1975). Some of the principles espoused by this movement, The Radical Psychiatry Manifesto, included the following statement:

> Extended individual psychotherapy is an elitist, outmoded, as well as non-productive form of psychiatric help. It concentrates the talents of a few on a few. It silently colludes with the notion that people's difficulties have their sources within them while implying that everything is well with the world. It

promotes oppression by shrouding its consequences with shame and secrecy. It further mystifies by attempting to pass as an ideal human relationship when it is, in fact, artificial in the extreme. People's troubles have their cause not within them but in their alienated relationships, in their exploitation, in polluted environments, in war, and in the profit motive. Psychiatry must be practiced in groups. One-to-one contacts, of great value in crises, should become the exception rather than the rule. The high ideal of I-Thou loving relations should be pursued in the context of groups rather than in the stilted consulting room situation.

(Steiner 1971: 3)

Further information about the radical psychiatry movement, along with the other sections of the manifesto, is available on Steiner's website and in Steiner (2001). Many of these ideas found their way into TA practice, in the form of an emphasis on working in groups, brief rather than extended therapy, collaborative contracting with clients, encouraging clients to learn therapy theory, willingness to allow clients to read clinical notes, and the development of ways of understanding power differences between individuals and gender relationships (Steiner 1981).

Transactional analysis is distinctive, in contrast to other approaches of counselling/psychotherapy, in that it is based on a formal set of theoretical propositions. Whole other approaches to therapy, such as person-centred/experiential, psychodynamic and CBT, can also draw upon rich sets of concepts, the tendency in these approaches is for theory to be organized in terms of a loose net, with various strands of conceptualization stretching out from ideas that were initially formulated by the founders of the model. Further, in these mainstream approaches there can be a fair degree of disagreement over the interpretation and meaning of core concepts. TA is not like that. There exists a unified theoretical framework, that is summarized in a series of key texts (Joines and Stewart 2002; Stewart and Joines 2012; Woollams and Brown 1978). While the ideas that comprise this framework are elaborated in the pages of the *Transactional Analysis Journal*, and in books, there are no major theoretical conflicts around core concepts (compare this situation, for example, with the debates in psychoanalysis around the true meaning of counter-transference, or the arguments in the person-centred tradition around the notion of non-directivity).

One of the reasons for the high degree of theoretical consensus within the TA world is because the theory itself is highly coherent. The theory is built around a set of basic assumptions, which are developed into specific models that can be applied to different levels of complexity in human interaction: the individual, the two-person dyad, group interaction, and the interaction between person and culture over a lifespan. A significant and distinctive feature of TA theory is concerned with the way that its ideas are expressed and communicated. TA theorists have striven to develop 'experience-near' theory, by using colloquial terms and imagery whenever possible, rather than using abstract technical terminology. Transactional analysis theorists also make frequent use of diagrams to display the links between theoretical entities. The diagrammatic presentation of TA concepts allows complex inter-relationships to be discussed without the danger of descending into over-abstruse and dense language.

Basic assumptions

The concept or image of the person that is used in TA is ultimately grounded in three simple yet powerful ideas – one relating to human motivation, the other two relating to values. The motivational concept is the idea of *strokes*. A 'stroke' can be defined as an act of recognition from one person to another. The communication of acceptance and liking is 'positive' stroking; rejection, criticism and discounting are forms of 'negative' stroking. The notion of stroking clearly has parallels with the concept of reinforcement, which is central to the operant/instrumental conditioning theory of learning espoused by B.F. Skinner. However, it also has parallels with existential ideas around affirmation and validation. One of the TA core concepts in the area of values is the idea of *OK-ness*. This idea refers to a basic attitude of acceptance toward self and others. The preferred position in TA, or to put it in different terms, the recipe for a good life, is to interact with other people from an 'I'm OK, You're OK' stance. In other words, if a person can accept and affirm him/herself, and also those other people with whom she is in contact, the possibilities for constructive, creative interaction are maximized. Adopting any of the alternative positions (i.e., I'm OK, You're not OK; I'm not OK, You're OK; I'm not OK, You're not OK) undermines the possibility of authentic relatedness in different ways (for instance, I'm OK, You're not OK reflects rejection and belittling of the other; I'm not OK, You're OK reflects avoidance of the other; I'm not OK, You're not OK reflects a depressive, hopeless attitude to life). The third basic assumption in TA refers to the value of different types of human action. This idea starts with the concept of *time structuring* – how do people use their time. From a TA perspective, there are six ways in which time can be structured: withdrawal, rituals, pastimes, activity, psychological games and intimacy. From a TA perspective, intimacy is intrinsically valuable and life-enhancing, as a mode of being with others.

These three core concepts (strokes, OK-ness and time structuring) provide a readily accessible way of understanding the goals of TA – the function of TA theory and therapy is to enable the person to create the conditions in which intimacy can be possible, from an I'm OK, You're OK position in which the person can give and receive positive strokes. The goal of TA therapy is achieved by learning about the many distinct ways in which individual psychology and social interaction can be organized in order to avoid or deny intimacy and 'OK-ness'. The simple, yet powerful basic assumptions of TA theory reflect an image of human strength and mutuality, that function as counter-balance, and source of hope, in contrast to the inevitable stories of dysfunction, hurt and disorder that are told by people who seek therapy.

Structural analysis

Structural analysis is the level of TA theory that attempts to make sense of the psychological functioning of the individual person. The TA perspective on personality is organized around the concept of the *ego state*, which can be defined as a pattern of thought, feeling and action, that represents a developmentally and functionally significant mode of relating to self and others. Transactional analysis theory specifies three main ego states – the Parent (P), Adult (A) and Child (C). The Parent ego state is the part of the personality that comprises rules and injunctions internalized from one's own mother and father, other significant figures during childhood and the wider culture. The Adult ego state is understood to operate as the rational, decision-making function in the personality. The Child ego state represents emotional experience and creativity. Usually, these ego states are visually represented in a traffic light configuration (Figure 8.1).

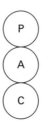

FIGURE 8.1 Structure of personality.

It is worth reflecting on some of the implications of this particular configuration, in contrast to other possible ways that three circles might be displayed – for example in a horizontal line, or in a triangle with each one touching the other. The vertical ordering of ego states chosen by Berne locates the Adult *between* Parent and Child. It also gives no possibility for direct contact between Parent and Child – their interaction is mediated by Adult. The parent appears, visually, to look over the other two ego states. Each of these factors has meaning, in terms of embodying implicit aspects of the model.

The traffic light image makes it easy to begin to visualize some significant facets of individual functioning. For example, are the boundaries between the three circles fixed and impermeable (implying that the person cannot readily engage all three states in response to external demands, but may be quite rigidly stuck in one or another of the states)? Or the boundary may be porous – one ego state may be *contagious*, and dominate the others (as when a person seems to approach all aspects of life from a critical, Parent, stance).

The depiction of the three ego states that has been considered so far is known as *first order* structural analysis. It is also possible to envisage the Parent and Child ego states each subdivided into *second order* structures. In other words, there is a hypothesized subsidiary Parent, Adult and Child embedded within each of these primary ego states. Figure 8.2 represents the second order – Parent, Adult and Child within the primary Child ego state.

The introduction of second order structural analysis makes it possible to diagrammatically represent the early developmental experiences that have contributed to current ego state functioning. For example the Parent-in-the-Child can be understood as comprising 'magical rules' that the person has unquestioningly internalized from their early years, such as 'if I don't eat all my dinner, Mother will go away and leave me and never come back' (Stewart and Joines 1987: 34). The Adult-in-the-Child has been described as a 'Little Professor', who generates intuitive, instance answers to problems, in the form of

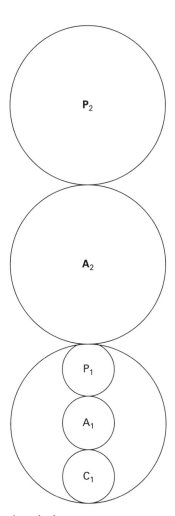

FIGURE 8.2 Second order structural analysis.

pseudo-rational responses. Finally, the Child-in-the-Child retains bodily memories of early experiences of pain and frustration, and also early experiences of pleasure and joy.

There is not space here to explore all of the uses and implications of the ego state model of personality structure. However, it is possible to comment on some of its features. It provides an easy-to-grasp representation of the multiplicity of human experiencing (see Rowan and Cooper 1998), and the ways in which different 'parts' of self may work together or be in conflict. It reflects one of the dominant themes in Western thought (since Freud) – the idea that the behaviour of the gown-up person is strongly influenced by what was learned or laid down in childhood. It also conveys an appreciation of the dynamic between pathology and strengths/assets in the life of a person – the Parent is both nurturing and protecting, and also critical and undermining; the Child is both hurt and avoidant, and fun-loving and curious.

Analysis of transactions

A further domain of TA theory is concerned with describing the nature of two-person interactions, or *transactions*. Note that the concept of 'transaction' is subtly different in meaning from 'interaction': the former term implies intentionality and purposefulness on the part of each protagonist, whereas 'interaction' makes no such assumption. Transactions are represented through arrowed lines between two side-by-side ego state diagrams. A *complementary* transaction consists of an episode in which one person is communicating from one of their ego states to the corresponding ego state in the other person, who in turn is responding with a reciprocal response. Complementary transactions are not problematic – they reflect situations in which interaction proceeds in an expected and predictable manner.

There are two forms of transaction that are psychological problematic. *Crossed* transactions occur when a person emits a communication that is intended to be received by an ego state in the other person, and the other responds from a different ego state. The first person is then left 'off balance' and wondering what has happened, because he or she has not received the expected response. An example of this would be if Person A asks 'what time is it' (Adult to Adult) and Person B replies 'Leave me alone – stop bothering me – can't you tell the time yourself?') (Critical Parent to Child). Finally, *ulterior* transactions refer to interaction sequences where the person may appear to be overtly communicating from one ego state, but in fact is sending an implicit or covert message from another ego state. An example would be: Person A: 'What time is it?' (overt Adult message; covert Child message 'Is it time to make the first gin and tonic of the evening'). If Person B responds to the overt message (by giving the time), then Person A may be annoyed and sulky (which leaves Person B feeling confused: 'what have I done, I just answered your question!' If Person B correctly interprets the implied message, and responds ('Oh, all right then, do you want ice?') then A and B could be regarded as engaging in a collusive transaction (i.e., pretence). It is easy to see how crossed and ulterior transactions can be associated with relationship difficulties – when counselling clients describe troubled relationships, TA counsellors use this framework to begin to make sense of what is happening, in a systematic manner.

Games

Probably the most widely read TA book has been *Games People Play* (Berne 1964); the idea of 'psychological games' has passed into everyday language usage. In relation to TA theory, Berne's ideas about games represent an attempt to make sense of aspects of human functioning and relationships that sit between the 'micro', moment-by-moment psychological states and interactions that are discussed within the theories that were developed to explain structure and transactions, and the more 'macro' level of script analysis (discussed in the following section). The theory of psychological games also makes it possible to make sense of the sometimes dramatic nature of human interactions; Berne was working on these ideas at the same time that the great sociologist Erving Goffman developing a broader 'dramaturgical' framework for understanding social life (Goffman 1955, 1956), and there are clear similarities between their ideas.

A game, in TA terms, can be defined as a repetitive sequence of transactions, between two or more people, that comprise a significant proportion of ulterior transactions (i.e., conducted out of Adult awareness), which incorporate a moment or moments of surprise and confusion, and which result in painful or inauthentic emotional states on the part of those who are involved. Berne (1964) suggested that each game proceeds through a set of stages. First there is the *con* (the invitation to play the game, or opening move). This is closely followed by the *gimmick* (the 'hook' that engages the other person at an emotional level). The *response* then consists of a series of transactions, through which the main part of the game (understood as a form of time-structuring) is played out. This phase may be completed in a few minutes, or can last for years. At some point there is a *switch,* which is characterized by cessation of the ritualized series of responses, and the introduction by the initial protagonist of a dramatically different type of interaction. This leads to a moment of confusion (the *crossup*) followed by the emotional *payoff*. The payoff is understood as reinforcing the underlying life position of each protagonist (e.g., I'm OK; You're not OK). Indeed, the unconscious purpose of games is that of enabling people to generate evidence for the validity of their life positions.

A simple example of a psychological game is *Why Don't You, Yes But* (Berne 1964). This game commences by Person A asking for advice: 'I am under a lot of stress at work and don't know what to do'. This request connects with the wish of Person B to be helpful and knowledgeable, so Person B begins to offer suggestions ('why don't you try to . . .'). Person B replied to each of these suggestions with the statement 'yes . . . but . . .'. Eventually, Person B runs out of suggestions, and is met by a sweet (but inauthentic) smile from Person A, and the statement 'thank you for trying to help me', uttered in a dismissive fashion. Person B feels confused – what has happened here? At this moment, each person enters an emotional state that is familiar to them. Person A feels isolated and indignant ('no one can help me; I'm not Ok and other people aren't OK either). Person B feels depressed and inadequate ('I'm no good at helping others').

The original TA thinking about games has been significantly elaborated by Karpman (1968), who suggested that games tend to be initiated by a person who adopts the role of *victim* ('please help me') and whose needs are responded to by another person who takes the role of *rescuer*. At the switch point, however, the victim becomes a *persecutor*, whereas the erstwhile rescuer is thrown into the role of victim. Karpman (1968) coined the term *drama triangle* to capture the way that each person moves around the triangle during the game.

The TA theory of games provides a powerful tool for understanding dysfunctional sequences that happen, over and over again, in the lives of people whose difficulties are enmeshed in patterns of unsatisfactory relationships with others, for example people who are addicted to alcohol, drugs or unhealthy eating (Steiner 1979). Typically, such people are surrounded by others, such as family members, who enact complementary roles in the games that they initiate. The theory of games is also a valuable analytic tool for making sense of how clients interact with each other in therapy groups (most of Berne's practice was based on working with groups).

Life scripts

The various TA concepts that have been described come together at the level of *script analysis* (Steiner 1974, 1976). Contemporary TA theory and practice is highly focused on using the idea of 'script' for two key therapeutic purposes. First, in TA terms, 'script' is how TA practitioners make sense of the client's personality as a whole. Secondly, script analysis is the TA equivalent of cognitive–behavioural case formulation – it provides a comprehensive plan for understanding the issues being experienced by the client, his or her strengths and weaknesses in relation to dealing with these issues, and a road-map for how to initiate positive change. Berne (1975: 418) defined a script as 'an ongoing program, developed in early childhood under parental influence, which directs the individual's behaviour in the most important aspects of his life'.

In the final book he published, *What Do You Say After You Say Hello: The Psychology of Human Destiny,* Berne (1975) suggested that a person's script was formulated in early childhood, as the young person looked around him/her and arrived at some basic deci-sions about his or her 'destiny'. Berne (1975) hypothesized that children need to find answers to existential questions such as 'what kind of a person am I?' and 'what happens to people like me?' In seeking answers to these questions, children are influenced by the example set by their parents, and by the way they are treated by parents and other signifi-cant grown-up figures. However, the young person is not in a position to make rational choices, but instead needs to draw on the conceptual resources that are available to him or her. Berne (1975) points out that fairy tales represent a rich source of answers to the question of 'what happens to different types of people?', because fairy stories comprise a form of distilled human wisdom, that has been refined and deepened through generations of storytelling. He therefore proposes that a good way to begin to make sense of the general outline of a person's life script is to ask him or her what was their favourite or most memorable fairy story (or, nowadays, their favourite or most memorable movie or cartoon drama). Within that story, there is likely to be a character with whom the person particu-larly identifies, and whose destiny has functioned as a template for the person's own life journey. For example, a woman who identifies with *Cinderella* might have spent her life as an unrecognized and oppressed princess, waiting for her prince to find her and take her away. Berne (1975) points out that people tend to remember their own personalized versions of fairy tales, in which they adapt and select key ideas and events, rather than necessarily identify with the precise detail of the tale as it is recorded in books.

In relation to the key goals of TA therapy, 'fairy tale' characters typically do not enjoy lives that are characterized by intimacy, OK-ness, and giving and receiving positive strokes. The purpose of therapy, therefore, is to enable the person to replace the fixed script that was written for them in childhood, with a more flexible personal story that reflects the life decisions that the person has made for himself or herself.

In practice, it is no easy matter to change a life script that may have operated as a guiding life plan for many decades. The primary TA strategy, in relation to working with script, is to seek to identify and challenge the moment-by-moment psychological pro-cesses through which the script is maintained, and reproduces itself in new relationships and situations. One of the most useful ideas, in this respect, are the concepts of *driver* (Kahler 1978) and *racket system* (Erskine and Zalcman 1979). A 'driver' can be understood as a fundamental life principle or survival strategy that guides the person's actions in life. A driver is derived from messages received in early life from one's parents, arising from their conditional acceptance of their offspring (i.e., 'you're OK *if . . .*'). Clinical experience in TA has enabled six different drivers to be identified:

- *be strong* (you're OK if you are strong and don't feel things);
- *try hard* (you're OK if you do your best and don't have fun);
- *please me* (you're OK if you do what I say, rather than follow your own initiative or take care of your own needs);
- *hurry up* (you're not OK until you have achieved the task I have set for you);
- *be perfect* (you're OK if you always get things right);
- *take it* (you're OK if you demand what you need; Tudor 2008).

It is assumed in TA that, for each individual, the script is 'driven' by one of these statements. The task of the therapist is to help the person to recognize when they are functioning according to this pattern, and to develop alternatives that allow a wider repertoire of responses to life situations. For example, a woman living a *Cinderella* life might always be striving to *please* her potential partners, thus not allowing them to relate to her at an authentic, intimate level.

The 'racket system' refers to the strategies that a person uses in order to keep himself or herself with an 'I'm not OK' position. A simple example of a racket might be if someone receives a positive and loving comment from another person, which in effect is saying to them 'You are OK'. A person who is not comfortable with intimacy and OK-ness needs to find some means of deflecting this comment, which threatens the whole basis on which he or she has built their approach to life. Such a person might respond in an angry fashion: 'you don't mean it, you are just trying to make yourself look good by dishing out compliments'. A racket system is based in one or two emotions that the person has acquired as strategies for avoiding intimacy – for example, feeling depressed and withdrawing from other people, getting angry and pushing people away, feeling afraid and seeing other people as threats, and so on. A racket feeling is strongly felt by the person, but experienced by others as not wholly appropriate to the situation, or exaggerated. The racket system represents a means through which the script is reinforced and maintained. For TA therapists, the aim is to enable the person to move beyond being 'specialists' in maybe one or two areas of feelings, and to be able to fulfil their potential to experience a range of feelings and emotions, appropriate to the situation that the person is in at the time.

TA in practice

As with any approach to counselling that has been in existence for any length of time, TA has been interpreted and applied in somewhat different ways by various groups of practitioners. The core characteristics of any form of TA therapy have been described by Woollams and Brown (1978: 243–5) as:

- using TA language and concepts, and where appropriate sharing these ideas with clients;
- working with ego states and life scripts;
- contracting: making an explicit agreement with the client around the goals of counselling, and keeping this contact under regular review. TA practitioners have

made significant contributions to good practice in contracting (see, for example, Lee 2006; Stewart 2006);

- a *decisional* approach, which emphasizes the early life decisions of the client, and his or her capacity to make new decisions;

- a *strengths* approach, based on an 'I'm OK – You're OK' stance: 'the therapist does not consider the client to be inadequate, defective, or incapable of modification, no matter what the diagnosis' (p. 245).

Within this set of general principles, there have emerged a number of contrasting 'schools' of TA: classical, redecison, cathexis, cognitive–behavioural and relational. These 'schools' (and others not listed here) overlap to a large extent, but nevertheless have each developed their own distinctive brand of TA practice.

The *classical* school of TA is based on the form of practice originally developed by Eric Berne, using the group as the primary medium for therapy. The therapist allows the group process to build up, and then points out to members the games, rackets and other 'script' behaviours that they are exhibiting. Participants in the group work together to understand these patterns, and then contract to change them.

The *redecison* school of TA is associated with the work of Bob and Mary Goulding (1979), who have incorporated ideas and methods from gestalt therapy into their approach. They work with groups, but do not focus on group process, preferring to work with one individual at a time (the gestalt 'hot seat' model) with the remaining members of the group functioning as observers, witnesses and supporters. Redecision TA therapists pay particular attention to the phenomenon of *impasse,* where the person is caught between two conflicting emotional forces or action tendencies. They also highlight the centrality of personal *responsibility* in the therapeutic process: the assumption is that the script decisions made by the person in early life can only be changed by 'redecisions' made when he or she is older.

The *Cathexis Institute* was formed by Jacqui and Shea Schiff in the 1970s, to provide intensive, inpatient treatment for people with severe and enduring mental health problems (e.g., schizophrenia) (Schiff 1971; Schiff *et al.* 1975). The distinctive feature of the cathexis model is that 'craziness' is the result of contradictory and destructive Parental messages to which the person was exposed during childhood, and that the cure involves 'reparenting' by a therapist 'mother' and 'father', to enable the person to acquire more benign and affirming Parent functions that will allow the person to feel safe enough to use Adult and Child effectively in responding to everyday situations. This kind of work is hugely intensive, and requires a high degree of commitment and professionalism from therapists. In the early years of the Cathexis Institute, therapists even went as far as legally adopting some of their client-children. Inevitably, it proved to be difficult for some therapists to maintain appropriate therapeutic boundaries when using this approach, and there have been ethical issues associated with the application of a full-scale reparenting model. Controversial issues in the use of the cathexis approach are discussed by Jacobs (1994) and Rawson (2002). Nevertheless, many TA (and other) therapists acknowledge the value of being willing to adopt a parenting stance in relation to clients who have only known destructive and undermining attitudes and behaviour from their actual early caregivers (Childs-Gowell 2000). A valuable account of the contemporary use of a reparenting approach in the context of a therapeutic community is provided by Rawson (2002).

Cognitive–behavioural TA reflects the close affinity between TA and some aspects of CBT, specifically the use of case formulation and contracting, and attention to cognitive information-processing (i.e., Adult functioning). Cognitive–behavioural and cognitive therapy strategies can readily be integrated into a broad TA framework for understanding (Mothersole 2002).

Relational TA has emerged over the last 20 years, largely influenced by the writings of Helena Hargaden and Charlotte Sills (Cornell and Hargaden 2005; Hargaden and Sills 2002). They describe the origins of their approach as arising from changing patterns of clinical practice:

> . . . when Berne first wrote, the common client was putatively an inhibited, rule-bound individual who needed the metaphorical 'solvent' of therapy to loosen the confines of his or her script. As we move into the twenty-first century, the 'typical' client is one who needs not solvent but 'glue' – a way of integrating and building his or her sense of self in the world . . . our client population frequently seemed to have a disturbance of sense of self . . . (reflecting) a schizoid process that referred to hidden, sequestered areas of the self.
>
> (Hargaden and Sills 2002: 3)

The *relational* approach draws on ideas from psychodynamic psychotherapy and psycho-analysis in its emphasis on the central importance of the therapeutic relationship as an arena within which the deeply buried personal conflicts of the client (i.e., 'sequestered areas of self' within the Child ego state) can be identified and worked through. A distinc-tive contribution of relational TA has been its re-working of psychoanalytic concepts of transference, counter-transference, attachment and self, within a TA framework. Compared with other schools of TA, the relational model explicitly highlights the process being expe-rienced by the therapist (counter-transference), and the use of this information as a means of exploring the relational patterns of the client.

This brief review of schools of TA practice supports a view that there is no single distinctive therapeutic intervention or method associated with this approach. Many other approaches have largely defined themselves in terms of a unique contribution to therapeutic method (for example: free association and interpretation in psychoanalysis; empathic reflection in client-centred therapy; two-chair work in gestalt therapy). Transactional analysis is not that type of therapy. Instead, TA comprises a rich theoretical system, which can be applied in therapy using a wide range of interventions and methods.

Box 8.2: *TA in action: the case of Martin*

A good example of how an integrative model of TA therapy, drawing on various schools of practice, works in practice can be found in the case of Martin (Tudor and Widdowson 2002). The client, Martin, was a young man who was angry, socially isolated, depressed, and self-harming, who was seen for 15 sessions by a counsellor in a youth work drop-in centre. He was unemployed, had recently come out as gay and felt uncomfortable about his sexuality, and had been experiencing panic attacks in his local supermarket.

The first three sessions were devoted to gathering information, and using cognitive–behavioural relaxation exercises to enable Martin to feel grounded enough to engage in therapy. The counsellor identified that Martin was alternating between 'pleasing others' and 'being strong' drivers, and gradually began to point out these patterns, thus enabling a process of 'decontamination' of Adult ego state functioning. At the same time, the counsellor was gently operating from a Nurturing Parent position, providing Martin with information and advice designed to enhance well-being and safety. By the third session, Martin was able to collaborate in the setting of a contract that specified a number of goals for change. The counsellor suggested a number of self-soothing activities, such as taking warm baths and eating healthily, that began to establish an internalized Nurturing Parent, which in turn allowed Martin to disclose that he had been sexually abused in childhood. This new information led to a process of 'deconfusion', comprising discussion of what this event had meant for Martin at Parent, Adult and Child levels. At each stage, the counsellor introduced Martin to more of the TA ideas behind the therapy. Over the next few sessions, Martin was able to enter a 'redecision' phase, where he looked at what he wanted to achieve in his life, and how he might realistically attain these goals.

The case of Martin is notable in demonstrating multiple ways in which TA conceptualization can be applied in therapy through the use of a wide range of interventions drawn from other therapy traditions. In this case, the counsellor used relaxation techniques, in-vivo exposure, homework assignments, two-chair work, interpretation, letter-writing, grief rituals and several other methods, while adhering to a set of basic TA principles around contracting and collaborative working.

The organizational structure of TA

Transactional analysis is unusual among contemporary approaches to therapy in having evolved a unified international structure. All TA therapists are members of the International Transactional Analysis Association (ITAA) or one of its constituent national or regional associations, all of which are formally registered as non-profit organizations. The ITAA has developed a rigorous framework for training and accreditation, which means that all TA therapists have achieved a high standard of knowledge and competence. Unlike other therapy orientations, which have been characterized by a proliferation of splinter groups and networks, TA has remained a unified approach, which has been able to contain and build on a tradition of lively debate around theory and method. The ITAA incorporates sections that deal with educational and organizational applications of TA, in addition to counselling/psychotherapy, and publishes the *Transactional Analysis Journal*.

Although Eric Berne and other founders of TA mainly conducted therapy within groups, current TA practice is largely focused on working with individuals. Compared with other approaches, TA counsellors and psychotherapists are more likely to be based in private practice, rather than employed in health or educational settings. There has been relatively little research into TA (see Box 8.3), which has meant that the approach has been largely invisible in relation to debates around evidence-based practice, and as a result has been marginalized by health-provision organizations such as the NHS in Britain.

Box 8.3: *Research into the effectiveness of TA therapy*

There has been limited research into either the outcomes or processes of TA counselling and psychotherapy. Emerson *et al.* (1994) showed that psychological disturbance, measured with standard symptom checklist, was associated with higher than average expression of Critical Parent and Adapted Child, and that effective therapy could reduce the predominance of these ego state functions in clients. Greene (1988) reviewed seven studies that had been carried out into the outcomes of TA therapy or training for marital problems. He found that most of the studies were of low methodological quality, and had yielded inconclusive evidence regarding the effectiveness of TA in relation to this client group. Greene (1988) suggested that it would be more appropriate for TA therapists to conduct systematic case studies into their marital therapy practice. To date, no such studies have been published.

McLeod (McLeod, Julia 2013) and Widdowson (2012a, 2012b, 2012c) have published rigorous systematic single case studies that have documented the effectiveness of TA therapy with depressed clients and clients with long-term health conditions. Ohlsson (2002) assessed the effectiveness of TA psychotherapy for clients with severe problems of drug misuse. Group TA therapy was delivered as part of a therapeutic community intervention in several centres in Sweden. Ohlsson (2002) reported that TA therapy had been highly effective with clients who had completed the course of therapy, particularly those who had received more than 80 sessions. Gains were maintained at 2-year follow-up. Novey (1999, 2002) carried out two studies in which clients who had completed TA therapy were invited to complete a retrospective questionnaire that asked them about their satisfaction with therapy, and the benefits they had experienced. The questionnaire that was used, was adapted from the *Consumer Reports* survey conducted by Seligman (1995). Novey (1999, 2002) found that over 60 per cent of clients who had received six months or more reported major improvements in symptoms, while around 45 per cent of those who had undergone therapy of six months or less reported similar gains. The level of change found in the clients in the Novey (1999, 2002) surveys was significantly higher than in the Seligman (1995) study. However, the design of the Seligman (1995) study was more inclusive, and thus probably more likely to elicit responses from less satisfied clients.

Although the studies briefly reviewed here are interesting and valuable, and open up many possibilities for further research, none of them achieve the standards of methodological rigour required to be incorporated into systematic reviews that would influence health care policy in the area of evidence-based practice. Van Rijn (2011) carried out a naturalistic outcome study of clients receiving TA therapy in a primary care clinic, and reported effectiveness rates equivalent to other therapies. A review of research on TA, up to 2010, has been compiled by Ohlsson (2010). It can be concluded that some evidence exists for the effectiveness of TA counselling and psychotherapy, but that further studies are needed.

An appraisal of the TA approach to counselling

The major strength of TA, as an approach to counselling, lies in its contribution to theory. Transactional analysis writers have constructed the richly creative and coherent set of ideas, that enable practitioners to think through the complex linkages, in the lives of their clients, between early experience and here-and-now personal and social functioning. Transactional analysis theory is based on close observation of how people think, feel and act in different situations. It probably represents the most fully articulated integrative model of human personality and functioning currently in use within the therapy community.

The direction in which TA has been developing in recent years, particularly the movement toward psychodynamic theory and practice represented by the work of Hargaden and Sills (2002) raises questions about the continuing distinctiveness of the approach. Is TA gradually evolving into a variant of psychodynamic counselling/psychotherapy? Associated with this direction of travel has been an increasing complexity in the theoretical structure of TA. A key element of Eric Berne's original project was to de-mystify the language of professional psychology, and explain psychological processes in a language that would be accessible to ordinary people. The language of ego states, games and rackets certainly went a long way towards achieving this goal. By contrast, the intricacies of some contemporary TA theorizing and diagrammatic representation are well beyond what a lay person might reasonably be expected to grasp.

There are a number of areas within which TA theory and practice might benefit from further development. It would be valuable to be able to make reference to research into the effectiveness of TA therapy with different client groups. At present, TA has created a sophisticated training and accreditation structure, but on the basis of little published evidence of efficacy. It would also be useful to carry out research into which aspects of TA are most relevant in working with different client groups and problem areas. At present, the TA literature gives relatively little consideration to cultural factors. Although Eric Berne himself was a second-generation immigrant cultural 'outsider', and Claude Steiner grew up in Spain and Mexico, TA theory pays little attention to the possibility of cultural diversity in relation to scripts, drivers or rackets, or to the compatibility between TA ideas and indigenous forms of healing. It is surprising, given the deliberate adoption of colloquial, humorous, accessible, jargon-free language by TA theorists, that TA has not been more widely disseminated in the context of self-help books and manuals. With the exception of Claude Steiner's popular writing on emotional literacy (Steiner 1997, 2003), there are few currently available TA self-help books. The production of such texts would be of assistance to TA therapy clients, as well as to the general public.

Conclusions

Transactional analysis represents a unique resource for counsellors, in providing a comprehensive theoretical system that provides both practitioners and clients with ways of making
sense of how and why personal problems occur, and what can be done about them. It is
essential for counsellors to learn to appreciate the contrast between TA as a set of ideas,
and how these ideas can be applied in practice. Eric Berne was fond of the image of the
therapist (or person who is 'cured') as a 'Martian':

> . . . the Martian comes to Earth and has to go back and 'tell it like it is' – not
> like the Earth people say it is, or want him to think it is. He doesn't listen to
> big words nor tables of statistics, but watches what people are actually doing
> to, for, and with each other, rather than what they say they are doing
>
> (Berne 1975: 40)

The TA theory that he was instrumental in devising, and which his colleagues and succes-
sors have continued to articulate using this style of thinking and expression, is a theory of
human personality and interaction, as it might have been created by a Martian: based on
careful observation, classification and categorization, for the perspective of a theory-maker
who is an outsider, interested only in what is truly happening. It is in its overt 'Martianism'
that there lies the fundamental strength of TA as an approach to therapy. The point of TA is
not to get lost in the intricacies of ego state diagrams or how many drivers there are. The
point, instead, is that TA ideas represent an invitation to step aside from the 'trash which has
accumulated in your head ever since you came home from the maternity ward' (Berne 1975:
4) and thereby to be able to 'see the other person, to be aware of him/her as a phenomenon,
to happen to him/her, and to be ready for him/her to happen to you'. This is the radical,
hopeful and life-affirming agenda that remains at the heart of all authentic TA therapy.

Topics for reflection and discussion

1   Reflect on the meaning of the concept of 'strokes' in your own life. What is your own
    'stroke economy'? To what extent are you able to give and receive negative and positive
    strokes? To what extent can areas of difficulty in your life be understood as associated
    with a tendency to 'discount' (i.e., deflect or deny) positive strokes that are directed to
    you by others? What are the origins, in your early life, of your current 'stroke pattern'?

2   Are Hargaden and Sills (2002) justified in characterizing classical/Bernian TA as 'essen-
    tially cognitive therapy'?

3   Transactional analysis theorists and practitioners place a strong emphasis on the
    capacity of TA theory to operate as an integrative framework, encompassing ideas from
    other mainstream approaches. However, how fully integrative is TA? When you
    consider the concepts and themes introduced in earlier chapters in this book, what are
    the ideas that do *not* readily fit into the TA system?

4 There is an obvious similarity between Freud's concepts of *superego, ego* and *id*, and the Parent, Adult and Child ego states of transactional analysis. What are the differences in emphasis between these alternative formulations? What is gained (or lost) by employing an ego state model, rather than the original psychoanalytic concepts?

Suggested further reading

The best introductory text on TA theory is *TA Today* by Stewart and Joines (2012), and a useful account of how TA is used in practice is *Transactional Analysis Counselling in Action*, by Stewart (2000). Anyone interested in understanding the spirit of TA needs to read some of Eric Berne's original writings. A good place to start is the book that he completed just before he died: *What Do You Say After You Say Hello?* (Berne 1975). The *Transactional Analysis Journal* publishes readable and practice-friendly articles that testify to the continued vitality of the TA tradition, and the willingness of the TA community to integrate and incorporate ideas from other therapeutic orientations. The *International Journal of Transactional Analysis Research* is the central point of contact for the rapidly expanding TA research literature.

9 Gestalt therapy

Introduction

Gestalt therapy is a widely used humanistically oriented approach to therapy, developed in the 1950s by Fritz and Laura Perls, Paul Goodman, Ralph Hefferline and others. As a form of therapy arising from the humanistic tradition, Gestalt therapy has some similarities with person-centred therapy in rejecting and yet at the same time being deeply influenced by psychoanalytic ideas, and in a shared commitment to humanistic values such as the celebration of individual freedom, creativity and expression of feeling. The spirit of gestalt therapy is captured in a passage written by the British Gestalt therapist Malcolm Parlett (2001: 44):

> Gestalt . . . provides a means for interrupting the flow of self-talk, inviting us to return to 'now', 'here', 'the actual', in order to be 'more present'. Thereby, individuals can learn to notice and capture subtle feeling states that easily go unnoticed. They register themselves as alive physical beings; sensing, moving and feeling. They are ready to engage fully with others.

The aim of the present chapter is to provide an introduction to the ideas and methods associated with this influential approach, review its strengths and limitations, and highlight resources for further exploration and learning.

Cultural and philosophical influences

There are several respects in which gestalt therapy is significantly different from other forms of 'talking therapy'. Organizationally and institutionally, gestalt therapy has tended to follow its own path, eschewing formal affiliation with academic departments in universities and therapy services provided by large health care systems. To understand the distinctiveness of gestalt therapy theory and practice, it is necessary to have an appreciation of its cultural and philosophical roots, and the way in which it has developed over the last half century.

The story of gestalt therapy continues to be dominated by the intellectual presence of its founder, Fritz Perls. It is instructive to compare the life trajectory of Perls with that of Carl Rogers, founder of person-centred therapy. Rogers was essentially the product of a conventional, small-town, upper-middle-class America upbringing, who worked for most of his life in salaried positions within social service and educational organizations. By contrast, Fritz Perls (1893–1970) was born in a Berlin Jewish ghetto. His father, a wine salesman, became financially successful, and Fritz Perls enjoyed a middle-class upbringing, albeit one in which he experienced considerable family tension. Although he was actively involved in theatre, he entered medical school. He was drafted into the German army in World War I, and spent nine months in the trenches as a medical orderly, narrowly escaping death. He qualified as an MD in 1920, and became part of the Bauhaus group of dissident artists and intellectuals.

After entering psychoanalysis in 1926, with Karen Horney, he decided to become an analyst. Within the psychoanalytic community of that era, he was particularly influenced by the ideas of Wilhelm Reich around the significance of bodily defences against authentic feeling. Fritz Perls made his living as an analyst between 1929 and 1950, first in Germany, then in South Africa (where he emigrated in 1936 as a result of the rise of fascism in Germany) and finally in New York. His mother and sister died in concentration camps.

Throughout his life, he openly experimented with different types of sexual experience, and was associated in the USA with 'counter-culture' figures such as Paul Goodman, and with radical theatre groups. He found it hard, throughout his life, to maintain close relationships. Compared with Carl Rogers, and indeed with almost any other leading figure in psychotherapy, the life of Fritz Perls was characterized by alienation, first-hand experience of death and cruelty, and what R.D. Laing has described as 'ontological insecurity'. It is hardly surprising that the therapy approach that he created placed a premium on the discovery and creation of moments of authentic contact, and paid little attention to issues of coping, or adjustment to social norms.

In the years following the death of Fritz Perls, the worldwide network of gestalt therapy practitioners and therapists needed to come to terms with his legacy. He had written relatively little, and it was left to others to articulate and explain the conceptual framework of gestalt therapy. His practice reflected what could be regarded as a somewhat extreme, individualist representation of gestalt principles. As a reaction to this, a major theme in subsequent gestalt theory, training and practice has been an emphasis on developing a more *relational* perspective. A key figure in the process of re-shaping gestalt therapy was Laura Perls (1905–1990) (Serlin 1992), who had been around from the start. Her less confrontational version of gestalt work, largely disregarded during the lifetime of her husband, became increasingly influential after his death.

Although recent gestalt writing contains little reference to psychoanalytic ideas, and appreciation of what gestalt therapy is about requires recognition of its psychoanalytic origins. Fritz and Laura Perls were both trained in psychoanalysis, underwent personal analyses, and practised as analysts for several years. Underpinning everything that happens in gestalt therapy is the notion of the 'unconscious': the assumption that the most important processes through which people relate to self and others are outside of conscious awareness, and that effective therapeutic work necessarily involves bringing these processes into awareness. The difference between gestalt therapy and psychoanalysis, in respect of their understanding of the unconscious, is that gestalt practitioners are primarily interested in the here-and-now expression of unconscious processes in bodily enactments, rather than in attempts to promote insight around the original causes of these processes in early childhood memories and experiences.

At the same time, it is essential to understand that psychoanalytic ideas comprise only one facet of gestalt theory and practice. Gestalt therapy also brings together important ideas from the German tradition of gestalt psychology and Lewin's field theory. The 'Gestalt' school of psychology had been an influential force in the psychology of perception and cognition in the period 1930–50 (Kohler 1929; Koffka 1935). 'Gestalt' is a German word that means 'pattern', and the key idea in this psychological model is the capacity of people to experience the world in terms of wholes, or overall patterns, and, more specifically, to have a tendency to complete unfinished patterns. The actual gestalt psychologists were primarily interested in studying human perception and thought, and were responsible for familiar ideas, such as 'mental set' (viewing later phenomena as if they were similar to the first configuration the viewer had originally encountered) and the 'Zeigarnik effect' (having a better recollection of tasks that had not been completed than of tasks that had been fully finished). The ideas of the social psychologist Kurt Lewin extended gestalt psychology into the sphere of social relationships, by proposing that each individual exists within a 'life space' or 'field' that is constructed along gestalt principles. Gestalt psychology has influenced gestalt therapy in a number of ways, for example in its emphasis on 'wholeness' and the inter-relatedness of all things, the view that the human mind actively makes meaning from whatever information is available to it, and sensitivity to the significance of boundaries, edges and points of contact between regions of experience.

In addition to these psychological concepts, the founders of gestalt therapy were also influenced by the phenomenological tradition in philosophy, spiritual and self-enlightenment practices from eastern religious traditions, such as Zen, the 'body therapy' methods of Wilhelm Reich, and an appreciation of the significance of the artistic, dramatic and aesthetic dimensions of life. Compared to most other therapy approaches, the theoretical 'hinterland' of gestalt therapy is exceptionally creative and diverse. Further discussion and explanation of the underlying philosophy of gestalt therapy can be found in Brownell (2008), Wagner-Moore (2004) and Woldt and Toman (2005).

Box 9.1: *The Gloria case: Fritz Perls at work*

One of the most famous psychotherapy cases of all time is the 'Gloria' tape (available on YouTube) in which a film was made of sequential therapy sessions between one client (Gloria) and three leading therapists: Carl Rogers, Albert Ellis and Fritz Perls. The Gloria tapes have been studied by thousands of counselling and psychotherapy trainees, and have generated an ever-expanding critical and research literature (see for example Magai and Haviland-Jones 2002). The recording of the session with Fritz Perls provides a vivid example of the confrontational way in which the early generation of gestalt therapists worked with the here-and-now embodied experience of the client. For example, Perls regularly directed Gloria's attention to her non-verbal behaviour through the use of statements such as:

> "What are you doing with your feet now?"
> "Are you aware of your smile?"
> "You didn't squirm for the last minute."
> "Are you aware that your eyes are moist?"
> "Are you aware of your facial expression?"

Immediately following the session with Perls, Gloria is reported to have said that she found these interventions to be helpful. However, some commentators have doubted whether these statements had a positive impact on Gloria within the actual session (Dolliver 1991). The ready access that is now available in respect to viewing the Gloria tapes means that it is possible for anyone to examine the recordings at their leisure, and make up their own mind. Important background information, which is not provided on the tapes themselves, included the fact that Gloria had been a gestalt therapy client for several years (not with Perls) before the recordings were made (Ellis 1991) and that Gloria developed a close and enduring friendship with Carl Rogers that lasted to the end of her life.

Theoretical framework for practice

The theoretical framework for the practice of gestalt therapy was established with the publication of *Ego, Hunger and Aggression* (Perls 1947) and *Gestalt Therapy* (Perls *et al.* 1951). The later writings of Perls (1969, 1973) mainly articulated the approach through examples of his work with clients, rather than through a formal theoretical presentation, although Perls also demonstrated his work extensively in training workshops. An essential feature of gestalt therapy as practised by Fritz Perls was an extreme hostility to over-intellectualization, or what he called 'bullshit'. His approach, therefore, focused rigorously on the here-and-now experiencing or awareness of the client, with the aim of removing the blocks to authentic contact with the environment caused by old patterns ('unfinished business').

The emphasis on working with immediate experience, combined with Fritz Perls' rejection of theorizing, meant that gestalt therapy has often been considered as a source of practical techniques for exploring current awareness, and enabling clients to express buried feelings, rather than as a distinctive theoretical model. There is some validity to this view, since gestalt has been responsible for a wide range of techniques and exercises, such as two-chair work, first-person language and ways of working with art materials, dreams and guided fantasies. Nevertheless, this approach includes a theoretical framework that contains many important ideas, and is notable for the degree to which it highlights existential issues.

It is important to acknowledge that the writings of Fritz Perls do not present a particularly balanced view of the gestalt approach as it is currently practiced. Perls has been described as a 'brilliant, dramatic, controversial and charismatic teacher' (Parlett and Page 1990: 239) who modelled a style of working with clients that was significantly more confrontational and anti-intellectual than that adopted by subsequent gestalt practitioners (see Shepard 1975; Masson 1992). More recently, gestalt practice has moved in the direction of work based on the relationship between client and therapist, and the development of awareness and understanding of contact disruptions within this relationship, and uses dramatic enactments rather less often than previously. Contemporary Gestalt practitioners tend to describe themselves as employing a *dialogical* approach (Wheeler 1991; Hycner and Jacobs 1995; Yontef 1995, 1998), which has the aim of developing conversation that enables the client to become aware of 'what they are doing and how they are doing it' (Yontef 1995).

Box 9.2: *The case of Rose*

The case of 'Rose' is an account of a woman who received gestalt therapy in a student counselling service over an 18-month period, from Bob Harman (1986). Rose was severely overweight, depressed, and had difficulties in forming close relationships. This case report includes several descriptions of ways in which a gestalt therapist might try to facilitate awareness of bodily actions and feeling states within the ongoing flow of conversation. For example:

> During our first session I was struck by two very unusual pieces of nonverbal behaviour that she exhibited. . . . when I spoke she pushed back in her chair as far as she could go, opened her eyes as wide as possible, and held her breath. So, this is what I saw – this huge woman pushed back in her chair with her eyes open as wide as they could possibly go and her chest inflated as far as it could possibly go. As I spoke she maintained this awkward position while exhaling with such force I could feel it across the room. I thought this would be something fine with which to work and so my first comment was, 'Are you aware of your expression?'
>
> 'No.'
>
> 'Well, would you be willing to stay as you are and focus your awareness on your face!'
>
> 'Yes.' Nothing.
>
> So, 'Well, Rose, what do you experience with your face!'

'Well, I can feel my eyes open.'

'Well, to me you look terrified or terror-stricken.'

Her response was, 'That's interesting.' which I later reframed to mean, 'That doesn't mean shit to me, Bob.'

(Harman 1986: 20)

This unwillingness to explore bodily meaning continued throughout the course of therapy. Harman (1986 :20) acknowledged that 'almost everything I did with her nonverbal behavior fell flat. She complied with every request I made . . . and she got nothing from it'. Yet, at the same time, Rose gradually became more able to be aware of her feelings, often through moments of humour, and to trust her therapist enough to use sessions as a safe place where she could talk about what she found hard in her everyday interactions with people. Gradually, she was able to construct more of the life that she wanted to live. Reflecting on the process of his work with Rose, Harman (1986: 29) suggests that what was most helpful was 'my presence and my personhood'. This case report incorporates other features that may be of interest to readers, including a brief account of Harman's own development as a therapist, and a critique of his work with Rose from several leading figures in the gestalt therapy community.

Gestalt strategies for facilitating awareness and change

Gestalt therapists have imported ideas from drama that involved the client physically *enacting* the emotional issues in their lives. A further distinctive aspect of the approach lies in an emphasis on *conflict* between parts of the self, mirroring the personal and social conflict experienced by Perls throughout his life. Clients are encouraged to participate in experiments that allow such conflict to be brought into the open. Wagner-Moore (2004: 184) argues that the rationale, within gestalt theory and practice, for the use of experiential experiments is that 'clients will more fully understand their own emotions and needs through a process of *discovery*, rather than through insight or interpretation'. Some of the specific strategies used in gestalt practice include:

- The practice of gestalt therapy represents, for the client, a training in the application of the methods of phenomenology. The client is invited to report directly on his or her present experiencing: what is being thought, felt and done here and now. This process creates the possibility of identifying aspects of existence ('I am alone', 'I am looking at you', 'I feel a pain in my chest') rather than merely talking or intellectualizing 'about' external problems.

- The concept of *contact* is used in gestalt therapy to refer to the quality of the person's capacity to be with another person. When two people are together, there is a *contact boundary* where they meet each other. Gestalt theorists have devised a set of concepts for making sense of what is experienced at this boundary. There can be *confluence* (fusion between the two people), in which the separation and distinction between self and other becomes so unclear that the boundary is lost. In *isolation*, the boundary is experienced as impermeable – there is an absence of connectedness. *Retroflection* represents the creation of internal boundaries by a person, who appears to be doing to self what he or she wants to do to someone else, or doing for self what he or she wants someone else to do for them (Yontef 1995). *Introjection* describes a process through which thoughts, emotions of actions from another person are absorbed or 'swallowed' whole by the person. *Projection* involves attributing to the other, emotions, thoughts or intentions that actually belong to the self. Finally, *deflection* is the avoidance of contact or of awareness by not paying attention to the other, or by expressing things in an indirect manner. These concepts help a therapist to make sense of the experience of what it is like to *be with* a client. By engaging in conversation that invites the client to be aware of these dimensions of his or her existence, the client is given opportunities to make choices around autonomy/connectedness.

- A great deal of attention is paid to *embodiment*, in terms not only of how the person is feeling at any moment, but how he or she uses their body to express meaning, through gesture, movement, voice quality and posture.

- The notion of *polarities* within personal experience and action is a central aspect of gestalt theory and practice, for example in the well-known gestalt technique of 'two-chair' work, in which the person is invited to engage in a dialogue between different aspects of self, each of which is placed on a separate chair, with the client shifting to and fro between one chair and the other as he or she gives voice to the pattern of thinking, feeling and action associated with each 'part' of the self.

- The use of first-person language (for instance 'I feel . . .' rather than 'it feels . . .') as a means of 'owning' experience and promoting authentic self-expression.

- Various exercises that make use of fantasy, dream imagery and art-making to shift the client out of his or her dominant rational/cognitive mode of being, and into moments of spontaneous self-discovery.

These therapeutic activities are all part of the intention, in gestalt therapy to assist the person to live an authentic life in which they take responsibility for their actions. It is therefore a form of therapy that places a great deal of emphasis on the discovery of personal truth, and the elimination of all forms of self-deception.

Box 9.3: *Two-chair work*

One of the therapy techniques that was developed by Fritz Perls and his colleagues is *two-chair* work. This method can be used when a person is stuck, or at a point of impasse, in relation to an issue in their life. From a gestalt perspective, the impasse arises because of a polarity or conflict in the self, in which one part of the self (the 'top dog') seeks to dominate and control the expression of another part (the 'bottom dog'). For example, a person may feel angry about something that is happening in his or her life, but the expression of this anger is suppressed by a belief that anger is bad and destructive. As a result of this impasse, the person withdraws from contact with the external environment and other people – the emotion that should really be directed outwards is held within.

In two-chair work, the therapist would invite the client to sit in one chair and '*be* the anger', and then move to an adjacent chair and '*be*' the controlling self and reply to what 'anger' has said. The client then moves back into the first chair, and responds again from 'anger'. Throughout this activity, the therapist is coaching the client to remain within each role, and to speak directly from that position. Typically, this dialogue leads to increasing emotional tension, and an eventual melting or dissolving of the impasse, as each part comes to accept the right of the other to exist, and arrives at a creative solution that satisfies each of them ('it is OK to be angry as long as you take care of yourself').

The origins of this technique in the lifelong interest that Perls had in theatrical perform-ance are easy to see – during two-chair dialogue, the therapist almost becomes a drama coach or director. Two-chair work (and variants of it) has been the focus of research by Les Greenberg, and this technique has been integrated into his EFT. The EFT literature contains a valuable analysis of the situations in which two-chair work is most appropriate, and the sequence of therapist and client actions that are associated with its effective deployment (Greenberg 2002; Elliott *et al.* 2003).

Box 9.4: *The case of Irvina*

A good example of contemporary gestalt therapy practice can be found in a case study written by Fabienne Kuenzli, an experienced gestalt therapist who worked in the USA. The case describes the process of therapy during the first four sessions of her work with Irvina, an 18-year-old Mexican–American woman who had been in care and been adopted, and had previously received multiple episodes of therapy over several years. Over the course of her life, Irvina had experienced emotional rejection and sexual abuse, and at the time of entering gestalt therapy had major difficulties around controlling her anger, and was suicidal. The case report constructed by Kuenzli (2009) provides several examples of what a gestalt therapist does to facilitate dialogue with a client. Several of these examples refer to episodes in therapy where the therapist was highly sensitive to the language of the client, for instance around use of psychiatric labels. She did her best to follow the client's word use – including one instance in which the therapist used swear words. Another episode of dialogue occurred when the client arrived for a session wearing sunglasses with blue lenses – the therapist asked if she could try them on, to experience what it was like to be in a 'blue' world. On a further occasion, when Irvina complained of feeling tired, the therapist invited her to lie down on a couch and close her eyes.

This case study is particularly notable in the extent to which it describes the awareness, reflexivity and inner dialogue of the therapist herself. It is very clear that the dialogical contact that was made with Irvina was made possible by a highly tuned self-awareness on the part of her therapist. This contact seemed to make it possible for Irvina to begin to make important changes in her life – get close to a boyfriend who was not sexually exploitative, get a job, write poetry. The case clearly illustrates the extent to which current gestalt therapy has moved away from the staging of dramatic therapeutic events or change moments, toward an application of gestalt principles that are expressed in conversation, spontaneous moments of creativity and a caring relationship.

Research into the process and outcome of gestalt therapy

One of the distinctive aspects of the gestalt therapy literature, in contrast to the bodies of writing that exist around other leading therapy approaches, is that it is characterized by an absence of research studies. The lack of research into gestalt therapy is an interesting phenomenon in its own right, because it is clear that gestalt theory and practice have continued to grow and develop over the past 30 years, even without a recognizable research base. It is not entirely clear why the gestalt therapy community has chosen to keep conventional empirical research at a distance. In a chapter in a recent book that argues that research on gestalt therapy is necessary, Gold and Zahm (2008) suggest that the reasons why gestalt therapy is 'not well researched' include:

- a reaction to what is regarded as the 'over-intellectualized' theory and practice of psychoanalysis;
- the radical, anti-establishment political views of the founders of gestalt therapy;
- it is obvious that it is effective: 'psychotherapists doing this work . . . see its power to evoke life-changing insights and awareness . . . result(ing) in less perceived need to explain gestalt therapy or to try to "validate" its worth' (p. 27).

Other gestalt therapy writers have argued that gestalt therapy represents a creative flexible approach to working with people – any attempt to standardize it for research purposes would therefore destroy what it sets out to investigate. Finally, there is also a view that evaluating change in terms of symptom reduction misses the point of what gestalt therapy seeks to achieve. The consequence of these attitudes has been 'a dearth of literature supporting the use of gestalt therapy in treating clinical populations, or specific disorders' (Gold and Zahm 2008: 28).

The situation in respect of research into gestalt therapy is in fact quite complex. Two of the leading figures in contemporary psychotherapy research, Larry Beutler and Les Greenberg, have published a considerable number of high-quality studies into specific gestalt interventions. Much of Beutler's work, over several decades, has centred on the question of whether certain therapeutic approaches are more effective for clients with different coping styles. In one study, Beutler et al. (1991) looked at whether the effectiveness of three contrasting therapies (CBT, supportive therapy or experiential therapy that included some gestalt interventions) depended on the ways that depressed clients dealt with their emotions, and the way that they related to their therapist. What he found was that the experiential/gestalt therapy was fairly effective for clients with all coping styles.

Greenberg and his colleagues have carried out several studies (see Greenberg 2008) that have examined the effectiveness of specific gestalt interventions, such as two-chair work, and have sought to identify the step-by-step sequence of activities that is associated with more impactful and less impactful deployment of these techniques. They have also carried out controlled studies that have evaluated the effectiveness of EFT (an integrative form of therapy that embraces ideas and methods from person-centred and gestalt approaches). What they found was that EFT was at least as effective as other leading forms of therapy, such as CBT, for conditions such as depression, and that two-chair work and other gestalt interventions are potent therapeutic interventions in their own right. A more detailed account of EFT can be found in Chapter 7 on pages 190–2.

Although the work of Beutler, Greenberg and their colleagues certainly provides support for the effectiveness of gestalt therapy, it is not possible to conclude, on the basis of this evidence, that gestalt therapy as it is routinely practised produces beneficial outcomes. Leading figures within the gestalt therapy community, such as Yontef (1993) have consistently argued that gestalt therapy cannot be reduced to techniques and interventions, and that anything other than the whole philosophical 'package' cannot be considered as representing the reality of gestalt therapy in action. From this perspective, the studies carried out by Beutler and Greenberg cannot be counted as evidence for gestalt therapy.

Research into the process and outcomes of gestalt therapy has been summarized and reviewed by Strümpfel (2004) and Strümpfel and Goldman (2001). Although these reviews managed to identify a large number of studies, many of them use methodologies that are idiosyncratic, or investigate the impact of gestalt therapy experiences for people seeking personal growth rather than those struggling with emotional difficulties. There is no evidence, from this body of literature, of the effectiveness (or otherwise) of gestalt therapy for the kinds of clients who attend most counselling centres and services. This does not mean that gestalt therapy lacks effectiveness – it just means that relevant evidence has not been collected.

Some groups within the gestalt therapy world network have pursued an alternative strategy in relation to what they regard as the philosophical limitations of conventional therapy research. Rather than employ established outcome and process measures, or standard techniques of qualitative analysis of interviews, these groups have sought to create a new approach to research that is consistent with the values and ideas of the gestalt tradition. An example of this kind of effort can be found in the work of Scheinberg and colleagues (2008), who draw on gestalt ideas such as the importance of dialogue, and the cycle of experience, to guide their research programme. The kind of findings that will emerge from this process have yet to be disseminated. However, it seems likely that a research approach that is congruent with gestalt principles will have more potential to mobilize the energies of gestalt trainers, practitioners and students.

It can be argued that the development of some kind of credible research base represents a major priority for the gestalt therapy community (Brownell 2008). It has proved possible for other therapy approaches to embrace research – even psychoanalysis and psychodynamic therapy. Most of the time, counsellors and psychotherapists who actually engage with research report that it enhances their understanding of their practice. From the point of view of colleagues from outside the world of gestalt therapy, there are possibly two major research questions that arise.

The first question relates to the extent to which the approach facilitates enduring change. The descriptions of two-chair work, and other gestalt interventions, that are available in books and videos, provide compelling evidence of the way that gestalt therapy can allow clients to have new experiences in the moment. But to what extent does this awareness become transferred to everyday life, and to what extent does it lead to improvement in the quality of life?

The second question relates to the limits of gestalt therapy, in relation to clients who just may not appreciate what it has to offer. Some case studies of EFT (Watson *et al.* 2007, 2011) have described experiences of clients who were so cut off from their emotions, or so afraid to express emotion in the therapy room, that they were unable to benefit from therapy from expert gestalt-oriented practitioners. This kind of result matters less in psychotherapy private practice settings in which clients actively opt for gestalt therapy, but raises difficult questions about the use of gestalt therapy in open access, frontline counselling services.

Training and practice

Gestalt therapy is mainly (but not entirely) conducted in private practice settings. Compared to other approaches, gestalt therapy has a minimal presence in university academic departments, or in large health care systems. Training and supervision is mainly organized through autonomous Gestalt Institutes, which can be found in most major cities, and supported by a number of practice-oriented journals. Gestalt therapy can be applied in individual, couple and group therapy, and there is a growing area of application in the field of organizational development (Barber 2012).

Box 9.5: *Can gestalt therapy be combined with other therapeutic approaches?*

The position of gestalt therapy in relation to therapy integration appears to be somewhat one sided. On the whole, leading figures within the gestalt therapy community seem to have shown little interest in assimilating concepts and practices from other approaches. On the other hand, for several decades the gestalt tradition has provided rich picking for practitioners from other approaches (see Thoma and Cecero 2009). Gestalt methods of active experimentation, creative dream work, first-person language, two-chair work, and much else, have been incorporated into the repertoires of many therapists. There are several points of convergence between person-centred/client-centred and gestalt approaches (see Watson *et al.* 1998). An influential and widely read book by James and Jongeward (1971) harnessed gestalt techniques as a means of applying transactional analysis theory. Amendt-Lyon (2001) has discussed the connections between art therapy and gestalt therapy, and Tonnesvang *et al.* (2010) has explored links with cognitive therapy.

Conclusions

It should be clear, from the material presented in this chapter, that gestalt therapy has a great deal to offer to anyone in a counselling role. Historically, there has been a tendency within the world of counselling and psychotherapy to view gestalt therapy as a repository of powerful change techniques: two-chair work, gestalt dreamwork, body awareness exercises, first-person language, and so on. In my view, this kind of appropriation of gestalt techniques is missing the point. Close attention to what gestalt therapists actually do in practice suggests that what is distinctive about this approach to therapy is a capacity to apply an intensely focused awareness of what is happening in the present moment. Rather than using the interaction with a client to collect information that can be used to arrive at a formulation of whether the client has negative automatic thoughts, or an external locus of evaluation (or whatever), gestalt therapists try to develop a sense of the quality of interpersonal contact that exists at that moment, and in particular what the client does to make contact, avoid contact, and keep safe. It is only possible to engage in this kind of work, as a therapist, on the basis of extensive training and practice. It is, perhaps, like walking a tightrope. Most people can do it for a moment or two, but then fall off because they start to think about other things, or get scared. To be able to stay on the tightrope requires a capacity to be still inside and to be responsive to tiny movements.

The gestalt therapy community has needed to develop a philosophical framework from which the present moment can be understood. The key element of this framework is phenomenology, which is built around the idea that truth can be found through staying with an experience to a sufficient extent that something of the essence of that experience or phenomenon can be disclosed. Willingness to follow the logic of phenomenology then leads in a number of directions that have become central to gestalt theory and practice.

Phenomenological philosophers such as Maurice Merleau-Ponty have demonstrated that the experience of embodiment, and the reality of one's own body and the bodily presentation of other people, is a central aspect of the 'essence' of personal experience. Other phenomenological philosophers have shown that experience always occurs in a 'field' or contact – there is always a sense of some kind of 'being-with'. Finally, the phenomenology exploration of the use of language shows that talk is always a dialogical, in the sense of being directed at or in response to a real or imagined 'other'. In these respects, it can be seen that gestalt therapy theory and practice is supported by important developments in twentieth-century philosophy.

Topics for reflection and discussion

1   One of the characteristic strategies of gestalt therapy is to invite the client to be aware of, and report on, what he or she is doing *now* – the moment-by-moment flow of his or her thoughts, feelings and actions. What might be the advantages and disadvantages of this therapeutic strategy?

2   Which elements of gestalt therapy and technique could be integrated into your own practice? In what ways might your practice be enhanced by these new ideas?

3   Who are the groups of clients or what are the types of problem for which gestalt therapy might be more effective? What are the areas in which it might be least effective?

4   To what extent, and in what ways, does gestalt therapy reflect the ideas and values of Western culture?

Suggested further reading

The classic texts that defined the direction of travel of post-Perlsian gestalt therapy are *The Healing Relationship in Gestalt Therapy* (Hycner and Jacobs 1995) and *Awareness, Dialogue and Process* by Gary Yontef (1993). The best sources of information around current developments in this approach are Ginger (2007), Mann (2010) and Sills *et al.* (2012).

CHAPTER 10

Existential therapy

Introduction

Counselling offers the person a space, outside the busy flow of everyday life, within which he or she can reflect on how things are going, and in particular engage in exploration around things that are going wrong, in the hope of resolving such problems in living. Much of the time, the reflective space provided by counselling is used to address practical problems: How can I have a more satisfying relationship with my partner? How can I be less anxious, and more confident when asked to give my opinion at a staff meeting? How can I reconstruct my life now that my mother has died? Many of the models of therapy that are most widely used, such as CBT and solution-focused approaches, are built around a powerful and consistent emphasis on helping the person to take practical action to deal with such difficulties. At the same time, however, the opportunity for reflection that arises in counselling almost always leads clients in the direction of thinking about the deeper issues that underpin their practical dilemmas: Not 'how to communicate better with my partner', but 'what does *love* mean to me?' Not 'how do I learn relaxation skills' but 'what is the *purpose* of my work?' Not 'what do I need to do to grieve and move on?' but 'what does *death* mean for me?' These underlying questions, about the basic meaning of central aspects of life, are *existential* in nature – they are questions about the quality of existence, the fundamental sense that I might have of *being* human. It is perhaps quite seldom that a counselling client will define his or her primary goal for therapy as that of exploring issues of existence and being. On the other hand, it is common for any client who attends more than a couple of therapy sessions to encounter existential issues in some shape or form.

Sensitivity to questions of being and existence is an essential counselling competence; an absence of awareness of core existential issues runs the risk of the therapy conversation becoming superficial. The aim of this chapter is to examine the significance of existential themes in counselling theory and practice. Following a brief account of some key existential themes, there is an overview of the theory and practice of existential therapy. The chapter concludes by reviewing some of the ways in which existential issues can be explored within counselling practice.

Existential themes

The understanding and analysis of existential themes, within Western culture, owes a great deal to the work of existential philosophers such as Martin Heidegger (1889–1976), Soren Kierkegaard (1813–55) and Jean-Paul Sartre (1905–80). These writers lived within a European culture, in the late nineteenth and early twentieth centuries, in which previous sources of meaning, largely derived from collection traditions organized around religion, family, community and place, were being eroded and undermined by the progress of modernity. As a result, they and others were faced with a stark question: what does life mean? In exploring their question, they employed the philosophical method of *phenomenology*, which involves setting aside, as much as possible, the pre-existing assumptions that one holds in relation to an area of experience, and through this strategy gradually arriving at a disclosure of the *essence,* or essential qualities of that experience. So, for example, a phenomenological inquiry into the experience of marital conflict might reveal a set of component meanings around essential qualities such as love, commitment and responsibility. It is easy to see that phenomenological inquiry is far from being an exact science, and that the search for essential qualities is never complete (how can one know that there is nothing left to bracket off?).

Further information about the challenges of phenomenological–existential inquiry, and its achievements, can be found in Moran (2000) and Moran and Mooney (2002). Nevertheless, despite these undoubted difficulties with this method, what has emerged over the course of time has been a reasonably degree of consensus on some key existential themes that run through human existence: being with others, multiplicity, living in time, agency and intentionality, embodiment, and truth (Wartenberg 2008). These themes are introduced in the following sections.

Being alone/being with others: autonomy and relatedness

Social being constitutes an irreducible aspect of human existence: we live our lives both in connection with others, and alone within our own private awareness. There are two basic questions, for each of us, that arise from this aspect of existence: What is the quality of my contact and connectedness with others? What is the quality of my experience of being with 'me', of being alone?

The modern world opens up staggering possibilities for individual autonomy. In traditional cultures, people depended on each other, for food, shelter and security, in very tangible and obvious ways. For the majority of people, there were very limited choices, even in relation to what they ate or where they lived. All this seems to be different in the modern world. We are individuals. We please ourselves. We have rights. We consume. As many people have observed, the growth of individualism and the growth of counselling and psychotherapy have gone hand in hand. As individual selves, we can only really deal with our anxiety, fear, depression and destiny on an individual basis, in the privacy of a confidential counselling room. Individualism is built into the fabric of society in such forms as the design of houses and cars, the organization of the tax system, the plotlines of novels, films and plays. Yet, in the end, the individualism of the modern world is false. We are all profoundly interdependent, at both personal and economic levels. Anxiety, depression and destiny are embedded in relationships with others, are understood through shared cultural conceptions, are assuaged through talking to someone who accepts and understands.

The most important relationships a person has are (usually) those of being a child and being a parent, and the most important group to which a person belongs is his or her family. In counselling, people talk about how they feel about these relationships, and try to find the best mix of giving and taking, caring and being cared for. Likewise, the existential issue of autonomy underpins conversations about how a person spends his or her time, and how they make decisions and choices, and the extent to which they accept who they are or perhaps wish to destroy a 'self' that cannot be tolerated.

To be a person in modern society is therefore to be caught in a field of great tension, simultaneously pulled in the direction of individual autonomy and alone-ness, and in the direction of connectedness, relatedness and the communal. All approaches to counselling, and all counsellors, have had to find their own way of addressing this question, of resolving this tension. Many approaches have attempted to deal with it by excluding or redefining the social. In person-centred theory, the social becomes a set of generalized 'conditions of worth'. In recent psychodynamic theory, the social is dealt with in terms of attachments and 'internalized objects'. By contrast, systemic and family-oriented approaches down-play the individual and highlight the communal. Other approaches, such as multicultural and feminist, strive to find ways of incorporating both the social and the individual within their models of the person. What all approaches share is the necessity of coming up with some means of talking about the tension between the individual and the collective, some way of carrying out a conversation – however stilted or partial – around this pervasive existential theme.

Living in time

As persons, we live in time. Our plans and aspirations stretch out into, and create, a future. The past is represented not only in our memories, our mental images and recollections, but through the meanings that external objects and places hold for us. One of the basic human dilemmas arises from the task of being able to locate oneself in time and history. There seems to be a basic human tendency or need to construct a story of one's life, with a beginning, middle and end (or possible endings). Many of the problems that people bring to counselling can be seen as distortions of the person's relationship with the time of their life: depression is a time with no hoped for future state, compulsive behaviour is warding off a feared future event, low self-esteem may entail returning again and again to a moment of failure in the past. Although different approaches to counselling must each be flexible enough to enable the client to move across past, present and future, each model has its own distinctive time slot.

Humanistic approaches emphasize 'here-and-now' experiencing. Behavioural approaches are much concerned with what will happen in the future: achieving behavioural *targets*; relapse *prevention*. On the whole, most counselling models operate within the time frame of the client's life. Some family therapy approaches stretch this personal time frame to encompass intergenerational influences. The more culturally oriented therapies, such as feminist, multicultural and narrative counselling, operate within an extended time frame that may include events well outside the family history of the individual client. For example, some multicultural counsellors would see relevance for some clients in studying the history of racism. In all of these approaches, counselling can be seen as a means of assisting people to construct an identity that is positioned in time and history.

A further crucial aspect of the experience of time, as a basic dimension of existence, arises from the question: 'When does time end?' The end of time, for each of us, is death. Although there are many meanings that death can have, for individuals and cultural groups, it remains a basic given of human experience. Contemporary industrial–scientific cultures have tended to seek to deny the reality of death, by truncating traditional death rituals and creating a detached viewpoint on death in the form of movie and television dramas in which death occurs somehow painlessly and without personal meaning. And yet it hardly needs to be said that the relationship that a person has with his or her inevitable death, and with the deaths of others, has a profound influence on the way in which that person lives their life.

Box 10.1: *Phenomenological research*

In recent years, there has been an increasing amount of research that makes use of methods of phenomenological inquiry to explore basic aspects of lived experience. Examples of this work include studies carried out by the group led by Steen Halling at the Seattle University, into topics such as despair (Beck *et al.* 2005) and forgiveness (Halling *et al.* 2006a). These research papers are written in an open dialogical style that invites the reader to enter into the phenomenon and reflect on its meaning for them in the context of both their personal life and professional role.

Agency

What does it mean to *intend* something, to act with intentionality and purpose? What does it mean to be *powerful*, to be able to exert influence and control? What does it mean to be powerless, to be a victim of oppression, to be controlled by others? What is the right balance in a life between powerfulness and powerlessness, between controlling others and allowing them to control oneself, domination and submission? As human beings, we possess many powers, and are confronted by the power of others. These aspects of experience can be regarded as arising from the core human experience of *agency*. There is an inevitability in any life to the experiencing of triumph, joy and achievement (the personal expression of agency), pain and suffering (being subjected to the malign agency of others), caring and nurturance (being subjected to the benign agency of others).

Within society, power differences are structured and institutionalized around fundamental demographic categories, such as class, race and gender. Dilemmas and issues around the nature of power, control and agency are intrinsic to counselling, for both counsellor and client. Does the counsellor adopt a position of expert (i.e., the powerful one who 'intervenes'), of client-centred equal or of 'not-knowing' witness? How much does the counsellor say in the counselling room? *What* kinds of statement does he or she make – reflection, instruction, interpretation? Is the aim of counselling self-control and self-management, or a self-fulfilment that reflects a celebration of personal power? How is the person who has been oppressed, as in childhood sexual abuse, encouraged to name their experience? Are they 'victims', 'survivors' or 'post-traumatic stress disorder sufferers'? Should this person seek to express their power through anger, or through forgiveness? How much responsibility does a person have, in respect of his or her actions and life difficulties? These are just some of the many examples of issues of human agency that emerge in counselling. In reality, questions of agency are always present in counselling: in the stories told by the client, in the counsellor–client relationship and in the relationship between both counsellor and client and the counselling organization.

Box 10.2: *Working with client agency: a cornerstone of therapy practice*

The writings of Art Bohart and Karen Tallman have had a major impact on therapy training and practice in recent years, in making explicit the many ways in which client are active co-participants in therapy (Bohart 2000; Bohart and Tallman 1996, 1998, 1999). The notion of the client as 'active self-healer' opens the attention of the therapist to the strengths of resources of the client, and the ways in which the client actively chooses from what is offered by their therapist. Further discussion of this topic, and how it has been explored in research, is available in Hoener *et al.* (2012), Mackrill (2009) and Rennie (2000b, 2001).

Bodily experience

To be a person is to be embodied, to have physical presence and sensations, to move. Living with, and within, a body presents a continual set of challenges. The person's relationship with his or her body is one of the central issues in many (perhaps all) counselling situations. The primary area in which aspects of the body dominate counselling is through the existence (or non-existence) of feeling and emotion. We feel in our bodies, and these feelings or emotions are indicators of what is most important to us. Our bodies tell us how we feel about things. And we live in a culture in which acknowledging, naming and expressing emotions is deeply problematic. Mass modern society places great value on rationality, self-control and 'cool'. For many people, the counselling room is the only place in which they have permission to allow themselves fully to feel. All approaches to counselling, in their very different ways, give emotion a high place on the therapeutic agenda. Another crucial dimension of bodily experiencing is sexuality. The person's relationship with himself or herself as a sexual being, as someone with sexual powers and energies, can often be a core issue in counselling.

Other counselling issues that centre on the body are concerns about eating, digesting, defecating, being big or small, being attractive or ugly. Finally, there are many highly meaningful experiences that people have around health, including fertility, being ill, dealing with loss of functioning or parts of the body and the encounter with death. The common thread through all these life issues is the experience of embodiment. We are all faced with the issue of what our body means to us, and how we accept or deny different aspects of our bodily functioning. Counselling is a setting in which some of these issues can be explored and reconciled, and all counsellors and theories of counselling adopt their own particular stance in relation to the body.

Truth and authenticity

How do we *know*? What counts as valid knowledge? What is the *right* thing to do? People act on the basis of what they believe to be true, and so the issue of what is to count as true knowledge is therefore a fundamental question with profound implications. However, knowing what is true and what is right is far from easy for members of modern technological societies. First, there are many competing sources of authoritative knowledge. In the past, most people would have accepted the teachings of their religious leader or text as the primary source of true knowledge. Now, the majority of people doubt the validity of religious knowledge, and look instead to science to provide certainty and a reliable guide to action. On the other hand, scientific knowledge can be questioned in terms of the areas of human experience which it excludes. There is a reawakening in some quarters of the value of spiritual experience as a source of knowledge. Other people look to art as a source of knowledge, claiming that insight and understanding are developed through the use of creative imagination and different modes of representing reality. Finally, through all this, many people maintain a belief in the truth of their own everyday common sense experience.

Counselling reflects this multiplicity of knowledge sources; different approaches to counselling can be viewed as encouraging their clients to specialize in one or another modes of knowing. For example, cognitive–behavioural therapies place great weight on objective, scientific knowing, psychodynamic and person-centred approaches emphasize the validity of personal feelings and memories, whereas transpersonal therapies attempt to create the conditions for spiritual learning. A central theme, in much counselling, concerns the quest of the individual for his or her own personal truth – for a sense of authenticity, genuineness and 'realness', in contrast to a sense of being 'false' or a 'fraud'. This theme reflects a search for an answer to questions such as: 'What is the truth about *me*? Who am *I*?'

The core existential issues that have been discussed above – being with others, agency/ power, time, embodiment, and truth – are inevitably interlinked in practice. These issues represent some of the basic questions or dilemmas that we face as members of the society in which we live; counselling is one of the few arenas in which we are allowed an opportunity to reflect on how we deal with them. All therapy theories provide frameworks that enable people to engage, to a greater or lesser extent, in a personal conversation about these issues.

Box 10.3: *The concept of* ontological insecurity

The existential psychiatrist and psychotherapist R. D. Laing used the term *ontological insecurity* to describe a state of fundamental self-doubt that can underpin many issues that are presented by those who seek counselling and psychotherapy. 'Ontology' refers to the person's sense or understanding of his or her own *being*. Laing (1960: 39) describes an ontologically secure person as someone who will 'encounter all the hazards of life, social, ethical, spiritual, biological, from a centrally firm sense of his own and other people's reality and identity'. By contrast, an ontologically insecure person lacks this 'firm sense of . . . reality and identity', and experiences him/herself, and the world, as unreal, insubstantial.

Laing (1960) identified three ways in which ontological insecurity is expressed by a person: *engulfment,* where the person fears that any relationship will completely overwhelm his or her fragile sense of identity; *implosion,* a sense of utter emptiness, a belief that all the person can ever be is an 'awful nothingness'; *petrification and depersonalization,* a dread of being turned from a living person into stone, or into a robotic state or a 'thing'. Laing (1961) argues that a state of ontological insecurity is gradually built up through relationships in which the person is exposed to repeated disconfirmation by significant others in his or her life, or trapped in collusive relationships.

Existential therapy

Existential therapy draws upon the ideas of existential philosophers such as Heidegger, Kierkegaard, Sartre and Merleau-Ponty (see Macquarrie 1972; Moran 2000). There have been several important strands within the development of this form of therapy. The first has evolved from the work of European therapists such as Boss (1957) and Binswanger (1963). This body of work influenced the work of the widely read Scottish psychiatrist and psychotherapist R. D. Laing (1960, 1961). Another significant strand consists of American therapists such as May (1950), Bugental (1976) and Yalom (1980). The work of Viktor Frankl, a European psychotherapist who lived for many years in the USA, is also a valuable resource for counsellors interested in an existential approach. Although the model of therapy developed by Frankl is described as 'logotherapy', it is in fact existentially informed. Finally, more recently the writings of Emmy van Deurzen, Ernesto Spinelli and Mick Cooper have comprised important contributions to existential psychotherapy and counselling. The *Society for Existential Analysis* functions as a vehicle for current developments within this approach, and operates a journal.

Within the broad tradition of existential therapy, there have been several different inter-pretations of how existential concepts can best be translated into therapeutic practice. Cooper (2003: 1) argues that existential therapy 'is best understood as a rich tapestry of inter-secting therapeutic practices, all of which orientate themselves around a shared concern: "human lived-existence"'. In the discussion that follows, no attempt has been made to differ-entiate between different styles of existential therapy. Instead, the aim is to identify those existential ideas and methods that can be most readily integrated into counselling practice.

The aim of existential philosophy is to understand or illuminate the experience of 'being-in-the-world'. Existential thinkers use the method of phenomenological reduction to 'bracket-off' their assumptions about reality, in an attempt to arrive closer to the 'essence' or truth of that reality. The aim is to uncover the basic dimensions of meaning or 'being' that underpin everyday life, and by doing this to be better able to live an *authentic* life. The results of existential inquiry appear to suggest a number of central themes to human existence or being.

First, human beings exist in time. The present moment is constituted by various horizons of meaning derived from the past. The present moment is also constituted by the various possibilities that stretch out into the future. Individual worlds are constructed with different orientations to past, present and future. The presence and acceptance of death is a factor in the capacity of a person to exist fully in time; people who deny death are avoiding living fully, because they are limiting the time horizon within which they exist.

A second key theme that derives from existential analysis is that to be a person is to exist in an *embodied* world. Our relationship with the world is revealed through our own body (our feelings and emotions, perception of the size or acceptability of our body, general awareness of parts of the body etc.) and the way we organize the space around us.

A third major theme emerging from existential philosophy is the centrality of *anxiety, dread* and *care* in everyday life. For existential philosophers, anxiety is not a symptom or sign of psychiatric disorder, but instead is regarded as an inevitable consequence of caring about others, and the world in general. From this perspective, it is a lack of anxiety (revealed as a sense of inner emptiness or alienation) that would be viewed as problem-atic. Existential philosophy emphasizes that to be a person is to be alone and at the same time to be always in relation to other people. Understanding the quality of a person's existential contact with the *other* is therefore of great interest to existentialists: is the person capable of being both alone and in communion with others? From an existential point of view, authentic being-in-the-world requires an ability to take responsibility for one's own actions, but also a willingness to accept that one is 'thrown' into a world that is 'given'. Much of the focus of existential analysis is on the 'way of being' of a person, the qualitative texture of his or her relationship with self (*Eigenwelt*), others (*Mitwelt*) and the physical world (*Umwelt*).

The brief summary of existential ideas offered here cannot claim to do justice to the richness and complexity of this body of thought. Unlike some other philosophical approaches, which perhaps emphasize a process of logical abstraction from the everyday world, existential philosophers seek to enter into the realm of everyday experience. In principle, existential philosophy should be accessible and understandable to everyone, because it is describing and interpreting experiences (anxiety, fear of death, taking responsibility) that are familiar to us all. In practice, much of the writing of existential philosophers such as Heidegger, Sartre and Merleau-Ponty is difficult to follow, because, in trying to reach beyond the ways in which we ordinarily speak of things, they frequently find it necessary to invent new terminology. Nevertheless, the insights of existential philosophy represent an enormously fertile resource for counsellors and psychotherapists, in providing a framework for enabling clients to explore what is most important for them in their lives.

Box 10.4: *The case of Louise*

Louise was a student from an affluent American family, studying in London and living away from home for the first time. When her new flatmates defrauded her of some money, she became hugely upset and unable to continue with her studies. Her tutor advised her to visit the college counsellor. Du Plock (1997a) describes how he used an existential approach in his work with Louise. This was a situation in which the client was certainly not attending therapy in order to explore existential issues. In addition, because of pressure of time, they had only one session. Nevertheless, a therapeutic process took place that was clearly informed by existential principles. Du Plock (1997a: 73) described his first impression of Louise in these terms:

> . . . she was of average height and build with a great deal of very blond hair. She wore a polo-necked jumper under a pale pink shirt, pearls and designer jeans – altogether the ubiquitous preppy image the majority of the female American students on campus seemed to sport. I recall an impression of self-confidence.

For Du Plock (1997a), an important step in being able to engage with the 'lived experience' that was troubling Louise, was to 'bracket off' these first impressions, and be open to what else was there. Louise was helped to express and be aware of the aspects of her way of 'being in the world' that were implicated in the incident with her flatmates, including her sense of herself as a person, and her way of relating to others. She became able to accept that the way she had been with her flatmates has resulted in them viewing her as an arrogant 'rich bitch' who deserved to be exploited. She came to a point of being able to understand the whole incident as an opportunity for learning that supported her sense of herself as being open and adventurous. By the end of one extended session, Louise had resolved her emotional turmoil around what had happened, and was ready to move on. This case is particularly interesting from a counselling perspective because it illustrates some of the ways in which an existential approach can be applied in a typical counselling encounter.

The goals of existential therapy have been described by van Deurzen (1990: 157) in the following terms:

1 To enable people to become truthful with themselves again.

2 To widen their perspective on themselves and the world around them.

3 To find clarity on how to proceed into the future while taking lessons from the past and creating something valuable to live for in the present.

It can be seen that this is an avowedly exploratory approach to counselling, with a strong emphasis on the development of authentic understanding and action, and the creation of meaning. One of the distinguishing features of the existential approach is its lack of concern for technique. As van Deurzen (2001: 161) observes: 'the existential approach is well known for its anti-technique orientation . . . existential therapists will not generally use specific techniques, strategies or skills, but . . . follow a . . . philosophical method of inquiry'. At the heart of this 'philosophical method' is the use of phenomenological reduction.

Phenomenology is a philosophical method, initially devised by Edmund Husserl, which aims to get beyond a 'taken-for-granted' way of looking at things, and instead achieve the 'essential' truth of a situation or feeling. Spinelli (1989, 1994) has described this method as comprising three basic 'rules'.

- The rule of *bracketing*, or putting aside (as best we can) our own assumptions in order to clear our perceptions and actually hear what the other person is expressing.

- The rule of *description* – it is important to *describe* what you have heard (or observed) rather than rushing into theoretical explanation.

- The rule of *horizontalization* – the therapist seeks to apply no judgement, but to try to hear *everything* before allowing importance to be attributed to any part of the experience.

Using a phenomenological approach, the goal of the existential counsellor or therapist is to explore the meaning for the client of problematic areas of experience. In line with some of the findings of existential philosophy, this exploration of meaning may focus on the significance for the person of broad categories of experience, such as choice, identity, isolation, love, time, death and freedom. Often, such exploration will be associated with areas of crisis or paradox in the current life situation of the person. The basic assumption being offered to the client is that human beings create and construct their worlds, and are responsible for their lives.

May *et al.* (1958) remains a core seminal text in existential psychotherapy, and offers a thorough grounding in the European roots of this approach. This book is, however, a difficult read, and more accessible introductions to the principles and practice of existential counselling are to be found in Bugental (1976), Yalom (1980) and van Deurzen (1988). Yalom (1989) has also produced a collection of case studies from his own work with clients. The growth of interest within British counselling and psychotherapy in existential ideas is reflected in books by Cohn (1997), Cohn and du Plock (1995), van Deurzen (1996), Strasser and Strasser (1997), Du Plock (1997b) and Spinelli (1997), and chapters by van Deurzen (1990, 1999) and Spinelli (1996). Useful introductions to the broader field of existential–phenomenological psychology, which provides an underlying framework for existential counselling, have been produced by Valle and King (1978) and Schneider and May (1995).

Although existential counselling and psychotherapy is an approach that is grounded in the philosophical traditions of phenomenology and existentialism, the majority of existential therapists would be reluctant to describe what they do as 'philosophical counselling'. There are basically two reasons for the adoption of this stance by existential therapists. First, the practice of existential therapy is informed by a highly developed theory of existential and phenomenological *psychology*, whereas the adherents of philosophical counselling are explicitly attempting to evolve a non-psychological mode of helping. Second, the philosophical counselling movement has drawn on a wide and eclectic range of philosophical sources, rather than being identified with any single philosophical 'school of thought'. Philosophical counselling represents the use of 'philosophizing' within the therapeutic context, rather than the application of a specific set of philosophical constructs. Existential therapy, therefore, can be seen as a therapeutic approach that, although philosophically oriented, has harnessed a particular set of philosophical ideas to a broadly exploratory, conversational approach to therapy, which is similar in many ways to contemporary psychodynamic, person-centred and constructivist models.

Box 10.5: *Yalom's 'missing ingredients'*

In the introduction to *Existential Psychotherapy*, Irvin Yalom tells the story of enrolling in a cooking class taught by an elderly Armenian woman who spoke no English. He found that, as much as he tried, he could not match the subtlety of flavouring that his teacher achieved in her dishes, and was unable to understand why. One day, he observed that, en route from the table to the oven, she 'threw in' to each dish various unnamed spices and condiments. Yalom (1980: 6) reports that he is reminded of this experience when he thinks about the ingredients of effective therapy:

> Formal texts, journal articles and lectures portray therapy as precise and systematic, with carefully delineated stages, strategic technical interventions, the methodical development and resolution of transference, analysis of object relations, and a careful, rational program of insight-offering interpretations. Yet, I believe deeply that, when no one is looking, the therapist throws in the 'real thing'.

What is the 'real thing', the essential 'missing ingredient' in counselling? Yalom suggests that the important 'throw-ins' include compassion, caring, extending oneself and wisdom. He characterizes these ingredients as central existential categories, and goes on to argue that the most profound therapy is that which addresses one or more of the four 'ultimate concerns' in life:

- confronting the tension between the awareness of the inevitability of death, and the wish to continue to be;

- acceptance of the possibilities of freedom, including the terrifying implication that each of us is responsible for our actions;

- the ultimate experience of isolation – 'each of us enters existence alone and must depart from it alone';

- meaninglessness – what meaning can life have, if there are no pre-ordained truths?

Yalom (1980) takes the view that all effective counsellors are sensitive to these 'ultimate concerns' and ingredients, but the study of existential thought enables a counsellor or psychotherapist to place these elements 'at the centre of the therapeutic arena'.

Box 10.6: *Existential touchstones*

Mearns and Cooper (2005) use the term 'existential touchstones' to refer to a source of personal knowing that is fundamental to the capacity to offer a counselling relationship. A personal or existential touchstone is a memory that has deep significance for a person, and from which he or she has learned something vital about the meaning of being human. Mearns and Cooper (2005: 137) define touchstones as 'events and self-experiences from which we draw considerable strength and which help to ground us in relationships as well as making us more open to and comfortable with a diversity of relationships'. An example of an existential touchstone might be the experience of the death of a parent in childhood, which led to a capacity both to accept the reality of intense emotional pain and to know that love and connectedness are possible even in the face of such despair.

Mearns and Cooper (2005) suggest that it is by making use of such personal experiences, and what has been learned from them, that counsellors are able to engage with people seeking help at a deeper level of meaning. The life histories that have been written by therapists provide a wealth of examples of childhood events that have sensitized the later-to-be-therapist to basic existential issues (see, for example, Dryden and Spurling 1989 and Goldfried 2001). The concept of 'existential touchstones' has important implications for counselling training, in drawing attention to the need for personal development activities to focus on positive aspects of early life, and the ways in which these events can be used as a therapeutic resource.

Conclusions

Ideas and methods of existential therapy have been highly influential within the world of counselling for many years. Existential therapy seeks to address 'ultimate concerns'. Whereas other forms of therapy may be more effective in helping the person to cope with the pressures of everyday life, and deal with symptoms, existentially informed therapies strive to enable a person do something else, which is to make fundamental *choices* about who they are and what direction their live will take. Every therapeutic intervention is accompanied by an implied existential choice. A client who works through a CBT anxiety-management programme, must choose, in the end, whether or not to take responsibility, and act with courage in the face of fear. A client who receives a consistent empathic response from a person-centred counsellor is faced with the choice of whether to say more, and allow his or her most painful emotions and memories to be known to another person. A client who is helped by a psychodynamic therapist to appreciate the extent to which his or her present life constitutes a repetition of past events and relationships, is faced with a choice of whether to step into the actual present moment. In each of these examples, it is possible to understand the action of therapy in terms of psychological processes: behaviour change, self-acceptance, insight. An existential perspective suggests that there can also be a more fundamental process at work, across all of these different therapeutic approaches.

Topics for reflection and discussion

1 Choose any *one* of the approaches to therapy discussed in earlier chapters (e.g., psychodynamic, CBT, person-centred therapy, etc.). To what extent, and in what ways, does the conceptual language provided by that approach encourage conversations about existential issues (the basic experience of: being with others, multiplicity, living in time, agency and intentionality, embodiment, authenticity, etc.).

2 What are the strengths and weaknesses of an existential approach to counselling in comparison with other approaches? Are there groups of clients, or problem areas, where existential therapy might be *more*, or *less* appropriate?

3 What are the existential issues in your own life? What are your strategies for managing, or living with, these issues?

Suggested further reading

Good sources of reading about existential ideas are *Existentialism* by John Macquarrie (1972) and *Existential-Phenomenological Perspectives in Psychology* by Ronald Valle and Steen Halling (1989). The best introductory text is *Existential Therapy,* by Mick Cooper (2003). The 'cross-over' existential therapy author, whose work is known to a wide audience, is Irving Yalom – everything he has written is worth reading.

Constructivist, narrative and collaborative approaches: counselling as conversation

Introduction

The psychologist Jerome Bruner (1990) has argued that there exist two quite different ways of knowing the world. There is what he calls *paradigmatic* knowing, which involves creating abstract models of reality. Then there is *narrative* knowing, which is based on a process of making sense of the world by telling stories. Bruner suggests that in everyday life we are surrounded by stories. We tell ourselves and each other stories all of the time. We structure, store and communicate our experiences through stories. We live in a culture that is saturated with stories – myths, novels, television soaps, office gossip, family histories and so on. Yet, Bruner points out, on the whole social science and psychology have until recently paid very little attention to stories. Social scientists and psychologists have been intent on constructing paradigmatic, scientific models of the world. The stories told by research subjects in psychological experiments, informants in sociological surveys or clients in counselling and psychotherapy sessions have been listened to [perhaps], but have then been converted into abstract categories, concepts or variables. The actual story has been largely ignored. For Bruner, true knowledge of the world requires interplay between both ways of knowing, between scientific abstractions and everyday stories. He suggests we should take stories more seriously.

The writings of Bruner and other key figures in what has become known as the 'narrative turn' in psychology (Sarbin 1986; Howard 1991) have stimulated an explosion of interest in narrative, which has found expression within the counselling and psychotherapy field in the idea that individuals and groups create social reality through the use of *language* – metaphors, stories, ways of talking. In terms of therapy practice, the implication is that problems can be understood as brought into being through language. This idea leads to the notion of therapy as *conversation* – the task of the therapist to facilitate a conversation within which new meaning can be found, new ways of talking that can result in new forms of action.

This chapter introduces some contemporary counselling and psychotherapy approaches that have developed ways of using a language-informed perspective in work with clients. These approaches each have somewhat different origins and influences, in terms of philosophy and practice, but they all share a central guiding conception that close attention to language, conversation and storytelling sits at the heart of effective therapy.

A radical philosophical position

The counselling approaches that are discussed in this chapter represent a significant philosophical shift away from the assumptions that underpin mainstream theories of counselling and psychotherapy such as psychodynamic and cognitive–behavioural. These mainstream approaches reflect, in their different ways, a common-sense or 'realist' view, widely held by people in modern societies that there exists a single objective, knowable reality. For a psychodynamic therapist, the unconscious, or transference, really exist. For a CBT therapist, dysfunctional cognitive schema really exist. However, it is possible to take a different view. It is possible to regard the unconscious, transference, or cognitive schema, as *constructions* that people place on experience. For example, if a client mistrusts his therapist, this is an event that can be described in many different ways. Some people (e.g., psychodynamic therapists) would describe what was happening in terms of transference. Other people might describe it as a matter of a reaction to the professional distance adopted by the counsellor, as an unremarkable and normal reaction to anyone in a position of power, as due to a biochemical imbalance in the client's brain, or in many other ways.

These different 'ways of seeing' are not neutral. They have consequence, and lead to different courses of action. For instance, a transference perspective on the part of a therapist might lead to questioning about the early experiences that predisposed the client to lack trust, while a biochemical perspective might lead to questioning about other symptoms of a depressive illness. By contrast, regarding lack of trust as a reaction to power might lead a therapist to look for ways of achieving more equality, perhaps by talking about her own experience. On a moment-by-moment basis, therefore, the ways in which we make sense of phenomena and events results in different ways of relating to each other, and different actions in the world.

This central insight – that reality and experience is 'constructed' – has itself been interpreted differently by various groups of philosophers. An appreciation of these philosophical standpoints is necessary in order to make sense of the alternative directions that have been followed by the various therapy approaches that are explored in this chapter. There are four philosophical perspectives that are particularly relevant here: constructivism, social constructionism, post-structuralism, and postmodernism.

Constructivism refers to the idea that reality is constructed at an individual level. Constructivists are interested in the processes by which individuals make sense of the world, through the words and metaphors they use, and the stories they tell. Constructivism has been highly influential in education, because it draws attention to the fact that students do not merely take on board everything that their teachers tell them, but actively choose to pay attention to ideas that interest them, and then assimilate these ideas into their own individual pre-understanding of the topic. Constructivist therapists are highly sensitive to the active ways that their clients create meaning (e.g., by paying attention to some areas of experience more than others) and to the client's use of language and metaphor. Within psychology and therapy, *personal construct theory* represents the most fully articulated constructivist approach (Butt 2008; Fransella 2005).

Social constructionism refers to the idea that the meaning of phenomena or events is constructed by people working together (Burr 2003; Gergen 1999; Lock and Strong 2010). Specifically, the way that a thing is understood will depend a great deal on historical factors – how it has been understood in the past – and how this 'archaeology' of understanding is expressed in the meanings of words. Social constructionists are particularly interested in talk and conversation, because it is in the interaction between speakers that certain constructions of reality are adopted, and while other constructions are set aside. Social constructionist therapists tend to focus on the types of conversation that clients hold with other people in their lives, and in the way that the client positions himself or herself in relation to cultural discourses.

Post-structuralism is a philosophical position that is complex and elusive to define. However, at its most straightforward level, it is a perspective that questions the assumptions of structuralist approaches to understanding. A structuralist way of understanding individuals or society is one that believes that it is possible to explain events and behaviour in terms of some kind of underlying structure. For example, on a superficial level the social world may seem complex and confusing, but at a deeper level this complexity can be explained in terms of an underlying class structure (a Marxist explanation). Similarly, the behaviour of an individual person can be explained in terms of an underlying personality structure (a psychological explanation). Post-structuralism, by contrast, questions any such 'totalizing' explanation based on an all-knowing 'God's eye view' of things, and instead seeks to understand people and events by carefully describing and analysing (or 'deconstructing') what people are actually doing. In relation to therapy, a valuable example of post-structuralist thinking can be found in Michael White's (2004) discussion of 'folk psychology' (the way that ordinary people think about what it means to be a person) as compared to the hypothetical psychological structures constructed by psychologists.

Postmodernism is a sociological perspective, rather than a philosophical position. Postmodernism characterizes contemporary society as moving in the direction of increasing scepticism about the validity of universal 'truths' such as psychoanalysis, Marxism or Christianity, and replacing these 'grand narratives' with a more pragmatic 'local knowledge' that reflects the interests of people in particular times and places.

In addition to these discrete 'schools' of philosophy, there are also a number of individual philosophers whose writings have influenced the therapy approaches discussed in this chapter. The work of Mikhail Bakhtin has elucidated the nature of conversation, in terms of drawing attention to the idea that different 'voices' are apparent in a person's speech, and that the act of talking implies the presence of an audience (Bakhtin 1981). The writings of John Shotter have been influential in integrating various philosophical perspectives on language, in terms of their relevance to psychology and psychotherapy (Shotter 1993).

The role that these philosophical positions play, in relation to the approaches to counselling outlined in this chapter, can be quite confusing for those who do not have a grounding in philosophy. One of the reasons for the difficulty of this philosophical literature is that much of it is not written in response to issues in psychotherapy (or even to issues in psychology), but has been primarily addressed to questions in the fields of art and literary criticism. Although each of these philosophical perspectives has some distinctive features, there is also a great deal of overlap between them – they all start from a constructivist and anti-realist standpoint, based on the idea that people construct or co-construct the realities that they live within. Further discussion of these philosophical ideas, and their relevance to counselling, can be found in White and Epston (1990), Kvale (1992), Lock and Strong (2012), McNamee and Gergen (1992) and Anderson and Gehart (2007).

The emergence of constructivist therapy

Having become established as the form of psychological therapy most favoured by health care providers in the USA and in many European countries, it is perhaps surprising that the cognitive–behavioural approach should then be shaken to its roots by a theoretical revolution. Over the past decade or more, key figures in the cognitive–behavioural tradition, such as Michael Mahoney and Donald Meichenbaum, have taken to calling themselves *constructivist* therapists. What does this mean?

Constructivism can be characterized as resting on three basic assumptions. First, the person is regarded as an active knower, as purposefully engaged in making sense of his or her world. Second, language functions as the primary means through which the person constructs an understanding of the world. Constructivist therapists are therefore particularly interested in linguistic products such as stories and metaphors, which are seen as ways of structuring experience. Third, there is a developmental dimension to the person's capacity to construct their world. These three core assumptions mark a significant contrast between the older cognitive and cognitive–behavioural therapies and the newer constructivist alternative. Some of the main points of contrast between cognitive and constructivist theories of therapy are depicted in Table 11.1.

TABLE 11.1 Comparison between cognitive–behavioural and constructivist approaches to counselling

Feature	Traditional cognitive therapies	Constructivist therapies
Target of intervention and assessment	Isolated automatic thoughts or irrational beliefs	Construct systems, personal narratives
Temporal focus	Present	Present, but more developmental emphasis
Goal of treatment	Corrective: eliminate dysfunction	Creative; facilitate development
Style of therapy	Highly directive and psycho-educational	Less structured and more exploratory
Therapist role	Persuasive, analytical, technically instructive	Reflective, intensely personal
Interpretation of emotions	Negative emotion results from distorted thinking; represents problem to be controlled	Negative emotion as informative signal of challenge to existing constructions; to be respected
Understanding of client 'resistance'	Lack of motivation, viewed as dysfunctional	Attempt to protect core ordering processes

Source: Neimeyer 1993, 1995.

The main historical precursor of constructivist therapy was *personal construct psychology,* originally devised by George Kelly (1955) and later developed by Don Bannister, Fay Fransella, Miller Mair and their colleagues, largely in Britain (Bannister and Fransella 1985; Fransella 2005). This theory proposes that people make sense of, or 'construe', the world through systems of personal constructs. A typical example of a personal construct might be 'friendly–unfriendly'. Such a construct enables the person to differentiate between people who are perceived as 'friendly' and those who are 'unfriendly'. This construct will function to channel the person's behaviour; he or she will behave differently towards someone construed as 'friendly', in comparison to how they might act towards someone who is 'unfriendly'. A construct is embedded within a system. In some circumstances, the 'friendly–unfriendly' construct would be subsumed under a core construct such as 'reliable–unreliable'. Each construct also has its own range of convenience. For instance, 'friendly–unfriendly' can be used to construe people, but not (presumably) food.

Kelly and his colleagues devised a technique known as the repertory grid to assess the unique structure and content of the construct systems of individuals, and also devised a number of methods for applying personal construct principles in therapeutic practice. The best known of the techniques is *fixed role* therapy. Clients are asked to describe themselves as they are, and then to create an alternative role description based on a different set of constructs. They are then encouraged to act out this role for set periods of time. A more detailed account of personal construct therapy can be found in Fransella *et al.* (2007) and Fransella (2005).

One of the unusual aspects of personal construct psychology was that Kelly published his ideas as a formal theory, with postulates and corollaries. The most important of these statements was Kelly's *fundamental postulate*:

a person's processes are psychologically channelized by the way in which he anticipates events.

(Kelly 1983: 7)

Later writers and theorists have gradually moved away from Kelly's formal system. The constructivist approach to counselling and therapy that has emerged over the last decade, can be viewed as true to the spirit of Kelly but including many new ideas and insights that did not appear in his original theory.

Box 11.1: *The creative possibility of therapy*

The Scottish psychologist and psychotherapist Miller Mair was a central figure in constructivist and personal construct therapy for several decades. His sensitivity to the ways in which everyday speech can convey a sense of mystery and enchantment, and the role of therapy in facilitating these possibilities, acted as a reminder to therapists to stay close to 'what is already there' in people's lives. The death of Miller Mair in 2011 represented a major loss to the field of counselling and psychotherapy. One of his final papers, Mair (2012), offers an introduction to his unique way of thinking, and an entry into his body of work as a whole.

A particularly clear statement of the theory and practice of constructivist therapy can be found in the writings of Michael Mahoney, particularly his book *Constructive Psychotherapy* (Mahoney 2003). His approach is based on the application of a set of key principles:

- the creation of a caring, compassionate relationship;
- a collaborative style, in which client and therapist work together to identify strategies for change;
- an action orientation: 'a high priority on what clients are actually doing in their lives' (Mahoney 2003: 19);
- a focus on the ways in which the person actively makes meaning, and creates order, out of the events of their life;
- attention to the processes of development through which meaning systems are constructed;
- sensitivity to cycles of experience that are involved in active meaning-making: opening/closing; comforting/challenging – productive therapy requires the occurrence of each pole of these cycles.

In practice, Mahoney's constructivist therapy is organized around the use of a very wide range of techniques. Some of these, such as relaxation skills training, problem-solving, cognitive restructuring and homework assignments, are based in Mahoney's own initial training and experience in behaviour therapy and CBT. Other techniques, such as reading and writing assignments, personal rituals, breathing and body exercises, voice work and dramatic re-enactment of problem scenarios, are borrowed from many therapeutic tradi-tions. The assumption is, however, not that the technique matters in itself, but that it creates an opportunity for the person to reflect on how he or she constructs the world or reality within which they live, and opens up possibilities for constructing that world in fresh ways.

An example of constructivist therapy in action is the use of *mirror time*. Mahoney (2003) describes how one of his clients had a strong emotional reaction to catching sight of himself in a mirror in the therapy room. This experience stimulated Mahoney to experiment, on himself and with colleagues, with the use of mirrors in therapy sessions, and eventually to develop a protocol for this technique (Mahoney 2003: 251–2). The decision to work with a mirror is jointly taken by the therapist and client together, and the client has a choice of the size of mirror that he or she will use. In advance of looking into the mirror, the client is invited to become centred, and open to his or her present experiencing, through a breathing and meditation routine. The timing of the mirror activity is organized to allow time to reflect on the experience before the end of the session. Mahoney describes the impact of mirror work on a client named Adam, who had presented with multiple problems including depression, bulimia and personality disorder. Adam crept toward the mirror:

> . . . like a frightened child about to encounter a huge monster in a dark place . . . he stood there for some time. The look on his face slowly changed from trepidation to puzzlement. . . . He grinned slightly and said, 'The guy in the mirror doesn't look as fucked up as I feel'. He sighed. Taking a step closer to the mirror, Adam smiled and said, 'In fact, I wouldn't mind *being him*!'
>
> (Mahoney 2003: 156–7)

This moment did not facilitate significant change in itself for this client, but it did mark a turning point in terms of his pattern of relating to himself, by allowing new meaning to emerge.

The version of constructivist therapy developed by Mahoney reflects his own curiosity, and effort to make meaning from life experience. In a similar fashion, other constructivist therapists have evolved their own style of working with clients. Examples of the range of ways in which constructivism has been applied as a framework for therapy practice, can be found in Neimeyer and Mahoney (1995) and Neimeyer and Raskin (2000). It is not possible to specify a set of core procedures or techniques that all constructivist counsellors and psychotherapists would use. In this respect it is quite different from the cognitive–behavioural approach, which possesses a toolkit of familiar techniques with known effectiveness. By contrast, constructivist therapy is principle-driven rather than technique-driven.

Box 11.2: *The use of metaphor in constructivist therapy for PTSD*

The behavioural and cognitive traditions in counselling and psychotherapy have been shaped by the behaviourist need to deal with tangible, preferably observable, behaviours and irrational thoughts. Counsellors operating from a constructivist perspective are more interested in *meaning*, and in the ways that people create or find meaning in their lives.

When a client in counselling talks about events that were traumatic and emotionally painful, it will usually be very difficult for him or her to find the words to capture just how they felt, or what happened. To convey to their counsellor or therapist some sense of the meaning of the event, the client will often use *metaphors*. Unable to articulate what happened directly, a metaphor at least makes it possible to say what the event was *like*. Attention to metaphor is an important theme in constructivist therapy. In his guide to therapy with people suffering from PTSD, Meichenbaum (1994: 112–14) places great emphasis on sensitivity to the role of metaphor and he gives long lists of metaphors employed by PTSD clients: 'I am a time bomb, ready to explode. I walk a thin red line. Over the edge. Enclosed in a steel ball. A spectator to life. Hole in my life. My life is in a holding pattern. Prisoner of the past and occasionally on parole. Vacuum in my history'.

Meichenbaum (1994: 96) also provides a list of healing metaphors that clients and therapists have used in their attempts to overcome PTSD. Among the therapist metaphors are:

> Someone who has experienced a traumatic event [is] like someone who *emigrates* to a new land and must build a new life within a new culture from the one left behind.

> When a flood occurs, the water does not continue forever. There is a rush, but it is temporary and eventually the storm stops, the land dries up, and everything begins to return to normal. Emotions can be viewed in the same way.

> Just as you can't force a physical wound to heal quickly, you can't force a psychological wound to heal either.

Other examples of the intentional use of metaphor in constructivist therapy can be found in Mahoney (2003).

Box 11.3: *Constructivist counselling for loss and bereavement*

Work with clients who are experiencing difficulties around loss and bereavement represents an area of counselling practice that has received a lot of attention from constructivist theorists and researchers. A person who has undergone significant loss needs to engage in a process of re-constructing their sense of self, their relationships, and the stories that they tell about who they are. The American constructivist therapist Robert Neimeyer has made a major contribution to this area (Neimeyer 2002; 2006a, 2006b; Neimeyer *et al.* 2006; Neimeyer *et al.* 2002).

Solution-focused therapy

In recent years, *solution-focused therapy* has become possibly the most influential of the various emergent constructivist approaches to counselling and psychotherapy. The range and scope of the approach is well illustrated in the *Handbook of Solution-focused Therapy* (O'Connell and Palmer 2003). Excellent overviews of solution-focused therapy can be found in Macdonald (2007), O'Connell (2005) and de Shazer *et al.* (2007).

Solution-focused brief therapy is mainly associated with the work of Steve de Shazer (1985, 1988, 1991, 1994) at the Brief Family Therapy Centre in Milwaukee, and a group of colleagues and collaborators, including Insoo Kim Berg (Miller and Berg 1995; Berg and Kelly 2000), Yvonne Dolan (1991) and Bill O'Hanlan (O'Hanlan and Weiner-Davis 1989; Rowan and O'Hanlan 1999). de Shazer has a background in social work and music, and in his training as a psychotherapist was strongly influenced by the theory and research carried out by the Mental Research Institute (MRI) in Palo Alto, California. The Palo Alto group were the first, during the 1950s, to study interaction patterns in families, and their approach borrowed heavily from anthropological and sociological ideas as opposed to a psychiatric perspective. de Shazer acquired from his exposure to the ideas of the Palo Alto group a number of core therapeutic principles found in systemic family therapy: a belief that intervention can be brief and 'strategic'; appreciation of the use of questioning to invite clients to consider alternative courses of action; and the use of an 'observing team', which advises the therapist during 'time out' interludes. Like many other family therapists (including members of the Palo Alto group), de Shazer became fascinated by the unique approach to therapy developed by Milton H. Erickson (see Box 11.4). The case studies published by Erickson convinced de Shazer that it was possible to work strategically and briefly with individual clients, not just with families, and that for each client there could exist a unique 'solution' to their own unique difficulties.

Over the course of a number of years, de Shazer came to develop his own coherent approach, which emphasized the role of language in constructing personal reality. In working out the implications of placing language ('words', 'talk') at the heart of therapy, de Shazer made use of the ideas of philosophers such as Wittgenstein and Lyotard, and the French psychoanalytic thinker Jacques Lacan. The essence of de Shazer's approach to therapy concentrates on the idea that 'problem talk' perpetuates the 'problem', maintains the centrality of the problem in the life and relationships of the person and distracts attention from any 'solutions' or 'exceptions' to the problem that the person might generate. The task of the therapist, therefore, is to invite the client to engage in 'solution' talk, while respectfully accepting (but not encouraging) the client's wish to talk about their distress and hopelessness, or the general awfulness of their problem. From de Shazer's point of view, therefore, solution-focused sessions are best thought of as conversations involving language games that are focused on three inter-related activities: namely, producing exceptions to the problem, imagining and describing new lives for clients and 'confirming' that change is occurring in their lives.

Box 11.4: *The enigma of Milton Erickson*

Milton H. Erickson MD (1902–80) was an intriguing figure who played a significant role in the history of psychotherapy. Erickson worked for most of his career in Phoenix, Arizona, seeing patients in the living room of his three-bedroom home. He made major contributions to the field of medical hypnosis in his early career, and in the 1950s wrote the *Encyclopaedia Britannica* entry on hypnosis. Erickson was considered by those who knew him to be a heroic and magical individual. He overcame polio twice in youth, and developed an approach to therapy that 'cured' clients in ways that were almost impossible to understand, let alone replicate.

Although he was originally best known for his use of hypnosis, it became clear to Erickson, and to those who studied with him, that the effectiveness of his approach to therapy did not rely on the use of suggestions made to patients while in trance states, but to his sensitive and creative use of language, metaphor and stories, his capacity to observe the fine detail of the client's behaviour and his ability to form a collaborative relationship with his clients.

Erickson's methods were popularized by the family therapist Jay Haley (1973), and have influenced many constructivist therapists (Hoyt 1994), as well as the solution-focused approach of Steve de Shazer. Further examples of Erickson's unique style of therapy can be found in Haley (1973), Rossi (1980), Rosen (1982) and Lankton and Lankton (1986).

The solution-focused approach to therapy is built up from a range of strategies designed to enable the client to articulate and act on the widest possible range of solutions to their problems. These strategies include the following.

Focusing on change. The idea that change is happening all the time is an important concept in solution-focused therapy. Solution-focused therapists assume therefore that change is not only possible but inevitable. In practice this means that therapists will usually ask new clients about changes in relation to their presenting concerns prior to their first session – often referred to as 'pre-session change'. During therapy the therapist will usually begin each session by asking the client about changes since the last session: for example, 'What's better even in small ways since last time?' If the client describes any changes, even apparently minor ones, then the therapist will use a range of follow-up questions to amplify the change and resourcefulness of the client: for instance, 'How did you do that?'; 'How did you know that was the right thing to do/best way to handle the situation?' Should the client not be able to identify any change, the therapist might use 'coping questions' to invite the client to talk about how they are managing to survive or cope despite the problem.

Problem-free talk. At the beginning of a session, a counsellor might engage the client in talk about everyday activities, as a means of gaining some appreciation of the client's competencies and positive qualities.

Exception finding. Fundamental to the solution-focused approach is a belief that no matter how severe or all-pervasive a person's problem may appear there will be times when it does not occur, is less debilitating or intrusive in their lives. Such instances again point to clients' strengths and self-healing abilities, which when harnessed allow clients to construct their own unique solutions to their difficulties and concerns. Practitioners will therefore deliberately seek out exceptions by asking clients questions like: 'When was the last time you felt happy/relaxed/loved/confident etc. etc.?' 'What have you found that helps, even a little?' Exception finding questions help to deconstruct the client's view of the problem and at the same time to highlight and build on the client's success in redefining themselves and their lives.

Use of pithy slogans. There are a number of short, memorable statements that help to communicate to clients (and trainee therapists) the basic principles of a solution-focused approach. Typical solution-focused messages include: 'If it isn't broken, don't fix it', 'If it's not working stop doing it', 'If it's working, keep doing it', 'Therapy need not take a long time', 'Small changes can lead to bigger changes'.

The 'miracle question'. Typically, in a first session, a solution-focused counsellor will ask the client to imagine a future in which their problem has been resolved: 'Imagine when you go to sleep one night a miracle happens and the problems we've been talking about disappear. As you were asleep, you did not know that a miracle had happened. When you woke up, what would be the first signs for you that a miracle had happened?' (de Shazer 1988). This catalytic question allows the person to consider the problem as a whole, to step into a future that does not include the problem and to explore, with the therapist, how they would know that the problem had gone, how other people would know and how such changes had been brought about. The image of a 'miracle' is also a potent cultural metaphor that helps the client to remember what they learned from this discussion that follows the asking of the question.

Scaling. Scaling questions are designed to facilitate discussion about and measure change, and are used to consider a multitude of issues in client's lives. For instance, to assess a client's readiness or motivation to change, their coping abilities, self-esteem, progress in therapy and so on. Typically, the client is asked to rate their problem (e.g., depression) on a 0–10 scale, where 0 is as bad as it can be ('rock bottom') and 10 is ideal. Once the client places themselves at a point on the scale (a 2, for example), the therapist will first of all enquire about what has helped to get them to a 2 or what the client is doing to prevent themselves from slipping back to 'rock bottom'. Subsequently the therapist will work with the client to negotiate further small goals by inviting them to consider what will be different when they are at 3 on the scale and so on in subsequent sessions until the client reaches a point where they are ready to end therapy.

Homework tasks – exploring resources. Towards the end of each session, the therapist will either leave the room to consult with co-workers who have been observing the session, or (if working alone) take a few minutes to reflect in silence. In the final segment of the session, the therapist restates his or her admiration for positive achievements that the client has made, and then prescribes a task to be carried out before the next session. The homework task is designed to enable the person to remain focused on solutions. An example of a homework task that might be used following the first session of therapy is: 'Until the next time we meet, I'd like you just to observe what things are happening in your life/family/work that you'd like to see continue, then come back and tell me about it'.

These are some of the many ways in which a solution-focused therapist will structure the therapeutic conversation to allow the client to identify and apply their own personal strengths and competencies. Some of the key points of contrast between a problem-focused and a solution-focused approach to therapy are highlighted in Table 11.2.

It is important to appreciate the wider issues associated with the solution-focused approach. Solution-focused therapy exists as a distinct approach to therapy, which is practised by Steven de Shazer, Insoo Kim Berg and many other practitioners that they have trained. However, the solution-focused approach also has a wider significance, in representing a radical perspective in relation to a number of the key issues that have dominated debates within counselling and psychotherapy during the past 50 years.

The historical account of the development of therapy offered in Chapter 2 described the emergence of psychoanalysis, the earliest form of psychotherapy, from a medical–psychiatric context that emphasized the necessity of diagnosing and assessing the patient's problem as the first step in effective treatment. In psychoanalysis, much of the effectiveness of therapy is attributed to the achievement of suitable levels of insight and understanding of the origins of the presenting problem: for example, its roots in childhood experience. The next generation of therapies that emerged in the mid-twentieth century – humanistic and cognitive–behavioural – retained an interest in understanding the roots of the person's problem, but, compared to psychoanalysis, paid much more attention to what the person might be seeking to be able to do in the future. Both self-actualization and behaviour change are 'future-oriented' constructs. Solution-focused therapy represents a radical further movement in this direction. In solution-focused therapy, the 'problem' is not particularly interesting. What is important is to focus on the solutions

TABLE 11.2 Comparison between a problem-focused and a solution-focused approach to counselling

Problem-focused	Solution-focused
How can I help you?	How will you know when therapy has been helpful?
Could you tell me about the problem?	What would you like to change?
Is the problem a symptom of something deeper?	Have we clarified the central issue on which you want to concentrate?
Can you tell me more about the problem?	Can we discover exceptions to the problem?
How are we to understand the problem in the light of the past?	What will the future look like without the problem?
How many sessions will be needed?	Have we achieved enough to end?

Source: O'Connell (1998: 21).

and strengths that the person already possesses, or is able to devise, in relation to living the kind of life they want to live.

Why is this a radical shift? Surely, it could be argued, even 'problem-focused' or 'assessment-oriented' therapies such as psychoanalysis use the process of analysing and understanding a problem as a means of arriving at the best solution to that problem? Even if the work of therapy concentrates largely on unravelling the connections between past experience and present troubles, in gaining insight the patient or client is effectively creating a space within which new options or solutions can be adopted. de Shazer does not share this view. For de Shazer, the concept of 'problem', as employed in counselling and psychotherapy theory, implies a notion of the person as structured in terms of a set of internal mechanisms (mind, unconscious, self, schemas) that have 'gone wrong' and need to be fixed. de Shazer, and other solution-focused therapists, *do not view people in these terms*. For them, the person exists within the way they talk, within the stories that they tell to themselves and other people. From this perspective, any attempt to explore and understand the 'problem' is merely encouraging 'problem talk', the maintenance of relationships characterized by a story-line of the 'I have a problem' type, and the suppression of stories that offer an account of the person as resourceful, capable, in control and so on. In addition, one of the by-products of an extended exploration of a 'problem' with a therapist is that the person begins to apply the language of psychology and psychotherapy not only as a means of accounting for this specific problem, but as a way of talking about other aspects of their life: the person becomes socialized into a 'problem-sensitive' way of talking about himself or herself. Moreover, de Shazer would reject any assumption that there is a necessary cause and effect relationship between studying a problem and arriving at its solution: a solution is a kind of unpredictable 'creative leap'. This way of looking at therapy seriously challenges any notion of the 'scientific' knowability of what happens in therapy. If clients get 'better' by following their own, idiosyncratic solutions, then what role is left for scientific models of dysfunction and change?

What de Shazer is doing can be seen as a rigorous attempt to conduct therapy from a postmodern standpoint. The idea that there exist internal psychological structures that determine behaviour is an essentially 'modern' way of making sense of the world. A postmodern sensitivity argues that these theories/structures are no more than another kind of story. They are stories that are associated with the power that professions and institutions have to define individuals as 'cases', as exhibiting 'deficits' (Gergen 1990). Like other postmodern writers, de Shazer adopts a role of challenging and questioning established ideas, with the aim of opening up possibilities for individuals to create their own personal or 'local' truths, rather than become assimilated into any theoretical framework that claims universal truth.

In contrast to the mainstream approaches to counselling (psychodynamic, cognitive–behavioural and person-centred), solution-focused therapy has never generated a formal theory, and has not cultivated a base within the university/research system. Although some research has been carried out into the effectiveness of solution-focused therapy (Gingerich and Eisengart 2000), there have been no large-scale studies of research programmes into this approach. As a result, although this research is generally supportive of the effectiveness of solution-focused therapy, it has received little attention within the psychotherapy research community. The published literature on solution-focused therapy mainly comprises fragments of philosophical analysis, rather than any attempt to assemble a definitive theoretical model or 'manual', supplemented by numerous case examples (which rely almost entirely on session transcripts) and dialogues between practitioners (see Hoyt 1994, 1996a).

It is important to acknowledge the difference between solution-focused therapy, which de Shazer describes as a *brief* therapy, and the imposition of limits on the number of sessions available to clients, associated with many workplace counselling schemes, managed care services in North America and counselling in primary care in the UK. The intention of solution-focused therapy is to respect the personal resourcefulness of the client by asking them whether they have achieved what they need, or inviting them to say what would need to happen for them to know they were ready to finish therapy. A solution-focused therapist would argue that it is a mark of their profound belief in the resourcefulness of people that they can accept that one session of therapy may be sufficient. However, they acknowledge that, for some people, *many* sessions may be required: it is up to the person. In this sense, solution-focused therapy is not time-*limited*, even though it is usually *brief*.

Perhaps because of the radical, 'outsider' status of solution-focused therapy, there is sometimes a sense that writers and practitioners operating within this approach are unwilling to accept the common ground between what they do and the practices of therapists from competing traditions, or to deviate from the cardinal 'rules' of solution-focused therapy, such as asking the 'miracle question' in the first session. Nylund and Corsiglia (1994) make the point that solution-focused therapy work can risk becoming solution-*forced* rather than solution-*focused*, and suggest that some clients may find its relentless future-oriented optimism persecutory and unhelpful. Bill O'Hanlan, one of the pioneers within this approach, now describes his method as *possibility* therapy (Hoyt 1996b), and argues that it is necessary to integrate Rogerian qualities of empathy and affirmation in order to offer a more caring relationship to clients.

It is difficult to predict the long-term impact of solution-focused therapy on the field of counselling and psychotherapy as a whole. Probably thousands of counsellors and psychotherapists in Europe and North America have attended workshops on solution-focused therapy, and have read de Shazer's books. It is impossible to know how many of these practitioners have attended workshops because they are curious about what may seem an odd or – in their eyes – mistaken way to conduct therapy. There are many others who would be drawn to specific techniques, such as the miracle question or scaling, that they might apply within a cognitive–behavioural, humanistic or integrative approach. It remains to be seen whether the contribution of de Shazer and his colleagues lies in the construction of a radically constructivist, postmodern approach to therapy, or whether their legacy is more properly understood in more modest (but nevertheless valuable) terms, as comprising the invention of a number of techniques for inviting clients to imagine desirable future scenarios.

Narrative therapy

Social constructionism is a philosophical position that regards personal experience and meaning as being not created merely by the individual (the constructivist position) but something embedded in a culture and shaped by that culture. People are social beings. Personal identity is a product of the history of the culture, the position of the person in society and the linguistic resources available to the individual. Social constructionism is mainly associated with the writings of Gergen (1985, 1994), although in fact it is more accurately understood as a broad movement within philosophy, humanities and the social sciences. From a social constructionist perspective, narrative represents an essential bridge between individual experience and the cultural system. We are born into a world of stories. A culture is structured around myths, legends, family tales and other stories that have existed since long before we are born, and will continue long after we die. We construct a personal identity by aligning ourselves with some of these stories, by 'dwelling within' them.

Applied to therapy, social constructionism does not look for answers in terms of change in internal psychological processes. Indeed, the whole notion that an inner psychological reality exists is questionable from a social constructionist stance. This is because the idea of a 'true, core self' is not seen as constituting a fixed truth, but is viewed instead as part of a romantic narrative that people in Western societies tell themselves about what it means to be a person (Gergen 1991). Instead of focusing on 'self', social constructionist therapists look at what is happening within a culture or community, and the relationship between a troubled person (or client) and that community. Narrative therapy is heavily influenced by the ideas of the French post-structuralist philosopher Michel Foucault, who advocates a critical stance in relation to expert knowledge claims, and the replacement of culturally dominant narratives (the stories told by those in power) by the 'insider' knowledge that is held by ordinary people.

The main inspiration for social constructionist narrative counselling or therapy has come from the work of Michael White and David Epston. Perhaps because they lived in Australia (White) and New Zealand (Epston), these therapists have been able to evolve an approach which is radically different from mainstream therapies. Although their initial training and background was in family therapy, their ideas can be, and have been, used in work with individuals, couples and groups. Following the publication of their main book, *Narrative Means to Therapeutic Ends*, in 1990, their approach was carried to new audiences by books from Parry and Doan (1994), Freedman and Combs (1996) and Monk *et al.* (1996). Narrative therapy has generated an international network of conferences, training programmes and publications, based around the Dulwich Centre in Adelaide, Australia, and associated centres in many other countries. It represents the most highly organized of all the 'constructionist' approaches to therapy. Recent developments in narrative therapy theory and practice are discussed in Brown and Augusta-Scott (2007), Duvall and Beres (2011) and White (2007).

The key ideas that underpin social constructionist narrative therapy can be summarized as:

- people live their lives within the dominant narratives or knowledges of their culture and family;
- sometimes, there can be a significant mismatch between the dominant narrative and the actual life experience of the person, or the dominant narrative can construct a life that is impoverished or subjugated;
- one of the main takes of a therapist is to help the client to externalize the problem, to see it as a story that exists outside of them;
- the therapist also works at deconstructing the dominant narrative, reducing its hold over the person;

- another therapist task involves helping the client to identify unique outcomes or 'sparkling moments' – times when they have escaped from the clutches of the dominant narrative;

- the therapist adopts a *not-knowing* stance in relation to the client; the client is the expert on his or her story and how to change it (Anderson and Goolishian 1992; Hoffman 1992); at the completion of therapy the client is invited back as a 'consultant', to share their knowledge for the benefit of future clients;

- a central aim of therapy is to assist the person to re-author their story and to perform this new story within their community;

- another aim of therapy is to help the person to complete important life transitions;

- although much of the therapy is based on conversation and dialogue, written or literary communications such as letters and certificates are used because they give the client a permanent and 'authoritative' version of the new story;

- where possible, cultural resources, such as support groups or family networks, are enlisted to help a person to consolidate and live a re-authored story, and to provide supportive audiences.

Many of these features can be observed in the case of Rose (Box 11.5) (Epston *et al.* 1992). Here it can be seen that this kind of narrative therapy tends to be of fairly short duration, with high levels of therapist activity. The therapist is clearly warm and affirming, adopting a style of relating to the client that is reminiscent of Carl Rogers in the degree of hope that is transmitted, and in the implicit belief in the client's capacity to grow and change in positive ways.

Box 11.5: *Re-authoring therapy: Rose's story*

An example of how the originally systemic, family-oriented approach of White and Epston can be applied in individual counselling is provided by the case of Rose (Epston *et al.* 1992). Rose had lost her job as a receptionist/video-camera operator at an advertising agency, because she would 'crack up' and burst into tears if interrupted while completing a work task. When she met David Epston, she told him that 'I don't have a base inside myself'. He replied, 'there must be a story behind this. Do you feel like telling me about it?' She then talked about the physical abuse she had received from her father, a well-respected parish minister. Following this first session, Epston sent her a lengthy letter, which began:

> Dear Rose,
> It was a very pleasing experience to meet up with you and hear some of your story, a story of both protest and survival against what you understood to be an attempt to destroy your life. And you furthered that protest yesterday by coming and telling me that story. I would imagine that you had not been able to tell anyone for fear of being disbelieved. I feel privileged that you shared it

with me and hope that sharing it relieved you of some of its weight. I can see how such a history could have left you the legacy you described – a sense of not seeming 'to have a base'.

(Epston et al. 1992: 103)

The rest of the letter retold the story that Rose had recounted during the counselling session, but retelling it as a story of courage, survival, and hope. The letter ended with:

> I look forward to meeting you again to assist you to write a new history of events in your life, a new history that could predict a very different kind of future than your old history.
>> Yours sincerely,
>> David

The next counselling session was one month later. During the interval, Rose had applied for and secured a job as a chef (her preferred occupation), and had been so successful in this role that the restaurant owner had left her in charge while he took his holidays. She had renewed her relationship with her mother, and had met with each of her siblings to talk through the message of the letter with them. She felt her life was 'on the right track'. After this second meeting, Epston sent another letter, which opened:

> Dear Rose,
> Reading the letter, which provided you with a different story, seems to have led to 'a sense of relief . . . it was normal I had problems . . . it wasn't my fault . . . I had previously felt weak and vulnerable . . . and that I should have got it all together by now.' Instead, you began to appreciate more fully that 'I felt I had made a start . . . I was definitely on the right track.' And I suspect now that you are realizing that you have been on the 'right track' for some time now; if not, as you put it, you would have become 'disillusioned . . . and ended my life'. Well, there is a lot of life in you, and it is there for all to see!

(Epston et al. 1992: 105)

There was one other counselling session, and then 6 months later Rose was invited to join her therapist as a 'consultant to others' so that 'the knowledges that have been resurrected and/or generated in therapy can be documented' (Epston *et al.* 1992: 106). During this consultation meeting, Rose gave her explanation of how she had been helped:

> Having the story [the first letter] gave me a point of reference to look back at, to read it through, to think about it and form my own opinions from what we had discussed and draw my own conclusions. I remember getting the letter from the letter box, making myself a nice cup of tea, sitting down and reading it. I had feelings of 'Yes . . . that's it . . . that's the whole story!' Thinking about it, re-reading it . . . and feeling a lot better about myself . . . Without it, I think I'd still be confused.

(Epston et al. 1992: 107)

Externalizing the problem

One of the distinctive features of narrative therapy is the procedure that White and Epston (1990) refer to as externalizing the problem. They argue that many clients enter counselling with a sense that the problem is a part of them, it is inherent in who they are as a person. When this happens, people can all too readily arrive at a 'totalizing' position where their whole sense of self, and the way they talk about themselves, is self-blaming and 'problem-saturated'. The process of externalizing the problem involves separating oneself and one's relationships from the problem, and frees up the person to take a lighter approach to what had previously been defined as a 'deadly serious' issue.

More than this, from a narrative point of view the 'problem' is understood as arising from the 'dominant narrative' that has shaped the client's life and relationships. It is as though the dominant narrative or story is being told or enacted through the life of the client, leaving no space for alternative narratives. Externalizing the problem opens up a space for telling new types of story about the problem, for re-authoring. But how is this achieved?

The first step in externalizing is naming the problem. Ideally, the problem should be defined or phrased in language used by the client. It is normally helpful to make the problem term as specific as possible, and to use humour or imagery. So, for example, with a client who begins therapy referring to a problem as 'panic attacks' or 'depression', it may be useful to agree on a more colloquial problem label, such as 'scary stories' or 'the influence of unreachable standards of perfectionism'. Terms such as 'anxiety', 'panic attacks' or 'depression' may be elements of the dominant discourse of mental health that might have oppressed the client, so even a shift of label away from diagnostic terminology in the direction of everyday language may have the effect of beginning a process of re-authoring.

The next step is to explore such issues as: how does the problem stay strong; and how does the problem influence your life? White and Epston (1990) refer to this phase as relative influence questioning. The purpose of these questions is to map out the influence of the problem, and in doing so increasingly to draw a distinction between the person and the problem story. While this is happening, the therapist is alert for the appearance of unique outcome stories, which are stories of times when the problem did not dominate the person, or was not strong. These new or 'sparkling moment' stories form the basis for re-authoring. The task of the narrative therapist is to enable the client to elaborate on these unique outcomes and find audiences for them.

In some of the writing of White and Epston (1990) there appears to be a tendency to represent externalizing as a matter of asking the client a lot of questions. This seems to be a legacy of the family therapy origins of their approach, and there does not seem to be any reason why externalizing should not take place equally well through conversation and dialogue, or through the use of ritual, artistic creations, poetry and music. Parry and Doan (1994) offer some useful examples of the flexible application of externalizing principles in therapy. Box 11.6 gives a summary of the Case of Sneaky Poo. Many famous therapists are associated with celebrated cases: for example, Freud with the Dora case, Rogers with the Gloria film. Sneaky Poo is the classic White and Epston case, and it provides a wonderful example of externalizing at its best.

Box 11.6: *The Sneaky Poo story*

Nick was six years old, and had a long history of encopresis. Hardly a day would go by without a serious incident of soiling: the 'full works' in his underwear. Nick had befriended the 'poo'. He smeared it on walls and hid it behind cupboards. His parents, Sue and Ron, were miserable, embarrassed, despairing. They went for therapy to Michael White's clinic. Through a series of 'relative influence' questions, he discovered that the poo was:

- making a mess of Nick's life by isolating him from other children;
- forcing Sue to question her ability to be a good parent;
- profoundly embarrassing Ron and as a result making him isolate himself by avoiding visiting friends and family;
- affecting all the relationships in the family.

However, in response to a further series of questions that mapped the influence of what they came to call Sneaky Poo on the family, they found that:

- there were some occasions when Nick did not allow Sneaky Poo to 'outsmart' him;
- there were also times when Sue and Ron did not allow Sneaky Poo to defeat them.

White built on these 'unique outcomes' by inquiring just how the individual family members managed to be so effective against the problem. Did their success give them any ideas about 'further steps they might take to reclaim their lives from the problem'? All three of them could think of ways forward. Nick said he was 'ready to stop Sneaky Poo from outsmarting him so much'. At their next session, two weeks later, much had changed. In that time, Nick had only had one very minor accident. He had 'taught Sneaky Poo a lesson'. Sue and Ron had started to shift from their states of stress, isolation and embarrassment. On the third meeting, three weeks later and at a six-month follow-up everything continued to go well. White encouraged them to reflect on what their success against Sneaky Poo said about their qualities as people, and the strength of their relationships (White and Epston 1990: 43–8).

Enlisting community resources and audiences

It cannot be emphasized enough that social constructionist narrative counselling or therapy is not primarily an individual-centred approach, but is a way of working in the space between the person and the community, drawing on each as necessary. Epston and White (1992) describe therapy as a *rite de passage*, through which the person negotiates passage from one status to another. In a *rite de passage*, the person first undergoes a separation stage, when they become detached from their previous niche or social role. They then enter a liminal stage, a time of exploration and confusion, and then finally proceed to reincorporation, when they re-enter society in a new role. The case of Rose (Box 11.5) illustrates this process well. At the start of therapy Rose was performing an almost child-like, dependent role in society, while at the end she had adopted a quite different, highly adult managerial role as head chef in a restaurant.

Sometimes considerable effort needs to be invested in supporting the continued existence of appropriate and life-enhancing audiences in situations where the client's problem story is enmeshed in all-pervasive cultural narratives. A good example of this kind of situation is work with women experiencing difficulties in controlling their eating (Maisel *et al.* 2004). The dominant cultural and family narratives around food, women's bodies and dieting are so powerful (a major international industry) that it can be very difficult for women to find a space to develop unique outcome stories. Epston *et al.* (1995) describe the foundation of the Anti-Anorexic/Bulimic League, which has been conceived not as a support group but as an 'underground resistance movement' or 'community of counter-practice', set up to promote anti-anorexic/bulimic knowledges. Epston *et al.* (1995: 82) give an account of a ritual designed to celebrate the person's liberation from anorexia/bulimia. The new member of the League is presented with:

> The Anti-Anorexic/Bulimic League T-shirt. The recipient is asked to remember all those women executed by anorexia, all those languishing in the private 'concentration camps' throughout the Western world, and is requested to walk forward into her own 'freedom' and if it suits her, to speak out against anorexia/bulimia and all those beliefs and social practices that support it. The mood is lightened when the League's logo is revealed to them on the front of the T-shirt: A circle inside of which is the word DIET with a slash bisecting the 'T'.
>
> (Epston *et al.* 1995: 82)

The point here is that resistance to the anorexia/bulimia narrative requires joint action, sharing knowledge and resources, and that individuals stand little chance against the huge oppressive power of anorexia/bulimia.

One of the consequences of the collectivist focus of social constructionist therapy has been a questioning of the value of traditional one-to-one therapy as an effective site for constructing new stories. There are many pressures on the therapist in individual counselling and therapy to resort to an expert role, and subtly (or not so subtly) to impose his or her dominant mental health narrative on the patient or client. Gergen and Kaye (1992) and Gergen (1996) have questioned whether the privileged position of the therapist that is intrinsic to traditional modes of therapy is, in the long run, consistent with a social constructionist perspective.

Research on narrative therapy

It has taken some time for research into narrative therapy to gain momentum and develop a sense of direction as a result of the research posture adopted within the narrative therapy professional community. Narrative therapy theory and practice draws on critical political discourse that questions and challenges the power relations that are reflected in most of the research that is published in mainstream journals. Specifically, the narrative therapy tradition questions the value of research in which the researcher is positioned as an expert who measures or interprets the meaning of the client's experience. Instead, narrative therapy has evolved a form of inquiry that is based on collaborative meaning-making and writing, and which views the products of therapy (e.g., letters and other documents produced by clients and therapists) as research data. The rationale for this way of thinking about research has been powerfully made by Crocket *et al.* (2004). So far, few studies of this type have been published.

However, there have been some studies of narrative therapy that have drawn on conventional methodologies. O'Connor *et al.* (1997) used qualitative methods to explore client experiences of narrative therapy in a child and family outpatient clinic in Canada. Interviews were carried out with members of families at different stages in their therapy. The main themes to emerge from this study was that clients valued the ways that therapists treated them with respect and regarded them as the 'experts' on their problems, and described the main outcome of therapy as being the development of personal agency and control over their lives. Some clients reported that they were uncomfortable with some aspects of the narrative therapy procedure, such as being observed.

A further study by the same research group examined therapist experiences of delivering narrative therapy (O'Connor *et al.* 2004). In this study, it was found that all the therapists at the clinic were enthusiastic about narrative therapy and believed that it was an effective way of working with their clients. However, they also described some limitations of narrative therapy: it was hard for therapists who had previous training to learn narrative therapy language and methods, it was costly in terms of staff time, and on occasions the information from reflecting teams (where a group of observers reports on their reactions to the family) could be overwhelming. The most significant difficulty, reported by half of the therapists in this study, was that it was hard to adopt a narrative therapy stance when clients reported family violence issues. In such situations, therapists found themselves retreating to a more controlling, rather than collaborative, stance.

Keeling and Nielson (2005) investigated the experiences of Asian Indian women in the USA, who were invited to take part in a brief online therapeutic intervention using expressive arts techniques and journal writing, based on a narrative therapy approach. This study documents the experiences of these participants and provides examples of the kinds of material that they produced during the programme. The main finding of this study was that Asian Indian women appreciated the opportunity to work privately on personal issues, as the intervention continued they also began to realize the value of face-to-face meetings. This study also provided evidence that clients from non-Western cultural backgrounds interpret the task of 'externalizing' a problem in ways that reflect their own cultural assumptions about self.

Young and Cooper (2008) carried out a qualitative study of the experiences of young people who had received single-session narrative therapy at a drop-in centre. In this study, participants were invited to 're-visit' the therapy clinic to watch a video of their therapy session. They were asked to stop the tape at any point of interest, and talk about what they recalled they had been experiencing at that moment in the session. Research participants reported that their single session therapeutic encounter had been helpful for them, and that the suggestion to externalize their problem had been particularly valuable. They also reported that the opportunity to watch their session again, and reflect further on what they had said on that earlier occasion, had been useful in itself.

A further example of a qualitative study of a narrative therapy intervention is the pragmatic case study published by Palgi and Ben-Ezra (2010), into a successful narrative-based approach to working with a client experiencing an acute traumatic stress response. Also, Munro *et al.* (2008) have reported positive results from a pilot study of narrative therapy in clients who were deaf.

There have been few quantitative studies of the outcomes of narrative therapy. However, a study by Vromans and Schweitzer (2011) found that depressed clients receiving narrative therapy reported benefits equivalent to the outcomes of CBT. This is an important piece of research, because Vromans and Schweitzer (2011) used a research approach that was based on standard investigations, and as a result was not particularly sensitive to the distinctive characteristics of narrative therapy. For narrative therapy to yield positive results in this kind of scenario is therefore of some significance.

Overall, the expanding research literature on the processes and outcomes of narrative therapy has provided evidence of the effectiveness of this approach, as well as some indications on how certain aspects of the model might be further developed.

Collaborative therapy

The term *collaborative therapy* has been used to describe an approach to therapy that emphasizes the co-constructed nature of the interaction between therapist and client (Anderson and Gehart 2007; Strong 2000). Collaborative therapy draws on social constructionist and postmodern perspectives in stressing the importance of *dialogue* between equal partners to enable conversations to take place within which new meanings can emerge. As Anderson (2007: 41) puts it: 'dialogue allows us to find ways of going on from here'. The attention that is given, within this form of therapy, to careful listening and responding on the part of the therapist, is reminiscent of client-centred therapy.

One of the best-known and most widely researched examples of collaborative therapy is the *open dialogue* approach to working with people experiencing severe mental health problems, developed by Jaakko Siekkula and his colleagues based at the Keropudas Psychiatric Hospital in Western Lapland, a province in the north of Finland (Haarakangas *et al.* 2007; Seikkula and Arnkil 2006; Seikkula *et al.* 2006). When a person, or their family, seeks help for a crisis in which one member is acting in a manner consistent with a diagnosis of schizophrenia a team of three therapists is convened. Depending on whether the person is hospitalized, or being helped at home, the team members (drawn from a pool of psychiatrists, nurses, psychologists, social workers and child guidance workers) will represent the helping networks that are most relevant for the person and his or her family. A first meeting is convened within 24 hours, attended by the person, their family, other key members of their social network, and workers from official agencies involved in the case. There may be daily meetings for the following 10 to 12 days. The focus of the meetings is 'on promoting dialogue . . . a new understanding is built up in the area between the participants in the dialogue' (Seikkula *et al.* 2006: 216). Rather than rush into the formulation of a treatment plan, or the prescription of medication, there is a high degree of tolerance of uncertainty: 'the psychotic hallucinations or delusions of the patient are accepted as one voice among others' (p. 216). The results of a five-year follow-up of patients who had received help through the open dialogue approach showed that over 80 per cent had returned to an active social life, with no recurrence of psychotic symptoms. These outcomes compare favourably with those obtained in other studies of first-onset psychosis. In addition, the introduction of the open dialogue model was cost-effective, with a 30 per cent reduction in psychiatric services costs over the time period when this approach was introduced, arising from reduced utilization of inpatient beds.

The factors that appear to be responsible for the success of the open dialogue approach are:

- a social network perspective – key members of the person's social network are invited to participate;
- flexibility – the therapeutic response is adapted to the specific and changing needs of each case;
- psychological continuity – the team that is originally convened retains responsibility for integrating the experiences of all participants, for the duration of the process;
- dialogue and tolerance of uncertainty – maximizes the active involvement of those who are participating, by ensuring that their views and suggestions are taken into account.

As in narrative therapy, open dialogue and other collaborative approaches are built around a strategy of enabling people to tell their stories, and to begin to create new stories that provide scaffolding for different ways of acting. There is also an emphasis on the process of enlisting community resources. A key difference between narrative therapy and collaborative therapy is that while the former specifies a sequence of therapist activities (e.g., externalizing the problem) that will lead to 're-authoring', the latter approach is a more open, dialogical process, in which the shape and structure of the therapy may be created anew in each case.

Box 11.7: *Open dialogue in action: the case of Martti*

Martti was 16 years of age, and attending a vocational college in a city separate from his parental home, when 'everything seemed to fall apart'. He became increasingly isolated and irritable, stopped taking care of his hygiene, talked only in a mumble, and made rocking movements. His parents took him to a primary care centre, and he was admitted for one night. An open dialogue team was assembled, and daily meetings were held with Martti and his parents. It was decided that he would return home, and all further meetings were held in his parents' home.

At first, Martti said little, and looked up at the sky; his parents cried a lot. His sister returned home to be with him. Medication was considered, but the parents did not like the idea, so no prescription was made. Gradually, Martti began to be able to sleep at nights, and to answer questions. After three months, there was a five-week break, at the request of the family. On resumption of weekly meetings, Martti reported that he wanted to return to college. The team members, and his parents, were concerned about this, and after consid-erable discussion it was agreed that open dialogue meetings would continue at the college, involving the principal of the school, Martti's closest teacher, and the school nurse. At the five-year follow-up meeting, Martti was in work and coping well with his life. He was considering entering individual psychotherapy to 'clarify to himself what had happened during his crisis'.

This case, reported in Seikkula *et al.* (2006), illustrates the way in which a collaborative caring network can be established around a person in crisis, which the person can use to begin to put his or her life back on track. The open dialogue approach has significant implications for the therapists who are involved. As Haarakangas *et al.* (2007: 232) put it:

> we have evolved from being 'experts' to becoming 'dialogicians' . . . the open
> dialogue approach has also transformed the patient into coworker and thera-
> pists into active listeners. In the Finnish language, we would call the work of
> supporting families caught in a mental health system 'walking together'.

The radical theatre tradition

Within the broad social constructionist and post-structuralist philosophical perspective that informs many of the therapies reviewed in this chapter can be found a radical critique of inequality and oppression in contemporary society. One of the consequences of taking stories seriously is to raise the question: 'in whose interest is this story being told?' The process of critically 'deconstructing' the concepts, assumptions and 'grand narratives' around which both everyday life and professional activity are constructed, opens up for scrutiny the ways in which powerful groups in society promote dominant narratives that control people's lives. The anti-anorexia league, developed within the narrative therapy approach (Maisel *et al.* 2004) is an example of how some therapists have found it necessary to go beyond merely working with the images of 'perfect thin-ness' that exist within the minds of their clients, and create a strategy for challenging the social machinery (the media, the food industry, the diet industry) that aggressively promote these images within modern culture.

There are some therapists who have moved further than this, in an attempt to position therapy more closely to social action. One of the strategies that they have adopted in order to achieve this goal, has been to make connections between therapy and the world of political theatre and community theatre. A key figure in this movement has been the Brazilian theatre director Augusto Boal, who in the 1960s developed an approach known at the *theatre of the oppressed* (Boal 1979, 1995). In a theatre of the oppressed event, a group of actors uses exercises and games to bring about a sense of involvement in the audience (who are described as 'spect-actors', to emphasize their active role in the produc-tion). The actors then stage brief dramatic enactments of problematic situations that are familiar to the audience. However, the audience are invited to interrupt the performance at any point, in order to join in and improvise their own solutions.

An example, taken from a family therapy project in a school in Australia, was based on a performance of a situation in which a teenage son tried to tell his father that he was gay (Proctor *et al.* 2008). The actors portrayed a scenario in which a boy enters his father's study, and asks to talk to him. The father is too busy to listen, and seems irritated. After a while, the boy loses his temper, and storms out. The audience then decided to replay the scene:

> A spect-actor from the audience, who happened to be the school's deputy principal, shouted 'Stop!' when the father was most obviously ignoring his son's overtures to him. (He) . . . leaped into the position of the oppressive father and began a more engaging conversation with his son, but still continued to work at his computer. Another spect-actor from the audience, a young teenage girl, clearly not yet happy with the 'solution', leaped into the position of the oppressed son, and demanded that her father listen to her, and in a most assertive way leaned across and turned off the computer . . .
>
> (Proctor *et al.* 2008: 45)

This improvised drama was then played out in a new way, with the father responding in a much more compassionate fashion. That audience discussion that followed included a great deal of personal sharing about the experience of 'coming out', and more general issues of parent–child relationships.

The practice of the theatre of the oppressed is based on a number of principles. First, the enactment of everyday dilemmas inevitably shifts the focus from an individualized conception of problems to a more social perspective – the problem is seen to occur in the interactions that take place *between* a group of people. Second, a therapeutic process is constructed that is organized around *action* – rather than just talk about an issue, the person or group has an opportunity to act, to try out different ways of responding to situations. Third, the theatre of the oppressed is an approach that maximizes the role of *dialogue* – the possibility of change is facilitated by the interplay between different positions that are taken in the drama. Finally, this approach takes it for granted that many problems arise because individuals are oppressed or silenced by the conscious or unconscious actions of others who are more powerful – the theatre environment that is created is designed to allow those who have been silenced to speak and to be heard.

A similar approach is reflected in the *social therapy* model that has been developed by Fred Newman and Lois Holzman at the East Side Institute for Group and Short Term Psychotherapy and the Castillo Theatre in New York, and associated projects such as the *All Stars Talent Show* (Holzman and Mendez 2003).

The use of techniques from theatre and the arts to dramatize and make visible the multivoiced nature of social reality has also been used within research into therapeutic processes. Notable in this domain has been the work of Jane Speedy (2008), whose research group uses creative writing and performance art to convey the findings of research studies.

Conclusions

There has been a tremendous excitement and energy surrounding the evolution of the new narrative and constructionist approaches to therapy. For many therapists and clients it has been a liberating experience to be given permission to talk and to tell stories. There is a great richness and wisdom in the everyday stories that people tell. However, until very recently, virtually anyone who claimed to be doing constructivist, solution-focused, narrative or collaborative counselling or psychotherapy would almost certainly have received their primary training in another approach. This situation raises a number of questions about the future of narrative therapy. Has the success of these therapies been due to the fact that their practitioners already possess a basis of skills and theory derived from other models, such as family therapy, psychoanalysis or cognitive therapy? Can training in a purely constructionist model be sufficient? Will the formalization and subsequent institutionalization of these therapy approaches stifle their creative edge?

Another challenging issue for this group of therapies lies in their relationship with research. There is some research evidence to support the effectiveness of solution-focused therapy and the open dialogue approach, but very little objective evidence relating to the effectiveness of narrative or constructionist therapies. Absence of evidence should not be taken to mean absence of effectiveness. However, in a professional environment that is increasingly organized around the tenets of evidence-based practice, the absence of a knowledge base that is supported by relevant research may turn out to be a hindrance to the long-term acceptance of these therapies.

A further challenge to the ongoing articulation of the approaches discussed here lies in the fact that three of the leading voices in this field recently died, while at the peak of their creative powers: Steve de Shazer (1945–2005), Michael Mahoney (1946–2006) and Michael White (1948–2008). It remains to be seen how this professional community moves forward in the absence of these inspirational figures.

It is important to acknowledge that the approaches to counselling and psychotherapy that have been discussed in this chapter reflect the articulation of philosophical and social concepts that have also been embraced by some theorists and practitioners in mainstream approaches such as psychodynamic and person-centred counselling, and CBT. The methods discussed within the chapter merely represent the most explicit and clear-cut examples of the influence of these ideas on therapeutic theory and practice. Nevertheless, in being so fundamentally grounded in philosophical and social concepts, the approaches explored here raise issues around counselling and psychotherapy training, and the need to introduce students to both basic ideas and current debates around constructivism, social constructionism, post-structuralism and postmodernity.

These approaches to counselling have made a significant contribution to the therapy field as a whole by bringing close attention to the nature of therapeutic conversations, and the potency of 'just talking'. Whereas earlier forms of therapy may have attended to language as a mirror of the inner state of the client, constructionist and collaborative approaches have gone beyond this in their appreciation of the ways in which *conversation* occurs between people, and has the possibility of bringing new meaning into existence. These contemporary approaches also recognize and make use of the fact that therapeutic conversations do not only (or even mainly) take place between a counsellor and a client, but can occur in interactions between family members and other significant persons in the life of the individual who is seeking help. As a result, practitioners have innovatively pushed the scope of participation in such conversations ever-wider, and in so doing have been able to bridge the gap that can often occur between the therapy room and the person's everyday life.

The intention to engage in conversation and collaboration with a person who is seeking help implies that the person has something positive to offer, in terms of ideas about how to resolve their problem. Conversational approaches to counselling and psychotherapy therefore imply a *strengths* perspective (Wong 2006). The critical, sceptical edge of social constructionist and post-structuralist thinking contributes to the establishment of a strengths perspective, by questioning and deconstructing the idea of the therapist as expert; in collaborative therapies, both the client and the therapist are experts.

Finally, the concept of *dialogue* represents a major and distinctive addition to the conceptual vocabulary of counselling. It is a concept that extends the concept of the therapeutic relationship, by suggesting that it relies on the existence of a two-way, responsive, active engagement of each person with the other. It is a concept that presents a constant challenge to counselling practitioners – if we reflect on the conversations we have with our clients, how often (or how seldom) can these be characterized as being truly dialogical?

Topics for reflection and discussion

1 What are your favourite fictional stories (novels, fairy stories, plays etc.)? Why do these stories appeal to you? Are there ways that these stories capture aspects of your own experience of life, or sense of self? How do you use these stories, in constructing your own life-story?

2 How satisfactory is the narrative therapy idea of 're-authoring', as a means of characterizing the outcomes of counselling? What other valued therapy outcomes can you identify that are not readily understandable as varieties of 're-authoring'? What are the implications of adopting a specific 're-authoring' focus – are there aspects of the therapy process that may be unhelpfully downplayed?

3 One of the key themes in all constructivist and constructionist therapies is an emphasis on the *strengths* and accomplishments of the person seeking help, rather than on his or her deficits or pathology. What are the advantages and disadvantages of this emphasis, for example when compared with a psychodynamic approach that explicitly seeks to make contact with the broken or disordered aspects of the client's personality?

Suggested further reading

There are two classic texts in this area of counselling. *Narrative Means to Therapeutic Ends* by Michael White and David Epston (1990) is essential reading for anyone interested in understanding more about the 'narrative turn' in therapy. *Constructive Psychotherapy* by Michael Mahoney (2003) is a *tour de force* expression of how constructivist philosophical principles can be allied to practical techniques to create an approach to therapy that is compassionate, caring and highly effective.

The best introduction to narrative therapy is Alice Morgan's (2000) book, *What is Narrative Therapy?* Recent developments in narrative therapy are discussed by Duvall and Beres (2011). A posthumous collection of previously unpublished papers by Michael White (2011) provides an insight into the political dimension of narrative therapy. A valuable overview of different strands of collaborative therapy has been published by Harlene Anderson and Diane Gehart (2007): *Collaborative Therapy: Relationships and Conversations that Make a Difference*. For those interested in the nature of current debates around the 'discursive' therapies, Strong and Pare (2003) and Lock and Strong (2012) provide a range of cutting-edge contributions.

A wide ranging set of articles on solution-focused brief therapy is available as an online open access 'virtual issue' of the *Journal of Marital and Family Therapy*.

CHAPTER 12

Working with family systems

Introduction

Most counselling has evolved as a response to individual suffering and individual needs. As discussed in Chapter 2, an historical analysis of Western societies suggests that there has been a trend during the 'modern' era, particularly during the highly industrialized, urbanized society of the twentieth and twenty-first centuries, to move in the direction of individualizing problems that had previously been dealt with at a community level. At the same time, however, the experience of living in the modern world is that of struggling to exist within large and complex social systems. So, at the same time that counselling and psychotherapy have been developing methods of working with individuals, a whole other branch of the social and physical sciences has been occupied with the problem of finding ways to understand the principles by which systems operate, and the types of intervention that can bring about change at a systemic level. The growth of a *systemic* perspective can be seen in a number of different fields, from the study of organizations through to research into the properties of living, ecological systems. In the field of counselling and psychotherapy, the systemic approach is mainly associated with family therapy. The basic assumption underpinning all versions of family therapy is that the distress or maladjusted behaviour of individual family members is best understood as a manifestation of something going wrong at a systemic level: for example, through ineffective communication between family members or some distortion of the structure of the family group.

It is difficult to integrate traditional family therapy into 'mainstream' models of counselling for a number of reasons, some philosophical, some practical. The emphasis of family therapists on the structural and systemic aspects of family life, on what goes on *between* people rather that what takes place *inside* them, does not sit easily with counsellors trained to work with self, feelings and individual responsibility. From the point of view of many counsellors, too, family therapists appeared to adopt strange and alien ways of relating to their clients, often seeming to eschew the possibility of relationship. Finally, the application of classical family therapy makes a range of demands that most counsellors could not countenance: attendance by all members of the family, intervention delivered by a team of therapists, therapy rooms equipped with one-way mirrors, telephones and video. In recent years, however, there has been a gradual *rapprochement* between family therapy (or at least some branches of it) and the more individual-oriented therapies, and there has been an increasing acknowledgement on the part of many counsellors that it is essential to include in their work an awareness of systemic influences on the lives of their clients. The aim of this chapter is to review some of these developments. The chapter begins with a brief account of some key ideas used in understanding human systems, before moving on to examine the legacy of family therapy, the issues involved in working systemically with couples and organizations, and then, finally, the nature of a systemic approach to generic counselling practice.

Understanding human systems

The analysis of systems of one kind or another has generated a vast literature. However, it seems clear that much systemic thinking originates from the ideas of Ludwig von Bertalanffy, the founder of cybernetics, Norbert Weiner, an information theorist, and Gregory Bateson, a philosopher and anthropologist. As Guttman (1981: 41) puts it:

> general systems theory had its origins in the thinking of mathematicians, physicist, and engineers in the late 1940s and early 1950s, when technological developments made it possible to conceive of and build mechanical models approximating certain properties of the human brain. At that time, it was recognised that many different phenomena (both biological and non-biological) share the attributes of a system – that is, a unified whole that consists of interrelated parts, such that the whole can be identified from the sum of its parts and any change in one part affects the rest of the system. General systems theory concerns itself with elucidating the functional and structural rules that can be considered valid for describing all systems, whatever their composition.

The key ideas here are that a system comprises a whole made up of inter-related parts, and that, crucially, change in any one part affects the rest of the system. These processes can be seen to operate in social, biological and mechanical systems. For example, a motor car is a whole system made up of many subsystems (the brakes, gear box, engine etc.). If even a minor change happens in one subsystem, such as the tyres being under-inflated, there will be consequences in other areas – in this instance higher strain on the engine leading eventually to breakdown. To take another example, a family can be viewed as a system containing, perhaps, a mother, father and two children. Each of them plays certain roles and fulfils specific tasks within the system. If, however, the mother becomes seriously ill and is not able to continue to discharge the same roles and tasks, then these functions will be redistributed among other members of the family, changing the balance of relationships.

There is another property of systems that is closely linked to the part–whole idea. Functioning systems tend to be *homeostatic* in the way that they operate. In other words, once a system is established, is 'up and running', it will tend to keep functioning in the same way unless some external event interferes: systems reach a 'stable state', where their parts are in balance. The most common example of homeostasis is the operation of a domestic central heating system. The room thermostat is set at a certain temperature. If the temperature rises above that level, the boiler and radiators will be turned off; if the temperature falls below, the boiler and radiators are switched on. The result is that the room, or house, is maintained at a steady temperature. This process can be understood as one in which feedback information is used to regulate the system (in the case of domestic central heating, the thermostat provides feedback to the boiler). Homeostasis and feedback also occur in human systems. To return to the example of the family in which the mother becomes seriously ill, there are likely to be strong forces within the family acting to prevent change in the system. For instance, the mother may not be physically able to wash and iron clothes but may have a belief that this is what a 'real mother' must do. Her children and spouse may share this belief. The sight of the father incompetently ironing the clothes can serve as feedback that triggers off a renewed effort on her part to be a 'real mother', but then her attempt to iron may make her more ill.

Another important idea found in general systems theory is the notion that all systems are based on a set of rules. In the example just given, the hypothetical family being described possessed powerful, unwritten rules about gender and parental roles and identities. These rules may function well for the family when it is in a state of equilibrium, but at times of change it may be necessary to revise the rules, to allow the system to achieve a new level of functioning. With this family, it would seem clear that unless they can shift their notion of 'mother', there will be a fundamental breakdown in the system brought about by the hospitalization of the mother.

A final key concept in systemic approaches relates to the notion of the *life cycle* of a system. To return to the example of the motor car, a vehicle such as this comes supplied with a detailed set of rules concerning when certain parts should be inspected, adjusted or replaced. Similarly, a human system such as a family tracks its way through a predictable set of transitions: leaving home, marriage, entering the world of work, the birth of a child, the death of a parent, retirement, the death of a spouse and so on. The issue here is that while some changes to the family system (e.g., illness, unemployment, disaster) are unpredictable, there are many other potential disruptions to the system that are normative and wholly predictable. This realization brings with it important ways of understanding what is happening in a system, by looking at how it reacts to life cycle transitions and what it has 'learned' from previous events of this sort.

It is necessary to be clear at this point that the systemic ideas presented here represent a simplified version of what is a complex body of theory. Readers interested in learning more about this perspective are recommended to consult Carr (2012), Dallos and Draper (2010), McGoldrick *et al.* (2012) or Rivett and Street (2009). Nevertheless, it is hoped that these core systemic principles are sufficient to map out the basic outline of a powerful and distinctive style of counselling and psychotherapy. It should be clear that a systemically oriented counsellor is not primarily interested in the intrapsychic inner life of his or her client. Instead, they choose to focus on the system within which the person lives, and how this system works. Essentially, if a person reports a 'problem', it is redefined by a systemic therapist as a failure of the system to adapt to change. The goal of the systemic therapist, therefore, is to facilitate change at a systemic level: for example, by rewriting implicit rules, shifting the balance between different parts of the system or improving the effectiveness of how communication/feedback is transmitted.

Box 12.1: *Responding to the complexity of the family system: reflecting teams*

When a family takes part in therapy, as a group, there is a lot happening – a multiplicity of interactions between individuals and within subgroups. It can be very hard for a therapist, or even a pair of therapists, to keep track of what is going on. In the early years of family therapy, additional members of the therapy team would sit behind a one-way mirror, or watch the session on live video feed, and provide feedback and guidance for the primary therapists in the room. A Norwegian psychiatrist, Tom Andersen, developed the idea of the 'reflecting team', a group of therapists or trainees who watch the session (now usually from within the therapy room), and share their reflections in the presence of the family. The family is not a part of the conversation with the reflecting team, but merely listens.

This technique continues to allow more of the family interaction to be captured, while at the same time creating an opportunity for family members to reflect on a range of different perceptions on what has been happening. It is also valuable that these perceptions are 'de-centred' – they are not associated with the authority of the primary therapists, and so family members are better able to accept or reject them as they see fit. The use of a reflecting team has been adapted and modified by different groups of family therapists, as well as by therapists working within the narrative therapy tradition. Examples of different ways of organizing the reflecting team process can be found in Friedman (1995).

The analysis and treatment of family systems

The systemic ideas described above have been applied in therapy in a variety of different ways by different groups of family therapists. It is generally agreed that there are three main schools of classical family therapy. First, there is structural family therapy, created by Salvador Minuchin (1974) and his colleagues in Philadelphia. The key concepts employed within this model to understand the structure and patterning of interaction in a family are subsystems, boundaries, hierarchies and alliances.

Second, the strategic approach to family therapy grew out of pioneering research carried out by Gregory Bateson, John Weakland, Don Jackson and Jay Haley at the Mental

Research Institute at Palo Alto, California, in the 1950s. Haley later became the central figure in this approach, and introduced some of the ideas of the hypnotherapist Milton Erickson. The distinctive features of this model are the use of techniques such as paradoxical injunction, reframing and the prescription of tasks, to bring about change in symptoms.

The third main grouping is known as the Milan group, featuring Palazzoli *et al.* (1978). The special contribution of this group has been to emphasize some of the philosophical aspects of family life, such as the collective construction of a family reality through shared beliefs, myths and assumptions. The Milan-systemic school makes particular use of the idea of circularity, which refers to an assumption of reciprocal causality: everything causes and is caused by everything else. All parts of the family system are reciprocally connected, and the therapy team will attempt to open up this aspect of family life through circular questions. For example, rather than ask a family member what he feels about something that has happened in the family, the therapist could ask how he feels about what his brother thinks about it, thus both introducing an awareness of the links between people and raising the possibility of generating multiple descriptions (double descriptions) of the same event. Other techniques introduced by the Milan school have been positive connotation (giving a positive meaning to all behaviour: for instance, 'how brave you were to withdraw from that situation to preserve your commitment to the family's core values . . .') and the use of therapeutic ritual. Jones (1993) offers an accessible account of the Milan-systemic approach. The similarities and differences between these models can be examined in more detail in Guttman (1981) and Hayes (1991). It should be noted, too, that there exist several well established non-systemic approaches to working with families, such as psychodynamic and behavioural.

It is probably fair to say that in recent years the divisions between these major schools of family therapy have gradually dissolved as increasing numbers of therapists have integrated different approaches within their own practice, and as new hybrid forms of systems-oriented therapy have emerged, such as the narrative therapy of White and Epston (1990) or the solution-focused model developed by de Shazer (1985) (see Chapter 11). Further, without wishing to deny the important ideological differences between these approaches, it is possible to see significant points of convergence in the way that they have been put into action. Omer (1994) has argued that the differences between family therapy practitioners are more matters of style than of substance. The common ground of contemporary family therapy can be taken to include:

- Active participation of all or most family members, to allow patterns of interaction to be observed and change to be shared.

- Interventions aimed at properties of the system rather than at aspects of the experiences of individuals. Techniques such as family sculpting (Satir 1972; Duhl *et al.* 1973; Papp 1976) or genograms (McGoldrick and Gerson 1985, 1989) allow the therapist to work with the family system as a whole.

- The therapist adopting a detached, neutral stance, to avoid being 'sucked in' to the system or seduced into forming an alliance with particular family members or subgroups.

- Therapists working as a team, with some workers in the room with the family and others acting as observers, to reinforce neutrality and the 'systems' orientation, and to enable the detection of subtle interaction patterns occurring in the complex dynamic of a family's way of being together.

- Use of a limited number of high-impact sessions, rather than an extended number of 'gentler' or more supportive sessions.

Another area of common ground between the competing traditions of family therapy is that many of them began as ways of attempting to carry out therapy with schizophrenic patients and their families. It is generally accepted that counselling and psychotherapy on a one-to-one basis with people diagnosed or labelled as schizophrenic is very difficult and has limited success. Basically, the behaviour and thought patterns of people who can be classified in this way make it hard to establish an effective therapeutic alliance. In addition, the experience of working with persons whose experience of the world is fragmented and highly fearful places a huge pressure on an individual therapist. To enter into such a world, to be empathic over an extended period of time, brings the counsellor or psychotherapist into close contact with feelings of terror, engulfment and overwhelming threat. It is hardly surprising, then, that the most effective types of therapeutic intervention for people assigned the label of 'schizophrenic' have been family therapy and therapeutic communities. But the cost, at least in family therapy, has been the development of a style of doing therapy that has, to a large extent, functioned to insulate the therapist from direct person-to-person contact. This aspect of family therapy practice has changed substantially in recent years, under the influence of writers such as Bott (1994), O'Leary (2011) and Reimers and Treacher (1995), who have argued for a more 'person-centred' stance.

Box 12.2: *Using a genogram to explore family patterns across generations*

For a counsellor working with a person in the context of their family system, it can be difficult to capture and makes sense of the complexity of the relationships between family members, particularly across generations. A technique that is widely used in family and couples counselling to depict intergenerational patterns of relationships is the genogram. This is similar to a family tree or family history. Usually, the information is gathered by the counsellor and the chart is co-constructed by counsellor and family members, although it is possible to give clients instructions on how to complete a self-administered genogram. There exist a set of conventional symbols that are employed in genograms: for example, a man is represented by a square and a woman by a circle. A close relationship is designated by a double line between the individuals, and a conflictual relationship by a jagged line. Details of these symbols can be found in McGoldrick and Gerson (1985, 1989) and Papadopoulos *et al.* (1997).

A genogram is used to map how a problem may have evolved over time, or be linked to family dynamics. The genogram can also help in highlighting events that have been significant for the family. A genogram is not only a method for gathering information, but also an intervention in itself, because participating in the construction of a genogram may well enable family members to achieve greater understanding of the role they play in the family, and the roles played by other family members.

In their account of the use of genograms in family work, McGoldrick and Gerson (1985, 1989) give many fascinating examples of analyses of the family structures of famous people. One of the most interesting of the cases they have examined is that of the family of Sigmund Freud. The genogram presented in Figure 12.1 (McGoldrick and Gerson 1989: 172) gives a sketch of the Freud family in 1859, when Sigmund Freud was three years old. Jacob and Amalia are Sigmund's parents; Schlomo, who died in 1856, is his paternal grandfather; Anna is his younger sister; John is a cousin with whom he had a close relationship.

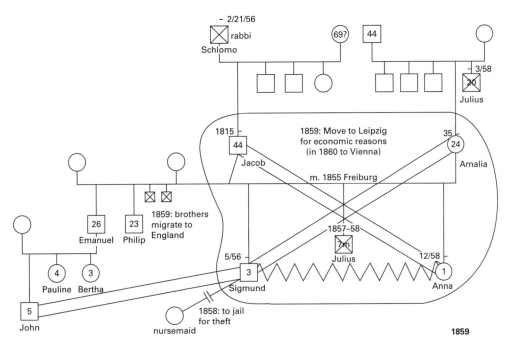

FIGURE 12.1 A genogram analysis of Freud's family.
Source: Adapted from McGoldrick and Gerson (1989).

In this genogram there are many signs of a family system under a great deal of stress. First, the family has experienced a series of losses. The grandfather, Amalia's brother Julius and the baby Julius died within the space of two years. Jacob's sons from his first marriage, Emanuel and Philip, emigrate to England. Sigmund thus loses his closest playmate, John. Moreover, the family move house twice, in 1859 and 1860, because of financial problems. Second, the Freud family constituted a mix or 'blend' of two family systems. Jacob had been married before, and had two adult sons, one of whom was older than his new wife. The age difference between Jacob and Amalia is further under-lined by the fact that Jacob is the same age as Amalia's father. The role of Sigmund as 'special', a family myth that was to have a profound effect on his life, can perhaps be explained by imagining that he was in some sense a replacement for Schlomo, the rabbi leader of the family, who died shortly after he was born. Finally, the family contained at least one secret at this point. Jacob's second wife Rebecca, whom he married in 1852, was apparently never mentioned.

This genogram makes it possible to see some of the family factors that made Freud the person he was. It is hardly surprising that he spent his professional life attempting to make sense of the earliest experiences in his patients' lives. Nor is it surprising that he evolved a psychological theory that portrayed women in a subservient role in relation to men.

The standard introduction to the use of genograms is McGoldrick and Gerson (1985). Papadopoulos *et al.* (1997) and Stanion *et al.* (1997) provide valuable reviews of further developments in the use of this technique, with a particular emphasis on its application in health settings.

Box 12.3: *What does it feel like to be in a family? Sculpting the experience of family life*

A very direct way in which family members can convey their experience of being in a family is to construct a family sculpture. This is an exercise through which one family member arranges the other people in the family to represent the way that he or she sees the family. The position of the people in the family, their facial expressions and posture, closeness or distance and direction of gaze all convey the sculptor's sense of what the family is like from their perspective. Sometimes, the therapist might ask the person to resculpt the family in terms of how they would ideally like it to function or how they imag-ined it might be in the future, or might invite other family members to create alternative sculpts.

Onnis *et al.* (1994) give an example of the use of sculpting with a family that had been referred because Gianni, aged ten, suffered from severe chronic asthma, which had shown little improvement in response to standard medical procedures and had been diagnosed as 'untreatable'. The family comprised Gianni, his mother and father and a seven-year-old younger sister, Sabrina. Asked to sculpt his family 'as it was presently', Gianni placed an empty chair between his parents, and situated his sister in front of his mother, looking at her. He placed himself in front of the other members of the family, facing the empty chair. After completing the sculpture, he quickly ran to sit down in the empty chair between his parents. Gianni was then asked to represent the family as he thought it would be in ten years. He placed his sister at a distance, facing away from them. He said that she was facing 'towards a friend'. He then placed himself in front of his parents, with himself as the apex of a triangle, at the centre of their attention. He announced that 'they are looking at me'. The therapist asked Gianni where he was looking, and he replied 'I'm looking at the mirror' (the one-way mirror on the wall in the therapy room). His parents interjected that they did not have a mirror like that at home, and Gianni turned to his parents and said 'I'm looking at them. They're looking at me, and I am looking at them, like three pillars!' He then began to cough as he was about to have an asthma attack.

These sculptures were interpreted by the family therapy team as expressing, first of all, Gianni's feeling that there was 'a distance between Mom and Dad', and that he had to capture his father's attention and check that he stayed in position. Gianni saw his role in relation to his parents as 'neither of the two will leave if I am between them'. The therapy team understood the second sculpture as representing Gianni's fear of change. Here, Gianni reinforces his earlier message by depicting his family as a kind of immobile eternal triangle, as if he was saying:

> I can't leave my parents alone. Sabrina can perhaps look outside, have her own life, but I must stay here. I would like to see myself, reflect on myself (the desire to look into the mirror), but I cannot. If we are no longer three pillars, everything will collapse.
>
> (Onnis *et al.* 1994: 347)

Based on these messages, the therapy team offered the family a reframing of their situation that suggested some possibilities for positive change. This reframing statement is typical of the kind of intervention made by many family therapists:

> the sculptures you made have proven very useful to us to better understand what is happening in your family. We were particularly impressed by how Gianni sees himself in the future. Sabrina can have a friend and begin to go her own way. But Gianni cannot! Gianni must stay near his parents to sustain the family. 'We are three pillars', he said. We now understand how great an effort Gianni is making, how heavy the burden he is bearing is, an excessive burden for a child, a burden which can suffocate him, cut off his air, take his breath away. But there is one thing which remains obscure to us: why does Gianni think that his parents, alone, cannot carry this burden or organise themselves to sustain it. We believe that there is another possibility: that his parents succeed in reassuring Gianni, proving to him that they are capable of this. Perhaps then Gianni will find it easier to breathe, to begin to look at himself and find his own way.
>
> (Onnis *et al.* 1994: 347)

Central to this formulation is positive connotation of the symptom. The asthmatic attacks are characterized not as a problem, but as a positive sacrifice that Gianni is making in order to preserve the family unit. In this case, the family was well able to develop the alternative strategy (the parents taking up the burden) implied in the reframing statement, and soon Gianni's asthmatic crises reduced considerably.

The concept of the person's social 'niche'

The *ecological* approach to therapy, pioneered in Switzerland by Jurg Willi and his colleagues (Willi 1999; Willi *et al.* 2000) represents an important integration of psycho-dynamic and systemic ideas. The key idea in this approach is that the individual shapes his or her environment into a personal *niche* that allows them to meet their emotional and interpersonal needs. However, a niche that may have been highly functional at an early stage in a person's life (for example, as a young adult) may become dysfunctional as the individual develops as a person and acquires different motives or needs.

Willi *et al.* (2000) present a case of a 29-year-old man who experienced frightening panic attacks, even when asleep. In his childhood and adolescence, the client had been exposed to insecurity in his relationships with his mother and father. As a result, on entering adult life he developed a niche for himself as an 'independent adventurer', through work as a sailor or odd-job man who had numerous affairs. He was generally admired by his friends in this role, and the niche he had created for himself allowed him to avoid the possibility of hurt through becoming attached to another person.

In therapy, he became aware that his panic attacks had started when he had entered a relationship with a new girlfriend, who was very devoted and affectionate towards him. He had moved in with her. Most of his friends by this time had 'settled down' and started families, and they expected him to do likewise. Over the course of therapy, he came to understand that his old niche was no longer fully appropriate for him – he wished to sustain a more settled relationship. At the same time, his persistent need for independence made living with his girlfriend intolerable. He was able to develop a new niche, which encompassed some of the features of his 'early adult' way of life, but which also enabled him to continue his relationship with his girlfriend on a more distanced basis.

The ecological framework devised by Willi (1999) is firmly based in the idea that a person exists within a social system, and that constructive change involves taking into account what is happening in the system as a whole. However, it is a model that goes beyond family systems, and allows the therapist to help the client to look at other social systems within which a client lives his or her life – housing, work, leisure, physical environment etc. It is also an approach that places emphasis on the ability of the individual to create (and re-create) his or her niche.

Box 12.4: *Healing through ritual*

One of the key features of families and other social systems is the use of ritual to mark the transition from one social role or status to another, to symbolize the bonds between group members and to express the relationship between individuals and a higher power. The family life cycle is marked by a series of rituals – marriages, Christmas or Thanksgiving celebrations, funerals. In a modern, largely secular world, many traditional rituals have lost their meaning, or may be inappropriate in situations where families comprise people from different religious or ethnic backgrounds. Some psychologists have suggested that it is important for people to be able to invent their own rituals (Imber-Black and Roberts 1992).

Family therapists have become interested in the ways that ritual occasions, such as mealtimes, exemplify the values and relationship patterns of a family, and have also developed ways of employing ritual to facilitate change in families.

Imber-Black and Roberts (1992) describe the case of Brian, 19, who went to live with his older brother when his mother died. This was a difficult time for Brian, who told his brother and sister-in-law that 'I feel I don't have a security blanket'. After reflecting on this statement, the older brother and his wife got together with other surviving members of the extended family to create a patchwork quilt for Brian, using pieces of his mother's nurse uniform, his father's marine shirt and other fabric that carried meaning for Brian. They presented the quilt to Brian on the occasion of his grandmother's eightieth birthday. It symbolized for Brian, and the family as a whole, that his brother and sister-in-law were able to give Brian the nurturing and 'security blanket' that he needed. This family ritual gave members of the family a structure through which to channel their concern for Brian, it brought them all together in a collective expression of grief and hope and, finally, it made use of a tangible physical object, a quilt, that could function as a symbol and reminder of what they had done and felt. Other physical symbols used in family rituals can include candles, places where objects or messages are buried or boxes that contain worries or joys.

Imber-Black and Roberts (1992) and Wyrostok (1995) are good sources for further reading about ways in which ritual has been employed by different therapists.

Conclusions: themes and issues in the application of systemic ideas in counselling

An appreciation of systemic concepts is invaluable for counsellors operating in any sphere. Any individual client is inevitably embedded within a social system. Usually this system is a family unit, but on some occasions it may be a work group, friendship network or hospital ward. The capacity of an individual client to make changes in his or her life will depend on the permeability of the system, on how much the pattern of relationships across that set of people can shift, or even on whether the system will allow the client to leave it. All good counsellors have an intuitive sense of these issues, whether they have studied them theoretically or not.

However, at another level systemic ideas introduce a radically different way of making sense of the goals and processes of counselling. The theoretical models of psychodynamic, cognitive–behavioural and person-centred counselling all place the counsellor in a direct personal relationship with the client. Systemic counselling demands a realignment of counsellor and client. There is still the necessity to form an alliance with the individual, but it is also necessary to see the individual as part of a bigger whole, and for the counsellor to relate to that system as a whole and to work with the client's relationship with it. The image of the person here is radically different from the one that underpins mainstream psychodynamic, cognitive–behavioural and person-centred counselling. These established approaches conceive of the person as a bounded, autonomous entity, essentially separate from the rest of the social world. Systemic counselling sees the person as fundamentally a *relational* being, as an entity that can only exist as part of a family, group or community. Alongside theoretical approaches that are introduced in other chapters of this book – feminist, narrative and multicultural – systemic therapy has taken up the challenge of implementing a relational philosophy based on an understanding that, in the end, individualism is not an adequate basis for living the good life.

Topics for reflection and discussion

1   Take a group in which you belong. This may be a work or friendship group, or a group on a college course. Analyse the dynamics of that group in terms of some of the systemic concepts described in this chapter. What have you learned from this analysis? What does it add to your understanding of your friends or colleagues, in comparison with thinking about these people in terms of their separate individual lives and personalities? What have you learned about yourself from this exercise?

2   What might be some of the ethical issues that could be raised when working with a family or other system? How might confidentiality and informed consent operate within a system? Is the ethical principle of respect for autonomy still relevant?

3   Reflect on the implications for the counsellor–client relationship of adopting a systemic perspective. For example, from a person-centred perspective a good relationship would

be characterized by high levels of congruence, empathy and acceptance. Are these concepts applicable in systemic work? How useful are psychoanalytic ideas of transference and counter-transference?

4 Are there particular counselling issues that might be more suited to a systemic approach, and other issues that might be better dealt with at an individual level?

5 What is your own personal 'niche'? How have you negotiated change in your niche, as your needs and desires have changed at different points in your development?

Suggested further reading

Well-established textbooks that contain a wealth of relevant material on systemic approaches to counselling and psychotherapy are: *An Introduction to Family Therapy* (Dallos and Draper 2010), and *Family Therapy: Concepts, Process and Practice* (Carr 2012). A chapter by Hoffman (1992) captures a spirit of 'person-centredness' that is increasingly adopted by many systemic therapists. A practical, down-to-earth account of the main skills and techniques used in *family* therapy can be found in *Family Therapy: 100 Key Points and Techniques* (Rivett and Street 2009). Both of the main research and professional journals in this field, *Family Process* and the *Journal of Family Therapy*, consistently publish papers that are stimulating and readable.

Multicultural counselling

Introduction

One of the defining characteristics of the contemporary world is the salience of cultural difference. In earlier times, it was much more possible to live as a member of a relatively isolated and self-contained social class or group, and remain relatively unaware of, and be unaffected by, the existence of different forms of life. In recent years, all this has changed. Increasingly, members of so-called 'ethnic minority' groups have become unwilling to be treated as a marginalized, disadvantaged and politically disenfranchised segment of the labour force, and have claimed their voice and their power within society. At the same time, the process of globalization, including the spread of global communications media such as satellite television and the growth of international air travel, have resulted in a huge increase in accessibility of information about other cultures. The images and sounds of other cultures are available in ways that they never have been before. It is impossible to deny that we live in a multicultural world.

Counselling has responded to the trend towards multiculturalism in two ways. The original, foundational approaches to counselling – for example, the psychodynamic, person-centred and cognitive–behavioural models – were clearly 'monocultural' in nature. They were designed and applied in the context of Western (mainly American) industrial society, and had little to say about culture or cultural difference. In the 1960s and 1970s, the counselling and psychotherapy community attempted to react to the political, legislative and personal pressures arising from the equal opportunities movement and debates over racism and equality by developing strategies for building a greater awareness of cultural issues into counselling training and practice. This phase, which generated a substantial literature on 'cross-cultural', 'transcultural' and 'intercultural' approaches to counselling and psychotherapy, represented an attempt to assimilate a cultural dimension into mainstream practice. Useful though these efforts have been in legitimating the experiences and needs of 'minority' clients and counsellors, it can be argued that they do not go far enough.

A second response to the issues raised by an awareness of cultural difference has been, therefore, to strive to construct an approach to counselling that places the concept of 'culture' at the centre of its 'image of the person', rather than leaving it to be 'tacked on' as an after-thought. This new, *multicultural* approach (Pedersen 1991) starts from the position that membership of a culture (or cultures) is one of the main influences on the development of personal identity, and that the emotional or behavioural problems that a person might bring to counselling are a reflection of how relationships, morality and a sense of the 'good life' are understood and defined in the culture(s) in which a person lives his or her life. Pedersen (1991) has argued that multiculturalism should be regarded as a *fourth force* in counselling, complementing behaviourism, psychoanalysis and humanistic psychology. The aim of this chapter is to offer an overview of the theory and practice of this important, emergent approach to counselling.

What do we mean by 'culture'?

It is important to avoid any temptation to oversimplify the concept of culture. At one level, culture can be understood simply as 'the way of life of a group of people'. In any attempt to understand 'culture', it is necessary to make use of the contribution made by the social science discipline that has specialized in the task of describing and making sense of different cultures: social anthropology. The tradition in social anthropological research has always been to take the view that it is only possible to do justice to the complexity of a culture by living within it for a considerable period of time, and carrying out a systematic and rigorous set of observations into the way that the members of that culture construct the world that they know through processes such as kinship networks, ritual, mythology and language. In the words of Clifford Geertz (1973: 89), possibly the most influential anthropologist of recent years, culture can be understood as a:

> historically transmitted pattern of meaning embodied in symbols, a system of inherited conceptions expressed in symbolic form by means of which [people] communicate, perpetuate, and develop their knowledge about and attitudes toward life.

Geertz and other anthropologists would argue that making sense of the culture or way of life of a group of people can only be achieved by trying to understand what lies beneath the surface, the web of meaning and 'inherited conceptions' that are symbolized and expressed in outward behaviour. This external behaviour can be literally anything, from work patterns to the design of Coke bottles to the performance of religious ritual. Everything that members of a culture do represents some aspect of what life means to them. And this meaning has historical roots, it has evolved and been shaped over many years. The image that Geertz (1973) uses to capture all this is that of culture as 'thick'; an appreciation of a culture requires the construction of a 'thick description'.

This idea that the culture within which a person exists is complex and, by implication, difficult to understand has important implications for counsellors. An anthropologist would spend months or years working towards an adequate appreciation of what things mean to a person from another culture. A counsellor attempts to achieve the same goal in a much shorter period of time. Moreover, a counsellor will seldom have an opportunity to observe his or her client interacting within their own cultural milieu; counselling takes place in the world of the counsellor. For these reasons, it is necessary for counsellors to be cautious, and modest, about the extent to which they can ever hope fully to enter the cultural reality inhabited by the client. Further discussion of the ways in which cultural factors intersect with counselling theory and practice can be found in Cornforth (2001) and Hoshmand (2006a, 2006b).

The basis for multicultural counselling is therefore *not* exhaustive training in the culture and norms of different groups of people; this is not realistic. Instead, multicultural counsellors should be able to apply a schematic model of the ways in which the personal and relational world of the client, and the client's assumptions about helping or 'cure', can be culturally constructed. The core of multicultural counselling is a sensitivity to the possible ways in which different cultures function and interact, allied to a genuine *curiosity* (Falicov 1995) about the cultural experience of other people.

In relation to the aims of counselling, the task is not to be able to analyse the 'objective' cultural world of a client, but to be able to appreciate his or her *cultural identity* – how the person sees himself or herself in cultural terms. Lee (2006: 179) has defined cultural identity in the following terms:

> . . . cultural identity refers to an individual's sense of belonging to a cultural group . . . cultural identity may be considered as the inner vision that a person possesses of himself as a member of a cultural group and as a unique human being. It forms the core of the beliefs, social forms and personality dimensions that characterize distinct cultural realities and worldview for an individual. Cultural identity development is a major determinant of a person's attitudes toward herself, others of the same cultural group, others of a different cultural group, and members of the dominant cultural group.

From this perspective, cultural identity plays a crucial role in shaping and maintaining the way that a person seeking counselling defines problems and solutions, and the assumptions that he or she holds about what it means to be a person, and what it means to be in relationships.

Although the lived experience of being a member of a culture is 'seamless' and unified, it is nevertheless useful for purposes of clarity to make a distinction between the underlying philosophical or cognitive dimensions of a culture and the expression of these beliefs in patterns of social behaviour. Some of the most important features of cultural identity in the area of underlying beliefs and assumptions are:

- how reality is understood, e.g., dualistic or holistic;
- concept of self (autonomous, bounded, referential versus social, distributed, indexical);
- sense of morality (e.g., choice versus fate, values);
- concept of time (linearity, segmented, future-oriented, respect for elders);
- sense of land, environment, place.

Salient aspects of externally observable dimensions of interpersonal and social life include:

- non-verbal behaviour, eye contact, distance, gesture, touch;
- use of language (e.g., reflexive and analytic versus descriptive; linearity of storytelling);
- kinship and relationship patterns (what is the most important relationship?);
- gender relationships;
- expression of emotion;
- role of healer and theory of healing.

For the multicultural counsellor, these features represent a kind of mental 'checklist' through which the world of the client can be explored, and an appropriate and helpful mutual client–counsellor world can be constructed.

The concept of reality

At the most basic level of understanding and comprehension, people in different cultures possess different ideas about the fundamental nature of reality. In Western cultures, people generally hold a *dualistic* view of reality, dividing up the world into two types of entity: mind and body. The mind is 'disembodied', and consists of ideas, concepts and thought. The physical world, on the other hand, is tangible, observable and extended in space. Many writers have argued that it is this mind–body split, originally formulated by the French philosopher Descartes in the sixteenth century, that has made possible the growth of science and the resulting highly technological way of life of people in Western industrial societies. It is also a philosophical position that limits the role of religious and spiritual experience and belief, since it assigns the study of the physical world to science, and therefore places it outside of the realm of the 'sacred'. In terms of social relationships, dualism has had the impact of increasing the division between self and object, or self and other. The 'self' becomes identified with 'mind', and set against and apart from the external world, whether this be the world of things or of other people.

People who belong in many other cultures do not have a dualist conception of the nature of reality, but instead experience the world as a wholeness, as a unity. The philosophical systems associated with Buddhism, Hinduism and other world religions all adopt this position, in which the physical, the mental and the spiritual are understood as aspects or facets of a single unified reality, rather than as separate domains of being.

It might appear as though discussions of the nature of reality are esoteric and obscure, and relate only to the interests of those few people who engage in philosophical discourse and debate. Far from it. The person's understanding of reality cuts through everything that happens in counselling. For example, a dualistic Western culture has generated many terms and concepts that refer solely to mentalistic phenomena: depression, anxiety, guilt. These terms do not exist in cultures where there is a more wholistic view of things. In these cultures, the person's response to a difficult life situation will be expressed in terms that are primarily physical. An Asian person experiencing loss, for instance, might go to a doctor and complain about physical aches and pains. A European undergoing the same life event might present himself or herself as depressed. The core elements of counselling, the words that the person uses to describe their 'troubles', reflect the underlying, implicit, philosophical viewpoint of the culture to which the person belongs. Not only that, but the concept of healing espoused in a culture depends on whether it is dualist or holist. In Western dualist cultures, it makes sense merely to talk about problems, to engage in a 'mental cure'. In cultures built around a unity of mind, body and spirit, healing practices will engage the person at all these levels, possibly encompassing activities such as meditation, exercise and diet. The Hindu discipline of yoga is an example of a method of healing, learning and enlightenment that operates in this kind of holistic manner.

The sense of self

The sense of what it means to be a person varies across cultures. As indicated in Chapter 2, counselling and psychotherapy have primarily developed within cultures that espouse an understanding of the person as being an autonomous, separate individual, with strong boundaries and an 'inner', private region of experience. Landrine (1992) has described this definition of self as *referential*. The self is an inner 'thing' or area of experience: 'the separated, encapsulated self of Western culture . . . is presumed to be the originator, creator and controller of behavior' (Landrine 1992: 402). Landrine (1992: 406) contrasts this notion with the *indexical* experience of self found in non-Western or 'sociocentric' cultures: ' "the self" in these cultures is not an entity existing independently from the relationships and contexts in which it is interpreted . . . the self is created and re-created in interactions and contexts, and exists only in and through these'.

Sampson (1988) is among many theorists who have commented on the difference between the *individualist* concept of self that predominate in Western societies, and the *collectivist* approach that is part of traditional cultures and ways of life. This distinction is similar to the concepts of *agency* and *communion* used by Bakan (1966). The person in a collectivist community is likely to regard himself or herself as a member of a family, clan or other social group, and to make decisions in the light of the needs, values and priorities of this social network. Concepts such as self-actualization or authenticity (being true to one's individual self) do not make a lot of sense in the context of a collectivist culture. Conversely, notions of honour, duty and virtue can seem archaic within modern individualist cultures. Individualist cultures emphasize the experience of guilt, referring to an inner experience of self-criticism and self-blame. People in collectivist cultures are more likely to talk about shame, referring to situations where they have been found wanting in the eyes of a powerful other person. It can be very difficult for people from extreme individualist or collectivist cultures to understand each other (Pedersen 1994). In practice, however, most cultures, and most individuals, comprise a mix of individualist and collectivist tendencies, so that, for example, a counsellor brought up in a highly individualist environment should be able to draw on some personal experiences of collective action when working with a client from a more collectivist background.

Sato (1998) has suggested that it may be valuable for individualist/agentic cultures (such as those in the West) to make use of therapy techniques from collectivist/communitarian cultures (for example, in Africa and Japan), and vice versa, as a means of counteracting a destructive overemphasis on one style of living rather than another. Nevertheless, despite these attempts to acknowledge the value of both polarities of the individualism–collectivism split, the tension between an individual self with 'depth' and a relational self that is 'extended' presents a real challenge for counsellors and psychotherapists. For reasons of training, selection and personal preference, as well as lifetime acculturation, there has been a tendency for many therapists to have a strong sense of the power and sanctity of the 'individual' and seek to initiate change at an individual level. However, this tension may be easing, as the fundamentally individualist mainstream therapies that emerged in the twentieth century, such as psychodynamic, person-centred and CBT, are being supplemented by more collectivist therapies such as narrative therapy, feminist therapy and constructionist approaches.

The construction of morality

Making moral choices, deciding between right and wrong, is central to life. However, the moral landscape is constructed quite differently in different cultures. The key characteristics of modern, Western morality are a belief in individual choice and responsibility, and a willingness to be guided by abstract moral principles such as 'fairness' or 'honesty'. By contrast, in traditional cultures moral issues are much more likely to be decided through consideration of the operation of *fate* (e.g., the Hindu notion of *karma*), and moral teachings or principles are embedded in stories rather than articulated through abstract concepts. The choice–fate distinction is crucial in many counselling situations. One of the goals of person-centred and other approaches to counselling is to help the person to discover or develop their 'internal locus of evaluation', their capacity to make moral choices on the basis of an individual set of values. It is not hard to make a connection between this definition of moral choice and the image of the present-day individual as consumer depicted by Cushman (1990, 1995) (see Chapter 2). Most counsellors would seek to challenge a client who continues to attribute his or her actions to fate, and denies any personal responsibility. Most traditional healers would, conversely, regard a person who insisted that his or her problems were due to individual choices as stubbornly self-centred and unwilling to admit the extent to which ancestors or spirit presences were determining his or her life.

Box 13.1: *Moroccan sense of self: the function of the* nisba

Morocco, Middle Eastern and . . . extrovert, fluid, activist, masculine, informal
to a fault, a Wild West sort of place without the barrooms and the cattle
drives, is another kettle of selves altogether. My work there, which began in
the mid-sixties, has been centered around a moderately large town or small
city in the foothills of the Middle Atlas, about twenty miles south of Fez. It's
an old place, probably founded in the tenth century, conceivably even earlier.
It has the walls, the gates, the narrow minarets rising to prayer-call platforms
of a classic Muslim town, and, from a distance anyway, it is a rather pretty
place, an irregular oval of blinding white set in the deep-sea-green of an olive
grove oasis, the mountains, bronze and stony here, slanting up immediately
behind it. Close up, it is less prepossessing, though more exciting: a labyrinth
of passages and alleyways, three quarters of them blind, pressed in by wall-
like buildings and curbside shops and filled with a simply astounding variety
of very emphatic human beings. Arabs, Berbers and Jews; tailors, herdsmen
and soldiers; people out of offices, people out of markets, people out of tribes;
rich, superrich, poor, superpoor; locals, immigrants, mimic Frenchmen,
unbending   medievalists,   and   somewhere,   according
to the official government census for 1960, an unemployed Jewish airline
pilot – the town houses one of the finest collections of rugged individuals I, at
least, have ever come up against. Next to Sefrou (the name of the place),
Manhattan seems almost monotonous.

(Geertz 1983: 64 –5)

This vivid description portrays a traditional society, one where the sense of self possessed
by people might be expected to be more collectivist than individualist. Yet Geertz argues
that the Moroccan sense of self is *both* individual *and* collective. When naming a person,
Arabic language allows the use of a device known as the *nisba*. This involves transforming
a noun into a relational adjective. For example, someone from Sefrou would be known as
Sefroui (native son of Sefrou). Within the city itself, the person would use a *nisba* that
located him or her within a particular group, for example *harari* (silk merchant). Geertz
reports that he had never known a case where a person was known, or known about, but
his or her *nisba* was not. He suggests that this cultural system functions to create 'contex-
tualized persons': people 'do not float as bounded psychic entities, detached from their
backgrounds and singularly named . . . their identity is an attribute that they borrow from
their setting' (p. 67). Geertz's study of the Sefroui illustrates how complex and subtle the
differences between Western and non-Western notions of self can be. For a Sefroui, a high
degree of rugged, flamboyant individuality is made possible by the fact that one can act in
virtually any way one wishes, '*without any risk of losing one's sense of who one is*' (p. 68,
emphasis added).

Another dimension of cultural contrast can be found in the area of *moral values*. Individualist cultures tend to promote values such as achievement, autonomy, independence and rationality. Collectivist cultures place more importance on sociability, sacrifice and conformity.

The concept of time

It has been one of the great contributions of existential philosophers to review the significance for individuals and cultures of the way that *time* is experienced. From the perspective of physics, time can be treated as a linear constant, segmentable into units such as seconds, minutes and hours. From the perspective of persons and social groups, time is one of the elements through which a way of being and relating is constructed. One of the defining characteristics of modern industrial societies is the extent to which they are *future-oriented*. The past is forgotten, destroyed, built over. Oral history, the story of what a family or community achieved in the past, survives only to the most minimal degree. The past is redefined, packaged and sold as 'heritage'. Traditional, collectivist societies, by contrast, are predominantly *past-oriented*. There is a strong continuity in the oral history that is available to members of traditional cultures. It is normal to imagine that ancestors are in some sense present and can communicate with the living. In modern cultures, the notion of *progress* is given a great deal of value. The practices, lifestyle and possessions of previous generations are considered 'old-fashioned' and 'dated'. In traditional cultures, 'progress' and development can often be perceived as threatening. The forms of communication and storage of information, and types of work tasks, in different cultural settings also have an impact on the experience of time. In pre-literate cultures it makes sense to assume that everyday life was lived largely in the moment, focused on tasks that required attention in the here-and-now. In modern technological societies there is a spectrum of activities, including reading and watching television, that unavoidably shift the consciousness of the person to 'there-and-then'. There is some irony in the attempts of humanistic psychologists and therapists, in the mid-twentieth century, to create methods of enabling people to rediscover the *present*.

The influence of modern attitudes to time lies at the very heart of therapy. Implicit, and often explicit, in the practice of much psychodynamic and humanistic counselling and psychotherapy is an invitation to the client to confront and reject the authority of his or her parents, who are regarded as responsible for the inculcation of repressive and life-restricting injunctions and patterns of behaviour. This way of seeing relationships between parents and children is consistent with the pervasive ageism of contemporary society and with the need for an advanced capitalist economy to encourage citizens to consume new and different products and adopt new work patterns and roles. It does not sit easily, however, with the past-centred reverence for parents and ancestors widespread in non-Western cultures. The construction of time in different cultural settings can have very practical consequences. In cultures where linear, segmented, clock-defined time is dominant, it makes sense for counselling clients to be given hour-long appointments at the same time each week. In some other cultures these arrangements just do not make sense, and clients would expect to be able to drop in to see a counsellor when it feels right to them, rather than when the clock or calendar dictates they should.

The significance of place

The final dimension of culture to be discussed here concerns the relationship between cultures and the physical environment, the land. It is clear that the bond between person and place has been largely severed in modern urban societies. Social and geographical mobility is commonplace. People move around in response to educational and work opportunities. Transport and relocation are relatively easy. As a result, there are few people who live as adults in the same neighbourhood or community in which they grew up, and even fewer who live in the neighbourhoods or communities where their parents or grand-parents grew up. In modern cultures there is an appreciation of place, but often this is detached and takes the form of tourism. All this means that it can be enormously difficult for counsellors and therapists socialized into the ways of modernity to understand the meaning of place for people from different cultural backgrounds. Some of the most compel-ling evidence for this come from studies of native American communities. For example, Lassiter (1987) reports on the widespread psychological damage caused to Navajo peoples by forced relocation resulting from the sale of their ancestral lands to mining companies.

Research into native American and other traditional cultures has established that place and land can have a powerful emotional and social significance for people. These aspects of human experience are, however, largely ignored by Western psychology and approaches to counselling and psychotherapy. It does not need much reflection to confirm that place is often extremely important for members of modern industrial–urban societies. People invest a great deal of energy in their homes and gardens, and in their relationship with the countryside.

Box 13.2: *The development of cultural identity*

One of the challenges for any counsellor who believes in the relevance of cultural factors in shaping and maintaining personal issues is to gain a clear understanding of the cultural identity of each client with whom he or she is working. There are two main areas of diffi-culty. First, the identities of many people in modern societies derive from multiple cultural sources – a grandmother who was Irish, a grandfather who was Jamaican, an interest in Buddhism acquired in adulthood (see Ramirez 1991; Josephs 2002). The other source of complexity is that people differ in the degree to which they have developed an awareness of their cultural identity – some people have never reflected on their cultural roots, whereas others have devoted a great deal of time and effort to exploring such issues.

Models of cultural identity development have been constructed by Helms (1995), Sue and Sue (2003) and others. A key facet of these models is that they describe different pro-cesses of development for people in dominant and subordinate cultural groups, respec-tively. At the first phase of cultural identity development, a person has limited awareness of himself/herself as a cultural being. At later phases, experiences of meeting people from different cultural backgrounds triggers an increasing awareness of cultural factors. For a person in a subordinate cultural group, this phase is characterized by increased identifica-tion with his or her own group, and a strong rejection of the values and worldview of the dominant group. For a member of a dominant cultural group, this phase is accompanied by guilt and questioning of his or her privileged position, and denigration of aspects of his or her own culture. At a final phase of cultural identity development, subordinate and dominant cultural group members are able to achieve a more balanced and nuanced view of the role of cultural factors in their lives. They become able to sustain meaningful and satisfying relationships with members of other cultural groups, and to appreciate the wider historical and sociopolitical factors that shape intergroup conflict, stereotyping and ignorance. This model has significant implications for counselling practice. For example, the relevance and impact of counsellor–client cultural differences will vary a great deal depending on the stage of cultural identity development at which each participant is currently functioning.

Externally observable dimensions of cultural identity

Turning now to more immediately observable and overt aspects of culture, it is clear that many of the underlying philosophical dimensions of different cultural 'worldviews' are expressed and visible in the ways that people behave. One of the observable aspects of cultural difference that has received substantial attention has been *non-verbal behaviour*. Cultures can be differentiated in terms of the way that people employ non-verbal cues such as touch, eye contact, gesture and proximity. Often, the difficulties of communication that can exist between members of separate cultural groups can be understood through an appreciation of non-verbal factors. For example, direct eye contact is considered in Western cultures as a sign of honesty and openness, but in many other cultures would be perceived as rude or intrusive. Similarly, each culture employs complex unwritten rules about who can be touched, and in what circumstances.

Important cultural differences can also be observed in patterns of *verbal behaviour*. Bernstein (1972), examining linguistic differences between working-class and middle-class subcultures in English society, found that, when asked to tell a story based on a series of pictures, middle-class people tended to use what he called an 'elaborated code', in which they explained the assumptions behind their understanding of the situation. Working-class participants in his study, by contrast, seemed to use a 'restricted code', in which they took for granted that the listener would 'know what they meant'. Landrine (1992) has suggested that people from 'referential self' cultures talk about themselves in abstract terms, as an object with attributes (e.g., 'I am female, a mother, middle-aged, tall, a librarian), whereas those immersed in 'indexical self' social life find it very difficult to do this. When asked to talk about themselves they are much more likely to recount stories of specific concrete instances and episodes that express these qualities in dramatic form. People from different cultures have quite distinct modes of storytelling. Western individuals tend to tell well ordered, logical, linear stories. People from more orally based traditional cultural groups tend to tell stories that are circular and never seem to get to the 'point'. These are just some of the many linguistic aspects of cultural difference. The key point here is that the way that a person talks, the way that he or she uses language, conveys a great deal about his or her cultural and personal identity.

A feature of social life to which anthropologists have given a great deal of attention is *kinship patterns*. There are a series of issues around this topic that are fundamental to the construction of identity in members of a culture: What is the size and composition of the family group? How are marriages arranged? Who looks after children? How is property passed on from one generation to another? From the point of view of a counsellor, the answers a person gives to these questions help to generate a picture of the kind of relational world in which he or she expects to live, or which is regarded as normal. A powerful way of illustrating differences in kinship ties is to ask: what is your most important relationship? In Western cultures the answer will often be that the most important relationship is with the spouse or life partner. In other parts of the world, the closest relationship is between parent and child.

Very much linked in with kinship patterns is the issue of *gender relationships*. The influence of gender on personal identity is immense, and some feminist theorists would even argue that gender is more central than culture to understanding the way that a person thinks, feels and acts. Nevertheless, it is also clear that gender identity and gender roles are constructed differently in different cultures. Included within the cultural definition of gender is the extent to which a culture represses, tolerates or celebrates homosexuality.

The *expression of emotion* is a facet of enculturation that is central to counselling. Different cultures have varying understandings of which emotions are 'acceptable' and are allowed expression in public. One way that the 'emotional rules' of a culture can be observed is through the range of words that a person has available to describe emotions and feelings. It is clear, from research carried out by anthropologists and cross-cultural psychologists, that emotion or feeling words or facial expressions in one culture do not map easily on to the language of another culture. For example, in the Shona (Zimbabwe) language the term *kufungisisa* (roughly translated as 'thinking too much') is widely used to account for psychological problems, but has no direct equivalent in English. Farooq *et al.* (1995), and many other researchers, have found that people from Asian cultures tend to express depression and anxiety through bodily complaints and ailments rather than in psychological terms. Marcelino (1990) suggests that an appreciation of emotion words in communities in the Philippines is only possible if Filipino concepts of relationships are understood first. These examples represent one of the key challenges for multicultural counselling. Counselling is based on purposeful, problem-solving conversation and communication around the meanings, goals, relationships and emotions that are troubling a person. Cultural difference strikes at the heart of this endeavour. To what extent can anyone know how someone from another language community *really* feels?

The final observable manifestation of cultural difference to be discussed is the area of attitudes and practices around healing. Every culture has its own understanding of well-being, illness and cure. The *theory of healing* espoused by members of a culture can be based on scientific knowledge, as in Western industrial societies, or can be grounded in supernatural beliefs. In many cultures, traditional/spiritual and modern/scientific approaches to healing may exist side by side. For example, in Malaysia, an Asian country with an economy and educational system modelled on Western ideas, a recent survey found that over half of patients attributed their illness to supernatural agents, witchcraft and possession, and were just as likely to use the services of a traditional healer (*bomoh*) as a Western-trained physician. In his review of different varieties of psychotherapy and counselling practised in different cultures, Prince (1980) found a range of methods that extended far beyond the domain of conventional counselling, including meditation, village meetings, shamanic ecstasy and social isolation. It is futile to expect that Western approaches to counselling and psychotherapy will be seen as relevant or acceptable to people who have been brought up to view any of these kinds of ritual as the way to deal with depression, anxiety or interpersonal conflict.

The value for counsellors of possessing a model of cultural identity arises from the fact that it is impossible for a counsellor to know about all cultures. What is more useful is to know the right questions to ask. It can be dangerous to imagine that it is even possible to build up a comprehensive knowledge base about a cultural group – for instance, through attending a module or workshop on a training course – because within that cultural group there will certainly be a myriad of varying strands of cultural experience. Probably the best that can be achieved by training workshops or book chapters on the counselling needs and issues of particular groups (see, for example, the relevant sections of Ponterotto *et al.* 1995; Pedersen *et al.* 1996) is to *sensitize* the counsellor to the structures, language and traditions of that group. When working with a client from another cultural background, information on relevant cultural experiences can be gleaned from the client, from reading, from other members of that culture or from living in that culture.

The cultural identity checklist presented above gives one way of making sense of the influence of various cultural factors in the life of an individual counselling client. Falicov (1995) offers an alternative way of structuring such a cultural map, focusing on family structure and life cycle, the living environment (ecological context) of the client and the person's experience of migration and acculturation. Hofstede (1980, 2003) has produced a way of categorizing cultures that some counsellors have found helpful (for instance, Draguns 1996; Lago 2006). The Hofstede model describes four main dimensions of cultural difference between cultures: power distance, uncertainty avoidance, individualism–collectivism and masculinity–femininity.

Power distance refers to the extent to which inequalities in power exist within a culture. Western industrial societies are (relatively) democratic, with power and authority being available, in principle, to all citizens. Many traditional cultures, and contemporary authoritarian regimes, are structured around major inequalities in power and privilege. *Uncertainty avoidance* distinguishes between cultures where 'each day is taken as it comes' and cultures with absolute rules and values. *Individualism–collectivism* captures the difference between cultures in which people exist as discrete, autonomous individuals, and those where there is a strong allegiance to family, clan or nation. Finally, *masculinity –femininity* reflects differences not only in the domination of conventional sex roles, but in the extent to which values of achievement and money (masculine) or quality of life and interdependence (feminine) are predominant. This model can be used to create a cultural mapping of approaches to therapy. For example, person-centred counselling is an orientation that is marked by low power distance, fairly high levels of individualism, low masculinity and uncertainty avoidance, and a mainly short-term (here and now) orientation. The person-centred approach may therefore be perceived by people within high power distance, collectivist and masculine cultures (for example, some Muslim societies) as lacking in credibility and relevance. Similar mapping exercises can be carried out for other therapy approaches.

There is no 'right' or 'wrong' way to understand culture, and the best that any of these guidelines or frameworks can achieve is to offer a means for beginning to make some sense of the enormous complexity of cultural identity. Effective multicultural counselling involves not only being able to 'see' people in cultural terms, but also having a capacity to apply this understanding to the task of helping people with their problems.

Box 13.3: *Using interpreters in counselling*

The role of language, as a means of communicating meaning and significance, is of enormous importance in any counselling situation where therapist and client have grown up in different language communities. The language that a person acquired during his or her childhood is likely to be the most immediately accessible way in which a person can simply and directly convey the emotional truth of their life.

Bowker and Richards (2004) interviewed therapists about their experience of working with bilingual clients who were receiving counselling in their second language. A central theme in the accounts of these therapists was a sense of emotional distance from these clients, and uncertainty about whether they were truly understanding all of what their client was telling them. Some of the therapists described cases in which clients had purposefully chosen to receive therapy in a second language, as a way of maintaining their own psychological distance from painful memories.

The role of language is even more acute in counselling with refugee or immigrant clients who require the involvement of an interpreter. The use of an interpreter brings another person into the counselling relationship, and the personal style and attitudes of the interpreter, and the extent to which both client and counsellor trust the interpreter, become critical factors in determining the effectiveness of the therapy.

Raval and Smith (2003) and Miller *at al.* (2005) interviewed therapists about their experiences of working with interpreters. It is clear that there are marked differences across therapists in terms of their way of working with interpreters. Some therapists view the interpreter as merely a translation machine, and are eager to dispense with the services of the interpreter at the earliest opportunity. For example, one therapist in the Miller *at al.* (2005: 30) study stated that:

> My rule of thumb is that I get the interpreter out of the room as fast as I can . . . Therapy turns on the nuances, there is a certain point after I have worked with somebody for a while and we have gotten to know each other and we have gotten the basic story, if they can understand half of what I am saying after a while, and I can understand half of what they are saying, I tell the interpreter to leave.

For other counsellors, by contrast, the interpreter becomes a central participant in the therapeutic process, a witness to the client's story, and a cultural consultant. A therapist who operated from this position recounted that:

> I remember countless times when you would hear something that would just
> be like a punch in the gut, and there would just be this shock, you would
> think, 'I could never hear something more shocking in my life.' It was trauma-
> tizing . . . and having the interpreter there with you was so immensely
> comforting because you knew that you could process it together. There was
> this implicit understanding between you that you had both witnessed some-
> thing very profound.
>
> (Miller *at al.* 2005: 33)
>
> These statements illustrate something of the complexity and challenge of conducting
> therapy through an interpreter. A comprehensive discussion of issues and strategies
> associated with this kind of work is available in Tribe and Raval (2003).

Multicultural counselling in practice

So far, we have mainly considered the question of how to make sense of culture, and how
to develop an appreciation of how the way that a person experiences the world is built up
through a multiplicity of cultural influences. We now turn to a discussion of how a multicultural approach can be applied in practice. What are the counselling techniques and
strategies that are distinctive to this approach? Some of the skills associated with multicultural counselling involve concrete, practical issues. For example, d'Ardenne and Mahtani
(1989) discuss the need to review with clients the implications of using appropriate names
and forms of address, deciding on whether to use an interpreter, and negotiating
differences in non-verbal communication and time boundaries. Behind these tangible
issues lie less concrete factors associated with the general therapeutic strategy or 'mind-set'
adopted by the counsellor.

Ramirez (1991) argues that the common theme running through all cross-cultural
counselling is the challenge of living in a multicultural society. He proposes that a
central aim in working with clients from all ethnic groups should be the development of
'cultural flexibility'. Ramirez (1991) points out that even members of a dominant, majority
culture report the experience of 'feeling different', of a sense of mismatch between who we
are and what other people expect from us. The approach taken by Ramirez (1991) involves
the counsellor matching the cultural and cognitive style of the client in initial meetings,
then moving on to encourage experimentation with different forms of cultural behaviour.
This approach obviously requires a high degree of self-awareness and cultural flexibility
on the part of the therapist.

Another important strategy in multicultural counselling is to focus on the links between
personal problems and political/social realities. The person receiving counselling is not
perceived purely in psychological terms, but is understood as being an active member of
a culture. The feelings, experiences and identity of the client are viewed as shaped by the
cultural milieu. For example, Holland (1990: 262) makes a distinction between loss and
expropriation:

> In my work . . . we return over and over again to the same history of being separated from mothers, rejoining mothers that they did not know, leaving grandmothers they loved, finding themselves in a totally different relationship, being sexually abused, being put into care, and so on: all the kinds of circumstances with which clinicians working in this field are familiar. That is loss, but expropriation is what imperialism and neo-colonialism does – it steals one's history; it steals all kinds of things from black people, from people who don't belong to a white supremacist race.

Holland is here writing about her work with working-class black women in Britain. But the experience of having things stolen by powerful others is a common theme in the lives of those who are gay, lesbian, religiously different, unemployed or sexually abused. Loss can be addressed and healed through therapy, but expropriation can only be remedied through social action. The theme of empowerment, within an individual life, through self-help groups or by political involvement, is therefore a distinctive and essential ingredient of multicultural counselling.

The unconscious dimension of the links between personal problems and sociohistorical realities is discussed by Kareem (2000: 32–3), a psychotherapist born in India and working in the UK:

> As most of the black and other ethnic peoples who have settled in the UK and other Western countries have come from areas which were once under colonial power, psychotherapy cannot be expected to operate and be meaningful without taking into consideration the effects of colonial rule on these individuals . . . (. . .) How was it possible for Britain to colonize India, for example, a much older civilization, and to undermine the value systems which had existed there for generations? It seems to me that in this situation psychological occupation was much more damaging and long-lasting than physical occupation. It destroyed the inner self. All occupying forces strive to find people in the occupied territories whose minds can be colonized, so that the colonization process can be continued through them, through thoughts rather than physical coercion. This process has a long-lasting effect which can continue through generations after colonization has ended.

The implication of Kareem's (2000) observations is to draw attention to the deeply buried, and deeply problematic, impact of historical events: how is it possible to repair the destruction of a cultural 'inner self'?

Box 13.4: *Working with the client's explanatory model*

The psychiatrist and social anthropologist Arthur Kleinman is one of the leading figures in the area of cross-cultural mental health (Kleinman 2004). His book *The Illness Narratives: Suffering, Healing and the Human Condition* (Kleinman 1988) is a classic within this field. One of the central themes in Kleinman's work has been to help health professionals to appreciate the very different ways in which people from different cultural groups make sense of illness and health. He suggests that it is essential for any helper to make the effort to understand the client or patient's 'explanatory model' (Kleinman 1988; Kleinman and Benson 2006), by collecting information in relation to the following questions:

- what do you call this problem?
- what do you believe is the cause of this problem?
- what course do you expect it to take? How serious is it?
- what do you think that this problem is doing to your body and mind?
- what do you most fear about this condition?
- what do you most fear about the treatment?

Kleinman argues that these questions open up an appreciation of 'what matters most' for the client, and enables the therapist to use his or her expert knowledge alongside that of the person seeking help.

Dyche and Zayas (1995) argue that in practice it is impossible for counsellors to enter the first session with comprehensive detailed knowledge of the cultural background of their client. They suggest, moreover, that any attempt to compile such knowledge runs the danger of arriving at an overtheoretical, intellectualized understanding of the culture of a client, and may risk 'seeing clients as their culture, not as themselves' (p. 389). Dyche and Zayas argue that it is more helpful to adopt an attitude of cultural naiveté and respectful curiosity, with the goal of working collaboratively with each client to create an understanding of what their cultural background means to them as an individual. Ridley and Lingle (1996) refer to a similar stance towards the client, but discuss it in terms of *cultural empathy*. David and Erickson (1990) argue that this quality of curiosity about, or empathy towards, the cultural world of others must be built upon a similar attitude towards one's own culture.

The work of Dyche and Zayas (1995), Holland (1990), Martinez (1991) and Ridley and Lingle (1996) demonstrates the point that the practice of multicultural counselling is largely driven by a set of principles or beliefs, rather than being based in a set of discrete skills or techniques. Multicultural counsellors may use different forms of delivery, such as individual, couple, family or group counselling, or may employ specific interventions such as relaxation training, dream analysis or empathic reflection. In each instance, the counsellor must take into consideration the cultural appropriateness of what is being offered. Multicultural counselling does not fit easily into any of the mainstream counselling approaches, such as psychodynamic, person-centred, cognitive–behavioural or systemic. There are some multicultural counsellors who operate from within each of these approaches; there are others who draw on each of them as necessary. Multicultural counselling is an *integrative* approach that uses a culture-based theory of personal identity as a basis for selecting counselling ideas and techniques.

One specific behaviour or skill that can be observed in effective multicultural counsellors can be described as *willingness to talk about cultural issues*. Thompson and Jenal

(1994) carried out a study of the impact on the counselling process of counsellor 'race-avoidant' interventions. In other words, when working with clients who raised concerns about race and culture, these counsellors responded in ways that addressed only those aspects of the client's issue that could relate to anyone, irrespective of race, rather than acknowledging the actual racial content of what was being said. Thompson and Jenal found that this kind of 'race neutralizing' response had the effect of disrupting or constricting the client's flow, and led either to signs of exasperation or to the client conceding or deferring to the counsellor's definition of the situation by dropping any mention of racial issues.

A further study by Thompson and Alexander (2006), where clients received ten sessions of counselling found no differences in process or outcome measures between clients who had worked with a 'race-avoidant' counsellor, and those whose counsellor actively invited conversation around racial and ethnic issues. However, Thompson and Alexander (2006) acknowledged that the measures that they used in their study may not have been sensitive enough to detect the impact of this aspect of counsellor style. It seems clear that this kind of research needs to be repeated with other groups and clients and counsellors, and in relation to a wider range of cultural issues. Nevertheless, the findings of the study seem intuitively accurate: if the counsellor is unwilling or unable to give voice to cultural issues, then the client is silenced.

Moodley (1998) uses the phrase 'frank talking' to describe the openness that is necessary in this kind of work. Cardemil and Battle (2003), in a review of the literature on the counsellor's willingness to be active in initiating discussion with clients about cultural issues, note that some clients may not like it if their therapist insists on talking about cultural matters, when they are wanting to talk about personal concerns – clearly, sensitivity and timing are essential skills in relation to this strategy. By contrast, Patterson (2004) argues that is not helpful for counsellors to pay any particular attention to issues of cultural difference in their conversations with clients, because this distracts from their capacity to respond to the client as a person. Despite the views of Patterson (2004), there appears to be a broad emerging consensus across the profession, influenced by the research of Thompson and Jenal (1994), Tuckwell (2001) and others, that it is necessary for counsellors to take the initiative in acknowledging and giving voice to possible areas of difference in cultural worldview and experience that may have a bearing on the counselling process and relationship.

Another distinctive area of competence for multicultural counsellors lies in being able to draw on therapeutic techniques and ideas from other cultures, in the service of client needs. The vignettes presented in Boxes 13.5, 13.6 and 13.7 provide examples of this kind of process operating in the context of a specific cultural milieu. The work of Walter (1996), in the field of bereavement counselling, provides a more general example of multicultural awareness functioning at a theoretical level. Walter (1996) notes that most Western models of grief propose that it is necessary for the bereaved person to work through their feelings of loss in order to arrive at a position where they are able to make new attachments. Within bereavement counselling, this process is facilitated by speaking to a stranger, the bereavement counsellor. Walter (1996) learned that in Shona culture, there is a tradition of keeping the spirit of the deceased person alive by continuing to acknowledge him or her as a continuing member of the family or community. This goal was achieved by a process of talking about the deceased person. People who knew the deceased spoke at length to each other about their memories of that person. At a time of his own personal bereavement, Walter (1996) tried out this approach, and found that it was helpful and satisfying both for him and for the other bereaved people around him. In his writing, he proposes some ways in which this Shona tradition can be integrated into Western counselling practice. Lee (2002) explores similar issues in his discussion of the integration of indigenous and Western therapies in his work with Singapore Chinese.

Box 13.5: *Counselling in the Chinese temple*

In Taiwan, people in crisis may choose to visit the temple to seek advice through *chou-chien* (fortune-telling through the drawing of bamboo sticks). The *chien* client makes an offering to the temple god, tells the god about his or her problems, then picks up and shakes a bamboo vase containing a set of *chien* sticks. One of the sticks becomes dislodged, and is selected. The client then throws a kind of die to determine whether he or she has drawn the correct *chien*. Once sure that they have chosen the right stick, they take it over to a desk in the temple and ask for the *chien* paper corresponding to a number inscribed on the stick. On the paper there is a classical short Chinese poem describing a historical event. Often the person consults an interpreter – usually an older man – whose role is to explain the meaning of the poem in a way that he feels is helpful to the supplicant.

A young man asked whether it was 'blessed' for him to change his job. The interpreter read to him the *chien* poem on the paper he had drawn and then asked several questions before he made any interpretation, including how long he had been on the present job, why he was thinking of changing his job and whether he had any opportunities for a new job. The young man replied that he had been in his present job for only a month or so, having just graduated from school. He did not like the job because of its long hours and low pay. He had made no plans for a new job and had no idea how to go about it. Upon hearing this, the interpreter said that it was not 'blessed' for the young man to change his job at that time, that young people should make more effort than demands, and that if he worked hard and long enough he would eventually be paid more.

This account is taken from Hsu (1976: 211–12), who observes that *chien* fulfils a number of important therapeutic functions: giving hope, eliminating anxiety, strengthening self-esteem and the reinforcement of adaptive social behaviour. Hsu suggests that *chien* counselling is particularly appropriate in the Chinese cultural milieu, in which deference to authority is highly valued, and in which it is considered rude to express emotion in a direct fashion. In addition to the use of *chien* sticks, there are several other forms of indigenous therapeutic ritual that are widely used in Chinese culture, for example shamanism and *feng-shui,* and traditional Chinese medicine. Lee (2002) provides a number of case examples of how counsellors trained in Western approaches can effectively incorporate these forms of healing into their practice, when clients find it meaningful to do so.

To summarize, it can be seen that multicultural counselling can take many forms. In responding to the needs and experiences of people from different cultural backgrounds, a multicultural counsellor must be creative and adaptive. Nevertheless, it is possible to suggest a set of guidelines for multicultural counselling practice, derived from the writings of Johnson and Nadirshaw (1993), Pedersen (1994) and LaRoche and Maxie (2003):

- There is no single concept of 'normal' that applies across all persons, situations and cultures. Mainstream concepts of mental health and illness must be expanded to incorporate religious and spiritual elements. It is important to take a flexible and respectful approach to other therapeutic values, beliefs and traditions: we must each of us assume that our own view is to some extent culturally biased.

- Individualism is not the only way to view human behaviour and must be supplemented by collectivism in some situations. Dependency is not a bad characteristic in all cultures.

- It is essential to acknowledge the reality of racism and discrimination in the lives of clients, and in the therapy process. Power imbalances between therapist and client may reflect the imbalance of power between the cultural communities to which they belong.

- Language use is important – abstract 'middle-class' psychotherapeutic discourse may not be understood by people coming from other cultures. Linear thinking/storytelling is not universal.

- It is important to take account of the structures within the client's community that serve to strengthen and support the client: natural support systems are important to the individual. For some clients, traditional healing methods may be more effective than Western forms of counselling.

- It is necessary to take history into account when making sense of current experience. The way that someone feels is not only a response to what is happening now, but may be in part a response to loss or trauma that occurred in earlier generations.

- Be willing to talk about cultural and racial issues and differences in the counselling room. Be actively curious about the social and cultural world in which the client lives his or her life, and his or her cultural identity.

- Check it out with the client – be open to learning from the client.

- Take time to explore and reflect on your own cultural identity, and associated attitudes and beliefs, and how these factors shape your interaction with clients.

These principles have informed the construction of lists of multicultural counselling competences. For example, Sue and Sue (2007) suggest that culturally competent counsellors possess knowledge and skill, and culturally sensitive attitudes in beliefs, in three broad areas: awareness of their own values and biases, awareness of client worldviews, and culturally appropriate intervention strategies. Instruments for assessing cultural competence in counsellors have been developed, such as the *Multicultural Counseling Inventory* (MCI; Sodowsky *et al.* 1994, 1998). Research into multicultural counselling competence has been reviewed by Worthington *et al.* (2007).

Box 13.6: *Naikan therapy: a distinctive Japanese approach*

The form of therapy known as *Naikan Therapy* reflects a distinctively Japanese integration of Western therapeutic practices and traditional Buddhist beliefs and rituals (Tanaka-Mastsumi 2004; Reynolds 1980, 1981a). Naikan is particularly effective with individuals who are depressed and socially isolated. The person spends several days in a retreat centre, engaging in a process of continuous meditation based upon highly structured instruction in self-observation and self-reflection. The role of the 'counsellor' is merely to interview the person briefly every 90 minutes to check that he/she has been following the specified therapeutic procedure, which consists of recollecting and examining memories of the 'care and benevolence' that the person has received from particular people at particular times in their life. Having recalled such memories, the client is then encouraged to move on to recollect and examine their memories of what they have *returned* or given to that person, and the troubles and worries that they have given that person. These questions provide a foundation for reflecting on relationships with others such as parents, friends, teachers, siblings, work associates, children, and partners. The person can reflect their self in relation to pets, or even objects such as cars and pianos. In each case, the aim is to search for a more realistic view of our conduct and of the give and take which has occurred in the relationship. The most common result of this therapeutic procedure is an improvement in the person's relationships, and an alleviation of levels of depression.

Murase (1976: 137) points out that in Buddhist philosophy:

> the human being is fundamentally selfish and guilty, and yet at the same time favoured with unmeasured benevolence from others. In order to acknowledge these existential conditions deeply, one must become open-minded toward oneself, empathic and sympathetic toward others, and courageously confront one's own authentic guilt.

Also, elders are received and respected in Japanese culture, to an extent that is not found in contemporary European cultures – to revisit the 'care and benevolence' of elders can be, for people who have grown up within Japanese culture, an antidote to depression and hopelessness. Naikan represents a vivid example of a way in which a healing practice that would be regarded as boring and useless by the majority of people in Europe and North America, can nevertheless be highly meaningful and effective within its own cultural context.

Culture-bound syndromes

It is important to appreciate that there exist different patterns of psychological and emotional problems in different cultures. It probably makes sense to regard the consequences of problems in living, in all cultures, as falling into broad patterns of thought, feeling and action associated with the experience of fear/anxiety, sadness/loss/depression and breakdown of meaning (psychosis). However, the form that these reactions take appears to be significantly influenced by cultural factors, with the result that a large number of distinct psychiatric 'culture-bound syndromes' have been identified within various communities. When considering the topic of culture-bound syndromes, it is useful to take into account the fact the way that patterns of psychological problems are understood in contemporary Western society does not in fact remain static. For example, Cushman and Gilford (1999) have discussed some of the ways in which revisions to the Diagnostic and Statistical Manual (DSM) of the American Psychiatric Association, over the last 30 years, have reflected shifts in the cultural milieu. A striking example of this is the inclusion, then exclusion, of homosexuality as a category of psychiatric disorder. It is possible to see, therefore, that there are no fixed definitions of patterns of psychological and emotional problems, but that ideas about these topics depend on values and ideas that prevail in a particular community or society at a particular point in time.

A well-studied example of a culture-bound syndrome is *shinkeishitsu*. This is a pattern of distress and dysfunction reported by people in Japan (Ishiyama 1986; Russell 1989), characterized by self-preoccupation, high levels of sensitivity to health symptoms, perfectionist self-expectations and high achievement motivation, and a rigid worldview. Although *shinkeishitsu* has some similarities to the Western concept of anxiety disorder, it also encompasses unique features arising from the trends toward conformity and social acceptance that are found in Japanese culture. Japan enjoys a strong and long-established tradition of psychotherapeutic practice, which includes a specific form of therapy, Morita therapy (Ishiyama 1986; Reynolds 1981b), which has been developed to address this specific type of problem. If a counsellor or psychotherapist is working with a Japanese client, it may be that the client understands his or her problem in terms of the concept of *shinkeishitsu,* and will be likely to benefit from therapeutic strategies that have been shown to be effective in tackling this syndrome.

Another example of a culture-bound syndrome is *ataques de nervios,* which is prevalent in some Latin American areas such as Puerto Rica. *Ataques de nervios* is characterized by a sense of being out of control. The person may shout, cry, engage in verbal or physical aggression, or exhibit seizures or fainting episodes. This patter tends to occur when a person has learned of bad news concerning his or her family, such as a tragic bereavement or accident. The person may not remember what they did during the attack, and will typically return to normal after a short time (Guarnaccia and Rogler 1999).

Shinkeishitsu and *ataques de nervios* are just two of the dozens of culture-bound syndromes that have been identified and studied; there exists an extensive literature on this topic. Knowledge of culture-bound syndromes is valuable for counsellors, because it makes it possible to grasp the connections between cultural factors, and manifestations of personal and psychological problems, in ways that can be hard to achieve in relation to one's own culture, in which the reality of psychiatric categories is largely taken for granted. In relation to working with clients from other cultures, knowledge and curiosity around culture-bound syndromes is a means of expressing respect for the language, culture and worldview of the individual, and potentially a route toward finding therapeutic strategies that are most effective, and make most sense for that person.

Box 13.7: *A culturally sensitive approach to counselling in a case of traumatic bereavement*

In the winter of 1984, about 12,000 *Falashas* (Jews of Ethiopia) were driven out of their villages in northern Ethiopia by a combination of hunger, fear of war and a desire to emigrate to Israel. On their long march through the desert and in refugee camps about 3,000 died. Eventually, the Israeli government managed to airlift the survivors to safety, but only after enormous trauma and disruption to family groups.

Some two years later, M, a 31-year-old Ethiopian woman, married with four children, and who spoke only Amharic, was referred to a psychiatric unit in Jerusalem. Although it was difficult to obtain adequate translation facilities, it emerged that she had wandered for many weeks in the desert, during which time her baby had died. She continued to carry the dead body for several days, until she arrived in Israel, when the strong-smelling corpse was taken from her and buried. For the previous two years she had been repeatedly hospitalized following 'asthmatic attacks'. Now she was agitated, fearful and depressed, and complained of 'having a snake in her leg'. She was diagnosed as suffering from an acute psychotic episode. The staff in the psychiatric unit were able to find an anthropologist familiar with M's culture and language, and it emerged that she experienced herself as 'impure' because she had never been able to undergo the purification ritual required by her religious sect for all those who have come into contact with a human corpse. Her mother-in-law had not allowed her to talk about her feelings surrounding her bereavement: 'snake in the leg' turned out to be a Falasha idiom for referring to disagreement with a mother-in-law. M received counselling that encouraged her to talk about the death of her baby, and a purification ritual was arranged. At 30-month follow-up, she was doing well and had a new baby, although admitting to still mourning her dead child.

The case of M, and the issues it raises, are described more fully in Schreiber (1995). It is a case that demonstrates the strengths of a multicultural approach. Although the person in need presented with physical, somatic symptoms that could in principle be treated by medication and conventional Western psychiatry, the therapists involved in the case took the trouble to explore the *meaning* of these symptoms, and then to construct a form of help that brought together indigenous and psychotherapeutic interventions in a way that was appropriate for this individual person.

Adapting existing services and agencies to meet the needs of client groups from different cultures

Counsellor awareness training is of fundamental importance, given that ethnocentric counsellor attitudes are sure to impede the formation of a good working relationship with clients from other cultures or social groups. There are, however, limits to what can be achieved through this strategy. No counsellor can acquire an adequate working knowledge of the social worlds of all the clients he or she might encounter. In any case, many clients prefer to have a counsellor who is similar to them in sexual orientation, social class or gender, or they may not believe that they will find in an agency someone who will understand their background or language. In response to these considerations, some counsellors have followed the strategy of aiming for organizational, as well as individual, change. To meet the needs of disadvantaged clients, they have attempted to adapt the structure and operation of their agencies.

Rogler *et al.* (1987) and Gutierrez (1992) describe a range of organizational strategies that have been adopted by counselling and therapy agencies to meet the needs of ethnic minority clients, and that are also applicable in other situations. One approach they describe focuses on the question of access. There can be many factors (financial, geographical, attitudinal) that prevent people from seeking help. Agencies can overcome these barriers by publicizing their services differently, employing outreach workers, hiring bilingual or bicultural staff, opening offices at more accessible sites and providing crèche facilities. A second level of organizational adaptation involves tailoring the counselling to the target client group. Services are modified to reflect the issues and problems experienced by a particular set of clients. One way of doing this is to offer courses or groups that are open to these people only: for example, a bereavement group for older women, an assertiveness class for carers or a counselling programme for women with drink problems.

Rogler *et al.* (1987) describe the invention of *cuento*, or folklore therapy, as a therapeutic intervention specifically designed to be of relevance to a disadvantaged group, in this case disturbed Hispanic children. This approach is based on cognitive–behavioural ideas about modelling appropriate behaviour, but the modelling is carried out through the telling of Puerto Rican folktales, followed up by discussion and role-play. A useful paper by Le *et al.* (2010) explains the procedures followed by one therapy centre to adapt a well-established therapy model for use with clients from a different cultural group.

A further stage in the adaptation of a counselling agency to the needs of minority clients occurs when the actual structure, philosophy or aims of the organization are changed in reaction to the inclusion within it of more and more members of formerly excluded groups. When this happens, initiatives of the type described above can no longer be marginal to the functioning of the organizations, but come to be seen as core activities. Gutierrez (1992: 330) suggests that without this kind of organizational development, 'efforts toward change can be mostly symbolic and marginal'.

There has been a considerable amount of research into the impact of adapting counselling and psychotherapy services and procedures for cultural minority clients. A review of this literature by Benish *et al.* (2011) concluded that culturally adapted therapy was significantly more effective than standard therapy.

Box 13.8: *How relevant are Western ideas about counselling to people living in Islamic societies?*

In many predominantly Islamic societies, such as Saudi Arabia, Kuwait, Qatar and Malaysia, counselling has become an accepted component of health and social services provision (Al-Issa 2000a). In these countries, exposure to Western ideas through trade, education, travel and the global media has resulted in the adoption of ideas about counselling and psychotherapy taken from European and North American sources.

Nevertheless, some leading Muslim psychologists have argued that it is essential to acknowledge the necessity to adapt therapeutic approaches to the needs and worldview of people who follow traditional Islamic teachings. Al-Issa (2000b) points out that there exists a rich history of Islamic psychiatry and psychotherapy, which pre-dates Western psychiatry, and which in general is more accepting of abnormal behaviour than its Western equivalent. As a result, counselling clients who have an Islamic cultural identity will bring into counselling distinct images and expectations regarding the role of the healer, and process of help.

Al-Abdul-Jabbar and Al-Issa (2000) also suggest that 'insight-oriented' approaches to therapy, and therapy that involves questioning parental values and behaviour, may be hard to accept for many Islamic clients brought up in a strongly patriarchal culture. They offer a case history of Nawal, a 28-year-old married woman who complained of being constantly anxious and losing control of her emotions. In therapy, Nawal disclosed that she had entered into an affair with another man, and was feeling guilty about this situation. The therapist used mainly open-ended questions to help the client to explore and reflect on her feelings and choices in this situation. However, her symptoms deteriorated the longer therapy continued. Al-Abdul-Jabbar and Al-Issa (2000: 280–1) reported that:

> At this stage, the therapist decided to use direct guidance to address her pressing problem. The therapist now considered the problem as an approach-avoidance conflict: she had to choose between keeping her despised husband or her lover. Although she was left to make the final choice, the therapist as a patriarch (i.e., representing the father) suggested the alternative that is compatible with societal demands (i.e., staying with her husband). The patient decided with the help of the therapist that having a stable and good social front with her husband was more valuable to her than pursuing her sensual needs. This decision was followed by a gradual disappearance of her symptoms.

Al-Abdul-Jabbar and Al-Issa (2000) propose that non-Muslim counsellors working with Muslim clients need to be aware of the importance of religious and collective values for these clients. They emphasize that the role of the counsellor must involve a willingness to be assertive, direct and advisory: 'the learning experience during therapy is "teacher-based" rather than "student-based"' (p. 283). The counsellor should also be able to express his or her own emotions, and to console the client. Finally, the counsellor should remember that the client is seeking to find solutions that strengthen their interdependence with other family members, rather than promoting independence and self-actualization:

> The emphasis is not on the client's individuality or personal beliefs, but on the extent to which they conform to accepted norms . . . there is no expectation that the client's behaviour must be consistent with their own personal beliefs. They are expected to express the common beliefs and behave in a socially acceptable fashion . . . The outcome of treatment is often assessed by the ability of the clients to carry out their social roles and meet their social obligations. The emotional states of the client are given less attention by the family than daily functioning.
>
> (Al-Abdul-Jabbar and Al-Issa (2000): 283)

The values expressed in this statement present a significant challenge for any of the mainstream Western therapies – psychodynamic, humanistic, cognitive–behavioural. In using ideas and methods derived from mainstream Western therapies, if what an Islamic counsellor was seeking to do was basically to attempt to deflect the clients away from their personal beliefs and emotions, and move in the direction of fulfilling their social obligations (as in the case of Nawal), their practice would appear to be quite different from anything that a Western counsellor might intend. Yet, at the same time, surely there are parallels between the principles of Islamic therapy described by Al-Abdul-Jabbar and Al-Issa (2000) and the theme of 'connectedness' highlighted by feminist therapists such as Jean Baker Miller and Judith Jordan (see Chapter 14). And the definition of counselling as an activity that gives the client an opportunity to 'explore, discover and clarify ways of living more satisfyingly and resourcefully' (see Chapter 1) would apply well enough to an Islamic as a Western approach.

The literature on Islamic therapy reviewed in Al-Issa (2000a) is perhaps best seen not as an instance of the straightforward application of Western ideas in a different cultural context, but as an instance of active appropriation by Islamic individuals and groups of an approach to helping that they have assimilated into their way of life, and have made their own. Further discussion of this topic can be found in Raiya and Pargament (2010) and Weatherhead and Daiches (2010).

Another strategy that has been adopted in order to make counselling available to 'minority' clients, has been to set up specialist agencies that appeal to specific disadvantaged groups. There is a wide array of agencies that have grown up to provide counselling to women, people from different ethnic and religious communities, gay and lesbian people and so on. These services are based on the recognition that many people will choose to see a counsellor who is similar to them. One of the difficulties these agencies face is that, usually, they are small and suffer recurring funding crises. They may also find it difficult to afford training and supervision. Nevertheless, there is plentiful evidence that people who identify strongly with a particular set of cultural experiences often do choose to consult counsellors and psychotherapists who share these experiences. On these grounds it can be argued that it is vitally important to maintain a diversity of counselling provision, and to find ways of encouraging the development of effective specialist agencies. A study by Netto *et al.* (2001), based in the Asian community in the UK, found that their informants reported many barriers to access to counselling agencies. Their report includes a list of recommendations of strategies that agencies might employ to enhance access for Asian clients.

There are several examples of counselling agencies that have carefully planned and designed their services to reflect the needs of the culturally diverse communities that they serve. For instance, the *Just Therapy* centre in New Zealand has developed a form of practice that is consistent with the separate and interlocking strands of Maori, Samoan and European culture within that society (Waldegrave *et al.* 2003). The *My Time* counselling service in Birmingham, UK, is an example of a highly successful counselling practice that has developed in response to the needs of a multi-ethnic community (Lilley 2007;

Lilley *et al.* 2005). The key to the success of both *Just Therapy* and *My Time* has been the creation of culturally diverse staff teams offering a range of services that encompass not only counselling/psychotherapy but also practical forms of help. In addition, both of these agencies have carefully considered the theoretical basis of their work, and have developed theoretically integrative approaches that are appropriate to their client populations, and the service goals.

Research into multicultural counselling

Racial and ethnic minority research continues to be significantly under-represented in the professional literature (Ponterotto 1988; Delgado-Romero *et al.* 2005). One of the topics that have received most attention has been the question of client–therapist ethnic matching: do clients benefit more from seeing a counsellor or psychotherapist with a similar ethnic background to their own?

Findings from some studies suggest that black clients seeking help from 'majority culture' agencies will drop out of treatment more quickly than white clients (Sattler 1977; Abramowitz and Murray 1983). Thompson and Alexander (2006) found that African American clients assigned to an African American counsellor reported more perceived benefit than those who had been allocated to a European American counsellor. There is also evidence that in these situations black clients receive more severe diagnostic labels and are more likely than white clients to be offered drug treatment rather than therapy, or to be referred to a non-professional counsellor rather than a professional (Atkinson 1985).

Research studies have also shown that clients tend to prefer counsellors from the same ethnic group (Harrison 1975). In one study, Sue *et al.* (1991) checked the client files of 600,000 users of therapy services from the Los Angeles County Department of Mental Health between 1973 and 1988. Ethnic match between client and therapist was strongly associated with length of stay in treatment (i.e., fewer early drop-outs). For those clients whose primary language was not English, ethnic match was also associated with better therapy outcome. A systematic review of ten ethnic matching studies that had studied samples of African American and European American counsellors and clients in the USA, was carried out by Shin *et al.* (2005). This review found that overall, there were no differences between ethnically matched and unmatched therapist–client cases in terms of attrition (dropping out of therapy early), total number of sessions, or overall outcome at the end of therapy. However, Shin *et al.* (2005) noted that there were significant methodo-logical limitations in the students that they were able to identify, particularly around providing information on the basis on which matching was carried out. Also, within the studies included in their review, there were wide differences in findings, with some studies showing that matched clients did better, and other studies showing that there was more benefit for unmatched clients.

More recent research by Farsimadan *et al.* (2007), and a review by Farsimadan *et al.* (2011) have found that ethnic matching is associated with a stronger therapeutic alliance and outcomes, whereas mismatch tends to lead to a poorer alliance and less satisfactory outcomes. It seems likely that the somewhat ambiguous results of studies of ethnic matching can be explained in terms of counsellor multicultural competence. Owen *et al.*

(2012) and Imel *et al.* (2011) carried out research into the outcomes of counselling in situations where therapists saw some clients with similar ethnic backgrounds to their own and other clients with different ethnic backgrounds. Overall, there was a tendency for therapists to do better with clients who were culturally similar to them. However, in both studies there were big differences in the cross-cultural effectiveness of counsellors. Some of the counsellors in these studies were equally effective with matched and non-matched clients, whereas others only appeared to be able to work effectively with matched clients. These findings suggest that the mixed results in ethnic matching research may be attributable to the proportion of culturally competent counsellors included in the study: if most of the counsellors in a study are culturally competent, the 'matching effect' disappears. It is important to note, in this context, that in both the Owen *et al.* (2012) and Imel *et al.* (2011) studies, it was possible to differentiate between general counselling competence and specific cultural competence.

Research into the processes occurring in multicultural counselling have been described earlier in this chapter (e.g., Wade and Bernstein 1991; Thompson and Jenal 1994). There have also been several studies of client and therapist experiences of doing or receiving counselling with a person from a different cultural background (Thompson *et al.* 2004; Chang and Berk 2009; Chang and Yoon 2011; Ward 2005). In these studies, ethnic minority clients reported that they believed counselling could potentially be valuable for them, but believed that there were barriers to accessing therapy services, and that therapists were insensitive to their experience. Burkard *et al.* (2006) interviewed therapists about their experience of working with clients from different cultural backgrounds, and found that, for these practitioners, being open about differences appeared to be an effective strategy for building a constructive therapeutic relationship.

Box 13.9: *Microaggression: the invisible dynamics of cultural difference*

An important research-based development in multicultural theory and practice in recent years has focused on the phenomenon of *microaggression*: 'brief and commonplace daily verbal, behavioral, or environmental indignities, whether intentional or unintentional, that communicate hostile, derogatory, or negative racial slights and insults toward people of color' (Sue *et al.* 2007: 271). Three forms of microaggression can be identified: *microassault* (use of racist language or active discrimination against members of ethnic minority groups); *microinsult* (example: a minority employee is asked 'how did you get that job?'); and *microinvalidation* (nullifying the reality of the target person, for example by telling them they have over-reacted if they comment on having been subjected to negative attitudes).

Sue *et al.* (2008) suggest that members of low-status cultural groups are exposed to excluding and wounding responses on an everyday basis in ways that are largely outside of conscious awareness. The implication for counselling is that this kind of interaction occurs within the counselling sessions, and that counsellors may not be aware that it is occurring. It seems clear that microaggression undermines the establishment of productive and trusting counselling relationships.

To counteract this tendency, counsellors need to examine not only their attitudes and knowledge around cultural issues, but also the subtle ways in which they interact with people from different cultural groups. The existence of microaggressive interactions makes it possible to make sense of why it is hard to define how and why cross-cultural counselling can go wrong, and why it is hard for counsellors to fix things. The concept of microaggression draws attention to the fact that difficulties in cross-cultural interaction are not so much a question of *difference* but of *status*. It is not that one person just does not understand the other person. What is happening, instead, is that he or she implicitly believes that they are superior to the other. Microaggression occurs not only in situations of ethnic or cultural difference, but also in situations where differences are defined by gender, age, disability status, sexual orientation and other dimensions.

Conclusions

Each cultural group contains its own approach to understanding and supporting people with emotional and psychological problems. Counsellors can draw upon these resources, such as traditional healers, religious groups and social networks, when working with clients. The possibility of integrating indigenous and Western counselling approaches, to create a model of help that is tailored to meet the needs of a specific client group, offers great promise as a means of extending and renewing the practice and profession of counselling.

Multicultural counselling has received relatively little attention in the research literature. In addition, many counselling agencies and individual counsellors in private practice have so many clients applying from their majority cultural group that there is little incentive for them to develop expertise in multicultural work. The multicultural nature of contemporary society, and the existence of large groups of dispossessed exiles and refugees experiencing profound hopelessness and loss, make this an increasingly important area for future investment in theory, research and practice. There exist well-established guidelines for training and practice in culturally informed counselling. The espousal of a more culturally oriented approach to counselling represents an ongoing challenge to mainstream traditions in therapy, which persist in operating on the basis of a largely individualized and psychologized concept of the person, in which social and cultural factors are only of peripheral interest.

Topics for reflection and discussion

1 It can be argued that mainstream approaches to counselling (psychodynamic, person-centred, cognitive–behavioural) are so intrinsically bound up with Western assumptions about human nature that they are just not relevant to people from traditional, non-Western cultures. Do you agree?

2 How would you describe your own cultural identity? What stage of development have you attained, in relation to your cultural identity? How does your cultural identity influence your approach to counselling? For example, does it lead you to prefer to employ some ideas and techniques rather than others? Does it lead you to be more comfortable, or effective, with some clients than with others?

3 How justified was Paul Pedersen, in 1991, in suggesting that multiculturalism should be regarded as a 'fourth force'? To what extent has his vision of a multicultural counselling been supported by events over the past 20 years?

4 Reflect on the way that counselling agencies operate in your town or city. If appropriate, collect any leaflets that they use to advertise their services. How sensitive to multicultural issues are these agencies? What effect might their attitude to multiculturalism have on the clients who use their service, and on the way they are perceived in the community?

5 Is racism the real issue? Is there a danger that the term 'multicultural' might distract attention from the experiences of violence, oppression and expropriation that are caused by the ideology of racism?

6 Identify a culture-bound syndrome that is of particular interest for you, either because you have had some contact with that culture, or because you work with clients from that community. In what ways does the syndrome itself, and the indigenous therapies associated with it, reflect the beliefs and values of the culture within which they are embedded? In what ways does the study of this culture-bound syndrome enrich your understanding of the counselling process and relationship within your own cultural group?

Suggested further reading

There are two texts, which offer extended coverage of the themes introduced in this chapter, and are highly recommended. The *Handbook of Transcultural Counselling and Psychotherapy*, edited by Colin Lago (2011) offers a mainly British perspective. The *Handbook of Multicultural Counseling*, edited by Joseph Ponterotto and colleagues (2010) includes mainly North American authors. Valuable collections of papers on cultural issues in counselling have been assembled by Palmer (2002) and Moodley and Palmer (2006). An excellent summary of types of therapy in different cultures, and how they might be combined, can be found in Tseng (1999). The issue of how to integrate indigenous or culture-specific therapeutic procedures into 'mainstream' counselling approaches is a topic that has attracted a great deal of interest. Fascinating accounts of this type of work are available in Gielin *et al.* (2004) and Moodley and West (2005). An accessible and stimulating, but also carefully referenced, exploration of the relationship between culture and mental health is *Crazy Like Us: The Globalization of the Western Psyche*, by Ethan Watters (2010).

CHAPTER 14

Feminist therapy

Introduction

Feminist perspectives have represented one of the most significant areas of advance in counselling theory and practice over the past 20 years. The role of gender in counselling and psychotherapy has been the source of a great deal of important new theory and research. This work has explored three main areas of interest: the development of a feminist approach to counselling and psychotherapy; the impact on process and outcome of the gender match (or mismatch) of counsellor and client; and the creation of counselling models appropriate to specific areas of women's experience. The aim of this chapter is to provide an introduction to feminist counselling. First, the origins of this counselling orientation in feminist philosophy are described. This is followed by an account of how these ideas have been used to critique existing mainstream approaches to therapy. This critique sets the scene for a discussion of the nature of feminist counselling, and a review of the implications of this approach for theory, practice and research.

The basic assumption of feminism is that, in the great majority of cultures, women are systematically oppressed and exploited. Howell (1981) describes this state of affairs as 'the cultural devaluation of women'; other people would label it as 'sexism'. The ways in which a male-dominated social order is created and maintained have been subjected to critical analysis by many feminist scholars. A language for describing and understanding the experience of women has been created, leading to the development of new forms of practice, social action and institutions that have the aim of empowering women.

Within the broad social and political tradition of feminism there exist a number of discrete strands of thought. Enns (1992) has divided the 'complex, overlapping and fluid' perspectives that operate within feminism into four main feminist traditions: liberal, cultural, radical and socialist. *Liberal* feminism can be regarded as the 'mainstream' feminist tradition, and has its roots in the struggle of the Suffragettes to gain equal rights and access. *Cultural* feminism, by contrast, has placed greater emphasis on recognizing and celebrating the distinctive experience of being a woman and promoting the 'feminization' of society through legitimating the importance of life-affirming values such as cooperation, harmony, acceptance of intuition and altruism. *Radical* feminism centres on a systematic challenge to the structures and beliefs associated with male power or patriarchy, and the division of social life into separate male and female domains. Finally, *socialist* feminism is derived from a core belief that, although oppression may be influenced by gender, it is determined at a more fundamental level by social class and race. For socialist feminists, the fulfilment of human potential will only be possible when issues of control over production and capital, and the class system, have been adequately addressed. These groupings within the feminist movement have evolved different goals, methods and solutions, and have tended to apply themselves to different sets of problems.

It is essential to acknowledge that feminism is a complex and evolving system of thought and social action. Nevertheless, it is possible to identify a set of core beliefs concerning self and society that would receive broad support from the majority of feminist-oriented counsellors. In this vein, Llewelyn and Osborne (1983) have argued that feminist therapy is built on four basic assumptions about the social experience of women.

1   Women are consistently in a position of deference to men. For example, women tend to have less power or status in work situations. The leading feminist therapist, Jean Baker Miller (1987) argued that women who seek to be powerful rather than passive are viewed as selfish, destructive and unfeminine.

2   Women are expected to be aware of the feelings of others, and to supply emotional nurturing to others, especially men.

3   Women are expected to be 'connected' to, and controlled by men, so that the achievement of autonomy is difficult.

4   The issue of sexuality is enormously problematic for women. This factor arises from a social context in which images of idealized women's bodies are used to sell commodities, assertive female sexuality is threatening to many men and sexual violence against women is widespread.

It is possible to see that these statements map out a distinctive agenda for feminist counselling. None of the topics highlighted by Llewelyn and Osborne (1983) is given any significant emphasis in theories of counselling such as psychodynamic, person-centred or cognitive–behavioural. The agenda of a feminist-inspired counselling brings into the counselling arena an awareness of social and economic realities, the meaning of the body and the centrality of power in relationships that is quite unique within the counselling and psychotherapy world. The first task of those women committed to putting this agenda into action was to clear themselves a space, to show how and why the ways of doing therapy that prevailed in the 1960s and 1970s were just not good enough.

The feminist critique of psychotherapy theory and practice

Virtually all of the key historical figures in counselling and psychotherapy have been men, and they have written, whether consciously or not, from a male perspective. There have been extensive efforts by women writers and practitioners to envision theories and approaches in counselling and psychotherapy that are more consistent with the experiences and needs of women. Many of these efforts were inspired by the consolidation of feminism in the 1960s as a central force for social change. The work of feminist authors such as Simone de Beauvoir, Germaine Greer, Kate Millett and others encouraged female psychologists and therapists to look again at established ideas in these disciplines. It would be mistaken to assume, however, that women had no voice at all in counselling and psychotherapy before that time. Within the psychoanalytic movement, Melanie Klein and Karen Horney had played a crucial role in emphasizing the part of the mother in child development. Other women therapists, such as Laura Perls, Zerka Moreno and Virginia Axline, had been important contributors to the founding of gestalt therapy, psychodrama and client-centred therapy respectively, but had received much less attention than the men alongside whom they had worked.

The field of mental health affords multiple examples of the oppression and exploitation of women. There is ample evidence of experimentation on and sexual abuse of women clients and patients (Appignanesi 2008; Masson 1984; Showalter 1985). Studies of perceptions of mental health in women have shown that mental health workers view women in general as more neurotic and less well adjusted than men (Broverman *et al.* 1970). The psychiatric and mental health professions, which provide the intellectual and institutional context for counselling and psychotherapy, can be seen to be no less sexist than any other sector of society. It is therefore necessary to recognize that the occurrence of patriarchal and sexist attitudes and practices in counselling and psychotherapy are not merely attributable to the mistaken ideas of individual theorists such as Freud, but have been part of the taken-for-granted background to most mental health care.

The evolution of feminist counselling and psychotherapy has involved a powerful re-examination of theoretical assumptions, particularly those of psychoanalysis, from a feminist point of view. Two of the fundamental ideas in psychoanalysis have received special attention: the concept of penis envy, and the formulation of childhood sexuality. The notion of penis envy was used by Freud to explain the development of femininity in girls. Freud supposed that when a little girl first saw a penis, she would be 'overcome by envy' (Freud 1905/1977). As a result of this sense of inferiority, the girl would recognize that:

> this is a point on which she cannot compete with boys, and that it would be therefore best for her to give up the idea of doing so. Thus the little girl's recognition of the anatomical distinction between the sexes forces her away from masculinity and masculine masturbation on to new lines which lead to the development of femininity.

> (Freud 1924/1977: 340)

These 'new lines' included a motivation to look attractive to compensate for the missing penis, and a tendency to a less mature type of moral sensitivity due to the absence of castration anxiety, which Freud saw as such an important element in male moral development.

From a contemporary perspective the penis envy hypothesis seems incredible, ludicrous and objectionable. However, such was the domination of Freud that this doctrine remained in force within the psychoanalytic movement for many years after his death (Howell 1981). It was only in the writings of Mitchell (1974) that a thorough critique of this aspect of Freudian theory was carried out.

It is possible to regard the penis envy hypothesis as an example of a lack of understanding of women in Freudian theory, an ill-conceived idea that can be reviewed and corrected without threat to the theory as a whole. The other main feminist objection to psychoanalysis is, however, much more fundamental. In the early years of psychoanalysis, Freud had worked with a number of women patients who had reported memories of distressing sexual experiences that had taken place in their childhood. Freud was uncertain how to interpret these memories, but in the end came to the conclusion that the childhood events that these women were reporting could not have taken place. It has been claimed, by Masson (1984) and others, that Freud, in the end, could not believe that middle-class, socially respectable men could engage in this kind of behaviour. Freud therefore interpreted these reports as 'screen memories', or fantasies constructed to conceal the true nature of what had taken place, which was the acting out by the child of her own sexual motives. From a modern perspective, when so much more is known about the prevalence of child sexual abuse and the barriers of secrecy, collusion and adult disbelief that confront child victims, the classical Freudian approach to this issue can be seen to be deeply mistaken. Masson (1984), one of the leading critics of this aspect of Freudian theory, was driven to label this set of ideas an 'assault on truth'. Like so many aspects of Freud's work, the truth about what actually happened in Freud's work with these patients is open to alternative interpretations (Esterson 1998, 2002). Nevertheless, the consequences of the position that Freud took (interpreting 'scenes of seduction' described by patients as fantasies) were to be far-reaching in terms of systematic professional denial of the reality of victims of abuse. Through time, many women therapists came to agree with Taylor (1991: 96) that 'a careful reading of Freud's writings reveals that he thoroughly rejected women as full human beings'.

At a theoretical level, the feminist re-examination of psychoanalysis carried out by Mitchell (1974) and Eichenbaum and Orbach (1982, 1984) has been followed by a steady stream of publications devoted to integrating feminist principles with psychotherapeutic (usually psychodynamic) practice. These theoretical studies have involved carrying out a systematic critique of male-dominated approaches. The feminist critique of conventional sex therapy has drawn attention to the 'phallocentric' assumptions made by most sex therapists (Stock 1988; Tiefer 1988). Waterhouse (1993) provides a carefully argued feminist critique of the application of the person-centred approach with victims of sexual violence, pointing out that the Rogerian emphasis on personal responsibility, the authentic expression of feelings and empathy pays insufficient attention to the social and political reality of women's lives, and specifically to the effects of inequalities in power. Klein (1976) has argued that the methods used for evaluating the effectiveness of therapy do not adequately reflect feminist values and women's experience.

These are some of the ways in which feminist writers have contributed to a comprehensive critique of the dominant, male-oriented models of counselling. From and alongside this critique there has emerged an alternative body of feminist theory and practice.

Theory and practice of feminist counselling

The construction of a feminist model of counselling and psychotherapy has not been an easy matter. It is probably reasonable to suppose that the majority of counsellors who have been influenced by feminist ideas actually work in counselling agencies where they are not able to deliver 'pure' feminist therapy. These counsellors can perhaps do little more than work in feminist mode with those clients with whom it is applicable. This tendency is reflected in the contemporary literature on feminist counselling and psychotherapy, much of which is avowedly eclectic or integrative in nature, drawing on a variety of ideas and techniques already employed in the field. This version of feminist counselling is advocated in widely read texts such as those of Chaplin (1988) and Worell and Remer (2002). For example, Worell and Remer encourage their readers to evolve their own 'feminist-compatible' model, by examining the theory they presently employ in terms of the kinds of feminist principles and ideas discussed in earlier sections of this chapter. In effect, this approach constitutes a kind of feminist-informed integrationism.

Integrative feminist approaches have been successful in identifying the distinctive goals and characteristics of feminist practice. For example, many feminist practitioners would agree with the following guidelines (Worell 1981; Worell and Remer 2002), which suggest that a feminist approach should include:

- An egalitarian relationship with shared responsibility between counsellor and client. For example, being cautious about the imposition of interpretations on the client's experience.
- Using a consciousness-raising approach. For example, differentiating between personal problems and political or social issues.
- Helping women to explore and express their personal power.
- Helping women to identify their internalized sex-role messages and beliefs, replace sex-role stereotyped beliefs with more self-enhancing self-talk and develop a full range of behaviours that are freely chosen and not dictated by sex-role stereotypes.
- Enabling women to understand that individual women's experiences are common to all women.
- Helping women to get in touch with unexpressed anger.
- Assisting women to define themselves apart from their role relationships to men, home and children.
- Encouraging women to nurture themselves as well as others.
- Promoting skills development in areas such as assertiveness and employment.

Similar principles have been identified by Israeli and Santor (2000) in their analysis of 'effective components' of feminist therapy and by Hill and Ballou (1998) in a survey of feminist therapists. Tzou *et al.* (2012) provide an example of an integrative approach to feminist therapy, based on the Worell and Remer (2002) model, that was developed to address specific needs in women in a particular cultural group.

Box 14.1: *A feminist integrative approach to working with substance abuse*

A study by LaFave *et al.* (2008) used a combination of quantitative measures and qualitative interviews to evaluate treatment outcomes and perceived benefits of therapy in women with substance abuse problems who attended a feminist-oriented centre, 'A Woman's Place'. This report is of particular interest because it represents a flexible, integrative approach using feminist ideas alongside well-established substance abuse interventions such as motivational techniques and solution-focused therapy. The therapy programme that was on offer placed a strong emphasis on collaborative working and client empowerment. These therapeutic elements were reflected in the themes that emerged in interviews with clients at the end of therapy, who consistently mentioned the importance of the fact that the therapy they were offered gave them the opportunity to make their own choices and take responsibility for their own lives:

> I didn't have choices before. I didn't feel like I did. I knew that I had to get stoned and . . . that I had to drink liquor and beer to be able to cope with life and cope with [my boyfriend] and the kids. You know, that was my only choice. I didn't have any other choice but to stay wasted.
>
> (LaFave *et al.* 2008: 61)

What comes across very powerfully in this study is the extent to which feminist values made it possible for a team of counsellors to create an environment in which women were able to talk about the things that really concerned them, and actively expand their repertoire of coping strategies, rather than being passive recipients of a 'one size fits all' treatment package.

The Stone Center model of feminist counselling: relational–cultural therapy

Worell and Remer (2002) present an integrationist approach to constructing a feminist therapy. The other route towards a feminist model of counselling and psychotherapy has been to attempt to create a free-standing set of ideas and methods that is internally consistent and can be not only disseminated through training but also the focus of research. One group that has pursued this strategy consists of the network of practitioners associated with the Women's Therapy Centre in London (established 1976) and the Women's Therapy Centre Training Institute (established in New York in 1981). These organizations have developed a form of feminist psychoanalytic practice that is expressed in the writings of Luise Eichenbaum and Susie Orbach (Eichenbaum and Orbach 1982) and their colleagues (Gutwill *et al.*

2010). An informative and accessible study of the experiences of women who have received therapy from the Women's Therapy Centre can be found in Morris (2005).

The group that has been most successful in articulating a specific feminist approach to therapy is the team based at the Stone Center and Jean Baker Miller Training Institute at Wellesley College, in Cambridge, Massachusetts, drawing on the work of key figures such as Miller (1976), Chodorow (1978) and Gilligan (1982).

The theoretical framework developed by Miller and her colleagues has sought to make sense of the psychological dimensions of the social inequality and powerlessness experienced by women through the use of a core concept of 'relatedness' or 'self-in-relation' (Miller 1976). In her study of gender differences in moral reasoning, for example, Gilligan (1982) found that, in general, men make moral judgements based on criteria of fairness and rights, whereas women assess moral dilemmas according to a sense of responsibility in relationships. The male way of looking at things, in Gilligan's (1982) words, 'protects separateness', and the female way 'sustains connections'. Gilligan goes on from this finding to suggest that men and women use different styles of constructing social reality: men fear intimacy, women fear isolation.

Miller (Miller, A. 1976), Kaplan (1987) and other members of the Stone Center group have explored the implications of this 'relational' perspective for understanding patterns of development in childhood. They conclude that there is a basic difference between social development in boys and girls. For a girl, the relationship with the primary caretaker, the mother, is one of mutuality. Both are the same sex, both are engaged in, or preparing to be engaged in (Chodorow 1978), the tasks of mothering and nurturing. For boys the situation is one of achieving development and maturity only through increasing separation and autonomy from the mother. Men, as a result, are socialized into a separate, isolated way of being, and in counselling need help to understand and maintain relationships. Women, by contrast, spend their formative years in a world of relationships and connectedness, and in counselling seek help to achieve autonomy and also, crucially, to secure affirmation for their relatedness. The approach to therapy that has emerged from this perspective on human development has been summarized by Jordan *et al.* (1991) and Jordan (2000) in terms of a set of core ideas:

- people grow through and towards relationships throughout the lifespan;
- movement towards mutuality rather than movement towards separation characterizes mature functioning;
- relational differentiation and elaboration characterize growth;
- mutual empathy and mutual empowerment are at the core of growth-fostering relationships;
- in growth-fostering relationships, all people contribute and grow or benefit, development is not a one-way street;
- therapy relationships are characterized by a special kind of mutuality;
- mutual empathy is the vehicle for change in therapy;
- real engagement and therapeutic authenticity are necessary for the development of mutual empathy.

The basic assumptions that inform this approach have been summed up by Jordan (2004: 11) in the following terms:

> . . . the yearning for and movement toward connection are seen as central organizing factors in people's lives and the experience of chronic disconnection or isolation is seen as a primary source of suffering . . . When we cannot represent ourselves authentically in relationships, when our real experience is not heard or responded to by the other person, then we must falsify, detach from, or suppress our response . . . a sense of isolation, immobilization, self-blame and relational competence develops. These meaning systems and relational images of incompetence and depletion interfere with our capacity to be productive, as well as to be in a creative relationship.

More recent work of the Stone Center group has emphasized the *cultural* as well as interpersonal aspects of the experience of 'chronic disconnection', for example in such arenas as racism, the workplace, and family life (Jordan *et al.* 2004).

The Stone Center emphasis on the *relational* nature of women's development has led to a re-examination of some elements in the counselling process: empathy, mutuality, dependency, caring. Jordan (1991) points out that male-dominated therapy theory has tended to emphasize the goal of developing 'ego strength', defined in terms of strong boundaries between self and other. By contrast, the feminist notion of the relational self implies much more of a sense of interconnectedness between persons. This connection is maintained through a capacity to respond empathically to the other, and the concept of empathy is therefore a central element of the Stone Center approach. However, a distinctive aspect of the use of empathy within this approach to therapy is that it takes into account the empathic sensitivity of the client as well as that of the counsellor. In the classical Rogerian 'core conditions' model (Chapter 7), empathy is regarded as a counsellor-supplied condition that can facilitate understanding and self-acceptance on the part of the client. In the Stone Center theory, empathy is viewed as a fundamental characteristic of women's ways of knowing and relating. As a result, the client's empathic engagement with others, including with the counsellor, is one of the key areas for exploration in this type of counselling (Jordan 1997a). In recent years, the approach to therapy that originated from the Stone Center has become known as *relational–cultural therapy* (Walker and Rosen 2004), to acknowledge that effective practice requires attention to relationships within a cultural context.

Relational–cultural theory suggests that women are typically socialized into taking care of others, and participate in relationships where they give empathy but find it difficult to receive it back. The experience of mutuality is therefore one of the areas that relational–cultural counselling seeks to examine. As Jordan (1991: 96) puts it: 'in intersubjective mutuality . . . we not only find the opportunity of extending our understanding of the other, we also enhance awareness of ourselves'.

One of the key goals of counselling is to enable the client to become more able to participate in relationships marked by high levels of mutuality. Mutuality is also expressed in the counselling relationship itself, with feminist counsellors being willing to be 'real', self-disclosing and actively helpful in the counselling room (Jordan 2000). That mutuality, based on the counsellor's willingness to let the client see how she is affected by what the client is going through, helps clients to 'develop a realistic awareness of the impact of their actions and words on other people and on relationships'(Jordan 2000: 1015).

The theme of connectedness in relational–cultural theory is also applied through a reappraisal of the concept of dependency. In the counselling and psychotherapy literature as a whole, this quality is generally considered to reflect an inability on the part of the person to take adequate control of their own life. Many men find dependency threatening to their self-esteem (Stiver 1991a). From a feminist perspective, however, dependency is a basic aspect of everyday experience. The fact that it is pathologized by mental health professionals can be seen as another example of the dominance of patriarchal attitudes. In an effort to highlight the life-enhancing and constructive aspects of dependency, Stiver (1991a: 160) defines it as 'a process of counting on other people to provide help in coping physically and emotionally with the experiences and tasks encountered in the world when one has not sufficient skill, confidence, energy and/or time'. She adds that the experience of self can be 'enhanced and empowered through the very process of counting on others for help'. 'Healthy' dependency can be regarded as providing opportunities for growth and development.

Stiver (1991b) draws out some of the implications for counselling practice of a relational–cultural perspective on the concept of care. For her, traditional psychodynamic approaches to counselling and psychotherapy have been based on a principle of establishing relational distance between counsellor and client, in order to promote objectivity. Stiver argues that this is essentially a masculine model, which does not work well for women (or for some men), and proposes that counsellors should be willing to demonstrate that they care about their clients, that they express 'an emotional investment in the other person's well-being' (Stiver (1991b: 265).

This is a necessarily oversimplified account of a complex and powerful theoretical model. Nevertheless, it can be seen that it points the way towards a distinctive approach to feminist counselling. Relational–cultural theory places a psychodynamic theory of development alongside a person-centred understanding of the therapeutic relationship, but has reinterpreted both sets of ideas from a feminist perspective that looks at therapy as part of a social and cultural environment characterized by male domination. The notion of the relational, connected self serves as a way of effectively bridging these theoretical domains. The relational–cultural model has also been used to construct an analysis of the ways that women mask their power and anger (Miller 1991a, 1991b), and to develop a model of women's depression (Stiver and Miller 1997).

Another important theme running through the work of this group has been an appreciation of women's problems in the world of work, in environments where mutual, empathic, caring relationships are difficult to sustain. Recent writings have focused on the application of the model to ethnic minority and lesbian women (Jordan 1997b), substance abuse, therapy in prisons, and group therapy (Walker and Rosen (2004), the dynamics of power in relationships (Jordan 2008), self-injury (Trepal 2010), schools counselling (Tucker *et al.* 2011) and eating disorders (Trepal *et al.* 2012). Finally, it is important to note that, even though the relational–cultural model derives from the collaboration of a specific group of counsellors and psychotherapists, it nevertheless reflects many of the ideas and themes apparent in the writings of other feminist therapists: for example, the work of Taylor (1990, 1991, 1995, 1996) and the psychodynamic feminist approach represented by Lawrence and Maguire (1997).

Box 14.2: *Mutuality in feminist counselling*

After I had pursued a fleeting and fragile alliance with a fearful young female client, she revealed to me that she was not comfortable trusting me because she knew little about me and asked why she should have to reveal herself if I was not willing to do the same. I asked her what she would like to know that she did not know. She did not have an answer at that moment but said she would think about it.

One of the client's abiding concerns was her fear of the death of one or both of her parents. This fear, together with other stressors, resulted in a chronic, cyclical pattern of depressed mood. Three weeks after the aforementioned incident, my client asked me if I had ever lost a parent. I examined my immediate impulse, which was to inquire about why the client needed to know this. After a moment of deliberation, I decided to answer rather than inquire about her need to know. I already knew her meaning. She wanted to hear that someone who had survived this kind of loss could not only survive, but thrive. I gave her my reply, 'Yes, I have lost both of them.'

Tears appeared in my client's eyes, and she replied, 'That must feel very lonely to you sometimes'. Tearfully also, I replied, 'Yes. However, I learned to grieve, to move on and to bring other important people into my life'. We had a moment in which my client's isolation with her issues of loss was shattered and in which she felt the power and validation of her ability to empathize with me. I then added, 'And I believe that you also will learn to do that when the time comes'. Our focus then returned to my client and her fears. However, since that moment we had an alliance that permitted us to progress faster in a few weeks than we had in the previous several months.

I chose that intervention deliberately, based on therapeutic intent rather than personal need. I allowed my client to see my experience, which in turn gave her permission to reveal her own . . . In addition to allowing the client the opportunity to experience mutuality, the discrete use of counselor self-disclosure seems to promote the goal of feminist therapy that client and therapist remain as equal as possible on the power dimension.

Source: Nelson (1996: 343)

Radical feminist therapy

While being explicitly relational in emphasis, relational–cultural therapy concentrates mainly on the psychological processes surrounding relationships with immediate significant others, such as parents, siblings, partners and work colleagues. It is a model that shares the psychodynamic preoccupation with the relationship between mother and child, even if it then extracts a quite different understanding of the dynamics of that relationship. Miller, Jordan, Stiver and other relational–cultural practitioners start with intimacy, and then work out towards society. Radical feminist therapy, by contrast, is primarily interested in the social and material circumstances in which women live. It starts with the social, and works back from that to arrive at an appreciation of possibilities for intimate relationships.

Perhaps the clearest account of radical feminist therapy can be found in the writing of Burstow (1992). When Burstow reviews the experience of women in contemporary society, the major theme that emerges for her is violence. The fundamental assumptions around which her approach to counselling and therapy is based are:

> 1 Women are violently reduced to bodies that are for-men, and those bodies are then further violated.
> 2 Violence is absolutely integral to our experience as women.
> 3 Extreme violence is the context in which other violence occurs and gives meaning to the other forms, with which it inevitably interacts.
> 4 All women are subject to extreme violence at some time or live with the threat of extreme violence.
>
> (Burstow 1992: xv)

Childhood sexual abuse, rape and physical abuse are obvious examples of violence against women. Psychiatric treatment is a less obvious example. Depression, cutting, dissociation/splitting and problems with eating can be regarded as forms of women's responses to violence.

Radical feminist therapy understands the socialization of women as a process that is shaped by the domination of women by men, the power of men over women and the sexualization of women. A woman's experience of her body, as a sexualized object, is therefore a central topic for exploration in therapy. MacKinnon (1982: 16–17) explains the radical feminist view:

> the female gender stereotype is . . . in fact, sexual. Vulnerability means the appearance/reality of easy sexual access; passivity means disabled resistance, enforced by trained physical weakness; softness means pregnability by something hard. Incompetence seeks help as vulnerability seeks shelter, inviting the embrace that becomes the invasion . . . Socially, femaleness means femininity, which means attractiveness, which means sexual availability on male terms. Gender socialization is the process through which women internalize themselves as sexual beings, as beings that exist for men . . . Women who resist or fail, including those who never did fit – for example, Black and lower-class women who cannot survive if they are soft and weak and incompetent, assertively self-respecting women, women with ambitions of male dimensions – are considered less female, lesser women.

The argument here is that the image of women as sexual objects, as 'beings that exist for men', is at the heart of women's gender roles, even though it may be overlaid by liberal rhetoric.

The application of these ideas in radical feminist practice is illustrated by the kinds of questions that Burstow (1992: 44–5) suggests a feminist counsellor or therapist should ask herself on first meeting a new client. For example, Burstow would observe whether the woman looked exhausted or frightened, wore make up, high heels and tight clothing, or was extremely thin. These questions yield information about how oppressed the client might be. For example, a woman who wore lipstick, mascara, high heels and tight clothes could be considered to be overtly 'sexualized'. The aim of radical feminist therapy is to help the client to identify the ways in which she is oppressed, and to be empowered to bring about change. Often, the kinds of change processes that the client will be encouraged to pursue may well involve different forms of community action, and generally becoming more 'woman-identified'.

Radical feminist therapy also necessarily involves questioning the role of mainstream therapies in supporting oppressive attitudes. This is expressed particularly forcefully by McLellan (1999: 336):

> The institution of psychotherapy needs practitioners who have the courage to be fiercely independent of mainstream society, rather than its servants. Positioning ourselves apart from mainstream attitudes and culture allows us to analyse the socio-political dynamics of individual personal distress in a more objective way . . . and recognise the role of mystification and oppression . . . when honesty and the pursuit of justice are central to a therapist's work, emotional and psychological health is made possible.

A key concept here is the idea of *mystification*: the ideas and beliefs that are promoted by those in power are assimilated by those without power, in ways that lead them to deny the truth of their situation.

Box 14.3: *A feminist approach to depression*

From a feminist perspective, depression can be understood as a form of silencing, through which women's responses to oppressive social practices are suppressed (Jack 1991; Jack and Ali 2010). There are two therapeutic principles that have informed feminist counselling for depression. The first is to use women as a guide to what might be useful, rather than rely on general theoretical models. An example of using women as a guide is a study by Wilson and Giddings (2010), which collected women's stories of recovery from depression as a means of building a framework for counselling practice. The second therapeutic principle is to recognize that overcoming depression requires practical action (in relation to issues such as housing, employment, debt, education, parenting and domestic violence) as well as psychological insight. An example of a feminist approach to depression that combines practical action alongside personal development is the Feminist Relational Advocacy project (Goodman *et al.* 2009), in which low-income women who were depressed were paired with counsellor–advocates. In their analysis of follow-up interviews with clients, Goodman *et al.* (2009: 858) concluded that:

> . . . advocates could not be effective in addressing pragmatic needs unless they listened carefully and responded authentically . . . a problematic aspect of social services in general is the artificial separation of mental health interventions aimed at a woman's internal distress and advocacy interventions aimed at her external situation.

The findings of this study provided substantial evidence for the view that internalized oppression and external oppression are inextricably interlinked, and that moving on from depression requires attention to both at the same time.

The development of a feminist ethics for counselling practice

The practice of feminist counselling or psychotherapy involves the practitioner in acting not only from a therapeutic standpoint, but also espousing a set of values and a political agenda. This position has led most feminist counsellors to be highly aware of the ethical dilemmas arising from their work:

- Critics of feminism may accuse feminist practitioners of misusing the therapeutic relationship to promote feminist ideology or recruit members for feminist organizations.

- The political dimension of feminism makes women aware of power inequalities in general, but specifically the power difference inherent in any client–counsellor relationship.

- Feminist counsellors and psychotherapists and their clients may be drawn from relatively small communities of like-minded women, leading to greater possibilities for potentially destructive dual relationships.

- Women's moral decision-making makes use of intuition and feeling as well as logical analysis, and takes account of how moral actions have an impact on relationships. As a result, there are times when ethical codes and guidelines formulated from a male perspective may not be wholly appropriate to feminist practice.

- There can be occasions when the emphasis in feminist counselling theory on mutuality and the existence of a genuine, transparent relationship between counsellor and client may contribute to a lack of clarity in therapeutic boundaries.

These factors map out a significant area of difference between feminist practice and mainstream thinking, and have stimulated considerable debate within the feminist therapy literature.

It is important to note here that feminist counselling and psychotherapy has largely evolved in isolation from mainstream organizational and institutional settings. For many feminists, the office blocks of professional power and authority represent patriarchal structures to be subverted and opposed. As Wooley (1994: 320–1) has written, the experience of being a feminist practitioner can be similar to that of professional 'outlaw':

> many of our most fundamental values and sensibilities are at variance with the way things are 'supposed' to be . . . most female therapists have an assortment of fears related to the way they have quietly, often secretly, diverged from the dictates of their training and the official version of psychotherapy.

Taylor (1995: 109) perhaps expressed the same feelings when she wrote that: 'I reached the point in my work as a psychotherapist where I could no longer stand apart from my women clients and play dumb'. It is this unwillingness to be detached, to 'stand apart', that lies at the heart of the feminist ethical dilemma.

Feminist counsellors and psychotherapists have addressed these ethical issues in two ways. First, a great deal of feminist counselling takes place in the context of 'collective' feminist organizations, such as women's therapy centres or rape crisis centres. Typically, members of these organizations are well aware of moral and ethical dilemmas associated with feminist practice, and set up effective mechanisms for reviewing the operation of their agency in the light of such issues. Second, there have been some attempts to create a feminist ethical code. The following sections are part of the ethical guidelines used by the Feminist Therapy Institute in Denver, Colorado (Rave and Larsen 1995: 40–1):

> A feminist therapist increases her accessibility to and for a wide range of clients . . . through flexible delivery of services. Where appropriate, the feminist therapist assists clients in accessing other services.
>
> A feminist therapist discloses information to the client which facilitates the therapeutic process. The therapist is responsible for using self-disclosure with purpose and discretion in the interests of the client.
>
> A feminist therapist is actively involved in her community. As a result, she is especially sensitive about confidentiality. Recognizing that her clients' concerns and general well-being are primary, she self-monitors both public and private statements and comments.
>
> A feminist therapist actively questions other therapeutic practices in her community that appear abusive to clients or therapists, and when possible, intervenes.
>
> A feminist therapist seeks multiple avenues for impacting change, including public education and advocacy within professional organizations, lobbying for legislative actions and other appropriate activities.

These guidelines offer a useful supplement to the ethical codes published by established professional associations. The latter tend to focus mainly on the ethical implications of direct work with clients, and the impact of this work on immediate family members and significant others. The feminist code, by contrast, stresses the importance for counsellors of keeping in mind their broader social responsibilities and roles.

Box 14.4: *Becoming a feminist therapist*

There are few training programmes in feminist counselling and psychotherapy, and feminist ideas tend to be ignored or given scant respect in most training institutes and courses. It is therefore difficult for beginning counsellors and psychotherapists who find meaning in feminist perspectives, to obtain the support and guidance that is required in order to develop an identity as feminist practitioners. Studies by Horne *et al.* (2001) and Kannan and Levitt (2009) have analysed the personal accounts of counselling and psychotherapy trainees who have identified themselves as feminist. One participant in the Horne *et al.* (2001) study reported that 'I knew that feminism was something that I believed in but it was so hard to see how I could be a part of it. It seemed like something so far away from me. Well, how do I do that? Is this something I can look up in the phone book?' (p. 12). In addition to isolation and lack of information (there is unlikely to be an entry under 'F' for 'feminism' in any phone book), another key theme that emerged from these stories was the importance of finding a mentor, not only as a role model but also to act as a buffer against hostile anti-feminist remarks from colleagues and tutors.

Conclusions: the contribution of feminism to counselling and psychotherapy

Feminist counselling is a relatively recent addition to the range of therapy models on offer. It is an approach that fundamentally transforms, subverts and radicalizes therapy, by placing practice firmly and explicitly within a contact of social action and change. The progress of feminist counselling and psychotherapy over the past 20 years has been impressive, given the fact that it represents a radical perspective that is not likely to find any special favour in male-dominated universities and government agencies. There has been an explosion of new ideas and methods, books, and applications of feminist approaches to different client groups. Feminist practitioners have been in the vanguard of the movement to make counselling more socially aware and user-friendly. Feminist theory has provided a philosophical, historical and social dimension that has enabled feminist counselling to move beyond a purely psychological, individualized view of the person. Many counsellors (including male counsellors) have been influenced by these ideas and principles. At the same time, there appears to have been little research into feminist counselling and psychotherapy. The absence of research evidence may, in the longer term, have the effect of excluding feminist therapy from settings, such as health agencies, that increasingly will only support 'evidence-based' approaches.

Topics for reflection and discussion

1   How important do you believe that gender issues are, in relation to both the client–counsellor relationship, and the issues that clients want to work on?

2   What are the implications of feminist ideas for male counsellors and clients?

3   To what extent is feminist counselling only appropriate or helpful for women who already hold feminist beliefs? Does feminist counselling necessarily imply conversion to a feminist way of thinking?

Suggested further reading

The journal *Women and Therapy* is well worth reading for its coverage of feminist research and scholarship. Further exploration of the themes discussed in the present chapter can be found in *Feminist Therapy* by Laura Brown (2009) and *Introduction to Feminist Therapy* by Evans *et al.* (2010). Laura Brown is one of the leading figures in contemporary feminist therapy. She has produced many books, chapters and articles that are worth reading, and a video demonstration of feminist therapy in action, available through the American Psychological Association.

Art-making as a therapeutic practice

15

Introduction

The making of objects and performances that are of 'special' significance appears to be an intrinsic aspect of what it means to be human (Dissanayake 1988, 1992, 2000). Art is a mode of expression and communication that is found in all cultures, and artistic activity of some kind or another is used in all cultures to symbolize the core values of the culture, and its sense of what it means to be human. There is a long tradition of the use of art as a method of dealing with problems in living. Scheff (1980) described the role that dramatic performance played in ancient Greek culture, as a method of enabling the healing of emotional wounds. Hogan (2001) documents the important role that music, painting and architecture played in the 'moral treatment' for the insane that developed in England in the early nineteenth century. During the period in the twentieth century when counselling and psychotherapy became professionally established, the arts therapies evolved in parallel as separate forms of practice, with specific areas of application.

The main arts therapies to achieve professional status have been art therapy, dance therapy, drama therapy and music therapy. These therapy modalities are associated with specialist training programmes, and have tended to be used with clients who have difficulties in verbal expression – for example children, people with learning difficulties, or those who are traumatized or severely mentally ill (Malchiodi 2004a, 2004b). Typically, therapists who have received training in art, dance, drama or music therapy have tended to use only that specific medium in their work with clients. More recently, however, there has been an increasing recognition that 'expressive' methods can usefully be incorporated into mainstream 'verbal' counselling practice with all client groups. This broader use of art-based techniques is associated with the writings of Natalie Rogers (2000, the daughter of Carl Rogers), as well as other figures, and tends to involve the client being offered the opportunity to work with a range of expressive media, depending on their preference and on the specific issue being explored.

There exists a wide range of art-making practices that can be used in counselling. These include:

- autobiographical writing;
- dance and movement;
- dramatic performance;
- film-making;
- music;
- painting and drawing;
- photography;
- poetry writing;
- sand tray play;
- sculpting clay or other materials;
- storytelling;
- tapestry and quilting.

Within each of these (and other) art forms, the person can be encouraged to express his or her feelings, thoughts, sense of identity and relationships through the process of *making* objects and performances. This can be carried out in simple ways, with little equipment, for example offering a client a piece of paper and some coloured pens and inviting him or her to make a drawing of what their life is like at the present time. Alternatively, art objects that already exist (such as movies and novels) can be used as templates or triggers for the inner life of the person.

Box 15.1: *Using expressive techniques in counselling*

Several examples of how to embed expressive arts techniques into conventional verbal/conversational counselling can be found in Carrell (2001). The family memories exercise involves giving the client a large sheet of paper and some coloured markers. The client is asked to draw a line down the middle of the page. On one side, he or she is asked to draw an unhappy family memory; on the other side, a happy memory.

Carrell (2001) describes her use of this technique with Agneta, a woman experiencing a significant personal crisis. The unhappy image produced by Agneta portrayed a stick figure standing on a globe with outstretched hands reaching for an aeroplane flying in the sky. On being asked to talk about the picture, Agneta reported that it described a summer holiday as a child, where she had been left for several weeks with distant relatives in Europe, and had spent the whole time looking towards the sky for the plane that would take her home to the USA. This theme of abandonment, which emerged for the first time through the picture-making activity, turned out to be the key to this client's current difficulties.

In another example, Carrell (2001) gives an account of how she might ask each member in a troubled marriage to buy a disposable camera, and take a series of pictures that captured the way that he or she felt about the relationship. The clients are then invited to talk about their images. These ways of using art-making techniques within counselling are experienced by clients as challenging, but also as making sense in terms of how they might create and use images in their everyday lives.

Integrating art-making into the process of counselling: accessible forms of practice

Although in principle it is possible to draw on any form of art-making activity within a typical one-to-one, one-hour counselling session, there are some arts therapy traditions that probably work best in group or workshop settings (e.g., drama therapy, dance therapy) and some that call on specific expertise and skills (e.g., music therapy). This section introduces some examples of art-making techniques that do not require lengthy specialist training, and are commonly used by counsellors in frontline counselling and helping agencies. Many counsellors accumulate a handful of such techniques during their basic training or during post-qualification continuing professional development workshops. The use of such approaches is always enriched and enhanced by attending training events offered by experts in these areas. However, it is generally the case that counsellors gravitate toward art-based methods that resonate with their own personal interests and life experience, and are able to draw on their basic curiosity around the method to keep them open to new learning, wherever that learning may occur. The following sections highlight some examples of accessible art-making practices, that can be readily incorporated into counselling.

Drawing, painting and sculpting

Using images to express and convey meaning is a cultural universal. Almost everyone, at some time or another, makes diagrams, doodles, drawings, patterns or maps. Drawing, painting and sculpting are developmentally significant, because children learn to use these media before they are able to write. There will almost certainly be a piece of paper and a pen available in any counselling room. Many counsellors also like to have additional art-making materials at hand – coloured pens, chalk and crayons, rolls of paper, jars of buttons, bowls filled with stones or shells, sand trays, pieces of plasticine, and so on. The presence of such materials in the counselling room acts as an invitation and reminder for the client that other methods of communication are possible, beyond talk.

There are many ways of introducing art-making into the counselling process. In the early stage of therapy, when the counsellor is finding out about the client's world, a counsellor can say to the client that it could be helpful if he or she could create an image of all the people in the family and how they relate to each other, or construct a timeline that depicts where he or she is now, along with how they got there and where they are going to. At later stages in counselling, it may be useful to invite a client to create an image to convey their sense of a difficult and painful emotional state ('what it feels like to want to cut myself') or to capture the memory of a dream. There are many excellent books that suggest different types of visual art exercises and techniques that can be used in counselling (e.g., Buchalter 2009; Makin and Malchiodi 1999; Malchiodi 2004a, 2004b; Schroder 2004; Silverstone 2009). Further discussion of the underlying principles that inform this kind of approach can be found in Rogers (2000), Niff (2004) and Wood (2011).

Box 15.2: *Research into the client experience of making art*

It is important to realize that the use of art-making activity within counselling operates at a number of different levels. In a study by Van Lith *et al.* (2011), clients who had taken part in an art therapy group were interviewed about their experiences. Analysis of the interview transcripts identified three main themes. First, there was a sense of freedom, creativity and acceptance associated with the process of making art. In other words, art-making was regarded as an enjoyable, valued and meaningful experience in itself. Second, creating an image was a tangible task. The person could become absorbed in the task, and gain a sense of accomplishment when an image took shape in a satisfactory manner. Third, there was an intense relationship with the image itself. The image was a vehicle for self-expression and insight. It also functioned as a means of communicating with others, and an indicator of therapeutic progress. Participants also talked about how the image 'gave them something back'. One client said 'that's my picture on that wall'; it gives me an amazing sense of achievement' (Van Lith *et al.* 2011: 657). It was as though there was a point at which an image had a life of its own, and its creator could both learn from it and gain a sense of affirmation through the extent to which other people appreciated it. Similar themes have been found in other research into client experience of therapeutic art-making, for example by Griffiths (2008) and Reynolds *et al.* (2008).

Selecting and taking photographs

For many decades, photography has been an affordable part of everyday life. The recent development of cameras within mobile phones, coupled with the capacity to share pictures online, has further expanded the notion of photography as a routine activity. The use of photographs in counselling can be as simple as inviting a client to bring in some family photographs, and to use these to talk about their relationships with other family members (Berman 1993; Weiser 1999). It is also possible to encourage clients to take photographs that will be specifically used in therapy (see Box.15.3). A study by Smith and colleagues (2012) analysed the outcomes of 'photovoice' a project that combined individual and group counselling with community action. Young people in a deprived inner-city area were provided with disposable cameras and invited to take pictures that represented their definitions of 'success', and then discuss these images together in a group setting. There were two main benefits reported by participants in this project; they became more able to be 'agents' in their own lives, and they had an opportunity to reflect on, and make sense of, key dilemmas that they were facing in the process of growing up. These outcomes capture some of the central therapeutic possibilities of the use of photography in counselling. Further discussion of the therapeutic use of photography can be found in Loewenthal (2013).

Box 15.3: *Creating photo-self-narratives*

A photograph can be understood as a 'snapshot' or fragment of personal identity – who one was at one point in time. Assembling a series of photographs allows a person to build a more complete sense of identity, and to begin to explore how that identity changes and unfolds over time. Ziller (2000) has developed a technique for self-exploration, which he calls 'photo-self-narratives', based on the following instructions:

> This is a task that asks you to communicate with yourself about yourself. Ask yourself to take, or have taken 12 photographs that tell the story of yourself as you would tell the story to yourself. These photographs can be of anything as long as you feel that they are depicting yourself over time which may include the future. You will be talking to yourself about yourself and presenting to yourself the results in picture story form. Your photo-taking ability is not your task. You are trying to understand yourself, to yourself and to no one else through this photo-narrative. When you have finished you will have a 12 page book about yourself with only one photograph on each page.
>
> (Ziller 2000: 268)

Several months later the person is invited to revise or 're-author' the photo-self-narrative by repeating the procedure with a new set of pictures. Ziller (2000) presents a case study of the experiences of one young woman, Ann, who talked about the meaning of each picture, and wrote a reflective account about what she learned from the whole procedure. It is very clear that this structured photography exercise allowed Ann to explore and reflect on significant events in her life, such as the recent death of her father, in ways that made a positive contribution to her ability to move forward in preferred directions.

Writing

The use of creative writing in counselling and psychotherapy represents possibly the most widely deployed and comprehensively studied example of therapeutic art-making. Partly this is because we live in a literate society, in which the value and power of written language is taken for granted. There are also many different forms of writing that can be deployed: diaries, letters, poems, autobiography, etc. But the salience of therapeutic writing also owes a great deal to the impact of a highly influential programme of research carried out by James Pennebaker and his associates. In a series of studies, Pennebaker and his colleagues (see, for example, Pennebaker 2004a) invited participants simply to write for 15 minutes every day, over a period of four or five days, about the 'deepest emotions and thoughts about the most upsetting experience in your life'. Research participants who were randomly allocated to a control condition were asked to write about trivial matters. In various studies, the researchers tracked the impact of this brief writing intervention on a range of indicators of mental and physical health. What they found was that writing about mundane topics had no health impact. However, those who had written about stressful experiences exhibited a range of significant health benefits, including a reduction in number of visits to see their doctor.

This technique has subsequently been adopted as a stand-alone self-help method (Pennebaker 1997, 2004a), and means of helping people to cope with serious health conditions (Bolton 2008; Davidson *et al.* 2002; Lepore *et al.* 2002; Stanton and Danoff-Burg 2002), and as an adjunct to psychotherapy (Batten *et al.* 2002; Graf *et al.* 2008; Green Lister 2002, 2003; Kerner and Fitzpatrick 2007).

Because therapeutic writing has been examined in a number of carefully controlled studies, it has been possible to begin to identify the constituent healing elements of the writing process that contribute to the enhancement of well-being in the person doing the writing. There appear to be three main helpful aspects of this type of activity (Sloan and Marx 2004; Pennebaker 2004b).

1 *Physiological.* Inhibiting ongoing thoughts, feelings or behaviour is associated with expenditure of energy at a physiological level. Short-term inhibition is manifested in increased autonomic nervous system activity. Long-term inhibition serves as a low-level cumulative biological stressor that can cause or exacerbate a variety of health problems, ranging from colds and flu to heart disease and cancer.

2 *Cognitive.* Active inhibition of memories of stressful events is associated with deleterious changes in information processing. In holding back significant thoughts and feelings associated with an event, individuals do not process the event fully, and are left with ruminations, dreams and other intrusive cognitive symptoms. Confronting traumatic memories can help negate the effects of inhibition, by reducing the physiological work put into inhibition, and by enabling individuals to understand and assimilate the event.

3 *Social.* The stressful events that people write about often involve relationships with others, and the process of writing allows these relationship difficulties to be viewed in perspective, and to some degree resolved. When people write about a problem, they are also then more likely to talk to others about the issue, thus enlisting social support.

The research into the 'Pennebaker paradigm' has also clarified some of the conditions that need to be in place in order for therapeutic writing to be effective. The activity of writing needs to have an emotional dimension – the helpfulness of writing depends on whether the person has used writing as a means of accessing and expressing painful emotions. The writer needs to persist with the task. Typically, participants in the Pennebaker studies do not enjoy writing about stressful experiences, particularly at the outset. Finally, it seems to be helpful if there is no expectation that anyone else will necessarily read what has been produced, and the person can share the products of their writing with whom, and at a time, that is appropriate for them. The privacy dimension of the writing experience is also linked to the importance for the writer of having permission to ignore grammatical conventions and spelling rules, and just express things in their own way.

Box 15.4: *Structured writing therapy*

The Interapy package, developed in the Netherlands by Alfred Lange and his colleagues as a treatment for PTSD, represents an innovative combination of interaction with a therapist, alongside use of a structured internet learning programme. Potential clients are given access to a website, which provides information about the treatment protocol, a rationale for therapy, and screens participants to determine whether this particular therapy is appropriate for them.

Clients who proceed with therapy are then invited to create a schedule for engaging in intensive therapeutic writing tasks (ten 45-minute writing sessions over five weeks), organized around three phases of therapy: *self-confrontation, cognitive re-appraisal,* and *sharing with others*. Self-confrontation writing tasks involve describing the traumatic event in detail, and also writing about their thoughts and fears related to the event. A therapist provides brief feedback, within 24 hours following each writing assignment, for example:

> I would like you to select a more specific moment from the episode of your car accident; this moment might be very tough and frightening for you, and you may well prefer not to think about it at all. As I mentioned previously, this may be something you still have occasional flashbacks about, that arouses emotions and physical reactions such as sweating, cold hands or difficulty breathing. It could, for example, be the moment when you see the flames coming out of the vehicle, or when you say goodbye to John in hospital. In your next two essays I would like you to write about this.
>
> (Lange *et al.* 2003: 902)

To facilitate self-confrontation, clients are encouraged to use first person, present tense writing, to describe the sensory perceptions that they experienced at the time of the traumatic event in as much detail as possible, and not to worry about matters of writing, style, grammar, or spelling.

In the *cognitive reappraisal* phase of Interapy, clients are instructed in the principles of cognitive reframing, and are invited to apply these principles by writing as though they were offering 'encouraging advice for a hypothetical friend who had experienced a similar traumatic event' (Lange *et al.* 2003: 902). Finally, in the third phase of therapy, clients are asked to share their new learning by writing a letter (which may or may not be sent) to a significant other, outlining the ways in which the traumatic event had changed them, and how they had learned to cope with it.

A randomized controlled trial of Interapy, Lange *et al.* (2003) found that clients who received this therapy exhibited substantially more gains than clients in a matched waiting list control group. Around 50 per cent of those who completed Interapy experienced significant levels of clinical change, which was maintained at follow-up. This is a striking and encouraging result, given the initial high levels of PTSD in the client group recruited to this study. However, Lange *et al.* (2003) also found that around 30 per cent of clients dropped out of treatment, either because they were experiencing technical difficulties with the system, preferred face-to-face contact, or reported that the writing tasks were too threatening. Further development in this approach, in the form of a protocol for 'structured writing therapy' (SWT) have been reported by van Emmerik *et al.* (2008).

The research studies carried out by Pennebaker and others have mainly focused on a stripped-down or minimalist form of writing. It is clear that there are many ways in which therapeutic writing can be taken further, by drawing on long-established narrative and literary traditions. There are many genres of creative writing that have been used for therapeutic purposes, including journal writing, poetry writing (Tegner *et al.* 2009) and story writing. Within each of these genres, guidelines have been developed around specific writing tasks or exercises that can be used by individuals on their own, or in the context of counselling (see, for example, Adams 1998; Baldwin 1992; DeSalvo 2000; Fox 1997; Reiner 1998). It can be valuable to carry out therapeutic creative writing in a group setting, in which stories and other written outputs can function as a means of connection between members (Huss *et al.* 2009).

One of the major advantages of writing as a therapeutic activity is that it is a method that is available to the majority of people. In addition, there are many forms of writing that are possible, ranging from highly structured (e.g., thought diaries used in CBT) through to forms of writing that encourage improvisation and experimentation (e.g., certain types of poetry).

Kerner and Fitzpatrick (2007) have constructed a two-dimensional model of therapeutic creative writing. They suggest that creative writing techniques can be more cognitive-focused versus more emotion-focused and at the same time more structured versus more open-ended. For example, a client could explore emotional issues by using a mood diary (highly structured) or by writing a poem (unstructured). At a different time, that client might seek to make the cognitive meaning of his or her experiences by following the prompts in an online programmed writing package, or by writing an autobiography. Although it seems clear that some writing techniques are hard to categorize (for instance, the experience of writing an autobiography may move back and forwards between moments of high emotional intensity, and moments of analytic reflection). The Kerner and Fitzpatrick (2007) model offers at least the beginnings of a framework to guide counsellors and clients in their decisions around which writing approaches might be most relevant at particular points in therapy.

There is rich literature available on how to use creative writing in counselling – Bolton *et al.* (2004) provide a good entry point to this resource.

Box 15.5: *Reweaving the self: creative writing following the death of a child*

A paper by a psychotherapist, Judith Ryan, described how she used creative writing to 'reweave' the 'terrible rent in the fabric of the self' caused by the death of her 23-year-old son, Sean, in a climbing accident. In a state of profound dissociation following the loss, it took six months before she could write. Her first journal entry was:

> My memory and my sense of time are still impaired—there is a fluidity and confusion that I know is related to loss, but I don't know quite how . . . I still have difficulty remembering my dreams, and almost never dreams of Sean. I wake up often at night, but cut off from how I feel. I think instead. I woke up yesterday morning with such a clear visual image of him. It was such a relief to know that I can do that, but I was emotionally detached.
>
> (Ryan 2009: 532)

Within a few weeks, the writing began to shift into a more direct style of expression:

> I think I could go crazy—without knowing even what I mean. How can one accept what is intolerable? That a living, breathing, beautiful, vital son is reduced, first, to a body that has no meaning without him, and then to ashes. We can't deal with the ashes. They are still at the funeral home.
>
> (Ryan 2009: 532)

At around six months after the first journal entry, Ryan joined a writing group: writing became a means of connecting with others. After two years, her writing was able to celebrate her son's life, and its meaning for her:

> So many of my memories of Sean are physical. His joyful energy as his sturdy legs propelled him, full speed ahead, across our wood floor astride his Fisher-Price truck . . .
> The sound of his voice singing in the shower. . . . . . . The intensity and rhythm he exhibited on his skateboard . . .
>
> (Ryan 2009: 533)

Ryan (2009: 537) observed that, eventually, she arrived at a point where:

> I think of writing as Sean's legacy to me. Sean hungered for new experiences. He was a free spirit, unafraid of his own desire. I don't have him to be my free spirit anymore. The trauma of his death broke through my restraint, and uncovered more of my passion. I have learned to take risks of my own in the world of words.

This paper is a remarkable and unusual piece of work, because Judith Ryan is obviously a sensitive and skilled observer of her own emotional processes, and because she is willing to share her experience in a professional arena. What this case report shows us is the way that the meaning of writing can change over a period of time, from initially being a mechanism for coping with awful feelings and memories, then later becoming an integral part of a person's sense of who she is.

Singing

Most people can sing. A technique that has been used in group and community-based work has been to invite participants to work together to write and perform a song (Denborough *et al.* 2008). Singing is a bodily activity that encourages breathing, and allows people to be joined in shared rhythmic movement, as well as being a form of self-expression.

Responding to art: movies, novels and music

Most examples of art-based therapy involve active participation in art-making. It is also possible to make therapeutic use of the experience of being an audience. Some therapists suggest novels, poems and plays that their clients might read, or work on exploring the meaning of fictional writing or poetry that has special significance for the client. It is also possible for a therapist and client to listen to a piece of music that the client has chosen. Possibly the most widely used approach within this category is *movie therapy*, in which the therapist may 'prescribe' a movie or watch a movie suggested by the client (Hesley and Hesley 2001; Lampropoulos *et al.* 2004; Schulenberg 2003; Wedding and Niemiec 2003; Wolz 2010). The therapeutic possibility afforded by watching a movie (or reading a novel) is that the client can identify with a character who may represent a constructive way of resolving the client's problem. Some movies and fiction may allow emotional catharsis. A movie can also provide client and therapists with shared images, metaphors and narratives.

Box 15.6: *Reading a book: what is the therapeutic process?*

One of the few studies to look at the process of therapeutic reading was carried out by Cohen (1994). In this study, open-ended interviews were carried out with eight people who had benefited from self-guided reading, in the absence of intervention or support from a therapist. The interviews were subjected to phenomenological analysis, which yielded a number of key themes. A central factor for these readers was a process of *recognition of self*. For example, participants reported that:

> It felt like this person has experienced what I'm experiencing, has been through it and had crystallized my kind of sentiment into this passage and it was also as though I had been hit on the head with how I felt.
>
> (Cohen 1994: 39)

> You feel this could be you or this could be your sister or this could be your best friend.
>
> (Cohen 1994: 39)

Another core theme related to the sense of being validated, of feeling as though a difficult or stigmatizing life experience was acceptable:

> (The reading) made me feel part of a group. It validated my feelings. It validated the whole experience. . . . It made me feel as though it was okay to feel the way that I did . . . .
>
> (Cohen 1994: 40)

Other significant themes that emerged from the analysis were comfort, hope, inspiration, catharsis, information gathering and gaining understanding. All of the participants in the study described themselves as approaching their reading in a highly purposeful and determined fashion, often rereading sections of a book, and intentionally remembering key passages at moments of stress. The experience of reading was regarded as an individual process, which was difficult to explain to another person, or share. Finally, participants reported that they had a sense of losing themselves, of being *transported* and using the reading to escape for a time from their current life difficulties. It is essential to be aware of the limitations of the Cohen (1994) study, which was conducted with a small sample of people who all reported highly positive experiences with therapeutic reading. Nevertheless, the findings of this study have major implications for the way that therapists work with clients who are concurrently using self-help reading.

Therapeutic processes associated with the use of art in counselling

There are a number of therapeutic processes that are associated with the use of expressive arts methods in counselling. These techniques engage the imagination of the person, and allow him or her to begin to stand back from the concrete situation that is bringing pain into their life, and reflect on its meaning. Many arts techniques, such as painting, sculpting and dance, are carried out in the absence of talk, and provide opportunities for the emergence of pre-verbal, unconscious, implicit or hidden material – thoughts, feelings and fantasies that might otherwise be hard to articulate. The creation of an object, such as a picture, has the effect of 'externalizing' the problem, and allowing the client and therapist to look at it together, and consider it as something slightly separate from the client, but around which he or she has expert knowledge (Keeling and Bermudez 2006; Rubin 2005). Art-making also introduces activity and 'doing' into a therapy session, which can enable the person to break out of passive states of mind. The making of an art object also represents a ritual that demonstrates to the person that it is possible to do things that lead step by step from one state of mind or emotion, to another. Many art-making activities are highly embodied, and help the person to get 'out of their head', in the sense of cutting through the flow of negative self-talk, and into a more direct mode of making contact with the world. Finally, the objects that are made in therapy, or even the images of moments in dance or drama sessions, function as tangible reminders of personal issues and insights, and moments of change in therapy.

Box 15.7: *Learning involves moving through different levels of representation*

Jerome Bruner can be regarded as one of the most influential psychologists of the twentieth century. Among his many contributions to the discipline is a model of learning that has important implications for the way that we understand the role of art-making activities in counselling. Through extensive observation of infants and children, Bruner (1966, 1973) realized that learning involves moving through three quite distinct modalities of representation: *enactive, iconic* and *symbolic*. For example, in learning about the weight of objects, a child will first of all experiment with picking things up (action-based learning), then will be able to use mental or visual *images* (this toy car looks heavier than that one), and then will become able to use abstract symbols (words, numbers) to represent how much things weigh. Effective learning experiences allow the person to access all three modes of representation, as necessary. 'Ordinary therapy', where client and counsellor just talk to each other, takes place almost entirely in the domain of symbolic knowing. By contrast, drawing a picture or writing a story allows client to shift back and forward between enactive, iconic and symbolic realms. This is helpful.

Expressive methods provide a fertile arena for building and exploring the client–therapist relationship. The process of deciding on which media are to be used, how, for how long and for what purpose, opens up an array of opportunities for collaborative decision-making. There may be valuable exploration around the feelings that the client may hold regarding showing the eventual object to their therapist. Is the therapist regarded as a potential harsh critic of the art object, or as a loving parent welcoming her child's latest efforts? In either case, where do these feelings come from, and what might they mean. Is the therapist trusted to touch or to hold the art object? Is he or she sensitive enough to ask whether it is alright to touch or hold it? The interplay between client and therapist around the art object allows the latter many ways of offering (or failing to offer) the 'core conditions' of acceptance, empathy and congruence.

Because psychoanalysis was the earliest form of psychotherapy to be developed, and so was the first approach to 'discover' the therapeutic potential of the arts, but also because so much expressive work in the arts operates on the borderline between conscious and unconscious, much of the theory that has grown up around arts therapies has been psychoanalytic and psychodynamic in nature. The fascination of Carl Jung with imagery and the creative process has also meant that there exists a rich tradition of Jungian theorizing within art therapy. More recently, however, influenced by the writings of Natalie Rogers (2000), Silverstone (1997) and others, there has been a movement in the direction of a more theoretically integrationist approach to expressive therapy, drawing on theoretical ideas from person-centred, gestalt and CBT perspectives.

Conclusions

Expressive arts methods represent the assimilation into counselling of timeless cultural traditions and practices – the capacity to symbolize experience in art works, the motivation to make objects and moments that are 'special'. This approach brings back into therapy an aspect of what it means to be human that has been occluded by the purely psychological image of the person that has held sway over the profession. It is a relatively straightforward matter to integrate expressive arts methods into virtually any counselling situation.

Topics for reflection and discussion

1 Reflect on the significance that art-making has had in your own life. In what ways have writing, drawing, painting, music-making or other forms of artistic expression had a 'therapeutic' effect for you? What is it about these activities that has been helpful for you?

2 To what extent are the arts-based approaches described in this chapter generally applicable to *all* types of presenting problem? For each of the approaches, list two or three types of problem or client group, for which it would be likely to be *most* or *least* helpful.

Suggested further reading

To develop an appreciation of the significance of art-making in human living, it is worthwhile to become familiar with the ideas of Ellen Dissanayake, for example her classic book *Homo Aestheticus: Where Art Comes From and Why* (Dissanayake 1992). Marion Milner was a psychoanalyst who wrote about her own personal experience as an artist. Her book *On Not Being Able to Paint* (Milner 1957; originally published under a pseudonym in 1950) was highly influential in conveying an appreciation of the dynamics of art-making to therapists. Key books that describe current practice in expressive arts therapies are Rubin (2005), Warren (2008) and Weiner (2001). *The Arts in Psychotherapy* is a journal that is consistently interesting and worth reading and contains clinical and research articles on all forms of expressive arts therapies. A widely used workbook that provides many strategies for tapping into the basic human capacity for creativity and imagination that underpins all arts-oriented therapy, is *The Artist's Way*, by Julia Cameron (1994).

CHAPTER

16

Therapy in nature: using the outdoor environment

Introduction

One of the common factors in most forms of counselling and psychotherapy, which is seldom mentioned, is that it takes place indoors, usually in a fairly small room. There exists, however, an alternative that is increasingly widely used, which is to conduct therapy out of doors. The use of the natural environment as a setting for therapy has several advantages (as well as some disadvantages). The main advantages of therapy out of doors is that it provides an opportunity for the person to experience himself or herself in a different way, in contrast to his or her ordinary routine. Some proponents of the use of nature in therapy also believe that contact with nature has an intrinsic healing capacity.

The use of nature in therapy has been influenced by ideas from ecology and environmental studies. The Norwegian philosopher Arne Naess (1989) invented the phrase *deep ecology* to refer to the natural world and the ecological connections between all things as a profound source of wisdom, which is largely ignored and discounted in the modern urban world. Books such as *The Spell of the Sensuous* (Abram 1996) and *Coming Back to Life* (Macy and Brown 1998) have been highly influential in conveying the possibilities of a sense of connectedness to the natural world that is missing in many people's lives and the healing potentials that are triggered by making contact with this dimension of experience. An important strand within these writings has been the argument that there is a moral and ethical aspect to the relationship between human beings and nature: it is not ethically acceptable merely to 'use' nature, and there is an overarching ethical imperative to respect the right to exist of animals, plants and habitats. This perspective has been further developed by various *ecofeminist* writers, who suggest that there is a connection between the oppression of the Earth, and the oppression of women (Adams 1993; Plumwood 1993).

The aim of this chapter is to provide an overview of different strands of theory and practice in relation to counselling and psychotherapy that is conducted in outdoor settings. At the present time, there does not exist a unified model of outdoor therapy. There are many examples of this kind of work that involve collaboration between counsellors and practitioners of other disciplines (e.g., outdoor pursuits instructors or wilderness guides). As a result, 'outdoor' therapy has not yet found a single professional 'home', but instead straddles a number of professional domains.

The health benefits of being in an outdoor environment

One of the important aspects of outdoor therapy is there is plentiful evidence that spending even a small amount of time in the natural environment, or even being able to look at hills, trees and seascapes through a window, can have a powerful beneficial impact on health and well-being (Barton and Pretty 2010; Pinquart *et al.* 2007; Coon *et al.* 2011) and on the efficiency of cognitive functioning (Berman *et al.* 2008). Moreover, the majority of people believe that being outdoors, being in nature, and participating in exercise, are likely to be good for them (Parker and Crawford 2007). As a result there are many counselling clients who do not need to be convinced that there may be some merit in conducting all or part of their therapy outside of an office environment. People who seek counselling may already be engaged in outdoor activities, may have past experience of this kind of endeavour, or may be open to trying new types of nature-based experience. The challenge for counsellors has been to find safe, effective and affordable ways of channelling these tendencies to respond to the needs of different client groups.

Forms of outdoor therapy

There exist a range of strategies for conducting counselling and psychotherapy in outdoor settings. These different approaches reflect the huge diversity of possibilities that are opened up by moving counselling out of the office. For example, it becomes possible to think in terms of walking around a park that is close to a counselling office or clinic, or relocating entirely to a wilderness area. The different outdoor therapy approaches also reflect a variety of ideas about what is helpful for clients. For instance, some approaches emphasize the basic transformational power of merely interacting with nature, while other approaches emphasize the opportunity to overcome physical challenge, or the opportunity to be part of a group. These (and other) change processes are combined in different ways within different outdoor therapy traditions.

Ecopsychology

A significant source of theoretical influence on the development of approaches to counselling that makes reference to nature and the outdoor environment is *ecopsychology* (Higley and Milton 2008; Roszac *et al.* 1995; Totton 2003, 2005). The work of writers, theorists and practitioners within the ecopyschology movement extends far beyond the domain of counselling and psychology – ecopsychology represents an attempt to refocus the whole of psychology, including developmental psychology, social psychology and evolutionary psychology. Initially, ecopsychology adopted a largely psychoanalytic approach, in using terms such as the 'ecological unconscious'. More recently, ecopsychology has redefined itself as a broad field of inquiry, which does not give any specific priority to any particular psychological approach over others. Because ecopsychology, deep ecology and ecofeminism are broad philosophical and theoretical approaches, which embrace a variety of interdisciplinary interests, they have tended not to have generated much in the way of concrete therapeutic methods. Instead, the ideas and principles of ecopsychology have permeated different approaches to the practice of outdoor/nature-oriented therapy in a variety of ways.

Adventure/wilderness therapy

In terms of practical applications, the earliest approaches to use the outdoor environment for therapeutic purposes have been *adventure therapy* and *wilderness therapy*. Adventure therapy particularly emphasizes the use of physical and psychological challenge (Ray 2005; Richards and Smith 2003). For example, success in abseiling down a cliff, climbing a rock face, or traversing a high rope ladder may have a highly positive impact on a person who suffers from low self-esteem, and the memories of his or her achievement may help to maintain that gain in everyday life situations. The adventure therapy approach has its origins in the *Outward Bound* tradition developed in Britain in the 1950s.

Wilderness therapy makes similar use of challenge, but in this case the risk is not designed or planned by the facilitators, but is inherent in the experience of trekking through wild countryside or canoeing down a gorge (Greenway 1995; Plotkin 2001). The experience of undergoing a wilderness experience acts as a metaphor for the personal journey that the person is undertaking (Corazon *et al.* 2011; Hartford 2011). The person travels away from his or her normal routines and everyday reality, and further and further into a new and unknown reality (McDonald *et al.* 2009).

Typically, adventure therapy and wilderness therapy are conducted in groups, thus introducing therapeutic processes such as the experience of group cohesiveness and a sense of belonging, and receiving support and feedback from other group members. Adventure therapy and wilderness therapy have mainly been practised within educational organizations, with specific groups such as people with drug problems and young people with conduct disorders, rather than being applied to a wider population of people with anxiety, depression and relationship difficulties. These methods have also been applied in the field of counsellor training (Wheeler *et al.* 1998). However, many of the techniques developed within these approaches have been assimilated into more explicitly 'psychotherapeutic' forms of outdoor work (Gass *et al.* 2012). For example, Kyriakopoulos (2010, 2011) offered clients of a university student counselling service an opportunity to take part in a brief adventure therapy workshop. Clients were able to use their ongoing relationship with their counsellors (who did not take part in the workshop) to explore and work through the meaning of these experiences. In follow-up interviews, the majority of clients reported that the adventure activities had made a positive contribution to their therapy.

Box 16.1: *Adventure therapy in action: overcoming eating disorders*

An example of how outdoor therapy can operate is provided by Richards (2003) and Richards and Peel (2005), in their study of the effectiveness of adventure therapy with a group of women suffering from intractable eating disorders that had not been dealt with in previous episodes of conventional indoor therapy. These women spent five days engaged in a series of challenging outdoor activities, involving canoeing, climbing and walking. The programme was facilitated by outdoor pursuits experts working alongside counsellors, and the women were invited to talk about their experiences following each activity. The majority of the women who took part in the programme reported significant gains in terms of a lessening of their eating disorder symptoms. Some of the women found the experience to be transformational, and felt that they had been able to experience themselves in a completely different way, emerging with a greater sense of self-confidence. For their part, the therapists who were part of the team of facilitators observed that the women under-taking the programme were able to begin to explore significant personal issues much more quickly, and in more depth, than they would have expected in a conventional therapy relationship.

The results of this study illustrate some of the processes that can make outdoor therapy so effective. The person seeking help is exposed to new experiences that invite them to view themselves in a new light. They are invited to exhibit new behaviour and strengths. All this takes place in a context of high challenge and high group support, away from pre-existing everyday contexts that might trigger old patterns of feeling, thought and action. Taken as a whole, the experience is emotionally and physically intense and vividly memorable, and can readily become a turning point or epiphany moment in a person's life. Similar themes are also reported in a study by Hennigan (2010).

Nature therapy

A fully developed framework for the use of the natural world in therapy is the *nature therapy* approach created by the Israeli therapist Ronen Berger (Berger 2004, 2005; Berger and McLeod 2006). Nature therapy is an integration of creative arts therapies along with ideas from other therapeutic approaches such as psychodynamic, gestalt and Jungian. A key idea within nature therapy is the concept of the 'three-way relationship', between the client, the therapist, and nature. Each participant in this relationship can affect, and be affected by, the other. Nature is regarded as a force, which has a autonomous impact on persons. For example, during a nature therapy session, a person may walk up a hill in a strong wind and feel cold. This experience may trigger thoughts and fantasies about being vulnerable. A moment later, the sun may come out and the person may feel warm, which may evoke images of safety and nurturance. Part of the role of the therapist is to choose environments that have the possibility of stimulating particular types of experience in group participants. For example, the time of sunset and the onset of darkness has the potential to elicit feelings of loss, whereas a tidal shore has the potential to elicit an awareness of cyclical change and renewal. Nature therapy makes use of ritual to intensify the person's contact with the natural world. The client is encouraged to find and make a 'home in nature', which comes to represent a form of 'secure base' within which difficult personal issues can be explored.

Nature therapy has been applied to many people with a range of problems: PTSD, children with learning difficulties, anxiety, depression. The therapeutic process that takes place within nature therapy operates in two dimensions. Primarily, it offers clients the same kind of therapeutic experiences that they would find in other therapies, such as a relationship with a therapist, an opportunity to remember, to tell their story and reflect on their experience, the chance to experiment with different behaviour. Beyond this, however, nature therapy produces a sense of interconnectedness with the natural world, an awareness of something that lies beyond human-made objects and activities. This awareness can contribute to the development of a broader perspective on life, that can be valuable in many situations. In addition, for a person who has experienced nature therapy, the natural world becomes more of a resource in his or her life as a whole.

Horticulture therapy

A contrasting approach to outdoor therapy is to combine therapeutic work with gardening and horticultural activities. One of the best examples of this approach comes from the work of the Medical Foundation for the Care of Victims of Torture, in London, with people who have been exiled from countries and have been traumatized by the torture they have seen or received (Linden and Grut 2002). In this project, gardening experts and psychotherapists work alongside the person in his or her plot. The role of the therapist is to enable the person to use the process of gardening to express and reflect on his or her experience. For example, cultivating crops that were familiar to the person from his or her home country can have great meaning. The experience of growth and renewal that comes from starting with bare earth, and ending up with food that can be shared with the group, and used to feed one's own family, allows the person to begin to move beyond a sense of hopelessness and despair. Tending a memorial garden gives a tangible way of remembering those who have been left behind. The key to the therapy that is described by Linden and Grut (2002) is that the natural world, in the form of an allotment plot, has the capacity to evoke emotion and memory, which can then be shared and discussed with the therapist who is on the spot. A broader tradition of horticultural therapy is described by Simson and Straus (1997).

Animal-assisted therapy

Many therapists have encouraged clients to be interact with, or care for, animals for thera-peutic purposes. Being involved with animals helps to slow the person down, has the potential to expose them to unconditional acceptance, and puts the person in a situation in which they are called on to communicate in a direct and authentic manner. Involvement with animals may also take the person out of doors. There have been several different forms of animal-assisted psychotherapeutic initiative (Fine 2010). Probably the most widely used of these approaches is equine-assisted therapy (Trotter 2012), although the presence of dogs is certainly used on an informal basis by many counsellors and psychotherapists.

Taking ordinary counselling out of doors

There are several other approaches to using the outdoors in therapy that have been devel-oped in recent years. Burns (1998) has described a form of 'nature-guided' therapy that is largely based on conventional office consultation, but the person is encouraged to reflect on his or her involvement in nature, and to carry out a series of outdoor homework exer-cises that are designed to deepen the significance of nature as a source of personal meaning, and the use of outdoor activities as a way of coping with emotional problems. In similar fashion, the gestalt therapist William Cahalan (1995) mainly works with his clients in an office, but moves into outdoor spaces to explore specific issues, particularly in rela-tion to restoring the client's sense of *contact*, a key concept within gestalt theory. Doucette (2004) introduced the concept of 'walk and talk' counselling: young people receiving therapy were given the option of counselling sessions carried out while walking around the grounds of their school. Jordan and Marshall (2010) provide examples of their practice as therapists who give their clients the option of meeting in a range of outdoor contexts, as well as in a therapy office.

Jordan and Marshall (2010) also offer a valuable discussion of the practical and concep-tual issues involved in shifting the therapy 'frame' or 'space' into a setting such as an urban park. What happens if someone passes by while the therapist and client are in the middle of an intense conversation? What happens if a stray dog appears? What happens if the session runs over time because the client is walking very slowly? What happens if it rains? Jordan and Marshall (2010) suggest that it is essential for counsellors who move their prac-tice out of doors to consider these issues in advance, and engage in appropriate contracting with the client around how to respond to the unpredictable challenges of conducting therapy out of doors. Further discussion of these issues can also be found in Hays (1999).

Political dimensions of outdoor therapy

There are an increasing number of counsellors who take the view that their work has a significant political dimension. Although the primary purpose of counselling is to help individuals and families to resolve problems in living, it is clear that this kind of endeavour can be enhanced and strengthened by an attention to the political dimensions of these problems (see Chapter 21). From this perspective, the use of outdoor settings in counselling has the potential to make a positive contribution to individual and collective efforts to combat climate change and increase environmental awareness. Activities that enable counselling clients to appreciate the natural world, and to make connections between involvement in nature and personal well-being, are likely to lead to more awareness of the value of the natural environment, and willingness to act to conserve and preserve that environment. It also seems likely that engagement with nature will be associated with a reduction in consumerism.

Some counsellors and psychotherapists are actively exploring the interface between therapy and the environmental movement. Moir-Bussy (2009) and others have created theoretical bridges between these domains. Randall (2009) has used psychotherapeutic concepts to account for why the majority of the population are in denial about the threat of global warming, and uses therapeutic skills to facilitate groups in which participants can move in the direction of conscious acknowledgement and action. In turn, an understanding of the broader social and political meanings associated with concepts such as 'nature', 'wilderness' and 'landscape' has important implications for the conduct of outdoor therapy itself (Willis 2011). At one extreme, the outdoors represents a convenient, or large-scale setting for aerobic exercise, or doing adventurous things such as abseiling, that is no more than an alternative to carrying out the same activities in a gym or leisure centre. At the other extreme, being out of doors is a form of spiritual reconnection with an essential aspect of what it means to be human.

Conclusions

The use of the outdoor environment in counselling represents a significant emergent form of practice. It is a form of practice that is rapidly entering the mainstream, the leading UK mental health charity, MIND, evaluated a number of ecotherapy pilot projects and strongly supports an expansion of this way of working (MIND 2007). It is clear that counsellors intending to work out of doors with their clients need appropriate training. For example, there are issues of safety involved in taking clients canoeing, or hiking into wilderness areas where they might be injured. There is also a need for further research into outdoor therapies, in terms of their effectiveness for different client groups, and into the therapeutic processes that occur. Nevertheless, it seems certain that outdoor and nature-informed approaches to counselling will expand in the future, both in response to an increasing public awareness of the significance of the environment, and because these approaches generate important possibilities for innovative ways of working with people to bring about meaningful change in their lives.

Topics for reflection and discussion

1   Reflect on the significance that the outdoor environment has had in your own life. In what ways have walking, climbing, gardening or other ways of being with nature had a 'therapeutic' effect for you? What is it about these activities that has been helpful for you?

2   To what extent are the innovative approaches described in this chapter generally applicable to *all* types of presenting problem? For each of the approaches, list two or three types of problem or client group for which it would be likely to be *most* or *least* helpful.

3   What are the therapeutic processes that are more likely to occur when therapy involves some kind of outdoor activity? What are the processes that are *less* likely to occur, compared to 'indoor' therapy?

Suggested further reading

For a valuable selection of perspectives on the meaning and therapeutic potential of nature and the outdoors, it is still worth reading the classic edited book that was largely responsible for initiating the whole ecopsychology movement: *Eco-psychology: Restoring the Mind, Healing the Earth* (Roszak et al. 1995). To gain an appreciation of the unique quality of enchantment that is associated with the discovery that being human involves being part of the natural world there is no better book than *The Spell of the Sensuous: Perception and Language in a More-Than-Human World* by David Abram (1996). Recent developments in outdoor therapy are reviewed in *Adventure Therapy: Theory, Research, and Practice* (Gass et al. 2012).

Part 3
Integrating approaches

The challenge of therapeutic integration

Introduction

This chapter discusses the issues involved in combining ideas and methods from different theoretical approaches. Chapters 4 to 16 have reviewed the most widely used theories and approaches within contemporary therapy, ranging from the beginnings of psychotherapy in the work of Sigmund Freud, to the most recent developments in postmodern practice. These chapters on different approaches can be read as free-standing descriptions of distinctive and contrasting ways of understanding the aims and process of counselling. The theoretical literature represents a rich resource for counsellors. In the past, practitioners tended to be trained within a single theoretical orientation, and stuck with that set of ideas and methods throughout their career. In recent years, by contrast, there has emerged a growing tendency for practitioners to be exposed to a range of ideas in training, and to seek ways of combining different concepts and techniques in their work with clients.

Operating from an assumption that there are valuable 'truths' in many theories of therapy, more and more counsellors have adopted the aim of developing their own *personal* approach, consistent with their life experience, cultural values and work setting. However, it is no easy matter to combine theoretical ideas in practice. Each discrete theoretical orientation comprises a coherent set of principles and practices about how to do therapy. Some of these principles do not readily map on to each other, or may even appear to contradict each other. The task of combining theories therefore represents a significant challenge for all counsellors. The extent of this challenge can be appreciated by considering some of the key ideas that run through this book as a whole, in relation to the role of theory, and the differences between competing 'schools' or approaches within the field of counselling and psychotherapy:

- each of the 'pure' theoretical orientations discussed in earlier chapters represents a viable structure for practice – there is good work being done under the auspices of each of these approaches, and there are therapists who, over the entire span of their professional careers, find meaning and value within the orientation that they have espoused;

- an increasing proportion of therapists, probably more than half, define their approach as 'eclectic' or 'integrative', rather than espousing a 'pure' theoretical orientation;

- being able to offer a secure, confidential relationship, hopefulness and some kind of structure for exploring and resolving problems in living and becoming more connected with other people, is more important than theory;

- it is essential for effective counselling that the practitioner has a coherent framework for understanding what he or she is trying to achieve;

- in multicultural, pluralist democratic societies it is inevitable that competing value systems and cultural traditions will generate different ideas about human personality and the proper aims of counselling – some degree of theoretical diversity and debate is healthy and necessary;

- it can be argued that the success of all forms of therapy is due to the operation of a core of common factors or ingredients, for example the existence of a therapeutic relationship of trust and caring;

- theories of counselling and psychotherapy reflect the ideas and concerns that are most pressing at any particular point in history, therapy theories are continually undergoing *reconstruction* to reflect prevailing social issues and developments;

- almost all research into the effectiveness of therapy is based on the evaluation of specific, named theoretical approaches, there is little research evidence pertaining to the effectiveness of combined/integrative approaches;

- there is little evidence that any one theory of counselling is more valid, effective or 'true' than any other;

- there are many professional associations and journals that represent the interests of single-theory groups, but few networks or professional communities that are built around integrative approaches;

- the prevailing movement within counselling is in the direction of increased theoretical convergence and consensus;

- from the point of view of the client, the experience of counselling is much the same, no matter which theoretical orientation is being used by the counsellor.

These ideas serve as a reminder of the complexity of the task, for practitioners, of achieving an effective balance between ideas and methods from different mainstream therapy traditions. The purpose of the present chapter is to explore the strategies that counsellors and psychotherapists have developed to effectively and safely integrate different theories into their practice, to maintain a coherent and effective form of practice that is open to a range of influences and sources.

The underlying unity of theories of therapy

From the very beginnings of the emergence of counselling and psychotherapy as mainstream human service professions, there have been people who have pointed out that the similarities between theoretical approaches were much greater than the differences. For example, in 1940 the psychologist Goodwin Watson organized a symposium at which well-known figures such as Saul Rosenzweig, Carl Rogers and Frederick Allen agreed that factors such as support, a good client–therapist relationship, insight and behaviour change were common features of all successful therapy (Watson 1940). An early piece of research by Fiedler (1950) found that therapists of different orientations held very similar views regarding their conception of an ideal therapeutic relationship.

Perhaps the most influential writer in this area has been Jerome Frank (1993, 1974), whose book *Persuasion and Healing* (originally published in 1961; most recent edition 1993) has been a seminal text in the field of psychotherapy. Frank argued that the effectiveness of therapy is not primarily due to the employment of the specific therapeutic strategies advocated by approaches (e.g., free association, interpretation, systematic desensitization, disowning irrational beliefs, reflection of feeling), but is attributable instead to the operation of a number of general or 'non-specific' factors.

Frank (1974) identified the principal non-specific factors as being the creation of a supportive relationship, the provision of a rationale by which the client can make sense of his or her problems, the instillation of hope, the expression of emotion, and the participation by both client and therapist in healing rituals. Frank (1974: 272) wrote that although these factors are delivered in different ways by different counselling approaches, they all operate to 'heighten the patient's sense of mastery over the inner and outer forces assailing him by labeling them and fitting them into a conceptual scheme, as well as by supplying success experiences'. The model of non-specific therapeutic factors created by Jerome

Frank is all the more convincing in that his analysis was based not only on the study of psychological therapies in Western industrial societies, but also incorporated evidence from investigations of healing practices in all cultures.

Box 17.1: *'Demoralization' as a common factor in therapy*

One of the great gifts of Jerome Frank (1910–2005) was his capacity to describe the process of therapy in ways that transcend the limits of any one single approach, yet apply to all approaches. A good example of this strategy lies in his use of the concept of *demoralization* to account for the reasons why a person might seek therapy in the first place. Frank (1974: 271) asserts that:

> the chief problem of all patients who come to psychotherapy is demoraliza-tion and . . . the effectiveness of all psychotherapeutic schools lies in their ability to restore patients' morale . . . Of course, patients seldom present themselves to therapists with the complaint that they are demoralized; rather, they seek relief for an enormous variety of symptoms and behavior disorders, and both patients and therapists see relief or modification of these as the prime goal of therapy. However, surveys of general populations, confirmed by clinical experience, indicate that only a small proportion of people with psychopathological symptoms come to therapy; apparently something else must be added that interacts with their symptoms. This state of mind, which may be termed 'demoralization', results from the persistent failure to cope with internally or externally induced stresses that the person and those close to him expect him to handle. Its characteristic features, not all of which need be present in any one person, are feelings of impotence, isolation and despair. The person's self-esteem is damaged, and he feels rejected by others because of his failure to meet their expectations . . . The most frequent symptoms of patients in psychotherapy – anxiety and depression – are direct expressions of demoralization.

The concept of demoralization, as used here by Frank, not only accounts for widely accepted ideas about therapy (e.g., anxiety and depression in clients), but also helps to explain a fact that is generally ignored by therapy theories (why relatively few people who are anxious and depressed make use of therapy). The use of 'remoralization' or 'restoration of morale' as the primary goal of therapy also brings together apparently conflicting theo-retical points of view: restoring morale involves not only the recovery of self-esteem, but also developing the means to 'cope with internally or externally induced stresses that . . . those close to him expect him to handle' (Frank 1974: 271).

The 'non-specific' hypothesis has stimulated extensive debate within the field (Hill 1989; Parloff 1986; Strupp 1986), since it directly challenges the beliefs of most counsellors and therapists that their own specific techniques and intervention strategies do have a positive effect on clients. One of the outcomes of this scholarly activity has been the generation of a large number of suggestions regarding a whole range of non-specific factors not mentioned by Frank (1974).

The literature on non-specific or 'common' factors has been reviewed by Grencavage and Norcross (1990), who compiled a list of all the factors mentioned by at least 10 per cent of the fifty articles and books included in their review. They identified four broad categories of non-specific factors, reflecting client characteristics, therapist qualities, change processes and treatment methods. They found that the highest levels of consensus in this review of professional opinion were concerning the therapeutic alliance, the opportunity for catharsis and emotional relief, acquisition and practising of new behaviours, the client having positive expectations, the qualities of the therapist being a source of positive influence on the client, and the provision of a rationale for the client's difficulties.

There are three important sources of evidence that lend support to the non-specific hypothesis:

- research findings that demonstrate that different theoretical orientations, using different specific strategies, report similar success rates;
- non-professional counsellors, who have not received enough training to be able to claim mastery of specific techniques, appear to be as effective as highly trained professional therapists;
- participants in studies of the experiences of clients in therapy, when clients are asked what they find most helpful, tend to rate non-specific elements more highly than specific techniques.

In general, research into the existence of non-specific factors has pointed to a huge area of shared common ground between different therapies (Hubble *et al.* 1999). Indeed, one of the unintended and unexpected consequences of the expansion of research into the processes and outcomes of specific approaches to therapy, has been the discovery of an ever-expanding list of points of similarities between different approaches.

However, the strong evidence that points in the direction of the key role of non-specific factors, it is a misunderstanding of the non-specific hypothesis to conclude that effective counselling consists *only* of these common factors. There are all sorts of complex interactions between common factors, specific techniques and theoretical models. For example, the instigation of a specific CBT technique, such as exposure to a feared event, may have the effect of enhancing the potency of common or non-specific factors such as hope ('this is going to help me get better') and the therapy relationship ('my therapists understands and appreciates what I need, and cares enough to organize this intervention that is designed around my needs'). Nevertheless, it makes sense to acknowledge that at the heart of any counselling relationship there are a set of generic, common processes. The diversity of theories and approaches can therefore plausibly be viewed as different versions of one common activity, rather than as fundamentally different activities.

Box 17.2: *Non-specific factors in action: the performance of a non-professional counsellor*

In a carefully designed and controlled study, Strupp and Hadley (1979) were able to show that, under certain conditions, non-professional counsellors could be just as effective as highly trained professional therapists. The study was carried out in a university in the USA, with male clients being referred either to professional therapists or to members of academic staff with an interest in student well-being. In addition to the main report of the study published by Strupp and Hadley (1979), the research team completed intensive case study analyses in which they contrasted success and failure cases seen by the same therapist.

In Strupp (1980a), an analysis is presented of the work of a non-professional counsellor who participated in the study. Dr H was a professor of statistics in his early forties. His most successful client, assessed in terms of standard outcome measures, was Sam, who was 21, mildly depressed, moderately anxious and withdrawn, and describing himself as lacking in confidence. Sam received 20 sessions of therapy, and was significantly improved at termination and follow-up. Examination of recordings of these counselling sessions showed that Dr H adopted a robustly common-sense approach to the task. He talked a lot, took the initiative and was ready to offer advice and reassurance. For example, at the end of the first session, during which Sam had been discussing some problems with his relationship with his father, Dr H told him 'try to get along with your father over Thanksgiving weekend . . . just try . . . the world isn't lost if you don't succeed' (Strupp 1980a: 837). Although Dr H seemed quite happy to encourage Sam to talk about everyday topics such as courses, the university football team or campus politics, from time to time he would also guide him back to more conventionally therapeutic topics such as his difficulties in relating to girls or his parents, and his problems around controlling his anger. However, Sam frequently avoided talking about difficult issues, and on these occasions Dr H did not appear to possess any strategies or techniques for keeping Sam focused on therapeutic business. Dr H usually offered Sam a cup of tea. There were virtually no silences during sessions.

In many respects, therefore, Dr H did not behave in the style that might be expected from a trained counsellor. Strupp (1980a: 834) comments that, from the perspective of the research team analysing the tapes, 'many of the exchanges eventually became tedious and dreary, not unlike a conversation one might overhear in a barbershop'. Nevertheless, Sam improved. And the benefits he gained from the therapy can be attributed to a variety of non-specific factors. Strupp (1980a: 834) sums up the case in this way:

> [Dr H] displayed a benign, accepting, and supportive fatherly attitude that extended to Sam's life, academic pursuits, and worries about the choice of a career. This was in contrast to Sam's relationship to his parents . . . A camaraderie between the therapist and the patient was established, which Sam clearly enjoyed. While Dr H became Sam's ally and confidant, the therapist resisted Sam's occasional attempts to make him a partner in his cynical attitude toward the world.

Dr H's view of the case was that:

> I felt that I understood what his problems were right away and they were suffi-
> ciently minor so that they could be worked out with a little empathy and an
> older-brother type relationship. Mostly we just talked, and I'd encourage him
> to do things rather than just sit around his room. He responded fairly well to
> little suggestions. I think he just sort of hit a period in his life when he was
> lonely and just a bit depressed about breaking up with his girl . . . it was not
> difficult for me to put myself back at 18 or 19 and recall being in similar
> situations.
>
> (Strupp 1980a: 837–8)

The non-specific factors that appeared to be operating in this case were that the client was
able to enter a relationship in which he was offered a high degree of respect and acceptance and was valued by a high-status member of the culture in which he lived, where the
therapist acted as an effective model of how to cope with social situations, the client was
allowed to tell his story and the therapist provided a framework (his own personal philosophy of life) for making sense of troubles and how to resolve them.

The movement towards integration

Historically, the psychotherapy profession has been largely structured around distinct,
separate sets of ideas or theoretical models, each backed up by its own training institute or
professional association. Most therapy textbooks are organized around chapters on individual theorists, such as Freud, Rogers, Perls and Ellis, or are specifically devoted to single
schools of thought. The impression given by these characteristics is that counsellors would
in general be members of one or another of these subgroups, and adhere to one specific
approach. Increasingly, however, counsellors and therapists are looking beyond the
confines of theoretical purity. A series of studies in the 1960s and 1970s showed that more
and more practitioners were describing themselves as 'eclectic' or 'integrationist' in
approach, rather than being followers of any one single model. Garfield and Kurtz (1974),
for example, carried out a survey of 855 clinical psychologists in the USA, and found that
55 per cent defined themselves as eclectic, 16 per cent as psychoanalytic/psychodynamic,
10 per cent as behavioural and 7 per cent as Rogerian, humanistic and existential (the
remaining 12 per cent were divided between a wide range of other orientations).

Garfield and Kurtz (1977) followed up the eclectic clinical psychologists from their
1974 study and found that 49 per cent had at some time in the past adhered to a single
theory and 45 per cent had always seen themselves as eclectic. Of those who had once
been single-approach oriented, the main shift was from psychoanalysis and Rogerian to
eclecticism. Prochaska and Norcross (1983), in a survey of 410 psychotherapists in the
USA, reported figures of: eclectic 30 per cent, psychodynamic 18 per cent, psychoanalytic
9 per cent, cognitive 8 per cent, behavioural 6 per cent, existential 4 per cent, gestalt 3 per
cent, humanistic 4 per cent, Rogerian 2 per cent and other approaches 15 per cent.

O'Sullivan and Dryden (1990) found that 32 per cent of clinical psychologists in one region in Britain designated themselves as eclectic in orientation. Hollanders and McLeod (1999) carried out a survey of over 300 counsellors and psychotherapists in Britain, drawn from a number of professional associations. Participants were allowed to describe their theoretical orientation in a way that respected the complexity of their theoretical influences. For example, when asked about the intervention techniques they used, 95 per cent showed an eclectic mix of intervention strategies. Based on their theoretical framework, 49 per cent of participants in the survey reported themselves as *explicitly* eclectic/integrative, with another 38 per cent being *implicitly* eclectic/integrative (identifying themselves with a single theoretical model but also acknowledging being influenced by other models). Only 13 per cent of the practitioners included in the Hollanders and McLeod (1999) survey could be regarded as unequivocal followers of a 'pure' approach.

A membership survey conducted by the British Association for Counselling and Psychotherapy (2001a) indicated that 36 per cent of members defined themselves as predominantly person-centred in orientation, 25 per cent as psychodynamic and 13 per cent as integrative. However, the majority of those who aligned themselves with 'pure' approaches also reported that they had been influenced by other models. A survey of psychologists who were members of Division 12 (clinical psychology) of the American Psychological Association, revealed that 29 per cent selected eclectic/integrative as their primary theoretical orientation (Norcross *et al.* 2005).

One of the issues thrown up by these studies has been the sheer difficulty of finding meaningful ways of getting information about counsellors' theoretical orientations; there are so many different, often highly idiosyncratic, combinations of approaches that it is hard to design a questionnaire that will do justice to what counsellors want to say about themselves (Poznanski and McLennan 1995). It is therefore hard to compare, with any confidence, the findings of different studies, regarding proportions of therapists who espouse particular approaches, or to interpret historical trends that might be taking place. Findings are also highly dependent on the sample of therapists that is used, with distinctive profiles of therapeutic orientation reported by practitioners affiliated to different professional organizations. Nevertheless, the trend across all surveys of counsellors and psychotherapists has been that some form of eclecticism/integrationism has either emerged as the single most popular approach, or has been a significant source of influence even among those therapists who operate mainly within a single model. It also seems likely that the profession is gradually moving away from theoretical purity, and in the direction of eclecticism/integrationism. For example, the study by Norcross *et al.* (2005) asked respondents to indicate the trajectory of their theoretical development. They found that half of the eclectic integrationist therapists in their sample had previously defined themselves as committed to a single model, and had gradually added other methods and viewpoints into their original approach.

The debate over the merits of integrated versus 'pure' approaches

The roots of the trend towards eclecticism and integrationism can be found in some of the earliest writings in the field. For example, as behaviourism began to be influential in the

1930s and 1940s, a number of writers, such as Dollard, Miller and Rosenzweig, were beginning to explore ways in which parallels and connections could be made between behavioural and psychoanalytic ideas and methods (see Marmor and Woods 1980). As humanistic thinking achieved prominence in the 1950s the commonalities and divergences between it and existing approaches were widely debated. It could well be argued that there is no such thing as a 'pure' theory. All theorists are influenced by what has gone before. Freudian ideas can be seen as representing a creative integration of concepts from philosophy, medicine, biology and literature. The client-centred model encompasses ideas from psychoanalysis, existential and phenomenological philosophy and social psychology. The cognitive–behavioural approach is an example of an overt synthesis of two strands of psychological theory: behaviourism and cognitive psychology (and, more recently, constructivist philosophy). Nevertheless, even though there has been an integrationist 'underground' within the field of therapy, it is probably reasonable to suggest that the dominant view until the 1960s was that different models and approaches provided perfectly viable alternative ways of working with clients, and that, on the whole, theoretical 'purity' was to be preferred.

A significant number of influential writers have remained convinced that any form of theoretical combination would inevitably result in muddle and confusion, and that it was necessary to stick to one consistent approach. Voices speaking out against the integrationist trend included Eysenck (1970: 145), who vividly asserted that to follow in the direction of theoretical integration would lead us to nothing but a:

> mishmash of theories, a huggermugger of procedures, a gallimaufry of therapies and a charivaria of activities having no proper rationale, and incapable of being tested or evaluated. What are needed in science and in medicine are clear-cut theories leading to specific procedures applicable to specific types of patients.

Eysenck (1970) argued that, in his view, only behaviour therapy could provide the kind of logically consistent and scientifically evaluated approach he believed was necessary. Another critic of integrationism, but this time from a psychoanalytic perspective, has been Szasz (1974: 41):

> The psychotherapist who claims to practice in a flexible manner, tailoring his therapy to the needs of his patients, does so by assuming a variety of roles. With one patient, he is a magician who hypnotizes; with another, a sympathetic friend who reassures; with a third, a physician who dispenses tranquilizers; with a fourth, a classical analyst who interprets; and so on . . . The eclectic psychotherapist is, more often than not, a role player; he wears a variety of psychotherapeutic mantles, but owns none and is usually truly comfortable in none. Instead of being skilled in a multiplicity of therapeutic techniques, he suffers from what we may consider, after Erikson, 'a diffusion of professional identity'. In sum, the therapist who tries to be all things to all people may be nothing to himself; he is not 'at one' with any particular method of psychotherapy. If he engages in intensive psychotherapy, his patient is likely to discover this.

Theoretical purists argue that there are conflicting philosophical assumptions underlying different approaches, and that any attempt to combine them is likely to lead to confusion (Eysenck) or inauthenticity (Szasz). For example, within psychoanalysis the actions of a person are regarded as ultimately determined by unconscious motives arising from repressed childhood experiences. By contrast, humanistic theories view people as capable of choice and free will. It could be argued that these are irreconcilably opposing ways of making sense of human nature, and can only breed contradiction if combined into one approach to counselling (Patterson 1989).

Another type of confusion can be created by taking ideas or techniques out of context. For example, systematic desensitization is a therapeutic technique that has been developed within a behavioural perspective in which anxiety is understood in terms of a conditioned fear response to a stimulus. A humanistic counsellor who understood anxiety in terms of threat to the self-concept might invite the client to engage in a process that could superficially resemble systematic desensitization, but the meaning of the procedure would be radically different.

A final source of confusion that can result from an eclectic approach reflects the difficulties involved in mastering concepts and methods from different theories. It is hard enough, according to this line of argument, to be a competent counsellor within one approach, without attempting to achieve a depth of understanding and experience in them all.

If the main objection to eclecticism is that it can result in confusion and misunderstanding, a secondary objection is that it may undermine effective training, supervision and support. If a theoretical model provides a language through which to discuss and reflect on the complex reality of work with clients, it is surely helpful to work with trainers, supervisors and colleagues who share the same language. Similarly, research or scholarship in a field of study are facilitated when everyone involved can agree on the meaning of terminology. This is a strong argument in favour of at least a strong degree of theoretical purity. The language of psychoanalysis and the psychodynamic approach, for example, is over 100 years old, and constitutes a rich and extensive literature on just about every aspect of human psychological and cultural functioning that can be imagined. Only specialists within a psychodynamic approach, it is argued, can really make effective use of these resources. Integrationist practitioners with a more superficial grasp of psychodynamic language would be much less able to find their way through this material.

Despite the cogency of the critique of eclecticism and integration that has been mounted by writers such as Eysenck and Szasz, it is perhaps worth noting that the quotations cited above date back to the 1970s. There are few, if any, contemporary figures who would seek to mount such an outright condemnation of the integrationist movement. The current consensus would appear to be that integration is in principle a desirable aim, while remaining difficult to achieve in practice.

It can be seen, therefore, that for many years the field of counselling and psychotherapy has been involved in an internal debate over the relative merits of theoretical purity as against integration or eclecticism. Behind this debate is a much larger question, around how far integration can go. Is it possible, even in principle, to create a universally acceptable framework for understanding human behaviour? The experience of the 'hard' sciences, such as physics and biology, suggest that, at least in these domains, the creation of a dominant 'paradigm' (Kuhn 1962) has had huge advantages in terms of enabling systematic accumulation of practical knowledge. On the other hand, it is possible to argue that, in the domain of social life, the adoption of a single framework for understanding could be oppressive – the absence of debate over fundamental assumptions about human nature and society is associated with totalitarian and authoritarian states. From yet another point of view, the Western tendency to divide reality into competing dualisms (e.g., psychoanalysis versus behaviourism), rather than envisaging the world as a seamless whole, can be seen as equally dangerous.

In practice, the debate between theoretical purists and integrationists is being won by the latter group, in terms of the increasing proportion of practitioners who embrace at least some degree of integration in their work. However, for any therapist seeking to combine theories and concepts from different approaches, there remains a critical issue of *how* to achieve a satisfactory and coherent synthesis of ideas. As the following section demonstrates, there are several integrative strategies that can be adopted.

Strategies for achieving integration

How can different theories and techniques be combined? Within the counselling and psychotherapy professions, the urge to create a broader, more all-encompassing approach has taken a variety of forms. In practice, counsellors and psychotherapists interested in combining theories and methods have forged a number of different pathways towards integration: *technical eclecticism*, the *common factors* approach, *theoretical integration, disorder-based integration, assimilative integration, collective integration*, and *pluralism*.

Technical eclecticism

An eclectic approach to therapy is one in which the therapist chooses the best or most appropriate techniques from a range of theories or models, in order to meet the needs of each individual client. One of the distinctive features of eclecticism, as applied in therapy, is that it has focused almost entirely on the selection of therapeutic techniques or procedures, and has paid little attention to the question of the theoretical framework within which these interventions have been developed:

> . . . . to attempt a theoretical rapprochement is as futile as trying to picture the edge of the universe. But to read through the vast amount of literature on psychotherapy, *in search of techniques*, can be clinically enriching and therapeutically rewarding.
>
> (Lazarus 1967: 416)

> . . . . however interesting, plausible, and appealing a theory may be, it is techniques, not theories, that are actually used on people. Study of the effects of psychotherapy, therefore, is always the study of the effectiveness of techniques.
>
> (London 1964: 33)

Eclecticism is a highly pragmatic approach to therapy, which concentrates on 'what works' in practice rather than bothering to any great extent about the underlying images of the person or systems of theoretical constructs.

The term 'eclectic', as a description of a form of therapy practice, was fashionable in the 1960s, but subsequently has dropped out of favour. Although eclecticism is an attractive idea that makes a lot of intuitive sense, the weakness of a purely eclectic approach is that it does not define the criteria on which the choice of technique is to be based. The lack of interest in theory compounds this difficulty, because it eliminates a possible source of criteria that might inform the identification of suitable techniques. In the absence of such criteria, there can be a tendency for the practitioner to select interventions on weak grounds (e.g., 'I attended a weekend workshop on CBT, so all of my clients in the following week will be getting homework assignments'). In recent times, therefore, undefined or 'simple' eclecticism has been regarded by critics as comprising a muddle-headed approach: 'eclecticism connotes undisciplined subjectivity . . . many of these psychotherapists wander around in a daze of professional nihilism experimenting with new fad methods indiscriminately' (Norcross 2005: 15).

Those practitioners who have remained convinced of the potential value of eclecticism have been stimulated by these criticisms to develop a more systematic approach to the selection of techniques. This more rigorous version of eclecticism is called *technical eclecticism*. The practice of technical eclecticism is based on two key principles:

- careful assessment of the presenting problems, personality and therapeutic goals of the client;
- recourse to research evidence to guide the selection of an effective intervention package, tailored to the characteristics of the client.

There have been two key figures in the development of technical eclecticism, both highly influential clinical psychologists in the USA: Arnold Lazarus and Larry Beutler. The approach constructed by Lazarus is called *multimodal therapy* (Lazarus 1989a, 1989b, 2005; Eskapa 1992). Clients' presenting problems are assessed within seven discrete domains: behaviour, affect, sensation, imagery, cognition, interpersonal relationships, drugs/biology. Lazarus (1989a,1989b) uses the term *BASIC-ID* as a mnemonic for these domains. The task of the therapist is to identify the main focus for client work, using an assessment interview and a multimodal life history questionnaire, and then choose the most relevant intervention techniques, based on research findings. In practice, the technical eclecticism of Lazarus operates mainly within the cognitive–behavioural. A somewhat similar approach has been developed, within a humanistic/creative arts tradition, by the Israeli psychologist Mooli Lahad, with his *BASIC Ph* framework (belief, affect, social, imagination, cognitive, physiological) (Lahad 1992, 1995, 2002). The *BASIC Ph* system, which has been widely used in work with children, is less rigorously grounded in research evidence than is the multimodal therapy model.

The other significant contribution to technical eclecticism is the *systematic treatment selection* approach developed by Beutler and his colleagues (Beutler 1983; Beutler and Clarkin 1990; Beutler *et al.* 2005). The assessment matrix used in systematic treatment selection is organized around six key variables: problem complexity, chronicity, level of functional impairment, coping style, resistance level and distress. An attractive feature of this approach, for many practitioners, is the extent to which it is highly sensitive to the personality and moment-by-moment experiencing of the client. For example, clients whose personality structure is built around externalizing their problems, will respond better to interventions that provide a high degree of structure, whereas those who tend to internalize their problems will respond better to interventions that promote insight and self-awareness. Similarly the client's immediate level of distress functions as an indicator of whether the therapist should provide support or challenge. The approach goes beyond the original emphasis in technical eclecticism, on technique, and opens up a range of possibilities around shaping the client–therapist *relationship* in accordance with the client's needs. It is perhaps worth noting that the original training received by Larry Beutler was in client-centred therapy (see Beutler 2001).

A major advantage of technical eclecticism is that this perspective on integration is largely atheoretical and thus avoids pointless debate over the compatibility (or otherwise) of theoretical constructs. On the other hand, by focusing largely on technique rather than theory, there is a danger that this approach misses out on some, or all, of the valuable functions of theory in relation to supplying organizing principles for practice (see Chapter 4). A key challenge for technical eclecticism, is that, strictly speaking, it relies on the existence of sound research evidence concerning the effectiveness of particular techniques with particular categories of client. Such evidence is frequently not available, forcing the clinician to rely on his or her personal experience, which will have been at least partly shaped by theoretical assumptions, suppositions and other factors. A further challenge lies in the fact that technical eclecticism calls for a high level of knowledge and competence in the practitioner, in respect of assessment procedures, familiarity with the research evidence and the effective delivery of specific techniques.

Eclecticism has a great deal to offer, as a strategy for combining ideas and methods from different therapy traditions (Lazarus *et al.* 1992). The 'bad press' that eclecticism has received may be attributable to its status as the earliest form of therapy integration to receive widespread publicity – to a large extent, other approaches to integration (discussed below) have based their credibility on defining the ways in which they are 'better than' eclecticism. The abiding appeal of eclecticism, for counselling and psychotherapy practitioners, can be seen in the wide sales of books that provide catalogues of techniques, such as Carrell (2001), Seiser and Wastell (2002), and Yalom (2002).

Box 17.3: *The limitations of therapy based on a single approach*

The research literature on the effectiveness of therapy includes a large number of studies that demonstrate the effectiveness of 'pure', single-theory approaches (see Lambert 2004). However, there is also evidence that at least some clients are unhappy with what they experience as rigidly defined therapeutic regimes. In one study, based on in-depth interviews with clients who had received psychodynamic psychotherapy, Lilliengren and Werbart (2005) found that around 40 per cent of the clients felt that there had been 'something missing' in their therapy. Although most of these clients reported that they had benefited from what their therapist had been able to offer, they also believed that there had been an intrinsic limitation in what was provided, with the effect that their therapy was experienced as incomplete.

A collection of articles written by strongly dissatisfied clients, and edited by Bates (2006), provides a different kind of evidence. The recurring theme, in the stories of these clients who felt that they had been damaged by their therapy, was not necessarily that their therapist was exploitative or personality disordered, but that he or she was ideologically far too rigid – when a particular approach or line of intervention was clearly not working, they persisted in increasing the intensity of the intervention, rather than trying something different.

The common factors approach

The common factors approach to therapy integration is associated with the work of Scott Miller, Barry Duncan and Mark Hubble, and also more recently Bruce Wampold. The guiding principle in this form of integration is the writings of Jerome Frank (1974), which identified a number of therapeutic elements (or 'common factors') that were present in all forms of counselling and psychotherapy, and indeed in healing practices worldwide. Miller, Duncan and Hubble (Miller *et al.* 1997, 2005; Duncan and Miller 2000; Hubble *et al.* 1999) regard four common factors as particularly important: extratherapeutic events (helpful experiences that occur outside of the therapy room – for example, the client becoming friends with someone who is supportive to them); the therapy relationship; the instillation of hope and positive expectations for change; and specific 'therapy rituals' (the structure of the therapeutic work, the use of techniques). They argue that we live in a culture in which there are many competing and alternative theories about what causes personal problems, and how such problems can be resolved, and that it is therefore necessary to base therapy on the 'theory of change' espoused by each individual client: interventions should be complementary to the *client's* theory.

The secret of effective therapy, from a common factors perspective, is to pay attention to 'what works' for each client, by using the client's beliefs as a starting point, and subsequently obtaining regular feedback regarding the client's experience of the process and outcome of therapy. Feedback is collected during sessions ('what would be helpful now?' 'how helpful was that discussion we just had?') and across sessions. At the start of each session, the Session Rating Scale (SRS) is used to evaluate the quality of the therapeutic relationship, and the Outcome Rating Scale (ORS) is used to monitor the amount of change achieved by the client. These are brief scales, which take only a few minutes to complete. The aim is to give the client an explicit opportunity to communicate his or her views about what is working, and not working, in the therapy. Evidence that the therapy is working, is an indication to continue as before. Evidence that it is not working is a signal to pause and review what has been happening, and in particular to reflect on whether the four common therapeutic factors are being implemented to a sufficient degree.

Although the core members of the common factors group have been primarily influenced by ideas from solution-focused therapy (Miller *et al.* 1996), their approach can be readily adopted by any counsellor or psychotherapist, whatever their primary theoretical orientation may have been. From a common factors point of view, almost anything can be therapeutic – the essential criterion is whether it makes a positive difference to the client. The common factors group position themselves as radical critics of mainstream therapy; they describe what they do as a 'new way to think about therapy' (Miller, S.D. 2004), and maintain a website (http://scottdmiller.com/) that seeks to interpret a range of professional issues from a common factors perspective in which the client is portrayed as a heroic figure who is resourcefully seeking to improve his or her life (Duncan *et al.* 2004).

The common factors approach to therapy integration has been highly influential, in terms of providing a coherent counter-argument to the proponents of theoretical purity. The idea of common factors has served to liberate many practitioners from the intellectual confines of their initial, single-theory training. However, until now, the common factors model has not stimulated the formation of a professional community beyond the Miller, Duncan and Hubble group. This may be because the common factors model does not actually specify what a therapist should do, in terms of specific procedures and techniques (other than access the client's theory of change, and use outcome information). The common factors model operates as a kind of 'meta-perspective', which is useful for therapists who are already competent in a range of specific methods.

Box 17.4: *Hope as a common factor*

The instillation of hope was identified by Jerome Frank (1974) as a common factor in all forms of emotional healing. Since that time, there has been a substantial amount of research into the ways in which counselling can help clients to develop hope that their problems can be overcome. Larsen and Stege (2012) interviewed clients about what their counsellors did in early sessions that led to them feeling more hopeful. What they found was that ordinary counselling responses, such as inviting the client to talk about him/herself, could have a positive impact:

> I'm not accustomed to being asked about me . . . that's a hopeful thing. . . . It's hopeful that I would find the rejuvenation of my spirit in thinking about me and who I am and what I want, rather than focusing on what other people need . . . so the hope there lay in the fact that I was identifying things about myself, which would lead to a hopeful future.
>
> (Larsen and Stege 2012: 49)

This kind of finding, that what seems to happen in effective counselling is that a general hopeful stance on the part of the counsellor is subtly conveyed to the client in a myriad of different ways, is backed up by results from several other studies. A comprehensive overview of theory and research on the role of hope in counselling can be found in O'Hara (2013).

Theoretical integration

Theoretical integration can be defined as the construction of a new approach to therapy that draws upon concepts and methods from already existing approaches. A key strategy in achieving theoretical integration has been to find a central theoretical concept or framework within which some or all existing approaches can be subsumed. Barkham (1992) has suggested that successful implementation of this strategy involves the identification of higher-order constructs that can account for change mechanisms beyond the level of any single model. The aim is to produce a cognitive 'map' that will enable the links and connections between ideas and techniques to be understood. There are several examples of approaches to counselling and therapy that have effectively employed higher-order or transtheoretical constructs in this way, to create a new theoretical integration: reality therapy, the Egan 'skilled helper' model, the self-confirmation model and cognitive analytic therapy (CAT).

Reality therapy

Reality therapy represents one of the most theoretically interesting approaches to counselling and psychotherapy that can be found within the current literature, because it brings together ideas from several therapy traditions. Reality therapy was founded by William Glasser, a psychiatrist, in 1965, and has been widely adopted in many countries around the world, including Malaysia and Taiwan. It has been extensively used by schools counsellors, with Pryzwansky *et al.* (1984) reporting that it was the most widely applied specific model, in a survey of schools counsellors in the USA carried out in 1981. It has also been used in marital/couples counselling, and therapy for survivors of sexual abuse (Ellsworth 2007) as well as in general counselling practice. The use of reality therapy in counselling is supported by accredited training programmes, a journal and a programme of research (Wubbolding 2000).

The central or 'transtheoretical' construct that lies at the heart of reality therapy is the concept of *choice*. Glasser (2000: xv) contends that 'we choose essentially everything we do'. The main focus of therapy is therefore to encourage the client to stop choosing to do things that lead to unhappiness, and to begin to choose to do things that are consistent with their inner sense of what is right for them (their internal 'quality world'). The emphasis on choice, alongside a lack of interest in exploring how the client feels, might appear to locate reality therapy as a member of the cognitive therapy/CBT family of therapies. Reality therapy incorporates strategies for cognitive change that could, in fact, be seen as an improvement on standard CBT practice. For example, reality therapists do not require clients to spend time identifying irrational thoughts or negative automatic thoughts, as a precursor to changing these cognitive patterns. Rather, reality therapists get straight to the point of all this, which is to choose to see the world in a different way. In addition, reality therapy pays special attention to the language that the client uses to talk about their problems, and teaches clients to use 'choice language': for example, rather than 'being depressed', a person 'depresses' himself or herself. This new way of talking has the effect of taking the client a step closer to choosing not to 'depress' him/herself.

However, there are other elements of reality therapy theory and practice that are significantly different from cognitive therapy or CBT. The main difference lies in the emphasis in reality therapy on the importance of relationships. Reality therapy is a profoundly relational therapy, in that there is a general assumption that the reason why clients seek counselling is that they experience a specific relationship difficulty. Reality therapy includes a model of human needs, and how satisfying relationships depend on each partner's needs being satisfied. There is also a strong value position based on the principle that people should not try to control others. Overall, therefore, reality therapy consists of a creative synthesis of ideas and practices from both cognitively oriented and relationship-oriented approaches to therapy. Some reality therapy themes also reflect aspects of existential therapy, for instance around the importance of personal responsibility.

For reasons of space, this summary of reality therapy theory and practice inevitably reflects only a partial and incomplete account of what it has to offer. Further information is available from two contrasting sources. Glasser (2000) provides a highly accessible introduction to reality therapy, based on numerous case examples. By contrast, Wubbolding (2000) provides a more formal, structured introduction. Reality therapy represents a prime example of theoretical integration based on the bold and rigorous use of a central construct (choice) as an organizing principle for therapy practice.

The Egan 'skilled helper' model

An example of a theoretical approach to integration, which is widely used within the world of counselling, is the 'skilled helper' model constructed by Egan (2009). The key integrating concept chosen by Egan is that of *problem management*. Egan suggests that clients who seek assistance from counsellors and other helpers are experiencing difficulties in coping with problems in their lives, and that the primary task of the helper is to enable the person to find and act on appropriate solutions to these problems. The emphasis is therefore on a problem-solving process, which involves three stages.

First, the client is helped to describe and explore the 'present scenario', the problem situation that he or she is faced with at present. The second stage is to articulate a 'preferred scenario', which includes future goals and objectives. The third stage is to develop and implement action strategies for moving from the current to the preferred scenario.

Egan describes substages within each stage, and identifies the client tasks and helper skills necessary to facilitate this problem-solving process. The Egan model can usefully be viewed as a 'map' through which the usefulness of relevant elements of other approaches can be located and evaluated. For example, the concept of empathy is taken from client-centred theory and regarded as a communication skill essential to the helping process, and the idea of congruence is included under 'immediacy'. From a psychodynamic perspective, the aim of insight is included in Egan's goal of identifying and challenging 'blind spots' in the client.

Many counsellors and therapists have used the Egan model as a framework through which they can employ techniques and methods from a wide range of approaches: for example, gestalt exercises as a way of challenging blind spots or assertiveness training as a way of developing action strategies.

A valuable case study in Inskipp and Johns (1984) illustrates some of the ways in which various ideas can be included within the skilled helper model, and Wosket (2006) reviews recent developments and applications of the Egan model in a range of settings. The main strengths of the skilled helper model are that it offers an intensely practical and pragmatic approach to working with people, and that it is applicable to a wide variety of situations, ranging from individual counselling to organizational consultation. As an integrationist approach, its limitation is that it is primarily based on a cognitive–behavioural perspective. Although the model clearly encompasses some elements of humanistic and person-centred thinking, through such concepts as respect, immediacy and empathy, it includes very little from the psychodynamic approaches. Key concepts from psychodynamic approaches, such as the importance of childhood object relations, the idea of defence mechanisms and unconscious processing or the notion of transference, are all absent.

The self-confirmation model

The core idea in the self-confirmation model is that the individual acts in the world to reaffirm his or her self-concept (Andrews 1991). The process of self-confirmation involves a feedback loop consisting of a number of stages. The self-concept of the person represents the way he or she perceives his or her attitudes, feeling states, ways of acting in situations and all other dimensions of 'what is me'. This sense of self generates characteristic needs and expectations. For example, a person who views herself as 'dominant' may experience a need or drive to be powerful and controlling in relationships, and will expect other people to follow her directives. Patterns of behaviour and action will ensue that are consistent with the underlying needs and expectations of the person, and his or her basic self-concept. This behaviour is, in turn, perceived and reacted to by others, some of whom are people with whom the person is actually in relationship (e.g., friends, colleagues) but some being 'internalized others' (e.g., mental images of parents or other significant others). The person then perceives the response of these others and not only cognitively interprets that response but also has a feeling or emotional reaction to it. These inner experiences are assimilated into the self-concept, and the process resumes.

At the heart of the self-confirmation model is that at all these stages the person acts in order to prevent outcomes that are dissonant or in conflict with his or her self-concept. Problems in living occur when the person engages in distortion at one or more of the stages in the feedback loop, in order to protect the self-concept from contradictory information from the environment. The objective of counselling or psychotherapy is, therefore, to enable the client to understand how self-confirmation operates in his or her life, and to change what is happening at those stages of the loop where the most serious distortion is occurring. The model enables an integration of a wide variety of therapeutic concepts and strategies, by providing a model that combines all of the issues (self-concept, motivation, behaviour, object relations and so forth) from all other models.

Cognitive analytic therapy (CAT)

Cognitive analytic therapy (CAT) is an integrationist approach that is widely used in Britain. It was originally developed by Anthony Ryle (1990) and has been further articulated through a number of publications (Ryle and Cowmeadow 1992; Ryle 1995, 2005; Ryle and Kerr 2002). The key transtheoretical concept that underpins CAT is the idea of the *procedure*: a sequence of goal-directed behaviour that incorporates cognitive, emotional and social processes. Cognitive analytic therapy is based on ideas from cognitive psychology and cognitive therapy, psychoanalysis and developmental psychology. The cognitive dimension of the model concerns the ways that people engage in intentional activity through sequences of mental and behavioural acts. In pursuing their life goals, people run into trouble when they encounter traps, dilemmas and snags. The psychoanalytic dimension of this model includes the Freudian idea of defence mechanisms as examples of cognitive 'editing', and takes account of the origins of traps, dilemmas and snags in early parent–child interactions.

In practice, CAT is implemented through brief (16-session) therapy, which begins with an exploration of the life history and current functioning of the client. This leads on to a reformulation of the difficulties being experienced by the client, in which the counsellor or therapist identifies targets for change, using diagrams, and letters from the therapist to the client, to define the key ideas in a form that is visible and memorable. One of the significant features of CAT is the extent to which it has remained open to further sources of theoretical influence. For example, in recent years CAT theorists have integrated ideas concerning the dialogical nature of human communication (Hermans and DiMaggio 2004; Leiman 1997).

Issues in theoretical integration

The fundamental difficulties involved in theoretical integration, as well as its potential, can be examined through reflection on the approaches outlined above. Although all four models successfully integrate previously existing sets of ideas, they all arrive at a different result regarding a suitable overarching concept or principle. A notable feature of these integrative approaches is that they bring together some ideas but clearly reject others; they are *partial* integrations of previous theory. In effect, Glasser, Egan, Andrews and Ryle have arrived at new theories of therapy. In doing so, it could be argued that they have inevitably fragmented the counselling and psychotherapy world even further. On the other hand, each of these integrative approaches supplies a complete and detailed specification of how to do therapy. This means that people can be trained, from scratch, to deliver these interventions, and that research can be carried out into their effectiveness (see Schottenbauer *et al.* 2005).

The fate of approaches based on theoretical integration is exemplified through the history of these three approaches. The self-confirmation model of Andrews has received little attention, and does not appear to be in current use. The Egan model is widely used, particularly in the counselling community in Britain, but has remained largely static, in conceptual terms, has generated little research, and is not supported by a professional network. By contrast, both reality therapy and CAT have continued to evolve in terms of theory and practice, have generated a considerable amount of research, and are supported by a journal, conferences and a networks of adherents. The lesson here would appear to be that it may be relatively easy to arrive at a novel integration of theory (this is why so may new approaches have emerged in the past 30 years), but that it is much harder for an integrative approach to pass the test of broad professional acceptance that is required in order to become firmly established as a viable form of therapy.

For practitioners and trainees, theoretical integration supplies a relatively straightforward route toward broadening the theoretical base of their practice, through learning more about, and receiving training in, an integrative approach that has already been formulated by others. Full-scale theoretical integration on an individual basis is much harder to attain. It is more likely that individual practitioners seeking to move in the direction of theoretical integration are engaging in what has become known as *assimilative integration* (discussed below).

Box 17.5: *Symptom-oriented versus person-oriented approaches to therapy: a false dichotomy?*

Within the counselling and psychotherapy professional community, a strong source of resistance to forms of integration comes from practitioners who adhere to the idea that effective therapy, and in particular successful brief therapy, needs to stick to a single aim or focus.

Omer (1993) divides therapists into those who believe in the value of a symptom-orientated focus, for example cognitive–behavioural therapists who work with clients to identify cognitive or behavioural goals, and those who adopt a person-oriented focus, for example psychodynamic and person-centred practitioners who work with clients around relationship patterns. Omer (1993) argues that, in contrast to these polarized approaches, an integrative focus does not assume that there is any one basic level (i.e., symptomatic or relational) to which all other can be reduced, but that problems can always be understood from a variety of perspectives. He points out that, from the client's point of view, the problems with which they are struggling nearly always have a symptom dimension and a person dimension.

Omer (1993) describes the case of Sara, a 44-year-old woman who presented with symptoms of claustrophobia and agoraphobia, and could not enter elevators or aircraft, or drive in open areas. As Sara began to explore these problems, it emerged that she had grown up in a family in which there were constant worries about the dangers and catastrophes that lurked in the external world. She also described difficulties in her marriage – her husband indulged in extramarital affairs, and was highly critical of her fear of flying. In acknowledgement of both the symptomatic and personal–relational aspects of Sara's concerns, Omer (1993: 290) offered her the following formulation:

> All through your life you have wished for independence (both from your parents and your husband), but also feared to lose the apparently secure enclosure, first of your parental home, and now of your marriage. In many areas you have succeeded in doing what you wanted, as shown by your openness and curiosity, and by the free atmosphere in which you raise your children. In other areas, however, you carry your home jail with you, restricting yourself, and shunning the dangers of the world outside. Your life alternates between independent expansion and dependent constriction, and you are now at a crossing between the two. Your phobias and your personal autonomy are two sides of the same coin: any progress in dealing with the phobias will lead to personal expansion and autonomy; and any personal expansion and autonomy will make you stronger to fight your phobias.

This statement had a catalytic effect in mobilizing Sara's energies, and setting her on a path that would eventually result in a more satisfying life. Omer (1993) points out that formulations that link together symptoms and broader personal–relational themes make a lot of sense to clients, and typically remain in their minds and operate as a guide for action. He suggests that it also has the effect of liberating the therapist from the unnecessary constraint of refusing to give full attention to an issue (whatever side of the symptom versus person polarity that is being ignored) that is of great significance to the client. An *integrative* focus, therefore, can serve to enhance the quality of the therapist–client alliance.

Disorder-based integrative approaches

A variant of theoretical integration can be found in therapy protocols that have been developed to respond to the needs of specific client groups. The most influential example of this integrative strategy can be found in *dialectical behaviour therapy* (DBT: Heard and Linehan 2005; Linehan 1993a, 1993b), which is described in more detail on page 143. Dialectical behaviour therapy was a response to the widely recognized difficulties in conducting effective therapy with people who were diagnosed as having 'borderline personality disorder'. These are individuals who tend to have major problems in sustaining relationships, due to highly self-destructive patterns of behaviour up to and including suicide attempts. The founder of DBT, Marsha Linehan, worked out that clients in this category had been brought up in 'invalidating' family environments, in which they were harshly criticized, and had learned to suppress their awareness of their emotions. She realized that in addition to core CBT interventions around behaviour change, emotional self-regulation and social skills, such clients required a strongly affirming relationship with a therapist. Dialectical behaviour therapy therefore comprises an integration of ideas from both CBT and relationship-oriented therapy approaches such as person-centred and psychodynamic.

Another example of a disorder-based integrative model is the *understanding your eating* programme developed by Julia Buckroyd, aimed at people who engage in emotional eating. This approach makes use of family systems theory, and psychodynamic concepts such as attachment theory, as a means of helping participants to gain an understanding of the origins and interpersonal function of binge eating, alongside cognitive–behavioural strategies to provide support with eating patterns (Buckroyd 2011; Buckroyd and Rother 2007).

An integrative therapy for traumatized police officers developed by Gersons *et al.* (2000) appears to have been used in only one project. Further examples of integrative approaches constructed for specific client groups can be found in Norcross and Goldfried (2005).

Box 17.6: *The limits of theoretical integration*

What seems to be the case, in relation to attempts to accomplish theoretical integration across different therapy approaches, is that no one has managed to produce a theory of therapy that incorporates all of the ideas and techniques that are available within the literature. One reason for this might be that some therapy approaches are logically incompatible with other approaches. For example, it is very hard to envisage an integration of psychodynamic therapy and narrative therapy, because the underlying image of the person is so different in each tradition (White 2011). At the level of an individual therapist or client, both of these sets of ideas might have some meaning. But at a more abstract theoretical level, a psychodynamic transference relationship that bases the process of change in what is happening between client and therapist, and a narrative therapy 'de-centred' relationship that encourages the client to pay attention to what is happening for them outside the therapy room, are heading in quite different therapeutic directions.

Assimilative integration

A particularly fertile approach to understanding integrationism may be to view it as a personal process undertaken by individual counsellors and psychotherapists, arising from ongoing personal and professional development over the course of their careers. Several writers have commented that one of the central tasks for any counsellor is to develop his or her own personal approach. Smail (1978) and Lomas (1981) have been particularly insistent that theory and techniques must be assimilated into the person of the therapist.

Lomas (1981: 3) writes that the essence of counselling or therapy is 'the manifestation of creative human qualities' rather than the operation of technical procedures. From this perspective, eclecticism and integration can be regarded not as abstract theoretical exercises, but as *choices* intimately connected with the process of counsellor development. Significantly, the literature on theoretical integration is dominated by the writings of mature 'master therapists', usually holding academic positions, who have had the benefit of extensive training and research time, and are able to employ sophisticated and highly differentiated conceptual maps in making sense of the similarities and differences between alternative theories and techniques. Such individuals are not in the majority in the world of counselling. For most practitioners, integration is something that happens at a personal, local level.

The process of integration at an individual level has been described as *assimilative* integration (Messer 1992). Assimilative integration can be defined as 'a mode of integration (that) favors a firm grounding in any one system of psychotherapy, but with a willingness to incorporate or assimilate, in a considered fashion, perspectives or practices from other schools' (Messer 1992: 132). The key principle in this form of integration is that the therapist begins his or her career by being trained in a 'pure' single-theory approach (e.g., psychodynamic, person-centred, cognitive–behavioural). As the practitioner gains experience and confidence, he or she reads outside of their primary approach, and may attend training workshops and courses on other models and new techniques. Each of these new ideas is interpreted in the light of the primary model, and is either rejected or is found a place (i.e., assimilated) in the practitioner's initial theoretical structure of understanding and intervention. There is therefore a crucial difference between assimilative integration, and eclecticism:

> The assimilative approach . . . is not purely eclectic because a therapist's clinical decision making continues to be guided by a particular theoretical model. Using a sports metaphor . . . technical eclecticism is akin to compiling an all-star team, taking the best players from diverse squads, potentially sacrificing team chemistry (i.e., theoretical coherence) to assemble a squad composed of 'the best of the best'. Assimilative integration, on the other hand, is analogous to acquiring a talented free agent to fill a specific need within the team, but one who also complements the existing team chemistry.
>
> (Ramsay 2001: 23)

The driving force for assimilative integration is a sense that an existing approach can be enhanced or extended by the inclusion of new elements, as long as these new elements do not undermine the balance of the practitioner's previous network of ideas and methods. It is worth noting that, unlike technical eclecticism, assimilative integration encompasses the incorporation of new concepts as well as new techniques.

Some of the best examples of assimilative integration in action can be found in the writings of the psychodynamic psychotherapists, George Stricker and Jerry Gold (2005; Stricker 2006). In one case, Stricker and Gold (2006) describe the process of therapy with a man who was struggling with acute and severe anxiety. He was a tightly controlled, aggressive man, who initially showed little willingness to explore psychodynamic themes in his life. The therapist therefore initiated some cognitive–behavioural interventions, around monitoring of automatic thoughts and practising relaxation. These techniques were not particularly effective, because the client did not comply, and instead 'seemed to look for ways to subtly discredit the therapist' (p. 235). In response to this impasse, the therapist then challenged the client, which resulted in a growing awareness on his part of the contradiction between what he wanted (symptom relief), and his actual behaviour.

The therapy then moved into a phase in which the therapist and client examined, together, the ways in which therapy had re-activated memories of the client's relationship with an overly demanding father (i.e., transference interpretation). In turn, this successful psychodynamic work allowed the client to return to the CBT interventions, and make effective use of them to control his anxiety in a variety of social situations. However, even as he was practising CBT self-control techniques in this final phase of the therapy, the client became interested in the memories and dreams that seemed to be triggered by these activities, and discussed these experiences with the therapist. In effect, the therapist basically approached his work with this client from a psychodynamic perspective, but one that included some CBT methods that were used in order to address some specific issues. However, these CBT methods had been successfully assimilated by the therapist, into his style of working, so that he was able to retain an overall psychodynamic focus on developmental and relationship factors, even while instructing the client in the use of relaxation skills.

Assimilative integration is a process that unfolds over the working life of any therapist who is interested in expanding his or her repertoire. Messer (1992) suggests that there is a point where assimilation (into a pre-existing theory) becomes *adaptation* (the underlying theoretical structure is fundamentally changed, into something new). It may be, therefore, that the bend-point of assimilative integration, at least for some therapists, is a point of arrival at their own personal theoretical assimilation (i.e., construction of a distinctive new model).

The model of assimilative integration described by Messer (1992) represents, for many practitioners, an attractive and relevant pathway toward integration. It is a strategy that allows a therapist to remain grounded in a primary approach, while gradually trying out different ideas and techniques, and provides a secure set of criteria for evaluating these innovations ('are they consistent with what I already know?').

Box 17.7: *The permeability of therapy traditions*

Approaches to therapy differ in the extent to which they are open to new ideas. It seems clear that CBT has a highly permeable boundary, in terms of being open to influence from other therapy traditions. Indeed, one of the founders of cognitive therapy and CBT, Aaron Beck, is reputed to have asserted that 'if it works, its CBT'. Another approach that has been consistently hospitable to ideas from elsewhere has been transactional analysis (Tudor 2002) – the archives of the *Transactional Analysis Journal* includes articles describing how to assimilate almost every known therapy concept and technique into the TA tradition. By contrast, there has been a tendency for psychodynamic and person-centred approaches to be less welcoming of ideas and methods from other approaches, even though psychoanalytic concepts, and Rogers' understanding of the qualities of a facilitative therapeutic relationship, are universally known, and have demonstrably influenced theorists and practitioners within other traditions.

Collective integration

A form of assimilative integration that is seldom discussed in the literature, but which has a great deal of potential, is *collective integration*. This integrative strategy refers to situations in which groups of counsellors work closely together, and reach a point of developing a joint approach that is informed by the diversity of personal and professional backgrounds, training experiences and theoretical interests of members of the group. A good example of collective integration is the work of the *Just Therapy* centre in New Zealand (Waldegrave *et al.* 2003). Another example of collective integration is the approach to bereavement counselling for people with learning disabilities, developed by a group of counsellors in England (Read 2007). It seems likely that there are many collaborative initiatives of this type that have never been publicized, either because the group of practitioners did not ever reach a stage of defining or articulating their approach in formal terms, or because they did not believe that there would be an audience for this kind of writing.

Pluralism

A pluralistic perspective on counselling reflects a position that there are many plausible ways of doing therapy, and many different change processes that can be helpful for clients. A pluralistic approach therefore seeks to find ways to make use of the widest possible range of therapeutic strategies, with the aim of identifying what works best for each individual client. A pluralistic stance not only recognizes a multiplicity of valid therapeutic approaches, but also acknowledges the role of a multiplicity of ways of integrating these approaches. Pluralism can be regarded as a meta-perspective, that builds on the strengths and limitations of each of the integrationist models discussed in this chapter. The implications of pluralism, as a guiding framework for counselling training, practice and research, are explored in the next chapter.

Integrating spirituality into counselling practice

Earlier sections of this chapter have discussed integration in relation to *theory*: how to bring together ideas, theories and concepts from different therapeutic traditions. There is another meaning of integration, which is the focus of this final section: integrating aspects of human life that have been omitted from mainstream psychotherapeutic approaches and theories. In adopting a largely psychological and individualized perspective, the main 'brand name' therapy approaches that developed during the twentieth century (psychodynamic, CBT, person-centred) constructed ways of understanding people that ignored some dimensions of human existence, such as social class, gender, the body, cultural identity and spirituality. One of the main challenges for the counselling profession at the close of the twentieth century and into the twenty-first century, has been to devise ways to re-integrate these dimensions into counselling theory, training, research and practice. The nature of these challenges, in relation to social class, gender, the body, and cultural identity, are discussed elsewhere in this book. The topic of spirituality is discussed here.

A survey published in 2000 found that 75 per cent of adults in the UK reported personal awareness of a spiritual dimension to their lives (Hay and Hunt 2000). An earlier survey, conducted only slightly more than a decade previously, found that 48 per cent of respondents gave a positive answer to a similar question (Hay and Heald 1987). These results suggest that spirituality is significant for many people, and that the appreciation and awareness of spirituality is increasing (or is more readily admitted to a survey interviewer). It is important to make a distinction here between religion and spirituality. At the time when these surveys were being carried out, Church attendance in the UK was declining.

Although organized religion does provide a focus for the spiritual experience of many people, it is clear that there is also a large and growing proportion of the population whose spirituality is expressed through less formal means. Religion encompasses membership of an organization, and adoption of a set of moral rules, beliefs and values, in addition to the possibility of ritualized spiritual experience. Spirituality, by contrast, refers to a direct awareness of transcendent meaning, and/or some kind of sacred presence, which can occur whether or not the person espouses a religious belief system or not. Spirituality implies a form of *relational consciousness* – the person is in relationship with something that goes beyond the individual ego or self, and leads to an understanding that there is meaning that transcends individual needs and goals.

Spirituality is therefore, for many people, central to their sense of what it is to be human. Despite this, there is very little mention of the role of spirituality in counselling in the earlier chapters of this book that present mainstream theories of therapy. How can this absence be explained? Analysis of the history of counselling and psychotherapy tells us that these practices emerged from, and partially replaced, religion-based forms of helping and healing, during the period around the end of the nineteenth century and beginning of the twentieth century. Although many of the leading figures on the emergent therapy movement had personal backgrounds of involvement in religion, they were determined to position therapy as part of a new 'progressive' movement that aligned itself with secular, scientific values. The role of spirituality and religion was therefore expunged from the account of human personality offered by these early theorists, it was described as a form of psychopathology, in which religious visions might be interpreted as psychotic delusions, and a sense of merging with others would be viewed as evidence for poor ego boundaries.

Over the years, inevitably, spirituality has crept back into therapy practice. Some counsellors who were influenced by their experience of working with clients from traditional cultures, or certain Western subcultures, in which spiritual traditions were very much alive, began to recognize that any process of empathically entering the client's world, or engaging with the client's assumptions about healing and change, would require a willingness to pay serious attention to the spiritual experiences that the person might want to talk about. At the same time, a cluster of therapy approaches began to be developed by therapists who were themselves convinced of the importance of spirituality. These approaches include Jungian therapy, psychosynthesis, transpersonal therapy and various Buddhist-inspired methods (Boorstein 1996; Lines 2006; Rowan 2005; West 2000, 2004). However, these forms of therapy are not widely practised, and are largely used by clients for whom spirituality is a major part of life, and who want to use therapy to enhance their spiritual awareness and growth, rather than the majority of people for whom spirituality is part of life, but not a major preoccupation. Spiritually oriented therapies represent a thriving enclave within the wider therapy world, rather than a source of influence across the profession as a whole. A possible sign of a more general acceptance of spiritual experience in counselling and psychotherapy has been the widespread integration into therapy practice of aspects of Buddhist mindfulness meditation. In many instances, however, mindfulness has been redefined and packaged in such a way that its spiritual origins are effectively concealed, and thus not rejected by clients who are not spiritually inclined.

It would appear that counselling theory and practice will inevitably travel in the direction of a more general appreciation of the role of spiritual experience in people's lives (Smith *et al.* 2007; Sollod 2005; Sperry and Sharfranske 2005). At the present time, the form that this development will take is not clear. It may be that 'good ideas' from spiritual practice, such as mindfulness techniques or relaxation methods based on yoga, are gradually slotted into counselling. Or there may be a more fundamental rapprochement at a theoretical level. It is certainly likely that an enhanced place for spiritual dimensions would have a part to play in contributing to a resolution of other issues, for example the adoption of a more strengths-oriented stance in counselling, and the construction of forms of practice that enable people to address issues around their relationship with nature.

Conclusions

It should be clear that there is no one 'eclectic' or 'integrated' approach to counselling. There is, rather, a powerful trend towards finding ways of combining the many valuable ideas and techniques developed within separate schools and approaches. At the same time, however, there are also strong forces within the counselling and psychotherapy world acting in the direction of maintaining the purity of single-approach training institutes, professional associations and publications networks. The only prediction that would appear warranted would be that this tension between integration and purity is unlikely to disappear, and that it is to be welcomed as a sign of how creative and lively this field of study is at this time.

This chapter has necessarily provided a partial, incomplete and introductory overview of the issue of integration of therapy approaches. Two of the interesting and relevant areas that have not been covered, due to lack of space, are integration of delivery systems and sequential integration. Integration of delivery systems refers to the construction of therapy programmes that include different modalities (e.g., not just one-to-one therapy, but also group therapy, use of self-help reading, internet resources, etc). Some of the issues around this form of integration are discussed in Chapter 23. Sequential integration refers to programmes in which clients receive one form of therapy followed by another. For example, it may be useful, when working with a young person, to start off with family therapy (to address family processes that might be influencing the difficulties being experienced by the individual) and then move to CBT as an intervention that is targeted at specific behaviour change. Sequential integration is an important strategy, that is widely used within complex public health care systems, such as the NHS in Britain. However, it has not received much attention in terms of research. In addition, there are significant issues around training, supervision and research, that are hinted at, but not explored in any detail, in this chapter. At the present time, there exist some training programmes based on single models, whereas other programmes are organized around integrative principles. However, there is little research evidence or debate around how well these different training strategies operate, and whether they are equally appropriate for different groups of trainees (e.g., paraprofessionals, graduate trainees, etc.). Similarly, it is far from clear whether it is helpful or unhelpful to receive supervision based on the practitioner's primary theoretical approach, or from a supervisor using a different approach. In the field of research, although there have been some studies of integrationist approaches (Schottenbauer et al. 2005), there remain many unanswered questions around the process of integrative ways of working, and their effectiveness.

Beyond the current debates over eclecticism and integrationism is a broader historical perspective. The intellectual history of counselling and psychotherapy is not extensive. Psychoanalysis is about 100 years old, humanistic approaches have been established for 60 years, cognitive models came on the scene less than 40 years ago. If the founders of an approach, and their first generation of students, usually fight to establish the distinctiveness and uniqueness of their creation, and subsequent generations of adherents become secure enough to feel less threatened about making links with other approaches, then we are only just entering a period when such collaborations are even possible. This trend has, of course, been complicated and slowed down by the tendency towards splitting and factionalism in the therapy world. But it may well be that we are seeing the beginnings of an emergent consensus over the aims, concepts and methods of counselling and psychotherapy. Yet, true consensus is only possible when differences are acknowledged and respected. There is also a requirement within any profession or discipline that is intellectually alive and socially responsive, for a certain degree of creative tension.

Topics for reflection and discussion

1   How important are non-specific or common factors? Do you believe that they are more influential than the actual techniques used by therapists? What are the implications of this perspective for the ways that counsellors work with clients? What are the implications for counsellor training?

2   Where do you stand on the question of eclecticism and integration? In terms of your own current counselling work, do you find it more useful to keep to one approach, or to combine different approaches? Can you envisage circumstances under which your position might change in the future?

3   John Norcross (in Dryden 1991: 13) has stated that 'a single unifying theory for all psychotherapies is neither viable nor desirable'. Do you agree?

4   How useful do you find Frank's concept of 'demoralization' as a means of explaining why people enter therapy? Does it apply in all cases? What might be the advantages and limitations of adopting Frank's perspective?

5   This chapter has examined some different pathways to integration of therapy approaches. Which of these integration strategies seems most relevant and applicable to you? Why?

6   How important is it for the counselling profession to come to terms in an effective and consistent way with the spiritual needs of clients? How much of a priority would you give this task, in comparison with other issues?

7   How might counselling training need to change, in order to give serious attention to spirituality, and other 'forgotten' dimensions of human such as social class and cultural identity?

Suggested further reading

The classic, must-read book that has influenced a generation of counsellors and psychotherapists to take integration seriously, is *The Heart and Soul of Change. Delivering what Works in Therapy*, edited by Barry Duncan *et al.* (2010). One of the early chapters in the book is based on a fascinating interview with the grandfather of integrationism, Sol Rosenzweig (Duncan 2010). The *Handbook of Psychotherapy Integration*, edited by Norcross and Goldfried (2005), *Casebook of Psychotherapy Integration* (Stricker and Gold 2006) and *Journal of Psychotherapy Integration*, each represent comprehensive sources of current ideas about integration. The opening chapter in the *Handbook of Psychotherapy Integration* which is by Norcross (2005) includes a succinct summary of the argument in favour of integrationism. The chapter by

Trijsburg *et al.* (2007) in the *Oxford Textbook of Psychotherapy* covers similar territory. Highly recommended are a set of books that explore in some depth the issues involved in developing a personal approach to counselling/psychotherapy, drawing on the personal experiences of the authors: Corey (2000), Gilbert and Orlans (2010), Holmes and Bateman (2002), Lapworth *et al.* (2001) and O'Brien and Houston (2007).

CHAPTER 18

Pluralism: an organizing framework for counselling practice

Introduction

In previous chapters, we have looked at a wide range of models of therapy, each of which consists of a theoretical framework linked to practical methods for facilitating learning and change. We have also looked at a number of strategies for combining ideas and methods from different models of therapy. The existence of so many approaches to therapy creates a dilemma for counsellors. All of these approaches are credible, and several of them are supported by research evidence. Should a counsellor (or group of counsellors working together in an agency) stick to one approach, in the hope of becoming as effective as possible in applying that model? This is a reasonable position to take, but it leads to a major question: what about all these other ideas and methods, that I am not using? Might they be just what some of my clients need? Or should a counsellor adopt, or try to develop, an approach that combines ideas and methods from several theories? This is also a reasonable position to adopt, but in turn leads to other major questions: how do I know that what I am doing is not full of inconsistencies, and possibly confusing for a client? Can I be sufficiently competent in a range of methods to be sure that I am using them well enough to make a difference to my clients' lives?

The dilemma being described here can be summarized as: *the adoption of a position, or stance, that provides an organizing framework for practice*. This dilemma has generated problems for the counselling profession at all levels. How should training and supervision be organized? What kind of research should we do? How should services be delivered? Because different groups of counsellors have developed different answers to these questions, the field of counselling has remained fragmented, divided into a myriad of subgroups that are each pursuing their own answers to these questions. As a consequence of this fragmentation, counselling has been held back from making the contribution to individual well-being and social progress of which it is capable.

In recent years, it has become clear that the concept of *pluralism* offers a solution to this dilemma, and has the potential to provide an organizing framework that allows existing ideas and methods to be brought together in a way that will allow counselling to move forward in a coherent manner. This chapter provides an introduction to the concept of pluralism, and explores the implications of this perspective for theory, practice, training and research.

The concept of pluralism

Pluralism is a philosophical concept, which refers to the idea that there is no single truth. Pluralists argue that, in any significant dimension of human affairs, there are always multiple plausible ways of understanding and explaining what is happening. From a pluralistic perspective, human culture and history is characterized by 'dissensus' – a continual debate or dialogue between individuals and groups who espouse different beliefs or theories about what is 'true' or 'right'. Pluralism can be contrasted with 'monism', the position that there is a single theory to which all theories can ultimately be reduced.

The question of the adequacy of monism or pluralism as ways of making sense of the world has been a key issue throughout the history of philosophy. It is clear that human cultures have tended to adopt definite ideas about what is 'true', and that these ideas have often been predicated on the assumption of a single Supreme Being. More recently, modern science operates according to the assumption that, ultimately, a single agreed set of 'laws of nature' will be identified. On the other hand, the early Greek philosophers developed a powerful tradition of *scepticism*, which was grounded in the premise that it is not possible to establish, beyond doubt, the truth of any particular statement.

It can be argued that we are living in an era that is characterized by general recognition of the value of pluralism as a guiding principle for human affairs. There are two strong arguments in favour of pluralism. The first argument was articulated by William James (1842–1910), the American philosopher and one of the founders of modern psychology, in a book titled *A Pluralistic Universe* (1909/1977), based on a set of lectures at the University of Oxford in 1908 and 1909. In these lectures, James set out the case for pluralism, and in particular emphasized the point that if a theory represented an absolute singular truth, it would imply that it could not be improved or changed, because any new ideas would need to come from a competing theory (which could not be a source of valid ideas, because if it was valid, it would have already been part of the primary true theory). Given that theories do evolve and change, the monist idea that there can be single truth is therefore unsustainable.

The other strong argument for pluralism arises in the field of moral philosophy, in relation to the right of people to hold different beliefs. Events in recent history, such as the extermination of indigenous populations following European expansion into America and Australia, the holocaust, the gulag and the Rwandan massacre, have illustrated the implications of adopting a radical monist position in respect of cultural belief systems.

In exploring the meaning of the idea of pluralism, philosophers are generally agreed that it is important to make a distinction between pluralism and relativism. The concept of relativism refers to the idea that everything is true, depending on the context. Relativism is an expression of 'indifferentism' ('it does not matter what you believe') and scepticism ('nothing is true'). However, indifferentism and scepticism are not credible as descriptions of the way that human beings function. On the whole, individuals tend to hold strong beliefs around what is 'true' and 'right', at least in relation to some aspects of their lives. In addition, it seems clear that human progress is not fuelled by people who are sceptical and indifferent, but by those who have a passionate commitment to a particular theory. It is therefore unsatisfactory to equate pluralism with relativism. Instead, this line of argument leads to the hugely challenging conclusion that pluralism implies a willingness to (a) possess strong beliefs about what is true, while at the same time (b) accepting that the different strong beliefs held by other people are also true. In effect, pluralism implies *dialogue* – adopting a pluralistic perspective requires a willingness to build meaning bridges between one's own strong held truths, and the truths that are held by others.

In summary, the concept of pluralism suggests that there is no single truth to which we can aspire, and that it is more effective to base our lives on a willingness to be open to multiple perspectives on a problem. In terms of decision-making and problem-solving, pluralism invites a 'both/and' approach rather in place of the adoption of 'either/or' strategies. Finally, in the domain of social life, pluralism highlights the importance of constructing opportunities for dialogue (conversations between people who are open to each other, make good faith attempts to understand each other, and are willing to express their own positions as fully as they can, and to allow these positions to shift in response to new ideas). In this context, dialogue can be contrasted with debate (trying to persuade the other person that you are right and they are wrong).

This overview of the concept of pluralism can do no more than indicate some of the key aspects of philosophical thinking around this topic. The most accessible source of further discussion of the meaning of pluralism is Rescher (1993). Beyond that, other useful philosophical perspectives can be found in Ferrara (2010), Goertzen and Smythe (2010), Irving and Young (2002), McLennan (1995) and Stone (2006), and in a special issue of the *Journal of Mind and Behavior*, (Slife and Wendt 2009; Woody and Viney 2009) published to mark the hundredth anniversary of *A Pluralistic Universe*.

Why counselling is pluralistic

Like a missing last piece of a jigsaw, the concept of pluralism fits very easily into contemporary theory and practice of counselling, and has the effect of completing the picture. Some of the ways in which pluralism connects up existing aspects of counselling include the following.

As a philosophical construct, pluralism provides a meta-perspective that is not grounded in any single discipline, or specific set of ideas within that discipline. In Chapter 3, it was suggested that effective counselling draws on knowledge from a wide range of sources. Later chapters have introduced several specific sets of ideas (psychoanalysis, behaviourism, etc.) from within the discipline of psychology. It seems clear that whatever 'counselling' is, it straddles all of these areas of knowledge. Any attempt to organize counselling theory and practice around a specific concept from any of these areas would have the result of downplaying the relevance of other concepts. For example, defining counselling as a 'psychological therapy' downplays the social dimension of counselling; defining counselling as a form of relationship downplays the idea that counselling can involve helping people to make choices. By contrast, a pluralistic framework allows consideration to be given to the potential relevance of any ideas that may seem useful.

Counselling is a 'frontline' form of help, that needs to be responsive to the many different ideas about the origins and development of problems, and how they can be addressed, that exist within contemporary society. Counselling services are generally used by people who need urgent help, rather than by people who have made a decision to seek a specific brand of therapy. To engage effectively with their clients, counsellors need to understand and appreciate the ideas and strategies that the client already holds in relation to their problem. Counsellors typically work with people who are concurrently using other strategies for coping with their lives – for example medication, complementary therapies, diet, spiritual practices and so on. A counsellor needs to be able to appreciate the potential value of these resources.

Respect for diversity has always represented a core value of counselling. Although ideas around acceptance and 'unconditional positive regard' were first used by Carl Rogers in the 1940s, since that time they have permeated the culture of counselling as a whole, and can be regarded as intrinsic to the moral DNA of the profession. The active promotion of diversity has become an increasingly salient characteristic of counselling, exemplified in the extent to which it has embraced multiculturalism (Chapter 13) and social advocacy (Chapter 21).

A major strength of the counselling workforce lies in its capacity to make use of many different patterns of life experience. In many countries, the population of people who train as counsellors includes a high proportion of individuals with extensive prior experience in occupations such as nursing, teaching, social work and the clergy, as well as individuals who have been service users. Unlike other professions, where the workforce mainly comprises those who have entered the profession straight from school, the structure of counsellor training has always made it possible for people to learn with and from people with very different life histories and personal experience.

These factors represent some of the reasons why many counsellors are drawn to a pluralistic framework for practice – the concept of pluralism offers a means of making explicit a central theme within the experience of being a counsellor.

The implications of pluralism for counselling

The adoption of a pluralistic perspective on counselling is not merely a matter of 're-badging' counselling, in the sense of finding a new way of describing what is already happening. There are many aspects of current theory and practice of counselling that do not reflect a pluralistic ethos. The following sections explore some of the implications for counselling of taking pluralism seriously.

A pluralistic perspective on theory

The proliferation of theories of therapy represents both a challenge to pluralism, and an opportunity. The challenge to pluralism lies in the extent to which supporters of specific theoretical approaches operate from a monist position in which they assume that their own model is 'true' or 'effective', and other approaches are mistaken and ineffective. Because a large proportion of counselling and psychotherapy training and research is organized around competing 'schools' of therapy, there are many practitioners who have been systematically socialized into believing that their way is the right way. This tendency is reinforced by the existence of professional associations consisting solely of people who have been trained in a specific theoretical approach, and research studies that aim to provide evidence for the unique effectiveness of that approach. Within these single-orientation groups, there may be some form of 'internal pluralism', for example in the form of dialogue between contrasting versions of psychoanalysis, or CBT or person-centred theory. Most of the time, brand-name schools of therapy operate like renaissance city states, asserting their status and seeking to gain an advantage over their rivals. On the whole, the counsellors and psychotherapists who operate within these enclaves do not have much contact with colleagues from other approaches, and are unlikely to read the work of writers and researchers who are based in different traditions. The existence of *An Introduction to Counselling* (and other similar texts) creates dissonance for adherents of single schools of therapy, by making it clear that good ideas can be found in a wide range of therapy approaches.

At the same time, the proliferation of therapy approaches represents an opportunity for pluralism, because it has created a situation in which strong statements are available regarding the validity of different ways of thinking about therapy. It also means that much of the diversity of thinking about problems in living and their solution that can be found within the culture as a whole has been formally articulated. (However, it is also important to acknowledge that many indigenous and 'common-sense' ideas and strategies are currently excluded from the 'scientific' therapy literature.)

In order to open up the domain of therapy theory, so that more of the ideas that are available can be accessed by more clients and counsellors, it is first of all necessary to re-visit the question of 'what is a theory?' An outline of different ways in which theory can be used was provided in Chapter 4. The question of how theory operates in counselling has been further explored in a series of papers by Hansen (2004, 2006, 2007). What he suggests is that it is not helpful to regard therapy theories as being similar to scientific theories that allow scientists and technologists to predict and control aspects of the world. Instead, therapy theories function as potential narrative structures, that allow different types of story to be told about how problems develop, and how they can be handled: '. . . theories are useful not because they embody objective truth but because they equip the counselor with prepackaged narratives that can contribute to the meaning construction process in the counseling relationship' (Hansen 2006: 295).

In philosophical terms, what Hansen (2007) is advocating is the adoption of a *pragmatic* stance in relation to therapy theory (see also Fishman 1999). The client is looking for a way of making sense of his or her problems, and theories of therapy provide a stock of possible narrative story-lines that can be tried on for size. It is probable that the client will not find an 'off the shelf' theory that suits them, but will end up assembling a bespoke or personalized theory that meets his or her needs at the time and sufficiently reflects their values and worldview. From this perspective, therapies theories can be viewed as resources for understanding. An example of how this can work in practice can be found in a study by Polkinghorne (1992), summarized in Box 18.1. The pragmatic attitude to theory reported by Polkinghorne (1992) is consistent with the findings of several studies of the attributes of 'master therapists' (Jennings and Skovholt 1999), who exhibit a lifelong openness to new ideas.

Box 18.1: *Using theory: a postmodern, pragmatic perspective*

How do counsellors and psychotherapists actually use theory on a day-to-day basis? What are the strategies that are employed either to maintain a unitary theoretical stance or to integrate ideas from different theoretical models? Polkinghorne (1992) interviewed several therapists in Los Angeles, and carried out an analysis of books on therapy practice. He found that, on the whole, previous clinical experience was used as the primary source of knowledge. Although theories were seen to function as useful models and metaphors that 'assist in constructing cognitive order' (p. 158), there was no sense that any theory could ever capture the complexity of human existence. These therapists were 'comfortable with the diversity of theories' (p. 158). There was a feeling among several therapists that their theoretical knowledge was necessarily 'unfinished'. They might be able to anticipate how a client might respond to an intervention, but there was always the possibility that something different and unexpected might happen. They were aware that their theoretical ideas were personal constructions or 'templates', grounded in concrete instances and cases, rather than formal systems based on scientific thought and proof. The main criterion for assessing the value of a theoretical idea was pragmatic: does it work?

Polkinghorne (1992) argues that these features of the way that practitioners use theory are consistent with a postmodern perspective (Kvale 1992; Lyon 1994). The belief in progress, rationality and the ultimate validity of scientific theories is seen as characteristic of modernity. Philosophical and sociological writers such as Polkinghorne have suggested that, in contrast, the currently emerging postmodern era is associated with a movement towards foundationlessness, fragmentariness, constructivism and neo-pragmatism. Polkinghorne finds all these elements in the 'psychology of practice' employed by many contemporary psychotherapists. The implication here is that the movement in counselling and psychotherapy away from the modernist 'grand theories' of those such as Freud, Rogers and Berne, and towards a much more fragmented, locally or personally constructed integrationist or eclectic approach to knowledge, reflects a much broader social and cultural shift.

Pluralistic practice

Looking at what happens in the counselling room from a pluralistic perspective makes it possible to identify some important limitations of current counselling practice. In counselling, a person seeks help from someone who is outside their social circle to deal with some kind of emotional or relationship problem that is bothering them. What is immediately apparent, from a pluralistic perspective, is that there exists a multiplicity of ways in which the client's problem might be tackled. First, there are many ideas and methods within the counselling and psychotherapy literature that might be relevant. The counsellor will be aware of at least some of these ideas and methods. Second, the client will almost certainly have tried to deal with the problem in some fashion, in advance of consulting a counsellor. Some of the client's ideas may be useful, while other initiatives that the client has taken in the past may have had the effect of exacerbating the problem. The client may also know about, or have had experience with, other strategies that he or she has not yet tried to implement in relation to the current problem. Third, there are other problem-solving strategies that are available within the broader culture and society, that go beyond the immediate ideas that are in the awareness of the counsellor or client, or which cannot be accommodated or implemented within the therapy room. A pluralistic point of view invites consideration of all of these possibilities. By contrast, counselling that immediately engages with a single perspective on the client's problem, or a single change process, allows little or no space for this wider set of possibilities to be used.

A pluralistic approach to practice emphasizes the value of client–counsellor dialogue around how the problem is to be tackled. Most counsellors are good at exploring what the client wants, and how the client's goals for counselling make sense in the context of their life as a whole (i.e., the meaning of the problem). On the whole, counsellors are willing to spend quite a lot of time making sure that they understand what the client wants, and building a relationship of trust with the client within which painful or embarrassing problems and experiences can be discussed. The adoption of a pluralistic perspective invites the counsellor to go further than this, invite dialogue around:

- the client's way of making sense of the problem (i.e., the client's 'theory');
- the client's sense of what kind of change strategies would be most/least helpful for them;
- what the counsellor has to offer (the ideas and methods available to the counsellor);
- the resources within the client's cultural and social world that might be brought to bear on the problem.

A pluralistic approach to counselling involves using this kind of dialogue to co-construct a mutually agreeable way of working that brings together the various possibilities that arise, into a plan of action that is flexibly tailored to each individual client. Box 18.2 offers an example of how this can work in practice.

Box 18.2: *Pluralistic counselling in action: developing a shared understanding*

'B' (pseudonym chosen by client himself) had been living with HIV for 11 years, and was experiencing some persistent health conditions that affected his quality of life. He received counselling at a therapy organization that offered a limit of 12 sessions. At the start of counselling, B identified a number of therapeutic goals: more balance in his relationship with his partner, and the opportunity to make sense of some traumatic experiences. In early sessions, his counsellor invited him to share his ideas about how therapy might be helpful for him. Drawing on some previous experience of therapy, which had not been ideal for him, B stated that he wanted space to explore; he did not want to be challenged and he wanted to be the expert in the room.

B's counsellor was female, with a primary training in humanistic approaches and a commitment to working in a pluralistic way that reflected the client's sense of what was helpful. For the most part, the counsellor adopted a non-directive, empathic way of being with the client, as a means of allowing him to be the expert and to have the 'space' that he needed. B introduced some specific therapeutic strategies: writing his memoirs, constructing a time-line of his life. When the counsellor became too challenging or directive, B was able to tell her that what she was doing was not useful for him, and she was able to change her emphasis. In feedback sessions after the end of counselling, B reported that therapy had been helpful for him, and he had accomplished most of what he had hoped to achieve. Miller and Willig 2012: 40 concluded that:

> . . . without creating a shared understanding the work would have been entirely different . . . the therapy would have been similar to the experience he had undergone with 'other professionals' (e.g., doctors and pain specialists) where they tried to work with him and he became frustrated and defensive because he felt that they had not tried to understand his specific needs.

The case of B offers an example of how a client was able to teach a counsellor what he needed, and the counsellor in turn was able to create an environment and a relationship that the client was able to use to move on in his life.

A pluralistic approach to counselling draws attention to the significance of client *preferences* (McLeod 2012). For several decades, counselling and psychotherapy researchers have investigated various aspects of how clients perceive therapy, using constructs such as attitudes, beliefs, expectations and credibility. More recently, this line of inquiry has refocused around the notion of 'preference', in recognition of the idea that the client draws on his or her beliefs and attitudes to make an active choice around how far they are willing to engage with different aspects of the therapy process, or with different therapeutic techniques.

The findings of research suggest that client preferences have a bearing on the outcomes of counselling, in two main ways. First, when what happens in counselling matches the client's preferences there are lower rates of drop-out and unplanned ending (Swift and Callahan 2009). Second, clients who are offered a preferred way of working are more likely to benefit from therapy, in terms of problem reduction and attaining therapeutic goals (Berg *et al.* 2008). A detailed discussion of this area of research, and its implications for practice, can be found in McLeod (2012, 2013b). One of the most interesting aspects of this research is that it will be clear to most practising counsellors that, on the whole, when clients are asked at the start of therapy to describe their preferences for how they think their problem might best be approached they tend to be quite vague in what they say. What the research shows, on the other hand, is that, given a simple preference questionnaire to fill in, the relatively vague and uncrystallized ideas that are in the client's mind, do have significant predictive value.

The practice of pluralistic counselling therefore involves developing ways to encourage clients to share their inklings about what might be helpful for them, and to get feedback from clients concerning the value of strategies and directions of exploration that are initiated by the counsellor. There is good evidence that many clients are deferential in relation to their counsellor – when the counsellor makes a suggestion or comment that the client regards as mistaken or unhelpful, the client may be polite and defer to the perceived greater wisdom of the 'expert' (Rennie 1994).

As a means of assisting clients to play an active role in shaping what happens in counselling, pluralistically oriented counsellors may invite their clients to complete brief process and outcome scales on a regular basis. The use of such feedback or 'tracking' tools represents a major area of recent innovation within counselling practice (Lambert 2010). Sundet (2009) characterizes this kind of procedure as the use of 'conversational tools': the purpose of using a feedback scale is not to obtain a scientifically 'valid' measurement, but instead to create an opportunity for a client–counsellor conversation about whether counselling is helping, and how the counsellor could do better.

Box 18.3: *Pluralistic practice in medicine and health psychology*

The implications of pluralism are widely acknowledged within the field of health care. For many medical conditions, there can be several viable treatment options that are available to patients (for example, the choice of medication, surgery, heat therapy or massage for back pain). Beyond the range of conventional treatments that may be relevant, there can often exist a further set of indigenous remedies and complementary therapies that may be viewed as credible and useful by the patient. Doctors and other health professionals have needed to develop strategies for responding to 'medical pluralism' (see, for example, Kiesser *et al.* 2006; Maclachlan 2000; Stevenson *et al.* 2003). In a review of research and practice in this area, Mulley and colleagues (2012) have suggested that competence in 'preference diagnosis' represents an important means of reducing health costs and enhancing patient satisfaction, since patients are less likely to adhere to treatment regimes that do not correspond to their personal preferences.

It is clear that there are many ways in which a pluralistic perspective can be applied in counselling practice. At the present time, the most fully articulated version of pluralistic counselling that is available can be found in the work of Cooper and McLeod (2007, 2011) and McLeod and McLeod (2011). Their approach assumes that there exist multiple change processes, all of which seem to be effective at least some of the time, and that the decision about which change process to follow is not a matter solely for the therapist, but is best achieved through collaborative conversation between client and therapist. A central focus of pluralistic counselling is therefore to create opportunities for conversations between the client and therapist around the construction of a set of therapy procedures that best fit the client's needs. The idea is to create a unique therapy for each client. It is suggested it can be valuable to make sure that collaborative conversations address at least the following set of central issues:

- developing a *shared understanding* of the problem in living that has led the person to seek therapy;
- the *goals* of the client – in what direction are they moving in their life? What do they want to get from therapy? What are their purposes and intentions in relation to therapy?
- how can these goals be broken down into step-by-step *tasks*, the completion of which will contribute to the achievement of each goal?
- what are the *methods* through which tasks can be fulfilled? What activities can therapist and client engage in, to enable task completion?

Attention to these four domains (problem understanding, goals, tasks and methods) allows the client and therapist to form a productive collaborative relationship, which maximizes client agency and involvement (Bohart and Tallman 1999) through being firmly rooted in the client's construction of reality, and by being highly attuned to the client's existing and ongoing strategies for resolving his or her problems in living.

Within this form of collaborative pluralist therapy, it is the aim and intention of the counsellor to make use not only of concepts, techniques and interventions that have been described and investigated within the therapy literature, or are derived from psychological theory, but to be open to a wider sense of plural possibilities. For example, potentially valuable change mechanisms may be found within the *cultural resources* (McLeod 2005) that are accessible to the person. Cultural resources can encompass a vast array of opportunities for learning and healing, that are available within a culture, for instance, education classes, walking in the countryside, meditation, participation in sport, internet-based support groups, watching movies and much else. A particularly crucial cultural resource, in relation to finding meaning in life and making connection with others, is *art-making* (see Chapter 15). Collaborative pluralism also encourages an attitude of therapeutic improvisation – making use of whatever resources are at hand.

Collaborative pluralism assumes that, as counselling and psychotherapy become more and more deeply embedded into contemporary social life, people will become better informed about the different processes of learning/healing/change that are potentially on offer, and will become more discerning and active 'consumers' of therapy. What this means is that, while it would not necessarily have been relevant to clients in the 1960s to attempt to engage in discussion around 'how do you understand your problem?' or 'what are your ideas about how best we might work together on this problem?', these conversations are increasingly meaningful for those who seek therapy.

There are many other examples of forms of collaborative practice in counselling that are consistent with a pluralistic perspective. Anderson and Gehart (2007) have brought together a valuable collection of papers on collaborative and dialogical approaches to therapy. The work of Seikkula *et al.* (2006) demonstrates the use of a dialogical, community-based model of therapy with people undergoing a psychotic episode.

Box 18.4: *Exercise as a cultural resource*

Taking exercise is a resource that is available to almost everyone. Walking, jogging, playing sport, dancing – these are all forms of exercise. The physical and mental health benefits of exercise are well established. It can be helpful for counsellors to be interested in the ways that clients take exercise, and to encourage clients to undertake appropriate exercise. Hays (1999) describes several ways in which she, and other therapists, explore the meaning of exercise for clients, and enable them to be more aware of how the effect of exercise can contribute to therapeutic change.

For example, a client who is depressed may find that working out at the gym gives him a more positive outlook. A socially anxious and isolated client may find it possible to engage in brief conversations with fellow-dog walkers in the park. In these situations, the counsellor is not trying to be a coach or fitness trainer, but instead is working with the client's own strengths and resources. Exercise is not helpful for everyone: if a client is not interested at all in exercise, then there will be other cultural resources in his or her life that may be relevant.

Pluralistic service delivery

The pluralistic framework for practice outlined by Cooper and McLeod (2011) is particularly appropriate in situations where one-to-one counselling is offered in the context of a 'frontline' community counselling agency. In such a context, it is particularly important for the counsellor to be able to adopt a flexible approach that is responsive to the many different ideas about help that are held by different clients, establish a collaborative relationship from the outset, and engage the active participation of the client.

Frontline counselling agencies need 'generalist' counsellors who are able to work with whoever walks through the door. In such a situation, a specialist therapist who had expertise in only one therapeutic model could be very effective with clients for whom that model made sense, but might struggle with clients who had other ideas about what would help them. In adopting a pluralistic perspective, it is important for organizations to be aware that pluralism is not merely a matter of employing counsellors who take a collaborative approach. Pluralism also involves consideration of diversity issues, and practical aspects of a service such as flexibility in the length and timing of sessions, and being able to choose one's counsellor or change to another counsellor (Carey 2011).

The existence of generalist counsellors based in community agencies or primary health care does not necessarily reduce the need or demand for 'single-orientation' psycho-therapists working in private practice or in secondary care. There are many people who make an informed choice that a specific approach to therapy (e.g., person-centred, CBT, psychodynamic) is right for them, and will seek out a therapist who can offer that way of working. Sometimes, it may be valuable for a generalist counsellor to refer a client to a 'single-orientation' specialist colleague, if it turns out that client wishes to work more intensively within a particular change modality.

There are other models of service delivery that represent potentially valuable means of implementing a pluralistic approach. There are some organizations that offer a range of therapeutic experiences, for example individual counselling, group therapy, weekend workshops, psycho-educational groups on topics such as anger management, mindfulness training courses, access to a library of 'therapeutic' DVDs and books, and so on. Some of these organizations also encompass complementary therapy practitioners. This format for service delivery allows the client to try out different therapeutic experiences, and different combinations of activities, in a situation in which each practitioner with whom he or she interacts will have an appreciation of the nature of the other learning experiences that are on offer.

Another framework for pluralistic work can be found in the use of reflecting teams and 'consultants' in family therapy and narrative therapy. One counsellor works with an indi-vidual client, couple, or family group, in the presence of a group of observers. At a later point in the session, the counsellor and client pause in their work, and listen to the reac-tions and reflections of the observers, to what has been said up to that point. This proce-dure makes available a multiplicity of alternative perspectives and preferences around a problem in a form that allows the client to pick and choose between them, or adapt them to his or her needs, without any sense of being advised by the therapist, or whoever is assessing them, to pursue any particular course of action.

In recent years, many health care systems have started to use a 'stepped care' model to organize the delivery of counselling and psychotherapy (see pages 573–5). Within this kind of structure, the client is assessed and then (depending on the severity of the problem) referred to a low-intensity activity, such as supported reading or an online self-help package. If this first 'step' is not effective in addressing the problem, the client is then allocated to a higher intensity service, such as individual counselling or CBT. If this level of therapy is not effective, the client is referred again, perhaps to psychiatric care or to a specialist service that focuses on a particular disorder (e.g., eating disorders, alcohol dependency, bipolar disorder, etc). It is important to note that stepped care is not plural-istic from the point of view of the client. It may be pluralistic from the point of view of the health care organization, because from their perspective they are offering a range of thera-pies, linked to patient/client need. But in fact the client has little choice, because what they get is decided by the person who is assessing them. In principle, the array of services within a stepped care system could operate in a pluralistic fashion, for example if informa-tion about all the possible therapies and therapists was made available on a website and the client was able to choose, and if open dialogue was possible around the therapies that clients or user groups might wish to see included in the list.

Box 18.5: *The paradox of the founders of therapy approaches*

It can be a powerful experience to read case examples of client work carried out by leading figures in the field of counselling and psychotherapy, or to observe them in action on video or in live demonstrations. These men (usually men) who have pioneered new approaches to therapy, are self-evidently highly competent and masterful therapists, profoundly comfortable and competent in what they are doing with clients. We all aspire to be like them. But further exploration of the biographies of these figures (Freud, Rogers, Berne, Perls, Glasser, Beck, Greenberg, White) reveals a similar pattern within their careers. Each of them was initially trained in an approach to therapy that they did not consider to be entirely satisfactory. Each of them spent years developing a new approach to therapy that was consistent with their own personal values, temperament and life experience. This is why they are so competent and confident. They have arrived at a point of doing therapy is a manner that fits them like a glove. There is no uncertainty or hesitation in their performance. There is a paradox here. These individuals, and those around them who admire their work, then set up training institutes and programmes to help new therapists to learn to work according to the principles and techniques established by the founding father. The paradox is that the approach being taught by the founding father consists of (a) some ideas from their initial training, followed by (b) a reaction against that initial training, followed by (c) a long and arduous journey of discovery that led to the construction of a personal approach. What they teach new therapists, in their training institutes, is only the first step on this journey. The paradox is this: to *really* be an outstanding therapist such as Rogers or Berne it is necessary to reject key elements of whatever it is you have learned from your chosen founding father, and develop your own personal therapeutic style.

Training and supervision from a pluralistic standpoint

Traditionally, training in counselling and psychotherapy has focused on enabling students or trainees to become competent in a single approach, such as CBT, person-centred, psychodynamic, narrative therapy, gestalt, etc. There is a sparse literature on training in integrative or pluralistic approaches to counselling. Supporters of single-orientation training argue that training that seeks to encompass a multiplicity of therapy models and methods runs the risk of producing practitioners who may possess a broad-based knowledge, but are unable to implement any one particular intervention well enough to help clients in a meaningful way. In addressing these concerns, it may be helpful to be reminded of an important, but widely ignored, lesson from the history of counselling and psychotherapy research. Several studies carried out in the 1970s and 1980s into the effectiveness of therapy delivered by untrained or minimally trained volunteer counsellors consistently showed that untrained and minimally trained therapists could be just as effective as highly trained practitioners, as long as they were carefully selected and were offered appropriate supervisory support. It is possible to interpret these findings in different ways. However, it is hard to argue that they demonstrate that advanced expertise in specific interventions is a necessary part of being an effective counsellor.

A further historical lesson comes from initiatives within the psychology community in the USA in the 1930s and 1940s concerning the training needs of students entering the emerging field of clinical psychology. At that time there were few vested interests in the form of powerful single-orientation groups and associations. What emerged from these deliberations was an outline of a pluralistic and interdisciplinary model for training, including courses in philosophy, art, literature, politics and social anthropology, and experience of working alongside colleagues from other professional backgrounds (American Psychological Association, Committee of Training in Clinical Psychology 1947). From a contemporary perspective, it is possible to see that, over the years, the pluralistic elements of this training model have gradually been stripped away, while single-discipline (psychology) elements have been added.

It is possible to identify some key principles that can be used to guide and inform the design of pluralistic training programmes (see Cooper and McLeod 2011 as above). In addition to coverage of standard topics, such as professional issues and ethics, self-awareness, personal therapy and research skills, the nature and implications of a pluralistic approach to counselling can be emphasized by such activities as:

- attention to the philosophical rationale for pluralism;
- emphasis on training as a first step in lifelong learning;
- skills training to develop common factors competencies;
- learning to use cultural resources;
- dialogue between different theoretical perspectives;
- training in use of feedback tools to enable collaborative conversations with clients.

Similarly, while retaining the effective elements of current supervision approaches, pluralistically oriented supervision has an additional focus on exploring how best to maximize the resourcefulness of both client and counsellor.

Conclusions: counselling in a post-heroic era

There are substantial personal and organizational barriers to pluralism that operate within the counselling profession. There are personal barriers that arise from the deep and genuine commitment and belief that many counsellors hold in relation to specific therapy models. This commitment and belief is not without foundation – over the years, an enormous amount of good has been done by practitioners of psychodynamic, person-centred, cognitive–behavioural and other brand name therapies, and innumerable productive and satisfying careers have been lived out within these arenas. There are also organizational barriers in the form of enormous amounts of investment in training courses, journals, books, and bodies of research evidence that have been constructed around single models. Pluralism, as described in the present chapter, does not ask anyone to abandon ideas and methods that they already find useful. Pluralism merely invites serious consideration of other options, in addition to what is already familiar.

On the other hand, there are reasons to believe that we are approaching a period of change in relation to the theory and practice of counselling (Gergen 2000). There is a growing awareness of the fact that that we have reached a point where it is clear that there are many ways that issues such as anxiety, depression and relationship problems can be addressed. There is also an appreciation that good therapy involves collaboration and dialogue between client and counsellor, in a form that allows the strengths, resources and knowledge of the client to be brought to bear on whatever it is that troubles them. One of the indicators of the current sea-change in counselling is a shift in the image of the therapist. In almost all of the existing clinical literature and research the therapist is the hero of the story. The therapist is the potent one whose 'intervention' makes a difference. In pluralistic stories, by contrast, the client is the hero. The client is the one who has the courage to face up to things, to draw on his or her own capacities, and to use whatever it is that his or her therapist has to offer.

A pluralistic perspective in counselling opens up a whole series of challenges and agendas, in such areas as training, supervision and research. It creates possibilities for collaboration with practitioners and groups who have different skills and techniques, such as outdoor pursuits trainers, complementary therapists, poets and artists.

Topics for reflection and discussion

1   A pluralistic perspective suggests that there exist multiple change processes that can be equally helpful for clients. To what extent is this position consistent with your own counselling worldview? Do you believe that there is a single, universal healing process that is of fundamental importance in therapeutic work?

2   What is your own personal preferred approach for dealing with challenges that emerge in your own life? Which therapy models are most, or least, compatible with your own problem-solving style? What might be the advantages and disadvantages of seeing a therapist who used techniques and interventions that were significantly different from your existing personal coping strategies?

3 What are the cultural resources that have been most meaningful for you? In what ways have these resources enabled you to overcome periods of worry and low mood?

4 To what extent are you open and curious about the diversity of therapy theories and methods that are available? What form does this curiosity take (e.g., reading, talking with colleagues, attending training events)? What are the barriers that hold you back from learning more about different approaches? How might these barriers be overcome?

5 If you have had the experience of being a client in therapy, reflect on the degree to which your therapist(s) initiated or encouraged conversation around your ideas for how you could work most effectively together. Looking back, would it have been helpful to have had more of this type of conversation, or less?

Suggested further reading

Extended discussion of the ideas introduced in this chapter can be found in *Pluralistic Counselling and Psychotherapy*, by Mick Cooper and John McLeod (2011), and many of the chapters in *Adolescent Counselling Psychology: Theory, Research and Practice*, edited by Terry Hanley and colleagues (2012). One of the core assumptions of pluralistically oriented counselling is that the client is an active co-participant who has his or her own ideas about what will work. The concept of the 'active client' is explored in one of the classic therapy texts of recent years – *How Clients Make Therapy Work: The Process of Active Self-healing*, by Art Bohart and Karen Tallman (1999). An inspiring portrayal of a master pluralist in action (although he does not describe his work in these terms) can be accessed in Bruce Levine's (2007) book on *Surviving America's Depression Epidemic: How to find Morale, Energy, and Community in a World gone Crazy*.

19

The counselling relationship

Introduction

The actual contact between a counsellor and a person who is seeking help lies at the heart of what counselling is about. Although a counsellor may be able to use theory to make sense of the client's difficulties, and may have a range of techniques at his or her disposal for revealing and overcoming these difficulties, the fact remains that theory and technique are delivered through the presence and being of the counsellor as a person: the basic tool of counselling is the person of the counsellor. An interest in the nature of the therapeutic relationship represents a common concern of all therapy practitioners and theorists. Even if different approaches to counselling make sense of the client–therapist relationship in different ways they all agree that effective counselling depends on how this kind of relationship operates, what happens when it goes wrong and how to fix it.

The relationship between a client or patient and their therapist is probably unique for the majority of people who enter counselling. Even in short-term counselling, the person is exposed to a situation in which another person will listen to him or her for several hours, will make every effort to see issues and dilemmas from the speaker's perspective, will treat what is said with extreme respect and confidentiality and will abstain from seeking to gratify any of their own needs during this time. There is a deep caring, and sense of being 'special', that is unusual or even absent from the experience of most people in Western industrial societies. Of course, such an experience may be hard to accept: can the counsellor really be trusted? Is he or she genuinely interested in what I am saying? How can I take so much without giving something back? The intensity with which many therapy clients experience their relationship with their therapist is captured well in a study by Lott (1999), who interviewed women around their feelings about their therapists, and by Wachholz and Stuhr (1999), who found that, 12 years after the end of therapy, clients still held vivid memories of their therapist and the qualities of their relationship with him or her (see Box 19.1).

The importance of the counsellor–client relationship has been reflected in the findings of many research studies. Research that has invited clients to describe what has been helpful or unhelpful for them in counselling has consistently found that clients identify relationship factors as being more important than the use of therapist techniques. In the eyes of the client, it is the quality of their relationship with their therapist that has made the largest contribution to the value of therapy for them. Another line of research has involved measuring the strength of the client–therapist relationship early in therapy, and looking at whether a strong therapeutic alliance predicts a subsequent good outcome. This research, which is reviewed by Cooper (2008), repeatedly demonstrates a high positive correlation between the quality of the therapeutic relationship and the amount the client gains from therapy. These research findings have been interpreted as providing support for the role of *non-specific* factors in therapy: the relationship between client and therapist is a core non-specific factor existing in all forms of therapy.

Why is the therapeutic relationship so important? There are several ways of making sense of what happens in the relationship between a counsellor and a client. There are some counsellors, often influenced by the cognitive–behavioural tradition, or by ideas about professional–client relationships in occupations such as medicine, teaching or social work, who regard the building of 'rapport' to be an initial step in counselling, of significance mainly as a platform from which structured therapeutic interventions can be made. In contrast, there are other counsellors, working within the psychoanalytic tradition, who see the relationship as an arena in which the client acts out dysfunctional relationship patterns, thus enabling the therapist to observe these patterns and set about remediating them. Finally, there are counsellors operating within the humanistic tradition who regard authentic contact or encounter between persons as intrinsically healing. Some counsellors move between these types of relationship, depending on the client with whom they are working, or the stage of the work.

The aim of this chapter is to examine the different images of the therapeutic relationship that have been proposed in the counselling and psychotherapy literature, and to explore the ways in which these ideas have been applied in practice.

Box 19.1: *The intensity of the therapeutic relationship: the client's internalization of the counsellor*

Any therapy that continues for more than two or three sessions represents a situation in which an intense relationship between client and counsellor is likely to develop. The experience of being the focus of attention of another person, continuously for a whole hour at a time, and becoming more and more *known* to this person, in terms of highly personal and private information (but for the other person to remain largely unknown), is almost certain to be unique for the majority of people. For many clients, the experience is one of becoming exposed and vulnerable, of taking risks.

As a client one is highly sensitive to what the counsellor or therapist has to say. In all probability, the counsellor says little (compared with the client's output of words), so what he or she does say takes on a special significance. The client may wonder why the counsellor replies in a particular way, and what it signifies about the kind of person the counsellor might be, outside of the therapy room. And as a client, as one begins to speak of things that one may never have talked about before, things that have hitherto been held within an inner, private dialogue, the voice of the counsellor comes to be added to the voices within that inner space. Most of us can 'hear', within us, the voices of some or all of our parents, siblings, life partner and children. Being in therapy can often result in the addition of the voice of the therapist to this inner chorus.

In a qualitative study carried out by Knox *et al.* (1999), 13 people in long-term therapy were interviewed about their 'internal representation' of their therapist. These clients reported a range of different types of internal representation. Some described vivid, detailed internal 'conversations' with their therapist. For others, their inner therapist was described in more dream-like terms. The frequency of occurrence of these internal images varied a great deal, with some clients using their 'inner therapist' on a daily basis, and others only monthly. One of the main themes emerging from this study was the significant degree to which clients deliberately used such internal images to continue the therapeutic process outside of sessions. Examples of such usage included:

> One client invoked a literal and complete re-creation of the therapy setting in her mind when she felt anxious as she drove in heavy traffic. She repeated words that her therapist had told her about being a good problem solver. These words enabled her to avert a full-blown panic attack, and allowed her to do the things she wanted to do in her life . . .
>
> Another client reported envisioning her therapist extending her arms to the client, beseeching her to come for help when she considered self-mutilation.

(Knox *et al.* 1999: 248)

On the whole, the clients interviewed in this study regarded this process of internal representation of the therapist as a beneficial aspect of therapy, although some were concerned that it might indicate an overdependence on the therapist, or reflect the absence of other supportive individuals in their life. Few of these clients had mentioned these between-session experiences to their therapist, possibly because they believed that such occurrences were not 'normal'.

The Knox *et al.* (1999) study presents the internal representation of the therapist in a positive light. However, their study was carried out on a small sample of clients still in therapy, who probably volunteered to participate in the research because they were comfortable with their therapists and their progress in therapy. By contrast, Wachholz and Stuhr (1999; Stuhr and Wachholz 2001) interviewed 50 clients who had completed therapy 12 years previously, within the outpatient department of the Hamburg University Hospital. Half of these clients had received psychodynamic therapy, and half had received client-centred therapy. Some of the cases had been successful, whereas in other cases the therapy appeared to have only limited benefit for the client.

Wachholz and Stuhr (1999) found that the internalized 'images of the therapist' that emerged in the follow-up interviews could be analysed in terms of eight 'types':

1   *Therapist as 'mature mother' object.* There was a trusting relationship, which satisfied the client's needs. Over the course of therapy, however, the client developed a more differentiated image of the therapist, as someone who had both good and bad sides. The relationship at termination was therefore both realistic and honest.

2   *Therapist as 'symbiotic mother'.* The therapist is exclusively a 'good', warm voice that is wholly attuned to the client's needs and never challenges the client's attitudes.

3   *Therapist as 'insufficient mother'.* The therapist fails to accept the client's needs to be accepted and supported: 'this permanent frustration proves intolerable for patients . . . they react by breaking off therapy, or by subsequently searching for better and more understanding mothers in countless additional therapies' (p. 334).

4   *Therapist as 'unattainable father'.* At the outset of therapy, some women clients perceive their male therapist as the partner they have always longed for: loving, understanding, accepting. As therapy progresses, these clients become increasingly disappointed and angry, and 'regard themselves as the victims of an obscure game whose rules they do not understand' (p. 334).

5   *Therapist as 'stern demanding father'.* The client's inner image is of a father whose affection and esteem she vainly struggles to win.

6   *Therapist as 'devalued object'.* The client does not feel understood or accepted at all, and is internally critical of the therapist.

7   *Therapist as 'repressed object'.* The client finds it impossible to re-create a detailed image of the therapist at all.

8   *Therapist as 'unreachable, ideal object'.* The therapist is represented as an omniscient, wise figure who stands on a pedestal and is beyond reach.

The internalized images associated with therapists who had been 'motherly' in a constructive manner (types 1 and 2) were described by clients as 'warm memories' and 'what they had been looking for'. All of the other internalized images were, to a greater or lesser extent, relatively unhelpful for clients. The research carried out by Wachholz and Stuhr (1999) conveys a sense of the complexity of the therapeutic relationship, and the degree to which the client's internalized image of the therapist is a product of the therapist's style, the client's needs and the interaction between them both. Their findings also point towards fascinating aspects of the role of gender and theoretical orientation in therapy. Both types of therapy (psychodynamic and client-centred) and all combinations of client and therapist gender were found across all the 'image types' except two: the 'stern demanding fathers' (type 5) were all male psychodynamic therapists with female clients, and all the clients who had negative father images (types 4 and 5) were female, with male therapists.

Images of the therapeutic relationship

It is useful to think about the different types or style of therapeutic relationship in terms of *images*, rather than as lists of attributes or theoretical models. By reflecting on images of relationship, it is possible to consider a wide array of cultural images that lie behind, or may fuse with, the approach to the counsellor–client relationship advocated by different theorists. For example, images of the counsellor or helper as confessor, priest, healer, shaman or friend are also present in contemporary theory and practice, but are generally referred to in an implicit rather than explicit fashion. The notion of 'image' also reminds us that the ideas of Freud, Rogers and others arise from their imagination. Any relationship between two people is played out at a number of levels: social, emotional, linguistic, physical etc. Theories of what goes on between counsellor/therapist and client are inevitably a partial representation of the relationship, one among many possible versions of reality. It is important to recognize that ideas such as transference and empathy are *ways of describing* some of what is happening in therapy, rather than constituting objective truths. Finally, the idea of 'image' also reminds us that the intensity and focus of an image can vary. In short-term counselling there may not be time for an intense relationship to become established. In longer-term counselling the relationship may become stronger and more sharply defined, but may at the same time begin to be overlaid by other images, as counsellor and client get to know each other in different ways.

The psychoanalytic concept of transference: therapist as container

The earliest attempt to make sense of what was happening in the relationship between a psychotherapist and a patient was made by Freud. When Freud and Breuer, in the 1880s, began their experiments with what they called the 'talking cure', they became aware that their patients often responded to them in terms of strong emotional reactions: admiration, erotic attraction, anger, hatred. Initially, it was hard for Freud and Breuer to make sense of why this was taking place: these emotional responses did not seem to arise from anything in the therapy itself. Eventually, they reasoned that these reactions had their origins in unresolved childhood conflicts, desires and emotional needs, which were now finding expression, many years later, in the safe environment of the therapy session. Freud (1917/1973: 494–6) eventually came to use the term *transference* to describe this phenomenon:

> a phenomenon which is intimately bound up with the nature of the illness itself . . . known by us as *transference* . . . We mean a transference of feelings on to the person of the doctor, since we do not believe that the situation in the treatment could justify such feelings. We suspect, on the contrary, that the whole readiness for these feelings is derived from elsewhere, that they were already prepared in the patient, and upon the opportunity offered by the analytic treatment, are transferred on to the person of the doctor. Transference can appear as a passionate demand for love . . . a proposal for an inseparable friendship . . . jealousy of everyone close to [the doctor] in real life . . . It is out of the question for us to yield to the patient's demands deriving from the transference . . . We overcome the transference by pointing out to the patient that his feelings do not arise from the present situation and do not apply to the person of the doctor, but that they are repeating something that happened to him earlier. In this way we oblige him to transform his repetition into a memory. By that means the transference, which, whether affectionate or hostile, seemed in every case to constitute the greatest threat to treatment, becomes its best tool, by whose help the most secret compartments of mental life can be opened.

This discovery, by Freud, of how to unlock 'the most secret compartments of mental life' became a cornerstone of psychoanalytic, and later psychodynamic, therapy. One of the core tasks of the therapist was, according to this approach, to create a relationship within which transference reactions could be powerfully and consistently exhibited by the client.

Freud and his colleagues then observed that these expressions of feeling on the part of the patient often triggered off corresponding responses within the analyst. For example, if a patient was expressing hostility towards the therapist, he or she might find himself or herself being angry in return, or seeking to defend his or her actions. If a patient commented on the attractiveness of the analyst, it would be natural to feel flattered, or to become seduced. Freud and those who worked alongside him in the early years of the development of psychoanalysis came to describe these therapist reactions as *counter-transference*.

For a long time, psychoanalysts tended to view counter-transference as an unwelcome source of bias on the part of the therapist, and suggested that sufficient personal analysis would enable a therapist to be able to be free of these reactions, and achieve a state of absolute neutrality in response to the patient. Although the Hungarian analyst Sandor Ferenczi argued vigorously in the 1930s that the analyst should be willing to make active use of his or her counter-transference response to the client, it was only in the 1950s, through the work of British analysts such as Heimann and Symington (see Chapter 5), that counter-transference came to be regarded as a valuable source of therapeutic material.

The image that is used by many psychoanalytic and psychodynamic counsellors and psychotherapists to convey their sense of the type of relationship they seek to construct with clients is that of the *container*. The relationship becomes a place within which the most painful and destructive feelings of the client can be expressed and acted out, because they are held safe there. Psychodynamic counsellors also draw on the image of the *boundary*, or *frame*, to characterize the therapeutic relationship. It is only when the edges of the container are clearly defined that the client knows that they are there. If these edges are permeable or indistinct the client will be left with uncertainty about whether their desire or rage can in fact be contained and held effectively. The image of the container itself evokes and is associated with aspects of *parenting*: for example, the parent making sure that a toddler having a tantrum does not harm himself or herself, or the setting of limits for teenagers experimenting with sex or alcohol. The container image also implies that, as in parenting, one of the functions of the therapist is to *frustrate* the client/child. Within the therapeutic space, it is acceptable to express any kind of desire, but not to consummate it. It is therapeutically valuable to show anger with the therapist – for example, by being late for sessions, but if the therapist is provoked into an argument with the client ('You are wasting my time by being late every week') the client is merely repeating a destructive pattern, and has lost the opportunity to gain insight into it: the task of psychodynamic therapy is to arrive at an understanding of the meaning and origins of behaviour. The therapist therefore frustrates the unconscious desire of the client to get into a fight, and instead offers an interpretation of what has taken place between them.

The notion of the therapeutic relationship as a container or vehicle for emotional learning linked to the development of new insight into childhood patterns of relations with authority figures is described by Hans Strupp (1969: 209–10) in this passage:

> Learning in psychotherapy, almost by definition, occurs within the context of a personal relationship, in the course of which the patient typically becomes dependent on the therapist as an authority, teacher and mentor . . . Learning by identification and imitation is probably the single most important aspect of the therapeutic influence . . . the patient's learning is to a large part experiential but it is also cognitive. However, cognitive learning is seen as maximally effective when the feelings have become mobilized, most notably feelings about the therapist and the therapist–patient interaction . . . I am convinced that interpretation of resistances, that is, those roadblocks which the patient erects to prevent a more open and closer relationship with the therapist, are of the greatest significance and are tremendously important in facilitating the identificatory process . . . For therapeutic learning to occur, the most important precondition is the patient's *openness* to the therapist's influence . . . in an important sense he [the patient] also complies to earn the therapist's approval which becomes an excruciatingly crucial leverage . . . [in] the agonizing process of subordinating himself to a powerful parent figure whom (following his past experiences) he never fully trusts.

Here, although Strupp acknowledges that cognitive learning is important, he also implies that the core of psychodynamic work involves a re-experiencing, in the relationship with the counsellor or psychotherapist, of the emotional responses that the person typically has in relation to significant others, such as his or her parents. The sense of the *struggle* involved in this process, a struggle that needs to be contained if it is to reach a satisfactory conclusion, is conveyed in Strupp's use of terms such as 'roadblocks', 'excruciating' and 'agonizing'.

It is probable that the image of the container is so central to the psychodynamic tradition that any practitioner working within this approach will adopt this way of seeing the therapeutic relationship to a greater or lesser extent. However, contemporary psychodynamic therapists who believe in the usefulness of counter-transference are inevitably drawn in the direction of viewing the relationship as much more of a reciprocal process, with the wishes and feelings of both participants contributing to the creation of what Gill (1994) has called a 'two-person field'. If the therapist is actively involved in sharing what he or she feels, the relationship becomes less focused on holding and containing, and more attuned to processes of mutuality and collaboration. Nevertheless, it would appear that, for therapists working in this tradition, what is created is a mutuality that emerges out of boundaried containment rather than being an open collaboration from the start.

Box 19.2: *How clients view the formation of the therapeutic alliance*

A research study by Bedi *et al.* (2005) collected the views of 40 clients concerning incidents that had occurred during their therapy that they felt had contributed to the establishment of a productive relationship with their counsellor. In the interviews, clients rarely mentioned things that they themselves had done to foster a relationship – they clearly believed that relationship-building was primarily the responsibility of their counsellor. Some of the incidents that were described by clients corresponded to established ideas about the therapy relationship. For instance clients said that they had been helped to feel closer to the counsellor by the way that he or she had used active listening or sensitive non-verbal communication, or had introduced therapy techniques or exercises that were effective. But there were also many incidents that reflected aspects of relationship-building that are not part of existing theory. Clients said that the relationship was strengthened by the environment of the therapy room ('the therapist decorated her office with little objects'), the characteristics of the therapist ('he was always well groomed') and by the therapist being willing to 'go the extra mile' ('the therapist said "call anytime or come in anytime – there will always be somebody here, even if I'm not here"'). These findings suggest that the quality of the client–counsellor relationship can be affected by a myriad of factors, which extend well beyond those that have been identified by therapy theories. They also suggest that clients respond to the degree to which they believe that their counsellor genuinely *cares* about them.

Creating the conditions for growth: therapist as authentic presence

The emergence of humanistic psychology, and the development of the person-centred approach to counselling, have been discussed in Chapter 7. For Carl Rogers during the

1930s and 1940s, as he formed the key ideas of client-centred therapy and then for those who worked alongside him at the University of Chicago in the 1950s, the image of the psychoanalytic relationship was alien to their values and cultural experience. Rogers had been brought up in a Midwest American community that emphasized individual autonomy and equality between people, and as a result he was never comfortable with what he perceived as the expert-driven nature of psychoanalysis. So, although client-centred (and then person-centred) counselling is similar to the psychodynamic approach in emphasizing the disclosure of feelings and difficult experiences in the context of a trusting relationship, it has evolved a very different image of the kind of relationship that should exist between counsellor and client.

In contemporary writing about person-centred counselling much emphasis has been placed on what Rogers (1959) called the 'necessary and sufficient conditions' for therapeutic change, which have subsequently become known as the 'core conditions': the perception by the client of high enough levels of therapist-provided acceptance, congruence and empathy. Much effort has been devoted by person-centred theorists and researchers to the task of clarifying just what these concepts mean, and to identifying the various facets of the experience of congruence and empathy (see Chapter 7). However, it is important to recognize that the 'core conditions' model arose from an attempt by Rogers (1959), in response to an initiative headed by the psychologist Sigmund Koch, to devise a scientifically testable formulation of an approach to therapy that was already successful and widely used. For most of his career, Rogers worked within the professional environment of an academic psychological establishment that was grounded in a behavioural approach. The core conditions formula, and much of the other published work produced by Rogers and his colleagues, is expressed in a behavioural stimulus-response form of language. To understand the image of relationship that underpins this model, it is necessary to search around the edges of the literature on the client-centred/person-centred approach.

A fascinating glimpse of the root image of the person-centred relationship can be found in a section of *Client-centered Therapy* (Rogers 1951), which comprises a lengthy passage written by a junior colleague of Rogers, Oliver Bown. Here, it is suggested that 'love . . . is a basic ingredient of the therapeutic relationship' (Rogers 1951: 160). What is meant here is a non-sexual love that is reflected in a willingness to move beyond pretence and role-playing, to a relationship in which we are not threatened by the other person, and understand him or her. This involves openness on the part of the therapist to his or her own needs and feelings in the therapeutic situation. Rogers was strongly affected by the writings of the philosopher Martin Buber (see Kirschenbaum and Henderson 1990), who promoted the idea that authentic encounter depends on allowing oneself to 'meet' the other. Buber believed in the transformative power of the 'I–Thou' relationship, in which the other person is experienced without labels or conditions. An important paper by Schmid (1998) relates this dimension of person-centred thinking not only to the ideas of Buber, but also to the writings of Emmanuel Levinas and other philosophers.

The principal relationship qualities suggested by these ideas are *presence* and *contact*. It is through being present, in the current moment, with the client that the counsellor is able to be empathic, accepting and congruent. The commitment to be present, in the 'here-and-now', is a continual challenge to any counsellor, because it is easy to revert to evaluating the client in terms of professional and theoretical categories, to slip into thinking ahead ('What is the possible outcome?' 'Is this useful?'), or to lack the courage to respond honestly to the other. The image of the therapeutic relationship as being distinctive in its level of *authentic presence* lies at the heart of the humanistic tradition in psychology and psychotherapy (Mearns and Cooper 2005). It is consistent with the existentially informed therapy of key humanistic psychologists such as Bugental (1976), the adoption of meditative spiritual practices by some humanistic practitioners (Claxton 1996) and an emphasis on the importance of client agency (Bohart and Tallmann 1999; Rennie 2000b, 2001).

The role of therapist-offered *contact* has been summarized by Erskine (1993: 186) in the following terms:

> Contact between client and therapist is the therapeutic context in which the client explores his or her feelings, needs, memories and perceptions. Such contact is possible when the therapist is fully present, that is, attuned to his or her own inner processes and external behaviors, constantly aware of the boundary between self and client, and keenly aware of the client's psycho-dynamics. Contact within psychotherapy is like the substructure of a building: It cannot be seen, but it undergirds and supports all that is above ground. Contact provides the safety that allows the client to drop defenses, to feel again, and to remember.

Therapist as teacher, coach, scientist and philosopher

Within cognitive and cognitive–behavioural approaches to counselling, a good relationship between therapist and client is considered to be necessary for effective therapy to take place, but the relationship is not regarded as a central focus of the therapeutic process. Whereas psychodynamically and humanistically informed counsellors tend to see the relationship as both a here-and-now arena in which emotional issues are expressed and a source of healing, cognitive–behavioural therapists take a much more pragmatic view of what takes place between counsellor and client. The primary aim of cognitive–behavioural therapies is to help the person to change their performance in social situations in the external, 'real' world, typically through using structured exercises and interventions. Although the relationship between client and counsellor needs to be 'good enough' to enable these interventions to be applied appropriately, the focus of CBT is mainly on the interventions, rather than the relationship. Goldfried and Davison (1976: 55) put it in these terms:

> Any behavior therapist who maintains that principles of learning and social influence are all that one needs to know in order to bring about behavior change is out of contact with clinical reality. We have seen therapists capable of conceptualizing problems along behavioral lines and adept at the imple-mentation of the various behavior therapy techniques, but they have few opportunities to demonstrate their effectiveness; they often have difficulty keeping their clients in therapy, let alone getting them to follow through on behavioral assignments.

For Goldfried and Davison (1976), the bond between therapist and client is important because it helps to keep the client in treatment long enough for the intervention to take effect. The image that pervades much cognitive–behavioural practice is the counsellor–client relationship as similar to that of a coach or teacher and student. A coach is someone who supports a person in learning new skills, by demonstrating or modelling these skills, but also by reinforcing and celebrating achievements and successes, giving encouragement and acting as a source of motivation. A good coach also promotes positive expectations, by conveying their confidence in the capacity of the student to do well.

In addition, some cognitive–behavioural therapists, and many cognitive therapists, regard their role as being like that of a scientist or philosopher, who is trying to challenge the basic, dysfunctional beliefs and cognitive schemas held by the client. Homework assignments can be understood, within this perspective, as 'experiments' in observing the effects of new ways of behaving in social situations. Cognitive therapists, and practitioners using rational emotive behaviour therapy (REBT) often use the image of the 'Socratic dialogue' to describe the way they work. The counsellor takes on the role of the Greek philosopher Socrates, in engaging in a process of challenging, sometimes with humour, the irrationality or arbitrariness of the beliefs or patterns of logic that the client has used to create and maintain their state of anxiety or depression.

A central theme that runs through cognitive–behavioural thinking about the nature of the therapeutic relationship is *collaboration* (Raue and Goldfried 1994; Sanders and Wills 2002). The counsellor and client work *alongside* each other to find solutions to a problem that is 'out there'. Some of the metaphors that may be used by the counsellor to explain this way of working to the client are that therapy is a 'team effort' or that 'two heads are better than one'. Some interesting findings have emerged from research into the therapeutic relationship in cognitive–behavioural therapy (CBT). Comparative studies (e.g., where CBT is compared with psychodynamic therapy) have shown that the quality of the relationship in CBT is as strong as, and sometimes significantly stronger than, the ratings derived from the more 'relationship-oriented' therapies (see Raue and Goldfried 1994). There is also consistent evidence that the quality of the relationship in CBT is associated with outcome; CBT counsellors who fail to establish collaborative relationships with their clients end up with poor results (Raue and Goldfried 1994). The research results can perhaps be understood as consistent with the idea that clients experience the type of relationship that cognitive and cognitive–behavioural counsellors offer them as being fairly comfortable, in that it resembles other types of relationship they might have come across in their lives. Cognitive–behavioural therapy-oriented counsellors also provide clients with a relatively high degree of structure within sessions, and focus on developing solutions to problems and symptoms, rather than exploring the inner experience of painful issues to any great extent. All these factors may suggest that the therapeutic relationship in CBT is on the whole smoother and more predictable than it may at times become in psychodynamic and person-centred therapy.

The 'not-knowing' stance: therapist as editor

Developments in narrative therapy (White and Epston 1990) have been accompanied by a distinctive and different approach to the therapeutic relationship. One of the central principles of narrative therapy is the idea that the freedom and individuality of the person has been limited as a consequence of conformity to 'dominant narratives', which define the way the person 'should' behave in various circumstances. The goal of narrative therapy is, instead, to enable the person to be 'the author of their own story'. From this perspective, any theoretical perspective (such as psychodynamic or person-centred theory) can be viewed as a dominant narrative ready to be imposed on the person. The kind of relationship that is consistent with a narrative approach is described by Anderson and Goolishian (1992). They describe the therapist as a 'participant–facilitator of the therapeutic conversation' (p. 27). At the heart of this way of being a therapist is the concept of *not-knowing*:

> the excitement for the therapist is in learning the uniqueness of each individual client's narrative truth, the coherent truths in their storied lives . . . therapists are always prejudiced by their experience, but . . . they must listen in such a way that their pre-experience does not close them to the full meaning of the client's descriptions of their experience. This can only happen if the therapist approaches each clinical experience from the position of not-knowing. To do otherwise is to search for regularities and common meaning that may validate the therapist's theory but invalidate the uniqueness of the clients' stories and thus their very identity.
>
> (Anderson and Goolishian 1992: 30)

A 'not-knowing' stance may appear to be similar in intention to the empathic phenomenological listening found in person-centred counselling or the 'free-floating attention' of the psychoanalyst. However, whereas in person-centred counselling or psychoanalysis the open listening of the therapist is used to gather material that is then understood in terms of either respective theoretical model, in narrative therapy the aim is to not arrive at a final formulation or interpretation of the 'problem', but to 'keep understanding *on the way*'. What this means is that the therapist is 'led by the expertise of the client', and is seeking to work with the client to keep the dialogue open, as a means of creating an ever-richer narrative.

The role of the therapist here is to suggest strategies that the client might use to deconstruct, reconstruct and retell his or her story. These strategies can involve questioning, using metaphor or writing. The relationship between therapist and client is akin to that between a writer and his or her editor. It is the writer who *creates* and *imagines* the story into existence; the editor helps to give it shape, and nurture it into publication.

Integrative models: the all-purpose therapist

The images of the therapeutic relationship discussed so far have derived from attempts to fashion distinctive approaches to therapy. Each approach, in its own way, has sought to maximize the difference between itself and other competing 'brands' of therapy by specifying a different quality of relationship between counsellor and client. However, there have also been theorists who have tried to bring together apparently competing ideas about the therapeutic relationship, with the aim of producing an integrative understanding of the relationship.

Although currently regarded as providing an *integrative* framework for understanding the therapeutic relationship, the title of Bordin's (1979) paper – 'The generalizability of the psychoanalytic concept of the working alliance' – clearly indicates that the origins of his thinking lie within psychoanalysis. What Bordin was essentially able to do was to take psychoanalytic ideas about the therapeutic relationship and redescribe them in everyday language. The concept of the 'alliance' has been highly significant within psychodynamic counselling:

> The concept of the therapeutic alliance has historically played an important role in the evolution of the classic psychoanalytic tradition, insofar as it has provided a theoretical justification for greater technical flexibility . . . By highlighting the importance of the real, human aspects of the therapeutic relationship, the therapeutic alliance has provided grounds for departing from the idealized therapist stance of abstinence and neutrality.
>
> (Safran and Muran 2001: 165)

Bordin (1979) proposed that a functioning working alliance between a therapist and a client comprised three features: an agreement on *goals*; an assignment of a task or series of *tasks*; and the development of a *bond*. Bordin proposed that all forms of therapy were built around goals, tasks and bonds, even if the relative weighting of each element varied in different approaches. For example, he argued that: 'some basic level of trust surely marks all varieties of therapeutic relationships, but when attention is directed toward the more protected recesses of inner experience, deeper bonds of trust and attachment are required and developed' (p. 254).

The model outlined by Bordin has proved highly resilient in informing research and practice over a 30-year period. Although it is clear that goals, tasks and bonds are quite separate features of the therapeutic enterprise, it is also certain that they interconnect in complex and reciprocal ways. For example, the degree to which a painful therapeutic task can be successfully completed may depend on the quality of the bond between therapist and client. Yet, at the same time, the successful achievement of tasks may in itself contribute to a stronger bond. In his original paper, Bordin emphasized his three key features as representing *challenges* to both counsellor and client, and he speculated that the link between the personality of the counsellor or client and their performance in therapy was mediated through the way that their personality characteristics might influence their approach to each element of the working alliance. For example, he observes that a humanistic therapist might be a person who was drawn towards the therapeutic task of self-disclosure. Such a therapist might be effective with clients who had similar needs, while a behaviour therapist (low self-discloser) might be more helpful for a client who did not wish to disclose feelings and personal material.

Box 19.3: *The room as an active element of the therapeutic relationship*

The philosopher, social critic and co-founder of gestalt therapy, Paul Goodman (1962) commented on the significance of the seating arrangements associated with different approaches to therapy. For example, he suggested that the room layout in classical Freudian psychoanalysis, where the patient lies on a couch with the analyst sitting in a chair at the head of the couch, out of the patient's line of sight, had the effect of 'by-passing' the actual relationship between patient and therapist:

> the patient does not see the therapist . . . any social contact with the therapist as though he were a 'person' is frowned on . . . there is thus developed the transference, infantile relationship, and treatment is largely management of this transference.
>
> (Goodman 1962: 157–61)

The significance of the physical environment within which counselling takes place was investigated by Fenner (2011, 2012) through interviews with clients and therapists. What was very clear, in the findings of this study, was the extent to which both client and therapist had a relationship with the room. Clients talked about how they interpreted the decoration and furnishing in the room as evidence for similarities between their own taste and values, and those of their therapist. Clients felt deep connection with certain parts of the room, or objects in the room. The ability to look out of a window was important for some clients:

> Yes, it's really important to be able to look out and see the light and the green. In summer, as soon as I come in I open the window and get the air and the light out there. It gives me a bit of perspective. I just need to have that. I don't like being sort of closed into the situation. Looking out to see something fresh, something of wider horizons than just the room.
>
> (Fenner 2011: 855)

A comprehensive review of research into the physical attributes of therapeutic spaces (e.g., light, sound, smell, temperature, etc.) can be found in Pressly and Heesaker (2001).

It is of interest that Bordin developed his model of the working alliance in the mid-1970s, at a time when research into Rogers' necessary and sufficient conditions' theory was at its peak. Yet, although he definitely knew of this research, he did not refer to it in his classic 1979 paper. There were perhaps two reasons for this (Horvath 2000). First, Bordin was intent on developing a framework that would transcend any specific theoretical orientation; he regarded Rogers' theory as primarily relevant to client-centred therapy. Second, he wished to emphasize that the therapeutic alliance was truly *bidirectional*, and equally influenced by both client and therapist, whereas the 'core conditions' model focuses mainly on the attitudes and qualities of the therapist alone.

Another attempt to construct an integrated approach to working with the client–counsellor relationship, was developed by Howard *et al.* (1987). The significant contribution made by the authors has been to suggest that the therapist's style of relating to the client should be adapted to the needs of the client at that time. Their model is influenced by research into situational leadership in management. Howard *et al.* (1987) propose that it makes sense to analyse therapist behaviour, in respect of how he or she interacts with a client, in terms of two general dimensions: *directiveness* and *supportiveness*. These dimensions combine to form four therapist *relational styles*:

- *High direction/low support*. The therapist is in charge of what is happening. This style is appropriate when the client is unwilling or unable to move him/herself toward the goals of therapy.
- *High direction/high support*. The therapist adopts a teaching/psycho-educational role, in relation to a client who has indicated a willingness to learn. This is relational style commonly found in CBT approaches.
- *Low direction/high support*. The therapist using this style is essentially accompanying a client who is engaged in a process of exploration and growth. This is the relational style associated with person-centred counselling.
- *Low direction/low support*. The therapist functions mainly as an observer of the client's progress. This relational style is characteristic of classical psychoanalysis.

Howard *et al.* (1987) suggest that the majority of clients experience times when they need their therapist to relate to them in each of these different ways. They also suggest that the majority of therapists are comfortable and confident in only one or two of these relational styles, and that expansion of the relational style repertoire represents a key focus for training and supervision.

Clarkson (1990, 1995) has proposed an integrative framework for making sense of therapeutic relationships, which envisages five different kinds of therapeutic relationship, all potentially available to the counsellor and client. These are:

1 The working alliance.
2 The transferential/counter-transferential relationship.
3 The reparative/developmentally needed relationship.
4 The person-to-person relationship.
5 The transpersonal relationship.

Implicit in Clarkson's model is a sense that there is a developmental movement across these relationship types: an 'alliance' is viewed as a basic functional level of communication, whereas a 'transpersonal' relationship is characterized as a 'higher-level' type of contact. Her writing is poetic and creative, rather than research-informed, and seeks to convey the distinctive emotional environment created within each of these contrasting types of relationship. In her view, all of these relationships are possible and implicit in any therapy, and training should prepare practitioners to operate comfortably across the entire range.

Josselson (1996) constructed a model of relationship dimensions that is specifically oriented toward making sense of the types of relationship difficulties and issues that people might bring to counselling. Josselson (1996) suggests that there are eight main relationship dimensions:

- *Holding* – being there for another person, allowing another person to be there for oneself.

- *Attachment* – the emotional bonds, or enduring connection with another person.
- *Passionate involvement* – being aroused in a relationship, being excited, feeling pleasure, being physically touched.
- *Eye-to-eye validation* – affirmation, recognition of one's meaning and value in the eyes of another person.
- *Idealization and identification* – admiring another person, using them as a model or mentor, wanting to be like that person.
- *Mutuality and resonance* – being with another person, joining in together, doing things together, sharing the same feelings.
- *Embeddedness* – belonging, being a member of a group.
- *Tending and caring* – looking after, being dependent.

Josselson (1996) takes the position that an emotionally well-adjusted person will have the capacity to engage with others along any and all of these dimensions of relationship. Conversely, a person may develop relationship difficulties, or have an absence of capability, around any of the dimensions. It is easy to see that the models of relationship discussed earlier fail to address all of the dimensions identified by Josselson. For example, the person-centred approach provides a good framework for making sense of eye-to-eye validation and mutuality/resonance, while the psychodynamic model has a lot to say about attachment and idealization/identification. However, neither approach has a great deal to offer when it comes to understanding relationship issues arising from passion or tending/caring. It is perhaps significant, and not surprising, that counselling/psychotherapy theories of relationship mainly consider relationship dimensions that may be directly played out within the counselling room. Practitioners offering counselling that is embedded within other roles are possibly more likely to catch sight of the expression of passion and caring in the lives of people with whom they are working, and may be better placed to engage with these issues.

Another multidimensional model that can be used to analyse the client–counsellor relationship is the framework used in the Structural Analysis of Social Behavior (SASB; Benjamin 1987) and the Interpersonal Octagon (Birtchnell 1999) approach. This perspective specifically considers reciprocal patterns of behaviour that takes place between participants in a relationship. For example, a person who has a need for controlling and maintaining order is likely to seek out relationships with people who will reciprocate through having a need for care and protection. In terms of more negative or destructive forms of this pattern of relating, it could be argued that people who behave in ways that are intimidating and sadistic will gravitate toward people who may expect rejection and disapproval. Ultimately, these reciprocal patterns can be viewed as manifestations of the interaction between how close to others (or distant from others) a person prefers to be, and their preference for being powerful and dominant (as contrasted with submissive).

The examples outlined above demonstrate that there exist well-established theoretical frameworks that can be applied to the job of making sense of relationships in counselling situations. These models can be used in counselling in two main ways. First, it is helpful for a counsellor to be aware of their own strengths and weaknesses in terms of relating to others. For example, a counsellor may be very comfortable in relating to other people on the basis of mutuality and equality, but find it hard to respond when a person idealizes them, or demands to be taken care of. Each of the integrative frameworks outlined above, is essentially advocating relational flexibility on the part of therapists, to enable them to be maximally responsive to their clients' relational needs. The concept of counsellor *responsiveness* provides a useful means of making sense of this kind of flexibility.

Stiles and colleagues (1998) have proposed that therapists and clients are highly sensitive and responsive to the reactions of each other. Within the moment-by-moment interaction that occurs in a therapy session, there exist complex feedback loops through which the behaviour of one participant influences, and is influenced by, the behaviour of the other. Stiles *et al.* (1998) suggest that the reason why all forms of therapy are broadly equivalent in effectiveness is that therapists who are trained to relate to their clients in a specific way can be gradually pulled by their clients in the direction of other relational styles. Less effective therapists, by contrast, tend to continue to do the same thing, no matter what signals are sent out by the client.

A further way in which the integrationist approach to understanding relationships can be useful for counsellors is concerned with the task of making sense of patterns and themes in a client's life. When listening to the stories that a person seeking counselling tells about his or her life, it is valuable to be able to pick out recurring patterns of relating, particularly if the person's problems in living seem to involve relationship difficulties.

Box 19.4: *Beyond the alliance: the concept of* relational depth

The idea that effective counselling involves the creation of an *alliance* between client and therapist has proved to be a remarkably useful way of thinking about the therapy relationship. However, like any metaphor, the image of client and counsellors being 'allies' to fight a common cause has its limitations. In particular, it does not capture the quality of intense person-to-person contact that can sometimes occur in therapy. Mearns and Cooper (2005) have developed the concept of *relational depth* to begin to describe this kind of experience. They define relational depth as 'a state of profound contact and engagement between two people, in which each person is fully real with the Other' (p. xii).

Research into the experience of relational depth by therapists (Cooper 2005) and clients (Knox 2008; McMillan and McLeod 2006) has further articulated the dimensions of this concept. A participant in the Knox (2008: 185) study described a moment of relational depth in these terms: 'It felt as though my counsellor, without breaching boundaries, went beyond a professional level/interest – and gave me such a human, compassionate response – something I couldn't put a price on . . . It felt like she was giving from her core'. Clients report that these moments have a profound and enduring healing impact on them. However, they also report that such events rarely occur. Knox (2008) and McMillan and McLeod (2006) both interviewed clients who had experience of multiple episodes of therapy throughout their lives. These clients recounted that they had encountered relational depth events with less than half of the therapists with whom they had worked.

The practicalities of relationship competence: how to develop an effective therapeutic alliance

Although the images of the therapeutic relationship that have been reviewed above offer a valuable range of different ways of making sense of what happens between a client and a counsellor, they tend to be fairly silent on the question of what a counsellor should actually *do* to establish a robust alliance with a client. Some of the more recent theory and research around the topic of the therapeutic relationship has focused on identifying and developing practical strategies that can be applied by counsellors to build and maintain constructive relationships with clients.

Adopting a collaborative style: being congruent and using metacommunication

A limitation of much of the writing on the person-centred concept of congruence is that it has been described almost as a mystical state or 'way of being' (see Wyatt 2001). It is helpful to realize that, on a moment-to-moment basis, congruence can be expressed in the *way the counsellor talks*. Most of the time in counselling, both counsellor and client talk in a manner that refers to the topic of the client's 'problem'. By also including talk that refers to the process and activity of talking, it becomes possible to weave in to the conversation a continual flow of statements about aspects of the relationship between counsellor and client. This 'talking about the process of talking' has been discussed by Rennie (1998: 89) as the skill of *metacommunication*: 'the act of communicating about communication . . . stepping outside the flow of communication to appraise it'. Examples of therapist-initiated metacommunication would be when the therapist:

- talks about his or her own plans, strategies, assumptions;
- asks the client to focus on his or her plans, strategies, assumptions;
- shares his or her assumptions about what the client thinks and intends;
- invites the client to share his or her assumptions or fantasies about what the counsellor thinks or intends;
- reviews the relationship in all these ways when stuck, or in a therapy 'crisis';
- explores the impact of the client on the counsellor (the feelings, action tendencies and fantasies that are evoked by the client's behaviour);
- explores the impact of the counsellor on the client.

Each of these ways of talking opens up a layer of the 'unspoken' or implicit relationship between counsellor and client, and makes it possible for both participants in that relationship to reflect on what is happening between them, and if necessary change it. The use of metacommunication represents the application in therapy of the relationship framework developed by Laing *et al.* (1966).

On the whole, counsellors do not engage in metacommunication to any great extent within therapy – this is a neglected skill. Kiesler (1988: 127) concluded, as a result of his research into this topic, that 'therapist interventions incorporating metacommunicative feedback have been almost universally overlooked in the individual psychotherapy literature'.

Repairing ruptures in the alliance

It is seldom that a therapist and client meet, form a good working relationship and then continue through several sessions of therapy without any challenge or disruption to the bond between them, or their agreed goals and tasks. This kind of 'ideal' relationship (in therapy as in any other area of life) is a myth. What is more usual is for the relationship, and the therapeutic work, to 'hit the buffers' now and again. Participants in counselling – both clients and counsellors – may report that they have reached an 'impasse', or that there has been a 'rupture' in the relationship. In these circumstances it is necessary for the counsellor to be able to call on strategies for 'repairing' the relationship.

A significant amount of recent theory and research has begun to address the question of how best a therapist or counsellor can repair or retrieve the therapeutic relationship when it goes through a bad patch. The work of Jeremy Safran (Safran 1993a, 1993b; Safran and Muran 1996, 2000a, 2000b, 2001) has been at the forefront of attempts to investigate the processes and implications of 'ruptures' in the therapeutic alliance. For Safran, the single most important strategy for the therapist in such situations is *metacommunication* – it is necessary to stand back from what is happening, name and discuss the problem, and then negotiate around it.

Safran has identified a series of steps or stages that can be observed in the effective repair of a therapeutic alliance. First, the therapist needs to be sensitive to the presence of rupture in the alliance. Typically, a client will express confrontation (anger with the therapist or criticism of the progress of therapy), withdrawal (disengagement from the therapist or the therapeutic process) or a combination of these two responses. The task of the therapist at this point is to draw attention to what is happening within the here-and-now relationship, for example by asking 'What are you experiencing . . . ?' or 'I have a sense that you are withdrawing from me. Am I right?' The acknowledgement by both the therapist and the client that there is a difficulty moves the repair process on to the next stage, which involves helping the client to describe their negative feelings, or what it is they believe is blocking them or hindering progress. The therapist may need to acknowledge at this point, in an undefensive way, how he or she might be contributing to the rupture. The final stage involves encouraging the client to access their primary feelings (typically anger or sadness), and to express to the therapist their underlying needs or wishes. One of the tasks of the therapist at this stage is to affirm the importance of these needs and wishes.

Successfully resolving a rupture in a therapeutic alliance can have a number of benefits for the client. Clearly, it strengthens the relationship, and makes it possible to continue therapy in a productive direction. But it also gives the client an opportunity to learn about how to sort out relationship difficulties in general, and how to ask/demand what they need in a relationship. Finally, for people who may be more familiar with rivalrous conflict-ridden relationships, it provides a model of collaborative give-and-take relatedness.

A case study published by Agnew *et al.* (1994) explored the process of resolving a rupture in the therapeutic alliance within a case of psychodynamic therapy. This case took place in the context of a research study in which all sessions were taped and transcribed, and both client and therapist completed questionnaires on several aspects of process and outcome. It was possible, therefore, to examine the stages of rupture resolution in great detail. In this case, the breach between client and therapist emerged towards the end of Session 2, when the client angrily confronted the therapist with her uneasiness about their 'roles', specifically claiming that the therapist had adopted a role of an 'expert' and a 'superior' man. Agnew *et al.* (1994) were able to identify the following stages in the repair process:

1 *Acknowledgement.* Therapist acknowledges client's feelings.

2 *Negotiation.* Therapist and client develop a shared understanding of their roles and responsibilities.

3 *Exploration.* Client and therapist explore parallel situations outside therapy (e.g. the client's relationship with her father).

4 *Consensus and renegotiation.* Therapist and client develop a consensus over the origins of the client's dissatisfaction and renegotiate the terms of their working relationship.

5 *Enhanced exploration.* Further exploration of parallel situations outside therapy.

6 *New styles of relating.* Therapist and client discuss alternative styles of relating in these situations.

As in the Safran model, the therapist's willingness to accept responsibility for his part in the rupture (Stage 2 of the Agnew model) was a crucial element in overcoming the relationship breakdown. Agnew *et al.* (1994) emphasized that, in this case, it was also important that the therapist explained to the client *why* it might be useful to explore the similarities between their current dilemma and other relationship impasses that she had experienced in her life.

The work of Safran, Agnew and others contributes to an appreciation of the value in therapy of being able to face up to, and learn from, tensions within the client–counsellor relationship. These models reinforce the key idea that, for clients, the interpersonal arena of therapy provides unique opportunities for learning about needs and relationships in ways that can then generalize to everyday life.

The embodiment of the relationship: transition objects

The British psychoanalyst D. W. Winnicott carried out a great deal of observation of the emotional and social behaviour of young infants. He noted that, from about the age of six months, a young child may come to have a favoured possession, such as a teddy bear, blanket or bundle of wool, which appears to represent its 'emotional security'. If the object is lost or taken away, the child exhibits a grief reaction. Winnicott reasoned that the object represents the security of the mother's breast, and operates as a defence against anxiety during the period where the child is being asked to move away from its symbiotic relationship with the breast, and become a more autonomous individual. Winnicott coined the term *transition object*, in recognition of the important role of such objects at this crucial stage of transition in the child's life. Winnicott's account of the dynamics of transition objects is explained in his popular book *Playing and Reality* (Winnicott 1971).

A transition object represents a physical embodiment of a relationship. When the other person is not available, the object can remind us of his or her continuing existence and qualities. Sometimes, when a client in therapy develops a strong relationship with his or her therapist, he or she may wish to possess some object that will remind them of the therapist, and perhaps bring strength between sessions. This phenomenon is known to most experienced therapists (and clients), but has seldom been studied in a systematic manner. Arthern and Madill (1999) interviewed six experienced therapists (three gestalt therapists and three psychodynamic therapists) about their understandings of the role of transition objects in their relationships with clients. Although not selected on the basis of having been known to use or promote transition objects, all of them could recall examples of the use of transition objects by their clients.

These therapists considered that transition objects were particularly helpful for clients who experienced separation anxiety between sessions, and who were working on painful interpersonal issues, and needed to 'internalize a sense of a nourishing relationship'. They believed that the objects served not only to remind clients of the existence of a safe, constant relationship in their life, but also provided something to 'play' with, in the sense of reflecting on the meaning of the object, and using it as a trigger for learning about personal needs and relationship patterns.

What kinds of objects were used by clients? The therapists interviewed in this study reported a wide range of objects, including greetings cards and postcards (written from therapist to client), formal letters, books and pens, through to a soft toy, a therapist's cardigan and a piece of a therapist's jewellery. Arthern and Madill (1999) compared the characteristics of objects reported by gestalt therapists and those reported by psychodynamic clients. The psychodynamic transition objects tended to be verbal (cards, pens, messages); the gestalt objects tended to be soft, personal or wearable. All three of the psychodynamic therapists reported feeling that they had 'broken the rules' (i.e., violated a therapeutic boundary) by allowing a client to retain an object. None of the gestalt therapists mentioned rule violation.

It is important to note that the Arthern and Madill (1999) study refers only to instances in which therapists were aware that transition objects had been created. No doubt there are many clients who 'acquire' such objects without letting their therapist know that they are doing so.

One of the key conclusions drawn by Arthern and Madill (1999) is that transition objects can be hugely significant for clients and therapists. They suggest that these objects serve as a means of *embodying* the therapeutic relationship, and function as a practical means of supporting those clients for whom trusting relationships can be problematic.

The concept of boundary

One useful way to begin to make sense of the relationship between a therapist and client is to consider the way in which the *boundary* between the two participants is created and maintained. Although the concept of boundary was not used by any of the 'founders' of therapy (e.g., Freud, Jung, Rogers), it has become widely used in recent years as a means of describing important aspects of the therapeutic relationship. In common sense terms, a boundary marks the limits of a territory, and the line where one territory or space ends and another one begins. In counselling and psychotherapy, the concept of 'boundary' is clearly a metaphor – there are no actual boundary posts, markers or lines laid out in a therapy room. In therapy, the concept of boundary has been defined as: 'the envelope within which treatment takes place . . . to create an atmosphere of safety and predictability' (Gutheil and Gabbard 1998: 409–410).

In a therapy situation, boundaries can be identified in reference to a range of different dimensions of the relationship. For example, boundaries can be defined around:

- Time. The beginning and end of a therapy session.
- Physical space. How close (or far apart) should the client and counsellor sit; how extensive is each participant's 'personal space'?
- Information. How much should the client know about the counsellor?
- Intimacy. How emotionally close should the counsellor and client be? Does the level of intimacy within the relationship extend to touching, or even to sexual contact?
- Social roles. How does the counsellor acknowledge the client if they meet in another setting? How should the counsellor respond to a client's request to form a relationship outside of the therapy room?

The idea of boundary also allows other significant aspects of the therapeutic relationship to be discussed. Boundaries can be rigid or permeable. Counsellors differ in personal style, with some favouring strictly regulated boundaries, and others being more flexible. Some counsellors may 'loosen' their boundary in the later stages of therapy with a client. Many different forms of behaviour (the client being late or 'forgetting' to pay the fee; the counsellor touching the client) can be interpreted as boundary 'violations' or 'transgressions', and links can be made with other boundary issues reported by the client in his or her everyday life.

The concept of boundary has been particularly widely used within contemporary psychodynamic and psychoanalytic thinking. The psychoanalytic psychotherapist Robert Langs (1988) has been prominent in arguing for the strict imposition of clearly defined boundaries in therapy as a core principle of therapy. Langs believes that definite boundaries create a strong therapeutic frame within which the client will be safe to explore painful and threatening personal material.

Many humanistically oriented counsellors and psychotherapists have had reservations about the way in which the idea of 'boundary' is used within therapy as a justification for a distanced, detached stance in relation to the client. For example, Hermansson (1997: 135) has argued that 'the very nature of the counselling process demands a measure of boundary crossing . . . counsellor aloofness, often promoted by boundary rigidity, is in itself potentially abusive'. Jordan (2000:1015) acknowledges that she has: 'trouble with [a] "boundary language" . . . anchored in [a] view of separation as safety. We need to look at boundaries as places of meeting, and we need to think of safety as residing in the development of growth-fostering connections'. In a similar vein, Mearns and Thorne (2000: 50) have written that:

there are certainly psychodynamic practitioners who would have no difficulty in defining the person-centred attitude toward boundaries and the therapeutic relationship to be . . . unethical . . . The willingness of person-centred therapists to extend sessions, increase frequency of sessions, allow telephone contact, engage in home visits, and respond to client requests for mild physical contact like a hug, are all so manifestly inappropriate within other theoretical models that they are automatically taken as evidence of therapist inadequacy, or, indeed, *over-involvement*. It is fascinating that ethical challenges are made on the basis of over-involvement, yet there are no codes which describe a pattern of systematic therapist *under-involvement*. It seems strange that a profession which emphasises the power of relationship should not be prepared to challenge members who offer clients such a degree of detachment in the face of pain that the client experiences this as abusive.

The emphasis in person-centred and humanistic therapy, clearly evident in these passages, on the value of authentic contact or encounter between counsellor and client leads to a view of a boundary not as a 'rule for remaining separate' but as an indicator of a place where contact and 'meeting' might occur.

One of the disappointing features of much recent writing around the concept of boundary in therapy is that it has focused to a major extent on the issue of boundary violation, specifically on violations in relation to sexual exploitation of clients. This form of boundary violation is highly destructive, and undoubtedly deserves attention. However, a consequence of highlighting sexual boundary violations has been implicitly to promote a confusion and conflation of boundary issues and ethical issues. *Some* boundary issues (such as sex with clients) have definite ethical dimensions, but others (e.g., extending the length of a session) do not. Potentially, the metaphor of an interpersonal 'boundary' provides practitioners with a powerful conceptual tool with which the nature of the therapeutic relationship with a client can be examined. The construction and maintenance of boundaries present practitioners with a series of choices that have implications for the quality of the help that is offered to clients. There are, no doubt, dangers in both therapeutic relationships that are insufficiently boundaried and those that are overboundaried. But the more interesting question is: what is the optimal set of boundaries for each specific counsellor–client relationship? As Hartmann (1997) has shown in his research studies, individuals have different boundary needs or boundary 'thickness' or 'thinness': the boundary setting that may be right for one client (or counsellor) may not be right for another.

Box 19.5: *Making a distinction between boundary crossings and boundary violations*

It is generally agreed within the counselling and psychotherapy community that it is helpful for clients if the therapist defines a clear set of boundaries within which the work can proceed. There is less agreement around how best to make sense of occasions when these boundaries are not maintained. For some practitioners, any boundary lapse is viewed as highly problematic, and as an all-or-nothing *violation* of the therapeutic space. By contrast, other practitioners make a distinction between boundary violations and boundary *crossings*.

Glass (2003: 433) defines a boundary crossing as 'benign, discussable, nonprogressive departures from an established treatment framework that are creative and conscientious attempts to adapt the treatment to the individual patient'. He describes an example of a boundary crossing with one of his own clients, a man who had been in therapy with him for several years. The client invited him to attend his first poetry recital, a major event in his personal development. Glass (2003) discussed the situation with the client, and decided to accept the invitation. The therapist 'sat in the back row, and left without interacting with other attendees or formally greeting (the client), beyond making eye contact' (p. 437). This event was not 'progressive', it did not lead into a 'slippery slope' of ongoing social contact and erosion of the distinctiveness of the therapy relationship.

Glass (2003: 438) suggests that the profession should acknowledge that 'long-term . . . treatment relationships . . . almost always include an accumulation of boundary crossings that shape the unique relationship that evolves'.

Measuring the therapeutic relationship

A great deal of research has been carried out around the topic of the therapeutic relationship. This research is of interest to counsellors for three reasons. First, it confirms the importance of the therapeutic relationship as a factor that makes a significant contribution to the success of therapy with a client. Second, the statements used in questionnaires that have been employed to measure the therapeutic alliance and other aspects of the relationship provide a succinct summary of what the therapeutic relationship means in practice. Third, research has generated tools that can be used by counsellors to evaluate their own work.

Several questionnaires have been devised to measure dimensions of the therapeutic relationship. These questionnaires list a series of statements; the person completing the scale is required to indicate the extent to which they agree or disagree with each statement, typically using a five-point scale. Versions of most of these questionnaires have been developed for counsellors, clients and external observers (e.g., listening to a tape recording of the session) to complete. Normally, the questionnaire is completed by the counsellor or client immediately following the end of a session. The most widely used questionnaires are: the Working Alliance Inventory (WAI; Horvath and Greenberg 1986, 1994), which measures Bordin's bond, task and goal dimensions; the Barrett-Lennard Relationship Inventory (BLRI; Barrett-Lennard 1986), which assesses the Rogerian core conditions; and the Penn Helping Alliance Scales (HA; Alexander and Luborsky 1986), which evaluates the overall strength of the helping alliance between counsellor and client. The Session Rating Scale (SRS; Duncan *et al.* 2003; Miller *et al.* 2005) is an ultra-brief (four-item) visual analogue scale, designed to be easy to use within routine counselling practice.

The association between client–therapist relationship and outcome has been demonstrated in a number of studies (see Cooper 2004, 2008). In addition to documentation of the importance of the therapeutic alliance, the other striking finding to emerge from research has been that there are often low levels of agreement between the client, the counsellor and external observers on how they rate the therapeutic relationship in any individual case. It seems as though the different participants in therapy have quite different ways of interpreting the same events, or different criteria for judging these events. Another conclusion generated by research has been that there is a great deal of overlap between all of the therapeutic relationship scales, and between the subfactors (i.e., bond, goals and tasks) within these scales. The implication here is that clients, in particular, may have a sense that their relationship is 'good', but are vague about the various dimensions that may constitute that 'goodness'. An excellent review of research into the therapeutic relationship can be found in Agnew-Davies (1999).

The process of developing a valid and reliable questionnaire is time-consuming and intricate. Essentially, the aim is to create a questionnaire with the smallest possible number of carefully worded questions. The task of the test compiler, therefore, requires checking with many people in order to arrive at a set of statements that accurately capture the meaning of the factor that is being measured (or 'operationalized'). Table 19.1 gives examples of items taken from some of the more widely used relationship measures.

The role of money in the relationship

The issue of payment can have a significant impact on the relationship between a counsellor and a client. In a relationship in which a person talks about an emotional difficulty or crisis to a friend or family member, the question of payment does not arrive. The implicit assumption, when using a friend in this way, is that the relationship is reciprocal: at some point in the future the roles will be reversed. Clearly, counselling is not like this. Although the experience of being listened to, and being encouraged to explore feelings, may be very similar, in the end the counsellor is there not because of feelings of friendship or family loyalty, but because he or she is, in some way or another, being paid to be there.

In some voluntary agencies and self-help groups, the counsellor and client may be regarded as having a 'gift relationship': the helper is 'giving' because he or she believes they are making a contribution to the common good. In many (but not all) countries, being a blood donor is an example of a pure form of 'gift relationship'. When such a relationship is clearly understood by both parties in these terms, monetary issues may recede into the background. But even in many self-help groups and voluntary agencies in which helpers or counsellors are freely giving their time, the client may be asked to make a 'donation' to cover the running costs of the organization. And, of course, in the majority of counselling situations the issue of payment is highly salient: the counsellor is being paid a fee or salary to listen. So, it is probably reasonable to conclude that payment is a meaningful (if hidden) dimension of most counselling relationships.

The hidden nature of the financial relationship between counsellor and client ultimately derives from the high level of secretiveness and ambivalence that exists in most modern industrialized societies in relation to the topic of money. For most people, the incomes and savings of even their closest friends and family members remain unknown. Yet, at the same time, we live in a society in which financial success is highly valued.

TABLE 19.1 Defining the therapeutic relationship: statements from research questionnaires

---

Working Alliance Inventory

The therapeutic bond
I believe my counsellor is genuinely concerned for my welfare
*I have the feeling that if I say or do the wrong things, my counsellor will stop working with me

Therapeutic task agreement
I am clear on what my responsibilities are in therapy
*I find that what my counsellor and I are doing in therapy is unrelated to my concerns

Therapeutic goals
My counsellor and I are working toward mutually agreed goals
As a result of these sessions, I am clearer as to how I might be able to change

Barrett-Lennard Relationship Inventory

Positive regard
The counsellor cares for me
*I feel the counsellor disapproves of me

Empathy
The counsellor wants to understand how I see things
When I am hurt or upset, the counsellor can recognize my feelings exactly without becoming upset himself/herself

Unconditionality of regard
How much the counsellor likes or dislikes me is not altered by anything that I tell him/her about myself
I can (or could) be openly critical or appreciative of my counsellor without him/her really feeling any different towards me

Congruence
I feel that my counsellor is real and genuine with me
*I believe that my counsellor has feelings that he/she does not tell me about that are causing difficulty in our relationship

Penn Helping Alliance Questionnaire
I feel I am working together with my therapist in a joint effort
I believe we have similar ideas about the nature of my problems

Session Rating Scale
I felt heard, understood and respected
The therapist's approach is a good fit for me

Note: * Negatively phrased items; agreement with this statement indicates a *low* level of the factor.

Within the counselling and psychotherapy literature, a number of different ideas have been proposed concerning the effect of payment and fees on the therapeutic relationship (Herron and Sitkowski 1986; Cerney 1990). First, Freud and other psychoanalysts have argued for the 'sacrificial' nature of the fee. The assumption here is that, as a means of maximizing the motivation of the patient for therapy, and signalling the importance of their commitment to therapy, a fee should be set that is the maximum affordable by the patient. This implies that sliding fees should be operated: a fee that represented a major personal commitment for one client might be insignificant for another, more affluent client. From a psychoanalytic perspective, it has also been argued that the fee is a therapeutic tool which symbolizes the strict boundaries within which therapy is conducted: no matter what happens, the fee must be paid. The existence of the fee also makes a bridge between therapy and the 'real' world, and provides motivation for completing therapy rather than becoming dependent on the therapist. From a psychodynamic perspective, therefore, the fact of a client directly paying a fee makes a positive contribution to the therapeutic process.

However, it is also possible to argue that direct payment can have a counterproductive impact on the therapeutic relationship. A client who is paying for therapy may doubt the authenticity of their counsellor's acceptance: 'he/she is only pretending to value me because they are being paid' (Wills 1982). If a counsellor's income is contingent on a client remaining in therapy, he or she might subtly find ways to prolong treatment (Kottler 1988).

Being involved in the collection of fees is a role that many therapists find troubling. Some therapists experience 'fee guilt' (Herron and Sitkowski 1986) arising from the conflict between being wanted to be perceived as a 'helper' and being involved in a business that involves making a living and a profit. Counsellors and psychotherapists in private practice often report conflict around negotiating and charging fees, sending out reminders etc.

If psychoanalytic theory around the 'sacrificial' role of direct fee payment were correct, there should be evidence that therapy is more effective when fees are paid by clients, as compared to situations where there is a third-party paying (e.g., student counselling in a university, workplace counselling) or where the therapist is working for free. There is no evidence that any such a difference in effectiveness exists (Herron and Sitkowski 1986), in terms of studies that have made comparisons between fee payment and free services. Moreover, there is a huge amount of evidence that counselling and psychotherapy provided within workplace counselling schemes (McLeod 2008) or state-run health services in Britain and other European countries (which are free at the point of delivery) are just as effective as therapy that is delivered in classical private practice settings.

Does this mean that we should dismiss psychoanalytic ideas about the impact of fees on the therapeutic relationship? Not at all. The 'sacrifice' theory of payment predicted that the quality of the client's investment in the therapeutic relationship would depend on the level of fee they paid. Although there may be some truth in this idea in some cases, it fails to take account of the profound meaning that therapy has for many people, in terms of creating a worthwhile life, or in some instances even as a means of survival. The intrinsic meaningfulness and value of therapy is surely diminished by assuming that it can only be beneficial if it is being directly paid for. Instead, the question of money is important for the client–counsellor relationship because it represents a potentially vital area of 'things not said' (Cerney 1990). In counselling settings in which the client directly pays a fee to the counsellor, he or she may wonder 'am I worth it?', 'is my well-being or future worth it?' In settings where the counsellor's fee or salary is being paid by a third party, the client may reflect on 'does he or she really care about me, or is it just a job?', or 'if the university/hospital/company is paying his or her salary, won't they want to know about just how disturbed I am?' The counsellor, in either situation, may wonder 'am I worth what I'm being paid?' or even 'do I only tolerate this person because it's my job?'

In addition, the meaning of money may be linked to the cultural or social class background of the client and counsellor. Some people are brought up in environments where self-esteem and value are bound up with 'paying your own way' or using economic power always to have 'the best'. Others have grown up in collectivist cultures in which helping others is valued in its own terms, and 'profiting' from the distress of another person would be questionable. In addition, there are wide variations around the extent to which different social groups find it acceptable to talk openly about money. Bringing underlying issues about money into the therapy conversation can therefore represent an effective method for exploring cultural identities and assumptions.

There is some evidence of gender differences in therapist attitudes and behaviour around fee payment. Lasky (1999) found that women therapists tended to charge less than male colleagues of similar levels of experience, and Parvin and Anderson (1999) reported that women therapists were more flexible in negotiating fees than their male colleagues. Lasky (1999) also found that, among the therapists she interviewed, male practitioners were able to gloss over potential internal conflicts over fees, whereas female practitioners tended to be 'acutely aware' of such dilemmas, and saw themselves as trapped in a three-way conflict:

> (1) needing to support themselves and their families, (2) feeling torn between working additional hours to earn more money and wanting to spend the time with friends and family, and (3) focusing more on the client's financial needs than their own.
>
> (Lasky 1999: 9)

These studies are based on small samples of therapists in the USA and it would be interesting to learn the extent to which they generalize to other settings. Nevertheless, they illustrate the possibility that males and females approach this aspect of the therapeutic relationship in different ways.

The question of money represents a challenge to the therapeutic relationship because unspoken thoughts and feelings about money can impede full client–counsellor collaboration. For example, a workplace counselling client who assumes that their counsellor is, ultimately 'in the pocket' of management because that is who pays their wages may (consciously or unconsciously) screen out oversensitive information, and not permit the counsellor to learn about the depth of their despair or destructive behaviour. It is a particularly acute challenge for some counsellors, who experience 'fee guilt'. But it is also a difficulty for all counsellors, to the extent that the social and cultural meaning of money is an issue that has been largely neglected within therapy theory, research and training.

Implications of relationship theories for counsellor training and development

There is a substantial consensus within the counselling and psychotherapy literature that the quality of the relationship between client and counsellor is a central element in effective therapy, no matter what theoretical model is being applied. It is therefore essential that counsellor training takes seriously the issue of enabling trainees or students to acquire an understanding of how relationships function in general terms, and to develop an appreciation of their own style of relating. Most counselling training programmes promote student learning in these areas through a requirement to undertake personal therapy, participate in experiential groupwork and contribute to meetings of the whole course community. Mearns (1997) has argued that, in the past, counselling training courses have not done enough to facilitate trainee integration and reflection of learning across these different domains.

There is also a lack of reading and training materials that focus specifically on relationship issues. Josselson (1996) is one of the few texts explicitly to place therapeutic learning within a relationship context. On the whole, writers on counsellor training have tended to frame the experiential elements of training programmes in terms of *personal* development or *self*-awareness, rather than discussing these themes from a *relational* or *self-in-relation* perspective.

Box 19.6: *Hidden dimensions of relationship: Shlien on empathy*

For many counsellors, the attempt consistently to respond empathically to a client lies at the heart of the kind of relationship they seek to offer. Within the counselling and psychotherapy literature, empathy has generally been understood in terms of sensitivity to the language used by the client. Counsellor training has tended to emphasize the development of skill in responding appropriately to verbal cues. The recent writing of John Shlien (1997) opens up other dimensions of empathic relating. Shlien was a student, then colleague, of Carl Rogers who describes himself as 'privileged to be a participant observer, a sort of bystander and witness, to the development of the theory of empathy as it took place at the University of Chicago after World War II' (Shlien 1997: 67). Over a period of many years, Shlien was involved in the research on empathy and the 'core conditions' carried out by Rogers and his group. Drawing on this experience, he has arrived at the conclusion that responding fully to another person requires not merely a verbal response, but a 'whole body' reaction:

> empathy operates on such data as smell, sight, and sound: the smell of fear; the sight of tears, of blushing, and of yawning; and the sound of cadences, tones, sighs and howls. It operates at what we might think of as primitive levels, cellular, glandular, olfactory, chemical, electromagnetic, autonomic, postural, gestural, and musical-rhythmical, more than lexical.
>
> (Shlien 1997: 77)

Shlien argues that recent models of empathy have promoted the 'supremacy of brain over body', and that a proper understanding of this phenomenon will require the restoration of an appreciation of the 'whole person'. For Shlien, the experience of attunement to the kind of 'primitive' signals listed above is best described as *sympathy* rather than empathy. He suggests that sympathy involves a type of moral commitment to the other person: 'empathy alone, without sympathy, and even more, without understanding, may be harmful' (Shlien 1997: 67).

Shlien's ideas will be provocative and challenging for many counsellors. Even if only partially true, they carry the implication that the current ways in which counsellors and psychotherapists understand the therapeutic relationship may be inadequate, and possibly even unhelpful.

Conclusions: the complexity of the therapeutic relationship

The theory and research discussed in this chapter reflects the importance of the client–counsellor relationship in all approaches to therapy. It is clear that counsellors trained in the use of different theoretical models employ quite different ways of understanding the therapeutic relationship. It also seems clear, however, that there are fundamental 'truths' about the client–counsellor relationship, relevant for all approaches to counselling, captured in the ideas of Rogers (1957) and Bordin (1979), and in Freud's concepts of transference and counter-transference. It also seems likely that some clients respond better to some types of relationship than others, depending on their own personal history and needs. The therapeutic relationship *makes a difference* in counselling – the quality of the relationship has been shown to contribute significantly to the eventual outcome of counselling, and to the ability to help distressed people to stay in counselling. It is essential, therefore, for any counsellor to be aware of where his or her strengths lie, in terms of making and maintaining helpful ways of relating to clients, and also to keep striving to become more responsive to the endless variety of relationship patterns that may be presented by clients. Therapeutic relationships are complex, and operate at a number of different levels at the same time. It is difficult to 'decentre' sufficiently from one's own viewpoint to develop an accurate understanding of how one behaves in relationships. For any counsellor, building an understanding of how he or she engages in relationship with clients is greatly facilitated by the use of opportunities, such as training groups, or supervision, which provide feedback and challenge on his or her way of being with others.

Topics for reflection and discussion

1 Think about a person who has helped you to overcome or resolve an emotional issue in your life. How would you describe your relationship with this person? Think about someone you know but from whom you would be very reluctant to seek emotional support. How would you describe this relationship? How well can these personal experiences be explained in terms of the models and images of therapy relationships introduced in this chapter?

2 Research mentioned in this chapter has shown that a good relationship between therapist and client, in the early stages of counselling, is highly predictive of a good outcome at the end of therapy. Does this finding necessarily mean that the relationship is the *cause* of the eventual outcome? How else might you explain the fact that clients (and therapists) who give positive ratings of the strength of the 'therapeutic alliance' at the third or fourth session of therapy also report, several weeks later, that therapy has been successful?

3 Many counsellors and psychotherapists working in private practice operate a 'sliding fee' system, where what the client pays is adjusted according to their income and circumstances. In some situations, clients may suggest that they pay their therapist in goods and services rather than money. For example, a client who is a farmer may be able to offer produce of a higher value than any possible cash payment that he or she

could afford. What are the potential implications for the therapeutic relationship of establishing a barter contract? What ethical issues might need to be addressed? (A useful source of further reading on this topic is Hill 1999).

4 Safran and Muran (2001: 165) have suggested that: 'strains in the therapeutic alliance tap into a fundamental dilemma of human existence – the tension between the need for agency and the need for relatedness – and the process of working through these strains can provide patients with a valuable opportunity to constructively negotiate these two needs'. How useful do you find this way of understanding relationships? Reflect on a relationship you have experienced that has been difficult. (This could be a counselling relationship, or one in another area of your life.) What was the tension within that relationship between the need for agency (being in control, following your own purposes and intentions) and the need for relatedness (being in contact) for both you and the other person? Was this tension resolved (or could it have been resolved) through a process similar to Safran's model of resolution?

Suggested further reading

A short paper that thoughtfully explores many of the issues discussed in the present chapter, is Hill and Knox (2009). The question of how to decide how to respond to potential boundary issues, is succinctly and sensibly reviewed by Pope and Keith-Speigel (2008). Essential reading for anyone interested in counselling, is *Between Therapist and Client: The New Relationship*, by Michael Kahn (1997). Kahn captures the essence of psychodynamic and person-centred approaches to the relationship in a sensitive and highly readable manner, and demonstrates how Freudian and Rogerian ways of understanding the relationship have converged in the work of writers such as Merton Gill and Heinz Kohut.

Working at Relational Depth in Counselling and Psychotherapy, by Dave Mearns and Mick Cooper (2005), offers a unique insight into the central role of the relationship in therapeutic healing, and includes some compelling case examples. Further discussion of theory, research and practice around the concept of relational depth, can be found in a collection of papers edited by Knox *et al.* (2012).

The Space between Us: Exploring the Dimensions of Human Relationships by Ruthellen Josselson (1996) is not specifically a book about counselling and psychotherapy, but includes examples drawn from therapy, and will be of interest to both counsellors and users of counselling. Josselson suggests that many people lack a 'map' or conceptual framework for understanding relationship issues. Her book provides such a framework, based loosely on the ideas of the psychoanalytic theorist Erik Erikson but written in a way that makes sense to those who are not necessarily adherents of psychodynamic models.

Psychotherapy Relationships that Work, edited by Norcross (2011), provides authoritative reviews of research into key aspects of the therapy relationship, written by leading figures in the field.

The process of counselling

Introduction

In previous chapters, different approaches to making sense of counselling were introduced, and some of the issues involved in combining or integrating these approaches were discussed. One of the themes that emerged from this examination of competing theories and models of counselling was that, despite their undoubtedly contrasting emphases, there is in fact a fair amount of common ground. What actually happens in counselling and psychotherapy may depend less on the theoretical orientation of the

TABLE 20.1 Some process variables that have been studied in research

Goal consensus
Client role preparation
Client suitability
Personality, age, ethnic and gender match between client and therapist
Therapist willingness to talk about race and culture
Therapist skills
Extent of therapist adherence to a training manual
Focus during therapy on life problems and core personal relationships
Accuracy of transference interpretations
Frequency of transference interpretations
Client adherence to homework instructions
Therapeutic alliance
Ruptures in the therapeutic alliance
Impasse between client and therapist
Use of metaphor
Client expressiveness and openness
Therapist self-disclosure
Client deference to the therapist
Treatment duration
Fee structure

Main source: Orlinsky *et al.* (1994).

specific counsellor, than on a set of more general features of the counselling situation as a particular type of helping relationship. This sense that there may exist a common core to all forms of counselling has perhaps achieved its fullest expression in the growing research and theoretical literature on the *process* of counselling.

The concept of 'process' is defined and understood in several different ways in the literature, which can lead to confusion. Four main meanings of 'process' can be identified. First, there is a very broad sense in which any activity involving change can be described as being a 'process'. This meaning of the term merely refers to the idea that what happens in therapy is not static, and that there is some sort of sequence of events that takes place. A second meaning of 'process' has been employed mainly in the research literature, to refer to a very wide set of factors that may promote or inhibit therapeutic effects in clients. The use of the term contrasts 'process' with 'outcome': therapeutic 'processes' are the ingredients that contribute to outcomes. A list of some of the process factors investigated in research studies is given in Table 20.1. It can be seen that researchers have not lacked imagination in coming up with the widest possible list of what might be considered as 'process'.

A third meaning of 'process' is found mainly within humanistic perspectives on therapy. This definition characterizes process as an essential human quality of being and becoming. Rogers (1961: 27) captures this sense of process in writing that:

> Life, at its best, is a flowing, changing process in which nothing is fixed. In my
> clients and in myself I find that when life is richest and most rewarding it is a
> flowing process. To experience this is both fascinating and a little frightening.
> I find I am at my best when I can let the flow of my experience carry me, in a

> direction which appears to be forward, towards goals of which I am dimly aware . . . Life is . . . always in process of becoming.

This way of understanding process, almost as a value dimension, is also expressed by contemporary narrative social constructionist therapists. For example, Anderson and Goolishian (1992: 29) describe their aim in therapy as being 'to facilitate an emerging dialogic process in which "newness" can occur'. This sense of process, as moments of flowing newness where 'nothing is fixed', represents an important way in which the concept is used by many therapists.

A fourth sense of 'process' that is sometimes used by counsellors and psychotherapists describes the way that clients in therapy attempt to comprehend or assimilate difficult experiences in their lives. This use of the term can be likened to a metaphoric analogy. The work that clients and therapists do in making meaning out of raw feelings of loss, trauma or stress can be seen as similar to the manufacturing process, in which raw materials are transformed into finished, usable products. For instance, the *emotional processing* model employed by Greenberg *et al.* (1993) involves 'doing things' to and with emotions: naming them, expressing them, reflecting on their meaning.

There would appear to be little value in attempting to nominate any one of these definitions of 'process' as more valid than the others. Not only are all of these meanings of process used by practitioners and theorists, but they all refer, in different ways, to an underlying sense that counselling is concerned with change, and that at some level this change is created by the actions and intentions of both clients and counsellors working collaboratively. Finally, implicit in these various ideas of process is the notion that to be a counsellor it is necessary not only to be able to make sense of what is happening in an abstract, conceptual manner (e.g., knowing about 'the unconscious', or 'second order change') but to have a handle on the practicalities (e.g., making an interpretation, offering an empathic response, negotiating a therapeutic contract).

It is clear that counselling process represents a huge topic. There is also a range of different perspectives from which therapy process can be observed. For example, any of the processes listed in Table 20.1 could be explored from the point of view of the client or the therapist, or through the eyes of an external observer. Moreover, what takes place can occur simultaneously at different levels of awareness and visibility: there is always a hidden, covert process unfolding inside the consciousness of each participant. Therapeutic processes also vary in terms of their duration. Elliott (1991) suggests that it can be helpful to break down the ongoing flow of the process occurring in counselling into different types of units demarcated by their time boundaries:

- The speaking turn (interaction unit), encompassing the response of one speaker surrounded by the utterances of the other speaker. This can be regarded as a *micro-process* that lasts for perhaps no more than one or two minutes.
- The episode, comprising a series of speaking turns organized around a common task or topic. This process unit is sometimes described as a therapeutic *event*, and can last for several minutes.
- The session (occasion unit).
- The treatment (relationship unit): the entire course of a treatment relationship.

Each of the units identified by Elliott (1991) can be regarded as representing a different way of 'seeing' what takes place in counselling. Analysing microprocesses is like looking at counselling through a microscope; examining the process of a whole treatment is like constructing a map by using a telescope to view the furthest horizons.

This chapter introduces some of the theoretical and research material on counselling process that has been particularly influential in recent years. There is potentially a huge area to be covered here, and readers interested in learning more are recommended to consult Greenberg and Pinsof (1986), Hill and Lambert (2004) and Sachse and Elliott (2002) to gain access to the research literature on this topic. The issues involved in systematically studying the counselling process, including the demanding question of how it is possible to record, measure or otherwise observe process factors without intruding unhelpfully into the actual counselling relationship, are discussed in Chapter 25.

The process of counselling: beginnings and endings

It makes most sense to begin by looking at models for understanding the process of treatment in its entirety, since other, smaller-scale processes at the session, event or microprocess level are always embedded in the wider context supplied by the process of counselling as a whole. Many writers on counselling have tended to divide up the process of treatment into three broad phases. For example, Mearns and Thorne (2007) talk about 'beginnings', 'middles' and 'ends'. Egan's (1994) 'problem management' approach is structured around three main stages: helping clients to identify and clarify problem situations; developing programmes for constructive change; and implementing goals.

The opening and concluding phases of counselling can be split into further sets of discrete component elements or tasks. For example, the beginning phase may include negotiating expectations, assessment of suitability for counselling, the formation of a therapeutic alliance, agreeing a contract, helping the client to tell their story and so on. The final phase may entail negotiating the ending, referral, dealing with issues of loss, ensuring transfer of learning into real-life situations, anticipating and preventing relapse and planning follow-up meetings. Each of these aspects of the counselling process raises key issues for theory and practice.

Negotiating expectations and preparing clients for counselling

The question of client *expectations* has received a considerable amount of attention in the literature. An appreciation of the social and historical origins of counselling (see Chapter 2) suggests that there exist many other culturally available forms of help – for example, spiritual and religious guidance, medical intervention and even neighbourly advice – that are much more directive and overtly authoritarian than is counselling. In addition, people from non-Western cultures may hold beliefs about self that are very difficult to incorporate within counselling models. There is, therefore, often a need on the part of the counsellors and counselling agencies to take these factors into account.

Box 20.1: *Counsellors' images of the process of therapy*

It is clear that there are very different ways of making sense of the process of counselling, reflected in the range of counselling theories that are currently in use. However, what kinds of images or metaphors do counsellors and therapists themselves employ when thinking about their work? Najavits (1993) carried out a survey of 29 counsellors, working in a variety of settings and using a number of different theoretical models. In this study, counsellors were provided with a list of 16 metaphors derived from a review of the literature, and were asked to use a five-point scale to endorse the metaphors they thought were most or least applicable to their work, to circle their own favourite metaphor and finally to write in any additional metaphors of their own that they used. Analysis of results identified seven clusters of metaphors, or what Najavits (1993) labelled as 'meaning systems':

- *Task-oriented, professional*: counselling process likened to teaching, acting, science, selling.
- *Primal, fantasy*: play, a spiritual quest, handling wastes.
- *Taking responsibility*: hard labour, parenting.
- *Healing arts*: art, healing.
- *Intellectual*: writing a novel, philosophical dialogue.
- *Alteration of consciousness*: meditation, intuition.
- *Travel*: voyage, exploration.

No relationship was found between the metaphors endorsed by the counsellor and their theoretical orientation, work setting or satisfaction with their job. In general, counsellors gave higher ratings to the metaphors they generated themselves, rather than the ones in the list provided by Najavits (1993). Moreover, there were extreme disagreements between those who completed the questionnaire. For example, some counsellors rated 'art', 'healing', 'science' and 'spiritual quest' as *highly* appropriate metaphors for the therapy process, whereas others rated these metaphors as being completely irrelevant. The only metaphors that were generally seen as reasonably applicable, by the majority of counsellors, were 'teaching' and 'parenting'. The diversity of opinion uncovered by these results seems to imply that counsellors tend to hold relatively idiosyncratic views about the process of therapy, with little apparent linkage between their images and the theoretical model they describe themselves as using. Of course, this study is based on a small sample of counsellors in the USA – it would be interesting to know how counsellors in other countries, or drawn from a wider variety of backgrounds, 'imagined' their work. And it would be valuable, too, to know more about the images of counselling held by clients. How many clients see their counsellor as a parent or teacher? How many experience counselling in terms of images of war?

Research into expectations for counselling has shown significant differences in the extent to which people perceive different approaches as credible or preferable (Shapiro 1981; Rokke *et al.* 1990; Galassi *et al.* 1992; Pistrang and Barker 1992; Wanigaratne and Barker 1995; Bragesjo *et al.* 2004). There is also evidence that clients who receive a form of counselling that matches their expectations are more likely to do well, particularly in time-limited counselling (Morrison and Shapiro 1987; Hardy *et al.* 1995). It is also clear that people seek psychological help from a range of sources, and may enter counselling with expectations that have been shaped by a previous type of treatment. This is a major issue in cross-cultural counselling, where a client may have previously consulted an indigenous healer. Particular groups of clients can have very definite expectations about what they need. For example, Liddle (1997) found that many gay and lesbian clients put a great deal of time and effort into finding an 'affirmative' counsellor or therapist.

The realization that many potential clients may not understand the way that counselling operates has led some practitioners to develop and evaluate methods of providing appropriate pre-counselling information: for example, role induction videos or leaflets. For example, Reis and Brown (2006) showed clients a brief (12 minute) video presentation on what therapy is, and how one can benefit from it, and found that premature drop-out was reduced by a significant amount. Beutler and Clarkin (1990: 187–96) offer an excellent review of the use of client preparation techniques.

It can be argued that the importance of pre-counselling expectations and preferences is often underestimated by counsellors. The settings for counselling – the agency and the counselling room – are familiar to the counsellor. The counsellor is also thoroughly acquainted with the rules of the counselling encounter. Furthermore, most clients will regard counsellors as high-status 'experts'. For all these reasons, clients are likely to be dominated by the counselling situation, and find it hard to articulate their assumptions and wishes about what should happen. Often, the mismatch between client and counsellor expectations and definitions is only brought to light when a client fails to turn up for a session. In fact, as many as one in three counselling contracts end in this manner. In some of these cases, the client may well be satisfied with what he or she received. In other cases, however, the client does not return because he or she is not getting what he or she wants.

Assessment

The beginning of counselling is also marked by a process of *assessment*. Many counsellors and counselling agencies explicitly demarcate assessment or 'reception' sessions as separate from actual counselling. In some places, assessment is carried out by someone other than the eventual counsellor. Assessment can serve a wide variety of purposes (see Table 20.2), including evaluating whether the person will benefit from the counselling that is available, providing sufficient information for the client to make up his or her mind and agreeing times, scheduling and costs. Some counsellors employ standardized psychological tests as part of the assessment phase (Watkins and Campbell 1990; Anastasi 1992; Whiston 2000). These tests can be utilized to evaluate a wide range of psychological variables, such as anxiety, depression, social support and interpersonal functioning. Others use open-ended questionnaires that the person completes in advance of the actual assessment interview (Aveline 1995; Mace 1995a).

TABLE 20.2 Reasons for making a formal pre-counselling assessment

Establishing rapport
Making a clinical diagnosis
Assessing the strengths and weaknesses of the client
Giving information
Enabling the client to feel understood
Arriving at a case formulation or plan
Giving hope
Gathering information about cultural needs and expectations
Explaining the way that therapy works; obtaining informed consent
Opportunity for the client to ask questions
Giving a taste of the treatment
Motivating the client; preventing non-attendance
Arranging for any further assessments that might be necessary (e.g., medical)
Selecting clients for treatment
Selecting treatments or therapists for the client
Giving the client a basis for choice of whether to enter counselling
Making practical arrangements (time, place, access)
Providing data for research or audit

The nature of assessment depends a great deal on the theoretical model being used by the counsellor or counselling agency, and a wide spectrum of assessment practices can be found (Mace 1995b; Palmer and McMahon 1997). On the whole, psychodynamic counsellors and psychotherapists consider it essential to carry out an in-depth assessment of the client's capacity to arrive at a psychodynamic formulation of the key features of the case. Hinshelwood (1991), for example, proposes that such a formulation should explore three main areas of object relations: the current life situation, object-relationships in early life and the transference relationship with the assessor. Hinshelwood also suggests that other useful information that can be collected includes the assessor's counter-transference reaction to the client and the client's ability to cope with a 'trial interpretation' of some of the material that is uncovered. Coltart (1988) regards 'psychological mindedness' as a crucial criterion for entry into a long-term psychodynamic therapy.

Box 20.2: *Psychological mindedness: an indicator of readiness to engage in psychodynamic therapy*

It is widely believed among psychoanalytic and psychodynamic therapists and counsellors that it is difficult, or even impossible, to work effectively with clients who lack a capacity or willingness to make sense of their actions in psychological terms. The construct of *psychological mindedness* has been used as a means of measuring this capacity. Appelbaum (1973: 36) has defined psychological mindedness as 'a person's ability to see relationships among thoughts, feelings and actions, with the goal of learning the meaning of . . . experiences and behavior'. McCallum and Piper (1990: 412) have defined this quality in more explicitly psychodynamic terms: 'the ability to identify dynamic (intrapsychic) components and to relate them to a person's difficulties'. When they carry out assessment or intake interviews, psychodynamic counsellors are aiming to collect evidence of the level of psychological mindedness of a client, as an indicator of readiness to engage in dynamic 'work'. A number of assessment tools have also been developed to evaluate the client's level of psychological mindedness (Conte and Ratto 1997). The *insight test* (Tolor and Reznikoff 1960) presents the client with a series of hypothetical situations depicting the operation of various defence mechanisms. The client then chooses between a set of four possible explanations for the situation. An example of an item from this technique is:

A man who intensely dislikes a fellow worker goes out of his way to speak well of him.

1   The man doesn't really dislike his co-worker.

2   The man believes he will make a better impression on others by speaking well of him.

3   The man is overdoing his praise in order to cover up for his real feelings of dislike.

4   The man doesn't want to hurt anyone's feelings.

The situation is an example of the defence mechanism of 'reaction formation', so the third response represents the most insightful (or psychologically minded) response, whereas the first item represents the least insightful explanation.

McCallum and Piper (1997) have constructed a psychological mindedness assessment procedure that does not provide answers to the client, but instead requires them to give their own personal response. Clients are asked to watch two scenarios on video, and then asked to explain in their own words why they think the people they have observed were behaving in the way they were. McCallum and Piper (1997) then rate the person's answer in terms of nine levels of psychological mindedness. McCallum and Piper (1997) have carried out research that has shown that, in psychodynamic group therapy, clients who are more psychologically minded benefit more, and are less likely to drop out of the group prematurely.

Although psychological mindedness may be an important prerequisite for psychodynamic therapy, is it also a factor in the extent to which clients may benefit from other forms of therapy? No one really knows. Certainly, from a person-centred perspective, the client's capacity to *feel* (i.e., engage in experiential processing) might be considered to be more important than their capacity to identify defences. On the other hand, the basic ability to *reflect* on patterns of behaviour, implicit in the notion of psychological mindedness, may be a common factor in all therapies.

Behaviourally oriented counsellors, by contrast, regard assessment as necessary in order to identify realistic, achievable treatment goals (Galassi and Perot 1992). Finally, humanistic or person-centred counsellors tend to eschew formal assessment on the grounds that they do not wish to label the client or to present themselves in an 'expert' position. Some humanistically oriented counsellors may employ 'qualitative' methods of assessment, where the client will be invited to participate in learning/assessment exercises integrated into the flow of the counselling session itself. An example of this type of assessment would be the use of the Life Line as a means of eliciting the client's perceptions of significant points in his or her development, relationships with important others and values (Goldman 1992).

Halgin and Caron (1991) suggest a set of key questions that counsellors and psychotherapists should ask themselves when considering whether to accept or refer a prospective client:

- Does the person need therapy?
- Do I know the person?
- Am I competent to treat this client?
- What is my personal reaction to the client?
- Am I emotionally capable of treating the client?
- Does the client feel comfortable with me?
- Can the client afford treatment under my care?

There are times when the outcome of an assessment interview will be that the client is referred to another agency. This process can evoke powerful feelings in both clients and assessors (Wood and Wood 1990).

Cutting across these different approaches to assessment is the degree to which the counsellor will share his or her assessment with the client. Some counsellors and psychotherapists may provide the client with a written formulation (e.g., Ryle 1990), or may analyse test data together (Fischer 1978). In addition, external factors may determine the extent to which formal assessment is employed. In the USA, for instance, counsellors and psychotherapists are only able to claim payment from health insurance companies if they first of all diagnose their clients/patients, and then deliver a form of treatment shown through research to be suitable for that diagnostic category.

Box 20.3: *The role of diagnosis in counselling and psychotherapy*

Is it helpful for counsellors or psychotherapists to make a diagnosis of their clients' psychopathology? Within psychiatry and clinical psychology, it is usual to carry out a diagnostic interview at the point of assessment, and both patient statistics and research papers in these disciplines tend to be organized around diagnostic categories. There are two diagnostic systems that are currently in use. The International Classification of Diseases (ICD) diagnostic guide, published by the World Health Organization, is widely employed in Europe and many other countries. The *Diagnostic and Statistical Manual* (DSM), published by the American Psychiatric Association (1994), is exclusively used in North America, and has also been adopted elsewhere. There are many similarities between the two systems. An excellent counselling-oriented account of DSM-IV (the fourth and most recent edition of the manual) can be found in Whiston (2000).

There are strong arguments for and against the use of diagnosis in counselling and psychotherapy. Those who are *against* diagnosis argue that:

- there is a danger of labelling patients;
- there is little evidence that diagnostic information is of any use in planning or choosing the right therapy for any individual client;
- diagnostic procedures introduce an expert-dominated relationship that can undermine collaborative work between client and therapist;
- defining the problem as an 'illness' may make it harder for the client to commit themselves to a therapy, which always requires active participation and taking responsibility for personal change;
- the use of diagnosis introduces a medical/biological perspective that is not consistent with the aims and processes of counselling.

The factors *in favour* of using diagnosis include:

- it enables therapists working in medical settings to communicate effectively with colleagues;
- an increasing number of treatment manuals are structured in terms of diagnostic classifications, such as depression, anxiety and borderline personality disorder;
- in some environments (e.g., managed care services in the USA), a diagnosis is a necessary precondition for being accepted for treatment;
- it helps practitioners to be clear about the limits of their competence (for example, in identifying cases where clients may require specialist referral).

The debate around the use of diagnosis is therefore multifaceted, with strong arguments for both positions. In pragmatic terms, much counselling takes place in settings where clients attend for fewer than six sessions, and where formal diagnosis would constitute a waste of precious therapeutic time. In other settings, where counselling is delivered by volunteers or paraprofessionals, it would not be realistic to expect the counsellor to be a competent diagnostician. However, counsellors who lack information about diagnostic systems run the risk of cutting themselves off from the huge resources and accumulated knowledge of the therapies used in the medical domain.

A considerable amount of research evidence exists concerning the actual effects of assessment on client engagement in therapy, outcome or other variables. For example, Frayn (1992) examined the assessments carried out on 85 people who had applied for psychoanalysis or long-term psychoanalytic psychotherapy. About one-quarter of these clients were later to drop-out of therapy prematurely. Compared with the clients who had remained in therapy, those who had terminated prematurely were less motivated, possessed lower levels of psychological-mindedness and had a lower tolerance for frustration. In addition, at assessment their therapists had experienced more negative attitudes toward the clients who were later to leave early. The results of this study offer support for many of the assessment principles described earlier, including the importance of the criterion of the counsellor or therapist deciding whether he or she can accept the client sufficiently to work effectively with them.

The theme that emerges most clearly from research into the impact of assessment on subsequent therapy, is that a collaborative approach to assessment can have a significant impact on the quality of the client–therapist relationship, and the client's engagement in the therapy process (Finn and Tonsager 1997; Hilsenroth and Cromer 2007). The therapist activities during assessment that are positively related to the establishment of a strong therapeutic alliance include:

- conducting longer, depth-oriented assessment interviews;
- adopting a collaborative stance toward the client;
- using clear, concrete, experience-near language;
- allowing the client to initiate discussion of salient issues;
- actively exploring these issues;
- clarifying sources of distress
- facilitating client exploration of feelings;
- reviewing and exploring the meaning of assessment results (e.g., questionnaire scores);
- providing the client with new understanding and insight;
- offering psycho-educational explanations around symptoms and the treatment process;
- collaboratively developing therapy goals and a treatment plan.

Hilsenroth and Cromer (2007) point out that these activities are transtheoretical, and can be readily adopted within any approach to therapy.

In conclusion, it can be seen that there are many issues raised by the decision as to whether or not to assess, and the choice of mode of assessment. In many circumstances, practical factors may influence and limit the type of assessment that can be carried out. However, no matter how brief the assessment that is carried out, it is clear that careful assessment, appropriate to the model of therapy that is being provided, can do a great deal to prepare both client and therapist to work together in an effective manner.

Box 20.4: *How clients assess their counsellors*

In an interview study of the experiences of African American working class clients attending counselling in a community mental health centre in the USA, Ward (2005) found that all the clients who were interviewed described themselves as actively assessing their counsellor during initial meetings. Clients reported that their assessment covered three main areas: how effective the counsellor appeared to be, how safe they felt with the counsellor, and the degree of client–therapist match. Some of the statements made by research participants included:

> When I'm in counselling I mean to assess . . . to see who I'm talking to, that's what I'm looking for. I am looking to feel you and I know that I can feel things through pictures, through things and just being around the person's office and everything. So I'm looking to see who you are. That's what I'm looking for.

I'm looking to see who you are because I don't wanna share myself with someone that I can't see. So I'm looking to see you, to feel you.

. . . when I meet people (counsellors) I kind of ask myself do I feel comfortable with them?

First of all, you know, I have to look at some of your training. Cause you want some experience in this. Sometimes you don't even have a chance to ask these questions, you know, how many people of colour have you worked with?

Safe is the way you feel when you are talking to a friend.

It wouldn't make any difference if the counsellor was White or Black. Just as long as it was a female.

I really like my counsellor here because we have a lot of things in common . . . its like he's been where I am.

(Ward 2005: 476)

It seems likely that in this particular context, in which many clients may distrust the involvement of the courts in their therapy or may have had damaging experiences with previous therapists, is one in which the process of client appraisal of their counsellors is particularly salient. Nevertheless, the statements that were made by these clients do seem to capture something of the essence of the first meeting that any client has with his or her therapist.

Case formulation and contracting

Having carried out some kind of initial assessment of the problems for which the client is seeking help, and his or her goals for therapy, the next stage of the therapy process usually involves the construction of some kind of *case formulation*. A case formulation can be viewed as an overall framework that can be used to guide the activities of the client and counsellor. A typical case formulation might include the following elements:

1 Current issues/presenting problems/stated goals.

2 Underlying causes/vulnerability (why does the person have these problems?).

3 What are the mechanisms/actions/processes through which these difficulties are maintained? (why haven't they disappeared by now? What hasn't the person been able to deal with these problems already?) How do these mechanisms connect the underlying and the current problems?

4 Why now? What has precipitated the need for help now?

5 How can the problem be tackled in therapy? (treatment plan.)

6 What are the obstacles to therapy? What are the client's strengths?

Different therapy approaches give differing degrees of importance to the role of case formulation. Within most versions of CBT, and in TA, case formulation is taken extremely seriously, and is a defining characteristic of each of these approaches. By contrast, many psychodynamic and person-centred practitioners give more emphasis to the ongoing process of therapy, and allow their understanding of the case to emerge over time. However, even psychodynamic and person-centred counsellors would tend to discuss aspects of a formulation in supervision, or in their own personal reflection on their work with a client.

Practitioners also differ in the extent to which they explicitly share their formulation with the client. Some therapists, for example in CAT (Ryle 2005; Ryle and Kerr 2002) will provide the client with a written statement and diagram, outlining he formulation in some detail. Other therapists might merely introduce aspects of the formulation into the therapy conversation at appropriate moments. Further information on the variety of strategies for carrying out and using case formulations can be found in Eells (2007) and Johnstone and Dallos (2006).

Tracey Eells and his colleagues have carried out a series of studies into therapist competence in case formulation (Eells and Lombart 2003; Eells *et al.* 2005; Kendjelic and Eells 2007). This research programme has shown that there are marked differences in formulation quality associated with levels of experience. Compared with more experienced colleagues, novice therapists produce formulations that are less detailed and coherent, and which do not clearly specify the causal factors or mechanisms that link underlying conflicts with current presenting problems. This research also showed that brief training in the principles of case formulation could produce major shifts in competence (Kendjelic and Eells 2007).

Formulating an understanding of a case and developing a sense of where the counselling might go, is associated with the use of *contracting*. As with case formulation, there are major differences between therapists trained in different orientations, in relation to their use of contracting. Some therapists generate written contracts that their clients are asked to sign, whereas other therapists merely rely on a verbal agreement to work together, perhaps for a specified period of time. There are ethical issues associated with the use of contracting, because it is widely accepted that informed consent represents a basic principle of ethical good practice. The issues involved in making a contract with a client, and strategies for contracting, are discussed in Sills (2006).

Establishing a working alliance

One of the main tasks for counsellors in the initial phase of counselling, following assessment, formulation and contracting, is the establishment of a productive *working alliance* or *therapeutic alliance* with the client. The introduction of this concept is usually attributed to Bordin (1979), who suggested that there are three key aspects of the alliance that the counsellor needs to attend to in the early stages of contact with a client. First, there is agreement over the *goals* of therapy. Second, client and therapist need to reach a mutual understanding over *tasks*. What will each of the participants actually *do* during therapy, if it is to be successful? Third, there must be a good human relationship, or *bond*, between client and therapist. In Chapter 7, the origins of this model in Rogers' 'core conditions' theory was noted. There is considerable evidence that the therapeutic alliance comprises an essential element in all successful therapies (Orlinsky *et al.* 1994), even in behaviour therapy. A study by Saltzman *et al.* (1976) found that it is necessary to consolidate the alliance by the third session – if it is not established by then it is unlikely that it ever will be.

A significant body of recent research has explored the processes associated with *ruptures* in the therapeutic alliance (Safran *et al.* 1990). In another, similar, piece of research Hill *et al.* (1996) carried out a survey of counsellors concerning their experience of *impasse* in their work with clients. The findings of these studies are consistent with the view of Mearns (1994) that lack of therapeutic progress, or what he terms 'stuckness', is often associated with *over-* or *underinvolvement* on the part of the counsellor. The issues involved in creating an effective working relationship between counsellor and client, and different perspectives on this process, are discussed in more detail in Chapter 19.

The successful negotiation of expectations, the completion of assessment and the formation of a productive working alliance lead into the main 'working' phase of counselling. It is perhaps important to keep in mind that a significant number of clients do not turn up for their first appointment with a counsellor or psychotherapist, and there are many who only attend for one or two sessions before stopping. It seems reasonable to assume, therefore, that clients who commit themselves to more than four or five sessions are motivated to work, believe in the value of therapy as a means of helping them to overcome their problems and find their current therapist credible as a source of help. Why, under these circumstances, does therapy sometimes go wrong? Clearly, therapists can make mistakes in applying their chosen model. Research by Binder and Strupp (1997) has identified a number of common therapist sources of error. It is also useful to consider the client's view of what they have found *hindering* in therapy. In one recent study, Paulson *et al.* (2001) interviewed clients about things they believed had hindered or impeded their therapeutic progress. These clients generated a long list of hindering factors (see Table 20.3). Some of these items can be interpreted as errors in therapist technique, but others surely represented basic human weaknesses and foibles.

The existence of impasses, errors and hindrances is a reminder that, in many cases, progress in counselling does not follow a neat pathway; there can well be times when counsellor and client are forced to revisit the 'basics' of their relationship. Nevertheless, when counselling is going at least reasonably well, there will be a stage when the client and counsellor are working together to achieve productive learning, insight or behavioural change. There exist several different ways of making sense of the basic change process that occurs at this juncture. To do sufficient justice to this subject, these models of change are reviewed in a separate section below. We turn instead to the question of ending, and the processes occurring when therapy is completed.

TABLE 20.3 What clients find hindering in counselling

Concerns around vulnerability	*Lack of connection*
Feeling like I was going to be a guinea pig	The counsellor was going to stop seeing me because I was going to go to sessions elsewhere at the same time
Being concerned about confidentiality being broken	
Being expected to do homework exercises outside of session	One bad counselling session disrupting sessions after that
Being video-taped	Counselling ending before I was ready
Not being motivated to attend the appointments	Difficulty getting in contact with the counsellor
Not starting counselling soon enough	Not feeling connected from session to session
The counsellor and I tending to become sidetracked	Not having enough in-depth discussion
Doing exercises I didn't like	Not having enough exercises in session
The counsellor asking a strange question	

Uncertain expectations	*Barriers to feeling understood*
	The counsellor being paid to listen
Not knowing what I want from the counsellor	Feeling like part of an assembly line
Not knowing what I'm supposed to get from a counsellor	Being phoned by one counsellor, seen initially by another counsellor and finally assigned to somebody else
Not knowing what to expect from counselling	
Not knowing where I was going with counselling	Talking to somebody who doesn't have a shared cultural experience
Not feeling ready to open up fully	
I didn't ask the proper question	The counsellor not asking about the side effects of medication
Not liking where I was going in counselling	
Not being 100 per cent comfortable with the notion of counselling	The counsellor not being close to my age
	My counsellor not being worldly enough
Expecting more specific information that I didn't get	Being concerned about the counsellor's religious agenda
Not knowing what I was supposed to do in counselling	
Expecting the counsellor to give me answers to my questions	*Structure of counselling*
Sometimes wanting the counsellor to make the decision for me	Not having regular sessions
	An hour session is not long enough
Not being able to make the counsellor understand what I was feeling	Having long spaces between sessions
	Not having enough counselling sessions
	Not being able to have sessions more often when I wanted
Negative counsellor behaviours	Not being comfortable with the gender of my counsellor
Feeling that the counsellor wanted to get me out of the office as soon as possible	Being in the room with the two-way mirror
	Feeling like the counsellor was trying out a technique
The counsellor having too many other things on their mind	
Feeling like the counsellor didn't have the time for me	*Insufficient counsellor directiveness*
Thinking the counsellor didn't really care	Having more in me I wanted to say and my counsellor not asking
The counsellor leaving with no warning	
The counsellor not really listening	Not being pushed enough by my counsellor
The counsellor using words that felt judgemental	Saying something and having the counsellor summarize it differently than I want
The counsellor deciding to end counselling	
The counsellor not remembering details from the last session	Talking about the same thing but not moving forward with it
	The counsellor not really doing what I expected
	My counsellor not telling me what to do

TABLE 20.3 *Continued*

Negative counsellor behaviours	Lack of responsiveness from the therapist
Asking for books and resources and not getting them	The counsellor getting hung up on one pattern, and following it regardless – not tailoring counselling to my needs
The counsellor trying to be my friend, but it not seeming real	
The counsellor being unaccommodating to my work hours	The counsellor not being able to determine what the problem areas were
My counsellor not following up on suggestions made previously	The counsellor dealing with the specific concern I came in for, but not other concerns that come up
The counsellor being too concerned about fees	The counsellor not putting very much input into the conversation
The counsellor assuming I was no longer interested in counselling	
The counsellor seeming kind of closed	Being over an issue and the counsellor not realizing it
The counsellor not being very objective	The counsellor seeming more like a teacher
Feeling like just another statistic to the counsellor	The counsellor not taking a stand on a lot of things and sitting on the fence
The counsellor trying to tell me what to do	
My counsellor being too directive	
Talking for a couple of minutes and then being cut off by the counsellor	
The counsellor just keeps pushing and pushing	

Source: Paulson *et al.* (2001).

Ending counselling

The challenge for the counsellor at the *ending* phase is to use this stage of counselling to the maximum benefit of the client. The goals of this stage include the consolidation and maintenance of what has been achieved, the generalization of learning into new situations and using the experience of loss and/or disappointment triggered by the ending as a focus for new insight into how the client has dealt with such feelings in other situations. The most fully developed strategies for working with endings are to be found in the model of *relapse prevention* that has been devised within the cognitive–behavioural tradition (see Chapter 6), and in the rigorous exploration of themes of attachment and loss associated with brief dynamic therapy (see Chapter 5). The difficult question of client readiness to end counselling is discussed by Ward (1984).

Research by DeBerry and Baskin (1989) found that there were significant differences between the termination criteria used by public-sector and private-practice therapists. Therapists working in public clinics reported that the most common reasons for finishing therapy were the excessive caseload of the therapist or administrative factors. The therapists in private practice, by contrast, overwhelmingly reported that endings resulted from either the client or therapist (or both) believing that treatment goals had been achieved. It may be that the deep concerns that many counsellors and psychotherapists express over endings are overstated. There have been few studies of how clients feel about ending. In one survey Fortune *et al.* (1992) found that the majority of former clients felt pride and a sense of accomplishment. In a more recent study, where clients were interviewed, Knox *et al.* (2011) found that satisfaction with the ending of therapy tended to reflect the quality of the therapeutic relationship. Clients who had good relationships with their therapists were able to negotiate a satisfactory ending, whereas those with poor relationships reported that the ending had been stressful. A similar pattern emerged in an in-depth case study by Råbu and Haavind (2012).

In much counselling practice, however, endings are unplanned or relatively haphazard. Sometimes the client will just cease to turn up, because they are disillusioned with therapy, because they have got what they need or for practical reasons associated with housing, child care, transport or work. Sometimes the counsellor may initiate the ending. Counsellors get other jobs, move elsewhere on training rotation, are made redundant, get pregnant, get ill, die. Each of these reasons for ending will have its own unique impact on the counselling relationship and on the client (Penn 1990). There are also ethical issues arising from the process of ending, arising from the need to avoid the risk of leaving the client with a sense of abandonment (Davis and Younggren 2009).

Box 20.5: *How well do counsellors understand clients' reasons for ending?*

For many counsellors and their supervisors, one way of assessing how successful therapy has been for a client is to review the reason why the decision has been made to leave counselling. Some counselling agencies keep records on clients' reasons for finishing counselling, as a means of auditing the quality of the service that is delivered. Ideally, counselling terminates when the client has sufficiently resolved his or her presenting problems, or at least has made enough progress to feel better able to cope with life.

But how aware are counsellors of the true reasons why clients may decide to finish? Research by Hunsley *et al.* (1999) suggests that, in many cases, counsellors have a somewhat skewed and overoptimistic view of the state of mind of their clients at the point of termination. The study carried out by Hunsley *et al.* (1999) was based in a therapy clinic attached to a university in Canada. Clients who used this clinic were on average in their thirties and experiencing difficulties around anxiety, depression, relationships and self-esteem, and received an average of 12 sessions of counselling, using a variety of therapeutic approaches.

Reasons for termination, from the point of view of the counsellor, were identified on the basis of information held in the case files of 194 clients. Eighty-seven of these clients were interviewed by telephone and asked to describe their own perception of why they left counselling. A comparison was made between counsellors' and clients' perspectives on reasons for terminating therapy. Counsellors believed that around one-third of clients completed because they had achieved their goals, with most of the remainder stopping because of practical constraints such as moving house, lack of time and money or referral to another service. Counsellors recorded fewer than 5 per cent of cases in which clients finished because of dissatisfaction with therapy. The picture emerging from clients was quite different from the one presented by their therapists. Compared with their counsellors, a slightly higher proportion of clients (44 per cent) stated that they terminated counselling because they had achieved their goals. But a *much* higher proportion described themselves as dissatisfied. Around one in three told the interviewer that 'therapy was going nowhere', 'therapy did not fit my ideas about treatment' and they were 'not confident in my therapist's ability'. Nine per cent of these clients stated that 'therapy was making things worse'.

The findings of the Hunsley *et al.* (1999) study are consistent with results from other research into this issue. In one survey, by Dale *et al.* (1998), some clients even reported that they were afraid to leave counselling because they believed that their therapist would be angry with them if they announced that they wanted to finish. In another study, Murdock *et al.* (2010) concluded that therapists' explanations for premature ending were generally 'self-serving'. Research by Rennie (1994a, b) has drawn attention to the extent to which clients show deference to their counsellors, and refrain from telling them things they believe that the counsellor might not want to hear. These studies have implications for practice. As counselling comes to an end, it is important for counsellors to allow clients to be open about their disappointments, as well as to celebrate and reinforce their achievements. The possibility of being grateful to someone who has genuinely tried to help, yet being able to acknowledge openly to that person that their help has not made a difference, can be a significant learning experience in itself.

One special type of ending is *referral* to another counsellor or agency. Referral can occur after initial assessment, or may take place after several sessions of counselling. For example, in some counselling settings, clients may be allowed only a limited number of sessions (sometimes no more than six), and may need to be passed on to another therapist once the limit has been reached. The experience of referral is often difficult for both counsellor and client (Wood and Wood 1990). There are several ways in which counsellors can manage the ending of therapy. It can be valuable, from the start of therapy, to agree to conduct a review every few sessions (typically every six sessions). This means that the possibility of ending, or working toward an ending, is part of the ongoing conversation between counsellor and client, rather than comprising a topic that may be dreaded or avoided (Etherington and Bridges 2011). Another strategy, in long-term therapy, can be to use 'natural' breaks such as holidays as 'trial endings'. At the first session following a vacation break, the counsellor can explore with the client whether they had felt, during that time, able to cope in the absence of the therapist (Råbu and Haavind 2012; Råbu *et al.* (2012).

The middle part of counselling: the process of change

The aim of this section is to provide a framework for thinking about what happens within the crucial 'middle' stage of counselling, between the point where a therapeutic relationship and contract have been established, and before the ending of the work. Change is central to counselling, and every approach to counselling is built around a set of ideas regarding how and why change occurs, and what counsellors can do to promote change. It is generally assumed that therapeutic change mainly occurs during the middle stage of therapy, and is then reinforced and maintained during the final, ending stage. However, research has shown that in successful therapy, significant change can occur within the first few sessions (Stiles *et al.* 2003), and that the occurrence of therapeutic gains within early sessions helps to retain the client in therapy, and provide him or her with the confidence to continue. Nevertheless, despite the evidence for early therapeutic change, it remains the case that, for the most part, the benefits that clients accrue from counselling largely occur once the client and counsellor have settled into a productive way of working together.

Each of the approaches to counselling that were introduced in the opening chapters of this book are associated with their own distinctive ideas about the change process. For example, the seven-stage model of change proposed by Rogers, Gendlin and their colleagues (Chapter 7) describes a model of the change process that is consistent with the concepts and assumptions of the person-centred approach. Rather than attempt to review theories of change associated with each specific therapy approach, this section provides an integrative perspective on the change process, relevant to all theoretical orientations. First, the 'assimilation model' is described. The assimilation model is an integrative model of change that has been of value to many counselling practitioners. Then, the section moves on to consider a number of counselling methods for facilitating client change within the middle stage of therapy.

Assimilation of problematic experiences

The first model of change being considered here is the *assimilation model*, devised by Stiles and his associates (Stiles *et al.* 1990, 1992; Barkham *et al.* 1996; Honos-Webb *et al.* 1998, 1999; Stiles 1991, 2001, 2002, 2005, 2006). The key idea behind this model is that the individual possesses a model of the world, or a set of cognitive schemas that guides that person's behaviour. New experiences need to be assimilated into that model if they are to be understood and to make sense. Experiences that do not fit into the schema or model can lead to a process of change, or accommodation, in the model itself. This theory is basically adopted from Piagetian developmental psychology, but is consistent with most models of therapy. It therefore represents a transtheoretical or integrative model.

The assimilation model specifies a series of stages, or a process, that takes place when assimilation occurs (Table 20.4). In therapy, the most significant assimilation processes occur in relation to *problematic experiences*. The client reports an experience that is painful, or even not quite within awareness, and the task of the counsellor or therapist is to help the client to 'take it in' to their model of the world, to make it familiar, to become comfortable with an idea or feeling that initially was problematic. At the beginning of the process the problem is warded off, and the client does not report any strong emotion. However, as the problem begins to come into focus, through the emergence of unwanted thoughts leading to vague awareness, the client is likely to have very strong feelings. As the process continues into clarification, insight and working through, the feelings triggered off by the problem become more manageable and less intense.

The assimilation model brings together aspects of several different theoretical models. The notion that problems can be unconscious is reflected in the 'warded-off' stage. The

TABLE 20.4 Stages in the assimilation of a problematic experience in counselling

0	*Warded off*. Client is unaware of the problem; the problematic voice is silent or dissociated. Affect may be minimal, reflecting successful avoidance
1	*Unwanted thoughts*. Client prefers not to think about the experience; topics are raised by therapist or external circumstances. Affect involves strong but unfocused negative feelings; their connection with the content may be unclear. Problematic voices emerge in response to therapist interventions or external circumstances and are suppressed or avoided
2	*Vague awareness*. Client is aware of a problematic experience but cannot formulate the problem clearly. Affect includes acute psychological pain or panic associated with the problematic experience. Problematic voice emerges into sustained awareness
3	*Problem statement/clarification*. Content includes a clear statement of the problem – something that could be or is being worked on. Opposing voices are differentiated and can talk about each other. Affect is negative but manageable, not panicky
4	*Understanding/insight*. The problematic experience is formulated and understood in some way. Voices reach an understanding with each other (a meaning bridge). Affect may be mixed, with some unpleasant recognitions but also some pleasant surprise of the 'aha' sort
5	*Application/working through*. The understanding is used to work on a problem. Voices work together to address problems of living. Affective tone is positive, business-like, optimistic
6	*Problem solution*. Client achieves a successful solution for a specific problem. Voices can be used flexibly. Affect is positive, satisfied, proud of accomplishment
7	*Mastery*. Client automatically generalizes solutions. Voices are fully integrated, serving as resources in new situations. Affect is positive or neutral (i.e. this is no longer something to get excited about)

Source: Barkham *et al.* (1996); Stiles (2002).

humanistic or person-centred assumption that therapeutic change requires acceptance of feeling and working through emotion is consistent with the vague awareness stage. The importance of behavioural 'working-through' is also captured in the later stages of the model. It is important to note that not all of the problems clients work on in therapy will start at stage 0 and continue through to Stage 7 in the model. A client may well enter therapy with a vague awareness of what is troubling them, or could even have arrived at a problem statement. Equally, clients may leave therapy before they have achieved mastery of the problem, either because the therapy is not long enough or because insight or even stating the problem may be sufficient for them at that point in their life. Moreover, clients may be working on two or more problematic experiences in parallel, with perhaps one of these topics as the major theme for therapy.

Examples of how the assimilation model can be applied in individual cases can be found in Brinegar *et al.* (2008), Goldsmith *et al.* (2008), Honos-Webb *et al.* (1998, 1999) and Stiles *et al.* (1990, 1992). The attraction of the assimilation model for practitioners is that it makes it possible to gain a sense of where the client is, in relation to an overall sense of where they might be heading. It also makes it possible to understand what has happened when a client stops talking about a particular topic: it can be because he or she has assimi-lated the experience, and has no further need to discuss it. The assimilation model is a useful stimulus to counsellors to reflect on their repertoire of facilitative skills. Some coun-sellors may be wonderful at bringing a warded-off feeling into the light of day, but may be less effective at helping the client to achieve insight.

Recent developments in theory and research in relation to the assimilation model have resulted in a 'reformulation' of the model in terms of 'voices' (Honos-Webb and Stiles 1998). From this perspective, a warded-off experience can be viewed as a 'silenced' voice within the client's self. As this muted or silenced voice becomes more able to be expressed, it takes its place in the 'community of voices' that comprise the client's personal reality. An advantage of a 'voice' formulation is that it encourages the counsellor or psychotherapist to be sensitive to the actual physical characteristics and qualities of the submerged problematic experience, and thus more able to 'hear' this experience in the early stages of its emergence. A 'voice' perspective also draws attention to the existence of an underlying conflict (between dominant and silenced voices) that typically underlies the decision to seek therapy in the first place. Finally, the community of voices notion acts as a reminder to the counsellor and client that therapeutic change occurs not so much through the elimination or suppression of difficult experiences (e.g., 'just forget it') but through their acceptance.

Box 20.6: *The use of metaphor to deepen the therapeutic process*

At the moment of moving another step more fully into his or her experience of a problematic issue, a client may be literally 'lost for words'. The person may just not possess a phrase or image that they have used before, that could do justice to their sense of discovering something new about self. A programme of research by Lynne Angus and Brian Rasmussen (Angus and Rennie 1988, 1989; Rasmussen and Angus 1996; Rasmussen 2000) has made a unique contribution to our understanding of some of the ways in which the use of metaphor can facilitate the therapeutic process. In their research, Angus and Rasmussen tape-recorded therapy sessions, and then invited the client and the therapist to listen to sections of the tape in which vivid metaphors were used, commenting on their experience during these events. They have found that the use of metaphor strengthens the collaborative relationship between counsellor and client, and helps them both to represent important issues in therapy. They also found that the use of metaphor can help to *deepen* the client's engagement in the process. In one case described in Rasmussen and Angus (1996: 526), a client was tearfully recalling experiences in which she had felt that her mother had behaved towards her in a dismissive fashion. The counsellor offered the following reflection:

> It sounds very intense to me. The feelings in it. Like, cut right to the bone.

In the research interview conducted after the end of the therapy session, the client noted that, at this point in the session, she had been 'feeling completely lost in a sea of emotions'. When asked to comment on the counsellor's metaphor, 'cut to the bone', she stated that:

> That was a good way of putting it. Very much so. It really kind of epitomizes
> how I am feeling right now . . . kind of the heart of the matter at that point.

This simple statement by the therapist ('cut right to the bone') was able to pull together several crucial aspects of the client's experience (the pain of what had happened, the pain being inflicted by another person, the sense that it could go no further without breaking the bone itself . . .) and thereby allow the client to develop a more coherent perspective on the issue she had been exploring.

It is of interest that this metaphor, like so many other metaphors that arise in therapy, draws on an image derived from a domain of bodily experiencing. The pervasiveness of physical, embodied metaphors was originally noted by the psychoanalyst Sharpe (1940). Further research into the role of metaphor in the therapeutic process has been carried out by Angus (1996), Levitt *et al.* (2000), Long and Lepper (2008) and Shinebourne and Smith (2010).

Change: process or event?

There is a sense in which therapeutic processes can be viewed as inseparable, overlapping, and braided together. From this perspective, change can be viewed as a gradual unfolding of new awareness or mastery of new skills and behaviours. One of the most influential versions of a 'gradualist' perspective on change can be found in the writings of Carl Rogers and other person-centred theorists, who use the metaphor of biological growth, and the creation by the therapist of an environment within which growth can occur, as the basis for their therapeutic style. By contrast, however, many counsellors and therapists find it helpful to look at process in terms of a series of significant *change events*. These events can be regarded as particularly intense, meaningful and memorable episodes within sessions. They are the moments when 'something happens'.

The most complete analysis of change events carried out so far can be found in the work of Greenberg *et al.* (1993), working within the humanistic tradition. Their ideas are reported in Chapter 7, and are based on an assumption that when a client indicates a particular type of issue (e.g., a dilemma or a tendency to be self-critical), there is a specific sequence of therapist actions or tasks that are particularly helpful and appropriate. A further approach to comprehending helpful events has been created by Mahrer and his colleagues, who have attempted to understand the value of therapy in terms of 'good moments' (Mahrer *et al.* 1987). The *Helpful Aspects of Therapy* (HAT) client self-report form (Llewelyn 1988) provides a valuable method for clients to record and reflect on events that have been significant for them in therapy. An increasing amount of research has shown that when client symptom levels are tracked session-by-session, using a brief questionnaire such as the CORE-OM or OQ45, a wide range of types of individual 'growth curves' can be observed. Although the majority of clients who benefit from therapy appear to improve in small increments, around 25 per cent demonstrate a quite different pattern, marked by significant gains after particular sessions, followed by periods of no change/consolidation (Present *et al.* 2008; Stiles *et al.* 2003; Tang and DeRubeis 1999). These findings support the notion that, at least some of the time, therapeutic change is associated with the experience of powerful in-therapy events. Supporting clinical evidence is also available in the form of observations by therapists of 'quantum change' in some clients: 'sudden, dramatic, and enduring transformations that affect a broad range of personal, cognitive and emotional functioning' (Miller, W.R. 2004: 453).

It seems sensible to regard therapeutic change as mainly comprised of small steps, arising from a gradual process of exploring and resolving personal issues, which may be occasionally punctuated, for some clients, with more intense events or moments in which some kind of personal revelation or transformation occurs. It is important for practitioners to be able both to acknowledge and celebrate these events when they occur, and not to push their clients to achieve such 'Hollywood moments' if they do not arise naturally – most clients, with most therapists, accomplish meaningful and significant benefits from therapy in the absence of any such breakthroughs.

Facilitating change: being responsive to the client's agenda

The key characteristic of the 'middle' phase of counselling lies in the capacity of the client and counsellor to work productively together to achieve a deeper understanding of the issues that brought the client to counselling, and to translate that understanding into strategies and action that will allow the client to achieve his or her life goals. To accomplish this kind of productive therapeutic work it is essential that a counsellor should be *responsive* to the client's needs, way of communicating, and style of problem-solving (Stiles *et al.* 1998). Although each counsellor inevitably has a limited repertoire of skills, interventions and explanatory models, on which they draw during their work with clients, good therapists are able to adapt these ideas and methods to meet the needs of different clients. Researchers who have interviewed clients who have been disappointed with the therapy they have received, typically find that dissatisfied clients are those who have been exposed to therapists who are not flexible enough to find common ground with their clients, but persist with a fixed therapeutic approach even when this is not effective for their client (Lilliengren and Werbart 2005; Nilsson 2007). These therapists may be highly effective with clients whose way of working closely matches their own, but are not flexible enough to accommodate to the requirements of clients who have a different agenda.

It can be useful to think about the process of working collaboratively with clients, during the middle stage of counselling, in terms of negotiations around choices from a therapy *menu*. McLeod and McLeod (2011) have suggested that there are a set of core tasks that clients are looking to fulfil in counselling:

- making meaning: talking through an issue in order to understand things better;
- making sense of a specific problematic experience;
- problem-solving, planning and decision-making;
- changing behaviour;
- negotiating a life transition or developmental crisis;
- dealing with difficult feelings and emotions;
- finding, analysing and acting on information;
- undoing self-criticism and enhancing self-care;
- dealing with difficult or painful relationships.

A competent counsellor is someone who is able to respond to any of these tasks, in a form that makes sense to the client.

Box 20.7: *The impact of counsellor self-disclosure on the therapeutic process*

It seems clear to most people that counselling is a situation in which the client does the talking, and the counsellor listens and facilitates. Traditionally, counsellors have been trained to abstain from talking about themselves in the therapy room, sometimes even to the extent of not being willing to acknowledge whether they are married or single, gay or straight. There has been a tendency to regard the curiosity of the client about the counsellor as something to be interpreted, and any desire on the part of the counsellor to disclose personal material ('my mother died too, and I know that it affected me deeply') as an unhelpful departure from role, and possible boundary violation.

In recent years, however, research into the impact of counsellor self-disclosure on the therapeutic process has allowed a more nuanced appreciation of therapist self-disclosure to emerge. This research has made it possible to differentiate between self-involving statements and self-disclosure statements. A self-involving statement can be viewed as a form of immediacy or congruence, for example if a counsellor states that 'as you were talking, I was aware of feeling confused, then sad . . .' Here, the counsellor is making reference to a here-and-now personal response to the client. Self-disclosure, on the other hand, refers to situations where the counsellor shares personal biographical information ('I am married', 'I am gay').

Barrett and Berman (2001) conducted an experiment where they asked 18 counsellors in a university student counselling service to increase their self-disclosure with one client, and to limit their self-disclosure with another client. The clients who had received more counsellor self-disclosure showed more symptom change, and reported liking their counsellor more, compared with those who had received limited self-disclosure. It should be noted here that even in the high self-disclosure condition, the counsellors were still being cautious about the amount that they disclosed (five disclosures per session, compared to two per session in the limited disclosure condition).

Hanson (2005) interviewed 18 clients about their experience of therapist self-disclosure and non-disclosure (refusal to self-disclose at a moment when the client had expected the therapist to do so). In this study, clients described several ways in which disclosure had been helpful for them – fostering the alliance, validating or normalizing the client's experience, expressing moral solidarity. They also described ways in which non-disclosure could be unhelpful, for instance by leading to an avoidance of a particular topic. The findings of these (and other) studies have led to a reappraisal of the role of counsellor self-disclosure in the direction of an appreciation of the therapeutic value of skilful, sensitive and judicious self-disclosure on the part of the therapist. Further discussion of these issues, and guidelines for effective use of counsellor self-disclosure, can be found in Hanson (2005), Hill and Knox (2001), Knox and Hill (2003) and Farber (2006).

Innovative moments

Usually, the story told by the client will be fairly repetitive and 'problem-saturated'. One of the therapeutic strategies used in narrative therapy and solution-focused therapy

(Chapter 11), and indeed in any therapy that focuses on the strengths of the client, is to pay close attention to any client statements that represent solutions to their problem, or accounts of achievements or pleasure. Miguel Gonçalves and his colleagues have developed an approach to this phenomenon, which they describe as 'innovative moments' (Gonçalves *et al.* 2008, 2010, 2012). In their research, they have identified several different types of innovative moment: reflecting on patterns of experience; descriptions of new experiences; new types of action or behaviour; complaining or protesting about their problems; and reconceptualization. Each of these types of innovative moment represents a welcome development. However, Gonçalves *et al.* (2008) suggest that reconceptualization can be viewed as a particularly important marker of change, because it explicitly connects the past with the present and the future, and therefore reflects a new capacity on the part of the client to see his or her previous troubles in perspective. Other types of innovative moment also indicate change, but are forms of change that can be reversed. By contrast, reconceptualization is less easily reversed.

A key point here is that this approach assumes that the client is an active participant in the process of trying to move on in his or her life. It is therefore inevitable that the client will generate at least a few innovative moments in each therapy session. The task of the therapist is to take note of the moments, be curious about them, and see where they lead (Gonçalves *et al.* 2010).

Working with multiple parts of the self

A dimension of person-hood that appears to have emerged as particularly salient along with the growth of modern culture is that of a sense of personal *multiplicity* or fragmentation. It seems that whereas in traditional cultures people were able largely just to *be* whoever they were, in modern cultures people find themselves functioning in different social roles, in different settings, with different networks of other people. Modern culture presents the individual with a substantial range of choices around identity, career, lifestyle and location.

As a result of these cultural factors, a pervasive aspect of contemporary life is that of experiencing self as being comprised of a number of parts, which are to a greater or lesser extent separate and in conflict with each other. It seems probable that, in evolutionary terms, the development of language allowed human beings to have the potential for self-reflection, since language allows the possibility of referring to self as an object as well as an active subject, and encourages dialectical talk ('on the one hand . . . on the other hand . . .'). It is likely, therefore, that a sense of self-multiplicity has always been an aspect of being human (see, for example, the powerful inner conflicts exhibited by tragic figures in Shakespearean drama). However, the conditions of modern life have contributed massively to a splitting of the experience of being who one is. The publication in 1885 of the short story *The Strange Case of Dr Jekyll and Mr Hyde*, by Robert Louis Stephenson, which has enjoyed immediate and enduring popularity, has been regarded by some cultural historians as representing a marker of the appearance of self-multiplicity as a core existential issue.

The existential phenomenon of multiplicity encompasses the idea that there has been a time (within an individual life, or within the history of a cultural group) when there existed a sense of experience as being a unity (an enchanted time), which may be re-established through personal effort. For example, the Jungian idea of *individuation*, or the idea of a 'real' or 'core' self that occurs in some humanistic theories, reflect a sense of personal wholeness as a quest. Other therapy theories, by contrast, take the notion of a fragmented self as their starting point – for example the *ego state* structure used in TA, or the idea of *configurations of self* in contemporary person-centred theory. Psychoanalytic theory remains a highly influential and valuable framework for thinking about the dynamics of self-fragmentation.

In counselling and psychotherapy, there are two levels at which an appreciation of the multiplicity of experience can be practically relevant. At its most simple level, a sensitivity to multiplicity can enable a therapist to become attuned to the ways in which a person maintains a way of living that is unsatisfying for them. An example is the tendency in many people to be locked into a polarity in which a vulnerable and creative part of the self is criticized or suppressed by a conformist part. It can be very helpful for a person who is stuck in this kind of duality of existence to be facilitated to hold a more open dialogue between these parts of the self.

The other level at which self-multiplicity can be approached in therapy is to 'normalize' it, or consider it as a condition of existence – some people may believe that there is something wrong with them if they experience different impulses to act in different ways, and can be relieved to discover that self-multiplicity is just the way things are.

As with 'innovative moments', a key skill in relation to the process of therapy is to be able to *listen for* self-multiplicity, take note of when it is occurring, and reflect on what it might mean. Many interventions used by counsellors can be understood as ways of working with self-multiplicity. For example, good empathic reflection can encourage a client to give voice to silenced and vulnerable feelings, which then leads to a more open dialogue between these feelings and the dominant part of them that is saying 'pull yourself together'.

Box 20.8: *The community of self*

The idea that parts of a self might be viewed as constituting a *community* has been suggested by Miller Mair (1977). He describes the case of one client who imagined his 'community of self' to comprise a 'troupe of players'. Some of the main characters within this troupe were the 'producer', whose job was to take responsibility for what was happening 'on stage', the 'conversationalist', an actor who enjoyed relaxing in good company, the 'businessman', the 'country bumpkin', and several others. As he reflected on this way of thinking about himself, Peter realized that his 'dreamer' self, who generated a lot of ideas that were useful for other characters, was too easily silenced by the autocratic 'producer'. He also realized that the troupe as a whole was guided by a 'council', which had not been very effective in helping the different characters to communicate with each other. Peter initiated a programme of 'community development', to increase understanding and communication between members of his troupe, with the goal of preventing situations where the 'producer' would need to exert arbitrary authority. This was therapeutically helpful for Peter, in enabling him to be more resourceful in terms of how he dealt with stressful situations in his life.

Mair (1977) regards the notion of 'community of self' as a *metaphor* that effectively brings together various strands of how a person sees himself or herself, and the action tendencies that he or she exhibits. Mair (1977: 149) argues that it would be a mistake to reify the concept of 'community of self', by assuming that it provides a description of how things really are. Instead, as a metaphor, it opens up the possibility of choice in 'what we take ourselves to be'.

Using structured exercises and interventions

Both research and practical experience suggest that the most potent factors responsible for enabling therapeutic change to occur in counselling are 'non-specific': the experience of being in a supportive yet challenging relationship, the expression and exploration of feelings and emotions, the instillation of hope, the counsellor as a model of how someone might seek to engage authentically with another person. These non-specific factors are largely conveyed through generic counsellor responses such as sensitive, empathic listening, seeking clarification, encouragement, expression of caring and interpretation of meaning. However, there may be points in counselling, usually (but not always) in the middle, 'change' phase of the work, when it is helpful to use specific techniques and interventions to facilitate the development of the client.

An exercise or intervention may perhaps best be viewed as providing a catalyst that allows the client to focus on and work through a specific issue. Some interventions are highly embedded in the flow of therapeutic conversation: for example, the exploration of metaphors generated spontaneously by the client (see Box 20.5). Other interventions involve stopping the flow of interaction, and concentrating on specific, structured exercises. Some of these exercises are associated with particular theoretical approaches. Examples of theory-informed exercises include the use in CBT of the method of systematic desensitization, 'two-chair' work in gestalt therapy and experiential focusing in person-centred counselling. Other exercises are more idiosyncratic or eclectic, and are passed on from one therapist to another informally or on training courses, or are invented by individual counsellors themselves.

Examples of such exercises are the use of buttons or animal figures to represent members of a family, drawing a 'life-line', reflecting on the memories evoked by significant photographs and guided fantasy. There are several books available that offer collections of widely used therapeutic exercises (Burns 2010; Carrel 2001; Greenberg *et al.* 1993; Hall *et al.* 2006; Hecker and Deacon 2006; Hecker and Sori 2007; King 2001; Leahy 2003; Seiser and Wastell 2002; Sori and Hecker 2008; Timulak 2011; Yalom 2002). In some instances, exercises may encompass homework assignments, which the client carries out between sessions. Examples of homework assignments are: keeping a diary or personal journal; spending time each day pursuing a therapeutically valuable activity such as listening to one's partner, meditating quietly or exercising; doing research on one's family history; reading a self-help book or 'inspirational' novel or watching a 'therapeutic' film.

The importance and usefulness of structured exercises vary a great deal, depending on the preferences of the particular client and counsellor involved. Some counsellors work effectively without ever using such 'props'; others find them invaluable. Some clients appreciate the structure provided by an exercise; others seem to find that it creates a distance between them and their counsellor, and prevents them from talking about what is really on their minds.

Box 20.9: *Working with dreams: an example of the counselling process in action*

Working with clients' dream provides a good example of how different therapeutic processes are interwoven within a counselling session. A significant proportion of clients believe in the value of dream analysis, and expect some form of dreamwork to be part of the counselling 'menu'. Although the use of dreams in psychotherapy originated into the interpretive, psychoanalytic approach to dreamwork devised by Freud and Jung, many contemporary counsellors prefer to adopt a more collaborative style of working with dreams, such as the cognitive–experiential model developed by Clara Hill (1996, 2004). This model describes three stages of the interpretation of a dream: *exploration, insight* and *action*.

The exploration stage begins by explaining the procedure to the client, then inviting him or her to recount the dream in the first person present tense, as if it was being experienced in the moment. The client is then asked to describe the overall feelings associated with the dream, before being invited to explore the meaning of between five and ten major images in the dream, in terms of associations and waking life triggers. The therapist then summarizes what has emerged during the exploration process. During the insight stage, the client is encouraged to share his or her own interpretation of the meaning of the dream, and to deepen that interpretation by considering the relevance of the dream to waking life triggers and inner personality dynamics (for example, conflicts between parts of the self). Finally, in the action stage, the client is asked to change the dream, by imagining a different ending or sequel, and to identify behavioural changes that may be suggested by the dream interpretation.

The cognitive–experiential model of dreamwork brings together a wide range of therapeutic processes, for example providing an explanatory rationale, collaborative decision-making, here-and-now experiencing, empathic reflection, and cognitive problem-solving. The detailed descriptions of how therapists work with clients' dreams, provided by Hill (1996, 2004) demonstrates the extent to which a specific therapeutic intervention (in this case, dream interpretation) are comprised a myriad of constituent subprocesses.

What happens between sessions

Having a really good discussion, within a counselling session, of how and what to do differently, and how to change problematic behaviour, is of little value if the person then does not implement any changes in his or her everyday life. One of the useful strategies for bridging the gap between the counselling room and real life is the practice of agreeing on *homework* tasks. Homework tasks in counselling can be suggested by the person or by the counsellor, and can range from quite structured and formal tasks, such as writing a journal or completing worksheets, to more informal or flexible tasks such as 'listening to other people more', 'practising slow and deep breathing as a way of coping with my anxiety' or 'visiting my grandmother's grave'. There has been a substantial amount of research carried out into the process of agreeing homework tasks in counselling (see, for example, Mahrer *et al.* 1994; Scheel *et al.* 1999, 2004). Although homework is often considered as a method that is primarily employed by cognitive–behavioural therapists, there is plentiful evidence that counsellors using a wide variety of approaches are all likely to use homework with at least 50 per cent of their cases (Ronen and Kazantzis 2006).

Based on a review of the research evidence, Scheel *et al.* (2004) have developed some useful guidelines for using homework in counselling. These include: the homework assignment to be based on collaboration between counsellor and client; describing the task in detail; providing a rationale for why the task will benefit the person; matching the task to the person's ability; writing down the task; asking how confident the person is about fulfilling the task, and if necessary modifying the task accordingly; try out the task during the session; ask about how the person got on with the task, at the next meeting; celebrating or praising the person's achievement of the task.

In some counselling situations, it is also possible to use reminders to maximize the chances that the task is carried out. For example, a number of smoking cessation projects phone up patients between sessions to check on their progress. Also, counsellors who use email contact with clients, as an adjunct to face-to-face contact can quite easily send a brief email message between meetings.

The findings of research carried out by Dreier (2008) and Mackrill (2011a, 2011b) suggests that what happens between sessions goes far beyond homework. Their studies looked at the everyday lives of clients, and found that clients bring ideas from everyday life into therapy, in ways that are not visible to their therapists. It is not that learning from therapy is exported into everyday life (e.g., through homework tasks). Instead, what happens in therapy has to fit into the structures of the everyday world of the client, and what happens in therapy is a by-product of that process. This research represents a 180 degree shift away from the way that most therapists think about their work.

Finally, there is evidence that therapists do things between sessions, that have a bearing on the process of therapy. It is obvious that a therapist might see a supervisor or personal therapist, or might be stimulated to make a connection between a current client and a book or article that he or she is reading. However, research has found that therapists regularly think about their clients between sessions (Schröder *et al.* 2009), and will sometimes also dream about clients (Spangler *et al.* 2009). In one study, Flückiger and Holtforth (2008) found that if a therapist thought about their client's strengths and resources, for ten minutes before the start of each session, the client would be more likely to benefit from therapy.

The implication of all of these factors is that it is not sufficient to think about the process of counselling merely in terms of what happens in the counselling room. There are very significant parts of the process that also take place between sessions. However, the nature and impact of these intersession processes is still not very well understood and has not been adequately studied.

Process defined in terms of counsellor behaviour, actions and intentions

Yet another way of looking at the process of counselling is to focus on the behaviour of the counsellor, and how this behaviour can have an effect on the client. Clearly, if is possible to identify those counsellor actions that are consistently associated with good outcomes, then it should be possible to train and supervise counsellors in order to maximize the frequency of occurrence of these responses, and reduce the frequency of less helpful interactions. Clara Hill and her colleagues have devised widely used lists of both counsellor and client response modes (see Tables 20.5 and 20.6).

The taxonomies of therapist 'response modes' developed by Hill and others (Stiles 1992) in the 1980s tended to focus on simple, 'molecular' items of therapist behaviour. Although these lists provide a valuable means of categorizing aspects of therapeutic process, they yield a somewhat 'broad brush' picture of what is happening. In an attempt to look more closely at the complexity of therapist responsiveness, a number of researchers have created more detailed checklists, such as the *Therapeutic Procedures Inventory* (McNeilly and Howard 1991), *Comprehensive Therapeutic Interventions Rating Scale*

TABLE 20.5 Categories of therapist verbal responses

Approval. Provides emotional support, approval, reassurance or reinforcement. It may imply sympathy or tend to alleviate anxiety by minimizing the client's problems

Information. Supplies information in the form of data, facts or resources. It may be related to the therapy process, the therapist's behaviour or therapy arrangements (time, fee, place)

Direct guidance. These are directions or advice that the therapist suggests to the client for what to do either in the session or outside the session

Closed question. Gathers data or specific information. The client responses are limited and specific

Open question. Probes or requests for clarification or exploration by the client

Paraphrase. Mirrors or summarizes what the client has been communicating either verbally or non-verbally. Does not 'go beyond' what the client has said or add a new perspective or understanding to the client's statements or provide any explanation for the client's behaviour. Includes restatement of content, reflection of feelings, non-verbal referent and summary

Interpretation. Goes beyond what the client has overtly recognized and provides reasons, alternative meanings or new frameworks for feelings, behaviours or personality. It may: establish connections between seemingly isolated statements or events; interpret defences, feelings, resistance or transference; or indicate themes, patterns or causal relationships in behaviour and personality, relating present events to past events

Confrontation. Points out a discrepancy or contradiction but does not provide a reason for such a discrepancy. The discrepancy may be between words and behaviours, between two things a client has said or between the client's and therapist's perceptions

Self-disclosure. Shares feelings or personal experiences

Source: Hill (1989).

TABLE 20.6 Categories of client verbal responses

Simple response. A short, limited phrase that may indicate agreement, acknowledgement or approval of what the therapist has said, indicate disapproval or disagreement or respond briefly to a therapist's question with specific information or facts

Request. An attempt to obtain information or advice or to place the burden of responsibility for solution of the problem on the therapist

Description. Discusses history, events or incidents related to the problem in a storytelling or narrative style. The person seems more interested in describing *what* has happened than in communicating affective responses, understanding or resolving the problem

Experiencing. Affectively explores feelings, behaviours or reactions about self or problems, but does not convey an understanding of causality

Exploration of client–therapist relationship. Indicates feelings, reactions, attitudes or behaviour related to the therapist or the therapeutic situation

Insight. Indicates that the client understands or is able to see themes, patterns or causal relationships in his or her behaviour or personality, or in another's behaviour or personality. Often has an 'aha' quality

Discussion of plans. Refers to action-oriented plans, decisions, future goals and possible outcomes of plans. Client displays a problem-solving attitude

Silence. Pause of four or five seconds between therapist and client statements, or immediately after a client's simple response

Other. Statements unrelated to the client's problem, such as small talk or comments about the weather or events

Source: Hill (1989).

(Trijsburg *et al.* 2004), *Multitheoretical List of Therapeutic Interventions* (McCarthy and Barber 2009), *Therapist Techniques Survey Questionnaire* (Thoma and Cecero 2009) and the *Psychotherapy Process Q-Sort* (Jones 2000). It is of interest that, even though the authors of these scales were working independently, they have each arrived at lists that overlap to a substantial degree. McNeilly and Howard (1991: 232) suggested that there exists a basic structure that lies behind the apparent proliferation of therapy techniques:

> . . . our results indicate three targets or themes of therapeutic interventions. One is to enhance patient functioning through helping the patient understand the patterns and sources of his or her pathological functioning. A second is to help the patient gain mastery through the learning of alternative coping strategies. Yet a third is to encourage self-knowledge through moving the patient to a fuller experiencing of thoughts and feelings.

The categories of therapist interventions used by McNeilly and Howard (1991) are outlined in Table 20.7. The *Psychotherapy Process Q-Sort* has been widely used to compare the therapeutic processes that are associated with different approaches to therapy. Jones and Pulos (1993) found that approaches can be differentiated in terms

TABLE 20.7 Items from the *Therapeutic Procedures Inventory*

Directive/behavioural interventions:
1 Suggest changes in your client's behaviour
2 Offer explicit guidance or advice
3 Explore possible practical solutions to your client's current life problems
4 Confront or challenge your client's attitudes or reactions
5 Train your client in assertiveness, social skills or other lack of relevant skills
6 Directly teach or demonstrate a new way of responding to or acting with another person
7 Reframe your client's formulation of a problem
8 Try to calm or confront your client
9 Help your client resolve conflicting or incompatible wants, needs or goals
10 Discuss the effect of recent experiences in therapy on your client's behaviour outside of therapy
11 Acknowledge your client's gain in therapy or reassure him or her that gains will be forthcoming
12 Try to help your client stay focused on a particular theme or problem
13 Develop specific assignments for the client to carry out between sessions
14 Point out flaws or errors in your client's reasoning or assumptions
15 Discuss your client's reactions and feelings regarding termination
16 Encourage your client to identify his or her emotional reactions in this session
17 Engage in social conversation about activities or current events

Psychodynamic/past-focused interventions:
18 Help your client understand how childhood experiences influence his or her current life
19 Explore your client's childhood experiences
20 Link your client's reactions to his or her present or past reactions to parents
21 Try to direct your client's attentions to patterns or themes in his or her experience
22 Point out ways in which your client tries to avoid anxiety (i.e., interpret defences)
23 Encourage your client to keep a record of thoughts, feelings and/or activities between sessions
24 Discuss the desirability or effect of psychoactive medication with your client
25 Work on the interpretation of a dream

Affective, emotion-focused interventions:
26 Help your client express unexpressed feelings
27 Try to facilitate the client's focusing on inner feelings and experiences
28 Encourage your client to examine meanings of his or her thoughts, behaviour or feelings
29 Remind your client of material that has been discussed in previous sessions
30 Actively support your client's transference determined experience of you
31 Try to convey a sense of non-judgemental acceptance
32 Explore the meaning of your client's fantasies
33 Explore your client's reactions to procedural changes in treatment
34 Try to reflect your client's feelings
35 Encourage your client to engage in a dialogue between conflicting parts of his or her self
36 Explore the meaning or function of your client's symptoms
37 Pay attention to your own reactions as a way of better understanding your client
38 Work actively with your client's non-verbal communications
39 Attempt to correct your client's transference determined experience of you
40 Point out behaviours on the part of your client that interfere with the work of therapy (e.g., resistance)

Source: McNeilly and Howard (1991).

of characteristic errors that are associated with them (e.g., CBT therapists not being empathic enough, psychodynamic therapists being too distant, person-centred therapists not offering enough structure). Ablon and Jones (2002) reported that therapists frequently use interventions that they do not think they are using (and are more effective because of this).

The therapist as process facilitator

The taxonomies of counsellor or psychotherapist intentions, responses and interventions, reviewed in the previous section, provide a valuable resource in terms of making it possible to begin to identify the contribution of a therapist to the process that might be unfolding in any particular case. However, the limitation of these taxonomies is that they only supply a static picture of what is happening, and do not provide any insight into the impact that the therapist's actions have on the client. An important body of research, carried out by the German psychotherapist Rainer Sachse, has focused on the micro-analysis of 'triples': sequences of therapist–client interaction in which the client speaks, the counsellor responds, and then the client responds to the counsellor's intervention (Sachse and Elliott 2002). This research has examined the ways in which different types of therapist response can influence the depth of experiencing being displayed by the client.

For example, a client may say: 'Only yesterday I noticed again how terribly worried I get when I'm telling somebody a story and he is not listening to me at all' (example from Sachse and Elliott 2002: 94). In this statement, the client is speaking personally, but with relatively limited elaboration of the underlying meaning of this type of incident, or the feelings associated with it. The therapist can respond at any one of three levels, each of which may have a different impact on the way that the client continues to process his or her experience at that moment. For example, a *flattening* response, such as 'who was with you at the time?' would be likely to divert the client into factual detail, and away from further exploration of feelings and meaning. A *maintaining* response, such as 'you really feel that it bothers you' would have the probable effect of holding the client at the same level of processing as their initial statement. However, a *deepening* response, such as 'what does it mean to you, to get terribly worried?' will tend to influence the client in the direction of greater depth of experiential processing, at their subsequent speaking turn.

The findings of an extensive programme of research into the role of therapist as 'process facilitator' (Sachse and Elliott 2002), which has examined the impacts of different types of therapist responses, has found that:

- the level of processing exhibited by the therapist has a consistent impact on the depth of processing expressed by the client – around 60 per cent of the time, clients match the depth of processing embodied in the preceding therapist statement;
- clients relatively rarely shift in the direction of greater depth of processing, in the absence of the therapist modelling such behaviour;
- clients are more sensitive to 'flattening' responses than to 'deepening' ones.

The implications of this research suggest that, in attempting to understand the process of therapy it is essential to consider the effect on the client of preceding therapist interventions or statements. The evidence suggests that even if clients are 'on track' in the sense of actively exploring the emotional and personal meaning of an aspect of their experience (Rennie 1998), they can readily be brought to a halt by an over-concrete or factually-oriented therapist response. By contrast, clients who may appear to be stuck in a process of merely reporting everyday events, can be encouraged to explore the meaning of these events if the therapist responds in an appropriately 'deepening' manner. The implications of this perspective for counsellor training are discussed in Hammond *et al.* (2002).

The covert dimension of process: what is going on under the surface

One of the most fascinating aspects of counselling process arises from the fact that both client and counsellor *conceal* a great deal of information from each other. Basic theoretical concepts that counsellors often use to make sense of process, ideas such as transference, counter-transference, resistance, genuineness and congruence, are grounded in the reality that, for much of the time, both participants in any counselling relationship monitor what they think, select what they choose to say and attempt to control their non-verbal communication. If the aim of analysing process is to gain a fuller understanding of what is happening in a therapeutic encounter, in the interests of facilitating its effectiveness, one of the most productive strategies is to pay attention to what is *not* said. Regan and Hill (1992) carried out a number of studies in which they asked clients and counsellors at the end of each session to list 'things not said'.

In his programme of research into the client's experience of counselling, Rennie (1994a, b) found that there were many ways in which clients chose to conceal their thoughts, feelings and intentions. For example, clients might defer to the counsellor by saying nothing in a situation where they felt the counsellor had misunderstood them or asked an irrelevant question. Other clients reported to Rennie (1994b) that sometimes they overtly talked about things that were not really all that important, while covertly they might be running through another issue, or weighing up whether they felt ready to introduce into their story particular events or areas of experience that were painful or embarrassing.

The implication of these studies is to reinforce the idea that there is a lot going on 'behind the scenes' in any counselling encounter. To make sense of process, therefore, requires gaining as much access as possible to this hidden material. In training or research situations, it can be valuable to use the method of interpersonal process recall (IPR) (Kagan *et al.* 1963; Kagan 1984; Elliott 1986; Baker *et al.* 1990; Kagan and Kagan 1990), which is a systematic method for asking both participants to listen (usually separately) to the tape of a counselling session and comment on what they had been experiencing during the original interaction. If this task is carried out within 24 hours of the session, the informant is able directly to recall a lot of what went on. The longer the recall interview is delayed, the less the person will remember. In everyday ongoing counselling, ethical and practical constraints may preclude the use of IPR. In these situations the covert process of the client will only be recovered to the extent that they choose to disclose and explore it in sessions. However, it is feasible for counsellors to examine their inner experience during counselling by writing notes afterwards that focus on what they felt as well as what the client said and did, and by exploring this topic with their supervisor.

Using process analysis to inform practice

Many different aspects of counselling process have been discussed in this chapter. It is clear that the process of counselling is complex, multifaceted and comprising multiple layers or horizons of meaning. Making sense of this complexity, and using that understanding to inform practice, represents a key dimension of both initial training and ongoing supervision and professional development. Most counsellors will find that they will be required to carry out one or more 'process analyses' as part of their training. Experienced and qualified counsellors may be aware of a desire to understand more about the process of their own work with clients, perhaps in the context of supervision, or to write up for publication the process that has taken place around the use of a new technique, or in relation to working with a particularly significant or unusual client. The aim of this section is to describe some principles by which practitioners can systematically analyse the counselling process for themselves.

A valuable first step in making sense of the counselling process within one's own practice, is to record a counselling session (with the consent of the client), using either audio or video. Although it is possible, after the therapy session, to construct detailed process notes, or a 'verbatim' account of what was said, there is no doubt that even the best notes or verbatim select and 'smooth' the full reality of what happened. It is therefore usually better to work from recordings whenever possible. The next stage in process analysis is to transcribe the recording, or key parts of it, to make it easier to give detailed attention to particular words, phrases and sequences, and to make notes on interesting or significant aspects of the text.

For a counsellor, the aim of carrying out this kind of analysis is to arrive at a new appreciation of how one works. It is essential, therefore, to be able to see beyond one's pre-existing ideas about what one was trying to accomplish with the client, and learn from a dispassionate scrutiny of what was actually happening. Quite often, merely transcribing a session can in itself lead to new insights. Listening closely to a recording, and reading the words on a page, typically reveals that a lot of what the client is trying to convey, is not getting through to the counsellor, or that some of the counsellor's responses to the client are clumsy and off the mark. It can be helpful to listen to a recording, or work through a transcript, with a group of colleagues, for example other students on a training programme, or co-members of a supervision group. It is certain that other readers or listeners will pick up on aspects of the process that the therapist himself/herself was not aware of.

Beyond just reading or listening closely to the record of the session, it can be helpful to use some analytic strategies that have been developed by researchers who have carried out in-depth investigations of the process of therapy. These ideas can be used as start-points or sensitizing constructs for exploration of session transcripts. They are guides for 'where to look', without making any assumptions about what will be found.

1 *'Triples'*: sequences of client statement > therapist response > client further statement (Sachse and Elliott 2002). There are at least two aspects of 'triples' that are of interest. First, to what extent did the statement made by the counsellor fully acknowledge and reflect what the client had just said (or had said in earlier utterances)? Second, to what extent did the statement made by the therapist lead to a deepening of the client's exploration of the topic, or have the consequence of closing down that exploration?

2 *Events.* There may be a significantly helpful (or hindering) event that jumps out when reading a transcript. An important indicator of the significance of an event is if the event is memorable to the client or therapist (e.g., the client refers back to it in a later session, or the therapist talks about it in supervision). Understanding the unfolding process of a moment or event that was particularly helpful for a client may tell the counsellor a lot about 'what works' for that particular person, or about more generally

facilitative aspects of their own style as a therapist. In analysing an event it is valuable to define the beginning and end of the event, and carefully track just what it was that the counsellor and the client did, that made this such a useful few minutes. It can also be interesting to look back at what preceded the event (what led up to it and set the scene for it) and what followed it (what effect did it have on the therapeutic relationship, the client's problem, etc.).

3 *Topics.* Clients usually shift back and forward between different topics or themes. For example, a client may talk for a few minutes about feeling depressed, then shift to exploring her difficulties in her work role, then her plans for a forthcoming vacation. The evidence from research into the assimilation model (discussed earlier in this chapter), and other research studies, suggests that progress in therapy proceeds at a different pace for different topics. It is therefore particularly useful to look closely at what is happening in respect of the topic or topics that reflect the client's main therapeutic goals (e.g., depression) and temporarily set to one side the discussions around other topics. Another productive analytic strategy can be to pay special attention to what happens around topic shifts. For example, does the client change topic because he or she is uncomfortable with the painful feelings that are being evoked? If so, was the counsellor aware of these feelings? Or, did the counsellor change topic because he or she was uncomfortable with what was being said, or did not appreciate its significance?

4 *Metaphors.* There has been a substantial amount of research into the role of metaphor in therapy (discussed earlier in this chapter). Metaphors are rich in meaning, and provide opportunities for the client and counsellor to work together to generate new understandings of the client's problem, and to strengthen their sense of being on the same wavelength. It is relatively easy to identify metaphors within a session transcript, and to look at how and whether the metaphor is then picked up by the other person, and becomes a shared source of meaning.

5 *Emotion.* Feelings and emotions are indictors of what really matters to the client. It is unlikely that therapeutic change will occur in the absence of some form of acknowledgement and exploration of what the client feels about the issues that are bothering them. At the same time, counsellors may be somewhat selective in the emotions that they pick up on. It can be useful to listen to a session recording with the specific intention of identifying emotion words, phrases or images used by the client, or emotion expressed through voice quality. It is then possible to analyse the way that the counsellor responded to these emotions, and the impact of these responses on the subsequent direction of therapy.

6 *Covert processes.* Although a session recording contains an enormous amount of information, it is also obvious that there is a great deal of further information that is not captured in this way. Both counsellor and client will be aware of much that is 'not said'. One of the most useful learning strategies for any counsellor undertaking a process analysis of their own practice, is to pause the recording every time they recall what they were experiencing at that point in the original session, and write down what they remember. This material provides direct evidence around aspects of therapy that might be categorized as 'counter-transference' reactions, or therapist

'congruence'. It is often the case that the therapist is holding back on a response that could be of great potential value to the client. In training settings, for instance where students are being clients for each other, it is possible to collect similar information around the covert process of the client. Some research studios have also collected such data from real-life clients.

Further information on methods of analysing therapy process can be found in McLeod (2013a). A massive contribution to the development of methodologies for studying therapy process has been made by Robert Elliott, in the form of *Comprehensive Process Analysis* (CPA; Elliott 1984) of single sessions of therapy, and *Hermeneutic Single Case Efficacy Design* (HSCED; Elliott 2002) investigations of whole cases. Examples of process analyses carried out using these principles can be found in Balmforth and Elliott (2012), Elliott (1983), Elliott *et al.* (1990, 2009) and Elliott and Shapiro (1992). It is important to note that these published studies are rather more ambitious and time-consuming than the type of process analysis that would be feasible for a typical student or practitioner. Nevertheless, the same principles can be applied in small-scale process analyses conducted by trainees and practitioners.

Box 20.10: *It can also be valuable for clients to listen to recordings of their therapy sessions*

The use of process analysis of session recordings has proved to be an invaluable learning tool for counsellors. However, it can also be valuable for clients to listen to recordings of their counselling sessions. Shepherd *et al.* (2009) routinely made audio recordings of therapy sessions with clients, for purposes of training, supervision and research. After a while, they began to offer clients the option of taking home their own copy of the recordings each week. Later, they carried out a study into how clients felt about this procedure, and found that the majority of their clients regularly listened to the recordings and reported that doing this had been a positive contribution to their experience of therapy as a whole.

The third task in carrying out a process analysis is to scan the tape or text of the session to find a significant or interesting *event* that merits fuller interpretation and analysis. There exist a number of criteria on which events can be identified. Elliott (1984), for example, will often ask the client at the end of the session to nominate and describe the events that he or she felt were *most helpful* or *most hindering*. Mahrer *et al.* (1987) chose events considered by the therapist to represent 'good moments'. Angus and Rennie (1988, 1989), interested in the role of metaphor in therapy, directed their attention to events in which either client or counsellor employed a novel or striking metaphor. Elliott *et al.* (1990) wished to explore the meaning of insight in cognitive–behavioural and psychodynamic counselling, and so focused on 'insight' events drawn from each of these two therapeutic modalities. Although these are examples from research studies, it is striking, when reading case studies published by counsellors and therapists, or listening to counsellors present cases at supervision, that very often the discussion of a case hinges on the meaning and significance of key moments or events.

Having found an event that is, for either theoretical or practical reasons, significant or important, it is then useful to gather as much information as possible on the *covert* processes that were occurring during it, perhaps using IPR. Although in principle both client and counsellor may be invited to share their recollections of what they were thinking or feeling during the event, there are obvious ethical sensitivities involved in seeking client collaboration in this type of project. If the 'inquirer' is his or her actual counsellor there is a risk of setting up an unhelpful 'dual relationship' in which the client is caught between the roles of research participant and recipient of therapeutic help. However, it may be possible to use a tool such as the *Helpful Aspects of Therapy* (HAT) form (Llewelyn 1988) to collect information from the client on his or her perceptions of the session, without intruding on his or her privacy. However, there will usually be a great deal of covert material that can be added by the actual counsellor, for example around things not said, images or fantasies that occurred at various points, feelings and emotions that were experienced, and the intentions that guided their interventions and statements.

Once an event has been 'filled out' with the addition of what was 'not said', it is possible to move into the analysis of its constitutive meanings and processes. This involves careful consideration of the following questions:

- What actually happened? What was the sequence of counsellor and client interactions during the event itself?

- What are the micro-processes (e.g., counsellor responses and interventions, client responses) that comprised the elements or 'building blocks' of the event?

- Where does the event fit within the context of the session as a whole, the stage within the change process, or the therapy as a whole? What led up to the event, and what were its consequences?

- What is the significance of the event? What did it mean, in relation to the overall therapeutic goals of the client? How can the event be understood from a theoretical perspective?

- What are the conclusions that can be reached, from an analysis of this event? What has been learned? What are the implications of the analysis (e.g., for the therapist, for the conduct of therapy with this type of client)? What are the therapeutic principles that are highlighted by this event?

Once the answers to these key process questions have been identified, it may be helpful, in bringing together the different aspects of what has been found, to draw on a pre-existing theoretical framework. In other words, it is generally useful in analysing process to make a distinction between *observation* and *interpretation*. The first step is to describe, in as much detail as possible, what happened. Although any description or observation is to some extent shaped and guided by the underlying theoretical assumptions or conceptual language of the observer; nonetheless, it is still valuable to make an effort to 'bracket off' assumptions and see what is there.

In practice, there are two alternative techniques that can be helpful in organizing the material generated by a process analysis. The first is just to write a summary account of what happened during the event – the detailed 'story' of the event – and then in a separate section to work up the analysis and interpretation of the event. The second method is to divide the page into columns, with the transcript or descriptive account in the left-hand column and a commentary, or categorization of responses, in the right-hand column. With this method it can be helpful to number lines, so that any subsequent analysis or interpretation can refer back to what was said at specific points in the transcript.

Conclusions: making sense of process

Counselling process is really all about the *flow* of what happens in a therapy session. Most of this flow is probably beyond any conscious control, by either party, either because it occurs so quickly or because it is so multidimensional and complex. Yet this is the environment in which a counsellor must operate. It is no good (unless you are an old-style family therapist) asking the client to wait a minute while you leave the room to consult your colleagues about what to do next or run the video-tape back to check up on what was said or done. The value of understanding process is that it can sensitize counsellors to what may be happening, it can help them to *see*. Ivey (1995) has described counselling as an *intentional* activity. All of us have probably unwittingly learned during our lives some ways of being helpful and facilitative to other people. To be a good counsellor it is necessary to be able to extend this repertoire when necessary, to be aware of when to work harder at being empathic and when to move instead into collaborative problem-solving mode. Theories and models of process, and comprehensive process analyses, are all means of slowing down and stopping the flow of process long enough to gain an appreciation of what is involved in different courses of intentional action in relation to a client.

Topics for reflection and discussion

1 Looking back on your own experience as a client, or as someone being helped by another person in a less formal situation, can you identify particular *helpful* or *hindering* events? What were the main characteristics of these events that made them helpful or hindering?

2 In your view, is systematic assessment of clients necessary or useful? What might be some of the ways in which assessment might affect clients in terms of their motivation to participate in counselling?

3 Reflect on the different meanings that *ending* counselling might have for a client. How might the client be feeling about the ending? How might their behaviour change as the final session gets closer? How might the counsellor be acting and feeling? What might *not* be being said? How helpful would it be to bring the 'unsaid' into the conversation?

4 To what extent can the assimilation model be applied to all types of counselling? Is it a model that is most relevant to insight-oriented, exploratory approaches to counselling, such as psychodynamic and person-centred? Or is it equally relevant to CBT or family therapy?

5 How might a client's expectations affect the way they behave in counselling? What can a counsellor do to negotiate expectations with clients?

Suggested further reading

There is little to be said about the process of counselling that has not already been said by Carl Rogers in the 1950s and 1960s. Most people read 'A process conception of psychotherapy' in *On Becoming a Person* (Rogers 1961).

Part 4
Professional issues in counselling

The politics of counselling

Introduction

Counsellors and psychotherapists are generally considered to be members of society who enjoy prestige, status and respect. Most of the time, counselling takes place within a therapeutic space defined and dominated by the counsellor: the therapist is the one who knows the 'rules of the game'. Meanwhile, clients are by definition people in need, people who are vulnerable. This vulnerability is exacerbated when the client is a member of an oppressed or 'minority' group. The counselling encounter is therefore a situation that is characterized by potentially major differences in power. Yet for many practitioners and counselling agencies the goal of client positive *empowerment* lies at the heart of the counselling enterprise. How can this apparent tension be resolved? How can the power imbalance between client and counsellor be used to the advantage of the latter? What are the dynamics of power in the counselling room? This chapter focuses on the *politics* of counselling: the acceptance, understanding and respect afforded to diversity, and the ways in which political factors play a role in counselling practice.

Historically, the first wave of counselling approaches – psychodynamic, person-centred and cognitive–behavioural – paid little attention to issues of power in counselling. By contrast, more recently developed approaches – systemic, feminist, multicultural and narrative – have promoted an appreciation of the social role of counselling. The growing literature on ethical and moral issues in counselling (Chapter 22) reflects some of the efforts being made both within counselling itself and externally through the legal system, to regulate some of the potentially oppressive aspects of counselling. The question of power in counselling, and the notion that counselling is a social and political act, can therefore be understood as highlighting issues and themes found in other chapters in this book.

The chapter begins by mapping the contours of control and power within the counselling relationship. This is followed by an exploration of recent developments around the adoption of social justice and social advocacy as central values and objectives of counselling. Next, there is an exploration of the ways in which oppression and control operate within specific areas of counselling, focusing particularly on the domains of social class, sexual orientation, mental 'illness' and disability. The strategies that have been taken by counsellors to combat oppression and subjugation are considered. Finally, there is a brief account of the 'macro-politics' of counselling, in terms of the political landscape within which counselling organizations and professional associations are required to operate.

Box 21.1: *The political context of counselling: learning from extreme situations*

To understand the relationship between counselling and politics, it can be helpful to consider what happens in extreme situations. When a society is controlled by a totalitarian regime, it becomes very hard to do therapy. It is well known that many psychoanalysts were forced to flee from Nazi Germany because they were Jewish. What is less well known is that the psychotherapy that remained in Germany during the 1930s and 1940s was fatally compromised because clients and psychotherapists could not be honest with each other, for fear of being reported to the authorities for holding forbidden attitudes (Cocks 1997). Similar dilemmas have been reported by therapists working in the Soviet Union, Chile and Argentina, at the times when these societies were under totalitarian rule (Totton 2000). The Israeli psychotherapist Emanuel Berman (2006: 155), in reflecting on his struggle to oppose the impact of aggressive militarization on Israeli life, has reflected that:

> It is no coincidence that psychotherapy has developed in a democratic,
> pluralistic culture. Many of its basic assumptions are close to those of

democracy: the complex and paradoxical nature of human reality, which cannot be explained by an overriding single principle; the uniqueness of the experience of different individuals and different groups, which precludes the possibility of absolute truth; the power of words and verbal communication and resolving conflicts; the value of free choice and the difficulty of making it possible; the importance of attempting to 'step into the other's shoes' and taking his needs into account; the effort to avoid black-and-white thinking, drastic polarizations of good and evil and paranoid perceptions demonizing the other, individually or collectively.

By considering the role of counselling and psychotherapy in times of war and imposition of totalitarian rule it is possible to identify the extent to which genuine therapeutic relationships, and democratic egalitarian social life go hand in hand. The primary expansion of counselling and psychotherapy has occurred in North American and European post-World War II societies with strong democratic traditions and values.

The nature of social and interpersonal power

Politics is about power: who has control and who is in charge. It is no easy matter to understand the nature of interpersonal and social power. The concept of 'power' has many meanings, and is employed in different ways by different people. Nevertheless, it is perhaps useful to focus on three basic aspects of power as a phenomenon within social life:

- power differences are universal;
- power is socially constructed;
- power is a combination of individual and structural factors.

In drawing attention to these elements of power, it is important to acknowledge the existence of an extensive social science literature on this topic (see Dowding 2011), within which each of these themes has been articulated in great detail.

The idea that power differences comprise a universal feature of human social organization is supported by research findings from many different areas. The existence of status hierarchies or a 'pecking order' in animal groups has been reported in many ethological studies. It is harder to observe hierarchical structures in human social interaction, because of its greater complexity. Nevertheless, research into the social psychology of humans also overwhelmingly supports the notion that power differentials are an unavoidable feature of human social life.

However, although it might make sense to regard many of the status hierarchies observed in the animal world as determined by fairly simple genetic or biological mechanisms (e.g., size and strength), it is clear that in human groups power is socially constructed in complex ways. The power that a person is able to exert in a situation may depend on their gender, social class, ethnicity, age or role, or on combinations of these characteristics. The extent to which specific social attributes empower the individual is derived from the history of the social group concerned. For example, the oppression (disempowerment) of black people in Europe and North America can only be understood as the outcome of centuries of racism, which in turn can only be explained in terms of the religious beliefs and economic structures of Western society. Similarly, the oppression of lesbian, gay, bisexual and transgender persons, older people or physically disabled people can equally well be understood in a historical perspective.

One implication of the social and historical construction of oppression is the realization that power differences are not merely a matter of individual attitudes, but are embedded in actual social and institutional structures and practices. Power differences are not only 'in your head', but are 'out there'. This fact has been a problem for approaches to counselling based solely in psychology. Psychological perspectives on power and oppression attempt to explain racism, sexism and ageism in terms of factors such as attitudes, perceptions and individual psychopathology. In the real lives of people who seek counselling, by contrast, the experience of racism, sexism and ageism is a tangible component of everyday life. It happens. There is a physical side to interpersonal power. Being oppressed can involve violence, fear and hunger, or the threat of these things.

A person has the power to act in a certain way because he or she possesses authority within a social system. Most interpersonal power in everyday life is of this type. Within counselling and psychotherapy, by contrast, issues of power and control have been addressed by introducing the concept of *personal* power, for example the image of the therapist as being a 'powerful healer' or possessing a 'powerful presence'. The idea of personal power is described most clearly in some of the later writings of Carl Rogers. He regarded personal power as the reverse of authority power. First, in a personal relationship such as counselling or psychotherapy, the therapist *gives up* influence and control based in social structure and authority: 'the politics of the client-centered approach is a conscious renunciation or avoidance by the therapist of all control over, or decision-making for, the client. It is the facilitation of self-ownership by the client . . . it is politically centered in the client' (Rogers 1978: 14). Second, personal power involves developing a particular set of values and style of relating: the aim is to produce people who '. . . have a trust in their own experience and a profound distrust of all external authority' (p. 274). In other words, the sources of personal power come from within, rather than being drawn from external roles and statuses. Personal power depends on the capacity to be real, genuine and empathic. Rogers and many other counsellors regard themselves as 'quiet revolutionaries', and see their work as revolutionary and emancipatory. They see themselves as providing opportunities for clients to develop 'self-ownership', to make their own decision, to claim their own personal authority and voice. Ultimately, this is a form of power based in love rather than in fear.

There is no doubt a deep truth contained within the notion of personal power. However, there is also a deep contradiction. At the time that he wrote *On Personal Power*, at the age of 75, Carl Rogers was probably the most famous living psychologist in the world. During his career he had received all the honours that the American academic system could bestow. His books had sold in millions, and he was revered whenever he made a public appearance. Although Rogers did, by all accounts, have a powerful personal presence and positive, facilitative impact on the lives of those who knew him, he was also a person who possessed a huge amount of authority power. The sources of this authority power were clearly identifiable in the social system. He was a leader of a major professional group. He could claim the status of a successful scientist. His reputation and prestige were promoted and marketed by the publishing industry. Yet these factors were not included in his understanding of his own powerfulness as a person. In many ways Rogers was in an ideal position from which to reflect on these matters, but he could not recognize the social bases of much of his authority and influence. The fact that it was so difficult for him to appreciate the social, as well as the individual, dynamics of interpersonal power illustrates the extent to which social and political factors have been sidelined in the counselling and psychotherapy literature.

The institutionalization of power and oppression in counselling

The attempt by Rogers to depict counselling (or, at least, person-centred counselling) as a subversive activity that empowers clients to take charge of their own lives presents an attractive image of a set of values to which many counsellors would aspire. It can be argued, however, that there are a number of mechanisms of social control built into prevailing forms of counselling practice that are far from emancipatory or empowering in their effect. These mechanisms include:

- the language and concepts of counselling;
- acting as an agent of social control;
- control of space/territory/time;
- differential access to services;
- undermining existing systems of social support.

In Chapter 22, examples are discussed of specific types of oppressive or abusive events that can occur in counselling settings, such as sexual or financial exploitation of clients, or physical violence. These kinds of occurrences can be seen as being based in the more general power dynamics being discussed here. Although ethical codes and guidelines can often be effective in minimizing specific instances of mistreatment of clients, these more general issues to some extent lie beyond the remit of professional ethical codes, and are more correctly seen as intrinsic to the nature of counselling as it has developed over the past 50 years.

The language and concepts of counselling

Gergen (1990) has suggested that the way that counsellors and psychotherapists talk about their clients can be regarded as comprising a 'professionalized language of mental deficit'. He describes widely used therapeutic concepts such as 'impulsive personality', 'low self-esteem' or 'agoraphobia' as being 'invitations to infirmity', because they function in such a way that the person is identified with their 'problem'. The language of therapy, therefore, operates to:

> furnish the client a lesson in inferiority. The client is indirectly informed that he or she is ignorant, insensitive, or emotionally incapable of comprehending reality. In contrast, the therapist is positioned as the all-knowing and wise, a

model to which the client might aspire. The situation is all the more lamentable owing to the fact that in occupying the superior role, the therapist fails to reveal its weaknesses. Almost nowhere are the fragile foundations of the therapist's account made known; almost nowhere do the therapist's personal doubts, foibles, and failings come to light. And the client is thus confronted with a vision of human possibility that is unattainable as the heroism of cinematic mythology . . . each form of modernist therapy carries with it an image of the 'fully functioning' or 'good' individual; like a fashion plate, this image serves as a guiding model for the therapeutic outcome.

(Gergen 1990: 210)

The point being made by Gergen is that a language in which one person is characterized as a 'problem' and the other as 'problem-free' cannot help but be mirrored in the actual relationship between them. The inequality expressed in the language of counselling is carried over and acts as a 'guiding model' for the practice of counselling.

The language of counselling constitutes one of the means by which the power of a high-status professional group can be employed to control those who use their services. It is important to recognize that, here, the language of counselling and psychotherapy does not refer merely to technical terms and concepts found in textbooks, but is also reflected in the ways that counsellors speak to their clients in therapy sessions. Several studies of psychotherapeutic discourse (for example, Davis 1986; Madill and Doherty 1994; Madill and Barkham 1997) have revealed the subtle ways in which therapeutic conversation is shaped and directed by the therapist.

The counsellor as an agent of social control

One of the ways in which counsellors can exert power over their clients is by acting as agents of social control. Ideally, in most situations counsellors strive to be as 'client-centred' as possible, regarding themselves as acting solely on behalf of their client. There are some counselling settings, however, in which the approach taken by the counsellor or the attitude of the counsellor towards the client are defined and controlled in terms of external demands. Examples of these might include:

- working with drug or alcohol users referred by the court, with the explicit aim of eliminating their addiction;
- counselling sex offenders, to prevent them from re-offending;
- student counselling in a college where there is pressure on counsellors to maximize retention of students;
- workplace counselling where there is an expectation that clients who are absent from work on health grounds should return to work as soon as possible.

These are all instances where a counsellor might be expected by those who pay his or her salary to influence clients in a specific direction. In these situations the pressure may be fairly overt and explicit. In other cases, however, counsellors may find themselves responding to more subtle, covert social pressures.

The clearest examples of counsellors operating as agents of social control can be seen in the relationship between counselling and psychiatry. Psychiatrists have the power to impose custodial, compulsory treatment on people who are assessed as being at risk to themselves or to others. From a medical perspective, such a decision can be seen as a helpful response to illness and crisis. From a sociological perspective it can be seen as a means of control. People who cause trouble are locked up, or are forced to take drugs that control their behaviour. Counsellors who refer patients to psychiatrists are agents of a system that, in extreme cases, can make use of significant state powers (laws, police) to lock people up.

It has been argued by the radical psychoanalyst Thomas Szasz (1961, 1971, 1974, 1978) that any involvement whatsoever by counsellors and psychotherapists in the institutions of social control (which for him would include the medical system and social services) makes meaningful therapy impossible. Szasz contends that true therapy is only possible under conditions of absolute voluntary participation by a client paying for the services of a therapist. Hurvitz (1973) goes further, and argues that the theories and concepts of therapy represent an ideological position that serves to individualize social issues and subvert social action to address these issues. Hurvitz (1973: 234) contended that:

> . . . therapeutic ideology identifies success with personal worth and failure with one's own inherent limitations. . . . Psychotherapists tend to treat middle- and upper-class members who are dissatisfied with their place and achievement within the social system, but not with the system itself . . . They foster their clients' belief that they can live fulfilling lives without making basic social changes.

This kind of critique of counselling and psychotherapy was strongly influenced by the social unrest and radical political movements of the late 1960s and early 1970s. One of the leading voices in this movement was Russell Jacoby, who described counsellors and psychotherapists as suffering from a form of 'social amnesia' (Jacoby 1975) through which they were able to blank out any awareness of the power of social institutions to control the lives of their clients. Although this overt radicalism has faded as counselling has become more established within society, it is impossible to deny that these arguments retain their relevance in the context of many aspects of contemporary theory and practice.

Box 21.2: *Counselling in a 'surveillance society'*

One of the defining characteristics of the contemporary social world, according to many sociologists and political scientists, is the extent to which we live in a 'surveillance society' (Lyon 2007). Sophisticated surveillance technology, such as CCTV and the use of biometric data, came to be widely used in the 1980s and their adoption was then further reinforced by the fear of terrorism evoked by 9/11 and similar events. At some level, all counsellors participate in surveillance through the duty to report to the relevant authorities when a client exhibits a risk of harming others. In some instances, the surveillance role of counsellors is much more explicit. Moore (2011) observed the operation of 'drug treatment courts' in Canada, in which drug offenders were mandated to receive counselling, in conjunction with regular attendance at court to monitor their compliance. Failure to attend counselling, or court, or violation of the treatment contract, could result in a prison sentence. The information presented to the court consisted not only of factual records of participation in therapy. Instead, 'therapeutic surveillance is personal. . . . it is built on relationships and intimate knowledge of those being watched' (Moore 2011: 259). This kind of relationship between counsellors and the justice system raises many issues. At one level, it is intended to be benevolent, and undoubtedly does function in many instances in a caring and facilitative manner. On the other hand, it can obviously lead to situations where a client will choose to conceal information from their counsellor, and it places demands on the counsellor in respect of maintaining a balance between working for the client, and working for the court. The growing pervasiveness of surveillance systems in contemporary life means that counsellors may need to become more aware of the sensitivities of clients whose lives have been affected by such practices, or who may fear the possibility of such damage occurring in the future.

Control of space, territory and time

One of the most significant, but least mentioned, aspects of the politics of counselling concerns the practicalities of the typical counselling interview: where and when it happens, and how long it lasts. Counselling usually takes place on the counsellor's territory, in their office. The counsellor or a receptionist will often meet the client in a waiting area, and escort them to the counselling room. Appointments are usually made for 50-minute or 1-hour sessions every week. All of these factors are for the convenience of the counsellor or counselling agency, and are not necessarily what the user might wish, if given the choice. For example, telephone or e-mail counselling (see Chapter 23) is attractive to many people because they can contact the counsellor or counselling service at the time of their choosing, and finish the counselling session at the point where they feel they have had enough. The number of sessions that a client will receive is also often controlled by the agency. In some agencies, there can be a limit of six or eight sessions, regardless of the needs or preferences of clients. In other agencies it is made clear to clients at the time of assessment that they will only be accepted if they make a contract for long-term therapy lasting for a year or more.

Differential access to services

Even if a counselling agency, or counsellor in private practice, is able to carry out counselling in a rigorously empowering or non-oppressive manner, their work could still be regarded as contributing to political inequality if their client group was drawn from only relatively privileged members of the community. It seems fairly clear that access to counselling services is highly correlated with various indices of social power and status. There exists only the most meagre literature, or training opportunities, in relation to counselling with people with learning disabilities or physical disabilities, older people or people labelled as severely mentally ill. Although counselling services for members of ethnic minorities, gays, lesbians and religiously committed persons have improved in recent years, it is still the case that most mainstream counselling services are staffed by white, middle-class, heterosexual, non-disabled people who attract clients with similar social characteristics. In one piece of research into access to counselling services, Crouan (1994) traced the ethnic, geographical, gender and economic circumstances of a group of 97 clients who had used a British inner-city voluntary counselling agency. She found that, despite the location of the agency near a deprived area of the city, and despite its stated mission to meet the needs of the disadvantaged, the vast majority of clients were affluent white women. In addition, black and Chinese clients who did use the agency were more likely to drop out of counselling within the first few sessions. Similar findings were reported in a more recent study, by Self *et al.* (2005) (described below).

Undermining existing support structures

Research carried by Masson (1984, 1988, 1992) has uncovered a long list of examples of oppressive and abusive practice perpetrated by some of the leading members of the psychotherapy profession. Masson (1988: 24) concludes from this evidence that 'the very idea of psychotherapy is wrong', and goes on to assert that 'the structure of psychotherapy is such that no matter how kindly a person is, when that person becomes a therapist, he or she is engaged in acts that are bound to diminish the dignity, autonomy, and freedom of the person who comes for help'. Masson argues that what is wrong with therapy (and, by implication, counselling too) is that the client is offered a relationship that may appear to be a friendship, in that he or she is encouraged to share his or her closest secrets and feelings, but that is in reality a false friendship. The relationship between therapist and client, Masson points out, is a professional one, based on an inequality in power. The attempt to maintain a quasi-friendship in such conditions is, he suggests, in the end false and destructive for both therapist and client. He proposes that 'what we need are more kindly friends and fewer professionals' (Masson 1988: 30). Along similar lines, Kitzinger and Perkins (1993) have argued that:

> In seeking out the pseudo-friendship of a therapist, we run the risk of destroying our capacity for genuine. . . . friendships. Therapy offers us a let-out clause. With the institutionalization of therapy, we cease to expect to have to deal with each other's distress: it is consigned to the private realm of therapy. This deprives our communities of a whole realm of experience, deprives us of the strength and ability to support each other, and deprives us of understanding the context and meaning of our distress. Therapy privatizes pain and severs connections between us, replacing friendship in community with the private therapist–client relationship.
>
> (Kitzinger and Perkins 1993: 88)

It is not difficult to identify areas of social life in which long-established support structures and healing rituals have been undermined or replaced by professional counselling. For example, communities have always been able to draw on shared understandings of how to respond to bereavement, such as laying out the body to be viewed by visitors, wearing particular clothing for a period of time and communal remembrance. These practices enable an appreciation of how to make sense of death to be handed down to younger generations. In many sectors of contemporary society, these rituals and practices have been eroded and forgotten. Instead, those who are troubled by their loss may attend bereavement counselling. Although bereavement counselling can certainly be helpful for many clients, there seems little doubt that it contributes to the 'severing of connections' and 'privatization of pain' described by Kitzinger and Perkins (1993).

Social justice as a central aim of counselling

The politics of counselling have been discussed here in terms of a range of factors: language, control of time and space, surveillance, access and undermining existing support structures. These issues represent a serious and profound challenge to counselling and counsellors. In terms of formulating a strategy for responding to these challenges, and findings ways of acknowledging and working constructively with the underlying political dimension of counselling, an important lead has been taken by the Counselling Psychology Division of the American Psychological Association, and the American Counselling Association. Over the past decade, these professional communities in the USA have been in the vanguard of promoting *social justice* as a core value and goal of counselling. These initiatives have encompassed the formulation of position statements and dialogues around the nature and meaning of social justice work (Aldarondo 2007; Kiselica and Robinson 2001; Lewis 2011; Ratts 2009; Smith *et al.* 2009), the development of appropriate training in this area (Goodman *et al.* 2004; Lewis, Toporek and Ratts 2010; Weintraub and Goodman 2010), and research into the processes and outcomes of counselling that is informed by social justice principles (Erhard and Sinai 2012; Goodman *et al.* 2009; Singh *et al.* 2010; Smith *et al.* 2012).

The key principles of social justice-oriented counselling, that have emerged from the recent American literature, can be divided into two broad areas. First, the counsellor needs to develop a specific position or stance in relation to his or her work with clients, characterized by a set of core competencies (Goodman *et al.* 2004): *ongoing self-examination* of the counsellor's own knowledge, awareness and attitudes around social inequality; *sharing power* with clients and working in a collaborative manner that builds on client strengths; *facilitating consciousness-raising* in clients, to allow personal issues to be viewed in their social, political and historical context; and *leaving clients with the tools for social change*. An illustration of how these principles can be applied in practice can be found in Box 21.3. The other key domain of social justice counselling involves active *advocacy* on behalf of the needs and interests of client groups, or of individual clients within specific organizational contexts. An example of what advocacy work might mean in practice is described by Stotts and Ramey (2009). In a discussion of how counsellors might respond to the issue of human trafficking, Stotts and Ramey (2009) propose that counsellors need to become sensitized to the nature of modern slavery, be open to the possibility that some clients may have been victims of trafficking, and appreciate the ways in which individuals may be affected by these activities. However, they also suggest that counsellors should be willing to name this issue within the counselling room, but also use their position to enhance awareness of it within the communities that they serve. For instance, a schools counsellor could talk to young people about the risks of being lured into prostitution.

It is important to acknowledge the value of these developments within the North American counselling community, as an example of a coherent and research-informed approach to politically aware counselling. However, it is also essential to be willing to learn from similar initiatives that have taken place in other countries. In the UK, for example, Holland (1990) developed a form of 'social action therapy', in the context of a community-based project in which individuals could be involved in different roles. Holland (1990) argued that persons who are socially oppressed are often labelled as patients, and are allocated to forms of treatment, such as behaviour therapy or psycho-pharmacology, that can be viewed as essentially constituting forms of social control and as 'functionalist' in character. She suggested that it is necessary to help such a person to move to a position of accepting their own personal self, that they are indeed a worthwhile individual and that what has happened in their life has some meaning. This can be achieved by means of individual counselling or psychotherapy.

However, the limitation of individual counselling is that it does not offer a good arena for exploring sociopolitical issues, so within the project described by Holland (1990), there were opportunities for service users to participate in groups where they could uncover their shared, collective histories and make sense of their individual experiences within a social and cultural context. This stage drew on ideas of radical humanism, encouraging participants to encounter each other and free up their energies and desires. Finally, participants had the possibility of then working together to make demands on social institutions to gain access to resources that could make a difference to their lives.

Other examples of ways of working that bring together counselling skills and relationships, and social action, can be found in the work of narrative therapists (for example, Denborough et al. 2008; Waldegrave et al. 2003) and feminist therapists (see Chapter 14). Within the area of social advocacy, it is possible to find historical examples of situations in which counsellors and psychotherapists spoke out about issues. For instance, Freud was instrumental in contributing to resistance against nationalist militaristic treatment of shell-shocked Austrian soldiers in World War I (Brunner 2000), and Carl Rogers was a leading figure among psychologists in the USA who sought to humanize the treatment of traumatized military personnel in the years following World War II.

The extent to which a social justice stance is already evident in the everyday work of counsellors is reinforced by the findings of a survey of schools counsellors in Israel, conducted by Erhard and Sinai (2012). The majority of the counsellors who completed a survey questionnaire reported that around half of their time allocation was devoted to working with disadvantaged students, and that they perceived themselves as having a leadership and advocacy role in relation to promoting changes in their school, and in wider society as a whole, that would advance the academic and social status of disadvantaged students.

Box 21.3: *Social justice counselling in action: the* Reaching Out About Depression *project*

One of the most thoroughly reported and researched social justice counselling initiatives is the *Reaching Out About Depression* (ROAD) programme, which has operated in a number of urban communities in some eastern states in the USA (Goodman *et al.* 2004, 2009; Weintraub and Goodman 2010). The aim of the project has been to support low-income women with self-identified symptoms of depression. The programme comprises two stages. First, women participate in a series of workshops on topics related to depression and poverty. These workshops are run by women from within the community, and participants are eligible to train as facilitators for subsequent workshops. Second, participants are paired up with counselling students, who have received brief training in a feminist relational model of counselling (Goodman *et al.* 2004) and who act as 'advocates' for the depressed women who are seeking support. The advocacy partnership that ensues incorporates both practical support (e.g., helping a partner to complain to a landlord) and emotional/psychological (e.g., making sense of self-destructive patterns of behaviour). The advocate and partner meet for four to six hours each week over nine months, and the advocate receives regular supervision throughout this period.

Interviews with women who had been helped by the project (Goodman *et al.*2009) and counselling students who had served as advocates (Weintraub and Goodman 2010) indicated that offering a counselling relationship in the context of more practical forms of help was effective:

> . . . in addition to reporting concrete improvements (e.g., heating fixed), participants spoke eloquently about subtle shifts in their perceptions of themselves over the course of the advocacy process. Over time, they began to see themselves as deserving fair treatment, as being entitled to services and well-being, and as feeling able to act on the world effectively. Indeed, working with an advocate not only helped some participants feel better able to advocate for others but advocate more effectively for themselves.
>
> (Goodman *et al.* 2009: 869)

At the same time, it was clear that the advocate–partner relationship could be challenging on both sides. The role of counsellor–advocate required being able to face up to challenging real-world conflict. Being a partner called for a willingness to ask for and receive help, which was hard for many women whose previous life experience led them to have low expectations that professional helpers would take them, and their needs, seriously.

Counselling people from disadvantaged, marginalized and stigmatized groups

Earlier sections in this chapter have offered an introduction to some ways of making sense of political dimensions of the process of counselling. The following sections begin to examine how these factors are manifest in counselling with specific client groups. There are a wide range of disadvantaged, marginalized and stigmatized client groups that might have been discussed, including older people, immigrant and exile groups, people in prison and those who espouse minority religious beliefs but for reasons of space it is not possible to include coverage of all these groups. Instead, the following paragraphs explore the counselling issues and challenges that are associated with four specific client populations: economically disadvantaged people; gay, lesbian, bisexual and transgender people; people with disabilities; and people with mental health difficulties. When reading these accounts, it is important to keep in mind that categorizing a counselling client as 'homeless', 'gay', or 'schizophrenic' runs the risk of highlighting one facet of a person's identity at the expense of other facets that may be equally (or more) important to their sense of who they are and where they fit in the world. Nevertheless, these categories do possess some currency and leverage at a social and political level, and can function as ways of opening up conversations that are valuable and necessary for the counselling profession.

Counselling, social class, social status and poverty

Research in the USA, reviewed by Bromley (1983) and Garfield (1986), found that counselling and psychotherapy services are most widely used by people in middle- and upper-income and social class groups, either because others do not seek therapy or because when they do seek therapy they are more likely to be refused or offered drug treatment. These early studies also found that lower-class clients are also more likely to drop out of counselling prematurely. This pattern seems to be confirmed by contemporary research. For example, a study carried out by Self et al. (2005), into the attendance patterns of patients referred for psychotherapy in UK NHS clinics in a region of the north of England, found that clients who lived in neighbourhoods of high social deprivation were more likely to fail to attend their first appointment, and to quit therapy before their fifth session, compared with clients from more prosperous localities. On the other hand, Self et al. (2005) also found that there was no difference in attendance or benefit reported by working-class and middle-class clients who stayed in therapy beyond five sessions. The results of the Self et al. (2005) study illustrate what is perhaps the central issue in relation to the role of counselling with people who are economically disadvantaged – although therapy can be potentially beneficial, there are barriers to engagement in the therapy process.

Although the topic of social class and counselling has received little attention within the counselling and psychotherapy literature as a whole, there are some signs of a renewal of interest in this area (Krupnick and Melnikoff 2012; Smith 2005). The main themes within this reappraisal of the significance for counselling of factors such as social class and economic hardship are highlighted in an important set of recent research studies. Smith et al. (2011) carried out a quasi-experimental study in a large number (200) of students on a counselling training programme who were asked to read a package of information about a new client, and then respond to some questions regarding their views on how therapy might proceed with this client. The information package was the same for all participants, except for the fact that for half of the sample, the client was described as middle class, and in the other half the client was described as working class. The students who believed that the client was working class predicted that therapeutic progress would be slower and more difficult, compared to the ratings made by students who had been informed that the client was middle class.

Three studies have explored the experiences of clients in relation to working with a client from a different social class background. Balmforth (2006) interviewed working-class clients about their experiences of seeing therapists who they perceived as being upper or middle class. Many of these clients reported that they had felt uncomfortable, inferior and misunderstood, unable to form a productive relationship with their therapist, and unable to talk about these difficulties. A similar study by Thompson *et al.* (2012) found that low-income clients believed that their therapist just did not 'get it' in respect of the realities of economic and social disadvantage. However, this study also described some positive examples of middle-class therapists building productive therapeutic relationships with their low-income clients. Cormack (2009) interviewed homeless young people about their experiences of counselling and found that most of them were extremely negative about the help they had been offered. These young people described themselves as unwilling to trust their counsellor and experiencing themselves as 'trapped' in the counselling room.

Two studies have examined therapist experiences of working with clients from different social class backgrounds (Ballinger and Wright 2007; Ryan 2006). These studies indicate that counsellors are often aware of difficulties associated with social class barriers, but that their training and supervision have not sufficiently prepared them to address these issues. In reflecting on her research, Ryan (2006: 59–60) observed that:

> . . . my own experience of conducting these interviews was frequently of opening up a hidden subject, about which most of the interviewees had many thoughts and concerns, but with little or no framework for articulation or discussion. . . . The powerful, persistent and far-reaching psychic effects of class were evident in how many of the therapists understood both themselves and their patients; as one said: 'Class is in you'.

There were two broad patterns that emerged in the Ryan's (2006) study. Working-class therapists, with middle-class clients, had a sense of being a target of contempt, and described fears of inferiority and humiliation. They described their middle-class clients as engaged in the 'use of class as a defence, to create an illusion of superiority and false confidence, warding off fears of failure and inadequacy'(p. 60). By contrast, middle-class therapists, paired with working-class clients, were aware of an underlying sense of guilt, arising from privilege, and an inhibition around exploring certain topics in case they triggered 'class-based anger' on the part of their clients.

How can we make sense of these themes? Most counsellors and psychotherapists are middle class, and have undergone several years of professional education and training. Their worldviews, personal values and ways of using language are quite different from those of working-class clients. To some extent, the existence of social class issues in counselling can be regarded as an example of working with difference, or building meaning bridges and possibilities for connection across cultures (see Chapter 13). Arsenian and Arsenian (1948) suggested that it is necessary for therapists to grasp the difference between 'tough' and 'easy' cultures. In a 'tough' social environment, people have fewer options open for satisfying their needs, those options that are available do not reliably lead to desired outcomes and the link between action and goal achievement can be difficult to identify. Living in such a culture results in feelings of frustration and low self-esteem. The lack of positive expectations for the future and belief in the efficacy of personal action resulting from socialization in a tough culture would make counselling more difficult.

Meltzer (1978) has argued that social class differences in psychotherapy are as a result of linguistic factors. Research carried out by Bernstein (1972) found that communication in working-class cultures took place through a 'restricted' code, which is largely limited to describing concrete, here-and-now events rather than engaging in reflexive, abstract thought. The implication for counselling of this linguistic theory is that working-class language does not lend itself to 'insight' or exploratory therapies, and that clients from this group would be better served by behaviour therapy or family therapy (Bromley 1983).

It is necessary to treat these analyses of working-class culture, personality and communication style with considerable caution. The characteristics that are interpreted as deficits of working-class culture can equally well be seen as assets. For example, middle-class people who grow up in an 'easy' culture can become narcissistic and self-absorbed. Similarly, the capacity of middle-class people to engage in abstract intellectualization, rather than describing their concrete experience, is viewed by many counsellors as a barrier to effective work. It may be more correct to regard these ideas as indicative of potential areas of mismatch between working-class clients and their (predominantly) middle-class counsellors.

There is a further aspect of social class that is highlighted in recent research, particularly in the study by Ryan (2006): the experience of status difference. It makes sense, up to a point, to regard working-class and middle-class individuals as existing in separate cultural worlds. But it is also the case that these individuals actually exist in the same cultural world, and possess different levels of status within that world. Status is not merely a matter of 'difference' (not the same but equally valuable). Status implies that one group is 'better' than the other group in some sense. There has been a substantial amount of research in the field of health outcomes that demonstrates that societies with higher levels of economic inequality (e.g., USA) are more likely to report higher levels of physical and mental health problems in citizens, compared with societies with lower levels of inequality (e.g., Cuba, Sweden). Health outcomes do not depend, to such an extent, on average income levels or gross national productivity. Instead, health (including mental health) depends on how the national cake is divided (Marmot 2004; Wilkinson and Pickett 2010).

A study by Gilbert *et al.* (2009) begins to illustrate the way in which inequality is linked to emotional problems. In a study of people who were depressed, Gilbert *et al.* (2009) found that when people are aware of being subordinate, or losers, in a clearly defined hierarchy, they experience a fear of rejection that increases vulnerability to depression, anxiety and stress. This pattern holds for anyone at any level of a status hierarchy. Further examples of ways in which inequality and the fear of being a social 'loser' can impact on emotional well-being can be found in James (2010). The research by Ryan (2006) into therapist experiences of working with clients from different social backgrounds seems to indicate that the therapy relationship represents a microcosm within which painful class-based emotions, such as jealousy and contempt, can be triggered. The research by Smith *et al.* (2011) that showed unconscious, irrational and instant class-based rejection of clients can be understood as confirming that these feelings can be triggered by even the slightest of class-based cues. In this respect, it is relevant to note that, in her study *Therapy in the Ghetto*, Lener (1972) found a strong relationship between client improvement and 'democratic attitudes' in their therapists. The effective therapists in this study were those who were able to reach out across the class divide and accept their clients, and were willing to be proactive in acknowledging potential class-based dynamics in the therapy relationship.

Box 21.4: *Being homeless as a counselling issue*

The experience of being homeless, and its implication in relation to counselling, have been sensitively explored by Bentley (1994, 1997). In a series of interviews with homeless people in London, Bentley (1997) found a number of recurring themes. These homeless people perceived themselves as outsiders, invisible and unseen, 'a freak show on the streets'. Maintaining existence was a constant struggle. The daily threat of theft of possessions and the difficulty of accessing food and finding a quiet safe place to sleep were key issues. There was also a strong sense of helplessness and hopelessness. Bentley (1994) suggests that these factors make it very difficult for homeless people to commit themselves to counselling. She recounts the story of Ben, a formerly homeless man with drink and violence problems who had been resettled. His reason for accepting the offer of counselling was that 'otherwise I won't talk to anyone from one end of the week to the next'. Bentley (1994: 134) writes that:

> he continually punctuated his speech with phrases like 'I bet you're sick of me' or 'you don't have to listen to this. Do you want me to go now?' and would mask his vulnerability by cruelly mocking himself . . . On our fourth meeting he came to the session looking vibrant and alive. He announced that he'd 'given up', he'd begun drinking . . . and felt free of the pressures to master his life. He announced that I'd never have to see him again.

However, the counsellor's statement at this point that she would be willing to see him again had a deep effect on him, by letting him know that someone valued him. After a couple of weeks he resumed counselling.

Bentley (1994, 1997) suggests that effective counselling with homeless people requires either that the client has previously been found some kind of accommodation or that a 'pre-therapeutic' relationship be established first of all with a hostel or outreach worker.

A final dimension of social class that is not sufficiently acknowledge within counselling theory and training is the impact on people of lack of money, poor housing conditions, lack of work or absorption in exhausting, low-paid and degrading work. For example, there is considerable evidence that the loss of employment can have a significant negative impact on mental health and well-being, and for unemployed people, gaining employment can reduce symptoms of anxiety and depression (Allen 1999; Fryer and Fagan 2003; Murphy andAthanasou 1999). A review of research into the psychological effects of unemployment, carried out by Murphy andAthanasou (1999), suggests that, for someone who is unemployed, the effect of gaining a job is broadly equivalent to the effect of receiving therapy. There is some evidence that counselling is less effective with people who are unemployed, compared to those who are in work but in low-wage jobs (McLeod *et al.* 2000; Saxon *et al.* 2008). This is probably because being in work gives a person more opportunities to practice new behaviours (e.g., with work colleagues) that are discussed in counselling sessions. Similarly, living in a damp or overcrowded housing, having a poor diet, having no access to cultural life, and having little hope for the future, is likely to make most people feel depressed.

It is evident that there does not exist a coherent body of theory and research on the psychotherapeutic issues associated with either negative aspects of working-class life, such as lack of money, poor housing conditions or homelessness, job insecurity and unsatisfying work, and powerlessness, or positive aspects such as solidarity, direct language and family cohesiveness. It would seem that counsellors and psychotherapists have tended to regard working-class people as being primarily in need of practical help, such as social work, legal advice or debt counselling. Following Maslow, therapy is for those whose needs for security and safety have already been fulfilled. Storck (2002) suggests that a set of unhelpful myths have developed, within the counselling and psychotherapy professions, regarding the lack of interest in therapy in people from economically disadvantaged groups, and the difficulties involved in working with clients from these backgrounds. It is very hard to justify this state of affairs on either moral or pragmatic grounds. The seeds of a model of class-sensitive counselling practice are there, in the writings of Allen (1999), Freire *et al.* (2006), Hannon *et al.* (2001), Holland (1979, 1990), Kearney (1996) and many others. It is possible to integrate these ideas into training and practice, as a basis for a coherent and research-informed approach to working constructively in counselling with issues of social class and economic disadvantage.

Counselling with lesbian, gay, bisexual and transgender clients

The social world in which counselling has developed over the past century is a world marked by a high degree of homophobia. Many societies enforce laws that restrict or criminalize homosexual behaviour, and there is widespread stigmatization of gay and lesbian relationships even in societies where such behaviour is legal, despite the fact that around 10 per cent of the population is homosexual. Although gay and lesbian clients in counselling will seek help for the same wide range of general relationship, self-esteem and stress problems felt by heterosexual people, there are some distinctive issues that may be presented by clients from this group. These include dilemmas and anxieties about the process of 'coming out' and accepting a gay or lesbian identity. There may be additional problems for the heterosexual counsellor of being aware of his or her own possible homo-phobia, and achieving an understanding of the language and norms of gay and lesbian subcultures.

In recent years, the term 'LGBT' (lesbian, gay, bisexual, transgender) has become widely used as a term for categorizing individuals who do not espouse conventional heterosexual relationships. This terminology is valuable in acting as a reminder that, although there exists a substantial proportion of the population who are gay or lesbian, there are also people who represent different patterns of marginalized sexuality, for example being bisexual or transgender. In addition, some writers and commentators add the concept of 'queer' to this list (so that it becomes 'LGBTQ'). The re-appropriation by the gay community (and others) of the word 'queer' reflects an intentional act of political resistance to a dominant 'heteronormative' society. The concept of 'queer-ness' encom-passes all forms of 'deviant' sexuality, from bondage to asexuality. As a means of avoiding overcomplexity, the discussion within the present section will focus on counselling with people who are gay and lesbian. However, it is important to keep in mind that other forms of marginalized sexual identity do exist.

Many lesbian and gay counselling agencies have been set up to offer telephone or face-to-face counselling and self-help support networks. This trend has been motivated in part by the hostility to homosexuals shown by the mental health profession. It was only in 1974 that homosexuality ceased being classified as a psychiatric disorder by the American Psychiatric Association (Bayer 1987). The considerable opposition to this change included psychoanalysts and psychotherapists as well as 'medical model' psychiatrists. The founder of rational emotive therapy (REM), Albert Ellis, was also in the 1950s a proponent of the view that exclusive homosexuality was a neurotic disorder that could be resolved through effective psychotherapy (Bayer 1987). Mainstream counselling research, training and practice largely ignore the existence or needs of non-heterosexual clients. For example, in a survey of articles published between 1978 and 1989 in the six most widely read and prestigious counselling psychology journals, Buhrke et al. (1992) found that out of a total of 6,661 articles and reports, only 43 (0.65 per cent) focused on lesbian and gay issues in any way. The majority of these articles were theoretical discussions or reviews of the litera-ture, rather than empirical studies of counselling process or outcome. Over one-third of the articles over this 12-year period had appeared in one special issue of the *Journal of Counseling and Development* (Dworkin and Gutierrez 1989). It is clear that even research articles that are published can be written in an anti-homosexual manner. As recently as 1991, the American Psychological Association found it necessary to publish guidelines for 'avoiding heterosexist bias' in research (Herek et al. 1991).

Singh and Shelton (2011) suggest that it is particularly important to publish qualitative research into the lived experience of therapy clients who are gay, lesbian, bisexual, trans-gender and queer, as a way of allowing their voices to be heard within the literature. In a recent survey of leading counselling journals in the USA they found that only around one such article was being published each year. In a systematic review of research into affirma-tive therapy with LGBT clients, King et al. (2007) were able to identify 22 good-quality studies.

Counsellors working with gay men, lesbians and bisexual people have evolved an 'affirmative' (Hall and Fradkin 1992; Davies 1996; Walsh and Hope 2010) stance towards the problems presented by their clients, informed by the values and practices of the person-centred approach to counselling (Lemoire and Chen 2006). A key element in the approach is to reinforce the validity and acceptability of homosexual behaviour and relationships, and to celebrate the possibilities of same-sex relationships. To accomplish this, it is often necessary to challenge the homophobic attitudes that the client has internalized through socialization. The provision of accurate information about homosexuality can often be a part of this process, as can sensitive rehearsal with the counsellor of how the client will tell others about his or her decision to come out.

Many counsellors working with gay and lesbian clients adopt a developmental approach, viewing the experience of 'coming out' as a set of developmental tasks. The model of coming out constructed by Coleman (1982) has been widely utilized in counselling. Coleman (1982) postulates five developmental stages in the coming-out process: pre-coming out, coming out, exploration, first relationships and integration. Other issues that are often present in counselling gay and lesbian clients include: the traumatizing effects of exposure to homophobic attitudes, behaviour and violence; internalized homophobia; family conflicts; sexual problems; attitudes to ageing; and coping with AIDS/HIV. An important theme within this literature is the idea that effective therapy requires social empowerment, in addition to work on individual issues (Savage et al. 2005). Recent developments in theory, research and practice in counselling for lesbian and gay clients are discussed by Kort (2008), Langdridge (2007) and Moon (2008). The result of the 'gay affirmative' movement in counselling is that there exists a body of literature that can enable counsellors to work creatively with homosexual clients, in contrast to the situation in the 1960s and even 1970s where most of the published theory and research functioned to pathologize members of this group. There is evidence that LGBT people are more likely than heterosexual people to make use of therapy during their lifetime (Eubanks-Carter et al. 2005).

The field of counselling and psychotherapy in relation to sexual orientation has clearly advanced substantially since the times when homosexuality was regarded as an illness to be cured. However, the existence of problems as well as progress can be seen in a series of research studies carried out by Liddle (1995, 1996, 1997). In these studies, carried out in the USA, she found that a group of counselling trainees presented with a case vignette that described the client as either heterosexual or lesbian were just as likely to give high likeability ratings to the latter (Liddle 1995). In a large-scale survey of lesbian and gay male clients of counselling and psychotherapy, she found that the majority of those who answered the questionnaire reported themselves to be generally satisfied with the therapy they had received, even when it was delivered by a heterosexual therapist (Liddle 1996), and that lesbian and gay people were likely to stay in therapy longer than a matched sample of heterosexual clients.

These results suggest that the counselling profession may have overcome its earlier prejudices about homosexuality, leading to a greater trust of therapists on the part of gay and lesbian users. However, other aspects of the data collected by Liddle (1995, 1996, 1997) suggest that significant problems remain. When the sample of trainee counsellors in the Liddle (1995) study was divided into male and female subgroups, it became apparent that the women trainees liked and admired the lesbian client more than the heterosexual client, whereas the result for the male trainees was the opposite: they were less likely to accept the lesbian client.

In the Liddle (1996) study, even though the therapy experiences of the gay and lesbian clients was positive overall, there were still a significant minority who stated that their therapist pressurized them to renounce their homosexuality, or even terminated therapy once the client had disclosed their sexual orientation. Liddle (1997) observed that 63 per cent of gay and lesbian clients screened their therapist for gay-affirmative attitudes before committing themselves to therapy, and that the majority had a strong preference for a therapist with a similar sexual orientation. The therapy preferences of lesbian and gay clients have also been explored in research by Burckell and Goldfried (2006) and Jones *et al.* (2003), which confirms the value of an 'affirmative' stance on the part of therapists, and the destructive impact of therapist attitudes and practices that are based in a pathology model.

Research conducted by Liddle (1995, 1996, 1997), Annesley and Coyle (1998), Evans and Barker (2010) and Ryden and Loewenthal (2001) suggests that many gay and lesbian consumers of therapy are aware that they need to be careful about which therapist they choose. There is still a significant amount of anti-homosexual sentiment and behaviour around among heterosexual counsellors and psychotherapists (Shelton and Delgado-Romero 2011), and in counselling and psychotherapy training (Coyle *et al.* 1999). Eubanks-Carter *et al.* (2005) believe that, even though recent campaigns by professional associations and LGBT groups have resulted in lower levels of overt discrimination against LGBT clients, there still exists a 'subtle bias against non-heterosexual feelings and behaviours' (p.11) on the part of many therapists. There is also evidence of heterosexist bias in some counselling agencies (Matthews *et al.* 2005). Further information on current research and practice guidelines in relation to counselling with LGBT clients can be found in Pachankis and Goldfried (2004), Eubanks-Carter *et al.* (2005), King *et al.* (2007) and Butler *et al.* (2009). Recommended further reading, for anyone new to this topic, remains the 'Pink Therapy' trilogy (Davies and Neal 1996, 2000; Neal and Davies 2000).

It is of course essential to avoid assumptions that there exists a single coherent or unified LGBT experience or community, and that all lesbian, gay, bisexual or transgender clients will have the same needs. Same-sex orientation and gender change interact with ethnicity, social class, age and personal circumstances, in a wide range of ways. An important emerging area for theory, research and practice in counselling is concerned with the ways in which the significance of 'intersecting identities' may not be sufficiently acknowledged in therapy (das Nair and Butler 2012). Highly recommended, as an accessible, brief and moving introduction to the issues explored in this section, is a paper by an American gay therapist, Douglas Haldeman (2010) in which he reflects on the experiences over the course of his career as a gay practitioner.

Counselling with lesbian and gay clients probably represents the field of therapy with the most hard-edged political dimension. There are deep divisions within most societies concerning the acceptability of sexual behaviour that diverges from conventional heterosexual patterns. These are not divisions of relative indifference, but instead reflect the whole range from active celebration to violent persecution. There have been, and still are, counsellors and psychotherapists who make a living by promising to 'cure' people of their homosexual desires. An important study by Beckstead and Morrow (2004), into the experiences of 42 men and women in Utah, USA (a strongly religious community) who had undergone 'conversion therapy', and the ensuing debate (Gonsiorek 2004; Haldeman

2004; Miville and Ferguson 2004; Morrow *et al.* 2004; Phillips 2004; Worthington 2004), illustrate some of the complexities of this issue. Beckstead and Morrow (2004) found that none of the participants in their study reported that their basic pattern of social desire had been changed as a result of therapy. On the other hand, about half of the participants regarded their therapy as having been useful for them, in enabling them to accept a hetero-sexual lifestyle. These findings are consistent with the results of previous research into sexual reorientation/conversion therapy (Shidlo and Schroeder 2002; Throckmorton 2002). The ethical dilemmas associated with this area of work have created enormous difficulties for professional groups. If a profession is committed to respecting diversity, how should it respond when there is a fundamental clash between values stances of two 'diversities'? In 2012, the British Association for Counselling and Psychotherapy reaffirmed their stance that conversion therapy represented an unethical and unacceptable form of practice.

Box 21.5: *Experiences of lesbians and gay men in therapy*

The American Psychological Association has responded to initiatives from its membership by becoming involved in various campaigns to support the rights of gay men, bisexual men and women, and lesbians. For instance, the American Psychological Association has presented legal evidence in several court cases to the effect that homosexuality is not an illness (Herek *et al.* 1991). In 1984, the American Psychological Association set up a task force to investigate bias in psychotherapy with lesbians and gay men. The task force group surveyed a large number of psychologists concerning specific instances of biased and sensitive practice. Respondents in the survey were asked to describe incidents that they had experienced personally, or that had been reported to them by clients, that exemplified anti-homosexual attitudes or, alternatively, examples of informed, sensitive or gay-affirmative therapist behaviour. The survey revealed a wide variation of practitioner attitudes towards homosexuality (Garnets *et al.* 1991). For example, one therapist wrote that:

> I'm convinced that homosexuality is a genuine personality disorder and not merely a different way of life. Every one that I have known socially or as a client has been a complete mess psychologically. I think they are simply narcissistic personality disorders – see the description in the DSM-III – that's what they have looked and acted like – all of them.
>
> (Garnets *et al.* 1991: 966)

Other replies to the survey recounted stories that had been told by clients:

> A lesbian told me about her first therapist who encouraged her to date men and give up her ideas and feelings regarding women as intimate partners.

> A lesbian struggling with her sexual identity was challenged by her therapist, 'If you have a uterus, don't you think you should use it?'

A gay male couple seeking assistance with inhibited sexual desire on the part of one partner . . . were told the problem indicated the one partner probably wasn't really gay and that the recommended intervention was to break up their relationship.

(Garnets *et al.* 1991: 967)

There were also observations of discriminatory behaviour on the part of colleagues:

A colleague told me she 'couldn't help' expressing astonishment and disgust to a male client who 'confessed homosexuality'.

(Garnets *et al.* 1991: 967)

A gay clinical psychology student was required to get aversion therapy from a professor as a condition of his remaining in the program once he was discovered.

(Garnets *et al.* 1991: 968)

Although this survey also identified many examples of good practice, it is these instances of oppression and misuse of power that stick in the mind. These replies and observation come from a professional group that is highly trained and regulated. How much more bias is there in the counselling and psychotherapy profession outside of this select group?

Box 21.6: *The attitudes of psychoanalytic psychotherapists to working with gay and lesbian clients*

A central theme that has emerged from the literature on gay and lesbian counselling is that people who are gay and lesbian who decide to enter therapy find it important to work with a therapist who will actively support and *affirm* their sexuality. A survey among British psychoanalytic psychotherapists (Bartlett *et al.* 2001; Phillips *et al.* 2001) used a combination of questionnaires and in-depth interviews to explore the attitudes of a group of experienced and highly qualified therapists to working with gay and lesbian clients. A postal questionnaire was sent to 400 randomly selected members of the British Confederation of Psychotherapists, with completed questionnaires being received from 218 (55 per cent) respondents. The questionnaire asked whether the respondent would be willing to be interviewed: 33 indicated willingness, and of this group 15 were interviewed.

The quantitative data collected in this study revealed that there were issues for many of these therapists around acceptance of gay and lesbian experience. Of the 218 therapists who completed the questionnaire, 18 declined to answer a question that invited them to describe, in their own terms, their sexual orientation. Only 30 per cent of the sample agreed that gay and lesbian clients should have a right to see a gay or lesbian psychotherapist. The open-ended comments written in response to the questionnaire, and the recordings from interviews, provided a more detailed picture of these difficulties. For example, one psychotherapist, when asked about why he chose to use the term 'homosexual' rather than 'gay', stated that:

> I've never used the word 'gay' in my life. 'Lesbian', yes, but never the word 'gay'. I've never seen the point about it, its not my business – except to be very curious about what it means to the average homosexual who changes the fact of his homosexuality to refer to it as 'gay', and I think it's part of the new sort of twist that's going on in which we are invited to consider that homosexual people behave as if they've had a choice and chosen the homosexual way of life.
>
> (Phillips *et al.* 2001: 79)

When asked about the low number of gay and lesbian therapists within the training organization, this therapist replied:

> nobody sitting in the room that night at the (training organisation) was the result of a 'homosexual' love affair – each was the result of a heterosexual experience between a man and a woman, the woman becoming pregnant . . . in my opinion no homosexual person exists who can't be envious of such a procedure, because homosexual love doesn't produce anything creative . . . Homosexuality needs to be recognised as 'madness'; when it is presented as a fulfilling self choice, it is a delusion, which is about the 'impersonation' of ordinary heterosexual world, and of the heterosexual capacity for ordinary thinking.
>
> (Phillips *et al.* 2001: 79)

These statements are clearly grounded in a position in which heterosexual sexuality is regarded as 'normal' and 'mature', and gay or lesbian sexuality is defined as a form of 'arrested development' and clinical entity.

Many of the therapists in the study reported that they believed that their training organization would not accept gay or lesbian people for psychotherapy training, and that gay or lesbian trainees or members of the organization kept their sexual orientation secret (Phillips *et al.* 2001: 82):

> I would have thought that as far as the training organisation is concerned, it would be a fear of exposure, and a fear of being, what's the equivalent of struck off or defrocked? There's a deep distrust about actually continuing to be respected as a colleague.

> Terror, fear. There are a lot of people, I believe, in all the trainings, that refuse gay and lesbian people.

The majority of the therapists who were interviewed said that they knew of colleagues, whom they regarded as suitable for training, who had been refused a place on the grounds of sexuality. However, some of the interviewees agreed with the policy of excluding gay men and lesbians from psychotherapy training (Phillips *et al.* 2001: 82):

> We should not play the game of this collusive idea of normalising muck and rubbish.

> It's a bit like not taking people with drugs offences into the police force.

These statements suggest a bedrock of lack of acceptance of the capacity of gay and lesbian individuals to be effective psychoanalytic psychotherapists, no matter how much they may have achieved, or how competent they might be in fields such as psychiatry, social work, clinical psychology, nursing or teaching (the typical primary professions of members of the British Confederation of Psychotherapists).

It is important, in a study of this kind, to be careful not to allow conclusions to be biased by the extreme views of a minority of respondents. In an attempt to offer a balanced overview of their findings, Phillips *et al.* (2001: 82–3) wrote that:

> There was some polarization of the analysts' views in that women and younger therapists were more likely to regard gay men and lesbians as valuable members of society who should have access to training as analysts and should not be 'pathologized' in psychoanalysis. However, all therapists were equivocal at some point and were uncomfortable with the issues. The psychoanalysts interviewed found it difficult to accept gay and lesbian sexuality as one variant of the human condition. Although many of them held empathic views about gay men and lesbians and stated that they should have equal access to training as analysts, most were uncomfortable with the scenario whereby a heterosexual client may be aware that their therapist was gay. Furthermore, they were uncomfortable with the suggestion that gay people might choose a gay therapist with all that implied in terms of self-disclosure on the part of the analyst.

Phillips *et al.* (2001: 83) further concluded that, in their opinion, 'such a wholly negative approach to gay and lesbian sexuality is unlikely to help their clients adjust positively to their life circumstances'.

What are the implications of this study for counselling? There are many openly gay and lesbian individuals who are not only participants on counselling courses, but are respected trainers on courses and senior members of the profession. The kinds of negative homophobic attitudes expressed by some of the psychoanalytic psychotherapists in the Phillips *et al.* (2001) study would probably lead to the person being asked to leave a counselling training course. Similar prejudices exist in counselling, even if in a more muted form (Evans 2003). Finally, the findings of the Phillips *et al.* (2001) study need to be viewed in context – it is certainly the case that many psychoanalytic therapists are much more accepting and affirming with their LGBT clients (see, for example, Drescher *et al.* 2003).

Counselling people with disabilities

The concept of 'disability' encompasses a wide spectrum of human experience. In literal terms, disability refers to a lack of capacity to carry out basic human actions and functions that are regarded by the majority of people as taken for granted, such as seeing, hearing, speaking, remembering, learning, walking, feeding and holding. However, it is important, in any discussion of disability, to be clear that this concept can be understood and interpreted in radically different ways, each of which reflects a distinct political stance and mode of helping (Smart and Smart 2006).

A *biomedical* model of disability is deeply embedded in the way that disabled people are currently treated by social institutions. The biomedical perspective on disability focuses attention on the biological causes of the disability, on medical and physical solutions, and implies that there is something abnormal or 'wrong' with the person. In addition, a person with a disability may be eligible for 'sickness' benefits under health insurance schemes.

By contrast, a *functional* model of disability emphasizes the ways in which the person functions in the world, and displays relatively little interest in the causes of the disability. Most counsellors working with disabled clients implicitly or explicitly adopt a functional perspective, and seek to explore issues associated with the client's goals, and how these can be attained. Unlike a biomedical perspective, which views disability in entirely negative terms, as a set of deficits, a functional approach introduces the possibility that there can be positive learning and growth arising from the person's experience of their disability.

Finally, the *social* perspective on disability adopts the position that, for the most part, it is not the disability itself that causes difficulties for a person, but the way that other people respond to the disability (Reeve 2006). For example, a person with a learning disability, living in a traditional rural community in which people worked on the land, might not encounter any serious barriers to employment. The same person living in a society in which employment required literacy skills, might never find a job. The implication of a social perspective on disability is that effective helping on an individual basis is never sufficient, and needs to be supplemented by social action.

People with disabilities encounter all three of these perspectives in the course of their everyday lives, and will probably view each of them as relevant in some situations. It is essential, therefore, for counsellors equally to be able to interpret the experience of disability through these distinct frameworks.

In reflecting on the role of counselling in relation to people with disabilities, it is important to acknowledge two obvious truths. First, it is quite possible that a person who lives with a disability such as blindness or paralysis, and who seeks counselling, may not have any wish or need to discuss their disability with the therapist. People with disabilities have emotional and relationship problems, eating disorders, bereavements, and so on, just like anyone else. Second, there are significant differences between the experiences of people who have lived with a disability from birth, and those for whom the onset of the disability follows some years of 'normal' life. For this latter group, there are likely to be pressing emotional issues associated with the shock of the diagnosis and the process of readjustment in relationships, working life and self-concept.

One of the key challenges to effective counselling with clients who are disabled, lies in the attitudes and emotional reactions of the counsellor faced with a client who is physically 'different'. In a study by Kemp and Mallinckrodt (1996), two groups of experienced counsellors were shown a video of a client talking about problems arising from an incident of sexual abuse. In one condition, the client was portrayed in a wheelchair, whereas in the other condition, the client was shown walking to her seat. After viewing the video, the counsellors were asked to complete a questionnaire on their views of how therapy might proceed. The counsellors who had viewed the client as disabled were significantly less likely to mention that the clients might need to work on issues of sexual intimacy. Much research into the attitudes of counsellors toward disabled clients has largely used self-report questionnaire measures, such as the Attitudes Toward Disabled Persons Scale (ATDP; Yuker *et al.* 1960) and the Counseling Clients with Disabilities Scale (CCDS; Strike *et al.* 2004). These studies have tended to show that, although counsellors may possess good self-awareness in relation to disability issues, they do not feel competent in terms of knowing how to work with disabled clients in practice (Strike *et al.* 2004).

An important limitation of the use of self-report questionnaires in this research is that counsellors are likely to believe that they 'should' hold positive and accepting attitudes toward disabled people, and are therefore highly likely to seek to present a favourable impression in their questionnaire responses. As a means of addressing this source of bias, Pruett and Chan (2006) have developed a non-verbal attitude test that assessed the speed of response to reasoning tasks that involved images of disability. This technique appears to represent a promising way forward in terms of evaluating counsellor attitudes.

It is important to recognize that these research initiatives take place in the context of a situation in which many disabled people report low levels of acceptance and understanding on the part of the counsellors that they visit. Reeve (2002: 11) has argued that:

> counsellors are subject to the same negative images and stereotypes of disabled people as the rest of society . . . the attitudes and prejudices of counsellors toward disabled people can adversely affect the nature of the client–counsellor relationship when the client is a disabled person – there is sometimes oppression within the counselling room.

There may be a number of aspects of the communication and interaction process that need to be considered when the client is a disabled person. These range from difficulties in word-finding in people with brain injuries or illnesses, absence of communication channels such as sight, hearing or gesture, and ensuring appropriate physical facilities within a room or building. In situations where a disabled client has spent most of his or her life within a community that is organized around the disability, or has spent time in a rehabilitation centre, it may make sense for a counsellor to adopt a multicultural perspective (see Chapter 13). For example, Williams and Abeles (2004) point out that deaf people have their own language, and have often participated in a powerful shared experience of deaf schooling and membership of deaf families and friendship networks, and that a counsellor working with a deaf client needs to be sensitive to, and curious about, these cultural dimensions of the therapeutic process.

There are some psychological issues that appear to be consistently associated with the experience of disability. Because they may need to depend on other people to accomplish certain tasks, there can be tendency for some disabled people to undergo a process of 'infantilization', in which they are not treated as a grown-up adult with the ability to choose (Segal 1996). There can be many conscious and unconscious responses to infantilization, ranging from passive acceptance and depression through to anger, that may be expressed in the counselling room. There can be issues around sexuality that can be linked to infantilization – a disabled person is not expected to have sexual needs. There are also issues, such as loss, that able-bodied people *expect* disabled people to feel, but which may not in fact be high on a disabled person's emotional agenda (Reeve 2002).

Another key emotional issue concerns the capacity to achieve life goals. A programme of research carried out by Elliott *et al.* (2000) explored the role of life goals in adjustment to disability, and found that people who reported unstable goals (i.e., difficulties in maintaining and pursuing meaningful goals) tended to have higher levels of psychological problems than those who had been able to retain a sense of purpose in the face of the challenges thrown up by their disability. This finding was consistent across both people who had experienced sudden onset disability (e.g., spinal cord injury due to a sports accident) and those with long-term conditions. The challenge of being able to make a living, or play a role in the workforce, is another critical issue for many disabled people. In an interview-based study with women who had severe disabilities that prevented them from working, Moore (2005: 344) found that her informants sought to give meaning to life by 'being a part of something larger than oneself', for example through education, religion, unpaid work, and family involvement that provided connection to others.

There has been only a limited amount of research into the effectiveness of counselling with disabled clients. There is good evidence that behavioural and cognitive approaches can be effective with groups of people with mild learning disabilities, and in some clients with more severe learning disabilities (Willner 2005), and also for the effectiveness of psychodynamic psychotherapy (Beail *et al.* 2005) in learning disability. However, on the whole there is a dearth of research into the role of counselling and psychotherapy in disability. For further information on the topic of counselling and disability, readers are recommended to consult the excellent textbook by Olkin (1999), and her inspiring account of her career as a disabled therapist fighting for the rights of disabled clients (Olkin 2010). A useful summary of Olkin's guidelines for practice can be found in Artman and Daniels (2010).

The topic of counselling for people with disabilities illustrates several recurring political issues that are associated with the provision of therapy for people in disadvantaged groups. Just as people with disabilities are marginalized in modern society as a whole, their needs have been marginalized within counselling theory, practice and training. In an article that discusses the role of counselling in helping young people with spina bifida to develop more independent lives, Brislin (2008) highlights the complexity of this work, and the extent to which the counsellor needs to be able to explore a very wide range of issues with a client: the personal meaning of the condition, medical information and physical symptoms, family dynamics, peer relationships, social attitudes, the politics of disability and the adequacy of institutional service providers (see also, Livneh and Antonak 2005). A capacity to work effectively with such issues takes a counsellor well beyond the range of convenience of mainstream theories of therapy, and requires a reconceptualization of counselling as a pluralistic and politically informed activity. Within the field of counselling for people with learning difficulties, examples of creative and integrative approaches that have been developed in this spirit include the work of Lambie and Milsom (2010) and Read (2007).

Counselling for long-term users of psychiatric services

If disability is defined in functional terms, then people who experience 'severe and enduring' mental health problems, such as chronic depression, schizophrenia or bipolar disorder, can often be categorized as being highly disabled. Although it is certainly possible to debate the validity or helpfulness of the concept of *illness* to describe the problems of these people (see, for example, Szasz 1961), it is not possible to deny that these conditions are associated with issues around an ability to work, sustain satisfactory relationships, or, in extreme cases, even to engage in basic self-care. Many counsellors and counselling agencies are reluctant to offer therapy to people within this category, because they view such clients as possessing complex and deep-rooted problems that require a more intensive form of intervention, such as inpatient treatment in a psychiatric unit, or regular home visits from a support worker or mental health nurse. In contrast to this view, many users of mental health services regard counselling as a valuable alternative, or complement, to drug and residential treatments (e.g., Glass and Arnkoff 2000; Rogers *et al.* 1993). For example, Rogers *et al.* (1993) reported that mental health service users valued counselling above other treatments they had received, with 33 per cent of service users stating that they had wanted (but had been unable to get) counselling.

There is considerable evidence that it is possible to use standard counselling and psychotherapy approaches with clients who are long-term users of psychiatric services (Coursey *et al.* 1997). Caccia and Watson (1987) compared the demographic characteristics and clinical profiles of clients of a voluntary-sector counselling service and patients attending a psychiatric outpatient unit (both in London), and found 'levels of psychiatric morbidity in the (counselling) which were both considerable and similar to those found in psychiatric out-patient attenders' (p. 184). Archer *et al.* (2000), in a follow-up study based at the same counselling service, reported that clients improved significantly in psychological well-being.

Brief therapy that focuses on relationships and sense of self has been shown to be effective as an element in rehabilitation of patients with severe and enduring mental health problems (Coursey *et al.* 1997; Lysaker and France 1999), and to result in a decrease in health service costs in high utilizers of mental health services (Guthrie *et al.* 1999; Davenport *et al.* 2000). The effective use of person-centred counselling with clients who have been diagnosed with severe mental health problems is discussed by Sommerbeck (2003).

It is important to acknowledge that counselling with people with long-term mental health problems may be *difficult*: if someone has had a problem for a long time the chances are that they have experienced several unsuccessful attempts to deal with it in the past. It is also probable that the difficulties in relating to others, that represent a central characteristic of all long-term mental health conditions, are likely to be exhibited in a relationship with a counsellor or psychotherapist.

An important factor associated with the effectiveness of psychotherapeutic treatment for people who have been long-term users of mental health services is the opportunity given to the person to re-examine and re-construct their personal life narrative (or sense of self) in order to establish a new identity in relation to the social world in which they live (Corin 1988; Davidson and Strauss 1992). In many cases, people living with long-term mental health problems can be understood to turn to formal counselling when some aspect of their experience (e.g., strong emotions, hearing voices, memories of abuse) is consistently *excluded from expression* in their social world (i.e., they are *silenced*). The purpose of therapy is to enable the person to negotiate social inclusion and re-engagement in a form that is meaningful to them (McLeod 1999), and to achieve a more coherent life-story (Lysaker *et al.* 2003; Roe and Davidson 2006). The aim is not to achieve a 'cure' for schizophrenia, bipolar disorder or any other condition, but to contribute (along with other forms of help, such as medication, occupational therapy and self-help) to a process of *recovery* (Davidson *et al.* 2005, 2006; Ridgway, 2001).

The work of Lysaker and France (1999) provides a particularly good example of how psychotherapy can work alongside other interventions (in this case, a supported employment scheme). Another theme is counselling and psychotherapy with people who have been diagnosed with severe psychiatric problems is the experience of *loss*. It is probable that the person may have lost several years of their life, and many of their personal hopes and life goals, to their 'illness'. This sense of loss may be exacerbated by the experience of having been treated in an oppressive or abusive manner by professional helpers or family members, who may or may not have been trying to do their best, but whose interventions have come across as controlling and uncaring. These facets of a personal world may make a person who has survived a severe and enduring mental illness highly sensitive to situations and relationships that are stressful, and actively committed to effective self-care strategies. Many people who have undergone this kind of episode in their life find support and meaning in the network of peer support organizations that form the 'recovery movement'.

Box 21.7: *Psychotherapy with a case of 'incurable' schizophrenia*

The online journal *Pragmatic Case Studies in Psychotherapy* is a particularly valuable resource for counsellors because it publishes systematic, high-quality case studies in an accessible format. A case included in this journal is that of 'Mr X' (Karon 2008). At the point of entering psychodynamic psychotherapy, Mr X had undergone several years of unsuccessful psychiatric inpatient and outpatient treatment for schizophrenia. He had been categorized as 'incurable', and was not eating or sleeping, and constantly hallucinating.

The case report describes a process of therapy that was tailored to the specific needs of this client. The therapist began by seeing Mr X seven times each week for the first week, six times the second week, and then five times each week for several months. He arranged for Mr X's wife and friends to stay with him on a 24-hour basis, for the first few weeks, in order to ensure his safety. Karon described his therapeutic principles in these terms:

> The therapist must create a therapeutic alliance by being unequivocally helpful, tolerating incoherence, tolerating not understanding, and being realistically optimistic. The patient is usually surprised that you expect them to get better, with hard work . . . They do not believe you, because most of them have been told by professionals that they have a genetic disease whose

> biological defect is known and which is incurable . . . The therapist must give a feeling of strength in that you are willing and able to deal with anything and go anywhere the patient needs to go, no matter how scary.
>
> Karon 2008: 4–5

The issues that were worked through in therapy included not eating (fear of poisoning), the experience of hallucinating (burning in hell), sexual guilt, marital problems and childhood emotional abuse. The therapy continued for 14 years, although the client was able to go back to work after the first six months of treatment. This case study presents a detailed account of the process of therapy with a man diagnosed as incurably schizophrenic, and the rationale for the approach that was adopted. It provides evidence of the potential efficacy of psychotherapy with people who have suffered from severe and enduring mental health difficulties.

Themes in counselling people from disadvantaged and marginalized groups

It is possible to identify a set of key themes that have arisen in the discussion of counselling with clients who are economically disadvantaged, espouse a minority sexual orientation, or are disabled, or survivors of 'mental illness':

- there has been a general avoidance of these client groups by the counselling and psychotherapy professions;
- many counsellors describe themselves as feeling uncomfortable when working with disadvantaged clients, and unsure about how to proceed;
- members of disadvantaged groups report that they have difficulties in accessing services;
- members of these groups often report that the counselling they receive is not helpful, because the therapist does not appreciate their experience;
- historically, there has been an institutional tendency to apply negative labels to members of these groups, characterizing them as either mentally ill, or incapable of making use of counselling;
- the clinical and theoretical literature in relation to these groups is sparse;
- there is a lack of training opportunities for counsellors seeking to develop knowledge and expertise in this area of work;
- there is a lack of research into counselling and psychotherapy with disadvantaged groups;
- absence of research evidence results in an unwillingness on the part of health policy-makers and administrators to allocate resources to the provision of counselling for these populations.

Alongside these negative factors, there are also many examples of areas of good practice, where people from potentially oppressed groups have worked with the counselling and psychotherapy profession to develop effective and accessible services. However, it seems reasonable to conclude the overall picture is one in which the counselling profession has not found it at all easy to develop counselling services for people in disadvantaged, stigmatized and marginalized groups. There are possibly two reasons for this failure. First, counsellors and psychotherapists have been so preoccupied with individual 'psychological' problems in their clients that they have not given sufficient attention to the effects of what might be termed a 'disabling society'. Second, there has been a tendency for counsellors and psychotherapists to assume that they are the ones who are most truly accepting and 'person-centred in their approach to clients, and that it is other professions (such as psychiatry, social work and education) that engage in labelling and social control. This tendency has perhaps inhibited counsellors from critically examining their own practices around difference and diversity, and being more open to examples of enlightened practice within these other professions.

Practical guidelines for politically informed counselling

The earlier sections of this chapter have explored some of the ways in which political factors – mechanisms and structures of power and control within society – can influence the counselling process and the type of counselling services that are available. In some sections of the counselling literature, these issues are discussed in relation to the adoption of 'anti-oppressive' forms of practice. However, the collaborative and broadly 'person-centred' nature of most contemporary counselling means that it is not accurate to characterize counselling, as a whole, as a form of oppression. It makes more sense to take a position that counselling would be more effective, as a means of enabling individual clients to live satisfying and productive lives, and as a means of contributing to a more just society, if it could move in the direction of becoming more politically informed. But what does 'politically informed' counselling look like? What does it involve, as a practical level? Based on the examples that have been discussed already, it is possible to identify some important ways that a politically informed approach can be integrated into counselling practice.

'Re-thinking': critical reconceptualization and reformulation of counselling theories. It seems clear that one of the barriers to politically informed counselling is the fact that the theoretical frameworks (e.g., psychodynamic, person-centred, CBT) that are used by the majority of counsellors to guide their practice consist solely of psychological or interpersonal concepts, and make it hard for counsellors to think in terms of wider social forces. In recent years, new theoretical models, such as narrative therapy, feminist therapy and multicultural counselling, have begun to offer ways of thinking about counselling from a social and political perspective. Politically informed practice requires finding means of assimilating these new ideas into supervision, service planning and reflection on practice, appropriate to the interests and experience of the practitioner.

Becoming more aware of one's own social knowledge and attitudes. Politically sensitive areas of counselling, discussed in the present chapter, reflect areas of social life where there exist traditions of rejection of certain groups of people. Counsellors are not immune to, or apart from, these traditions. No matter how 'accepting' of clients a counsellor may strive to be it is inevitable that there are aspects of social life around which he or she may never have had any direct personal experience. It is significant that within the 'social justice' movement in North American counselling that students are not merely asked to talk about their social attitudes, but are required to go out into the community to spend time with people from social groups that they may previously have been able to avoid contact with. It may be useful for the personal therapy that is undertaken by the majority of counsellors to incorporate exploration of social and political attitudes.

Inviting clients to talk about social and political aspects of their problems. Social and political issues are likely to remain hidden in therapy if a counsellor focuses their client's attention solely on psychological themes. Politically informed counsellors are curious about the social worlds of their clients, and the ways that clients can re-shape these worlds. Weiner (1998) describes how she set the scene for politically oriented conversations in the therapy room by installing a bulletin board in the waiting area, displaying leaflets, posters and articles on political themes and examples of collective action, and ensuring that only recyclable beakers were available at the water fountain.

Making connections between counselling and social action. One of the strongest and most consistent themes to emerge in the present chapter is the realization that clients do not necessarily find it helpful to make a distinction between psychological insights and practical action. The work of Goodman *et al.* (2004, 2009) and Waldegrave *et al.* (2003) provide examples of counselling services that are wholly integrated into broader community change programmes. In many other settings, counsellors establish collaborative links with educational and social services, voluntary groups and community projects, in a more informal fashion.

Using counselling methods and strategies that encourage clients to initiate political change in their own lives and communities. It is unfortunate that, at the present time, research into the outcomes of counselling concentrates almost entirely on the collection of data concerning symptom reduction in areas such as anxiety and depression. If outcome were also to be assessed in terms of social change, it might help counsellors to pay more attention to how therapy can help clients to contribute to the good of society as a whole. There are many ways in which this can be achieved. Taking a client's strengths seriously, and looking for ways in which potential or existing strengths can be expressed in action can begin to set a person on a pathway of making a difference. Sometimes, counselling can help clients to re-frame or reconceptualize the meaning of negative events that have previously been seen only as weaknesses or examples of failure. For example, a person who was involved in violence or drug-taking in their youth may have a lot to offer in relation to guiding young people away from such trajectories.

Counselling can also help people to get to a point of speaking out about injustice, and joining with others to fight that injustice. There are undoubtedly many stories that could be told, of how counselling has enabled clients to move on in their lives in ways that contribute to the social good. It would be useful if research could be used to document more of these examples, and highlight this aspect of therapy. Bergner (1999; Torres and

Bergner 2012) has described these types of intervention and facilitation as forms of 'status enhancement', in which the counsellor supports the client in shifting from one social role (or 'status') to another, more valued role/status. An example of this kind of shift might be in an art therapy group for people with long-term mental health problems, when a group member realizes that they have stopped being a 'patient', and started being an 'artist', or in bereavement counselling when a client begins to see that she has stopped being 'lost in grief' and is now able to offer support to other members of her family.

The adoption of these practical strategies for politically informed counselling does not imply that existing counselling methods are no longer relevant. Clearly, counselling is not the place that people go in order to engage in political action – it is the place to go to deal with personal problems. The point is that de-politicized counselling ignores a dimension of life that is extremely significant for people, in relation to their capacity to deal with everyday problems in living. Conversely, showing an interest in the social and political context of a client's life, opens up many possibilities for constructive change.

The macro-politics of counselling

The main focus of this chapter is on what might be called the 'micro-politics' of counselling – the ways in which social, historical and political processes and institutions shape a person's identity, his or her way of relating to others, and their engagement with therapy. Taking a step or two back from the concrete reality of the counselling room it is possible to see that counselling and psychotherapy can be regarded as political institutions in their own right, and operate in a difficult political landscape. It is important to appreciate that what happens at this kind of 'macro-political' level can have a powerful impact on what happens in the counselling room.

A key aspect of the macro-politics of counselling and psychotherapy is the level of fragmentation that exists. There are a large number of counselling organizations that compete for influence and control. Some of these are built around specific therapy approaches, such as psychoanalysis, person-centred therapy, CBT, gestalt therapy and TA. Other organizations are built around specific disorders, such as schizophrenia or eating disorders. There are still other, larger, organizations that function as 'federations' or 'umbrella' groups, such as the British Association for Counselling and Psychotherapy or the American Psychological Association. Some of these organizations are transnational (e.g., the International Transactional Analysis Association and the Society for Psychotherapy Research), whereas others are nationally based. Some of them include service users as members. Some of them are recognized by the state, others are not. Some of them run training courses, others accredit courses and others have nothing to say about training. There are many different forms of linkage between these organizations and the university sector. At another level within society, are state-run or state-sponsored licensing bodies that regulate the profession as a whole. Operating in parallel to all this are other organizations in fields such as psychiatry, clinical psychology, social work, nursing and the ministry whose interests overlap to a greater or lesser extent with counselling, and who may be competing for the same resources.

Conclusions

This chapter has explored the politics of counselling, through reviewing the ways that different forms of power relationship can be played out in the counselling room. The chapter then examined political dimensions of counselling with client groups who, for one reason or another, are marginalized in society. It is clear that it is important for counsellors to be aware of these issues to avoid perpetuating injustice. At the present time, however, issues of politics and power are given little space within counselling theory and training. This chapter has therefore attempted to highlight the contribution of groups of counsellors who are trying to remedy that situation.

Topics for reflection and discussion

1 Critics of counselling and psychotherapy have argued that therapy comprises an over-individualized response to personal problems and ignores the social origins and conditions that ultimately produce these problems (Furedi 2004; Smail 1991; Pilgrim 1992). Do you agree? Take any one field of counselling with which you are familiar (student, marital, workplace etc.). To what extent does the practice of counselling in that area ignore underlying social factors? In what ways might the counselling that is offered be more (or less) effective if social factors were given more attention?

2 Discuss the strengths and weaknesses of different theoretical orientations in counselling with clients from disadvantaged or marginalized groups. Is there one theoretical perspective, or combination of perspectives, that you find most (or least) applicable in this context?

3 Think about the counselling agency where you work (or a counselling agency you have used as a client). How do you feel when you are there? Do you have a sense of being powerful and in control, or do you have a sense of being in the hands of others? What are the physical cues (e.g., notices, leaflets, layout, furniture, decoration, etc.) and behaviours that give you a feeling of being empowered, or a sense of being oppressed? Do you think a member of a different cultural group might feel differently about this agency?

4 In what ways might counselling theory and practice change over the next 20 years, in response to the pressures on individuals to learn how to cope with the challenges of global warming, environmental destruction and scarcity of key natural resources such as food, water and oil?

Suggested further reading

There are three edited books that include a wide range of valuable chapters on themes and topics introduced in the present chapter: *Politicizing the Person-centred Approach: An Agenda for Social Change* edited by Gillian Proctor and others (2006); *Difference and Diversity in Counselling: Contemporary Psychodynamic Approaches*, edited by Sue Wheeler (2006); and *The Politics of Psychotherapy: New Perspectives*, edited by Nick Totton (2006). A passionate and inspiring exploration of the ways in which political factors permeate all aspects of therapy can be found in Michael White's last book – *Narrative Practice* (White 2011).

Virtues, values and ethics in counselling practice

22

Introduction

The practice of counselling includes a strong moral and ethical dimension. It is clear that one of the central characteristics of the social groups in which counselling and psychotherapy have become established is the experience of living in a world in which it is difficult to know what is the 'right' way to live. In an increasingly secular society where there may be much questioning or rejection of tradition and authority, and where different moral or religious codes coexist, individuals are required to make choices about moral issues to an extent unknown in previous generations. In Chapter 2 it was argued that much of the need for psychotherapy is due to the fact that in modern society moral controls are for the most part internalized rather than externalized. Because we do not live in communities dominated by single, comprehensive moral codes, individuals must possess within them the means of deciding what is right and wrong, and also the means of punishment – for example, feeling guilty – if they transgress these rules.

Many, perhaps even most, people who seek counselling are struggling with moral decisions. Should I finish my course or quit college? Should I stay in a marriage that is making me unhappy? Should I have this baby or arrange for an abortion? Should I come out and acknowledge that I am gay? Shall I take my own life? These, and many other counselling issues, are problematic for people because they involve very basic moral decisions about what is right and what is wrong.

One of the fundamental principles of most approaches to counselling is that the counsellor is required to adopt an accepting or non-judgemental stance or attitude in relation to the client. In general, most counsellors would agree that the aim of counselling is to help people to arrive at what is right for them, rather than attempting to impose a solution from outside. Nevertheless, at the same time counselling is a process of influence. In the end, the client who benefits from counselling will look back and see that the counselling process made a difference, and influenced the course of his or her life. The dilemma for the counsellor is to allow herself to be powerful and influential without imposing her own moral values and choices. Good counsellors, therefore, need to possess an informed awareness of the different ways in which moral and ethical issues may arise in their work.

In most societies, the principal source of moral and ethical thinking has been organized religion. Historically, there have been strong links between therapy and religion (discussed in Chapter 2). However, although Christian ideas about morality have been influential in the counselling world it is also apparent that at least some of the people who have come into counselling from a previous religious background have done so because they have rejected elements of traditional religious thinking, or have been seeking something beyond these traditions. There has also been a steady influence on counselling and psychotherapy of non-religious moral philosophy, particularly existentialism, and of political and social movements, such as feminism. Finally, there has been a growing interest in non-Western religious thinking, particularly Buddhism.

Counsellors need to be aware of the moral dilemmas faced by their clients, and of the moral or ethical assumptions they themselves bring to their practice. However, as professionals accredited by society to deal with clients who may be vulnerable, needy and ill-informed, counsellors also have a responsibility to act towards their clients in an ethical manner. There are, therefore, two broad areas in which ethical and moral considerations are particularly relevant to counselling. The first is rooted in the actual counselling process. Clients may need help to resolve the moral issues involved in the life crises or problems that have brought them to counselling. The counsellor must also be sensitively aware of her own moral stance, and its interaction with the value system of the client. The second area is in behaving towards the client in an ethical and responsible manner.

It seems to have taken a long time for the counselling and psychotherapy professions to face up to the ethical and moral dimensions of therapeutic practice. The editor of what was probably the first comprehensive text on ethical issues in psychotherapy, Rosenbaum (1982: ix), wrote of his experience in compiling the book:

> many professionals had simply not thought about the larger issues involved in
> the practice of psychotherapy. This was borne out when I invited friends and

colleagues who are considered major figures in the field of psychology and psychiatry to participate in my project. They reacted for the most part with anxiety and confusion. These honorable people, while aware of what they believed to be right or wrong, had great difficulty in setting this down in a form that would enable other professionals to benefit from their experiences.

The lack of attention paid to ethical issues within the profession is illustrated in the observations in Box 22.1 and can also be found in many anecdotal accounts around the edges of the literature. For instance, Masson (1991: 161) quoted the famous psychoanalyst Masud Khan as saying that 'I never sleep with other analysts' patients, only my own'. Khan was living with a former patient while continuing to see her husband in analysis, and was apparently unconcerned about the ethical implications of these domestic arrangements. It was only when the consumer movement and the women's movement gained ground in the 1980s that professional associations in counselling and psychotherapy, as well as other fields, started to see the need to develop codes of ethical standards and procedures. The tendency for clients and patients in the USA to seek redress in the courts gave added urgency to these developments.

In addition, many therapists experience significant levels of stress in relation to ethical dilemmas; Austin *et al.* (2005) have documented the 'moral distress' felt by mental health workers in situations where their moral integrity has been compromised by institutional demands and disagreements with colleagues over ethical issues.

Box 22.1: *Abuse in a training context*

There can be situations where the potential for abuse of counselling and psychotherapy does not simply involve the mistreatment of one person by another, but takes place within a complex network of interacting social and organizational pressures and forces. McLean (1986), an anthropologist, studied training workshops run in the 1970s and 1980s in which well-known family therapy experts gave 'live' therapy to an actual family in front of an audience. The advantage to the family was that it received treatment from an acknowledged expert. In addition, many therapists and trainees were able to learn at first hand how a 'master therapist' put his or her ideas into practice. Ethical problems were covered by an informed consent release signed by the family, and by the fact that proceedings were video-taped, and only presented to the audience after a two or three minute delay. McLean (1986: 180) describes events in one of these workshops, which feature two internationally renowned family systems therapists:

> During the morning of the first day, one of the therapists treated one family. In the afternoon, the second therapist treated the other family. On the second day, they exchanged families, although at points both therapists appeared together with each of the families . . . In being encouraged to participate, the families were undoubtedly informed of the rare chance they were offered to receive family therapy from two of the most recognized experts in the field. They were requested their written 'informed' consent to permit the recordings

of their therapy sessions to be used in the future for professional and training purposes. They were not told, however, that for all practical purposes, their therapy sessions were being observed 'live' by several hundred people . . . [A]t breaks and at the end of each session, the therapist left the room and discussed the 'case' with the audience while the family were still in the clinic, unaware that they were currently being 'studied' by a large audience who had purchased the opportunity to observe them. This fact was almost revealed to one of the families when several persons from the audience swarmed into a rest room, discussing the morning 'case', only to discover some members of the family there. On the second day, one of the doctors, upon reviewing the situation of one family, observed the powerful position of control that the mother enjoyed in the family. He blithely declared that if the son were to be saved from becoming schizophrenic, the mother would have to 'go crazy', as would the father eventually. He then proceeded to conduct therapy with the family in a way that successfully provoked a hysterical outburst from the mother. This irate woman was understandably reacting to the demeaning manner in which she was being treated. She cried profusely, insistently demanding an explanation from the therapist for his behavior toward her. He replied smugly, '*I'm* the doctor; I don't *have* to explain myself', only intensifying her rage, as he promptly walked out with the other therapist who was present for this scene. Their exit was accompanied by support throughout the audience, as evidenced by vigorous applause.

McLean discusses the social and economic factors that have led to the treatment of a family in need as a 'commodity'. She concludes that this sort of workshop is dehumanizing for both patient and therapist. One might add that, ultimately, the audience are equally participating in a dehumanizing spectacle. Yet no one objected, no one put a stop to it. Presumably the majority of the hundreds of therapists who attended these workshops believed that what was happening was right.

Values in counselling

Ethical and moral issues in counselling are closely connected to questions of *values*. One of the important contributions made by the founders of humanistic psychology, such as Maslow and Rogers, has been to highlight the importance of the concept of value. A value can be defined as an enduring belief that a specific end-state or mode of conduct is preferable. Rokeach (1973) differentiates between 'instrumental' and 'terminal' values. The latter refer to desirable end-states, such as wisdom, comfort, peace or freedom. Instrumental values correspond to the means by which these goals are to be achieved: for example, through competence, honesty or ambition. Rokeach (1973) argues that most people will be in favour of a value such as 'equality', and that the best way to uncover the personal value system that guides the behaviour of an individual is to inquire about his or her value preferences. For example, one person might value equality higher than freedom, whereas another might place these two values in the other order. The study of values is, therefore, a complex matter. However, several studies have shown that the values of the counsellor influence the values held by clients. The trend shown in most studies has been for the values of the client to converge with those of the counsellor (Kelly 1989). This finding raises questions for the practice of counselling. Are counsellors imposing their values on clients? Should counselling be seen as a form of socialization into a particular set of values?

Bergin (1980) claimed that the espousal by psychology of scientific beliefs and attitudes was associated with a rejection of religious values. His view is that, since many people in the general population hold strong religious views, there is a danger that therapy will be seen as irrelevant or even damaging. Bergin (1980) has carried out a systematic analysis of the differences between what he calls 'theistic' and 'clinical–humanistic' value systems (Table 22.1). The contrasts made by Bergin highlight divergences rather than acknowledging possible points of similarity and convergence, and his formulation has been criticized by Walls (1980), Ellis (1980) and Brammer *et al.* (1989). Nevertheless, his work makes it possible to see that there can be radically different views of what is 'right' or 'good'.

Counsellors, trained in institutions that may embody clinical–humanistic values, may perhaps lose touch with the values of their clients. The power imbalance of the counselling situation may make it impossible for the client to assert his or her values except by deciding not to turn up. The issue of value differences is particularly relevant in multicultural counselling, or when the client is gay or lesbian. It is significant that many clients from these groups deliberately seek out counsellors whom they know to have a similar background and values.

In a survey carried out in the USA, Kelly (1995) found that, compared with the population as a whole, counsellors were high in the values of benevolence (concern for the welfare of others), self-direction, autonomy and self-expression, but much lower in power (defined as an aspiration towards social status and authority over others) and tradition (acceptance of and respect for customs). Almost 90 per cent of these counsellors indicated some degree of religious or spiritual orientation. Finally, there was a high degree of broadmindedness and tolerance of the beliefs and sexual choices of others, indicating that counsellors are well able to distinguish between their own value positions and those adopted by their clients. There was a high degree of consensus among the counsellors answering this questionnaire. This might indicate the existence of a distinctive 'clinical–humanistic' value profile, as proposed by Bergin (1980), or it might be the result of political correctness

TABLE 22.1 Comparison of religious and therapeutic value systems

Religious/theistic	Clinical–humanistic
God is supreme; humility and obedience to the will of God are virtues	Humans are supreme; autonomy and the rejection of authority are virtues
Relationship with God defines self-worth	Relationships with others define self-worth
Strict morality; universal ethics	Flexible morality; situational ethics
Service and self-sacrifice central to personal growth	Self-satisfaction central to personal growth
Forgiveness of others who cause distress completes the restoration of self	Acceptance and expression of accusatory feelings are sufficient
Meaning and purpose derived from spiritual insight	Meaning and purpose derived from reason and intellect

Source: Bergin (1980).

leading to an implied 'right' set of answers to the survey questionnaire. However, the 'clinical–humanistic' value pattern found by Kelly (1995) included a strong religious dimension, even if for many counsellors this dimension was expressed through spiritual values rather than through conventional religious observance. The finding that counsellors are not power-oriented, and are the type of people who would question traditional morality, reinforces the idea introduced in Chapter 2 that counselling represents a set of moral values that are somewhat outside the mainstream of Western capitalist society, and gives credence to the notion that one of the effects of counselling and psychotherapy might be to socialize clients into this set of values.

The research that has been carried out into the distinctive moral values of therapy practitioners, and the differences between these values and the values held by many clients has largely been conducted by administering questionnaires to groups of therapists and clients. However, by using research approaches such as discourse analysis and conversation analysis it is also possible to explore the process through which moral issues are negotiated between therapists and clients within actual therapy sessions.

The work of Jarl Wahlstrom and his colleagues has investigated the ways in which clients may be helped by their therapists to reflect on their moral standpoint in relation to problematic issues in their life. For example, Kurri and Wahlstrom (2005) analysed the attribution of moral responsibility in a case of couple counselling. They found that each spouse initially adopted a fixed position of blaming the other for causing the problem that was under discussion. In the therapeutic conversation, the therapist consistently reframed what the couple were saying in terms of what Kurri and Wahlstrom (2005) described as a *principle of relational autonomy*, within which each spouse was invited to accept responsibility for his or her own actions, while at the same time acknowledging that what he or she was doing happened in the context of what their partner had done or said. This new moral position allowed the couple to create a moral space within which they could begin to find ways to change their actions, rather than being locked into a cycle of mutual blame.

In another study, Holma *et al.* (2006) analysed changes in the moral reasoning of men taking part in a therapy group for perpetrators of domestic violence. Initially, the men would not accept responsibility for assaulting their wives or partners, claiming that what happened was beyond their control, and due to alcohol, genetics, the emotional nagging of their wife, and other factors. In other words, they were victims. By contrast, the therapists facilitating the group viewed the men as entirely responsible for what they had done. The therapists used two strategies to encourage these men to accept responsibility. First, they created a group environment within which the men could share their experiences in an open and honest manner. This had the effect of bringing feelings of guilt into the open. The second strategy was to invite the men to describe in detail the minutes and seconds leading up to the assault, and to reflect on the choices that were available to them during these moments.

The research into moral reasoning in therapy suggests that issues of moral responsibility permeate the majority of counselling sessions, and that it is important for practitioners to be aware of this process, and to possess strategies for resolving moral dilemmas. Cushman (1995) argues that moral issues, in the form of questions and decisions around how to live a good life, are intrinsic to all therapy practice, but that most practitioners side-step these issues or reinterpret them in psychological terms.

> ## Box 22.2: *The legal and ethical implications of refusing to provide counselling to a lesbian client*
>
> A legal case that was pursued in the USA raises important issues around the influence that a counsellor's beliefs and values can have on the process of therapy. The case, described in detail by Hermann and Herlihy (2006), concerned the actions of a counsellor who was employed by an Employee Assistance Programme (EAP) to provide therapy to staff in a range of local businesses. After several sessions, a female client asked this counsellor for assistance in improving her relationship with her same-sex partner. The counsellor refused to do this, on the grounds that homosexuality was inconsistent with her religious beliefs. The client complained, and the situation was reviewed by the vice-president of the EAP, who offered to transfer her to another position, in which value conflicts were less likely to occur. However, no such position could be found, and the counsellor lost her job. The counsellor then sued her employer, on the basis that the company had failed to accommodate her religious beliefs – a human rights issue.
>
> An initial hearing by jury found in favour of the counsellor, but a subsequent appeal reversed these findings and supported the action taken by the employer. The appeal court ruling pointed out that employers only had to make *reasonable* accommodations for the religious beliefs of an employee, and that the introduction of an assessment procedure that ensured that this counsellor would never need to work with a client issue that was inconsistent with her religious beliefs, would have represented an unreasonable burden for the counselling agency and on her team of colleagues. The appeal court also ruled that refusing to counsel a client on certain issues could have a negative impact on the client. Although this case did not result in a complaint to the professional body to which the counsellor was affiliated, and consideration in the light of a professional ethics code, Hermann and Herlihy (2006) argue that any such referral would also have yielded a negative outcome for the counsellor.

Ethics guidelines and their basis in moral reasoning

The remainder of this chapter focuses on the issue of ethical practice. As with any other profession, counsellors are required and expected to act towards their clients in a manner that corresponds to the highest ethical standards. For example, it is clearly wrong to exploit a client for one's own gain, for example by manipulating a private practice client to remain in therapy long after he or she was well, in order to continue to collect a fee. Similarly, it would clearly be wrong to continue to implement a therapy intervention that was demonstrably doing harm to a client. However, these are examples of fairly straightforward ethical situations, where the right course of action would be obvious to most people. In practice, the complexity of therapeutic work can lead to the emergence of ethical dilemmas that are much less clear-cut. In situations where an ethically valid course of action is less obvious, how does a practitioner decide what to do? In responding to moral and ethical questions that arise in their work, counsellors can make reference to a variety of levels of moral wisdom or knowledge. Kitchener (1984) has identified four discrete levels of moral reasoning that are drawn by counsellors: personal intuition; ethical guidelines established by professional organizations; ethical principles; and, finally, general theories of moral action. These sources of moral reasoning are discussed in the following sections. The chapter then moves on to consider how these moral principles can be applied in practice.

Personal intuition

People generally have a sense of what feels right in any situation. This personal moral or ethical response is best understood as intuitive, since it is implicit rather than explicit, and taken for granted rather than systematically formulated. Most of the time, and particularly during an actual counselling session, counsellors rely on their intuitive moral judgement of 'what feels right' rather than on any more explicit guidelines. There are, however, a number of limitations or dangers involved in relying only on this way of responding to moral choices.

The first difficulty is that this kind of intuitive response is accumulated at least partially through experience, and beginning counsellors may need to have some other way of dealing with moral issues: for example, by reference to supervision or professional codes of ethics. Even for experienced counsellors, there may always be a sense in which their personal intuition is incomplete, especially in unusual or unforeseen situations. Other difficulties arise when the personal moral belief or choice of the client is outside the personal experience of the counsellor: for example, the Christian counsellor working with an Islamic client. Finally, it must be recognized that personal intuition can lead to unethical or immoral action as well as to more desirable behaviour. A counsellor in private practice, for instance, may persuade herself that a client who pays well would benefit from another ten sessions of therapy.

Despite the limitations of personal, intuitive moral reasoning, its presence is absolutely essential in counsellors. Trainers or tutors assessing candidates for counsellor training are concerned that the people they select are trustworthy, have developed a firm moral position for themselves and are capable of respecting boundaries. Counselling is an occupation in which external monitoring of ethical behaviour is extremely difficult, and therefore much depends on personal moral qualities.

Ethical guidelines developed by professional organizations

Counselling in most countries has become increasingly regulated by professional bodies. One of the functions of professional organizations such as the British Association for Counselling and Psychotherapy or the British Psychological Society is to ensure ethical standards of practice, and to achieve this objective both have produced ethical guidelines for practitioners, accompanied by procedures for dealing with complaints about unethical behaviour. In the USA, ethical guidelines have been published by the American Psychiatric Association, the American Psychological Association, the American Association for Marital and Family Therapy and the American Association for Counseling and Development (1988). In addition, some state legislatures in the USA have constructed ethical codes, as have numerous other professional groupings and agencies. All trained and competent counsellors currently in practice should be able to indicate to their clients the specific ethical guidelines within which they are operating.

Although these guidelines are undoubtedly helpful in placing on record a consensus view on many of the ethical dilemmas in counselling, they are by no means unambiguous. Each code highlights (and omits) different sets of issues, reflecting the fact that it is extremely difficult to formulate an ethical code that can cover *all* eventualities. It is important to note that these ethical codes have been developed not only to protect clients against abuse or malpractice by counsellors, but also to protect the counselling profession against state interference and to reinforce its claims to control over a particular area of professional expertise. Ethics committees and codes of practice serve a useful function in demonstrating to the outside world that the counselling house is in order, that counsellors can be relied upon to give a professional service.

Ethical principles

On occasions when neither personal intuition nor ethical codes can provide a solution to a moral or ethical issue, counsellors need to make reference to more general philosophical or ethical principles. These are the ideas or more general moral injunctions that underpin and inform both personal and professional codes. Kitchener (1984) has identified five moral principles that run through most thinking about ethical issues: autonomy, non-maleficence, beneficence, justice and fidelity.

One of the fundamental moral principles in our culture is that of the *autonomy* of individuals. People are understood as having the right to freedom of action and freedom of choice, in so far as the pursuit of these freedoms does not interfere with the freedoms of others. The concept of the autonomous person is an ideal that has clearly not been achieved in many societies, in which coercion and control are routine. Nevertheless, in the societies where counselling and psychotherapy have become established, individual freedom and rights are usually enshrined in law. This concept of autonomy has been so central to counselling that many counsellors would assert that counselling cannot take place unless the client has made a free choice to participate. Another implication for counselling of the concept of autonomy lies in the notion of informed consent: that it is unethical to begin counselling, or initiate a particular counselling intervention, unless the client is aware of what is involved and has given permission to proceed.

Although it may be morally desirable to act as though clients are autonomous people capable of freedom of thought and action, there are many counselling situations in which the concept of autonomy is problematic. From a theoretical perspective, counsellors working from a psychoanalytic or radical behaviourist position would question the very possibility of individual autonomy, arguing that most of the time the behaviour of individual people is controlled by powerful external or internal forces. Counsellors influenced by feminist or family therapy perspectives would argue that in many instances autonomy may not be an ideal, and that very often clients need to move in the direction of greater relatedness or interdependence.

The freedom of choice and action of clients is also limited by a variety of practical circumstances. For example, few people would suppose that young children are capable of informed consent regarding the offer of counselling help, but it is difficult to decide at just what age a young person is able to give consent. Even with adult clients it may be hard to explain just what is involved in counselling, which is an activity that is centred on first-hand experiential learning. Furthermore, the limits of client autonomy may be reached, at least for some counsellors, when the client becomes 'mentally ill', suicidal or a danger to others. In these situations, the counsellor may choose to make decisions on behalf of the client.

To summarize, the principle of freedom of choice and action is a theme that lies at the heart of much counselling practice. However, it is also evident that the concept of personal autonomy is not a simple one, and certainly not sufficient as a guide to action and good practice in all circumstances.

Non-maleficence refers to the instruction to all helpers or healers that they must 'above all do no harm'. Beneficence refers to the injunction to promote human welfare. Both these ideas emerge in the emphasis in codes of practice that counsellors should ensure that they are trained to an appropriate level of competence, that they must monitor and maintain their competence through supervision, consultation and training, and that they must work only within the limits of their competence.

One of the areas in which the principle of non-maleficence arises is the riskiness or harmfulness of therapeutic techniques. It would normally be considered acceptable for a client to experience deeply uncomfortable feelings of anxiety or abandonment during a counselling session, if such an episode were to lead to beneficial outcomes. But at what point does the discomfort become sufficient to make the intervention unethical? Some approaches to counselling advocate that clients be encouraged to take risks in experimenting with new forms of behaviour. The principle of autonomy might suggest that, if the client has given informed consent for the intervention to take place, then he or she has responsibility for the consequences.

However, in practice it can be difficult explicitly to agree on every step in the therapy process. The counsellor or therapist may well not know about the potential riskiness of a technique, given the lack of research on many aspects of practice and the infrequency with which practitioners are influenced by research studies. Research studies also tend to focus on what works rather than on what does not work, and rarely draw attention to procedures that go badly wrong.

Moral dilemmas concerning *beneficence* are often resolved by recourse to utilitarian ideas. The philosopher John Stuart Mill defined ethical behaviour as that which brought about 'the greatest good for the greatest number'. The question of whether, for example, it was ethical to refer a highly socially anxious client to group counselling might depend on whether it could be predicted that, on balance, the benefits of this type of therapy outweighed the costs and risks. Quite apart from the uncertainty involved in ever knowing whether a therapeutic intervention will be helpful or otherwise in a particular case, the application of utilitarian ideas may conflict with the autonomous right of the client to make such decisions for himself or herself, or might lead to paternalism.

The principle of *justice* is primarily concerned with the fair distribution of resources and services, on the assumption that people are equal unless there is some acceptable rationale for treating them differently. In the field of counselling, the principle of justice has particular relevance to the question of access to services. If a counselling agency has a lengthy waiting list, is it ethical for some clients to be offered long-term counselling while others go without help? If the agency introduces a system of assessment interviews to identify the clients most in need of urgent appointments, can it be sure that its grounds for making decisions are fair rather than discriminatory? Is it just for a counselling agency to organize itself in such a way that it does not attract clients from minority or disadvantaged groups? Kitchener (1984: 50) points to the special significance of justice for counselling in writing that:

> psychologists ought to have a commitment to being 'fair' that goes beyond that of the ordinary person. To the extent we agree to promote the worth and dignity of each individual, we are required to be concerned with equal treatment for all individuals.

The point here is that the conditions of trust and respect that are fundamental to the counsellor–client relationship are readily undermined by unjust behaviour.

The principle of *fidelity* relates to the existence of loyalty, reliability, dependability and acting in good faith. Lying, deception and exploitation are all examples of primary breaches of fidelity. The rule of confidentiality in counselling also reflects the importance of fidelity. One aspect of counselling that is very much concerned with fidelity is the keeping of contracts. The practitioner who accepts a client for counselling is, either explicitly or implicitly, entering into a contract to stay with that client and give the case his or her best efforts. Situations in which the completion of the contract is not fulfilled, because of illness, job change or other counsellor factors, need to be dealt with sensitively to prevent breaches of fidelity.

This discussion of moral principles of autonomy, non-maleficence, beneficence, justice and fidelity has provided several illustrations of the fact that although these moral ideas are probably always relevant, they may equally well conflict with each other in any particular situation. Beauchamp and Childress (1979) have suggested that, following legal terminology, such principles should be regarded as prima facie binding. In other words, they must be abided by unless they conflict with some other principle, or there are extenuating circumstances. But when they are in conflict, or when such special circumstances do exist, what should be done?

General moral theories

Kitchener (1984) reviews some of the general theories of moral philosophy that can be called upon to resolve complex ethical dilemmas. Utilitarianism, the theoretical perspective that was mentioned in relation to beneficence, can be useful in this respect. The application of a utilitarian approach would be to consider an ethical decision in the light of the costs and benefits for each participant in the event: for example, the client, the family of the client, other people who are involved and the counsellor. Another core philosophical approach is derived from the work of Kant, who proposed that ethical decisions should be universalizable. In other words, if it is right to breach confidentiality in this case, it must be right to do so in all similar cases in the future.

A practical approach to applying Kant's principle of universality to resolving ethical issues in counselling has been put forward by Stadler (1986). She advocates that any ethical decision should be subjected to tests of 'universality', publicity' and 'justice'. The decision-maker should reflect on the following questions:

1 Would I recommend this course of action to anyone else in similar circumstances? Would I condone my behaviour in anyone else? (Universality)

2 Would I tell other counsellors what I intend to do? Would I be willing to have the actions and the rationale for them published on the front page of the local newspaper or reported on the evening news? (Publicity)

3 Would I treat another client in the same situation differently? If this person was a well known political leader, would I treat him or her differently? (Justice)

An alternative position developed within moral philosophy has been to argue that it is just not possible to identify any abstract moral criteria or principles on which action can be based. For example, in debates over abortion some people support the moral priority of the rights of the unborn child whereas others assert the woman's right to choose. Philosophers such as MacIntyre (1981) argue that such debates can never be resolved through recourse to abstract principles. MacIntyre (1981) suggests instead that it is more helpful always to look at moral issues in their social and historical context. Moral concepts such as 'rights' or 'autonomy' only have meaning in relation to the cultural tradition in which they operate. MacIntyre suggests that a tradition can be seen as a kind of ongoing debate or conversation within which people evolve moral positions that make sense to them at the time, only to see these positions dissolve and change as social and cultural circumstances move on. Within any cultural tradition, certain *virtues* are identified as particularly representing the values of the community. For example, in many counselling circles, authenticity is regarded as a primary virtue. In the academic community, by contrast, the key virtue is intellectual rigour or rationality.

From a 'virtues' perspective on moral decision-making, the important thing is to keep the conversation open, rather than to suppose that there can ever be an ultimately valid, fixed answer to moral questions. The implications for counselling of adopting a virtues perspective are explored in more detail by Meara *et al.* (1996), Dueck and Reimer (2003) and Wong (2006). The British Association for Counselling and Psychotherapy (2001b: 4) *Ethical Framework for Good Practice* explicitly draws on a 'virtues' perspective by identifying a set of *personal qualities* that all practitioners should possess.

- Empathy: the ability to communicate understanding of another person's experience from that person's perspective.
- Sincerity: a personal commitment to consistency between what is professed and what is done.
- Integrity: personal straightforwardness, honesty and coherence.
- Resilience: the capacity to work with the client's concerns without being personally diminished.
- Respect: showing appropriate esteem to others and their understanding of themselves.
- Humility: the ability to assess accurately and acknowledge one's own strengths and weaknesses.

- Competence: the effective deployment of skills and knowledge needed to do what is required.
- Fairness: the consistent application of appropriate criteria to inform decisions and actions.
- Wisdom: possession of sound judgement that informs practice.
- Courage: the capacity to act in spite of known fears, risks and uncertainty.

The British Association for Counselling and Psychotherapy Ethical Framework additionally suggests that these qualities should be 'deeply rooted in the person concerned and developed out of personal commitment rather than the requirement of a personal authority' (2001b: 4).

Finally, it is perhaps worth noting that the tension in the field of moral philosophy between abstract, generalized moral systems (such as utilitarianism or Kantian ethics) and the more recent tradition-based 'virtue' approach to moral inquiry is mirrored in the debate over differences between men's and women's modes of moral decision-making. Chodorow (1978) and other feminist writers have suggested that men aspire to make moral decisions on the basis of abstract principles, whereas women's moral decision-making is grounded in consideration of the impact different decisions would have on the network of relationships within which the woman lives her life. The impact of different systems of moral thinking can also be detected in debates over multiculturalism. To some extent, it can be said that Western moral and legal systems are built around utilitarian or other ideas about moral rules, understood in abstract theoretical terms, whereas most non-Western cultures approach morality from a position in which moral virtues are invested in qualities of persons. It can be seen, then, that debates over how to make sense of moral issues in fact underpin or lie behind many of the other debates and issues in counselling and psychotherapy.

Applying moral principles and ethical codes: from theory to practice

It would be reassuring to be able to take for granted that someone who is a counsellor is inevitably a person of integrity and virtue who acts in accordance with an impeccable ethical code. This is far from being the case. There is ample evidence of ethical malpractice among counsellors and psychotherapists. A survey of ethical complaints against credentialed counsellors in the USA, carried out by Neukrug *et al.* (2001), found that 24 per cent of complaints were for an inappropriate dual relationship, 17 per cent for incompetence, 8 per cent misrepresentation of qualifications, 7 per cent sexual relationship with a client, and 5 per cent breach of confidentiality. These statistical data are brought to life in the many cases of therapist abuse of clients vividly described by Bates (2006), Masson (1988, 1991, 1992) and Singer and Lalich (1996).

On the other hand, the overall rate of ethical transgression appears to be low. An analysis carried out on the records of the complaints department of the British Association for Counselling and Psychotherapy found that only around an average of 15 actionable complaints were received each year (Khele *et al.* 2008; Symons *et al.* 2011). Male counsellors were more likely to be complained against compared with their female colleagues, and the source of more than half of the complaints was a member of the profession or trainee, rather than a member of the public. This low rate of complainant, and the fact that complaints predominantly came people in the profession who were familiar with the system, raises questions about whether the procedure for making a complaint (at the British Association for Counselling and Psychotherapy and other similar bodies) acts as a barrier that prevents some aggrieved clients from taking action.

Symons (2012) carried out a survey of therapy clients who had been the subject of an ethical breach by their therapist, but had chosen not too make a complaint. When asked to talk about what had stopped them from pursing their complaints, many of them stated that what they would have wanted was some form of mediation rather than a formal tribunal, and that it would just be 'his word against mine'. The British Association for Counselling and Psychotherapy is to be commended for its transparency in commissioning this research. What it shows is that it is in fact hard to determine, with any certainty, the extent of ethical misconduct in counselling. The cases discussed in the present chapter are the tip of the iceberg, because they have received wide publicity. Beyond that, the records of professional associations represent the visible part of the iceberg. It is inevitable that there is more beneath the surface – but no one knows how much more.

The question of the ethical basis of counselling practice is not merely a topic for theoretical debate, but a matter of immediate concern for many counsellors, clients and managers of counselling agencies. In order to function in an ethically acceptable manner, there are a series of key issues that counsellors need to consider:

- clarity around accountability;
- negotiating consent;
- the limits of persuasion;
- dual relationships;
- sexual attraction between counsellor and client;
- using touch.

Ethical practice requires that counsellors and counselling agencies need to be aware of the kinds of ethical challenge associated with each of these areas, and develop strategies for responding to them if and when they occur.

Whose agent is the counsellor?

One of the key ethical questions that can arise in the day-to-day practice of counselling is that of counsellor accountability. On whose behalf is the counsellor working? Is the counsellor only the agent of the client, only acting on behalf of the client? Or can there be other people who have legitimate demands on the allegiance of the counsellor? Traditionally, many counsellors have attempted to espouse a rigorous 'client-centred' ethos. Nevertheless, there are many situations where absolute client-centredness may not be morally and ethically the correct course of action. For instance, a client who is HIV positive may be engaging in unsafe sex that puts his or her partners or family at risk. A workplace counsellor being paid by a company may be under pressure to achieve a particular type of result with a client. A counsellor working with an adolescent may find the parents giving suggestions or seeking information. Agency is very often an issue in relationship or marital counselling. Some practitioners and researchers would argue that conducting therapy with one spouse is likely to lead to feelings of alienation and rejection in the other spouse, and eventually to separation and divorce. Even in work with both spouses, the interests of the children of the marriage can become a central consideration.

Conflict between fidelity to the client and other demands on the counsellor can also occur in 'third party' counselling settings, such as employee counselling or employee assistance programmes (Wise 1988). In these situations, the counsellor may be paid or employed by an organization, and may in fact be viewed by the organization as being primarily responsible to it rather than to the client (Bond 1992). There may be both overt and subtle pressures on the counsellor to disclose information about the client, or to ensure that the counselling arrives at a predetermined outcome (e.g., a troublesome employee being 'counselled' to take early retirement). Sugarman (1992) makes a number of recommendations concerning the maintenance of ethical standards in workplace counselling:

- discover the objectives the organization is attempting to fulfil by providing a counselling service;
- identify any points at which the counselling provision might benefit the organization at the expense of the individual;
- identify any points at which the organization exceeds its right to control aspects of the employee's behaviour;
- negotiate with the organization about what is to be understood by 'confidentiality', and the conditions under which it will or will not be maintained;
- discover whether the resources being allocated to counselling are sufficient to do more good than harm;
- develop a written policy statement concerning the provision of counselling within the organization.

Further discussion of the issue of accountability in workplace counselling can be found in Carroll (1996) and Shea and Bond (1997).

Another area of counselling that is associated with major dilemmas around accountability and agency is the domain of work with people who have been, or are being, sexually abused (Daniluk and Haverkamp 1993). In many countries there is a legal requirement on the counsellor to report instances of child sexual abuse to the appropriate legal authority. If a client tells the counsellor that he or she has been abused as a child, or that his or her children are being abused, the counsellor must then make a difficult decision about when and how to report this information to the authorities. Any move of this type clearly has profound implications for the relationship between client and counsellor. It also has implications for the ways that counsellors and counselling agencies carry out their work. For example, it becomes necessary to inform clients at the start of counselling that the counsellor would need to breach confidentiality in these circumstances.

Levine and Doueck (1995) carried out a thorough study of the impact of 'mandated reporting' on counselling practice in the USA. Their book offers a comprehensive analysis of the issues involved in this kind of work. They found that there are many different strategies that counsellors adopt in an attempt to preserve the therapeutic relationship at the point of reporting, including anonymous reporting, shifting responsibility to their supervisor, child protection agency or the law and encouraging the client to self-report. Kennel and Agresti (1995) found a greater reluctance to report among female than male therapists.

Some of the most painful and difficult dilemmas over accountability arise in relation to the counsellor's 'duty to warn and protect' in cases where their client threatens violence to another person. The difficulties arising from this kind of situation are illustrated in the well known *Tarasoff* case (Box 22.3).

Box 22.3: *The 'duty to protect and warn': ethical dilemmas arising from the Tarasoff case*

In August 1969, Prosenjit Poddar was a voluntary outpatient at the university health service in Berkeley, California, receiving therapy from a psychologist, Dr Lawrence Moore. Poddar had informed his therapist of his intention to kill his girlfriend, Tatiana Tarasoff, when she returned from a trip to Brazil. In consultation with two psychiatrist colleagues, Dr Moore recommended that Poddar be committed to hospital for observation. This decision was overruled by the chief of psychiatry. Poddar moved into an apartment with Tatiana's brother, near to where she stayed with her parents. Dr Moore wrote to the chief of police asking him to confine Poddar, and verbally asked the campus security service to detain him if he was seen. They did so. Poddar assured the campus officers that he meant no harm, and they released him. Poddar subsequently murdered Tatiana Tarasoff. No warning had been given to either the victim or her family. The chief of psychiatry asked the police to return the letter written by Dr Moore and directed that the letter and case notes be destroyed. The University of California was sued by the parents of Tatiana Tarasoff, on the grounds that they should have been warned of the danger to their daughter. The defence stated that, after Poddar had been involved with the police, he had broken off all contact with the hospital, and was no longer one of their patients. A lower court rejected the case, but on appeal a higher court found for the parents.

The outcome of this case clearly carries a number of implications for counsellors and psychotherapists. Counsellors need to be willing to breach client–therapist confidentiality when the safety of others is at risk. Counsellors need to do everything possible to 'warn and protect' those in danger from their clients. Many states in the USA have enacted laws that make the failure to protect a criminal offence (Fulero 1988; Austin *et al.* 1990). Counsellors should be able to assess accurately and reliably the potential dangerousness of clients. Finally, counselling agencies must enact specific policies and procedures for dealing with such cases.

The Tarasoff case demonstrates some of the complexities of ethical decision-making in counselling, and how ethical considerations can affect the counselling process itself. The right of the client, Prosenjit Poddar, to respect for his autonomy and for the confidentiality of his disclosures to his therapist was in conflict with the fundamental duty to protect life. The information about his intention to kill his girlfriend was shared with his therapist because they had a strong therapeutic relationship, but this relationship was destroyed by the action taken in an attempt to prevent violence. The therapist himself was faced with contradictory advice and guidance from professional colleagues. The situation necessitated him liaising with the police, a course of action that he had not been trained to undertake effectively.

Many clients express anger and resentment towards others in their counselling sessions. From some theoretical perspectives, such episodes can be interpreted as 'cathartic' and beneficial. On the other hand, as the Tarasoff case and many other such cases (see Austin *et al.* 1990 for details of 17 similar cases heard in courts in the USA between 1975 and 1986) reveal, there are occasions when such client intentions are turned into action.

The Tarasoff case and the ensuing discussions over the 'duty to protect and warn' are part of a broader ethical issue relating to the problem of agency. Is the counsellor an agent only of the client, or is he or she also accountable to other people with an interest in the case?

Issues associated with the 'duty to warn' of the counsellor are also encountered in AIDS counselling, mainly around the disclosure of HIV status to sexual partners of the client. Research by McGuire *et al.* (1995) suggests that counsellors working in this field are in fact very likely to seek to warn partners, and in some cases may even go as far as physically to detain clients who refuse to cooperate. Costa and Altekruse (1994) have compiled a valuable set of duty-to-warn guidelines for counsellors working in the HIV/AIDS field.

The accountability of counsellors can stretch beyond situations that concern the immediate provision of therapy. In 2008, Kenneth Pope, a psychologist who is a leading international figure carrying out research into ethical issues in therapy, resigned from the American Psychological Association in protest against what he regarded as its inadequate response to the involvement of psychologists in detainee interrogation in settings like the Guantanamo Bay Detainment Camp and the Abu Ghraib prison (see Pope, no date). Pope, and others, have argued that the American Psychological Association had not been sufficiently forthright in protesting against the use of psychological methods in interrogation, for fear of risking Department of Defence contracts for psychological research, and employment of psychologists within the US intelligence services (Bond 2008). The debate that has taken place within the US psychological community over this issue, and the action taken by Kenneth Pope, function as a reminder that there exists a level of collective responsibility, within a professional group, that operates in addition to the personal responsibility of individual members.

In conclusion, it is important to keep in mind that, in most counselling theory, there is an implicit assumption that throughout the counselling process the therapist acts solely as an agent of the client. The examples discussed in this section demonstrate that this view oversimplifies the situation – practice always takes place in a social and organizational context. An important task for any counsellor, therefore, is to be aware of these relationships and systems, and to be willing to explore, and at times defend, the appropriate boundaries. Nevertheless, there are some occasions on which the counsellor has a duty to the wider social good, and has no choice but to breach the boundary of accountability in relation to an individual client.

Negotiating informed consent

The use of *informed consent* represents one of the main strategies for ensuring that ethical principles are reflected in practice. Informed consent involves providing the client with accurate and adequate information about the therapy that they are being offered, and other alternative therapies that might be available. The person is then allowed sufficient time to make up his or her own mind, is offered an opportunity to ask questions, is not subjected to any kind of coercive pressure, and then makes a decision that forms a contract or binding agreement between himself/herself and the therapist. The importance of informed consent in counselling and psychotherapy was underscored by the outcome of the *Osheroff* legal action in the USA. Osheroff had received unsuccessful inpatient psychodynamic therapy in a private psychiatric facility, and later sued the centre that had not obtained his consent for the treatment that had been provided, and specifically that he had not been offered the choice of pharmacological treatment.

In practice, there are a number of difficulties involved in achieving a satisfactory consent procedure (Barnett *et al.* 2007; Beahrs and Gutheil 2001). These include:

- making information available in a form that the client will understand;
- using time that could otherwise be devoted to therapy;
- providing information that will cover every eventuality in therapy (i.e., all the different techniques or therapeutic strategies that might be employed);
- collecting up-to-date accurate information about the alternative treatments that are (a) in principle available, and (b) available within the locality;
- conveying information about alternatives in an even-handed manner, rather than steering the client in the direction of the therapist's preferred approach;
- knowing whether the client is genuinely agreeing, or is merely deferring to what they regard as the superior wisdom of an expert therapist.

A valuable principle, in relation to these issues, is to adopt a strategy of *process consent*: rather than assuming that informed consent is only a matter to be dealt with at the start of therapy, the practitioner routinely checks out with the client, on a regular basis, whether he or she feels they have sufficient information, and are satisfied with the course that is being taken in therapy. For example, Marzillier (1993) has suggested that informed consent should be seen as a process or dialogue, extending over more than one meeting, and being reviewed at later stages in ongoing therapy. Pomerantz (2005) carried out a survey of psychotherapists in the USA, which asked them to indicate the point in therapy at which they typically discussed a range of consent issues. These therapists reported that they would usually discuss contractual/business issues, such as payment, missed appointment arrangements and confidentiality with clients in the meeting, would negotiate most other consent issues in the second session, but would not be in a position to agree the length of therapy until at least the end of the third session.

Full informed consent is an ideal that is difficult to achieve in reality. It is difficult for some clients to enter a counselling relationship at all, and there is a danger that some people might be deterred by receiving a mass of detailed information during or at the end of their first meeting with a counsellor. Some clients may be too upset or traumatized to assimilate informed consent information. Other clients may not understand what it means. Many counsellors and counselling agencies provide clients with a leaflet explaining the principles of their therapy, outlining practical arrangements and informing them of complaints procedures. Handelsman and Galvin (1988) and Pomerantz and Handelsman (2004) have proposed that therapists and therapy agencies should give clients a list of questions that they should ask their therapist, with time being set aside to discuss these questions (see Table 22.2).

TABLE 22.2 Information you have a right to know

When you come for therapy, you are buying a service. Therefore, you need information to make a good decision. Below are some questions you might want to ask. We've talked about some of them. You are entitled to ask me any of these questions, if you want to know. If you don't understand my answers, ask me again.

I.   Therapy
- What is the name of your kind of therapy?
- How did you learn how to do this therapy? Where?
- How does your kind of therapy compare with other kinds of therapy?
- How does your kind of therapy work?
- What are the possible risks involved? (like divorce, depression)
- What percentage of clients improve? In what ways? How do you know? (e.g., published research? your own practice experience? discussions with your colleagues?)
- What percentage of clients get worse? How do you know?
- What percentage of clients improve or get worse without this therapy? How do you know?
- About how long will it take?
- What should I do if I feel therapy isn't working?
- Will I have to take any kind of tests? What kind?
- Do you follow a therapy manual with predetermined steps?
- Do you do therapy over the phone? Over the Internet?

II. Alternatives
- What other types of therapy or help are there for my problem? (like support groups)
- How often do they work? How do you know?
- What are the risks and benefits of these other approaches? What are the risks and benefits of NO therapy?
- How is your type of therapy different from these others?
- Do you prescribe medication? Do you work with others who do?
- (If I am taking medications:) Will you be working together with the doctor who prescribed my medication? How much do you know about the medications I am taking?

III. Appointments
- How are appointments scheduled?
- How long are sessions? Do I have to pay more for longer ones?
- How can I reach you in an emergency?
- If you are not available, who is there I can talk to?
- What happens if the weather is bad, or I'm sick?

IV. Confidentiality
- What kind of records do you keep? Who has access to them? (insurance companies, supervisors, etc.)
- Under what conditions are you allowed to tell others about the things we discuss? (suicidal or homicidal threats, child abuse, court cases, insurance companies, supervisors, etc.)
- Do other members of my family, or the group, have access to information?
- How do governmental regulations influence how you handle the confidentiality of my records? Under these regulations, is confidentiality equal for all types of information?

TABLE 22.2 *Continued*

V.   Money
 ● What is your fee?
 ● How do I need to pay? At the session, monthly, etc.?
 ● Do I need to pay for missed sessions?
 ● Do I need to pay for telephone calls, letters, or emails?
 ● What are your policies about raising fees? (for example, How many times have you raised them in the past two years?)
 ● If I lose my source of income, can my fee be lowered?
 ● If I do not pay my fee, will you pursue legal or debt collection activity? Under what circumstances?

VI.   General
 ● What is your training and experience? Are you licensed by the state? Supervised? Board certified?
 ● Are you a psychologist? Psychiatrist? Family therapist? Counsellor? What are the advantages and limitations of your credentials?
 ● Who do I talk to if I have a complaint about therapy which we can't work out?

I have already given you some written information. This included a contract, privacy statement, brochure, and/or consent form. We have also talked about some aspects of our work together. This information dealt with most of these questions. I will be happy to explain them, and to answer other questions you have. This will help make your decision a good one. You can keep this information. Please read it carefully at home. We will also look this over from time to time.

Sources: Handelsman and Galvin (1988); Pomerantz and Handelsman (2004).

Braaten *et al.* (1993) carried out a study in which members of the public were invited to write down the questions that they would like to ask a therapist. Half of the participants in the study were invited to respond spontaneously; the other half were provided with a copy of a list of questions. In both groups, people wanted to know about how the therapy would work, and the personal characteristics (e.g., values, previous experience) of the therapist. The main differences arising from providing participants with a list of questions was to stimulate more queries about confidentiality and fees.

Box 22.4: *Informed consent in action*

Informed consent is one of the bedrock principles of ethical best practice in health care, business and may other sectors of life in addition to counselling. The literature on informed consent highlights the key principles around which meaningful informed consent is constructed. But what happens in practice? How do therapy practitioners actually deal with the informed consent process? O'Neill (1998) interviewed a number of therapists and clients in Canada, around their experiences of negotiating consent. What he found was a broad spectrum of practices. For example, in the field of eating disorders, one therapist appeared to base her whole approach around a collaborative consensual stance:

> I negotiate. I hear their story and then I interpret it back to them from how I've heard it. Then I ask them what they expect or what they want from therapy – what they want from therapy. Then I exchange with them, or tell them what I think, how I would work with them, with their problem. Even when they

agree, and most do, nothing is carved in stone. I don't know if its going to work either. . . . The important thing is knowing that they're not a failure if it doesn't work. You can suggest something, and if it doesn't work, we'll try something else.

(O'Neill 1998: 58)

By contrast, another therapist, running a group-based residential programme for people with eating disorders, stated that:

It's a group therapy programme, and everybody has to eat the same way otherwise nobody would eat. So they have to eat off the hospital menu, which means they have to eat meat . . . We ask people not to exercise until their eating is normal, because . . . we can't tell how much of their exercise is purging and how much of it is, whatever.

(O'Neill 1998: 74)

The clients who were interviewed by O'Neill (1998) overwhelmingly wanted more choice, more information, and a greater degree of involvement in the process of deciding on what kind of therapy was best for them. One client pointed out that:

We know our own selves and we should be able to figure out what is best for us. Its like when you go into a clothing store – you know which clothes you're going to feel comfortable in and what you like. I think it's the same with therapy.

(O'Neill 1998: 68)

Another client observed that:

Should a therapist just say, 'This is what I offer,' instead of saying, 'These are the possibilities?' It seems that that really just serves the therapist . . . It just seems like that might be a way for therapists to sort of keep clients – rather than mentioning alternatives.

(O'Neill 1998: 68)

The study by O'Neill (1998) offers a rich account and discussion of the complexities of informed consent in practice. Overall, his findings suggest that the majority of therapists do not adequately address consent issues, and that as a result, a sizeable minority of clients are either dissatisfied with the therapy they receive, or drop out.

How far should the client be pushed or directed? The use of persuasion, suggestion and challenge

One of the fundamental tensions in counselling and psychotherapy arises from the definition and perception of the role of the therapist. In the client-centred/person-centred and psychodynamic traditions, the position is generally taken that the role of the therapist is to be reflective and patient, and on the whole to allow the client to use the time to arrive at his or her own understandings and insights. There is another tradition, represented by gestalt therapy, the 'body' therapies and cognitive–behavioural approaches, which favours a much more active stance on the part of the therapist through the use of interventions that attempt to accelerate the pace of change or force breakthroughs. It is essential not to exaggerate the dichotomy between these positions: client-centred counsellors challenge clients and gestalt therapists engage in empathic listening. However, the use of confrontative and manipulative tactics in therapy has been seen by many (Lakin 1988) as raising a number of ethical issues.

A central ethical issue here is the principle of informed consent. The ethical value of autonomy implies that clients should have a choice regarding treatment. The notion of choice rests on the idea that the person responds to information in a rational manner. The aim of confrontation techniques, by contrast, is to break through the rationalizations and intellectualized defences that the client has erected. To tell the client exactly what will happen would nullify the effectiveness of the intervention. Moreover, some techniques, such as 'paradoxical' methods, require giving the client contradictory information; for example, asking an insomniac client to check the time on an alarm clock every hour through the night.

These techniques also raise questions regarding beneficence. There is little research evidence to support the effectiveness of approaches that are highly confrontative. In fact, in their tightly controlled study of encounter groups, Lieberman et al. (1973) found that there were more casualties in the groups run by leaders who were high on challenge and emphasized catharsis. Lakin (1988: 3) considers that confrontation may at times be performed to meet the needs of the therapist rather than those of the client: 'active and aggressive interviewing may be based on egotistical wishes to prove one's effectiveness'.

An extreme example of a brand of highly active therapy that went beyond any acceptable limit to become overtly abusive is given by Masson (1988) in his account of the history of 'direct psychoanalysis' developed by the psychiatrist John Rosen, which included the use of physical violence, verbal assault, deception and imprisonment. Lakin (1988) describes a similar case, relating to the Centre for Feeling Therapy, where therapists again engaged in physical and verbal violence, and also encouraged extra-marital affairs among couples who were in therapy. The leading figures in both these enterprises were sued by patients, and debarred from practice. Although the levels of abuse and cruelty to clients exhibited in these cases may seem outrageous, it is important to note, as Masson (1988) and Lakin (1988) both point out, that the founders of these therapies were highly qualified and trained, had published widely and had been commended by leaders in their profession for their pioneering work.

These examples of confrontation and challenge illustrate very direct and overt attempts to control clients, to modify their beliefs and behaviour. A much more subtle form of control is implied in the issue of *false memories* of childhood sexual abuse. Most therapists are familiar with the experience of working with a client who seems suddenly to remember events from the past – for instance, memories of abuse or humiliation – that had been hidden for many years. Given that the events being recalled are in the distant past, and that quite possibly no independent or objective evidence exists concerning whether they actually happened or not, there is often an issue over whether these memories are genuine or are perhaps false and manufactured. Some people who wish to deny the prevalence of child sexual abuse in general, or are defending accusations in specific cases, have argued that some counsellors and therapists are too eager to suggest to their clients that they have been abused. These counsellors are said to be too ready to interpret feelings and images of childhood as indicators of abuse.

This is not the place to review the vast literature on the veracity or otherwise of recovered memories of childhood. The interested reader is recommended to consult Enns *et al.* (1995) and Spence (1994). The point is that there are powerful moral issues here. If a therapist does plant false memories, then he or she can end up being the instigator of great harm to an individual and their family. If, on the other hand, a therapist avoids drawing conclusions about abuse, or naming the abuse, the effect on the client can be equally damaging. The connection between the use of a counselling technique and its moral consequences is very clear in this type of case. How actively should a counsellor interpret the client's experience? Should the counsellor wait until there is overwhelming evidence to support the interpretation? Under what circumstances are clinical intuition and 'hunches' allowable?

Dual relationships

Dual relationships in counselling and psychotherapy occur when the therapist is also engaged in another, significantly different, relationship with a client (Syme 2003). Examples of dual relationships include: being a counsellor to someone who is a neighbour, friend or business partner; accepting payment from a client in the form of services (e.g., child-minding); or being the landlord to a client. Pope (1991) identifies four main ways in which dual relationships conflict with effective therapy.

First, dual relationships compromise the professional nature of the relationship. Counselling depends on the creation of an environment of emotional safety created in part by the construction of reliable professional boundaries. The existence of dual relationships makes these boundaries unclear. Second, dual relationships introduce a conflict of interest. No longer is the counsellor there solely for the client. Third, the counsellor is unable to enter into a business or other non-therapy relationship on an equal footing, because of the personal material the client has disclosed and the likelihood of transference reactions, such as dependence. Finally, if it became acceptable for counsellors to engage in dual relationships after counselling had terminated it would become possible for unscrupulous practitioners to use their professional role to set up relationships engineered to meet their needs.

Research on the prevalence of dual relationships (Pope 1991; Salisbury and Kinnier 1996; Lamb and Catanzaro 1998) has shown that around one-third of therapists have at some time developed non-sexual non-therapy relationships with current or former clients. Lamb and Catanzaro (1998) found that more than half of the therapists in their survey had engaged in 'going to a client's special event' (e.g., wedding, funeral of family member, art show).

The possibility that dual relationships might have a highly destructive impact on the capacity to conduct effective therapy, has resulted in many counsellors and psychotherapists adopting a stance that therapy is impossible if there is a dual relationship. For these practitioners, any relationship with a client beyond the therapy room, is 'unspeakable' (Gabriel 2005). On the other hand, there are many situations in which dual relationships are unavoidable. Bond (1992) points out that many counsellors in schools and colleges are also employed as teachers or tutors, so it is essential to be clear about the boundaries between these roles. Doyle (1997) has discussed the dual relationship dilemmas that arise when counsellors in recovery from addictions are engaged in working with clients with the same set of problems. For example, the counsellor and client may meet at a 'twelve step' meeting.

Schank and Skovholt (1997) interviewed counsellors who lived and worked in rural areas, and had no way of avoiding encountering their client in the supermarket or at a social event. These practitioners described a range of strategies that they had developed for maintaining appropriate professional boundaries while engaging in everyday social interaction with clients. Brown (2005) has described her experience as the most experienced feminist therapist in her city and the inevitability that younger colleagues would approach her for personal therapy. Lazarus (1994: 260) has forcibly argued that the taboo against any form of dual relationship has resulted in therapy that lacks compassion and common-sense: 'one of the worst professional or ethical violations is that of permitting current risk-management principles to take precedence over humane interventions'.

The recognition that it is feasible to carry out ethical and effective therapy in the contact of a dual relationship has resulted in a reappraisal in recent years of an absolute ban on this kind of practice (Gabriel 2005; Moleski and Kiselica 2005; Lazarus and Zur 2002). Moleski and Kiselica (2005) have introduced the useful concept of a *continuum* of dual/complex client–counsellor relationships, ranging from the therapeutic to the destructive. Gabriel (2005) and Moleski and Kiselica (2005) provide valuable guidelines for monitoring and assessing the functioning of dual relationships.

Sexual exploitation of clients

A number of surveys of psychologists and psychotherapists in the USA have discovered that sexual contact between therapists and their clients is not uncommon, despite being explicitly prohibited by all the professional associations in that country. Holroyd and Brodsky (1977), in a survey of 1,000 psychologists, found that 8.1 per cent of the male and 1.0 per cent of the female therapists had engaged in sex with clients. Some 4 per cent of their sample believed that erotic contact with clients might in some circumstances be of therapeutic benefit to the client. Pope *et al.* (1979) carried out a similar anonymous questionnaire survey of 1,000 psychotherapists, and found that 7 per cent reported having had sex with a client. Finally, Pope *et al.* (1986), in another large-scale survey of American practitioners, revealed admission of erotic contact with clients in 9.4 per cent of male and 2.5 per cent of female therapists.

The meaning of these figures is open to interpretation. The estimates made by the surveys cited must be regarded as representing a minimum estimate of the prevalence of client sexual abuse by therapists because of the many factors that would lead respondents to conceal or under-report their involvement.

Bates and Brodsky (1989) have given a detailed account of one case of sexual exploitation of a client (see Box 22.5). This case, and other cases that have been studied in depth, support the following general conclusions regarding such events:

1 Effective therapy can include phases when the client is highly dependent on the counsellor, and open to such suggestion or manipulation.

2 Within the confidential, secretive environment of the counselling relationship it is possible for counsellors to engage in unethical behaviour with little likelihood of being found out.

3 The focus of counselling on the personality and inner life of the client may readily result in the client blaming himself or herself and his or her own inadequacies for what has happened.

4 Clients who have been sexually abused by professionals encounter great difficulty in achieving redress.

These principles make it possible to understand how sexual abuse of clients can occur, and why it is under-reported.

Box 22.5: *A case of 'professional incest'*

Carolyn Bates was a client in psychotherapy who was sexually abused by her therapist over a period of months. Her story is told in a book, *Sex in the Therapy Hour*, co-written with a psychologist, Barbara Brodsky (Bates and Brodsky 1989). Their account offers a unique insight into the ways in which therapy can become transformed into a sexually abusive situation that is unethical and destructive.

Carolyn Bates was a shy, overweight teenager whose father had died after a long illness when she was 15. She 'staved off' her feelings of grief and loss by immersing herself in a church group. On leaving home to enter college, she met Steve, a Vietnam War veteran, who became her boyfriend and first sexual partner. She became dependent on him 'to ward off the feelings of depression that were nearly always encroaching upon me'. At the same time, she experienced intense guilt about engaging in premarital sex, in opposition to the teachings of her church. She stopped attending church. The emotional pressure built up, exacerbated by a deteriorating relationship with her mother:

> As the tenuous relationship between Steve and me progressed through the first year, my control over these newly emerging, volatile emotions began to break down. I brimmed over with disillusionment, anger, frustration, and, above all, a pervasive sense of desperation. My reactions to any hints from Steve of ending our relationship were of such inordinate proportions that, in hindsight, I know they were related to my ongoing grief over the separation by death from my father.
>
> (Bates and Brodsky 1989: 18)

After two years in this situation, with college grades dropping, Carolyn Bates entered therapy with a psychologist, Dr X, who had been recommended by one of her friends.

For the first five months of therapy, Carolyn felt a 'sense of hope and safety', and gradually opened up and explored her feelings about the death of her father and her relationship with Steve. At that point, her relationship with her therapist was close:

> I have no doubt that much of the trust and love I had for my father was directed toward Dr X, for I perceived him as having both wisdom and an unconditional concern for my well-being. I did not recognize at the time that this transference of feelings was occurring, but I did come to perceive him as a parental figure. And so I remained very dependent, working hard in therapy, in my eagerness for his acceptance and approval, believing him to be my sole source of affirmation.
>
> (Bates and Brodsky 1989: 24)

However, as time went on Dr X began to focus more and more on sexual issues during therapy sessions, encouraging Carolyn to talk about her own sexual behaviour, and explaining his own positive attitude to casual sexual intercourse. He offered an interpretation that perhaps Carolyn was repressing her sexual feelings for him. She described this later as 'the sexualization of the therapeutic relationship'. He began hugging her at the end of sessions, then kissing her goodbye. In one session he suggested that her denial of attraction to him indicated homosexuality.

During the ninth months of therapy Dr X introduced relaxation exercises, which involved Carolyn lying down on the floor of the office. During one of these sessions he raped her. She reports 'terror', 'dissociation' and 'humiliation'. Sexual intercourse continued during eight or ten sessions over the next 12 months, always at the start of a session. During therapy, Dr X began talking more about his own problems. Eventually, some two years after entering therapy, Carolyn Bates was able to overcome her dependency and numbness and leave.

The next few months were a period of 'depression and confusion beyond hope': 'I carried with me a dark secret – I believed myself a failure in therapy . . . and blamed myself for what had occurred' (Bates and Brodsky 1989: 41). There were nightmares and suicidal thoughts. When Carolyn entered therapy with another counsellor, it became possible to confront what had happened, and to file a complaint against Dr X. Despite the fact that six other women clients of Dr X came forward to testify that they had been the victims of similar sexual exploitation, the case in the civil courts took almost five years before an out-of-court settlement was made. Court appearances involved detailed cross-examination, which was additionally humiliating and distressing. There were other painful experiences arising from appearances before the State Licensing Board, which was considering whether to revoke the professional accreditation of Dr X. The process of achieving some limited redress against this practitioner was also accompanied by media attention. At the end of it all, he reapplied for, and was granted, a licence to practise.

The damage that this type of abuse does to clients has been documented in a number of studies. For example, in her research Durre (1980: 242) observed:

many instances of suicide attempts, severe depressions (some lasting months), mental hospitalizations, shock treatment, and separations or divorces from husbands . . . Women reported being fired from or having to leave their jobs because of pressure and ineffectual working habits caused by their depression, crying spells, anger and anxiety.

One way of making sense of the prevalence of sexual acting out between clients and therapists is to regard it as an inevitable, if unfortunate, consequence of the high levels of intimacy and self-disclosure that occur in therapy. An example of this approach can be found in the work of Edelwich and Brodsky (1991), who regard sex with clients as a professional issue for which therapists should be trained to cope. They take a position of encouraging practitioners to view feelings for clients as normal: 'anyone who ministers to the needs of others is bound to have unsettling experiences with emotional currents that run outside the bounds of professional propriety. These crosscurrents arise from normal, universal human feelings' (Edelwich and Brodsky 1991: xiii). Difficulties arise not because counsellors have these feelings, but because they act on them inappropriately.

Edelwich and Brodsky identify a number of guidelines for recognizing seductiveness in themselves and in their clients, and suggest strategies for dealing ethically with feelings of attraction:

- acknowledge your own feelings;
- separate your personal feelings from your dealings with the client;
- avoid over-identifying – the client's problems are not your own;
- do not give your problems to the client;
- talk to someone else about what is happening (e.g., colleagues or supervisor);
- set limits while giving the client a safe space for self-expression;
- do not be rejecting;
- express non-sexual caring;
- avoid giving 'double messages'.

They also point out that most sexual misconduct begins with other 'boundary violations', such as touching the client, seeing him or her socially or inappropriate counsellor self-disclosure to the client, and recommend that these apparently less significant boundaries be treated with great respect.

An alternative perspective on sexual misconduct can be developed from a Jungian–feminist standpoint. Almost all therapist–client sexual behaviour takes place between male therapists and female clients, and the professional organizations that make it difficult for women to bring perpetrators to justice are dominated by men. In his book *Sex in the Forbidden Zone*, Rutter (1989) agrees with many of the practical guidelines put forward by Edelwich and Brodsky (1991), but profoundly disagrees with their analysis of underlying causes. Rutter argues that sex between professional men (not just therapists and counsellors, but also clergy, teachers, doctors and managers) and women over whom they are in a position of power or authority results from deeply held cultural myths about what it means to be male or female. Many men, according to Rutter, suppress and deny their own emotional pain and vulnerability, but hold on to a fantasy that they can be made whole through fusion with an understanding and accepting woman. The experience of sex with a woman client is, therefore, part of an unconscious search for healing and wholeness. It is, of course only a temporary means of resolving this male dilemma, and soon the sexual intimacy will seem false and the woman will be rejected.

This interpretation of the dynamics of therapist sexual behaviour is consistent with the findings of a study carried out by Holtzman (1984), who interviewed women who had been sexually involved with their therapists. Several of these women spoke of taking care of the therapist, of being aware of gratifying his emotional needs. Searles (1975) has described this process as the client unconsciously acting as therapist to the therapist.

According to Rutter (1989), women bring to this situation a lifetime of assaults to their self-esteem, of being told they are not good enough, particularly by their fathers. The experience of being in a working relationship with a powerful man who appreciates their abilities and qualities, and seeks to help them achieve fulfilment, is, for the woman, a potentially healing encounter. The betrayal of this closeness and hope brought about by sexual exploitation is, therefore, deeply damaging. Chesler (1972) interviewed ten women who had had sexual relationships with their therapists. All were described as being insecure, with low self-regard, and all blamed themselves for what had happened. Pope and Bouhoutsos (1986) suggest that women at particularly high risk of sexual exploitation from therapists are those who have previously survived incest or sexual abuse in earlier life. This point is reinforced by Mann (1989).

Rutter (1989) is perhaps, more simply, making the point that men have a strong tendency to sexualize relationships marked by high degrees of trust and intimacy. He goes further in regarding the public silence of male colleagues in the face of sexual misconduct as evidence of the pervasiveness of the underlying myth:

> Although the majority of men holding positions of trust behave ethically in the sense that they will never have sexual contact with a woman under their care, they nevertheless hold on to the hope that one day it may actually happen . . . Men who do not engage in forbidden-zone sex participate in it vicariously through the exploits of men who do. In a tribal sense, it is as if men who violate the forbidden zone are the designated surrogates for the rest of the men in the tribe.
>
> (Rutter 1989: 62)

For Rutter, then, the existence of therapist–client sexual contact is not merely a professional issue, to be contained and addressed within the boundary of training programmes and professional associations, but something that arises from fundamental issues of gender relationships in Western culture. It is, as a result, something from which we can all learn and which casts light on all therapeutic encounters between men and women.

The issue of sexual abuse of clients has been examined at some length, to demonstrate that ethical problems in counselling are not just occasional extreme events, like the Tarasoff murder, that suddenly arise to trap the practitioner in a web of competing moral demands and practical dilemmas. Moral, ethical and value issues are there in each counselling room, in each session. Whatever the counsellor does, or does not do, is an expression of values.

Ethical issues involved in the use of touch

In her review of the views of psychoanalysts concerning the use of touch in therapy, Mintz (1969: 367) quotes a famous analyst as asserting that 'transgressions of the rule against physical contact constitute . . . evidence of the incompetence or criminal ruthlessness of the analyst'. This strong rejection of the possibility of touching the client pervades the therapy literature; even therapists who *do* touch their clients find it difficult to admit to this practice (Tune 2001). The main underlying fear appears to be that touch will lead to sexual gratification on the part of the client, the therapist or both. Another ethical concern is that the client may feel violated, and accept being touched against his or her true wishes. For example, a person who has been physically or sexually abused may have a great terror of being touched, but may have little or no capacity to assert their own needs. Other people may have cultural or religious prohibitions in relation to being touched by a stranger, or by a member of the opposite sex.

An additional concern, for some counsellors, arises from anxiety about being accused by clients of being over-intimate or exploitative. This can result in the adoption of a defensive policy of never offering a gesture of comfort or physical contact. In contrast to all of these concerns about the use of touch, it also needs to be acknowledged that touching is a basic expression of human caring and compassion, and that the unwillingness of their therapist to hold or hug them, or even to shake hands, can be experienced as cold and distancing. It is clear, therefore, there are a number of legitimate ethical issues associated with the use of touch.

Box 22.6: *Impaired professional or sexual abuser?*

Within the professional literature, the discussion of therapist sexual exploitation of clients has tended to focus on the development of ways of understanding and preventing this type of unethical behaviour, and on the possibility of rehabilitating those who engage in it (for example, through requiring further training or supervision). Pilgrim and Guinan (1999) have argued that the adoption of an 'impaired professional' framework detracts attention from activities that are more appropriately defined as sexual abuse.

Pilgrim and Guinan (1999) examined the cases of ten British mental health professionals (nurses, psychiatrists, psychologists and hypnotherapists) who had been found guilty by their professional associations of sexual misconduct. The majority of these professionals had committed multiple abuse, were senior members of their organizations and had elected to work with vulnerable groups of patients. Pilgrim and Guinan suggest that the profile of these mental health professionals was similar to that of sex offenders, and the consequences of their actions were similar to those suffered by victims of sexual abuse. However, Pilgrim and Guinan found that the professional associations that dealt with these cases applied an 'ideology of empathic tolerance toward errant colleagues', and allowed some of them to continue practising. They point out that:

> rehabilitation of ... paedophiles aims, at best, at their community re-integration without re-offending. It does not aim to restore or encourage their continued contact with children ... By contrast, a rehabilitation emphasis in TSA [therapist sexual abuse] aims to restore therapists to their role and place them back once more in patient contact. The commonest scenario in this regard is the use of suspension rather than expulsion from professional bodies.
>
> (Pilgrim and Guinan 1999: 163)

For Pilgrim and Guinan, it is important to acknowledge that professional groups tend to operate a process of collective self-preservation that can result in sexually exploitative colleagues being viewed as 'patients-to-be-understood', and treated with leniency and mitigation. They question whether such an approach is publicly justifiable.

In relation to the ethics of touch in therapy, the book by Hunter and Struve (1998) affords a wise pathway through these dilemmas. Hunter and Struve (1998) base their analysis on a comprehensive discussion of the physiology and meaning of touching in human beings, and the history of touch in therapy. They make a number of recommendations, which are summarized below.

Touch is clinically appropriate when:

- the client wants to touch or be touched;
- the purpose of touch is clear;
- the touch is clearly intended for the client's benefit;
- the client understands concepts of empowerment and has demonstrated an ability to use these concepts in therapy;
- the therapist has a solid knowledge base about the clinical impact of using touch;
- the boundaries governing the use of touch are clearly understood by both client and therapist;
- enough time remains in the therapy session to process the touch interaction;
- the therapist–client relationship has developed sufficiently;
- touch can be offered to all types of clients;
- consultation/supervision is available and used;
- the therapist is comfortable with the touch.

It is clinically advisable *not* to use touch when:

- the focus of therapy involves sexual content prior to touch;
- a risk of violence exists;

- the touch occurs in secret;
- the therapist doubts the client's ability to say no;
- the therapist has been manipulated or coerced into the touch;
- the use of touch is clinically inappropriate;
- the touch is used to replace verbal therapy;
- the client does not want to touch or be touched;
- the therapist is not comfortable using touch.

These guidelines provide a useful framework for evaluating the use of touch in counselling situations. It is clear, however, that much depends on the integrity of the therapist, and on the extent to which he or she has explored the meaning of touch for them personally, and indeed has arrived at an acceptance of his or her embodiment. There can be extreme disagreements between practitioners around the use of touch, as illustrated in the case presented in Box 22.7.

Box 22.7: *To touch or not to touch? The case of Mrs B*

The well-known British psychoanalyst Patrick Casement has written at length about one of his patients, 'Mrs B' (Casement 1982, 1985, 2000). He summarized the key features of his account of this case in the following words:

> The patient . . . had been seriously scalded when she was 11 months old. At the age of 17 months she had been operated on (under local anaesthetic) to release scar tissue from the surrounding skin. During this procedure the patient's mother was holding her hand until the mother had fainted. In re-living this experience, of being left alone with the surgeon who continued to operate on her regardless of her mother's absence, the patient asked and later demanded to hold the analyst's hand if the anxiety were to become too intolerable to bear. Without this possibility she felt she would have to terminate the analysis. In considering this demand the analyst decided that it would amount to a collusive avoidance of the central aspect of the original trauma, the absence of the mother's hand after she had fainted. The restoration of the analytic 'holding', without any physical contact, and the eventual resolution of the near-delusional transference at this time in the analysis is examined in detail. The interpretation, which eventually proved effective in restoring contact with the patient's readiness to continue with the analysis, emerged from a close following of the counter-transference responses to the patient and the projective-identificatory pressures upon the analyst during the clinical sequence described.
>
> (Casement 1982: 279)

At a moment of acute psychological pain, during the reliving of an unbearably harrowing experience from childhood, a client asks her therapist to hold her hand. What would you do? Patrick Casement decided against acceding to her request, and clearly believed that he had adopted the correct course of action.

The case of Mrs B was taken as the focus for a special issue of the journal *Psychoanalytic Inquiry*, in which ten experienced analysts were invited to comment on their reading of the case. One of these commentators, Breckenridge (2000), manages to convey, within the constraints imposed by professional discourse, her contempt for the stance taken by Casement. She comments that his celebration of a 'successful' interpretation 'is an appalling, inverted justification for his having failed her'. She concludes that:

> used within ethical, cultural, and common sense constraints, physical touch communicates with a subtlety and believability that words cannot carry. Not to touch . . . also communicates; however, the communication is, I fear, about unavailable rigidity, or even worse.

> (Breckenridge 2000: 10)

The case of Mrs B raises two important issues in relation to the ethics of touch in counselling and psychotherapy. First, under what circumstances can it be unethical *not* to touch a client? Under what circumstances (even if not in the case of Mrs B) might withholding touch be morally wrong? Second, where is the line to be drawn between application of therapeutic theory and technique, and adherence to the highest moral values. It would be difficult to argue that, in the case of Mrs B, Casement was *technically* in error. But, even while acting as a competent analyst, was he *morally* in error?

Ethical issues in research on counselling

Increasingly, counsellors and counselling agencies are carrying out research into the processes and outcomes of therapy, as a means of enhancing the effectiveness of practice and in response to the expectation that all practice will be accountable. Research training always includes a strong emphasis on ethics, and professional bodies such as the British Association for Counselling and Psychotherapy, and the American Psychological Association, have published ethical guidelines specifically oriented toward the kinds of issues that can arise in the field of counselling and psychotherapy research. Some of the ethical dilemmas that can arise include:

- the client agreeing to participate in research because he or she is concerned that lack of cooperation would jeopardize their therapy;
- a client completes a research questionnaire, and uses it to convey information that has not been disclosed to the therapist (e.g., suicidal thoughts) – can the client be confident that the therapist will receive the information?

- completing questionnaires before and after every session can have a negative impact on the therapy process, by interfering with the normal therapeutic process *or* completing questionnaires can have a positive impact, by giving the client an opportunity to reflect on important issues and monitor progress towards their goals;
- a client reads a book written by a therapist they saw a few years ago, and recognizes himself in one of the case descriptions;
- a client agrees to take part in a study of therapy, then finds herself randomized into a control group that will not receive therapy until after a six-month waiting period;
- a research study involves recording being made of therapy sessions – a client agrees to this but nevertheless remains cautious about what he says to this therapist;
- a therapist gains the assent of a client to allow recordings of their work to be used in a case study – the therapist is particularly interested in the role of dreams in therapy, and consistently encourages this client to recall dream material.

As in other areas of ethical good practice, the resolution of these ethical dilemmas involves the application of principles and procedures around informed consent, confidentiality and avoidance of harm. However, the introduction of research data collection and analysis, and eventual publication of results, introduces an additional dimension of ethical complexity into a situation in which people may be emotionally vulnerable and open to manipulation. Ethical issues in counselling research are discussed in more detail in McLeod (2013a).

Strategies for maintaining ethical standards

Increasing attention has been devoted by professional organizations in recent years to the question of how to maintain and enforce ethical standards. To some extent, these efforts have been motivated, particularly in the USA but also in other countries, by the recognition that media coverage of cases of misconduct was reducing public confidence and leading government agencies to impose legal penalties, thereby reducing professional autonomy. All professional organizations require their accredited members to abide by a formal code of ethics, and all enforce procedures for disciplining members who violate these codes. Increasingly, however, aspects of the enforcement of counselling standards are being taken over by the courts. In turn, some counsellors and psychotherapists have begun to develop an area of research, called 'therapeutic jurisprudence', that focuses on the impact of the law on therapy (Wexler 1990). The relationship between the therapeutic professions and the law appears to be growing in importance (Jenkins 1997). Some counsellors, however, would argue that the intrusion of legal considerations can in some cases interfere with the creation of a productive therapeutic relationship (see Box 22.8).

Box 22.8: *Should counsellors be covered by professional indemnity insurance?*

One of the ways in which the relationship between counselling and the law is made tangible is through the existence of professional indemnity insurance. Many counsellors pay insurance premiums that cover them against the costs of civil action on grounds of professional malpractice. Counsellors in some countries, such as the USA, are required by their professional associations to carry such cover. In other countries, such as Britain, indemnity insurance is at present optional for counsellors. Mearns (1993) has argued strongly against the spread of indemnity insurance. He points out that insurance companies insist that the counsellor should deny liability if challenged by a client. Mearns (1993: 163) points out that 'this dishonesty is likely to alienate the client and at worst it could create mystification and the compounding of any abuse the client may have experienced'. He suggests, moreover, that the idea of indemnity insurance originates in professions such as law and medicine where it is accepted that the practitioner is an *expert* on the client's problem, whereas in counselling the practitioner takes the role of *facilitator*. Insurance may therefore threaten the nature of responsibility in the counselling relationship. Although Mearns supports the value of ethical codes and procedures in counselling, he suggests that it is possible to 'go too far' in the direction of institutional regulation; indemnity cover represents that step too far.

Even in the USA, where professional insurance is mandatory, some practitioners share Mearns' misgivings. Wilbert and Fulero (1988) carried out a survey of psychologists (clinical and counselling) in the state of Ohio, inviting them to complete a questionnaire on their perceptions of malpractice litigation and how it had affected their work. Many of these therapists reported that the threat of malpractice lawsuits had encouraged them to improve certain areas of their practice: for example, by using informed consent procedures and release of information forms, keeping better records, evaluating evidence of suicidal intent and making more use of supervision. However, there were other areas in which they felt that the threat of malpractice litigation had diminished their practice. Some of them said that they excluded clients who looked as though they might sue, or that they had limited their practice to a specialized clinical domain. Around one in three agreed with the statement that 'there are many times in my practice when what I do is motivated more by the need to protect myself legally than what I feel is good practice clinically'.

Ethical codes can at best only supply broad guidelines for action. There are always 'grey areas', and situations where different ethical rules might be in conflict. It is therefore necessary for counsellors to acquire an understanding of the broader ethical, moral and value considerations that inform and underpin the statements made in formal codes. Most counselling courses give considerable attention to awareness of ethical issues, drawing on standard texts such as Bond (2000), Corey *et al.* (1993) and Pope and Vasquez (2007). Bashe *et al.* (2007) have described innovative methods for training in ethical issues, based around the use of an ethics autobiography that invites the trainee to reflect on ethical and moral issues that they have encountered at different points in their life, and the strategies they have used to resolve them. There has also been some movement in the direction of providing continuing professional development training for experienced practitioners, designed to enable them to revisit ethical questions. The field is also served by an increasing amount of research on ethical issues (Miller and Thelen 1987; Lakin 1988; O'Neill 1998). Another development within the field has been the construction of ethical codes designed to reflect the moral concerns of practitioners working within approaches such as multicultural and feminist counselling, which introduce moral positions and dilemmas that may not be adequately addressed within mainstream ethics codes. There has also been considerable attention devoted to areas of practice, such as working with people with HIV/AIDS, that present practitioners with highly complex and challenging ethical situations.

One of the main techniques for addressing ethical issues in counselling practice, which has already been referred to earlier in this chapter, is the use of *informed consent*. Effective informed consent can prevent or minimize difficulties arising over issues such as disclosure of confidential information to a third party, fees and cancellation arrangements, the risks of dual relationships and the emotional or practical demands of treatment.

Some counsellors have contributed to the development of ways of helping clients who have been the victims of malpractice. This work has been mainly concentrated on the needs of clients who have been sexually exploited by therapists, and has included advocacy services, setting up self-help groups and therapy for victims (Pope and Bouhoutsos 1986). There have been serious suggestions that the best way to prevent therapist sexual abuse of clients is for all women to be seen by women therapists (Chesler 1972). What is perhaps more realistic and achievable is to ensure that all clients are informed of their rights, and that when they attempt to complain their views will be treated with respect and acted upon quickly.

The research evidence on counsellor and psychotherapist malpractice suggests that errant therapists are likely to engage in multiple acts of misconduct (Gabbard 1989). It is difficult to bring charges of professional conduct against counsellors and psychotherapists, and even harder to pursue these charges to the point at which the perpetrator is forced to quit practising. It is therefore useful for the profession to establish means of rehabilitation through which damaged and damaging counsellors can work through their problems and resume practising in a safe and facilitating manner. Strean (1993) gives some interesting case examples of his therapeutic work with therapists (male and female) who have sexually exploited their clients. This kind of intervention can also yield valuable insights into the root causes of ethical misconduct. Hetherington (2000: 275) has argued that therapists who abuse their clients not only suffer from unresolved sexual identity issues, but also harbour 'a deep antipathy toward the practice of psychotherapy'.

It is not easy to accept the idea that counsellors and psychotherapists who exploit and humiliate their clients can get away with it, or even that they might be rehabilitated. It is in the nature of counselling, particularly long-term counselling, that from time to time the practitioner will experience strong feelings towards his or her client – love, lust, anger, despair. Using these feelings in the service of the client is a constant challenge for any counsellor. It is not surprising that counsellors who fail to use these feelings constructively, and instead act them out in their relationship with their clients, inspire anger and outright rejection from their colleagues.

Conclusions

The discussion in this chapter of moral, ethical and value dimensions of counselling needs to be read in the context of all the other chapters in the book: moral issues are relevant to all aspects of therapy. In the early years of the counselling profession, moral and ethical issues were largely taken for granted. Now, there is a thriving literature on ethical ideas and dilemmas that is increasingly being taken into account within routine counselling practice. The history of counselling shows that therapy evolved to fill the vacuum left by the erosion of religion in a largely secular, scientific modern world. What is surely needed now is the reintegration of moral thinking into therapy, what MacIntyre (1981) or Meara *et al.* (1996) would call the rediscovery of the 'virtues'.

Ethical counselling is more effective counselling. For example, a study by Woods and McNamara (1980) revealed that people were likely to be more open and honest about what they said about themselves if they were convinced that the information would be heard in confidence. There are many areas of counselling practice that would repay further examination from an ethical perspective. There are important moral and ethical questions to be asked about the theories that counsellors use, the kinds of research that is carried out and the way that counsellors are trained and supervised. There is also a need for further research into the effectiveness of different strategies for addressing ethical dilemmas. Morals and ethics in counselling are not just a matter of deciding whether or not it is unethical to ask a client out on a date. Most of the time, the answers to this sort of question are obvious. What is more important, and what is starting to emerge within the counselling profession, is that *all* counselling is fundamentally concerned with dialogue between competing and contrasting moral visions (Christopher 1996; Cushman 1995).

Topics for reflection and discussion

1 Consult at least two codes of ethics published by established counselling or psychotherapy professional bodies. Compare what they say on any one ethical issue (e.g., confidentiality, dual relationships, informed consent). What are the main differences between the statements you have read? How do you make sense of the different styles and emphases of these three sets of statements? What ambiguities can you identify in these guidelines – are there any situations you can imagine where one or all of these codes would not provide you with a clear-cut recommendation for action? What suggestions do you have for improving these codes?

2 What counselling situations can you imagine in which your values would be in conflict with those held by a client? What might you do in such a situation?

3 What is your reaction to the list of 'personal virtues' identified by the British Association for Counselling and Psychotherapy (pp. 518–19)? Do these qualities have meaning for you? Would you wish to add further virtues?

Suggested further reading

The topics introduced in this chapter are explored in more depth by Bond (2000) and Pope and Vasquez (2007). Jones *et al.* (2000) is a useful book, structured around the discussion of specific moral dilemmas by a group of experienced practitioners representing different theoretical traditions in counselling. Many of the current debates about moral philosophy and its relationship to counselling and psychotherapy can be tracked in the review paper by Meara *et al.* (1996), published in a special issue of *The Counseling Psychologist* that includes commentaries on their views from other leading writers in this area. The work of Alan Tjeltveit (2000, 2004) represents an invaluable source for anyone interested in exploring the place in therapy of an awareness of moral and ethical issues that goes beyond ethical codes. The journal *Ethics and Behavior* published research papers and review articles on a range of current ethical issues in therapy.

Different formats for the delivery of counselling services

Introduction

The image of counselling that has remained, since Freud, in the forefront of the public and professional imagination has been that of a therapist in his or her own consulting room, holding a person-to-person conversation with a client or patient on a weekly basis over a period of several months. Within the context of contemporary practice, however, there exist many alternative images of where and how counselling can take place. As core therapeutic principles and methods have been identified and refined, it has become clear that these processes can be delivered through many channels. The aim of this chapter is to explore the many differing shapes and forms that counselling can take, encompassing variants of one-to-one counselling, group counselling, telephone counselling, working with couples, using the internet and self-help. The chapter also considers strategies for integrating different modes of delivery into coherent service delivery systems, such as the use of stepped care. One of the key challenges for counsellors primarily trained in face-to-face individual work is to learn how to embrace the possibilities of alternative modes of delivery that will enable the benefits of counselling to achieve a wider impact in society.

Time-limited counselling

A considerable amount of research evidence has demonstrated that most counselling and therapy takes place within a fairly limited number of sessions, and that clients seem to benefit more from earlier than from later sessions (Howard *et al.* 1986). The average number of sessions that clients receive, even when an open-ended contract is offered, is around six to eight. These findings, as well as other theoretical and pragmatic considerations, have led to a growth in interest in developing forms of 'brief therapy' or 'time-limited counselling' in which the number of sessions available to the client is defined from the outset. Brief therapy approaches have been developed within all of the major orientations to counselling – psychodynamic, cognitive–behavioural and person-centred (Budman and Gurman 1998). The decision to adopt a time-limited rather than open-ended approach to working with clients has been viewed by Budman and Gurman (1988) as reflecting a shift in underlying counsellor or therapist values (see Table 23.1).

Some researchers and practitioners have addressed the question of how few sessions are necessary to enable effective counselling to take place. The attraction of very brief counselling is that its implementation can avoid the necessity for long waiting lists. In addition, clients may also be encouraged and given hope by the assumption that they can

TABLE 23.1 A comparison of the values underlying long-term and short-term counselling

The long-term therapist	The short-term therapist
Seeks change in basic character	Pragmatic, does not believe in concept of 'cure'
Sees presenting problems as indicative of underlying pathology	Emphasizes client's strengths and resources
Wants to be there as client makes significant change	Accepts that many changes will occur after termination of therapy, and will not be observable by therapist
Is patient and willing to wait for change	Does not accept the 'timelessness' of some approaches
Unconsciously recognizes the fiscal convenience of maintaining long-term clients	Fiscal issues often muted by the nature of the organization for which the therapist works
Views therapy as always benign and useful	Views therapy as sometimes useful and sometimes harmful
Being in therapy is the most important part of the client's life	Being in the world is more important than therapy

Source: Budman and Gurman (1988).

make progress quickly. Research into very brief therapy has included examining the efficacy of a '2 + 1' model. In this approach, clients are offered two sessions one week apart, then a follow-up meeting around three months later (Barkham and Shapiro 1989, 1990a, 1990b; Dryden and Barkham 1990). One of the aims of the study was to identify the types of client most likely to benefit from this approach. Initial results, based on counselling offered to white-collar workers referred for job-related stress and relationship difficulties, suggest that at six-month follow-up, around 60 per cent of clients exhibited significant benefits (Barkham and Shapiro 1990a).

A study of even shorter counselling by Rosenbaum (1994) focused on the effects on clients of offering single-session counselling. At the beginning of the first session, clients were told:

> We've found that a large number of our clients can benefit from a single visit here. Of course, if you need more therapy, we will provide it. But I want to let you know that I'm willing to work hard with you today to help you resolve your problem quickly, perhaps even in this single visit, as long as you are ready to work hard at that today. Would you like to do that?
>
> (Rosenbaum 1994: 252)

At the end of the session (which was allowed to extend to 90–120 minutes), clients were asked if they needed further sessions. Fifty-eight per cent of clients opted for the single session. When contacted at one-year follow-up, 88 per cent of these clients rated their problems as improved or much improved. Important features of the Rosenbaum (1994) approach are that it empowers clients by giving them choice in relation to the number of sessions, and that the initial introductory statement conveys positive expectations and hope, and sets the scene for an intense exploration of the client's problem. Further discussion of the possibilities of single-session therapy can be found in Talmon (1990) and also further discussion of the possibilities of single-session therapy can be found in a later section in the present chapter.

Another variant on time-limited counselling has been to 'front-load' sessions, with perhaps three sessions in the first week, one in the second week and then a final session one month later (Zhu and Pierce 1995). The '2 + 1' model mentioned above takes this strategy. Turner *et al.* (1996) report a successful experiment, in a student counselling service, in which they retained the same number of sessions, but reduced the length of each session to 30 minutes. They found that clients seemed to gain just as much from these shorter sessions.

The practice of structuring counselling around time limits makes special demands on counsellors, and requires careful training and supervision. Counsellors and counselling agencies employing time-limited approaches also need to organize themselves to enable effective and sensitive selection of clients, and appropriate referral of clients who turn out to require longer-term work. From the wide array of theory and research into brief therapy, some central principles for time-limited counselling have emerged. These include:

- initial assessment of clients in terms of readiness for short-term work;
- engaging the active involvement and cooperation of the client, for example through using homework assignments or behavioural experiments;
- finding a specific focus for the therapy, rather than seeking to address underlying personality issues;

- an active approach by the counsellor, which provides the client with new perspectives and experiences;
- structuring the therapeutic process in terms of stages or phases;
- making strategic use of the ending of therapy to consolidate gains and integrate the experience of loss.

Further information about time-limited counselling can be obtained from a number of excellent sources (Bor and Miller 2003; Budman and Gurman 1998; Elton-Wilson 1996; Feltham and Dryden 2006; Steenberger 1992).

One of the key questions in relation to time-limited counselling concerns the issue: how much is enough? In response to waiting lists and funding constraints, many counselling services have adopted a policy of imposing a fixed limit of six, or even three sessions. It is unlikely, for the majority of clients, that this amount of sessions will be sufficient to bring about meaningful benefit. Hansen *et al.* (2002) reviewed a large number of studies that tracked the number of sessions that were required to achieve clinically significant change in 50 per cent of clients. What they found was that for people with moderate levels of problem severity, between 10 and 20 sessions were required on average. For clients dealing with more severe problems (e.g., early trauma or multiple diagnoses) more than 20 sessions were necessary to ensure that meaningful and lasting clinical benefit ensued. Hansen *et al.* (2002) conclude, on the basis of these findings, that some therapy providers may be risking harm to clients by creating the hope of effective help but then not providing enough sessions for that help to be delivered. There are complex ethical and moral issues here. In practice, the consequence of allowing some clients to stay in therapy for a long time may be growing waiting lists, with ensuing distress for potential clients and their families. In addition, long-term therapy may be more comfortable (and, in private practice, more lucrative) for therapists – short-term therapy is harder work.

It is important for counsellors and service managers to be clear about the reasons for adopting a brief therapy mode of delivery. Brief therapy seems to be most appropriate where: the counselling agency is dealing with clients who mainly present with problems arising from life events; assessment or intake procedures are in place to identify clients who require long-term therapy contact; counsellors themselves have received training in brief therapy and are ideologically in tune with this approach; the agency seeks to maintain a brisk turnover of clients and avoid long waiting lists (i.e., there are few other therapy resources available to clients).

Introducing time-limited counselling solely because of resource factors is *not* a sensible or cost-effective option. Csiernik (2005) reviewed the policies of a large sample of workplace counselling and employee assistance providers in Canada, in respect of 'capping' of the number of counselling sessions allocated to clients. What he found was that there was no difference in the average number of sessions (about five) in providers with session limits, and those where the client and counsellor were free to negotiate the length of therapy. One of the implications of Csiernik's (2005) results is that, where session limits are introduced, there may be a tendency for some clients to take up *more* sessions than they need; for some clients, beneficial change may happen in the first one or two sessions, but if they have been told that counselling consists of a six-session package, they may continue to come in for later sessions that are not actually necessary.

Intermittent counselling

An assumption that informs the majority of counselling and psychotherapy practice is that the aim is to offer each client a complete therapy 'episode' that seeks wholly to resolve the fundamental problem for which the person is seeking help. The American psychotherapist Nicholas Cummings, has argued for many years that this assumption is misguided in most cases. He suggests, instead, that it is more realistic to take the view that a person with a problem will address aspects of that difficulty in a piecemeal fashion, at different times, depending on their life situation and opportunities for change at that particular moment. (Cummings and Sayama 1995; Cummings 2007, 2008). This approach has been described as brief, intermittent therapy throughout the life cycle, and is based on a concept of 'interruption, not termination' – from the outset, the client is told that the therapy will pause when he or she believes that they have gained enough to proceed with their life at that point, but that they are welcome to return whenever they might wish to continue. Cummings and Sayama (1995) describe cases in which there have been gaps of as long as 20 years between therapy sessions. Although the intermittent therapy developed by Cummings (2007, 2008) adopts a highly active approach to therapeutic change, based on behavioural experiments, Smith (2005) has written an account of a form of intermittent therapy that draws on psychodynamic principles.

There would appear to be at least two significant advantages associated with intermittent therapy. First, the client is positioned as a person who is empowered, who has the ability to make important decisions about his or her treatment. Second, the incompleteness of the therapy experience, and the fact that the person knows that they can return to see their therapist at a future time, seems to help clients to remember what it was that they learned in therapy, and make use of this learning on a day-to-day basis, rather than sealing off the therapy in their memory as something that is complete and over and done with. The practice of intermittent therapy has a number of implications for practitioners. Obviously, it is not possible for any one therapist to commit to remain working in the same locality over his or her whole career, and so a form of record keeping needs to be implemented that would make it feasible for a colleague from the same agency to pick up on the work with a client at the point where he or she returned for further therapy. In effect, the model of intermittent therapy invites counsellors and psychotherapists to be more like general practitioners or family physicians, rather than surgeons – in other words, to build their practice around an assumption of ongoing contact with a person through different stages of his or her life.

Single-session counselling and walk-in centres

No matter how a counselling service is organized, there will be many clients who only attend once. In general, counsellors tend to believe that such clients have failed to engage with the therapy process, and have not been helped. However, studies that have followed up single-session clients have found that at least half of them have been satisfied with the counselling they have received (Talmon 1990). In addition, there is a public demand for counselling that is available on demand, without the need or expectation for continued attendance. These factors have led some counselling and psychotherapy organizations to offer 'walk-in' services, that are specifically designed to provide one intensive session. Perkins (2006; Perkins and Scarlett 2008) found that a single-session therapy service for young people in Australia produced outcomes that were equivalent to those achieved in long-term therapy, and that clients and their families were satisfied with what they had received.

In designing a single-session service, it is usually necessary to work on the possibility of the session carrying on for up to two hours. The therapist also needs to use strategies for identifying a focus for the session, and ensuring the safety and well-being of the client. A useful description of the types of issue that need to be taken into consideration in operating such a service can be found in Miller and Slive (2004). Key sources for further information on this topic are Talmon (1990) and Slive and Bobele (2011). It is important for all counsellors to be aware of the possibilities of single-session work, because it is probable that a substantial proportion of their clients will fall into this category.

Non-professional counsellors

The use of non-professional, paraprofessional or lay counsellors in one-to-one work has attracted a great deal of controversy in recent years, following the publication by Karlsruher (1974) and Durlak (1979) of reviews of studies assessing the therapeutic effectiveness of non-professional helpers. Durlak (1979), in a review of 42 studies, reported that research evidence indicated that lay or non-professional counsellors tended to be more effective than highly trained expert practitioners. This conclusion, not unexpectedly, provoked a strong reaction within the profession (Durlak 1981; Nietzel and Fisher 1981). The accumulation of further evidence has, however, supported the original position taken by Durlak (1979). In two more recent reviews of the research literature, Hattie *et al.* (1984) concluded that paraprofessionals were more effective than trained therapists, and Berman and Norton (1985), using more rigorous criteria for accepting studies as methodologically adequate, concluded that there were no overall differences in effectiveness between professional and non-professional therapists. Since the Berman and Norton (1985) review, there have been further research studies (Burlingame and Barlow 1996; Bright *et al.* 1999) and reviews (Christensen and Jacobson 1994; den Boer *et al.* 2005; Faust and Zlotnick 1995), which have essentially arrived at the same conclusion. A review by Stein and Lambert (1995) reported that training did have an effect on effectiveness, but the studies they reviewed mainly looked at the effectiveness levels of psychologists at different levels of training, rather than comparing paraprofessional and professional helpers. On the whole, therefore, the research evidence does appear to confirm that non-professional/paraprofessional counsellors are as effective as trained professional therapists in terms of the benefits that their clients gain from counselling.

Although the general trend in these studies does not confirm the prediction that most people would make, that years of professional training should lead to positive advantages, it is necessary to be cautious in interpreting the results. The studies cover a wide range of client groups, including psychiatric patients, people with schizophrenia in the community, people in crisis, students with study problems and children with behavioural difficulties. The non-professional helpers have included adult volunteers, parents of children and college students. Modes of treatment have encompassed one-to-one and group counselling, behavioural methods and telephone counselling. So although the general effectiveness of non-professionals has been demonstrated, there are insufficient studies in specific areas to allow the claim that the efficacy of using volunteers for that specific client group has been established. Moreover, when the factors that are associated with effective non-professional counselling are considered, some interesting results emerge. Non-professionals who are more experienced and have received more training achieve better results (Hattie *et al.* 1984). Non-professionals did better with longer-term counselling (over 12 weeks), whereas professionals were comparatively more effective with short-term work (one to four weeks) (Berman and Norton 1985).

Box 23.1: *Research into the effectiveness of paraprofessional counsellors: the Vanderbilt study*

Probably the most detailed piece of research comparing professional and non-professional counsellors is the study at Vanderbilt University carried out by Strupp and Hadley (1979). In this study, male college students seeking counselling were assessed using a standardized personality questionnaire. Those who exhibited a profile characterized by depression, isolation and social anxiety were randomly allocated either to experienced therapists or to college professors without training in counselling who were 'selected on the basis of their reputation for warmth, trustworthiness, and interest in students' (Strupp and Hadley 1979: 1126). A comparison group was formed from prospective clients who were required to wait for treatment. The effectiveness of the counselling (twice weekly, up to 25 hours) was evaluated using standard questionnaires and ratings administered at intake, termination and a one-year follow-up. In addition, sessions were either video- or audio-taped.

Both treatment groups showed more improvement than the control group, but there was no difference in outcome between those clients seen by experienced therapists and those counselled by untrained college professors. The non-professional counsellors proved to be just as helpful as their professional colleagues. However, there were marked differences in the counselling style of the two sets of helpers. The non-professionals were more likely to give advice, discuss issues other than feelings and conflicts, and run out of relevant material to explore (Gomes-Schwartz and Schwartz 1978).

In a detailed examination of counselling carried out by one of the college professors in the study, Strupp (1980a) presents a picture of a professor of statistics who was genuinely interested in his clients, offered high levels of encouragement and acceptance and communicated a sincere belief in their capacity to change for the better. With a client who was ready to try out new behaviours he proved to be a highly effective therapist. With one of his more difficult clients, a young man who turned out to have deep-rooted difficulties arising from his relationship with his father, therapy broke down because of the counsellor's inability to understand or challenge high levels of client resistance and negative transference. The overall conclusion that can be drawn from this study is that volunteer, non-professional counsellors can achieve a great deal through 'the healing effects of a benign human relationship' (Strupp and Hadley 1979: 1135), but are less well equipped to cope with some of the dilemmas and difficulties that can occur in particular cases.

Why do non-professionals, such as volunteer counsellors, achieve such good results? The discussion of this issue has generated a number of suggestions for contributory factors:

- perceived by clients to be more genuine;
- less likely to apply professional labels to clients;
- restrict themselves to straightforward, safe interventions;
- clients will attribute success and progress to self rather than to the expertise of their therapist;
- able to refer difficult cases to professionals;
- limited case-load;
- highly motivated to help;
- may be more likely to come from similar cultural background to client;
- able to give more time to clients.

This list, derived from the writings of Durlak (1979) and Wills (1982), indicates that there are advantages in non-professional status and relative lack of experience that balance the advantages conferred by professional authority, experience and advanced training. There are also disadvantages associated with expertise, such as the danger of burnout due to overwork, and the development of professional distancing or detachment from clients. One possible explanation for the effectiveness of non-professional counsellors may be that they are selected from a pool of naturally talented, untrained listeners and helpers in the community.

Barker and Pistrang (2002) have suggested that psychotherapeutic help can be viewed as existing on a continuum, with highly trained professional therapists at one end, supportive family and friends at the other, and paraprofessional helpers somewhere in the middle. In a unique piece of research, Towbin (1978) placed an advertisement in the personal column of his local paper to seek out non-professional 'confidants'. The entry began, 'Do people confide in you?' Towbin interviewed 17 of those who replied. These people were self-confident and open, and had felt deeply loved as children. With regard to the relationships with those who confided in them, they saw themselves as trustworthy and able to be fully present in the situation.

Another factor that is significant in at least some paraprofessional counselling is that the counsellor is drawn from the same social and cultural group as are the clients whom they see, and as a result are readily able to appreciate the life challenges being faced by their clients, and the possible solutions that are available. This kind of counsellor–client social matching was a key element in the well-known Vanderbilt study (Strupp and Hadley 1979). It was also central to the success of a project in which depressed women in Karachi, Pakistan were provided with counselling from minimally trained volunteers from the same community (Ali *et al.* 2003).

An important area requiring further research is the relationship between professional and volunteer counsellors. For example, in Strupp and Hadley's (1979) study, the college professors acting as counsellors were all carefully selected by professional therapists, and had the option of passing clients on to the university counselling service. Clearly, professionals are heavily involved in volunteer counselling schemes through delivering training and supervision, and in taking referrals for clients whose difficulties are beyond the competence of volunteer counsellors to handle.

Unfortunately, little is known about the distinct training and supervision needs or the development of skills and awareness in volunteer counsellors. Another useful area of inquiry concerns the theoretical basis for volunteer counselling. Non-professionals with limited time to attend courses or explore the literature often lack a consistent theoretical orientation, even though they may possess good counselling skills, and may struggle when asked to deliver technically complex protocol-driven interventions (Bright *et al.* 1999). It is significant that theoretical models employed in training courses for volunteers, such as the Egan (2009) skilled helper model, are broadly integrative and action-oriented rather than exploratory in nature.

Telephone counselling

In terms of numbers of client contacts made each year, telephone counselling agencies such as the Samaritans, Childline, Nightline, Breathing Space and Gay Switchboard do much more counselling than any other type of counselling agency. For example, Childline alone answers over 1,000 calls each day. Despite the overwhelming importance of telephone counselling as a means of meeting public needs for emotional support, there has been relatively little effort devoted to theory and research in this area. The task of supplying counselling help over a telephone raises several fundamental questions. In what ways do counselling techniques and approaches need to be modified? Do telephone counsellors have different training and support needs? How much, and in what ways, do users benefit from telephone counselling? Which problems are amenable to telephone counselling and which require ongoing face-to-face contact with a counsellor?

The circumstances of telephone counselling make it difficult to evaluate the benefits that callers may experience. In studies that have asked callers, either at the end of the conversation or at subsequent follow-up, to assess their satisfaction with the service it has been found that consistently two-thirds or more of clients have reported high levels of satisfaction (Stein and Lambert 1984). The types of counsellor behaviour that are perceived by callers to be helpful include understanding, caring, listening, offering feedback, exhibiting a positive attitude, acceptance, keeping a focus on the problem, and giving suggestions (Slaikeu and Willis 1978; Young 1989). These counsellor behaviours are similar to effective counsellor interventions in face-to-face counselling.

In an important, carefully designed study of the effectiveness of telephone counselling, Reese *et al.* (2002, 2006) conducted a survey of client experiences around receiving telephone counselling from an employee assistance programme (EAP). They found that 80 per cent of clients reported that the specific problem that led them to counselling had improved, with 68 per cent being 'very satisfied' or 'completely satisfied' with the telephone counselling they had received. Those whose original problem was most severe were helped less than those whose original problems were less severe. Of the 236 participants who responded to the survey, 96 per cent would be willing to seek telephone counselling again (compared to 63 per cent being willing to seek face-to-face counselling again); of those who had received both telephone and face-to-face counselling, 58 per cent preferred telephone counselling. Moreover, telephone counsellors were perceived as expert and trustworthy, and clients reported developing a strong bond with their counsellor.

Reese *et al.* (2006) carried out a factor analysis of clients' perceptions of the value of telephone counselling. Three main factors emerged: *control* (e.g., 'I felt I could hang up if I did not like it'; 'I liked that the counsellor could not see me'); *convenience* ('I liked that I could call when I wanted to'), and absence of *inhibiting* influences (e.g., 'I liked that telephone counselling was free').The methodology developed by Reese *et al.* (2002, 2006) has the potential to be used in other studies of the process and outcome of this mode of delivery of counselling (Kenny and McEachern 2004). A valuable brief review of research into telephone counselling is available in Mallen *et al.* (2005a).

There does, however, appear to be one important process dimension along which telephone counselling differs from face-to-face work. Lester (1974) has suggested that telephone counselling is a situation that increases the positive transference felt by the caller. The faceless helper is readily perceived as an 'ideal', and can be imagined to be anything or anyone the caller needs or wants. Grumet (1979) points out the elements of the telephone interview that contribute to increased intimacy: visual privacy, the speaker's lips being, in a sense, only inches from the listener's ear and a high level of control over the situation. Rosenbaum (1974: 488) has written that 'the ringing of the phone symbolically represents the cry of the infant and there was an immediate response, namely my voice itself being equivalent to the immediate response of the mother'.

One consequence of the positive transference found in telephone counselling would appear to be to make the caller tolerant of counsellor errors. Delfin (1978) recorded the way clients responded to different types of statements made by telephone counsellors. It was found that clients appeared to react positively to counsellor responses that were viewed by trained observers as clichéd or inaccurate.

Zhu *et al.* (1996) describe a telephone counselling service set up in California to help people to quit smoking. They observed a number of advantages in operating a service of this type by telephone, rather than in more traditional one-to-one or group formats. The telephone contact allowed the counsellor to focus specifically on the needs of the individual client, something that could be difficult in many group-based smoking cessation programmes. Second, they noted, as have other counsellors, that the anonymity of the telephone enabled clients to be very honest, and therefore speeded up the counselling process. Third, they noted that the telephone format lent itself to using a standard counselling protocol, which the counsellor could add to, depending on the initial client. The existence of the protocol or manual was an effective way of ensuring counsellor competence and quality of service. Finally, they felt that the telephone allowed the counsellor to take the initiative much more:

> the telephone makes it possible to conduct proactive counseling. Once a smoker has taken the step of calling for help, all subsequent contacts can be initiated by the counselor. The fact that the counselor makes an appointment for each call and then follows through by calling at the appointed time seems to foster accountability and support. The proactive approach also reduces the attrition rate because the counselor does not share the client's possible ambivalence about following through with the sessions as planned.
>
> (Zhu *et al.* 1996: 94)

This element of proactivity is clearly a major advantage in counselling with smokers, where maintaining motivation to change is a high priority.

Most telephone counselling agencies are staffed by part-time volunteer workers who receive only very limited training and supervision, although there are increasing numbers of commercially run telephone helplines: for example, the California Smokers' Helpline described in the previous paragraph, or lines run by EAP providers. It would appear, from the research evidence already reviewed, that the personal qualities and presence of the counsellor are more important in telephone work than are technical skills. Most clients will have one contact with any individual counsellor, so some of the complexities of other forms of counselling, such as action planning, overcoming resistance to change and building a therapeutic alliance, are not present to the same extent. On the other hand, telephone counsellors need to work quickly, to be flexible and intuitive and to be able to cope with silence. Hoax calls and sex calls draw on skills that are less frequently used in face-to-face counselling. Telephone counsellors are required to enter into the personal worlds of people actually in the middle of crisis, and are thereby exposed to strong emotions. They may become remote participants in suicide. Not only are telephone counsellors involved in a potentially raw and harrowing type of work, they are also less liable to receive feedback on the results of their efforts. Indeed, they may never know whether a caller did commit suicide, or did escape from an abusive family environment. The rate of turnover and burnout in telephone counselling agencies, and the provision of adequate support and supervision, are therefore topics of some concern, which require further study and research.

From the point of view of the caller or client, telephone counselling has two major advantages over face-to-face therapy: access and control. It is easier to pick up a phone and speak directly to a counsellor than it is to make an appointment to visit a counselling agency at some time next week. Telephone counselling therefore has an important preventative function in offering a service to people who would not submit themselves to the process of applying for other forms of help, or whose difficulties have not reached an advanced stage. Moreover, most people are ambivalent about seeking help for psychological problems. The telephone puts the client in a position of power and control, able to make contact and then terminate as he or she wishes.

Clearly, this section can offer only a brief introduction to the issues associated with telephone counselling. This is a mode of delivery that tends to be highly valued by users, who appreciate its flexibility, anonymity and accessibility. Readers interested in learning more about telephone counselling are recommended to seek out the excellent book by Rosenfield (1997).

Counselling by email

One of the fastest growing modes of delivery of counselling within the past decade has involved the use of the internet. There are many counsellors who advertise their services on the internet, on a variety of different types of home pages, and it is possible for a client in any country to access a counsellor anywhere in the world, at any time of the day or night. Murphy and Mitchell (1998) have outlined some of the advantages of email counselling:

- there is a permanent record of the whole of the counselling contact (this is useful for the client, and also for the counsellor and counselling supervisor);
- typing is an effective means of 'externalizing' a problem;
- the act of writing helps the person to reflect on their experience;
- power imbalances are reduced – the internet is an intensely egalitarian medium;
- the client can express their feelings in the 'now', they can write email messages when in the middle of a depression or panic attack, rather than waiting for the next counselling session to come round.

Even the briefest of explorations on the internet will reveal a wide range of email counselling services and chat rooms. The diversity and creativity of uses of internet counselling for therapeutic purposes is reviewed by Anthony (2003), Fink (1999), Kraus et al. (2004), Mallen and Vogel (2005), Mallen et al. (2005b) and Rochlen et al. (2004).

Chechele and Stofle (2003) suggest that there are two main technical means of conducting individual therapy over the internet – *email therapy*, which involves asynchronous (i.e., time delayed) communication between therapist and client, and internet Relay Chat (IRC), which involves synchronous contact in real time. The process of internet therapy requires knowledge and awareness on the part of the counsellor, in respect of such issues as technical requirements of different internet service providers, skills in assessing clients as suitable for online therapy, and an appreciation of the impact on computer-mediated communication on the expression of emotion and formation of relationship.

There are a number of ethical issues associated with online counselling, such as:

- the capacity of the client to assess the professional status and qualifications of the counsellor, or to make a complaint if a breach of confidentiality or other ethical issue arises;
- the ability of the counsellor to respond if there is risk of suicide or self-harm on the part of the client;
- ensuring the security and confidentiality of written material – what happens if an email goes astray, or a stranger enters a chat room?
- maintaining contact if the internet link is broken.

Shaw and Shaw (2006) carried out a survey in 2002 of the ethical procedures followed by 88 counselling websites, and found that 88 per cent of the sites provided the full names of counsellors, with 75 per cent listing counsellor qualifications. However, only 49 per cent made use of intake/assessment procedures, and 27 per cent used a secure site or encryption software. The authors described these results as 'alarming'. However, this study merely considered the ethical policies and intentions of online counselling providers – there is currently a lack of information regarding the number of actual ethical complaints brought against such services.

At this time, relatively few research studies have been published into the processes or outcome of online counselling (Rochlen et al. 2004). A review of research into the effectiveness of online therapy, Barak et al. (2008) identified 92 studies. Taken as a whole, the outcomes reported in these studies were broadly comparable with those found in research into face-to-face therapy. The evidence suggested that results of online treatment of psychological problems, such as anxiety, panic and PTSD, were more positive than for psychosomatic conditions. In addition, there was some evidence that younger clients benefitted more than older clients from online interventions. Barak *et al.* (2008) located 14 studies in which clients had been randomly allocated to either online or face-to-face counselling, and found equivalent outcomes across both conditions.

Another important line of research has considered the characteristics of those clients who prefer online counselling. In one study, Kurioka *et al.* (2001) examined the acceptability and use of email counselling for employees in a Japanese manufacturing company. Employees were offered health counselling by email, telephone, ordinary mail or face-to-face contact. Email counselling was particularly popular with younger employees, and with those who had mental health issues. Email consultations were proportionally more likely to relate to prevention issues, compared with other methods. It would be interesting to know whether these findings, which suggest that there is a distinctive subgroup of clients who are drawn to online therapy, are generalizable to other counselling settings and cultural contexts. The present dearth of research on online therapy seems likely to be addressed in the near future: it appears that many studies are currently being carried out, with the promise that the research base for this form of therapy will significantly expand in future.

Self-help reading

The idea that people can engage in therapeutic activities on their own initiative, in the absence of a professional therapist, has gained in emphasis within the counselling and psychotherapy literature over the past decade. As therapy has become more widely accepted within modern industrial societies it has become inevitable that psychotherapeutic concepts and methods have become repackaged and marketed within different formats, such as books, websites and videos. There is also a significant force within contemporary counselling and psychotherapy, represented by the 'active client' approach of Bohart and Tallman (1999) that regards the effectiveness of any type of therapy as resting on the person's capacity for self-healing. In addition, there exists a portion of the population that is wary of professional helpers, and who prefer to sort out their difficulties alone or in the company of those who have directly shared the challenges that they are facing.

Woven through these forces, in recent years, has been the desire of governments and health service providers to deliver low-cost therapy, unburdened by the salaries of professionally trained therapists. The self-help literature embraces all of these themes, and reflects some of the most critical areas of debate around contemporary practice in counselling.

There has been an explosion of interest in recent years in the potential role of self-help books in counselling and psychotherapy (Norcross 2006). Partially, the basis of this interest lies in a huge public appetite for learning about psychological and psychotherapeutic topics – there were more than 3,500 new English-language self-help books published in 2003 (Menchola *et al.* 2007), and there are many thousands of reading groups in existence, stimulated by mass media fiction recommendations by figures such as Oprah Winfrey in the USA and Judy Finnegan and Richard Madeley in the UK. A further significant aspect of the attention being paid to self-help reading materials is a recognition by counselling and psychotherapy professionals and policy-makers that self-help books may represent a cost-effective response to increasing waiting lists for therapeutic treatments.

Starker (1988) carried out a questionnaire survey of psychologists in the USA, asking them about their prescription of self-help books in therapy. Some 69 per cent of these therapists reported that some of their clients had been 'really helped' by such books. More than half of the practitioners at least occasionally recommended self-help books to supplement treatment. Psychodynamic therapists were less likely to use bibliotherapy than were therapists from other orientations. The most popular bibliotherapy texts reported in the Starker (1988) survey were in the areas of parenting, assertiveness, personal growth, relationships, sexuality and stress.

In general, there are three categories of book that are used in bibliotherapy. The first category consists of explicit self-help manuals, which are designed to enable people to understand and resolve a particular area of difficulty in their lives. Self-help books will usually contain exercises and suggestions for action, and are typically grounded in a cognitive–behavioural theoretical orientation (however, the remarkable *Barefoot Psychoanalyst* booklet by Rosemary Southgate and John Randall (1978) demonstrates that it is possible to employ even Kleinian and Reichian ideas in a self-help mode). Examples of widely-used self-help mental health books are:

- Burns, D.D. (2000) *The Feeling Good Handbook.*
- Fennell, M. (1999) *Overcoming Low Self-Esteem: A Self-Help Guide using Cognitive–Behavioural Techniques.*
- Greenberger, D. and Padesky, C.A. (1995) *Mind Over Mood: Change how you Feel by Changing the Way you Think.*
- Jeffers, S. (2007) *Feel the Fear and do it Anyway: How to Turn your Fear and Indecision into Confidence and Action.*
- Ingham, C. (2000) *Panic Attacks: What They Are, Why They Happen, and What you can do about Them.*
- Mason, P.T. and Kreger, R. (2010) *Stop Walking on Eggshells: Taking your Life Back when Someone you Care about has Borderline Personality Disorder.*
- Rowe, D. (2003) *Depression: The Way Out of your Prison.*
- Williams, M., Teasdale, J., Segal, Z. and Kabat-Zinn, J. (2007) *The Mindful Way through Depression: Freeing yourself from Chronic Unhappiness.*

There are also texts that essentially discuss ideas and experiences rather than being explicitly oriented towards behaviour change. These may be originally written for a professional audience, but become taken up by the general public or achieve 'cult' status. Examples of this type of book, which have become appropriated into the self-help domain, are: *The Road Less Traveled* by Scott Peck (1978) and Alice Miller's (1987) *The Drama of Being a Child*. A review of mental health self-help books (and other self-help materials) can be found in Norcross *et al.* (2003). In addition to self-help books distributed by commercial publishing houses, there are also a large number of pamphlets, leaflets and workbooks produced by individual therapists and counselling agencies.

A second category of bibliotherapy texts comprises of autobiographical or biographical works by people who have experienced specific mental health problems. Individuals who are troubled by particular problems may often gain a great deal of support, insight and hope through being able to identify with the lives and feelings of others who have been faced by similar challenges. Examples of influential texts in this category are *An Unquiet Mind*, by Kay Jamison (1995), which describes the experience of mood disorder, *Elegy for Iris* by John Bayley (2001), which recounts the experience of caring for a spouse suffering from Alzheimer's disease, and *A Man Named Dave* by Dave Pelzer (2004, surviving child abuse). An overview of the issues involved in using autobiography in psychotherapy can be found in Sommer (2003).

Finally, a third category of bibliotherapy works consists of fictional texts, such as novels that depict life stories, behavioural patterns, choices and coping strategies that may be relevant to those undergoing therapy, such as *The Bell Jar* by Sylvia Plath (1963) or *The Trick is to Keep Breathing*, by Janice Galloway (1989).

Although there exists a wealth of written self-help materials readily available in the public domain through libraries and bookshops, there remain some challenging issues for counsellors and psychotherapists seeking to make use of this type of resource. The use of self-help manuals and books raises a number of theoretical issues (Craighead *et al.* 1984). Much theory and research in counselling emphasizes the importance of the therapeutic relationship, yet in bibliotherapy there is no direct relationship. Self-help manuals also assume that the same techniques will be effective for all people who experience a particular problem, rather than individualizing the intervention for separate clients. Finally, there may be concerns around the potential harm caused by self-help reading.

Useful guidelines for integrating self-help into counselling have been prepared by Fuhriman *et al.* (1989), Campbell and Smith (2003) and Norcross (2006). These authors suggest that therapists seeking to capitalize on self-help resources should:

- familiarize themselves with relevant self-help books, in advance of recommending them to clients;
- offer tangible support and encouragement to clients using self-help materials;
- tailor their recommendations to the needs of the individual client;
- pay attention to reading level and interests;
- as far as possible, use self-help texts that are backed up by research evidence;
- consider the relevance of the self-help book to the phase of therapy that the client has reached;
- guard against 'intellectualization of a self-help book as a diversion from the therapy' (Campbell and Smith 2003: 232).

However, it is clear that many people make use of self-help books without ever consulting a professional counsellor or psychotherapist. It is likely, therefore, that at least some clients may prefer that their therapist abstains from asking them to discuss the books they have been reading – they may wish to retain their reading as a private, independent therapeutic strategy.

There is an increasing amount of research that has looked at the effectiveness of bibliotherapy. In one study, Ogles *et al.* (1991) supplied self-help books for coping with loss to 64 people who had recently experienced divorce or the break-up of a relationship. Levels of depression and psychiatric symptoms were assessed before and after reading the book. Clinically significant benefits were reported by the majority of these participants. It was also found that greater gains were reported among those readers who initially had high positive expectations that the book would help, which might imply that a book or self-help manual received on the recommendation of a therapist might be particularly valuable. Some projects have combined the prescription of self-help manuals with telephone counselling, either using a telephone hotline that clients can phone or calling clients at regular intervals to encourage them to use the manual (Orleans *et al.* 1991; Ossip-Klein *et al.* 1991). Craighead *et al.* (1984) found that, although totally self-administered manuals may be effective for some people, most clients want or need some additional personal contact with a helper. Research by Scogin *et al.* (1990) suggested that bibliotherapy appeared to be more effective with older, more highly educated clients. There have been several meta-analytic reviews of the effectiveness of self-help reading. The most comprehensive of these reviews, carried out by Den Boer *et al.* (2005), Hirai and Clum (2006), Main and Scogin (2003) and Menchola *et al.* (2007), have found convincing evidence that self-help reading is moderately helpful for the majority of people with problems, across a wide range of presenting difficulties. However, self-help was found to be not as effective as treatment by a counsellor or therapist, or as effective as 'guided self-help' in which minimal contact was provided from a helper who supported and encouraged the client in their involvement with self-help materials.

Although the research evidence provides positive support for the use of self-help, it is nevertheless important to be aware that the value of self-help depends to a great extent on the context in which it is used. The most encouraging evidence for the effectiveness of self-help reading comes from studies using volunteer participants, who have actively sought self-help resources. By contrast, two studies carried out within the UK NHS, in which patients have expectations for face-to-face personal care, have reported less positive results. In well-controlled studies in which participants were allocated to a self-help condition, Mead *et al.* (2006) and Salkovskis *et al.* (2006) found that NHS patients were resistant to taking up the offer of self-help care, often did not make active use of the texts that were provided, and showed only marginal symptom improvement when compared with control patients who had not received self-help workbooks, even when the workbook was individually tailored to their needs (Salkovskis *et al.* 2006) or their use of the materials was facilitated by a mental health worker (Mead *et al.* 2006). The results of these studies suggest that the *meaning* of self-help reading may be intrinsic to its helpfulness. People who actively seek out self-books from their library or bookshop, or are encouraged to use such books by their therapist, may benefit from the fact that their sense of agency or self-efficacy is being reinforced through their reading (Bohart and Tallman 1999). By contrast, those who are offered 'institutionalized' self-help materials in the absence of more desirable and credible treatments, may take the view that they are being 'fobbed-off' with a form of help that is second best and principally driven by a desire to cut costs.

Self-help online packages

Compared with self-help books and manuals, internet packages have the advantage of greater flexibility, in terms of the use of interactivity, which can maximize active client engagement, and video materials, which can enhance client identification with real-life narratives portrayed on-screen. There have been a number of initiatives that have involved the construction of websites designed to deliver therapy online, usually informed by CBT principles. The history of the development of increasingly sophisticated computerized psychotherapy programmes, made possible by advances in technology, is discussed by Cavanagh *et al.* (2003). A widely used current self-help package is *Beating the Blues*, which comprises a structured course of CBT treatment for depression, and is licensed to general practitioners and family physicians for use in their surgeries. It includes innovative use of characterization (stories of people who have struggled to overcome depression), alongside more conventional self-help exercises. A detailed account of the thinking that informed the design of *Beating the Blues* is available in Cavanagh *et al.* (2003). A series of studies have established the effectiveness of *Beating the Blues* as an intervention for mild and moderate levels of depression (Cavanagh and Shapiro 2004; Cavanagh *et al.* 2006; Grime 2004; McCrone *et al.* 2004; Proudfoot *et al.* 2004). A similar package, developed for use in anxiety, is *FearFighter* (Gega *et al.* 2004; Schneider *et al.* 2005). Both *Beating the Blues* and *Fearfighter* have been approved by the UK National Institute for Health and Clinical Excellence (NICE 2006) as effective treatments. The *MindGym* site, by contrast, consists of an eclectic blend of self-help exercises intended to promote psychological well-being as well as enable users to deal with problems. A less structured, and not overtly 'psychotherapeutic' internet source is the *DipEX site*, which has been developed as a repository for autobiographical accounts of people who have experienced various health problems, including mental health issues such as depression. Finally, there are many therapy and mental health sites, such as John Grohol's *psychcentral.com*, which provide information, sources, and links.

Self-help internet packages can be seen as falling into three categories. First, there are sites, such as *Beating the Blues* and *FearFighter* that are only accessible through health profession gatekeepers, but are then used by clients without any professional support. Second, there are internet packages that involve a certain degree of self-help activity, but which essentially operate as adjuncts to therapist-provided treatment. This category of internet resource has been discussed above, in the section on online counselling. Finally, there are wholly self-help sites, which are accessible to anyone with an internet connection. It is of some interest that, at present, the more resource-rich sites such as *Beating the Blues* and *FearFighter* are only available to relatively small groups of people, no doubt due to the substantial development costs involved in creating these packages and the resulting need to recoup costs through commercial licensing. By contrast, freely available mental health internet sites are hugely popular – a survey conducted in 2003 by Anderson *et al.* (2004) reported that some anxiety-information sites were then receiving six million hits each month. This level of demand will probably mean that there will be increasing pressure to make more sophisticated psychotherapeutic packages more readily available online. It will undoubtedly mean, too, that the general population will become increasingly 'therapy-literate', and more discerning as consumers of conventional face-to-face therapy.

A basic dilemma for counsellors and psychotherapists, in relation to online resources, is that there is minimal quality control on the internet, and that clients may be making use of sites that are giving them poor information and misleading or biased advice. It is therefore necessary for therapists to be aware of what is around on the internet, in terms of the client groups with whom they work, and to be prepared to guide clients to the most useful sites. Valuable guidance on internet self-help resources, and how to incorporate them into counselling, is available in Grohol (2004) and Zuckerman (2003).

Self-help groups

A great deal of the group counselling that occurs within contemporary society takes place in self-help groups that consist of people with similar problems who meet together without the assistance of a professional leader. The appeal of the self-help movement can be seen to rest on two main factors. The first is that self-help groups can be created in the absence of professional resources, and can thereby transcend the budgetary limitations of health and welfare agencies. The second is that people who participate in self-help groups appreciate the experience of talking to others who 'know what it feels like' to have a drink problem, to have lost a child in a road accident or to be a carer of an infirm elderly parent.

The effectiveness of self-help groups for a variety of client groups has been well documented. In the field of alcohol dependence there is even evidence that Alcoholics Anonymous is on the whole more effective than individual or group counselling offered by professional experts (Emrick 1981). However, many mental health professionals remain sceptical about the value of self-help groups, and view them as opportunities for socializing, or at best emotional support, rather than as arenas for serious therapeutic work (Salzer *et al.* 1999).

One of the issues that can lead to difficulties in self-help groups is the establishment of an unhelpful or inappropriate group culture. For example, the group may come to be dominated by one or two people who have covert needs not to change, and who create groups where people collude with each other to remain agoraphobic, overweight or problem drinkers.

Another difficulty may be that the group does not evolve clear enough boundaries and norms, so that being in the group is experienced as risky rather than as a safe place to share feelings. Antze (1976) has suggested that the most effective self-help groups are those that develop and apply an explicit set of ground rules or an 'ideology'. Women's consciousness-raising groups, for example, can draw upon an extensive literature that details the philosophy and practice of feminist approaches to helping. Alcoholics Anonymous uses a clearly defined 'twelve-step' rulebook.

Research carried out by Davidson *et al.* (2000) indicates the most widely used self-help groups are those based around conditions that are perceived by sufferers as stigmatizing, for example Alzheimer's disease, alcoholism, AIDS, breast and prostate cancer. It would appear that one of the factors behind this tendency is the possibility that the self-help group can enable a person to develop a new self-narrative, and sense of identity, at a point of life crisis during which they feel that their previous identity has been irredeemably destroyed (Rappaport 1993). A self-help group provides a person with multiple examples, or role models, of people who have come to terms with a painful or debilitating illness or condition, and can thereby operate as a source for hope, practical support and coping strategies. Within the world of people who struggle with severe and enduring mental health difficulties, there exist a wealth of highly effective self-help groups, such as the Hearing Voices network (Romme and Escher 2000) and the global recovery movement (Davidson *et al.* 2005, 2006; Stricker 2000).

Apart from simply encouraging clients to make use of self-help groups that are available to them, and providing information where necessary, professional counsellors may be involved in enabling self-help groups to get started, either through taking a proactive role within their organization or because people in the group seek guidance about where to meet and how to proceed. For example, student counsellors may encourage the formation of self-help groups among mature students or overseas students. Counsellors in hospitals may work with self-help groups of nursing staff suffering from work stress, or of patients with cancer. The relationship between the 'expert' and the group requires sensitive handling, with the counsellor being willing to act as external consultant rather than coming in and taking charge (Powell 1994; Robinson 1980).

Reflections on self-help

The use of self-help activities has received a great deal of attention within the counselling and psychotherapy profession because it represents a very significant, and potentially cost-effective and accessible mode of delivery of therapeutic learning and care. It may be useful to place these developments within a broader cultural perspective. A central characteristic of any culture is that it tends to provide both a range of self-care remedies that people learn to employ in order to deal with everyday distress and discomfort *and* specialist expertise intended to be called upon in more extreme situations.

The organization of such self-care strategies in contemporary society is illustrated in a survey carried out by Jorm *et al.* (2004) in the Canberra area of Australia. Participants in the survey were asked to complete a brief depression scale, and a questionnaire inviting them to indicate their current usage of a range of self-help sources. The results of the survey showed that a very wide set of self-care procedures were used by individuals reporting low or mild levels of depression. For example, the following actions were endorsed by more than 10 per cent of those with mild depression: aromatherapy, avoiding caffeine, being with pets, cutting out alcohol, exercise, vitamins, dance. However, those with severe distress from depression used these activities *less* often than did those with mild-moderate symptoms. Survey respondents who were more distressed were significantly more likely to call for professional help, in the form of a GP, counsellor or psychologist. These findings need to be confirmed in other populations. However, if they are valid, Jorm *et al.* (2004) argue that the results of this study imply that there are three distinct 'waves of action' associated with psychological distress.

In the first wave, individuals with mild problems draw upon strategies that are already in everyday use, such as exercise, music and interaction with family and friends. As distress becomes more severe, the use of these everyday strategies declines, as individuals search for specific remedies, such as self-help books and complementary therapies. Finally, if the problem becomes even more troubling, the person seeks professional help. This model suggests that the meaning of self-help will be different for individuals at differing levels of distress. Specifically, at least some of those who are troubled enough to have recourse to a professional therapist may regard reading a self-help book as a strategy that they have tried, and which has failed for them, and as a result these people may be resistant to a 'prescription' of self-help. This model also explains why self-help books read by 'volunteers' (Main and Scogin 2003) appear to have a more beneficial impact than those recommended by health care professionals (Mead *et al.* 2006; Salkovskis *et al.* 2006).

It may be valuable to regard self-help books, groups and websites as part of a broad category of 'cultural resources' (McLeod 2005) that can be used therapeutically by individuals in a variety of ways. From this point of view, self-help and self-care are always to be encouraged, but individuals can be understood as engaging with these resources in quite different ways if they are trying to live a healthy life and prevent problems from arising, or are coping with low-level difficulties, are in the throes of a major 'breakdown', or are in a post-therapy recovery phase of their life. By seeking the appropriate self-help activities as an adjunct to formal therapy, counsellors and psychotherapists run the risk that individuals may come to perceive these strategies as in some sense 'owned' by professionals, and therefore as less openly accessible to them as self-care activities with which they might wish freely to experiment. Another way of looking at this area is that self-help and self-care, in relation to psychological and emotional difficulties, is a domain that is only partially influenced by professionalized therapists and therapy, and is much more under the control of voluntary networks of sufferers (e.g., Alcoholics Anonymous), commercial publishing companies and the efforts of individuals seeking to share their experiences.

Self-help activities are widely used in the general population; more than 20 per cent of those in the Jorm *et al.* (2004) study reported that they regularly used self-help books or meditation to enable them to cope with emotional problems. One of the implications of this phenomenon is that it is necessary for counselling and psychotherapy training to prepare practitioners to understand the advantages and disadvantages of various forms of self-help materials and activities, and to develop an informed position from which to facilitate client use of these resources when appropriate.

Group counselling

Group counselling and therapy represents a major area of theory, research and practice in its own right. The aim here is merely to identify some of the possibilities and issues arising from this mode of delivery of counselling help, rather than attempting a comprehensive review of this area of specialization. Interested readers who wish to know more are recommended to consult some of the excellent introductory texts that have been published on the topic of group counselling (Brabender *et al.* 2004; Corey 2010; Corey *et al.* 2004; DeLucia-Waack *et al.* 2004; Jacobs *et al.* 2006; Paleg and Jongma 2005; Yalom 2005a), and also the background literature on theories of group dynamics (Forsyth 1990; Poole and Hollingshead 2004). A fascinating insight into the process that can occur in a therapy group, and the experience of being a group therapist, can be found in the novel *The Schopenhauer Cure*, written by the celebrated group therapist Irvin Yalom (2005b).

There are several parallel historical sources of the origins of group therapy. Early forms of groupwork were pioneered by Jacob Moreno with psychodrama, by Kurt Lewin through the invention of 'T-groups' and by Wilfred Bion in his psychoanalytic groups. These various initiatives came together in the late 1940s and early 1950s to form what has become a strong tradition in the various branches of the helping professions. Group-based approaches are used in counselling, psychotherapy, social work and organizational development. The three main theoretical orientations in counselling – psychodynamic, humanistic and cognitive–behavioural – are all represented in distinctive approaches to the theory and practice of working with groups.

The first systematic psychodynamic group theory was formulated by Bion, Foulkes and Jacques, initially during World War II through work with psychologically disturbed and traumatized soldiers at the Northfield Hospital in Birmingham, and later at the Tavistock Institute in London. The key idea in psychodynamic groupwork is its focus on the 'group-as-a-whole'. Bion (1961) argued that, just as individual patients in psychoanalysis exhibit defences against reality, so do groups. He coined the phrase 'basic assumptions' to describe these collective patterns of defence and avoidance in groups. At the heart of a 'basic assumption' is a shared, unconscious belief that the group is acting 'as if' some imaginary state of affairs were true. For example, a group can act 'as if' the leader was all-knowing and all-powerful (dependency), 'as if' the only option in a group was to engage in conflict with others (fight–flight), or 'as if' the main purpose of the group was the formation of two-person friendships or sexual liaisons (pairing). The role of the group leader was similar to that of the analyst in individual psychoanalysis, in saying little and thereby acting as a blank screen on to which members could project their fantasies.

The benefits to be gained from therapy in this kind of group lie in gaining personal insight from participating in a group that was learning to understand issues concerning authority, boundaries, sexuality and aggression, which emerged in the culture of the group-as-a-whole. Whitman and Stock (1958) introduced the notion of the 'group focal conflict' as a way of making sense of the link between group process and individual learning. If the group becomes emotionally engaged in, for instance, the question of whether it is acceptable for members to meet outside of sessions, this issue will resonate in each individual member of the group in so far as it resembles similar issues in their own lives. One member may bring strong feelings about betrayal, another anger about having been controlled by his parents and so on.

The process of a psychodynamic group takes time, and it may be possible to see phases or stages in the life of the group. Bennis and Shepard (1956) have constructed a model that envisages two general stages in the life of a group. The first stage is concerned with issues of control and authority, the second with issues of intimacy and interdependence. During the first stage, group members behave in the group in line with previously learned ways of coping with authority: some may be conformist, others rebellious. In the process of the group as an entity sorting out how it can reconcile these tensions, there is the opportunity for individual insight and therapeutic change. The practical implications, in terms of running counselling groups, of these ideas about group dynamics are fully explored in Agazarian and Peters (1981) and Whitaker (1985), and current issues in the theory and application of this approach are discussed in Behr and Hearst (2005), Pines (1983) and Roberts and Pines (1991).

The humanistic approach to group counselling devotes particular attention to ideas of growth and encounter. The main aim of this approach is the personal development or self-actualization of group members, and traditionally there have been two contrasting methodologies employed by practitioners. Some group facilitators utilize a high degree of structure in their groups, providing the group with exercises and tasks to promote exploration and growth. This tradition has its origins in psychodrama and the T-group, or sensitivity training group, movement. The other tradition is to offer very little structure, and for the facilitator to strive to create a group environment characterized by respect, empathy and congruence. This latter tradition is associated with the work of Rogers and the person-centred approach. A central aim in much groupwork informed by humanistic thinking is the creation of a 'cultural island' where people can experiment with different behaviour, share experiences and receive feedback from others in a setting that is outside everyday life and thereby allows greater freedom (Corey 2008).

A third approach to group counselling has evolved from the cognitive–behavioural tradition, and is primarily concerned with using the group to deliver CBT in a group format to foster behavioural change in clients (Bieling *et al.* 2006; Free 2007; Heimberg and Becker 2002; Sharry 2007; White and Freeman 2000). Examples of this type of groupwork are social skills groups (Trower *et al.* 1978), assertiveness training and short-term groups focused on a specific problem behaviour, such as alcohol abuse, eating, social anxiety or offending. This form of group counselling typically embraces a strongly didactic approach, with the group leaders supplying information, and teaching and modelling appropriate skills. Group members practise skills through exercises, simulations and role-play, and will usually be given homework assignments to encourage generalization of the skill to ordinary life situations. The emphasis is on action and behaviour change rather than reflection and encounter, and there is relatively little attention paid to the dynamics of the group (e.g., relationships between group members).

As in other areas of therapeutic practice, there has been a significant movement within the area of group counselling in the direction of theoretical integration. Two notable examples of group interventions that incorporate ideas and methods from psychodynamic, humanistic and CBT approaches are the structured group therapy for obese women, developed by Buckroyd and Rother (2007), and group therapy for women with breast cancer, pioneered by Spira and Reed (2002).

The three main approaches to working with groups, described above, each have different aims, along a continuum with insight and personal development at one end and behaviour change at the other. The form of group that is set up will also reflect the needs of clients and the agency or organization within which it takes place; Agazarian and Peters (1981) propose a categorization of helping groups into three levels of challenge, depending on clients' needs. However, organizational factors can also have a bearing on group practice. Psychodynamic, Tavistock-oriented groups and Rogerian encounter groups, for example, will usually need to meet over many hours, to allow the dynamics of the group to develop. If the agency can only afford to allocate 10 or 20 hours of staff time to running a group, then a more behaviourally oriented experience will probably be selected.

Most counsellors are initially trained to work with individual clients, and group facilitation involves learning new skills. A group facilitator must monitor the relationships between himself or herself and the group members, but also those occurring between group members. The facilitator also needs to have a sense of what is happening to the group as a whole system. The emotional demands, or transference, that the facilitator absorbs from the group may at times be much more intense than in individual counselling. Bennis and Shepard (1956), for example, identify the 'barometric event' in the life of a group as the moment when all group members combine together to reject the authority of the leader. There are case management issues unique to groupwork: for example, designing and forming the group, selecting members, combining group and individual counselling, introducing new members once the group is under way and dealing with the process of people leaving the group (Whitaker 1985). There are distinctive ethical issues arising in groups, mainly concerning the conformity pressure that can be exerted on individuals and the difficulty of maintaining confidentiality (Lakin 1988). Finally, it is common practice to work with a co-leader or co-facilitator when running a group, as a way of dealing with some of the complexities of the task. There is, therefore, a distinctive knowledge base and set of requirements for effective group leadership. It is unfortunate that very few formal training courses exist to prepare people to be group facilitators. Most practitioners working with groups have acquired their groupwork competence through being members of groups and acting in a co-facilitator role as an assistant or apprentice.

Groups offer a number of ways of helping clients that are not readily available in individual counselling. The group provides an arena in which the client can exhibit a much broader range of interpersonal behaviour than could ever be directly observed in a one-to-one relationship with a counsellor. In individual counselling, a client may tell a male counsellor about how he has problems in communication with women. In a group these problems can be expressed in his relationships with the women in the group. Oatley (1980, 1984) has described this process as the acting out of 'role-themes'. Group counselling, therefore, presents the counsellor with a different quality of information about the client, and different opportunities for immediacy and working with the here-and-now. In groups, moreover, there are chances for clients to help each other through clarification, challenge and support. This is useful not only in that there is more help available, but also in that the client who is able to be helpful to another will benefit in terms of enhanced self-esteem. The group setting can be viewed as akin to a drama, where the interaction between group members is a means of acting out personal and collective issues (McLeod 1984). In this drama, not all participants are on centre stage at the same time. Some will be in the role of audience, but this ability to be able to observe how other people deal with things can in itself be a powerful source of learning.

One of the most fertile lines of research into group counselling and therapy in recent years has developed out of the work of Yalom (2005a) in identifying and defining the 'curative' or 'therapeutic' factors in groups. Struck by the complexity of what went on in his groups, Yalom set about reviewing the literature with the aim of bringing together ideas about the factors or processes in groups that help people. He arrived at a set of 12 factors:

- group cohesiveness;
- instillation of hope;
- universality;
- catharsis;

- altruism;
- guidance;
- self-disclosure;
- feedback;
- self-understanding;
- identification;
- family re-enactment;
- existential awareness.

The presence of these factors in a group can be assessed through questionnaire or Q-sort (a kind of structured interview) techniques devised by Yalom and others. Bloch *et al.* (1981) have developed a similar approach based on asking group members at the end of each group session to write briefly about what they found helpful. The 'curative factors' research is of particular interest to many group facilitators because it is grounded in the perceptions of clients regarding what is helpful or otherwise, and because it provides valuable pointers to how the group might be run.

The work of Yalom (2005a) and Bloch *et al.* (1981) focuses on what is helpful in groups but it is also valid to take account of group processes that may be harmful or damaging. In a large-scale, comprehensive study of 20 encounter groups run for students at Stanford University, Lieberman *et al.* (1973) found that around 10 per cent of the people who had participated in the groups could be classified at the end as 'casualties'. Being in the group had caused more harm than good to these people. This piece of evidence stimulated a lively debate in the literature, with some critics claiming that there were aspects of the Stanford study that would exaggerate the casualty estimate. Nevertheless, it is fair to say that the Lieberman *et al.* (1973) research does draw attention to some of the potentially worrying aspects of group approaches. Situations can arise in groups where individual members are put under pressure to self-disclose or take part in an exercise despite their resistance or defences against doing so. The reactions of other members of the group may be destructive rather than constructive: for example, when a group member shares his fears over 'coming out' as gay and is met by a homophobic response from others. The ensuing distress may be hidden or difficult to detect. These are some of the factors that lead group leaders to be careful about selecting people for groups, and group leaders are often keen to set up arrangements for providing support outside the group session for group members (e.g., individual counselling). There are also implications for the supervision of group facilitators themselves.

Couple counselling

A substantial number of people seek counselling as a couple, because they recognize that their problems are rooted in their relationship rather than being attributable to individual issues. Counselling agencies specifically devoted to working with couples or with individuals on relationship issues have been established in many countries. Many of these agencies, such as RELATE in the UK, began life as a result of fears about the sanctity of married life, and were in their early years mainly 'marriage saving' organizations. In recent years, however, the realities of changing patterns of marriage and family life have influenced these agencies in the direction of defining their work as being more broadly based in relationship counselling in general.

The field of couple counselling is dominated by three major approaches: psychodynamic, cognitive–behavioural and emotion-focused. The psychodynamic approach aims to help couples gain insight into the unconscious roots of their marital choice, and into the operation of projection and denial in their current relationship. One of the fundamental assumptions of psychodynamic couples counselling is that each partner brings to the relationship a powerful set of ideas about being a spouse and being a parent, which originate in his or her family of origin. Each partner also brings to the relationship a set of interpersonal needs shaped by experience in early childhood. For example, the person whose mother died at a critical age in childhood may have a need for acceptance but a fear of allowing himself to trust. A person who was sexually abused in childhood may express needs for intimacy through sexualized relationships. The job of the counsellor is, just as in individual work, to help the couple to achieve insight into the unconscious roots of their behaviour, and to learn to give expression to feelings that had been repressed.

The psychodynamic counsellor in marital or couples work also brings to the task a set of ideas about relationships. The dynamics of the Oedipal situation, with its triangular configuration of child, same-sex parent and opposite-sex parent, can serve as a template for understanding difficulties currently experienced by the couple, such as husband, wife and wife's mother, or husband, wife and first child. Another triangular pattern in couples work is that consisting of husband, wife and the person with whom one of them is having an affair. Many counsellors find object relations theory (Chapter 5) valuable in disentangling the processes of jealousy, attachment, loss and rivalry that can occur in couples work. The concepts of marital 'choice' and marital 'fit' help in making sense of the basis for the emotional bond between a couple. According to psychodynamic theory, a couple will choose each other because, at least partially, the unconscious needs of each will be met by the other. So, for example, a man who gets angry may find a partner who is even-tempered. However, this marital fit may become less and less comfortable as one or both of the partners develops in such a way as to claim back the unconscious territory ceded to the other. Some couples are able to renegotiate the basis of their relationship as and when such changes occur. Others are not able to do so, and after some time there is an explosion as the pressure becomes too great and the original pattern of the relationship is torn apart in a crisis of violence, splitting up or conducting an affair. It is often in such a crisis that the couple will come for help.

A psychodynamic perspective brings to couples counselling a sophisticated model of personality development. Behind the conflict and dissent projected by many couples who arrive for counselling are fundamental developmental issues. A woman who married at 16 finds herself experimenting with new partners and nightclubs when her daughter reaches the same age. A man in his mid twenties is terrified by the transition to parenthood; his wife is ready to have a child now. The Educating Rita scenario, where a woman who has missed out on her opportunity to fulfil her potential in the world of study or work, is not uncommon as a source of marital conflict.

The technique of psychodynamic couples work involves the same careful listening and exploration as in individual counselling. Some couples counsellors recommend that the counselling is provided by a pair of counsellors, a man and a woman, to facilitate different types of transference, but this is an option that is only feasible in well-resourced counselling centres. On the whole, it is necessary for counsellors working in this way to be more active and interventionist than they might be with individual clients, to keep the focus of the couple on the therapeutic work rather than on acting out arguments in the counselling room. Further information about the theory and practice of psychodynamic work with couples is available in Clulow (2000), Clulow and Mattinson (1989), Crawley and Grant (2007) and Skynner and Cleese (1993).

The cognitive–behavioural approach to couples counselling is quite different. There is relatively little theoretical baggage, little exploration of the past and a predominant emphasis on finding pathways to changed behaviour. The central assumption in this approach is that people in an intimate relationship act as a source of positive reinforcement for each other. At the time of first meeting each other, and through courtship, there is usually a high level of positive reinforcement or reward associated with the relationship. Later on, as the couple perhaps live together, work together or bring up children, the opportunities for rewarding contact diminish and the costs of the relationship, the compromise and stress, increase. As a result, the 'reward–cost ratio' reduces, and there is a loss of satisfaction. At the same time, the couple may encounter difficulties in such areas as communication, problem-solving and sexuality. The remedy for these problems, in a cognitive–behavioural mode, is to apply behavioural principles to initiate change, such as the use of contracts between spouses. Cognitive–behavioural methods have been particularly successful in couples work in the area of sex therapy. Further information about CBT-oriented couples therapy can be found in Epstein and Baucom (2002).

The third major contemporary approach to counselling with couples is emotion focused couples therapy (EFT; Greenberg and Johnson 1988), which takes an experiential approach that is also informed by attachment theory. Johnson *et al.* (1999) provide a useful review and summary of research and practice in this approach, and further information about the clinical practice of EFT for couples can be found in Greenberg and Goldman (2008), and Johnson (2004).

Other approaches to working with couples include models based in family therapy theory and practice (Bobes and Rothman 2002), the person-centred approach (O'Leary 2011) and narrative therapy (Percy 2007). An overview of issues and methods in couple counselling is available in Harway (2005).

Whatever theoretical model is adopted, one of the central debates in couples counselling concerns the decision to work with partners individually, or to see them together as a couple. There are many occasions when this decision is made by the clients, when only one member of the couple is willing to see the counsellor. Even in these circumstances, however, there is an issue about how much to involve the absent partner or spouse (Bennun 1985). There are also notable dilemmas associated with couple work around such issues as responding to domestic violence, adapting practice to meet the needs of same-sex couples and differing cultural assumptions about gender roles and marriage. This brief introduction to couple counselling can do little more than provide a preliminary sketch of some of the ideas, methods and topics arising from this area of work. Interested readers wishing to know more are recommended to consult Harway (2005) for an authoritative overview of current themes in couples counselling, and to explore the insights into the process of working with couples afforded by Scarf (1987) and Skynner and Cleese (1993).

Working with families

For most people who turn to counselling or psychotherapy for assistance with problems in living, the difficulties for which they are seeking help are connected, in some way or another, with their experience of family life. The family context of counselling issues is particularly striking when the client is a child or young person – in these cases it is all but impossible to disentangle the difficulties being faced by the individual child or adolescent from the web of family beliefs and relationships within which they live their life. For these reasons, one of the oldest established traditions of counselling practice has involved work with families rather than with individual clients. Family counselling presents a set of unique challenges to a counsellor, and a rich array of theory and method has emerged from the field of family therapy. Further information and discussion around this mode of delivery of counselling is available in Chapter 12.

Preventative interventions

On the whole, counselling is made available to people only once a problem has developed, and has become severe enough for the person actively to seek help from a professional source or organization. It has been very obvious, for a long period of time, to many observers, that there would be huge advantages in finding ways to effectively *prevent* psychological and emotional problems, rather than merely intervening only once the problem has become established. The principle of prevention, in relation to health care, is espoused at a fundamental level by all societies that lay down strict regulations for the purity of drinking water, standards for sewage treatment, and sell-by dates for food sold in shops – these are some of the basic preventative mechanisms used in the domain of public health.

Within the field of mental health, Caplan (1964) has identified three levels of prevention:

- *Primary prevention*. Interventions intended to reduce the future incidence of a problem. Example: social education in schools with the aim of developing coping strategies and limiting future relationship and marital difficulties.

- *Secondary prevention*. Targeting those at risk, or who have started to show early signs of a problem. Example: enriched induction and welcoming programmes in universities for international students who are at risk of 'culture shock' and adjustment stress.

- *Tertiary prevention*. Interventions designed to minimize the negative impact of an existing disorder or problem. Example: counsellors attached to accident and emergency departments to make contact with, and follow up, individuals who present with signs of domestic abuse.

In practice, it can be difficult to differentiate neatly between these three levels of prevention. For instance, a tertiary intervention (designed for people who already have a problem) may pick up people at risk, or knowledge of the existence of the intervention may have a wider primary prevention effect.

The concept of prevention presents a major challenge for the counselling profession. Down the years, keynote articles by leading figures such as Albee (1999), Romano and Hage (2000) and Hage *et al.* (2007) have drawn attention to (a) encouraging examples of good practice in prevention within the counselling profession; and (b) the general lack of attention paid to prevention by the profession as a whole. When considering preventative programmes, it is essential to give careful consideration to the possible unintended consequences that can arise from meddling with 'natural' coping and support systems. For example, Stroebe *et al.* (2005) found that 'outreach' initiatives, that made early contact with people who had been bereaved, could be harmful (in contrast to services in which individuals troubled by their bereavement actively sought help, which they found to be generally quite effective). Rose *et al.* (2003) reviewed the findings of research that had been carried out into the effectiveness of critical incident stress debriefing for people who had undergone a traumatic event such as a car crash or armed robbery. They discovered that, although debriefing had been designed as a secondary prevention intervention, with the goal of identifying those at risk of developing PTSD, in many cases it worked in the reverse direction, and actually increased the likelihood of future PTSD.

In both the bereavement and debriefing examples, it would appear that overzealous early intervention by counsellors or psychologists had the effect, at least in some cases, of cutting across and undermining naturally occurring psychological mechanisms (e.g., avoiding thinking about what had happened) and social support networks (e.g., relying on family and loved ones). The lesson would appear to be that the design of an effective and appropriate preventative intervention needs to take contextual factors into account. It is not enough just to provide counselling to more people, or to provide counselling as early as possible. Effective prevention requires careful analysis of just what it is that might be helpful for a person or group. In this respect, the best preventative initiatives are probably those that make use of models and insights from the field of community psychology (Prilleltensky and Nelson 2005).

Other modes of delivery

Earlier chapters in this book have explored other formats for the delivery of counselling, such as outdoor therapy with individuals and groups, creative writing and expressive arts workshops and one-to-one therapy. Readers are encouraged to consider these developments as further examples of the themes being addressed in the present chapter.

The use of technology

Many of the modes of delivery of counselling that have been outlined in the chapter make use of various forms of technology. Some of this technology is well-established, such as books, writing implements, art materials and even telephones. Other pieces of technology that have been used by therapists, such as computers and the internet, are of more recent origin. In addition to the technologies that have already been mentioned, there are a range of other technological systems and devices that have also been incorporated in therapeutic practice:

- *communication by video link*: some counsellors particularly in rural or island communities where clients may need to travel considerable distances to see a therapist have adopted videoconference links with clients (Simpson 2003);

- *computer-based and online assessment*: questionnaires and other scales that are used for assessment purposes can be delivered on-screen, rather than through a traditional paper and pencil format (Emmelkamp 2005);

- *palmtop computers*: small portable personal computers (palmtop devices) have been supplied to clients to enable them to monitor their behaviour and cognitions and collect assessment data while engaged in everyday activities and to deliver behaviour change guidance (Anderson *et al.* 2004; Przeworski and Newman 2004);

- *virtual reality systems*: in cognitive–behavioural approaches, a central therapeutic goal may be to enable the person to experience the situation that he or she has previously found as anxiety-provoking (the principle of *exposure*). One of the limitations of this therapeutic strategy is that it can be hard for the therapist to reproduce, in the therapy room, the situations that are anxiety-provoking for the client. Alternatively, if the client engages in exposure experiments in the real world, it may be impossible for the therapist to monitor the severity of the threat being faced by the client, or the coping strategies that the client is using to control his or her fear. Virtual reality environments, usually delivered through a head-mounted display, can be used to create a virtual world that immerses the client in a scenario that has been designed to stimulate specific fear responses. This technique has been used extensively in CBT interventions for fear of flying, and also in therapy for sexual dysfunction, eating disorders and addictions (Anderson *et al.* 2004; Emmelkamp 2005).

There are undoubtedly many other technologies that will be brought to bear, in time, on the process of therapy. For example, it is possible to envisage real-time brain scanning and emotional arousal monitoring devices that might contribute information that could be highly relevant to counsellors and clients, or computer games that could allow clients to practise different strategies for social problem-solving.

However, there are a number of issues that arise when advanced technologies are used in therapy. One dilemma that can often arise is cost – palmtops and virtual reality headsets are expensive items, not likely to be affordable by the majority of counselling agencies. The effective use of technology may draw on skills and knowledge that are not available within the counselling professional community. Although some clients may embrace a specific technology and find that it fits easily into their learning style, there will always be others who find the same device (even a pen or a book) to be alien and anxiety-provoking for them. There may be unexpected side-effects associated with technology; Anderson *et al.* (2004) have suggested that some clients may use technology as a means of avoiding relationships and emotions – in a similar fashion to people who appear to become 'addicted' to computer games at the cost of friendships and family life. Finally, some therapists fear that an over-reliance on technology may undermine the depth of the client–counsellor relationship. As always, these are issues that can be resolved through training, research, supervision and reflection on practice.

Stepped care: coordinating modes of delivery to provide maximally effective services

The concept of *stepped care* refers to a model for organizing the delivery of health care, in which the client or patient is first of all offered the least intensive form of potentially effective intervention, and only offered more complex or intensive interventions if the 'frontline' treatment proves not to be effective (Davidson 2000; Haaga 2000). The principle of stepped care is widely accepted within the mental health professional community in the UK and other countries. For example, in the UK, the National Institute for Health and Clinical Excellence (NICE 2006) has published an influential set of guidelines for the treatment of depression, based on a stepped care approach. In principle, stepped care can involve a wide variety of different treatments. However, in practice, not all treatments are likely to be available or affordable in one locality; the real-world stepped care systems that have been developed tend to be based on some variant of the following structure:

Step 1: access to self-care materials, such as books, manuals, leaflets and websites;

Step 2: counselling or time-limited psychotherapy, of a generic nature;

Step 3: long-term, specialist psychotherapy focused on a specific disorder, often based
on a manualized, empirically validated form of treatment;

Step 4: inpatient hospital treatment, involving medication supervised by a psychiatrist.

Typically, Steps 2 and 3 may be accompanied by a prescription for medication, such as antidepressants, prescribed by a GP or family doctor.

Stepped care is an attractive option for policy-makers and service managers, because it appears to address the challenge of enabling large-scale access to psychological care while not being able to afford to employ sufficient numbers of professional therapists. Essentially, stepped care offers low-intensity therapy (e.g., guided self-help, delivered by a minimally trained paraprofessional) to large numbers of patients, while retaining more expensive, specialist forms of help for those who are most in need.

Despite the interest in self-care models of service delivery exhibited by policy-makers in recent years, there are few examples of effective stepped care mental health/psychotherapy systems currently in operation, due to the formidable difficulties involved in successfully meshing together different elements of an integrated system. The issues involved in this enterprise are fully discussed by Bower and Gilbody (2005), and include:

- developing robust methods of assessment to ensure that each 'step-up' occurs at the right time for each client;

- identifying client groups for whom stepped care is appropriate. For example, Bower and Gilbody (2005) argue that, within the field of eating disorders, stepped care may be more suitable for binge eating, where 'failure' at the initial step may have relatively minor consequences, compared with anorexia, where early treatment failure may have life-threatening implications;

- assessing the acceptability of stepped care for both service users and health professionals, many of whom may regard immediate access to a fully qualified, specialist counsellor or psychotherapist as a basic right.

The most thorough trial of stepped care that has been published comprised a study carried out in Santiago, Chile, in which low-income depressed women were provided with either treatment as usual from a primary care doctor, or with a psycho-educational group experience (Step 1), followed by medication if necessary (Step 2) (Araya *et al.* 2006). The results of this study were that, compared with usual care, the stepped care package was significantly more effective and only marginally more expensive. It is important to be clear about the meaning of this study. The women who received stepped care were given much *more* care than those who received normal treatment – three additional group-workers were employed for the duration of the project. However, these additional costs could be set against savings arising from reduced medication costs. It is essential to interpret the findings of the Araya *et al.* (2006) study with caution – this was a single piece of research, carried out within an environment of urban poverty in which alternative health resources were scarce. Nevertheless, it does suggest that it may be possible to utilize carefully designed stepped care packages to enhance the quality and effectiveness of treatment in depression.

There is a key ethical/moral issue for counsellors operating within stepped care systems. The requirement within stepped care packages that the client must progress through the programme one step at a time, and the fact that the decision about 'stepping up' is made by the health professional both create dilemmas for any therapist who works from a stance of 'client-centredness' (broadly defined) and client choice. For example, what happens when a client allocated to guided self-help demands immediate access to a professional therapist? In principle, it is possible to envisage stepped-care systems that are built around collaborative decision-making at each stage. However, there have been no published examples of such systems, to date.

It is useful to consider the development of stepped care from within a wider sociological perspective. On the one hand, stepped care is a product of the postmodern acknowledgement that there is no one single 'truth', but that instead there exist multiple truths, each of which has meaning and credibility for particular groups of people. Within the field of psychotherapy and mental health, stepped care is a reflection of the underlying theme of the present chapter, which is that there are many different modes for delivering 'counselling', each of which has its own distinctive strengths and weaknesses. However, stepped care represents one specific response to postmodern diversity and playfulness, which is that of seeking to control multiplicity within a centralized 'top–down' bureaucratic system that is controlled by the state or (in the USA) by a massive health care corporation. One of the risks of stepped care is that of the construction of unwieldy psychotherapy/mental health bureaucracies that may undermine the quality of the relationship between counsellor and client. By contrast, it is possible to imagine ways of promoting client-led stepped care pathways, in which people seeking help are provided with the information that is necessary for them to make the choices that are best for them, in relation to modes and intensity of therapy that might be most effective. The research carried out by Jorm *et al.* (2004), and the case examples described by Bohart and Tallman (1999) suggest that many people adopt this strategy already – in all likelihood far more people than have ever bene-fited from formal stepped care. The disadvantages of client-led stepped care are the finan-cial costs involved in making such personal choices, and the fact that, at present, it is far from easy for individuals seeking therapy to get access to reliable information about different kinds of therapy that are on offer. Despite these barriers, it is clear that a signifi-cant proportion of the population already make use of multiple strategies for self-care (Elkins *et al.* 2006; Jorm *et al.* 2004).

Finally, it is clear that stepped care can take the form of creative locally organized sequences of interventions, rather than always necessarily comprising large-scale 'managed' health care systems. In Scotland, the *Doing Well by Depression* initiative (Scottish Executive 2006) consisted of seven locally organized projects, each of which involved provision of different forms of guided self-help, based on local resources. In Germany, Golkaramnay and colleagues (2007) have reported on a project in which clients who had received time-limited group therapy were offered ongoing support and contact through an internet chat room. Their study found a significantly lower proportion of those in the chat room condition were assessed at 12-month follow-up as poor outcome cases, compared with those who had received group therapy alone. The existence of these projects, alongside the pervasive reality of client-led care packages, suggest that stepped care need not always be interpreted as implying the imposition of externally defined evidence-based protocols, but can also represent a broader principle, which is that of not assuming that any single intervention is sufficient in itself. On the contrary, many people appear to find it helpful to combine help from diverse modes of delivery, in ways that best meet their individual needs, and respond positively when therapists create opportunities for them to operate in this fashion.

Conclusions

This review of alternative modes of providing counselling help for people in need indicates that there is a wide diversity of therapeutic formats that are available. It also appears as though the range of modes of delivery of counselling is expanding year-by-year, as new technologies become available, and as therapists creatively devise new ways of working. There is therefore plentiful scope for counsellors and counselling agencies to be expansive in their use of therapeutic resources and modalities – it is clear that face-to-face individual therapy is only one among many possible ways of providing a therapeutic experience. Moreover, it would appear that the approaches described in this chapter have the potential to reach people who might be reluctant to seek out conventional one-to-one counselling or therapy. For example, email and internet-based services allow high levels of anonymity and control to clients who may be fearful or shameful about engaging with therapy. The principle of *stepped care* offers a framework for beginning to make sense of how different modes of delivery may be combined. However, it is also clear that clients are capable of constructing their own assemblages of therapeutic experiences, to reflect their own personal predilections and circumstances – there is certainly more that needs to be understood about how different modes of counselling can be brought together most effectively.

Each of these modes of delivery discussed in this chapter requires training, based in an acknowledgement that they demand specific skills and knowledge on the part of practitioners. There are also underlying issues concerning the integration of face-to-face work with other modes of therapy. There exist valuable literatures on how individual therapy can be linked to group therapy, and how bibliotherapy can be incorporated into face-to-face work, but there are many other modality permutations that do not appear to have been critically examined. Finally, there is a lack of research into the therapeutic processes associated with alternative modes of delivery, their effectiveness, and how they fit together. The drive towards evidence-based practice in the psychological therapies (see Chapter 25) is almost entirely based on research into individual, face-to-face work – there is relatively little evidence concerning the effectiveness of other modalities, or of stepped care permutations of different modalities.

Topics for reflection and discussion

1 Reflect on the work of a face-to-face counselling agency with which you are familiar. How could the service offered by that agency be enhanced by introducing some of the other modes of delivery of counselling discussed in this chapter?

2 Do different modes of counselling help (e.g., groups, bibliotherapy, telephone counselling, individual face-to-face work) produce different outcomes in clients? Is the learning process for clients the same whatever type of intervention is used or are there change elements unique to each format?

3 Discuss the extent to which alternatives to traditional individual counselling represent attempts to deal with power issues in the helper–helpee relationship. How successful are these alternative approaches in empowering clients?

4 You have been asked to run a training course intended to enable counsellors who work with individual clients in face-to-face settings to undertake telephone counselling, groupwork or couples counselling. What would you include in the course?

5 Reflect on the experience of reading a self-help book, preferably one that you consulted some time ago. Why did you decide to use the book? Did you discuss it with anyone else, or merely work through it on your own? What impact, either in the short-term or of a more lasting nature, has the book made on you? What was it about the book that you felt was most and least helpful?

6 Do alternative modes of delivery present new ethical dilemmas? What might these be, and how could they be addressed?

7 An important theme running through the counselling literature, and certainly something that is apparent to many experienced counsellors, is the different ways in which men and women use counselling. Are there particular modes of delivery that are likely to be more attractive or appropriate for men or for women?

8 What is your own preferred mode of delivery of counselling? In terms of developing your career as a counsellor, which delivery formats are most likely to capitalize on your personal skills and interests?

Suggested further reading

This chapter deals with a diverse set of topics, and readers interested in learning more are recommended to follow up sources referenced in specific sections of the chapter. It is perhaps worth noting that at present there does not seem to be any unified model of the advantages and disadvantages of differing modes of delivery of counselling.

Being and becoming a counsellor

Introduction

In previous chapters, some fundamental questions were asked about the theory and practice of counselling. Ultimately, though, counselling is an activity carried out by people. Theoretical insights or research findings can only be expressed through the actions of counsellors in their responses to the immediate challenges presented by specific clients. The aim of this chapter is to explore what is involved in being a competent counsellor. The role of counsellor is multifaceted, requiring a range of different types of skill and knowledge. This chapter begins by considering the process of becoming a counsellor, and the type of training that is required. Finally, the chapter considers issues related to the challenge of maintaining effectiveness in a counselling role, and coping with the stresses of the work.

Themes in the childhood experience of counsellors

It is not obvious that being a counsellor would necessarily represent an attractive occupational choice. Counselling involves sitting in a fixed position, in a small office, for many hours, listening to people talk about bleak and depressing issues. Quite a lot of the time it is difficult to know whether a client has gained anything from their time with you. It is hard to get a paid job, salaries are low and there are few opportunities for professional advancement. So, given all this, why are so many people willing to invest substantial amounts of time and money on being trained as counsellors?

There are probably three main reasons why people seek to become counsellors. First, it is a type of work that can be immensely satisfying. There can be a huge sense of privilege associated with the opportunity to have been part of the process through which someone has turned their life around. Second, counselling is a highly flexible type of work, which appeals to people who wish to combine different work roles, or combine work with child care. Third, people are driven to be counsellors. It is an activity that they 'need' to do, no matter how many hurdles they need to overcome. This drive, or need, arises from relationship patterns and emotional needs established in childhood. Exposure to certain types of childhood experience can be viewed as the source of the passion and commitment that most counsellors bring to their work. At the same time, it is also the source of many of the troubles that can befall counsellors.

It is taken for granted within the field of counselling that one of the primary tasks of both initial training and ongoing professional development involves developing an appreciation and understanding of the ways in which life experience has shaped how one is as a therapist. The importance of this topic has also generated a large amount of research into the early family life of therapists (Barnett 2007; Burton 1970; Burton and Topham 1997; DiCaccavo 2002; Guy 1987; Henry 1966; Spurling and Dryden 1989; Sussman 2007; Racusin *et al.* 1981).

There are a number of factors that appear to be related to a later career choice as a counsellor or psychotherapist. It is essential to interpret these findings with a great deal of caution. It is clear that each person follows their own unique developmental pathway within which some themes may be highly salient whereas other factors may be entirely absent. Also, most of this research has been carried out on full-time psychotherapists in the USA. Research is lacking on the motivational patterns and developmental processes of non-professional or voluntary counsellors, and on the experiences of therapists from non-white ethnic or working class backgrounds.

The evidence shows that many therapists describe childhoods in which they had the experience of being cultural 'outsiders'. This sense of being an outsider might be as a result of belonging to a cultural minority group (for example, the high proportion of Jewish therapists), living for some time in another country, or having parents who are exiles or immigrants. As Henry (1977: 49) puts it, in childhood many therapists 'have been exposed to more than one set of cultural influences'. 'Outsiderness' can also arise from childhood experience of illness, loneliness (perhaps through being an only child or living in an isolated location), abuse or bereavement. People who have grown up with a strong sense of belonging to a culture or social group readily develop an intuitive understanding of social rules and norms. By contrast, the experience of being a social 'outsider' motivates a child to learn about and understand relationships and interactions that are puzzling or threatening. As Henry (1977) noted, the motive to care can lead to a wide range of potential careers (e.g., social work, nursing). However, being a therapist requires a wish to care for others allied to a strong interest in making sense of the inner worlds and relationships of clients. An exposure in childhood to periods of loneliness, isolation or outsider status provides fertile soil for the development of such skills and interests.

Another childhood theme that is frequently reported in interviews with therapists is conflict in family life, with the therapist as child taking the role of mediator or substitute parent. Consistent with this role, therapists often reported that they were the dominant sibling in the family. Brightman (1984: 295) suggests that 'the role of therapist itself may constitute a reenactment of an earlier situation in which a particularly sensitive and empathic child has been pressed into the service of understanding and caring for a parent (usually depressed mother) figure'. The child in this situation grows up with a need to care for others. As the sibling most involved in the family drama, from an early age he or she needs to become a 'junior psychologist' who is adept at picking up behavioural cues of impending family conflict and skilled in findings ways to deflect or resolve difficult situations.

The pattern of childhood experience is unique for every therapist, but the more that it contains some of the elements described above, the more likely it is to lead to a motivation to enter counselling as a career. Marston (1984) and Farber et al. (2005) observe that there are multiple motives for becoming a therapist, such as contact, helping others, discovery, social status, power and influence, and self-therapy, and there are multiple pathways into this line of work. For perhaps the majority of counsellors, the routes into this area of work unfolds over time. It is common for people to enter professions such as nursing, social work and teaching and then find themselves more and more attracted to and involved in the counselling components of their job. Undergoing personal therapy or counselling as a client may also function as a catalyst for the decision to enter counselling training. The experience of meeting therapists or trainers who become influential role models can also be a factor. It is important to acknowledge that the decision to become a counsellor is not made lightly by people. It constitutes a significant developmental stage in its own right, and many very talented counsellors do not complete this stage, and enter training, until well into their middle years.

For counsellors, the significance of what happened in their early childhood represents a strength and asset, and also a potential source of vulnerability. It is a strength because it provides a deep knowledge, understanding and curiosity around aspects of life to which most people give relatively little attention. There are perhaps three main ways in which these childhood themes can cause difficulties for counsellors. Children who have been family peacemakers and detached observers of the foibles of others, may develop a grandiose sense of their own self-importance. Children who have had troubled lives may grow up to be troubled adults, and lack emotional soundness and resilience. Being a therapist may function as a way of avoiding dealing with painful personal issues: clients become a substitute for real-world relationships, and the therapist may unconsciously seeks to learn how to resolve personal issues by watching how their clients do it.

Box 24.1: *Narcissism as a professional hazard*

The concept of *narcissism* comes from the Greek myth of Narcissus, a handsome youth who eventually perished because he fell in love with his own reflection. The precursors of narcissism are present in the way that babies and infants are generally adored and regarded as perfect in all that they do. An element of narcissism is a necessary component of a healthy personality, as a counterbalance to harsh self-criticism. The patterns of childhood experience that are found in the early lives of many counsellors create the potential for subsequent narcissistic personality structures. Being an outsider can cultivate a belief that one is better than those 'mere mortals'. Being a family peacekeeper at an early age can lead to a sense that one possesses special gifts and powers.

In some respects, therapist narcissism is institutionally reinforced within the counselling and psychotherapy professional literature and within popular culture: 'the stereotype of the psychotherapist as all-knowing, all-loving, a fusion of the artist and scientist setting forth to battle the dark forces of the human soul' (Brightman 1984: 295). Almost all therapy case studies portray the therapist (not the client) as the hero of the story, and textbooks tend to devote little attention to discussing or describing cases of failure. Nevertheless, the reality is that counsellors are continually confronted by the limits of their understanding, empathy and capacity to help. As a means of coping with an inner sense of inadequacy, some thera-pists evolve what Brightman (1984) has called a 'grandiose professional self' – an image of an all-powerful and all-loving therapist. The earliest observation of this phenomenon was made by Ernest Jones, the psychoanalyst who was student and biographer of Freud. Jones (1951) wrote that some analysts kept themselves aloof and mysterious, acted as if they knew everything and never admitted mistakes. He coined the term 'God complex' to describe such therapists. Marmor (1953) described this pattern as a 'feeling of superiority'.

The consequences of therapist narcissism have been explored by Glickauf-Hughes and Mehlman (1995) and Halewood and Tribe (2003). Narcissistic counsellors do not readily accept feedback, and are deeply threatened by any manifestation of client anger toward them or criticism from colleagues. They may be driven by perfectionist tendencies and seek to impose their version of truth on others. Behind an apparently confident external image, the narcissistic counsellor may hide a fear of being an imposter who is unable to be of any value to anyone. These narcissistic and grandiose qualities are the opposite of the characteristics of effective therapists. Any counsellor needs to arrive at an answer to the question 'Am I good enough?' To be 'good enough' to help people who are deeply damaged by life is to make a strong statement about one's own sanity, knowledge and competence. There are likely to be many episodes within a counselling career when the evidence points in the direction of inadequacy rather than sufficiency. The resolution of grandiose and narcissistic responses to these crises can be facilitated by appropriate supervision and personal therapy. The transition to a more realistic self-appraisal may be accompanied by depression and a sense of mourning for an idealized state that has been left behind.

The wounded healer model

The 'wounded healer' model (Guggenbuhl-Craig 1971; Nouwen 1979; Rippere and Williams 1985) proposes that the power of the healer (the priest or shaman in primitive societies, the counsellor or psychotherapist in modern society) derives from his or her inner experience of pain, loss or suffering. The presence of a 'wound' in the healer gives him or her an excellent basis from which to understand and empathize with the wounds of clients: '. . . making one's own wounds a source of healing . . . does not call for a sharing of superficial personal pains but for a constant willingness to see one's own pain and suffering as rising from the depth of the human condition which all men share' (Nouwen, 1979: 88).

The wounded healer concept makes it possible to understand the 'search for wholeness and integration' (Spurling and Dryden 1989: 252), which characterizes the lives of many counsellors and therapists as a strategy for transforming the pain of negative life experiences into a resource for helping others.

For several decades, the wounded healer model has remained in the shadows of the counselling and psychotherapy literature. Privately, many therapists will acknowledge the relevance of making practical use of their 'woundedness'. However, the mainstream literature and professional discourse has been dominated by models of therapy that attribute successful outcomes to the application of specific theories or evidence-based treatment protocols. The personality or life experience of the therapist has been regarded as at best irrelevant, and at worst a source of error. More recently, an increasing acceptance of the findings of research showing that effective therapy is heavily influenced by therapist characteristics (discussed in a later section of the present chapter), has resulted in a resurgence of interest in the implications of the wounded healer metaphor.

One of the key factors in this debate has been a realization that many counsellors and psychotherapists can clearly be understood as being wounded healers. For example, drug and alcohol counsellors may have struggled with substance dependency issues in their lives, marriage and family counsellors may have experienced divorce, domestic violence or family breakdown, rape and sexual abuse counsellors may be survivors of sexual abuse. There has been little research on this phenomenon.

A valuable study, which could usefully be replicated in other fields of counselling practice, was carried out by Costin and Johnson (2002) into the backgrounds of counsellors and psychotherapists working in specialist eating disorder services in the USA. In a survey of service managers, Costin and Johnson (2002) found that on average over a half of therapy staff were known to be recovering from eating problems of one kind or another. These managers could identify a number of ways in which these life patterns might make their staff vulnerable, for example through risk of relapse or by being overinvolved in the work and not taking care of themselves. However, on balance service managers regarded prior personal experience of an eating disorder as being an advantage for therapists, in making them more grounded and realistic, more empathic, and better able to instil hope.

An important review paper by Zerubavel and Wright (2012) offers a reappraisal and reconceptualization of the wounded healer model in the light of current research. Zerubavel and Wright (2012) suggest that the wariness that exists within the professional regarding the concept of the wounded healer can be addressed by introducing the notion of 'trajectories' of relapse and growth. They identify four possible trajectories. The 'chronic dysfunction' pattern describes instances in which a person is affected by a negative life experience, and continues to struggle to cope with its impact. The 'relapse' trajectory occurs when a person oscillates between periods of recovery and effective functioning, and periods of breakdown. The idea of a 'recovery' trajectory is used by Zerubavel and Wright (2012) to characterize the experience of people who overcome a difficult life experience and are able to return to a stable level of functioning. Finally, the 'post-traumatic growth' pattern reflects the experiences of people who are able to make positive use of difficult life experiences.

Reframing the image of the wounded healer in terms of a set of dynamic and potentially alterable trajectories makes it possible to make sense of both the positive and negative aspects of difficult life experiences. Clearly, a wounded healer who is on a post-traumatic growth trajectory has the potential to be a really special therapist. On the other hand, a student or trainee who attempts to conceal a pattern of chronic dysfunction or relapse, may turn out to be a poor therapist, particularly for clients whose problems overlap with or re-evoke the counsellor's own issues. The Zerubavel and Wright (2012) model does not make any assumptions that a chronic dysfunction trajectory is immutable and fixed: with appropriate support, supervision and therapy a trainee or practitioner who demonstrates this pattern may be enabled to move to a different path.

Almost all counsellors undertake personal therapy at some point in their career. An extensive discussion of the role of personal therapy is provided later in this chapter. To some extent, personal therapy for therapists can be regarded as a means of articulating the wounded healer model in a way that enhances the competence of the practitioner. Personal therapy helps to transform negative life experiences into sources of insight and wisdom that can be called upon in the service of clients. In the terminology of Zerubavel and Wright (2012), personal therapy promotes a post-traumatic growth trajectory. But there is also a sense in which personal therapy forces counsellors to be aware of and confront areas of experience that had previously been warded-off or boxed up. Personal therapy may therefore heighten the 'woundedness' of therapists, by expanding the extent to which they acknowledge difficulties in their lives. The phenomenon of enhanced sensitivity to woundedness means that it is important to be cautious when interpreting the findings of studies such as Burton and Topham (1997) and Halewood and Tribe (2003), that report higher levels of childhood abuse and trauma in therapists compared with people in other professions: therapists may have harder childhoods, but their training may have made them more aware of any hardship that was around.

There have been many initiatives within counsellor training to develop strategies for helping students and trainees actively to embrace the wounded parts of themselves. One example can be found in the idea of 'existential touchstones' (Mearns and Cooper 2005), which refers to unique personal strengths that have their roots in specific childhood experiences. For instance, a counsellor who has been brought up in a family in which emotional sharing and support was not available, and has then been able to develop emotional connectedness in their life is likely to be readily able to appreciate and work with clients who have had similar experiences. By contrast, a counsellor who has grown up in a more emotionally expressive family environment may have to work harder to engage with a client who has not had that kind of upbringing. Encouraging trainees to identify their 'existential touchstones' can be an effective means of learning to make therapeutic use of 'everyday woundedness'.

A further initiative, along similar lines, can be found in the training programme devised by Aponte and Kissil (2012: 4), who ask students to identify their personal 'signature theme', defined as a 'lifelong struggle [that] shap(es) the person's relationships with self and others'. Examples of signature themes generated by members of one class included: 'it's hard for me to stay in my emotions and be vulnerable', 'I am always thinking the worst; not being able to enjoy the good things but always waiting for the worst to happen' and 'I am afraid that I am alone or that I will be alone' (Aponte and Kissil 2012: 4). Students are then invited to consider the ways in which their signature themes represent personal resources. Finally, they engage in counselling practice role-play sessions where they actively draw on these resources in their work with clients.

These training initiatives are perhaps particularly valuable in acting as a reminder that the wounded healer model consists of two main elements. An effective healer is someone who has been able to overcome their wounds, and therefore appreciates what the process of healing is all about. But, what this then does, according to Nouwen (1979: 88) is to give the healer an enhanced 'willingness to see one's own pain and suffering as rising from the depth of the human condition which all men share'. A focus on personal therapy, and research that examines the impact on therapists of specific difficulties such as childhood abuse, or the experience of psychiatric hospitalization, draws attention to the first of these elements. By contrast, when students work in groups to explore their signature themes, they are learning to make sense of wounds as potential openings into areas of shared experience, and as ways of deepening their connection with clients.

The qualities of exceptional counsellors

Over the past decade, a series of research studies has examined the characteristics of senior and 'master therapists' – practitioners nominated by their peers as the 'best of the best' – the therapists that they would recommend a family member to consult. The value of these studies lies in their capacity to use the broader perspective available to highly successful practitioners, who have survived the hazards of practice and thrived, as a means of highlighting the attitudes and strategies that are associated with excellence in the field of counselling and psychotherapy.

Several research studies have reported wide differences in levels of effectiveness across individual therapists. A study by Okiishi et al. (2003) is an example of this kind of research – in their sample, the clients of the least successful counsellors tended to get worse, on average, whereas more than 80 per cent of the clients of the most effective therapists were completely recovered by the end of therapy. Similar findings have been reported by Kraus et al. (2011).

This kind of evidence has led many people to wonder about the characteristics of those practitioners who are maximally effective. There has always been a lot of attention given to analysing the work of Carl Rogers, as an exemplar of an effective therapist (see Farber et al. 1996). The work of Len Jennings, Thomas Skovholt and Helge Ronnestad has sought to take this topic further by using interviews with master therapists and experienced practitioners to find out just what makes a good therapist. Jennings and Skovholt (1999) interviewed ten master therapists (seven women and three men), aged between 50 to 72 years, representing a wide range of theoretical orientations. All of these therapists worked full time in private practice. The conclusions that emerged from this study were that master therapists are:

- voracious learners;
- sensitive to, and value cognitive complexity and the ambiguity of the human condition;
- emotionally receptive, self-aware, reflective, non-defensive, and open to feedback;
- mentally healthy and mature individuals who attend to their own emotional well-being;
- aware of how their emotional health affects the quality of their work;
- in possession of strong relationship skills;
- convinced that the foundation for therapeutic change is a strong working alliance;
- experts at using their exceptional relationship skills in therapy.
- able to use their accumulated life and professional experiences as a major resource in their work.

In a further study, Ronnestad and Skovholt (2001) interviewed 12 senior therapists with an average age of 74 years, and 38 years of post-qualification experience. Four major themes emerged from the data:

- the impact of early life experience;
- the cumulative influence of professional experience;
- the influence of professional elders;
- personal experiences in adult life.

Taken together, these studies show that there are a number of characteristics that appear to be common in 'master' therapists. They are practitioners who are not bound to one approach or set of assumptions. Even if they nominally demonstrate allegiance to a particular therapy approach, they read widely, and are open to new learning and new sources of influence. Master therapists are interested in other people and are comfortable in relating to others in an open and non-defensive manner. Finally, master therapists take care of themselves emotionally, and devote energy and attention to making sense of their personal life experience.

A study carried out by Goldfried *et al.* (1998) confirms many of these findings. Goldfried *et al.* (1998) invited master therapists (CBT and psychodynamic), nominated by their peers, to provide a tape of a good session with an ongoing client and to indicate the portion of the session that was particularly significant. The tapes were analysed using a coding system for therapist interventions that had been developed in order to differentiate between different therapists. The researchers coded therapist interventions such as support, focus on emotions, self-disclosure, and much else (over 40 different factors), and then compared the CBT and psychodynamic therapists, the special versus routine parts of the sessions, and also the performance of these master therapists with the results from a previous study of 'ordinary' therapists in a controlled study. What they found was there were relatively few differences between the CBT and psychodynamic master therapists, and that the master therapists were more similar to each other than were the comparison groups of 'ordinary' therapists. Finally, the results showed that both subgroups of master therapists were most alike during the significant sections of the session that was analysed, and were more different in the 'routine' parts of the sessions. These findings provide some evidence for the convergence of styles in master therapists from quite distinct theoretical orientations, and support the conclusions of Jennings and Skovholt (1999) that expertise in therapy is largely a matter of generic interpersonal skills and personal qualities, rather than the application of specific techniques.

Two studies that have examined the characteristics of therapists who are highly effective, defined in terms of success rates assessed by change in symptom scores before and after therapy, (Anderson, T. et al. (2009) found that what was distinctive about the best therapists in their sample was that they possessed exceptional interpersonal skills that they were able to exhibit even when under pressure from clients. This result is consistent with the findings of other research that has found that poor outcomes in therapy are often associated with situations in which a client becomes angry with their therapist, for whatever reason, and the latter is unable to find a way to resolve the situation (Binder and Henry 2010; Dalenberg 2004). Anderson and colleagues' study (Anderson, T et al. 2009) highlights the reverse of this: most therapists possess interpersonal skills that are sufficient for dealing with whatever might come in therapy most of the time whereas, by contrast, the best therapists are sufficiently resilient and resourceful, in their way of being with clients, that they can also handle what comes up when the going gets rough.

This pattern can be seen to reflect the characteristics of early childhood experience that lead people to become therapists. On the whole, therapists are people who function best when they are in a position of being able to be helpful to others, and are appreciated for their efforts. They are not comfortable when conflict and anger is directed at them. People who can tolerate or enjoy conflict, or situations where they are not popular, are more likely to be found in the police, or in senior management roles.

Another research study that examined the differences between therapists who were highly effective, and those who had average outcomes, was conducted by Nissen-Lie et al. (2010). In this study, it was found that the most effective therapists were more professionally self-effacing, and reported higher levels of self-doubt, than those who were less helpful to their clients. This finding supports one of the key conclusions from the studies of 'master therapists' (Jennings and Skovholt 1999), and also reflects themes in the early life experience of those who become therapists. Basically, what Nissen-Lie et al. (2010) found was that the most effective therapists are those who are least grandiose and narcissistic, and most open to feedback from others.

The significance of research on master therapists, and highly effective therapists, is that it provides an image of what to aspire to, for both counsellors in training and more experienced practitioners. This body of research is the counselling equivalent of a 'master class' – an opportunity to get a glimpse of what is possible in a therapeutic role. In other fields, such as music, it is taken for granted that some performers are much better than others, and can be used as sources of learning and inspiration. The intention is not that everyone who attends a master class with a famous musician will attain that level of expertise. The aim instead is that they might move a little bit in that direction. The situation is less clear-cut in the world of counselling and psychotherapy, because until recently it was not possible to determine with any confidence who was actually a 'master therapist' and who was not. The existence of research that is beginning to be able to identify exceptional performance in counselling with some degree of reliability, has begun to open up new sources for counsellor learning and development. The implications of this area of work, for counselling training and practice, is explored by Skovholt and Jennings (2004).

Box 24.2: *The psychology of expertise*

The issue of how to differentiate between 'novice', 'competent' and 'expert' practitioners has been explored in a wide range of occupational contexts. It can be valuable to make connections between the process of counsellor professional development, and the conclusions that can be drawn from this broader literature. One of the most influential models of professional expertise was developed by the philosopher Hubert Dreyfus (1989). Within this framework, the activities of novice practitioners exhibit a tendency to stick to taught rules, and a lack of flexibility in relation to contextual factors. The key difference that can be observed in more experienced, competent practitioners, is that they possess and are able to use, some kind of theoretical or conceptual scheme that provides them with a broader perspective on what they are doing and a capacity to take more information into account when deciding how to respond to situations. Finally, expert practitioners are able to drawn on a tacit or intuitive understanding of situations, which allows them to generate creative or novel solutions. This further dimension of competence gives expert practitioners the belief and confidence that they can handle the most challenging situations, the ones that competent and novice practitioners may have a tendency to avoid. A more detailed account of the Dreyfus model can be found in Flyvbjerg (2001), and a valuable discussion of the implications of the model for counsellor training and development is available in Skovholt and Ronnestad (2013).

An appreciation of the psychology of expertise provides insight into many issues in counselling. For example, therapists of differing levels of expertise may be equally effective with clients who present moderate levels of difficulty, even though they seem to be working in quite different ways. It is only with particularly challenging clients that the special qualities of expert therapists come into their own. Also, counsellor training can be regarded as a battle between the novice mind-set ('give me a recipe for how to respond to clients') and the cognitive styles of trainers and tutors who are either competent practitioners ('you need to base your work on a theoretical framework') or experts ('skills and theory are not where the action is – what matters is that you learn to develop your own approach, which reflects who you are as a person'). In this context, it is significant that the training approaches that have been shown to be most effective in producing competent counsellors, all start by drilling trainees in basic micro-skills.

Developing and supporting counsellor competence

So far, in this chapter we have considered various ways of describing and defining what counsellor competence looks like: the attributes associated with effective counselling practice. It is clear that counsellors need to have skills and knowledge in a range of areas, and that these characteristics need to be underpinned by a commitment to the development of self-awareness and strong interpersonal skills. Being a competent counsellor requires willingness to take responsibility for personal learning in these areas. However, counsellors do not work in a vacuum. Being a counsellor involves being part of a network or system of education, training and support that exists in order to develop and maintain the quality of counselling services. The main elements of this system are: training, supervision, personal therapy, well-being programmes and organizational development. The role of these activities in ensuring counsellor competence is explored in the following sections.

Training

In order to understand the structure of current training programmes in counselling, it is necessary to know about the history of training in psychotherapy. The primary training medium for psychoanalysts has been the training analysis. Trainees in psychoanalytic institutes enter analysis with a senior member of the institute. Through the period of training they may undergo training analyses with two or more analysts in this way. A training analysis was considered to be the only way in which an analyst could learn about what psychoanalysis was really like, although theoretical seminars, case discussions and child observation studies came eventually to be added to the psychoanalytic training programme in many institutes. The assessment of suitability of candidates for qualification as analysts was largely determined by the training analyst. The privacy and secretiveness of these arrangements precluded public discussion of training issues; the suitability of a candidate was assessed solely on the professional judgement, with no appeal possible. The potential oppressiveness of this kind of training has been documented by Masson (1988).

The emergence of client-centred therapy in the 1940s and 1950s brought with it a whole set of new ideas about how to train counsellors. Rogers and his colleagues brought in students to act as co-therapists in sessions with clients. Students practised counselling skills on each other. The 'T-group' or personal growth group was applied to counsellor training, with trainees participating in small experiential groups. Students watched films of sessions and analysed recordings and transcripts. This phase of development of approaches to counsellor training featured a more open and multifaceted approach to learning technique, and the introduction of other means of facilitating self-awareness (for example, encounter groups), rather than a reliance solely on personal therapy. There was also a degree of democratization in the training process, with student self-evaluations being used alongside staff appraisals.

During the 1960s and 1970s the main innovation in counsellor training consisted of the introduction of structured approaches to skills training. These approaches were used not only on counsellor training courses but also in the context of shorter skills courses designed for people in other helping or human service professions, such as teaching, nursing and management.

The first of these structured approaches was the human resource development model devised by Carkhuff (1969). Other packages of a similar nature were the micro-skills model (Ivey and Galvin 1984), the skilled helper model (Egan 1984) and interpersonal process recall (Kagan *et al.* 1963). Although these models and approaches differed in certain respects they all contained carefully structured training materials in the form of handouts, exercises and video or film demonstrations, which would take trainees through a standard programme for learning specific counselling skills.

More recently, significant developments in counsellor training have included increased attention to the role of supervision and personal therapy in training programmes (Mearns 1997; Thorne and Dryden 1991). There currently exists a broad consensus concerning the elements that need to be included in training courses (Dryden and Thorne 1991; Dryden *et al.* 1995; Mearns 1997). Different courses may emphasize some of these activities at the expense of others, but all courses will probably include substantial coverage of theory, skills, personal development, professional issues, supervised practice and research awareness.

Box 24.3: *The paradox of counselling and psychotherapy training*

It is generally accepted that at least three years of training is required in order to become a professional counsellor or psychotherapist. Typically, therapist training is highly demanding, and requires considerable commitment to supervised experience with clients and personal therapy in addition to academic study and research. What is somewhat surprising and paradoxical, therefore, is that there is very little evidence that training has much impact on the effectiveness of therapy that is provided for clients. A number of studies have compared the effectiveness of paraprofessional counsellors with fully trained professional therapists, or looked at the outcomes achieved by professional therapists at different points in their training. Overall, these studies reveal only minimal differences in effectiveness associated with training status. Recent reviews and discussion of this body of research can be found in Beutler *et al.* (2004), Lambert and Ogles (2004) and Ronnestad and Ladany (2006). The only consistent result that favoured trained therapists was that they had fewer clients who prematurely dropped out of therapy.

The meaning of these findings can be understood in many different ways. The most likely explanation is that all effective therapy depends on the provision of a set of common factors (such as a warm relationship and the instillation of hope), which depend on basic human qualities that are relatively unaffected by training. On the other hand, there are many commentators from within the professional community who question the validity of these studies and argue that over a mixed caseload of difficult clients a properly trained therapist will always do better than a minimally trained volunteer. However, no definitive study that confirms this position has yet been published. The key point here is that it is by no means obvious that the training practices that are currently being followed are necessarily optimal: there is a great deal to be learned about how therapy trainees can be helped to achieve their maximum potential.

Acquiring a theoretical framework. It is widely accepted that counsellors need to be equipped with a theoretical perspective through which to understand their work with clients. The theory component of courses may include models of counselling, basic psychological theories in areas such as developmental psychology, interpersonal behaviour and group dynamics, an introduction to psychiatric terminology and some aspects of sociology relating to social class, race and gender. There is potential in counselling courses, therefore, for extensive coverage of theoretical topics, particularly when it is taken into account that specialist areas of counselling, such as marital and couples counselling or bereavement work, have their own well-articulated theoretical models. The challenge of theoretical learning in counselling is further increased by the general recognition that students should not merely know about theory, but should be able to apply it in practice. The aim is to be able to use theory actively to understand clients and the reactions of the counsellor to these clients. One of the issues that arises in this area of counsellor training is whether it is more appropriate to introduce students to one theoretical orientation in depth, or to expose them to an integration of several theoretical models. To some extent this issue is linked to the nature of the organization that is offering the training. Independent institutes are often created around proponents of a particular theoretical approach, so that students being trained in these institutes will inevitably be primarily taught that set of ideas. Courses operating in institutions of higher education, such as colleges and universities, are likely to be influenced by academic values concerning the necessity for critical debate between theoretical positions, and will therefore usually teach theory from an integrationist or multiple perspective stance.

Counselling skills. Training in counselling skills has been associated more with person-centred and cognitive–behavioural than with psychodynamic approaches to counselling. The concept of *skill* refers to a sequence of counsellor actions or behaviours carried out in response to client actions or behaviours. Implicit in the idea of skill is an assumption that it makes sense to break down the role of counsellor into discrete actions or behaviours, and this has been an assumption that is difficult to reconcile with psychoanalytic ways of thinking. Many counsellor training programmes have adopted or adapted some version of the micro-skills training approach originally developed by Ivey and Galvin (1984), which breaks down the task of counselling into a number of discrete skills such as attending, open and closed questions, encouraging, paraphrasing, confrontation, etc. Trainees are given written descriptions of positive and negative examples of each skill, watch an expert demonstrating the skill on video, then engage in videotaped practice of the skills with other trainees acting as clients. Feedback is provided, and then the trainee attempts the skill once more. This sequence is repeated until the trainee reaches an appropriate level of competence in the skill.

One of the primary aims of the micro-skills approach is to enable counsellors to function in an 'intentional' rather than 'intuitive' manner, in other words to be able to select an appropriate response from a wide repertoire rather than being restricted to only one or two modes of communication and intervention. Another area of emphasis has been the identification of skills congruent with particular cultural settings (Ivey *et al.* 1987). Further discussion of approaches to teaching counselling skills can be found in Hill and Lent (2006) and McLeod and McLeod (2011).

Personal development. The importance of self-knowledge and self-awareness in counsellors is accepted by all of the established approaches to therapy. In psychodynamic work, for example, the counsellor must be able to differentiate between counter-transference reactions that are triggered by client transference, and those that are projections of unresolved personal conflicts. In person-centred work, the congruence of the counsellor, his or her ability to be aware of and act appropriately upon personal feelings, is considered a core condition in creating an effective therapeutic environment. Self-awareness is also necessary in a more general sense, in enabling the counsellor to survive without burning out through the experience of holding and sharing the pain, fear and despair of clients. Most ordinary people to whom clients turn deny the depth of the emotional suffering that is presented to them, or repress their own reactions to it. Effective counsellors cannot afford these defences, but must find ways of staying with clients in their distress. Finally, it is essential for counsellors to be aware of their own motivations and pay-offs for engaging in this kind of work, in order to prevent different types of client exploitation or abuse.

Traditionally, training courses in psychodynamic counselling, or influenced by psychodynamic approaches, have insisted that counsellors in training undergo personal therapy during the period of training. The number of sessions stipulated varies widely, from ten sessions to twice weekly over several years. The rationale for therapy is not only to promote personal development, but to give the student some experience in the role of client, and to enable first-hand observation of a therapist in action. An additional objective, in some training courses, is to enable assessment of the potential of the trainee.

Another approach to personal development work that is included in many courses is experiential work in groups. These groups may be run by external consultants or leaders, course tutors or even on a self-help or leaderless basis. The aims of such groupwork are similar to those of personal therapy, with the added dimension that the quality of relationships and support developed in the groups will benefit the learning that takes place in other areas of the course as a whole. Work in small groups can also enable counsellors to identify and clarify the values that inform their approach to clients.

Personal learning diaries and journals are employed in several courses to facilitate personal learning and to record the application of learning in practice. The diary or journal is particularly helpful in assisting the transfer of learning and insight beyond the course itself into the rest of the personal and professional life of the trainee. Reading and commenting on diary or journal material can, however, be a time-consuming business for trainers and tutors. The quality and depth of personal exploration and learning on counsellor training courses can often be facilitated through the creation of suitable physical surroundings. Training groups may use residentials, which are often held in countryside settings away from the usual training premises, to construct a 'cultural island' where relationships are strengthened and new patterns of behaviour tried out. The personal meaning of counsellor training for many trainees is that it is a time of intense self-exploration and change, which has implications for partners, family and work roles.

Box 24.4: *A baptism of fire*

Although people who complete counsellor training usually describe their learning experience as meaningful and satisfying, there is no doubt that at times training can also be highly stressful. One of the most terrifying moments in training can arise when the student for the first time meets a real client. Folkes-Skinner *et al.* (2010) published a detailed case study of the experience of Margaret, a student on a leading university-based counsellor training programme in the UK. In many respects, Margaret was well prepared for seeing her first client. She was 50 years of age, and could draw on a wealth of life experience including a successful professional background in a business environment. She was well able to handle interactions and form relationships with people from all walks of life. Margaret was in a stable and supportive relationship, and had personal experience of being a therapy client. She had worked on a telephone helpline, and had completed a two-year pre-clinical part-time training qualification. However, despite these qualities and attributes, when interviewed soon after starting to see clients, she reported that:

> . . . the client work has been quite painful, (to an extent that) that I wasn't expecting, the way the client impacts on you . . . I'm very able to go on a guilt trip, let's put it that way, so I thought it was me . . . I really was quite upset when I got home from work, it's just the sudden realisation that this is what it means to work with a client . . . what I really do question now is, is that something I'm going to have to cope with always? Or is it something I'm going to get a handle on? I really don't know the answer to that.
>
> (Folkes-Skinner *et al.* 2010: 89)

Margaret was able to work through this crisis, by drawing on her own personal resources and the support of tutors and fellow trainees. But this example illustrates the level of emotional intensity and personal challenge that is associated with counsellor training, even when the student is well-suited to a counselling role and has adequate support.

Professional issues. Training courses should include careful consideration of a wide range of professional issues. Principles of ethical practice are usually given substantial attention on courses, mainly through discussion of cases. Other professional issues that are covered are: power and discrimination in counselling, particularly with respect to race, gender, disability and sexual orientation; case management and referral; boundary issues; professional accountability and insurance; interprofessional working; and the organization and administration of counselling agencies. Bond (2009) provides a thorough discussion of these areas. A valuable discussion of training issues in relation to multicultural competence can be found in Kim and Lyons (2003).

Supervised practice. At some point in training students will begin work with real clients, rather than practising with course colleagues. It is generally considered essential that participants on training courses should be involved in some supervised practice, to provide them with material to use in other parts of the course, and to give them opportunities to apply skills and concepts. A broader discussion of the nature of supervision is introduced later in this chapter, but at this point it can be mentioned that the delivery of supervision to trainees can be either through regular one-to-one meetings with a supervisor or through group supervision. The quality and frequency of supervision is of vital importance to people learning to be counsellors. There are, however, aspects of training that make effective supervision difficult to achieve. The first of these arises from the anxieties and dependency that most people experience when first confronted by clients. A further issue concerns the relationship between the supervisor and the primary trainers or tutors. It is desirable for supervisors to work with their supervisees in ways that are consistent with the aims and philosophy of a course. It is also desirable, on the other hand, for the trainee to know that he or she can be open with the supervisor, with no fear that disclosures will find their way back to those deciding who will pass or fail the course. The role of the supervisor in relation to a training course represents a challenge to achieve an appropriate balance between involvement with the course and autonomy in service of the student.

Using research to inform practice. An exploration of the contribution of research to an understanding of the counselling process is included in many courses. This may take the form of sessions on research awareness, the ability to read research papers and draw appropriate conclusions from them, through training in research methods and ultimately to designing and implementing a piece of research.

Box 24.5: *The influence of training on the identity of the counsellor*

The process of undergoing counsellor training can have a profound effect on participants. Often, people on training courses have a sense of being asked to look at who they are from a different perspective, through the framework of the therapy approach that they are learning. This can be an exciting and liberating experience, but it can also be felt as a threat to the basis of one's pre-existing sense of self. Jafar Kareem (2000: 32), who was later to become one of the leaders of the intercultural therapy movement, described his experience of training in these terms:

> . . . during the time I was developing (my approach to therapy), I found that one of the most difficult things for me was to look deep into myself and to realize from what point I was starting and where I was, and to re-examine how much my analysis, my training process, and the process of acquiring a new skill, had affected me . . . Intensive training can be compared to a kind of colonization of the mind and I constantly had to battle within myself to keep my head above water, to remind myself at every point who I was and what I was. It was a painful and difficult battle not to think what I had been told to think, not to be what I had been told to be and not to challenge what I had been told could not be challenged and at the same time not become

alienated from my basic roots and my basic self . . . My authenticity was almost lost in favour of this 'new knowledge'.

This kind of tension between 'basic roots and basic self', and 'new knowledge' is reported by many who undergo training, and can have significant repercussions on the trainee's relationship with their partner, friends and other family members. Further accounts of the experience of counselling and psychotherapy training can be found in Harding-Davies *et al.* (2004), Rath (2008) and Truell (2001).

Issues and dilemmas in counsellor training. Although it might be said that there exists a fair measure of agreement over the broad shape and outline of counsellor training, this apparent consensus should not conceal the fact that there is a wide range of dilemmas and issues to be resolved. In terms of issues arising from the practicalities of operating courses, the two most common dilemmas are balance and time. There are always difficult choices to be made about how much emphasis to give some course elements at the expense of others. No matter how long a course is, the time available could be filled with theory, or could be taken up wholly by experiential work. The other fundamental dilemma is related to time. The process of counsellor development takes a lot of time. People training to be counsellors need to assimilate counselling theory and skills into their own personal way of relating. It probably takes at least four years for most people to become competent as counsellors, and very few courses allow that much time. Other issues that present challenges for those designing training programmes are selection of trainees and assessment of competence. Some of the emerging possibilities in counsellor training, arising from the use of digital media, are discussed by Manring *et al.* (2011).

Box 24.6: *Strengthening the counsellor's capacity to deal with difficult issues*

For the most part, research into counsellor training has tended to investigate the effectiveness of overall programmes of training, rather than look at training in relation to specific competencies. An exception to this general trend has been a handful of studies that have assessed the impact of training that is designed to overcome discrete areas of counsellor difficulties. Two such studies are the investigation of Crits-Christoph *et al.* (2006) into a training programme to improve the capacity of therapists to offer an effective therapeutic alliance, and the study of Hess *et al.* (2006) that examined the value of training in how to respond to angry clients.

In the Crits-Christoph *et al.* (2006) study, a group of therapists attended a workshop on methods of enhancing their therapeutic alliance with clients, and then received weekly supervision intended to reinforce the key themes of the workshop. The effectiveness of these therapists was assessed in relation to clients that they saw before and following the training phase, and it was found that the training package produced improved therapeutic alliance ratings, as well as better overall client outcomes.

In the Hess *et al.* (2006) study, a group of counsellors were asked to respond to three sets of video vignettes that portrayed angry clients (e.g., the client expressing anger because the therapist had fallen asleep during the session). Following each video presentation, the counsellor received a different form of training: (a) meeting individually with a supervisor to discuss strategies for responding to client anger; (b) self-study of written guidelines for responding to client anger; (c) individual self-reflection. Not surprisingly, the majority of participants perceived supervisor-delivered training as most helpful. However, all three forms of training produced a positive effect in terms of counsellor competence in responding to anger, with only a slight difference in favour of the supervisor condition. These studies exemplify a potentially significant area for further research into targeted training for counsellors who already possess basic skills.

Personal therapy

Personal therapy, when a counsellor of psychotherapist attends therapy as a client, to facilitate his or her development and well-being, and to address personal issues, represents a unique means of learning about the therapeutic process. Personal therapy can give insight into the role of client and can contribute to a general heightening of self-awareness in both trainees and experienced practitioners. Personal therapy can be a valuable means of coping with the stress of the counsellor role. Within the counselling and psychotherapy professions as a whole, there is a broad consensus regarding the value of personal therapy.

Box 24.7: *How does personal therapy affect a therapist's practice?*

The debate over the role of personal therapy in counselling and psychotherapy training, and the maintenance of good practice, has been hampered by the quality of the evidence that has been available. The position on personal therapy adopted by many therapists and trainers tends to be based largely on their personal experience of whether therapy has been helpful for them individually, or for colleagues they have known. This kind of 'testimonial' evidence is important, but can never be grounded in systematic analysis or sampling. The research evidence is largely derived from questionnaire surveys of therapists, which ask about their use of personal therapy and attitude to it. However, questionnaire surveys are unable to explore the *meaning* of an event or experience with any depth or complexity.

In recognition of these issues, Macran *et al.* (1999) conducted in-depth interviews with seven experienced therapists in Britain, representing a variety of approaches (psychodynamic, person-centred, body-oriented, eclectic). Their research sought to combine the authentic testimony of participants with a process of rigorous analysis of what these informants had to say.

These interviews generated a substantial list of ways in which personal therapy had affected day-to-day practice for these therapists. Three main themes were identified in the analysis of this interview material: *orienting to the therapist (humanity, power, boundaries), orienting to the client (trust, respect, patience)* and *listening with the third ear*. The report by Macran *et al.* (1999) provides a detailed account of these findings, illustrated by quotes from the interviews. These therapists described many examples of the effect of personal therapy on their awareness and practice:

> I think that some therapists . . . find it very difficult to understand that somebody can exhibit severe physical pain when it might actually be about something else. Because to be absolutely honest with you, I'd never have believed it if it hadn't happened to me. (p. 423)

> Have a much greater trust in being able to use the transference . . . and the significance of it . . . I don't think I understood until I understood the way I transferred myself and what I experienced onto my therapist. (p. 423)

> The point of getting therapy yourself is to actually remind you that you are a human being and your client is a human being, and the only difference between you is the roles that you're in in this particular interaction. (p. 424)

> I think what a lot of my therapy has helped me to do is to just be more ordinary in some way with other people. It's like . . . I don't have to put on a face so much or a mask or a professional role, do you know what I mean? It's like I . . . can trust in me. (p. 424)

> I think a client picks up, a client knows how far you've gone. At the unconscious level, they know if you're the kind of person who can take their rage, take their hostility, take their seductiveness . . . Unless you've been in the position of knowing about your own seductiveness, your own rage, your own hatred and whatever, it's quite difficult to sit with certain kinds of clients who will stir in you those sorts of feelings. (p. 425)

> I've been embroiled sexually with a couple of clients. Not in the sense of actually breaking the boundaries, but it was getting rather sort of hot and steamy and uncomfortable . . . I was getting confused . . . wasn't really able to step back and see the wood for the trees . . . [Therapy] helped me be true about what was mine and what was theirs and to actually process my own feelings and my own needs on my own and not try to get my needs met in therapy. (p. 426)

Macran *et al.* (1999) suggest that therapists *translate* their experiences as clients into the 'language' of their practice. In doing this, they use observations of their personal experience (self as client) but also observations they have made of how their therapist operated. It was clear that interviewees were not merely imitating or modelling themselves on their therapists – they learned as much from negative examples as from positive ones. An important source of learning was to figure out how to avoid making the mistakes with their own clients that their therapists had made with them.

One of the intriguing aspects of this study lies in what was *not* said by these therapists. There was little sense in what was reported in the Macran *et al.* (1999) paper that any of these people had entered therapy in order to resolve troublesome and distressing 'problems in living'. There did not appear to be any comments around a theme of learning from personal therapy about how to resolve or live with a problem (depression, panic attacks, eating disorder, surviving abuse etc.) of the type presented by clients in everyday therapy (rather than 'personal' therapy). Macran *et al.* (1999) presents a picture of personal therapy as a profoundly instructive and helpful learning experience, which contributes greatly to an improved awareness of the process of therapy and the role and experience of both client and therapist. But their study also implies that there is a difference between 'personal' therapy and 'everyday' therapy. The latter is typically focused more on surviving than on thriving. Of course, there are many therapists who have experienced 'everyday' therapy: for example, at a period of their life prior to deciding to train as a counsellor or psychotherapist. It would be interesting to know whether what they have learned from their therapy is similar to, or perhaps different from, the learning themes reported in Macran *et al.* (1999).

A review of several surveys of counsellors and psychotherapists, concerning their use of personal therapy, found that 75 per cent of therapists in the USA (Norcross and Guy 2005) had made use of personal therapy at some point in their career. Within these samples, there was some variation across theoretical orientations, with almost all of psychodynamic practitioners having been in therapy at some point and around 50 per cent of behaviour therapists, with practitioners of other approaches reporting prevalence rates between these figures. A recent international survey found that this pattern was found in all countries with mature psychotherapy professions (Orlinsky *et al.* 2005a, 2005b). On balance, the highest use of personal therapy occurs during training, with only around half of therapists re-entering therapy once they had qualified (Norcross and Guy 2005). In these surveys, the reasons that therapists give for first seeking therapy are fairly evenly divided between training requirements, personal growth and dealing with personal problems (Bike *et al.* 2009).

Many training programmes and professional associations require trainees to receive ongoing personal therapy throughout their period of training. There are, however, some fundamental difficulties that are raised by this practice. First, a situation is created where the client is required to attend, rather than depending on voluntary participation. This can create tensions in terms of the trainee/client's commitment to the therapy process. Second, if the trainee becomes deeply caught up in therapeutic work, it may diminish her own emotional availability for her clients. Third, in some traditional psychoanalytic training institutes the personal therapist is a member of the training staff, and not only reports on the progress of the trainee in therapy, but, if the trainee completes the programme, will then subsequently become a colleague of the person who was a client. This situation can create difficult boundary and dual relationship issues. However, the use of personal therapy as an evaluated training component is less prevalent now than in the past. Contrasting approaches to the use of personal therapy in training have been developed within different theoretical traditions, such as psychoanalytic (Lasky 2005), Jungian (Kirsch 2005), humanistic (Elliott and Partyka 2005), cognitive–behavioural (Laireiter and Willutzki 2005) and systemic/family therapy (Lebow 2005).

What is the impact of personal therapy on therapy practice? There are reasons to expect personal therapy to be associated with greater counsellor competence (for example, because of greater sensitivity to the client's experience), but also reasons to expect the reverse (for example, because therapists become preoccupied with their own problems). Studies of personal therapy reflect this balance of views. Although, for example, Buckley *et al.* (1981) found that 90 per cent of the therapists in their sample reported that personal therapy had made a positive contribution to their personal and professional development, Norcross *et al.* (1988) found that 21 per cent felt that, for them, personal therapy had been harmful in some way. Peebles (1980) reported that personal therapy was associated with higher levels of empathy, congruence and acceptance in therapists, whereas Garfield and Bergin (1971) concluded from a small-scale study that the therapists who had not received personal therapy were more effective than those who had.

In an important study of psychoanalytic psychotherapists in Sweden, Sandell *et al.* (2000) were able to compare the personal characteristics and training, supervision and personal therapy profiles of therapists who were found to be either more or less clinically effective in their work with clients. This study discovered that the *less* effective therapists reported having had *more* personal therapy than their more effective colleagues. Sandell *et al.* (2000) interpreted this result as suggesting the possibility that therapists who feel that they are not doing very well with their clients may enter person therapy as a means of enhancing their sensitivity and performance. Reviews of research into the outcomes of personal therapy, carried out by Macran and Shapiro (1998) and Orlinsky *et al.* (2005b) found that the overwhelming majority of therapists believed that their personal therapy had been extremely valuable for them, with only a small proportion (around 2 per cent) believing that it had been harmful. In terms of results from studies that observed the impact of personal therapy on therapists' actual performance in their work with clients, there is some evidence that personal therapy contributes to higher levels of empathy, and a stronger therapeutic relationship. However, the evidence around the impact of personal therapy on client outcomes is inconclusive.

Although surveys of psychotherapists have found that around three-quarters have received at least one course of personal therapy, similar surveys have not been carried out with practitioners who describe themselves as 'counsellors'. With non-professional counsellors, in particular, the financial and emotional cost of personal therapy might be more difficult to justify in the light of lower caseloads and generally more limited training. None of the research evidence that is currently available addresses issues related to *how many* sessions of personal therapy should be recommended or required for either trainees or practitioners. There is also a lack of evidence concerning the consequences of *when* such therapy might take place (before, during or after training), or of the relative effectiveness of models of personal therapy adopted by different theoretical orientations. At present, the personal therapy requirements stipulated by professional associations and licensing bodies are based on custom and practice and clinical wisdom, rather than on research evidence. Given that personal therapy is such a potentially important element of training and continuing professional development in counsellors, and also because it is so costly, the absence of research-informed policy-making is unfortunate.

Box 24.8: *The diversity of experiences of personal therapy*

Counsellors and psychotherapists are discerning consumers of therapy. In particular, more experienced therapists are well able to differentiate between the value of different episodes of therapy that they may have received at different stages in their professional career. *The Psychotherapist's own Psychotherapy: Patient and Clinician Perspectives,* edited by Jesse Geller and colleagues (2005), includes first-person accounts written by well-known therapists, concerning their use of personal therapy throughout their careers. Windy Dryden (2005) describes a series of short-term therapy episodes, ranging from psychodynamic group therapy as an undergraduate student, through to Jungian therapy at mid-life. Although he found the majority of these therapies to be unhelpful, in terms of addressing certain personal issues, he is also clear that he learned a great deal from this series of therapists, in respect of learning about what to do and not to do as a therapist. By contrast, Clara Hill (2005) writes about seeing a single therapist for 28 years for a total of 580 sessions, across several therapy episodes. In reflecting on a recent visit, after a lengthy gap, during which her therapist had retired from full-time practice, Hill (2005: 136) noted that:

> I wanted to see her . . . and be reassured that she was still there if I needed her. . . . It was good to see her and to fill her in on what had happened in the interim. One thing I was struck by was her memory for all the things that have happened to me over the years. It is truly comforting to know that she remembers so much of my history and can remind me of why I get stuck and anxious (e.g., she always remembers an image of me hiding under the table in the middle of the kitchen when I was a small child). Her reassurance and caring have kept me grounded.

William Pinsof (2005: 146) describes how he entered psychodynamic therapy at the age of 13: '. . . members of my family had been in analysis before I was born, the works of Freud occupied a central place in our family library'. This therapy was not helpful, and it was not until 15 years later that some sessions of family therapy, attended by his wife and parents, allowed him to achieve a breakthrough in his life. Rather than this therapy being part of his training, the choice of family therapy was the result of previous training in that orientation, and using it with his own patients – it was almost as though he needed to see how it worked for other people, before he could be ready to try it out for himself.

The biographical accounts of therapy experiences provided by Dryden, Hill and Pinsof, and other contributors to this book, act as a reminder that the value of personal therapy, and the meaning it has for the person engaged in therapy, is far from straightforward. To understand and appreciate how and what these individuals have learned from therapy, it is necessary to look at their therapy experiences in the context of their lives as a whole.

Box 24.9: *How therapists change*

Responding to the pain and confusion of other people's lives, in the role of counsellor, can have a profound impact on the practitioner. Kottler and Carlson (2005) interviewed several well-known therapists about their recollections of 'the client who changed me'. Robert Neimeyer described how he had been a cognitive–behavioural therapist when he met Carol, who he experienced as a 'frozen woman', 'not there' and 'empty inside'. Carol would not talk, but pounded the chair with her fists and arms, causing serious bruising. It emerged that she had been sexually abused, first by her father from the age of seven, and then by the leaders of a religious cult to which she had fled for sanctuary.

Neimeyer quickly found that his CBT techniques were of little value in helping him to make contact with this client, or to go more deeply into the core of her troubles. Gradually, he learned what to do. Carol allowed herself to communicate with him through her journal. Neimeyer began to appreciate that the way into Carol's experience was to listen to her metaphors and images, and to trust his own intuition. He talked in his interview about how his work with this client represented a turning point in his development as a therapist, in the direction of a more constructivist and philosophical orientation to practice.

Alan Marlatt was already a well-established figure in the alcohol counselling field when he met Tina, who had marital difficulties, a serious drink problem, and was depressed. After several months of therapy, marked by a number of relapses, Marlatt suggested that Tina might try a form of meditation with which he himself was familiar. She ended up spending some time in a spiritual retreat centre, where she finally came to terms with her drinking and made a commitment to lead a different life. Marlatt recalled this case as the trigger for his own deeper investigation into Buddhist psychology, and the role of mindfulness meditation in therapy. He went on to describe himself as a 'Buddhist psychologist', and became prominent in promoting the acceptance of spiritual experience and values in therapy theory and practice.

Kottler and Carlson (2005) found that a number of recurring themes emerged from interviewing with therapists about 'clients who changed them': being taken beyond the limits of their competence and usual practice, moments of 'empathic transcendence', being a witness to profound change, and being involved in a caring relationship that stretched over a lengthy period of time. All of these therapists acknowledged that these clients had changed them as people, not just as professionals.

Further examples of practice-induced therapist change can be found in Dryden (1987), Goldfried (2001) and Kahn and Fromm (2000). When reading these accounts, it is essential to keep in mind that these therapists have been asked to focus on specific, dramatic instances of being changed through work with a client. Behind these accounts are other stories of the routine and everyday ways in which counsellors learn about themselves through their work.

Supervision

An important element in counsellor development, not only during training but also throughout the working life of the counsellor, is the use of supervision. It is a requirement of most professional associations that counsellors accredited by them should receive regular supervision from a qualified person. In this context, it is necessary to emphasize that supervision has a different meaning from that in other work settings. Supervision in counselling is not primarily a management role in which the supervisee is given directions and allocated tasks, but is aimed at assisting the counsellor to work as effectively as possible with the client (Carroll 1988). The supervision role in counselling is similar to that of the tutor or consultant. Hawkins and Shohet (2012) have identified three main functions of supervision in counselling. The first is educational, with the aim of giving the counsellor a regular opportunity to receive feedback, develop new understandings and receive information. The second aspect is the supportive role of supervision, through which the counsellor can share dilemmas, be validated in his or her work performance and deal with any personal distress or counter-transference evoked by clients. Finally, there is a management dimension to supervision, in ensuring quality of work and helping the counsellor to plan work and utilize resources.

There are a number of different formats for providing supervision (Hawkins and Shohet 2012). Probably the most common arrangement is to make a contract for individual sessions over a period of time with the same person. A variant on this approach is to use separate consultants to explore specific issues: for example, going to an expert in family work to discuss a client with family problems, and using a mental health counsellor for consultation on a client who is depressed (Kaslow 1986). Another possibility is group supervision, where a small group of supervisees meet with a supervisor. The case discussion group is a type of group supervision that gives particular attention to understanding the personality or family dynamics of the client. Peer supervision groups involve a group of counsellors meeting to engage in supervision of each other, without there being a designated leader or consultant. Finally, supervision networks (Houston 1990) consist of a set of colleagues who are available for mutual or peer supervision, on either a one-to-one or a small group basis.

Each of these modes of supervision has its advantages and disadvantages. Regular individual supervision facilitates the development of a good working relationship between supervisor and supervisee. On the other hand, specific consultants will have a greater depth of experience in particular areas. Group and peer group supervision enable the counsellor to learn from the cases and issues presented by colleagues. In these supervision settings, however, there may be problems in maintaining confidentiality and in dealing with the dynamics of the group. The choice of mode of supervision depends on a wide range of factors, including personal preference, cost, availability, agency policy and organization, and counselling philosophy.

The supervision process is highly dependent on the quality of information that supervisees bring to the supervision setting. Most often, the supervisee will report what he or she has been doing with clients, using notes taken after counselling sessions to augment his or her recollection. Dryden and Thorne (1991) argue that, if the focus of the supervision is to be on the skills employed by the counsellor, the supervisor needs 'actual data' from sessions. These data can be obtained from detailed process notes written immediately after a session, and video- or audio-tapes of sessions. In some situations supervisors may even be able to make live observations of the supervisee working with a client.

One of the principal dilemmas in supervision is deciding on what it would be helpful to discuss. Potentially, the supervisee might need to explore his or her understanding of the client, the feelings he or she holds in reaction to the client, the appropriateness of different interventions or techniques and many other topics. Hawkins and Shohet (2012) have constructed a model of the supervision process that usefully clarifies some of these issues. They suggest that at any time in supervision there are six levels operating:

1 *Reflection on the content of the counselling session*. The focus here is on the client, what is being said, how different parts of the life of the client fit together and what the client wants from counselling.

2 *Exploration of the techniques and strategies used by the counsellor*. This level is concerned with the therapeutic intentions of the counsellor, and the approach he or she is taking to helping the client.

3 *Exploration of the therapeutic relationship*. The aim at this level is to examine the ways in which the client and counsellor interact, and whether they have established a functioning working alliance.

4 *The feelings of the counsellor towards the client*. In this area of supervision the intention is to identify and understand the counter-transference reactions of the counsellor, or the personal issues that have been re-stimulated through contact with the client.

5 *What is happening here and now between supervisor and supervisee*. The relationship in the supervision session may exhibit similar features to the relationship between the counsellor and his or her client. Paying attention to this 'parallel process' (McNeill and Worthen 1989) can give valuable insights.

6 *The counter-transference of the supervisor*. The feelings of the supervisor in response to the supervisee may also provide a guide to some of the ways of seeing the cases that are not yet consciously articulated by supervisor or supervisee, as well as contributing to an understanding of the quality of the supervisor–supervisee relationship.

7 *Organizational issues*. Supervision may need to involve discussion around constraints on counselling arising from organizational protocols, the level of support received by the counsellor, confidentiality issues and similar topics.

Hawkins and Shohet (2012) argue that good supervision will involve movement between all these levels. Supervisors tend to have a personal style of supervision in which they stick mainly to a particular set of levels, and the model can be used as a framework for both supervisors and supervisees to reflect on their work together and if necessary to negotiate change. The Hawkins and Shohet model has been widely used in training, but has not yet generated research.

An approach that can be used to complement the Hawkins and Shohet framework is the 'cyclical model' developed by Page and Wosket (2001). The cyclical model pays particular attention to the creation of a 'reflective space' in which the supervisee can explore dilemmas arising from his or her work, and to the crucial task of applying supervision insights in practice. Page and Wosket (2001) suggest that the work of supervision can be divided into five stages:

Stage 1: *Establishing a contract.* The counsellor and supervisor negotiate such matters as ground rules, boundaries, accountability, mutual expectations and the nature of their relationship.

Stage 2: *Agreeing a focus.* An issue is identified for exploration and the counsellor's objectives and priorities in relation to the issue are specified.

Stage 3: *Making a space.* Entering into a process of reflection, exploration, understanding and insight around the focal issue.

Stage 4: *The 'bridge' – making the link between supervision and practice.* Consolidation, goal setting and action planning in order to decide how what is to be learned can be taken back into the counselling arena.

Stage 5: *Review and evaluation.* Supervisor and counsellor assess the usefulness of the work they have done, and enter a phase of recontracting.

Page and Wosket (2001) emphasize that this series of stages is cyclical, with each completion of the cycle leading to a strengthening of the counsellor–supervisor relationship, and concluding with the negotiation of a new contract. An appreciation of the different levels at which learning in supervision may occur, as specified by Hawkins and Shohet (2012), can inform the awareness of counsellor and supervisor at all stages of this cycle.

The Hawkins and Shohet (2012) and Page and Wosket (2001) models primarily focus on what happens within a single supervision setting. There are also processes in supervision that occur over a much longer time-span, which concern the ways in which the stage of development of the counsellor can have an impact on the counselling process. Counsellors of different degrees of experience and maturity have different supervision needs, and numerous models have been devised to portray this developmental track (see Hess 1980 or Stoltenberg and Delworth 1987 for a review of these ideas). One such model is the six-stage model of development of professional identity constructed by Friedman and Kaslow (1986). The stages, which may take several years to pass through, are described as:

1 *Excitement and anticipatory anxiety.* This phase describes the period before the counsellor has seen his or her first client. The task of the supervisor is to provide security and guidance.

2 *Dependency and identification.* The second stage commences as soon as the counsellor begins work with clients. The lack of confidence, skill and knowledge in the counsellor results in a high degree of dependency on the supervisor, who is perceived as having all the answers. The trainee counsellor at this stage will use the supervisor as a model. However, anxiety about being seen as incompetent may lead the supervisee to conceal information from the supervisor. The personality and dynamics of the client, rather than the therapeutic relationship or counter-transference, is the most common focus of supervision at this stage, reflecting the lack of confidence and awareness of the counsellor in exploring his or her own contribution to the therapeutic process.

3 *Activity and continued dependency*. This phase of development is triggered by the realization of the counsellor that he or she is actually making a difference to clients. This recognition enables the counsellor to be more active with clients, and to try out different strategies and techniques. The counsellor is beginning to be more open to his or her own feeling response to clients, and may discuss counselling issues with colleagues and family members as a means of 'spilling affect' (Friedman and Kaslow 1986: 38). In this burst of enthusiasm for therapy, the counsellor may experiment by applying therapeutic skills and concepts to friends and family members. The primary task of the supervisor at this stage is to be able to accept the needs for dependency as well as active autonomy, and to allow the counsellor to explore different options.

4 *Exuberance and taking charge*. Friedman and Kaslow (1986: 40) write that 'the fourth phase of development is ushered in by the trainee's realization that he or she really is a therapist'. Having acquired considerable experience in working with clients, having read widely in the field and probably having embarked on personal therapy, the counsellor is actively making connections between theory and practice, and beginning to identify with one theoretical perspective rather than trying out diverse ideas and systems. In supervision, there is a willingness to explore counter-transference issues and to discuss theoretical models. The counsellor no longer needs as much support and warmth in supervision, and is ready for a higher degree of challenge. In becoming less dependent on the supervisor, the counsellor comes to view the latter more as a consultant than as a teacher.

5 *Identity and independence*. This is described as the stage of 'professional adolescence'. In beginning to envisage life without the protection and guidance of the supervisor, the counsellor becomes more willing and able to express differences of opinion. Counsellors at this stage of development are often attracted to peer supervision with others at a similar stage. The supervisee has by this time internalized a frame of reference for evaluating client work, and is in a position to accept or reject the advice or suggestions of the supervisor. The counsellor may be aware of areas in which his or her expertise exceeds that of the supervisor. It is necessary for the supervisor at this stage to remain available to the counsellor, and to accept a lack of control.

6 *Calm and collegiality*. By this stage the counsellor has acquired a firm sense of professional identity and belief in his or her competence. The counsellor is able to take a balanced view of the strengths and weaknesses of different approaches to therapy, and is able to use peers and supervisors as consultants, 'from a spirit of genuine respect among colleagues' (Friedman and Kaslow 1986: 45). At this stage counsellors begin to take an interest in taking on the supervisor role.

The process involved in the formation of a professional identity has the consequence that the focus of supervision can be qualitatively different at succeeding stages. It is helpful for both supervisors and supervisees to be aware that this kind of developmental sequence can take place, and to adjust their behaviour and expectations accordingly.

Throughout this account of the supervision process, it can be observed that the quality of the relationship between supervisor and supervisee is of paramount importance (Shohet and Wilmot 1991). Charny (1986: 20) has written that the 'greatest possibilities of growth in supervision . . . [lie] in tapping candidly just what is going on in the heart, mind and body of a therapist in relation to a given case'. He adds that, for him, the most valuable question in supervision is: 'what about this case really worries me?'. To undertake this kind of open exploration of self in relation to the client requires the same degree of emotional safety and the same 'core conditions' that are offered to clients. As in counselling, the freedom to choose an appropriate helper is valuable, as is the freedom to terminate. The sensitivity to relationship issues that is found in much effective supervision can also lead to the danger of straying over the boundary that separates supervision from actual therapy. The role of supervision in counsellor training and ongoing development is, therefore, closely linked to issues of how and when to structure counsellor personal therapy or work on self.

There is also an increasing appreciation that, although counselling supervision consists primarily of a secure, confidential relationship between a supervisor and an individual counsellor (or group of counsellors), the organizational context within which supervision takes place can have a profound influence on the quality and nature of what takes place. For example, a supervisor may have responsibility to report to the counselling agency management on the competence or effectiveness of the counsellor, or to ensure that the counsellor complies with agency regulations around risk assessment or the number of counselling sessions that can be offered. Further discussion of the issues associated with the interplay between supervisor, counsellor and the organization which employs (and manages) them both can be found in Hawkins and Shohet (2012) and Copeland (2000).

The requirement to engage in regular supervision has become one of the cornerstones of the commitment to the provision of quality therapy services in Britain. In other countries, supervision may be mandatory during training, with regular 'consultation' required following completion of training. Although the precise regulatory arrangements may differ in countries and within different professional groups, there can be no denying the immense commitment of time and energy that is currently devoted to supervision within the therapy professions. Recently, however, an increasing number of questions have been asked about the value of mandatory supervision. Critics have argued that supervision has the potential to be counterproductive in some circumstances (see Box 24.10). In contrast to these critical voices, there is also a great deal of research evidence that supports the value of supervision in enhancing counsellor effectiveness and well-being (Wheeler and Richards 2007).

Box 24.10: *The value of supervision: critical voices*

The most widely adopted format for supervision is based on the counsellor describing his or her work with a client to an individual supervisor, or to a peer group or supervision group. It has become apparent that there are a number of potentially serious limitations inherent in this approach. Some studies have shown that supervisees are typically selective in the material they present in supervision (Ladany *et al.* 1996; Webb 2000), and may not disclose information that they feel might reflect poorly on their competence. Other research has shown that, fairly often, supervisees report that their supervision has been counterproductive (Lawton 2000; Gray *et al.* 2001), or even that they feel that they have been locked into a supervision relationship that is conflict-ridden (Nelson and Friedlander 2001) or even abusive (Kaberry 2000). In contrast, there is no research evidence to back up the claim, made by advocates of mandatory supervision, that regular supervision is associated either with improved client outcomes or with lower levels of ethical violation on the part of practitioners.

Feltham (2000) has identified the current position in counselling in Britain, in relation to supervision, as reflecting what he calls 'the dynamics of the mandatory'. He argues that:

> The logic of regular, mandatory supervision is that, along with ever-rising costs of training, personal therapy, membership fees, accreditation, registration, continuing professional development and insurance, the counselling professional closes its doors to all but the relatively affluent . . . the dynamics of the mandatory within supervision itself [also requires that] the supervisee must attend for regular supervision whether he or she usually finds this useful or not. If the supervisee does not always find it particularly useful, there is an implication that something is wrong with the supervisee, since supervision is apparently found universally and invariably helpful.
>
> (Feltham 2000: 10)

The central concern for Feltham (2000: 21) is that 'there is currently little evidence, but much emotional rhetoric, supporting the value or clarifying the purposes of supervision'. The adoption of regular supervision as a mandatory requirement for counsellors can be viewed, therefore, as pre-empting other methods of achieving a number of important goals, such as ensuring the effectiveness of therapy that is provided for clients, maximizing adherence to ethical standards and preventing counsellor burnout. There are many other ways in which these goals might be facilitated. For example, within family therapy (see Chapter 12), there is a tradition of 'reflecting teams', in which colleagues observe the work of a therapist and immediately feed back their comments to him or her (and often to the clients as well). In the early years of client-centred counselling, trainee counsellors would sit in on therapy cases of more experienced colleagues, gradually playing a more active role as an actual therapist to the client (Rogers 1951). Either of these approaches give a much more direct form of consultation than would ever be available in conventional supervision. It may be that the task of monitoring the effectiveness of therapy could be better carried out by asking clients to complete questionnaires such as the CORE outcome measure on a regular basis. The use of information technology makes it possible for such data to be analysed and accessible to the counsellor in advance of the following session, and also for the counsellor to compare the rate of 'progress' of the client with that reported by other clients with similar presenting problems.

Among these critical voices, there is no suggestion that it is not helpful to have opportunities to reflect on work with clients in the context of a supportive relationship with an experienced colleague. The debate that has emerged over the past few years is about the formats within which such opportunities can be made available, and the wisdom of adopting a mandatory system of professional regulation built around a particular format. If a system of supervision is mandatory, there is a danger that it can degenerate into a bureaucratic ritual that evokes resistance, and that lacks sensitivity to individual needs. If, on the other hand, a system is wholly voluntary, it runs the risk of denying the all too real hazards of practice, and the grandiose fantasy of being able, on one's own, to take care of everything (Chapter 19).

Well-being programmes

As with all organizations, working in a counselling agency can affect the health and well-being of staff. Studies of many different types of organizations have demonstrated that stress and emotional and physical ill-health can be caused by overwork, unplanned change and a poor working environment. In human service organizations, a specific type of stress has been identified, which has been labelled *burnout* (Freudenberger 1974; Farber 1983a; Leiter and Maslach 2005; Maslach and Jackson 1984; Maslach and Leiter 1997). The phenomenon of burnout occurs when workers enter a human service profession (such as social work, nursing, the police or counselling) with high and unrealistic aspirations regarding the degree to which they will be able to help other people. In many instances the amount of help that can be offered, or the effectiveness of an intervention, is limited. There are also, usually, too many clients for them all to be dealt with in an ideal manner. The result is that the helper becomes caught between his or her own high standards and the impossibility of fulfilling these standards, and after a while is unable to maintain the effort and energy required in functioning at such a high level. This is the state of burnout.

Maslach and Jackson (1984) identified three main dimensions of the burnout syndrome. People experiencing burnout report emotional exhaustion, a persistent fatigue and a state of low motivation. They also exhibit depersonalization, gradually coming to see their clients not as unique people with individual problems but as 'cases' or representatives of diagnostic categories. Finally, burnout is associated with feelings of lack of personal accomplishment, or powerlessness. Prevention of burnout has been shown, in a number of studies of different groups of human services personnel, to be correlated with the presence of support from colleagues, realistic workloads, clarity about job roles and demands, variety and creativity in the job specification and recognition and positive feedback from clients and management (Leiter and Maslach 2005).

A number of studies of burnout with counsellors and therapists have been carried out. Farber and Heifetz (1982) interviewed 60 psychotherapists about their experiences of job-related stress. The primary source of stress reported by these therapists was 'lack of therapeutic success'. Other burnout factors included overwork, work with clients raising personal issues and isolation. Most of the interviewees stated that they could only see four to six clients a day before becoming depleted, although male therapists claimed they could see greater numbers before being affected. The therapists in this study also felt they were particularly prone to burnout when under stress at home.

Hellman and Morrison (1987) administered a 350-item stress questionnaire to psychologists engaged in therapy, and found that those working with more disturbed clients were likely to experience more professional doubt and personal depletion. Therapists working in institutions reported more stress from organizational factors, whereas those in private practice found it more stressful to deal with difficult clients.

Jupp and Shaul (1991) surveyed the stress experiences of 83 college counsellors in Australia, and found that more experienced counsellors reported more burnout symptoms than their less experienced colleagues. In all of these studies, the existence of effective social support networks was associated with lower levels of stress and burnout. Lawson (2007) conducted a survey of a large sample of counsellors in the USA. He found that a substantial proportion of the clients being seen by these counsellors were highly challenging – about half presented with trauma issues and around 15 per cent with suicide and self-harm issues. Around 20 per cent of this group of counsellors reported that they were stressed or distressed by their work.

A review of research into therapist burnout was carried out by Lee *et al.* (2011), specifically aiming to identify patterns of stress. This review identified that counsellor over-involvement with clients was associated with both burnout and high job satisfaction. It would appear that overinvolved counsellors go through a period of enjoying the fruits of successful work with clients, but are then unable to sustain this level of commitment, and burn out. These findings are consistent with the discussion of counsellor motivation earlier in the present chapter.

Another type of occupational stress experienced by some counsellors is *vicarious traumatization* (Neumann and Gamble 1995; Pearlman and Mclan 1995), sometimes described as *secondary traumatization* (Morrissette 2004). This can happen when counsellors work with clients who are suffering from extreme trauma: for example, survivors of sexual or physical abuse, refugees who have been tortured, disaster victims or Holocaust survivors. Counsellors working in these areas can often find that they begin to experience intrusive images linked to scenes described by their clients, and other symptoms of PTSD: for example, loss of trust in a safe world. This is an area in which there is a very clear link between the work counsellors are doing and the impact it has on their own personal lives. It is important for agencies offering services to these clients to be aware of the danger of vicarious traumatization, and to offer appropriate support to staff (Sexton 1999).

The potential for burnout in counselling work is considerable. Counsellors are routinely exposed to clients who are in great distress and whose problems do not readily resolve themselves in the face of therapeutic interventions. There are many references in the therapy literature to therapists who have been driven to the very depths of their personal resources through working with particular clients (e.g., Hobson 1985). The high suicide rate of psychiatrists, who are more likely to be involved with highly disturbed clients, has been noted in a number of studies (Farber 1983b). Many counselling agencies have long waiting lists and are under external pressure regarding continued funding. Feedback concerning the effectiveness of the work can sometimes be meagre.

Preventing burnout is therefore of immense importance. There are a range of organizational strategies designed to prevent stress and burnout, including regular supervision, opportunities for career development, and involvement in non-clinical roles in training, supervision, writing and research. Peer support, either within an agency (Scully 1983) or through training workshops and conferences, also contributes to burnout prevention. Cherniss and Krantz (1983) have argued that burnout results from the loss of commitment and moral purpose in the work. This absence of meaningfulness can be counteracted by the establishment of 'ideological communities' comprised of groups of colleagues sharing a set of beliefs and values. Boy and Pine (1980) similarly advocate the benefits of associating with committed, concerned colleagues. In the survey carried out by Lawson (2007), counsellors in fact gave relatively low ratings to these organizational wellness strategies, and reported instead that what kept them sane was maintaining a sense of humour, spending time with family, maintaining a work–life balance and engaging in quiet leisure activities. In this context, it is important to acknowledge that the stressful impact of a counselling role may also have an effect on the families of counsellors (Pack 2010).

Being able to deal with the stress that accompanies the combined pressures of client work and organizational life represents a core area of counsellor competence. In recent years there has been a wide range of books published that offer guidelines for counsellors on how to cope with the stress of the job (Kottler 1998; Rothschild 2006; Skovholt 2008).

Organizational development

It is not sufficient to view counselling purely as a process that takes place in the immediate encounter between helper and client. When a counsellor and client meet, it is not merely two individuals, but in fact two social worlds that engage with each other. Two sets of expectations, assumptions, values, norms, manners and ways of talking must accommodate each to the other. Usually it is the client who is required to enter the social world of the counsellor by visiting his or her consulting room or office. The physical and emotional environment in which counselling takes place forms a context for the counselling process that takes place. Counselling organizations can exert a strong influence on both their clients and their staff. The type of agency or setting, and the way it is organized and managed, can have a significant impact on how effective a counsellor is able to be.

One of the most valuable concepts to have emerged from the field of organizational studies has been the idea of the 'open system' (Hatch and Cunliffe 2006; Robbins and Judge 2007). From this perspective, an organization is seen as consisting of a set of overlapping and interconnecting parts, which combine to form an organizational *system*. Change in any element or part of the system will affect what happens elsewhere in the system. Furthermore, the system exists in an environment, and is open to influence from external factors. The purpose of the organizational system is to produce 'throughput': there is an input of 'raw materials', which are processed and then leave the system as 'output'. A typical counselling agency, therefore, could be viewed as a system made up of clients, counsellors, supervisors, managers and administrators, receptionists and fundraisers. The throughput of the agency is represented by the number of clients seen, and the external environment may include funding agencies, professional bodies and members of the general public. A systems perspective is particularly useful in providing a framework for beginning to understand the ways in which other parts in the system may have an impact on the client–counsellor relationship. For example, successful publicity and outreach work may increase the number of clients applying for counselling. The long waiting lists that may then result can lead to pressure to place a limit on the number of sessions offered to clients. Some of the counsellors may find this policy unacceptable and leave. This very brief, simplified (but not fictional) example gives a sense of how an organizational system might operate.

Two further concepts that are useful in terms of making sense of organizational factors in counselling are organizational *structure* and *culture* (Morgan 2006). The structure of an organization refers to the way in which it consists of different parts, and how these parts interconnect. For example, some agencies have a formal hierarchical structure, in which a great deal of authority is held by a director and there are clear lines of control and supervision from the leader through to frontline workers. Additionally, a hierarchical structure can involve subdivision of the workforce into subgroups or departments, each of which is in turn controlled by a manager. Typically, larger organizations operate in terms of formal hierarchical structures, with written protocols defining the role of each worker. The majority of large counselling agencies, and certainly those that provide services from more than one office or clinic, are structured along hierarchical lines. A contrasting form of organizational structure is found in therapy agencies that define themselves as *collectives*. In a collective, there is a 'flat' hierarchy, with decisions and procedures being agreed in open meetings of all workers. The role of manager or director tends to exist more as a point of reference for the external world, rather than as a privileged source of authority within the group. Many counselling agencies begin life as small collectives, and some retain a collective structure for ideological reasons. The *Just Therapy* centre in New Zealand and The *Psychotherapy Cooperative* in Seattle are examples of long-established centres that function along collective lines (Waldegrave *et al.* 2003; Halling *et al.* 2006b).

Whereas the structure of an organization can be readily easily mapped out in terms of a chart or decision-making diagram, the concept of organizational *culture* refers to factors that are less tangible (Schein 2004). The culture (or 'climate') of an organization can be defined as the 'feel' of the agency – what it is like to be there. The culture of any group of people is expressed in a myriad of ways: how people talk to each other, the use of touch, humour and emotion, and the physical 'look' of the space (and the 'look' of the people – what they wear). Underpinning these facets of culture there is a set of deeply held beliefs about the purpose of the organization, typically conveyed through stories and myths about the founding of the group and key landmark events in its history. The culture of any organization is strongly defined by its leader, supported by various 'culture carriers' who initiate new members into the informal rules of the group and maintain important cultural rituals ('the person who always sends round a card to be signed, when a colleague is off sick').

Expectations about 'what is supposed to happen here' are also communicated by the culture of an agency. Crandall and Allen (1981), for example, found in one study that different drug abuse therapy agencies embodied quite different levels of demand regarding client change. In some agencies there was a strong expectation that clients' behaviour would change in basic ways. In other agencies there were low therapeutic demands on clients. The promotion of a 'culture of excellence' can be expressed through various aspects of organizational culture, such as allocation of rewards and praise, availability of training and provision of support and resources.

The culture of an organization is reflected in the use of language within the organization. People in formal, hierarchical organizations, for example, address each other by title or surname; people in informal, 'flat hierarchy' organizations are more likely to be on first name terms. There may be shared images of the agency or unit that express a sense of the organizational culture: the agency may be a 'family', a 'team', a 'sinking ship'. People are usually consciously aware of the meanings of these uses of language.

Some writers on organizations have suggested, however, that a group or organizational culture operates largely at an unconscious level. These theorists have borrowed from Freud the idea that the most powerful motives in people are deeply hidden and emerge only indirectly in patterns of behaviour and in fantasies and dreams. Members of organizations may hold powerful fantasies about other people or groups in the organization, or their clients. According to this theory, the most fundamental elements of the culture of an organization are unconscious and are revealed only through fantasies, jokes and other non-conscious processes.

The structure and culture of a counselling agency can have a major impact on both clients and therapists. For example, a high degree of formal structure may be reflected in the initial 'intake' or assessment procedures that are applied to new clients, or in a lack of flexibility on the part of the counsellor in relation to the way that he or she works with a client, or the number of sessions that can be provided. Some counselling agencies convey a culture of hope and positive expectations ('deciding to come here is a positive step in your life'), whereas others convey a message of failure ('making an appointment with us is a sign of how bad things are for you'). The culture of an agency is also reflected in the open-ness of that agency to new ideas. For example, Hemmelgarn and Glisson (2006) discuss organization culture as a factor in the capacity of therapy agencies to adopt evidence-based practice.

Historically, the task of caring for people has been work for women. In counselling and other human service organizations, women predominate in frontline service delivery roles, although men are proportionally more heavily represented in management roles. This pattern is even more apparent in voluntary counselling agencies, where male counsellors can be thin on the ground. In general, female occupations enjoy lower status and rates of pay than male occupations, and this tendency can be seen in the field of counselling (Philipson 1993).

Another issue arising from the gendered nature of counselling is the influence of feminist values on counselling organizations. Taylor (1983: 445) has suggested that organizations dominated by women are more likely to espouse values such as 'egalitarianism rather than hierarchy, co-operation rather than competition, nurturance rather than rugged individualism, peace rather than conflict'. This set of values is congruent with the values of counselling as a whole, and can lead to misunderstanding, tension or difficulty when counselling agencies attempt to develop hierarchical structures or operate in host organizations that embody different beliefs.

A final perspective for making sense of the experience of working in a counselling organization is the theory of *institutional defence mechanisms*. The analysis of organizational life in terms of unconscious processes was originally developed by the psychoanalyst and organizational consultant Isabel Menzies Lyth and her colleagues at the Tavistock Institute (Menzies 1959; Menzies Lyth 1988, 1989; Obholzer and Roberts 1994). The first studies into unconscious processes in organizations were conducted with groups of hospital nurses. The very nature of the nursing task involves nurses in intimate contact with patients, through being exposed to physical and sexual bodily functions that are usually private, and to pain, anxiety and death. Menzies argued that this kind of contact can be emotionally threatening to nurses, and as a consequence they have evolved, on a collective or group basis, organizational defence mechanisms with which to cope with their emotional reactions to the job. These collective defences include 'objectifying' the patient, denying his or her humanity (e.g., 'the appendix in bed fourteen') and projecting their vulnerabilities on to other colleagues. Menzies found that more senior nurses, for example, tended to view student nurses as irresponsible and unreliable, thereby projecting their unconscious fears over their own ability to cope on to this group. These two processes – objectifying patients and blaming colleagues rather than acknowledging personal feelings of vulnerability – are of general relevance and can be found in many counselling agencies.

The aim of this section has been to explore some of the ways in which organizational factors can influence the effectiveness of the work that counsellors do, and the way that they think and feel about themselves. In organizations that function well, considerable effort is devoted, in the form of support structures, teambuilding and other activities, to making sure that the organization functions as well as it can. The consequences of failing to address these issues are poor quality of service to clients, high staff turnover and employee stress.

A model of counsellor competence

The issues explored in earlier sections of this chapter all converge on the key issue of *counsellor competence*. The concept of competence refers to any skill or quality exhibited by a competent performer in a specific occupation. In recent years there has been an increasing amount of research interest devoted to identifying the competencies associated with success in the counselling and psychotherapy. For example, Larson *et al.* (1992) constructed a model that breaks down counsellor competence (which they term 'counsellor self-efficacy') into five areas: micro-skills, process, dealing with difficult client behaviours, cultural competence and awareness of values. Beutler *et al.* (1986), in a review of the literature, identified several categories of 'therapist variables' that had been studied in relation to competence: personality, emotional well-being, attitudes and values, relationship attitudes (e.g., empathy, warmth, congruence), social influence attributes (e.g., expertness, trustworthiness, attraction, credibility and persuasiveness), expectations, professional background, intervention style and mastery of technical procedures and theoretical rationale. More recently, Roth and Pilling (2007; see also www.ucl.ac.uk/clinical-psychology/CORE/core_homepage.htm) have published the findings of expert reference groups that have identified the competencies required of practitioners of a range of therapies: cognitive–behavioural, humanistic, psychodynamic and systemic. The British Association for Counselling and Psychotherapy (2009) has disseminated a competency-based curriculum for counselling training. In addition, specific frameworks have been developed for multicultural competence (Pope-Davis *et al.* 2003).

Drawing on all of these initiatives, it is possible to identify seven broad areas of counsellor competence:

1 *Interpersonal skills.* Competent counsellors are able to demonstrate appropriate listening, communicating, empathy, presence, awareness of non-verbal communication, sensitivity to voice quality, responsiveness to expressions of emotion, turn-taking, structuring time, use of language.

2 *Personal beliefs and attitudes*. Capacity to accept others, belief in the potential for change, awareness of ethical and moral choices. Sensitivity to values held by client and self.

3 *Conceptual ability*. Ability to understand and assess the client's problems, to anticipate future consequences of actions, to make sense of immediate process in terms of a wider conceptual/theoretical scheme, to remember information about the client, to construct a case formulation. Cognitive flexibility. Skill in problem-solving.

4 *Personal 'soundness'*. Absence of personal needs or irrational beliefs that are destructive to counselling relationships, self-confidence, capacity to tolerate strong or uncomfortable feelings in relation to clients, secure personal boundaries, ability to be a client. Absence of social prejudice, ethnocentrism and authoritarianism.

5 *Mastery of technique*. Knowledge of when and how to carry out specific interventions, ability to assess effectiveness of interventions, understanding of rationale behind techniques, possession of a sufficiently wide repertoire of interventions or methods.

6 *Ability to understand and work within social systems*. Awareness of the family and work relationships of the client, the impact of the agency on the client, the capacity to use support networks and supervision. Sensitivity to the social worlds of clients who may be from a different gender, ethnic, sexual orientation or age group.

7 *Openness to learning and inquiry*. A capacity to be curious about clients' backgrounds and problems. Being open to new knowledge. Using research to inform practice.

This list of competencies comprises a set of characteristics that are partly based in the life experience of a person *before* he or she decides to be trained as a counsellor, and partly on what the person learns in training and over the course of their career. Effective training and supervision needs to address all of these areas, and a deficit in one or more area runs the risk that the practitioner will fail to respond in a facilitative manner to his or her client. Being a competent counsellor, therefore, is always a balancing act that involves paying attention to a range of personal and professional issues.

Conclusions

Working as a counsellor is an unusual kind of job, which involves a high degree of individual responsibility combined with limited external supervision or management. It also involves high levels of exposure to the sometimes harrowing stories that clients tell about their emotional pain. This chapter has introduced some of the issues associated with embarking on a career in counselling, and being a counsellor. It seems reasonable to imagine that there are some people whose life experience has enabled them to possess the potential for engaging effectively in healing relationships with troubled people. In relation to training, these individuals only need to be pointed in the right direction, quickly absorb all they need to know, and remain curious and open to new learning throughout their careers. There are other people attracted to the counselling profession and who may have great strengths and personal qualities but whose personality makes them vulnerable to getting enmeshed in unhelpful interpersonal conflict with some clients, or whose personal style may be off-putting to clients. These individuals may be quite successful with some of their clients, with whom they have a good personality 'fit', but be ineffective with the majority. It is far from clear whether training and personal therapy can ever be sufficient to remedy the limitations of this latter group – they are simply in the wrong job.

It is essential for anyone embarking on counsellor training to appreciate that the counselling role can have a powerful influence to shape the lives and relationships of those who dwell within it. Counselling practice can be highly stressful, and even traumatizing, for example when a client shares the experience of sexual abuse, torture, or deep and hopeless despair. However, even counselling that focuses on more everyday problems of relationships and life choices has the effect of reinforcing a particular way of being with people, based on intense attention to the personal. It can be hard for many counsellors to separate themselves from this way of being and engage in ordinary or superficial relationships and activities. This can represent a personal cost if the practitioner allows himself or herself to become socially isolated. In some respects, the dominant professional ideology within counselling and psychotherapy, which is largely based on an individualist image of the person, can serve to exacerbate the tendency to isolation, by leading therapists to believe that the pressure of their work is because of unresolved personal issues.

Being a counsellor can be an enormously satisfying and meaningful activity. It is constantly stimulating, because every client is different and represents a fresh challenge. There is always something more to learn. There is the satisfaction, perhaps two-thirds of the time, of having made a real difference to someone else's life, and possibly also to the lives of their family, friends and work colleagues. Occasionally, there is also even the knowledge that a life has been saved. Beyond all this, however, is the fact that virtually every person who sits in the client's chair expresses their own individual version of eternal and essential human struggles around love, death, autonomy, responsibility and relatedness. It is a great privilege to be able to be alongside people as they find the courage and resourcefulness to deal with what they find hardest in their life. Each time the counsellor inevitably has the opportunity to learn more about his or her own life, as well as about the nature of our shared humanity.

Topics for reflection and discussion

1 To what extent, and in what ways, have your early life experiences predisposed you to have an interest in counselling? Have these childhood and adolescent events and experiences influenced your choice of theoretical orientation, or your commitment to work with particular client groups?

2 Does the metaphor of the counsellor's 'journey' apply to your life? Where are you now in terms of that journey? What might be involved in the next stage of the journey? What other images or metaphors might also be relevant in conveying your sense of your development as a counsellor?

3 How valid is Sussman's (2007: 25) view that 'behind the wish to practice psychotherapy lies the need to cure one's inner wounds and unresolved conflicts'? What are the implications of this statement for counsellor training?

4 How would you know whether someone is a competent counsellor?

5 Consider one counselling or psychotherapy agency or practice with which you are familiar. In what ways do organizational factors influence the capacity of the therapists who work within this setting to offer the best possible service to clients?

6 What are the most important factors for you, in the choice of a supervisor?

7 Mair (1989: 281) has portrayed counselling and therapy as a 'trade in secrets':

> . . . therapists occupy a remarkable position in society. We daily have access to the secrets of our clients, and therefore of the society of which they and we are part. We are secret agents, being told what others try to hide . . . We are ambiguous and liable to be suspect by many in the ordinary world.

Do you agree? What are the implications of this statement for counsellor training and supervision, the way that counselling agencies are organized, and the maintenance of counsellor well-being?

Suggested further reading

An invaluable source of further information and deep insight on the issues addressed in this chapter, is *The Developing Practitioner: Growth and Stagnation of Therapists and Counselors* by Thomas Skovholt and Helge Ronnestad (2013). Weingarten (2010) and Marzillier (2010) have constructed powerful and moving autobiographical accounts of the links between their personal lives and their work as therapists. A series of books by Jeffrey Kottler and Jon Carlson explore the stresses and satisfactions of being a counsellor (Kottler 2003; Kottler and Carlson 2003a, 2003b, 2005, 2006, 2008, 2009). A text that has fundamentally shaped the way that people think about supervision and training, is *Supervision in the Helping Professions*, by Hawkins and Shohet (2012). A good way of learning about the value of personal therapy is to read accounts written by therapists of their own experiences as clients. Examples of this kind of autobiographical writing can be found in *The Psychotherapist's own Psychotherapy: Patient and Clinician Perspectives,* edited by Geller *et al.* (2005), and a special issue of the *Journal of Clinical Psychology*, edited by Geller (2011). Valuable collections of papers by leading trainers can be found in the *Journal of Family Therapy* (2005, issue 3 and 2007, issue 4) and the *New Zealand Journal of Counselling* (special issue, 2011).

Introduction

A great deal of research has been carried out into counselling and psychotherapy, particularly in the past 40 years. The existence of this body of research may seem to imply a paradox: the counselling relationship is private and confidential, whereas the research process involves external access to information. But it is just this hidden or secret dimension to counselling that has made research so important. Good research should, ultimately, allow the development of a better understanding of events and processes that are experienced by individual counsellors and clients and therefore enable practitioners to learn from each other. Research can also promote a critical and questioning attitude in practitioners, and help them to improve the quality of service offered to clients. Research allows the voice of clients and service users to be heard, and to influence the ways in which therapy is organized and delivered. Research is an international activity, and research journals are read by a world audience. Participation in such an international community of scholars helps counsellors to achieve a broader perspective on their work.

Some of the factors that can motivate people to conduct research in this field are:

- testing the validity of theory;
- evaluating the effectiveness of different approaches or techniques;
- demonstrating to a third-party funding agency (e.g., government department, insurance company, private company) the cost-effectiveness of counselling or psychotherapy;
- enabling an individual practitioner to monitor his or her work;
- allowing individual practitioners to resolve 'burning questions';
- to get a Masters degree or PhD;
- letting colleagues know about particularly interesting cases or innovations;
- establishing the academic credibility of counselling as a subject taught in universities;
- enhancing the professional status of counsellors in relation to other professional groups.

It can be seen that there are many different reasons for doing research. Some research studies are inspired by the practical concerns of practitioners. Other studies emerge from the interests of groups of people working together on a set of ideas or theory. Yet other studies are set up to meet external demands. Often, there can be more than one factor motivating a study.

Within the social sciences in general there has been considerable debate over the issue of what constitutes valid research. This debate has generated an enormous literature, which in part can be characterized as an argument between advocates of quantitative approaches and those who would favour qualitative methods of research. Quantitative research involves careful measurement of variables, with the researcher taking a detached, objective role. Qualitative research, by contrast, has as its aim the description and interpretation of what things mean to people, and to achieve this goal, a researcher must develop a relationship with the research informants or co-participants. The differences between the quantitative and qualitative research traditions are displayed in Table 25.1.

TABLE 25.1 The contrast between qualitative and quantitative approaches to research

Qualitative	Quantitative
Description and interpretation of meanings	Measurement and analysis of variables
Quality of relationship between researcher and informants important	Aims for neutral, objective relationship
Necessity for self-awareness and reflexivity in researcher	Aims for value-free researcher
Uses interviews, participant observation, diaries	Uses tests, rating scales, questionnaires
Researchers interpret data	Statistical analysis of data
Strongest in sociology, social anthropology, theology and the arts	Strongest in psychiatry and psychology
Many similar ideas to psychoanalysis and humanistic therapies	Many similar ideas to behavioural and cognitive therapies

Both approaches to research have a lot to offer in the field of counselling and psychotherapy research, and they can be combined effectively (see, for example, Hill 1989; Stiles *et al.* 1990; Stiles 1991). Nevertheless, the split between qualitative and quantitative approaches has been significant for the field as a whole, and remains a source of conflict and tension. The disciplines that have had the strongest professional and institutional influence on counselling have been psychology and psychiatry. These are both disciplines that have been associated with 'hard', quantitative research. On the other hand, the philosophy of the person and values of the qualitative research tradition are very close to those of most counselling and psychotherapy practitioners (McLeod 2011).

The breadth and scope of research in counselling and psychotherapy is immense, and it would be impossible to attempt meaningful discussion of all aspects of the field in this chapter. Particular attention will therefore be given to three types of research study that have been of central importance: outcome studies, process studies and case studies. Readers interested in pursuing other aspects of research in counselling, or to explore in more depth the topics covered in this chapter, are recommended to consult Cooper, (2008), Lambert (2004) and Timulak (2008), each of which provides an authoritative review of research findings on a wide range of topics. Readers interested in learning more about research design and the practicalities of carrying out research studies should consult Barker *et al.* (2002) and McLeod (2013a). More advanced discussions of methodological issues in research can be found in Aveline and Shapiro (1995), Lambert *et al.* (2004), Hill and Lambert (2004), Kendall *et al.* (2004), McLeod (2010b, 2011) and Kazdin (2003).

Outcome and evaluation research

Outcome and evaluation studies have the primary aim of finding out how much a particular counselling or therapy intervention has helped or benefited the client. The earliest systematic research into counselling and therapy concentrated entirely on this issue. In the 1930s and 1940s several studies were carried out into the effects of psychoanalysis. The results of these investigations suggested that, overall, around two-thirds of the psychoanalytic patients followed up improved, with one-third remaining the same or deteriorating after treatment.

These findings appeared highly encouraging for psychoanalysis and, by implication, for other forms of the 'talking cure'. However, in 1952 Eysenck published a devastating critique of this early research. Eysenck pointed out that studies of neurotic people who had not received therapy but had been followed up over a period of time also produced an improvement rate of around 60 per cent. He argued that psychoanalysis could not be considered effective if it produced the same amount of benefit as no therapy at all. Eysenck suggested that there existed a process of 'spontaneous remission', by which psychological problems gradually became less severe over time owing to non-professional sources of help in the community or because the person had learned to deal with a crisis situation that had provoked a breakdown.

The psychotherapy world reacted strongly to Eysenck's critique, but the main effect of his attack was to force researchers to design more adequate studies. In particular, it became accepted that outcome studies should include a control group of clients who do not receive treatment, so that the impact of the counselling or therapy can be compared with the levels of improvement brought about by spontaneous remission. The usual method of creating a comparison group of this kind has been to use a 'waiting list' group of clients who have applied for therapy but who are not offered their first appointment for some time, and are assessed at the beginning and end of that period to detect changes occurring in the absence of professional help.

A good example of outcome research is the Sloane et al. (1975) study that compared the effectiveness of psychodynamic therapy with that of a behavioural approach. The study was carried out in a university psychiatric outpatient clinic, and applicants for therapy were screened to exclude those too disturbed to benefit or who required other forms of help. Ninety-four clients were randomly allocated to behaviour therapy, psychodynamic therapy or a waiting list group. The people on the waiting list were promised therapy in four months, and were regularly contacted by telephone. Clients paid for therapy on a sliding scale, and received an average of 14 sessions over four months. Before the beginning of therapy, each client was interviewed and administered a battery of tests. In addition, clients identified three target symptoms, and rated the current intensity of each symptom. Ratings of the level of adjustment were also made by the interviewer and a friend or relative of the client. These measures were repeated at the end of the therapy, and at one-year and two-year follow-up. Every fifth session was audio-recorded and rated on process measures of therapist qualities, such as empathy, congruence and acceptance. Speech patterns of therapists and clients were also analysed from these tapes.

The results of the Sloane et al. (1975) study indicated that, overall, more than 80 per cent of clients improved or recovered at the end of therapy, with these gains being maintained at follow-up. Both treatment groups improved more than the waiting list group. The quality of the therapist–client relationship was strongly associated with outcome, for both types of therapy. Behaviour therapists were rated on the whole as being more congruent, empathic and accepting than the psychodynamic therapists. There was no evidence for symptom substitution.

Many other studies have been carried out along similar lines to the Sloane et al. (1975) investigation, and most have arrived at similar conclusions regarding the relative effectiveness of different approaches. With the aim of determining whether the apparent equivalence of approaches was confirmed across the research literature as a whole, several literature reviews have been conducted. The first comprehensive and systematic of these literature reviews was the 'meta-analysis' carried out by Smith et al. (1980). Meta-analysis involves calculating the average amount of client change reported for each approach in each separate study, then adding up these change scores to give an overall estimate of how much benefit a particular approach (such as psychoanalysis, client-centred therapy or behaviour therapy) yields over a set of studies comprising a large number of clients. In their report, Smith et al. (1980) conclude that they could find no consistent evidence that any one approach to counselling or therapy was any more effective than any other.

More recent meta-analyses of therapy outcome studies have been published by Roth and Fonagy (2005), Elliott et al. (2004), Lambert and Ogles (2004) and many other authors. Taken together, these analyses suggest that counselling and psychotherapy as a whole are highly effective, with clients who have received treatment reporting much more benefit than those in waiting list or other control conditions. The pattern of outcome in relation to specific disorders or problem areas is more mixed. There is strong evidence for the efficacy of CBT for most psychological problems, but this is because there have been many more outcome studies carried out on CBT interventions than on other approaches. Where relevant outcome studies have been conducted there also tends to be good evidence for the efficacy of psychodynamic and person-centred/experiential approaches to therapy. An accessible summary of the findings of outcome research and meta-analyses can be found in Cooper (2008).

The story of the development of outcome research might suggest that there is little more to be learned about the effectiveness of counselling and therapy. This is far from being the case. One of the important and significant aspects of studies such as Sloane *et al.* (1975) is that they are difficult to organize and expensive to implement, and as a result have tended to be carried out in 'elite' therapy institutions, such as university psychiatry or counselling clinics. The therapists in these studies are usually experienced, highly trained and conducting therapy in accordance with 'treatment manuals' that tightly specify how they should work with their clients as a means of monitoring their adherence to the therapeutic model being evaluated. All these factors mean that controlled studies of the *efficacy* of therapy (i.e., how well it does under ideal circumstances) can often be criticized as unrepresentative of everyday practice (Westen *et al.* 2004). There is a need, therefore, for more studies to be carried out into the effectiveness of the work done in agencies that are less well resourced and that may well serve clients who present with a wider range of problems or have less counselling sophistication. Relatively few naturalistic studies of this kind have been carried out, and those that have been completed have not been able to use control groups or to follow up large numbers of clients.

Another gap in the outcome research literature arises from the lack of specificity of many studies. Paul (1967: 111) has made the point that research should be able to identify 'what treatment, by whom, is most effective for this individual with that specific problem, and under which set of circumstances'. At the present time, research evidence is not precise enough to answer these questions. There are many client groups, and many therapy approaches, that have not been studied in terms of effectiveness research.

Box 25.1: *The researcher's own therapeutic allegiance: a factor in outcome research*

The concept of the 'experimenter effect' is familiar to anyone who has studied psychology. In a psychology experiment carried out in a laboratory the expectations of the researcher in relation to what he or she believes the experiment will show can be subtly communicated to subjects, and influence their responses to stimuli or tasks (Rosnow and Rosenthal 1997). The impact of 'experimenter effects' is to skew results so that the experimenter's hypothesis will be confirmed. As a result, laboratory researchers are extremely careful to standardize what they say to subjects, how they respond to questions etc. Does the experimenter effect apply in psychotherapy outcome studies? It seems unlikely that it would, because therapy is a 'real-world' situation, and clients have strong motivation to get what they need from therapy, rather than trying to 'second guess' the expectations of the person or team running the study.

The well-known therapy researcher Lester Luborsky, along with a group of colleagues (Luborsky *et al.* 1999) decided to try to find out the extent to which researchers' expectations and biases might be operating in psychotherapy outcome research. They reviewed 29 studies in which the relative effectiveness of two forms of therapy was compared. They then carried out a painstaking analysis of what was known about the therapeutic allegiances of the researchers who conducted the studies. They found a significant positive relationship between allegiance and outcome. For example, in a study carried out by a psychodynamic researcher, comparing cognitive–behavioural and psychodynamic therapy, it would be virtually certain that the results would favour the psychodynamic approach. In a study carried out by a researcher positively oriented towards cognitive–behavioural approaches, CBT would be likely to emerge as the most effective therapy. Luborsky *et al.* (1999) argue that researcher allegiances can seriously distort the findings of outcome studies, and make a number of suggestions for eliminating this possible source of bias.

The outcome and evaluation studies mentioned so far have all comprised the assessment of change in groups of clients receiving counselling or therapy from a number of practitioners. It has already been noted that these studies are complex, expensive and difficult to arrange. Several writers have advocated, by contrast, that it is desirable for individual counsellors to monitor or evaluate their own work in a systematic way. Barlow *et al.* (1984) have called for counsellors and therapists to adopt the role of 'scientist–practitioner' and to use research routinely to help them reflect on their work with clients. They point out that research instruments such as psychological tests or questionnaires may provide clinicians with invaluable information that can be used in therapy. The use of the scientist–practitioner approach normally involves gathering baseline information on the level of problem behaviour in a client, before the commencement of counselling, then continuing to monitor the level of that behaviour throughout counselling and then at follow-up.

Examples of some of the many different types of assessment tool that can be used in outcome and evaluation studies are:

- Self-monitoring of problem behaviours (e.g., eating, smoking, occurrence of paranoid or obsessional thoughts) using a notebook or diary.
- Self-ratings of moods or feelings. Examples: rating scales to assess level or intensity of tension, pain, sadness or anxiety.
- Questionnaire measures of general psychological adjustment. Examples: General Health Questionnaire (GHQ), Minnesota Multiphasic Personality Inventory (MMPI), Symptom Checklist 90 (SCL–90); Clinical Outcome Routine Evaluation Outcome Measure (CORE-OM); Outcome Questionnaire 45 (OQ45).
- Questionnaire measures of specific variables. Examples: Beck Depression Inventory (BDI), Spielberger State-Trait Anxiety Inventory (STAI).

- Client-defined variables. Examples: Personal Questionnaire (Phillips 1986), client ratings of target symptoms (Sloane *et al.* 1975).
- Client satisfaction questionnaires (Berger 1983).
- Direct observation of the client. Examples: counting frequency of stuttering or negative self-statements during counselling session, observation of social skills performance during role-play, measuring sleep duration of insomniacs.
- Post-therapy ratings of outcome from client, therapist or friends and family members of the client.

A very wide range of measures and techniques have been employed, reflecting a diversity of aims, client groups and theoretical rationales. Further information on these techniques can be found in Nelson (1981), Lambert *et al.* (1983), Bowling (2001, 2004) Ogles *et al.* (2002) and McDowell (2006).

A final type of research that can be carried out in the area of evaluation concerns the assessment of quality of service provided by a counselling agency or organization. In this kind of study, many other factors are investigated in addition to the impact of counselling on individual clients. Maxwell (1984) has suggested six criteria for evaluating service provision: relevance/appropriateness, equity, accessibility, acceptability, effectiveness and efficiency. The question of acceptability introduces the perceptions and judgements of consumers of the service. The issue of efficiency brings in considerations of cost-effectiveness and cost–benefit analysis (Tolley and Rowland 1995; Miller and Magruder 1999). For example, in the area of counselling in primary care (family medicine), studies have examined the relative costs and benefits of counselling as compared with routine GP care (Friedli *et al.* 2000).

Box 25.2: *Are all counsellors equally effective?*

Most research into the effectiveness of counselling and psychotherapy has looked at the overall, or average, effectiveness of a group of therapists participating in a research study. Seldom do researchers publish an analysis of the differential success rates of individual therapists. Sometimes this may be because the number of clients seen by each counsellor is small, so that differences in success rates might be due to random allocation of one or two 'good' clients to one counsellor, and one or two 'difficult' clients to another. However, there are also political and even ethical barriers to research into individual success rates: who would volunteer to be a counsellor in such a study? Despite these problems, there have been a number of studies that have looked at the relative effectiveness of individual counsellors and therapists.

McLellan *et al.* (1988) analysed the relative effectiveness of four counsellors employed on a substance abuse rehabilitation research project, and found marked and consistent differences in outcome. The clients of one counsellor showed significant decreases in drug use, arrest rates and unemployment. The clients seen by another counsellor, by contrast, reported higher drug use and criminality, despite the fact that their training, level of experience, supervision and client profiles were equivalent. From examining the notes and records kept by each of the counsellors in the study, McLellan *et al.* (1988) concluded that the more effective counsellors were those who were more highly motivated, concerned about clients and well organized, and who tended to anticipate future problems rather than merely reacting to crises.

Blatt *et al.* (1996) carried out a similar study, this time in the area of psychotherapy for people suffering from depression. The 28 therapists participating in this study could be placed at all points across a range of effectiveness rates. The clients seen by the most successful therapists reported clinically significant improvements; the clients seen by the least successful practitioners reported equally large levels of clinical deterioration. The more successful therapists also had a much higher percentage of clients completing therapy. The main differences between the more successful and less successful groups of therapists were that the former adopted a more psychological (rather than biological) perspective on depression, and were much better at forming a warm, empathic relationship with their clients. There was also a tendency for the more effective therapists to be female.

Okiishi *et al.* (2003) have reported on the findings from a large-scale survey of the effectiveness rates of counsellors in a range of therapy agencies in the USA, working in everyday practice settings rather than within the perhaps somewhat artificial setting of controlled research studies. They found that the clients of the least successful counsellors tended to get worse, on average, whereas more than 80 per cent of the clients of the most effective therapists were completely recovered by the end of therapy. Further studies by Lutz *et al.* (2007) and Kraus *et al.* (2011) on similarly large samples, have supported findings that supported the conclusions of Okiishi *et al.* (2003).

The results of research into what is known as 'therapist effects' has had a major impact on the counselling and psychotherapy profession as a whole. For example, Wampold (2001) has argued that these findings suggest that differences in outcome between therapy approaches (e.g., psychodynamic, person-centred, CBT) are minimal compared with differences between individual therapists, and that the whole field of therapy outcome research has been pursuing a mistaken strategy, in terms of understanding the factors that are responsible for effective therapy. Other commentators have disagreed, and have claimed that the data can be interpreted in different ways (Crits-Christoph and Gallop 2006; Elkin 1999; Elkin *et al.* 2006; Kim *et al.* 2006; Luborsky *et al.* 1997). All of the protagonists in the debate are in agreement that more research needs to be carried out. It is clear that the eventual resolution of this issue will have massive implications for counselling and psychotherapy theory, research and practice.

> # Box 25.3: *The CORE outcome measure – an essential evaluation tool*
>
> There are significant difficulties faced by practitioners seeking to evaluate the outcomes of their own practice. There are a large number of different questionnaires that have been used by previous researchers, and it can be hard to decide which is the most appropriate. In addition, the majority of outcome scales are copyrighted by publishing companies, with the result that they may be expensive to purchase, or access to them may be restricted to people who have completed specific training courses. As a response to these barriers to research, the Mental Health Foundation in Britain commissioned a team at the Psychological Therapies Research Centre, University of Leeds, to produce a new outcome questionnaire that embodied 'best practice' from existing scales, and could be made widely available to practitioners and researchers. The CORE (Clinical Outcomes Routine Evaluation) scale is a 34-item self-report questionnaire that measures client distress in terms of four dimensions: well-being, symptoms, functioning and risk (Mellor-Clark *et al.* 1999; Evans *et al.* 2000). It can be copied without charge, and a low-cost software package is available to facilitate data analysis.
>
> The CORE questionnaire has been widely adopted by counselling, psychotherapy and clinical psychology service providers, and is part of a range of measures and information management tools developed by the CORE group (see www.coreims.co.uk). The CORE scale has been widely used to collect naturalistic data on the progress of therapy with clients in a range of settings, and to build up a data-set and norms that enable 'benchmarking' of standards of effectiveness in different settings (Barkham *et al.* 2001; Mellor-Clark *et al.* 2001; Mellor-Clark and Barkham 2006a). One of the achievements of this project has been the publication of two studies by Stiles *et al.* 2006, 2008) on large data-sets of several thousand clients receiving counselling in the UK NHS, which have shown high levels of effectiveness, and equivalence in effectiveness across the three main therapy approaches used in that setting – CBT, psychodynamic and person-centred. Further detailed information on the use of CORE is available in special issues of *Counselling and Psychotherapy Research* (Mellor-Clark 2006) and the *European Journal of Psychotherapy, Counselling and Health* (Mellor-Clark and Barkham 2006b).

Process research

Whereas outcome studies mainly examine the difference in the client before and after counselling, without looking at what actually happens during sessions, process studies take the opposite approach. In a process study, the researcher is attempting to identify or measure the therapeutic elements that are associated with change. Following the conclusions of reviewers such as Smith *et al.* (1980) that counselling and psychotherapy is, on the whole, effective, the energies of many researchers have focused more on questions of process. Having established that therapy 'works', they are seeking to learn *how* it works (Elliot 2010).

Studies of process from a client-centred perspective

The client-centred approach to counselling and therapy developed by Rogers and his colleagues (Rogers 1942, 1951, 1961) has been characterized by a consistent emphasis on the process of change in clients, and the process of the client–counsellor relationship. Rogers and his colleagues at the University of Ohio (1940–5) were the first investigators to make recordings of therapy sessions, and the first to study process in a systematic way. The earliest studies within the client-centred framework explored changes in the ways that clients made references to self at different points in their therapy, and the 'directiveness' of counsellor statements, by analysing transcripts of counselling sessions (Snyder 1945; Seeman 1949). Other studies from this period focused on the experience of the client in counselling, for example through the exploration of diaries kept by clients (Lipkin 1948; Rogers 1951).

In a major piece of research carried out at the University of Chicago, Rogers and Dymond (1954) and their colleagues examined different aspects of change in clients' self-concepts during and after therapy. Self-acceptance, a key concept in Rogerian theory, was assessed using a technique known as the 'Q-sort', in which clients arrange a set of self-statements to describe 'how I see myself now' and 'how I would ideally like to be' (the difference between actual and ideal self being taken as a measure of self-acceptance). Taking a group of 29 clients, they administered the Q-sort, and a range of other tests, at a pre-therapy interview, regularly throughout therapy and at follow-up. Results showed that changes in self-perception were closely associated with good outcomes. One of the main achievements of this phase of research was to demonstrate that research could be undertaken that was phenomenological, respecting the experience of the client, yet at the same time rigorous and quantitative. For the first time, an important aspect of process, change in self-acceptance, had been measured and tracked across a course of therapy. The Rogers and Dymond (1954) report was also noteworthy in containing a systematic analysis of failure and attrition cases.

Towards the end of his stay at Chicago, Rogers integrated the fruits of research and practice in client-centred therapy and counselling into two key papers, one on the 'necessary and sufficient' relationship conditions of empathy, congruence and unconditional positive regard (Rogers 1957), the other on the process of change in therapy (Rogers 1961). These papers are discussed more fully in Chapter 7. In their next major piece of research, Rogers and his collaborators set out to test these ideas in a study of client-centred therapy with hospitalized schizophrenic patients (Rogers et al. 1967). Rating scales were devised to measure the levels of therapists' unconditional positive regard, congruence, empathy and experiencing level observed in recordings of sessions with clients. Barrett-Lennard developed a questionnaire, the Relationship Inventory, to assess these 'core conditions' as perceived by clients, counsellors or external observers. Although the results of the schizophrenia study were ambiguous, largely due to the difficulty in achieving any degree of substantial change in disturbed clients, the Relationship Inventory and the various rating scales developed during the project have remained standard instruments in process studies (Greenberg and Pinsof 1986).

The research team around Rogers split up after he moved to California following the Wisconsin study, but the hypothesis of Rogers that the 'core conditions' of adequate levels of acceptance, empathy and congruence once perceived by the client represented not only necessary but also sufficient conditions for positive personality change in clients received a great deal of further study. Reviews of the work on this important theoretical claim (Patterson 1984; Watson 1984; Cramer 1992) suggest that Rogers was largely correct, even though there have been severe practical difficulties in adequately testing his model. Currently the most active research within the client-centred process model has been that concerned with 'depth of experiencing' in clients and counsellors.

The process research carried out by Rogers and his collaborators has made a significant contribution to the field, for a number of reasons. First, it demonstrated that the phenomena and processes of the counselling relationship were not something mysterious and elusive, but could appropriately and effectively be opened up for external scrutiny and research. Second, it represents what is probably still the most successful attempt in counselling and therapy to use research to test theoretical assumptions and evolve new concepts and models. Third, it supplied an example of the fruitful integration of research with practice, since all the people taking part in the research were practitioners as well as researchers. Finally, Rogers and his colleagues showed that it was possible and profitable to give the client a voice, and to explore the experience and perceptions of the client in therapy.

Studies of process from a psychodynamic perspective

Psychodynamic theory contains a wealth of ideas about the process of therapy. For example, the counselling process in psychodynamic work is likely to include instances of free association, interpretation, transference, counter-transference, analysis of dream and fantasy material, and episodes of resistance. Research that could help practitioners to understand more fully the mode of operation of these factors would be of substantial practical utility. However, research that is consistent with the basic philosophical assumptions of psychoanalysis presents a number of distinctive methodological problems. From a psychoanalytic point of view, the meaning of a client statement, or interaction between client and counsellor, can only be understood in context, and can only be interpreted by someone competent in psychodynamic methods. It is insufficient, therefore, to conduct process studies that rely on tape-recordings of segments of an interview, or to use a standardized rating scale administered by research assistants, as in other process research. Psychodynamic process studies are carried out by expert, trained practitioners, and are based on the investigation of whole cases.

One of the best examples of psychodynamic process research is to be found in the use of the core conflictual relationship theme (CCRT) method developed by Luborsky *et al.* (1986) as a technique for exploring transference. In this technique, a number of expert judges first read a transcript of an entire session. They are then asked to focus on episodes in the transcript where the client makes reference to relationships, and to arrive at a statement of three components of each episode: the wishes or intentions of the client towards the other person; the responses of the other person; and the response of the client himself or herself. Taken together, these components yield a picture of the kind of conflictual relationships, or transference patterns, experienced by the client in his or her life. The formulations of different judges are checked against each other to arrive at a consensus view.

The CCRT method has been used to investigate a number of hypotheses regarding the transference process in therapy. For example, Luborsky *et al.* (1986) compared the transference themes displayed towards other people and those expressed in relation to the therapist. Results provided strong evidence to confirm the Freudian assumption that the transference relationship with the therapist is a reflection of the way the client characteristically relates to people in everyday life. Crits-Christoph *et al.* (1988), also using the CCRT technique, showed that accuracy of interpretation, assessed by comparing CCRT formulations with therapist interpretations of relationship issues, was positively correlated with client benefit in therapy. Similar studies, in which expert readers have been employed to identify psychodynamic themes in session transcripts, have been carried out by Malan (1976), Silberschatz *et al.* (1986) and Kachele (1992).

The psychodynamic tradition in counselling has generated a great deal of research activity, of which the examples discussed in this section represent only a small sample. Person *et al.* (2005) and Miller *et al.* (1993) are good sources for further information on psychoanalytic and psychodynamic process and outcome research.

The 'events paradigm'

Process-oriented research carried out within the client-centred perspective has become less fashionable in recent years, owing to a variety of factors that resulted in diminishing interest in the person-centred approach in the USA. Currently, researchers exploring therapy process are more likely to be working within what has become known as the 'events paradigm' (Rice and Greenberg 1984a). This approach concentrates on finding change events within therapy sessions, and identifying the therapist's or counsellor's actions or strategies that enabled these events to occur. This is quite different from the client-centred view of process, which focuses not so much on discrete events as on general conditions or the creation of a therapeutic environment.

One of the key figures in events research has been Robert Elliott, based at the University of Toledo in Ohio, who has adapted the interpersonal process recall (IPR) method for use in research (Kagan *et al.* 1963; Kagan 1984). In this approach, a video- or audio-tape of a therapy session is played back to either the therapist or the client, with the aim of stimulating their recall of the experience of being in the session, and collecting information about their evaluation or perception of events within it. Early studies using this method looked at process elements, such as client perceptions of what is helpful and dimensions of therapist intentions (Elliott 1986). However, later research has focused on identifying and analysing actual events, with the aim of describing 'the nature and unfolding of particular types of significant change event' (Elliott 1986: 507). Another approach to studying significant events has been evolved by Mahrer *et al.* (1987). In these studies, Mahrer and his co-researchers listened to audio-tapes of therapy sessions in order to identify 'good moments' where the client showed movement, progress, process improvement or change. The distribution of these moments over the session, and the therapist's behaviour that appeared to facilitate good moments, have been explored. In yet another series of studies of events, Rice and Greenberg (1984b) have looked at the tasks the therapist must carry out in order to facilitate change in different circumstances.

It is worth noting that, unlike the Rogerian studies, which were explicitly informed by theory, the events studies are largely non-theoretical in nature, and so far at least have been devoted to describing change events and processes rather than to developing a theoretical framework for understanding them.

The process as experienced by the client

One of the fundamental issues in research into counselling and psychotherapy concerns the question of who is observing what is happening. Rogers and Dymond (1954) pointed out that different conclusions on process and outcome could be reached depending on whether the perspective of the client, the therapist or an external observer was taken. Most research has relied on either the perspective of the therapist or that of an external observer, since to involve the client could intrude on his or her therapy, or cause distress. Most studies that have involved collecting data from clients have used standardized questionnaires or rating scales. In these studies, the experience of the client is filtered through categories and dimensions imposed by the researcher. There have been relatively few studies into the client's experience of the process of counselling as defined by the client (McLeod 1990).

Maluccio (1979) carried out intensive interviews with clients who had completed counselling. This piece of research illustrates the difficulties inherent in inviting people to talk retrospectively about the whole of their counselling experience. The informants interviewed by Maluccio produced large amounts of complex material that was difficult to interpret. Maluccio found that, on the whole, clients experienced their counselling as having passed through discrete stages. Another significant finding from this study was that clients often attributed changes in psychological and emotional well-being not to anything that was happening with their therapist, but to external events such as getting a job or moving house. This finding indicates one of the important differences between the client's and therapist's experience of counselling. The client experiences counselling as one facet of a life that may encompass many other relationships; the counsellor has no first-hand involvement with these other relationships and is limited to his or her experience of the actual sessions. The two types of experience therefore have quite different horizons.

The work of Maluccio (1979), and of other researchers such as Timms and Blampied (1985), has looked at the experience of the client over an extended time, which may span several months of counselling. Clearly, a lot can happen over the course of therapy, and this kind of research will not be able to pick up the fine-grained detail of what the client experiences on a moment-by-moment basis. In a series of studies, Rennie (1990) focused on the experiences of clients in single sessions. Rennie used a version of the Interpersonal Process Recall technique (Kagan 1984) to enable clients to re-live or re-experience what they thought and felt during the session. An audio- or video-tape is made of the session, and as soon as possible after the end of the session the client reviews the tape in the presence of the researcher, stopping the tape whenever he or she remembers what was being experienced at that point. The researcher then sorts through the transcript of the inquiry interview to identify themes and categories of experience.

The client experience studies carried out by Rennie and his associates (Angus and Rennie 1988, 1989; Rennie 1990, 1992) have opened up for research an area of the counselling process that is normally inaccessible to counsellors, and have produced some striking results. One of the conclusions Rennie arrives at is that clients are responding to the counsellor on different levels. They may be telling the counsellor about some event in their life but underneath that narrative may be considering whether or not to take the risk of talking about some previously secret piece of information. They may agree with an interpretation or intervention from the counsellor while knowing that it is inaccurate or inappropriate.

Exploration of the world of the client, as pioneered by Maluccio (1979) and Rennie (1990), requires sensitive, ethically aware contact between researcher and client, as well as much painstaking work categorizing and interpreting themes derived from interview transcripts. The aim of this type of work is to produce 'grounded theory' (Glaser and Strauss 1967; Glaser 1978; Rennie *et al.* 1988), or generalizations and models that are demonstrably rooted in actual experience rather than imposed by the researcher. Rennie (2002) has reviewed the substantial contribution that studies of this kind have made to appreciating the extent to which the client is an active, reflexive participant in therapy.

Box 25.4: *Using process research to generate principles for practice*

A good example of how research can be used to inform practice can be found in a study by Levitt *et al.* (2006). In this piece of research, 26 clients who had recently completed therapy (average length of therapy – 16 months), were interviewed in depth about what had been significant for them in their experience of therapy. The transcripts of these interviews were carefully analysed in terms of emergent therapeutic principles that might provide practical direction for therapists. Some of the principles that were identified in the study included the following:

- Initially, clients may enter therapy with expectations or fears that work against their engagement. If a commitment to therapy does not develop, it may be helpful if clients are guided to frankly discuss their shame or fear of examining threatening topics, or if the relationship is mutually examined.

- The therapeutic environment is experienced as a reflection of therapist care, and can facilitate clients' relating in a more relaxing way.

- Initially in therapy an increasing dependency on the therapist appeared to allow the client to individuate from significant others, and then it tapered off as the client became more self-reliant.

- Clients tended to develop trust after scrutinizing therapists for displays of caring, especially when vulnerable issues arose. Therapists can convey caring by appearing genuine, showing respect for the client's process, and demonstrating faith and expertise in the therapeutic process.

Although the ultimate validity of these principles needs to be evaluated through further research with different groups of clients, the Levitt *et al.* (2006) study is notable in providing clients with an opportunity to 'speak' to the professional community of therapists, and tell them what they find helpful. It is striking that, at least in this study, clients valued aspects of therapy that tend not to be highlighted in mainstream therapy theory – the therapist as someone who cares, the significance of the therapist's room and the positive value placed on the experience of feelings of dependency toward the therapist.

Case studies

Traditionally, case studies have been the primary vehicle for research and theory construction in psychodynamic approaches to counselling and psychotherapy. Many of the cases published by Freud, for example, have been widely debated and reinterpreted by other therapists and theorists and represent some of the basic building blocks of psychoanalytic knowledge and training. It would be unusual to find a trained and experienced psychodynamic counsellor or therapist who had not carefully read the cases of Dora (Freud 1901/1979), the Rat Man (Freud 1909/1979) or Schreber (Freud 1910/1979).

From a research point of view, however, there are many methodological issues raised by the manner in which Freud and his colleagues carried out case studies. Freud saw several patients each day, and wrote up notes of his consultations in the evening. Some of these notes were subsequently worked up as papers presented to conferences or published in books and journals. At each stage of this process of producing a case study, there was no possible check on the validity of the conclusions reached by Freud, or on any bias in his recollection or selection of evidence. Critics could put forward the argument that Freud distorted the evidence to fit his theories. For example, Spence (1989) argued that in a typical psychoanalytic case study, there is a strong tendency for the author to 'smooth' the data (i.e., ignore contradictory evidence) to make it fit the theory. There is little that psychoanalysts can do to counter this charge, given the way their case studies have been carried out.

The dilemma that is apparent in this debate over case studies is that, on the one hand, detailed examination of individual cases is invaluable for the development of theory and practice, but, on the other hand, finding a rigorous and unbiased way of observing and analysing individual cases is difficult. The construction of methods for *systematic* case study research has been a recurrent concern for researchers in the field of personality for many years (Murray 1938; DeWaele and Harré 1976; Rabin *et al.* 1981, 1990). Within the field of counselling and psychotherapy research, there have been four distinctive approaches to systematic case study investigation: 'N=1' studies, theory-building case studies, quasi-judicial case analysis, narrative case studies and pragmatic case studies.

Behavioural case studies are sometimes known as 'N=1' studies and are associated with the 'scientist–practitioner' model discussed earlier in this chapter. These case studies concentrate on tracking changes in a limited number of key variables predicted to change as a result of counselling: for example, amount of time spent studying or the score on a depression inventory. The principal aim of the study is to demonstrate the effectiveness of a particular type of intervention with a particular category of client; broader process issues are not usually considered. Morley (2007) provides a detailed account of the procedures involved in this type of case study. 'N=1' *case studies,* or 'single subject' designs, have played a central role in the development of CBT, by offering practitioners a means of documenting and analysing the effectiveness of innovative interventions, in advance of carrying out large scale studies.

Other case study researchers have used case studies in the development of theory (Stiles 2007). A powerful example of this type of work has been the series of eight case studies of brief therapy with depressed women clients carried out by Hill (1989), with the aim of identifying the relative contribution to outcome made by non-specific factors and therapist techniques. This study is unique in the exhaustive and comprehensive information that was gathered on each case (see Table 25.2). Bill Stiles and his colleagues have used systematic analysis of case data in the development of the assimilation model of therapeutic change (Stiles 2005, 2006). A number of other case studies have recently been published in which cases of special interest have been selected from large-scale extensive investigations. For example, Strupp (1980a, 1980b, 1980c, 1980d) presented four comparative pairs (one success and one failure case) of cases drawn from Strupp and Hadley (1979), in order to generate a comprehensive understanding of the factors associated with good and poor outcomes.

Quasi-judicial case studies represent an attempt to introduce rigour into the analysis of case data by introducing ideas from the legal system. In court cases, the true interpretation of what happened in a crime is determined by the presentation of prosecution and defence arguments, with the final decision being taken by a judge or jury. In similar fashion, in his psychotherapy case studies, Elliott (2002) employs two teams of researchers, with one group given the task of arguing that the outcome of the case is due to the therapy that was delivered, and the other group arguing that any changes that occurred were as a result of extra-therapeutic factors. Elliott (2002) suggests that the final conclusions arrived at through this kind of adjudication process are particularly credible, in comparison with conventional clinical case studies.

Narrative case studies use methods of qualitative inquiry to allow the client and/or the counsellor to tell his or her story of taking part in therapy. Etherington (2000) provides an example of this genre of case study research. If carried out carefully and rigorously, autobiographical, first-person writings may also fit into this category. The question being explored in this type of case research is 'what does therapy mean to a client or therapist,

TABLE 25.2 The intensive case study method

Pre-therapy, at termination and follow-up

Minnesota Multiphasic Personality Inventory
Hopkins Symptom Checklist (SCL–90-R)
Tennessee Self-Concept Scale
Target complaints
Hamilton depression and anxiety scales
Interview

After each session researchers rated

Counsellor verbal response modes
Counsellor activity level
Client reactions during session
Client level of experiencing

Client and therapist completed

Post-session questionnaire or interview
Working Alliance Inventory
Session Evaluation Questionnaire

Client and therapist separately

Watched video of session to recall feelings and rate helpfulness of each counsellor statement

Note: Information gathered on each case by Hill (1989).

in the context of his or her life as a whole?'; or alternatively, 'how do we understand the richness of how a particular case unfolds?'

A further approach to case study research in counselling and psychotherapy is represented by the *pragmatic case study*. An influential book by Fishman (1999) argued that case studies comprise a basic form of practical knowledge for therapists, because the work of therapy inevitably involves dealing with individual lives. Fishman (1999) proposed that a pragmatically useful body of research knowledge could be created by practitioners writing up their case experiences in a standardized fashion, and collecting these cases in a single database. The online, open access journal *Pragmatic Case Studies in Psychotherapy* has been established to enable such a database to be created, and has published series of detailed case analyses that provide an invaluable resource for therapists.

There has been a resurgence of interest in case study research in counselling and psychotherapy in recent years. Although the potential value of case-based evidence has always been recognized within the counselling profession, there has been a sense that case studies have too often been used almost as promotional vehicles for authors seeking to market new approaches to therapy, rather than as serious contributions to the research literature. There has also been a concern that, even if a case study in itself provides evidence that is convincing and credible, it is impossible to generalize from single examples. The development of new methods of systematic case analysis, using quasi-judicial, time-series and theory-building approaches, and the construction of databases of series of case studies, has gone a long way toward alleviating these concerns.

Box 25.5: *An everyday life perspective on the meaning of therapy*

One of the limitations of research into counselling and psychotherapy is that it remains primarily 'therapist-centred', in the sense of concentrating on what happens in the therapy room, and regarding the therapy process as the major source of change in a client's life. Some recent research carried out in Denmark by Dreier (2000, 2008) and Mackrill (2007, 2008a, 2008b) takes a 180 degree shift in perspective by looking at therapy from the point of view of the everyday life of the client. This research has identified some of the complex ways in which 'everyday' or 'extra-therapeutic' learning interacts with what happens in counselling sessions. In one striking example, Mackrill (2008a) describes a male client who reported that the main outcome of his therapy had been the development of a capacity to engage in 'positive thinking'. On further inquiry, it emerged that the issue of positive thinking was only mentioned once in 12 sessions of therapy, and that the client had picked up this idea from a lecture that he had attended while at school. However, he had interpreted his conversations with his therapist in the light of this construct, which for him functioned as a bridge between his therapy and his everyday life. This example, and many other observations recorded within this research programme, paints a picture of clients as active consumers of therapy, who selectively makes use of what is offered by their therapist in the context of other strategies for coping and change that they have acquired from a myriad of other sources.

Ethical dilemmas in counselling research

The purpose of counselling is to help people, or to empower them to help themselves, and the process of counselling can often require disclosure of confidential information, experience of painful memories and emotions, and the taking of decisions that affect other people. Counsellors take great care to ensure that this sometimes risky process does not bring harm to clients. It is easy to see that research into counselling introduces additional possibilities of harm. Research may lead to information about clients being disclosed, painful feelings being restimulated or the relationship of trust with the therapist being damaged.

Most forms of counselling research contain ethical dangers. For example, in outcome studies in which there is a control group of 'waiting list' clients, the decision is taken to offer help immediately to some people, but to withhold it from others. In studies of new types of counselling intervention clients may be exposed to therapy that is harmful. If the researcher contacts the client to request that he or she takes part in the study the knowledge that this person is a client is transmitted beyond the counsellor or agency. If the counsellor asks the client to participate in a study the client may be unwilling to do so but may nevertheless comply for fear of antagonizing someone upon whom he or she feels emotionally dependent. In studies where former clients are interviewed about their experience of therapy, the interview itself may awaken a need for further counselling.

For these reasons, counselling and psychotherapy research studies carried out in government agencies, such as hospitals or social services departments, or submitted for funding to charitable trusts will normally need to be assessed by ethical committees, and will need to document in detail their procedures for dealing with ethical issues. However, all research should be designed with ethical considerations in mind, and research training for counsellors and therapists should emphasize awareness of ethical factors.

Box 25.6: *The Consumer Reports study*

Consumer Reports is a popular consumer affairs magazine in the USA that routinely distributes survey questionnaires to its extensive readership, to gauge their views on a range of products and services. In 1994, the magazine include a series of questions in its survey concerning the use of counselling and psychotherapy, and the benefits that readers had experienced from any therapy in which they had participated. A summary of the findings of this therapy survey was published by the well-known American psychologist Martin Seligman in *American Psychologist* (Seligman 1995). In this article, he argued that surveys of how people feel about the real-life therapy they had received provides valuable evidence of how therapy works in everyday circumstances, in contrast to the artificial context of the randomized controlled trial. The main results of the survey were:

- over 80 per cent of those who had used therapy got better (a much higher proportion than in controlled studies);

- there was no difference in effectiveness between different therapy approaches;
- those who had received long-term therapy did significantly better than those who had received brief therapy;
- externally imposed limits on the number of sessions was associated with poorer outcomes;
- broadly equivalent outcomes to formal psychotherapy were reported by those people who had sought psychological help from clergy, their family doctor or Alcoholics Anonymous.

The publication of the *Consumer Reports* study raised a storm of controversy. On the whole, the psychotherapy research establishment were aghast at this attempt to short-circuit the careful research procedures that they had developed. The various strands of the critical debate are summarized in the introductory section of Nielsen *et al.* (2004). The critics complained that the *Consumer Reports* survey used a questionnaire that had not been properly validated, had recruited a biased sample (i.e., those who were particularly happy with the therapy they had received), and that the responses made by participants were inevitably inaccurate because they were being asked to retrospectively report on therapy that had taken place months or years previously.

A later, parallel study using the same questions was carried out in Germany, yielding similar results (Hartmann and Zepf 2003). A study by Howard *et al.* (2001) compared some of the *Consumer Reports* data with answers that clients in their controlled outcome study had given to the same, or similar, questions, and found a large degree of concordance between the two data-sets. VandenBos (1996) and Howard *et al.* (2001) produced analyses that suggested that the *Consumer Reports* sample represented a reasonably good reflection of the population of therapy users in the USA as a whole.

However, in a particularly significant follow-up study, Nielsen *et al.* (2004) went further, and asked a large sample of clients who had previously completed pre- and post-therapy questionnaires, to fill in the whole *Consumer Reports* survey questionnaire six months after their therapy had finished. What Nielsen *et al.* (2004) found was that it appeared that the way that the *Consumer Reports* questions were phrased seemed to lead people to overestimate their distress pre-therapy, and overestimate their well-being post-therapy, compared with their responses to questionnaires that they had completed at the time, thus producing an overpositive picture of the effectiveness of therapy.

The debate over the *Consumer Reports* study illustrates three things. First, estimates of the effectiveness of therapy depend on the methodology that is used. Second, research is a cumulative and collective endeavour – it may take years for the true meaning of a set of findings to be clarified. Third, there is some reluctance on the part of the research community to give credence to the views of clients.

The impact of research on the client

Connected with ethical issues, but also distinct from them, is the problem of reactivity in counselling research. Reactivity, or the impact of research on the client or therapist, occurs when the research process interferes with or alters what is happening in counselling. In the study by Hill (1989), for example, clients were asked to participate in a great many activities that involved self-exploration and learning (such as watching a video of the therapy session) but were not part of the actual therapy. Hill (1989: 330) acknowledged that 'the research probably influenced the results of all eight cases . . . the [research activities] were probably therapeutic in and of themselves'. In the Sheffield Psychotherapy Research Project (Firth *et al.* 1986), which compared the effectiveness of brief 'exploratory' or 'prescriptive' therapy, all questionnaires and other data gathering were carried out by a clinic secretary or by interviewers who were independent of the therapists. However, although they knew this, many clients wrote comments on the questionnaires as though they expected their counsellors to read them. Some also admitted sabotaging the research, by completing questionnaires at random, when feeling hostile towards their counsellor.

Anderson and Strupp (1996) interviewed clients who had taken part in a randomized study. Several of those who had perceived themselves as having been allocated to the 'control' or less-preferred condition reported that they had been aware of how the research had influenced the therapy they had received, and were resentful about it. Marshall (2001) used a questionnaire to collect client views on a range of research data collection procedures with which they had been involved, including completing questionnaires, being interviewed, and having their therapy sessions recorded. He found that, on the whole, clients quickly adjusted to any interference in the therapy process brought about by recording, and tended to describe the interview and questionnaire as being quite facilitative, by providing them with opportunities to think and reflect on themselves in new ways. The implications of these studies appears to be that, in general, clients are quite positive about the experience of taking part in research if the questions they are being asked make sense to them, and act as a stimulus to self-reflection. Clients in therapy research are also similar to people who take part in other forms of social and health research, in feeling good about any opportunity to make a contribution to the common good. However, it seems to be the case that a research design that involves manipulating clients, such as a randomized controlled trial, can lead to a negative reaction.

When interpreting these studies of the impact of research participation on clients, it is essential to keep in mind that the findings that have been described are formulated in terms of average or overall responses, and that individuals may react quite differently. For example, even if 95 per cent of clients in a research study are comfortable with completing questionnaires, there may be 5 per cent who feel threatened or confused about these procedures. Good ethical practice clearly involves taking account of the needs of this minority.

Another dimension of reactivity is the effect of the research on the counsellor. Many counsellors can be anxious about exposing their work to colleagues, and perhaps risking criticism or censure. For example, in process studies, transcripts of therapy sessions may be read and rated by a number of judges. Research has shown that there can be wide differences between counsellors and therapists in their levels of effectiveness, so there is a basis in reality for these fears. In some studies, the research design requires counsellors or therapists to provide standardized treatment, and to conform to the guidelines of a treatment manual, or to offer clients a limited number of sessions. There may be times when these constraints conflict with the professional judgement of the counsellor regarding how to proceed or how many sessions the client might need. It is possible, therefore, that when therapy is being investigated in the context of a research study, the practitioner may be inhibited in ways that affect the quality of service that he or she is able offer to his or her clients.

The consensus among therapists who are also researchers is that data collection procedures such as questionnaires and interviews have the potential to enhance the effectiveness of therapy. In recent years, there have been various attempts to more fully integrate research into routine practice. The most notable example of this area of development has been the 'client tracking' studies conducted by Michael Lambert and his colleagues in the USA, and then subsequently by researchers in other centres around the world (Lambert 2007). In these projects, the client completes an outcome questionnaire at each session, and the results are fed back to either the therapist, or to both the therapist and his or her client, in the form of a graph that charts improvement, or in the form of alarm signals (e.g., a red flag means that the client is deteriorating, a green flag means that the client is making good progress). When the progress of these 'feedback' clients is contrasted with results from a comparison group that has not received feedback, there is evidence of a small but meaningful impact on the outcome of therapy. Specifically, the use of this kind of feedback brings about a marked reduction in the proportion of poor outcome cases that are observed. In other words, the feedback gives the therapist (and possibly also the client) a clear signal that the work is 'stuck', and provides a trigger to review what is happening and make whatever changes are necessary. Another example of the use of client tracking tools to provide feedback that informs the therapy process, can be found in the work of Barry Duncan, Scott Miller and their colleagues (Duncan *et al.* 2004; Miller *et al.* 2005).

The relevance of research for practitioners

Although there may be a lot of research being carried out, the relevance or utility of that research for practitioners has been extensively questioned. In a study of psychotherapists in the USA, even though 88 per cent of a sample of 279 therapists had PhDs (which meant that they had received extensive training in research, and had carried out research), 24 per cent reported that they never read articles or books about research, and 45 per cent reported that none of the research articles they read had a significant influence on the way they worked with clients (Morrow-Bradley and Elliott 1986). It would seem highly probable that groups of practitioners in countries with less academically oriented training programmes, or therapists trained in independent institutes rather than in university departments, would report even lower levels of research utilization.

The perceived lack of relevance of much counselling and psychotherapy research has been labelled the 'researcher–practitioner gap', and has been attributed to the differing roles and professional interests and values of researchers and clinicians. Counsellors and therapists typically view research as not giving enough information about the methods of treatment used, looking at groups of clients rather than individuals and assessing differences between treatment groups on the basis of statistical rather than practical or clinical criteria for significance (Cohen *et al.* 1986; Morrow-Bradley and Elliott 1986). In addition, many practitioners may not have access to research libraries or facilities.

Behind the research–practice gap can be detected even more fundamental issues regarding the nature of knowledge about counselling. As mentioned at the beginning of this chapter, counselling and therapy research has been largely dominated by quantitative methods and assumptions borrowed from mainstream psychology and psychiatry, even though many of the ideas and assumptions of qualitative research are probably more congenial to counsellors. This situation will not be resolved until counselling achieves a more explicitly interdisciplinary approach, rather than continuing to define itself as a subdiscipline of psychology.

Box 25.7: *The debate over evidence-based practice*

The most significant issue to have emerged within counselling and psychotherapy research in recent years has focused on the question of which types of therapy are supported by research evidence, and which are not. Professional associations and government bodies in North America and Europe have sought to restrict therapeutic training and practice only to those approaches that are 'evidence-based' or (in North America) 'empirically validated' in terms of quantitative, randomized controlled trials. In the UK, the National Institute for Health and Clinical Excellence (NICE) is an independent organization that has responsibility for recommending to the government whether specific health interventions (including therapy approaches for particular disorders) should be made available through the NHS. The National Institute for Health and Clinical Excellence has adopted a 'hierarchy' of evidence that gives the highest weighting to findings from randomized controlled studies, and minimal weighting to large-scale naturalistic effectiveness studies such as those published by Stiles *et al.* (2006, 2008). There are several important questions linked to this debate:

- Are 'controlled', quantitative studies the best, or the only way to evaluate the effectiveness of therapy?

- How adequately do controlled trials reflect everyday therapeutic practice (Westen *et al.* 2004)?

- Does the lack of positive research evidence mean that an approach to therapy is invalid, or merely that those who practice it do not have access to the resources necessary to carry out rigorous research?

- Should clients be given a choice of which kind of therapist they see, regardless of the research evidence?

- How important, in the context of this debate, is the research evidence that suggests that the quality of relationship between client and therapist is a better predictor of good outcome than is the type of therapy being offered (Wampold 2001)?

In a social and political climate in which all forms of medical, nursing and social care are required to be 'evidence-based', it is surely reasonable that counselling and psychotherapy should be fully accountable. But the decisions that are taken will affect both therapists' livelihoods and clients' choices, and represent a crucial test of the trustworthiness and value of the research that has been carried out. Good sources of further reading around this critical issue are the book edited by Rowland and Goss (2000), and the special issue of *Psychotherapy Research* edited by Elliott (1998).

Another fundamental issue concerns the integration of research with theory and practice. For example, during the period spanning 1941 to *c*.1965, client-centred counselling and therapy was centred on a group of people headed by Rogers who were all active in seeing clients, teaching students, carrying out research and developing theory (McLeod 2002). The integration of these activities gave their research a high degree of coherence and impact. In more recent times, there has been a greater fragmentation of professional roles and fewer opportunities to create that kind of research environment.

The image of the person in therapy research

To return to some of the themes and issues introduced in Chapter 2, it can be argued that most research into counselling and therapy draws upon a medical/biological image of the person. Counselling or therapy is regarded as 'treatment' that is administered to the client, just as a drug is administered to a patient in hospital. The various dimensions of the counselling process, such as empathy or interpretation, can be seen as ingredients of the drug, and process research becomes a search for the best blend of ingredients. Howard *et al.* (1986) have written about the 'dose–effect relationship', meaning the link between the number of sessions (dose) and client improvement.

Stiles and Shapiro (1989) have criticized what they call the 'abuse of the drug metaphor' in research. They argue that counselling and therapy involve active, intentional participation on the part of the client rather than passive and automatic responding to ingestion of a drug. The ingredients of therapy, such as empathic reflection, are not fixed and inert, but consist of meanings negotiated between people. These are essential aspects of therapy that do not fit a drug model. Stiles and Shapiro (1989) observe further that even if the drug metaphor is accepted, its use in therapy research is less subtle than in pharmacological research. In studies of real drugs, it is not assumed that 'more is better': some drugs are most effective in small doses, or within certain parameters. Similar effects may well apply in counselling and therapy. For example, a little self-disclosure on the part of the counsellor may be beneficial, but a lot just gets in the way. The kinds of issues raised by Stiles and Shapiro (1989) have contributed to the need felt by many in the field of counselling and therapy research to construct research informed by alternative metaphors and images of the person.

Conclusions

The aim of this chapter has not been to attempt to provide a comprehensive account of the state of research-based knowledge in counselling and psychotherapy. Previous chapters have made plentiful reference to research evidence that has been relevant to specific topics that have been discussed. Instead, the aim of this chapter has been to offer an overview of some of the main themes and methodological issues in research on counselling. When exploring the counselling research literature it is essential to keep in mind that it sits within a wider context of scholarship and inquiry. There are two aspects of this wider context that are of particular relevance. First, there exists a massive research literature that is helpful for counsellors, that is concerned not with counselling processes and outcomes as such, but with the nature of the problems and issues that people bring to counselling. For example, many counselling clients describe their problems as 'depression', and there is a wealth of research into the effectiveness of different approaches to therapy for depression. But there is also a wealth of research into what it is like to be depressed, on different patterns of depression, and on the causes of depression. Being a research-informed practitioner involves being willing to make use of the valuable insights that can be obtained from this kind of 'background' research, which has a key role to play in sensitizing counsellors to the complexity of factors that may be associated with the problems reported by clients.

A second context within which counselling research operates is the literature on research methodology. Acquiring valid knowledge on something like counselling is never an easy matter. There are many facets to any issue that might be investigated, and hard choices to be made about how to approach the topic, what kind of data to gather, and how to analyse it when it has been collected. This chapter has sought to illustrate some of the methodological debates within current counselling and psychotherapy research, for example regarding the role of qualitative research (stories) versus quantitative research (numbers), or regarding the best way to evaluate outcomes. There is never a clear-cut definitive answer to methodological questions – each way of 'knowing' has its place. It is a matter of being able to appreciate the strengths as well as the limitations of all research methodologies, and realizing that reliable knowledge is attained through open conversation in which all points of view are respected.

We are at a time in the history of counselling and psychotherapy when research has greater significance than ever before. Up until quite recently, therapy research has operated as a kind of virtual 'R&D' department or think-tank for the therapy industry. Researchers have tested out ideas and 'therapy products' and there has been a slow and gradual filtering through of their findings into practice. Within the past decade or so, all this has changed. Governments and other large-scale health providers such as insurance companies have been faced with a situation in which there is an ever-expanding list of new health interventions, in the form of new drugs and other physical treatments at the same time as an ever-expanding patient need arising from an ageing population. Health providers therefore have a pressing need to prioritize the delivery of treatments that are shown to work, which are evidence-based in terms of hard research evidence. Applied to counselling and psychotherapy, this policy has meant that policy-makers have looked long and hard at the counselling and psychotherapy outcome literature. What they have found there is lots of studies on CBT, because CBT has developed within a research environment, and lots of studies on the effectiveness of time-limited therapy (because it is much easier to carry out research on brief therapy than on open-ended therapy). They have therefore, inevitably, decided to invest in time-limited CBT, and to restrict the availability of other forms of therapy. These decisions make good sense in the context of the way that evidence-based health care is organized. But they do not make good sense to many counsellors, who know (but cannot demonstrate in research terms) that many forms of therapy can be helpful, and that some clients will only benefit from long-term work. What has emerged in recent years is a real sense of urgency and crisis around the role of research in counselling and psychotherapy.

Topics for reflection and discussion

1 Imagine that a counselling agency (for example, a student counselling service in a college, an employee counselling unit, a branch of RELATE couple counselling) has asked you to carry out a study of how much benefit their clients gained from counselling. What would you do? How much would it cost them? How much person time would it require? What ethical issues would need to be considered? How would these ethical issues be dealt with in the design of your study?

2 What research would you like to see carried out? List three research questions that would be of particular interest to you. Consider how you would investigate these questions from both a qualitative and a quantitative perspective.

3 How relevant is counselling research for you in your work as a counsellor, or how relevant do you think it might be in your future counselling career? In what ways do you see research positively influencing your practice, or in what ways could you see it possibly leading to confusion and poor practice?

4 Read a research article published in one of the research journals. What are the strengths and weaknesses of this particular study? Does the author arrive at conclusions that are fully justified by the evidence, or can you think of other plausible interpretations of the data that the author has not taken into account? How valuable is this piece of research in terms of informing or guiding counselling practice?

Suggested further reading

An expanded account of the topics covered in this chapter can be found in my book *An Introduction to Research in Counselling and Psychotherapy* (McLeod 2013a) and in *Understanding Counselling,* edited by Barker *et al.* (2010). Books that explore the contribution that research can make to practice include: *Essential Research Findings in Counselling and Psychotherapy: The Facts are Friendly* (Cooper 2008); *Research in Counselling and*

Psychotherapy (Timulak 2008); *Counselling Based on Process Research: Applying What we Know* (Tryon 2002).

There are several excellent research journals in counselling and psychotherapy. The most consistent sources of good quality research articles are: the *Journal of Counseling Psychology*, the *Journal of Clinical Psychology, Psychotherapy; Psychology and Psychotherapy;* and *Counselling and Psychotherapy Research*.

The future of counselling: international perspectives

Introduction

For the most part, the earlier chapters of this book have been written as though 'counselling' can be understood as an activity that functions in more or less the same way, anywhere in the world. This kind of assumption is reinforced by the reality that counselling theory and practice is massively dominated by what happened in North America, which can be viewed as the global 'home' of counselling and psychotherapy. It is further reinforced by the fact that the author of the book lives and works in Britain, and is inevitably highly influenced by the particular ways in which counselling has evolved in that country. In an attempt to move beyond these limitations, the intention in this final chapter is to look at other regions in the world map of counselling, to try to develop a sense of what is happening elsewhere.

The global interconnectedness of counselling is an interesting phenomenon. From the visits of Carl Rogers, early in his career, to China and Japan, there have been many leading figures in counselling who have been profoundly affected by time spent in very different cultural environments. Some of the most significant developments in counselling and psychotherapy theory and practice have been developed at the margins. For example, narrative therapy came to life in Adelaide, Australia and in New Zealand. Open dialogue therapy and the use of reflecting teams came to life in Lapland. Mindfulness meditation was brought to the West by a handful of Buddhist priests from Japan. Counsellors like to know about what goes on in other places. Table 26.1 provides a list of some recent papers that have been published in recent years in order to share information about the state of

TABLE 26.1 Counselling around the world

Country	Publications
Belize	Smith-Augustine and Wagner (2012).
Botswana	Stockton *et al.* (2010)
Brazil	Hutz-Midgett and Hutz (2012)
China	Lim *et al.* (2010)
Costa Rica	Collier (2013)
Czech Republic	Simons *et al.* (2012)
Denmark	Dixon and Hansen (2010)
Greece	Malikiosi-Loizos and Ivey (2012)
India	Carson *et al.* (2009)
Ireland	O'Morain *et al.* (2012)
Israel	Israelashvili and Wegman-Rozi (2012)
Italy	Remley *et al.* (2010)
Jamaica	Palmer *et al.* (2012)
Japan	Grabosky *et al.* (2012)
Kenya	Atieno Okech and Kimemia (2012)
Lebanon	Ayyash-Abdo and Mukallid (2010)
Malaysia	See and Ng (2010)
Mexico	Portal *et al.* (2010)
Nigeria	Okocha and Alika (2012)
Palestine	Shawahin and Çiftçi (2012)
Philippines	Tuason *et al.* (2012)
Romania	Szilagyi and Paredes (2010)
Russia	Currie *et al.* (2012)
Singapore	Yeo *et al.* (2012)
South Africa	Maree and van der Westhuizen (2011)
South Korea	Lee *et al.* (2012)
Switzerland	Thomas and Henning (2012)
Thailand	Tuicomepee *et al.* (2012)
Turkey	Dogan (2000)
Uganda	Senyonyi *et al.* (2012)
United Kingdom	Dryden *et al.* (2000)
United States of America	Kaplan and Gladding (2011); Neimeyer and Diamond (2011)
Venezuela	Montilla and Smith (2009)
Zimbabwe	Richards *et al.* (2012)

counselling in different countries. The following sections of this chapter are based on an analysis of the main themes occurring in these papers. It is unfortunate that not all countries are represented in this list. Nevertheless, there is a sufficient coverage to provide a reasonable picture of the current international status of counselling.

The struggle for recognition

A consistent theme that emerges from almost all of the accounts of counselling in different countries, is the challenge to ensure that the professional role and status of counselling is recognized by the public, the legal system and the state. In some countries, such as Costa Rica and Denmark, counselling services are well established, but are largely subsumed into other professional domains, such as psychology or social work. In the UK, counselling is also well established, and has a distinct identity, but has yet to be awarded statutory recognition. In many other countries, counsellors are struggling to achieve any kind of recognition or status at all, whether formal or informal. In many of these countries, such as China or India, there are examples of local initiatives that have been successful in raising the profile of counselling in a specific city or region without leading to developments on a national scale.

The situation in the USA is of particular interest. In the USA, counselling as a professional is highly regulated, widely used by the public and effectively integrated into education, health and welfare services. However, Kaplan and Gladding (2011) report that an American Counseling Association taskforce found that there is a perception within the profession that it is too fragmented. Potential clients are confused by the existence of different professional associations and job titles for marital counselling, drug counselling, school counselling and so on. In the USA, therefore, even though a high level of external recognition and status has been achieved, it would appear that there is still a need to consolidate and defend that position.

The importance of counselling in schools

A review of international patterns of counselling practice reveals that counselling is provided in a wide range of settings, and in response to a wide range of problems: marital, drug and alcohol dependency, family violence, HIV/AIDS, bereavement, refugees, private practice, etc. However, the area of counselling specialism that is most widely represented is counselling in schools. The pattern seems to be that the initial development of a counselling profession in a country is almost always based on counselling in schools. The existence of a schools counselling service then serves to underpin the further growth of counselling in a country, by providing a nucleus of reasonably well-paid jobs and professional recognition. In addition, people who have received counselling at school, or who have met counsellors and been able to observe how counselling may have helped their friends, enter adult life with the attitude that counselling is a normal thing to do, and not the province of people who are 'mentally ill'.

Similarly, counselling in schools plays into the strengths of counselling as a specialism, because effective work with young people is likely to take a flexible, pluralistic stance rather than being locked into a specific model or treatment protocol. Counselling in schools is also not dominated by diagnostic labels, and instead adopts a developmental perspective. Looking, again, at the example of the USA as the most mature counselling professional environment, it can be seen that the recent emphasis on social advocacy within the profession in the USA has been largely driven (but not entirely) by schools counsellors working with disadvantaged children in deprived neighbourhoods.

Counselling as a response to social breakdown

There are some striking examples within the counselling international literature of the rapid development of counselling services in response to crisis. For instance, in Botswana, Kenya, South Africa and Uganda the HIV/AIDS epidemic was a trigger for the development of counselling for people with AIDS and their partners, and then for AIDS orphans. A lot of the time, these new counselling services were funded and organized by international charities and non-governmental organizations. Over time, the existence of these services contributed to the professionalization of counselling, the availability of training and the eventual expansion of counselling into other areas of social life.

Similar trajectories can be observed in countries affected by acts of war (such as Palestine) or internal oppression and economic collapse (such as Zimbabwe). These examples can be regarded as present-day case studies that mirror the conditions for the initial emergence of counselling in North America and Europe in the first half of the twentieth century. In the 'first world', the earliest forms of counselling comprised responses to crises in education and marriage. The more recent 'third world' examples represent responses to different sorts of crises. Nevertheless, the same basic process seems to be occurring: there is some form of social change that disrupts the functioning of relationships between people and causes emotional distress. The pre-existing sources of support (such as religious groups, or the government) are unable, for whatever reason, to construct a satisfactory solution to these difficulties. The provision of counselling, as an inexpensive, non-judgemental form of help that basically tries to activate mutual support, hope and resourcefulness in those who are enmeshed in the crisis, then becomes an obvious step to take. Over time, counselling then becomes institutionalized as a routine service that is not only available to people who are the victims of social crises, but is open to anyone.

The need to adapt to local cultural norms

A further recurring theme in accounts of the state of counselling in different parts of the world, is the assertion that it is necessary to adapt established models of counselling to local cultural beliefs and norms. For instance, counselling in Thailand is strongly influenced by Buddhist ideas and practices. Counselling in Costa Rica aims to build a 'progressive third-world psychology'. In some countries, there are substantial cultural barriers to the acceptance of Western counselling methods. Carson et al. (2009: 51–2), writing about counselling in India, compiled a long list of reasons why people in their country were unlikely to use counselling:

- a concern that people who work with welfare and social service related agencies are not necessarily trustworthy;

- widespread stigma in Indian society associated with mental health problems; mental illness in India is associated with shame and guilt, and as a result families will try to keep others from learning of their problems;

- the prevalent belief among many Indians that things do not really change (fatalism), either within people or in family systems ('no matter what you do, the outcome will be the same');

- rural versus urban differences among clients and/or between clients and counsellors, as well as the hierarchical nature of relationships (caste, family, marital, gender-based and vocational), can be detrimental to the counselling process;

- the assumption that only women and children (not men) would attend counselling in a society that is still generally patriarchal;

- the long history of Indians using traditional healers and healing methods (e.g., yoga, gurus, shamans, and temple rituals);

- fear of having Western values imposed on citizens of an Eastern culture when employing therapeutic approaches that have largely originated in the West.

This list cannot be understood as merely reflecting the difference between Western 'individualist' culture and the more 'collectivist' cultures that still exist elsewhere in the world. Instead, many of the issues highlighted by Carson *et al.* (2009) refer to specific cultural factors, that are associated with a particular cultural group. The challenge of adapting counselling to cultural belief and norms is not merely an issue in developing countries and non-Christian countries. For at least 20 years, reviews of the priorities for the counselling profession in the USA have clearly identified responsiveness to cultural diversity as an area for improvement.

Optimism about the future

Most of the international contributors whose papers have been cited in this chapter are optimistic about the future. No matter how great the cultural or economic barriers, there is a sense that counselling has something important to offer, and will continue to go from strength to strength. There is probably less optimism in countries such as the UK and USA, where counselling is well established but is under threat in two ways. Counselling in these countries has been badly affected by the financial crisis that began in 2008. Particularly in the UK, where a great deal of counselling has been delivered by not-for-profit charitable agencies, the economic squeeze has tipped many agencies over the line between 'just getting by' and 'sinking'.

In addition, health care systems in the UK and USA, and then other therapy providers influenced by these organizations, have adopted evidence-based practice policies that favour forms of therapy that are based on protocols developed for specific psychiatric disorders. As a flexible, client-focused, frontline service, counselling has increasingly been squeezed out of some areas of work.

Conclusions

It is, of course, necessary to be cautious when interpreting the material presented in the studies reported in this chapter. It is hard to do justice to the past, present and future of counselling in a country in the space of a journal article, and it is possible that the conclusions reached by some authors may not be shared by colleagues in their country. There is also a great deal of fascinating information included in these articles that could not be included in this brief chapter. What can be learned from the study of counselling in different countries? One obvious conclusion is that counselling approaches as a whole have not yet developed a satisfactory way of taking account of cultural factors and cultural identity. It is as though some kind of fundamental shift needs to take place at a theoretical level, in the direction of a more culturally informed image of the person and the healing process.

A further area of learning is that there appear to be cycles of development and change within the evolution of counselling in each country or region. Some countries are at the stage reached by counselling in the USA about 100 years ago – lots of energy and optimism, many people wanting to be involved, a clear sense of mission. By contrast, the longest established counselling professional groups may be viewed as being involved in a bit of a struggle to find sources of energy and passion, and are perhaps waiting for a renewed sense of mission to become apparent.

Suggested further reading

An extended discussion of themes and issues explored in this chapter can be found in: Moodley *et al.* (2012) *Handbook of Counselling and Psychotherapy in an International Context*.

References

Ablon, J.S. and Jones, E.E. (2002) Validity of controlled clinical trials of psychotherapy: findings from the NIMH treatment of depression collaborative program, *American Journal of Psychiatry*, 159, 775–83.

Ablow, R. (2008) Introduction: victorian emotions, *Victorian Studies*, 50, 375–7.

Abram, D. (1996) *The Spell of the Sensuous: Perception and Language in a More-than-Human World*. New York: Vintage Books.

Achenbach, G.B. (1995) Philosophy, philosophical practice, and psychotherapy. In R. Lahav (ed.) *Essays on Philosophical Counseling*. Lanham, MD: University Press of America.

Adams, C. (ed.) (1993) *Ecofeminism and the Sacred*. New York: Continuum.

Adams, K. (1998) *The Way of the Journal: A Journal Therapy Workbook for Healing*. Brooklandville, MD: Sidran Press.

Agazarian, Y. and Peters, R. (1981) *The Visible and Invisible Group: Two Perspectives on Group Psychotherapy and Group Process*. London: Tavistock/Routledge.

Agnew, R.M., Harper, H., Shapiro, D.A. and Barkham, M. (1994) Resolving a challenge to the therapeutic relationship: a single-case study, *British Journal of Medical Psychology*, 67, 155–70.

Agnew-Davies, R. (1999) Learning from research into the counselling relationship. In C. Feltham (ed.) *Understanding the Counselling Relationship*. London: Sage.

Ainsworth, M.D.S., Blehar, M.C., Waters, E. and Wall, S. (1978) *Patterns of Attachment: A Psychological Study of the Strange Situation*. Hillsdale, NJ: Erlbaum.

Al-Abdul-Jabbar, J. and Al-Issa, I. (eds) (2000) Psychotherapy in Islamic society. In I. Al-Issla (ed.) *Al-Junon: Mental Illness in the Islamic World*. Madison, IN: International Universities Press.

Albee, G.W. (1977) The Protestant ethic, sex and psychotherapy, *American Psychologist*, 32, 150–61.

Aldarondo, E. (ed.) (2007) *Advancing Social Justice through Clinical Practice*. New York: Routledge.

Aldridge, S. (2011) *Counselling – An Insecure Profession? A Sociological and Historical Analysis*. PhD thesis, University of Leicester. Available at https://lra.le.ac.uk/handle/2381/10261 (accessed 5 March 2013).

Alexander, F. and French, T.M. (1946) *Psychoanalytic Therapy. Principles and Applications*. New York: Ronald Press.

Alexander, L.B. and Luborsky, L. (1986) The Penn Helping Alliance scales. In L.D. Greenberg and W.M. Pinsot (eds) *The Psychotherapeutic Process: A Research Handbook*. New York: Guilford Press.

Al-Issa, I. (ed.) (2000a) *Al-Junon: Mental Illness in the Islamic World*. Madison, WI: International Universities Press.

Al-Issa, I. (2000b) Mental illness in medieval Islamic society. In I. Al-Issla (ed.) *Al-Junon: Mental Illness in the Islamic World*. Madison, WI: International Universities Press.

Allen, J. (1999) Responding to unemployment and inqualities in income and health, *European Journal of Psychotherapy, Counselling and Health*, 2, 143–52.

Allen, J.G. and Fonagy, P. (eds) (2006) *Handbook of Mentalization-Based Treatment*. Chichester: Wiley.

Amendt-Lyon, N. (2001) Art and creativity in Gestalt Therapy, *Gestalt Review*, 5, 225–48.

American Association for Counseling and Development (1988) *Ethical Standards*. Alexandria, VA: AACD.

American Counseling Association (2013) *Counseling Knowledge Centre*. Alexandria, VA: American Counseling Association. Available at http://www.counseling.org/knowledge-center/counseling-knowledge-center (accessed 3 March 2013).

American Psychiatric Association (1994) *Diagnostic and Statistical Manual of Mental Disorders*, 4th edn. Washington, DC: American Psychiatric Association.

American Psychological Association, Committee of Training in Clinical Psychology (1947) Recommended graduate training program in clinical psychology, *American Psychologist*, 2, 539–58.

Anastasi, A. (1992) What counselors should know about the use and interpretation of psychological tests, *Journal of Counseling and Development*, 70, 610–15.

Anderson, H. (2007) Dialogue: people creating meaning with each other and finding ways to go on. In H. Anderson and D. Gehart (eds) *Collaborative Therapy: Relationships and Conversations that Make a Difference*. New York: Routledge.

Anderson, H. and Gehart, D. (eds) (2007) *Collaborative Therapy: Relationships and Conversations that Make a Difference*. New York: Routledge.

Anderson, H. and Goolishian, H. (1992) The client is the expert: a not-knowing approach to therapy. In S. McNamee and K.J. Gergen (eds) *Therapy as Social Construction*. London: Sage.

Anderson, P., Jacobs, C. and Rothbaum, B.O. (2004) Computer-supported cognitive-behavioral treatment of anxiety disorders, *Journal of Clinical Psychology*, 60, 253–87.

Anderson, S. and Brownlie, J. (2011) Build it and they will come? Understanding public views of 'emotions talk' and the talking therapies, *British Journal of Guidance and Counselling*, 39, 53–66.

Anderson, S., Brownlie, J. and Given, L. (2009) Therapy culture? Attitudes toward emotional support in Britain. In A. Park, J. Curtice, K, Thomson, M. Phillips and E. Clery (eds) *British Social Attitudes: The 25th Report*. London: Sage.

Anderson, T. and Strupp, H.H. (1996) The ecology of psychotherapy research, *Journal of Consulting and Clinical Psychology*, 64, 776–82.

Anderson, T., Ogles, B.M., Patterson, C.L., Lambert, M.J. and Vermeersch, D.A. (2009) Therapist effects: facilitative interpersonal skills as a predictor of therapist success, *Journal of Clinical Psychology*, 65, 755–68.

Angus, L. (1996) An intensive analysis of metaphor themes in psychotherapy. In J.S. Mio and A. Katz (eds) *Metaphor: Pragmatics and Applications*. New York: Erlbaum.

Angus, L.E. and Rennie, D.L. (1988) Therapist participation in metaphor generation: collaborative and noncollaborative styles, *Psychotherapy*, 25, 552–60.

Angus, L.E. and Rennie, D.L. (1989) Envisioning the representational world: the client's experience of metaphoric expressiveness in psychotherapy, *Psychotherapy*, 26, 373–9.

Ankarberg, P. and Falkenstrom, F. (2008) Treatment of depression with antidepressants is primarily a psychological treatment, *Psychotherapy Theory, Research, Practice, Training*, 45, 329–39.

Annesley, P. and Coyle, P. (1998) Dykes and psychs: lesbian women's experience of clinical psychology, *Changes*, 16, 247–58.

Anthony, K. (2003) The use and the role of technology in counselling and psychotherapy. In S. Goss and K. Anthony (eds) *Techology in Counselling and Psychotherapy: A Practitioner's Guide*. London: Palgrave Macmillan.

Antony, M., Ledley, D.R. and Heimberg, R.G. (eds) (2005) *Improving Outcomes and Preventing Relapse in Cognitive-Behavioral Therapy*. New York: Guilford Press.

Antze, P. (1976) The role of ideologies in peer psychotherapy organisations, *Journal of Applied Behavioral Science*, 12, 323–46.

Aponte, H.J. and Kissil, K. (2012) "If I can grapple with this I can truly be of use in the therapy room": using the therapist's own emotional struggles to facilitate effective therapy, *Journal of Marital and Family Therapy*, 15 Dec (Epub ahead of print).

Appelbaum, A. (1973) Psychological mindedness: word, concept and essence, *International Journal of Psychoanalysis*, 54, 35–46.

Appignanesi, L. (2008) *Mad, Bad and Sad: A History of Women and the Mind Doctors from 1800*. London: Virago.

Araya, R., Flynn, T., Rojas, G., Fritsch, R. and Simon, G. (2006) Cost-effectivenss of a primary care treatment programme for depression in low-income women in Santiago, Chile, *American Journal of Psychiatry*, 163, 1379–87.

Archer, R., Forbes, V., Metcalfe, C. and Winter, D. (2000) An investigation of the effectiveness of a voluntary sector psychodynamic counselling service, *British Journal of Medical Psychology*, 73, 401–2.

Argyle, M. and Kendon, A. (1967) The experimental analysis of social performance. In L Berkowitz (ed.) *Advances in Experimental Social Psychology*, Vol 3. New York: Academic Press.

Aries, P. (1962) *Centuries of Childhood*. New York: Vintage Books.

Aronson, T.A. (1989) A critical review of psychotherapeutic treatments of the borderline personality: historical trends and future directions, *Journal of Nervous and Mental Disease*, 177, 511–28.

Arsenian, J. and Arsenian, J.M. (1948) Tough and easy cultures: a conceptual analysis, *Psychiatry*, 11, 377–85.

Arthern, J. and Madill, A. (1999) How do transition objects work? The therapist's view, *British Journal of Medical Psychology*, 72, 1–21.

Artman, L.K. and Daniels, J.A. (2010) Disability and psychotherapy practice: cultural competence and practical tips, *Professional Psychology: Research and Practice*, 41, 442–8.

Atieno Okech, J.E. and Kimemia, M. (2012) Professional counseling in Kenya: history, current status, and future trends, *Journal of Counseling and Development*, 90, 107–12.

Atkinson, D.R. (1985) Research on cross-cultural counseling and psychotherapy: a review and update of reviews. Pedersen, P. (ed.) *Handbook of Cross-Cultural Counseling and Psychotherapy*. New York: Praegar.

Atwood, G. and Stolorow, R.D. (1993) *Faces in a Cloud: Intersubjectivity in Personality Theory*, 2nd edn. Northvale, NJ: Jason Aronson.

Austin, K.M., Moline, M.E. and Williams, G.T. (1990) *Confronting Malpractice: Legal and Ethical Dilemmas in Psychotherapy*. London: Sage.

Austin, W., Rankel, M., Kagan, L., Bergum, V. and Lemermeyer, G. (2005) To stay or to go, to speak of to stay silent, to act or not to act: moral distress as experienced by psychologists, *Ethics and Behavior*, 15, 197–212.

Aveline, M.O. (1995) How I assess for focal therapy. In C. Mace (ed.) *The Art and Science of Assessment in Psychotherapy*. London: Routledge.

Aveline, M. and Shapiro, D.A. (eds) (1995) *Research Foundations for Psychotherapy Practice*. Chichester: Wiley.

Axline, V. (1971) *Dibs: In Search of Self*. Harmondsworth: Penguin.

Ayllon, T. and Azrin, N.H. (1965) The measurement and reinforcement of behavior of psychotics, *Journal of the Experimental Analysis of Behavior*, 8, 357–83.

Ayllon, T. and Azrin, N.H. (1968) *The Token Economy*. New York: Appleton Century Crofts.

Ayyash-Abdo, H. and Mukallid, S. (2010) School counseling in Lebanon: past, present, and future, *Journal of Counseling and Development*, 88, 13–17.

Bados, A., Balaguer, G. and Saldaña, C. (2007) The efficacy of cognitive–behavioral therapy and the problem of drop-out, *Journal of Clinical Psychology*, 63, 585–92.

Bakan, D. (1966) *The Duality of Human Existence: An Essay on Psychology and Religion*. Chicago, IL: Rand McNally.

Baker, S.B., Daniels, T.G. and Greeley, A.T. (1990) Systematic training of graduate level counselors: narrative and meta-analytic reviews of three programmes, *Counseling Psychologist*, 18, 355–421.

Bakhtin, M. (1981) *The Dialogical Imagination: Four Essays* (M. Holquist, trans.). Austin, TX: University of Texas Press.

Baldwin, C. (1992) *One to One: Self-Understanding Through Journal Writing*. New York: Evans Publisher.

Ballinger, L. and Wright, J. (2007) 'Does class count?' Social class and counselling, *Counselling and Psychotherapy Research*, 7, 157–63.

Balmforth, J. (2006) Clients' experiences of how perceived differences in social class between a counsellor and client affect the therapeutic relationship. In G. Proctor, M. Cooper, P. Sanders and B. Malcolm (eds) *Politicizing the Person-centred Approach: An Agenda for Social Change*. Ross-on-Wye: PCCS Books.

Balmforth, J. and Elliott, R. (2012) 'I never talked about, ever': a comprehensive process analysis of a significant client disclosure event in therapy, *Counselling and Psychotherapy Research*, 12, 2–12.

Bandura, A. (1971) Psychotherapy based upon modeling principles. In A.E. Bergin and S.L. Garfield (eds) *Handbook of Psychotherapy and Behavior Change: An Empirical Analysis*. New York: Wiley.

Bandura, A. (1977) *Social Learning Theory*. Englewood Cliffs, NJ: Prentice Hall.

Bannister, D. and Fransella, F. (1985) *Inquiring Man*, 3rd edn. London: Routledge.

Barak, A., Hen, L., Boniel-Nissim, M. and Shapira, N. (2008) A comprehensive review and meta-analysis of the effectiveness of internet-based psychotherapeutic interventions, *Journal of Technology in Human Services*, 26, 109–60.

Barber, J.P., Liese, B.S. and Abrams, M.J. (2003) Development of the Cognitive Therapy Adherence and Competence Scale, *Psychotherapy Research*, 13, 205–18.

Barber, P. (2012) *Facilitating Change in Groups and Organisations – A Gestalt Approach to Mindfulness*. Oxford: Libri Press.

Barker, C. and Pistrang, N. (2002) Psychotherapyand social support: integrating research on psychological helping, *Clinical Psychology Review*, 22, 363–81.

Barker, C., Pistrang, N. and Elliott, R. (2002) *Research Methods in Clinical Psychology: An Introduction for Students and Practitioners*. Chichester: Wiley.

Barker, M., Vossler, A. and Langbridge, D. (eds) (2010) *Understanding Counselling*. London: Sage.

Barkham, M. (1992) Research on integrative and eclectic therapy. In W. Dryden (ed.) *Integrative and Eclectic Therapy: A Handbook*. Buckingham: Open University Press.

Barkham, M. and Shapiro, D.A. (1989) Towards resolving the problem of waiting lists: psychotherapy in two-plus-one sessions, *Clinical Psychology Forum*, 23, 15–18.

Barkham, M. and Shapiro, D.A. (1990a) Brief psychotherapeutic interventions for jobrelated distress: a pilot study of prescriptive and exploratory therapy, *Counselling Psychology Quarterly*, 3, 133–47.

Barkham, M. and Shapiro, D.A. (1990b) Exploratory therapy in two-plus-one sessions: a research model for studying the process of change. In G. Lietaer, J. Rombauts and R. Van Balen (eds) *Client-centered and Experiential Psychotherapy in the Nineties*. Leuven: Leuven University Press.

Barkham, M., Stiles, W.B., Hardy, G.E. and Field, S.F. (1996) The assimilation model:theory, research and practical guidelines. In W. Dryden (ed.) *Research in Counselling and Psychotherapy: Practical Applications*. London: Sage.

Barkham, M., Guthrie, E., Hardy, G.E., Margison, F.R. and Shapiro, D.A. (eds) (1998) *Psychodynamic-interpersonal Therapy: Foundations of Research-based Practice*. London: Sage.

Barkham, M., Margison, F., Leach, C. *et al.* (2001) Service profiling and outcomes benchmarking using the CORE OM: toward practice based evidence in the psychological therapies, *Journal of Consulting and Clinical Psychology*, 69, 184–96.

Barkham, M., Connell, J., Stiles, *et al.* (2006) Dose-effect relations and responsive regulation of treatment duration: the good enough level. *Journal of Consulting and Clinical Psychology*, 74, 160–7.

Barlow, D.H. and Cerny, A. (1988) *Psychological Treatment of Panic*. New York: Guilford Press.

Barlow, D.H., Allen, L.B. and Choate, M.L. (2004) Toward a unified treatment for emotional disorders. *Behavior Therapy*, 35, 205–30.

Barlow, D.H., Hayes, S.C. and Nelson, R.O. (1984) *The Scientist Practitioner: Research and Accountability in Clinical and Educational Settings*. New York: Pergamon.

Barnett, J.E., Wise, E.H., Johnson-Greene, D. and Bucky, S. (2007) Informed consent: too much of a good thing or not enough? *Professional Psychology: Research and Practice*, 38, 179–86.

Barnett, M. (2007) What brings you here? An exploration of the unconscious motivations of those who choose to train and work as psychotherapists and counselors, *Psychodynamic Practice*, 13, 257–74.

Barrett, M.S. and Berman, J.S. (2001) Is psychotherapy more effective when therapists disclose information about themselves? *Journal of Consulting and Clinical Psychology*, 69, 597–603.

Barrett-Lennard, G. (1962) Dimensions of therapist response as causal factors in therapeutic change, *Psychological Monographs*, 76 (whole number 562).

Barrett-Lennard, G. (1979) The client-centered system unfolding. In F.J. Turner (ed.) *Social Work Treatment: Interlocking Theoretical Approaches*, 2nd edn. New York: Free Press.

Barrett-Lennard, G. (1981) The empathy cycle – refinement of a nuclear concept, *Journal of Counseling Psychology*, 28, 91–100.

Barrett-Lennard, G.T. (1986) The Relationship Inventory now: issues and advances in theory, method and use. In L.S. Greenberg and W.M. Pinsof (eds) *The Psychotherapeutic Process: A Research Handbook*. New York: Guilford.

Barrett-Lennard, G. (1998) *Carl Rogers' Helping System: Journey and Substance*. London: Sage.

Bartlett, A., King, M. and Phillips, P. (2001) Straight talking: an investigation of the attitudes and practice of psychoanalysts and psychotherapists in relation to gays and lesbians, *British Journal of Psychiatry*, 179, 545–9.

Barton, J and Pretty, J. (2010) What is the best dose of nature and green exercise for improving mental health? A multi-study analysis, *Environmental Science and Technology*, 44, 3947–55.

Bashe, A., Anderson, S.K., Handelsman, M.M. and Klevansky, R. (2007) An acculturation model for ethics training: the ethics autobiography and beyond, *Professional Psychology: Science and Practice*, 38, 60–7.

Bates, C.M. and Brodsky, A.M. (1989) *Sex in the Therapy Hour: A Case of Professional Incest*. New York: Guilford Press.

Bates, Y. (ed.) (2006) *Shouldn't I be Feeling Better by Now? Client Views of Therapy*. London: Palgrave.

Batten, S.V. (2011) *Essentials of Acceptance and Commitment Therapy*. London: Sage.

Batten, S., Follette, V., Hall, M. and Palm, K. (2002) Physical and psychological effects of written disclosure among sexual abuse survivors, *Behavior Therapy*, 33,107–22.

Bauman, Z. (2004) *Wasted lives. Modernity and its Outcasts*. Cambridge: Polity Press

Baumeister, R. F. (1987) How the self became a problem: a psychological review of historical research, *Journal of Personality and Social Psychology*, 52(1), 163–76.

Bayer, R. (1987) *Homosexuality and American Psychiatry: The Politics of Diagnosis*, 2nd edn. Princeton, NJ: Princeton University Press.

Bayley, J. (2001) *Elegy for Iris*. New York: Picador.

Beahrs, J.O. and Gutheil, T.G. (2001) Informed consent in psychotherapy, *American Journal of Psychiatry*, 158, 4–10.

Beail, N., Warden, S., Morsley, K. and Newman, D. (2005) Naturalistic evaluation of the effectiveness of psychodynamic psychotherapy with adults with intellectual disabilities, *Journal of Applied Research in Intellectual Disabilities*, 18, 245–51.

Beauchamp, T.L. and Childress, J.F. (1979) *Principles of Biomedical Ethics*. Oxford: Oxford University Press.

Beck, A. (1976) *Cognitive Therapy and the Emotional Disorders*. Harmondsworth: Penguin.

Beck, A. and Weishaar, M. (1989) Cognitive therapy. In A. Freeman, K.M. Simon, L.E. Beutler and H. Arkowitz (eds) *Comprehensive Handbook of Cognitive Therapy*. New York: Plenum Press.

Beck, A.T. and Emery, O. (1985) *Anxiety Disorders and Phobias: A Cognitive Perspective*. New York: Basic Books.

Beck, A.T. and Freeman, A.F. (1990) *Cognitive Therapy of Personality Disorders*. New York: Guilford Press.

Beck, A., Rush, A.G., Shaw, B.F. and Emery, G. (1979) *Cognitive Therapy of Depression*. New York: Guilford Press.

Beck, A., Wright, F.D., Newman, C.P. and Liese, B.S. (1993) *Cognitive Therapy of Substance Abuse*. New York: Guilford Press.

Beck, B., Halling, S., McNabb, M., Miller, D., Rowe, J.O. andSchulz, J. (2005) On navigating despair: stories from psychotherapists, *Journal of Religion and Health*, 44, 187–205.

Beckstead, A.L. and Morrow, S.L. (2004) Mormon clients' experiences of conversion therapy: the need for a new treatment approach, *The Counseling Psychologist*, 32, 651–90.

Bedi, R.P., Davis, M.D. and Williams, M. (2005) Critical incidents in the formation of the therapeutic alliance from the client's perspective, *Psychotherapy: Theory, Research, Practice, Training*, 41, 311–23.

Behr, H. and Hearst, L. (2005) *Group-analytic Psychotherapy: A Meeting of Minds*. New York: Wiley.

Benish, S.G., Quintana, S. and Wampold, B.E. (2011) Culturally adapted psychotherapy and the legitimacy of myth: A direct-comparison meta-analysis, *Journal of Counseling Psychology*, 58, 279–89.

Benjamin, J. (2004) Beyond doer and done to: an intersubjective view of thirdness. *Psychoanalytic Quarterly*, 73, 5–46.

Benjamin, L.S. (1987) The use of Structural Analysis of Social Behavior (SASB) to guide intervention in psychotherapy. In J.C.Anchin and D.J. Kiesler (eds) *Handbook of Interpersonal Psychotherapy*. New York: Pergamon.

Bennett-Levy, G., Butler, M., Fennell, M., Hackmann, A., Mueller, M. and Westbrook, D. (eds) (2004) *Oxford Guide to Behavioural Experiments in Cognitive Therapy*. Oxford: Oxford University Press.

Bennis, W. and Shepard, H. (1956) A theory of group development, *Human Relations*, 9, 415–57.

Bennun, I. (1985) Unilateral marital therapy. In W. Dryden (ed.) *Marital Therapy in Britain, Volume 2. Context and Therapeutic Approaches*. London: Harper and Row.

Bentley, A. (1997) The psychological effects of homelessness and their impact on the development of a counselling relationship, *Counselling Psychology Quarterly*, 10(2), 195– 210.

Bentley, A. (1994) Counselling and homelessness, *Counselling*, 5, 132–4.

Berg, A.L., Sandahl, C. and Clinton, D. (2008) The relationship of treatment preferences and experiences to outcome in generalized anxiety disorder (GAD), *Psychology and Psychotherapy: Theory, Research and Practice*, 81, 247–59.

Berg, I.K. and Kelly, S. (2000) *Building Solutions in Child Protective Services*. New York: Norton.

Berger, M. (1983) Toward maximising the utility of consumer satisfaction as an outcome. In M.J. Lambert, E.R. Christensen and S.S. DeJulio (eds) *The Assessment of Psychotherapy Outcome*. New York: Wiley.

Berger, R. (2004) Therapeutic aspects of nature therapy, *Therapy through the Arts – the Journal of the Israeli Association of Creative and Expressive Therapies*, 3, 60–9.

Berger, R. (2005) Using contact with nature, creativity and rituals as a therapeutic medium with children with learning difficulties, *Emotional and Behavioural Difficulties*, 11(2), 135–46.

Berger, R. and McLeod, J. (2006) Incorporating nature into therapy: a framework for practice, *Journal of Systemic Therapies*, 25(2), 80–94.

Bergin, A.E. (1980) Psychotherapy and religious values, *Journal of Consulting and Clinical Psychology*, 48, 95–105.

Bergner, R.M. (1999) Status enhancement: A further path to therapeutic change, *American Journal of Psychotherapy*, 53, 201–14.

Berman, E. (2006) Israeli psychotherapists and the Israeli-Arab conflict. In N. Totton (ed.) *The Politics of Psychotherapy: New Perspectives*. Maidenhead: Open University Press.

Berman, G., Jonides, J. and. Kaplan, S. (2008) The cognitive benefits of interacting with nature, *Psychological Science*, 19, 1207–12.

Berman, J.S. and Norton, N.C. (1985) Does professional training make a therapist more effective? *Psychological Bulletin*, 98, 401–7.

Berman, L. (1993) *Beyond the Smile: the Therapeutic Use of the Photograph*. London: Routledge.

Berne, E. (1964) *Games People Play*. London: Penguin.

Berne, E. (1961/2001) *Transactional Analysis in Psychotherapy*. London: Souvenir Press.

Berne, E. (1975) *What Do You Say After You Say Hello? The Psychology of Human Destiny*. London: Corgi.

Bernstein, B. (1972) Social class, language and socialization. In P.P. Giglioli (ed.) *Language and Social Context*. Harmondsworth: Penguin.

Bettelheim, B. (1983) *Freud and Man's Soul*. London: Chatto and Windus.

Beutler, L.E. (1983) *Eclectic Psychotherapy: A Systematic Approach*. New York: Pergamon.

Beutler, L.E. (2001) From experiential to eclectic psychotherapist. In M.R.Goldfried (ed.) *How Therapists Change: Personal and Professional Reflections*. Washington, DC: American Psychological Association.

Beutler, L.E. and Clarkin, J.F. (1990) *Systematic Treatment Selection: Toward Targeted Therapeutic Interventions*. New York: Brunner/Mazel.

Beutler, L.E., Crago, M. and Arizmendi, T.G. (1986) Therapist variables in psychotherapy process and outcome. In S.L. Garfield and A.E. Bergin (eds) *Handbook of Psychotherapy and Behavior Change*, 3rd edn. New York: Wiley.

Beutler, L.E., Engle, D., Daldrup, D. Bergan, R., Meredith, J. and Merry, K. (1991) Predictors of differential response to cognitive, experiential, and self-directed psychotherapeutic procedures, *Journal of Consulting and Clinical Psychology*, 59, 333–40.

Beutler, L.E., Malik, M., Alimohamed, A. and Harwood, T.M. (2004) Therapist variables. In M.J. Lambert (ed.) *Bergin and Garfield's Handbook of Psychotherapy and Behavior Change*, 5th edn. New York: Wiley.

Beutler, L.E., Consoli, A.J. and Lane, G. (2005) Systematic treatment selection and prescriptive psychotherapy. In J.C. Norcross. and M.R. Goldfried (eds) *Handbook of Psychotherapy Integration*. New York: Oxford University Press.

Bieling, P.J. and Kuyken, W. (2003) Is cognitive case formulation science or science fiction? *Clinical Psychology: Science and Practice*, 10, 52–69.

Bieling, P.J., McCabe, R.E. and Antony, M.M. (2006) *Cognitive-behavioural Therapy in Groups*. New York: Guilford Press.

Bike, D.H., Norcross, J.C and Schatz, D.M. (2009) Processes and outcomes of psychotherapists' personal therapy: replication and extension 20 years later, *Psychotherapy Theory, Research, Practice, Training*, 46, 19–31.

Binder, J.L. and Henry, W.P. (2010) Developing skills in managing negative process. In J.C. Muran and J.P. Barber (eds) *The Therapeutic Alliance: An Evidence-Based Approach to Practice*. New York: Guilford Press.

Binder, J.L. and Strupp, H.H. (1997) 'Negative process': a recurrently discovered and underestimated facet of therapeutic process and outcome in the individual psychotherapy of adults, *Clinical Psychology: Science and Practice*, 4, 121–39.

Binswanger, L. (1963) *Being-in-the-World*. New York: Basic Books.

Bion, W. (1961) *Experiences in Groups*. London: Tavistock.

Birtchnell, J. (1999) *Relating in Psychotherapy: The Application of a New Theory.* London: Brunner Routledge.

Blackburn, S. (1999) *Think.* Oxford: Oxford University Press.

Blagys, M. and Hilsenroth, M.J. (2000) Distinctive features of short-term psychodynamic-interpersonal psychotherapy: a review of the comparative psychotherapy process literature, *Clinical Psychology: Science and Practice,* 7, 211–23.

Blatt, S.J., Sanislow, C.A., Zuroff, D.C. and Pilkonis, P.A. (1996) Characteristics of effective therapists: further analysis of data from the National Institute of Mental Health Treatment of Depression Collaborative Research Program, *Journal of Consulting and Clinical Psychology,* 64(6), 1276–84.

Bloch, S., Crouch, E. and Reibstein, J. (1981) Therapeutic factors in group psychotherapy, *Archives of General Psychiatry,* 38, 519–26.

Boal, A. (1979) *Theatre of the Oppressed.* London: Pluto Press.

Boal, A. (1995) *The Rainbow of Desire.* London: Routledge.

Bobes, T. and Rothman, B. (2002) *Doing Couple Therapy: Integrating Theory with Practice.* New York: Norton.

Bohart, A. (1990) Psychotherapy integration from a client-centered perspective. In G. Lietaer, J. Rombauts and R. Van Balen (eds) *Client-centered and Experiential Therapy in the Nineties.* Leuven: Leuven University Press.

Bohart, A. (1995) The person-centred psychotherapies. In A. Gurman and S. Messer (eds) *Essential Psychotherapies: Theory and Practice.* New York: Guilford Press.

Bohart, A. (2000) The client is the most important common factor: clients' self-healing capacities and psychotherapy, *Journal of Psychotherapy Integration,* 10, 127–48.

Bohart, A. and Tallman, K. (1996) The active client: therapy as self-help, *Journal of Humanistic Psychology,* 3, 7–30.

Bohart, A.C. and Tallman, K. (1998) The person as an active agent in experiential therapy. In L.S. Greenberg, J.C. Watson and G. Lietaer (eds) *Handbook of Experiential Psychotherapy.* New York: Guilford Press.

Bohart, A.C. and Tallman, K. (1999) *How Clients Make Therapy Work: The Process of Active Self-healing.* Washington, DC: American Psychological Association.

Bohart, A., Humphrey, A., Magallanes, M., Guxman, R., Smiljanich, K. and Aguallo, S. (1993) Emphasizing the future in empathy responses, *Journal of Humanistic Psychology,* 33, 12–29.

Bolton, G. (2008) "Writing is a way of saying things I can't say"— therapeutic creative writing: a qualitative study of its value to people with cancer cared for in cancer and palliative healthcare, *Medical Humanities,* 3, 40–6.

Bolton, G., Howlett, S., Lago, C. and Wright, J.K. (eds) (2004) *Writing Cures: An Introductory Handbook of Writing in Counselling and Psychotherapy.* London: Brunner-Routledge.

Bond, T. (1992) Ethical issues in counselling in education, *British Journal of Guidance and Counselling,* 20, 51–63.

Bond, T. (2000) *Standards and Ethics for Counselling in Action,* 2nd edn. London: Sage.

Bond, T. (2008) The Elephant at Gitmo. *Counterpunch,* 12 February.

Bond, T. (2009) *Standards and Ethics for Counselling in Action,* 3rd edn. London: Sage.

Boorstein, S. (ed.) (1996) *Transpersonal Psychotherapy,* 2nd edn. Albany, NY: State University of New York.

Bor, R. and Miller, R. (2003) *Doing Therapy Briefly.* London: Palgrave Macmillan.

Bordin, E.S. (1979) The generalizability of the psychoanalytic concept of working alliance, *Psychotherapy: Theory, Research and Practice,* 16, 252–60.

Borrill, J. and Foreman, E.I. (1996) Understanding cognitive change: a qualitative study of the impact of cognitive-behavioural therapy on fear of flying, *Clinical Psychology and Psychotherapy,* 3(1), 62–74.

Borthwick, A., Holman, C., Kennard, D., McFetridge, M., Messruther, K. and Wilkes, J. (2001) The relevance of moral treatment to contemporary health care, *Journal of Mental Health,* 10, 427–39.

Boss, M. (1957) *Psychoanalysis and Daseinanalysis.* New York: Basic Books.

Bott, D. (1994) A family systems framework for intervention with individuals, *Counselling Psychology Quarterly,* 7(2), 105–15.

Bourguignon, E. (1979) *Psychological Anthropology: An Introduction to Human Nature and Cultural Differences.* New York: Holt, Rinehart and Winston.

Bower, P and Gilbody, S. (2005) Stepped care in psychological therapies: access effectiveness and efficiency. Narrative literature review, *British Journal of Psychiatry,* 186, 11–17.

Bowker, P. and Richards, B. (2004) Speaking the same language?: A qualitative study of therapists' experiences of working in English with proficient bilingual clients, *Psychodynamic Practice,* 10, 459–78.

Bowlby, J. (1969) *Attachment*. London: Hogarth.

Bowlby, J. (1973) *Separation, Anxiety and Anger*. London: Hogarth.

Bowlby, J. (1980) *Loss, Sadness and Depression*. London: Hogarth.

Bowlby, J. (1988) *A Secure Base: Clinical Applications of Attachment Theory*. London: Routledge.

Bowlby, J., Robertson, J. and Rosenbluth, D. (1952) A two year old goes to hospital, *Psychoanalytic Studies of the Child*, 7, 82–94.

Bowling, A. (2001) *Measuring Disease: A Review of Disease Specific Quality of Life Measurement Scales: A Review of Disease-specific Quality of Life Measurement Scales*. Maidenhead: Open University Press.

Bowling, A. (2004) *Measuring Health. A Review of Quality of Life Scales*. Maidenhead: Open University Press.

Boy, A.V. and Pine, G.J. (1980) Avoiding counselor burnout through role renewal, *Personnel and Guidance Journal*, 59, 161–3.

Boy, A.V. and Pine, G.J. (1982) *Client-centered Counseling: A Renewal*. Boston, MA: Allyn and Bacon.

Bozarth, J. (1984) Beyond reflection: emergent modes of empathy. In R.F. Levant and J.M. Shlien (eds) *Client-centered Therapy and the Person-centered Approach: New Directions in Theory, Research and Practice*. New York: Praeger.

Bozarth, J. (1998) *Person-Centered Therapy: A Revolutionary Paradigm*. Ross-on-Wye: PCCS Books.

Bozarth, J. (2002) Nondirectivity in the person-centered approach: critique of Kahn's critique, *Journal of Humanistic Psychology*, 42, 78–83.

Braaten, E.B., Otto, S. and Handelsman, M.M. (1993) What do people want to know about psychotherapy? *Psychotherapy*, 30, 565–70.

Brabender, V., Smolar. A. and Fallon, A. (2004) *Essentials in Group Therapy*. New York: Wiley.

Bragesjo, M., Clinton, D. and Sandell, R. (2004) The credibility of psychodynamic, cognitive, and cognitive-behavioural psychotherapy is a randomly selected sample of the general public, *Psychology and Psychotherapy: Theory, Research and Practice*, 77, 297–307.

Brammer, L., Shostrom, E. and Abrego, P.J. (1989) *Therapeutic Psychology: Fundamentals of Counseling and Psychotherapy*. Englewood Cliffs, NJ: Prentice Hall.

Breckenridge, K. (2000) Physical touch in psychoanalysis: a closet phenomenon? *Psychoanalytic Inquiry*, 20, 2–20.

Breger, L. and McGaugh, J. (1965) Critique and reformulation of 'learning-theory' approaches, *Psychological Bulletin*, 63, 338–58.

Bretherton, I. and Waters, E. (eds) (1985) Growing points of attachment theory and research, *Monographs of the Society for Research in Child Development*, 50 (Serial 209). Chicago, IL: Chicago Univesity Press.

Bright, J.I., Baker, K.D. and Neimeyer, R.A. (1999) Professional and paraprofessional group treatments for depression: a comparison of cognitive-behavioral and mutual support interventions, *Journal of Consulting and Clinical Psychology*, 67, 491–501.

Brightman, B.K. (1984) Narcissistic issues in the training experience of the psychotherapist, *International Journal of Psychoanalytic Psychotherapy*, 10, 293–371.

Brinegar, M.G., Salvi, L.M., Stiles, W.B. and Greenberg, L.S. (2008) The case of Lisa and the assimilation model: The interrelatedness of problematic voices, *Psychotherapy Research*, 18: 657–66.

Brink, D.C. and Farber, B.A. (1996) Analysis of Carl Rogers' therapeutic interventions. In B. A. Farber, D.C. Brink and P.M. Raskin (eds) *The Psychotherapy of Carl Rogers: Cases and Commentary*. New York: Guilford Press.

Brislin, D.C. (2008) Reaching for independence: counseling implications for youth with spina bifida, *Journal of Counseling and Development*, 86, 34–8.

British Association for Counselling (1977) *Counselling News No. 16*. Rugby: BAC.

British Association for Counselling (1992) *16th Annual Report 1991/92*. Rugby: BAC.

British Association for Counselling and Psychotherapy (2001a) *Membership Survey*. Rugby: British Association for Counselling and Psychotherapy.

British Association for Counselling and Psychotherapy (2001b) *Ethical Framework for Good Practice in Counselling and Psychotherapy*. Rugby: British Association for Counselling and Psychotherapy.

British Association for Counselling and Psychotherapy (2009) *Accreditation of Training Courses*. Lutterworth: British Assoication for Counselling and Psychotherapy.

British Association for Counselling and Psychotherapy (2012) *Statement of Ethical Practice (1). 18 September 2012*. Lutterworth: BACP. Available at http://www.bacp.co.uk/admin/structure/files/pdf/10302_sep_1_p2_web.pdf (accessed 5 April 2013).

British Association for Counselling and Psychotherapy (2013) *BACP Definition of Counselling*. Lutterworth: BACP. Available at http://www.bacp.co.uk/ (accessed 3 March 2013).

Britton, R. (1989) The missing link: parental sexuality in the Oedipus complex. In J. Steiner (ed.) *The Oedipus Complex Today*. London: Karnac.

Bromley, E. (1983) Social class issues in psychotherapy. In D. Pilgrim (ed.) *Psychology and Psychotherapy. Current Issues and Trends*. London: Routledge.

Broverman, I.K., Broverman, D., Clarkson, F.E., Rosencrantz, P.S. and Vogel, S.R. (1970) Sex-role stereotypes and clinical judgements of mental health, *Journal of Consulting and Clinical Psychology*, 34, 1–7.

Brown, C. and Augusta-Scott, T. (eds) (2007) *Narrative Therapy: Making Meaning Meaning, Making Lives*. Thousand Oaks, CA: Sage.

Brown. L.S. (2005) Feminist therapy with therapists: egalitarian and more. In J.D. Geller, J.C Norcross and D.E.Orlinsky (eds) *The Psychotherapist's own Psychotherapy: Patient and Clinician Perspectives*. New York: Oxford University Press.

Brown, L.S. (2007) Empathy, genuineness – and the dynamics of power: a feminist responds to Rogers, *Psychotherapy: Theory, Research, Practice, Training*, 44, 257–9.

Brown, L.S. (2009) *Feminist Therapy*. Washington, DC: American Psychological Association.

Brownell, P. (ed.) (2008) *Handbook for Theory, Research and Practice in Gestalt Therapy*. Newcastle: Cambridge Scholars Publishing.

Bruner, J.S. (1966) *Toward a Theory of Instruction*. Cambridge, MA: Harvard University Press

Bruner, J.S. (1973) *Beyond the Information Given*. New York: Norton.

Bruner, J. (1990) *Acts of Meaning*. Cambridge, MA: Harvard University Press.

Brunner, J. (2000) Will, desire and experience: etiology and ideology in the German and Austrian medical discourse on war neuroses, 1914–1922, *Transcultural Psychiatry*, 37, 295–320.

Buchalter, S.I. (2009) *Art Therapy Techniques and Applications*. London: Jessica Kingsley.

Buckley, P., Karasu, T.B. and Charles, E. (1981) Psychotherapists view their personal therapy, *Psychotherapy: Theory, Research and Practice*, 18, 299–305.

Buckroyd, J. (2011) *Understanding your Eating. How to Eat and not Worry about It*. Maidenhead: Open University Press.

Buckroyd, J. and Rother, S. (2007) *Therapeutic Groups for Obese Women: A Group Leader's Handbook*. Oxford: Wiley-Blackwell.

Budman, S. and Gurman, A. (1988) *Theory and Practice of Brief Psychotherapy*. London: Hutchinson.

Bugental, J. (1964) The Third Force in psychology, *Journal of Humanistic Psychology*, 4, 19–25.

Bugental, J. (1976) *The Search for Existential Identity*. San Francisco, CA: Jossey-Bass.

Buhrke, R.A., Ben-Ezra, L.A., Hurley, M.E. and Ruprecht, L.J. (1992) Content analysis and methodological critique of articles concerning lesbian and gay male issues in counseling journals, *Journal of Counseling Psychology*, 39, 91–9.

Bunting, M. (2004) *Willing Slaves: How the Overwork Culture is Ruling our Lives*. London: HarperCollins.

Burckell, L.A. and Goldfried, M.R. (2006) Therapist qualities preferred by sexual-minority clients, *Psychotherapy: Theory, Research, Practice, Training*, 45, 32–49.

Burgess, M. (2005) *Overcoming Chronic Fatigue: A Self-help Guide using Cognitive-Behavioural Techniques*. London: Constable and Robinson.

Burkard, A.W., Knox, S., Groen, M., Perez, M. and Hess, S. (2006) European American therapist self-disclosure in cross-cultural counseling, *Journal of Counseling Psychology*, 53, 15–25.

Burke, B.L., Arkowitz, A. and Menchola, M. (2003) The efficacy of motivational interviewing: a meta-analysis of controlled clinical trials, *Journal of Consulting and Clinical Psychology*, 71, 843–61.

Burks, H.M. and Stefflre, B. (1979) *Theories of Counseling*, 3rd edn. New York: McGraw-Hill.

Burlingame, G.M. and Barlow, S.H. (1996) Outcome and process differences between professional and nonprofessional therapists in time-limited group psychotherapy, *International Journal of Group Psychotherapy*, 46, 455–78.

Burns, D.D. (2000) *The Feeling Good Handbook*. New York: Penguin.

Burns, G. (1998) *Nature-Guided Therapy: Brief Intervention Strategies for Health and Well-Being*. London: Taylor and Francis.

Burns, G. (ed.) (2010) *Happiness, Healing, Enhancement: Your Casebook Collection for applying Positive Psychology in Therapy*. New York: Wiley.

Burr, V. (2003) *Social Constructionism*. London: Routledge.

Burstow, B. (1992) *Radical Feminist Therapy: Working in the Context of Violence*. Newbury Park, CA: Sage.

Burton, A. (1970) The adoration of the patient and its disillusionment, *American Journal of Psychoanalysis*, 29, 194–204.

Burton, M.V. and Topham, D. (1997) Early loss experiences in psychotherapists. Church of England clergy, patients assessed for psychotherapy, and scientists and engineers, *Psychotherapy Research*, 7, 275–300.

Butler, C., O'Donovan, A. and Shaw, E. (eds) (2009) *Sex, Sexuality and Therapeutic Practice: A Manual for Therapists and Trainers*. London: Routledge.

Butler, G. (1999) *Overcoming Social Anxiety and Shyness: A Self-Help Guide using Cognitive-Behavioural Techniques*. London: Constable and Robinson.

Butt, T. (2008) *George Kelly: the Psychology of Personal Constructs*. London: Palgrave Macmillan.

Caccia, J. and Watson, J.P. (1987) A counselling centre and a psychiatric out-patient clinic, *Bulletin of the Royal College of Psychiatrists*, 11, 182–4.

Cahalan, W. (1995) The earth is our real body: Cultivating ecological groundedness in Gestalt therapy, *Gestalt Journal*, 18, 99–100.

Cain, D.J. (2002) Defining characteristics, history and evolution of humanistic psychotherapies. In D.J. Cain and J. Seeman (eds) *Humanistic Psychotherapies: Handbook of Research and Practice*. Washington, DC: American Psychological Association.

Cain, D.J. and Seeman, J. (eds) (2002) *Humanistic Psychotherapies: Handbook of Research and Practice*. Washington, DC: American Psychological Association.

Cameron, J. (1994) *The Artist's Way. A Course in Discovering and Recovering your Creative Self*. London: Souvenir Press.

Campbell, L.F. and Smith, T.P. (2003) Integrating self-help books into psychotherapy, *Journal of Clinical Psychology*, 59, 177–86.

Caplan, E. (1998) *Mind Games: American Culture and the Birth of Psychotherapy*. Berkeley, CA: University of California Press.

Cardemil, E.V. and Battle, C.L. (2003) Guess who's coming to therapy? Getting comfortable with conversations about race and ethnicity in psychotherapy, *Professional Psychology: Research and Practice*, 34, 278–86.

Carey, T.A. (2011) As you like it: adopting a patient-led approach to psychological treatments, *Journal of Public Mental Health*, 10, 6–16.

Carey, T.A. and Mullan, R.J. (2004) What is Socratic questioning? *Psychotherapy: Theory, Research and Practice*, 41, 217–26.

Carkhuff, R. (1969) *Helping and Human Relations*, Volume 2. New York: Holt, Rinehart and Winston.

Carr, A. (2012) *Family Therapy: Concepts, Process and Practice*, 3rd edn. Oxford: Wiley-Blackwell.

Carrell, S.E. (2001) *The Therapist's Toolbox*. Thousand Oaks, CA: Sage.

Carroll, M. (1988) Counselling supervision: the British context, *Counselling Psychology Quarterly*, 1, 387–96.

Carroll, M. (1996) *Workplace Counselling*. London: Sage.

Carson, D.K., Jain, S. and Ramirez, S. (2009) Counseling and family therapy in India: evolving professions in a rapidly developing nation, *International Journal for the Advancement of Counseling*, 31, 45–56.

Carvalho, R. (1990) Psychodynamic therapy: the Jungian approach. In W. Dryden (ed.) *Individual Therapy: A Handbook*. Milton Keynes: Open University Press.

Casement, P. (1982) Some pressures on the analyst for physical contact during the reliving of an early childhood trauma, *International Review of Psycho-Analysis*, 9, 279–86.

Casement, P. (1985) *On Learning from the Patient*. London: Tavistock.

Casement, P. (1990) *Further Learning from the Patient: The Analytic Space and Process*. London: Tavistock/Routledge.

Casement, P. (2000) The issue of touch: a retrospective overview, *Psychoanalytic Inquiry*, 20, 160–84.

Cashdan, S. (1988) *Object Relations Therapy: Using the Relationship*. New York: W. W. Norton.

Cassidy, J. and Shaver, P.R. (eds) (1999) *Handbook of Attachment: Theory, Research and Clinical Applications*. New York: Guilford.

Cavanagh, K. and Shapiro, D.A. (2004) Computer treatment for common mental health problems, *Journal of Clinical Psychology*, 60, 239–51.

Cavanagh, K., Zack, J.S., Shapiro, D.A. and Wright, J.H. (2003) Computer programs for psychotherapy. In S. Goss and K. Anthony (eds) *Techology in Counselling and Psychotherapy: A Practitioner's Guide*. London: Palgrave Macmillan.

Cavanagh, K., Shapiro, D.A., Van Den Berg, S., Swain, S., Barkham, M. and Proudfoot, J. (2006) The effectiveness of computerized cognitive behavioural therapy in routine care, *British Journal of Clinical Psychology*, 45, 499–514.

Cepeda, L.M. and Davenport, D.S. (2006) Person-centered therapy and solution-focused brief therapy: an integration of present and future awareness, *Psychotherapy: Theory, Research, Practice, Training*, 43, 1–12.

Cerney, M.S. (1990) Reduced fee or free psychotherapy: uncovering the hidden issues, *Psychotherapy Patient*, 7, 53–65.

Chang, D.F. and Berk, A. (2009) Making cross-racial therapy work: A phenomenological study of clients' experiences of cross-racial therapy, *Journal of Counseling Psychology*, 56, 521–36.

Chang, D.F. and Yoon, P. (2011) Ethnic minority clients' perceptions of the significance of race in cross-racial therapy relationships, *Psychotherapy Research*, 21, 567–82.

Chaplin, J. (1988) *Feminist Counselling in Action*. London: Sage.

Charny, I.W. (1986) What do therapists worry about? A tool for experiential supervision. In F.W. Kaslow (ed.) *Supervision and Training: Models, Dilemmas and Challenges*. New York: Haworth Press.

Chechele, P.J. and Stofle, G. (2003) Individual therapy online via email and Internet Relay Chat. In S. Goss and K. Anthony (eds) *Techology in Counselling and Psychotherapy: A Practitioner's Guide*. London: Palgrave Macmillan.

Cherniss, C. and Krantz, D.L. (1983) The ideological community as an antidote to burnout in the human services. In B.A. Farber (ed.) *Stress and Burnout in the Human Service Professions*. New York: Pergamon.

Chesler, P. (1972) *Women and Madness*. New York: Doubleday.

Childs-Gowell, E. (2000) *Reparenting Schizophrenics: The Cathexis Experience*. New York: iUniverse.

Chodorow, N. (1978) *The Reproduction of Mothering*. Berkeley: University of California Press.

Christensen, A. and Jacobson, N.S. (1994) Who (or what) can do psychotherapy: the status and challenge of nonprofessional therapies, *Psychological Science*, 5, 8–14.

Christopher, J.C. (1996) Counseling's inescapable moral visions, *Journal of Counseling and Development*, 75, 17–25.

Clark, D.M. (2011) Implementing NICE guidelines for the psychological treatment of depression and anxiety disorders: The IAPT experience, *International Review of Psychiatry*, 23, 318–27.

Clarkson, P. (1990) A multiplicity of psychotherapeutic relationships, *British Journal of Psychotherapy*, 7(2), 148–63.

Clarkson, P. (1995) *The Therapeutic Relationship*. London: Whurr.

Claxton, G. (ed.) (1996) *Beyond Therapy: The Impact of Eastern Religions on Psychological Theory and Practice*. Sturminster Newton: Prism Press.

Clulow, C. (ed.) (2000) *Adult Attachment and Couple Psychotherapy: The 'Secure Base' in Practice and Research*. London: Brunner Routledge.

Clulow, C. and Mattinson, J. (1989) *Marriage Inside Out. Understanding Problems of Intimacy*. Harmondsworth: Penguin.

Cocks, G. (1997) *Psychotherapy in the Third Reich: The Goring Institute*, 2nd edn. New Brunswick, NJ: Transaction.

Cohen, L.H., Sargent, M.H. and Sechrest, L.B. (1986) Use of psychotherapy research by professional psychologists, *American Psychologist*, 41, 198–206.

Cohen, L.J. (1994) Phenomenology of therapeutic reading with implications for research and practice of bibliotherapy, *The Arts in Psychotherapy*, 21(1), 37–44.

Cohn, H.W. (1997) *Existential Thought and Therapeutic Practice*. London: Sage.

Cohn, H.W. and du Plock, S. (eds) (1995) *Existential Challenges to Psychotherapeutic Theory and Practice*. London: Society for Existential Analysis Press.

Coleman, E. (1982) *Developmental Stages of the Coming Out Process*. New York: Haworth.

Collier, C. (2013) Counseling in Costa Rica: a comparative study, *International Journal for the Advancement of Counseling*, 35: 64–70.

Coltart, N. (1988) Diagnosis and assessment for suitability for psycho-analytical psychotherapy, *British Journal of Psychotherapy*, 4(2), 127–34.

Coltart, N.E.C. (1986) 'Slouching towards Bethlehem' . . . or thinking the unthinkable in psychoanalysis. In G. Kohon (ed.) *The British School of Psychoanalysis: The Independent Tradition*. London: Free Association.

Combs, A.W. (1989) *A Theory of Therapy. Guidelines for Counseling Practice*. London: Sage.

Conte, H.R. and Ratto, R. (1997) Self-report measures of psychological mindedness. In M. McCallum and W.E. Piper (eds) *Psychological Mindedness: A Contemporary Understanding*. Mahwah, NJ: Lawrence Erlbaum.

Coon, J.T., Boddy, K., Stein, K., Whear, R., Barton, J. and Depledge, M.H. (2011) Does participating in physical activity in outdoor natural environments have a greater effect on physical and mental wellbeing than physical activity indoors? A systematic review, *Environmental Science and Technology*, 45, 1761–72.

Cooper, M. (2003) *Existential Therapies*. London: Sage.

Cooper, M. (2004) Towards a relationally-oriented approach to therapy: empirical analysis, *British Journal of Guidance and Counselling*, 32, 451–60.

Cooper, M. (2005) Therapists' experiences of relational depth: a qualitative interview study, *Counselling and Psychotherapy Research*, 5, 87–95.

Cooper, M. (2008) *Essential Research Findings in Counselling and Psychotherapy: The Facts are Friendly*. London: Sage.

Cooper, M. and McLeod, J. (2007) A pluralistic framework for counselling and psychotherapy: implications for research, *Counselling and Psychotherapy Research*, 7, 135–43.

Cooper, M. and McLeod, J. (2011) *Pluralistic Counselling and Psychotherapy*. London: Sage.

Cooper, Z. Fairburn, C.G. and Hawker, D.M. (2004a) *Cognitive-Behavioral Treatment of Obesity: A Clinician's Guide*. New York: Guilford Press.

Cooper, M., Mearns, D., Stiles, W.B., Warner, M. and Elliott, R. (2004b) Developing self-pluralistic perspectives within the person-centered and experiential approaches: a round-table dialogue, *Person-Centered and Experiential Psychotherapies*, 3, 176–191.

Cooper, M., O'Hara, M., Schmid, P.F. and Bohart, A. (eds) (2013) *The Handbook of Person-centred Psychotherapy and Counselling*. London: Palgrave Macmillan.

Cooter, R. (1981) Phrenology and the British alienists: 1825–1845. In A. Scull (ed.) *Mad-houses, Mad-doctors and Madmen*. Philadelphia, PA: University of Pennsylvania Press.

Copeland, S. (2000) New challenges for supervising in organisational contexts. In B. Lawton and C. Feltham (eds) *Taking Supervision Forward: Enquiries and Trends in Counselling and Psychotherapy*. London: Sage.

Corazon, S., Schilhab, T. and Stigsdotter, U. (2011) Developing the therapeutic potential of embodied cognition and metaphors in nature-based therapy: lessons from theory to practice, *Journal of Adventure Education and Outdoor Learning*, 11, 161–71.

Corey, G. (2000) *The Art of Integrative Counseling*. Belmont, CA: Wadsworth.

Corey, G. (2008) *Theory and Practice of Group Counseling*, 8th edn. Belmont, CA: Wadsworth.

Corey, G. (2010) *Theory and Practice of Group Counseling*, 8th edn. San Francisco, CA: Broadman and Holman.

Corey, G., Corey, M. and Callanan, P. (1993) *Issues and Ethics in the Helping Professions*, 4th edn. Pacific Grove, CA: Brooks/Cole.

Corey, G., Corey, M.S., Callanan, P. and Russell, J.M. (2004) *Group Techniques*, 3rd edn. Belmont, CA: Wadsworth.

Corin, E. (1998) The thickness of being: intentional worlds, strategies of identity, and experience among schizophrenics, *Psychiatry*, 61, 133–46.

Cormack, J. (2009) Counselling marginalised young people: a qualitative analysis of young homeless people's views of counselling, *Counselling and Psychotherapy Research*, 9, 71–7.

Cornell, A.W. (1993) Teaching focusing with five steps and four skills. In D. Brazier (ed.) *Beyond Carl Rogers*. London: Constable.

Cornell, A.W. (1996) *The Power of Focusing: A Practical Guide to Emotional Self-Healing*. Oakland, CA: New Harbinger.

Cornell, W.F. and Hargaden, H. (2005) *From Transactions to Relations: The Emergence of a Relational Tradition in Transactional Analysis.* London: Haddon Press.

Cornforth, S. (2001) Culture: the song without words, *Counselling and Psychotherapy Research*, 1, 194–9.

Costa, L. and Altekruse, M. (1994) Duty-to-warn guidelines for mental health counselors. *Journal of Counseling and Development*, 72, 346–50.

Costin, C. and Johnson, C.L. (2002) Been there, done that: clinicians' use of personal recovery in the treatment of eating disorders, *Eating Disorders*, 10, 293–303.

Coursey, R. Alford, J. and Safarjan, B. (1997) Significant advances in understanding and treating serious mental illness, *Professional Psychology: Research and Practice*, 28, 205–16.

Coyle, A., Milton, M. and Annesley, P. (1999) The silencing of gay and lesbian voices in psychotherapeutic texts and training, *Changes*, 17, 132–41.

Craighead, L.W., McNamara, K. and Horan, J.J. (1984) Perspectives on self-help and bibliography: you are what you read. In S.D. Brown and R.W. Lent (eds) *Handbook of Counseling Psychology*. New York: Wiley.

Cramer, D. (1992) *Personality and Psychotherapy: Theory, Pratice and Research.* Buckingham: Open University Press.

Crandall, R. and Allen, R. (1981) The organisational context of helping relationships. In T.A. Wills (ed.) *Basic Processes in Helping Relationships*. New York: Academic Press.

Crawley, J. and Grant, J. (2007) *Couple Therapy: The Self in the Relationship.* London: Palgrave Macmillan.

Crits-Christoph, P. and Gallop, R. (2006) Therapist effects in the National Institute of Mental Health Treatment of Depression Collaborative Research Program and other research studies, *Psychotherapy Research*, 16, 173–5.

Crits-Christoph, P., Cooper, A. and Luborsky, L. (1988) The accuracy of therapists' interpretations and the outcome of dynamic psychotherapy, *Journal of Consulting and Clinical Psychology*, 56, 490–5.

Crits-Christoph, P., Gibbons, M.B.C., Crits-Christoph, K., Narducci, J., Schamberger, M. and Gallop, R. (2006) Can therapists be trained to improve their alliances? A preliminary study of alliance-fostering psychotherapy, *Psychotherapy Research*, 16, 268–81.

Crocket, K., Drewery, W., McKenzie, W., Smith, L. and Winslade, J. (2004) Working for ethical research in practice, *International Journal of Narrative Therapy and Community Work*, 3, 61–6.

Crouan, M. (1994) The contribution of a research study toward improving a counselling service, *Couseling*, 5(10), 32–4.

Csiernik, R. (ed.) (2005) *Wellness and Work: Employee Assistance Programming in Canada.* Toronto: Canadian Scholars Press.

Cuijpers, P., Andersson, G., Donker, T. and van Straten, A. (2011) Psychological treatment of depression: Results of a series of meta-analyses, *Nordic Journal of Psychiatry*, 65, 354–64.

Cullen, C. (1988) Applied behaviour analysis: contemporary and prospective agenda. In G. Davey and C. Cullen (eds) *Human Operant Conditioning and Behaviour Modification*. London: Wiley.

Cummings, N.A. (2007) Interruption replaces termination in focused, intermittent psychotherapy throughout the life cycle. In W.T. O'Donohue, N.A. Cummings and J.T. Cummings (eds) *Clinical Strategies for Becoming a Master Psychotherapist*. San Diego, CA: Academic Press.

Cummings, N.A. (2008) Interruption replaces termination in focused, intermittent psychotherapy throughout the life cycle. In W.T. O'Donohue and M. Cucciare (eds) *Terminating Psychotherapy: A Clinican's Guide*. New York: Routledge.

Cummings, N.A. and Sayama, M. (1995) *Focused Psychotherapy: A Casebook of Brief, Intermittent Psychotherapy.* New York: Psychology Press.

Currie, C.L., Kuzmina, M.V. and Nadyuk, L. (2012) The Counseling Profession in Russia: Historical Roots, Current Trends, and Future Perspectives, *Journal of Counseling and Development*, 90, 488–92.

Cushman, P. (1990) Why the self is empty: toward a historically-situated psychology, *American Psychologist*, 45, 599–611.

Cushman, P. (1992) Psychotherapy to 1992: a historically situated interpretation. In D.K. Freedheim (ed.) *History of Psychotherapy: A Century of Change*. Washington, DC: American Psychological Association.

Cushman, P. (1995) *Constructing the Self, Constructing America: A Cultural History of Psychotherapy.* Reading, MA: Addison-Wesley.

Cushman, P. and Gilford, P. (1999) From emptiness to multiplicity: the self at the year 2000, *Psychohistory Review*, 27, 15–31.

Daines, B., Gask, L. and Howe, A. (2007) *Medical and Psychiatric Issues for Counsellors*, 2nd edn. London: Sage.

Dale, P., Allen, J. and Measor, L. (1998) Counselling adults who were abused as children: clients' perceptions of efficacy, client–counsellor communication, and dissatisfaction, *British Journal of Guidance and Counselling*, 26, 141–58.

Dalenberg, C.J. (2004) Maintaining the safe and effective therapeutic relationship in the context of distrust and anger: countertransference and complex trauma, *Psychotherapy: Theory, Research, Practice, Training*, 41, 438–47.

Dallos, R. and Draper, R. (2010) *An Introduction to Family Therapy: Systemic Theory and Practice*, 3rd edn. Maidenhead: Open University Press.

Daniluk, J.C. and Haverkamp, B.E. (1993) Ethical issues in counseling adult survivors of incest, *Journal of Counseling and Development*, 72, 16–22.

D'Ardenne, P. and Mahtani, A. (1989) *Transcultural Counselling in Action*. London: Sage.

das Nair, R. and Butler, C. (eds) (2012) *Intersectionality, Sexuality and Psychological Therapies: Working with Lesbian, Gay and Bisexual Diversity*. Oxford: Wiley-Blackwell.

Davanloo, H. (ed.) (1980) *Short-term Psychodynamic Psychotherapy*. New York: Jason Aronson.

Davenport, S., Hobson, R. and Margison, F. (2000) Treatment development in psychodynamic-interpersonal psychotherapy for chronic treatment-resistant schizophrenia: two single case studies, *British Journal of Psychotherapy*, 16, 287–312.

David, A.B. and Erickson, C.A. (1990) Ethnicity and the therapist's use of self, *Family Therapy*, 17, 211–16.

Davidson, K.P., Pennebaker, J.W., and Dickerson, S.S. (2000) Who talks? The social psychology of illness support groups, *American Psychologist*, 55, 205–17.

Davidson, K., Schwartz, A.R., Sheffield, D., McCord, R.S., Lepore, S.J. and Gerin, W. (2002) Expressive writing and blood pressure. In S.J. Lepore and J.M. Smyth (eds) *The Writing Cure*. Washington, DC: American Psychological Association.

Davidson, L., Harding, C. and Spaniol, L. (eds) (2005) *Recovery from Severe Mental Illnesses: Research Evidence and Implications for Practice*, Volume 1. Boston, MA: Boston University Center for Psychiatric Rehabilitation.

Davidson, L., Harding, C. and Spaniol, L. (eds) (2006) *Recovery from Severe Mental Illnesses: Research Evidence and Implications for Practice*, Volume 2. Boston, MA: Boston University Center for Psychiatric Rehabilitation.

Davidson, L. and Strauss, J.S. (1992) Sense of self in recovery from mental illness, *British Journal of Medical Psychology*, 65, 131–45.

Davies, D. (1996) Towards a model of gay affirmative therapy. In D. Davies and C. Neal (eds) *Pink Therapy: A Guide for Counsellors Working with Lesbian, Gay and Bisexual Clients*. Buckingham: Open University Press.

Davies, D. and Neal, C. (eds) (1996) *Pink Therapy: A Guide for Counsellors Working with Lesbian, Gay and Bisexual Clients*. Buckingham: Open University Press.

Davies, D. and Neal, C. (eds) (2000) *Therapeutic Perspectives on Working with Lesbian, Gay and Bisexual Clients*. Buckingham: Open University Press.

Davis, D.D. and Younggren, J.N. (2009) Ethical competence in psychotherapy termination, *Professional Psychology: Research and Practice*, 40, 572–8.

Davis, K. (1986) The process of problem (re)formulation in psychotherapy, *Sociology of Illness and Health*, 8, 44–74.

DeBerry, S. and Baskin, D. (1989) Termination criteria in psychotherapy: a comparison of private and public practice, *American Journal of Psychotherapy*, 43, 43–53.

Defife, D.A., Conklin, C.Z., Smith, J.A. and Poole, J. (2010) Psychotherapy appointment no-shows: rates and reasons, *Psychotherapy Theory, Research, Practice, Training*, 47, 413–17.

Delfin, P.E. (1978) Components of effective telephone intervention: a critical incidents analysis, *Crisis Intervention*, 9, 50–68.

Delgado-Romero, E.A., Galvan, N., Machino, P. and Rowland, M. (2005) Race and ethnicity in counselling and counseling psychology research: a 10-year review, *The Counseling Psychologist*, 33, 419–48.

DeLucia-Waack, J.L., Gerrity, D.A., Kalodner, C.R. and Riva, M. (eds) (2004) *Handbook of Group Counseling and Psychotherapy*. Thousand Oaks, CA: Sage.

Demos, J. (1997) Oedipus and America: historical perspectives on the reception of psychoanalysis in the United States. In J. Pfister and N. Schnog (eds) *Inventing the Psychological: Toward a Cultural History of Emotional Life in America*. New Haven, CN: Yale University Press.

den Boer, P.C., Wiersma, D., Russo, S., van den Bosch, R.J. (2005) Paraprofessionals for anxiety and depressive disorders. *Cochrane Database of Systematic Reviews* 2005, Issue 2. Art. No.: CD004688.

Denborough, D., Freedman, J. and White, C. (2008) *Strengthening Resistance: The Use of Narrative Practices in Responding to Genocide Survivors*. Adelaide: Dulwich Centre Publications.

DeSalvo, L.A. (2000) *Writing As a Way of Healing: How Telling Our Stories Transforms Our Lives*. Boston, MA: Beacon Press.

de Shazer, S. (1985) *Keys to Solution in Brief Therapy*. New York: Norton.

de Shazer, S. (1988) *Clues: Investigating Solutions in Brief Therapy*. New York: Norton.

de Shazer, S. (1991) *Putting Difference to Work*. New York: Norton.

de Shazer, S. (1994) *Words Were Originally Magic*. New York: Norton.

de Shazer, S., Dolan, Y. and Korman, H. (2007) *More than Miracles: The State of the Art of Solution-focused Therapy*. New York: Haworth Press.

DeWaele, J.P. and Harré, R. (1976) The personality of individuals. In R. Harre (ed.) *Personality*. Oxford: Blackwell.

Dewe, P. and Cooper, C.L. (2004) *Stress: A Brief History*. Oxford: Blackwell.

Dewe, P.J., O'Driscoll, M. and Cooper, C.J. (2010) *Coping with Work Stress: A Review and Critique*. Oxford: Wiley-Blackwell.

DiCaccavo, A. (2002) Investigating individuals' motivations to become counselling psychologists: the influence of early caretaking roles within the family, *Psychology and Psychotherapy: Theory, Research and Practice*, 75, 463–72.

Dickson, W. (1945) The Hawthorne Plan, *American Journal of Orthopsychiatry*, 15, 343–7.

Dickson, W. and Roethlisberger, F.J. (1966) *Counselling in an Organization*. Cambridge, MA: Harvard University Press.

Dissanayake, E. (1988) What Is Art For? Seattle, WA: University of Washington Press.

Dissanayake, E. (1992) *Homo Aestheticus: Where Art Comes From and Why*. New York: Free Press.

Dissanayake, E. (2000) *Art and Intimacy: How the Arts Began*. Seattle, WA: University of Washington Press.

Dixon, A.L. and Hansen, N.H. (2010) *Fortid, Ñutid, Fremtid* (past, present, future): professional counseling in Denmark, *Journal of Counseling and Development*, 88, 38–42.

Dobson, J.K.S. and Dozois, D.J.A. (2001) Historical and philosophical bases of the cognitive-behavioral therapies. In K.S. Dobson (ed.) *Handbook of Cognitive-behavioral Therapies*, 2nd edn. New York: Guilford Press.

Dobson, K. (ed.) (2001) *Handbook of Cognitive-Behavioral Therapies*. New York: Guilford Press.

Dobson, K. and Craig, K.D. (1996) *Advances in Cognitive–Behavioral Therapy*. London: Sage.

Dobson, K. and Khatri, N. (2000) Cognitive therapy: looking backward, looking forward, *Journal of Clinical Psychology*, 56, 907–23.

Dogan, S. (2000) The historical development of counseling in Turkey, *International Journal for the Advancement of Counselling*, 22, 57–76.

Doidge, N. (2007) *The Brain that Changes Itself. Stories of Personal Triumph from the Frontiers of Brain Science*. London: Penguin.

Dolan, Y.M. (1991) *Resolving Sexual Abuse: Solution Focused Therapy and Ericksonian Hypnosis for Adult Survivors*. New York: Norton.

Dolliver, R.H. (1991) Perls with Gloria re-viewed, *Journal of Counseling and Development*, 69, 299–304.

Doucette, P. (2004) Walk and talk: an intervention for behaviourally challenged youths, *Adolescence*, 39, 373–88.

Dowding, K. (ed.) (2011) *The Encyclopedia of Power*. Thousand Oaks, CA: Sage.

Downing, J.N. (2000) *Between Conviction and Uncertainty: Philosophical Guidelines for the Practicing Psychotherapist*. Albany, NY: State University of New York Press.

Doyle, K. (1997) Substance abuse counselors in recovery: implications for the ethical issue of dual relationships, *Journal of Counseling and Development*, 75, 428–32.

Draguns, J.G. (1996) Humanly universal and culturally distinctive: charting the course of cultural counseling. In P.B. Pedersen, J.G. Draguns, W.J. Lonner and J.E. Trimble (eds) *Counseling across Cultures*. London: Sage.

Dreier, O. (2000) Psychotherapy in clients' trajectories across contexts. In C. Mattingly and L. Garro (eds) *Narratives and the Cultural Construction of Illness and Healing*. Berkeley, CA: University of California Press.

Dreier, O. (2008) *Psychotherapy in Everyday Life*. New York: Cambridge University Press.

Drescher, J., D'Ercole, A. and Shoenberg, E. (2003) *Psychotherapy with Gay Men and Lesbians: Contemporary Dynamic Approaches*. New York: Routledge.

Dreyfus, H.L. (1989) The Dreyfus model of skill acquisition. In J. Burke (ed.) *Competency Based Education and Training*. London: Falmer Press.

Dryden, W. (ed.) (1987) *Key Cases in Psychotherapy*. London: Croom Helm.

Dryden, W. (ed.) (1991) *A Dialogue with John Norcross: Towards Integration*. Maidenhead: Open University Press.

Dryden, W. (ed.) (1996) *Developments in Psychotherapy: Historical Perspectives*. London: Sage.

Dryden, W. (2004a) *Rational Emotive Behavioural Counselling in Action*, 3rd edn. London: Sage.

Dryden, W. (2004b) *The Rational Emotive Behavioural Approach to Therapeutic Change*. London: Sage.

Dryden, W. (2005) The personal therapy experience of a Rational Emotive Therapist. In J.D. Geller, J.C Norcross and D.E.Orlinsky (eds) *The Psychotherapist's own Psychotherapy: Patient and Clinician Perspectives*. New York: Oxford University Press.

Dryden, W. and Barkham, M. (1990) The two-plus-one model: a dialogue, *Counselling Psychology Review*, 5, 5–18.

Dryden, W. and Spurling, L. (eds) (1989) *On Becoming a Psychotherapist*. London: Tavistock/Routledge.

Dryden, W. and Thorne, B. (1991) Approaches to the training of counsellors. In W. Dryden and B. Thorne (eds) *Training and Supervision for Counselling in Action*. London: Sage.

Dryden, W., Horton, I. and Mearns, D. (1995) *Issues in Professional Counsellor Training*. London: Cassell.

Dryden, W., Mearns, D. and Thorne, B. (2000) Counselling in the United Kingdom: past, present and future, *British Journal of Guidance and Counselling*, 8, 467–83.

Du Plock, S. (1997a) An innocent abroad? An example of brief student counselling. In S. Du Plock (ed.) *Case Studies in Existential Psychotherapy and Counselling*. Chichester: Wiley.

Du Plock, S. (ed.) (1997b) *Case Studies in Existential Psychotherapy and Counselling*. Chichester: Wiley.

Dudley, R. and Kuyken, W. (2006) Formulation in cognitive-behavioural therapy. In L. Johnstone and R. Dallos (eds) *Formulation in Psychology and Psychotherapy: Making Sense of People's Problems*. London: Routledge.

Dueck, A. and Reimer, K. (2003) Retrieving the virtues in psychotherapy: thick and thin discourse, *American Behavioral Scientist*, 47, 427–41.

Duhl, F.J., Kantor, D. and Duhl, B.S. (1973) Learning space and action in family therapy. In D. A. Bloch (ed.) *Techniques of Family Psychotherapy: A Primer*. New York: Grune and Stratton.

Duncan, B.L. (2010) Prologue. Saul Rosenzweig: the founder of common factors. In B.L. Duncan, S.D. Miller, B.E.Wampold and M.A. Hubble (eds) *The Heart and Soul of Change. Delivering what Works in Therapy*, 2nd edn. Washington, DC: American Psychological Association.

Duncan, B.L. and Miller, S.D. (2000) The client's theory of change: consulting the client in the integrative process, *Journal of Psychotherapy Integration*, 10, 159–87.

Duncan, B.L., Miller, S.D., Sparks, J.A., Claud, D.A., Reynolds, L.R., Brown, J. and Johnson, L.D. (2003) The Session Rating Scale: preliminary psychometric properties of a "working" alliance measure, *Journal of Brief Therapy*, 3, 3–12.

Duncan, B.L., Miller, S.D. and Sparks, J.A. (2004) *The Heroic Client: A Revolutionary Way to Improve Effectiveness Through Client-Directed, Outcome-Informed Therapy*. San Francisco, CA: Jossey-Bass.

Duncan, B.L., Miller, S.D., Wampold, B.E. and Hubble, M.A. (eds) (2010) *The Heart and Soul of Change. Delivering what Works in Therapy*, 2nd edn. Washington, DC: American Psychological Association.

Durlak, J.A. (1979) Comparative effectiveness of paraprofessional and professional helpers, *Psychological Bulletin*, 86, 80–92.

Durlak, J.A. (1981) Evaluating comparative studies of paraprofessional and professional helpers: a reply to Nietzel and Fisher, *Psychological Bulletin*, 89, 566–9.

Durre, L. (1980) Comparing romantic and therapeutic relationships. In K.S. Pope (ed.) *On Love and Losing. Psychological Perspectives on the Nature and Experience of Romantic Loss*. San Francisco, CA: Jossey-Bass.

Duvall, J. and Beres, L. (2011) *Innovations in Narrative Therapy. Connecting Practice, Training, and Research*. New York: W.W. Norton.

Dworkin, S.H. and Gutierrez, F. (1989) Introduction to special issue. Counselors be aware: clients come in every size, shape, color and sexual orientation, *Journal of Counseling and Development*, 68, 6–8.

Dyche, L. and Zayas, L.H. (1995) The value of curiosity and naivete for the cross-cultural psychotherapist, *Family Process*, 34, 389–99.

Eames, V. and Roth, A. (2000) Patient attachment orientation and the early working alliance: a study of patient and therapist reports of alliance quality and ruptures, *Psychotherapy Research*, 10, 421–34.

Edelwich, J. and Brodsky, A. (1991) *Sexual Dilemmas for the Helping Professional*, 2nd edn. New York: Brunner/Mazel.

Eells, T.D. (ed.) (2007) *Handbook of Psychotherapy Case Formulation*, 2nd edn. New York: Guilford Press.

Eells, T.D. and Lombart, K.G. (2003) Case formulation and treatment concepts among novice, experienced and expert cognitive-behavioural and psychodynamic therapists, *Psychotherapy Research*, 13, 187–204.

Eells, T.D, Lombart, K.G., Kendjelic, E.M., Turner, L.C. and Lucas, C.P. (2005) The quality of psychotherapy case formulations: a comparison of expert, experienced, and novice cognitive-behavioral and psychodynamic therapists, *Journal of Consulting and Clinical Psychology*, 73, 579–89.

Egan, G. (1984) People in systems: a comprehensive model for psychosocial education and training. In D. Larson (ed.) *Teaching Psychological Skills: Models for Giving Psychology Away*. Monterey, CA: Brooks/Cole.

Egan, G. (1994) *The Skilled Helper: A Systematic Approach to Effective Helping*, 5th edn. Belmont, CA: Brooks/Cole.

Egan, G. (2009) *The Skilled Helper: A Systematic Approach to Effective Helping*, 9th edn. Belmont, CA: Brooks/Cole.

Egan, S.J., Wade, T.D. and Shafran, R. (2011) Perfectionism as a transdiagnostic process: a clinical review, *Clinical Psychology Review*, 31, 203–12.

Eichenbaum, L. and Orbach, S. (1982) *Outside in, Inside out. Women's Psychology: A Feminist Psychoanalytic Approach*. Harmondsworth: Penguin.

Eichenbaum, L. and Orbach, S. (1984) *Understanding Women: A Feminist Psychoanalytic Approach*. London: Basic Books.

Elkin, I. (1999) A major dilemma in psychotherapy outcome research: disentangling therapists from therapies, *Clinical Psychology: Science and Practice*, 6, 10–32.

Elkin, I., Falconnier, L., Martinovich, Z. and Mahoney, C. (2006) Therapist effects in the National Institute of Mental Health Treatment of Depression Collaborative Research Program, *Psychotherapy Research*, 16, 161–72.

Ellenberger, H.F. (1970) *The Discovery of the Unconscious: The History and Evolution of Dynamic Psychiatry*. London: Allen Lane.

Elliott, R. (1983) 'That in your hands . . .': a comprehensive process analysis of a significant event in psychotherapy, *Psychiatry*, 46, 113–29.

Elliott, R. (1984) A discovery-oriented approach to significant change events in psychotherapy: interpersonal process recall and comprehensive process analysis. In L.N. Rice and L.S. Greenberg (eds) *Patterns of Change: Intensive Analysis of Psychotherapy Process*. New York: Guilford Press.

Elliott, R. (1986) Interpersonal Process Recall (IPR) as a psychotherapy process research method. In L.S. Greenberg and W.M. Pinsof (eds) *The Psychotherapeutic Process: A Research Handbook*. New York: Guilford Press.

Elliott, R. (1991) Five dimensions of therapy process, *Psychotherapy Research*, 1, 92–103.

Elliott, R. (1998) A guide to the empirically supported treatments controversy, *Psychotherapy Research*, 8, 115–25.

Elliott, R. (2002) The effectiveness of humanistic therapies: a meta-analysis. In D.J. Cain and J. Seeman (eds) *Humanistic Psychotherapies: Handbook of Research and Practice*. Washington, DC: American Psychological Association.

Elliott, R. (2010) Psychotherapy change process research: realizing the promise, *Psychotherapy Research*, 20, 123–35.

Elliott, R. and Freire, E. (2007) Classical person-centered and experiential perspectives on Rogers (1957), *Psychotherapy: Theory, Research, Practice, Training*, 44, 285–8.

Elliott, R. and Greenberg, L.S. (1997) Multiple voices in process-experiential therapy: dialogues between aspects of the self, *Journal of Psychotherapy Integration*, 7, 225–39.

Elliott, R. and Partyka, R. (2005) Personal therapy and growth work in experiential humanistic therapies. In J.D. Geller, J.C Norcross and D.E.Orlinsky (eds) *The Psychotherapist's own Psychotherapy: Patient and Clinician Perspectives.* New York: Oxford University Press.

Elliott, R. and Shapiro, D.A. (1992) Client and therapist as analyst of significant events. In S. G. Toukmanian and D.L. Rennie (eds) *Psychotherapy Process Research: Paradigmatic and Narrative Approaches.* London: Sage.

Elliott, R., Clark, C., Kemeny, V., Wexler, M.M., Mack, C. and Brinkerhoff, J. (1990) The impact of experiential therapy on depression: the first ten cases. In G. Lietaer, J. Rombauts and R. Van Balen (eds) *Client-centered and Experiential Psychotherapy in the Nineties.* Leuven: University of Leuven Press.

Elliott, R., Suter, P., Manford, J., Radpour-Markert, L., Siegel-Hinson, R., Layman, C. and Davis, K. (1996) A process-experiential approach to post-traumatic stress disorder. In R. Hutterer, G. Pawlowsky, P.F. Schmid and R. Stipsits (eds) *Client-centered and Experiential Psychotherapy: A Paradigm in Motion.* Frankfurt am Main: Peter Lang.

Elliott, R., Davis, K. and Slatick, E. (1998) Process-experiential therapy for post-traumatic stress difficulties. In L.S. Greenberg, G. Lietaer and J. Watson, *Handbook of Experiential Psychotherapy.* New York: Guilford Press.

Elliott, R., Watson, J., Goldman, R.N., and Greenberg, L.S. (2003) *Learning Emotion-Focused Therapy: The Process-Experiential Approach to Change.* Washington, DC: American Psychological Association.

Elliott, R., Greenberg, L.S. and Lietaer, G. (2004) Research on experiential psychotherapies. In M.J. Lambert (ed.) *Bergin and Garfield's Handbook of Psychotherapy and Behavior Change,* 5th edn. New York: Wiley.

Elliott, R., Partyka, R., Wagner, J., et al. (2009) An adjudicated hermeneutic single case efficacy design study of experiential therapy for panic/phobia, *Psychotherapy Research,* 19, 543–57.

Elliott, R., Greenberg, L.S., Watson, J., Timulak, L. and Freire, E. (2013) Research on experiential psychotherapies. In M.J. Lambert (ed.) *Bergin & Garfield's Handbook of Psychotherapy and Behavior Change,* 6th edn. New York: Wiley.

Elliott, T.E., Uswatte, G., Lewis, L. and Palmatier, A. (2000) Goal instability and adjustment to physical disability, *Journal of Counseling Psychology,* 47, 251–65.

Ellis, A. (1962) *Reason and Emotion in Psychotherapy.* New York: Lyle Stuart.

Ellis, A. (1973) *Humanistic Psychotherapy.* New York: McGraw-Hill.

Ellis, A. (1980) Psychotherapy and atheistic values: a response to A. E. Bergin's 'Psychotherapy and religious values', *Journal of Consulting and Clinical Psychology,* 48, 635–9.

Ellis, A. (1989) The history of cognition in psychotherapy. In A. Freeman, K.M. Simon, L.E. Beutler and H. Arkowitz (eds) *Comprehensive Handbook of Cognitive Therapy.* New York: Plenum Press.

Ellis, A. (1991) Comment on "Perls with Gloria re-viewed", *Journal of Counseling and Development,* 70, 353.

Ellsworth, L. (2007) *Choosing to Heal: Using Reality Therapy in the Treatment of Sexually Abused Children.* London: Routledge.

Elton-Wilson, J. (1996) *Time-conscious Counselling and Therapy.* Chichester: Wiley.

Emerson, J., Bertoch, M.R. and Checketts, K.T. (1994) Transactional Analysis ego state functioning, psychological disturbance, and client change, *Psychotherapy,* 31, 109–13.

Emmelkamp, P. (2005) Technological innovations in clinical assessment and psychotherapy, *Psychotherapy and Psychsomatics,* 74, 336–43.

Emrick, C. (1981) Nonprofessional peers as therapeutic agents. In M.H. Bean and N.E. Zinberg (eds) *Dynamic Approaches to the Understanding and Treatment of Alcoholism.* New York: Free Press.

Enns, C.Z. (1992) Toward integrating feminist psychotherapy and feminist philosophy, *Professional Psychology: Theory and Practice,* 23(6), 453–66.

Enns, C.Z., McNeilly, C.L., Corkery, J.M. and Gilbert, M.S. (1995) The debate about delayed memories of child sexual abuse: a feminist perspective, *The Counseling Psychologist,* 23, 181–279.

Epstein, N.B. and Baucom, D.H. (2002) *Enhanced Cognitive-behavioural Therapy for Couples: A Contextual Approach.* Washington, DC: American Psychological Association.

Epston, D. and White, M. (eds) (1992) *Experience, Contradiction, Narrative and Imagination.* Adelaide: Dulwich Centre Publications.

Epston, D., White, M. and Murray, K. (1992) A proposal for a re-authoring therapy: Rose's revisioning of her life and a commentary. In S. McNamee and K.J. Gergen (eds) *Therapy as Social Construction.* London: Sage.

Epston, D., Morris, F. and Maisel, R. (1995) A narrative approach to so-called anorexia/ bulimia. In K. Weingarten (ed.) *Cultural Resistance: Challenging Beliefs about Men, Women and Therapy*. New York: Haworth Press.

Erhard, R.L. and Sinai, M. (2012) The school counselor in Israel: an agent of social justice? *International Journal for the Advancement of Counselling*, 34, 159–73.

Erikson, E. (1950) *Childhood and Society*. New York: W.W. Norton.

Erskine, R.G. (1993) Inquiry, attunement, and involvement in the psychotherapy of dissociation, *Transactional Analysis Journal*, 23, 184–90.

Erskine, R. and Zalcman, M. (1979) The racket system: a model for racket anlysis, *Transactional Analysis Journal*, 23, 184–90.

Eskapa, R. (1992) Multimodal therapy. In W. Dryden (ed.) *Integrative and Eclectic Therapy: A Handbook*. Buckingham: Open University Press.

Esterson, A. (1998) Jeffrey Masson and Freud's seduction theory: a new fable based on old myths, *History of the Human Sciences*, 11, 1–21.

Esterson, E. (2002) The myth of Freud's ostracism by the medical community in 1896–1905: Jeffrey Masson's assault on truth, *History of Psychology*, 6, 115–34.

Etherington, K. (2000) *Narrative Approaches to Working with Adult Male Survivors of Child Sexual Abuse: The Client's, the Counsellor's and the Researcher's Story*. London: Jessica Kingsley.

Etherington, K. and Bridges, N. (2011) Narrative case study research: on endings and six session reviews, *Counselling and Psychotherapy Research*, 11, 11–22.

Eubanks-Carter, C., Burckell, L.A. and Goldfried, M.R. (2005) Enhancing therapeutic effectiveness with lesbian, gay, and bisexual clients, *Clinical Psychology: Science and Practice*, 12, 1–15.

Evans, C., Mellor-Clark, J., Margison, F. *et al.* (2000) CORE: Clinical Outcomes in Routine Evaluation, *Journal of Mental Health*, 9, 247–55.

Evans, K.M., Kincade, E.E. and Seem, S.R. (2010) *Introduction to Feminist Therapy: Strategies for Social and Individual Change*. Thousand Oaks, CA: Sage.

Evans, M. (2003) Christian counsellors' views on working with gay and lesbian clients: Integrating religious beliefs with counselling ethics, *Counselling and Psychotherapy Research*, 3, 55–60.

Evans, M. and Barker, M. (2010) How do you see me? Coming out in counselling, *British Journal of Guidance and Counselling*, 38, 375–91.

Eysenck, H.J. (1952) The effects of psychotherapy: an evaluation, *Journal of Consulting Psychology*, 16, 319–24.

Eysenck, H.J. (1970) A mish-mash of theories, *International Journal of Psychiatry*, 9, 140–6.

Fairbairn, R.D. (1958) On the nature and aims of psycho-analytical treatment, *International Journal of Psychoanalysis*, 39, 374–85.

Falicov, C.J. (1995) Training to think culturally: a multidimensional comparative framework, *Family Process*, 34, 373–88.

Farber, B.A. (1983a) Dysfunctional aspects of the psychotherapeutic role. In B.A. Farber (ed.) *Stress and Burnout in the Human Service Professions*. New York: Pergamon.

Farber, B.A. (ed.) (1983b) *Stress and Burnout in the Human Service Professions*. New York: Pergamon.

Farber, B.A. (2006) *Self Disclosure in Psychotherapy*. New York: Guilford Press.

Farber, B.A. (2007) On the enduring and substantial influence of Carl Rogers' not-quite necessary nor sufficient conditions, *Psychotherapy: Theory, Research, Practice, Training*, 44, 289–94.

Farber, B.A. and Heifetz, L.J. (1982) The process and dimensions of burnout in psychotherapists, *Professional Psychology*, 13, 293–301.

Farber, B.A., Brink, D.C. and Raskin, P.M. (eds) (1996) *The Psychotherapy of Carl Rogers: Cases and Commentary*. New York: Guilford Press.

Farber, B.A., Manevich, I., Metzger, J. and Saypol, E. (2005) Choosing psychotherapy as a career: why did we cross that road? *Journal of Clinical Psychology*, 61, 1009–31.

Farooq, S., Gahir, M.S., Okyere, E., Sheikh, A.J. and Oyebode, F. (1995) Somatization: a transcultural study, *Journal of Psychosomatic Research*, 39, 883–8.

Farsimadan, F., Draghi-Lorenz, R. and Ellis, J. (2007) Process and outcome of therapy in ethnically similar and dissimilar therapeutic dyads, *Psychotherapy Research*, 17, 567–75.

Farsimadan, F., Khan, A. and Draghi-Lorenz, R. (2011) On ethnic matching: a review of the research and considerations for practice, training and policy. In C. Lago (ed.) *Handbook of Transcultural Counselling and Psychotherapy*. Maidenhead: Open University Press.

Faust, D. and Zlotnick, C. (1995) Another Dodo Bird verdict? Revisiting the comparative effectiveness of professional and paraprofessional therapists, *Clinical Psychology and Psychotherapy*, 2, 157–67.

Feldman, L.B. and Feldman, S.L. (1997) Integrating psychotherapy and pharmacotherapy in the treatment of depression, *In Session: Psychotherapy in Practice*, 3, 23–38.

Feltham, C. (1995) *What Is Counselling?* London: Sage.

Feltham, C. (2000) Counselling supervision: baselines, problems and possibilities. In B. Lawton and C. Feltham (eds) *Taking Supervision Forward: Enquiries and Trends in Counselling and Psychotherapy*. London: Sage.

Feltham, C. and Dryden, W. (1993) *Dictionary of Counselling*. London: Whurr.

Feltham, C. and Dryden, W. (2006) *Brief Counselling: A Practical Guide for Beginning Practitioners*. Maidenhead: Open University Press.

Fennell, M. (1999) *Overcoming Low Self-esteem: A Self-help Guide using Cognitive-behavioural Techniques*. London: Constable and Robinson.

Fenner, P. (2011) Place, matter and meaning: Extending the relationship in psychological therapies, *Health and Place*, 17, 851–7.

Fenner, P. (2012) What do we see?: Extending understanding of visual experience in the art therapy encounter, *Art Therapy*, 29, 11–18.

Ferrara, A. (2010) Reflexive pluralism, *Philosophy and Social Criticism*, 36, 353–64.

Fiedler, F.E. (1950) A comparison of psychoanalytic, nondirective and Adlerian therapeutic relationships, *Journal of Consulting Psychology*, 14, 436–45.

Fine, A. (ed.) (2010) *Handbook on Animal-Assisted Therapy: Theoretical Foundations and Guidelines for Practice*, 3rd edn. New York: Academic Press.

Fink, J. (1999) *How to Use Computers and Cyberspace in the Clinical Practice of Psychotherapy*. Northvale, NJ: Jason Aronson.

Finn, S.E. and Tonsager, M.E. (1997) Information-gathering and therapeutic models of assessment: complementary paradigms, *Psychological Assessment*, 9, 374–85.

Firth, J., Shapiro, D.A. and Parry, G. (1986) The impact of research on the practice of psychotherapy, *British Journal of Psychotherapy*, 2, 169–79.

Fischer, C.T. (1978) Personality and assessment. In R.S. Valle and M. King (eds) *Existential– Phenomenological Alternatives for Psychology*. New York: Oxford University Press.

Fishman, D.B. (1999) *The Case for a Pragmatic Psychology*. New York: New York University Press.

Fitzpatrick, M.R., Kovalak, A.L. and Weaver, A. (2010) How trainees develop an initial theory of practice: A process model of tentative identifications, *Counselling and Psychotherapy Research*, 10, 93–102.

Flückiger, C. and Holtforth, M.G. (2008) Focusing the therapist's attention on the patient's strengths: a preliminary study to foster a mechanism of change in outpatient psychotherapy, *Journal of Clinical Psychology*, 64, 876–90.

Flyvbjerg, B. (2001) *Making Social Science Matter. Why Social Inquiry Fails and How it can Succeed Again*. New York: Cambridge University Press.

Folkes-Skinner, J., Elliott, R. and Wheeler, S. (2010) 'A baptism of fire': a qualitative investigation of a trainee counsellor's experience at the start of training, *Counselling and Psychotherapy Research*, 10, 83–92.

Fonagy, P. (1999) Psychoanalytic theory from the viewpoint of attachment theory and research. In J. Cassidy and P.R. Shaver (eds) *Handbook of Attachment: Theory, Research and Clinical Applications*. New York: Guilford Press.

Fonagy, P. and Bateman, A.W. (2006) Mechanisms of change in mentalization-based treatment of BPD, *Journal of Clinical Psychology*, 62, 411–30.

Fonagy, P. and Target, M. (2006) The mentalization-focused approach to self pathology, *Journal of Personality Disorders*, 20, 544–76.

Fonagy, P., Gergely, G., Jurist, E. and Target, M. (2002) *Affect regulation, Mentalization and the Development of the Self*. New York: Other Press.

Fordham, M. (1986) *Jungian Psychotherapy*. London: Karnac.

Forsyth, D.R. (1990) *Group Dynamics*, 2nd edn. Pacific Grove, CA: Brooks/Cole.

Fortune, A.E., Pearlingi, B. and Rochelle, C.D. (1992) Reactions to termination of individual treatment, *Social Work*, 37(2), 171–8.

Foucault, M. (1967) *Madness and Civilization: A History of Insanity in the Age of Reason*. London: Tavistock.

Fox, J. (1997) *Poetic Medicine: The Healing Art of Poem-Making*. New York: Tarcher Putman.

Frank, J.D. (1993) *Persuasion and Healing: A Comparative Study of Psychotherapy*. Baltimore, MD: Johns Hopkins University Press.

Frank, J.D. (1974) Psychotherapy: the restoration of morale, *American Journal of Psychiatry*, 131, 271–4.

Fransella, F. (ed.) (2005) *The Essential Practitioner's Handbook of Personal Construct Psychotherapy*. Chichester: Wiley Blackwell.

Fransella, F., Dalton, P. and Weselby, G. (2007) Personal construct therapy. In W. Dryden (ed.) *Handbook of Individual Therapy*, 5th edn. London: Sage.

Frayn, D.H. (1992) Assessment factors associated with premature psychotherapy termination, *American Journal of Psychotherapy*, 46(2), 25–61.

Free, M.L. (2007) *Cognitive Therapy in Groups: Guidelines and Resources for Practice*, 2nd edn. New York: Wiley.

Freedman, J. and Combs, G. (1996) *Narrative Therapy: The Social Construction of Preferred Identities*. New York: Norton.

Freeman, A., Simon, K.M., Beutler, L.E. and Arkowitz, H. (eds) (1989) *Comprehensive Handbook of Cognitive Therapy*. New York: Plenum Press.

Freire, E.S., Koller, S.H., Piason, A., da Silva, R.B. and Giacomelli, D. (2006) Person-centred therapy with child and adlosecent victims of pverty and social exclusion in Brazil. In G. Proctor, M.Cooper, P. Sanders and B. Malcolm (eds) *Politicizing the Person-centred Approach: An Agenda for Social Change*. Ross-on-Wye: PCCS Books.

Freud, A. (1936/1966) *The Ego and the Mechanisms of Defense*, revised edn. New York: International Universities Press.

Freud, S. (1900/1997) *The Interpretation of Dreams*.Ware: Wordsworth Editions.

Freud, S. (1901/1979) The case of Dora. *Pelican Freud Library Volume 8: Case Histories I*. Harmondsworth: Penguin.

Freud, S. (1905/1977) Three essays on the theory of sexuality. *Pelican Freud Library Volume 7: On Sexuality*. Harmondsworth: Penguin.

Freud, S. (1909/1979) Notes upon a case of obsessional neurosis (the 'Rat Man'). *Pelican Freud Library Volume 9: Case Histories II*. Harmondsworth: Penguin.

Freud, S. (1910/1963) *Five Lectures on Psycho-analysis*. Harmondsworth: Penguin.

Freud, S. (1910/1979) Psychoanalytic notes on an autobiographical account of a case of paranoia (Dementia Paranoides) (Schreber). *Pelican Freud Library Volume 9. Case Histories II*. Harmondsworth: Penguin.

Freud, S. (1917/1973) *Introductory Lecture on Psychoanalysis*. Harmondsworth: Penguin.

Freud, S. (1924/1977) The dissolution of the Oedipus complex. *Pelican Freud Library Volume 7: On Sexuality*. Harmondsworth: Penguin.

Freud, S. (1933/1973) *New Introductory Lectures on Psycho-Analysis*. Harmondsworth: Penguin.

Freud, S. (1976) *The Complete Psychological Works of Sigmund Freud (The Standard Edition) (Vols 1–24)*. New York: W. W. Norton and Company.

Freudenberger, H.J. (1974) Staff burn-out, *Journal of Social Issues*, 30, 159–65.

Friedli, K., King, M.B. and Lloyd, M. (2000) The economics of employing a counsellor in general practice: analysis of data from a randomised control trial, *British Journal of General Practice*, 50, 276–83.

Friedman, D. and Kaslow, N.J. (1986) The development of professional identity in psychotherapists: six stages in the supervision process. In F.W. Kaslow (ed.) *Supervision and Training: Models, Dilemmas and Challenges*. New York: Haworth Press.

Friedman. S. (ed.) (1995) *The Reflecting Team in Action. Collaborative Practice in Family Therapy*. New York: Guilford Press.

Fryer, D. and Fagan, R. (2003) Toward a critical community psychological perspective on unemployment and mental health research, *American Journal of Community Psychology*, 32, 89–96.

Fuhriman, A., Barlow, S.H. and Wanlass, J. (1989) Words, imagination, meaning: towards change, *Psychotherapy*, 26, 149–56.

Fulero, S.M. (1988) Tarasoff: 10 years later, *Professional Psychology: Research and Practice,* 19, 184–90.

Furedi, F. (2004) *Therapy Culture: Cultivating Vulnerability in an Uncertain Age.* London: Routledge.

Gabbard, G. (ed.) (1989) *Sexual Exploitation in Professional Relationships.* Washington, DC: American Psychiatric Press.

Gabriel, L. (2005) *Speaking the Unspeakable: The Ethics of Dual Relationships in Counselling and Psychotherapy.* London: Routledge.

Galassi, J.P. and Perot, A.R. (1992) What you should know about behavioral assessment, *Journal of Counseling and Development,* 70, 624–31.

Galassi, J.P., Crace, R.K., Martin, G.A., James, R.M. and Wallace, R.L. (1992) Client preferences and anticipations in career counseling: a preliminary investigation, *Journal of Counseling Psychology,* 39, 46–55.

Galloway, J. (1989) *The Trick is to Keep Breathing.* London: Polygon.

Garfield, S. (1986) Research on client variables in psychotherapy. In S.L. Garfield and A.E. Bergin (eds) *Handbook of Psychotherapy and Behavior Change,* 3rd edn. London: Wiley.

Garfield, S. and Bergin, A.E. (1971) Personal therapy, outcome and some therapist variables, *Psychotherapy,* 8, 251–3.

Garfield, S. and Kurtz, R. (1974) A survey of clinical psychologists: characteristics, activities and orientations, *The Clinical Psychologist,* 28, 7–10.

Garfield, S. and Kurtz, R. (1977) A study of eclectic views, *Journal of Consulting and Clinical Psychology,* 45, 78–83.

Garfield, S.F., Smith, F.J. and Francis, S. (2003) The paradoxical role of antidepressant medication – returning to normal functioning while losing the sense of being normal, *Journal of Mental Health,* 12, 521–35.

Garnets, L., Hancock, K.A., Cochran, S.D., Goodchilds, J. and Peplau, L.A. (1991) Issues in psychotherapy with lesbians and gay men, *American Psychologist,* 46(9), 964–72.

Gass, M.A., Gillis, H.L. and Russell, K.C. (eds) (2012) *Adventure Therapy: Theory, Research, and Practice.* New York: Routledge.

Gay, P. (1988) *Freud. A Life for Our Times.* London: Dent.

Geertz, C. (1973) *The Interpretation of Cultures.* New York: Basic Books.

Geertz, C. (1983) *Local Knowledge: Further Essays in Interpretive Anthropology.* New York: Basic Books.

Gega, L., Marks, I. and Metaiz-Cols, D. (2004) Computer-aided CBT for anxiety and depressive disroders: experience of a London clinic and future directions, *Journal of Clinical Psychology,* 60, 147–57.

Geller, J.D., Norcross, J.C. and Orlinsky, D.E. (eds) (2005) *The Psychotherapist's own Psychotherapy: Patient and Clinician Perspectives.* New York: Oxford University Press.

Geller, J.S. (2011) The psychotherapy of psychotherapist, *Journal of Clinical Psychology,* 67, 759–65.

Gendlin, E.T. (1962) *Experiencing and the Creation of Meaning.* New York: Free Press.

Gendlin, E.T. (1967) Subverbal communication and therapist expressivity: trends in clientcentered therapy with schizophrenics. In C. Rogers and B. Stevens (eds) *Person to Person: The Problem of Being Human.* San Francisco, CA: Real People Press.

Gendlin, E.T. (1969) Focusing, *Psychotherapy,* 6, 4–15.

Gendlin, E.T. (1974) Client-centered and experiential psychotherapy. In D.A. Wexler and L.N. Rice (eds) *Innovations in Client-centered Therapy.* New York: Wiley.

Gendlin, E.T. (1981) *Focusing,* revised edn. New York: Bantam.

Gendlin, E.T. (1984a) The client's client: the edge of awareness. In R.F. Levant and J.M. Shlien (eds) *Client-centered Therapy and the Person-centered Approach: New Directions in Theory, Research and Practice.* New York: Praeger.

Gendlin, E.T. (1984b) Imagery, body and space in focusing. In A.A. Sheikh (ed.) *Imagination and Healing.* New York: Baywood.

Gendlin, E.T. (1996) *Focusing-oriented Psychotherapy: A Manual of the Experiential Method.* New York: Guilford Press.

Gergen, K.J. (1985) The social constructionist movement in modern psychology, *American Psychologist,* 40, 266–75.

Gergen, K.J. (1990) Therapeutic professions and the diffusion of deficit, *Journal of Mind and Behavior,* 11, 353–68.

Gergen, K.J. (1991) *The Saturated Self: Dilemmas of Identity in Modern Life.* New York: Basic.

Gergen, K.J. (1994) *Toward Transformation in Social Knowledge,* 2nd edn. London: Sage.

Gergen, K.J. (1996) Beyond life narratives in the therapeutic encounter. In J.E. Birren, G.M. Kenyon, J.-K. Ruth, J.F. Schroots and T. Svensson (eds) *Aging and Biography: Explorations in Adult Development*. New York: Springer.

Gergen, K.J. (1999) *An Invitation to Social Construction*. London: Sage.

Gergen, K.J. (2000) The coming of creative confluence in therapeutic practice, *Psychotherapy*, 37, 364–9.

Gergen, K.J. and Kaye, J. (1992) Beyond narrative in the construction of therapeutic meaning. In S. McNamee and K. Gergen (eds) *Therapy as Social Construction*. London: Sage.

Gersons, B.P.R., Carlier, I.V.E., Lamberts, R.D. and van der Kolk, B.A. (2000) Randomized clinic trial of brief eclectic psychotherapy for police officers with posttraumatic stress disorder, *Journal of Traumatic Stress*, 13, 333–47.

Giddens, A. (1991) *Modernity and Self-Identity: Self and Society in the Late Modern Age*. Cambridge: Polity Press.

Gilbert, M. and Orlans, V. (2010) *Integrative Therapy: 100 Key Points and Techniques*. London: Routledge.

Gilbert, P. (2000) *Overcoming Depression: a Self-help Guide using Cognitive-Behavioural Techniques*, 2nd edn. London: Constable and Robinson.

Gilbert, P. and Leahy, R.L. (eds) (2007) *The Therapeutic Relationship in the Cognitive-Behavioural Psychotherapies*. London: Routledge.

Gilbert, P., McEwan, K., Bellew, R., Mills, A. and Gale, C. (2009) The dark side of competition: how competitive behaviour and striving to avoid inferiority are linked to depression, anxiety, stress and self-harm, *Psychology and Psychotherapy: Theory, Research and Practice*, 82, 123–36.

Gill, M.M. (1994) *Psychoanalysis in Transition*. Hillsdale, NJ: Analytic Press.

Gilligan, C. (1982) *In a Different Voice*. Cambridge, MA: Harvard University Press.

Ginger, S. (2007) *Gestalt Therapy, the Art of Contact*. London: Karnac.

Gingerich, W.J. and Eisengart, S. (2000) Solution-focused brief therapy: a review of the outcome research, *Family Process*, 39, 477–98.

Gitlin, M.J. (2007) *Psychotherapist's Guide to Psychopharmacology*. New York: Free Press.

Glaser, B.G. (1978) *Theoretical Sensitivity: Advances in the Methodology of Grounded Theory*. Mill Valley, CA: The Sociology Press.

Glaser, B.G. and Strauss, A. (1967) *The Discovery of Grounded Theory*. Chicago, IL: Aldine.

Glass, C.R. and Arnkoff, D.B. (2000) Consumers' perspectives on helpful and hindering factors in mental health treatment, *Journal of Clinical Psychology*, 56, 1467–80.

Glass, L.L. (2003) The gray areas of boundary crossings and violations, *American Journal of Psychotherapy*, 57, 429–44.

Glasser, W. (2000) *Counseling with Choice Theory. The New Reality Therapy*. New York: HaperCollins.

Glickauf-Hughes, C. and Mehlman, E. (1995) Narcissistic issues in therapists: diagnostic and treatment considerations, *Psychotherapy*, 32, 213–21.

Goertzen, J.R. and Smythe, W.E. (2010) Theorising pluralism: an introduction, *New Ideas in Psychology*, 28, 199–200.

Goffman, E. (1955) On face-work: an analysis of ritual elements in social interaction, *Psychiatry*, 18, 213–31.

Goffman, E. (1956) *The Presentation of Self in Everyday Life. Social Sciences Research Centre, Monograph no. 2*. Edinburgh: University of Edinburgh.

Gold, E. and Zahm, S. (2008) The need for Gestalt Therapy research. In P. Brownell (ed.) *Handbook for Theory, Research and Practice in Gestalt Therapy*. Newcastle: Cambridge Scholars Publishing.

Goldberg, D. and Huxley, P. (1992) *Common Mental Disorders: A Bio-social model*. London: Tavistock.

Goldberg, D.P., Hobson, R.F., Maguire, G.P. et al. (1984) The classification and assessment of a method of psychotherapy, *British Journal of Psychiatry*, 144, 567–75.

Goldfried, M.R. (2001) *How Therapists Change: Personal and Professional Reflections*. Washington, DC: American Psychological Association.

Goldfried, M.R. (2007) What has psychotherapy inherited from Carl Rogers? *Psychotherapy: Theory, Research, Practice, Training*, 44, 249–52.

Goldfried, M.R. and Davison, G.C. (1976) *Clinical Behavior Therapy*. New York: Holt, Rinehart and Winston.

Goldfried, M., Raue, P. and Castonguay, L. (1998) The therapeutic focus in significant sessions of master therapists: a comparison of cognitive-behavoural and psychodynamic-interpersonal interventions, *Journal of Consulting and Clinical Psychology*, 66, 803–10.

Goldman, L. (1992) Qualitative assessment: an approach for counselors, *Journal of Counseling and Development*, 70, 616–21.

Goldsmith, J.Z., Mosher, J.K., Stiles, W.B. and Greenberg, L.S. (2008) Speaking with the client's voices: how a person-centered therapist used reflections to facilitate assimilation, *Person-Centered and Experiential Psychotherapies*, 7, 155–72.

Golkaramnay, V., Bauer, S., Haug, S. *et al.* (2007) The exploration of the effectiveness of group therapy through an internet chat as aftercare: a controlled naturalistic study, *Psychotherapy and Psychosomatics*, 76, 219–25.

Gomes-Schwartz, B. and Schwartz, J.M. (1978) Psychotherapy process variables distinguishing the 'inherently helpful' person from the professional psychotherapist, *Journal of Consulting and Clinical Psychology*, 46, 196–7.

Gomez, L. (1997) *An Introduction to Object Relations*. London: Free Association Books.

Gonçalves, M., Matos, M. and Santos, A. (2008) Narrative therapy and the nature of "innovative moments" in the construction of change, *Journal of Constructivist Psychology*, 22, 1–23.

Gonçalves, M., Mendes, I., Cruz, C. *et al.* (2012) Innovative moments and change in client-centred psychotherapy, *Psychotherapy Research*, 22, 389–401.

Gonçalves, M., Mendes, I., Ribeiro, A., Angus, L. and Greenberg, L. (2010) Innovative moments and change in emotion-focused therapy: the case of Lisa, *Journal of Constructivist Psychology*, 23, 267–94.

Gonsiorek, J.C. (2004) Reflections from the conversion therapy battlefield, *The Counseling Psychologist*, 32, 750–9.

Goodman, L.A., Helms, J.E., Latta, R.E., Sparks, E. and Weintraub, S.R. (2004) Training counseling psychologists as social justice agents: feminist and multicultural principles in action, *Counseling Psychologist*, 32, 793–837.

Goodman, L.A., Glenn, C., Bohlig, A., Banyard, V. and Borges, A. (2009) Feminist relational advocacy: processes and outcomes from the perspective of low-income women with depression, *Counseling Psychologist*, 37, 848–76.

Goodman, P. (1962) *Utopian Essays and Practical Proposals*. New York: Vintage Books.

Gortner, E.T., Gollan, J.K., Dobson, K.S. and Jacobson, N.S. (1998) Cognitive-behavioral treatment for depression: relapse prevention, *Journal of Consulting and Clinical Psychology*, 66, 377–84.

Goulding, R. and Goulding, M. (1979) *Changing Lives through Redicision Therapy*. New York: Brunner-Mazel.

Grabosky, T.K., Ishii, H. and Mase, S. (2012) The development of the counseling profession in Japan: past, present, and future, *Journal of Counseling and Development*, 90, 221–5.

Graf, M.C., Gaudiano, B.A. and Geller, P.A. (2008) Written emotional disclosure: a controlled study of the benefits of expressive writing homework in outpatient psychotherapy, *Psychotherapy Research*, 18, 389–99.

Grafanaki, S. and McLeod, J. (1999) Narrative processes in the construction of helpful and hindering events in experiential psychotherapy, *Psychotherapy Research*, 9, 289–303.

Grafanaki, S. and McLeod, J. (2002) Experimental congruence: qualitative analysis of client and counsellor narrative accounts of significant events in time-limited person-centred therapy, *Counselling and Psychotherapy Research*, 2, 20–32.

Granvold, D. (ed.) (2004) *Cognitive and Behavioural Treatment Methods*. Belmont, CA: Brooks/Cole.

Gray, L.A., Ladany, N., Walker, J.A. and Ancis, J.R. (2001) Psychotherapy trainees' experience of counterproductive events in supervision, *Journal of Counseling Psychology*, 48, 371–83.

Greenberg, L. (2002) *Emotion-Focused Therapy: Coaching Clients to Work Through Feelings*. Washington, DC: American Psychological Association.

Greenberg, L. (2008) Quantitative research. In P. Brownell (ed.) *Handbook for Theory, Research and Practice in Gestalt Therapy*. Newcastle: Cambridge Scholars Publishing.

Greenberg, L.S. and Geller, S. (2001) Congruence and therapeutic presence. In G. Wyatt (ed.) *Rogers' Therapeutic Conditions: Evolution, Theory and Practice. Volume 1: Congruence*. Ross-on-Wye: PCCS Books.

Greenberg, L.S. and Goldman, R.N. (2008) *Emotion-focused Couples Therapy: The Dynamics of Emotion, Love, and Power*. Washington, DC: American Psychological Association.

Greenberg, L.S. and Johnson, S. (1988) *Emotionally Focused Therapy for Couples*. New York: Guilford Press.

Greenberg, L.S. and Pinsof, W.M. (eds) (1986) *The Psychotherapeutic Process: A Research Handbook*. New York: Guilford Press.

Greenberg, L.S., Elliott, R. and Foerster, F.S. (1990) Experiential processes in the psychotherapeutic treatment of depression. In C.D. McCann and N.S. Endler (eds) *Depression: New Directions in Theory, Research and Practice*. Toronto: Wall and Emerson.

Greenberg, L.S., Rice, L.N. and Elliott, R. (1993) *Facilitating Emotional Change: The Moment-by-moment Process*. New York: Guilford Press.

Greenberg, L.S., Watson, J.C. and Lietaer, G. (eds) (1998) *Handbook of Experiential Psychotherapy: Foundations and Differential Treatment*. New York: Guilford Press.

Greenberg, L.S. and Watson, J.C. (2005) *Emotion-Focused Therapy for Depression*. Washington, DC: American Psychological Association.

Greenberger, D. and Padesky, C.A. (1995) *Mind over Mood: Change how you Feel by Changing the Way you Think*. New York: Guilford Press.

Greene, G. (1988) Analysis of the effectiveness of Transactional Analysis for improving marital relationships: toward close encounters of the single side, *Transactional Analysis Journal*, 18, 238–48.

Green Lister, P. (2002) Retrieving and constructing memory: the use of creative writing by women survivors of child sexual abuse. In C. Horrocks, K. Milnes, B. Roberts and D. Robinson (eds) *Narrative Memory and Life Transitions*. Huddersfield: University of Huddersfield Press.

Green Lister, P. (2003) Feminist dilemmas in data analysis: researching the use of creative writing by women survivors of sexual abuse. *Qualitative Social Work*, 2, 45–59.

Greenway, R. (1995) The wilderness effect and ecopsychology. In T. Roszak, M.E. Gomes, and A.D. Kanner (1995) *Eco-psychology: Restoring the Mind, Healing the Earth*. San Francisco, CA: Sierra Club Books.

Grencavage, L.M. and Norcross, J.C. (1990) Where are the commonalities among the therapeutic common factors? *Professional Psychology: Research and Practice*, 21, 372–8.

Griffiths, S. (2008) The experience of creative activity as a treatment medium, *Journal of Mental Health*, 17, 49–63.

Grime, P.R. (2004) Computerized cognitive behavioural therapy at work: a randomized controlled trial in employees with recent stress-related absenteeism, *Occupational Medicine*, 54, 353–9.

Grohol, J.M. (2004) *The Insider's Guide to Mental Health Resources Online*, revised edn. New York: Guilford Press.

Grumet, G.W. (1979) Telephone therapy: a review and case report, *American Journal of Orthopsychiatry*, 49, 574–84.

Guarnaccia, P.J. and Rogler, L.H. (1999) Research on culture-bound syndromes: new directions, *American Journal of Psychiatry*, 156, 3122–7.

Guay, S., O'Connor, K.P., Gareau, D. and Todorov, C. (2005) A single belief as a maintaining factor in a case of obsessive-compulsive disorder, *Journal of Cognitive Psychotherapy*, 19, 369–78.

Guggenbuhl-Craig, A. (1971) *Power in the Helping Professions*. Dallas, TX: Spring Publications.

Gummere, R.M. (1988) The counselor as prophet: Frank Parsons, 1854–1908, *Journal of Counseling and Development*, 66, 402–5.

Gustafson, J.P. (1986) *The Complex Secret of Brief Psychotherapy*. New York: W.W. Norton.

Gutheil, T. and Gabbard, G. (1998) Misuses and misunderstandings of boundary theory in clinical and regulatory settings, *American Journal of Psychiatry*, 155, 409–14.

Guthrie, E. (1991) Brief psychotherapy in patients with refractory irritable bowel syndrome, *British Journal of Psychotherapy*, 8(2), 175–88.

Guthrie, E, Moorey, J., Barker, H., Margison, F. and McGrath, G. (1998) Brief psychodynamic-interpersonal therapy for patients with severe psychiatric illness which is unresponsive to treatment, *British Journal of Psychotherapy*, 15, 155–66.

Guthrie, E., Moorey, J., Marigson, F. et al. (1999) Cost-effectiveness of brief psychodynamic-interpersonal therapy in high utilizers of psychiatric services, *Archives of General Psychiatry*, 56, 519–26.

Guthrie, E., Kapur, N., Mackway-Jones, K. et al. (2001) Randomised control trial of brief psychological intervention after deliberate self poisoning, *British Medical Journal*, 323, 212–19.

Gutierrez, L.M. (1992) Empowering ethnic minorities in the twenty-first century: the role of human service organizations. In Y. Hasenfeld (ed.) *Human Services as Complex Organizations*. London: Sage.

Guttman, H.A. (1981) Systems theory, cybernetics, and epistemology. In A.S. Gurman and D.P. Kniskern (eds) *Handbook of Family Therapy*. New York: Brunner/Mazel.

Gutwill, S., Gitter, A. and Rubin, L. (2010) The Women's Therapy Centre Institute: the personal is political, *Women and Therapy*, 34, 143–58.

Guy, J.D. (1987) *The Personal Life of the Psychotherapist.* New York: Wiley.

Haaga, D.A. (2000) Introduction to the special section on stepped care models in psychotherapy, *Journal of Consulting and Clinical Psychology*, 68, 547–8.

Haarakangas, K. Seikkula, J., Alakare, B. and Aaltonen, J. (2007) Open dialogue: an approach to psychotherapeutic treatment of psychosis in Northern Finland. In H. Anderson and D. Gehart (eds) *Collaborative Therapy: Relationships and Conversations that Make a Difference.* New York: Routledge.

Hage, S.M., Romano, J.L. Conyne, R.K. *et al.* (2007) Best practice guidelines on prevention practice, research, training and social adocacy for psychologists, *The Counseling Psychologist*, 35, 493–566.

Haldeman, D.C. (2004) When sexual and religious orientation collide: considerations in working with conflicted same-sex attracted male clients, *The Counseling Psychologist*, 32, 691–715.

Haldeman, D.C. (2010) Reflections of a gay male psychotherapist, *Psychotherapy Theory, Research, Practice, Training*, 47, 177–85.

Halewood, A. and Tribe, R. (2003) What is the prevalence of narcissistic injury among trainee counselling psychologists? *Psychology and Psychotherapy: Theory, Research and Practice*, 76, 87–102.

Haley, J. (1973) *Uncommon Therapy: The Psychiatric Techniques of Milton H. Erickson, M.D.* New York: Norton.

Halgin, R.P. and Caron, M. (1991) To treat or not to treat: considerations for referring prospective clients, *Psychotherapy in Private Practice*, 8, 87–96.

Hall, A.S. and Fradkin, H.R. (1992) Affirming gay men's mental health: counseling with a new attitude, *Journal of Mental Health Counseling*, 14, 362–74.

Hall, E., Hall, C., Stradling, P. and Young, D. (2006) *Guided Imagery: Creative Interventions in Counselling and Psychotherapy.* London: Sage.

Halling, S., Leifer, M. and Rowe, J.O. (2006a) Emergence of the dialogal approach: forgiving another. In C.T. Fischer (ed.), *Qualitative Research Methods for Psychologists: Introduction through Empirical Examples.* New York: Academic Press.

Halling, S., McNabb, M. and Rowe, J.O. (2006b) Existential-phenomenological psychotherapy in the trenches: a collaborative approach to serving the underserved, *Journal of Phenomenological Psychology*, 37, 171–96.

Halmos, P. (1965) *The Faith of the Counsellors.* London: Constable.

Hammond, D.C, Hepworth, D.H. and Smith, V.G. (2002) *Improving Therapeutic Communication: A Guide for Developing Effective Techniques*, 2nd edn. New York: Jossey-Bass.

Handelsman, M.M. and Galvin, M.D. (1988) Facilitating informed consent for out-patient psychotherapy, *Professional Psychology: Research and Practice*, 19, 223–5.

Hanley, T., Humphrey, N. and Lennie, C. (eds) (2012) *Adolescent Counselling Psychology: Theory, Research and Practice.* London: Routledge.

Hannon, J.W., Ritchie, M. and Rye, D.R. (2001) Class; the missing discourse in counselling and counsellor education in the USA, *Journal of Critical Psychology, Counselling and Psychotherapy*, 1, 137–54.

Hansen, J. (2004) Thoughts on knowing: epistemic implications of counseling practice. *Journal of Counseling and Development*, 82, 131–8.

Hansen, J. (2006) Counseling theories within a postmodernist epistemology: new roles for theories in counseling practice, *Journal of Counseling and Development*, 84, 291–7.

Hansen, J. (2007) Counseling without truth: toward a neopragmatic foundation for counseling practice, *Journal of Counseling and Development*, 85, 423–30.

Hansen, J. (2012) Extending the humanistic vision: toward a humanities foundation for the counseling profession, *Journal of Humanistic Counseling*, 51, 133–44.

Hansen, N.B., Lambert, M.J. and Forman, E.M. (2002) The psychotherapy dose–response effect and its implications for psychotherapy services, *Clinical Psychology: Science and Practice*, 9, 329–43.

Hanson, J. (2005) Should your lips be zipped? How therapist self-disclosure and non-disclosure affects clients, *Counselling and Psychotherapy Research*, 5, 96–104.

Harding-Davies, V., Hunt, K., Alred, G. and Davies, G. (eds) (2004) *Experiences of Counsellor Training.* London: Palgrave Macmillan.

Hardy, G.E., Barkham, M., Shapiro, D. A. *et al.* (1995) Credibility and outcome of cognitivebehavioural and psychodynamic-interpersonal psychotherapy. *British Journal of Clinical Psychology*, 34, 555–69.

Hare, E. (1962) Masturbatory insanity: the history of an idea. *Journal of Mental Science*, 108, 1–25.

Hargaden, H. and Sills, C. (2002) *Transactional Analysis: a Relational Perspective.* London: Brunner Routledge.

Harman, J. (1986) A case presentation in Gestalt Therapy: II, *The Gestalt Journal*, 9, 16–35. Available at www.gestalttherapy.net/gpatwork/harman1.pdf (accessed 19 March 2013).

Harrison, D.K. (1975) Race as a counselor–client variable in counseling and psychotherapy: a review of the research, *Counseling Psychologist*, 5, 124–33.

Hart, J.T. and Tomlinson, T.M. (eds) (1970) *New Directions in Client-centered Therapy.* Boston, MA: Houghton Mifflin.

Hartford, G. (2011) Practical implications for the development of applied metaphor in adventure therapy, *Journal of Adventure Education and Outdoor Learning*, 11, 145–60.

Hartmann, E. (1997) The concept of boundaries in counselling and psychotherapy, *British Journal of Guidance and Counselling*, 25, 147–62.

Hartmann, S. and Zepf, S. (2003) Effectiveness of psychotherapy in Germany: a replication of the *Consumer Reports* study, *Psychotherapy Research*, 13, 235–42.

Harway, M. (ed.) (2005) *Handbook of Couples Therapy.* New York: Wiley.

Hatch, M. and Cunliffe, A.L. (2006) *Organization Theory: Modern, Symbolic, and Postmodern Perspectives,* 2nd edn. New York: Oxford University Press.

Hattie, J.A., Sharpley, C.F. and Rogers, H.J. (1984) Comparative effectiveness of professional and paraprofessional helpers, *Psychological Bulletin*, 95, 534–41.

Hawkins, P. and Shohet, R. (2012) *Supervision in the Helping Professions,* 4th edn. Maidenhead: Open University Press.

Hay, D. and Heald, G. (1987) Religion is good for you, *New Society,* 17 April.

Hay, D. and Hunt, K. (2000) *Understanding the Spirituality of People who don't go to Church. Final Report of the Adult Spirituality Project, Nottingham University.* London: Mission Theological Advisory Group.

Hayashi, S., Kuno, T., Morotomi, Y., Osawa, M., Shimizu, M. and Suetake, Y. (1998) Client-centered therapy in Japan: Fujio Tomoda and Taoism, *Journal of Humanistic Psychology*, 38, 103–24.

Hayes, A.M. and Goldfried, M.R. (1996) Carl Rogers' work with Mark: an empirical analysis and cognitive-behavioral perspective. In B.A. Farber, D.C. Brink and P.M. Raskin (eds) *The Psychotherapy of Carl Rogers.* New York: Guilford Press.

Hayes, H. (1991) A re-introduction to family therapy: clarification of three schools, *Australia and New Zealand Journal of Family Therapy*, 12(1), 27–43.

Hayes, S.C. (2004) Acceptance and commitment therapy, relational frame theory, and the third wave of behavior therapy, *Behavior Therapy*, 35, 639–65.

Hayes, S.C., Strosahl, K. and Wilson, K. (1999) *Acceptance and Commitment Therapy: an Experiential Approach to Behavior Change.* New York: Guilford Press.

Hayes, S.C., Luoma, J.B., Bond, F.W., Masuda, A. and Lillis, J. (2006) Acceptance and Commitment Therapy: model, processes and outcomes, *Behaviour Research and Therapy*, 44, 1–25.

Hays, K.F. (1999) *Working it out. Using Exercise in Psychotherapy.* Washington, DC: American Psychological Association.

Heard, H.L. and Linehan, M.M. (2005) Integrative therapy for Borderline Personality Disorder. In J.C. Norcross. and M.R. Goldfried (eds) *Handbook of Psychotherapy Integration.* New York: Oxford University Press.

Hecker, L.L. and Deacon, S.A. (eds) (2006) *The Therapist's Notebook. Homework, Handouts, and Activities for Use in Psychotherapy.* New York: Routledge.

Hecker, L.L. and Sori, C.F. (eds) (2007) *The Therapist's Notebook, Volume 2. More Homework, Handouts, and Activities for Use in Psychotherapy.* New York: Routledge.

Heimann, P. (1950) On countertransference, *International Journal of Psycho-Analysis*, 31, 81–4.

Heimberg, R.G. and Becker, R.E. (2002) *Cognitive-behavioural Group Therapy for Social Phobia: Basic Mechanisms and Clinical Strategies.* New York: Guilford Press.

Heller, M.C. and Duclos, M. (2012) *Body Psychotherapy: History, Concepts, and Methods.* New York: Norton.

Hellman, I.D. and Morrison, T.L. (1987) Practice setting and type of caseload as factors in psychotherapist stress, *Psychotherapy*, 24, 427–33.

Helms, J. (1995) An update of Helms' white and people of color racial identity models. In J.G. Ponetrotto, J.M. Casas, L. Suzuki and C. Alexander (eds) *Handbook of Multicultural Counseling.* Thousand Oaks, CA: Sage.

Hemmelgarn, A.L. and Glisson, C. (2006) Organizational culture and climate: implications for services and interventions research, *Clinical Psychology: Science and Practice*, 13, 73–89.

Hennigan, K. (2010) Therapeutic potential of time in nature: implications for body image in women, *Ecopsychology*, 2, 135–40.

Henry, W.E. (1966) Some observations on the lives of healers, *Human Development*, 9, 47–56.

Henry, W.E. (1977) Personal and social identities of psychotherapists. In A.S. Gurman and A.M. Razin (eds) *Effective Psychotherapy: A Handbook of Research*. Oxford: Pergamon.

Herek, G.M., Kimmel, D.C., Amaro, H. and Melton, G.B. (1991) Avoiding heterosexist bias in psychological research, *American Psychologist*, 46(9), 957–63.

Hermann, M.A. and Herlihy, B.R. (2006) Legal and ethical implications of refusing to counsel homosexual clients, *Journal of Counseling and Development*, 84, 414–18.

Hermans, H.J.M. and DiMaggio, G. (eds) (2004) *The Dialogical Self in Psychotherapy*. London: Brunner-Routledge.

Hermansson, G. (1997) Boundaries and boundary management in counselling: the neverending story, *British Journal of Guidance and Counselling*, 25, 133–46.

Herron, W.G. and Sitkowski, S. (1986) Effect of fees on psychotherapy: what is the evidence? *Professional Psychology: Research and Practice*, 17, 347–51.

Hesley, J.W. and Hesley, J.G. (2001) *Rent Two Films and Let's Talk in the Morning: Using Popular Movies in Psychotherapy,* 2nd edn. New York: Wiley.

Hess, A.K. (ed.) (1980) *Psychotherapy Supervision. Theory, Research and Practice*. New York: Wiley.

Hess, S.A., Knox, S. and Hill, C.E. (2006) Teaching graduate trainees how to manage client anger: a comparison of three types of training, *Psychotherapy Research*, 16, 282–92.

Hesse, E. (1999) The Adult Attachment Interview: historical and current perspectives. In J. Cassidy and P.R. Shaver (eds) *Handbook of Attachment: Theory, Research and Clinical Applications*. New York: Guilford Press.

Hetherington, A. (2000) A psychodynamic profile of therapists who sexually exploit their clients, *British Journal of Psychotherapy*, 16, 274–86.

Higley, N. and Milton, M. (2008) Our connection to the Earth – a neglected relationship in counselling psychology? *Counselling Psychology Review* 23: 31–5.

Hill, C.E. (1989) *Therapist Techniques and Client Outcomes: Eight Cases of Brief Psychotherapy*. London: Sage.

Hill, C.E. (1996) *Working with Dreams in Psychotherapy*. New York: Guilford Press.

Hill, C.E. (ed.) (2004) *Dream Work in Therapy: Facilitation Exploration, Insight and Action*. Washington, DC: American Psychological Association.

Hill, C.E. (2005) The role of individual and marital therapy in my development. In J.D. Geller, J.C Norcross and D.E.Orlinsky (eds) *The Psychotherapist's own Psychotherapy: Patient and Clinician Perspectives*. New York: Oxford University Press.

Hill, C.E. (2007) My personal reactions to Rogers (1957): the facilitative but neither necessary nor sufficient conditions of therapeutic personality change, *Psychotherapy: Theory, Research, Practice, Training*, 44, 260–4.

Hill, C.E. and Knox, S. (2001) Self-disclosure, *Psychotherapy: Theory, Research, Practice, Training*, 38, 413–25.

Hill, C.E. and Knox, S. (2009) Processing the therapeutic relationship, *Psychotherapy Research*, 19, 13–29.

Hill, C.E. and Lambert, M.J. (2004) Methodological issues in studying psychotherapy processes and outcomes. In M.J. Lambert (ed.) *Bergin and Garfield's Handbook of Psychotherapy and Behavior Change,* 5th edn. New York: Wiley.

Hill, C.E. and Lent, R.W. (2006) A narrative and meta-analytic review of helping skills training; time to revive a dormant area of inquiry, *Psychotherapy: Theory, Research, Practice, Training*, 43, 154–72.

Hill, C.E. and Nakayama, E.Y. (2000) Client-centered therapy: where has it been and where is it going? A commentary on Hathaway (1948), *Journal of Clinical Psychology*, 56, 861–75.

Hill, C.E., Nutt-Williams, E., Heaton, K.J., Thompson, B.J. and Rhodes, R.H. (1996) Therapist retrospective recall of impasses in long-term psychotherapy: a qualitative analysis. *Journal of Counseling Psychology*, 43, 207–17.

Hill, M. (1999) Barter: ethical considerations in psychotherapy, *Women and Therapy*, 22(3), 81–92.

Hill, M. and Ballou, M. (1998) Making therapy feminist: a practice survey, *Women and Therapy*, 21, 1–16.

Hilsenroth, M.J. and Cromer, T.D. (2007) Clinican interventions related to alliance during the initial interview and psychological assessment, *Psychotherapy: Theory, Research, Practice, Training*, 44, 205–18.

Hinshelwood, R.D. (1991) Psychodynamic formulation in assessment for psychotherapy, *British Journal of Psychotherapy*, 8(2), 166–74.

Hirai, M. and Clum, G.A. (2006) A meta-analytic study of self-help interventions for anxiety problems, *Behavior Therapy*, 37, 99–111.

Hobson, R.E. (1985) *Forms of Feeling: The Heart of Psychotherapy*. London: Tavistock.

Hoener, C., Stiles, W.R., Luka, B.J. and Gordon, R.A. (2012) Client experiences of agency in therapy, *Person-Centered and Experiential Psychotherapies*, 11, 64–82.

Hoffman, L. (1992) A reflexive stance for family therapy. In S. McNamee and K.J. Gergen (eds) *Therapy as Social Construction*. London: Sage.

Hofmann, S.G., Sawyer, A.T. and Fang, A. (2010) The empirical status of the "new wave" of CBT, *Psychiatric Clinics of North America*, 33, 701–10.

Hofstede, G. (1980) *Culture's Consequences: International Differences in Work-related Values*. London: Sage.

Hofstede, G. (2003) *Culture's Consequences, Comparing Values, Behaviors, Institutions, and Organizations Across Nations*, 2nd edn. Newbury Park, CA: Sage.

Hogan, S. (2001) *Healing Arts: The History of Art Therapy*. London: Jessica Kingsley.

Holifield, E.B. (1983) *A History of Pastoral Care in America: From Salvation to Self-realization*. Nashville, TN: Abingdon Press.

Holland, S. (1979) The development of an action and counselling service in a deprived urban area. In M. Meacher (ed.) *New Methods of Mental Health Care*. London: Pergamon.

Holland, S. (1990) Psychotherapy, oppression and social action: gender, race and class in black women's depression. In R.J. Perelberg and A.C. Miller (eds) *Gender and Power in Families*. London: Tavistock/Routledge.

Hollanders, H. and McLeod, J. (1999) Theoretical orientation and reported practice: a survey of eclecticism among counsellors in Britain, *British Journal of Guidance and Counselling*, 27, 405–14.

Holma, J., Partanen, T., Wahlstrom, J., Laitila, A. and Seikkula, J. (2006) Narratives and discourses in groups for male batterers. In M. Libschitz (ed.) *Domestic Violence and its Reverberations*. New York: Nova Science.

Holmes, J. (2000) Attachment theory and psychoanalysis: a rapprochement, *British Journal of Psychotherapy*, 17, 157–72.

Holmes, J. (2001) *The Search for the Secure Base: Attachment, Psychoanalysis, and Narrative*. London: Routledge.

Holmes, J. (2005) Notes on mentalizing – old hat, or new wine? *British Journal of Psychotherapy*, 22, 170–97.

Holmes, J. and Bateman, A. (eds) (2002) *Integration in Psychotherapy: Models and Methods*. New York: Oxford University Press.

Holmqvist, R. (2001) Patterns of consistency and deviation in therapists' countertransference feelings, *Journal of Psychotherapy Practice and Research*, 10, 104–16.

Holmqvist, R. and Armelius, B.A. (1996) Sources of therapists' countertransference feelings, *Psychotherapy Research*, 69(1), 70–8.

Holroyd, J.C. and Brodsky, A. (1977) Psychologists' attitudes and practices regarding erotic and nonerotic physical contact with patients, *American Psychologist*, 32, 843–9.

Holtzman, B.L. (1984) Who's the therapist here? Dynamics underlying therapist-client sexual relations, *Smith College Studies in Social Work*, 54, 204–24.

Holzman, L. and Mendez, R. (eds) (2003) *Psychological Investigations: A Clinician's Guide to Social Therapy*. New York: Brunner-Routledge.

Honos-Webb, L. and Stiles, W.B. (1998) Reformulation of assimilation analysis in terms of voices. *Psychotherapy*, 35, 23–33.

Honos-Webb, L., Stiles, W. B., Greenberg, L.S. and Goldman, R. (1998) Assimilation analysis of process – experiential psychotherapy: a comparison of two cases, *Psychotherapy Research*, 8, 264–86.

Honos-Webb, L., Surko, M., Stiles, W.B. and Greenberg, L.S. (1999) Assimilation of voices in psychotherapy: the case of Jan, *Journal of Counseling Psychology*, 46, 448–60.

Horne, S., Mathews, S., Detrie, P., Burke, M. and Cook, B. (2001) Look it up under "F": dialogues of emerging and experienced feminists, *Women and Therapy*, 23, 5–18.

Horvath, A.O. (2000) The therapeutic relationship: from transference to alliance, *In Session: Psychotherapy in Practice*, 56, 163–73.

Horvath, A.O. and Greenberg, L.S. (1986) The development of the Working Alliance Inventory. In L.D. Greenberg and W.M. Pinsot (eds) *The Psychotherapeutic Process: A Research Handbook*. New York: Guilford Press.

Horvath, A.O. and Greenberg, L. (eds) (1994) *The Working Alliance: Theory, Research and Practice*. New York: Wiley.

Hoshmand, L.T. (2006a) Thinking through culture. In L.T. Hoshmand (ed.) *Culture, Psychotherapy and Counseling: Critical and Integrative Perspectives*. Thousand Oaks, CA: Sage.

Hoshmand, L.T. (2006b) Culture and the field of psychotherapy and counseling. In L.T. Hoshmand (ed.) *Culture, Psychotherapy and Counseling: Critical and Integrative Perspectives*. Thousand Oaks, CA: Sage.

Houghton, S. (1991) A multi-component intervention with an Olympic archer displaying performance related anxiety: a case study, *Behavioural Psychotherapy*, 19, 289–92.

Houston, G. (1990) *Supervision and Counselling*. London: The Rochester Foundation.

Howard, A. (2000) *Philosophy for Counselling and Psychotherapy: Pythagoras to Postmodernism*. London: Macmillan.

Howard, G.S. (1991) Culture tales: a narrative approach to thinking, cross-cultural psychology and psychotherapy, *American Psychologist*, 46, 187–97.

Howard, G.S., Nance, D.W. and Myers, P. (1987) *Adaptive Counseling and Therapy: A Systematic Approach to Selecting Effective Treatments*. San Francisco, CA: Jossey-Bass.

Howard, K.I., Kopta, S.M., Krause, M.S. and Orlinsky, D.E. (1986) The dose–effect relationship in psychotherapy, *American Psychologist*, 41, 159–64.

Howard, K.I., Krause, M.S., Caburney, C.A. and Noel, S.B. (2001) Syzygy, science, and psychotherapy: the *Consumer Reports* study, *Journal of Clinical Psychology*, 57, 865–74.

Howell, E. (1981) Women: from Freud to the present. In E. Howell and M. Bayes (eds) *Women and Mental Health*. New York: Basic Books.

Hoyt, M.F. (ed.) (1994) *Constructive Therapies*. New York: Guilford.

Hoyt, M.F. (ed.) (1996a) *Constructive Therapies 2*. New York: Guilford.

Hoyt, M.F. (1996b) Welcome to PossibilityLand. A conversation with Bill O'Hanlan. In M.F. Hoyt (ed.) *Constructive Therapies 2*. New York: Guilford.

Hsu, J. (1976) Counseling in the Chinese temple: a psychological study of divination by *chien* drawing. In W.P. Lebra (ed.) *Culture-bound Syndromes, Ethnopsychiatry and Alternative Therapies. Volume IV of Mental Health Research in Asia and the Pacific*. Honolulu, HI: University Press of Hawaii.

Hubble, MA, Duncan, B.C. and Miller, S.D. (eds) (1999) *The Heart and Soul of Change: What Works in Therapy*. Washington, DC: American Psychological Assocation.

Hunsley, J., Aubry, T.D., Verservelt, C.M and Vito, D. (1999) Comparing therapist and client perspectives on reasons for psychotherapy termination, *Psychotherapy*, 36, 380–8.

Hunter, M. and Struve, J. (1998) *The Ethical Use of Touch in Psychotherapy*. Thousand Oaks, CA: Sage.

Huss, E., Tekoa, S.D. and Cwikel, J.G. (2009) "Hidden treasures" from Israeli women's writing groups: exploring an integrative, feminist therapy, *Women and Therapy*, 32, 22–39.

Hutz-Midgett, A. and Hutz, S. (2012) Counseling in Brazil: past, present, and future, *Journal of Counseling and Development*, 90, 238–42.

Hycner, R. and Jacobs, L. (1995) *The Healing Relationship in Gestalt Therapy: A Dialogical/Self Psychology Approach*. New York: The Gestalt Journal Press.

Ilardi, S.S. and Craighead, W.E. (1994) The role of nonspecific factors in cognitive-behavior therapy for depression, *Clinical Psychology: Science and Practice*, 1, 138–56.

Ilardi, S.S. and Craighead, W.E. (1999) Early response, cognitive modification, and nonspecific factors in cognitive behavior therapy for depression: a reply to Tang and DeRubeis, *Clinical Psychology: Science and Practice*, 6, 295–9.

Imber-Black, E. and Roberts, J. (1992) *Rituals for Our Times: Celebrating, Healing and Changing Our Lives and Our Relationships*. New York: HarperCollins.

Imel, Z.E., Baldwin, S., Atkins, D.C., Owen, J., Baardseth, T. and Wampold, B.E. (2011) Racial/ethnic disparities in therapist effectiveness: a conceptualization and initial study of cultural competence, *Journal of Counseling Psychology*, 58, 290–7.

Ingham, C. (2000) *Panic Attacks: What They Are, Why They Happen, and What you can do about Them*. London: Thorsons.

Inskipp, F. and Johns, H. (1984) Developmental eclecticism: Egan's skills model of helping. In W. Dryden (ed.) *Individual Therapy in Britain*. Milton Keynes: Open University Press.

Irving, A. and Young, T. (2002) Paradigm for pluralism: Mikhail Bakhtin and social work practice. *Social Work*, 47, 19–29.

Ishiyama, F.I. (1986) Morita therapy: its basic features and cognitive intervention for anxiety treatment, *Psychotherapy*, 23, 375–81.

Israelashvili, M. and Wegman-Rozi, O. (2012) Formal and applied counseling in Israel, *Journal of Counseling and Development*, 90, 227–32.

Israeli, A.L. and Santor, D.A. (2000) Reviewing effective components of feminist therapy, *Counselling Psychology Quarterly*, 13, 233–47.

Ivey, A.E. (1995) Psychotherapy as liberation: toward specific skills and strategies in multicultural counseling and therapy. In J.G. Ponterotto, J.M. Casas, L.A. Suzuki and C.M. Alexander (eds) *Handbook of Multicultural Counseling*. London: Sage.

Ivey, A.E. and Galvin, M. (1984) Microcounseling: a metamodel for counseling, therapy, business and medical interviews. In D. Larson (ed.) *Teaching Psychological Skills: Models for Giving Psychology Away*. Monterey, CA: Brooks/Cole.

Ivey, A.E., Ivey, M.B. and Simek-Downing, L. (1987) *Counseling and Psychotherapy: Integrating Skills, Theory and Practice,* 2nd edn. Englewood Cliffs, NJ: Prentice Hall.

Jack, D.C. (1991) *Silencing The Self: Women and Depression*. Cambridge, MA: Harvard University Press.

Jack, D.C. and Ali, A. (eds) (2010) *Silencing the Self Across Cultures: Depression and Gender in the Social World*. New York: Oxford University Press.

Jacobs, A. (1994) Theory as ideology: reparenting and thought reform, *Transactional Analysis Journal,* 24, 39–55.

Jacobs, E.E., Masson, R.L. and Harvill, R.L. (eds) (2006) *Group Counseling: Strategies and Skills,* 5th edn. Belmont, CA: Wadsworth.

Jacobs, M. (1992) *Sigmund Freud*. London: Sage.

Jacobs, M. (1995) *DW Winnicott*. London: Sage.

Jacobs, M. (2010) *Psychodynamic Counselling in Action,* 4th edn. London: Sage.

Jacobson, N.S., Dobson, K.S., Truax, P.A. and Prince, S.E. (1996) A component analysis of cognitive-behavioral treatment for depression, *Journal of Consulting and Clinical Psychology,* 64, 295–304.

Jacoby, R. (1975) *Social Amnesia: A Critique of Conformist Psychology from Adler to Laing*. New York: Beacon Press.

Jaison, B. (2002) Integrating experiential and brief therapy models: a guide for clinicians. In J.C. Watson, R.N. Goldman and M.S. Warner (eds) *Client-centred and Experiential Psychotherapy in the 21st Century: Advances in Theory, Research and Practice*. Ross-on-Wye: PCCS Books.

James, W. (1909/1977) *A Pluralistic Universe*. Cambridge, MA: Harvard University Press.

James, M. and Jongeward, D. (1971) *Born to Win: Transactional Analysis with Gestalt Experiments*. Reading, MA: Addison-Wesley.

James, O. (2010) *Britain On The Couch: How keeping up with the Joneses has depressed us since 1950*. London: Vermilion.

James, W. (1890) *Principles of Psychology*. New York: Holt.

Jamison, K.R. (1995) *An Unquiet Mind*. New York: Vintage.

Jeffers, S. (2007) *Feel the Fear and do it Anyway: How to Turn your Fear and Indecision into Confidence and Action*. London: Vermilion.

Jenkins, P. (1997) *Counselling, Psychotherapy and the Law*. London: Sage.

Jennings, L. and Skovholt, T.M. (1999) The cognitive, emotional and relational characteristics of master therapists, *Journal of Counseling Psychology*, 46, 3–11.

Johnson, A.W. and Nadirshaw, Z. (1993) Good practice in transcultural counselling: an Asian perspective, *British Journal of Guidance and Counselling*, 21(1), 20–9.

Johnson, S. (2004) *Practice of Emotionally Focused Couple Therapy: Creating Connection,* 2nd edn. New York: Brunner-Routledge.

Johnson, S.E., Hunsley, J., Greenberg, L. and Schindler, D. (1999) Emotionally focused couples therapy; status and challenges, *Clinical Psychology: Science and Practice*, 6, 67–79.

Johnstone, L. and Dallos, R. (eds) (2006) *Formulation in Psychology and Psychotherapy: Making Sense of People's Problems*. London: Routledge.

Joines, V. and Stewart, I. (2002) *Personality Adaptations*. Nottingham: Lifespace.

Jones, C., Shillito-Clarke, C., Syme, G., Hill, D., Casemore, R. and Murdin, L. (2000) *Questions of Ethics in Counselling and Therapy*. Buckingham: Open University Press.

Jones, E. (1951) *Essays in Applied Psychoanalysis,* Volume II. London: Hogarth Press.

Jones, E. (1955) *Life and Work of Sigmund Freud,* Volume 2. London: Hogarth Press.

Jones, E. (1993) *Family Systems Therapy: Developments in the Milan-systemic Therapies*. Chichester: Wiley.

Jones, E.E. (2000) *Therapeutic Action: A Guide to Psychoanalytic Therapy*. Northvale, NJ: Jason Aronson.

Jones, E.E. and Pulos, S.M. (1993) Comparing the process in psychodynamic and cognitive-behavioral therapies, *Journal of Consulting and Clinical Psychology*, 61, 306–16.

Jones, M.A., Botsko, M. and Gorman, B.S. (2003) Predictors of psychotherapeutic benefit of lesbian, gay, and bisexual clients: the effects of sexual orientation matching and other factors, *Psychotherapy: Theory, Research, Practice, Training*, 40, 289–301.

Jongsma, I. (1995) Philosophical counseling in Holland: history and open issues. In R. Lahav and M. da Venza Tillmanns (eds) *Essays on Philosophical Counselling*. Lanham, MD: University Press of America.

Jordan, J.V. (1991) Empathy, mutuality and therapeutic change: clinical implications of a relational model. In J.V. Jordan, A.G. Kaplan, J.B. Miller, I.P. Stiver and J.L. Surrey (eds) *Women's Growth in Connection*. New York: Guilford Press.

Jordan, J.V. (1997a) A relational perspective for understanding women's development. In J.V. Jordan (ed.) *Women's Growth in Diversity: More Writings from the Stone Center*. New York: Guilford Press.

Jordan, J.V. (ed.) (1997b) *Women's Growth in Diversity: More Writings from the Stone Center*. New York: Guilford Press.

Jordan, J.V. (2000) The role of mutual empathy in relational/cultural therapy, *Journal of Clinical Psychology*, 56, 1005–16.

Jordan, J.V. (2004) Toward competence and connection. In J.V. Jordan, M. Walker and L.M. Hartling (eds) *The Complexity of Connection: Writings from the Stone Center's Jean Baker Miller Training Institute*. New York: Guilford Press.

Jordan, J.V. (ed.) (2008) *The Power of Connection: Recent Developments in Relational-Cultural Theory*. New York: Haworth Press.

Jordan, J.V., Kaplan, A.G., Miller, J.B., Stiver, I.P. and Surrey, J.L. (eds) (1991) *Women's Growth in Connection: Writings from the Stone Center*. New York: Guilford Press.

Jordan, J.V., Walker, M. and Hartling, L.M. (eds) (2004) *The Complexity of Connection: Writings from the Stone Center's Jean Baker Miller Training Institute*. New York: Guilford Press.

Jordan, M. and Marshall, H. (2010) Taking counselling and psychotherapy outside: Destruction or enrichment of the therapeutic frame? *European Journal of Psychotherapy and Counselling*, 12, 345–59.

Jorm, A.F., Griffiths, K.M., Christensen, H. *et al.* (2004) Actions taken to cope with depression at different levels of severity: a community survey, *Psychological Medicine*, 34, 293–9.

Josephs, I.E. (2002) 'The Hopi in me' The construction of a voice in the dialogical self from a cultural psychological perspective, *Theory and Psychology*, 12: 161–73.

Josselson, R. (1996) *The Space Between Us: Exploring the Dimensions of Human Relationships*. Thousand Oaks, CA: Sage.

Jung, C.G. (1963) *Memories, Dreams, Reflections* (edited by A. Jaffe). New York: Pantheon Books.

Jung, C.G. (1964) *Man and His Symbols*. New York: Doubleday.

Jupp, J.J. and Shaul, V. (1991) Burn-out in student counsellors, *Counselling Psychology Quarterly*, 4, 157–67.

Kabat-Zinn, J. (1990) *Full Catastrophe Living: Using the Wisdom of your Body and Mind to Face Stress, Pain and Illness*. New York: Delacorte.

Kabat-Zinn, J. (1994) *Wherever you go, there you are: Mindfulness Meditation in Everyday Life*. New York: Hyperion.

Kaberry, S. (2000) Abuse in supervision. In B. Lawton and C. Feltham (eds) *Taking Supervision Forward: Enquiries and Trends in Counselling and Psychotherapy*. London: Sage.

Kachele, H. (1992) Narration and observation in psychotherapy research: reporting on a 20 year long journey, *Psychotherapy Research*, 2, 1–15.

Kachele, H., Richter, R., Thoma, H. and Meyer, A.-E. (1999) Psychotherapy services in the Federal Republic of Germany. In N. E. Miller and K. M. Magruder (eds) *Cost-effectiveness of Psychotherapy: A Guide for Practitioners, Researchers and Policymakers.* New York: Oxford University Press.

Kagan, N. (1984) Interpersonal Process Recall: basic methods and recent research. In D. Larson (ed.) *Teaching Psychological Skills: Models for Giving Psychology Away.* Monterey, CA: Brooks/Cole.

Kagan, N. and Kagan, H. (1990) IPR – a validated model for the 1990s and beyond, *Counseling Psychologist,* 18, 436–40.

Kagan, N., Krathwohl, D.R. and Miller, R. (1963) Stimulated recall in therapy using videotape – a case study, *Journal of Counseling Psychology,* 10, 237–43.

Kahler, T. (1978) *Transactional Analysis Revisited.* Little Rock, AR: Human Development.

Kahn, E. (1999) A critique of nondirectivity in the person-centered approach, *Journal of Humanistic Psychology,* 39, 94–110.

Kahn, M. (1997) *Between Therapist and Client: The New Relationship,* 2nd edn. New York: W. H. Freeman.

Kahn, S. and Fromm, E. (eds) (2000) *Changes in the Therapist.* Wokingham: Lea Publishing.

Kanfer, A. and Goldstein, A. (eds) (1986) *Helping People Change,* 3rd edn. New York: Pergamon.

Kannan, D. and Levitt, H.M. (2009) Challenges facing the developing feminist psychotherapist in training, *Women and Therapy,* 32, 406–22.

Kaplan, A.G. (1987) Reflections on gender and psychotherapy. In M. Braude (ed.) *Women, Power and Therapy.* New York: Haworth Press.

Kaplan, D.M. and Gladding, S. (2011) A vision for the future of counseling: the 20/20 principles for unifying and strengthening the profession, *Journal of Counseling and Development,* 89, 367–72.

Karasu, T.B. (1986) The specificity against nonspecificity dilemma: toward identifying therapeutic change agents, *American Journal of Psychiatry,* 143, 687–95.

Kareem, J. (2000) The Nafsiyat Intercultural Therapy Centre: ideas and experiences in Interncultural therapy. In Kareem, J. and Littlewood, R. (eds) *Intercultural Therapy,* 2nd edn. Oxford: Blackwell.

Karlsruher, A.E. (1974) The nonprofessional as psychotherapeutic agent, *American Journal of Community Psychology,* 2, 61–77.

Karon, B.P. (2008) An "incurable" schizophrenic: the case of Mr. X, *Pragmatic Case Studies in Psychotherapy,* 4, 1–24. Available at http://pcsp.libraries.rutgers.edu/index.php/pcsp/article/view/923/2325 (accessed 19 March 2013).

Karpman, S. (1968) Fairy tales and script drama analysis, *Transactional Analysis Bulletin,* 7(26), 39–43.

Kaslow, F.W. (1986) Supervision, consultation and staff training – creative teaching/ learning processes in the mental health profession. In F.W. Kaslow (ed.) *Supervision and Training. Models, Dilemmas and Challenges.* New York: Haworth Press.

Kaufmann, Y. (1989) Analytical psychotherapy. In R.J. Corsini and D. Wedding (eds) *Current Psychotherapies,* 4th edn. Itasca, IL: F.E. Peacock.

Kazantzis, N., McEwan, J. and Dattilio, F.M. (2005) A guiding model for practice. In Kazantzis, N. Deane, F.P., Ronan, K.R. and L'Abate, L. (eds) *Using Homework Assignments in Cognitive Behavior Therapy.* London: Routledge.

Kazdin, A.E. (1978) *History of Behavior Modification: Experimental Foundations of Contemporary Research.* Baltimore, MD: University Park Press.

Kazdin, A.E. (ed.) (2003) *Methodological Issues and Strategies in Clinical Research.* Washington, DC: American Psychological Association.

Kearney, A. (1996) *Counselling, Class and Politics: Undeclared Influences in Therapy.* Ross-on-Wye: PCCS Books.

Keeling, M.L. and Bermudez, M. (2006) Externalizing problems through art and writing: Experiences of process and helpfulness, *Journal of Marital and Family Therapy,* 32, 405–19.

Keeling, M.L. and Nielson, L.R. (2005) Indian women's experience of a narrative intervention using art and writing, *Contemporary Family Therapy,* 27, 435–55.

Kelly, E.W. (1995) Counselor values: a national survey, *Journal of Counseling and Development,* 73, 648–53.

Kelly, G.A. (1955) *The Psychology of Personal Constructs,* Volumes 1 and 2. New York: W.W. Norton.

Kelly, G.A. (1983) A brief introduction to personal construct theory. In F. Fransella (ed.) *International Handbook of Personal Construct Psychology.* Chichester: Wiley.

Kelly, T.A. (1989) The role of values in psychotherapy: a critical review of process and outcome effects, *Clinical Psychology Review*, 10, 171–86.

Kemp, N.T. and Mallinckrodt, B. (1996) Impact of professional training on case conceptualization of clients with a disability, *Professional Psychology: Research and Practice*, 27, 378–85.

Kendall, P.C., Holmbeck, G. and Verduin, T. (2004) Methodology, design and evaluation in psychotherapy research. In M.J. Lambert (ed.) *Bergin and Garfield's Handbook of Psychotherapy and Behavior Change,* 5th edn. New York: Wiley.

Kendjelic, E.M. and Eells, T.D (2007) Generic psychotherapy case formulation training improves formulation quality, *Psychotherapy: Theory, Research, Practice, Training*, 44, 66–77.

Kennel, R.G. and Agresti, A.A. (1995) Effects of gender and age on psychologists' reporting of child sexual abuse, *Professional Psychology: Research and Practice*, 26(6), 612–15.

Kennerley, H. (1997) *Overcoming Anxiety: A Self-help Guide using Cognitive-behavioural Techniques*. London: Constable and Robinson.

Kenny, M.C. and McEachern, A.G. (2004) Telephone counselling: are the offices becoming obsolete? *Journal of Counseling and Development*, 82, 199–202.

Kernberg, O.F. (1975) *Borderline Conditions and Pathological Narcissism*. New York: Aronson.

Kernberg, O.F. (1976) *Object Relations Theory and Clinical Psychoanalysis*. New York: Jason Aronson.

Kernberg, O.F. (1984) *Severe Personality Disorders: Psychotherapeutic Strategies*. New Haven, CT: Yale University Press.

Kerner, E. and Fitzpatrick, M. (2007) Integrating writing into psychotherapy practice: a matrix of change processes and structural dimensions, *Psychotherapy: Theory, Research, Practice, Training*, 44, 333–46.

Khele, S., Symons, C. and Wheeler, S. (2008) An analysis of complaints to the British Association for Counselling and Psychotherapy, 1996–2006, *Counselling and Psychotherapy Research*, 8, 124–32.

Kiesler, D. (1988) *Therapeutic Metacommunication: Therapist Impact Disclosure as Feedback in Psychotherapy*. Palo Alto, CA: Consulting Psychologists Press.

Kiesser, M., McFadden, J. and Belliard, J.C. (2006) An interdisciplinary view of medical pluralism among Mexican-Americans, *Journal of Interprofessional Care*, 20, 223–34.

Kilmann, P.R., Laughlin, J.E., Carranza, L.V., Downer, J.T., Major, S. and Parnell, M.M. (1999) Effects of an attachment-focused group preventive intervention on secure women, *Group Dynamics*, 3, 138–47.

Kim, B.S.K. and Lyons, H.Z. (2003) Experiential activities and multicultural counseling training, *Journal of Counseling and Development*, 81, 400–8.

Kim, D.-M., Walmpold, B.E. and Bolt, D.M. (2006) Therapist effects in psychotherapy: a random-effects modeling of the National Institute of Mental Health Treatment of Depression Collaborative Research Program data, *Psychotherapy Research*, 16, 144–60.

King, A. (2001) *Demystifying the Counseling Process. A Self-help Handbook for Counselors*. Needham Heights, MA: Allyn and Bacon.

King, J.H. and Anderson, S.M. (2004) Therapeutic implications of pharmacotherapy: current trends and ethical issues, *Journal of Counseling and Development*, 82, 329–36.

King, M., Semylen, J., Killaspy, H., Nazareth, I. and Osborn, D. (2007) *A Systematic Review of Research on Counselling and Psychotherapy for Lesbian, Gay, Bisexual and Transgender People*. Lutterworth: British Association for Counselling and Psychotherapy.

King-Spooner, S. (1999) Editorial: introduction to special issue on philosophy and psychotherapy, *Changes*, 17(3), 159–60.

Kirkwood, C. (2000) *The Development of Counselling in Shetland*. Stirling: COSCA.

Kirkwood, C. (2012) *The Persons in Relation Perspective: In counselling, Psychotherapy and Community Adult Learning*. Rotterdam: Sense Publishing.

Kirsch, I. (1978) Demonology and the rise of science: an example of the misperception of historical data, *Journal of the History of the Behavioral Sciences*, 14, 149–57.

Kirsch, T.B. (2005) The role of personal therapy in the formation of a Jungian analyst. In J.D. Geller, J.C Norcross and D.E.Orlinsky (eds) *The Psychotherapist's own Psychotherapy: Patient and Clinician Perspectives*. New York: Oxford University Press.

Kirschenbaum, H. (1979) *On Becoming Carl Rogers*. New York: Dell.

Kirschenbaum, H. (2007) *The Life and Work of Carl Rogers*. Ross-on-Wye: PCCS Books.

Kirschenbaum, H. and Henderson, V. L. (eds) (1990) *Carl Rogers: Dialogues*. London: Constable.

Kiselica, M.S. and Robinson, M. (2001) Bringing advocacy counselling to life: the history, issues, and human dramas of social justice work in counseling, *Journal of Counseling and Development*, 79, 387–97.

Kitchener, K.S. (1984) Intuition, critical evaluation and ethical principles: the foundation for ethical decisions in counseling psychology, *Counseling Psychologist*, 12, 43–55.

Kitzinger, C. and Perkins, R. (1993) *Changing Our Minds: Lesbian Feminism and Psychology*. London: Onlywomen Press.

Kivlighan, D.M., Patton, M.J. and Foote, D. (1998) Moderating effects of client attachment on the counselor experience–working alliance relationship, *Journal of Counseling Psychology*, 45, 274–8.

Klein, M.H. (1976) Feminist concepts of therapy outcome, *Psychotherapy: Theory, Research and Practice*, 13(1), 89–95.

Klein, M.H., Mathieu-Coughlan, P. and Kiesler, D.J. (1986) The Experiencing Scales. In L.S. Greenberg and W.M. Pinsof (eds) *The Psychotherapeutic Process: A Research Handbook*. New York: Guilford Press.

Kleinman, A. (1988) *The Illness Narratives: Suffering, Healing and the Human Condition*. New York: Basic Books.

Kleinman, A. (2004) Culture and depression, *New England Journal of Medicine*, 351, 951–2.

Kleinman, A. and Benson, P. (2006) Anthropology in the clinic: the problem of cultural competency and how to fix it, *PLoS Med*, 3(1): e294.

Knox, R. (2008) Clients' experience of relational depth in person-centred counselling, *Counselling and Psychotherapy Research*, 8, 182–8.

Knox, R. and Cooper, M. (2011) A state of readiness: an exploration of the client's role in meeting at relational depth, *Journal of Humanistic Psychology*, 51, 61–81.

Knox, R. Murphy, D. Wiggins, S. and Cooper, M. (eds) (2012) *Relational Depth: New Perspectives and Developments*. London: Palgrave Macmillan.

Knox, S. and Hill, C.E. (2003) Therapist self-disclosure: research-based suggestions for practitioners, *Journal of Clinical Psychology*, 59, 529–39.

Knox, S., Goldberg, J.L., Woodhouse, S.S. and Hill, C.E. (1999) Clients' internal representations of their therapists, *Journal of Counseling Psychology*, 46, 244–56.

Knox, S., Adrians, N., Everson, E., Hess, S., Hill, C. and Crook-Lyon, R. (2011) Clients' perspectives on therapy termination, *Psychotherapy Research*, 21, 154–67.

Koffka, K. (1935) *Principles of Gestalt Psychology*. New York: Harcourt, Brace.

Kohler, W. (1929) *Gestalt Psychology*. New York: Liveright.

Kohon, G. (ed.) (1986) *The British School of Psychoanalysis: The Independent Tradition*. London: Free Association Books.

Kohut, H. (1971) *The Analysis of the Self*. London: Hogarth.

Kohut, H. (1977) *The Restoration of the Self*. Madison, CT: International Universities Press.

Kopp, S. (1972) *If You Meet the Buddha on the Road, Kill Him!* Palo Alto, CA: Science and Behavior Books.

Kopp, S. (1974) *The Hanged Man*. Palo Alto, CA: Science and Behavior Books.

Kort, J. (2008) *Gay Affirmative Therapy for the Straight Clinician: the Essential Guide*. New York: W.W. Norton.

Kottler, J. (1988) *The Imperfect Therapist*. San Francisco, CA: Jossey-Bass.

Kottler, J.A. (1998) *The Therapist's Workbook: Self-Assessment, Self-Care, and Self-Improvement Exercises for Mental Health Professionals*. New York: Jossey-Bass.

Kottler, J.A. (2003) *On Being a Therapist*, 3rd edn. San Franscisco, CA: Jossey-Bass.

Kottler, J. and Carlson, J. (2003a) *Bad Therapy: Master Therapists Share their Worst Failures*. New York: Brunner-Routledge.

Kottler, J.A. and Carlson, J. (2003b) *The Mummy At the Dining Room Table: Eminent Therapists Reveal Their Most Unusual Cases and What They Teach Us About Human Behavior*. San Francisco, CA: Jossey-Bass.

Kottler, J.A. and Carlson, J. (eds) (2005) *The Client who Changed Me: Stories of Therapist Personal Transformation*. New York: Routledge.

Kottler, J.A. and Carlson, J. (2006) *The Client Who Changed Me: Stories of Therapist Personal Transformation*. New York: Brunner-Routledge.

Kottler, J.A. and Carlson, J. (2008) *Their Finest Hour: Master Therapists Share Their Greatest Success Stories*, 2nd edn. Bethel, CT: Crown Publishing.

Kottler, J.A. and Carlson, J. (2009) *Creative Breakthroughs in Therapy: Tales of Transformation and Astonishment.* New York: Wiley.

Kovel, J. (1981) The American mental health industry. In D. Ingleby (ed.) *Critical Psychiatry: The Politics of Mental Health.* Harmondsworth: Penguin.

Kraus, D.R., Castonguay, L., Boswell, J.F., Nordberg, S.S. and Hayes, J.A. (2011) Therapist effectiveness: implications for accountability and patient care, *Psychotherapy Research,* 21, 267–76.

Kraus, R., Zack, J. and Stricker, G. (eds) (2004) *Online Counseling: A Handbook for Mental Health Professionals.* San Diego, CA: Academic Press.

Krupnick, J.L. and Melnikoff, S.E. (2012) Psychotherapy with low-income patients: lessons learned from treatment studies, *Journal of Contemporary Psychotherapy,* 42, 7–15.

Kuehnel, J. and Liberman, P. (1986) Behavior modification. In I. Kutush and A. Wolf (eds) *A Psychotherapist's Casebook.* San Francisco, CA: Jossey-Bass.

Kuenzli, F. (2009) Turning away from difficult problems with gentle solutions: therapy with a teenager battling with anger, *The International Gestalt Journal,* 32, 138–164. Available at http://www.reflexivepractices.com/ (accessed 19 March 2013).

Kuhn, T.S. (1962) *The Structure of Scientific Revolutions.* Chicago, IL: University of Chicago Press.

Kurioka, S., Muto, T. and Tarumi, K. (2001) Characteristics of health counselling in the workplace via email, *Occupational Medicine,* 51, 427–32.

Kurri, K. and Wahlstrom, J. (2005) Placement of responsibility and moral reasoning in couple therapy, *Journal of Family Therapy,* 27, 352–69.

Kurtz, R. and Grummon, D. (1972) Different approaches to the measurement of therapist empathy and their relationship to therapy outcomes, *Journal of Consulting and Clinical Psychology,* 39, 106–15.

Kuyken, W., Padesky, C.A. and Dudley, R. (2009) *Collaborative Case Conceptualization: Working Effectively with Clients in Cognitive-Behavioral Therapy.* New York: Guilford Press.

Kvale, S. (ed.) (1992) *Postmodernism and Psychology.* London: Sage.

Kyriakopoulos, A. (2010) Adventure based counselling, individual counselling and object relations: a critical evaluation of a qualitative study, *European Journal of Psychotherapy and Counselling,* 12, 311–22.

Kyriakopoulos, A. (2011) How individuals with self-reported anxiety and depression experienced a combination of individual counselling with an adventurous outdoor experience: a qualitative evaluation, *Counselling and Psychotherapy Research,* 11, 120–8.

Lacan, J. (1977) *Ecrits: A Selection.* New York: W.W. Norton.

Lacan, J. (1979) *The Four Fundamental Concepts of Psycho-Analysis.* London: Penguin.

Ladany, N., Hill, C.E., Corbett, M.M. and Nutt, E.A. (1996) Nature, extent and importance of what psychotherapy trainees do not disclose to their supervisors, *Journal of Counseling Psychology,* 43, 10–24.

LaFave, L., Desportes, L. and McBride, C. (2008) Treatment outcomes and perceived benefits: A qualitative and quantitative assessment of a women's substance abuse treatment program, *Women and Therapy,* 32, 51–68.

Lago, C. (2006) *Race, Culture and Counselling: The Ongoing Challenge,* 2nd edn. Maidenhead: Open University Press.

Lago, C. (ed.) (2011) *Handbook of Transcultural Counselling and Psychotherapy.* Maidenhead: Open University Press.

Lahad, D. (2002) *Creative Supervision.* London: Jessica Kingsley.

Lahad, M. (1992) Story-making in assessment method for coping with stress: six-piece story-making and BASIC Ph. In S. Jennings, (ed.), *Dramatherapy: Theory and Practice 2.* London: Routledge.

Lahad, M. (1995) Interviews with pioneers and practitioners. In S. Jennings, A. Cattanach, S. Mitchell, A. Chesner and B.Meldrum (eds) *The Handbook of Dramatherapy.* London: Routledge.

Lahav, R. (1995a) Introduction. In R. Lahav and M. da Venza Tillmanns (eds) *Essays on Philosophical Counseling.* Lanham, MD: University Press of America.

Lahav, R. (1995b) A conceptual framework for philosophical counseling: worldview interpretation. In R. Lahav and M. da Venza Tillmanns (eds) *Essays on Philosophical Counselling.* Lanham, MD: University Press of America.

Lahav, R. and da Venza Tillmanns, M. (eds) (1995) *Essays on Philosophical Counselling.* Lanham, MD: University Press of America.

Laing, R.D. (1960) *The Divided Self.* Harmondsworth: Penguin.

Laing, R.D. (1961) *Self and Others.* Harmondsworth: Penguin.

Laing, R.D., Phillipson, H. and Lee, A.R. (1966) *Interpersonal Perception – A Theory and a Method of Research.* London: Tavistock.

Laireiter, A.-R. and Willutzki, U. (2005) Personal therapy in cognitive-behavioral tradition and current practice. In J.D. Geller, J.C Norcross and D.E.Orlinsky (eds) *The Psychotherapist's own Psychotherapy: Patient and Clinician Perspectives.* New York: Oxford University Press.

Lakin, M. (1988) *Ethical Issues in the Psychotherapies.* New York: Oxford University Press.

Lam, D.C.K. and Gale, J. (2004) Cognitive behaviour therapy: an evidence-based clinical framework for working with dysfunctional thoughts, *Counselling Psychology Quarterly,* 17, 53–67.

Lamb, D.H. and Catanzaro, S.J. (1998) Sexual and nonsexual boundary violations involving psychologists, clients, supervisees, and students: implications for professional practice, *Professional Psychology: Research and Practice,* 29, 498–503.

Lambert, M.J. (ed.) (2004) *Bergin and Garfield's Handbook of Psychotherapy and Behavior Change,* 5th edn. New York: Wiley.

Lambert, M.J. (2007) What we have learned from a decade of research aimed at improving psychotherapy outcome in routine care, *Psychotherapy Research,* 17, 1–14.

Lambert, M.J. (2010) "Yes, it is time for clinicians to routinely monitor treatment outcome". In B.L. Duncan, S.D. Miller, B.E.Wampold and M.A. Hubble (eds) *The Heart and Soul of Change. Delivering what Works in Therapy,* 2nd edn. Washington, DC: American Psychological Association.

Lambert, M.J. and Ogles, B.M. (2004) The efficacy and effectiveness of psychotherapy. In M.J. Lambert (ed.) *Bergin and Garfield's Handbook of Psychotherapy and Behavior Change,* 5th edn. New York: Wiley.

Lambert, M.J., Christensen, E.R. and DeJulio, S.S. (eds) (1983) *The Assessment of Psychotherapy Outcome.* New York: Wiley.

Lambert, M.J., Bergin, A.E. and Garfield, S.L. (2004) Introduction and historical overview. In M.J. Lambert (ed.) *Bergin and Garfield's Handbook of Psychotherapy and Behavior Change,* 5th edn. New York: Wiley.

Lambie, G.W. and Milsom, A. (2010) A narrative approach to supporting students diagnosed with learning disabilities, *Journal of Counseling and Development,* 86, 196–203.

Lampropoulos, G.K., Kazantzis, N. and Deane, F.P. (2004) Psychologists' use of motion pictures in clinical practice, *Professional Psychology: Research and Practice,* 35, 535–41.

Landrine, H. (1992) Clinical implications of cultural differences: the referential vs the indexical self, *Clinical Psychology Review,* 12, 401–15.

Langdridge, D. (2007) Gay affirmative therapy: a theoretical framework and defence, *Journal of Gay and Lesbian Psychotherapy,* 11 (1/2), 27–43.

Lange, A., Rietdijk, D., Hudcovicova, M., van de Ven, J-P., Schrieken, B. and Emmelkamp, P.M.G. (2003) Interapy: a controlled randomized trial of the standardized treatment of posttraumatic stress through the internet, *Journal of Consulting and Clinical Psychology,* 71, 901–9.

Langman, P.F. (1997) White culture, Jewish culture, and the origins of psychotherapy, *Psychotherapy,* 34, 207–18.

Langs, R.J. (1988) *A Primer of Psychotherapy.* New York: Gardner.

Lankton, S. and Lankton, C. (1986) *Enchantment and Intervention in Family Therapy.* New York: Brunner/Mazel.

Lapworth, P., Sills, C. and Fish, S. (2001) *Integration in Counselling and Psychotherapy: Developing a Personal Approach.* London: Sage.

LaRoche, M.J. and Maxie, A. (2003) Ten considerations in addressing cultural differences in psychotherapy, *Professional Psychology: Research and Practice,* 34, 180–6.

Larsen, D.J and Stege, R. (2012) Client accounts of hope in early counseling sessions: a qualitative study, *Journal of Counseling and Development,* 90, 45–54.

Larson, D. (ed.) (1984) *Teaching Psychological Skills: Models for Giving Psychology Away.* Monterey, CA: Brooks/Cole.

Larson, L.M., Suzuki, L.A., Gillespie, K. N. et al. (1992) Development and validation of the counseling self-estimate inventory, *Journal of Counseling Psychology,* 39, 105–20.

Lasky, E. (1999) Psychotherapists' ambivalence about fees: male–female differences. *Women and Therapy,* 22(3), 5–14.

Lasky, R. (2005) The training analysis in the mainstream Freudian model. In J.D. Geller, J.C Norcross and D.E.Orlinsky (eds) *The Psychotherapist's own Psychotherapy: Patient and Clinician Perspectives.* New York: Oxford University Press.

Lawrence, M. and Maguire, M. (eds) (1997) *Psychotherapy with Women: Feminist Perspectives*. London: Macmillan.

Lawson, G. (2007) Counselor wellness and impairment: a national survey, *Journal of Humanistic Counseling*, 46, 20–34.

Lawton, B. (2000) 'A very exposing affair': explorations in counsellors' supervisory relationships. In B. Lawton and C. Feltham (eds) *Taking Supervision Forward: Enquiries and Trends in Counselling and Psychotherapy*. London: Sage.

Lazarus, A.A. (1967) In support of technical eclecticism, *Psychological Reports*, 21, 415–16.

Lazarus, A.A. (1989a) *The Practice of Multimodal Therapy*. Baltimore, MD: Johns Hopkins University Press.

Lazarus, A.A. (1989b) Multimodal therapy. In R.J. Corsini and D. Wedding (eds) *Current Psychotherapies,* 4th edn. Itasca, IL: F E Peacock.

Lazarus, A.A. (1994) How certain boundaries and ethics diminish therapeutic effectiveness, *Ethics and Behavior*, 4, 253–61.

Lazarus, A.A. (2005) Multimodal therapy. In J.C. Norcross. and M.R. Goldfried (eds) *Handbook of Psychotherapy Integration*. New York: Oxford University Press.

Lazarus, A.A. (2007) On necessity and sufficiency in counseling and psychotherapy (revisited), *Psychotherapy: Theory, Research, Practice, Training*, 44, 253–6.

Lazarus, A.A. and Zur, O. (eds) (2002) *Dual Relationships in Psychotherapy*. New York: Springer.

Lazarus, A.A., Beutler, L.E. and Norcross, J.C. (1992) The future of technical eclecticism, *Psychotherapy*, 29, 11–20.

Le, H., Zmuda, J., Perry, D.F. and Munoz, R. (2010) Transforming an Evidence-Based Intervention to Prevent Perinatal Depression for Low-Income Latina Immigrants, American *Journal of Orthopsychiatry*, 80, 34–45.

Leahy, R. (2003) *Cognitive Therapy Technique: A Practitioner's Guide*. New York: Guilford Press.

Lebow, J. (2005) The role and current practice of personal therapy in systematic/family therapy traditions. In J.D. Geller, J.C Norcross and D.E.Orlinsky (eds) *The Psychotherapist's own Psychotherapy: Patient and Clinician Perspectives*. New York: Oxford University Press.

Ledley, D.R., Marx, B.P. and Heimberg, R.G. (2005) *Making Cognitive-Behavioral Therapy Work: Clinical Process for New Practitioners*. New York: Guilford Press.

Lee, A. (2006) Process contracts. In C. Sills (ed.) *Contracts in Counselling and and Psychotherapy*. London: Sage.

Lee, B.-O. (2002) Chinese indigenous psychotherapies in Singapore, *Counselling and Psychotherapy Research*, 2, 2–10.

Lee, J., Lim, N., Yang, F. and Min Lee, S. (2011) Antecedents and consequences of three dimensions of burnout in psychotherapists: a meta-analysis, *Professional Psychology: Research and Practice*, 42, 252–8.

Lee, S.M., Suh, S., Yang, E. and Jang, Y.J. (2012) History, current status, and future prospects of counseling in South Korea, *Journal of Counseling and Development*, 90, 494–8.

Leijssen, M. (1993) Creating a workable distance to overwhelming images: comments on a session transcript. In D. Brazier (ed.) *Beyond Carl Rogers*. London: Constable.

Leijssen, M. (1998) Focusing microprocesses. In L.S. Greenberg, J.C. Watson and G. Lietaer (eds) *Handbook of Experiential Psychotherapy*. New York: Guilford Press.

Leijssen, M. (2006) Validation of the body in psychotherapy, *Journal of Humanistic Psychology*, 46, 126–46.

Leiman, M. (1997) Procedures as dialogical sequences. A revised version of the fundamental concept in cognitive analytic therapy, *British Journal of Medical Psychology*, 67, 97–106.

Leiter, M. P. and Maslach, C. (2005) *Banishing Burnout: Six Strategies for Improving your Relationship with Work*. San Francisco, CA: Jossey-Bass.

Lemoire, S.J. and Chen, C.P. (2005) Applying person-centred counseling to sexual minority adolescents,*Journal of Counseling and Development*, 83, 146–54.

Lener, R. (1972) *Therapy in the Ghetto*. New York: Wiley.

Lepore, S.J., Greenberg, M. A., Bruno, M. and Smyth, J.M. (2002) Expressive writing and health: self-regulation of emotion-related experience, physiology, and behavior. In S.J. Lepore and J.M. Smyth (eds) *The Writing Cure*. Washington, DC: American Psychological Association.

Lester, D. (1974) The unique qualities of telephone therapy, *Psychotherapy*, 11, 219–21.

Levant, R.F. and Shlien, J.M. (eds) (1984) *Client-centered Therapy and the Person-centered Approach: New Directions in Theory, Research and Practice*. New York: Praeger.

Levinas, E. (1969) *Totality and Infinity: An Essay on Exteriority* (A. Lingis, trans.). Pittsburgh, PA: Duquesne University Press.

Levine, B.E. (2007) *Surviving America's Depression Epidemic. How to find Morale, Energy, and Community in a World Gone Crazy*. White River Junction, VT: Chelsea Green Publishing.

Levine, M. and Doueck, H.J. (1995) *The Impact of Mandated Reporting on the Therapeutic Process: Picking up the Pieces*. London: Sage.

Levinson, H. (1956) Employee counselling in industry: observations on three programs, *Employee Counselling in Industry*, 20, 76–84.

Levitt, B. (ed.) (2005) *Embracing Non-directivity: Re-assessing Person-centred Theory and Practice for the 21st Century*. Ross-on-Wye: PCCS Books.

Levitt, H., Korman, Y. and Angus, L. (2000) A metaphor analysis in treatments of depression: Metaphor as a marker of change, *Counselling Psychology Quarterly*, 13, 23–35.

Levitt, H., Butler, M. and Hill, T. (2006) What clients find helpful in psychotherapy: developing principles for facilitating moment-to-moment change, *Journal of Counseling Psychology*, 53, 314–24.

Lewin, K. (1952) *Field Theory in Social Science: Selected Theoretical Papers by Kurt Lewin*. London: Tavistock.

Lewis, I.A., Toporek, R.L. and Ratts, M. (2010) Advocacy and social justice: Entering the mainstream of the counseling profession. In M.I. Ratts, R.L. Toporek and J.A. Lewis (eds) *ACA Advocacy Competencies: A Social Justice Framework for Counsellors*. Alexandria, VA: American Counseling Association.

Lewis, J., Clark, D. and Morgan, D. (1992) *Whom God Hath Joined Together: The Work of Marriage Guidance*. London: Routledge.

Lewis, J. (2011) Operationalizing social justice counseling: paradigm to practice, *Journal of Humanistic Counseling*, 50, 183–91.

Liddle, B.J. (1995) Sexual orientation bias among advanced graduate students of counseling and counseling psychology, *Counselor Education and Supervision*, 34, 321–31.

Liddle, B.J. (1996) Therapist sexual orientation, gender, and counseling practices as they relate to ratings of helpfulness by gay and lesbian clients, *Journal of Counseling Psychology*, 43(4), 394–401.

Liddle, B.J. (1997) Gay and lesbian clients' selection of therapists and utilization of therapy. *Psychotherapy*, 34, 11–18.

Lieberman, M., Yalom, I. and Miles, M. (1973) *Encounter Groups: First Facts*. New York: Basic Books.

Lietaer, G. (1990) The client-centered approach after the Wisconsin project: a personal view on its evolution. In G. Lietaer, J. Rombauts and R. Van Balen (eds) *Client-centered and Experiential Therapy in the Nineties*. Leuven: Leuven University Press.

Lietaer, G. (1993) Authenticity, congruence and transparency. In D. Brazier (ed.) *Beyond Carl Rogers*. London: Constable.

Lietaer, G. (2001) Becoming genuine as a therapist: congruence and transparency. In G. Wyatt (ed.) *Rogers' Therapeutic Conditions: Evolution, Theory and Practice, Volume 1: Congruence*. Ross-on-Wye: PCCS Books.

Lietaer, G., Rombauts, J. and van Balen, R. (eds) (1990) *Client-centered and Experiential Therapy in the Nineties*. Leuven: Leuven University Press.

Lilley, M. (2007) My time, *Therapy Today*, 18(5), 34–5.

Lilley, M., Twigg, E. and Keane, M. (2005) My time: widening and increasing participation of hard-to-read learners through provision at the interface of education and primary health care. In Y. Hillier and A. Thompson (eds) *Readings in Post-compulsory Education: Research in the Learning and Skills Sector*. London: Continuum.

Lilliengren, P. and Werbart, A. (2005) A model of therapeutic action grounded in the patients' view of curative and hindering factors in psychoanalytic psychotherapy, *Psychotherapy: Theory, Research, Practice, Training*, 3, 324–99.

Lim, S.L., Lim, B.K.H., Cai, R. and Schock, C.K. (2010) The trajectory of counseling in China: past, present, and future trends, *Journal of Counseling and Development*, 88, 4–8.

Linden, S. and Grut, S. (2002) *The Healing Fields: Working with Psychotherapy and Nature to Rebuild Shattered Lives*. London: Frances Lincoln.

Linehan, M.M. (1993a) *Cognitive-behavioral Treatment of Borderline Personality Disorder*. New York: Guilford Press.

Linehan, M.M. (1993b) *Skills Training Manual for Treating Borderline Personality Disorder*. New York: Guilford Press.

Linehan, M.M. (1994) Acceptance and change: the central dialectic in psychotherapy. In S.C. Hayes, N.S. Jacobson, V.M. Follette and M.J. Dougher (eds) *Acceptance and Change: Content and Context in Psychotherapy*. Reno, NV: Context Press.

Lines, D. (2006) *Spirituality in Counselling and Psychotherapy*. London: Sage.

Lipkin, S. (1948) The client evaluates nondirective therapy, *Journal of Consulting Psychology*, 12, 137–46.

Livneh, H. and Antonak, R. F. (2005) Psychosocial adaptation to chronic illness and disability: A primer for counselors, *Journal of Counseling and Development*, 83, 12–20.

Llewelyn, S. (1988) Psychological therapy as viewed by clients and therapists, *British Journal of Clinical Psychology*, 27, 223–38.

Llewelyn, S. and Osborne, K. (1983) Women as clients and therapists. In D. Pilgrim (ed.) *Psychology and Psychotherapy: Current Trends and Issues*. London: Routledge.

Lock, A. and Strong, T. (2010) *Social constructionism: sources and stirrings in theory and practice*. Cambridge: Cambridge University Press.

Lock, A. and Strong. T (eds) (2012) *Discursive Perspectives in Therapeutic Practice*. New York: Oxford University Press.

Locke, A. (1971) Is behavior therapy 'behavioristic'? *Psychological Bulletin*, 76, 318–27.

Loewenthal, D. (2013) *Phototherapy and Therapeutic Photography in a Digital Age*. London: Routledge.

Loewenthal, D. and Snell, R. (2003) *Post-Modernism for Psychotherapists: A Critical Reader*. London: Brunner-Routledge.

Logan, R.D. (1987) Historical change in prevailing sense of self. In K. Yardley and T. Honess (eds) *Self and Identity: Psychosocial Perspectives*. Chichester: Wiley.

Lomas, P. (1981) *The Case for a Personal Psychotherapy*. Oxford: Oxford University Press.

Lomas, P. (1994) *Cultivating Intuition: An Introduction to Psychotherapy*. Harmondsworth: Penguin.

London, P. (1964) *The Modes and Morals of Psychotherapy*. New York: Holt, Rinehart and Winston.

Long, P.S. and Lepper, G. (2008) Metaphor in psychoanalytic psychotherapy: a comparative study of four cases by a practitioner-researcher, *British Journal of Psychotherapy*, 24, 343–64.

Lott, D.A. (1999) *In Session: The Bond between Women and Their Therapists*. New York: W. H. Freeman.

Lovering, A. (2002) Person-centred and feminist theories: how we connect them in our work with groups of Mexican women. In J.C. Watson, R. Goldman and M.S. Warner (eds) *Client-centered and Experiential Therapy in the 21st Century: Advances in Theory, Research, and Practice*. Ross-on-Wye: PCCS Books.

Luborsky, L. and Crits-Christoph, P. (eds) (1990) *Understanding Transference: The CCRT Method*. New York: Basic Books.

Luborsky, L., Singer, B. and Luborsky, L. (1975) Comparative studies of psychotherapies: is it true that 'everyone has one and all must have prizes'? *Archives of General Psychiatry*, 32, 995–1008.

Luborsky, L., Crits-Christoph, P. and Mellon, J. (1986) Advent of objective measures of the transference concept, *Journal of Consulting and Clinical Psychology*, 54, 39–47.

Luborsky, L., Barber, J.P. and Diguer, L. (1992) The meanings of narratives told during psychotherapy: the fruits of a new observational unit, *Psychotherapy Research*, 2, 277–90.

Luborsky, L., Popp, C., Luborsky, E. and Mark, D. (1994) The core conflictual relationship theme, *Psychotherapy Research*, 4, 172–83.

Luborsky, L., McLellan, A.T., Diguer, L., Woody, G. and Seligman, D.A. (1997) The psychotherapist matters: comparison of outcomes across twenty-two therapists and seven patient samples, *Clinical Psychology: Science and Practice*, 4, 53–65.

Luborsky, L., Diguer, L., Seligman, D. A. *et al.* (1999) The researcher's own therapy allegiances: a 'wild card' in comparisons of treatment efficacy, *Clinical Psychology: Science and Practice*, 6, 95–106.

Lundahl, D., Tollefson, D., Gambles, C. and Brownell, C. (2010) A meta-analysis of motivational interviewing: twenty five years of empirical studies, *Research in Social Work Practice*, 20, 137–60.

Lutz, W., Leon, S.C., Martinovich, Z., Lyons, S.J. and Stiles, W.B. (2007) Therapist effects in outpatient psycho-therapy: a three-level growth curve approach, *Journal of Counseling Psychology*, 54, 32–9.

Lyddon, W.J. (1989a) Personal epistemology and preference for counseling, *Journal of Counseling Psychology*, 36, 423–39.

Lyddon, W.J. (1989b) *Root metaphor theory: A philosophical framework for counseling and psychotherapy*, Journal of Counseling and Development, 67, 442–8.

Lyddon, W.J. (1991) Epistemic style: implications for cognitive psychotherapy. *Psychotherapy*, 28, 588–97.

Lyddon, W.J. and Adamson, L.A. (1992) Worldview and counseling preference: an analogue study, *Journal of Counseling and Development*, 71, 41–5.

Lyddon, W.J. and Bradford, E. (1995) Philosophical commitments and therapy approach preferences among psychotherapy trainees, *Journal of Theoretical and Philosophical Psychology*, 15, 1–15.

Lynch, D., Laws, K.R. and McKenna, P.J. (2010) Cognitive behavioural therapy for major psychiatric disorder: does it really work? A meta-analytical review of well-controlled trials, *Psychological Medicine*, 40, 9–24.

Lyon, D. (1994) *Postmodernity*. Buckingham: Open University Press.

Lyon, D. (ed.) (2007) *Surveillance Studies: An Overview*. London: Polity Press.

Lyotard, J.F. (1984) *The Postmodern Condition*. Manchester: Manchester University Press.

Lysaker, P.H. and France, C.M. (1999) Psychotherapy as an element in supported employment for persons with severe and persistent mental illness, *Psychiatry*, 62, 209–21.

Lysaker, P.H. Lancaster, R.S., Lysaker, J.T. (2003) Narrative transformation as an outcome in the psychotherapy of schizophrenia, *Psychology and Psychotherapy*, 76, 285–99.

Macdonald, A. (2007) *Solution-Focused Therapy: Theory, Research and Practice*. London: Sage.

MacDougall, C. (2002) Rogers's person-centered approach: consideration for use in multicultural counseling, *Journal of Humanistic Psychology*, 42, 48–65.

Mace, C. (1995a) When are questionnaires helpful? In C. Mace (ed.) *The Art and Science of Assessment in Psychotherapy*. London: Routledge.

Mace, C. (ed.) (1995b) *The Art and Science of Assessment in Psychotherapy*. London: Routledge.

Mace, C. (ed.) (1999) *Heart and Soul: the Therapeutic Face of Philosophy*. London: Routledge.

MacIntyre, A. (1981) *After Virtue: A Study in Moral Theory*. London: Duckworth.

MacIntyre, A. (2007) *After Virtue: A Study in Moral Theory*, 3rd edn. Notre Dame: University of Notre Dame Press.

Mackay, H.C., West, W., Moorey, J., Guthrie, E. and Margison, F. (2001) Counsellors' experiences of changing their practice: learning the psychodynamic-interpersonal model of therapy, *Counselling and Psychotherapy Research*, 1, 29–40.

MacKinnon, C. (1982) Feminism, Marxism, method and the state: an agenda for theory. In N. Keohane, M. Rosaldo and B. Gelpi (eds) *Feminist Theory: A Critique of Ideology*. Chicago: University of Chicago Press.

Mackrill, T. (2007) Using a cross-contextual qualitative diary design to explore client experiences of psychotherapy, *Counselling and Psychotherapy Research*, 7, 233–9.

Mackrill, T. (2008a) Exploring psychotherapy clients' independent strategies for change while in therapy, *British Journal of Guidance and Counselling*, 36, 441–53.

Mackrill, T. (2008b) Solicited diary studies of psychotherapeutic practice – pros and cons, *European Journal of Psychotherapy and Counselling*, 10, 5–18.

Mackrill. T. (2009) Constructing client agency in psychotherapy research, *Journal of Humanistic Psychology*, 49, 193–206.

Mackrill. T. (2011a) A diary-based, cross-contextual case study methodology: background for the case of "Jane and Joe", *Pragmatic Case Studies in Psychotherapy*, 7, 156–86.

Mackrill. T. (2011b) The case of "Jane and Joe": a diary-based, cross-contextual case study. *Pragmatic Case Studies in Psychotherapy*, 7, 187–229.

Maclachlan, M. (2000) Cultivating pluralism in health psychology, *Journal of Health Psychology*, 5, 373–82.

Macquarrie, J. (1972) *Existentialism*. Harmondsworth: Penguin.

Macran, S. and Sharpiro, D.A. (1998) The role of personal therapy for therapists: a review, *British Journal of Medical Psychology*,71, 13–26.

Macran, S., Stiles, W.B. and Smith, J.A. (1999) How does personal therapy affect therapists' practice? *Journal of Counseling Psychology*, 46, 419–31.

Macy, J. and Brown, M.Y. (1998) *Coming Back to Life: Practices to Reconnect Our Lives, Our World*. New York: New Society.

Madill, A. and Barkham, M. (1997) Discourse analysis of a theme in one successful case of brief psychodynamic-interpersonal psychotherapy, *Journal of Counseling Psychology*, 44, 232–44.

Madill, A. and Doherty, K. (1994) 'So you did what you wanted then': discourse analysis, personal agency, and psychotherapy, *Journal of Community and Applied Social Psychology*, 4, 261–73.

Magai, C. and Haviland-Jones, J. (2002) *The Hidden Genius of Emotion: Lifespan Transformations of Personality.* Cambridge: Cambridge University Press.

Magee, B. (2010) *The Story of Philosophy.* London: Dorling Kindersley.

Maguire, G.P., Goldberg, D.P., Hobson, R.F. *et al.* (1984) Evaluating the teaching of a method of psychotherapy, *British Journal of Psychiatry*, 144, 575–80.

Mahler, M.S. (1968) *On Human Symbiosis and the Vicissitudes of Individuation: Infantile Psychosis.* New York: International Universities Press.

Mahler, M.S., Pine, F. and Bergman, A. (1975) *The Psychological Birth of the Human Infant.* New York: Basic Books.

Mahoney, M.J. (1995) Theoretical developments in the cognitive psychotherapies. In M.J. Mahoney (ed.) *Cognitive and Constructive Psychotherapies: Theory, Research and Practice.* New York: Springer.

Mahoney, M.J. (1974) *Cognition and Behavior Modification.* Cambridge, MA: Ballinger.

Mahoney, M.J. (2003) *Constructive Psychotherapy: Theory and Practice.* New York: Guilford Press.

Mahrer, A.R. (2007) To a large extent, the field got it wrong: new learnings from a new look at an old classic, *Psychotherapy: Theory, Research, Practice, Training*, 44, 274–8.

Mahrer, A.R., Nadler, W.P., Dessaulles, A., Gervaize, P.A. and Sterner, I. (1987) Good and very good moments in psychotherapy: content, distribution and facilitation, *Psychotherapy*, 24, 7–14.

Mahrer, A.R., Gagnon, R., Fairweather, D.R., Boulet, D.B. and Herring, C.B. (1994) Client commitment and resolve to carry out postsession behaviors, *Journal of Counseling Psychology*, 41, 407–44.

Main, J.A. and Scogin, F.R. (2003) The effectiveness of self-adminstered treatments: a practice-friendly review of research, *Journal of Clinical Psychology*, 59, 237–46.

Main, M. (1991) Metacognitive knowledge, metacognitive monitoring, and singular (coherent) versus multiple (incoherent) model of attachment: findings and directions for future research. In C.M. Parkes, J. Stevenson-Hinde and P. Marris (eds) *Attachment across the Life-cycle.* London: Routledge.

Mair, J.M.M. (1977) The community of self. In D. Bannister (ed.) *New Perspectives in Personal Construct Theory.* London: Academic Press.

Mair, M. (1989) *Between Psychology and Psychotherapy: A Poetics of Experience.* London: Routledge.

Mair, M. (2012) Enchanting psychology: the poetry of personal inquiry, *Journal of Constructivist Psychology*, 25, 184–209.

Maisel, R., Epston, D. and Borden, A. (2004) *Biting the Hand that Starves you: Inspiring Resistance to Anorexia/Bulimia.* New York: Norton.

Makin, S.R. and Malchiodi, C. (1999) *Therapeutic Art Directives and Resources: Activities and Initiatives for Individuals and Groups.* London: Jessica Kingsley.

Malan, D.H. (1976) *The Frontiers of Brief Psychotherapy.* New York: Plenum.

Malan, D.H. (1979) *Individual Psychotherapy and the Science of Psychodynamics.* London: Butterworths.

Malchiodi, C.A. (2004a) *Art Therapy Sourcebook,* 2nd edn. New York: McGraw-Hill.

Malchiodi, C.A. (ed.) (2004b) *Expressive Therapies.* New York: Guilford Press.

Malikiosi-Loizos, M. and Ivey, A.E. (2012) Counseling in Greece, *Journal of Counseling and Development*, 90, 113–18.

Mallen, M.J., Vogel, D.L., Rochlen, A.B. and Day, S.X. (2005a) Online counselling: reviewing the literature from a counseling psychology framework, *The Counseling Psychologist*, 33, 819–71.

Mallen, M.J. Vogel, R.D. and Rochlen, A.B. (2005b) The practical aspects of on-line counseling: training, technology and competency, *The Counseling Psychologist*, 33, 776–818.

Malloch, S. and Trevarthen, C. (eds) (2010) *Communicative Musicality: Exploring the Basis of Human Companionship.* New York: Oxford University Press.

Maluccio, A. (1979) *Learning from Clients. Interpersonal Helping as Viewed by Clients and Social Workers.* New York: The Free Press.

Mann, D. (1989) Incest: the father and the male therapist, *British Journal of Psychotherapy*, 6, 143–53.

Mann, D. (2010) *Gestalt Therapy. 100 Key Points and Techniques.* London: Routledge.

Mann, J. (1973) *Time-limited Psychotherapy.* Cambridge, MA: Harvard University Press.

Manring, J., Greenberg, R.P., Gregory, R. and Gallinger, L. (2011) Learning psychotherapy in the digital age, *Psychotherapy*, 48, 119–26.

Mansell, W., Harvey, A., Watkins, E. and Shafran, R. (2009) Conceptual foundations of the transdiagnostic approach to CBT, *Journal of Cognitive Psychotherapy*, 23, 6–19.

Marcelino, E.P. (1990) Toward understanding the psychology of the Filipino, *Women and Therapy*, 9, 105–28.

Maree, J.G. and van der Westhuizen, C.N. (2011) Professional counseling in South Africa: a landscape under construction, *Journal of Counseling and Development*, 89, 105–11.

Marlatt, G.A. and Gordon, J.R. (eds) (1985) *Relapse Prevention: Maintenance Strategies in the Treatment of Addictive Behaviors*. New York: Guilford Press.

Marlatt, G.A. and Kristeller, J.L. (1999) Mindfulness and meditation. In W.R. Miller (ed.) *Integrating Spirituality into Treatment*. Washington, DC: American Psychological Association.

Marmor, J. (1953) The feeling of superiority: an occupational hazard in the practice of psychotherapy, *American Journal of Psychiatry*, 110, 370–6.

Marmor, J. and Woods, S.M. (eds) (1980) *The Interface Between the Psychodynamic and Behavioral Therapies*. New York: Plenum.

Marmot, M. (2004) *Status Syndrome: How your Social Standing directly affects your Health*. London: Bloomsbury.

Maroda, K.J. (2004) *The Power of Counter-Transference: Innovations in Psychoanalytic Technique*, 2nd edn. Hillsdale, NJ: Psychology Press.

Maroda, K.J. (2010) *Psychodynamic Techniques: Working with Emotion in the Therapeutic Relationship*. New York: Guildford Press.

Marrow, A. (1969) *The Practical Theorist: The Life and Work of Kurt Lewin*. New York: Basic Books.

Marshall, R.D., Spitzer, R.L., Vaughan, S.C. et al. (2001) Assessing the impact of research: the experience of being a research subject, *American Journal of Psychiatry*, 158, 319–21.

Marston, A.R. (1984) What makes therapists run? A model for the analysis of motivational styles. *Psychotherapy*, 21, 456–9.

Marzillier, J. (1993) Ethical issues in psychotherapy: the importance of informed consent. *Clinical Psychology Forum*, 54, 33–7.

Marzillier, J. (2010) *The Gossamer Thread: My Life as a Psychotherapist*. London: Karnac.

Maslach, C. and Jackson, S.E. (1984) Burnout in organisational settings. In S. Oskamp (ed.) *Applied Social Psychology Annual 5: Applications in Organizational Settings*. London: Sage.

Maslach, C. and Leiter, M.P. (1997) *The Truth about Burnout: How Organizations Cause Personal Stress and What to Do about It*. San Francisco, CA: Jossey-Bass.

Maslow, A. (1943) A theory of human motivation, *Psychological Review*, 50, 370–96.

Mason, P.T. and Kreger, R. (2010) *Stop Walking on Eggshells: Taking your Life Back when Someone you Care about has Borderline Personality Disorder,* 2nd edn. Oakland, CA: New Harbinger Publications.

Masson, J. (1984) *The Assault on Truth: Freud's Suppression of the Seduction Theory*. New York: Farrar, Straus and Giroux.

Masson, J. (1988) *Against Therapy: Emotional Tyranny and the Myth of Psychological Healing*. Glasgow: Collins.

Masson, J. (1991) *Final Analysis: The Making and Unmaking of a Psychoanalyst*. London: HarperCollins.

Masson, J. (1992) The tyranny of psychotherapy. In W. Dryden and C. Feltham (eds) *Psychotherapy and Its Discontents*. Buckingham: Open University Press.

Matthews, C.R., Selvidge, M.M.D. and Fisher, K. (2005) Addiction counselors' attitudes and behabiors toward gay, lesbian, and bisexual clients, *Journal of Counseling and Development*, 83, 57–65.

Maxwell, R.J. (1984) Quality assessment in health, *British Medical Journal*, 288, 1470–2.

May, R. (1950) *The Meaning of Anxiety*. New York: W. W. Norton.

May, R., Angel, E. and Ellenberger, H. (1958) *Existence: A New Dimension in Psychology and Psychiatry*. New York: Basic Books.

McAdams, D.P. (1985) *Power, Intimacy, and the Life Story: Personological Inquiries into Identity*. New York: Guilford Press.

McAdams, D.P. (1993) *The Stories We Live By: Personal Myths and the Making of the Self*. New York: William Murrow.

McAdams, D.P. (2006) *The Redemptive Self: Stories Americans Live By*. New York: Oxford University Press.

McAdams, D.P. (2009) *The Person: An Introduction to the Science of Personality Psychology,* 5th edn. New York: Wiley.

McAdams, D.P. and Pals, J.L. (2006) A new Big Five: fundamental principles for an integrative science of personality, *American Psychologist,* 61, 204–17.

McCallum, M. and Piper, W. (1990) The psychological mindedness assessment procedure. *Psychological Assessment*, 2, 412–18.

McCallum, M. and Piper, W. (1997) The psychological mindedness assessment procedure. In M. McCallum and W. Piper (eds) *Psychological Mindedness: A Contemporary Understanding*. Mahwah, NJ: Lawrence Erlbaum.

McCarthy, K.S. and Barber, J.P. (2009) The Multitheoretical List of Therapeutic Interventions (MULTI): initial report, *Psychotherapy Research*, 19, 96–113.

McCrone, P., Knapp, M., Proudfoot, J. et al. (2004) Cost effectiveness of computerized cognitive behavioural therapy for anxiety and depression in primary care: randomized controlled trial, *British Journal of Psychiatry*, 185, 55–62.

McDonald, M.G., Weaing, S. and Ponting, J. (2009) The nature of peak experience in wilderness, *The Humanistic Psychologist*, 37, 370–85.

McDowell, I. (2006) *Measuring Health: A Guide to Rating Scales and Questionnaires*. Maidenhead: Open University Press.

McGoldrick, M. and Gerson, R. (1985) *Genograms in Family Assessment*. New York: Norton.

McGoldrick, M. and Gerson, R. (1989) Genograms and the family life cycle. In B. Carter and M. McGoldrick (eds) *The Changing Family Life Cycle: A Framework for Family Therapy*, 2nd edn. Boston, MA: Allyn and Bacon.

McGoldrick, M., Carter, B. and Garcia-Preto, N. (2012) *The Expanded Family Life Cycle: Individual, Family, and Social Perspectives*, 4th edn. New York: Pearson.

McGuire, J., Nieri, D., Abbott, D., Sheridan, K. and Fisher, R. (1995) Do *Tarasoff* principles apply in AIDS-related psychotherapy? Ethical decision making and the role of therapist homophobia and perceived client dangerousness, *Professional Psychology: Research and Practice*, 26(6), 608–11.

McLean, A. (1986) Family therapy workshops in the United States: potential abuses in the production of therapy in an advanced capitalist society, *Social Science and Medicine*, 23(2), 179–89.

McLellan, A.T., Woody, G.E., Luborsky, L. and Gohl, L. (1988) Is the counselor an 'active ingredient' in substance abuse rehabilitation? An examination of treatment success among four counselors, *Journal of Nervous and Mental Disease*, 176, 423–30.

McLellan, B. (1999) The prostitution of psychotherapy: a feminist critique, *British Journal of Guidance and Counselling*, 27, 325–31.

McLennan, G. (1995) *Pluralism*. Maidenhead: Open University Press.

McLeod, J. (1984) Group process as drama, *Small Group Behavior*, 15, 319–32.

McLeod, J. (1990) The client's experience of counselling: a review of the research literature. In D. Mearns and W. Dryden (eds) *Experiences of Counselling in Action*. London: Sage.

McLeod, J. (1999) Counselling as a social process, *Counselling*, 10, 217–26.

McLeod, J. (2001) *Qualitative Research in Counselling and Psychotherapy*. London: Sage.

McLeod, J. (2002) Research policy and practice in person-centered and experiential therapy: restoring coherence, *Person-Centered and Experiential Psychotherapies*, 1, 87–101.

McLeod, J. (2005) Counseling and psychotherapy. In L.T. Hoshmand (ed.) *Culture, Psychotherapy and Counseling: Critical and Integrative Perspectives*. Thousand Oaks, CA: Sage.

McLeod, J. (2008) *Counselling in the Workplace: A Comprehensive Review of the Research Literature*, 2nd edn. Lutterworth: British Association for Counselling and Psychotherapy.

McLeod, J. (2010a) *The Counsellor's Workbook: Developing a Personal Approach*, 2nd edn. Maidenhead: McGraw-Hill.

McLeod, J. (2010b) *Case Study Research in Counselling and Psychotherapy*. London: Sage.

McLeod, J. (2011) *Qualitative Research in Counselling and Psychotherapy*, 2nd edn. London: Sage.

McLeod, J. (2012) What do clients want from therapy? A practice-friendly review of research into client preferences, *European Journal of Psychotherapy, Counselling and Health*, 14, 19–32.

McLeod, J. (2013a) *An Introduction to Research in Counselling and Psychotherapy*. London: Sage.

McLeod, J. (2013b) Developing pluralistic practice in counselling and psychotherapy: using what the client knows, *European Journal of Counselling Psychology*, 2, 51–64.

McLeod, J. and McLeod, J. (2011) *Counselling Skills. A Practical Guide for Counsellors and Helping Professionals*, 2nd edn. Maidenhead: Open University Press.

McLeod, J., Johnston, J. and Griffin, J. (2000) A naturalistic study of the effectiveness of time-limited counselling with low-income clients, *European Journal of Psychotherapy, Counselling and Health*, 3, 263–78.

McLeod, Julia (2013) Process and outcome in pluralistic transactional analysis counselling for long-term health conditions: a case series, *Counselling and Psychotherapy Research*, 13, 32–43.

McManus, F., Shafran, R. and Cooper, Z. (2011) What does a 'transdiagnostic' approach have to offer the treatment of anxiety disorders? *British Journal of Clinical Psychology*, 49, 491–505.

McMillan, M. and McLeod, J. (2006) Letting go: the client's experience of relational depth, *Person-centred and Experiential Psychotherapies*, 5, 277–92.

McNamee, S. and Gergen, K.J. (ed.) (1992) *Therapy as Social Construction*. London: Sage.

McNeill, B.W. and Worthen, V. (1989) The parallel process in psychotherapy supervision, *Professional Psychology: Research and Practice*, 20, 329–33.

McNeill, J.T. (1951) *A History of the Cure of Souls*. New York: Harper and Row.

McNeilly, C.L. and Howard, K.I. (1991) The Therapeutic Procedures Inventory: psychometric properties and relationship to phase of treatment, *Journal of Psychotherapy Integration*, 1, 223–34.

Mead, N., MacDonald, W., Bower, P., et al. (2006) The clinical effectiveness of guided self-help versus waiting-list control in the management of anxiety and depression: a randomized controlled trial, *Psychological Medicine*, 36, 1633–44.

Meadow, A. (1964) Client-centered therapy and the American ethos, *International Journal of Social Psychiatry*, 10, 246–60.

Meara, N.M., Schmidt, L.D. and Day, J.D. (1996) Principles and virtues: a foundation for ethical decisions, policy and character, *Counseling Psychologist*, 24(1), 4–77.

Meares, R. and Hobson, R.F. (1977) The persecutory therapist, *British Journal of Medical Psychology*, 50, 349–59.

Mearns, D. (1993) Against indemnity insurance. In W. Dryden (ed.) *Questions and Answers for Counselling in Action*. London: Sage.

Mearns, D. (1994) *Developing Person-centred Counselling*. London: Sage.

Mearns, D. (1996) Working at relational depth with clients in person-centred therapy, *Counselling*, 7(4), 307–11.

Mearns, D. (1997) *Person-centred Counselling Training*. London: Sage.

Mearns, D. (2004) The humanistic agenda: articulation, *Journal of Humanistic Psychology*, 43, 53–65.

Mearns, D. and Cooper, M. (2005) *Working at Relational Depth in Counselling and Psychotherapy*. London: Sage.

Mearns, D. and Thorne, B. (2000) *Person-centred Therapy Today: New Frontiers in Theory and Practice*. London: Sage.

Mearns, D. and Thorne, B. (2007) *Person-centred Counselling in Action*, 3rd edn. London: Sage.

Mearns, D. and Thorne, B. (2013) *Person-centred Counselling in Action*, 4th edn. London: Sage.

Meichenbaum, D. (1977) *Cognitive-Behavior Modification: An Integrative Approach*. New York: Plenum.

Meichenbaum, D. (1985) *Stress Innoculation Training*. New York: Pergamon.

Meichenbaum, D. (1986) Cognitive-behavior modification. In A. Kanfer and A. Goldstein (eds) *Helping People Change*, 3rd edn. New York: Pergamon.

Meichenbaum, D. (1994) *Treating Post-traumatic Stress Disorder. A Handbook and Practical Manual for Therapy*. Chichester: Wiley.

Mellor-Clark, J. (2006) Developing CORE performance indicators for benchmarking in NHS primary care psychological therapy and counselling services: an editorial introduction, *Counselling and Psychotherapy Research*, 6(1), 1–2.

Mellor-Clark, J. and Barkham, M. (2006a) The CORE system: quality evaluation to develop practice-based evidence base, enhanced service delivery and best practice management. In C. Feltham and I. Horton (eds) *Handbook of Counselling and Psychotherapy*. London: Sage.

Mellor-Clark, J. and Barkham, M. (2006b) Using clinical outcomes in routine evaluation, *European Journal of Psychotherapy, Counselling and Health*, 8(2), 137–40.

Mellor-Clark, J., Barkham, M., Connell, J. and Evans, C. (1999) Practice based evidence and standardized evaluation: Informing the design of the CORE system, *European Journal of Psychotherapy, Counselling and Health*, 2, 357–74.

Mellor-Clark, J., Connell, J., Barkham, M. and Cummins, P. (2001) Counselling outcomes in primary health care: a CORE system data profile, *European Journal of Psychotherapy, Counselling and Health*, 4, 65–86.

Meltzer, J.D. (1978) A semiotic approach to suitability for psychotherapy, *Psychiatry*, 41, 360–76.

Menchola, M., Arkowitz, H.S., and Burke, B.L. (2007) efficacy of self-administered treatments for depression and anxiety, *Professional Psychology: Research and Practice*, 38, 421–9.

Menzies Lyth, I. (1988) *Containing Anxiety in Institutions: Selected Essays*. London: Free Association.

Menzies Lyth, I. (1989) *The Dynamics of the Social: Selected Essays*. London: Free Association.

Menzies, I. (1959) A case-study in the functioning of social systems as a defence against anxiety: a report on a study of the nursing service of a general hospital, *Human Relations*, 13, 95–121.

Merry, T. (1999) *Learning and Being in Person-centred Counselling*. Ross-on-Wye: PCCS Books.

Merry, T. and Brodley, B.T. (2002) The nondirective attitude in client-centered therapy: a response to Kahn, *Journal of Humanistic Psychology*, 42, 66–77.

Messer, S.B. (1992) A critical examination of belief structures in integrative and eclectic psychotherapy. In J.C. Norcross and M.R. Goldfried (eds) *Handbook of Psychotherapy Integration*. New York: Basic Books.

Miller, A. (1987) *The Drama of Being a Child and the Search for the True Self*. London: Virago.

Miller, D.J. and Thelen, M.H. (1987) Confidentiality in psychotherapy: history, issues and research, *Psychotherapy*, 24, 704–11.

Miller, E. and Willig, C. (2012) Pluralistic counselling and HIV-positive clients: the importance of shared understanding, *European Journal of Psychotherapy and Counselling*, 14, 33–45.

Miller, J.B. (1976) *Toward a New Psychology of Women*. Harmondsworth: Penguin.

Miller, J.B. (1987) Women and power. In M. Braude (ed.) *Women, Power and Therapy*. New York: Haworth Press.

Miller, J.B. (1991a) The construction of anger in women and men. In J.V. Jordan, A.G. Kaplan, J.B. Miller, I.P. Stiver and J.L. Surrey (eds) *Women's Growth in Connection: Writings from the Stone Center*. New York: Guilford Press.

Miller, J.B. (1991b) Women and power. In J.V. Jordan, A.G. Kaplan, J.B. Miller, I.P. Stiver and J.L. Surrey (eds) *Women's Growth in Connection: Writings from the Stone Center*. New York: Guilford Press.

Miller, J.K. and Slive, A.B. (2004) Breaking down the barriers to clinical service delivery: the process and outcome of walk-in family therapy, *Journal of Marital and Family Therapy*, 30, 95–103.

Miller, K.E., Zoe, L.M., Pazdirek, L., Caruth, M. and Lopez, D. (2005) The role of interpreters in psychotherapy with refugees, *American Journal of Orthopsychiatry*, 75, 27–39.

Miller, N.E. and Magruder, K.M. (eds) (1999) *Cost-effectiveness of Psychotherapy: A Guide for Practitioners, Researchers and Policymakers*. New York: Oxford University Press.

Miller, N., Luborsky, L. and Barber, J. (eds) (1993) *Psychodynamic Treatment Research: A Handbook for Clinical Practice*. New York: Basic Books.

Miller, R. and Rose, G. (2009) Towards a theory of motivational interviewing, *American Psychologist*, 64, 527–37.

Miller, S.D. (2004) Losing faith: arguing for a new way to think about therapy, *Psychotherapy in Australia*, 10, 44–51.

Miller, S.D. and Berg, I.K. (1995) *The Miracle Method: A Radically New Approach to Problem Drinking*. New York: Norton.

Miller, S.D., Hubble, M.A. and Duncan, B.L. (1996) *Handbook of Solution-focused Brief Therapy*. San Francisco, CA: Jossey-Bass.

Miller, S.D., Duncan, B.L. and Hubble, M.A. (1997) *Escape from Babel: Toward a Unifying Language for Psychotherapy Practice*. New York: W.W. Norton.

Miller, S.D., Duncan, B.L. and Hubble, M.A. (2005) Outcome-informed clinical work. In J.C. Norcross. and M.R. Goldfried (eds) *Handbook of Psychotherapy Integration*. New York: Oxford University Press.

Miller, W.R. (1983) Motivational interviewing with problem drinkers, *Behavioural Psychotherapy*, 1, 147–72.

Miller, W.R. (2004) The phenomenon of quantum change, *Journal of Clinical Psychology*, 60, 453–60.

Miller, W.R. and Rollnick, S. (1991) *Motivational Interviewing: Preparing People to Change Addictive Behaviour*. New York: Guilford.

Miller, W.R. and Rollnick, S. (2002) *Motivational Interviewing: Preparing People for Change*, 2nd edn. New York: Guilford.

Miller, W.R. and Rollnick, S. (2009) Ten things that motivational interviewing is not, *Behavioural and Cognitive Psychotherapy*, 37, 129–40.

Milner, M. (1957) *On Not Being able to Paint*. London: Heinemann.

MIND (2007) *Ecotherapy: The Green Agenda for Mental Health*. London: Mind.

Minton, K., Ogden, P. and Pain, C. (2006) *Trauma and the Body: A Sensorimotor Approach to Psychotherapy*. New York: Norton.

Mintz, E.E. (1969) Touch and the psychoanalytic tradition, *Psychoanalytic Review*, 56, 365–76.

Minuchin, S. (1974) *Families and Family Therapy*. London: Tavistock.

Mitchell, J. (1974) *Psychoanalysis and Feminism: A Radical Reassessment of Freudian Psychoanalysis*. London: Allen Lane.

Mitchell, S.A. (1986) *Relational Concepts in Psychoanalysis*. Cambridge, MA: Harvard University Press.

Miville, M.L. and Ferguson, A.D. (2004) Impossible "choices": identity and values at a crossroads, *The Counseling Psychologist*, 32, 760–70.

Moir-Bussy, A. (2009) The greening of our earth: ecopsychological and ecofeminist perspectives. In K. Gow (ed.) *Meltdown: Climate Change, Natural Disasters and Other Catastrophes: Fears and Concerns for the Future*. New York: Nova Science.

Moleski, S.M. and Kiselica, M.S. (2005) Dual relationships: a continuum ranging from the destructive to the therapeutic, *Journal of Counseling and Development*, 83, 3–11.

Monk, G. Winslade, J., Crocket, K. and Epston, D. (eds) (1996) *Narrative Therapies in Action: The Archeology of Hope*. San Francisco, CA: Jossey-Bass.

Monte, C.F. (1998) *Beneath the Mask: An Introduction to Theories of Personality*. New York: Thomson.

Montgomery, A. (2013) *Neurobiology Essentials for Clinicians. What every Therapist needs to Know*. New York: Norton.

Montilla, R.E. and Smith, R.L. (2009) Counseling in the República Bolivariana de Venezuela (Bolivarian Republic of Venezuela), *Journal of Counseling and Development*, 87, 122–6.

Moodley, R. (1998) 'I say what I like': frank talk(ing) in counselling and psychotherapy, *British Journal of Guidance and Counselling*, 26, 495–508.

Moodley, R and Palmer, S (eds) (2006) *Race, Culture and Psychotherapy: Critical Perspectives in Multicultural Practice*. London: Routledge.

Moodley, R. and West, W. (eds) (2005) *Integrating Indigenous Healing Practices into Counselling and Psychotherapy*. London: Sage.

Moodley, R., Gielen, U.W. and Wu, R. (eds) (2012) *Handbook of Counselling and Psychotherapy in an International Context*. London: Routledge.

Moon, L. (ed.) (2008) *Feeling Queer or Queer Feelings? Radical Approaches to Counselling Sex, Sexualities and Genders*. London: Routledge.

Moore, D. (2005) Expanding the view: the lives of women with severe work disabilities in context, *Journal of Counseling and Development*, 83, 343–8.

Moore, D. (2011) The benevolent watch: therapeutic surveillance in drug treatment court, *Theoretical Criminology*, 15, 255–68.

Moran, D. (2000) *Introduction to Phenomenology*. London: Routledge.

Moran, D. and Mooney, T. (eds) (2002) *The Phenomenology Reader*. London: Routledge.

Morgan, A. (2000) *What is Narrative Therapy? An Easy-to-read Introduction*. Adelaide: Dulwich Centre Publications.

Morgan, G. (2006) *Images of Organization*, revised edn. London: Sage.

Morley, R. (2007) *The Analysand's Tale*. London: Karnac.

Morrall, P. (2008) *The Trouble with Therapy: Sociology and Psychotherapy*. Maidenhead: Open University Press.

Morris, B. (2005) *Discovering Bits and Pieces of Me: Research exploring Women's Experiences of Psychoanalytical Psychotherapy*. London: Women's Therapy Centre. Available at: http://www.womenstherapycentre.co.uk/Documents/Uploads/11.pdf (accessed 20 March 2013).

Morrison, L.A. and Shapiro, D.A. (1987) Expectancy and outcome in prescriptive vs. exploratory psychotherapy, *British Journal of Clinical Psychology*, 26, 59–60.

Morrissette, P.J. (2004) *The Pain of Helping: Psychological Injury of Helping Professionals*. London: Routledge.

Morrow, S.L., Beckstead, A.L., Hayes, J.A. and Haldeman, D.C. (2004) Impossible dreams, impossible choices, and thoughts about depolarizing the debate, *The Counseling Psychologist*, 32, 778–85.

Morrow-Bradley, C. and Elliott, R. (1986) Utilization of psychotherapy research by practicing psychotherapists, *American Psychologist*, 41, 188–97.

Mothersole, G. (2002) TA as short-term cognitive therapy. In K.Tudor (ed.) *Transactional Analysis Approaches to Brief Therapy*. London: Sage.

Mulley, A., Trimble, C. and Elwyn, G. (2012) *Patients' Preferences Matter. Stop the Silent Misdiagnosis*. London: The King's Fund.

Munley, P.H., Duncan, L.E., McDonnell, K.A. and Sauer, E.M. (2004) Counseling psychology in the United States of America, *Counselling Psychology Quarterly*, 17, 247–71.

Munro, J., Knox, M. and Lowe, R. (2008) Exploring the potential of constructionist therapy: deaf clients, hearing therapists and a reflecting team, *Journal of Deaf Studies and Deaf Education*, 13, 307–23.

Murase, T. (1976) Naikan therapy. In W.P. Lebra (ed.) *Culture-bound Syndromes, Ethnopsychiatry, and Alternate Therapies, Volume IV of Mental Health Research in Asia and the Pacific*. Honolulu, HI: University Press of Hawaii.

Murdock, N.L., Edwards, C. and Murdock, T.B. (2010) Therapists' attributions for client premature termination: are they self-serving? *Psychotherapy Theory, Research, Practice, Training*, 47, 221–34.

Murphy, G.C. and Athanasou, J.A. (1999) The effect of unemployment on mental health, *Journal of Occupational and Organisational Psychology*, 72, 83–99.

Murphy, L.J. and Mitchell, D.L. (1998) When writing helps to heal: e-mail as therapy, *British Journal of Guidance and Counselling*, 26, 21–32.

Murray, H.A. (1938) *Explorations in Personality: A Clinical and Experimental Study of Fifty Men of College Age*. New York: Oxford University Press.

Myers-Shirk, S.E. (2000) 'To be fully human': US protestant psychotherapeutic culture and the subversion of the domestic ideal, 1945–1965, *Journal of Women's History*, 12, 112–36.

Naess, A. (1989) *Deep Ecology, Community and Lifestyle*. Cambridge: Cambridge University Press.

Najavits, L.M. (1993) How do psychotherapists describe their work? A study of metaphors for the therapy process, *Psychotherapy Research*, 3, 294–9.

National Institute for Health and Clinical Excellence (2006) *Computerised Cognitive Behaviour Therapy for Depression and Anxiety – Review of Technology Appraisal 51*. London: NICE.

Neal, C. and Davies, D. (eds) (2000) *Issues in Therapy with Lesbian, Gay, Bisexual and Transgender Clients*. Buckingham: Open University Press.

Neenan, M. and Dryden, W. (2004) *Cognitive Therapy: 100 Key Points and Techniques*. London: Routledge.

Neimeyer, G.J. and Diamond, A.K. (2011) The anticipated future of counselling psychology in the United States: a Delphi poll, *Counselling Psychology Quarterly*, 14, 49–65.

Neimeyer, R.A. (1993) Constructivist psychotherapy. In K.T. Kuehlwein and H. Rosen (eds) *Cognitive Therapies in Action: Evolving Innovative Practice*. San Francisco, CA: Jossey-Bass.

Neimeyer, R.A. (1995) Constructivist psychotherapies: features, foundations, and future directions. In R.A. Neimeyer and M.J. Mahoney (eds) *Constructivism in Psychotherapy*. Washington, DC: American Psychological Association.

Neimeyer, R.A. (2002) Traumatic loss and the reconstruction of meaning, *Journal of Palliative Medicine*, 5, 935–42.

Neimeyer, R.A. (2006a) Re-storying loss: fostering growth in the posttraumatic narrative. In L.G. Calhoun and R.G. Tedeschi (eds) *Handbook of Posttraumatic Growth: Research and Practice*. New York: Routledge.

Neimeyer, R.A. (2006b) Complicated grief and the quest for meaning: a constructivist contribution, *Omega*, 52, 37–52.

Neimeyer, R.A. and Mahoney, M.J. (eds) (1995) *Constructivism in Psychotherapy*. Washington, DC: American Psychological Association.

Neimeyer, R.A. and Raskin, J.D. (2001) Varieties of constructivism in psychotherapy. In K. Dobson (ed.) *Handbook of Cognitive-behavioral Therapies*. New York: Guilford Press.

Neimeyer, R.A. and Raskin, J.D. (eds) (2000) *Construction of Disorder: Meaning-making Frameworks for Psychotherapy*. Washington, DC: American Psychological Association.

Neimeyer, R.A., Prigerson, H.G. and Davies, B. (2002) Mourning and meaning, *American Behavioral Scientist*, 46, 235–51.

Neimeyer, R.A., Herrero, O. and Botella, L. (2006) Chaos to coherence: psychotherapeutic integration of traumatic loss, *Journal of Constructivist Psychology*, 19, 127–45.

Nelson, M.L. (1996) Separation versus connection: the gender controversy: implications for counseling women, *Journal of Counseling and Development*, 74, 339–44.

Nelson, M.L. and Friedlander, M.L. (2001) A close look at conflictual supervisory relationships: the trainee's perspective, *Journal of Counseling Psychology*, 48, 384–95.

Nelson, R.O. (1981) Realistic dependent measures for clinical use, *Journal of Consulting and Clinical Psychology*, 49, 168–82.

Nelson, S.H. and Torrey, E.F. (1973) The religious functions of psychiatry, *American Journal of Orthopsychiatry*, 43, 362–7.

Netto, G., Gaag, S., Thanki, M., Bondi, E. and Munro, M. (2001) *A Suitable Space: Improving Counselling Services for Asian People*. Bristol: The Policy Press.

Neugebauer, R. (1978) Treatment of the mentally ill in medieval and early modern England: a reappraisal, *Journal of the History of the Behavioral Sciences*, 14, 158–69.

Neugebauer, R. (1979) Early and modern theories of mental illness, *Archives of General Psychiatry*, 36, 477–83.

Neukrug, E., Milliken, T. and Walden, S. (2001) Ethical complaints against credentialed counselors: an updated survey of State Licensing Boards, *Counselor Education and Supervision*, 41, 57–70.

Neumann, D.A. and Gamble, S.J. (1995) Issues in the professional development of psychotherapists: counter-transference and vicarious traumatization in the new trauma therapist, *Psychotherapy*, 32, 341–7.

Nielsen, S.R., Smart, D.W., Isakson, R.L., Worthen, V.E., Gregersen, A.T. and Lambert, M.J. (2004) The *Consumer Reports* effectiveness score: what did consumers report? *Journal of Counseling Psychology*, 51, 25–37.

Nietzel, M.T. and Fisher, S.G. (1981) Effectiveness of professional and paraprofessional helpers: a comment on Durlak, *Psychological Bulletin*, 89, 555–65.

Niff, S. (2004) *Art Heals: How Creativity Cures the Soul*. London: Shambhala.

Nilsson, T., Svensson, M., Sandell, R. and Clinton, D. (2007) Patients' experiences of change on cognitive-behavioral therapy and psychodynamic therapy: a qualitative comparative study, *Psychotherapy Research*, 17: 553–66.

Nissen-Lie, H.A., Monsen, J.T. and Ronnestad, M.H. (2010) Therapist predictors of early patient-rated working alliance: a multilevel approach, *Psychotherapy Research*, 20, 627–46.

Norcross, J.C. (2005) A primer on psychotherapy integration. In J.C. Norcross. and M.R. Goldfried (eds) *Handbook of Psychotherapy Integration*. New York: Oxford University Press.

Norcross, J.C. (2006) Integrating self-help into psychotherapy: 16 practical suggestions, *Professional Psychology: Research and Practice*, 37, 683–93.

Norcross, J.C. (ed.) (2011) *Psychotherapy Relationships that Work*. New York: Oxford University Press.

Norcross, J.C. and Goldfried, M.R. (eds) (2005) *Handbook of Psychotherapy Integration*. New York: Oxford University Press.

Norcross, J.C. and Guy, J.D. (2005) The prevalence and parameters of personal therapy in the United States. In J.D. Geller, J.C Norcross and D.E.Orlinsky (eds) *The Psychotherapist's own Psychotherapy: Patient and Clinician Perspectives*. New York: Oxford University Press.

Norcross, J.C., Strausser, D.J. and Missar, C.D. (1988) The processes and outcomes of psychotherapists' personal treatment experiences, *Psychotherapy*, 25, 36–43.

Norcross, J.C., Santrock, J.W., Campbell, L.F. Smith, T.P., Sommer, R. and Zuckerman, E.L. (2003) *Authoritative guide to self-help resources in mental health*, 2nd edn. New York: Guilford Press.

Norcross, J.C., Karpiak, C.P. and Lister, K.M. (2005) What's an integrationist? A study of self-identified integra-tive and (occasionally) eclectic psychologists, *Journal of Clinical Psychology*, 61, 1587–94.

Nouwen, H.J.M. (1979) *The Wounded Healer*. New York: Image.

Novey, T.B. (1999) The effectiveness of transactional analysis, *Transactional Analysis Journal*, 29, 18–30.

Novey, T.B. (2002) Measuring the effectiveness of transactional analysis: an international study, *Transactional Analysis Journal*, 32, 8–20.

Nylund, D. and Corsiglia, V. (1994) Being solution-focused forced in brief therapy: remembering something important we already knew, *Journal of Systemic Therapies*, 13, 5–12.

Oatley, K. (1980) Theories of personal learning in groups. In P.B. Smith (ed.) *Small Groups and Personal Change*. London: Methuen.

Oatley, K. (1984) *Selves in Relation: An Introduction to Psychotherapy and Groups*. London: Methuen.

Obholzer, A. and Roberts, V.Z. (eds) (1994) *The Unconscious at Work: Individual and Organizational Stress in the Human Services*. London: Routledge.

O'Brien, K.M. (2001) The legacy of Parsons: career counselors and vocational psychologists as agents of social change, *Career Development Quarterly*, 50, 124–32.

O'Brien, M. and Houston, G. (2007) *Integrative Therapy: A Practitioner's Guide*, 2nd edn. London: Sage.

O'Connell, B. (1998) *Solution Focused Therapy*. London: Sage.

O'Connell, B. (2005) *Solution Focused Therapy*, 2nd edn. London: Sage.

O'Connell, B. and Palmer, S. (eds) (2003) *Handbook of Solution-focused Therapy*. London: Sage.

O'Connor, T.S., Meakes, E., Pickering, R. and Schuman, M. (1997) On the right track: client experience of narrative therapy, *Contemporary Family Therapy*, 19, 479–96.

O'Connor, T.S., Davis, A., Meakes, E., Pickering, R. and Schuman, M. (2004) Narrative therapy using a reflecting team: an ethnographic study of therapists' experiences, *Contemporary Family Therapy*, 26, 23–39.

Ogden, P. and Fisher, J. (2012) *The Body as Resource. A Therapist's Manual for Sensorimotor Psychotherapy*. New York: Norton.

Ogden, P. and Minton, K. (2000) Sensorimotor psychotherapy: one method for processing traumatic memory, *Traumatology*, 6, 149–73.

Ogles, B.M., Lambert, M.J. and Craig, D.E. (1991) Comparison of self-help books for coping with loss: expectations and attributions, *Journal of Counseling Psychology*, 38, 387–93.

Ogles, B.M., Lambert, M.J. and Fields, S.A. (2002) *Essentials of Outcome Assessment*. Chichester: Wiley.

O'Hanlon, W.H. and Weiner-Davis, M. (1989) *In Search of Solutions: A New Direction in Psychotherapy*. New York: Norton.

O'Hara, D. (2013) *Hope in Counselling and Psychotherapy*. London: Sage.

Ohlsson, T. (2002) Effectiveness of transactional analysis psychotherapy in the community treatment of drug addicts, *Transactional Analysis Journal*, 32, 153–77.

Ohlsson, T. (2010) Scientific evidence base for transactional analysis in the year 2010, *International Journal of Transactional Analysis Research*, 1, January.

Okiishi, J., Lambert, M.J., Nielsen, S.L. and Ogles, B.M. (2003) Waiting for supershrink: an empirical analysis of therapist effects, *Clinical Psychology and Psychotherapy*, 10, 361–73.

Okocha, A.A.G. and Alika, I.H. (2012) Professional counseling in Nigeria: past, present, and future, *Journal of Counseling and Development*. 90, 362–6.

O'Leary, C. (2011) *The Practice of Person-Centred Couple and Family Therapy*. London: Palgrave Macmillan.

Olfson, M. and Pincus, H.A. (1999) Outpatient psychotherapy in the United States: the national Medical Expenditure survey. In N.E. Miller and K.M. Magruder (eds) *Costeffectiveness of Psychotherapy: A Guide for Practitioners, Researchers and Policymakers*. New York: Oxford University Press.

Oliver, L.E. and Ostrofsky, R. (2007) The ecological paradigm of mind and its implications for psychotherapy, *Review of General Psychology*, 11, 1–11.

Olkin, R. (1999) *What Psychotherapists should Know about Disability*. New York: Guilford.

Olkin, R. (2010) Limping toward Bethlehem: a personal history. In J. Ponterotto, J.M. Casas, L.A. Suzuki and C.M. Alexander (eds) *Handbook of Multicultural Counseling*, 3rd edn. Thousand Oaks, CA: Sage.

Omer, H. (1993) The integrative focus: coordinating symptom- and person-oriented perspectives in therapy, *American Journal of Psychotherapy*, 47, 283–95.

Omer, H. (1994) *Critical Interventions in Psychotherapy: From Impasse to Turning Point*. New York: Norton.

O'Morain, P., McAuliffe, G.J., Conroy, K., Johnson, J.M. and Michel, R.E. (2012) Counseling in Ireland, *Journal of Counseling and Development*, 90, 367–72.

O'Neill, P. (1998) *Negotiating Consent in Psychotherapy*. New York: New York University Press.

Onnis, L., Gennaro, A.D., Cespa, G. et al. (1994) Sculpting present and future: a systemic intervention model applied to psychosomatic families, *Family Process*, 33, 341–55.

Orleans, C.T., Schoenbach, C.J., Wagner, E. H. et al. (1991) Self-help quitting smoking interventions: effects of self-help manuals, social support instructions and telephone counselling, *Journal of Consulting and Clinical Psychology*, 59, 439–48.

Orlinsky, D.E. and Ronnestad, M.H. (2000) Ironies in the history of psychotherapy research: Rogers, Bordin, and the shape of things that came, *Journal of Clinical Psychology*, 56, 841–51.

Orlinsky, D.E, Grawe, K. and Parks, B.K. (1994) Process and outcome in psychotherapy – noch einmal. In A.E. Bergin and S.L. Garfield (eds) *Handbook of Psychotherapy and Behavior Change*, 4th edn. Chichester: Wiley.

Orlinsky, D.E. Ronnestad, M.H., Willutzki, U., Wiseman, H. and Rotermans, J-F. (2005a) The prevalence and parameters of personal therapy in Europe and elsewhere. In J.D. Geller, J.C. Norcross and D.E.Orlinsky (eds) *The Psychotherapist's own Psychotherapy: Patient and Clinician Perspectives*. New York: Oxford University Press.

Orlinsky, D.E., Norcross, J.C., Ronnestad, M.H. and Wiseman, H. (2005b) Outcomes and impacts of the psychotherapist's own psychotherapy: a research review. In J.D. Geller, J.C Norcross and D.E.Orlinsky (eds) *The Psychotherapist's own Psychotherapy: Patient and Clinician Perspectives*. New York: Oxford University Press.

Ossip-Klein, D.J., Giovino, G.A., Megahed, N. *et al.* (1991) Effects of a smokers' hotline: results of a ten-county selfhelp trial, *Journal of Consulting and Clinical Psychology*, 59, 325–32.

O'Sullivan, K.R. and Dryden, W. (1990) A survey of clinical psychologists in the South East Thames Region: activities, role and theoretical orientation, *Clinical Psychology Forum*, 29, 21–6.

Overholser, J.C. (2010) Psychotherapy according to the Socratic method: integrating ancient philosophy with contemporary cognitive therapy, *Journal of Cognitive Psychotherapy*, 24, 354–63.

Owen, J., Imel, Z., Adelson, J. and Rodolfa, E. (2012) 'No-show': therapist racial/ethnic disparities in client unilateral termination, *Journal of Counseling Psychology*, 59, 314–20.

Pachankis, J.E. and Goldfried, M.R. (2004) Clinical issues in working with lesbian, gay, and bisexual clients, *Psychotherapy: Theory, Research, Practice, Training*, 41, 227–46.

Pack, M. (2010) Transformation in progress: the effects of trauma on the significant others of sexual abuse therapists, *Qualitative Social Work*, 9, 249–65.

Page, S. and Wosket, V. (2001) *Supervising the Counsellor: A Cyclical Model*, 2nd edn. Hove: Brunner-Routledge.

Palazzoli, M., Cecchin, G., Boscolo, L. and Prata, G. (1978) *Paradox and Counter Paradox*. New York: Aronson.

Paleg, K and Jongma, A.E. (2005) *The Group Therapy Treatment Planner*, 2nd edn. New York: Wiley.

Palgi, Y. and Ben-Ezra, M. (2010) "Back to the future": narrative treatment for post-traumatic, 1 acute stress disorder in the case of paramedic Mr.G, *Pragmatic Case Studies in Psychotherapy*, 6 (1), 1–26. Available at http://pcsp.libraries.rutgers.edu/index.php/pcsp/article/view/1012/2406 (accessed 20 March 2013).

Palmer, S. (ed.) (2002) *Multicultural Counselling: A Reader*. London: Sage.

Palmer, S. and McMahon, G. (eds) (1997) *Handbook of Counselling*, 2nd edn. London: Routledge.

Palmer, G.J., Palmer, R.W. and Payne-Borden, J. (2012) Evolution of counseling in Jamaica: past, present, and future trends, *Journal of Counseling and Development*, 90, 97–101.

Papadopoulos, L., Bor, R. and Stanion, P. (1997) Genograms in counselling practice: a review (part 1), *Counselling Psychology Quarterly*, 10(1), 17–28.

Papp, P. (1976) Family choreography. In P.J. Guerin Jr (ed.) *Family Therapy: Theory and Practice*. New York: Gardner Press.

Parker, G. and Crawford, J. (2007) Judged effectiveness of differing antidepressant strategies by those with clinical depression, *Australian and New Zealand Journal of Psychiatry*, 41, 32–7.

Parlett, M. (2001) On being present at one's own life (Gestalt Psychotherapy). In E. Spinell and S. Marshall (eds) *Embodied Theories*. London: Continuum.

Parlett, M. and Page, F. (1990) Gestalt therapy. In W. Dryden (ed.) *Individual Therapy: A Handbook*. Buckingham: Open University Press.

Parloff, M.B. (1986) Frank's 'common elements' in psychotherapy: nonspecific factors and placebos, *American Journal of Orthopsychiatry*, 56, 521–30.

Parry, A. and Doan, R.E. (1994) *Story Re-visions: Narrative Therapy in the Post-modern World*. New York: Guilford.

Parsons, F. (1909) *Choosing a Vocation*. Boston, MA: Houghton Mifflin.

Parvin, R. and Anderson, G. (1999) What are we worth? Fee decisions of psychologists in private practice, *Women and Therapy*, 22(3), 15–26.

Patterson, C.H. (1984) Empathy, warmth and genuineness in psychotherapy: a review of reviews. *Psychotherapy*, 21, 431–8.

Patterson, C.H. (1989) Eclecticism in psychotherapy: is integration possible? *Psychotherapy*, 26, 157–61.

Patterson, C.H. (2004) Do we need multicultural counseling competencies? *Journal of Mental Health Counseling*, 26, 67–73.

Patterson, J., Albala, A.A., McCahill, M.E. and Edwards, T.M. (2009) *The Therapist's Guide to Psychopharmacology*, revised edn. New York: Guilford Press.

Paul, G.L. (1967) Strategy of outcome research in psychotherapy, *Journal of Consulting Psychology*, 31, 109–18.

Paulson, B., Everall, R.D. and Stuart, J. (2001) Client perceptions of hindering experiences in counselling, *Counselling and Psychotherapy Research*, 1, 53–61.

Pearlman, L.A. and McIan, P.S. (1995) Vivarious traumatisation: an empirical study of the effects of trauma work on trauma therapists, *Professional Psychology: Research and Practice*, 26, 558–65.

Peck, M.S. (1978) *The Road Less Traveled: A New Psychology of Love, Traditional Values and Spiritual Growth*. New York: Simon and Schuster.

Pedersen, P.B. (1991) Multiculturalism as a generic approach to counseling, *Journal of Counseling and Development*, 70, 6–12.

Pedersen, P.B. (1994) Multicultural counseling. In R.W. Brislin and T. Yoshida (eds) *Improving Intercultural Interactions: Modules for Cross-cultural Training Programs*. London: Sage.

Pedersen, P.B., Draguns, J.G., Lonner, W.J. and Trimble, J.E. (eds) (1996) *Counseling across Cultures*. London: Sage.

Peebles, M.J. (1980) Personal therapy and ability to display empathy, warmth and genuineness in therapy, *Psychotherapy*, 17, 252–62.

Pelzer, D. (2004) *A Man Named Dave*. London: Orion.

Penn, L.S. (1990) When the therapist must leave: forced termination of psychodynamic therapy, *Professional Psychology: Research and Practice*, 21, 379–84.

Pennebaker, J.W. (1997) *Opening Up: The Healing Power of Expressing Emotions*, revised edn. New York: Guilford Press.

Pennebaker, J.W. (2004a) *Writing to Heal. A Guided Journal for Recovering from Trauma and Emotional Upheaval*. Oakland, CA: New Harbinger Press.

Pennebaker, J.W. (2004b) Theories, therapies, and taxpayers: on the complexities of the expressive writing paradigm, *Clinical Psychology: Science and Practice*, 11, 138–42.

Percy, I. (2007) Composing our lives together: narrative therapy with couples. In E. Shaw and J. Crawley (eds) *Couple Therapy in Australia: Issues Emerging from Practice*. Victoria: PsychOz Publications.

Perkins, R. (2006) The effectiveness of one session of therapy using a single-session therapy approach for children and adolescents with mental health problems, *Psychology and Psychotherapy: Theory, Research and Practice*, 79, 215–27.

Perkins, R. and Scarlett, G. (2008) The effectiveness of single session therapy in child and adolescent mental health. Part 2: An 18-month follow-up study, *Psychology and Psychotherapy: Theory, Research and Practice*, 81, 143–56.

Perls, F.S. (1947) *Ego, Hunger and Aggression*. London: Allen and Unwin.

Perls, F.S. (1969) *Gestalt Therapy Verbatim*. Lafayette, CA: Real People Press.

Perls, F.S. (1973) *The Gestalt Approach and Eye-witness to Therapy*. Ben Lomond, CA: Science and Behavior Books.

Perls, F.S., Hefferline, R.F. and Goodman, P. (1951) *Gestalt Therapy: Excitement and Growth in the Human Personality*. New York: Julian Press.

Person, E.S., Cooper, A.M. and Gabbard, G.O. (eds) (2005) *Textbook of Psychoanalysis*. New York: American Psychiatric Press.

Persons, J.B. (1993) Case conceptualization in cognitive–behavior therapy. In K.T. Kuehlwein and H. Rosen (eds) *Cognitive Therapies in Action: Evolving Innovative Practice*. San Francisco, CA: Jossey-Bass.

Persons, J.B. and Davidson, J. (2001) Cognitive-behavioral case formulation. In K. Dobson (ed.) *Handbook of Cognitive-behavioral Therapies*. New York: Guilford Press.

Persons, J.B. and Tompkins, M.A. (2007) Cognitive-behavioral case formulation. In T.D. Eells (ed.) *Handbook of Psychotherapy Case Formulation*, 2nd edn. New York: Guilford Press.

Persons, J.B., Curtis, J.T. and Silberschatz, G. (1991) Psychodynamic and cognitive-behavioral formulations of a single case, *Psychotherapy*, 28, 608–17.

Pervin, L. and Johns, O. (2000) *Personality*, 8th edn. New York: Wiley.

Peters, H. (1999) Pretherapy: a client-centered/experiential approach to mentally handicapped people, *Journal of Humanistic Psychology*, 39, 8–30.

Peters, H. (2005) Pretherapy from a developmental perspective, *Journal of Humanistic Psychology*, 45, 62–81.

Petersen, T.J. (2006) Enhancing the efficacy of antidepressants with psychotherapy, *Journal of Psychopharmacology*, 20, 19–28.

Pfister, J. (1997) On conceptualizing the cultural history of emotional and psychological life in America. In J. Pfister and N. Schnog (eds) *Inventing the Psychological: Toward a Cultural History of Emotional Life in America*. New Haven, CN: Yale University Press.

Philipson, I.J. (1993) *On the Shoulders of Women: the Feminization of Psychotherapy*. New York: Guilford Press.

Phillips, A. (2007) *Winnicott*. Harmondsworth: Penguin.

Phillips, J.C. (2004) A welcome addition to the literature: nonpolarized approaches to sexual orientation and religiosity, *The Counseling Psychologist*, 32, 771–7.

Phillips, J.P.N. (1986) Shapiro Personal Questionnaire and generalized personal questionnaire techniques: a repeated measures individualised outcome measurement. In L.S. Greenberg and W.M. Pinsof (eds) *The Psychotherapeutic Process: A Research Handbook*. New York: Guilford Press.

Phillips, P., Bartlett, A. and King, M. (2001) Psychotherapists' approaches to gay and lesbian patients/clients: a qualitative study, *British Journal of Medical Psychology*, 74, 73–84.

Pilgrim, D. (1992) Psychotherapy and political evasions. In W. Dryden and C. Feltham (eds) *Psychotherapy and Its Discontents*. Buckingham: Open University Press.

Pilgrim, D. and Guinan, P. (1999) From mitigation to culpability: rethinking the evidence about therapist sexual abuse, *European Journal of Psychotherapy, Counselling and Health*, 2, 153–68.

Pines, M. (ed.) (1983) *The Evolution of Group Analysis*. London: Tavistock/Routledge.

Pinquart, M., Duberstein, P. and Lyness, J. (2007) Effects of psychotherapy and other behavioural interventions on clinically depressed older adults: a meta-analysis, *Aging and Mental Health*, 11, 645–57.

Pinsof, W.M. (2005) A Shamanic tapestry: my experiences with individual, marital and family therapy. In J.D. Geller, J.C Norcross and D.E.Orlinsky (eds) *The Psychotherapist's own Psychotherapy: Patient and Clinician Perspectives*. New York: Oxford University Press.

Pistrang, C. and Barker, C. (1992) Clients' belief about psychological problems, *Counselling Psychology Quarterly*, 5, 325–35.

Plath, S. (1963) *The Bell Jar*. London: William Heinemann.

Plotkin, B. (2001) *Soulcraft: Crossing into the Mysteries of Nature and the Psyche*. Novato, CA: New World Library.

Plumwood, V. (1993) *Feminism and the Mastery of Nature*. London: Routledge.

Polanyi, M. (1958) *Personal Knowledge*. London: Routledge.

Polkinghorne, D.E. (1992) Postmodern epistemology of practice. In S. Kvale (ed.) *Psychology and Postmodernism*. London: Sage.

Pomerantz, A.M. (2005) Increasing informed consent: discussing distinct aspects of psychotherapy at different points in time, *Ethics and Behavior*, 15, 351–60.

Pomerantz, A.M. and Handelsman, M.M. (2004) Informed consent revisited: an updated written question format, *Professional Psychology: Research and Practice*, 35, 201–5.

Ponterotto, J.G. (1988) Racial/ethnic minority research in the Journal of Counseling Psychology: a content analysis and methodological critique, *Journal of Counseling Psychology*, 35, 410–18.

Ponterotto, J.G., Casas, J.M., Suzuki, L.A. and Alexander, C.M. (eds) (1995) *Handbook of Multicultural Counseling*. London: Sage.

Ponterotto, J.G., Casas, J.M., Suzuki, L.A. and Alexander, C.M. (eds) (2010) *Handbook of Multicultural Counseling*, 3rd edn. London: Sage.

Poole, M.S. and Hollingshead, A.B. (eds) (2004) *Theories of Small Groups: Interdisciplinary Perspectives*. Thousand Oaks, CA: Sage.

Pope, K.S. (no date) *Psychologists' & Physicians' Involvement in Detainee Interrogations*. Available at http://kspope.com/interrogation/index.php (accessed 14 March 2012).

Pope, K.S. (1991) Dual relationships in psychotherapy, *Ethics and Behavior*, 1, 21–34.

Pope, K.S. and Bouhoutsos, J.C. (1986) *Sexual Intimacy between Therapists and Patients*. New York: Praeger.

Pope, K.S. and Vasquez, M.J.T. (2007) *Ethics in Psychotherapy and Counseling: A Practical Guide, Third Edition.* San Francisco, CA: Jossey-Bass.

Pope, K.S. and Keith-Speigel, P. (2008) A practical approach to boundaries in psychotherapy: making decisions, bypassing blunders, and mending fences, *Journal of Clinical Psychology*, 64, 638–52.

Pope, K.S., Levenson, H. and Schover, L.R. (1979) Sexual intimacy in psychology training: results and implications of a national survey, *American Psychologist*, 34, 682–9.

Pope, K.S., Keith-Speigel, P. and Tabachnick, B.G. (1986) Sexual attraction to clients: the human therapist and the (sometimes) inhuman training system, *American Psychologist*, 41, 147–58.

Pope-Davis, D.B., Coleman, H., Liu, W.M. and Toporek, R.L. (eds) (2003) *Handbook of Multicultural Competencies in Counseling and Psychology.* Thousand Oaks, CA: Sage.

Portal, E.L., Suck, A.T. and Hinkle, J.S. (2010) Counseling in Mexico: history, current identity, and future trends, *Journal of Counseling and Development*, 88, 33–6.

Porter, R. (ed.) (1985) *The Anatomy of Madness*, Volumes 1 and 2. London: Tavistock.

Powell, T.J. (ed.) (1994) *Understanding the Self-help Organization: Frameworks and Findings.* Thousand Oaks, CA: Sage.

Poznanski, J.J. and McLennan, J. (1995) Conceptualizing and measuring counselors' theoretical orientation, *Journal of Counseling Psychology*, 42, 411–22.

Present, J., Crits-Christoph, P., Connolly Gibbons, M.B., *et al.* (2008) Sudden gains in the treatment of generalized anxiety disorder, *Journal of Clinical Psychology*, 64, 119–26.

Pressly, P.K. and Heesaker, M. (2001) The physical environment and counselling: a review of theory and research, *Journal of Counseling and Development*, 79, 148–60.

Prilleltensky, I and Nelson, G.B. (2005) *Communityy Psychology: In Pursuit of Liberation and Well-being.* Basingstoke: Palgrave Macmillan.

Prince, R. (1980) Variations in psychotherapeutic procedures. In H.C. Triandis and J.G. Draguns (eds) *Handbook of Cross-cultural Psychopathology*, Volume 6. Boston, MA: Allyn and Bacon.

Prochaska, J. and Norcross, J. (1983) Contemporary psychotherapists: a national survey of characteristics, practices, orientations and attitudes, *Psychotherapy*, 20, 161–73.

Proctor, G., Cooper, M., Sanders, P. and Malcolm, B. (eds) (2006) *Politicizing the Person-centred Approach: An Agenda for Social Change.* Ross-on-Wye: PCCS Books.

Proctor, K., Perlesz, A., Moloney, B., McIlwaine, F. and O'Neill, I. (2008) Exploring theatre of the oppressed in family therapy clinical work and supervision, *Counselling and Psychotherapy Research*, 43–52.

Proudfoot, J., Ryden, C., Everitt, B., *et al.* (2004) Clinical efficacy of computerised cognitive-behavioural therapy for anxiety and depression in primary care: randomised controlled trial, *British Journal of Psychiatry*, 185, 46–54.

Prouty, G. (1976) Pre-therapy, a method of treating pre-expressive psychotic and retarded patients, *Psychotherapy: Theory, Research and Practice*, 13, 290–4.

Prouty, G. (1990) Pre-therapy: a theoretical evolution in the person-centered/experiential psychotherapy of schizophrenia and retardation. In G. Lietaer, J. Rombauts and R. Van Balen (eds) *Client-centred and Experiential Psychotherapy in the Nineties.* Leuven: University of Leuven Press.

Prouty, G. (1998) Pre-therapy and pre-symbolic experiencing: evoluations in personcentred/ experiential approaches to psychotic experience. In L.S. Greenberg, J.C. Watson and G. Lietaer (eds) *Handbook of Experiential Psychotherapy.* New York: Guilford Press.

Prouty, G. and Kubiak, H. (1988) The development of communicative contact with a catatonic schizophrenic, *Journal of Communication Therapy*, 4(1), 13–20.

Prouty, G., Van Werde, D. and Pörtner, M. (2002) *Pre-Therapy: Reaching Contact-impaired Clients.* Ross-on-Wye: PCCS Books.

Pruett, S.R. and Chan, F. (2006) The development and psychometric validation of the Disability Attitude Implicit Association Test, *Rehabilitation Psychology*, 51, 202–13.

Pryzwansky, W.B., Harris, J.L. and Jackson, J.H. (1984) Therapy/counseling practices of urban school psychologists, *Professional Psychology: Science and Practice*, 15, 396–404.

Przeworski, A and Newman, M.G. (2004) Palmtop computer-assisted group therapy for social phobia, *Journal of Clinical Psychology*, 60, 178–88.

Purton, C. (2004) *Person-centred Therapy: The Focusing-oriented Approach.* London: Palgrave.

Raabe, P. (ed.) (2006) *Philosophical Counselling and the Unconscious*. Amherst, NY: Trivium.

Raabe, P.B. (2001) *Philosophical Counseling: Theory and Practice*. Westport, CT: Praeger.

Rabin, A.I., Aronoff, J., Barclay, A. and Zucker, R. (eds) (1981) *Further Explorations in Personality*. New York: Wiley.

Rabin, A.I., Zucker, R.A., Emmons, R.A. and Frank, S. (eds) (1990) *Studying Persons and Lives*. New York: Springer.

Råbu, M. and Haavind, H. (2012) Coming to an end: a case study of an ambiguous process of ending psychotherapy, *Counselling and Psychotherapy Research*, 12, 109–17.

Råbu, M., Haavind, H. and Binder, P. (2012) We have travelled a long distance and sorted out the mess in the drawers: metaphors for moving toward the end in psychotherapy, *Counselling and Psychotherapy Research*, 13, 71–80.

Racusin, G.R., Abramowitz, S.I. and Winter, W.D. (1981) Becoming a therapist: family dynamics and career choice, *Professional Psychology*, 12, 271–9.

Raiya, H.A. and Pargament, K. (2010) Religiously integrated psychotherapy with Muslim clients: from research to practice, *Professional Psychology: Research and Practice*, 41, 181–8.

Ramirez, M. III (1991) *Psychotherapy and Counseling with Minorities: A Cognitive Approach to Individual and Cultural Differences*. Oxford: Pergamon Press.

Ramsay, J.R. (2001) The clinical challenges of assimilative integration, *Journal of Psychotherapy Integration*, 11, 21–42.

Randall, R. (2009) Loss and climate change: the cost of parallel narratives, *Ecopsychology*, 1, 118–29.

Rapaport, D. and Gill, M. (1959) The points of view and assumptions of metapsychology, *International Journal of Psycho-Analysis*, 40, 153–62.

Rappaport, J. (1993) Narrative studies, personal studies, and identity transformation in the mutual help process, *Journal of Applied Behavioural Sicience*, 29, 239–56.

Rasmussen, B. (2000) Poetic truths and clinical reality: client experiences of the use of metaphor by therapists, *Smith College Studies in Social Work*, 27, 355–73.

Rasmussen, B. and Angus, L. (1996) Metaphor in psychodynamic psychotherapy with borderline and non-borderline clients: a qualitative analysis, *Psychotherapy*, 33, 521–30.

Rath, J. (2008) Training to be a volunteer Rape Crisis counsellor: a qualitative study of women's experiences, *British Journal of Guidance and Counselling*, 36, 19–32.

Ratts, M.J. (2009) Social justice counseling: toward the development of a fifth force among counseling paradigms, *Journal of Humanistic Counseling*, 48, 160–72.

Raue, P.J. and Goldfried, M.R. (1994) The therapeutic alliance in cognitive-behavior therapy. In A.O. Horvath and L.S. Greenberg (eds) *The Working Alliance: Theory, Research and Practice*. New York: Wiley.

Raval, H. and Smith, J.A. (2003) Therapists' experiences of working with language interpreters, *International Journal of Mental Health*, 32, 6–31.

Rave, E.J. and Larsen, C.C. (eds) (1995) *Ethical Decision Making in Therapy: Feminist Perspectives*. New York: Guilford Press.

Rawson, D. (2002) Cathexis: brief therapy in a residential setting. In K.Tudor (ed.) *Transactional Analysis Approaches to Brief Therapy*. London: Sage.

Ray, N. (2005) Transactions on the rock face, *Therapy Today*, 16(10), 15–17.

Rayner, E. (1990) *The Independent Mind in British Psychoanalysis*. London: Free Association Books.

Read, S. (2007) *Bereavement Counselling for People with Learning Disabilities: A Manual to Develop Practice*. London: Quay Books.

Reese, R.J., Conoley, C.W. and Brossart, D.F. (2002) Effectiveness of telephone counseling: a field-based investigation, *Journal of Counseling Psychology*, 49, 233–42.

Reese, R.J., Conoley, C.W. and Brossart, D.F. (2006) The attractiveness of telephone counseling: an empirical investigation, *Journal of Counseling and Development*, 84, 54–60.

Reeve, D. (2002) Oppression within the counselling room, *Counselling and Psychotherapy Research*, 2, 11–19.

Reeve, D. (2006) Towards a psychology of disability: the emotional effect of living in a disabling society. In D. Goodley and R. Lawthom (eds) *Disability and Psychology: Critical Introductions and Reflections*. Basingstoke: Palgrave Macmillan.

Regan, A. and Hill, C.E. (1992) Investigation of what clients and counsellors do not say in brief therapy, *Journal of Counseling Psychology*, 38, 168–74.

Reimers, S. and Treacher, A. (1995) *Introducing User-friendly Family Therapy*. London: Routledge.

Reis, B.F. and Brown, L.G. (2006) Preventing therapy dropout in the real world: the clinical utility of videotape preparation and client estimate of treatment duration, *Professional Psychology: Research and Practice*, 37, 311–16.

Remley Jr., T.P., Bacchini, E. and Krieg, P. (2010) Counseling in Italy, *Journal of Counseling and Development*, 88, 28–32.

Rennie, D.L. (1998) *Person-centred Counselling: An Experiential Approach*. London: Sage.

Rennie, D.L. (1990) Toward a representation of the client's experience of the psychotherapy hour. In G. Lietaer, J. Rombauts and R. Van Balen (eds) *Client-centered and Experiential Therapy in the Nineties*. Leuven: University of Leuven Press.

Rennie, D.L. (1992) Qualitative analysis of the client's experience of psychotherapy: the unfolding of reflexivity. In S. Toukmanian and D. Rennie (eds) *Psychotherapy Process Research*. London: Sage.

Rennie, D.L. (1994a) Clients' deference in psychotherapy, *Journal of Counseling Psychology*, 41, 427–37.

Rennie, D.L. (1994b) Storytelling in psychotherapy: the clients' subjective experience, *Psychotherapy*, 31, 234–43.

Rennie, D.L. (2000a) Grounded theory methodology as methodological hermeneutics: reconciling realism and relativism, *Theory and Psychology*, 10, 481–512.

Rennie, D.L. (2000b) Aspects of the client's conscious control of the psychotherapeutic process, *Journal of Psychotherapy Integration*, 10, 151–67.

Rennie, D.L. (2001) Clients as self-aware agents, *Counselling and Psychotherapy Research*, 1, 82–9.

Rennie, D.L. (2002) Experiencing psychotherapy: grounded theory studies. In D.J. Cain and J. Seeman (eds) *Humanistic Psychotherapies: Handbook of Research and Practice*. Washington, DC: American Psychological Association.

Rennie, D.L., Phillips, J.R. and Quartaro, J.K. (1988) Grounded theory: a promising approach for conceptualization in psychology? *Canadian Psychology*, 29, 139–50.

Rescher, N. (1993) *Pluralism: Against the Demand for Consensus*. Oxford: Oxford University Press.

Reynolds, D.K. (1980) *The Quiet Therapies*. Honolulu: University Press of Hawaii.

Reynolds, D.K. (1981a) Naikan psychotherapy. In R.J. Corsini (ed.) *Handbook of Innovative Psychotherapies*. New York: Wiley.

Reynolds, D.K. (1981b) Morita psychotherapy. In R.J. Corsini (ed.) *Handbook of Innovative Psychotherapies*. New York: Wiley.

Reynolds, F., Lim, K.H. and Prior, S. (2008) Narratives of therapeutic art-making in the context of marital breakdown: older women reflect on a significant mid-life experience, *Counselling Psychology Quarterly*, 21, 203–14.

Rice, L.N. (1974) The evocative function of the therapist. In D.A. Wexler and L.N. Rice (eds) *Innovations in Client-centered Therapy*. New York: Wiley.

Rice, L.N. (1984) Client tasks in client-centered therapy. In R.F. Levant and J.M. Shlien (eds) *Client-centered Therapy and the Person-centered Approach: New Directions in Theory, Research and Practice*. New York: Praeger.

Rice, L.N. and Greenberg, L.S. (1992) Humanistic approaches to psychotherapy. In D.K. Freedheim (ed.) *History of Psychotherapy: A Century of Change*. Washington, DC: American Psychological Association.

Rice, L.N. and Greenberg, L.S. (eds) (1984a) *Patterns of Change: Intensive Analysis of Psychotherapy Process*. New York: Guilford Press.

Rice, L.N. and Greenberg, L.S. (1984b) The new research paradigm. In L.N. Rice and L.S. Greenberg (eds) *Patterns of Change: Intensive Analysis of Psychotherapy Process*. New York: Guilford Press.

Rice, N.M., Grealy, M.A., Javaid, A. and Serrano, R.M. (2011) Understanding the social interaction difficulties of women with unipolar depression, *Qualitative Health Research*, 21, 1388–99.

Richards, K. (2003) Self-esteem and relational voices: eating disorder interventions for young women in the outdoors. In K. Richards (ed.) *Self-esteem and Youth Development*. Ambleside: Brathay Hall Trust.

Richards, K. and Peel, J. (2005) Outdoor cure, *Therapy Today*, 16(10), 4–8.

Richards, K. and Smith, B. (eds) (2003) *Therapy within Adventure*. Augsberg: Ziel Publications.

Richards K.A.M., Zivave, A.T., Govere, S.M., Mphande, J. and Dupwa, B. (2012) Counseling in Zimbabwe: history, current status, and future trends, *Journal of Counseling and Development*, 90, 102–6.

Richards, P.S. and Bergin, A.E. (eds) (2000) *Handbook of Psychotherapy and Religious Diversity*. Washington, DC: American Psychological Association.

Richards, P.S. and Bergin, A.E. (eds) (2004) *Casebook for a Spiritual Strategy in Counseling and Psychotherapy*. Washington, DC: American Psychological Association.

Richards, P.S. and Bergin, A.E. (eds) (2005) *A Spiritual Strategy for Counseling and Psychotherapy*, 2nd edn. Washington, DC: American Psychological Association.

Ridge, D. and Ziebland, S. (2006) "The old me could never have done that": how people give meaning to recovery following depression, *Qualitative Health Research*, 16, 1038–63.

Ridge, D. and Ziebland, S. (2011) Understanding depression through a 'coming out' framework, *Sociology of Health and Illness*, 34, 730–45.

Ridgway, P. (2001) Experiencing recovery: a dimensional analysis of recovery narrative, *Psychiatric Rehabilitation Journal*, 24, 335–43.

Ridley, C.R. and Lingle, D.W. (1996) Cultural empathy in multicultural counseling: a multidimensional process model. In P.B. Pedersen, J.G. Draguns, W.J. Lonner and J.E. Trimble (eds) *Counseling across Cultures*. London: Sage.

Riesman, D., Glazer, N. and Denny, R. (1950) *The Lonely Crowd*. New Haven, CT: Yale University Press.

Rippere, V. and Williams, R. (eds) (1985) *Wounded Healers: Mental Health Workers' Experiences of Depression*. New York: Wiley.

Rivett, M. and Street, E. (2009) *Family Therapy: 100 Key Points and Techniques*. Hove: Routledge.

Robbins, S.P. and Judge, T.A. (2007) *Organizational Behavior*, 12th edn. Englewood Cliffs, NJ: Prentice Hall.

Roberts, J. and Pines, M. (eds) (1991) *The Practice of Group Analysis*. London: Tavistock/ Routledge.

Robinson, D. (1980) Self-help health groups. In P.B. Smith (ed.) *Small Groups and Personal Change*. London: Methuen.

Rochlen, A.B., Back, J.S. and Speyer, C. (2004) Online therapy: review of relevant definitions, debates, and current empirical support, *Journal of Clinical Psychology*, 60, 269–83.

Rodman, F.R. (2003) *Winnicott: Life and Work*. Cambridge, MA: Perseus.

Roe, D. and Davidson, L. (2006) Self and narrative in schizophrenia: time to author a new story, *Medical Humanities*, 31, 89–94.

Rogers, A., Pilgrim, D. and Lacey, R. (1993) *Experiencing Psychiatry: Users' Views of Services*. London: Macmillan.

Rogers, C.R. (1942) *Counseling and Psychotherapy*. Boston, MA: Houghton Mifflin.

Rogers, C.R. (1951) *Client-centered Therapy*. Boston, MA: Houghton Mifflin.

Rogers, C.R. (1957) The necessary and sufficient conditions of therapeutic personality change, *Journal of Consulting Psychology*, 21, 95–103.

Rogers, C.R. (1959) A theory of therapy, personality, and interpersonal relationships, as developed in the client-centered framework. In S. Koch (ed.) *Psychology: A Study of a Science. Volume 3. Formulations of the Person and the Social Context*. New York: McGraw-Hill.

Rogers, C.R. (1961) *On Becoming a Person*. Boston, MA: Houghton Mifflin.

Rogers, C.R. (1963) The concept of the fully functioning person, *Psychotherapy: Theory, Research and Practice*, 1, 17–26.

Rogers, C.R. (1968) Interpersonal relationships: USA 2000, *Journal of Applied Behavioral Science*, 4, 265–80.

Rogers, C.R. (1978) *Carl Rogers on Personal Power: Inner Strength and its Revolutionary Impact*. London: Constable.

Rogers, C.R. (1980) *A Way of Being*. Boston, MA: Houghton Mifflin.

Rogers, C.R. and Dymond, R.F. (eds) (1954) *Psychotherapy and Personality Change*. Chicago, IL: University of Chicago Press.

Rogers, C.R. and Stevens, B. (eds) (1968) *Person to Person: The Problem of Being Human*. Lafayette, CA: Real People Press.

Rogers, C.R., Gendlin, E.T., Kiesler, D.J. and Truax, C.B. (eds) (1967) *The Therapeutic Relationship and its Impact: A Study of Psychotherapy with Schizophrenics*. Madison, WI: University of Wisconsin Press.

Rogers, N. (1993) *The Creative Connection: Expressive Art as Healing*. Palo Alto, CA: Science and Behavior Books.

Rogers, N. (2000) *The Creative Connection: Expressive Arts as Healing*. Ross-on-Wye: PCCS Books.

Rogler, L.H., Malgady, R.G., Costantino, G. and Blumenthal, R. (1987) What do culturally sensitive mental health services mean? The case of Hispanics, *American Psychologist*, 42, 565–70.

Rokeach, M. (1973) *The Nature of Human Values*. New York: The Free Press.

Rokke, P.D., Carter, A.S., Rehm, L.P. and Veltum, L.G. (1990) Comparative credibility of current treatments for depression, *Psychotherapy*, 27, 235–42.

Rollnick, S. and Allison, J. (2004) Motivational interviewing. In N. Heather and T. Stockwell (eds) *The Essential Handbook of Treatment and Prevention of Alcohol Problems*. Chichester: Wiley.

Romano, J.L. and Hage, S.M. (2000) Prevention and counseling psychology; revitalizing commitments for the 21st century, *The Counseling Psychologists*, 28, 733–63.

Romme, M. and Escher, S. (2000) *Making Sense of Voices: A Guide for Mental Health Professionals Working with Voice Hearers*. London: Mind Publications.

Ronan, K.R. and Kazantzis, N. (2006) The use of between-session (homework) activities in psychotherapy: conclusions from the *Journal of Psychotherapy Integration* special series, *Journal of Psychotherapy Integration*, 16, 254–9.

Ronnestad, M.H. and Ladany, N. (2006) The impact of psychotherapy training: Introduction to the special section, *Psychotherapy Research*, 16, 261–7.

Ronnestad, M.H. and Skovholt, T.M. (2001) Learning arena for professional development: retrospective accounts of senior psychotherapists, *Professional Psychology: Research and Practice*, 32, 181–7.

Rorty, R. (1979) *Philosophy and the Mirror of Nature*. Princeton, NJ: Princeton University Press.

Rose, S., Bisson, J. and Wessely, S. (2003) A systematic review of single-session psychological interventions ('debriefing') following trauma, *Psychotherapy and Psychosomatics*, 72,171–5.

Rosen, G.M. (1987) Self-help treatment books and the commercialization of psychotherapy, *American Psychologist*, 42, 46–51.

Rosen, S. (ed.) (1982) *My Voice Will Go with You: The Teaching Tales of Milton H. Erickson*. New York: W.W. Norton.

Rosenbaum, M. (1974) Continuation of psychotherapy by 'long distance' telephone, *International Journal of Psychoanalytic Psychotherapy*, 3, 483–95.

Rosenbaum, M. (ed.) (1982) *Ethics and Values in Psychotherapy: A Guidebook*. New York: Free Press.

Rosenbaum, R. (1994) Single-session therapies: intrinsic integration, *Journal of Psychotherapy Integration*, 4, 229–52.

Rosenfield, M. (1997) *Counselling by Telephone*. London: Sage.

Rosnow, R.L. and Rosenthal, R. (1997) *People Studying People: Artifacts and Ethics in Behavioral Research*. New York: W. H. Freeman.

Rossi, E.L. (ed.) (1980) *The Collected Papers of Milton H. Erickson on Hypnosis. Volume 1: The Nature of Hypnosis and Suggestion*. New York: Irvington.

Roszak, T., Gomes, M.E., and Kanner, A.D. (1995) *Eco-psychology: Restoring the Mind, Healing the Earth*. San Francisco, CA: Sierra Club Books.

Roth, A.D. and Fonagy, P. (2005) *What Works for Whom?* 2nd edn. New York: Guilford Press.

Roth, A.D. and Pilling, S. (2007) *Competencies Required to Deliver Effective Cognitive and Behaviour Therapy for People with Depression and with Anxiety Disorders*. London: Department of Health.

Rothman, D. (1971) *The Discovery of the Asylum: Social Order and Disorder in the New Republic*. Boston, MA: Little Brown.

Rothschild, B. (2000) *The Body Remembers: The Psychophysiology of Trauma and Trauma Treatment*. New York: Norton.

Rothschild, B. (2006) *Help for the Helper: The Psychophysiology of Compassion Fatigue and Vicarious Trauma*. New York: W.W. Norton.

Rowan, J. (2005) *The Transpersonal*. London: Routledge.

Rowan, J. and Cooper, M. (eds) (1998) *The Plural Self: Multiplicity in Everyday Life*. London: Sage.

Rowan, T. and O'Hanlon, B. (1999) *Solution-oriented Therapy for Chronic and Severe Mental Illness*. New York: John Wiley and Sons.

Rowe, D. (2003) *Depression: The Way Out of your Prison*, 3rd edn. Hove: Routledge.

Rowland, N. and Goss, S. (eds) (2000) *Evidence-based Counselling and Psychological Therapies: Research and Applications*. London: Routledge.

Rubin, J.A. (2005) *Artful Therapy*. Hoboken, NJ: Wiley.

Rubino, G., Barker, C., Roth, T. and Fearon, P. (2000) Therapist empathy and depth of interpretation in response to potential alliance ruptures: the role of patient and therapist attachment styles, *Psychotherapy Research*, 10, 408–20.

Russell, J.G. (1989) Anxiety disorders in Japan: a review of the Japanese literature on shinkeishitsu and taijinkyofusho, *Culture, Medicine and Psychiatry*, 13, 391–403.

Rutter, P. (1989) *Sex in the Forbidden Zone*. London: Mandala.

Ryan, J. (2006) 'Class is in you': an exploration of some social class issues in psychotherapeutic work, *British Journal of Psychotherapy*, 23, 49–62.

Ryan, J.L. (2009) Reweaving the self: creative writing in response to tragedy, *Psychoanalytic Review*, 96, 529–38.

Rycroft, C. (1966) Causes and meaning. In C. Rycroft (ed.) *Psychoanalysis Observed*. London: Constable.

Ryden, J. and Loewenthal, D. (2001) Psychotherapy for lesbians: the influence of therapist sexuality, *Counselling and Psychotherapy Research*, 1, 42–52.

Ryle, A. (1978) A common language for the psychotherapies? *British Journal of Psychiatry*, 132, 585–94.

Ryle, A. (1987) Cognitive psychology as a common language for psychotherapy, *Journal of Integrative and Eclectic Psychotherapy*, 6, 191–212.

Ryle, A. (1990) *Cognitive-Analytic Therapy: Active Participation in Change. A New Integration in Brief Psychotherapy*. Chichester: Wiley.

Ryle, A. (ed.) (1995) *Cognitive Analytic Therapy: Developments in Theory and Practice*. Chichester: Wiley.

Ryle, A. (2005) Cognitive Analytic Therapy. In J.C. Norcross. and M.R. Goldfried (eds) *Handbook of Psychotherapy Integration*. New York: Oxford University Press.

Ryle, A. and Cowmeadow, P. (1992) Cognitive-analytic therapy (CAT). In W. Dryden (ed.) *Integrative and Eclectic Therapy: A Handbook*. Buckingham: Open University Press.

Ryle, A. and Kerr, I.B. (2002) *Introducing Cognitive Analytic Therapy: Principles and Practice*. Chichester: Wiley.

Sachse, R. and Elliott, R. (2002) Process-outcome research on humanistic outcome variables. In D.J. Cain and J. Seeman (eds) *Humanistic Psychotherapies: Handbook of Research and Practice*. Washington, DC: American Psychological Association.

Safran, J.D. (1993a) The therapeutic alliance rupture as a transtheoretical phenomenon: definitional and conceptual issues, *Journal of Psychotherapy Integration*, 3, 33–49.

Safran, J.D. (1993b) Breaches in the therapeutic alliance: an arena for negotiating authentic relatedness, *Psychotherapy*, 30, 11–24.

Safran, J.D. and Muran, J.C. (1996) The resolution of ruptures in the therapeutic alliance, *Journal of Consulting and Clinical Psychology*, 64, 447–58.

Safran, J.D. and Muran, J.C. (2000a) *Negotiating the Therapeutic Alliance: A Relational Treatment Guide*. New York: Guilford Press.

Safran, J.D. and Muran, J.C. (2000b) Resolving therapeutic alliance ruptures: diversity and integration, *In Session: Psychotherapy in Practice*, 56, 233–43.

Safran, J.D. and Muran, J.C. (2001) The therapeutic relationship as a process of intersubjective negotiation. In J.C. Muran (ed.) *Self-relations in the Psychotherapy Process*. Washington, DC: American Psychological Association.

Safran, J.D., Crocker, P., McMain, S. and Murray, P. (1990) Therapeutic alliance rupture as a therapy event for empirical investigation, *Psychotherapy*, 27, 154–65.

Salisbury, W.A. and Kinnier, R.T. (1996) Postermination friendship between counselors and clients, *Journal of Counseling and Development*, 74, 495–500.

Salkovskis, P.M. (1985) Obsessional-compulsive problems: a cognitive-behavioural analysis, *Behaviour Research and Therapy*, 23, 571–83.

Salkovskis, P.M. (ed.) (1996) *Frontiers of Cognitive Therapy*. New York: Guilford Press.

Salkovskis, P.M. (2010) Cognitive behavioural therapy. In M. Barker, A. Vossler and D. Langdridge (eds) *Understanding Counselling and Psychotherapy*. London: Sage.

Salkovskis, P., Rimes, K., Stephenson, D., Sacks, G. and Scott, J. (2006) A randomized controlled trial of the use of self-help materials in addition to standard general practice treatment of depressuion compared to standard treatment alon, *Psychological Medicine*, 34, 325–33.

Saltzman, C., Luetgert, M.J., Roth, C.H., Creaser, J. and Howard, L. (1976) Formation of a therapeutic relationship: experiences during the initial phase of psychotherapy as predictors of treatment duration and outcome, *Journal of Consulting and Clinical Psychology*, 44, 546–55.

Salzer, M.S., Rappaport, J. and Segre, L. (1999) Professional appraisal of self-help groups, *American Journal of Orthopsychiatry*, 69, 536–40.

Sampson, E.E. (1988) The debate on individualism: indigenous psychologies of the individual and their role in personal and social functioning, *American Psychologist*, 43, 15–22.

Samstag, L.W. (2007) The necessary and sufficient conditions of therapeutic personality change: reactions to Rogers' 1957 article, *Psychotherapy: Theory, Research, Practice, Training*, 44, 295–9.

Sandell, R., Blomberg, J., Lazar, A. *et al.* (2000) Varieties of long-term outcome among patients in psychoanalysis and long-term psychotherapy. A review of findings of the Stockholm Outcome of Psychoanalysis and Psychotherapy Project (STOPPP), *International Journal of Psychoanalysis*, 81, 921–42.

Sanders, D. and Wills, F. (2002) *Counselling for Anxiety Problems*. London: Sage.

Sanders, P. (ed.) (2004) *The Tribes of the Person-Centred Nation: A Guide to the Schools of Therapy Related to the Person-centred Approach*. Ross-on-Wye: PCCS Books.

Sanders, P. (ed.) (2006) *The Contact Work Primer: An Introduction to Pre-Therapy and the Work of Garry Prouty*. Ross-on-Wye: PCCS Books.

Sarbin, T.R. (1986) The narrative as a root metaphor for psychology. In T.R. Sarbin (ed.) *Narrative Psychology: The Storied Nature of Human Conduct*. New York: Praeger.

Sass, L.A. (1988) Humanism, hermeneutics, and the concept of the human subject. In S.B. Messer, L.A. Sass and R.L. Woolfolk (eds) *Hermeneutics and Psychological Theory: Interpretive Perspectives on Personality, Psychotherapy and Psychopathology*. New Brunswick, NJ: Rutgers University Press.

Satir, V. (1972) *Peoplemaking*. Palo Alto, CA: Science and Behavior Books.

Sato, T. (1998) Agency and communion: the relationship between therapy and culture, *Cultural Diversity and Mental Health*, 4, 278–90.

Sattler, J.M. (1977) The effects of therapist–client racial similarity. In A.S. Gurman and A.M. Razin (eds) *Effective Psychotherapy: A Review of Research*. New York: Pergamon.

Savage, T.A., Harley, D.A. and Nowak, T.M. (2005) Applying social empowerment strategies as tools for self-advocacy in counseling lesbian and gay male clients, *Journal of Counseling and Development*, 83, 131–7.

Saxon, D., Ivey, C. and Young, C. (2008) Can CORE assessment data identify those clients less likely to benefit from brief counselling in primary care? *Counselling and Psychotherapy Research*, 8, 223–30.

Sayers, J. (1991) *Mothering Psychoanalysis: Helene Deutsch, Karen Horney, Anna Freud and Melanie Klein*. Harmondsworth: Penguin.

Scarf, M. (1987) *Intimate Partners*. New York: Century.

Schafer, R. (1992) *Retelling a Life*. New York: Basic Books.

Scheel, M.J., Seaman, S., Roach, K., Mullin, T. and Mahoney, K.B. (1999) Client implementation of therapist recommendations predicted by client perception of fit, difficulty of implementation, and therapist influence, *Journal of Counseling Psychology*, 46, 308–16.

Scheel, M.J., Hanson, W.E. and Razzhavaikina, T.I. (2004) The process of recommending homework in psychotherapy: a review of therapist delivery methods, client acceptability, and factors that affect compliance, *Psychotherapy: Theory, Research and Practice*, 41, 38–55.

Scheff, T.J. (1980) *Catharsis in Healing, Ritual and Drama*. San Francisco, CA: University of California Press.

Schein, E.H. (2004) *Organizational Culture and Leadership*, 3rd edn. San Franciso, CA: Jossey-Bass.

Scheinberg, S., Johansson, A., Stevens, C. and Conway-Hicks, S. (2008) Research communities in action: three examples. In P. Brownell (ed.) *Handbook for Theory, Research and Practice in Gestalt Therapy*. Newcastle: Cambridge Scholars Publishing.

Schiff, A.W. and Schiff, J.L. (1971) Passivity, *Transactional Analysis Journal*, 1(1), 71–8.

Schiff, J.L., Schiff, A.W., Mellor, K. *et al.* (1975) *Cathexis Reader: Transactional Analysis Treatment of Psychosis*. New York: Harper.

Schmid, P.F. (1998) On becoming a person-centred approach: a person-centred understanding of the person. In B. Thorne and E. Lambers (eds) *Person-centred Therapy: A European Perspective*. London: Sage.

Schmid, P.F. (2001) Acknowledgement: the art of responding. Dialogical and ethical perspectives on the challenge of unconditional personal relationships in therapy and beyond. In J. Bozarth and P. Wilkins (eds) *Unconditional Positive Regard*. Ross-on-Wye: PCCS Books.

Schmid, P.F. (2007a) A personalizing tendency. Philosophical perspectives on the actualizing tendency axiom and its dialogical and therapeutic consequences. In B. Levitt (ed.) *A Positive Psychology of Human Potential. The Person-centred Approach*. Ross-on-Wye: PCCS Books.

Schmid, P.F. (2007b) The anthropological and ethical foundations of person-centred therapy. In Cooper, M., O'Hara, M., Schmid, P.F. and Wyatt, G. (eds) *The Handbook of Person-centred Psychotherapy and Counselling*. Ross-on-Wye: PCCS Books.

Schneider, A.J., Mataix-Cols, D., Marks, I.M. and Bachofen, M. (2005) Internet-guided self-help with or without exposure therapy for phobic and panic disorders, *Psychotherapy and Psychosomatics*, 74, 154–66.

Schneider, K.J. (1998) Existential processes. In L.S. Greenberg, J.C. Watson and G. Lietaer (eds) *Handbook of Experiential Psychotherapy*. New York: Guilford Press.

Schneider, K.J. and May, R. (1995) *The Psychology of Existence: An Integrative, Clinical Perspective*. New York: McGraw-Hill.

Schneider, K.J., Bugental, J.F.T. and Pierson, J.F. (eds) (2001) *The Handbook of Humanistic Psychology: Leading Edges in Theory, Research and Practice*. Thousand Oaks, CA: Sage.

Schneider, K.J. and Längle, A. (2012) The renewal of humanism in psychotherapy: a roundtable discussion, *Psychotherapy*, 49, 427–9.

Schottenbauer, M.A., Glass, C.R. and Arnkoff, D.B. (2005) Outcome research on psychotherapy integration. In J.C. Norcross. and M.R. Goldfried (eds) *Handbook of Psychotherapy Integration*. New York: Oxford University Press.

Schreiber, S. (1995) Migration, traumatic bereavement and transcultural aspects of psychological healing: loss and grief of a refugee woman from Begamer County in Ethiopia, *British Journal of Medical Psychology*, 68, 135–42.

Schroder, D. (2004) *Little Windows into Art Therapy: Small Openings for Beginning Therapists*. London: Jessica Kingsley.

Schröder, T., Wiseman, H. and Orlinsky, D. (2009) "You were always on my mind": Therapists' intersession experiences in relation to their therapeutic practice, professional characteristics, and quality of life, *Psychotherapy Research*, 19, 42–53.

Schulenberg, S.E. (2003) Psychotherapy and the movies: on using films in clinical practice, *Journal of Contemporary Psychotherapy*, 33, 35–48.

Schuster, S.C. (1999) *Philosophy Practice: An Alternative to Counseling and Psychotherapy*. Westport, CT: Praeger.

Scogin, F., Bynum, J., Stephens, G. and Calhoon, S. (1990) Efficacy of self-administered treatment programmes: meta-analytic review, *Professional Psychology: Research and Practice*, 21, 42–7.

Scott, M.J., Stradling, S.G. and Dryden, W. (1995) *Developing Cognitive–Behavioural Counselling*. London: Sage.

Scottish Executive (2006) *National Evaluation of the 'Doing Well by People with Depression' Programme*. Edinburgh: Scottish Executive.

Scull, A. (1975) From madness to mental illness: medical men as moral entrepreneurs, *European Journal of Sociology*, 16, 218–61.

Scull, A. (1979) *Museums of Madness: The Social Organization of Insanity in Nineteenth Century England*. London: Allen Lane.

Scull, A. (ed.) (1981a) *Mad-houses, Mad-doctors and Madmen*. Philadelphia, PA: University of Pennsylvania Press.

Scull, A. (1981b) Moral treatment reconsidered: some sociological comments on an episode in the history of British psychiatry. In A. Scull (ed.) *Mad-houses, Mad-doctors and Madmen*. Philadelphia, PA: University of Pennsylvania Press.

Scull, A. (1989) *Social Order/Disorder: Anglo-American Psychiatry in Historical Perspective*. London: Routledge.

Scull, A. (1993) *The Most Solitary of Affleictions: Madness and Society in Britain, 1700–1900*. New Haven: Yale University Press.

Scully, R. (1983) The work-settings support group: a means of preventing burnout. In B.A. Farber (ed.) *Stress and Burnout in the Human Service Professions*. New York: Pergamon.

Searles, H. (1975) The patient as therapist to his analyst. In R.C. Givaccini (ed.) *Tactics and Techniques in Psychoanalytic Treatment*, Volume II. New York: Jason Aronson.

See, C.M. and Ng, K.M. (2010) Counseling in Malaysia: history, current status, and future trends, *Journal of Counseling and Development*, 88, 18–22.

Seeman, J. (1949) A study of the process of nondirective therapy, *Journal of Consulting Psychology*, 13, 157–68.

Segal, H. (1964) *Introduction to the Work of Melanie Klein*. London: Hogarth.

Segal, J. (1985) *Phantasy in Everyday Life: A Psychoanalytical Approach to Understanding Ourselves*. Harmondsworth: Penguin.

Segal, J. (1992) *Melanie Klein*. London: Sage.

Segal, J. (1996) Whose disability? Countertransference in work with people with disabilities, *Psychodynamic Counselling*, 2(2), 152–66.

Segal, Z.V., Williams, J.M.G. and Teasdale, J.D. (2001) *Mindfulness-Based Cognitive Therapy for Depression: A New Approach to Preventing Relapse*. New York: Guilford Press.

Seikkula, J. and Arnkil, T.E. (2006) *Dialogical Meetings in Social Networks*. London: Karnac.

Seikkula, J., Aaltonen, J., Alakare, B., Haarakangas, K., Keranen, J. and Lehtinen, K. (2006) Five-year experience of first-treatment nonaffective psychosis on open-dialogue approach: treatment principles, follow-up outcomes, and two case studies, *Psychotherapy Research*, 16, 214–28.

Seiser, L. and Wastell, C. (2002) *Interventions and Techniques*. Maidenhead: Open University Press.

Self, R., Oates, P., Pinnock-Hamilton, T. and Leach, C. (2005) The relationship between social deprivation and unilateral termination (attrition) from psychotherapy at various stages of the health care pathway, *Psychology and Psychotherapy: Theory, Research and Practice*, 78, 95–111.

Seligman, M.E.P. (1975) *Helplessness*. San Francisco, CA: Freeman.

Seligman, M.E.P. (1995) The effectiveness of psychotherapy. The *Consumer Reports* study, *American Psychologist*, 50, 965–74.

Seligman, M.E.P. and Csikszentmihalyi, M. (2000) Positive psychology – an introduction, *American Psychologist*, 55, 5–14.

Sennett, R. (1998) *The Corrosion of Character: The Personal Consequences of Work in the New Capitalism*. New York: W.W. Norton.

Sennett, R. (2003) *Respect in a World of Inequality*. New York: W.W. Norton.

Senyonyi, R.M., Ochieng, L.A. and Sells, J. (2012) The development of professional counseling in Uganda: current status and future trends, *Journal of Counseling and Development*, 90, 500–4.

Serlin, I.A. (1992) A tribute to Laura Perls, *Journal of Humanistic Psychology*, 32, 57–66.

Sexton, L. (1999) Vicarious traumatisation of counsellors and effects on their workplaces, *British Journal of Guidance and Counselling*, 27, 393–404.

Shamdasani, S. (2005) 'Psychotherapy': the invention of a word, *History of the Human Sciences*, 18, 1–22.

Shapiro, D.A. (1981) Comparative credibility of treatment rationales: three tests of expectancy theory, *British Journal of Clinical Psychology*, 28, 111–22.

Shapiro, D.A., Barkham, M., Rees, A. et al. (1994) Effects of treatment duration and severity of depression on the effectiveness of cognitive-behavioral and psychodynamicinterpersonal psychotherapy, *Journal of Consulting and Clinical Psychology*, 62, 522–34.

Shapiro, F. (2001) *EMDR: Eye Movement Desensitization and Reprocessing: Basic principles, protocols and procedures*, 2nd edn. New York: Guilford Press.

Sharpe, E.F. (1940) Psycho-physical problems revealed in language: an examination of metaphor, *International Journal of Psycho-Analysis*, 21, 21–43.

Sharry, J. (2007) *Solution-focused Groupwork*, 2nd edn. London: Sage.

Shaw, H.E. and Shaw, S.F. (2006) Critical ethical issues in online counseling: assessing ethical practices with an ethical intent checklist, *Journal of Counseling and Development*, 84, 41–53.

Shawahin, L. and Çiftçi, A. (2012) Counseling and mental health care in Palestine, *Journal of Counseling and Development*, 90, 378–82.

Shea, C. and Bond, T. (1997) Ethical issues for counselling in organizations. In M. Carroll and M. Walton (eds) *Handbook of Counselling in Organizations*. London: Sage.

Shedler, J. (2006) *That was Then, This is Now: Psychoanalytic Psychotherapy for the Rest of Us*. Available at http://psychsystems.net/shedler.html (accessed 19 March 2013).

Shedler, J. (2010) The efficacy of psychodynamic psychotherapy, *American Psychologist*, 65, 98–109.

Shelton, K. and Delgado-Romero, E.A. (2011) Sexual orientation microaggressions: the experience of lesbian, gay, bisexual, and queer clients in psychotherapy, *Journal of Counseling Psychology*, 58, 210–21.

Shepard, M. (1975) *Fritz*. New York: Bantam Books.

Shepherd, L., Salkovskis, P.M. and Morris, M. (2009) Recording therapy sessions: an evaluation of patient and therapist reported behaviours, attitudes and preferences, *Behavioural and Cognitive Psychotherapy*, 37, 141–50.

Shidlo, A. and Schroeder, M. (2002) Changing sexual orientation: A consumers' report, *Professional Psychology: Research and Practice*, 33, 249–59.

Shin, C.-M., Chow, C., Camacho-Gonsalves, T., Levy, R.J., Allen, I.E. and Leff, H.S. (2005) A meta-analytic review of racial-ethnic matching for African American and Causasian American clients and clinicians, *Journal of Counseling Psychology*, 52, 45–56.

Shinebourne, P. and Smith, J.A. (2010) The communicative power of metaphors: an analysis and interpretation of metaphors in accounts of the experience of addiction, *Psychology & Psychotherapy: Theory, Research and Practice*, 83, 59–73.

Shipton, G. (1999) Self-reflection and the mirror. In C. Mace (ed.) *Heart and Soul: The Therapeutic Face of Philosophy*. London: Routledge.

Shlien, J. (1997) Empathy in psychotherapy. A vital mechanism? Yes. Therapist's conceit? All too often. By itself enough? No. In A.C. Bohart and L.S. Greenberg (eds) *Empathy Reconsidered: New Directions in Psychotherapy*. Washington, DC: American Psychological Association.

Shohet, R. and Wilmot, J. (1991) The key issue in the supervision of counsellors: the supervisory relationship. In W. Dryden and B. Thorne (eds) *Training and Supervision for Counselling in Action*. London: Sage.

Shotter, J. (1993) *Conversational Realities: Constructing Life through Language*. London: Sage.

Showalter, E. (1985) *The Female Malady: Women, Madness and English Culture, 1830–1980*. New York: Pantheon Books.

Siegel, D.J. (2006) An interpersonal neurobiology approach to psychotherapy: how awareness, mirror neurons and neural plasticity contribute to the development of well-being, *Psychiatric Annals*, 36, 248–58.

Siegel, D.J. (2009) Mindful awareness, mindsight, and neural integration, *The Humanistic Psychologist*, 37, 137–58.

Siegel, D.J. (2012) *Pocket Guide to Interpersonal Neurobiology. An Integrative Handbook of the Mind*. New York: Norton.

Sifneos, P. E. (1979) *Short-term Dynamic Psychotherapy*. New York: Plenum.

Silberschatz, G. (2007) Comments on "the necessary and sufficient conditions of therapeutic personality change", *Psychotherapy: Theory, Research, Practice, Training*, 44, 265–7.

Silberschatz, G., Fretter, P.B. and Curtis, J.T. (1986) How do interpretations influence the process of psychotherapy? *Journal of Consulting and Clinical Psychology*, 54, 646–52.

Sills, C. (ed.) (2006) *Contracts in Counselling and Psychotherapy*. London: Sage.

Sills, C., Lapworth, P. and Desmond, B. (2012) *An Introduction to Gestalt*. London: Sage.

Silove, D. and Manicavasagar, V. (1997) *Overcoming Panic: A Self-Help Guide using Cognitive-Behavioural Techniques*. London: Constable and Robinson.

Silverstone, L. (1997) *Art Therapy: The Person-centred Way*, 2nd edn. London: Jessica Kingsley.

Silverstone, L. (2009) *Art Therapy Exercises: Inspirational and Practical Ideas to Stimulate the Imagination*. London: Jessica Kingsley.

Simons, J.D., Hutchison, B. and Baštecká, Z. (2012) Counseling in the Czech Republic: history, status, and future, *Journal of Counseling and Development*, 90, 233–7.

Simpson, S. (2003) Video counselling and psychotherapy in practice. In S. Goss and K. Anthony (eds) *Techology in Counselling and Psychotherapy: A Practitioner's Guide*. London: Palgrave Macmillan.

Simson, S. and Straus, M.C. (1997) *Horticulture as Therapy: Principles and Practice*. New York: Food Products Press.

Sinacola, R.S. and Peters-Strickland, T.S. (2011) *Basic Psychopharmacology for Counselors and Psychotherapists*, 2nd edn. London: Pearson.

Singer, M.T. and Lalich, J. (1996) *Crazy Therapies: What are They? Do they Work?* San Francisco, CA: Jossey-Bass.

Singh, A.A. and Shelton, K. (2011) A content analysis of LGBTQ qualitative research in counseling: a ten-year review, *Journal of Counseling and Development*, 89, 217–26.

Singh, A.A.,Urbano, A., Haston, M. and McMahon, E. (2010) School counselors' strategies for social justice change: a grounded theory of what works in the real world, *Professional School Counseling*, 13, 135–45.

Skinner, B.F. (1953) *Science and Human Behavior*. New York: Macmillan.

Skovholt, T.M. (2008) *The Resilient Practitioner: Burnout Prevention and Self-Care Strategies for Counselors, Therapists, Teachers, and Health Professionals*, 2nd edn. New York: Allyn and Bacon.

Skovholt, T.M. and Jennings, L. (2004) *Master Therapists: Exploring Expertise in Therapy and Counseling*. New York: Allyn and Bacon.

Skovholt, T.M. and Ronnestad, M.H. (2013) *The Developing Practitioner. Growth and Stagnation of Therapists and Counselors*. New York: Routledge.

Skynner, R. and Cleese, J. (1993) *Families and How to Survive Them*, 2nd edn. London: Vermillion.

Slade, A. (1999) Attachment theory and research: implications for the theory and practice of individual psycho-therapy with adults. In J. Cassidy and P.R. Shaver (eds) *Handbook of Attachment: Theory, Research and Clinical Applications*. New York: Guilford Press.

Slaikeu, K.A. and Willis, M.A. (1978) Caller feedback on counselor performance in telephone crisis intervention: a follow-up study, *Crisis Intervention*, 9, 42–9.

Slife, B.D. (2004) Theoretical challenges to therapy practice and research: the constraint of naturalism. In M.J. Lambert.(ed) *Bergin and Garfield's Handbook of Psychotherapy and Behavior Change*, 5th edn. New York: Wiley.

Slife, B.D. and Wendt, D.C. (2009) Editors' introduction: the modern legacy of William James's *A Pluralistic Universe, Journal of Mind and Behavior*, 30, 30–33.

Slife, B.D. and Williams, R.N. (1995) *What's Behind the Research? Discovering Hidden Assumptions in the Behavioral Sciences*. Thousand Oaks, CA: Sage.

Slive, A. and Bobele, M. (2011) *When One Hour is all You Have: Effective Therapy for Walk-in Clients*. Phoenix, AZ: Zeig, Tucker and Thiesen.

Sloan, D.M. and Marx, B.P. (2004) Taking pen to hand: Evaluating theories underlying the written disclosure paradigm, *Clinical Psychology: Science and Practice*, 11, 121–37.

Sloane, R.B., Staples, F.R., Cristol, A.H., Yorkson, N.J. and Whipple, K. (1975) *Psychotherapy versus Behavior Therapy*. Cambridge, MA: Harvard University Press.

Smail, D. (1978) *Psychotherapy: A Personal Approach*. London: Dent.

Smail, D. (1991) Towards a radical environmentalist psychology of help, *The Psychologist*, 2, 61–5.

Smail, D. (2001) *Why Therapy doesn't Work: and What you should Do about it*. London: Robinson.

Smail, D. (2005) *Power, Interest and Psychology: Elements of a Social Materialist Understanding of Distress*. Hay-on-Wye: PCCS Books.

Smart, J.F. and Smart, D.W. (2006) Models of disability: implications for the counseling profession, *Journal of Counseling and Development*, 84, 29–40.

Smith, L. (2005) Psychotherapy, classism and the poor: conspicuous by their absence, *American Psychologist*, 60, 687–96.

Smith, L., Bratini, L. and Appio, L.M. (2012) "Everybody's teaching and everybody's learning": Photovoice and youth counseling, *Journal of Counselling and Development*, 90, 3–12.

Smith, L., Mao, S., Perkins, S. and Ampuero, M. (2011) The relationship of clients' social class to early therapeutic impressions, *Counselling Psychology Quarterly*, 24, 15–27.

Smith, M., Glass, G. and Miller, T. (1980) *The Benefits of Psychotherapy*. Baltimore, MD: Johns Hopkins University Press.

Smith, T.B., Bartz, J. and Richards, P.S. (2007) Outcomes of religious and spiritual adaptations to psychotherapy: a meta-analytic review, *Psychotherapy Research*, 17, 643–55.

Smith, S.D., Reynolds, C.A. and Rovnak, A. (2009) A critical analysis of the Social Advocacy Movement in counselling, *Journal of Counseling and Development*, 87, 483–91.

Smith-Augustine, S. and Wagner M. (2012) School Counseling in Belize: poised for great development, *International Journal for the Advancement of Counseling*, 34, 320–30.

Snyder, C.R., Ilardi, S.S., Cheavens, J., Scott, M.T., Yamhure, M. and Sympson, S. (2000) The role of hope in cognitive-behavior therapies, *Cognitive Therapy and Research*, 24, 747–62.

Snyder, W.U. (1945) An investigation of the nature of non-directive psycho-therapy, *Journal of Genetic Psychology*, 13, 193–223.

Sodowsky, G.R., Taffe, R.C., Gutkin, T.B. and Wise, S. (1994) Development of the Multicultural Counseling Inventory (MCI): a self-report measure of multicultural competencies, *Journal of Counseling Psychology*, 41, 137–48.

Sodowsky, G.R., Kuo-Jackson, P.Y., Frey-Richardson, M. and Corey, A.T. (1998) Correlates of self-reported multicultural competencies: counselor multicultural social desirability, race, and social inadequacy, locus of control racial ideology, and multicultural training, *Journal of Counseling Psychology*, 45, 256–64.

Sollod, R.N. (1978) Carl Rogers and the origins of client-centered therapy, *Professional Psychology*, 9, 93–104.

Sollod, R.N. (1982) Non-scientific sources of psychotherapeutic approaches. In P.W. Sharkey (ed.) *Philosophy, Religion and Psychotherapy: Essays in the Philosophical Foundations of Psychotherapy*. Washington, DC: University Press of America.

Sollod, R.N. (2005) Integrating spirituality into psychotherapy. In J.C. Norcross. and M.R. Goldfried (eds) *Handbook of Psychotherapy Integration*. New York: Oxford University Press.

Sommer, R. (2003) The use of autobiography in psychotherapy, *Journal of Clinical Psychology*, 59, 197–205.

Sommerbeck, L. (2002) Person-centered or eclectic? A response to Kahn, *Journal of Humanistic Psychology*, 42, 84–7.

Sommerbeck, L. (2003) *The Client-Centred Therapist in Psychiatric Contexts: A Therapist's Guide to the Psychiatric Landscape and its Inhabitants*. Ross-on-Wye: PCCS Books.

Sori, C.F. and Hecker, L.L. (eds) (2008) *The Therapist's Notebook Volume 3. More Homework, Handouts, and Activities for Use in Psychotherapy*. New York: Routledge.

Southgate, J. and Randall, R. (1978) *The Barefoot Psychoanalyst: An Illustrated Manual of Self-help Therapy*. London: Association of Karen Horney Psychoanalytic Counsellors.

Spangler, P., Hill, C.E., Mettus, C., Huajing Guo, A. and Heymsfield, L. (2009) Therapist perspectives on their dreams about clients: a qualitative investigation, *Psychotherapy Research*, 19, 81–95.

Spanos, I. (1978) Witchcraft in histories of psychiatry: a critical analysis and alternative conceptualisation, *Psychological Bulletin*, 85, 417–39.

Sparks, J.A., Duncan, B.L. and Miller, S.D. (2006) Integrating psychotherapy and pharmacotherapy: myths and the missing link, *Journal of Family Psychotherapy*, 17, 83–108.

Speedy, J. (2008) *Narrative Inquiry and Psychotherapy*. London: Palgrave Macmillan.

Spence, D.P. (1982) *Narrative Truth and Historical Truth: Meaning and Interpretation in Psychoanalysis*. New York: Norton.

Spence, D.P. (1989) Rhetoric vs. evidence as a source of persuasion: a critique of the case study genre. In M.J. Packer and R.B. Addison (eds) *Entering the Circle: Hermeneutic Investigation in Psychology*. Albany, NY: State University of New York Press.

Spence, D.P. (1994) Narrative truth and putative child abuse, *International Journal of Clinical and Experimental Hypnosis*, 42, 289–303.

Sperry, L. and Sharfranske, E.P. (eds) (2005) *Spiritually-oriented Psychotherapies*. Washington, DC: American Psychological Association.

Spinelli, E. (1989) *The Interpreted World: An Introduction to Phenomenological Psychology*. London: Sage.

Spinelli, E. (1994) *Demystifying Therapy*. London: Constable.

Spinelli, E. (1996) The existential-phenomenological paradigm. In R. Woolfe and W. Dryden (eds) *Handbook of Counselling Psychology*. London: Sage.

Spinelli, E. (1997) *Tales of Unknowing: Therapeutic Encounters from an Existential Perspective*. London: Duckworth.

Spira, J.L. and Reed, G.M. (2002) *Group Psychotherapy for Women with Breast Cancer*. Washington, DC: American Psychological Association.

Spurling, L. (2009) *An Introduction to Psychodynamic Counselling*, 2nd edn. London: Palgrave Macmillan.

Spurling, L. and Dryden, W. (1989) The self and the therapeutic domain. In W. Dryden and L. Spurling (eds) *On Becoming a Psychotherapist*. London: Tavistock/Routledge.

Stadler, H.A. (1986) Making hard choices: clarifying controversial ethical issues, *Counseling and Human Development*, 19, 1–10.

Stanion, P., Papadopoulos, L. and Bor, R. (1997) Genograms in counselling practice: constructing a genogram (part 2), *Counselling Psychology Quarterly*, 10(2), 139–48.

Stanton, A.L. and Danoff-Burg, S. (2002) Emotional expression, expressive writing, and cancer. In S.J. Lepore and J.M. Smyth (eds) *The Writing Cure*. Washington, DC: American Psychological Association.

Starker, S. (1988) Do-it-yourself therapy: the prescription of self-help books by psychologists, *Psychotherapy*, 25, 142–6.

Stearns, C. and Stearns, P. (1986) *Anger: The Struggle for Emotional Control in America's History*. Chicago, IL: University of Chicago Press.

Steenberger, B.N. (1992) Toward science–practice integration in brief counseling and therapy, *Counseling Psychologist*, 20, 403–50.

Stein, D.M. and Lambert, M.J. (1984) Telephone counseling and crisis intervention: a review, *American Journal of Community Psychology*, 12, 101–26.

Stein, D.M. and Lambert, M.J. (1995) Graduate training in psychotherapy: are therapy outcomes enhanced? *Journal of Consulting and Clinical Psychology*, 63, 182–96.

Steiner, C. (1971) Radical psychiatry manifesto, *The Radical Therapist*, 2, 3–4.

Steiner, C. (1974) *Scripts People Live*. New York: Grove Press.

Steiner, C. (ed.) (1976) *Beyond Games and Scripts*. New York: Grove Press.

Steiner, C. (1979) *Healing Alcoholism*. New York: Grove Press.

Steiner, C. (1981) *The Other Side of Power*. New York: Grove Press.

Steiner, C. (1997) *Achieving Emotional Literacy*. New York: Avon Books.

Steiner, C. (2001) Radical psychiatry. In R. Corsini (ed.) *Handbook of Innovative Psychotherapies*. New York: Wiley.

Steiner, C. (2003) *Emotional Literacy; Intelligence with a Heart*. Fawnskin, CA: Personhood Press.

Steiner, C. and Wyckoff, H. (1975) *Readings in Radical Psychiatry*. New York: Grove Press.

Stephenson, R.L. (1885/1999) *The Strange Case of Dr Jekyll and Mr Hyde*. Ware: Wordsworth Editions.

Stevenson, F.A., Britten, N., Barry, C.A., Bradley, C.P. and Barber, N. (2003) Self-treatment and its discussion in medical consultations: how is medical pluralism managed in practice? *Social Science and Medicine*, 57, 513–27.

Stewart, I. (1992) *Eric Berne*. London: Sage.

Stewart, I. (2000) *Transactional Analysis Counselling in Action*, 2nd edn. London: Sage.

Stewart, I. (2006) Outcome-focused contracts. In C. Sills (ed.) *Contracts in Counselling and Psychotherapy*. London: Sage.

Stewart, I. and Joines, V. (1987) *TA Today*. Nottingham: Lifespace Publishing.

Stewart, I. and Joines, V. (2012) *TA Today: A New Introduction to Transactional Analysis*, 2nd revised edn. Nottingham: Lifespace Publishing.

Stiles, W.B. (1991) Longtitudinal study of assimilation in exploratory psychotherapy, *Psychotherapy*, 28, 195–206.

Stiles, W.B. (1992) *Describing Talk: A Taxonomy of Verbal Response Modes*. Thousand Oaks, CA: Sage.

Stiles, W.B. (2001) Assimilation of problematic experiences, *Psychotherapy: Theory, Research, Practice and Training*, 38, 462–5.

Stiles, W.B. (2002) Assimilation of problematic experiences. In J.C. Norcross (ed.) *Psychotherapy Relationships that Work*. New York: Oxford University Press.

Stiles, W.B. (2005) Extending the Assimilation of Problematic Experiences Scale: commentary on the special issue, *Counselling Psychology Quarterly*, 18, 85–93.

Stiles, W.B. (2006) Assimilation and the process of outcome: introduction to a special section, *Psychotherapy Research*, 16, 389–92.

Stiles, W.B. (2007) Theory-building case studies of counselling and psychotherapy, *Conselling and Psychotherapy Research*, 16, 389–92.

Stiles, W.B. and Shapiro, D.A. (1989) Abuse of the drug metaphor in psychotherapy process-outcome research, *Clinical Psychology Review*, 9, 521–43.

Stiles, W.B. and Glick, M.J. (2002) Client-centered therapy with multi-voiced clients: empathy with whom? In J.C. Watson, R. Goldman and M.S. Warner (eds) *Client-centered and Experiential Therapy in the 21st Century: Advances in Theory, Research, and Practice*. Ross-on-Wye: PCCS Books.

Stiles, W.B., Elliott, R., Llewelyn, S.P. *et al.* (1990) Assimilation of problematic experiences in psychotherapy, *Psychotherapy*, 27, 411–20.

Stiles, W.B., Meshot, C.M., Anderson, T.M. and Sloan, W.W. (1992) Assimilation of problematic experiences: the case of JohnJones, *Psychotherapy Research*, 2, 81–101.

Stiles, W.B., Honos-Webb, L. and Surko, M. (1998) Responsiveness in psychotherapy, *Clinical Psychology: Science and Practice*, 5, 439–58.

Stiles, W.B., Honos-Webb, L. and Knobloch, L.M. (1999) Treatment process research methods. In P.C. Kendall, J.N. Butcher, and G.N. Holmbeck (eds) *Handbook of Research Methods in Clinical Psychology*. New York: Wiley.

Stiles, W.B., Leach, C., Barkham, M. *et al.* (2003) Early sudden gains in psychotherapy under routine clinic conditions: practice-based evidence, *Journal of Consulting and Clinical Psychology*, 71, 14–21.

Stiles, W.B., Barkham, M., Twigg, E., Mellor-Clark, J. and Cooper, M. (2006) Effectiveness of cognitive-behavioural, person-centred and psychodynamic therapies as practiced in UK National Health Service settings, *Psychological Medicine*, 36, 555–66.

Stiles, W.B., Barkham, M., Mellor-Clark, J. and Connell, J. (2008) Effectiveness of cognitive-behavioural, person-centred, and psychodynamic therapies in UK primary-care routine practice: replication in a larger sample, *Psychological Medicine*, 38(5), 667–88.

Stinckens, N., Lietaer, G. and Leijssen, M. (2002a) The inner critic on the move: analysis of the change process in a case of short-term client-centred/experiential therapy, *Counselling and Psychotherapy Research*, 2, 40–54.

Stinckens, N., Lietaer, G. and Leijssen, M. (2002b) Working with the inner critic: fighting the 'enemy' or keeping it company. In J.C. Watson, R. Goldman and M.S. Warner (eds) *Client-centered and Experiential Therapy in the 21st Century: Advances in Theory, Research, and Practice*. Ross-on-Wye: PCCS Books.

Stiver, I.P. (1991a) The meanings of 'dependency' in female–male relationships. In J.V. Jordan, A.G. Kaplan, J.B. Miller, I.P. Stiver and J.L. Surrey (eds) *Women's Growth in Connection: Writings from the Stone Center*. New York: Guilford Press.

Stiver, I.P. (1991b) The meaning of care: reframing treatment models. In J.V. Jordan, A.G. Kaplan, J.B. Miller, I.P. Stiver and J.L. Surrey (eds) *Women's Growth in Connection: Writings from the Stone Center*. New York: Guilford Press.

Stiver, I.P. and Miller, J.B. (1997) From depression to sadness in women's psychotherapy. In J.V. Jordan (ed.) *Women's Growth in Diversity: More Writings from the Stone Center*. New York: Guilford Press.

Stock, W. (1988) Propping up the phallocracy: a feminist critique of sex therapy and research. In E. Cole and E.D. Rothblum (eds) *Women and Sex Therapy: Closing the Circle of Sexual Knowledge*. New York: Harrington Park Press.

Stockton, R., Nitza, A. and Bhusumane, D.B. (2010) The development of professional counseling in Botswana, *Journal of Counseling and Development*, 88, 9–12.

Stoltenberg, C.D. and Delworth, U. (1987) *Supervising Counselors and Therapists*. San Francisco, CA: Jossey-Bass.

Stone, R. (2006) Does pragmatism lead to pluralism? Exploring the disagreement between Jerome Bruner and William James regarding pragmatism's goal, *Theory and Psychology*, 16, 553–64.

Storck, L.E. (2002) Hearing, speaking and doing class-aware psychotherapy: a group-analytic approach, *Group Analysis*, 35, 437–46.

Stotts, E.L. and Ramey, L. (2009) Human trafficking: a call for counselor awareness and action, *Journal of Humanistic Counseling*, 48, 36–47.

Strasser, F. and Strasser, A. (1997) *Time Limited Existential Therapy: the Wheel of Existence*. Chichester: Wiley.

Strean, H.S. (1993) *Therapists Who Have Sex with Their Patients: Treatment and Recovery*. New York: Brunner and Mazel.

Stricker, G. (2000) Listening to the voice of the C/S/X: Consumer/Survivor/Expatient, *Journal of Clinical Psychology*, 56, 1389–94.

Stricker, G. (2006) Assimilative psychodynamic psychotherapy integration. In G. Stricker and J. Gold (eds) *A Casebook of Psychotherapy Integration*. Washington, DC: American Psychological Association.

Stricker, G. and Gold, J. (2005) Assimilative psychodynamic psychotherapy. In J.C. Norcross. and M.R. Goldfried (eds) *Handbook of Psychotherapy Integration*. New York: Oxford University Press.

Stricker, G. and Gold, J.R. (eds) (2006) *A Casebook of Psychotherapy Integration*. New York: Plenum.

Strike, D.L., Skovholt, T.M. and Hummel, T.J. (2004) Mental health professionals' disability competence: measuring self-awareness, perceived knowledge, and perceived skills, *Rehabilitation Psychology*, 49, 321–7.

Stroebe, W., Schut, H. and Stroebe, M. (2005) Grief work, disclosure and counselling: do they help the bereaved? *Clinical Psychology Review*, 25, 395–414.

Strong, T. (2000) Six orienting ideas for collaborative counsellors, *European Journal of Psychotherapy, Counselling and Health*, 3, 25–42.

Strong, T. and Pare, D. (eds) (2003) *Furthering Talk: Advances in the Discursive Therapies*. New York: Springer.

Strümpfel, U. (2004) Research on gestalt therapy, *International Gestalt Journal*, 27, 9–54.

Strümpfel, U. and Goldman, R. (2001) Contacting gestalt therapy. In D.J. Cain and J. Seeman (eds) *Humanistic Psychotherapies: Handbook of Research and Practice*. Washington, DC: American Psychological Association.

Strupp, H.H. (1969) Toward a specification of teaching and learning in psychotherapy, *Archives of General Psychiatry*, 21, 203–12.

Strupp, H.H. (1972) On the technology of psychotherapy, *Archives of General Psychiatry*, 26, 270–8.

Strupp, H.H. (1980a) Success and failure in time-limited therapy: with special reference to the performance of the lay counselor, *Archives of General Psychiatry*, 37, 831–41.

Strupp, H.H. (1980b) Success and failure in time-limited psychotherapy. A systematic comparison of two cases: comparison 2, *Archives of General Psychiatry*, 37, 708–16.

Strupp, H.H. (1980c) Success and failure in time-limited psychotherapy. A systematic comparison of two cases: comparison 1, *Archives of General Psychiatry*, 37, 595– 603.

Strupp, H.H. (1980d) Success and failure in time-limited psychotherapy. Further evidence: comparison 4, *Archives of General Psychiatry*, 37, 947–54.

Strupp, H.H. (1986) The nonspecific hypothesis of therapeutic effectiveness: a current assessment, *American Journal of Orthopsychiatry*, 56, 513–20.

Strupp, H.H. and Binder, J.L. (1984) *Psychotherapy in a New Key: A Guide to Time-limited Dynamic Psychotherapy*. New York: Basic Books.

Strupp, H.H. and Hadley, S.W. (1979) Specific vs nonspecific factors in psychotherapy: a controlled study of outcome, *Archives of General Psychiatry*, 36, 1125–36.

Stuhr, U. and Wachholz, S. (2001) In search for a psychoanalytic research strategy: the concept of ideal types. In J. Frommer and D. Rennie (eds) *Qualitative Psychotherapy Research: Methods and Methodology*. Lengerich: Pabst.

Sturmey, P. (2007) *Behavioural Case Formulation: A Functional Analytic Approach*. Chichester: Wiley.

Sue, D.W. and Sue, D. (2003) *Counseling the Culturally Different*, 4th edn. New York: Wiley.

Sue, D.W. and Sue, D. (2007) *Counseling the Culturally Diverse: Theory and Practice*, 5th edn. New York: Wiley.

Sue, D.W., Capodilupo, C.M., Torino, G.C. et al. (2007) Racial microaggressions in everyday life: implications for clinical practice, *American Psychologist*, 62, 271–86.

Sue, D.W., Nadal, K.L., Capodilupo, C.M., Lin, A.I, Torino, G.C and Rivera, D.P. (2008) Racial microaggressions against Black Americans: implications for counseling, *Journal of Counseling and Development*, 86, 330–8.

Sugarman, L. (1992) Ethical issues in counselling at work, *British Journal of Guidance and Counselling*, 20, 64–74.

Sussman, M. (2007) *A Curious Calling: Unconscious Motivation for Practicing Psychotherapy*, 2nd edn. New York: Jason Aronson.

Swift, J.K. and Callahan, J.L. (2009) The impact of client treatment preferences on outcome: a meta-analysis, *Journal of Clinical Psychology*, 65, 368–81.

Syme, G. (2003) *Dual Relationships in Counselling and Psychotherapy*. London: Sage.

Symington, N. (1983) The analyst's act of freedom as an agent of therapeutic change, *International Review of Psycho-Analysis*, 10, 83–91.

Symons, C. (2012) *Complaints and Complaining in Counselling and Psychotherapy: Organisational and Client Perspectives*. PhD thesis, Institute for Lifelong Learning,, University of Leicester.

Symons, C., Khele, S., Rogers, J., Turner, J. and Wheeler, S. (2011) Allegations of serious professional misconduct: an analysis of the British Association for Counselling and Psychotherapy's Article 4.6 cases, 1998–2007, *Counselling and Psychotherapy Research*, 11, 257–65.

Szasz, T.S. (1961) *The Myth of Mental Illness*. New York: Hoeber-Harper.

Szasz, T.S. (1971) *The Manufacture of Madness: A Comparative Study of the Inquisition and the Mental Health Movement*. London: Routledge and Kegan Paul.

Szasz, T.S. (1974) *The Ethics of Psycho-Analysis: The Theory and Method of Autonomous Psychotherapy*. London: Routledge and Kegan Paul.

Szasz, T.S. (1978) *The Myth of Psychotherapy*. Oxford: Oxford University Press.

Szilagyi, A. and Paredes, D.M. (2010) Professional counseling in Romania: an introduction, *Journal of Counseling and Development*, 88, 23–7.

Talmon, S. (1990) *Single Session Therapy: Maximising the Effect of the First (and often only) Therapeutic Encounter*. San Franciso, CA: Jossey-Bass.

Tanaka-Mastsumi, J. (2004) Japanese forms of psychotherapy: Naikan Therapy and Morita Therapy. In U.P. Gielen, G.M. Fish, GM. and J.G. Draguns (eds) *Handbook of Psychotherapy, Culture and Healing*. New York: Routledge.

Tang, T.Z. and DeRubeis, R.J. (1999) Sudden gains and critical sessions in cognitive– behavioural therapy for depression, *Journal of Consulting and Clinical Psychology*, 67, 894–904.

Taylor, C. (1989) *Sources of the Self: The Making of Modern Identity*. Cambridge, MA: Harvard University Press.

Taylor, M. (1990) Fantasy or reality? The problem with psychoanalytic interpretation in psychotherapy with women. In E. Burman (ed.) *Feminists on Psychological Practice*. London: Sage.

Taylor, M. (1991) How psychoanalytic thinking lost its way in the hands of men: the case for feminist psychotherapy, *British Journal of Guidance and Counselling*, 19, 93–103.

Taylor, M. (1995) Feminist psychotherapy. In M. Walker (ed.) *Peta: A Feminist's Problems with Men*. Buckingham: Open University Press.

Taylor, M. (1996) The feminist paradigm. In R. Woolfe and W. Dryden (eds) *Handbook of Counselling Psychology*. London: Sage.

Taylor, V. (1983) The future of feminism in the 1980s: a social movement analysis. In L. Richardson and V. Taylor (eds) *Feminist Frontiers: Rethinking Sex, Gender and Society*. Reading, MA: Addison-Wesley.

Teasdale, J.D., Segal, Z.V., Williams, J.M.G., Ridgeway, V., Lau, M. and Soulsby, J. (2000) Reducing risk of recurrence of major depression using mindfulness-based cognitive therapy, *Journal of Consulting and Clinical Psychology*, 68, 615–23.

Tegner, I., Fox, J., Philipp, R. and Thorne, P. (2009) Evaluating the use of poetry to improve well-being and emotional resilience in cancer patients, *Journal of Poetry Therapy*, 22, 121–31.

Thoma, N.C. and Cecero, J.J. (2009) Is integrative use of techniques in psychotherapy the exception or the rule? Results of a national survey of doctoral-level practitioners, *Psychotherapy*, 46, 405–17.

Thomas, R. and Henning, S. (2012) Counseling in Switzerland: past, present, and future, *Journal of Counseling and Development*, 90, 505–9.

Thompson, C. and Jenal, S. (1994) Interracial and intraracial quasi-counselling interactions: when counselors avoid discussing race, *Journal of Counseling Psychology*, 41, 484–91.

Thompson, M.N., Cole, O.D. and Nitzarim, R.S. (2012) Recognizing social class in the psychotherapy relationship: a grounded theory exploration of low-income clients, *Journal of Counseling Psychology*, 59, 208–21.

Thompson, V.L.S. and Alexander, H. (2006) Therapists' race and African American clients' reactions to therapy, *Psychotherapy: Theory, Research, Practice and Training*, 43, 99–110.

Thompson, V.L.S., Bazile, A. and Akbar, M. (2004) African Americans' perceptions of psychotherapy and psychotherapists, *Professional Psychology: Research and Practice*, 35, 19–26.

Thomson, M. (2007) *Psychological Subjects: Identity, Culture, and Health in Twentieth-Century Britain*. Oxford: Oxford University Press.

Thoresen, C. and Mahoney, M. (1974) *Behavioral Self-control*. New York: Holt, Rinehart and Winston.

Thorne, B. (1991) *Person-centred Counselling: Therapeutic and Spiritual Dimensions*. London: Whurr.

Thorne, B. (2012) *Counselling and Spiritual Accompaniment: Bridging Faith and Person-centred Therapy*. Oxford: Wiley-Blackwell.

Thorne, B. and Dryden, W. (1991) Key issues in the training of counsellors. In W. Dryden and B. Thorne (eds) *Training and Supervision for Counselling in Action*. London: Sage.

Thorne, B. and Dryden, W. (eds) (1993) *Counselling: Interdisciplinary Perspectives*. Buckingham: Open University Press.

Thorne, B. and Sanders, P. (2012) *Carl Rogers*, 3rd edn. London: Sage.

Throckmorton, M. (2002) Initial empirical and clinical findings concerning the change process for ex-gays, *Professional Psychology: Research and Practice*, 33, 242–7.

Tiefer, L. (1988) A feminist critique of the sexual dysfunction nomenclature. In E. Cole and E.D. Rothblum (eds) *Women and Sex Therapy: Closing the Circle of Sexual Knowledge*. New York: Harrington Park Press.

Timms, N. and Blampied, A. (1985) *Intervention in Marriage: The Experience of Counsellors and Their Clients*. Sheffield: University of Sheffield Joint Unit for Social Services Research.

Timulak, L. (2008) *Research in Counselling and Psychotherapy*. London: Sage.

Timulak, L. (2011) *Developing your Counselling and Psychotherapy Skills and Practice*. London: Sage.

Tjeltveit, A.C. (2000) There's more to ethics than codes of professional ethics: social ethics, theoretical ethics, and managed care, *Counseling Psychologist*, 242–52.

Tjeltveit, A.C. (2004) The good, the bad, the obligatory, and the virtuous: the ethical contexts of psychotherapy, *Journal of Psychotherapy Integration*, 14, 149–67.

Tolley, K. and Rowland, N. (1995) *Evaluating the Cost-effectiveness of Counselling in Health Care*. London: Routledge.

Tolor, A. and Reznikoff, M. (1960) A new approach to insight: a primary report, *Journal of Nervous and Mental Disease*, 130, 286–96.

Tonnesvang, J., Sommer, U., Hammink, J. and Sonne, M. (2010) Gestalt Therapy and cognitive therapy – contrasts and complexities? *Psychotherapy Theory, Research, Practice, Training*, 47, 586–602.

Torres, W.J. and Bergner, R.M. (2012) Severe public humiliation: Its nature, consequences, and clinical treatment, *Psychotherapy*, 49, 492–501.

Torron, N. (2005) Wild at heart: another side of ecopsychology, *Therapy Today*, 16(10), 18–21.

Totton, N. (2000) *Psychotherapy and Politics*. London: Sage.

Totton, N. (2006) *The Politics of Psychotherapy: New Perspectives*. Maidenhead; Open University Press.

Towbin, A.P. (1978) The confiding relationship: a new paradigm, *Psychotherapy*, 15, 333–43.

Trepal, H.C. (2010) Exploring self-injury through a relational cultural lens, *Journal of Counseling and Development*, 88, 492–9.

Trepal, H.C., Boie, J. and Kress, V.E. (2012) A relational cultural approach to working with clients with eating disorders, *Journal of Counseling and Development*, 90, 346–56.

Tribe, R. and Raval, H. (eds) (2003) *Working with Interpreters in Mental Health*. Hove: Brunner-Routledge.

Trijsburg, R.W., Lietaer, G., Colijn, S., Abrahamse, R.M., Joosten, S. and Duivenvoorden, H.J. (2004) Construct validity of the Comprehensive Therapeutic Interventions rating scale. *Psychotherapy Research*, 14, 346–66.

Trijsburg, W., Colijn, L. and Holmes, J. (2007) Psychotherapy integration. In G.O. Gabbard, J.S. Beck and J. Holmes (eds) *Oxford Textbook of Psychotherapy*. New York: Oxford University Press.

Trotter, K.S. (2012) *Harnessing the Power of Equine Assisted Counseling: Adding Animal Assisted Therapy to Your Practice*. London: Routledge.

Trower, P., Bryant, M. and Argyle, M. (1978) *Social Skills and Mental Health*. London: Tavistock.

Truax, C.B. (1966) Reinforcement and nonreinforcement in Rogerian psychotherapy, *Journal of Abnormal Psychology*, 71, 1–9.

Truax, C.B. and Carkhuff, R.R. (1967) *Toward Effective Counseling and Psychotherapy*. Chicago, IL: Aldine.

Truell, R. (2001) The stresses of learning counselling: six recent graduates comment on their personal experience of learning counselling and what can be done to reduce associated harm, *Counselling Psychology Quarterly*, 14, 67–89.

Tryon, G.S. (ed.) (2002) *Counselling Based on Process Research: Applying What we Know*. Boston, MA: Allyn and Bacon.

Tseng, W.-S. (1999) Culture and psychotherapy: review and practical guidelines, *Transcultural Psychiatry*, 36, 131–79.

Tuason, M.T.G., Fernandez, K.T.G., Catipon, M.A.D.P., Trivino-Dey, L. and Arellano-Carandang, M.L. (2012) Counseling in the Philippines: past, present, and future, *Journal of Counseling and Development*, 90, 373–8.

Tucker, C., Smith-Adcock, S. and Trepal, H.C. (2011) Relational-cultural theory for middle school counselors, *Professional School Counseling*, 14, 310–16.

Tuckwell, G. (2001) 'The threat of the Other': using mixed quantitative and qualitative methods to elucidate racial and cultural dynamics in the counselling process, *Counselling and Psychotherapy Research*, 1, 154–62.

Tudor, K. (ed.) (2002) *Transactional Analysis Approaches to Brief Therapy*. London: Sage.

Tudor, K. (2008) "Take it": a sixth driver, *Transactional Analysis Journal*, 38, 43–57.

Tudor, K. and Widdowson, M. (2002) Integrating views of TA brief therapy. In K. Tudor (ed.) *Transactional Analysis Approaches to Brief Therapy*. London: Sage.

Tuicomepee, A., Romano, J.L. and Pokaeo, S. (2012) Counseling in Thailand: development from a Buddhist perspective, *Journal of Counseling and Development*, 90, 357–61.

Tuke, S. (1813/1964) *Description of the Retreat* (edited by R. Hunter and I. Macalpine). London: Dawsons.

Tune, D. (2001) Is touch a valid therapeutic intervention? Early returns from a qualitative study of therapists' views, *Counselling and Psychotherapy Research*, 1, 167–71.

Turner, B.S. (1995) *Medical Power and Social Knowledge*, 2nd edn. London: Sage.

Turner, P.R., Valtierra, M., Talken, T.R., Miller, V.I. and DeAnda, J.R. (1996) Effect of session length on treatment outcome for college students in brief therapy, *Journal of Counseling Psychology*, 43, 228–32.

Turner, V. (1964) A Ndembu doctor in practice. In A. Kiev (ed.) *Magic, Faith and Healing: Studies in Primitive Psychiatry Today*, New York: Free Press.

Turner, V. (1982) *From Ritual to Theatre: the Human Seriousness of Play*. New York: Performing Arts Society Publications.

Tursi, M.M. and Cochran, J.L. (2006) Cognitive-behavioral tasks accomplished in a person-centered relational framework, *Journal of Counseling and Development*, 84, 387–96.

Tyndall, N. (1985) The work and impact of the National Marriage Guidance Council. In W. Dryden (ed.) *Marital Therapy in Britain*, Volume 1. London: Harper and Row.

Tyrrell, C.L., Dozier, M., Teague, G.B. and Fallot, R.D. (1999) Effective treatment relationshops for persons with serious psychiatric disorders: the importance of attachment states of mind, *Journal of Consulting and Clinical Psychology*, 67, 725–33.

Tzou, J.Y., Kim, E. and Waldheim, K. (2012) Theory and practice of positive feminist therapy: a culturally responsive approach to divorce therapy with Chinese Women, *International Journal for the Advancement of Counselling*, 34, 143–58.

Valle, R.S. and King, M. (eds) (1978) *Existential-phenomenological Alternatives for Psychology*. New York: Oxford University Press.

Valle, R.S. and Halling, S. (eds) (1989) *Existential-Phenomenological Perspectives in Psychology: Exploring the Breadth of Human Experience*. New York: Plenum.

van Balen, R. (1990) The therapeutic relationship according to Carl Rogers: only a climate? a dialogue? or both? In G. Lietaer, J. Rombauts and R. van Balen (eds) *Client-centered and Experiential Therapy in the Nineties*. Leuven: Leuven University Press.

van Belle, H.A. (1990) Rogers' later move toward mysticism: implications for client-centered therapy. In G. Lietaer, J. Rombauts and R. van Balen (eds) *Client-centered and Experiential Therapy in the Nineties*. Leuven: Leuven University Press.

van Deurzen, E. (1988) *Existential Counselling in Practice*. London: Sage.

van Deurzen, E. (1990) Existential therapy. In W. Dryden (ed.) *Individual Therapy: A Handbook*. Buckingham: Open University Press.

van Deurzen, E. (1996) *Everyday Mysteries: Existential Dimensions of Psychotherapy*. London: Routledge.

van Deurzen, E. (1999) Existentialism and existential psychotherapy. In C. Mace (ed.) *Heart and Soul: The Therapeutic Face of Philosophy*. London: Routledge.

van Deurzen, E. (2001) *Existential Counselling and Psychotherapy in Practice*, 2nd edn. London: Sage.

van Emmerik, A.A.P., Kamphuis, J.H. and Emmelkamp, P.M.G. (2008) Acute Stress Disorder and Posttraumatic Stress Disorder with Cognitive Behavioral Therapy or Structured Writing Therapy: a randomized controlled trial, *Psychotherapy and Psychosomatics*, 77, 93–100

Van Lith, T., Fenner, P. and Schofield, M. (2011) The lived experience of art making as a companion to the mental health recovery process, *Disability and Rehabilitation*, 33, 652–60.

van Rijn, B. (2011) Evaluating the outcomes of transactional analysis and integrative counselling psychology within UK primary care settings, *International Journal of Transactional Analysis Research*. 2(2), July.

van Werde, D. (1994) An introduction to client-centred pre-therapy. In D. Mearns (ed.) *Developing Person-centred counselling*. London: Sage.

Vanaerschot, G. (1990) The process of empathy: holding and letting go. In G. Lietaer, J. Rombauts and R. van Balen (eds) *Client-centred and Experiential Psychotherapy in the Nineties*. Leuven: University of Leuven Press.

Vanaerschot, G. (1993) Empathy as releasing several micro-processes in the client. In D. Brazier (ed.) *Beyond Carl Rogers*. London: Constable.

Vanaerschot, G. (2004) It takes two to tango: on empathy with fragile process, *Psychotherapy: Theory, Research, Practice, Training*, 41, 112–24.

VandenBos, G. (1996) Outcome assessment of psychotherapy, *American Psychologist*, 51, 1005–6.

Veale, D. and Wilson, R. (2005) *Overcoming Obsessive Compulsive Disorder: A Self-help Guide using Cognitive-behavioural Techniques*. London: Constable and Robinson.

Viens, M.J. and Hranchuk, K. (1992) The treatment of bulimia nervosa following surgery using a stimulus control procedure: a case study, *Journal of Behaviour Therapy and Experimental Psychiatry*, 23, 313–17.

Vromans, L.P. and Schweitzer, R. (2011) Narrative therapy for adults with major depressive disorder: Improved symptom and interpersonal outcomes, *Psychotherapy Research*, 21, 4–15.

Wachholz, S. and Stuhr, U. (1999) The concept of ideal types in psychoanalytic follow-up research. *Psychotherapy Research*, 9, 327–41.

Wachtel, P.L. (2007) Carl Rogers and the larger context of therapeutic thought, *Psychotherapy: Theory, Research, Practice, Training*, 44, 279–84.

Wade, P. and Bernstein, B. L. (1991) Cultural sensitivity training and counselors' race: effects on black female clients' perceptions and attrition, *Journal of Counseling Psychology*, 38, 9–15.

Wagner-Moore, L.E. (2004) Gestalt Therapy: past, present, theory, and research, *Psychotherapy: Theory, Research, Practice, Training*, 41, 180–9.

Waldegrave, C., Tamasese, K., Tuhaka, F. and Campbell, W. (2003) *Just Therapy: A Journey. A Collection of Papers from the Just Therapy Team, New Zealand*. Adelaide: Dulwich Centre.

Walker, M. and Rosen, W.B. (eds) (2004) *How Connections Heal. Stories from Relational-Cultural Therapy*. New York: Guilford Press.

Wallace, A.F.C. (1958) Dreams and the wishes of the soul: a type of psychoanalytic theory among the seventeenth century Iroquois, *American Anthropologist*, 60, 234–48.

Walls, G. B. (1980) Values and psychotherapy: a comment on 'Psychotherapy and Religious Values', *Journal of Consulting and Clinical Psychology*, 48, 640–2.

Walsh, K. and Hope, D.A. (2010) LGB-Affirmative cognitive behavioral treatment for Social anxiety: a case study applying evidence-based practice principles, *Cognitive and Behavioral Practice*, 17, 56–65.

Walter, T. (1996) A new model of grief: bereavement and biography, *Mortality*, 1, 7–25.

Wampold, B.E. (2001) *The Great Psychotherapy Debate: Models, Methods and Findings*. Mahwah, NJ: Erlbaum.

Wanigaratne, S. and Barker, C. (1995) Clients' preferences for styles of therapy, *British Journal of Clinical Psychology*, 34, 215–22.

Wanigaratne, S., Wallace, W., Pullin, J., Keaney, F. and Farmer, R. (1990) *Relapse Prevention for Addictive Behaviours: A Manual for Therapists*. Oxford: Blackwell.

Ward, D.E. (1984) Termination of individual counseling: concepts and strategies, *Journal of Counseling and Development*, 63, 21–5.

Ward, E.C. (2005) Keeping it real: a grounded theory study of African American clients engaged in counseling at a community mental health agency, *Journal of Counseling Psychology*, 52, 471–81.

Warner, M.S. (2000a) Person-centred psychotherapy: one nation, many tribes, *Person-Centred Journal*, 7, 28–39.

Warner, M.S. (2000b) Person-centred therapy at the difficult edge: a developmentally-based model of fragile and dissociated process. In D. Mearns and B. Thorne, *Person-centred Therapy Today: New Frontiers in Theory and Practice*. London: Sage.

Warner, M.S. (2002a) Luke's dilemmas: a client-centered/experiential model of processing with a schizophrenic thought disorder. In J.C. Watson, R. Goldman and M.S. Warner (eds) *Client-centered and Experiential Therapy in the 21st Century: Advances in Theory, Research, and Practice*. Ross-on-Wye: PCCS Books.

Warner, M.S. (2002b) Psychological contact, meaningful process and human contact. In G. Wyatt and P. Sanders (eds) *Rogers' Therapeutic Conditions: Contact and Perception*. Ross-on-Wye: PCCS Books.

Warner, R. (2003) *Recovery from Schizophrenia: Psychiatry and Political Economy*, 3rd edn. New York: Routledge.

Warren, B. (ed.) (2008) *Using the Creative Arts in Therapy and Healthcare: A Practical Introduction*, 3rd edn. London: Routledge.

Wartenberg, T. (2008) *Existentialism: a Beginner's Guide*. London: OneWorld.

Waterhouse, R. (1993) 'Wild women don't have the blues': a feminist critique of 'person-centred' counselling and therapy, *Feminism and Psychology*, 3(1), 55–71.

Watkins, C.E. Jr and Campbell, V.L. (1990) *Testing in Counseling Practice*. Hillsdale, NJ: Lawrence Erlbaum.

Watson, G. (1940) Areas of agreement in psychotherapy, *American Journal of Orthopsychiatry*, 10, 698–709.

Watson, J. B. (1919) *Psychology from the Standpoint of a Behaviorist*. Philadelphia, PA: J.B. Lippincott.

Watson, J.C., Greenberg, L.S. and Lietaer, G. (1998) The experiential paradigm unfolding: relationship and experiencing in therapy. In L.S. Greenberg, J.C. Watson and G. Lietaer (eds) *Handbook of Experiential Psychotherapy*. New York: Guilford Press.

Watson, J.C. (2006) A reflection on the blending of person-centered therapy and solution-focused therapy, *Psychotherapy: Theory, Research, Practice, Training*, 43, 13–15.

Watson, J.C. (2007) Reassessing Rogers' necessary and sufficient conditions of change, *Psychotherapy: Theory, Research, Practice, Training*, 44, 268–73.

Watson, J.C., Goldman, R.N. and Greenberg, L.S. (2007) *Case Studies in Emotion-focused Treatment of Depression: A Comparison of Good and Poor Outcomes*. Washington, DC: American Psychological Association.

Watson, J.S., Goldman, R.N. and Greenberg, L.S. (2011) Contrasting two clients in Emotion-Focused Therapy for depression 1: The Case of 'Tom,' 'Trapped in the Tunnel', *Pragmatic Case Studies in Psychotherapy*, 7(2), 268–304. Available at http://pcsp.libraries.rutgers.edu/index.php/pcsp/issue/view/98 (accessed 19 March 2013).

Watson, N. (1984) The empirical status of Rogers's hypotheses of the necessary and sufficient conditions for effective psychotherapy. In R.F. Levant and J.M. Shlien (eds) *Client-centered Therapy and the Person-centered Approach: New Directions in Theory, Research and Practice*. New York: Praeger.

Watters, E. (2010) *Crazy like Us: The Globalization of the Western Psyche*. New York: Free Press.

Watts, R.E. (1998) The remarkable parallel between Rogers' core conditions and Adler's social interest, *Journal of Individual Psychology*, 54, 4–9.

Weatherhead, S. and Daiches, A. (2010) Muslim views on mental health and psychotherapy, *Psychology and Psychotherapy: Theory, Research and Practice*, 83, 75–89.

Webb, A. (2000) What makes it difficult for the supervisee to speak? In B. Lawton and C. Feltham (eds) *Taking Supervision Forward: Enquiries and Trends in Counselling and Psychotherapy*. London: Sage.

Wedding, D. and Niemiec, R.M. (2003) The clinical use of films in psychotherapy, *Journal of Clinical Psychology*, 59, 207–15.

Weiner, D.N. (1988) *Albert Ellis: Passionate Skeptic*. New York: Praeger.

Weingarten, K. (2010) Intersecting losses: working with the inevitable vicissitudes in therapist and client lives, *Psychotherapy Theory, Research, Practice, Training*, 47, 371–84.

Weintraub, S.R. and Goodman, L.A. (2010) Working with and for: student advocates' experience of relationship-centered advocacy with low-income women, *American Journal of Orthopsychiatry*, 80, 46–60.

Weiser, J. (1999) *PhotoTherapy Techniques: Exploring the Secrets of Personal Snapshots and Family Albums*, 2nd edn. Vancouver, BC: PhotoTherapy Centre Press.

Weiss, M., Nordlie, J.W. and Siegel, E.P. (2005) Mindfulness-based stress reduction as an adjunct to outpatient psychotherapy, *Psychotherapy and Psychosomatics*, 74, 108–12.

Wenger, E. (1998) *Communities of Practice: Learning, Meaning, and Identity*, Cambridge: Cambridge University Press.

West, W.S. (2000) *Psychotherapy and Spirituality: Crossing the Line between Therapy and Religion*. London: Sage.

West, W.S. (2004) *Spiritual Issues in Therapy, Relating Experience to Practice*. London: Palgrave Macmillan.

Westbrook, D., Kennerley, H. and Kirk, J. (2011) *An Introduction to Cognitive Behaviour Therapy: Skills and Applications*, 2nd edn. London: Sage.

Westbrook, D. and Kirk, J. (2005) The clinical effectiveness of cognitive behaviour therapy: Outcome for a large sample of adults treated in routine practice, *Behaviour Research and Therapy*, 43, 1243–61.

Westen, D., Novotny, C.M. and Thompson-Brenner, H. (2004) The empirical status of empirically-supported psychotherapies: assumptions, findings, and reporting in controlled clinical trials, *Psychological Bulletin*, 130, 631–63.

Westra, H.A. and Arkowitz, H. (2011) Integrating motivational interviewing with cognitive behavioral therapy for a range of mental health problems, *Cognitive and Behavioural Practice*, 18, 1–4.

Wexler, D.A. and Rice, L.N. (eds) (1974) *Innovations in Client-centered Therapy*. New York: Wiley.

Wexler, D.B. (1990) *Therapeutic Jurisprudence: The Law as Therapeutic Agent*. Durham, NC: Carolina Academic Press.

Wheatley, J. and Hackman, A. (2011) Using imagery rescripting to treat major depression: theory and practice, *Cognitive and Behavioral Practice*, 18, 444–53.

Wheeler, G. (1991) *Gestalt Reconsidered*. New York: Gardner Press.

Wheeler, S. (ed.) (2006) *Difference and Diversity in Counselling: Contemporary Psychodynamic Approaches*. Basingstoke: Palgrave Macmillan.

Wheeler, S. and Richards, K. (2007) *The Impact of Clinical Supervision on Counsellors and Therapists, their Practice and their Clients: A Systematic Review of the Literature*. Lutterworth: BACP.

Wheeler, S., Goldie, J. and Hicks, C. (1998) Counsellor training: an evaluation of the effectiveness of a residential outdoor pursuits activity weekend on the personal development of trainee counsellors, *Counselling Psychology Quarterly*, 11, 391–405.

Whiston, S.C. (2000) *Principles and Applications of Assessment in Counseling*. Belmont, CA: Brooks/Cole.

Whitaker, D. (1985) *Using Groups to Help People*. London: Tavistock/Routledge.

White, J.R. and Freeman, A.S. (eds) (2000) *Cognitive–behavioural Group Therapy for Specific Problems and Populations*. Washington, DC: American Psychological Association.

White, M. (2004) Folk psychology and narrative practice. In L. Angus and J. McLeod (eds) *Handbook of Narrative Psychology*. Thousand Oaks, CA: Sage.

White, M. (2007) *Maps of Narrative Practice*. New York: Norton.

White, M. (2011) *Narrative Practice.Continuing the Conversations*. New York: Norton.

White, M. and Epston, D. (1990) *Narrative Means to Therapeutic Ends*. New York: Norton.

Whiteley, J.M. (1984) A historical perspective on the development of counseling psychology as a profession. In S.D. Brown and R.W. Lent (eds) *Handbook of Counseling Psychology*. New York: Wiley.

Whitman, R. and Stock, D. (1958) The group focal conflict, *Psychiatry*, 21, 267–76.

Whittal, M.L. and O'Neill, M.L. (2003) Cognitive and behavioral methods for obsessive-compulsive disorder, *Brief Treatment and Crisis Intervention*, 3, 201–15.

Widdowson, M. (2012a) TA treatment of depression – a hermeneutic single case efficacy design study – 'Peter', *International Journal of Transactional Analysis Research*, 3(1), January.

Widdowson, M. (2012b) TA treatment of depression – a hermeneutic single case efficacy design study – 'Tom', *International Journal of Transactional Analysis Research*, 3(2), July.

Widdowson, M. (2012c) TA treatment of depression – a hermeneutic single case efficacy design study – 'Denise', *International Journal of Transactional Analysis Research*, 3(2), July.

Wiener, D. (2001) *Beyond Talk Therapy: Using Movement and Expressive Technique in Clinical Practice*. Washington, DC: American Psychological Association.

Wilbert, J.R. and Fulero, S.M. (1988) Impact of malpractice litigation on professional psychology: survey of practitioners, *Professional Psychology: Research and Practice*, 19(4), 379–82.

Wild, J. and Clark, D.M. (2011) Imagery rescripting of early traumatic memories in social phobia, *Cognitive and Behavioral Practice*, 18, 433–43.

Wilensky, J.L. and Wilensky, H.L. (1951) The Hawthorne case, *American Journal of Sociology*, 25, 269–80.

Wilkins, P. (1994) Can psychodrama be 'person-centred'? *Person-Centred Practice*, 2, 8–17.

Wilkinson, R.G. and Pickett, K. (2010) *The Spirit Level: Why Equality is Better for Everyone*. London: Penguin.

Willi, J. (1999) *Ecological Psychotherapy: Developing by Shaping the Personal Niche*. Seattle, WA: Hogrefe and Huber.

Willi, J., Frei, R. and Gunther, E. (2000) Psychotherapy of panic syndrome: focusing on ecological aspects of relationships, *American Journal of Psychotherapy*, 54, 226–42.

Williams, C.R. and Abeles, N. (2004) Issues and implications of deaf culture in therapy, *Professional Psychology: Research and Practice*, 6, 643–8.

Williams, J.M.G. (1996) Memory processes in psychotherapy. In P.M. Salkovskis (ed.) *Frontiers of Cognitive Therapy*. New York: Guilford Press.

Williams, J.M.G., Duggan, D.S., Crane, C. and Fennell, M.J.V. (2006) Mindfulness-based cognitive therapy for prevention of recurrence of suicidal behavior, *Journal of Clinical Psychology*, 62, 201–10.

Williams, M., Teasdale, J., Segal, Z. and Kabat-Zinn, J. (2007) *The Mindful Way through Depression: Freeing yourself from Chronic Unhappiness*. New York: Guilford Press.

Willis, A. (2011) Re-storying wilderness and adventure therapies: healing places and selves in an era of environmental crises, *Journal of Adventure Education and Outdoor Learning*, 11, 91–108.

Willner, P. (2005) The effectiveness of psychotherapeutic interventions for people with learning disabilities: a critical overview, *Journal of Intellectual Disability Research*, 49, 73–85.

Wills, F. and Sanders, D. (1997) *Cognitive Therapy: Transforming the Image*. London: Sage.

Wills, T.A. (1982) Nonspecific factors in helping relationships. In T.A. Wills (ed.) *Basic Processes in Helping Relationships*. New York: Academic Press.

Wilson, J. and Giddings, L. (2010) Counselling women whose lives have been seriously disrupted by depression: what professional counsellors can learn from New Zealand women's stories of recovery, *New Zealand Journal of Counselling*, 30, 23–39.

Winnicott, D.W. (1958) *Collected Papers: Through Paediatrics to Psychoanalysis*. London: Hogarth.

Winnicott, D.W. (1964) *The Child, the Family and the Outside World*. Harmondsworth: Penguin.

Winnicott, D.W. (1965) *The Maturational Process and the Facilitating Environment*. London: Hogarth.

Winnicott, D.W. (1971) *Playing and Reality*. London: Hogarth.

Winnicott, D.W. (1977) *The Piggle. An Account of the Psychoanalytic Treatment of a Little Girl*. London: Hogarth Press.

Wise, E.A. (1988) Issues in psychotherapy with EAP clients, *Psychotherapy*, 25, 415–19.

Wittchen, H. and Jacobi, F. (2005) Size and burden of mental disorders in Europe—a critical review and appraisal of 27 studies, *European Neuropsychopharmacology*, 15, 357–76.

Woldt, A.L. and Toman, S.M. (eds) (2005) *Gestalt Therapy: History, Theory, and Practice*. Thousand Oaks, CA: Sage.

Wollheim, R. (1971) *Freud*. London: Fontana.

Wolpe, J. (1958) *Psychotherapy by Reciprocal Inhibition*. Stanford, CA: Stanford University Press.

Wolz, B. (2010) Cinema as alchemy for healing and transformation: using the power of cinema in psychotherapy and coaching. In M.B. Gregerson (ed.) *The Cinematic Mirror for Psychology and Life Coaching*. New York: Springer.

Wong, Y.J. (2006) Strength-centered therapy: a social constructionist, virtues-based psychotherapy, *Psychotherapy: Theory, Research, Practice, Training*, 43, 133–46.

Wood, C. (ed.) (2011) *Navigating Art Therapy: A Therapist's Companion*. London: Routledge.

Wood, E.C. and Wood, C.D. (1990) Referral issues in psychotherapy and psychoanalysis, *American Journal of Psychotherapy*, 44, 85–94.

Woods, K.M. and McNamara, J.R. (1980) Confidentiality: its effect on interviewee behavior, *Professional Psychology*, 11, 714–21.

Woody, W.D. and Viney, W. (2009) A pluralistic universe: an overview and implications for psychology, *Journal of Mind and Behavior*, 30, 107–20.

Wooley, S.C. (1994) The female therapist as outlaw. In P. Fallon, M.A. Katzman and S.C. Wooley (eds) *Feminist Perspectives on Eating Disorders*. New York: Guilford Press.

Woollams, S. and Brown, M. (1978) *Transactional Analysis*. Dexter, MI: Huron Valley Institute.

Worell, J. (1981) New directions in counseling women. In E. Howell and M. Bayes (eds) *Women and Mental Health*. New York: Basic Books.

Worell, J. and Remer, P. (2002) *Feminist Perspectives in Therapy: Empowering Diverse Women*, 2nd edn. New York: Wiley.

Worthington, R.L. (2004) Sexual identity, sexual orientation, religious identity, and change: is it possible to depolarize the debate? *The Counseling Psychologist*, 32, 741–9.

Worthington, R.L., Soth-McNett, A.M. and Moreno, M.V. (2007) Multicultural counseling competencies research: a 20-year content analysis, *Journal of Counseling Psychology*, 54, 351–61.

Wosket, V. (2006) *Egan's Skilled Helper Model: Developments and Applications in Counselling*. London: Routledge.

Wubbolding, R.E. (2000) *Reality therapy for the 21st century*. Philadelphia, PA: Brunner-Routledge.

Wyatt, G. (ed.) (2001) *Rogers' Therapeutic Conditions: Evolution, Theory and Practice. Volume 1: Congruence*. Ross-on-Wye: PCCS Books.

Wyrostok, N. (1995) The ritual as a psychotherapeutic intervention. *Psychotherapy*, 32, 397– 404.

Yalom, I.D. (1980) *Existential Psychotherapy*. New York: Basic Books.

Yalom, I.D. (1989) *Love's Executioner and Other Tales of Psychotherapy*. Harmondsworth: Penguin.

Yalom, I.D. (2002) *The Gift of Therapy: Reflections on Being a Therapist*. London: Piatkus.

Yalom, I.D. (2005a) *Love's Executioner and Other Tales of Psychotherapy*. London: Penguin.

Yalom, I.D. (2005b) *The Schopenhauer Cure*. New York: HarperCollins.

Yeo, L.S., Tan, S.Y. and Neihart, M.F. (2012) Counselling in Singapore, *Journal of Counseling and Development*, 80, 243–8.

Yontef, G.M. (1993) *Awareness, Dialogue And Process: Essays on Gestalt Therapy*. Highland, NY: Gestalt Journal Press.

Yontef, G.M. (1995) Gestalt therapy. In A.S. Gurman and S.B. Messer (eds) *Essential Psychotherapies: Theory and Practice*. New York: Guilford Press.

Yontef, G.M. (1998) Dialogic Gestalt therapy. In L.S. Greenberg, J.C. Watson and G. Lietaer (eds) *Handbook of Experiential Psychotherapy*. New York: Guilford Press.

Young, J.E., Klosko, J.S. and Weishaar, M. (2003) *Schema Therapy: A Practitioner's Guide*. New York: Guilford Press.

Young, K. and Cooper, S. (2008) Toward co-composing an evidence base: the narrative therapy re-visiting project, *Journal of Systemic Therapies*, 27, 67–83.

Young, R. (1989) Helpful behaviors in the crisis center call, *Journal of Community Psychology*, 17, 70–7.

Young, S., Cashwell, C.S. and Ciordano, A.L. (2010) Breathwork as a therapeutic modality: an overview for counselors, *Counseling and Values*, 55, 113–25.

Yuker, H.E., Block, J.R. and Campbell, W.J. (1960) *A Scale to Measure Attitudes toward Disabled Persons*. Albertson, NY: Human Resources Center.

Zajonc, R. (1980) Feeling and thinking: preferences need no inferences, *American Psychologist*, 35, 151–75.

Zerubavel, N. and Wright, M.O. (2012) The dilemma of the wounded healer, *Psychotherapy*, 49, 482–91.

Zhu, S.-H. and Pierce, J. P. (1995) A new scheduling method for time-limited counseling. *Professional Psychology: Research and Practice*, 26, 624–5.

Zhu, S.-H., Tedeschi, G.J., Anderson, C.M. and Pierce, J.P. (1996) Telephone counseling for smoking cessation: what's in a call? *Journal of Counseling and Development*, 75, 93–102.

Ziller, R.C. (2000) Self-counselling through re-authored photo-self-narratives, *Counselling Psychology Quarterly*, 13, 265–78.

Zuckerman, E. (2003) Finding, evaulation, and incorporating internet self-help resources into psychotherapy practice, *Journal of Clinical Psychology*, 59, 217–25.

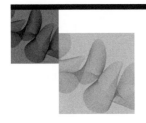

Index

Locators shown in *italics* refer to tables, figures and boxes.